The Encyclopedia of Religion

The Encyclopedia of Religion

Mircea Eliade

EDITOR IN CHIEF

Volume 8

MACMILLAN PUBLISHING COMPANY
New York

Collier Macmillan Publishers
London

MACMILLAN PUBLISHING COMPANY
866 Third Avenue, New York, NY 10022

Collier Macmillan Canada, Inc.

Library of Congress Catalog Card Number: 86-5432

PRINTED IN THE UNITED STATES OF AMERICA

printing number
1 2 3 4 5 6 7 8 9 10

Library of Congress Cataloging-in-Publication Data

The Encyclopedia of religion.

Includes bibliographies and index.
1. Religion—Dictionaries. I. Eliade, Mircea, 1907–1986. II. Adams, Charles J.
BL31.#46 1986 200'.3'21 86-5432
ISBN 0-02-909480-1 (set)
ISBN 0-02-909790-8 (v. 8)

Acknowledgments of sources, copyrights, and permissions to use previously published materials are gratefully made in a special listing in volume 16.

Abbreviations and Symbols Used in This Work

abbr. abbreviated; abbreviation
abr. abridged; abridgment
AD *anno Domini,* in the year of the (our) Lord
Afrik. Afrikaans
AH *anno Hegirae,* in the year of the Hijrah
Akk. Akkadian
Ala. Alabama
Alb. Albanian
Am. *Amos*
AM *ante meridiem,* before noon
amend. amended; amendment
annot. annotated; annotation
Ap. *Apocalypse*
Apn. *Apocryphon*
app. appendix
Arab. Arabic
ʿArakh. *ʿArakhin*
Aram. Aramaic
Ariz. Arizona
Ark. Arkansas
Arm. Armenian
art. article (pl., arts.)
AS Anglo-Saxon
Asm. Mos. *Assumption of Moses*
Assyr. Assyrian
A.S.S.R. Autonomous Soviet Socialist Republic
Av. Avestan
ʿA.Z. *ʿAvodah zarah*
b. born
Bab. Babylonian
Ban. Bantu
1 Bar. *1 Baruch*
2 Bar. *2 Baruch*
3 Bar. *3 Baruch*
4 Bar. *4 Baruch*
B.B. *Bava' batra'*
BBC British Broadcasting Corporation
BC before Christ
BCE before the common era
B.D. Bachelor of Divinity
Beits. *Beitsah*
Bekh. *Bekhorot*
Beng. Bengali
Ber. *Berakhot*
Berb. Berber
Bik. *Bikkurim*
bk. book (pl., bks.)
B.M. *Bava' metsiʿa'*
BP before the present
B.Q. *Bava' qamma'*
Brāh. *Brāhmaṇa*
Bret. Breton
B.T. Babylonian Talmud
Bulg. Bulgarian
Burm. Burmese
c. *circa,* about, approximately
Calif. California
Can. Canaanite
Catal. Catalan
CE of the common era
Celt. Celtic
cf. *confer,* compare
Chald. Chaldean
chap. chapter (pl., chaps.)
Chin. Chinese
C.H.M. Community of the Holy Myrrhbearers
1 Chr. *1 Chronicles*
2 Chr. *2 Chronicles*
Ch. Slav. Church Slavic
cm centimeters
col. column (pl., cols.)
Col. *Colossians*
Colo. Colorado
comp. compiler (pl., comps.)
Conn. Connecticut
cont. continued
Copt. Coptic
1 Cor. *1 Corinthians*
2 Cor. *2 Corinthians*
corr. corrected
C.S.P. Congregatio Sancti Pauli, Congregation of Saint Paul (Paulists)
d. died
D Deuteronomic (source of the Pentateuch)
Dan. Danish
D.B. Divinitatis Baccalaureus, Bachelor of Divinity
D.C. District of Columbia
D.D. Divinitatis Doctor, Doctor of Divinity
Del. Delaware
Dem. *Demaʾi*
dim. diminutive
diss. dissertation
Dn. *Daniel*
D.Phil. Doctor of Philosophy
Dt. *Deuteronomy*
Du. Dutch
E Elohist (source of the Pentateuch)
Eccl. *Ecclesiastes*
ed. editor (pl., eds.); edition; edited by
ʿEduy. *ʿEduyyot*
e.g. *exempli gratia,* for example
Egyp. Egyptian
1 En. *1 Enoch*
2 En. *2 Enoch*
3 En. *3 Enoch*
Eng. English
enl. enlarged
Eph. *Ephesians*
ʿEruv. *ʿEruvin*
1 Esd. *1 Esdras*
2 Esd. *2 Esdras*
3 Esd. *3 Esdras*
4 Esd. *4 Esdras*
esp. especially
Est. Estonian
Est. *Esther*
et al. *et alii,* and others
etc. *et cetera,* and so forth
Eth. Ethiopic
EV English version
Ex. *Exodus*
exp. expanded
Ez. *Ezekiel*
Ezr. *Ezra*
2 Ezr. *2 Ezra*
4 Ezr. *4 Ezra*
f. feminine; and following (pl., ff.)
fasc. fascicle (pl., fascs.)
fig. figure (pl., figs.)
Finn. Finnish
fl. *floruit,* flourished
Fla. Florida
Fr. French
frag. fragment
ft. feet
Ga. Georgia
Gal. *Galatians*
Gaul. Gaulish
Ger. German
Giṭ. *Giṭṭin*
Gn. *Genesis*
Gr. Greek
Ḥag. *Ḥagigah*
Ḥal. *Ḥallah*
Hau. Hausa
Hb. *Habakkuk*
Heb. Hebrew
Heb. *Hebrews*
Hg. *Haggai*
Hitt. Hittite
Hor. *Horayot*
Hos. *Hosea*
Ḥul. *Ḥullin*
Hung. Hungarian
ibid. *ibidem,* in the same place (as the one immediately preceding)
Icel. Icelandic
i.e. *id est,* that is
IE Indo-European
Ill. Illinois
Ind. Indiana
intro. introduction
Ir. Gael. Irish Gaelic
Iran. Iranian
Is. *Isaiah*
Ital. Italian
J Yahvist (source of the Pentateuch)
Jas. *James*
Jav. Javanese
Jb. *Job*
Jdt. *Judith*
Jer. *Jeremiah*
Jgs. *Judges*
Jl. *Joel*
Jn. *John*
1 Jn. *1 John*
2 Jn. *2 John*
3 Jn. *3 John*
Jon. *Jonah*
Jos. *Joshua*
Jpn. Japanese
JPS Jewish Publication Society translation (1985) of the Hebrew Bible
J.T. Jerusalem Talmud
Jub. *Jubilees*
Kans. Kansas
Kel. *Kelim*

Ker. *Keritot*
Ket. *Ketubbot*
1 Kgs. *1 Kings*
2 Kgs. *2 Kings*
Khois. Khoisan
Kil. *Kil'ayim*
km kilometers
Kor. Korean
Ky. Kentucky
l. line (pl., ll.)
La. Louisiana
Lam. *Lamentations*
Lat. Latin
Latv. Latvian
L. en Th. Licencié en Théologie, Licentiate in Theology
L. ès L. Licencié ès Lettres, Licentiate in Literature
Let. Jer. *Letter of Jeremiah*
lit. literally
Lith. Lithuanian
Lk. *Luke*
LL Late Latin
LL.D. Legum Doctor, Doctor of Laws
Lv. *Leviticus*
m meters
m. masculine
M.A. Master of Arts
Ma'as. *Ma'aserot*
Ma'as. Sh. *Ma'aser sheni*
Mak. *Makkot*
Makh. *Makhshirin*
Mal. *Malachi*
Mar. Marathi
Mass. Massachusetts
1 Mc. *1 Maccabees*
2 Mc. *2 Maccabees*
3 Mc. *3 Maccabees*
4 Mc. *4 Maccabees*
Md. Maryland
M.D. Medicinae Doctor, Doctor of Medicine
ME Middle English
Meg. *Megillah*
Me'il. *Me'ilah*
Men. *Menahot*
MHG Middle High German
mi. miles
Mi. *Micah*
Mich. Michigan
Mid. *Middot*
Minn. Minnesota
Miq. *Miqva'ot*
MIran. Middle Iranian
Miss. Mississippi
Mk. *Mark*
Mo. Missouri
Mo'ed Q. *Mo'ed qaṭan*
Mont. Montana
MPers. Middle Persian
MS. *manuscriptum,* manuscript (pl., MSS)
Mt. *Matthew*
MT Masoretic text
n. note
Na. *Nahum*
Nah. Nahuatl
Naz. *Nazir*
N.B. *nota bene,* take careful note
N.C. North Carolina
n.d. no date
N.Dak. North Dakota
NEB New English Bible
Nebr. Nebraska
Ned. *Nedarim*
Neg. *Nega'im*
Neh. *Nehemiah*
Nev. Nevada
N.H. New Hampshire
Nid. *Niddah*
N.J. New Jersey
Nm. *Numbers*
N.Mex. New Mexico
no. number (pl., nos.)
Nor. Norwegian
n.p. no place
n.s. new series
N.Y. New York
Ob. *Obadiah*
O.Cist. Ordo Cisterciencium, Order of Cîteaux (Cistercians)
OCS Old Church Slavonic
OE Old English
O.F.M. Ordo Fratrum Minorum, Order of Friars Minor (Franciscans)
OFr. Old French
Ohal. *Ohalot*
OHG Old High German
OIr. Old Irish
OIran. Old Iranian
Okla. Oklahoma
ON Old Norse
O.P. Ordo Praedicatorum, Order of Preachers (Dominicans)
OPers. Old Persian
op. cit. *opere citato,* in the work cited
OPrus. Old Prussian
Oreg. Oregon
'Orl. *'Orlah*
O.S.B. Ordo Sancti Benedicti, Order of Saint Benedict (Benedictines)
p. page (pl., pp.)
P Priestly (source of the Pentateuch)
Pa. Pennsylvania
Pahl. Pahlavi
Par. *Parah*
para. paragraph (pl., paras.)
Pers. Persian
Pes. *Pesahim*
Ph.D. Philosophiae Doctor, Doctor of Philosophy
Phil. *Philippians*
Phlm. *Philemon*
Phoen. Phoenician
pl. plural; plate (pl., pls.)
PM *post meridiem,* after noon
Pol. Polish
pop. population
Port. Portuguese
Prv. *Proverbs*
Ps. *Psalms*
Ps. 151 *Psalm 151*
Ps. Sol. *Psalms of Solomon*
pt. part (pl., pts.)
1 Pt. *1 Peter*
2 Pt. *2 Peter*
Pth. Parthian
Q hypothetical source of the synoptic Gospels
Qid. *Qiddushin*
Qin. *Qinnim*
r. reigned; ruled
Rab. *Rabbah*
rev. revised
R. ha-Sh. *Ro'sh ha-shanah*
R.I. Rhode Island
Rom. Romanian
Rom. *Romans*
R.S.C.J. Societas Sacratissimi Cordis Jesu, Religious of the Sacred Heart
RSV Revised Standard Version of the Bible
Ru. *Ruth*
Rus. Russian
Rv. *Revelation*
Rv. Ezr. *Revelation of Ezra*
San. *Sanhedrin*
S.C. South Carolina
Scot. Gael. Scottish Gaelic
S.Dak. South Dakota
sec. section (pl., secs.)
Sem. Semitic
ser. series
sg. singular
Sg. *Song of Songs*
Sg. of 3 *Prayer of Azariah and the Song of the Three Young Men*
Shab. *Shabbat*
Shav. *Shavu'ot*
Sheq. *Sheqalim*
Sib. Or. *Sibylline Oracles*
Sind. Sindhi
Sinh. Sinhala
Sir. *Ben Sira*
S.J. Societas Jesu, Society of Jesus (Jesuits)
Skt. Sanskrit
1 Sm. *1 Samuel*
2 Sm. *2 Samuel*
Sogd. Sogdian
Soṭ *Soṭah*
sp. species (pl., spp.)
Span. Spanish
sq. square
S.S.R. Soviet Socialist Republic
st. stanza (pl., ss.)
S.T.M. Sacrae Theologiae Magister, Master of Sacred Theology
Suk. *Sukkah*
Sum. Sumerian
supp. supplement; supplementary
Sus. *Susanna*
s.v. *sub verbo,* under the word (pl., s.v.v.)
Swed. Swedish
Syr. Syriac
Syr. Men. *Syriac Menander*
Ta'an. *Ta'anit*
Tam. Tamil
Tam. *Tamid*
Tb. *Tobit*
T.D. *Taishō shinshū daizōkyō,* edited by Takakusu Junjirō et al. (Tokyo, 1922–1934)
Tem. *Temurah*
Tenn. Tennessee
Ter. *Terumot*
Ṭev. Y. *Ṭevul yom*
Tex. Texas
Th.D. Theologicae Doctor, Doctor of Theology
1 Thes. *1 Thessalonians*
2 Thes. *2 Thessalonians*
Thrac. Thracian
Ti. *Titus*
Tib. Tibetan
1 Tm. *1 Timothy*
2 Tm. *2 Timothy*
T. of 12 *Testaments of the Twelve Patriarchs*
Ṭoh. *Ṭohorot*
Tong. Tongan
trans. translator, translators; translated by; translation
Turk. Turkish
Ukr. Ukrainian
Upan. *Upaniṣad*
U.S. United States
U.S.S.R. Union of Soviet Socialist Republics
Uqts. *Uqtsin*
v. verse (pl., vv.)
Va. Virginia
var. variant; variation
Viet. Vietnamese
viz. *videlicet,* namely
vol. volume (pl., vols.)
Vt. Vermont
Wash. Washington
Wel. Welsh
Wis. Wisconsin
Wis. *Wisdom of Solomon*
W.Va. West Virginia
Wyo. Wyoming
Yad. *Yadayim*
Yev. *Yevamot*
Yi. Yiddish
Yor. Yoruba
Zav. *Zavim*
Zec. *Zechariah*
Zep. *Zephaniah*
Zev. *Zevahim*

* hypothetical
? uncertain; possibly; perhaps
° degrees
\+ plus
− minus
= equals; is equivalent to
× by; multiplied by
→ yields

J

(CONTINUED)

JEREMIAH (c. 640–580 BCE), or, in Hebrew, Yirmiyah(u); biblical prophet. Jeremiah, son of Hilkiah, was born in Anathoth, some 3 miles (4.8 km) northeast of Jerusalem. The English name *Jeremiah* is based on the Greek *Hieremias* from the Septuagint and not on the received Hebrew Masoretic text. The Septuagint reflects a correct original Hebrew *Yarim-Yahu* ("Yahveh grants"), a name type whose antecedents can be traced to the third millennium BCE.

The Book of Jeremiah and the Biography of Jeremiah. Most of our knowledge about Jeremiah's life comes from the biblical *Book of Jeremiah.* The book is not arranged chronologically, with the result that contemporary scholarly reconstructions of the prophet's life are highly subjective. Important background information is found in the Hebrew scriptures, in *1 Kings, 2 Kings, 2 Chronicles, Zephaniah, Nahum, Habakkuk,* and *Obadiah.* Other important sources are the Hebrew letters from Lachish, primary documents from Egypt and Mesopotamia, and the histories of Herodotus and Josephus Flavius. However, *2 Kings,* which describes in great detail events contemporary with Jeremiah, does not mention him.

Later generations regarded Jeremiah very highly. According to the Chronicler, the prophet was the author of a lament over Josiah, king of Judah (*2 Chr.* 35:25). His prophecies about the duration of the exile were cited in *2 Chronicles* 36:15–21 and by the author of the ninth chapter of *Daniel.* Later writers composed pious fictions about Jeremiah. The apocryphal *Letter of Jeremiah,* allegedly written by Jeremiah to the Jewish exiles in Babylonia, is styled in the manner of *Jeremiah* 29. According to the second chapter of *2 Maccabees,* Jeremiah secreted the Ark and Tabernacle, a tradition based on *Jeremiah* 3:16. In the New Testament, Jeremiah is named in *Matthew* 2:17, and his vision of the "new covenant" (*Jer.* 31:31–34; cf. *Jer.* 32:38–40) is quoted in *Hebrews* 8:8–12 and 10:16–17. Jewish Talmudic tradition (B.T., *B.B.* 15a) ascribes to the prophet the authorship of *Jeremiah, Kings,* and *Lamentations* (the last probably on the basis of *2 Chronicles* 35:25).

Jeremiah was of priestly stock (*Jer.* 1:1) and probably of the Abiathar family, which had been banished to Anathoth by Solomon (c. 960) and had served at the Shiloh sanctuary before 1050. Yet there is no indication that Jeremiah ever functioned as a priest. Nonetheless, he generally had free access to the Temple and its chambers (*Jer.* 35:4). Apparently he was well off. He was able to spend seventeen shekels to buy a piece of property as a symbolic act (*Jer.* 32:9), and he was able to hire as a personal secretary one Baruch, son of Neriah, who thought the job would be lucrative and whose own brother was a high official (*Jer.* 45:2–5, 51:59). In addition, during the reigns of Jehoiakim (609–598) and Zedekiah (597–586), Jeremiah's counsel was regularly sought by the kings and their advisers. The powerful Shaphan family was particularly close to him (*Jer.* 26:24, 29:3, 36:10–12, 39:14, 40:5), and the Babylonian conquerors offered him special protection (*Jer.* 40:1–6). The high-ranking avengers of Gedaliah, son of Ahikam, sought him out as well, although they disregarded his counsel and forced him to accompany them to Egypt (*Jer.* 42). Perhaps a further indication of his affluence and influence is his relative lack of concern for the poor. Although he demanded justice for the oppressed (*Jer.* 7:6, 22:16), his denunciations of their suffering at the hands of the rich and powerful are not as frequent or as fervent as those of the prophets Amos and Isaiah. Josiah is praised as one who "ate and drank" at the same time as he dispensed justice and equity (*Jer.* 22:15). No particular class in society is singled out for condemnation (*Jer.* 5:1–5).

Among the details of his life, we hear that Jeremiah did not marry (*Jer.* 16:1–4), that he avoided social gatherings (*Jer.* 16:5–9), that he perceived himself as a man of strife and contention (*Jer.* 15:10), that he wished he had never been born (*Jer.* 20:15–17), and that his relatives had attempted to kill him (*Jer.* 10:21, 11:6), as had

Jehoiakim (*Jer.* 36:26), the audience in the Temple court (*Jer.* 26:24), and some of Zedekiah's ministers (*Jer.* 38:4–6). Sometime after 586 Jeremiah and his amanuensis were forcibly taken to Egypt, which is probably where he died.

It is difficult to treat Jeremiah's thought systematically for a number of reasons. First, Israelite prophets did not write systematic treatises. Second, the textual history of the book is very complicated. The present book is found in two major recensions, the Masoretic text and the Septuagint, which is about one-eighth shorter. In addition to the divergence in size, the recensions differ in arrangement. The Masoretic text of *Jeremiah* consists of prophecies directed to Jeremiah's own people (*Jer.* 1–25), narratives about him (*Jer.* 26–45), prophecies directed to the gentiles (*Jer.* 46–51), and a historical appendix (*Jer.* 52). The Septuagint, in contrast, places the oracles to the gentiles in the middle of the book, following chapter 25, verse 13. The Hebrew fragments of *Jeremiah* from Qumran demonstrate that in the late pre-Christian era, the Hebrew text was circulating in shorter and longer forms. It is not always certain whether the longer is an expansion or the shorter an abridgment. In both recensions, there is material that can hardly be from the hand of the prophet. For example, the prophecy against Damascus (*Jer.* 49:23–27) dates from the eighth century BCE. Other sections, such as *Jeremiah* 33:14–16 (not found in the Septuagint), are later additions. In this same category are *Jeremiah* 15:4b, which attempts to harmonize Jeremiah's theology with that of *2 Kings* by blaming the fall on Manasseh, and the injunction to keep the Sabbath (*Jer.* 18:21–27), which recalls *Nehemiah* 10:15–21. Other suspicious prophecies are the Edomite oracle (*Jer.* 49:7–16; cf. *Ob.*) and the Moabite oracle (*Jer.* 48:45–46; cf. *Nm.* 21:28–29).

Some clues to the book's composition are provided in the text itself. In each case, a religious motivation is given. According to *Jeremiah* 30:2–3, which begins the section generally known as "The Little Book of Consolation," Jeremiah was told by Yahveh: "Commit to writing all the words I have spoken to you, for days are coming when I will restore the fortunes of my people . . . and bring them back to the land." The prophecies were to be written so that later generations would know that all had been foretold. Unfortunately, no date is given for this action. The prophecies themselves contain genuine Jeremianic utterances as well as later interpolations. More specific information is provided in *Jeremiah* 36, which is dated to the fourth year of the reign of Jehoiakim, synchronized in *Jeremiah* 25:1 with 605 BCE, the first regnal year of Nebuchadrezzar II, king of Babylon (605–562). In that year Yahveh commanded Jeremiah, "Get a scroll and write in it all the words concerning Israel, Judah and all the nations that I have spoken to you, from the days of Josiah until now. Perhaps when the house of Judah hear all the terrible designs I have on them they will turn away from their wicked ways so that I might pardon their wicked sins" (*Jer.* 36:2–3). The specific reason for writing the prophecies of twenty-three years was to demonstrate to the people that they had been warned early and frequently and that there was still time to avert disaster. Though Jeremiah knew how to write (*Jer.* 32:10), he found a secretary, Baruch. By the ninth month of Jehoiakim's fifth year, at the latest (*Jer.* 36:9), the scroll was complete. It was read three times on a public fast day. First Baruch read it to a crowd at the Temple (*Jer.* 36:10) and then to a group of royal officials (*Jer.* 36:15). Finally, it was read to King Jehoiakim, who destroyed it section by section (*Jer.* 36:22–23). The scroll probably contained no more than ten thousand words.

After the destruction of the original scroll, Jeremiah purchased a second, on which Baruch rewrote the destroyed prophecies. To this scroll were added prophecies similar in content to the original ones (*Jer.* 36:32). The text gives no information about the time period in which this second edition was produced. Our present book of Jeremiah most likely had its origin in this edition.

Historical Background and the Prophet's Position. It is impossible to understand the man Jeremiah or his prophecies apart from the turbulent historical period in which he lived. When Jeremiah was born, the Assyrian empire was the single most important political power in the Middle East and, consequently, in the life of the southern kingdom of Judah. By the time Jeremiah was in his early thirties, Assyria had disappeared as a political entity, and Judah's fate had become contingent on Egypt and on the Neo-Babylonian empire and its allies. Before Jeremiah turned sixty, Judah had lost its political independence entirely, and the prophet himself had become part of the Jewish Diaspora in Egypt.

Assyrian foreign policy had been important to Judah as early as the ninth century BCE, but the fall of the closely related northern kingdom of Israel and the establishment of the Assyrian province of Samaria on Judah's northern border was momentous. Judah maintained nominal political autonomy by becoming an Assyrian vassal, an arrangement that required the regular payment of tribute and the provision of troops for Assyrian campaigns. Between 720 and 627, Judah's political policy was very much in the Assyrian shadow. King Hezekiah of Judah (715–686) had attempted a revolt in collaboration with the Babylonian king Merodachbaladan II (Marduk-apla-iddina, 721–710) and with

Egypt and various Philistine and Phoenician cities. The forces of the Assyrian king Sennacherib (704–681) quashed the rebellion, although they failed to take Jerusalem and left Hezekiah on his throne with a smaller domain and a larger tribute obligation.

If Jerusalem's deliverance appeared miraculous to some (*Is.* 37:33–38), it had a different moral for Manasseh, son and successor of Hezekiah. For most, and perhaps all, of his long reign (c. 692–639), Manasseh was a loyal Assyrian vassal. According to *2 Kings* 21:11, he was equally loyal in the service of foreign gods, outdoing everyone, the aboriginal Amorites included, in idolatry and wickedness. Some scholars have argued that Manasseh's religious and political policies were closely related, and have understood the worship of foreign gods as Assyrian vassal obligations. More recently, however, it has been noted that Assyria generally did not impose its forms of worship on its vassals. Even if we understand Manasseh's paganism as a somewhat voluntary attempt to curry favor with Assyria, we must keep in mind that the majority of the cults introduced or encouraged during his reign were not Assyrian (*2 Kgs.* 21:2–7). The bloodiness of his reign (*2 Kgs.* 21:16) surely reflects internal struggles, but we cannot tell what these concerned. Manasseh's death brought to the throne his son Amon, who was assassinated in a palace revolt of unknown motivation (*2 Kgs.* 21:23).

Amon's assassins were slain by *ʿam ha-arets* ("people of the land"), an influential body of Judahites who put on the throne his young son Josiah. The biblical books *2 Kings* (22–23) and *2 Chronicles* (34–35) have only praise for Josiah and devote much attention to his religious reforms, though each gives a different account. According to *2 Kings,* Josiah's reforms were initiated by Hilkiah's discovery of "the book of the *torah*" in the Jerusalem Temple (*2 Kgs.* 22:8). When the book, which is generally considered to be some form of *Deuteronomy,* was given by the scribe Shaphan to Josiah, the king rent his garments in contrition. In keeping with the book's message, the king centralized all sacrificial worship in the country, restricting it to Jerusalem. That same year (622 BCE), Josiah removed all traces of the foreign worship that Manasseh had encouraged. In addition, he abolished ancient rituals and institutions, which he considered antithetical to the cult of Yahveh.

In contrast, the Chronicler depicts a gradual reform in which important steps were taken in the king's eighth and twelfth years. Though chronologically more attractive, in this scheme the book is discovered in 622, by which time the major elements of the reform had been accomplished, with the exception of binding all the people of Judah by covenant to obey the book's provisions.

The wisest course is to combine elements from both our sources. The reforms must have been implemented gradually. At the same time, "the book of the *torah* [of the covenant]" must have been available at an early stage of the reform, when its reading would have had the greatest effect (cf. *Jeremiah* 36:24 with *2 Kings* 23:11). This is likely because, in the opinion of most current scholarship, the kernel of *Deuteronomy* was a northern Israelite work that had been brought to Judah after 720 BCE.

The political motivations for the Josianic reform have occasioned much debate. Some scholars have viewed the reform as a religious expression of anti-Assyrian nationalism; they have noted especially that Josiah destroyed the altar at Bethel, which was in Assyrian territory. Other scholars have remarked that neither *2 Kings* nor *2 Chronicles* imputes anti-Assyrian rebellion to Josiah, though both books describe revolts by "good" and "bad" kings of Israel and Judah (*2 Kgs.* 18:7, 24:1, 24:20; *2 Chr.* 32:10–11, 36:13). It is likely that Josiah's destruction of the Bethel altar had the motive of consolidating Davidic rule, for its original construction had been with the opposite intent (*1 Kgs.* 12:26–29, 13:2), but this could have been done with Assyrian acquiescence.

The role of Jeremiah in the Josianic reform has aroused much controversy. Some scholars depict the prophet as an early, ardent proponent of the reform who became disillusioned. At the other extreme, some scholars have revised the chronology of the prophet's life so that he begins to prophesy only after the death of Josiah in 609. If the Chronicler's chronology of the reform is accepted, then Jeremiah would have been an unlikely choice to consult about the book because of his tender age, and the prophetess Huldah a better candidate (*2 Kgs.* 22:14). It appears that sometime in the midtwenties of the seventh century, during the reign of Josiah, whom he considered a just and righteous king (*Jer.* 22:12–15), Jeremiah preached "return" (repentance) to the northerners (*Jer.* 3:6, 3:11–18; cf. 31:2–23). If so, then he must have been enthusiastic at the outset, only to be disappointed later.

It is probably correct to say that for Jeremiah, the people's return could never be sufficient. He was too much of an idealist. He considers Judah's return to Yahveh "deceitful" (*Jer.* 3:10), whereas the people complain, "I have been cleansed. Surely his anger is turned away from me. . . . Will he be angry forever? Will he rage for all time?" (*Jer.* 2:35, 3:5). The author of *2 Kings* 23 is in fundamental agreement with the people rather than with Jeremiah. According to *2 Kings,* Josiah "returned to Yahveh with all his heart and soul and might, in complete accord with the teaching of Moses" (23:25).

There is no indication that Josiah's contemporaries had not done enough or had been deceitful. Instead, the verse following says that although Josiah had repented *(shav)*, Yahveh had not repented of his anger, because of the sins of Manasseh. For the writer of *2 Kings*, Manasseh's generation was so irredeemably wicked that the following generations were doomed no matter how they acted (*2 Kgs*. 21:1–16).

Some of Jeremiah's contemporaries expressed this same pessimistic attitude in the proverb "The ancestors ate sour grapes but the children's teeth are clean" (*Jer.* 31:29; cf. *Ez.* 18:1). That is, they believed that because the ancestors ate forbidden food, their children go hungry. But Jeremiah disagrees. He believes that his contemporaries are worse because they have returned *(shavu)* to the ancestral sins after supposedly repudiating them, and thus have broken the ancient covenant that demanded Yahveh's exclusive worship (*Jer.* 11:9–10, 16:10–12). The notion that returning to sin after allegedly repenting is worse than sinning without repentance is characteristic of Jeremiah. In *Jeremiah* 34, for example, the prophet rebukes the people who had first reinstated the provision for the release of Hebrew slaves under the leadership of Zedekiah, but then turned around *(va-yashuvu)* and enslaved them a second time.

The sin of insincere repentance underlies Jeremiah's attitude toward the cult of his time. Josiah's reforms had made the Jerusalem Temple the only legitimate Yahvistic shrine in the country, so that it could truly be called "Yahveh's palace" (*Jer.* 7:4) by the people, echoing the prophecies of the eighth-century prophet Isaiah (*Is.* 2:1–4, 31:4–5, 37:32–35). In contrast, Jeremiah taught, as had others (*Jer.* 26:18–20), that the Temple was not inviolable, nor was it any more permanent than the anciently destroyed Shiloh sanctuary (*Jer.* 7:14). Probably at the same time, he made the statement, "Add your whole burnt offerings to your other sacrifices and eat the meat. For when I brought your ancestors out of Egypt I did not speak with them to command them about burnt offerings and sacrifices. This rather is what I commanded them: Hearken to my voice so that I can be your God and you can be my people" (*Jer.* 7:21–22).

It would be inaccurate to say that Jeremiah advocated a cultless religion. He did not disagree that the Temple is God's place. Indeed, if the people mend their ways, then Yahveh will dwell with them in the Jerusalem Temple (*Jer.* 7:3, 7:7). But, for a number of reasons, the people's offerings are not "pleasing" (*Jer.* 6:20); the word used, *leratson,* is a technical term for an acceptable sacrifice (see also *Leviticus* 1:3, 19:5, 22:29; *Isaiah* 56:7). Most important, the popular view had it that other gods might be worshiped by Israelites as long as their worship of Yahveh was in purity. As Jeremiah says in his indictment, "Will you steal and murder and commit adultery and swear falsely and sacrifice to Baal and follow other gods with whom you have no [rightful] relation and then come and stand before me in this house which is called by my name and say 'we are saved' and then continue to commit all these abominations?" (*Jer.* 7:9–10).

It is clear that the people believed the cult could purify them of all their sins. If such violations as theft, murder, adultery, and false oaths could succumb to purificatory rituals, why could not the worship of foreign gods? In fact, such temporary rejection of foreign gods is ascribed to Jacob (*Gn.* 35:4) and to Joshua (*Jos.* 24). According to *Leviticus* 16:30, the priesthood claimed that its atonement rituals could remove all impurity caused by sin. (A priesthood could hardly claim otherwise.) Jeremiah did not accept this view because he saw it as insincere. In his eyes, Israel had been faithful to Yahveh only in the wilderness (*Jer.* 2:1). The people strayed as soon as they entered the promised land and so profaned it (*Jer.* 2:8, 3:2). Borrowing an image from Hosea, Jeremiah depicts the people of Judah as a faithless wife who had pretended to mend her ways (*Jer.* 3:1ff.). She knows that Yahveh has divorced the northern kingdom of Israel for infidelity (*Jer.* 3:8), but her heart is still uncircumcised (*Jer.* 4:4, 9:25). The entire people is guilty, for none has practiced true repentance—neither priests, teachers, kings, nor prophets (*Jer.* 2:8, 21:11–23:5, 23:9–40, 27–29). Jeremiah's mission is to bring the people to true repentance (*Jer.* 3:14, 3:22, 4:1). If he fails, then destruction of the land is inevitable, and even the gentiles will know the cause (*Jer.* 22:8–9; cf. *Dt.* 29:21–29, *1 Kgs.* 9:8–9).

Compared with sincere repentance, the obligations of the cult are secondary. Inasmuch as Jeremiah agrees with Amos that there was no organized sacrificial cult in Israel's forty-year wandering in the desert (*Am.* 5:25), the covenant between Yahveh and his people could not have been made through the cult. Conversely, the cult must be insufficient to sustain the bond.

In the tradition of those prophets who influenced him, notably Hosea, the political events of his time were to Jeremiah an indication of Yahveh's disfavor. In his early prophecies, Yahveh's judgment was described as being through the agency of an unnamed northern foe. The kings of the north would come "and set their thrones at Jerusalem's gates," where Yahveh would pronounce sentence against Judah for serving other gods (*Jer.* 1:14–16). It does not seem that Jeremiah actually identified the northern foe as Babylon until the Babylonian victory over the Egyptians at Carchemish in Syria in 605 (cf. *Jer.* 36:29). It is also likely that the description of the Babylonian officers sitting in the gate in Jerusalem (*Jer.* 39:3) is a "fulfillment" of the early prophecy.

At first Jeremiah teaches that Yahveh's punishment of the people at the hands of their foes can be averted by true repentance. The death of Josiah and the accession of Jehoiakim to the throne mark a turning point. Jeremiah does not accuse Jehoiakim of the worship of foreign gods but of social abuses. The king was unjustly impressing laborers into service so that he could build himself a lavish palace. He was shedding innocent blood and perpetrating fraud and violence (*Jer.* 22:13–17). In consequence, predicted Jeremiah, perhaps inaccurately (*2 Kgs.* 24:6), Jehoiakim would have a donkey's funeral rather than a king's.

During Jehoiakim's reign, Jeremiah first began to commit his prophecies to writing in order to bring the people to repentance. Baruch was sent to read the scroll publicly in the Temple on a fast day (*Jer.* 36:9). The reading did not have the desired effect: Jehoiakim destroyed the scroll and attempted to kill Jeremiah and Baruch (*Jer.* 36:26) just as he had slain Uriah, who preached a similar message (*Jer.* 26:23). The writer of *Jeremiah* 36 remarks pointedly that Jehoiakim and his courtiers "showed no fear and did not tear their garments," in order to contrast Jehoiakim with his pious father, Josiah, who had torn his garments upon hearing Yahveh's word from a book (*2 Kgs.* 22:11, 22:19). Jehoiakim's unjust behavior, coupled with the rise of Babylon, was proof enough to Jeremiah that the required change of heart had not taken place, that Jehoiakim was not the man to bring it about, and that Yahveh would use Babylon to punish Judah, just as he had used Assyria to punish northern Israel.

In consequence, Jeremiah began to preach submission to Babylonia as Yahveh's will. This was particularly offensive to Jehoiakim, who had rebelled against Nebuchadrezzar II after three years of vassalage (*2 Kgs.* 23:26). The counsel of submission of Babylonia intensified after the death of Jehoiakim, in 597. Jehoiakin, Jehoiakim's son and successor, was deposed after three months, following a siege of Jerusalem. He and many other Judahites were deported. Jeremiah thought little of Jehoiakin and predicted that he would die in exile (*Jer.* 22:24–30).

In the reign of Zedekiah, the last king to occupy the throne of Judah, Jeremiah articulated Yahveh's plan. Yahveh had given all the lands over to Nebuchadrezzar and would punish those people who would not submit to Babylonian rule. Nebuchadrezzar was Yahveh's servant (*Jer.* 27:6) whose rule had been ordained for three generations (*Jer.* 27:7), or seventy years (*Jer.* 25:11). Those people who submitted to Nebuchadrezzar and, consequently, to Yahveh's word would be permitted by Yahveh to remain on their own land, while those who resisted would be exiled (*Jer.* 27:10–11). For Jeremiah, people like the Yahveh prophet Hananiah, son of Azzur, who preached the speedy return of Jeconiah, son of Jehoiakim, and the Temple vessels (*Jer.* 28:3–4) and who counseled rebellion were no better than the pagan diviners who offered the same message (*Jer.* 27:9, 27:15). Just as false were those prophets from Judah in Babylonia who taught that the exile would be short (*Jer.* 29:8–9). Yahveh had not sent them. The exiled Judahites should consider themselves "good figs" and should do Yahveh's will by building homes and families in Babylonia (*Jer.* 24:5, 29:4–7). Those people of Judah who had not been captured and exiled in 597 and who continued to resist Nebuchadrezzar were "bad figs." Flight to Egypt in order to escape Babylonian rule was just as bad, as far as Jeremiah was concerned (*Jer.* 24:8, 42:10–16). Yahveh himself had turned against Judah (*Jer.* 21:4–8). This meant that the "way of life" was surrender and the "way of death" was resistance (*Jer.* 21:8–10). Jeremiah's insistence on surrender landed him in the stocks (*Jer.* 20:1–6), caused him to be accused of treason and subversion, and nearly cost him his life (*Jer.* 38:3–6).

Pessimism and Hope in Jeremiah. The *Book of Jeremiah* provides more information about its subject's inner life than does any other biblical book. Even if some elements, such as the disinclination to prophecy, are felt elsewhere, they are more articulate in *Jeremiah*. Jeremiah does not want to prophesy (*Jer.* 1:6), but he cannot contain himself with Yahveh's anger (*Jer.* 6:11, 20:9). Though a prophet is normally supposed to intercede (*Gn.* 20:7, 20:17), Jeremiah is told not to (*Jer.* 7:16, 15:1). At least once, Yahveh was about to remove him from his prophetic office (*Jer.* 15:19). In Jeremiah's eyes, Yahveh seduced and even raped him (*Jer.* 20:7). Jeremiah prayed for the death of his relatives (*Jer.* 12:3) and cursed the day of his own birth (*Jer.* 20:15–18). He depicted himself as a man of strife and contention (*Jer.* 15:10) who lacked the comfort of family and social gatherings (*Jer.* 16:1–13). Yahveh's word has been, he says ironically, his joyful wedding tune (*Jer.* 15:16).

Yet the moroseness of the man and the generally pessimistic tone of his prophecy give us only one side of his personality. For at least twenty-three years, he believed that Yahveh might avert disaster if the people would repent. Even afterward, he prophesied hope. Perhaps the most optimistic of his prophecies is that of the *berit ḥadashah* (new covenant or testament), which must be understood in terms of the sixth century BCE.

According to the authors of the Pentateuch, especially *Deuteronomy*, Yahveh and Israel were joined by covenant, or treaty. Yahveh had taken Israel as his people, and they had accepted him as their god and had assumed the obligation to worship him alone. Violation of the covenant would bring all manner of curses on the people (*Dt.* 28; cf. *Jer.* 11). Modern research has shown that the covenant form employed by *Jeremiah* and *Deuteronomy* is based on ancient Near Eastern political documents whereby a minor king becomes a vassal of a greater one. In such treaties, the suzerain promises land and protection to the vassal in return for the vassal's exclusive and undivided loyalty. The biblical religious covenants conceive of Israel as the vassal of Yahveh, who is, therefore, entitled to exclusive worship. Israel was entitled to remain on the land given it by Yahveh only as long as it served Yahveh alone (*Jer.* 11:5). Jeremiah was certain that his people had broken their covenant with Yahveh by following other gods (*Jer.* 11:10) and were therefore doomed to suffer the expected consequences. In *Jeremiah* 31, however, inspired by Hosea's teaching, the prophet arrives at a new idea.

Hosea speaks of Israel as a faithless wife who was to be cast out and divorced. But Yahveh realized that her inability to be faithful was inherent in her constitutional lack of the qualities of justice, equity, loyalty, compassion, and steadfastness. Yahveh would remarry Israel and would give her these qualities as betrothal gifts so that she would be able to be truly intimate with Yahveh (*Hos.* 2:18–21). He would even make it inherently impossible for her to pronounce the name *Baal.*

Jeremiah follows the same line of thinking, but he employs a political rather than a marital metaphor:

> In days to come I will make a new covenant with the house of Israel and the house of Judah. It will not be like the covenant which I made with their ancestors . . . a covenant which they broke, so I rejected them. . . . I will put my teaching inside of them and inscribe it upon their hearts. Then I will be their god and they will be my people. No longer will they need to teach one another "heed Yahveh," for all of them . . . shall heed me. (*Jer.* 31:31–34)

A similar notion is found in *Jeremiah* 32:38–41: "They shall be my people and I will be their god. I will give them an undivided heart and nature to revere me for all time. I will make an everlasting covenant with them and put reverence for me in their hearts so that they cannot turn away from me. . . . Then I will plant them permanently in this land."

The new covenant is necessary because Israel and Judah lacked the innate ability to keep the old one. Yahveh's recognition of the deficiency of his people inspires him to remedy it by a change of their nature. Once Yahveh has effected the change, his people will be able to keep his covenant and remain permanently on his land.

The new covenant itself was designed for the salvation of Israel and Judah. Yet its implications that a radical change of human nature is possible became universal. In a great irony of religious history, the words of the prophet who spent much of his career prophesying doom became to his direct and indirect descendants a legacy of hope.

BIBLIOGRAPHY

Bright, John, trans. and ed. *Jeremiah.* Anchor Bible, vol. 21. Garden City, N.Y., 1965. A readable translation with commentary, notes, historical introduction, and bibliography. A scholarly work but accessible to the nonspecialist.

Childs, Brevard S. *Introduction to the Old Testament as Scripture.* Philadelphia, 1979. Excellent bibliography and a succinct treatment of Jeremiah from the viewpoint of canon criticism.

Cogan, Morton. *Imperialism and Religion: Assyria, Judah and Israel in the Eighth and Seventh Centuries B.C.E.* Missoula, Mont., 1974. An examination of primary Assyrian sources to determine religious policy in Assyrian provinces and vassal states.

Ehrlich, Arnold B. *Miqra' ki-feshuṭo.* 3 vols. Berlin, 1899–1901. An excellent and erratic philological commentary.

Fohrer, Georg. *History of Israelite Religion.* Translated by David E. Green. Nashville, 1972.

Ginsberg, H. L. "Hosea, Book of." In *Encyclopaedia Judaica.* Jerusalem, 1971. An extremely important account of the background of northern Israelite prophetic thought and of Hosea's influence on *Deuteronomy.*

Kaufmann, Yeḥezkel. *The Religion of Israel, from Its Beginnings to the Babylonian Exile.* Translated and abridged by Moshe Greenberg. Chicago, 1960. An attempt to demonstrate that there was no great gap between prophetic and popular religion. Kaufmann argues that prophetic polemics against idolatry are mostly rhetorical exaggerations by idealists.

Nelson, Richard. "Realpolitik in Judah, 687–609 B.C.E." In *Scripture in Context,* edited by William W. Hallo, James C. Moyer, and Leo G. Perdue, vol. 2, pp. 177–189. Winona Lake, Ind., 1982. A critique of the theory that Josiah's religious policies were part of his anti-Assyrian nationalism.

Rowley, H. H. "The Prophet Jeremiah and the Book of Deuteronomy." In his *From Moses to Qumran,* chap. 6. London, 1963. A good summary of the problems involved in the relation between the prophet and the book. Good bibliography to 1950.

Soden, Wolfram von. *Akkadisches Handwörterbuch,* vol. 2. Wiesbaden, 1972. See the index, s.v. *rimu(m).*

S. David Sperling

JEREMIAS II (1530 or 1535–1595), Greek prelate, scholar, and patriarch of Constantinople. Jeremias II was born in the ancient city of Anchialus, Thrace (present-day Pomorie, Bulgaria), on the Black Sea; he was a descendant of the important Tranos family. Since there were no organized Greek schools in the Turk-dominated area, Jeremias was privately educated. In 1565 he was elected metropolitan of Larissa, and in 1572 he became patriarch of Constantinople at an uncommonly early age. As a result of the policy of the Ottoman rulers of changing patriarchs, Jeremias was deposed twice, in 1579 and again in 1584, but he was restored to his post by popular demand. He was patriarch from 1572–1579, 1580–1584, and from 1586 until his death in 1595.

While Jeremias was patriarch, he raised the standards of ecclesiastical and cultural life, both of which were at extremely low levels. He condemned simony among the clergy, and he undertook to restore the former austerity of the monastic life by abolishing the idiorrhythmic monasteries and strengthening the more centralized cenobitic life. He also forbade the establishment of monastic houses in secular environments without prior ecclesiastical consent. The authority of the patriarchate itself was strengthened as a result of his frequent visits to other Orthodox churches. At the insistence of Tsar Feodor I Ivanovich (r. 1584–1598), Jeremias raised the Russian church to the status of patriarchate, placing it in fifth place in the pentarchy after Jerusalem.

Jeremias would not accept the calendar sought by Pope Gregory XIII and suggested that the Orthodox church in the West should also follow the old calendar. For the Orthodox living in Italy, he transferred the see of Philadelphia to Venice, and Gabriel Severus, the scholar, was appointed the first metropolitan. Jeremias's reaction to the establishment of Western schools for proselytism during the period of Turkish occupation was to advise his bishops to establish Greek schools in their territories. He thereby made a contribution to the development of education.

Jeremias is, for the most part, remembered for his contacts and theological dialogues with the Protestant theologians of Tübingen. The Lutherans and the Greek Orthodox sought support in their disagreements with the church of Rome and therefore turned to one another for assistance. In 1573, two professors from Tübingen, Martin Crusius and Jakob Andreä, sent a copy of the Augsburg Confession (1531) to Jeremias. In his correspondence with the Lutheran theologians, Jeremias pointed out the serious differences in dogma that precluded any union of the Protestant and Orthodox churches. This correspondence went on for some time, and it was published as *The Three Dogmatic Answers to the Theologians of Tübingen*. In his various other works, Jeremias presented Orthodoxy as a continuation of the ancient catholic church, stressing, in particular, faithfulness and adherence to the original traditions of the church and avoidance of new doctrines and practices. Although his dialogues with the Lutheran theologians eventually deteriorated, Jeremias began the dialogues in a climate of love and friendship, and thus they became the forerunner of today's ecumenical dialogues.

BIBLIOGRAPHY

No English work on Jeremias II is readily available. Readers of Greek may consult Iōannēs N. Karmirēs' *Ta dogmatika kai sumbolika mnēmeia tēs Orthodoxou Katholikēs Ekklēsias*, vol. 1 (Athens, 1960), pp. 437–503. German readers are directed to *Wort und Mysterium: Der Briefwechsel über Glauben und Kirche, 1573 bis 1581 zwischen den Tübinger Theologen und dem Patriarchen von Konstantinopel* (Witten, 1958).

THEODORE ZISSIS

Translated from Greek by Philip M. McGhee

JEROME (c. 347–420), properly Eusebius Hieronymus; church father and biblical scholar. Born at Stridon in Dalmatia (present-day Yugoslavia) of a prosperous Christian family, Jerome was educated at Rome under Aelius Donatus, the most eminent grammarian of the fourth century. With Donatus he studied the principal Latin authors, of whom Cicero and Vergil exerted a lasting influence on him. His rhetorical training included the rudiments of philosophy, which held little interest for him, except for dialectics. Rhetoric and dialectics became the tools of his polemics. While in Rome he enjoyed those youthful indiscretions that he would later bitterly lament as immorality. Jerome was nevertheless baptized, perhaps in the year 366.

In his twentieth year Jerome continued his studies at Trier, where the ideal of monasticism took hold of him forever. In 374 he made a pilgrimage to Antioch in Syria, where he mastered Greek and began in earnest his lifelong study of the Bible. Recovery from a serious illness strengthened his resolve to become an anchorite in the nearby desert of Chalcis. While practicing asceticism, he learned Hebrew so that he could read the Old Testament without recourse to the Septuagint. Suspected of religious heterodoxy, he returned to Antioch in 378.

Ordained a priest at Antioch, Jerome was introduced to biblical exegesis by Apollinaris of Laodicea. Around the year 381 Jerome traveled to Constantinople, where he met the theologians Gregory of Nazianzus and Gregory of Nyssa and began his translations of Origen's works on the Bible. Origen was both Jerome's blessing and his bane. From Origen, Jerome derived substantially his own approach to biblical exegesis, but later he was often suspected of sharing Origen's heretical views.

In 382 Jerome returned to Rome and soon became secretary to Pope Damasus, who set him to revising the Old Latin versions of the New Testament. Jerome left

Rome for the East in 389, soon to be joined by Paula and Eustochium, two religious Roman women. Together they established two monasteries at Bethlehem. Thereafter, Jerome lived the ascetic life of a monk and continued his study of the Bible. During these years there poured from his pen a river of Latin translations of the Bible from the Greek and Hebrew, translations of Origen's works on the Bible and commentaries of his own, polemical works, and letters to people throughout the Roman world. Although Jerome befriended Augustine of Hippo and the historian Paulus Orosius, he scorned Ambrose of Milan and hounded John Chrysostom. He died in 420. An obstinate monk, Jerome was combative, vindictive, and cantankerous. Nonetheless, as a biblical scholar he was the most learned of church fathers.

Jerome's voluminous writings fall into four broad groups: translations and studies of the Bible, polemics, historical works, and letters. By far the most important category deals with scripture, his towering achievement being his Latin translation of the Bible. Known as the Vulgate, it became the authorized version of the Bible in the Latin church. For the New Testament, Jerome corrected the Old Latin versions of the Gospels in the light of earlier Greek manuscripts. His work on the Old Testament took a more complicated course. He began by relying on the Septuagint, but the more familiar he became with Hebrew the more determined he was to base his translations on the Hebrew text. The result was a far more accurate version of the Old Testament than anything theretofore available in Latin.

Translation was only part of Jerome's biblical interests. In his quest to determine and understand the text, he wrote sixty-three volumes of commentaries and some one hundred homilies primarily concerned with explaining the Bible to the religious community at Bethlehem. Some of Jerome's commentaries are little more than Latin translations of Origen's Greek originals. In the areas of exegesis and homiletics, Jerome was influenced primarily by Apollinaris, Origen, and rabbinical thought, including the work of Akiva ben Joseph, one of the founders of rabbinical Judaism. From Apollinaris, Jerome learned the value of historical commentary and concrete interpretation of the Bible. Jewish exegesis also emphasized the literal sense of the Old Testament. In addition, his Hebrew teachers acquainted Jerome with Jewish oral traditions, a source unknown to most of his Christian contemporaries. Increasingly, Jerome respected the Hebrew text of the Old Testament, in his words, the *veritas Hebraica,* which ultimately led him to doubt the accuracy of the Septuagint. Origen influenced Jerome to go beyond literal and historical interpretation of scripture to discover its allegorical and symbolic meaning. Although Jerome often criticized Origen's approach, he too felt that under the literal text lay a level of deeper spiritual meaning.

Intellectually eclectic, Jerome used all three approaches to biblical exegesis. His usual method of exposition consisted of a literal explanation of every verse, including citations of variant readings and interpretations, frequently followed by an allegorical interpretation. For the Old Testament, he translated passages from Hebrew and from the Septuagint before commenting on them in turn. His treatment of the Hebrew text was generally historical and included discussion of Hebrew words, names, and grammar. Despite his high regard for rabbinical exegesis, Jerome never preferred it to orthodox Christian interpretation. The Septuagint was also often subjected to spiritual exegesis. Here especially Jerome relied heavily on Origen, whom he defended as a learned and gifted biblical scholar. Nonetheless, he often attacked Origen and steadfastly rejected his theology and dogmas. Origen's influence can be seen further in Jerome's tendency to give his own, original spiritual interpretation of the Septuagint.

The second major category of Jerome's writings is polemics. His early studies in Rome made their contribution in this area as well. The training in rhetoric and dialectics equipped him for controversy, and his mastery of Latin prose style gave him a clear, sometimes elegant, means of expression. Moreover, the young student had frequented the law courts and had enjoyed listening to the violent verbal exchanges of eminent lawyers. In addition to his well-turned Latin phrases, Jerome employed caustic and even disreputable abuse, his opponents generally being branded fools, charlatans, heretics, or all three. He was particularly adept at disparaging his opponents' literary style, which was all the more effective because he of all the church fathers wrote a Latin that was almost classically pure. These tools were valuable because Jerome was unimpressive as a theologian and a philosopher. His contribution was as a scholar, not as an original thinker.

Jerome employed his polemical works either to combat current heresies or to defend himself from the charge of heresy. His rebuttals often provide the best information about the nature of his opponents' views. Jerome unswervingly upheld the cause of orthodoxy. He entered the field of controversy in 378–379 with his *Altercatio Luciferiani et Orthodoxi* (Debate of a Luciferian and an Orthodox), in which he attacked the views of the Sardinian bishop Lucifer. Using the orthodox believer as a soundingboard for his own views, Jerome argued in favor of Arian bishops' retaining their clerical positions upon recantation and defended the validity of Arian baptism. Chief among Jerome's religious views are his abiding faith in the Christian church and its apostolic authority, and his opposition to heresy as destructive to Christian unity. He never wavered from these beliefs.

In 383 Jerome combated the views of the Roman layman Helvidius, who denied the virginity of Mary after the birth of Jesus and who argued that the married and celibate states were equal in dignity. In *Adversus Helvidium,* a spirited pamphlet, Jerome used exegetical and scholarly arguments, along with his usual verbal abuse, to defend the perpetual virginity of Mary and to exalt the value of celibacy in Christian life. Jerome's triumph over Helvidius helped to establish the orthodox views of the Latin church on Mariology and celibacy. Next, in *Adversus Iovinianum* (Against Jovinian), written in 393, Jerome marshaled all his skills in exegesis, dialectics, rhetoric, satire, and obloquy to defend again the doctrines of Mary's virginity, the virgin birth of Jesus, the superiority of celibacy over marriage, and the advocacy of asceticism. In 404 Jerome wrote *Contra Vigilantium* (Against Vigilantius), a response to the polemics of Vigilantius, a priest from Aquitaine. In this controversy, Jerome defended devotion to the relics of martyrs and saints and the offering of prayers to them, and he endorsed all-night vigils at their shrines as acts of piety. He also again championed the ascetic way of life, including celibacy, monasticism, and fasting, and he approved sending alms to monasteries in Jerusalem as Paul had urged.

In two polemical works Jerome defended himself against the charge of sharing Origen's heresy, first in 397 with his *Contra Ioannem Hierosolymitanum* (Against John of Jerusalem) and again in 401, when his old friend Rufinus of Aquileia openly accused him of being a follower of Origen. In effect, Rufinus attacked Jerome's whole approach to the Bible. Jerome's response, *Apologia adversus Rufinum* (Apology against Rufinus), was a terrible counterattack, violent, satirical, scurrilous, and learned. Jerome successfully defended his life's work, including his use and translations of Origen's commentaries, his reliance on the Hebrew original of the Old Testament, and his respect for the Septuagint. Not denying his debt to Origen's learning, Jerome steadfastly denied sharing Origen's theology.

Jerome's last polemical work, *Dialogus adversus Pelagianos* (Dialogue against a Pelagian), written in 415, attacked the tenets of the Pelagian heresy, which was primarily concerned with the concepts of sin and grace. Against the Pelagian position that people can live free of sin, Jerome countered that humans constantly need divine help. He further insisted that humanity is given to sin, despite its possession of free will. Jerome also defended Augustine's concept of original sin and accepted the need for infant baptism. *Against a Pelagian* exhibits the hallmarks common to the rest of Jerome's polemical works: personal abuse, biblical scholarship, and orthodoxy.

The last two categories of Jerome's work are more historical than religious in importance. Jerome either translated or wrote several historical treatises valuable for his study of the Bible. The first, published in 382, was his translation of Eusebius of Caesarea's *Chronikoi kanones* (Chronological Canons), an annalistically arranged work that combined biblical and Near Eastern chronology with Greco-Roman chronology. Jerome added to its contents and continued its coverage to his own times, ending with the Battle of Adrianople in 378. *Chronicle* became the historical framework of his exegetical studies. In wider terms, Jerome's *Chronicle* became the standard authority in western Europe for the chronology of the ancient world.

In 392–393 Jerome published *De viris illustribus* (On Famous Men), a historical catalog of Christian literature in which he surveyed the lives and writings of 135 authors, overwhelmingly Christian with a sprinkling of Jewish authors, beginning with the apostle Peter and ending with himself. Although he relied heavily on Eusebius for the early part, and although he inserted authors whom he had never read, in the later part he contributed much information derived from his own reading. The work was continued by others into the fifteenth century.

For religious purposes, a trilogy of biblical studies is Jerome's most significant historical work. Between 389 and 391 Jerome produced his *Onomastikon* (Hebrew Names), derived from Origen. *Hebrew Names* is an etymological dictionary of proper names in the Bible, alphabetically arranged. Next came his *Liber locorum* (Book of Places), a translation of Eusebius's *Onomastikon,* with meager additions drawn from his own knowledge of Palestine. The *Book of Places* is an alphabetical listing of the place names and descriptions of the geographical features of the sites mentioned in the Bible. Last came his *Liber hebraicarum quaestionum* (Hebrew Questions), a discussion of various problems in the text of the *Book of Genesis,* heavily dependent on rabbinical exegesis. The treatment is essentially linguistic, historical, and geographical. Rounding out Jerome's historical work are hagiographies of Paul, Malchus, and Hilarion.

Jerome's 154 letters also illuminate the religious climate of the time. In his correspondence, Jerome discussed prominent church leaders, satirized the Christian clergy, discussed the burning religious issues of the day, and provided much information about himself and his intellectual development. All his written work influenced the subsequent course of the Latin church. His greatest contribution can be put simply: when later generations read the Vulgate, they read the translation of Jerome and reaped the finest fruits of his superb scholarship.

BIBLIOGRAPHY

J. N. D. Kelly's *Jerome: His Life, Writings, and Controversies* (London, 1975) is easily the best treatment of Jerome's career. It is firmly based in the sources, and its approach is consistently sane. Philip Rousseau's *Ascetics, Authority, and the Church in the Age of Jerome and Cassian* (Oxford, 1978) is a much broader study of the religious and intellectual climate of the time. An excellent study of Jerome's polemics can be found in Ilona Opelt's *Hieronymus' Streitschriften* (Heidelberg, 1973), an exhaustive analysis of this genre. David S. Wiesen's *Saint Jerome as a Satirist* (Ithaca, N.Y., 1964) concentrates on one of the most salient aspects of Jerome's polemics and correspondence. Similarly, Harald Hagendahl's *Latin Fathers and the Classics* (Göteborg, 1958) devotes part 2, the heart of his book, to Jerome's use of classical writers. Francis X. Murphy, in *A Monument to Saint Jerome: Essays on Some Aspects of His Life, Works, and Influence* (New York, 1952), has assembled ten essays that discuss Jerome both as a religious figure and as an intellectual figure. The quality of the essays, however, is quite uneven.

JOHN BUCKLER

JERUSALEM, an old Canaanite settlement in the uplands of Judaea, enters history rather offhandedly in the biblical narrative: David, king of Israel, then resident at nearby Hebron, decides to make this Jebusite city his capital. No reason is given—even today the site has obvious security advantages—and indeed Jerusalem shows no particular religious associations until David buys a Jebusite threshing floor atop Mount Moriah just north of his new "City of David" and builds an altar there, where the Lord had stayed the hand of his avenging angel. This spot may have been an earlier Canaanite high place, but it now became the site of a grandiose temple possibly planned by David and certainly built by his son Solomon.

The Temple of Solomon was an enormous structure with interior courtyards of progressively limited access, in the midst of which stood an ornately adorned sanctuary. Outside it stood the great altar of sacrifice, and within, in a curtained inner chamber, the Holy of Holies, was installed the Ark of the Covenant containing the Tablets of the Law and other tokens of the Israelites' deliverance from Egypt and sojourn in the wilderness of Sinai. And there too were reinstituted all the cultic acts commanded to Moses on Sinai, the daily sacrifices, the feasts of the New Moon and the New Year, the Day of Atonement, and the three great pilgrimage feasts of Passover, Shavu'ot (Weeks), and Sukkot (Tabernacles), all performed and managed by a body of Aaronite priests and ministering Levites.

There is no sign of this building today, since it was destroyed by the Babylonians in 587/6 BCE. Solomon's son Rehoboam could not maintain his father's empire intact, and the schism between the northern kingdom of Israel, with its own priests and shrines and its own rival temple atop Mount Gerizim in Samaria, and the southern kingdom of Judah, ruled from Jerusalem, persisted down to the fall of Samaria to the Assyrians in 721 BCE. Although the days of Judah were likewise numbered, the southern kingdom sustained itself under royal saints (e.g., Hezekiah) and royal sinners (e.g., Manasseh) long enough for the reformer king Josiah to centralize all Israelite cult practices in Jerusalem. This was in 621 BCE, and thereafter Jerusalem had few political rivals and no religious peers; for Jews, whether in Palestine or abroad, in what was known as the Diaspora, the Temple in Jerusalem was the unique site of Jewish sacrificial worship of God, and the divine presence dwelt there in a special way. [*See* Biblical Temple.]

The Babylonians, then, took Jerusalem in 587/6 BCE, razed the Temple, and carried off many of the Jews into exile. And it is likely that at that time the Ark of the Covenant disappeared as part of the spoils; the Holy of Holies of later versions of the Jerusalem Temple was, at any rate, empty. Sometime after 538 BCE the Persian shah Cyrus II and his Achaemenid successors allowed the exiled Jews to return to Jerusalem. The city was rebuilt by Nehemiah, the Mosaic Law was repromulgated through the efforts of the priestly scribe Ezra, and under the auspices of Zerubbabel a reduced version of Solomon's Temple was constructed on the same site. The priesthoods were purified and God's cult restored. Jerusalem itself was rewalled and resettled and began to resume the growth that was already notable in the eighth century BCE. In the wake of Alexander the Great, Greeks succeeded to Persians in the late fourth century in Palestine, and after 200 BCE the Greco-Macedonian dynasty of the Seleucids ruled over what was a politically modest temple-state at Jerusalem.

The political straitening of Jerusalem was accompanied by an equally notable broadening of the religious character of the city. The chastening of the Israelites before, during, and immediately after their Babylonian exile produced a new type of religious leader in their midst, the prophet, and in their inspired visions Jerusalem became the symbol of and indeed identical with the Children of Israel and the Land of Israel, now cast down for its idolatry and fornication, now exalted, renewed, and glorified in the new age that would follow the present travails. Thus the historical Jerusalem, which often lay in ruin and misery, was transformed by Isaiah and Ezekiel, among others, into a heavenly and eschatological Jerusalem, a city whose holiness transcended the mere presence of the Temple but was rather coterminous with the glory of the Chosen People and served as a pledge of the presence of God.

The historical Jerusalem revived under Greek sovereignty, and a newly affluent upper class, including many priestly families, eased the way for the introduction there of the ideals and institutions of Hellenism. Under Antiochus IV Epiphanes (r. 175–164 BCE), the hellenized Jews in Jerusalem requested and were granted permission by their sovereign to convert the city into a polis, a genuine Greek-style city. Subsequently, Antiochus and a significant number of Jews grew disenchanted with this Jerusalem experiment in cultural and political Hellenism, Antiochus because he scented treachery in the city, and Jewish pietists because they correctly perceived that Hellenism brought more than paved streets and gymnasiums; they saw that it was heavily freighted with spiritual values that constituted an attractive alternative and so a grave threat to Mosaic Judaism. The king instituted a full-scale attack on Judaism in Judaea and installed a Macedonian garrison and foreign cults in the Temple precinct. The outraged Jews mounted a bold resistance, and under the priestly family called the Maccabees they eventually drove most of the Greeks from Judaea and Jerusalem and in 164 BCE rededicated the Temple there to the cult of the Lord.

The Hasmonean dynasty survived until 37 BCE, when its own weaknesses permitted, and Roman choice dictated, the passage of power to the Idumaean Herod I (r. 37–34 BCE). Jerusalem was still growing—it now covered the western hill as well as the eastern hill where Solomon's Temple and the City of David had been located—and Hasmonean kingship had done nothing to inhibit its assimilation to a Hellenic-style settlement with notable public buildings and a regular street plan. The prodigious building activity of Herod increased the tempo of Greco-Roman urbanization. He extended the street plan, built an immense citadel at the western gate of the city, erected his own palace nearby, and sought to crown his labors by undertaking in 20 BCE a reconstruction of the Temple. This mammoth Herodian temple complex, with its newly extended platform, not only doubled the size of Solomon's installation, it dwarfed every known temple assemblage in the Greco-Roman Near East. Today only the platform and some of its gates are extant, having survived the Roman destruction of 70 CE. For Jews, the Western Wall, a retaining wall of the platform, has been a potent symbol of Jewish historical continuity since Talmudic times. [*See* Pilgrimage, *article on* Contemporary Jewish Pilgrimage.] The platform itself has been venerated by Muslims as the Ḥaram al-Sharīf, the Holy Sanctuary, since the late seventh century.

Jewish sovereignty over Jerusalem did not last very long; the Romans by contrast held the city, although they never ruled from it, for six and a half centuries, and different Muslim dynasties, who likewise preferred to put their palaces elsewhere, held sway over Jerusalem from the mid-seventh to the early twentieth century. But however brief the span, Jewish kings ruled over a Jewish state *in* Jerusalem; Roman governors, some pagan, some Christian, ruled *over* Jerusalem; and for a very long time the city was a part, often not a very important part, of some form or other of a Muslim political organization, although never its capital. Nor was it under any circumstances the capital of "the Christian people" or "the Muslim people" simply because there never were such.

Jesus was born under Herodian and died under Roman sovereignty. Although at home in Galilee, he taught, performed miracles, died, and was buried in Herodian Jerusalem. He worshiped in Herod's Temple, with which he identified himself and whose destruction he openly predicted. As he had foreseen, it happened in 70 CE, at the end of a Jewish insurrection against the Romans, but only after Jesus himself had been tried in Jerusalem, crucified outside the western wall of the city, and buried nearby, having said that he would rise again in three days. A century thereafter Jerusalem, too, had its resurrection. In 132 CE the Roman emperor Hadrian published his plans for a new, very Roman Jerusalem. This may have been the provocation for a new revolt; what was left of the city was razed in 135 CE, and it was only then that Hadrian was free to construct his new Aelia Capitolina, named after his house and his god. The Jews for their part were banned from the city and its near vicinity.

We have a good idea of what Aelia Capitolina looked like from the Madeba map, a sixth-century mosaic map that lays out Jerusalem's plan and chief buildings in that era. But there are major new installations visible on that map. They were the work of Constantine and his Christian imperial successors. In 330 CE Constantine, with the urging or the assistance of his mother Helena, set about identifying the chief sites of Jesus' redemptive activity in Palestine. He enshrined them with major basilicas, notably the cave of the nativity in Bethlehem and the places, by then inside Jerusalem's walls, of Jesus' execution, burial, and resurrection. Jesus' tomb was housed under a splendid rotunda, and the site of the execution was enshrined at the corner of an open courtyard; abutting both was an extremely large basilica. The work was capped with both celebrity and authority when in the course of the construction Helena discovered the remains, verified by miracle, of Jesus' own cross.

It was Constantine's initiative that began the conversion of Jerusalem into a Christian holy city, or perhaps better, of Palestine into a Christian holy land, since the Christians held no brief for the city as such. For the early Christians the historical Jerusalem had been destroyed because of the perfidy of the Jews, and if Christians too, following Paul and the *Book of Revelation*, could savor the notion of a heavenly Jerusalem as the symbol of the New Covenant, it had no visible or even sentimental connection with the earthly Jerusalem. Nevertheless, in the wake of Constantine's building program, Christian pilgrims, particularly those from overseas, began to arrive in increasing numbers. What those visitors came to see, and to experience, was not Jerusalem, but the entire network of Palestinian sites connected with Jesus, his apostles, and the early Christian saints, who were being identified with enthusiastic liturgical and architectural celebration from the fourth century onward. [*See* Pilgrimage, *article on* Christian Orthodox Pilgrimage.]

One Jerusalem holy place was not celebrated in either fashion: the site of Herod's Temple, twice reduced to ruins by the Romans, was left in that sad state in graphic and continuous fulfillment of Jesus' prophecy. Christian visitors went up onto the platform and looked about and reflected, but the only liturgy marked there was the piteous Jewish return once a year on Tish'ah be-Av, the anniversary of its destruction, to mourn the fallen sanctuary. In the rest of the city, meanwhile, the effect of imperial investment began to manifest itself in the network of churches, shrines, hospices, and even hospitals as marked on the Madeba map. Now, with no claim to either political or commerical eminence—even in the ecclesiastical hierarchy the city lost ground to nearby Caesarea and distant Antioch—Jerusalem was assuming a role it would have until 1967: that of a holy city supported and adorned for its holiness, and for the political benefits accruing from the official recognition of that holiness.

But throughout most of its history Jerusalem was also a contested city. The Jews were in no position to contest it with the Christians at this stage—they continued to be prohibited residence there by the Christian as well as by the pagan Roman emperors—but in 638 CE the Muslims came up from the south and took the city from them and their Christian Roman empire in almost perfunctory fashion. Among the Muslims' first acts was to build a mosque on the deserted Temple mount and, within a century, to erect in the middle of that same platform an extraordinary Muslim shrine called the Dome of the Rock.

Although subsequently rebuilt, the mosque on the Temple mount is still called al-Masjid al-Aqṣā ("the distant sanctuary," i.e., mosque), as it was from the beginning, and the reason carries us back to the Qur'ān itself, where God describes how he "carried his servant by night from the Sacred Sanctuary to the Distant Sanctuary" (surah 17:1). The servant was of course Muḥammad, and the "Sacred Sanctuary" was easily identified as al-Masjid al-Ḥaram and the Ka'bah at Mecca. But the "Distant Sanctuary" provoked more discussion from the early commentators until here too a consensus developed that the reference was to Jerusalem and its Temple area. Quickly another tradition was worked into the first, that of Muḥammad's ascension into heaven where the mysteries of the prophets and of revelation were disclosed to him.

The Aqṣā, then, was the congregational mosque of Jerusalem, a prayer place that also commemorated that "Distant Sanctuary" mentioned in God's book and visited by the Prophet in the course of his "night journey." And what of the Dome of the Rock? It is in fact an ornate octagonal shrine over a rock, a bedrock outcropping of Mount Moriah, which, according to the Muslim tradition, marked part of the foundation of the Temple. The Muslim connection with Jerusalem, for them simply "the Holy" (al-Quds) or "the Holy House," runs back, then, both through the Bible to the Temple and through the Qur'ān to Muḥammad, and it centers precisely and exclusively on the Temple mount. Some Muslims, not a great many surely, settled in what was now their holy city in the years after 638 CE, and some Jews as well, since the Muslims permitted the latter to resettle in the city that had been forbidden to them for five centuries. The Jews did so with alacrity; they moved their chief rabbinical *yeshivah* from Tiberias to Jerusalem and may even have prayed somewhere on the Temple platform itself.

The relationship of Jews, Christians, and Muslims in Jerusalem, where a majority of the population was Christian and the political sovereignty Muslim, was more or less harmonious. But this holy city was and is a narrow place where emulation breeds envy, and envy, arrogance. In 1009 the assuredly arrogant and possibly envious Fatimid caliph al-Ḥākim burned down the Christians' Church of the Holy Sepulcher. It was eventually rebuilt, although on the reduced scale that separates the present church from its Constantinian predecessor, but some deep harm had been done. That harm was chiefly experienced in Christian Europe, which eventually launched a Crusade that took the city back from the Muslims in 1099. [*See* Crusades.]

The Western Crusade, with its religious propaganda and bloody violence, and the Muslims' response, which festooned the city with legends and blessings not unlike the Christians' own indulgences, poisoned relations between the two groups, and nowhere more disastrously than in Jerusalem itself. After the Muslim reoccupation of the city in 1187, Christians continued to come on pilgrimage, still following Jesus' "Way of the Cross" across the city, but now under the grimmest of circumstances; and the Muslim rulers, charged with the administration of an increasingly impoverished city, resorted to extortion against Jerusalem's only source of income, those same pilgrims. Between them were the Jews, too powerless as yet to be a political threat—the Christian pilgrims came from newly aggressive Christian nation-states, while the Jews found no European protectors until the nineteenth century—and almost too poor to be squeezed.

But power and poverty are not all. The Jews have always regarded themselves as a people, a single historical people, and so they alone, not the Christians or the Muslims, were capable of possessing, and did actually possess, a national capital, which was Jerusalem. No Christian pope or Muslim caliph—both quite different from a national king to begin with—ever had Jerusalem as his seat. Christian and Muslim governors Jerusalem has had and, during the Crusades, even a number of Christian kings, but that was either sectarian sovereignty or rule by delegated authority.

We are merely moving along the surface here, however. Jerusalem is more than a city or even a national capital; it is an idea. And it is safe to say that it is a biblical idea. As the Bible unfolds, one can easily follow the progressive identification being drawn between the people of Israel, or the Land of Israel, and Jerusalem and its Temple. People, city, and Temple become one, linked in destiny and God's plan, and then transformed, apotheosized, into the Heavenly Jerusalem. By the time the Jews returned from their Babylonian exile and were granted limited sovereignty in Judaea and permission to rebuild the Temple in Jerusalem, the idea was firmly in place, so firmly indeed that even though the city was again lost to the Jews and then both the city and the Temple destroyed, the idea survived. It survived not as a vaguely conceived and fitfully remembered nostalgia but as a symbol solid as Jerusalem stonework built into the thought and liturgy of Judaism. Rabbis sitting in Galilean and Iraqi *yeshivot* two centuries and more after the actual Temple had disappeared could still cite the physical measurements of the entire complex and were still debating questions of priestly ritual performed there with as much vigor and conviction as if the Temple still stood in its glory. As indeed it did, in a tradition more perennial than stones or mortar or golden fretting.

The theme that Jerusalem is perennial was taken up and repeated in the synagogue liturgy that all Jews recite as part of their ordinary worship and that recurs throughout the art and literature, pious or prosaic, of the Middle Ages. "If I forget thee, O Jerusalem . . ." rolls like an anthem across Jewish history, and in the sense of those words of the psalmist all Jews have always been Zionists, whether they believed that the restoration of Jerusalem could be achieved by political means—as very few did from the final debacle of 135 CE down to the late nineteenth century—or that it would occur in some long-distant eschatological context. And their spiritual descendants inherited the notion from them, although without the same nationalist and tribal overtones: Christians and Muslims are both eschatological Zionists. Jesus saw as in a vision the eschatological destruction of Jerusalem and John's *Book of Revelation* saw its restoration as a heavenly city; in Islam the Ka'bah itself will travel from Mecca to Jerusalem for the Day of Judgment.

BIBLIOGRAPHY

On the integration of the Jewish city into both ideology and the popular consciousness, see W. D. Davies's *The Territorial Dimension of Judaism* (Berkeley, 1982); *The Temple of Solomon: Archaeological Fact and Medieval Tradition in Christian, Islamic and Jewish Art*, edited by Joseph Gutmann (Missoula, Mont., 1976); *Zion in Jewish Literature*, edited by Abraham S. Halkin (New York, 1961); and Zev Vilnay's *Legends of Jerusalem*, vol. 1, *The Sacred Land* (Philadelphia, 1973). Vilnay's work includes many of the Muslim legends. On the conversion of Jerusalem to a Christian holy city, see W. D. Davies's *The Gospel and the Land: Early Christianity and Jewish Territorial Doctrine* (Berkeley, 1974); E. D. Hunt's *Holy Land Pilgrimage in the Later Roman Empire, A.D. 312–460* (Oxford, 1982); *Peregrinatio Aetheriae: Egeria's Travels to the Holy Land*, rev. ed., translated by John Wilkinson (London, 1981); and John Wilkinson's *Jerusalem Pilgrims before the Crusades* (Warminster, England, 1977).

On Muslim Jerusalem, the best introduction is the double article in *The Encyclopaedia of Islam*, new ed., vol. 5, fasc. 83–84 (Leiden, 1980), under "al-Ḳuds"—"Part A: History," by S. D. Goitein, and "Part B: Monuments," by Oleg Grabar. Many of the Muslim historians' and travelers' accounts of the city are collected in *Palestine under the Moslems*, translated by Guy Le Strange (New York, 1890). Sections of this book dealing specifically with Jerusalem have recently been reprinted under the title *Jerusalem under the Moslems* (Jerusalem, n.d.).

For the most revealing travel accounts of the post-Crusader era, consult *Jewish Travellers: A Treasury of Travelogues from Nine Centuries*, 2d ed., edited by Elkan N. Adler (New York, 1966); *The Wanderings of Felix Fabri*, 2 vols., translated by Aubrey Stewart (1892–1893; New York, 1971); and *The Travels of*

Ibn Battūta, A.D. 1325–1354, 2 vols., translated and edited by H. A. R. Gibb (Cambridge, 1958–1962).

On the ninteenth- and twentieth-century city, see Meron Benvenisti's *Jerusalem: The Torn City* (Jerusalem, 1976); N. A. Silberman's *Digging for God and Country: Exploration, Archeology and the Secret Struggle for the Holy Land, 1799–1917* (New York, 1982); and Walter Zander's *Israel and the Holy Places of Christendom* (New York, 1971). Finally, for visitors to the Holy City of all the faiths and in all eras, see my *Jerusalem: The Holy City in the Eyes of Chroniclers, Visitors, Pilgrims and Prophets from the Days of Abraham to the Beginnings of Modern Times* (Princeton, 1985).

F. E. PETERS

JESUITS is the popular name for members of the Society of Jesus (S.J.), a religious order of clerics regular, founded by Ignatius Loyola (1491–1556) and canonically established by Pope Paul III in 1540.

Purpose and Organization. The order's purpose is twofold: to promote the salvation and perfection both of individual Jesuits and of all humankind. Jesuit organization, manner of life, and apostolic ministries are all designed to further this very broad goal. For the same reason, all Jesuits are expected to be ready to go to any part of the world and to engage in any work assigned to them, laboring always for the greater glory of God—hence the order's motto, "Ad Majorem Dei Gloriam" (A.M.D.G.). Much in the original structure was borrowed from existing orders, but several features were novel. These included the very extensive authority and lifelong tenure of the superior general; the lengthy training period and gradation of members; a distinct spirituality based on the *Spiritual Exercises* of Ignatius Loyola; and stress on the vow of religious obedience. Official directives can be found in a large body of writings, known collectively as the Institute, which includes pertinent papal documents; the *Spiritual Exercises* and the Jesuit Constitutions (also composed by Ignatius Loyola); decrees of the society's thirty-three general congregations; and instructions of superiors general.

Supreme authority, subject always to the pope, rests in an elective body, the general congregation, which selects the superior general (the sole elected superior) and which alone has full legislative power. Day-to-day government is highly centralized under the superior general, resident in Rome, who has complete authority over the entire order. In practice, however, much of this authority is delegated to superiors throughout the world and to others whom the superior general appoints. Members are priests, candidates for the priesthood (scholastics), or temporal coadjutors (brothers). After priestly ordination and a final period of spiritual training (tertianship), priests receive their final grade as spiritual coadjutors or they are professed of four solemn vows (poverty, chastity, obedience, and special obedience to the pope). No special privileges attach to this last group, although certain posts are open only to them.

Early History and Suppression. The combating of Protestantism was a major preoccupation of Jesuits up to the mid-seventeenth century, although the order was not founded with this goal in mind. Education, both of young laymen and clerics (whose seminary training was largely in Jesuit hands), was the principal area of activity in Europe and in mission lands. The society accomplished its most effective work in the Counter-Reformation by means of its schools, all of which were tuition-free and which concentrated on the humanities. Uniform pedagogical norms were supplied by the *Ratio studiorum,* first published in 1599. By 1749 the order, with 22,589 members, was operating 669 secondary schools *(collegia)* and 176 seminaries; 24 universities were wholly or partly under its control. The academic renown of these institutions won Jesuits the reputation of being the "schoolmasters of Europe." Scholarship was also diligently pursued, especially in the ecclesiastical sciences. In theology those who gained lasting fame include Peter Canisius and Roberto Bellarmino (both doctors of the church), Francisco Suárez, Luis de Molina, Denis Petau (Petavius), Gregory of Valencia, Gabriel Vázquez, Leonard Lessius, and Juan de Ripalda. The Bollandists, a group of Belgian Jesuits, are renowned for their contributions to Christian hagiography.

Pastoral ministries were very diverse. The Jesuits placed special emphasis on preaching, popular missions, administration of the sacraments, retreat direction according to the method of the *Spiritual Exercises,* guidance of Marian Congregations (sodalities), and promotion of devotions, especially to the Sacred Heart. They had almost a monopoly on the post of royal confessor throughout Catholic Europe.

Next to education, missionary work was the chief preoccupation of the Jesuits. By the mid-eighteenth century the society was evangelizing more territory and sending out more missionaries than any other order. The overwhelming majority labored in the vast Spanish or Portuguese lands in the New World and Asia, with some also in Africa. Others toiled in the French possessions in North America. Jesuits first arrived in the present-day limits of the United States in 1566, along the southeastern coast. Up to the American Revolution almost all the Catholic clergy in the English colonies were Jesuits. In the Americas their missionary establishments, called Reductions, became famous. [*See* Christianity, *articles on* Christianity in North America *and* Christianity in Latin America.] In Asia, however, the Jesuits' missiological method of accommodation to native cultures, beneficial as it proved in many ways, involved the order in long, bitter disputes over Chinese and Malabar rites of worship, the greatest of all mission controversies. [*See* Christianity, *article on* Christianity in Asia; Missions, *article on* Christian Missions; *and the biography of Matteo Ricci.*]

The Society of Jesus has never lacked opponents. During the third quarter of the eighteenth century disparate groups of enemies combined forces to engage the order in a losing battle for life. French Gallicans and supporters of monarchical absolutism resented Jesuit championship of the papacy. [*See also* Gallicanism.] Jansenists were bent on the ruin of the group that had long supplied their chief theological critics. Most hostile of all were radical devotees of the rationalistic Enlightenment, whose ranks numbered highly placed government officials as well as such gifted authors as Voltaire. Between 1759 and 1768, governments expelled the society from Portugal and Spain and their overseas possessions, from the Kingdom of the Two Sicilies, and from the Duchy of Parma. France outlawed the order. In 1773, Pope Clement XIV bowed to the demands and threats of the Bourbon courts, and by virtue of his supreme apostolic authority, dissolved the entire order. Complete suppression never actually occurred, for Russia refused the necessary official publication of the papal brief *Dominus ac Redemptor.* This permitted the society in Belorussia to continue its canonical existence. Pope Pius VII restored the order in the Kingdom of the Two Sicilies in 1804 and allowed Jesuits everywhere to affiliate with their brethren in Russia. In 1814, Pius VII revoked the brief of suppression and completely restored the Society of Jesus.

Activities since 1814. After its restoration, the Society of Jesus spread throughout the world and came to exceed by far the numbers it had counted before 1773. Its membership totaled 36,038 in 1965, with 8,393 members in the United States. Educational and missionary endeavors continued to be its main areas of ministry. Scholarly traditions were revived, with more attention devoted to the social and physical sciences. The turbulence that has characterized life in the Catholic church since Vatican II has not escaped the order, as is evident by its decline in total membership (to 25,952 in 1983) and among young scholastics (from 9,865 in 1965 to 3,347 in 1983). Efforts to meet the challenges of the age were the major preoccupations of the thirty-first general congregation (1965–1966) and the thirty-second (1974–1975), which decreed changes in the order's government, in the training and life of members, and in the choice of ministries. These general congregations also called for more emphasis on the struggle against atheism, on ecumenism, on closer relations with the laity, on the social apostolate, on use of the mass media, on service of faith, and on promotion of justice.

[*See also the biographies of Bellarmino, Canisius, Ignatius Loyola, Suárez, and Xavier.*]

BIBLIOGRAPHY

The literature concerning the Jesuits is enormous and often controversial. The best recent bibliographies for source materials and for writings about all phases of Jesuit life and history, including works about individual Jesuits, are *Bibliography of the History of the Society of Jesus* by László Polgár, S.J. (Saint Louis, Mo., 1967), with 963 entries, and the same author's *Bibliographie sur l'histoire de la Compagnie de Jésus, 1901–1980,* 2 of 7 projected vols. to date (Rome, 1981–). Complete and well-ordered annual bibliographies appear in *Archivum historicum Societatis Iesu,* published since 1932. Important secondary works include *A History of the Society of Jesus* by William V. Bangert, S.J. (Saint Louis, Mo., 1972); *The Jesuits in History* by Martin P. Harney, S.J. (New York, 1941; reprint, Chicago, 1962); *Jesuiten-Lexikon: Die Gesellschaft Jesu einst und jetzt* by Ludwig Koch, S.J. (Paderborn, 1934; reprint, with a few additions by M. Dykmans, S.J., Louvain, 1962); and *The Jesuits: Their Spiritual Doctrine and Practice; A Historical Study* by Joseph de Guibert, S.J. (Chicago, 1964), an authoritative study. The reader should also consult Ludwig von Pastor's *The History of the Popes from the Close of the Middle Ages,* 40 vols. Volumes 12 through 39 devote in all several hundred pages to the Jesuits, giving a very detailed and lengthy treatment of the suppression.

JOHN F. BRODERICK, S.J.

JESUS (c. 7/6 BC–c. AD 30), more fully Jesus of Nazareth, called Christ; founder of Christianity.

Life and Work

Jesus left no writings and lived in almost complete obscurity except for the brief period of his public ministry. According to the evidence provided by the synoptic Gospels *(Matthew, Mark,* and *Luke),* that ministry could have lasted only about a year. The *Gospel of John* implies a period of two to three years.

The Sources. Knowledge of Jesus depends principally upon the four Gospels, but other sources confirm some of the points attested by Matthew, Mark, Luke, and John.

Non-Gospel sources. Such first- and second-century non-Christian sources as the Roman writers Tacitus, Suetonius, and Pliny the Younger, the Jewish historian Josephus Flavius (whose testimony suffers from later interpolations), the Cynic philosopher Lucian of Samosata, as well as the Babylonian Talmud, formed in the fifth century, yield but few data about Jesus: he was put to death under the procurator Pontius Pilate during the reign of the emperor Tiberius; some Jewish leaders in Palestine were involved in the execution; his followers called him "Christ" and regarded him as the divine founder of a new way of life.

The letters of the apostle Paul, which were written between 51 and 64 (or 67) and hence before the four Gospels, provide some details. Jesus was born a Jew (*Gal.* 3:16, *Rom.* 9:5), a descendant of King David (*Rom.* 1:3); he exercised a ministry to the people of Israel (*Rom.* 15:8); he forbade divorce (*1 Cor.* 7:10–11); he celebrated the Last Supper "on the night he was betrayed" (*1 Cor.* 11:23–25); he died by crucifixion (*Gal.* 2:20, 3:1; *1 Cor.* 1:23; *Phil.* 2:8); as risen from the dead, he appeared to Cephas (i.e., Peter), "the twelve," over five hundred followers, James (a leader of the church in Jerusalem), and Paul himself (*1 Cor.* 15:4–8; see also *1 Cor.* 9:1, *Gal.* 1:12, 1:16).

Other books of the New Testament occasionally allude to the story of Jesus. These references mainly concern his suffering and death (e.g., *1 Pt.* 2:24; *Heb.* 6:6, 13:12). For our limited knowledge of Jesus' life and work, however, we are almost totally dependent on the Gospels.

The four Gospels. In using the Gospels (*Mark,* written c. AD 70, *Matthew* and *Luke,* c. 80, and *John,* c. 90), we deal with material that has gone through three stages of development. Stage one covers the period of Jesus' ministry and the other events concerning him as they actually unfolded. Stage two was the time of preaching and various traditions (both oral and written) about him, which ran through the 30s to the early 60s. The form criticism pioneered by Rudolf Bultmann (1884–1976), Martin Dibelius (1883–1947), and others is concerned with this second stage. The contribution of the evangelists, or gospel writers, themselves in selecting, shaping, modifying, and embellishing the material they inherited made up stage three. This work of editing the Gospels is studied by redaction and composition criticism (developed after World War II).

Can we get back historically through stages three and two and reach some reliable conclusions about what Jesus said, did, and suffered? Or is any substantial access to stage one blocked forever by the work of the evangelists (stage three) and the needs of the Christian communities, who freely created pronouncement stories (short narratives ending with Jesus pronouncing on some issue), miracle stories, and other units developed in a stylized form to answer questions or support practices of the early church (stage two)?

Many arguments converge to make a case for the basic trustworthiness of the accounts that *Mark, Matthew,* and *Luke* give of Jesus' earthly activity. To begin with, what these Gospels say about the Herod family, the Pharisees, Pontius Pilate, the Sadducees, and so forth tallies well with the information about first-century Palestine and Judaism coming from Josephus (37–c. 100), Philo Judaeus (d. 45–50), and other such non-Christian sources. [*See also* Gospel; Pharisees; *and* Sadducees.]

For the evangelist Luke, we can verify many details in his *Acts of the Apostles* through Roman records and other non-Christian sources of information. In such matters as the complex system of titles for the kings, governors, magistrates, and petty officials he mentions, Luke shows a reasonable standard of historical accuracy in this second work. We can logically conclude that this level of accuracy holds also for his gospel and that he does carry out his promise to give a reliably authentic account of Jesus' story (*Lk.* 1:1–4). Of course, in writing history Luke took his standards at least partly from the conventions of his time. Yet the practice of Greek, Jewish, and Roman historians, even if freer than that of their modern counterparts, nevertheless maintained some fidelity to sources and facts.

Scholarship has developed a number of criteria for assessing the historical authenticity of particular items about Jesus' ministry and preaching. For instance, the criterion of dissimilarity or discontinuity argues that where the Gospels report Jesus' saying or doing things that have no background in Judaism or no follow-up in the life of the emerging church, we can conclude that at least such traditions come from Jesus himself. An example would be his language about the reign of God. The formulations are Semitic, but the language itself is characteristic neither of contemporary Judaism nor of the early church. It seems reasonable to maintain that this language derives from Jesus. This criterion of dissimilarity is a limited principle, useful only for things that were decisively original in Jesus' words or deeds. It should not be misused to exclude automatically as historically inauthentic other traditions where Jesus could have drawn on his Jewish heritage or influenced developments in emerging Christianity. To make dissimilarity an exclusive criterion would be to cut Jesus off from his environment and imply that he was curiously discontinuous from his past and without impact on his future followers.

A further criterion, that of multiple attestation, suggests that where something about Jesus is recorded in different forms and layers of early traditions, we may assert its historical authenticity more confidently than if it were reported by only one source. Such multiple attestation establishes, for example, that Jesus performed miraculous deeds and that at some point in his ministry he chose a core group of twelve from the wider ranks of his disciples.

These and other criteria and considerations, which I, like many other scholars today, have applied in studying Jesus (O'Collins, 1983), support the conclusion that the early Christian community and the first three evangelists passed on with substantial fidelity what was remembered from Jesus' ministry. We are not simply left with pious legends or irresponsible fabrications about him.

Undoubtedly, the mission of the early church, the persecutions and conflicts it suffered, its developing Christology (i.e., doctrines about the person of Jesus Christ), and sheer hindsight colored and affected stage two. At stage three, the synoptic Gospels adapted their sources to present and interpret the story of Jesus according to their own theological insights and for the particular audiences they addressed. They aimed to elicit, or at least develop, faith on the part of those who read and heard their works. Nevertheless, although these three gospels and the traditions behind them never purported to report simply factual, objective history (if there ever could be such), the broad center of contemporary scholarship holds that we can use these sources as substantially reliable accounts of Jesus' sayings and doings.

What of *John* as a source of historical information about Jesus? In this final gospel, long, symbolic discourses, fashioned by decades of interpretive and prayerful reflection, express directly theological beliefs about Jesus' divine identity and mission. All the same, a skepticism that would deny all historical value to *John* is not justified and has been widely replaced by a more nuanced attitude. For example, this gospel may be historically correct in reporting both Galilee and Jerusalem as the setting for Jesus' activity. Where the synoptic Gospels seemingly present the ministry as lasting for about a year and including only one, final journey to Jerusalem, *John* has Jesus attending three Passover feasts in Jerusalem (2:13, 6:4, 11:55) and making four journeys there (2:13, 5:1, 7:10, 12:12). The prolonged exposure to the Jerusalem public reported by John explains more plausibly the hostility toward Jesus shown by the authorities in the capital.

Physical data about Jesus is almost nil. However, one famous source is the Shroud of Turin, a piece of cloth measuring 14 × 3½ feet (4.3 × 1.06 meters) and bearing the image of a man. Kept as a holy relic in the Cathedral of Turin, it is memorialized as the shroud used to wrap the body of Jesus after his crucifixion. If it was indeed Jesus who was buried in this shroud, then we know something of his physical appearance: he was bearded, had long hair, weighed about 175 pounds (80 kilograms), stood about 6 feet (1.82 meters) tall, and—as the marks of the body indicate—was right-handed.

The Story. A basic history of Jesus would include at least the following items. He was a Galilean Jew, the son of a woman called Mary who was married to Joseph, a carpenter. Jesus was baptized by John, began to preach and teach, associated in a special way with public sinners and other outcasts, called disciples to follow him, worked miracles, and taught some memorable parables. His challenge to given forms of piety (*Mt.* 6:1–18), his desire to correct certain traditions (*Mk.* 7:1–23), his violation of some Sabbath observances (*Mk.* 2:23–27), his attitude toward the Temple in Jerusalem (*Mk.* 14:58, 15:29 and parallels), and other offenses aroused the antagonism of some Jewish leaders and teachers. In Jerusalem (where he had come for the Passover celebration) he was betrayed, arrested, interrogated by members of the Sanhedrin, condemned by Pontius Pilate, executed on a cross (which bore an inscription giving the charge against Jesus as a messianic pretender), and buried later the same day.

Ministry. Hardly anything is more certain about Jesus' ministry than that through his words and deeds he proclaimed the kingdom, or rule, of God. He understood his activity to be initiating a new, powerful, and final offer of salvation (e.g., *Mt.* 4:23, 9:35, 12:28). Faced with this offer, his audience was called to repent (e.g., *Mk.* 1:15) and accept the divine pardon that Jesus himself communicated in his own person (*Mk.* 2:17 and parallels). Through words of forgiveness (*Mk.* 2:5, *Lk.* 7:48), parables of mercy (e.g., *Lk.* 15:11–32), and table fellowship with outcasts (e.g., *Mt.* 11:19), he aimed to bring sinners back into God's company.

In doing all this, Jesus acted with a striking sense of personal authority (*Mk.* 1:22) that did not hesitate to go beyond the divine law received by Moses (*Mk.* 10:2–9). His call for radical conversion (e.g., *Mt.* 5:1–7:27, *Lk.* 6:20–49) entailed transforming in his own name that law and carrying to the ultimate its inmost spirit (*Mt.* 5:21–48).

Unlike both former prophets and contemporary teachers, Jesus repeatedly linked the divine offer of salvation not simply to his preaching but also to his own person. Accepting Jesus himself emerged as the decisive criterion for human destiny before God (*Mk.* 8:35 and parallels, *Lk.* 12:8–9 and parallel). What was the basis for this extraordinary sense of being the final agent of salvation and for the whole personal authority that Jesus claimed? It seems that a uniquely intimate relationship with the God whom he called "Abba, Father" (*Mk.* 14:36; a distinctive and unusual name connoting "father dear"), underlay Jesus' conviction of being absolutely reliable in mediating the divine will and grace to others (*Mt.* 11:27 and parallel).

As far as Jesus' miraculous deeds are concerned, these "works" or "signs," as John's gospel calls them, expressed the divine power breaking into history to conquer evil (*Mt.* 12:28 and parallel; see also *Mk.* 3:23–27). Like his preaching, they were utterly religious in their aim and significance. Jesus never performed miracles either to satisfy curiosity or to promote his own immediate interests (e.g., *Mk.* 6:5, 8:11–13; 15:31–32; *Lk.* 23:8–9). Rather, he associated his miraculous deeds with his call to faith and conversion. No less than his preaching, these deeds were meant to manifest the reign of God and the divine promise to deliver people from the forces that afflicted them.

How did Jesus assess and describe his own identity? To begin with, he thought of himself as a spiritual physician (*Mk.* 2:17), a shepherd to his people (*Mt.* 15:24), and a divinely authorized prophet (*Lk.* 13:33). Then around seventy times in the synoptic Gospels Jesus calls himself (the) "Son of man," a term that in its Semitic background either was a circumlocution for oneself as speaker (e.g., *Mt.* 8:20) or simply meant "a human being" or "someone." What is not quite certain is whether by the time of Jesus himself "Son of man" was also a clearly defined title associated with a deliverer expected to come in the last times. However, the three contexts in which Jesus designated himself as "Son of man" carried their own distinct meanings. This self-designation was used of Jesus' earthly work and condition (e.g., *Mk.* 2:10, 2:28; *Mt.* 11:19 and parallel); of his suffering, death, and resurrection (*Mk.* 8:31, 9:31, 10:33–34); and of his coming in future glory as a redeemer-judge (e.g., *Mk.* 8:38, 13:26; *Mt.* 24:27 and parallel).

From the outset his followers called Jesus "messiah" (Heb., *mashiaḥ*), as being both God's anointed agent of salvation and a kingly deliverer of David's house. This title, in its Greek form, *christos*, was so widely employed to express Jesus' functions and person that it became simply a second proper name for Jesus (e.g., *1 Thes.* 1:1), as frequently happens now when people refer to "Jesus Christ." But did Jesus identify himself in messianic terms during his lifetime? The evidence from the ministry outlined above suggests that at the very least he thought of himself as God's final agent of salvation. Did he also identify himself as a royal deliverer from David's line? It seems unlikely that Jesus would have been crucified on the charge of being a royal messianic pretender (*Mk.* 15:26 and parallels) if he had never even implicitly made such a claim. At the same time, however, he did not directly announce his messianic identity, and he reacted to Peter's confession "You are the Christ" by speaking of the Son of man being destined to suffer (*Mk.* 8:29, 8:31). [*See also* Messianism.]

Crucifixion. Jesus' ministry ended in Jerusalem when he was betrayed by Judas, put on trial before members of the Sanhedrin, convicted (for despising the law and blasphemously claiming messianic authority?), handed over to Pilate, and executed as a threat to the public order. Did Jesus anticipate and interpret in advance such a violent death?

It was, or at least became, obvious to Jesus—and for that matter to any moderately intelligent observer—that fidelity to his mission would bring deadly opposition from the public authorities (e.g., *Lk.* 11:47, 11:49–50, 13:33–34). Among other things, the fate of John the Baptist suggested such a danger. Then Jesus' demonstrative entry into Jerusalem (*Mk.* 11:1–11) and cleansing of the Temple (*Mk.* 11:15–18) increased the danger from Caiaphas and other leading Sadducees, who under the Roman army retained some power in the capital. This and further evidence (e.g., from the Last Supper and the agony in the garden of Gethsemane) point to the conclusion that Jesus anticipated and accepted his violent end. It seems that at least to the core group of his disciples he had at some stage announced his death and affirmed his hope of being vindicated through resurrection (*Mk.* 8:31, 9:31, 10:33–34). [*See also* Apostles *and the biography of John the Baptist.*]

But what benefits did he expect or intend his death to bring? It appears that he understood his suffering fate to be an ordeal through which God's rule was to come (*Mk.* 14:25). Having lived "not to be served but to serve" (*Mk.* 10:45; see also *Lk.* 22:27), Jesus interpreted his suffering death as a saving service for others—for the many who would "come from east and west and sit at table with Abraham, Isaac, and Jacob in the kingdom of heaven" (*Mt.* 8:11 and parallel). In *The Atonement* (1981) Martin Hengel plausibly argues that Jesus applied to himself the widespread conviction of his time—that the violent death of a just person could representatively atone for the sins of others.

Resurrection. Paul's letters (e.g., *1 Cor.* 15:3b–5), *Acts* (e.g., 2:22–24, 2:32–33, 2:36, 3:13–15), and other New Testament books (e.g., *Mk.* 16:6) incorporate traditional formulas about Jesus' resurrection that go back to the earliest years of Christianity. As far as the historical evidence goes, the Christian movement began with the simple announcement that the crucified Jesus had been raised to new life and had appeared to some witnesses. At first, individuals who had seen him risen from the dead guaranteed the truth of the resurrection (e.g., *1 Cor.* 15:5, 15:7, 15:8; *Lk.* 24:34), Then the Christian community as such professed this truth (see, for example, the formulations cited in *1 Thessalonians* 4:14, *Romans*

1:3–4, and *Romans* 10:9). The discovery of the empty tomb by Mary Magdalene, accompanied perhaps by other women (*Mk.* 16:1–8; *Jn.* 20:1, 20:11–13; *Lk.* 24:10, 24:23), served as a confirmatory sign. But the New Testament shows a clear awareness that an empty tomb simply by itself did not establish Jesus' resurrection (e.g., *Jn.* 20:2, *Mt.* 28:11–15).

It is not surprising that, together with their claims about Jesus' resurrection, Christians defined God in terms of the risen Christ. Repeatedly Paul cited a formula from the early tradition that identified God as "having raised Jesus from the dead" (e.g., *Gal.* 1:1, *Rom.* 10:9, *1 Cor.* 6:14). Hence, to be wrong about the resurrection would be to "misrepresent" God (*1 Cor.* 15:15). [*See also* Resurrection.]

Jesus' person and meaning. In the post-Easter situation, Christians named Jesus Lord (Gr., *kurios*) and Son of God. From the record of the ministry there are hints that Jesus thought of himself as being in a quite distinct way the son of the God whom he called "father dear" (cf. *Mk.* 13:32, *Mt.* 11:27). It is difficult to specify just what this "blasphemy," of which Jesus was accused, meant (see, e.g., *Mk.* 2:7, 14:64), but it seems that this accusation was a reaction to an impression given by Jesus that he had a certain unique relationship to Yahveh, or even that he was somehow on a level with Yahveh. At any rate, Jesus' resurrection and its aftermath led the early Christians to call him "Son of God" as being uniquely related to the Father for the salvation of the world (*1 Thes.* 1:10, *Rom.* 1:3–4, *Gal.* 4:4–7). This title pointed to an intimate link between Jesus and his Father revealed in those events that communicated divine salvation to human beings. The God "who did not spare his Son but gave him up for us all" will "also give us all things with him" (*Rom.* 8:32).

Their experience of him when they met for prayer made the early Christians name Jesus as their exalted and divine "Lord" (*1 Cor.* 12:3, *Rom.* 10:9, *Phil.* 2:9–11). An expression from the worship of Aramaic-speaking Christians, *maranatha* (*1 Cor.* 16:22), might have been a creedal statement ("Our Lord is come; he is here and present with us") or it could have been a prayer asking for the Parousia to occur soon ("Our Lord, come quickly"). Either way, *maranatha* referred to the risen and divine Lord who was acknowledged to be present in the church both with his Father and through his Spirit, especially when communities gathered for worship.

Both these titles, "Son of God" and "Lord," refer to the risen, exalted Christ as having a life, power, and authority after death (a "postexistence") on the divine level. The starting point for Christology was Christ's existence after death. From there Christians moved back through his baptism (Mark), his conception, and his birth and childhood (Matthew and Luke) to his preexistence (see *John,* 1:1–2, the Council of Nicaea, etc.), when they sought to clarify and express his origins.

Finally, the Christians of the New Testament used a wide variety of images to interpret the salvation (e.g., *Lk.* 2:11, 2:30) brought by Jesus, but much of this material can be grouped under three headings: liberation, expiation, and transforming love.

First, he had come to set people free from sin, death, and other evil forces that oppressed them (e.g., *Lk.* 4:18, 13:16; *1 Cor.* 15:25; *Gal.* 5:1, 5:13; *Col.* 2:15). Since he died at the time of the Passover, the Exodus from bondage in Egypt was quickly seen to foreshadow the liberation he had brought (*1 Cor.* 5:7). In the language of the *Revelation to John,* "the Lamb who was slain" had paradoxically conquered and effected a deliverance from the powers of evil (e.g., *Rv.* 3:21, 5:5–10, 6:2). He had rescued people from death for new and lasting life (*1 Cor.* 15:45 and John's gospel).

Second, Jesus' dying and rising was recognized to be a sacrificial act that representatively expiated the sins of others (*Rom.* 3:21–26), repaired a disturbed moral order, and established a new covenant between God and humankind (e.g., *1 Cor.* 11:25, *Mk.* 14:24). Christ was the priest and victim whose "blood cleansed us from all sin" (*1 Jn.* 1:7) and whose once-and-for-all act of atonement had been foreshadowed by the annual ceremony of the Day of Atonement (*Heb.* 2:17–18, 4:14–10:39, esp. 9:6–14, 9:25–26). Third, Jesus' death and resurrection revealed a love that could transform human hearts (*Jn.* 3:16, 13:1, 15:13; *2 Cor.* 5:14–15). He died to reconcile sinners with God (*Rom.* 5:6–11, *2 Cor.* 5:18–20). [*See* God, *article on* God in the New Testament; Atonement; Justification; *and* Redemption.]

Christological Developments

For the early Christians the union of activity between Jesus and God for the salvation of the world implied a union of being. They believed Jesus to be personally identified with God. Some passages in the New Testament apply the term *God* to Jesus Christ (*Jn.* 1:1, 1:18, 20:28; *Heb.* 1:8–9). Other passages probably also do the same (*Rom.* 9:5, *Ti.* 2:13, *2 Pt.* 1:1, *1 Jn.* 5:20). John distinguishes the type of sonship that Jesus communicates to those who believe in him and become *tekna* (*Jn.* 1:12) from Jesus' own divine sonship, which remains unique to him as *huios* (1:14). Paul likewise attributes adoptive sonship to Christians (*Rom.* 8:15, *Gal.* 4:5), but he speaks of Jesus as God's "own Son" (*Rom.* 8:32). The prologue of John's gospel (1:1–18) crowned the christological thought of the first century by announcing the incarnation of the divine Word become flesh. It also ushered in centuries of wrestling with ways for expressing this union of humanity and divinity in the one person of Jesus Christ.

Councils of the Church. In the development of Christology, progress often occurred in reaction to views rejected as heterodox. Thus the occasion for the first ecumenical council, the Council of Nicaea (325), came with the teachings of Arius (c. 250–336). To preserve the oneness of God, while at the same time affirming the uniqueness of Jesus Christ, Arius asserted that the Son was a perfect creature, at most a kind of demigod subordinated to the Father. To combat Arius, the council adopted a term that had been used by Origen (c. 185–c. 254) to indicate that Christ shared one common divine being with the Father: *homoousios* ("of one substance"). This teaching on Christ's divinity raised a question: how could believers then maintain Christ's true humanity? One supporter of Nicaea, Apollinaris of Laodicea (c. 310–c. 390), reduced Christ's full humanity by apparently suggesting that at the incarnation the divine Logos (or Word of God) assumed only a body and itself took the place of the human spirit. Against Apollinaris the First Council of Constantinople (381) taught that Christ had a true human soul.

But how then were Christ's being human (Constantinople) and being divine (Nicaea) related? An archbishop of Constantinople, Nestorius (d. 451?), refused to endorse the title for Mary, *theotokos* ("mother of God"), that was introduced to articulate the personal unity of divinity and humanity in Jesus right from his conception and birth. This term aimed to express the belief that the child born from Mary was truly the Son of God. Nestorius apparently held that there was a moral rather than a personal union between Christ's divinity and humanity. A divine being (the Logos) coexisted side by side with a human being (the man Jesus). A third ecumenical council, the Council of Ephesus (431), condemned Nestorius and upheld the title of *theotokos* for Mary. [*See also* Mary.]

In the aftermath of the Council of Ephesus, however, defenders of the unity between Christ's divinity and humanity went to another extreme. Eutyches of Constantinople (c. 378–454) seemed to maintain that Christ's divinity absorbed his humanity—the so-called monophysite heresy, according to which the one divine nature *(phusis)* swallowed up Christ's humanity. The Council of Chalcedon (451) reacted by acknowledging in Christ "two natures in one person [*prosōpon*] or acting subject [*hupostasis*]." This personal unity left the divine and human natures quite intact and in no way confused or intermingled them with each other.

Chalcedon said nothing about Christ's crucifixion and resurrection. In the centuries that followed, an all-absorbing theology of the incarnation generally monopolized attention. In one important development the Third Council of Constantinople (680) condemned monothelitism, or the view that acknowledged only one will in Christ. The council held for a divine and human will; the duality of Christ's natures entailed a duality of wills.

Controversy over the Holy Spirit also affected post-Chalcedonian Christology. In Spain and then elsewhere the Western church unilaterally changed the Nicene-Constantinopolitan creed by adding the term *filioque*, indicating thereby that the Holy Spirit "proceeds from the Father *and the Son*." Photios (c. 820–891), patriarch of Constantinople, insisted that the Holy Spirit proceeds "from the Father alone." These different notions of the relationship between the eternally preexistent Son and the Holy Spirit carried over into thinking about the incarnation and resurrection of Christ. [*See also* Councils, *article on* Christian Councils, *and* Creeds, *article on* Christian Creeds.]

The Middle Ages. After the christological controversies that supplied the agenda for early church councils, Thomas Aquinas (c. 1225–1274) and other theologians of the Middle Ages employed stricter philosophical categories to explore further the union between divinity and humanity in the one person of Christ (i.e., the hypostatic union) and the types of knowledge, grace, and freedom he possessed. Christology eventually made such high claims for Christ that his genuinely human life became suspect. For instance, in his human consciousness Jesus was credited with enjoying the beatific vision. Like the blessed in heaven, he saw God directly and hence could not be a believer. He lived his earthly life by vision, not by faith. This vision made his human existence somewhat implausible, or at least very distant from the experience of normal men and women.

When theology tended to represent Christ largely in terms of his divinity, church art, popular belief, and widespread devotions often defended his truly human existence and experience. Icons, the Christmas crib, carols, the stations of the cross, and later the success of Luther's hymns and Roman Catholic devotion to the Sacred Heart witnessed to the instinctive attachment of ordinary Christians to the real humanity of Jesus.

I have sketched above three mainline New Testament interpretations of salvation: salvation as liberation, salvation as expiation, and salvation as transforming love. In his *Cur Deus homo* (1098), Anselm of Canterbury developed the second interpretation in terms of satisfaction and became the first Christian writer to devote a whole work to the redemptive activity of Christ. According to Anselm, sin offended God's honor, and either satisfaction or punishment had to follow that offense. By making satisfaction, Jesus restored the divine honor, and punishment was not involved. Unfortunately, those who drew on *Cur Deus homo*—from Thomas Aquinas, through John Calvin (1509–1564), down to Karl Barth (1886–1968) and others—added punitive elements to Anselm's version of redemption. Nowadays his soteriology, or doctrine of salvation, has fallen on hard times and is often dismissed as legalistic and concerned with the divine honor rather than with God's love. However, John McIntyre, Gispert Greshake, and Walter Kasper have defended Anselm's theology of satisfaction for appreciating the divine fidelity to creation and the moral order. Taken within his feudal context, Anselm's appeal to God's honor implied rather than excluded love. The defects of *Cur Deus homo* lay elsewhere—for example, in the fact that it could discuss redemption while completely ignoring Christ's resurrection.

Modern Times. The mainline Reformation and the Counter-Reformation were primarily concerned with church issues and for the most part did not immediately affect doctrines about Jesus Christ. However, the sixteenth century also saw the rise of Socinianism and Unitarianism, which rejected the divinity of Jesus and the doctrine of the Trinity. Deism, which frequently did the same, arose in the following century. Then from the eighteenth century onward Christology began to be deeply affected by the rise of critical methods in historical and biblical research. Scientific history became and in many ways has remained the dominant partner in dialogue with theological thinking about Jesus' person and saving work.

The historical Jesus. In the classical period for the historical study of Jesus' life, writers like David Friedrich Strauss (1808–1874), Ernest Renan (1823–1892), and Adolf von Harnack (1851–1930) attempted to penetrate behind the christological doctrines of Paul and the early church and get back to Jesus of Nazareth as he actually was. They hoped to recover by scientific, unprejudiced use of the earliest sources—in particular Mark's gospel—an authentic picture of the real Jesus. Frequently this search was carried on by the unorthodox—by rationalists (who removed the miraculous element from Jesus' story and denied his divinity), by humanitarians (who stressed his ethical teaching at the expense of everything else), or by liberal Christians (for whom church membership was often unimportant).

Despite the work of these scholars, however, no common, scientifically established picture of Jesus emerged. By the time Albert Schweitzer wrote his classic study of this nineteenth-century enterprise, *The Quest of the Historical Jesus* (1906), it had become clear that many had been portraying Jesus largely in the light of their own personal presuppositions and the convictions of their society. Schweitzer protested against all these attempts to modernize Jesus and insisted that the key was to be found in Jesus' eschatology, or views about the end of history.

As Schweitzer read the evidence, Jesus held that the final coming of God's kingdom would happen in the imminent future (known as futurist or consistent eschatology). Later, C. H. Dodd was to react by arguing that Jesus proclaimed the *eschaton* as already there in his own person (realized eschatology). Others have held the mediating position of an inaugurated eschatology. Jesus announced an end that was in the process of being realized and hence was both present and future (so, with varying nuances, Oscar Cullmann, Joachim Jeremias, W. G. Kümmel, and others). In this view, Jesus expected that after his death and resurrection some kind of interval would elapse before the end. In this debate much turned on the interpretation of *Mark* 13 and such passages as *Mark* 9:1. One point that was often ignored is the symbolic nature of Jesus' eschatological utterances, which should not be taken as exact predictions that looked forward to some precise fulfillment. In their different ways, Anthony Harvey and Ben Meyer have insisted that such prophetic language offered a symbolic vision of the future, not an exact forecast of events.

After Schweitzer. The work of Schweitzer tended to dissuade scholars from continuing earlier efforts to write a life of Jesus. This reluctance was reinforced by the development of form criticism (see above, section on "The Four Gospels"), which showed that traditions about Jesus' words and deeds seemed to have been passed on mainly as separate units or small groups of units. Because the chronological order of these units and their original contexts are frequently unknown, no detailed biographical framework—even for Jesus' ministry in the last year or two of his life—can be established. In addition, the sources rarely mention Jesus' motivations or deal with his state of mind, so it is difficult to penetrate, or at least say much about, his inner life—a fact that nineteenth- and sometimes twentieth-century writers glossed over in their desire to elaborate on Jesus' psychology. After Bultmann's *Jesus* (1926), many New Testament scholars, at least in Europe, not only declined to produce lives of Jesus but would not even attempt studies on his historical ministry.

Bultmann himself reduced to a minimum the theological relevance (for Christians) of Jesus' human history, arguing that it is not the person of the historical Jesus who is the object of their faith but the Christ preached here and now by the church. A 1953 lecture by Ernst Käsemann ("The Problem of the Historical Jesus") led many who had hitherto adopted Bultmann's position to return to a position held (whether articulately or inarticulately) by the overwhelming majority of Christians: what can be known about Jesus' life is relevant for faith in him. A renewed scholarly interest in the history of Jesus produced works like Günther Bornkamm's *Jesus of Nazareth* (1956) and Hans Conzelmann's long article in *Religion in Geschichte und Gegenwart,* "Jesus Christus" (1959), which appeared in English in expanded and updated form as *Jesus* (1973). Such authors realized that disagreement with the classical life-of-Jesus enterprise should not lead to the other extreme of underrating or ignoring what historical sources establish about Jesus' ministry.

Cullmann, Jeremias, Hans Küng, and others went much further than the former disciples of Bultmann. In various ways they have implied or even explicitly maintained that beliefs about Christ's person and mission depend on establishing that the historical Jesus so identified himself and his work.

Many other exegetes, or at least many Christian theologians, adopt a middle ground. While admitting that only the crucifixion, resurrection, gift of the Holy Spirit, and experiences of the early church were the means to disclose the full truth about Jesus' person and work, they argue that historical conclusions about Jesus' activities, claims, and intentions show a basis or at least a starting point for the post-Easter beliefs that developed about his identity and mission.

During his brief ministry something had already been disclosed concerning his status as Son of God and savior of the world. Hence exponents of this view would talk about the implicit Christology and soteriology recorded by the synoptic Gospels unfolding into the explicit Christology and soteriology of the emerging church. This was not a movement from a low to a high Christology (and soteriology), as if Jesus had made only minimal and modest claims, which were later maximized. Rather, the development was from something indirectly implied to something directly proclaimed.

Contemporary approaches. From Thomas Aquinas in the Middle Ages down to Karl Barth in the twentieth century, classic Christology began its theological interpretation with God. The essential question for this approach was "How did the preexistent Son of God 'come down' and enter this world?" In place of this Christology "from above," much recent thinking has begun "from below," using as its starting point the historical, human situation of Jesus in this world. The key question for such a Christology "from below" is "What does it mean to say that a particular man from Nazareth was both universal savior and 'God among us'?" How could a human being have been such and been recognizable as such?

The difference between the two approaches can be traced back to opposed methodologies in the patristic period. The school of Alexandria, which included such figures as Origen and Cyril of Alexandria (c. 375–444), pursued a descending, Johannine Christology "from above." This "Logos-sarx" (Word-flesh) approach centered on the preexistent Logos who descended into the world, became flesh, and then returned to the place from which he came. Both then and now such a Christology normally succeeds well in maintaining the unity of Christ as subject, but it has trouble indicating how the eternal Logos could take on a genuinely and fully human way of acting. The school of Antioch, to which Theodore of Mopsuestia (c. 350–428) and Nestorius belonged, endorsed an ascending Christology "from below." This "Logos-anthropos" (Word-man) approach, which found its New Testament support in the synoptic Gospels, aimed to safeguard the full human nature of Jesus but had difficulty showing that his humanity and divinity were united in one acting subject.

Wolfhart Pannenberg, who originally championed a Christology "from below" in *Jesus: God and Man* (1964), in the second volume of *Grundfragen systematischer Theologie* (1980) came to question the correctness of setting up sharp alternatives. In *Jesus the Christ* (1974) Walter Kasper sees the two approaches as complementing each other. Such a position is not really new. The New Testament itself made room for both John's gospel and the synoptic Gospels. Then in the fifth century the Council of Chalcedon aimed at a compromise between the current Christologies "from above" and "from below." It took from Alexandria the insistence on Christ's unity and from Antioch a clear regard for the duality of distinct natures.

A second major distinction in contemporary Christology concerns its center. For some (e.g., John Robinson and Pierre Teilhard de Chardin), evolving creation provides the primary focus. Jean Galot, Karl Rahner, and others organize matters around the incarnation. In their varying ways, yet other scholars (e.g., Hans Küng, James Mackey, Edward Schillebeeckx, and Jon Sobrino) have taken the synoptic Gospels' account of the ministry as the center. Kasper, Jürgen Moltmann in *The Crucified God* (1972), and Pannenberg, despite their differences, maintain Jesus' crucifixion and resurrection as the central mystery around which christological thinking takes shape. Finally, Moltmann's *Theology of Hope* (1964), which was not as such a formal Christology, focused matters through the divine promises that have not yet been realized but await the future and final end of all things.

Right from the birth of Christianity the convictions embodied in worship supported the centrality of the Easter mystery. Believers expressed liturgically, especially through baptism (*Rom.* 6:3–5) and the Eucharist (*1 Cor.* 11:26), the sense that Jesus' crucifixion and resurrection were the heart of the matter. From such a midpoint, Christology can look in one direction (through Jesus' life, the incarnation, and the history of the Israelites) back to creation, and in the other direction (through the coming of the Holy Spirit, the life of the church, and the history of humanity) forward to the future consummation of all things. Christian worship supports the choice made by Kasper and Pannenberg.

A further variant in modern Christology comes from the diversity in philosophical presuppositions. Thus Martin Heidegger's brand of existentialism fed into Bultmann's major theological interpretations of Jesus and the Christian message (*The Gospel of John*, 1941; *Theology of the New Testament*, 1953) and into his demythologizing hermeneutics ("New Testament and Mythology," 1941). German idealist philosophy influenced the Christologies of Kasper and Rahner. The neo-Marxism of Ernst Bloch raised issues and provided categories for Moltmann's *Theology of Hope*. Neo-Thomism continues to serve some Roman Catholic Christologies.

Although different philosophical systems help to bring about a pluralism in systematic religious reflection, on one issue most contemporary authors agree: what is presented on Jesus' person and work must be correlated with human questions, hopes, aspirations, and sufferings. How this has been done (by Bultmann, Moltmann, Rahner, Schillebeeckx, Teilhard de Chardin, Tillich, and others, including various Latin American writers) varies. Some may not want to admit the term, but the method of correlation (elaborated by Tillich in his *Systematic Theology*, 1951–1963) runs through much contemporary reflection on Jesus. Whatever precise description is given of the human condition and human experience, Jesus is regularly proposed as the one who illuminates the first and integrates the second.

Issues

Below are outlined some major issues for reflection on Jesus of Nazareth's history, identity, and function. Many questions arise about his resurrection, redemptive work, knowledge, faith, and virginal conception.

The Resurrection. In the late nineteenth and early twentieth century Wilhelm Bousset, James G. Frazer, and others connected Jesus with myths of dying and rising gods, frequently those of the mystery religions of Greece and the ancient Near East. Belief in the resurrection of the crucified Jesus was taken to be simply another projection of the human need to cope with the changing seasons and common challenges of life. However, the religious parallels and possible historical connections between the story about Jesus and such figures as Adonis, Attis, and Osiris proved too tenuous to remain convincing.

Subsequently it was maintained that the message of the resurrection was not a statement that claimed to present a fact about Jesus himself but simply functioned to declare a personal commitment of the early Christians to a new way of life (e.g., Paul M. Van Buren in *The Secular Meaning of the Gospel*, 1963). Alternatively, it has been argued that the claims concerning resurrection did no more than express the inner value of Jesus' earthly history, or at least the real meaning of his death (e.g., Bultmann). The basic problem with taking "resurrection" merely to express such commitment and/or meaning is that the ordinary conventions covering the use of language indicate that the Easter message of the first Christians primarily offered some factual information about the destiny of Jesus himself after his death and burial. Only secondarily were new commitments and value judgments about the significance of Jesus' life and death associated with or implied by the Easter message. The first point of Christian witness to his resurrection was to claim a new event (distinct from and subsequent to the crucifixion) that brought Jesus himself from the condition of death to that of a new and lasting life.

Paul and the gospel writers report that the major catalysts of this claim about the resurrection were encounters with the risen Jesus and the confirmatory discovery of the empty tomb. These postresurrection meetings with Jesus are presented primarily in the language of sight: "he appeared" (e.g., *1 Cor.* 15:4–8, *Lk.* 24:34, *Acts* 13:31), or "they/I/we have seen him" (e.g., *Mt.* 28:17; *Lk.* 24:37, 24:39; *Jn.* 20:14, 20:18; *1 Cor.* 9:1).

It has sometimes been argued that the disciples "saw" and announced Jesus risen from the dead simply because they needed his resurrection to cope psychologically and religiously with the horror of his crucifixion. Yet to proclaim the crucified Jesus as risen from the dead and as messianic Lord (*Acts* 2:36) neither matched the actual psychological state of the disciples (radical disillusionment) nor emerged naturally from the religious possibilities of their Jewish faith. As Küng points out in *On Being a Christian* (1977), "The idea of a resurrection of the Messiah—still more of a failed Messiah—was an absolute novelty in the Jewish tradition" (p. 372).

In *The Resurrection of Jesus of Nazareth* (1968), Willi Marxsen takes "resurrection" to have been no more than one possible way of interpreting the experience of "seeing" Jesus and finding faith. Admittedly the disciples did not speak of resurrection in describing an event they claimed to have directly witnessed. They spoke of Jesus' resurrection as a result of meeting him alive after his crucifixion and burial. But was this a necessary inference from their new experience of him or just an optional interpretation?

In *Jesus* (1974) Schillebeeckx argues that the appearances were merely literary ways of expressing what the risen but invisible Jesus had done for the disciples: in offering them forgiveness, effecting their conversion, initiating their mission, and thus leading them to the conclusion that he must be alive. If this reconstruction of events is correct, the evangelists and Paul prove to be remarkably incompetent and confusing writers. The normal conventions for their use of language suggest just the opposite sequence from the one proposed by Schillebeeckx. These conventions indicate that the appearances of the risen Jesus effected the disciples' conversion and mission, not that their conversion and mission were eventually verbalized by reporting appearances that as such never took place.

Of course, any fully developed study of Jesus' resurrection would need also to report a number of related themes that have attracted the attention of modern scholars: (1) efforts to achieve a proper balance between Jesus' crucifixion and resurrection, neither absorbing one into the other nor allowing them to stand as two quite separate events (Kasper and Moltmann); (2) the ways in which exaltation language (e.g., *Phil.* 2:9, *1 Tm.* 3:16) complements the New Testament language of resurrection (Pheme Perkins); (3) interpretations of the risen body and the personal continuity between the crucified Jesus and the risen Christ (O'Collins); (4) reflections on the connections between his destiny, the resurrection of others, and the fate of the cosmos (e.g., in their different ways, Teilhard de Chardin and Pannenberg); (5) the significance of the empty tomb for a Christian theology of redemption centered on the transformation of this material world (with its history of sin and suffering) rather than on a flight (of the soul) to another, better world (O'Collins); and (6) the motivation and grounds for Easter faith (e.g., the transcendental hope as described by Rahner), which go beyond the mere historical testimony provided by the resurrection witness.

Suffering and Redemption. Moltmann (in *The Crucified God*) and other theologians have developed various kinds of post-Holocaust Christologies that draw partly on the theme of God's pain and sorrow over human sin, which is to be found in the Hebrew scriptures (e.g., *Gen.* 6:6, *Is.* 63:10) and in rabbinic literature. This approach was anticipated by certain English and Russian kenotic Christologies of the nineteenth and early twentieth centuries, in which the Son of God's self-emptying (*Phil.* 2:7) enabled him to enter into a radical solidarity with the alienated and dehumanized of this world. G. W. F. Hegel's view that the idea of God included "the pain of the negative" and "the suffering of abandonment" has encouraged Moltmann and others to develop a trinitarian theology of the cross: in the event of Calvary this history of God climaxed in the love of the abandoned Son and the grief of the Father, who also suffered the pain of abandonment; the Holy Spirit, however, opened up the future and created liberating life.

The interpretation of the scriptural texts to which these Christologies appeal (e.g., *Mk.* 15:34, *Rom.* 8:32, *Jn.* 3:16) has been widely challenged. The notion of God being open as such to suffering and change through an event of this world (the crucifixion) runs into philosophical and theological difficulties, at least for many schools of thought. The alternative to Moltmann's history of the triune God's suffering is not necessarily a detached God who remains indifferent to human pain and misery. Rather, it can be a belief in a compassionate God whose boundless love freely revealed itself in human history—above all, in the passion and death of Jesus.

Under the heading "Jesus' Person and Meaning," above, I recalled three characteristic New Testament images for salvation: liberation, expiation, and transforming love. In current theology the second image is frequently neglected (e.g., by Mackey, Moltmann, Schillebeeckx, and Sobrino) or drastically modified. In place of Jesus' accepting his passion to atone representatively for human guilt and repair a disturbed moral order, expiation is still sometimes explained this way. His Father treated Jesus as a sinful substitute for guilty humanity, condemning and punishing him not only with death but even with the pains of the damned. Thus an angry God was propitiated and redemption was accomplished. This penal-substitution view, which was partly endorsed by Thomas Aquinas, flourished in the hands of Calvin and J.-B. Bossuet (1627–1704) and in various forms has lingered on in the writings of Barth, Pannenberg, and Hans Urs von Balthasar, not to mention many popular preachers and writers. Although this theory claims to be based on the New Testament, it has little in common with the parable of the prodigal son (*Lk.* 15:11–32). In that story the father does not need to change from anger to gracious love. He is not waiting to be appeased but is waiting for the return of his son. The penal-substitution view frequently misuses the cry of abandonment (*Mk.* 15:34) and is not supported by accurate exegesis of the Pauline texts to which it mostly appeals (*Rom.* 3:25, 8:3; *2 Cor.* 5:21; *Gal.* 3:13). Further, the New Testament never links the divine "anger" with the suffering and death of Jesus. Rather, it uses that term to express the incompatibility between God and sin that coming judgment will reveal (e.g., *Rom.* 1:18, 2:5).

Jesus' Knowledge and Faith. Above, under "The Story," I included some data from the synoptic Gospels which concerned Jesus' knowledge of his personal identity and mission. Medieval theology maximized the scope of Jesus' human knowledge. It attributed to him not only ordinary knowledge gained by human experience *(scientia experientiae)* but also the infused knowledge *(scientia infusa)* proper to angels and even a direct, face-to-face beatific vision of God and all created realities *(scientia visionis)*. I do not know any contemporary Christian theologians of stature who still speak of Jesus' infused knowledge. Many have been led by the gospel evidence and theological reasons to acknowledge that he had some direct knowledge of his Father and of his own identity and work, but they interpret such immediate knowledge as a primordial, intuitive consciousness rather than a beatific vision. If the earthly Jesus did enjoy such a vision, that would have required some constant interference to prevent the vision from having its proper effect. Otherwise such a vision would have excluded genuine human experiences like fear, suffering, free obedience to the divine will, and the struggles in prayer that the agony in the garden of Gethsemane attests (*Mk.* 14:32–42 and parallels).

Because they attributed to Jesus' human consciousness a full and direct vision of the divine reality, medieval theologians logically denied that he walked by faith: Jesus did not believe, he simply *knew*. Once the hypothesis of his beatific vision was dropped, however, the way was open for many contemporary theologians to recognize a life of faith in the earthly Jesus.

Here an adequate Christian theology wants to exclude narrow alternatives. Imitating his life of faith or believing *like* the Jesus recorded by the synoptic Gospels does not rule out believing *in* the Jesus presented by John's gospel. He can be both the model and the object of Christian faith. Further, some reflection is needed on the basis of those three distinguishable but not separable dimensions of faith to which Paul bears witness: confession or judgments about the way things are (*Rom.* 10:9), commitment or obedient decisions about courses of action (*Rom.* 1:5), and confidence or trust for the future (*Rom.* 6:8). With regard to confession or "believing *that*" *(fides quae)*, there were some limitations in the content of Jesus' faith. He could confess the history of revelation and salvation in the story of the Jewish people, but—granted that he had a primordial awareness of his personal identity and mission—his judgments about these items were matters of knowledge, not of faith. With regard to commitment to action and confidence about the future, the Gospels witness to Jesus' obedient commitment and to the confidence that Jesus showed when faced with the human failure of his mission (e.g., *Mk.* 14:25). In this way characteristic attitudes of Jesus displayed a commitment, confidence, and (limited) confession that deserved the name of faith. To deny that the historical Jesus had faith or needed to have faith would in any case cast doubt on his real humanity.

Virginal Conception. On the basis of the infancy narratives of Matthew and Luke (*Mt.* 1–2, *Lk.* 1–2), Christian tradition has held that Jesus had no human father but was conceived through the power of the Holy Spirit. Challenges to this tradition have come on a number of grounds. Some rule it out as part of their general rejection of any such miraculous intervention by God. Others maintain that early Christians were under pressure to invent the story of the virginal conception, once Jewish critics began to claim that Jesus was illegitimate. Still others have argued that myths about male gods impregnating earthly women prompted Christians (who already believed in Jesus' divinity) to develop the legend of this virginal conception. Then there are those who think that Christians have misinterpreted the intentions of Matthew and Luke in their infancy narratives. Through the device of the virginal conception, those evangelists did not want to communicate some historical truth about the miraculous way Jesus was conceived but merely aimed to state their faith in him as Son of God and as Messiah.

These challenges to the tradition of the virginal conception are balanced by other arguments. Any adequate discussion of the rejection of divine miraculous intervention would require an enormous parenthesis on the nature and role of miracles. The challenge that the doctrine is a defense against the charge of illegitimacy is weakened by the argument of Raymond E. Brown in *The Birth of the Messiah* (1977). Brown shows that the charge of illegitimacy, which appeared in the second century, may have emerged only after the composition of the gospels of Matthew and Luke and perhaps even as a reaction to their narratives of the virginal conception. In that case the story of the virginal conception would not have arisen as a Christian response to a charge of illegitimacy that was already in circulation. The alleged parallels to the doctrine of the virginal conception in ancient mythology (or in legends about the marvelous conceptions of religious figures, emperors, and even philosophers like Plato) are by no means close to the nonsexual virginal conception that is at the heart of the infancy narratives of both Matthew and Luke. These so-called parallels consistently involve something different: "a type of *hieros gamos* where a divine male, in human or other form, impregnates a woman, either through normal sexual intercourse or through some substitute form of penetration" (Raymond E. Brown,

The Virginal Conception and Bodily Resurrection of Jesus, 1973, p. 62).

With regard to the challenge that Christians have misinterpreted the intentions of Matthew and Luke, Brown argues that while we cannot scientifically trace the way the tradition(s) of the virginal conception originated, were transmitted in the early Christian communities, and reached the evangelists, it seems that "both Matthew and Luke regarded the virginal conception as historical," even if "the modern intensity about historicity was not theirs" (*Birth of the Messiah*, p. 517). The two evangelists refer to the conception of Jesus from different standpoints—Matthew from that of Joseph, Luke from that of Mary—but both agree that the conception came about without human intercourse and through the power of the Holy Spirit.

At the same time, difficulties at the level of meaning continue to lead some Christians (not to mention others) to question and reject the virginal conception. Does it derogate Jesus' full humanity not to have been conceived in the normal way? Does the virginal conception imply that sexual intercourse is impure? And, in general, what religious message can the biological manner of Jesus' conception really deliver today? Ultimately any conclusions here will depend on the conviction carried by those major patterns of meaning to be found in *Matthew* and *Luke*. The virginal conception expresses Jesus' divine filiation and his relationship to the Holy Spirit. In these terms, the virginal conception will prove credible (historically and religiously) only to those who see in that story how right from his conception Jesus' total history disclosed a God who is Father, Son, and Holy Spirit. (Here the Muslims take an essentially different view inasmuch as they accept the virginal conception of Jesus but believe him to be a mere creature, one of the prophets, and not the only Son of God.) [*See also* Virgin Birth.]

Prospects

Several new and old points set the principal agenda for religious reflection on Jesus of Nazareth in the coming years. These include drawing together Eastern and Western Christologies; using Jewish, Muslim, Hindu, and other non-Christian works on Jesus; preserving the appropriate tensions in Christology; and wrestling with the traditional questions of humanity, divinity, and personhood.

An Ecumenical Approach. Western thinking on Jesus needs to be complemented and corrected with perspectives that have prevailed in Eastern Christian traditions. Western Christology has often spent its energies describing, interpreting, and explaining the person and mission of Jesus. With a more contemplative, poetic, worship-centered, and at times mystical stance, Eastern theologians have generally avoided constructing purely intellectual systems. Icons celebrate Jesus in the reality of the incarnation and the transformation of his resurrection. Eastern theology does not forget that the whole saving activity of Christ is inseparable from the Holy Spirit. Fedor Dostoevskii's short story "The Grand Inquisitor," for example, is a classic warning against the temptation of the institutional church to misrepresent Jesus and refuse him true obedience.

A wider ecumenical approach to Jesus entails using reflections on him and reactions to him coming from those who do not as such share Christian faith in him. This means drawing on Jewish writers (like Eugene Borowitz, Schalom Ben-Chorin, David Flusser, and Josef Klausner), Muslim sources (not only what the Qur'ān says about Jesus but also interpretations of him coming from contemporary authors), Hindu thinkers (such as Keshab Chandra Sen, Mohandas Gandhi, and Ramakrishna Paramahamsa), Marxist authors, and so forth. Christians maintain that sharing their belief is essential for any adequate understanding of Jesus' person and work, but at times outsiders can have a sharp perception of who he was and what he stood for. Gandhi's appreciation of the Sermon on the Mount and its teaching on nonretaliation is a classic example. Political interpretations of Jesus from Ernst Bloch, Leszek Kolakowski, and Milan Machovec̆ may have been rightly criticized for their partial use of the evidence, but they have served as useful counterweights to utterly nonpolitical presentations of Jesus that ignored his preference for the poor and marginalized people in Palestinian society. Such Marxist approaches, incidentally, are not to be confused with the official Soviet thesis (which appears to have been recently abandoned) that Jesus never existed and was a purely mythological figure. In all cases, non-Christian reflections of Jesus belong to the total picture of his place in human history and religious belief.

Furthermore, the data for such a total approach includes the artistic images of Jesus developed in painting, sculpture, music (both serious and popular), films, drama, and literature in general. Such depictions may at times exploit the story of Jesus, misrepresent the gospel testimony to his identity and function, and do little more than mirror the religious spirit (or prejudices) of the present age. Nevertheless, the images of Jesus in fiction, on the screen, and so forth are not always wrong. In any event, they belong among the most influential ways in which he continues to be interpreted and appreciated.

Polarities. In making religious sense of Jesus' person and mission, contemporary thinkers and, in particular, Christian theologians have started to preserve certain tensions that have often been presented as, or more often presumed to be, a choice between real alternatives. For example, Christian thinkers have already begun to retrieve a doctrine of creation in which the entire world is acknowledged to image forth the traces of Christ, the creative Word of God (e.g., *Jn.* 1:1–4, 1:10; *Col.* 1:16–17). This is to hold together the creation and the redemption and vindicate a view that reaches back through Teilhard de Chardin (1881–1955) and Charles Gore (1853–1932) to Duns Scotus (c. 1266–1308) and ultimately to Irenaeus (c. 130–c. 200). In this approach the creation and the incarnation/redemption are taken to be two phases in the one process of God's self-giving and self-expression.

The proper tension between the crucifixion and the resurrection has often slipped out of the picture. Generally speaking, Western theologians have proved loyal successors to Anselm of Canterbury. Often they have ascribed redemption to Jesus' death and reduced his resurrection to being a highly useful (if not strictly necessary) proof for Christian claims. A sound balance here is still being developed.

Above, under "Suffering and Redemption," some criticisms of Moltmann's trinitarian theology of the cross were noted. Nevertheless, that theology has the merit of bringing together two matters that are still often kept separate: reflection on Jesus' cross and the Christian doctrine of the Trinity. There is need for a renewed trinitarian understanding of Jesus' passion and death that would hold in unity the most characteristic Christian sign and symbol, the cross, and the central doctrine of Christianity, the Trinity.

In the wake of Philipp Melanchthon's classic dictum, "To know Christ is to know his benefits," Christology has at times been reduced to being at least largely a function of soteriology (e.g., Bultmann, Cullmann, Tillich). Beliefs about Jesus in himself *(in se)* took second place to beliefs about what he is for us *(pro nobis)* or were even dismissed as of little practical importance. Kasper, Pannenberg, and others have set themselves against such an alternative that would one-sidedly privilege soteriology at the expense of Christology. For them, doctrines about Jesus' person and function are distinguishable but not properly separable.

Liberation Christologies coming from Leonardo Boff, Juan Luis Segundo, and Jon Sobrino serve as strong reminders about the mutual relationship between political, social, and religious practice and theory, which can be lost by ignoring and/or suppressing the fact that Jesus died because of the historical sins of his society. For these Latin American writers, systematic discussion of his person and work entails analyzing concretely the present situation in a way that emerges from and then leads back into the struggle for justice now. Without engaging in debates about the nature of such analyses, one point is clear: any theoretical statements about Jesus will inevitably betray something of what the authors in question have experienced, hoped for, done, or failed to do in their lives. Here practice definitively gives shape to theory. Christian theology would add that the practice of conversion and dedicated discipleship are decisive for real knowledge of Jesus.

Humanity and Divinity. A perennial task for those who study the life and influence of Jesus concerns the full humanity and the full divinity that Christians acknowledge in his person. Ways of articulating and expressing the divine reality, the nature of human beings, and the essence of personhood vary according to culture, philosophy, and religious modes of thought. But in all cases, prior responses to three questions (What/who is God? What is it to be human? What is a person?) will come into play when anyone reflects on Christian beliefs about what Jesus is (the human and divine natures), who he is (divine person), and how he is what he is (the union between the natures in this one person). At the same time, Christians add that they not only bring to their reflection on Jesus some provisional notions on divinity, humanity, and personhood but also find that the data of their faith shape their fully developed answers to the three questions given above. Above all, the history of Jesus provides the specifically Christian idea of God.

Many others who do not share a faith in Jesus' divinity are aware of ways in which his story has affected their sense of what human existence is. Here too a mutual conditioning comes into play. They bring to their reflections on Jesus a prior understanding of humanity. But, in turn, reflection on him will feed back into their understanding and interpretation of human existence.

[*For further discussion of Christian reflection on the life and ministry of Jesus, see* Theology, *article on* Christian Theology; Trinity; *and the biographies of the theologians mentioned herein.*]

BIBLIOGRAPHY

The best available studies on the history of Jesus include A. E. Harvey's *Jesus and the Constraints of History* (London, 1982); Joachim Jeremias's *New Testament Theology: The Proclamation of Jesus*, translated by John Bowden (New York, 1971); Howard Clark Kee's *Jesus in History: An Approach to the Study of the Gospels*, 2d ed. (New York, 1977); and Ben F. Meyer's *The Aims of Jesus* (London, 1979). Joseph A. Fitzmyer's *A Christological Catechism: New Testament Answers* (Ramsey, N.J., 1982) accurately sums up the New Testament's presentation of Jesus' story and person. Hans Küng, in *On Being a Christian* (New York, 1977), marshals evidence to show the distinctiveness of the historical Jesus over against other founders of world religions. Pheme Perkins's *Resurrection* (New York, 1984) provides a detailed exegetical study of the New Testament witness to the resurrection of Jesus. The development of doctrines about Jesus in primitive Christianity is covered well by Martin Hengel's *The Son of God* (Philadelphia, 1976) and C. F. D. Moule's *The Origin of Christology* (Cambridge, 1977). Aloys Grillmeier's *Christ in Christian Tradition* (London, 1965) traces the development of Christology from the first century to the Council of Chalcedon. Contemporary Christologies include Walter Kasper's *Jesus the Christ* (New York, 1976); James P. Mackey's *Jesus, the Man and the Myth* (New York, 1979); my *Interpreting Jesus* (Ramsey, N.J., 1983); Wolfhart Pannenberg's *Jesus: God and Man*, 2d ed. (Philadelphia, 1977); Richard P. McBrien's *Catholicism*, vol. 1 (Minneapolis, 1980), pp. 367–563; and Karl Rahner's *Foundations of Christian Faith* (New York, 1978), pp. 176–321. Edward Schillebeeckx, in *Christ: The Experience of Jesus as Lord* (New York, 1980), reconstructs Christian belief in Jesus as Savior within the context of human suffering and the quest for salvation. A notable Jewish study on Jesus is Samuel Sandmel's *We Jews and Jesus* (New York, 1965). Géza Vermès's *Jesus the Jew: A Historian's Reading of the Gospels* (Philadelphia, 1981) presents a Jesus who as prophet, healer, exorcist, and agent of forgiveness belonged to the tradition of charismatic Judaism. M. M. Thomas's *The Acknowledged Christ of the Indian Renaissance* (London, 1969) surveys ways in which some spiritual leaders in Neo-Hinduism interpret the meaning of Jesus and Christianity for religion and society in modern India. Milan Machoveč's *A Marxist Looks at Jesus* (Philadelphia, 1976) is the best study on Jesus by a Marxist. Wismer Don's *The Islamic Jesus: An Annotated Bibliography of Sources in English and French* (New York, 1977) guides the reader to many Muslim studies on Jesus.

GERALD O'COLLINS, S.J.

JEVONS, F. B. (1858–1936), English classical scholar. Frank Byron Jevons played a significant role in popularizing the comparative study of religion in the English-speaking world during the two decades before World War I. Jevons, who was classical tutor at the University of Durham from 1882 to 1910, joined R. R. Marett, Andrew Lang, Gilbert Murray, and other Edwardians in applying the theoretical formulas of British evolutionist anthropology to the interpretation of Greco-Roman texts.

Magic was his special area of interest; he questioned the conclusion of James G. Frazer and others that magic necessarily preceded religion along a unilineal, evolutionary pathway. As he put it in his *Idea of God in Early Religions* (1910), magic and religion were "two moods" that were different from the beginning. Likewise, prayers and the worship of gods were phenomena that were originally separate from (and apparently as ancient as) spells and fetishism.

Jevons's most widely read work in England was *An Introduction to the History of Religion* (1896; 2d ed., 1902), complemented in the United States by his Hartford-Lamson Lectures on comparative religion for the American Board of Foreign Missions in 1908 (revised and published in 1910 under the title *Comparative Religion*). A liberal Anglican, Jevons thought that the religious quest of humanity reflected the divine will, and he maintained that all religions had their fulfillment in Christianity. He argued that Buddhism was not a religion but an etiolation of tendencies already present in ancient Brahmanism. Religious evolution, he believed, was above all the process by which the truth of monotheism came to be discerned. Following his appointment as professor of philosophy at the University of Durham in 1910, his books on *Evolution* (1910), *Personality* (1913), and *Philosophy* (1914) all find him espousing a species of nonmaterialist, creative, and dispersive (i.e., social) evolutionism influenced by Henri Bergson.

Jevons was principal of Hatfield Hall, Durham, from 1896 to 1923, and from there he corresponded with many scholars. His obvious theological orientation and evolutionism have led to a decline of interest in his work since World War I.

BIBLIOGRAPHY

Two important works by Jevons not discussed above are *Religion in Evolution* (London, 1906) and *An Introduction to the Study of Comparative Religion* (Cambridge, Mass., 1909). For works about Jevons, I refer the reader to Eric J. Sharpe's *Comparative Religion: A History* (London, 1975) and Jacques Waardenburg's *Classical Approaches to the Study of Religion*, 2 vols. (The Hague, 1973–1974).

GARRY W. TROMPF

JEWELRY. The wearing of jewelry is as old as civilization itself. Necklaces and bracelets of bone, pebbles, shells, and teeth have been found from the Paleolithic period (c. 25,000–18,000 BCE). Jewelry is used by primitive societies as a badge of office or demonstration of some personal achievement, as with necklaces made from the teeth of dangerous animals or enemies. This function survives in the developed world today in the form of medals and mayoral chains, for example.

The orifices of the human body require magic protection since, like any other openings, they invite entry by demons or evil spirits. Anything shiny, noisy, or colorful, or having dangling movement, is especially effective in frightening away evil spirits. In many traditional societies, people protect their nostrils with bone, stone, metal, or feather ornaments. Modern Hindu women may wear jeweled nose rings, if their wealth permits.

Ear entrances are almost universally protected by earrings or ear spools. Some people also protect the mouth by wearing lip plugs or lip plates.

The sexual orifices must also be guarded; in times past this was ensured by jeweled girdles and codpieces. In modern times ornate belts and large showy buckles are a substitute, especially as used by women; the belts may also feature dangling ornaments.

Necklaces and jeweled collars are particularly important because they guard the throat (the seat of the voice) and the neck, which represents the vital connection between the head (mind, psyche, spirit) and the rest of the body. The broad collars worn by the ancient Egyptians possessed powerful amuletic function, and mummies were customarily buried with many layers of collars to protect the important neck and throat.

An important form of necklace is the pectoral type, in which the suspended item (crucifix, gem, amulet, etc.) lies more or less directly over the heart, thereby bringing a close association between the item and the seat of life. On a deeper level, necklaces or chains worn around the neck represent diversity in unity: the separate beads or links are the multiplicity of manifestation, while the connecting thread represents the unity and the nonmanifest.

Rings are probably the item of jewelry most often and most heavily invested with symbolic import. The ring, with its circular shape, having neither beginning nor end, is a natural symbol for completion and eternity. The complete circle is regarded by the Chinese as denoting the combination of all divine principles as these move in an everlasting and unbroken circle.

One origin ascribed to the ring is the knot. A knotted cord or piece of wire twisted into a knot was a favorite charm in ancient times. Frequently this was used to cast a spell over a person. Even today rings are often made in the form of a knot. This symbol undoubtedly signified the binding or attaching of the spell to its object, and the same idea is present in the "true-lover's knot." [*See* Knots.]

The use of a ring to bind is reflected in Pliny's story *(Natural History)* of the origin of the ring: for his impious daring in stealing fire from heaven, Prometheus had been doomed by Zeus to be chained for thirty thousand years to a rock during which time a vulture fed daily on his liver. Eventually Zeus relented and liberated Prometheus; nevertheless, in order to avoid a violation of the original judgment, it was ordained that the Titan should wear a link of his chain on one of his fingers as a ring, and in this ring was set a fragment of the rock to which he had been chained, so that he might still be regarded as bound to the rock.

Romans were the first to use the "binding" of rings for betrothals, a custom that survives today in the wedding ring. The ring is placed on the third finger of the left hand, due to an ancient belief that a vein or nerve runs from this finger directly to the heart. The Roman writer Macrobius says, "Because of this nerve, the newly betrothed places the ring on this finger of his spouse, as though it were a representation of the heart."

Similarly, the mystic significance of the episcopal ring is the union of Christ with his church. When a ring is conferred upon a bishop, this formula is used: "Receive the ring of faith as a sign that thou wilt guard the Bride of God, Holy Church, with undaunted faith." The seal ring is also seen as a sign that priests keep the many secrets confided to them, as though beneath a seal. When a nun is consecrated, the priest places a ring that has been previously blessed on her finger and declares her to be the spouse of Christ. The Coronation Ring of English kings is sometimes called "the wedding ring of England," for the king is regarded as married to the nation over which he has sovereignty.

The employment of rings as religous symbols is sometimes bound up with their use in some other way, as in the case of many seal rings, for instance. Unquestionably, many of the engraved scarabs set in Egyptian rings had a specifically religious significance. The wearing of seal rings by the episcopate may actually have developed out of the use of the signet ring which was used to seal documents by officials of the Roman empire. Also, it was customary for senators, chief civil magistrates, and ambassadors to receive a gold ring upon their appointment. After the Peace of the Church in the fourth century the bishop became in some sense an official of the empire, and Constantine gave him the power to arbitrate in certain cases. By the sixth or seventh century in the West the ring was given at the consecration of a bishop as one of the ensigns of his office. Abbots and abbesses were also permitted to wear such rings. In the Eastern church this custom was never adopted, except among the Armenians.

The "Fisherman's Ring" is the gold seal ring of the pope. A new one is made for each successive pontiff, for immediately upon the pope's death the previous ring is purposely broken by the papal chamberlain, who is permitted to keep the fragments, although they may be buried with the pontiff. The design on the seal depicts the apostle Peter in a boat holding a net; the name of the reigning pope is inscribed above.

In ancient Rome the rings worn by the high priests of Jupiter, the *flamines Diales*, were hollow and openworked. This form was said to have been chosen for mystical or symbolic reasons, as showing that everything indicating harshness or severity, restriction, or arduous labor was to be kept away from these priests.

In the classical world, rings were often dedicated to a particular deity, especially to Apollo at Delos. An image of Mars on a ring's stone was popular with Roman soldiers. Members of one gnostic sect often wore a ring bearing the word *Abraxas,* the favorite designation of the creative energy.

In Rome on days of national mourning, gold rings were laid aside and iron rings substituted, as a mark of respect and sorrow. Occasionally, as a mark of disapproval, senators would remove their gold rings at a public sitting. Roman supplicants took off their rings as a mark of humility.

Tacitus states in his *Germania* that a warrior of the German tribes had to wear an iron ring until he had killed an enemy, and then he could divest himself of it. Such iron rings were looked upon as badges of slavery. Among the other cheap materials that have been used on occasion for making rings are horseshoe nails, which are thought to possess some of the talismanic power accorded to the horseshoe.

Some wealthy Romans wore rings set with ten different precious stones representing Minerva and the nine Muses. These were called "Ten Maidens rings." This ring of the Ten Maidens suggests the decade, or rosary, rings common in the Middle Ages. Usually there were ten bosses, or knobs, which could be turned around the finger, though occasionally there were eleven, for counting ten Ave Marias and one Paternoster.

There are many legends and tales of rings that appear to be irretrievably lost and are then found or returned after a long period of time; perhaps their shape suggests the idea of "coming full circle." A typical legend of this type is that of King Solomon, who was successful in all his undertakings because he possessed a wonderful ring given to him by four angels. It was set with a marvelous stone, which served as a mirror in which Solomon was able to see reflected the image of any place or person he wished. Stolen away by an evil *jinnī,* the ring reappeared forty years later in the body of a fish served at the king's table.

Jewelry has always played a large role in gift giving. Twentieth-century anthropological research has demonstrated that gift giving is essentially aggressive, since it puts the recipient into one's debt, hence into one's power. In Western culture during recent centuries jewelry is most often the gift of a man to a woman, perhaps an expression of a wish for physical possession. It is not uncommon, therefore, to see jewelry designs that are ambiguous—chokers that resemble collars for pets or slaves, and bracelets that look like manacles.

[*See also* Amulets and Talismans.]

BIBLIOGRAPHY

Black, J. Anderson. *The Story of Jewelry.* New York, 1974.

Kunz, George Frederick. *Rings for the Finger.* Philadelphia, 1917.

DIANA LEE JAMES

JEWISH ETHICAL LITERATURE. *See under* Jewish Thought and Philosophy.

JEWISH LAW. *See* Halakhah.

JEWISH PEOPLE. [*This entry discusses the nature of Jewish corporate identity, from the biblical period to the present. For further discussion of the religious dimension of the Jewish people, see* Judaism.]

The Jews are both a historical people in their own right and a social body required and sustained by the Jewish religious tradition. In what sense the Jewish people is to be considered a nation or ethnic group depends on how these terms are defined—the traditional Hebrew concepts for nation, *goi, le'um,* and above all *'am,* apply to the Jews collectively, but the extent to which the peoplehood of the Jews is amenable to definition by nineteenth- and twentieth-century concepts of nationality has been a matter of controversy, to be discussed later. This article seeks to explore the meanings attributed to Jewish peoplehood from ancient to modern times, with special attention to the relationship of Jewry to other faith communities that have emerged from the Israelite religious matrix.

That the Jews are at the same time a people and a religious fellowship is attested by the complex interplay between nationhood and religion in the course of Jewish history. Historical circumstances have periodically intruded on the parameters of membership and the idealized meaning of collective Jewish existence. During periods of rapid change affecting contemporaneous branches of the Diaspora differently, uncertainty and even conflict have emerged as to who is a Jew and what religious actions or principles of faith are required of a Jew. Jewish religious authorities have been forced to take up the task of clarifying the criteria for inclusion in the people and the theological significance of Jewish survival as a group "like all the nations" (*1 Sm.* 8:5), yet "a people dwelling alone and not reckoning itself among the nations" (*Nm.* 23:9). Eventually these confusions subside, only to reappear in later historical eras.

The nature of Jewish religious peoplehood can in part

be illuminated by comparative considerations. A similar congruence of peoplehood and religion is found in certain national forms of Christianity (e.g., the Armenian and Coptic churches) and in the "nation" of Islam as corporate body and subject of religious law, especially in the early history of Islam, when it was a religion of the Arabs only and before it became the religion of the Persian, Turkish, and other peoples. Unlike the Christian instances, however, Judaism stands quite separate from its scions and siblings. The line between Judaism and Christianity has remained firm, despite occasional allusion to a "Judeo-Christian" tradition, and, in contrast to Christianity, Judaism has resisted definition by creedal formulation. The centrality of salvation through Christ and related creedal and doctrinal formulations facilitated the theological idea of a multinational church quite different from the bonds that maintained the unity of the Jewish people. In its emphasis on the centrality of law rather than salvation through faith in Christ and sacramental grace, Judaism shows a much closer structural affinity to Islam. The cultural variation between the various branches of Jewry for many centuries was virtually as great as that of Christendom and Islam, but the political situation of Judaism and the Jews was overall quite different. The Jewish people was a nation before its religion achieved its mature form, and the religious tradition maintained the integrity of the people's identity when the Jews were a minority in all the lands of their residence.

Other peoples and religions have had diasporas, but the Jewish Diaspora is remarkable for its global dispersion and its ability to survive. At least since the end of antiquity the Jews were essentially a diaspora people. After the Israelite and Judean kingdoms of the eleventh to the sixth century BCE and the Hasmonean kingdom of the second and first centuries BCE, and despite exceptional situations where the ruling class of a society converted to Judaism, there was not a Jewish state until 1948; for almost nineteen centuries, the political factor in Jewish history has been more indirect, involving semiautonomous communal institutions and leaders of various types not possessing absolute sovereign power but buttressed by the gentile state and by Jewish figures accorded authority in matters of exegesis and legal interpretation. The need to adjust to the objective status of a Diaspora minority has surely contributed to Jewish unity and continuity.

During the long course of Jewish history in the Diaspora, common destiny and cohesiveness were maintained by external and internal forces working in tandem. Consciousness of living in *galut* ("exile") and awaiting ultimate redemption has been a key subjective element in the self-identity inculcated by the tradition and constantly reinforced by the Jewish liturgy. At the same time, however, this distinctive identity has been maintained by the conspicuous presence of the Jewish people in the formative narratives of Christianity and Islam. In the New Testament the Jewish people is depicted as having rejected Jesus as the Messiah, even though he and his disciples were Jews; in the Qur'ān the Jews are depicted as having rejected Muḥammad as the "seal of the prophets" even though he acknowledged the divine source of their sacred book and certain other features of Jewish worship. (In both cases these charges have a historical basis.)

Acknowledgment by Christianity and Islam that the Jewish people has played an extraordinary role in the history of salvation, even when accompanied by doctrines that God rejected the Jews and bestowed grace on another elect people, expressed the ambivalent attitudes toward Jewry of Christian and Muslim religious authorities: confirmation of Jewish specialness and anger at "stiff-necked" Jewish obstinate denial of the (Christian or Muslim) truth. Conviction of possessing the truth and anger at the Jews lay behind the social and legal restrictions on Jewish status and were easily available to rationalize anti-Jewish persecutions. But the peculiar conspicuousness of the Jewish people also serves to confirm the singularity of the Jewish people, which is a cardinal element of the Jewish tradition itself and a main reason for Jewish survival.

Another issue sometimes raised in connection with Jewish peoplehood is whether Judaism should be characterized as a universal or an ethnic faith. Judaism—more properly, Torah in its broad sense as holy teaching and action—is both universalistic and particularistic. Gaining ultimate authority from the conviction that it is derived from divine revelation, Torah includes all forms of Jewish religious practice (*mitsvot,* or commandments; *halakhah,* the correct way, or religious law; and *minhag,* or custom)—but Torah also comprises the values inculcated by Jewish law and preaching, as well as the understandings of reality and the human situation expressed in Jewish religious literature. Torah articulates concepts about the nature of deity in relation to cosmos and history: that deity is one, eternal, creative, transcendent as well as immanent, revelatory, and personal—although Jewish religious thought has brought forth a variety of sometimes quite complex formulations of these and other fundamental principles of faith.

At the same time, the very idea of Torah requires that there be a certain people among the nations of the world that is to study and practice Torah as the *raison d'être* of its existence (and of the existence of the universe, at least in its present form). The notion of a people elected by God to receive the commandments of the Torah hallows the people and locates its special role in the context of world history. The Jewish tradition conceives of this election not solely as a preordained, passive reception of revelation but as an active electing by the people to accept the "yoke" of the commandments. Thus Jewish religious thought transforms the mundane historical fact of the people's social existence into a joyful, voluntarily assumed obligation and responsibility. These introductory remarks indicate some of the complexities of Jewish peoplehood as fact and ideal, which will be dealt with separately in the following.

Names for the Jews and Judaism. In the Jewish tradition, the Jewish people as a socioreligious entity is designated *'am Yisra'el* (the "people of Israel"), *benei Yisra'el* ("children of Israel," Israelites), *beit Yisra'el* ("house of Israel"), *keneset Yisra'el* ("assembly of Israel," in rabbinic literature), or simply as *Yisra'el* (Israel). The biblical patriarch Jacob, renamed Israel in *Genesis* 32:28, is the eponymous ancestor of the people of Israel through his sons, who are considered the founders of the twelve Israelite tribes. In contrast, a native of the modern state of Israel *(medinat Yisra'el)*, which possesses Christian and Muslim, as well as Jewish, citizens, is usually rendered by the modern Hebrew adjective *Israeli (Yisra'eli)*. The term *Jew* (Heb., *Yehud*) is etymologically derived from *Judah (Yehudah)*, the eponym of the biblical tribe of Judah.

After the death of King Solomon around 922 BCE, when the majority of the Israelite tribes rejected his son as ruler and formed a kingdom called the kingdom of Israel *(mamlekhet Yisra'el)*, the southern kingdom of Judah, comprising the tribal territories of Judah and Benjamin and the Davidic capital of Jerusalem, remained loyal to the Davidic dynasty. The northern kingdom of Israel came to an end in 722 BCE; the southern kingdom of Judah *(mamlekhet Yehudah)* was destroyed in 587/6 BCE, but the Aramaic cognate *yahud* remained the name for the region around Jerusalem in the Persian empire. (In *Esther* 2:5 the term *Jew* refers to a member of the whole people, even someone of the tribe of Benjamin; in *Esther* 8:17 and 9:27 it refers to the act of gentiles joining the Jews in some unspecified way.) The Greek form *Ioudaia* was used by the Ptolemaic and Seleucid kingdoms and for the independent commonwealth established by the Hasmoneans in the second century BCE. The latinized form was Judaea.

By Hellenistic times the term *Jew* (Gr., *Ioudaios*, Heb., *Yehudi*) had become a name not only for subjects of the Hasmonean state but throughout the Diaspora for those who were members of the Jewish people and adherents of its religious tradition. While accepting the term *Yehudi*, the rabbinic literature continued to prefer *Yisra'el*, *benei Yisra'el*, and so forth. (In the context of the Jewish liturgy, an "Israelite" is a Jew called to the reading of scripture who is not a priest or a Levite.) Yet another relevant term is *'Ivri* ("Hebrew"), which probably at first referred to a social status rather than to ethnic or gentilic identification (this primary usage of *Hebrew*, as, for example, in *Exodus* 21:2, may have had a philological relationship to the second-millennium social category called in Akkadian the *habiru*). Several biblical instances when *Hebrew* can be construed as referring to an Israelite or to the ancestor of an Israelite (*Jon.* 1:8, *Gn.* 4:13) and as recalling Eber, a descendant of Noah's son Shem (*Gn.* 10:21, 11:14), may have led to its eventually becoming a synonym for the Israelites and their language. In the nineteenth century in some European countries, *Hebrew* became a polite equivalent for *Jew*, which had acquired negative connotations; in the twentieth century the positive force of *Jew* has been regained in English, German, and other languages.

Corporate Existence in Ancient Israelite Religion. The Hebrew scriptures represent a selection of the literature produced by and for the people of Israel, mainly in the Land of Israel and over as many as eight or ten centuries. A main theme of the Pentateuch is how the people came into being, a chain of narratives that sets the stage for the enumeration of Israel's corporate duties to its God, YHVH (probably vocalized as *Yahveh*). Accordingly, the ancestors of the children of Israel had lived in the land of Canaan as patriarchal clans for several generations until they settled in Egypt, were enslaved, and, after Moses' confrontation with Pharaoh, were redeemed by YHVH, who brought them to the wilderness of Sinai. There they entered a binding agreement with their God—a covenant that included a taboo against worshiping other gods (*Ex.* 20:2–6). The modern historiography on the origins of the people in the context of the nations and social movements of the second millennium BCE involves many speculative uncertainties: the exact relationship of the direct ancestors of the Israelites to such ancient groups as the Amorites and the Hyksos; whether the proto-Israelites worshiped YHVH before the Exodus (compare *Exodus* 6:3 with *Genesis* 4:26); the extent to which Canaanite peasants or tribes joined the Israelite federation in the thirteenth or twelfth centuries BCE, accepted its God, and were absorbed in the people.

The exclusive divine authority of YHVH in relation to the collective existence of Israel is reflected in various and fundamental aspects of ancient Israelite religion. For example, Israelite tradition went to considerable lengths to disassociate ownership of the land of Canaan from the right of conquest as such. Israelite settlement was said to have been made possible by YHVH as Israel's supreme ruler; the Land of Israel was a territory on which the people could become a nation akin to other nations but devoted to carrying out its covenantal duties. The corporate aspect of land ownership can be seen in the provision that land sold by individuals was to be returned periodically to the family to whom it was "originally" allocated (*Lv.* 25:2, 25:23).

Moral and legal obligations included many stipulations that regulated individual behavior as well as relations between sectors of Israelite society, but the framework and a substantial portion of the covenantal duties preserved in the Pentateuch refer to Israel as a collective entity. In addition to sacrifices to be offered by Israelites as expressing personal thanksgiving or contrition, an elaborate series of sacrifices is to be offered to God by the priests on behalf of the people to express collective gratitude or to expiate collective sin (e.g., *Nm.* 28:2, *Lv.* 16:30). Besides ethical duties incumbent on the Israelites individually and as members of families, there are responsibilities to the "widow, orphan, and stranger" for which Israel as a whole is responsible (*Ex.* 22:21–22).

Throughout the history of the Israelite kingdoms prophetic messengers warned the people that if these collective obligations were not fulfilled, YHVH could take away the land he had given them and force them into exile (e.g., *Am.* 3:2, 7:11). The destruction of the northern kingdom of Israel by Assyria in 722 BCE was interpreted in this manner by the so-called Deuteronomic movement, which probably acquired the opportunity to carry out an extensive program of religious reforms in the kingdom of Judah in the 620s (*2 Kgs.* 22–23, *2 Chr.* 34). The heart of the *Book of Deuteronomy* very likely reflects the position of this group, which emphasized that the corporate responsibility of Israel that had been voluntarily accepted at Sinai was binding on all generations of the people: to love YHVH, obey his commandments, avoid any taint of idolatry, worship him in the place—Jerusalem—that he would "cause his name to dwell," where his only house and sacrificial altar were to be constructed (e.g., *Dt.* 6:4–5, 12:1–14).

When Judah was destroyed by Babylonia in 587/6 BCE, the explanation offered was that the idolatry of the past had condemned the people to exile but that God continued to love them and held out a sure promise of redemption (*2 Kgs.* 24:3–4, *Jer.* 29). The experience of Babylonian exile brought to the fore the prophetic theme of the eternal nature of the covenant between YHVH and Israel. The religiosity of the exilic community was most likely marked by an acceptance of the divine causation for the people's exile, a pervasive regret for the sins of the ancestors, and a heightening of the idealized role of the people in history. While sustaining the concepts of a specific holy mountain (e.g., *Jl.* 4:1), city (*Is.* 2:3), and land of YHVH, that is, of Zion (*Is.* 10:24), a precedent emerged for autonomous Israelite survival outside the precincts of sacred space. (Contrast David's complaint that Saul banished him so that he could no longer serve YHVH, *1 Sm.* 26:19.) The exilic prophecies in the latter part of the *Book of Isaiah* portray the people as God's servant, as "light to the nations" (*Is.* 49:6) that God's salvation be known to the ends of the earth, and they anticipate that gentiles will worship YHVH, the author of good and evil (*Is.* 2:1–4; *Mi.* 4:1–4; *Is.* 45:14, 45:22–24, 56:3–8; *Zec.* 8:20–23).

The decisive difference between Israel's historical evolution and that of other ancient Near Eastern peoples was Israel's elevation of its God to the status of the sole deity, creator of heaven and earth, ruler of the world, and judge of all history. Pre-Mosaic sources of the Israelite cult of YHVH are quite uncertain, and perhaps unlikely. Unlike other Near Eastern deities (Sin, Adad, Ishtar, and so forth), YHVH did not have temples and shrines dedicated to him in various widely scattered localities around the Near East, and he was not incorporated into any other pantheon, confirming the attitude of the biblical authors that YHVH's name and reputation in the world depended solely on Israel. The dating of a full-fledged biblical monotheism is a matter of considerable scholarly controversy. For our purposes, determining when in Israelite history "other gods" came to be viewed as nondivine (in the biblical terminology, mere "idols") is less important than the fact of the eventual emergence, in the course of the intellectual development of ancient Israel, of an explicit, sweeping, and radical demotion of other deities and elevation of one God, an action unprecedented in the history of religion (*Is.* 45:5–7). This transformation was accompanied by the reinterpretation of traditions concerning the past from a monotheistic perspective rather than an abrupt break with the received traditions concerning that past.

The final redaction and reworking of the traditional material concerning human origins and the formative eras of Israelite history from the standpoint of radical monotheism may not have occurred until the postexilic period. The return to Zion of a large portion (but not all) of the Babylonian exiles in the late sixth century and again in the mid-fifth century BCE laid the groundwork for the revival of Jerusalem, its Temple, and the land of Judaea in late Persian and Hellenistic times. By then Judaism had become a world religion, centered on a scripture that defined the Jews as God's treasured possession, "a kingdom of priests and a holy people" (*Ex.*

19:4–6), necessary for his universal plan and goals. [*For further discussion, see* Israelite Religion.]

From Biblical Israel to the Christian and Rabbinic Israels. Both the corporate and the individual dimensions of Israelite faith were to be extensively developed in succeeding centuries. Closely associated with the corporate aspect of salvation is the messianic idea (buttressed by various scriptural verses and prophecies concerning the End of Days, the permanence of the Davidic dynasty, and the kingship of God) that there would be a completely just, God-inspired king to rule Israel and establish everlasting peace and harmony in the world.

The individualistic dimension of postscriptural Judaism took the form of each person's accountability to carry out the *mitsvot*, including many that had primarily been the duty of the priesthood earlier. Individual immortality became a central doctrine of Judaism perhaps in the second century BCE (a late biblical allusion to the resurrection of the dead is *Daniel* 12:2, most likely dating from the Maccabean Revolt; compare *2 Maccabees* 7:9, 7:14, 9:29). Personal immortality was soon absorbed into most branches of Judaism (except the Sadducees) and was made binding in the second of the Eighteen Benedictions (Shemoneh ʿEsreh or ʿAmidah) that Jewish males are to recite three times daily. Jewish eschatological teachings of the last centuries BCE and the first century CE, for all their flux and uncertainty, emphasized the crucial significance of Israel ("And the kingdom and the dominion and the greatness of the kingdoms under the whole heaven shall be given to the people of the saints of the Most High," *Dn.* 7:27) and the transcendent value of membership in it ("All Israel has a share in the world to come" with some notable exceptions, *San.* 10.1). This world *(ha-ʿolam hazeh)* of history will be climaxed by the coming of the King-Messiah and a utopian messianic age. And this world is transcended by another realm, the world to come *(ha-ʿolam ha-baʾ)*, where the guilty will be consigned to a merited punishment for their sins and the righteous of all generations will be eternally rewarded with the radiance of the divine presence.

Not only theology but also membership in the people of Israel was enlarged during the last centuries BCE and the first century CE. By the time of the Jewish revolt of 66–70 CE against the Romans in Judaea, a majority of Jews were probably residing in the Diaspora, either in Persia under the Parthians (the Jewish community of Babylonia, dating from the exile of the sixth century BCE) or in communities in the Hellenistic kingdoms and later the Roman empire (Antioch, the cities of Asia Minor and European Greece, Alexandria and elsewhere in Egypt, as well as Rome and other locations around the Mediterranean). These new communities had been founded by Jewish settlers who had left Judaea for a variety of political and economic reasons, but they had been augmented by a considerable number of conversions to Judaism in the Diaspora.

Formal conversion to Judaism was a new phenomenon in Jewish life. Previously, non-Israelites had been accepted into Israel on an individual basis (the *Book of Ruth,* which may date from postexilic times, contains one such account). A contrary instance of the rejection of "foreigners" is given by Ezra and Nehemiah, who demanded that the Judahites of their time separate themselves from their non-Israelite wives (*Neh.* 9:2, 13:3) and who rejected the inhabitants of Samaria (the heartland of the former northern kingdom of Israel) who worshiped YHVH but were considered by the Bible not to be of the seed of preexilic Israel (*2 Kgs.* 17:29–34). (The Samaritans became the first religious tradition that stemmed from the biblical matrix but was separate from the Jewish people. [*See* Samaritans.]) At the turn of the common era, however, proselytism seems to have become a common occurrence (see, for example, *Mt.* 23:15, *Acts* 2:5, and B. T., *Shab.* 31a). In addition to formal conversion, which probably entailed circumcision for males, immersion, and the offering of a special Temple sacrifice, there is reference to pagans who followed one or another element of the Jewish tradition (Josephus, *Against Apion* 2.39; Tacitus, *Histories* 5.5).

The last two centuries BCE and the first century CE was a period of intense Jewish religious ferment, when new schools of thought and new elites competed with each other: Pharisees, Sadducees, Essenes, Zealots, early Judeo-Christians, apocalyptic visionaries and sects in Judaea, and hellenized "philosophies" in the Diaspora. By the end of the first century CE or at least by the late second century after the last of the Jewish revolts against the Romans, the rabbinic Judaism that had developed out of the Pharisaic movement had become predominant, and Christianity had become fully separated from the Jewish people. By the end of the first century CE, the rabbis had added a benediction against sectarians *(birkat ha-minim),* apparently to indicate that Christians were unwelcome in the synagogue. Christian writings held that the Jews ignored the messiah and were collectively responsible for his death (*Mt.* 13:57, 27:25). In any event, by then most Christians were not of Jewish descent but were converted pagans.

After the Samaritans, Christianity was the second religious tradition that remained loyal to the witness of the Hebrew scriptures but came to constitute a distinct community of faith. A crucial element in the parting of the ways between Judaism and Christianity was the former's rejection of Jesus of Nazareth as Messiah and the latter's rejection (after a few years of uncertainty) of Jewish law. In what became the dominant Christian formulation, Torah law was held to have been divinely inspired but superseded by the coming of the Messiah, who made available a full salvation that had been prophesied in the Hebrew scriptures and that was not possible under "the law" (*Gal.* 3 and 4). [*For further discussion of the emergence of Christianity from Judaism, see* Judaism *and* Christianity *and the biography of Paul.*]

This principled negation of Jewish law, especially ritual law, ceremonial practice, and *kashrut,* meant that the experience of Jesus, accompanied by baptism, was a sufficient portal into the Christian people, now defined as the "new Israel" of the spirit (e.g., *Acts* 10, *Rom.* 9–11). In particular, the Jewish requirement of circumcision was rejected and baptismal immersion redefined as one's spiritual rebirth as a Christian. (According to rabbinic law, conversion is also a rebirth; the convert to Judaism terminates former family ties and is considered in the category of a newborn child. See *Gerim* 2.6.) For rabbinic Judaism, the Torah as divine law was a permanent feature of creation, a dynamic and ongoing process of articulating the tasks of God's people in history. In the New Testament, Christianity viewed the Hebrew scriptures through the concept of its fulfillment in Christ. Judaism viewed the written law of the Hebrew scriptures as part of a more comprehensive Torah that contained an oral law as well—an oral law that was partly redacted in the Mishnah, God's "mystery" given only to Israel (*Pesiqta' Rabbati* 14b). [*For discussion of this revelation in Judaism, see* Torah.]

Eventually Christianity did not reject the idea of religious law as such (it developed its own religious law to regulate creeds, holy days, family status, religious hierarchies, and so forth), but the Christian theological rejection of the eternally binding character of Torah law meant the sharp separation of *'am Yisra'el* by the Jewish self-definition and the "new Israel" according to the Christian viewpoint. The two conceptions of holy peoplehood thus reflect the two contrasting modes of relating to the Hebrew scripture as holy; Christianity pushed much further than Judaism the figural, allegoric, and symbolic interpretation of Old Testament figures, institutions, and prophecies.

Peoplehood in Rabbinic Judaism and Medieval Jewish Thought. According to rabbinic Judaism, the Jews were the direct, physical descendants of the remnant of preexilic Israel, augmented by those who had accepted the commandments and were adopted into the Jewish people through the rituals required by Torah as interpreted by the rabbis. The biblical term *ger* ("stranger, resident alien, sojourner") was understood to refer to a proselyte—a *ger tsedeq* in contrast to a *ger toshav,* who had rejected idolatry but not accepted the full burden of the *mitsvot.*

Conversion remained a legitimate mode of acquiring the status of Jew, even though most Jews were Jews by birth. Despite traditions that some of the most eminent rabbis were proselytes or their descendants and that God had special love for *gerim,* there were also Talmudic sages who expressed suspicion of the motives and behavior of proselytes. For their own good, prospective converts were to be warned that "this people was debased, oppressed, and degraded more than all other peoples." Only if they persisted were they to be accepted with joy: "To whom are you cleaving? Happy are you! To him who spoke and the world came into being" (*Gerim* 1.1–5).

From the early fourth century on, Jewish proselytizing was anathema to the christianized or islamicized state; the Roman emperor Constantine made conversion to Judaism punishable by death according to Roman law, and a similar prohibition was part of the so-called Pact of Omar defining the status of Christians and Jews under Islam. Certainly external obstacles were determinative in discouraging large-scale conversion to Judaism from the early Middle Ages until recently.

There were also, however, internal factors. Christianity viewed proselytism as its mission in the world with a far greater intensity than did Judaism, and the church fathers insisted with far more rigor that there was no salvation outside the church. The rabbinic doctrine held that only the Jewish people had knowledge of, and was bound by, the full complement of divine commandments, but that there were seven Noahic laws binding on all humanity (usually enumerated as the prohibitions of idolatry, blasphemy, bloodshed, sexual sins, theft, and eating a limb of a living animal, together with a positive commandment to establish a legal system; B.T., *San.* 56a). On the salvation of non-Jews, the normative Jewish doctrine became the opinion of Yehoshu'a that the "righteous of all nations have a share in the world to come" (Tosefta, *San.* 13.2).

According to rabbinic law since the second century CE, the child of a Jewish mother and a gentile father is a Jew, but the child of a gentile mother and a Jewish father is a gentile. This matrilineal principle is alluded to in the Mishnah (*Qid.* 3.12), which deals with marriages valid and invalid according to *halakhah* and the status of the offspring thereof. The relevant Talmudic ruling was Yonatan's that "thy son by an Israelite woman is called thy son, but thy son by a heathen woman is not called thy son but her son" (B.T., *Qid.* 68b); the commentators emphasize the positive conclusion that the offspring of a Jewish woman is a Jew (see Moses Maimonides' *Code of Law,* Forbidden Intercourse 12.7). Various explanations, sociological and historical, have been offered for this principle of matrilineal descent. Apart from the influence of Roman law or the impossibility of confirming paternity, in premodern times the ruling most likely was not often of widespread practical consequence, since it was unlikely that many Jewish men would marry non-Jewish women who did not formally convert yet would rear their children as members of the people of Israel.

What of abandoning the status of Jew? Jews who converted to another religion were still considered Jews, although there are differences of opinion among the authorities over their specific halakhic rights. The relevant Talmudic principle was that such a person was a sinful Jew: "An Israelite, even though he sinned, remains an Israelite" (B.T., *San.* 44a). Thus the Jewish community accepted the return of Jews who had been forcibly baptized during the First Crusade in Europe, but acts of penitence and rituals of purification were required.

Impossible as it was in theory to leave the Jewish people, it was not so in fact. Although there might be psychological costs in apostasy, there were tangible advantages to leaving a group that was of subordinate legal status and subject to persecution. Individual Jewish converts were welcomed by Christian and Muslim authorities. Only in certain situations when large numbers of Jews were pressed into converting, such as in the Iberian Peninsula in the 1390s and again in the 1490s, was there a backlash against these New Christian, or Marrano, families, whose Christian faith was for many centuries considered suspect by virtue of their Jewish bloodline.

Supplementing the halakhic problem of who was and was not a Jew was the aggadic problem of why there was a people of Israel. The determination to idealize the chosenness of the Jewish people is quite evident in this material, epitomized in the benediction recited in the synagogue before the reading of the Torah: "Blessed art thou, Lord our God, ruler of the universe, who chose us from all the nations and gave us the Torah."

The sheer givenness or brute factuality of being a Jew—that Jews found themselves thrown into a Jewish destiny—was acknowledged in some coolly realistic Talmudic statements. Expounding the biblical verse "And they stood at the nether part of the mount" (i.e., Israel at Mount Sinai; *Exodus* 19:17), Avdimi bar Ḥama' bar Ḥasa' explained that the Holy One, blessed be he, tilted the mountain over the Israelites like a cask and said, "If you accept the Torah, well and good; and if not, there shall be your burial" (B.T., *Shab.* 88a). Most other scholars reject this notion on the grounds that receiving the Torah under coercion could nullify the obligation to observe it. The rabbinic *aggadah* continues in the line of a theological idealization of the people by emphasizing the collective responsibility of all members of the people both to each other and to God and the absolute centrality of Israel's collective presence in universal history. In a discussion concerning divine punishment, the principle is proposed that "all Israel is surety one for the other" (B.T., *Shav.* 39a). Israel conciliates God only when it is one unity (B.T., *Men.* 27a). The Jewish people fulfills God's plan that his presence indwells in the world.

A homily in *Ruth Rabbah* (1.1) ascribes to God the statement that if Israel had not accepted the Torah, he would have caused the world to revert to void and destruction. A homily in *Exodus Rabbah* (47.3) attributes to God the statement that if this people had not accepted his Torah, he would not look upon them more than other idol worshipers. (The Talmudic dictum that "anyone who repudiates idolatry is called a Jew" [B.T., *Meg.* 13a], based on the biblical identification of Mordecai of the tribe of Benjamin as a *Yehudi* [Judean] in *Esther* 2:5, uses the term *Jew* in a theologically idealized, nonethnic, purely homiletic sense.) It was a merit for the Jews to have accepted the Torah, but ever since Sinai it was Israel's *raison d'être* to obey the 613 commandments it contained. In contrast to the distinction in Christianity of late antiquity and the Middle Ages between the "religious" and the laity, the goal of rabbinic Judaism was to raise all Israel to the level of masters of Torah, transforming the community into an academy, as it were, for the study and practice of Torah.

Despite a Diaspora stretching from the Atlantic to Central Asia and eastward, and from the Baltic to the Sahara and beyond to Ethiopia, medieval Judaism did not become a multinational religion in the sense that Christianity or Islam did. (Christianity was transformed into a multinational faith after becoming the religion of the Roman empire in the fourth century and the conversion of the Franks, the Germanic, Nordic, and Slavic peoples in the Middle Ages; Islam after the conversion of the Persians and Turks. There were only two medieval instances where Judaism was adopted as the religion of a state: sixth-century Yemen briefly and the Khazar kingdom on the Volga between the eighth and tenth centuries.) A wide diversity of Jewish subcultures did emerge: Jewries in the Middle East that were largely the continuation of the ancient homeland and Diaspora communities; Iranian and Kurdish Jews; Jewish tribal groups in the Caucasus Mountains; the various Jewish communities of India and China; Berber

Jews in the Maghreb; Sefardic Jews in the Iberian Peninsula; Provençal and Italian Jews; Ashkenazic Jews in northern France, the Rhineland, and later in eastern Germany, Poland, and Lithuania; and other communities with their own distinctive customs, dialectics, liturgies, and halakhic practices. As a result, in daily life medieval Jews spoke a wide variety of languages—Greek and Aramaic; Persian and Arabic; Spanish, French, and German—and they developed distinctive Jewish dialects of these languages, such as Ladino (a Jewish form of Spanish) and Yiddish (a Jewish form of Middle High German), Hebrew being maintained for literary and liturgical purposes.

Some branches of medieval and early modern Jewry produced sophisticated courtier and banking classes and intellectual elites trained in the natural sciences and Aristotelian and Neoplatonic philosophies, whereas other Jewries were folk cultures of a population overwhelmingly engaged in menial occupations. Although in some regions the Jewish population was large, compact, and had a sizable agricultural or village component (e.g., the Galilee and Babylonia in late antiquity), political conditions under Christian and Muslim rulers necessitated that Judaism sustain itself increasingly as the religion of an urbanized minority mostly limited to crafts and trade (the specific list of the economic roles open to Jews differed widely from land to land and from era to era). In certain areas, such as northwest and eastern Europe, Jewish communities were founded or augmented by Jews invited to settle in frontier areas where the rulers considered them to be economically useful. However, given the interweaving of religion and the state in the countries in which medieval and early modern Jews resided, a Jewry could maintain itself only if permitted considerable legal autonomy—although the extent to which the Jewish leadership was dependent on the gentile rulers or derived its authority solely from the consent of local Jewish communities varied considerably.

The principal cause, therefore, of the mononational character of the Jewish people was not cultural or economic homogeneity. The national unity of the Jews was conditioned by the common psychological situation of being a minority everywhere: a minority with a profound, if disputed, connection to the formative narratives of the ruling religion; a minority enjoying a precarious social status inasmuch as it was always susceptible to persecution but was for considerable stretches of time better off than the local peasants and serfs; a minority with considerable training (especially through the Babylonian Talmud) in adjusting to living under gentile governments while preserving the continuity of Jewish law; a minority possessing a far-flung Diaspora network linked together by traders, scholars, and other Jewish travelers, and a steady stream of Jewish migration, sometimes westward, sometimes eastward; and, above all, a minority that defined itself as central to the history of creation.

The religious self-definition of the Jewish tradition, transmitted through scriptures, rabbinic law and lore, and the *siddur*, reiterated the sanctity of being *Yisra'el*, *'amkha* ("your people," as addressed to God who "has chosen his people Israel in love"). This God, who "because of our sins exiled us from our land," nevertheless "remembers the pious deeds of the patriarchs and in love will bring a redeemer to their children's children for his name's sake." He will "gather the dispersed of your people Israel . . . break the enemies and humble the arrogant . . . rebuild Jerusalem as an everlasting building and speedily set up therein the throne of David" (from the Shemoneh 'Esreh, basic to the Jewish liturgy) and "will remove the abominations from the earth, and the idols will be utterly cut off when the world will be perfected under the kingdom of the Almighty and all the children of flesh will call upon your name, when you will turn unto yourself all the wicked of the earth . . . for the kingdom is yours and to all eternity you will reign in glory" (from the 'Aleinu prayer at the conclusion of each service).

Indicative of the force of religion in maintaining Jewish peoplehood until modern times is the major instance of Jewish schism involving the Karaite movement of the eighth and ninth centuries in the Middle East. Calling for a return to the literal meaning of the scriptures and denying the authority of the Talmud and rabbinic law, the Karaites became a distinct tradition separate from mainstream Judaism, with their own religious law based on biblical precedents. Religious authority and the sources of divine law were the cruxes of the Karaite-Rabbinite conflict, although there may have been socioeconomic forces operating as well. There were attempts, by Maimonides and others, to encourage close contacts between the two religious communities. In modern times some Karaite groups have closely identified with the Jews (the Karaites in Egypt), whereas others emphatically disassociated themselves (the Karaites in Russia).

Theorizing about the nature of Jewish peoplehood was not an especially important theme in medieval Jewish philosophy, but it was implied in various formulations of the purpose of Jewish existence. Speculative Jewish thought, with a few outstanding exceptions, moved as far away as possible from the idea of the Jewish people as a natural ethnic bond to its being a group embedded in a theology. In the rationalist stream Judaism was treated as an eminently logical faith, its doctrines of the oneness of God, the createdness of the universe, the rational component of prophecy, and the reasonableness of the commandments all being justified by categories and arguments derived from ancient Greek philosophy and glossed by Jewish, Muslim, and Christian writers. For Sa'adyah Gaon, "our nation of the children of Israel is a nation only by virtue of its laws" that, because they are divine, can never be abrogated; "the Creator has stated that the Jewish nation was destined to exist as long as heaven and earth would exist, its law would, of necessity, have to endure as long as would heaven and earth" (*The Book of Beliefs and Opinions*, trans. Samuel Rosenblatt, New Haven, 1948, p. 158). Torah, as consonant with right reason and authentic revelation, provided the most reliable, expeditious, and truthful means to serve God.

Maimonides presented Judaism as derived from Abraham's great insight into the divine nature:

> His father and mother and the entire population worshiped idols . . . but his mind was busily working and reflecting until he had attained the way of truth, apprehending the correct line of thought, and knew that there is One God, that He guides the celestial Sphere and created everything. . . . When the people flocked to him [in the land of Canaan] and questioned him regarding his assertions, he would instruct each one according to his capacity till he had brought him to the way of truth. . . . And so it went on with ever increasing vigor among Jacob's children and their adherents till they became a people that knew God.
>
> (*Mishneh Torah*, Idolatry 1.2)

Addressing a proselyte who asked if he could pray to the God of Abraham, Isaac, and Jacob as the "God of his fathers" (the first of the Eighteen Benedictions), Maimonides wrote that "Abraham our Father, peace be with him, is the father of his pious posterity who keep his ways, and the father of his disciples and of all proselytes who adopt Judaism" *(Letter to Obadiah the Proselyte)*. He who believes in the basic principles of the Jewish faith, as Maimonides defined them, "is then part of that 'Israel' whom we are to love, pity, and treat, as God commanded, with love and fellowship"—otherwise he is an atheist, heretic, and unbeliever (Introduction to Pereq Ḥeleq [*Sanhedrin* 10.1]). For Maimonides, those who affirm the unity of God as the cause of causes come as close as humanly possible to grasping divinity as such.

A second tendency in medieval Jewish thought was to emphasize the supermundane nature of Jewish peoplehood. In the philosophical tradition the exemplary exponent of this position was Yehudah ha-Levi, who suggested that "Israel among the nations is like the heart amid the organs of the body," at once the sickest and the healthiest of entities, exposed to all sorts of diseases and yet possessing through its relationship to the "divine influence" a unique proclivity that manifested itself as the gift of prophecy (*Kuzari*, trans. Hartwig Hirschfeld, New York, 1964, p. 109). In another of ha-Levi's images, Israel is the seed "which transforms earth and water into its own substance," carrying this substance from stage to stage until it brings forth fruit capable of bearing the divine influence, so that the nations who at least follow part of God's law pave the way for the Messiah and will become God's fruit (ibid., p. 227).

This version of Israel reached its apogee in Qabbalah, the medieval mystical tradition. Thus, in a discussion of the *mitsvot* in the basic qabbalistic text, the *Zohar*, circumcision is a prequisite for carrying out the surface meaning of the divine regulations (although to be circumcised only and not carry out the precepts of the Torah is to be like a heathen); the deeper mystery is to understand that Torah, God, and Israel are indissolubly linked together (*Zohar, Leviticus*, 73b). Drawing on the ancient Midrashic teachings about Israel's central role in the cosmos and on medieval Neoplatonic metaphysics, the qabbalists taught as esoteric doctrine that Israel's carrying out of the commandments has direct, puissant effects on the highest spheres of being as such. When Israel fulfilled the commandments with the proper intention *(kavvanah)*, they overcame forces making for cosmic disharmony, effecting unifications *(yiḥudim)* in the realm of divinity itself. After the expulsions from the Iberian Peninsula in the 1490s, Qabbalah spread like wildfire, protecting Judaism against loss of morale and providing a solace in times of outward degradation. In the sixteenth-century Lurianic version of Qabbalah, the exile of Israel reflected the tragic exile of God, while the ingathering of the sparks of divinity achieved by fulfilling the *mitsvot* was the metaphysical analogue of the eventual ingathering of Israel at the climax of history. The implications of these qabbalistic doctrines were felt in the seventeenth-century messianic movement surrounding Shabbetai Tsevi and, in a different way, in eighteenth-century Hasidism. [*See* Qabbalah *and* Hasidism.]

The Modernization of Jewish Peoplehood. The crisis of traditional Jewish peoplehood coincided with the overwhelming transformation of modernizing societies and the drastic shift in meaning of the term *nation* in Western and westernized societies. Previously, *nation* in many Western languages had loosely designated a community connected by ties of birth and common geographical origin. Toward the end of the eighteenth century and especially during the era of the French Revolution, *nation* acquired a more specific connotation in relation to sovereignty and citizenship: the *nation* came to apply to the citizenry as a whole, in contrast to the "political nation" of the *ancien régime,* which was limited to the wellborn and the elite.

Inasmuch as revolutionary France and, later, other modernizing countries forged the unity of the nation by dissolving the remnants of traditional estates and semi-autonomous corporate entities, the extension of legal equality to all citizens had profound implications for the Jews. As modern nationalist movements and ideologies called for the self-determination of one nation after the other on geographical, cultural, linguistic, and historical grounds, the status of the Jews, now on the road to legal and political emancipation and, apparently, to economic and social integration, became exceptional and problematic. The almost seamless web of sociology, *halakhah,* and *aggadah* that had supported traditional Jewish peoplehood for centuries began to unravel.

The French Revolution acknowledged the citizenship rights of all French Jewry in September 1791. In 1807 Napoleon invited a body of lay leaders and rabbis to clarify the status of the Jews of his realm with respect to the accusation that they were a "nation within the nation." In defense of their rights, the Assembly of Jewish Notables (and the following year a group given the grandiloquent title of Sanhedrin) distinguished between the religious requirements of Judaism, which were held to be timeless and absolute, and the political dispositions of biblical society, which were held not to be applicable "since Israel no longer forms a nation." In effect, large areas of Torah law that dealt with civil and criminal matters were declared inoperative, and the fiscal and semipolitical autonomies that the Jewish communities had been awarded were acknowledged as no longer feasible—all this occurring at a time when the assumptions in which traditional religious faith was grounded could no longer be taken for granted.

The course of Jewish emancipation in one Western country after another had to overcome considerable opposition by those who held to the Christian basis of the state or who continued to insist on the alienness of the Jews. During the first three-quarters of the nineteenth century, Jews in Central Europe tended to define Jewry as a purely religious body whose positive mission in the Diaspora was to preserve the doctrines of pure ethical monotheism. The national or ethnic component seemed to many, especially in Germany, to be obsolete. In their rejection of the traditional messianic notion of a particularistic Jewish redemption (the ingathering of the exiles to Zion, the rebuilding of the Temple in Jerusalem, the reinstitution of the Davidic monarchy), the German Jewish Reformers preferred to eliminate these symbols from the liturgy, just as they preferred the language of the land in worship at the expense of Hebrew and otherwise sought to assure Jews and their neighbors that they were "Germans of the Jewish faith."

To support this redefinition it was argued that nationhood had been a necessary aspect of the emergence of ethical monotheism in biblical times and had been the preservative of the truths of Judaism in the Middle Ages, but in an enlightened age, when Judaism would come into its own as a progressive, universalistic faith, it did not need an ethnic integument. Jewish unity was not of a political but of a spiritual character that in no way contravened the loyalty of Jews to their secular fatherlands. Such ideas were echoed in almost all the trends of nineteenth-century Jewish thought in Europe and America that welcomed emancipation as a just and humane move to rectify the humiliation and segregation inflicted on Jewry for centuries and recognize the historical role and intrinsic worth of Judaism. [*For discussion of the Jewish Enlightenment movement, see* Haskalah.]

These conceptions of Jewish peoplehood were influenced not only by the new political situation of the Jews but also by the growth of Jewish historical scholarship that accompanied the emergence of *Wissenschaft des Judentums.* Having gained an appreciation of how Jewish religious institutions and ideas had undergone development in the course of time, some historians, and especially Jewish intellectuals in eastern Europe toward the end of the nineteenth century, turned to the Jewish collectivity as a social fact in its own right. Just as the earlier phase of modern Jewish thinking had been influenced by the struggle for emancipation, so this phase was influenced by the rise of modern anti-Semitism, the growth of nationalist movements among the peoples of eastern Europe, and the emergence of modern Zionism.

The term *anti-Semitism* was coined in the 1870s to indicate that dislike and fear of the Jews supposedly was not the result of religious reasons but a defense against the Jews as "Semitic" aliens acting as a corrupting, dominating force in the national organisms of Europe. Drawing on the medieval negative image of the Jews as Christ-killers and allies of Satan, the new anti-Semitic ideologies assumed a variety of forms, economic, political, and cultural; racist anti-Semitism insisted that the sinister characteristics of the Jews could not be improved through cultural or theological reform because these traits were psychobiological in origin and that Christianity itself was infected with the Jewish virus. [*See* Anti-Semitism.]

The period between 1881 and 1914 also saw the reappearance of physical attacks on the Jews (the pogroms in Russia), restrictive quotas in education, blood libels in which Jews were accused of killing Christian children for ritual purposes, and anti-Semitic congresses and political parties. These and other elements were to be synthesized by Adolf Hilter's National Socialist German Workers' Party (Nazis), which was founded in Germany and came to power in 1933, with fatal results for the six million European Jews caught in the Nazi Holocaust during World War II. [*See* Holocaust, The.]

Zionism gained urgency from the spread of modern anti-Semitism, but it had deep roots in the Jewish tradition as well. Zionism can be considered a recovery of Jewish peoplehood in a tangible sense rather than in the ethereal theological sense of much previous nineteenth-century Jewish thought. Zionist ideologues argued that Jewishness was not based on the mission of Israel to convey pure ethical monotheism to the world but a natural pride in one's heritage and a healthy desire to identify with one's people rather than assimilating to one or another of the chauvinistic nationalisms of Europe. [*See* Zionism.]

This reassertion of Jewish ethnic unity in a secular rather than religious sense produced a broad continuum of movements in eastern Europe by the turn of the century. It engendered a Jewish socialist movement that championed economic justice as well as emancipation for the Jewish working class and came to advocate secular Jewish cultural rights; an ideology of Diaspora Jewish nationalism that called for legally recognized rights of the Jews as a European cultural minority; a Jewish "territorialist" organization that looked for a land other than Palestine as the setting for a Jewish state; a new interest in Jewish social and economic history and in the folklore of east European Jews and of the Sefardic communities; and a literary renaissance in Hebrew and Yiddish that produced a rich body of novels, drama, poetry, and prose in those languages.

In 1897 the world Zionist movement was established by Theodor Herzl to create a modern Jewish commonwealth in the ancient land of Israel. Zionism embraced the ideas that a Jewish homeland would serve as a creative center for the revitalization of Jewish cultural values in modern form; that anti-Semitism was a symptom of the abnormality of Jewish life in the Diaspora that could only be cured with the self-emancipation of a Jewish state; that cooperative Jewish farming communities and the labor movement in the Land of Israel was the expression of a social revolution among the Jewish masses. In post–World War I Europe, and especially after the Nazis came to power in Germany, the need for a Jewish refuge—a home that the Jews could go to by right when threatened with political persecution, economic discrimination, or physical extermination—became a dominant concern.

The thrust of modern thinking around the theme of Jewish peoplehood of Israel in the twentieth century has been marked, therefore, by a recovery of the notion of *kelal Yisra'el* (the wholeness of the people of Israel). An influential Jewish ideology that emphasizes cultural pluralism, Judaism as a civilization, and the centrality of Zion together with the international character of the Jewish people is that of Mordecai Kaplan, who insisted on the continued relevance of Jewish religious values but denied on principle the notion of the Jews as a chosen people. [*See the biography of Kaplan.*] Most Jewish theologians have rejected the effort to normalize fully the Jewish tradition by stripping it of its supernatural uniqueness and mystery. Since World War II the power of ethnicity has been acknowledged as a positive force in Jewry in and of itself, as it has among other groups, while Jewish identity has assumed a far more voluntaristic character, which can be expressed in a wide range and intensity of ways. With the decline of anti-Semitism after the Holocaust has come noticeable improvement in Jewish-Christian understanding. And with the greater acceptance of Judaism and the social integration of Jews has come a considerable increase, at least in America, in the numbers of converts to Judaism.

As a result of the establishment of the state of Israel in 1948 a new series of issues has come to the fore concerning Jewish membership and meaning. Will Israel, as a secular Jewish state, be recognized as a legitimate member of the international society of nations? And in what does the Jewishness of the state of Israel consist? What is to be its relation to the religious dimension of the Jewish heritage? The question of personal Jewish status has been raised several times in Israel's courts of law in connection with the Law of Return, which grants all Diaspora Jews immediate Israeli citizenship upon their immigration there. In the case of Oswald Rufeisen, a born Jew who became a Catholic priest, the supreme court of Israel ruled that although Rufeisen was a Jew by *halakhah* his acceptance of Catholicism excluded him from the Jewish people and therefore he was not to be granted automatic Israeli citizenship. In the 1968 Shalit case, involving children of a non-Jewish mother who were raised as nonreligious Jews, it was not allowed that the children be registered, on purely secular grounds, as Jews on their identity cards.

The current definition of "who is a Jew" in Israel reflects a precarious mix of halakhic principles and Jewish folk attitudes. Yet another issue involves whether the state of Israel will continue to recognize as authentically Jewish those Jews converted in the Diaspora not according to Orthodox authorities or strict halakhic procedures, that is, by Reform and Conservative rabbis. This in turn directs attention to the legitimacy of religious pluralism within the Jewish people—a conspicuous fact in parts of the Diaspora but not in the state of

Israel. In America the question of who is a Jew has been raised in connection with children of intermarriages where the non-Jewish mother does not convert to Judaism; the Reform and Reconstructionist movements, but not the Conservative and Orthodox, have argued for a recognition of patrilineal descent under certain circumstances. Underlying the question of who is a Jew is the issue of the authority of *halakhah* in contemporary Jewish life: how, to what extent, and by whom will Jewish religious law be adapted to modern times. Behind all these specifics, however, is the question of the transcendent meaning of Jewish peoplehood, which will surely remain a delicate and profound subject for Jewish theologians.

[*For further discussion of groups that were offshoots or branches of the Jewish people, see the independent entries* Essenes; Karaites; Marranos; Pharisees; Sadducees; Samaritans; *and* Zealots.]

BIBLIOGRAPHY

Three classic histories of the Jewish people are Heinrich Graetz's *Geschichte der Juden von den ältesten Zeiten bis auf die Gegenwart,* 11 vols. (Leipzig, 1853–1876), translated by Bella Löwy and others as *History of the Jews,* 6 vols. (Philadelphia, 1891–1898); Simon Dubnow's *Vsemirnaia istoriia evreiskogo naroda* (1924–1939), 10 vols., translated by Moshe Spiegal as *History of the Jews,* 5 vols. (South Brunswick, N.J., 1967–1973); and Salo W. Baron's *A Social and Religious History of the Jews,* 2d ed., 18 vols. to date (New York, 1952–). An overview of the historiography of the origins of the people up to and including the settlement in Canaan is George W. Ramsey's *The Quest for the Historical Israel* (Atlanta, 1981).

The uniqueness of Israelite monotheism is defended by Yehezkel Kaufmann in his *The Religion of Israel: From Its Beginnings to the Babylonian Exile,* translated and abridged by Moshe Greenberg (Chicago, 1960). An earlier work by Kaufmann explains the primary role of religion in Jewish survival until modern times: *Golah ve-nekhar,* 2d ed., 2 vols. (Tel Aviv, 1954). On Jewish and Christian self-definition in antiquity, see Lawrence H. Schiffman's *Who Was a Jew?: Rabbinic and Halakhic Perspectives on the Jewish-Christian Schism* (Hoboken, N.J., 1985). On biblical, Jewish, and Christian uses of the name *Israel,* also see Samuel Sandmel's *The Several Israels* (New York, 1971). Early halakhic aspects are treated by Shaye J. D. Cohen in "The Origins of the Matrilineal Principle in Rabbinic Law," *Association for Jewish Studies Review* 10 (Spring 1985): 19–53. The theological views of classic rabbinic Judaism are thoroughly treated in E. E. Urbach's *The Sages: Their Concepts and Beliefs,* 2d enl. ed., 2 vols. translated by Israel Abrahams (Jerusalem, 1979), in which see especially chapter 16.

Medieval Jewish views of Jewish identity in a Christian environment are discussed in Jacob Katz's *Exclusiveness and Tolerance: Studies in Jewish-Gentile Relations in Medieval and Modern Times* (Oxford, 1961). A history of Jewish proselytism is found in Joseph R. Rosenbloom's *Conversion to Judaism: From the Biblical Period to the Present* (Cincinnati, 1978). The branches of the Jewish people around the world are surveyed in Raphael Patai's *Tents of Jacob: The Diaspora; Yesterday and Today* (Englewood Cliffs, N.J., 1971). Among the books on Jewish modernization are Jacob Katz's *Out of the Ghetto: The Social Background of Jewish Emancipation, 1770–1870* (Cambridge, Mass., 1973), Calvin Goldscheider and Alan S. Zuckerman's *The Transformation of the Jews* (Chicago, 1984), and Simon N. Herman's *Jewish Identity: A Social Psychological Perspective* (Beverly Hills, 1977).

Secular approaches to Jewish nationhood are defended in the following ideological works, among many: Simon Dubnow's *Nationalism and History: Essays on Old and New Judaism,* edited by Koppel S. Pinson (Philadelphia, 1958), and Ben Halpern's *The American Jew: A Zionist Analysis* (New York, 1956). A gamut of Zionist views, secular and religious, can be found in *The Zionist Idea: An Historical Analysis and Reader,* edited by Arthur Hertzberg (Philadelphia, 1959). Most books that treat the main aspects of Jewish faith discuss the religious significance of Jewish peoplehood, but among the few important Jewish works that have taken it as their central theme are Mordecai Kaplan's *Judaism as a Civilization: Toward a Reconstruction of Jewish-American Life* (New York, 1934), and Michael Wyschogrod's *The Body of Faith: Judaism as Corporeal Election* (New York, 1983). A scholarly account of peoplehood in twentieth-century American Jewish religious thought is Arnold M. Eisen's *The Chosen People in America: A Study in Jewish Religious Ideology* (Bloomington, Ind., 1983). For a collection of statements on "who is a Jew," as this question has come to the fore since the establishment of the state of Israel, see *Jewish Identity: Modern Response and Opinions,* edited by Baruch Litvin (New York, 1956). A philosophically sensitive, coherent picture of the nature of Judaism is Leon Roth's *Judaism: A Portrait* (New York, 1960). A succinct treatment of Judaism in the context of the dilemmas of modernizing religions is R. J. Zwi Werblowsky's "Sacral Particularity: The Jewish Case," in his *Beyond Tradition and Modernity: Changing Religions in a Changing World* (London, 1976).

ROBERT M. SELTZER

JEWISH PHILOSOPHY. *See* Jewish Thought and Philosophy.

JEWISH RELIGIOUS YEAR. The Hebrew word *ḥodesh,* used in the Bible for "month," means "that which is renewed" and refers to the renewal of the moon. Hence the Jewish calendar is lunar, the first day of each month being Ro'sh Ḥodesh ("head of the month"). Some months have twenty-nine days, others thirty. When the previous month has twenty-nine days, Ro'sh Ḥodesh is celebrated as a minor festival for two days; when the previous month has thirty days, it is celebrated for one day. In the Pentateuch (*Ex.* 12:2), the month on which the Israelites went out of Egypt is counted as the first month of the year, so when the Bible speaks of the third month, the seventh month, and so on, these are counted from the month of the Exodus. But the festival of Passover, celebrating the Exodus, is said in *Deuteronomy* 16:1 to fall in the month Aviv ("ripening"). This is understood to mean that Passover must always fall in spring, and thus the Jewish lunar calendar presupposes a natural solar calendar like that used in most ancient societies. A process of intercalation was consequently introduced to enable the lunar year to keep pace with the solar. The method is to add an extra month to seven out of nineteen lunar years. During the Babylonian captivity, after the destruction of the First Temple, the Babylonian names of the months were adopted and are still used. These are Nisan, Iyyar, Sivan, Tammuz (its origin in the name of a Babylonian deity was either unknown or ignored), Av, Elul, Tishri, Marḥeshvan, Kislev, Ṭevet, Shevaṭ, Adar. When, in a leap year, an extra month is introduced at the end of the year, there is an Adar Sheni, or "second Adar."

The Development of the Calendar. There was no uniform method of dating years until the Middle Ages, when the current practice was adopted of reckoning from the (biblical) creation of the world. The French commentaries to the Talmud (*tosafot* to B.T., *Giṭṭin* 80b) observe that in twelfth-century France it was already an established practice to date documents from the creation. In the Talmudic literature it is debated whether the creation took place in Nisan (the first month) or in Tishri (the seventh month), but for dating purposes the latter view is followed, so that the new year begins on the first day of Tishri. This day is the date of the festival Ro'sh ha-Shanah (New Year). Thus the year 1240 CE is the year 5000 from the creation. Thus 1986 CE from 1 January to 3 October is the year 5746 from the creation; from 4 October (the date of Ro'sh ha-Shanah) it is 5747. This method of dating is used in legal documents, letters, and newspapers but has no doctrinal significance, so that it does not normally disturb traditionalists who prefer to interpret the biblical record nonliterally to allow for a belief in the vast age of the earth implied by science.

It is generally accepted in the critical study of the Bible that the recurring refrain in the first chapter of *Genesis*—"and it was evening and it was morning"—means that when daylight had passed into evening and then night had passed into morning, a complete day had elapsed. But the Talmudic tradition understands the verses to mean that night precedes the day. For this reason the day, for religious purposes, begins at nightfall and lasts until the next nightfall. The Sabbath begins at sunset on Friday and goes out at nightfall on Saturday. The same applies to the festivals. The twilight period is a legally doubtful one, and there is also an obligation to extend the Sabbaths and festivals at beginning and end. Jewish calendars, consequently, give the time of the Sabbath as beginning just before sunset and as ending when it is fully dark. Pious Jews, in the absence of a calendar, will keep the Sabbath until it is sufficiently dark to see three average-sized stars in close proximity in the night sky.

Before the present fixed calendar was instituted (in the middle of the fourth century CE), the date of the new moon was arrived at by observation. If witnesses saw the new moon on the twenty-ninth day of the month, they would present their testimony to the high court and that day would be declared Ro'sh Ḥodesh, the beginning of the next month. If the new moon had not been observed on the twenty-ninth day, the thirtieth day automatically became Ro'sh Ḥodesh. Since the festivals falling in the month are counted from Ro'sh Ḥodesh, there was always some doubt as to which of two days would be the date of the festival. Except on Ro'sh ha-Shanah, which falls on the actual day of the new moon, special messengers could always inform the Jews of Palestine of the correct date of the festival. But for the Jews of the Diaspora, who resided in lands too distant for them to be informed in time, it became the practice to keep both days as the festival and thus avoid any possibility of error. Even after the calendar was fixed, the Talmudic sources state, the Jews of the Diaspora were advised by the Palestinian authorities to continue to hold fast to the custom of their ancestors and keep the "two days of the Diaspora." A post-Talmudic rationale for the two days of the Diaspora is that outside the Holy Land the extra festival day compensates for the absence of sanctity in the land. The practice in the state of Israel is thus to keep only one day (with the exception of Ro'sh ha-Shanah), whereas Jews living elsewhere keep two days. There is much discussion in the legal sources on the practice to be adopted by a Jew living outside Israel who visits Israel for the festival or vice versa. Reform Jews prefer to follow the biblical injunctions only, and they do not keep the two days of the Diaspora. Some Conservative Jews, too, have argued for the abolition of the second day because of the anomaly of treating as a holy day a day that is not observed as sacred in Israel.

The Holy Days. Similar festivals in the ancient Near East suggest that the biblical festivals were originally agricultural feasts transformed into celebrations of historical events. The most striking aspect of the Jewish religious calendar is this transfer from the round of the seasons to the affirmation of God's work in human history—the transfer, as it were, from space to time.

The holy days of the Jewish year can be divided into two categories: the biblical and the postbiblical, or the major and the minor. (Purim, though based on *Esther,* a book from the biblical period, is held to be a postbiblical festival from this point of view and hence a minor festival.) The first and last days of Passover and Sukkot, Shavu'ot, Ro'sh ha-Shanah, and Yom Kippur are major festivals in that all labor (except that required for the preparation of food and even this on Yom Kippur) is forbidden. On the days between the first and last days of Passover and Sukkot, necessary labor is permitted. All labor is permitted on minor festivals such as Purim and Ḥanukkah.

Each of the festivals has its own rituals and its own special liturgy. On all of them the Hallel ("praise"), consisting of *Psalms* 113–118, is recited in the synagogue, except on Ro'sh ha-Shanah, Yom Kippur, and Purim. Only part of Hallel is said on Ro'sh Ḥodesh, when labor is permitted, and the last six days of Passover, it being held unseemly to rejoice by singing the full praises of God since the Egyptians, who were also God's creatures, were destroyed. Festive meals are the order of the day on the festivals (except, of course, on Yom Kippur), and the day is marked by the donning of one's best clothes. It is considered meritorious to study on each festival the relevant passages in the classical sources of Judaism. On the fast days neither food nor drink is taken from sunrise to nightfall (on Yom Kippur and Tish'ah be-Av, from sunset on the previous night).

Following are major dates of the religious year, month by month.

- 15–22 Nisan (15–23 in the Diaspora): Passover, celebrating the Exodus from Egypt.
- 6 Sivan (6–7 in the Diaspora): Shavu'ot, anniversary of the theophany at Sinai.
- 17 Tammuz: Fast of Tammuz, commemorating the breaching of the walls of Jerusalem at the time of the destruction of the First Temple (587/6 BCE) and the Second Temple (70 CE).
- 9 Av: Tish'ah be-Av (Ninth of Av), fast day commemorating the destruction of the First and Second Temples and other national calamities.
- 1–2 Tishri: Ro'sh ha-Shanah, the New Year festival.
- 3 Tishri: Tsom Gedalyah (Fast of Gedaliah), commemorating the slaying of Gedaliah as told in *Jeremiah* 41:1–2 and *2 Kings* 25:25, an event that marked the end of the First Commonwealth.
- 10 Tishri: Yom Kippur (Day of Atonement), the great fast day.
- 15–23 Tishri (15–24 in the Diaspora): Sukkot (Feast of Tabernacles), celebrating the dwelling in booths by the Israelites in their journey through the wilderness after the Exodus.
- 25 Kislev: first day of Ḥanukkah (Feast of Rededication), celebrating the victory of the Maccabees and the rededication of the Temple. Ḥanukkah lasts for eight days.
- 10 Ṭevet: 'Asarah be-Ṭevet (Fast of the Tenth of Ṭevet), commemorating the siege of Jerusalem by Nebuchadrezzar before the destruction of the First Temple in 587/6 BCE.
- 15 Shevaṭ: Ro'sh ha-Shanah le-Ilanot (New Year for Trees), a minor festival reminiscent of the laws of tithing in ancient times. Nowadays, this is a celebration of God's bounty, of thanksgiving for the fruit of the ground.
- 13 Adar: Ta'anit Ester (Fast of Esther), based on the account in *Esther* (4:16).
- 14 Adar: Purim (Lots), the festival celebrating the victory over Haman, who cast lots to destroy the Jews, as told in *Esther.*
- 15 Adar: Shushan Purim (Purim of Shushan), based on the account in *Esther* (9:18) that the Jews in the capital city of Shushan celebrated their deliverance on this day.

Major Festivals and Fast Days. The three festivals of Passover, Shavu'ot, and Sukkot form a unit in that, in Temple times, they were pilgrim festivals, when the people came to worship and offer sacrifices in the Temple. The connection between these three festivals is preserved in the liturgy in which there are references to the place of each festival in the yearly cycle. Thus, on Passover the reference is to "the season of our freedom," on Shavu'ot to "the season of the giving of our Torah," and on Sukkot to "the season of our rejoicing," since Sukkot, as the culmination of the cycle, is the special season of joy. The three major festivals of the month of Tishri have been seen as a unit of a different kind. Ro'sh ha-Shanah, the first of the three, is seen as the festival of the mind, when man reflects on his destiny and resolves to lead a better life in the coming year. Yom Kippur, the day when the emotions are stirred, is seen as the festival of the heart, because it is the day of pardon and reconciliation with God. Sukkot, the third in this triad, involves active participation in the building of the booth and eating meals there, and is seen therefore as the festival of the hand. Thus, head, heart, and hand are demanded in the service of God.

The days between Ro'sh ha-Shanah and Yom Kippur, inclusive, are known as the Ten Days of Penitence. This is a solemn season of reflection on life's meaning and sincere repentance. Similarly, the whole month of Elul, the last month of the old year, is a penitential season in preparation for the solemn period at the beginning of the new year. Ro'sh ha-Shanah and Yom Kippur are consequently known as Yamim Nora'im, the Days of Awe.

Minor Festivals and Fast Days. In the annual cycle there are two periods of mourning during which marriages are not celebrated and tokens of mourning are observed. The first of these is the three-week period from the seventeenth of Tammuz to Tish'ah be-Av, the period of mourning for the destruction of the Temple and the sufferings of the people in subsequent ages. In many places the period becomes more intense from the first of Av in that the consumption of meat and wine is proscribed. The other, lesser, period of mourning is known as the ʿOmer period, forty-nine days from the second day of Passover to the festival of Shavu'ot (though, of course, there is no mourning during Passover itself). The *ʿomer* was a measure of meal brought as an offering in Temple times, and there is a biblical injunction to count these forty-nine days (*Lv.* 23:9–16; known as "counting the ʿOmer"). It has been suggested that the custom of mourning during the ʿOmer has its origin in the ancient belief, held by many peoples, that it is bad luck to marry during the month of May. The traditional sources state that the mourning is over the death by plague of many of the disciples of ʿAqiva' ben Yosef in the second century CE. The mystics introduce a different note. There are seven lower potencies or powers in the godhead, the *sefirot,* that become flawed as a result of human sin. Each one of these contains the others as well, so that each of the forty-nine days of the ʿOmer calls for repentance for the purpose of putting right these flaws. The mystics of Safad in the sixteenth century held that the eighteenth of Iyyar, the thirty-third day of the ʿOmer—Lag ba-ʿOmer—is the anniversary of the death of the great mystic Shimʿon bar Yoḥ'ai, a disciple of ʿAqiva' and the alleged author of the *Zohar.* The belief that at the saint's death his soul became united with its source on high is referred to as "the marriage of Shimʿon bar Yoḥ'ai." This day, then, became a minor festival, and marriages are celebrated on the day.

The day of the new moon, Ro'sh Ḥodesh, is also a minor festival. From the juxtaposition of Ro'sh Ḥodesh with the Sabbath in a number of biblical passages, many biblical scholars conclude that in ancient times Ro'sh Ḥodesh was a major festival on a par with the Sabbath. Nowadays, however, the day is marked only by festivities in a minor key and by liturgical additions. An old custom frees women from the obligation to work on Ro'sh Ḥodesh, and this might be a vestige of the ancient sanctity the day enjoyed. The official reason given is that women refused to participate in the making of the golden calf and were, therefore, given an extra holiday. In the mystical tradition the moon symbolizes the Shekhinah, the female element in the godhead, the counterpart on high of the community of Israel, awaiting the redemption of the Jewish people and of all mankind with harmony restored throughout all creation. The waxing and the waning of the moon is thus a powerful mythological symbol. The Safad mystics consequently introduced a new ritual for the eve of Ro'sh Ḥodesh. This day is known as Yom Kippur Qaṭan (Minor Yom Kippur). As the name implies, it is a time of repentance and, for some, fasting.

There are a number of other lesser feasts and fast days. The Fast of the Firstborn has its origins in the early Middle Ages. In *Exodus* (13:1–16) it is related that the firstborn of the Israelites have a special sanctity because God spared them when he killed the firstborn of the Egyptians. Thus the custom of fasting on the eve of Passover, 14 Nisan, developed. Generally, nowadays, the firstborn, instead of fasting, attend a study session during which a tractate of the Talmud is completed. To partake of a festive meal on this occasion is held to be a religious obligation that overrides the obligation to fast.

Some pious Jews fast on the Monday, Thursday, and following Monday after the festivals of Passover and Sukkot—Beit He' Beit ("Two, Five, Two," referring to the days of the week). The reason given is that it is to atone for any untoward frivolity during the lengthy festival period.

In many Jewish communities the burial of the dead is attended to by a voluntary organization, whose membership is granted only to the most distinguished applicants. This organization is known as the *ḥevrah qaddisha'* ("holy brotherhood"). The members of the *ḥevrah' qaddisha'* observe a fast on the seventh of Adar, the anniversary of the death of Moses, to atone for any disrespect they may have shown to the dead. But on the night following the fast they celebrate their privileged position by holding a special banquet.

There are also minor festivals observed by particular groups. For instance, on the analogy of Purim, many communities delivered miraculously from destruction celebrate ever after their day of deliverance as a "Purim." For example, the Hasidic master Shne'ur Zalman of Lyady (1745–1813), founder of the Habad school of Hasidism, was released from prison in Russia on the nineteenth of Kislev, after his arrest on a charge of treason, and his followers observe this day as a festival.

Two modern institutions are Yom ha-Sho'ah (Holocaust Day) on 27 Nisan, marking the destruction of six million Jews during the Nazi period, and Yom ha-Atsma'ut (Independence Day) on 5 Iyyar, the celebration, especially in the state of Israel, of the Israeli declaration of independence on that date. In many religious circles this day is treated as a full *yom ṭov,* and the *Hallel* is recited.

[*For more detailed discussion of specific Jewish holidays, see* Shabbat; Ro'sh ha-Shanah and Yom Kippur; Passover; Shavu'ot; Sukkot; Purim; *and* Ḥanukkah. *For non-Western Jewish traditions, see* Judaism, *article on* Judaism in Asia and Northeast Africa.]

BIBLIOGRAPHY

The articles "Calendar, History of" and "Calendar" in the *Jewish Encyclopedia* (New York, 1906) are still the best general accounts. The article "Calendar" in *Encyclopaedia Judaica* (Jerusalem, 1971) contains more detail but is so technical as to be incomprehensible to all but the experts, who will have no need for it. Hayyim Schauss's *Guide to the Jewish Holy Days,* translated by Samuel Jaffe (New York, 1962), is a survey, from the rationalistic standpoint, with critical and historical notes. More traditional are Abraham P. Bloch's *The Biblical and Historical Background of the Jewish Holy Days* (New York, 1978) and Abraham Chill's *The Minhagim: The Customs and Ceremonies of Judaism, Their Origins and Rationale* (New York, 1979). A useful introduction to the traditionalist mood of thought on the significance of the festivals is *Seasons of the Soul: Religious, Historical and Philosophical Perspectives on the Jewish Year and Its Milestones* (New York, 1981), edited by Nisson Walpin. Similar meditations on the Jewish calendar year by a famous nineteenth-century Orthodox theologian are to be found in *Judaism Eternal: Selected Essays from the Writings of Rabbi Samson Raphael Hirsch,* vol. 1, translated from the German original by Isidor Grunfeld (London, 1956), pp. 3–152. *Ha-mo'adim ba-halakhah* (Jerusalem, 1980) by Shlomo Y. Zevin is a particularly fine and popular treatment of the legal principles behind the observances of the festivals and fast days. Part of this work has been published in English translation: *The Festivals in Halachah,* translated by Meir Fox-Ashrei and edited by Uri Kaploon (New York, 1981). Solomon Ganzfield's *Code of Jewish Law (Qitsur Shulḥan 'arukh): A Compilation of Jewish Laws and Customs,* vol. 3, annot. & rev. ed., translated by Hyman E. Goldin (New York, 1961), is a comprehensive and clearly written but very pedestrian account.

LOUIS JACOBS

JEWISH STUDIES.

[*This entry consists of two articles. The first examines the evolution of Jewish studies from their beginnings in the Wissenschaft des Judentums movement among nineteenth-century German Jewish intellectuals to a full-fledged academic discipline at the turn of the twentieth century. The second article discusses the further development of Jewish studies to the present day.*]

Jewish Studies from 1818 to 1919

Although Judaism has long valued the study of sacred texts as an instrument of piety, the field of Jewish studies as an academic discipline is a product of the emancipation process and the westernization of Judaism in the nineteenth century. Born of a sense of the profound changes in the context of Jewish life and imbued with the academic ethos of the newly founded University of Berlin (1810) and with the philosophic rhetoric of German Idealism, *Wissenschaft des Judentums* heralded a series of disorienting intellectual shifts: from Christian to Jewish scholarship on Judaism; from dogmatic to undogmatic, but not value-free, scholarship on Judaism; from a partial to a comprehensive conception of Jewish creativity; and from an exegetical to a conceptual mode of thought. What stands out in the subsequent development of the discipline over the next century, beyond its ceaseless growth and bifurcation, is the continued centrality of the German provenance down to the 1930s.

Early Academic Context. As launched by Leopold Zunz (1794–1886) and his friends in the Verein für Kultur and Wissenschaft der Juden (1819–1824), the application of the historical method to the study of Judaism by university-educated Jews challenged the undisputed Christian monopoly on the subject. Since economic utility had largely dictated the peripheral legal status of pre-emancipation Jews, their spokesmen had scarcely felt the need to transcend the insularity of the ghetto with an "insider's" depiction of Judaism for Christian consumption. In consequence, according to Zunz, "Rarely has the world been presented with more damaging, erroneous, and distorted views than on the subject of the Jewish religion; here, to render odious has been turned into a fine art" *(Etwas über die rabbinische Litteratur,* 1818). Against this backdrop, *Wissenschaft des Judentums* embodied a novel and sustained effort by Jews themselves to recount their history and expound their religion for non-Jews, to dissipate the miasma of misconceptions and prejudice with facts and empathy. From the outset, Zunz intuited the political payoff of the enterprise: public respect for Judaism would be the only secure ground for lasting social intergration.

Symptomatic of the prevailing denigration was the exclusion of ancient Jewry from the vaunted field of *Altertumswissenschaft.* Admission was restricted to the Greeks and Romans, for they alone of the nations of antiquity had achieved the level of a learned culture. In his lectures on the discipline, Friedrich August Wolf, famed Homer scholar and one of Zunz's teachers, dismissed Israel's historical claim to equal treatment:

> The Hebraic nation did not raise itself to the level of culture, so that one might regard it as a learned, cultured people. It does not even have prose, but only half poetry. Its writers of history are but miserable chroniclers. They could never write in full sentences; this was an invention of the Greeks.
>
> (*Vorlesungen über die Altertumswissenschaft,* vol. 1, 1831, p. 14)

Thus, academically as well as philosophically, Judaism was relegated to a preliminary and long-surpassed stage of Oriental history, and hence was consigned to the periphery of Western consciousness.

The absence of any countervailing Jewish scholarship at the time is graphically illustrated by the plight of the young Heinrich Heine, then a member of the Verein, when he tried to convey an image of the attractiveness and pathos of medieval Judaism through the medium of a historical novel. The reasons for his failure to complete *Die Rabbi von Bacharach* (1840) are no doubt many, but among them surely is the total absence of empathetical historical works by Jews in German. With the primary Hebrew sources closed to him, Heine, under Zunz's tutelage, was forced to feed on the standard Christian fare, with the result that his imagination soon foundered. By way of contrast, Michael Sachs's evocative *Die religiöse Poesie der Juden in Spanien,* which appeared in 1845, did trigger Heine's poetic fantasy and led directly to his richly inventive and deeply felt collection, *Hebräische Melodien* (1851), an eloquent testimony to what he, and German academics, had lacked in 1824.

Wissenschaft des Judentums. In terms of method, *Wissenschaft des Judentums* raised an equally formidable challenge to the principles and parameters of traditional Jewish learning. Unfettered by dogmatic considerations, the alienated intellectuals of the Verein, at bitter odds with rabbinism but not prepared to convert, had formed "an association of consciousness" to begin conceptualizing Judaism afresh. Toward that end it embraced the research program enunciated in 1818 by Zunz in his profound, prescient, and determinative work *Etwas über die rabbinische Litteratur.* Convinced that emancipation spelled the end of the Hebraic-rabbinic period of Jewish history, Zunz called for its dispassionate historical assessment. In the process, he demonstrated with stunning detail its dimly realized cultural expanse and diversity. Postbiblical Hebrew literature was authored by Jews of all kinds, not only rabbis, and embraced all the interests of the human mind, not only matters of Jewish law. Given that scope, only the historian was equipped to speak of its genesis and character with any authority. The anticlerical thrust was unmistakable: the canons of modern scholarship were to be enlisted "in order to know and sort out the old which is useful, the antiquated which is detrimental, and the new which is desirable." History presumed to usurp the role of *halakhah* and philosophy as both the arbiter and expositor of Judaism. At issue was a grievously flawed method of learning overgrown with historical myth and error, indifferent to time and contextual analysis, hostile to all non-Hebraic and non-Jewish sources, and crippled by a truncated view of Jewish literature and a static concept of sacred texts.

The comprehensiveness of this vision of the Jewish experience extended into the present. As conceived by Zunz and amplified by Immanuel Wolf in his opening essay for the Verein's ephemeral *Zeitschrift für die Wissenschaft des Judentums* (1823), from whence the name, the field comprised not only the study of a remote past but of a living present. Both as an inner idea and a religious culture, Judaism was still of vital concern to a living community, which itself deserved scholarly attention. In the words of Wolf, "The history of the past is directly followed by the second main division of the subject, i.e., Judaism in the living form in which it lies before us—the general statistical position of the Jews in every country, with special reference to their religious and political circumstances" (*Leo Baeck Institute Year Book,* vol. 2, 1957, p. 202). It is precisely this sense of continuity and connectedness that distinguished the practitioners of *Wissenschaft des Judentums* from those of *Altertumswissenschaft.* For all its appeal and meaning to German neohumanists, *Altertumswissenschaft* was not the uninterrupted cultural legacy of a contemporary community. A century after the Verein, Ismar Elbogen (1874–1943), Weimar's premier Jewish historian, again emphasized this existential dimension of the field by defining it as "the academic study of a vital Judaism, standing in the stream of development, as a sociological and historical unity" (*Festschrift . . . der Hochschule für die Wissenschaft des Judentums,* 1922, p. 141). Its proper academic analogue, claimed Elbogen, was not the study of Greece and Rome but the world of Islam. Given this degree of contemporaneity, *Wissenschaft des Judentums* became the major medium for thinking through the dilemmas generated by Judaism's confrontation with modernity.

Zunz's contribution. What facilitated that use was the shift to a conceptual mode of thought. For all their anticipation of modern scholarship, the pathbreaking Hebrew commentaries accompanying Moses Mendelssohn's translation of the Torah and Wolf Heidenheim's edition of the German cycle of festival prayerbooks both adhered to the traditional exegetical mode, which bespoke the centrality of sacred texts. In consonance with the secular temper of the age, modern scholarship would render the text subordinate to larger issues that required thematic and synthetic treatment. No one searched for new sources more zealously or read old ones more trenchantly than Zunz, but all in the service of questions and constructs that defied the limitations of disjointed analysis. The modern scholarship of eastern European autodidacts, steeped in the thought patterns of rabbinic culture, often failed to reach the level of conceptualization, coherence, and systematization achieved by university-trained practitioners of *Wissenschaft* in the West.

Of the original members of the Verein, Zunz alone remained true to the promise of *Wissenschaft.* Years later Heine would celebrate him as one "who stood firm, constantly and unshakably, in a period of transition, hesitation, and vacillation. . . . A man of words and a man of action, he worked unceasingly, he did what needed doing, at a time when others lost themselves in dreams and sank to the ground, bereft of courage" (quoted in S. S. Prawer's *Heine's Jewish Comedy,* 1983, p. 470). For much of his productive life, Zunz focused his scholarly energy on a history of the synagogue, the institution which he regarded as "the expression of Jewish nationality and the guarantee of its religious existence." In 1832, his *Die gottesdienstlichen Vorträge der Juden* was published, which first exhibited the full sweep of Midrashic creativity in the synagogue from the third century BCE down to his own day, and from 1855 to 1865 he complemented that work with three volumes: *Die synagogale Poesie das Mittelalters* (1855), *Die Ritus des synagogalen Gottesdienstes* (1859), and *Literaturgeschichte der synagogalen Poesie* (1865), which unveiled the synagogue's undreamed of liturgical richness. The final volume alone included the treatment of some six thousand liturgical poems along with the identification of nearly one thousand poets.

That devotion to the history of the synagogue derived from Zunz's conviction that a culture deserved to be studied at its core, in its more quintessential expressions and not on the fringes of its creativity. Not only did he fearlessly refuse to dilute the "parochial" character of Jewish culture, but by portraying it with insight and warmth he meant to raise the self-respect and level of commitment of contemporary Jews. "Genuine scholarship," ran his motto, "gives rise to action." Historical consciousness could serve to augment the depleted forces for Jewish survival.

Concept of development. The upshot of Zunz's massive research on the synagogue was to introduce the concept of development, the trademark of modern historical thought, into the study of rabbinic literature. The urgency of the hour dictated the early agenda of *Wissenschaft* scholars: emancipation seemed to challenge the very nature of a Judaism more rabbinic than biblical. Could subjects entangled in a seamless web of ritual obligations meet the demands of citizenship? Scholars soon moved beyond the inviting freedom of aggadic exegesis to the more problematic realm of rabbinic law to explore its genesis, evolution, and authority. Within two decades, works such as Levi Herzfeld's *Geschichte des Volkes Iisrael* (3 vols., 1847–1857), Naḥman Krochmal's *Moreh nevukhei ha-zeman,* edited by Zunz (1851), Heinrich Graetz's *Geschichte der Juden von den ältesten Zeiten bis auf die Gegenwart,* volume 4 (1853), Abraham Geiger's *Urschrift und Uebersetzungen der Bibel* (1857), Zacharias Frankel's *Darkhei ha-Mishnah* (1859), and Joseph Derenbourg's *Essai sur l'histoire et la géographie de la Palestine* (1867) had pierced the darkness of the Persian and Greco-Roman periods of Jewish history to illumine the dynamic origins of the halakhic system. For all the disagreement in detail and interpretation, the cumulative effect of their prodigious research was to dissolve a corpus of literature that had long been venerated as a single harmonious entity into its many historical components: namely, early sources, literary forms, exegetical modes, stages of complexity and composition, conflicting protagonists, and formative external influences. While it discomforted Orthodox spokesmen such as Samson R. Hirsch, and although it rested heavily on later rabbinic sources, the research served to show Christian scholars the unabated vitality of Judaism after the Babylonian exile and the responsive nature of rabbinic leadership.

Jewish sectarianism. At the same time, *Wissenschaft* chipped away at the static rabbinic monolith from yet another direction. As early as 1816, Krochmal, living in the midst of a still-unpunctured traditional society in eastern Galicia, had publicly defended the legitimacy of investigating the literature of the Karaites, who despite their halakhic deviance, had never distanced themselves from Jewish suffering. A few years later, Peter Beer of Prague published his *Geschichte, Lehren und Meinungen aller bestandenen und noch bestehenden religiösen Sekten der Juden und der Geheimlehre, oder Cabbalah* (2 vols., 1822–1823), an unabashedly antirabbinic history of Jewish sects (including medieval mystics), which provided a glimpse of the recurring resistance to Talmudic hegemony. At first, much of the interest in Jewish sectarianism focused on the era of the Second Commonwealth, but the steady publication of Karaite manuscripts in the ensuing decades, especially the rich cache by Simhah Pinsker in 1860, prompted works such as Isaak M. Jost's *Geschichte des Judenthums und seiner Sekten* (3 vols., 1857–1859), Heinrich Graetz's *Ge-*

schichte der Juden von den ältesten Zeiten bis auf die Gegenwart, volume 5 (1860), and Julius Fürst's *Geschichte des Karärthums* (3 vols., 1862–1869), which reflect a renewal of the effort at a synthesis of Karaite history, though with insufficient attention to the Islamic ambiance. In Geiger's *Urschrift und Uebersetzungen der Bibel* (1857) and *Das Judentum und seine Geschichte* (3 vols., 1864–1871) the inherent link between sectarianism and halakhic development and the possible continuity of sectarian praxis were ingeniously integrated into a single overarching theory. Still more important, Geiger rehabilitated the Pharisees as the progressive party in ancient Judaism and claimed their patrimony for his own movement. The effect was to undercut the penchant among Reform leaders to connect their cause with the Sadducean-Karaite line, an affinity without much benefit.

Rabbinic and biblical literature. The absorption with rabbinic literature was a function of conception as well as need. When Zunz unfurled the agenda of *Wissenschaft des Judentums* in 1818, it was restricted to *"neuhebräische oder jüdische Literature."* By design he seemed to exclude, for the moment, the study of biblical literature, a subject firmly ensconced in the German university. If scholarship was to facilitate legislation, it had to concentrate on what was least known and most problematic: the nature and history of rabbinic Judaism. And, in fact, the modest amount of biblical scholarship produced by Jews in the nineteenth century bespeaks an avoidance intensified by dogmatic inhibitions but also born of political considerations.

Against this background, what was achieved, while not generally original, was not undistinguished. In *Die gottesdienstlichen Vorträge der Juden* (1832), Zunz already argued for a single author of *Ezra, Nehemiah,* and *Chronicles* and a postexilic date for *Ezekiel.* In later essays, he analyzed the Pentateuch in terms of numerous constituent sources with none earlier than 900 BCE and *Leviticus* following *Ezekiel.* Though Geiger preferred to date *Leviticus* before *Deuteronomy,* he matched Zunz's documentary analysis of the Pentateuch and insisted on the fluidity of the biblical text long after composition. More conservative scholars like Krochmal and Graetz confined their research to the Prophets and the Writings, often taking leave of traditional views.

The most substantial and lasting Jewish contribution of the century to biblical research, however, came not from Berlin or Breslau but from Padua, where Shemu'el David Luzzatto, with an unsurpassed knowledge of the Hebrew language, renewed the long-disrupted genre of medieval Jewish exegesis of the Bible. Independent of Protestant scholarship and rooted in the distinctive style of Italian Judaism, Luzzatto's Hebrew commentaries were anything but doctrinaire. Unfortunately, by the last quarter of the century the rising tide of German anti-Semitism also seeped into the halls of the university and retarded the acceptance of the documentary hypothesis by Jewish scholars for decades. In 1910, the rabbinical seminary in Breslau still excluded modern biblical criticism from its curriculum.

Spanish Judaism. Zunz's modest proposal of 1818 ended with the charge to undertake the publishing of largely unknown but classical specimens of "rabbinic literature" in order to begin to banish the contempt in which it was held. By way of example, he declared his intention to bring out a scholarly edition with Latin translation of a Hebrew philosophical treatise by Shem Ṭov ibn Falaquera, a thirteenth-century Spanish Jew. The identification of the best of Hebrew literature with medieval Spain epitomized the Sefardic bias so vital to emancipated Ashkenazim in search of legitimacy. With roots going back to the seventeenth century, the attraction of Spanish Jewry and its descendants became a pervasive cultural force in nineteenth-century German Jewry, finding diverse expression in liturgy, synagogue architecture, literature, and, of course, scholarship.

Young scholars, whose own intellectual emancipation often started with Moses Maimonides' *Guide of the Perplexed* and the Hebrew literature of the Haskalah, gravitated naturally to the poetic and philosophical legacy of Spain. Ironically, the term *golden age,* which is used to highlight Jewish cultural creativity in Muslim Spain, is not of Jewish provenance. It was first bestowed by Franz Delitzsch, the greatest Christian scholar of Judaism in the nineteenth century, in his *Zur Geschichte der jüdischen Poësie* (1836), in which he depicted the two centuries from 940 to 1140 as the golden and silver ages respectively of Jewish poetic achievement. But the term accorded fully with the needs and perceptions of German Jewry, and despite the heroic effort by a penitent Zunz not to ignore the dissimilar but equally impressive cultural achievements of medieval Ashkenazic Jewry, the *Wissenschaft* of a long line of scholars served to deepen and solidify the bias. At the same time, their failure to generate much sympathy for the mystical side of Spanish Judaism was a consequence of their own rational bent, compounded by outrage at the unfounded historical claims of the mystics themselves.

The attraction to cultural history was reinforced by a decided aversion to political history. To work out a conceptualization that would have done justice to the unconventional political history of Diaspora Jewry would have produced more flak than self-esteem. The embattled position of German Jewry militated against the subject. When Michael Sachs decided to produce *Die religiose Poësie der Juden in Spanien* (1845), a volume of medieval religious poetry in translation, he settled on Spain because of the widely held view, going back to Shlomoh Yehudah Rappoport, that Sefardic poets addressed God as lonely believers, whereas Ashkenazic poets only lamented the fate of the nation. Sachs specifically asked of Luzzatto, who had agreed to supply him material, not to send any "national poems." Somewhat later, in volume five of his *Geschichte der Juden*, Graetz did declaim with courage that the medieval Jewish experience betrays a political dimension, but he failed completely to demonstrate it. Neither he nor his colleagues moved beyond the older Spanish conception of Jewish political history as one of recurring persecution, though they amplified it factually and emotionally. On occasion, isolated works of political history such as Selig Cassel's "Geschichte der Juden" in the *Allgemeine Encyklopädie der Wissenschaften und Künste* (1850), Otto Stobbe's *Die Juden in Deutschland während des Mittelalters in politischer, socialer und rechtlicher Beziehung* (1866), and a volume of *Regesten zur Geschichte der Juden in Deutschland während des Mittelalters* (1862) by Meir Wiener did reveal just how much the systematic use of non-Jewish archival sources could enlarge and enrich the conception of the subject, but Graetz, with whom Stobbe worked closely, remained skeptical about their large-scale utility.

Institutional standing. By the mid-1870s when the founders of *jüdische Wissenschaft* had completed most if not all of their work (only Zunz, Steinschneider, and Graetz were still living, though Zunz was no longer productive), the study of Judaism had all the signs of an academic discipline except one: inclusion in the structure of the German university, the premier research institution of the century. Though a direct product of its research imperative, *Wissenschaft des Judentums* matured entirely outside the framework of the university. Jewish scholars as its primary practitioners were never accorded the university's recognition and support. The occasional appointment of a *Privatdozent* or *Honorarprofessor* in a cognate field was but the trappings of academic respectability. Of course, that was exactly the kind of institutional affiliation, given their commitment to undogmatic scholarship and their resentment of rabbinic leadership, for which the founders yearned. Typical of faculty and bureaucratic resistance to the idea was the rebuff administered to Zunz in 1848 by the philosophy faculty of the University of Berlin to his request to create a chair in Jewish history and literature. Such a chair, it was felt, smacked of confessional interests and would merely strengthen Jewish parochialism. Misreading Zunz's intent, the faculty declared that it was not the function of the university to train rabbis. In the German context, such exclusion, which was, to be sure, experienced for a time by other nascent fields (such as history), meant the denial of the discipline's universal significance and doomed hardy aficionados to eke out a living in circumstances that were often trying. Increasingly, young scholars had little choice but to enter the ranks of a rabbinate in transition and to "make" the time for sustained research.

The creation of the Jewish Theological Seminary in Breslau in 1854 from the largesse of a single Jewish benefactor finally provided an institutional base for the floundering field and cemented its connection with the modern rabbinate. With a curriculum informed by *Wissenschaft des Judentums*, a small faculty immersed in it, and a scholarly journal promoting it, Breslau became the model for all modern rabbinical seminaries established during the next half-century in central and western Europe and the United States. Despite denominational differences, these institutions determined the scholarly character of the modern rabbinate, until it was modified again at the turn of the century by the changing social and political needs of the Jewish community. Its graduates brought to the pulpit a lively commitment to deepen as well as to disseminate the new mode of Jewish learning.

But Zunz and Moritz Steinschneider viewed these developments with dismay, regarding much of the scholarship coming out of Breslau as dogmatic and pretentious. Twice in the 1870s, Steinschneider, a man of awesome learning, prodigious output, and extensive personal contacts with non-Jewish scholars, preferred to turn down invitations from new seminaries in Berlin and Budapest and to stay at his modest post as director of the girls' school of the Berlin Jewish community. In 1876, he reaffirmed the original integrationist vision with typical acerbity:

> Institutions to preserve the rabbinate in the form acquired during the last centuries promote systematic hypocrisy and scholarly immaturity. What is scholarly about Jewish history and literature has no need to avoid the atmosphere of the university and must be made accessible to Christians. The task of our time seems to me, above all, to call for the temporary funding [obviously with Jewish money—I.S.] of unpaid instructorships for Jewish history and literature at philosophical faculties, so that governments will be prompted to create professorships and institutions in which matriculated Gymnasium students might prepare themselves for the study of Hebrew literature.
>
> (*Jewish Studies in Memory of George A. Kohut*, ed. Salo W. Baron and Alexander Marx, 1935, p. 521)

When Steinschneider shared his reasons for refusal with his old mentor and lifelong friend, Heinrich L. Fleischer, Germany's leading Orientalist, the latter, sensing the futility of such expectations, chided him for his errant purism: "If men like you deny your cooperation, have you then still a right to complain about the new institution's lack of success? Why not get involved from the outset in the hope that in this way the better will triumph?" (letter of 1 July 1875, Fleischer correspondence from the "Steinschneider Papers," archives of the Jewish Theological Seminary).

No scholar among the *Wissenschaft* pioneers contributed more to validating the right to university admission for Jewish studies than Steinschneider himself. With his matchless command of unpublished sources, he painstakingly reconstructed the unsuspected and seminal role that medieval Jews in the Islamic world had played in the transmission of Greco-Roman culture to the Christian West. His oeuvre, especially his massive *Die hebraeischen Übersetzungen des Mittelalters und die Juden als Dolmetscher* (2 vols., 1893), demonstrated for the first time the existence of a cultural unity in the medieval world that transcended religious differences, a theme that would continue to exercise Jewish scholars in the twentieth century. For instance, at Harvard, Harry A. Wolfson would try to integrate the parallel traditions of medieval religious philosophy into a single universe of discourse that operated from Philo to Spinoza. And at Princeton, on the basis of the inexhaustible documentary wealth of the Cairo Geniza, Shlomo D. Goitein would portray the social, economic, and material contours of a medieval Mediterranean society through the prism of Jewish life.

Turn of the Century. The engagement of Jewish scholarship with the vital concerns of a dynamic community was, if anything, intensified by the unsettling events of Jewish history in the twentieth century. In particular, the resurgence and diffusion of anti-Semitism at the turn of the century added to the inherent momentum toward specialization and institutionalization which the discipline had already generated in the course of the century. Even without this intrusion, the remarkable sweep of early *Wissenschaft* works would hardly have survived the growing technical complexity of the field. In 1897 alone, Solomon Schechter brought back to Cambridge from the Cairo Geniza, which he had emptied, some 100,000 literary fragments pertaining to nearly fifteen hundred years of Jewish history in the Greco-Roman and Islamic worlds. Thus, new sources, interests, and anxieties expanded Jewish scholarship into a movement of international proportions.

Historical Societies. The last decades of the nineteenth century give evidence of a chain reaction across the Jewish world in the formation of national Jewish historical societies. With the overt intention of stimulating research on the antiquity, fate, and contribution of Jews in their respective lands of settlement, these societies betray all the anxiousness of insecurity. But they also testify to the emergence of a cadre of indigenous scholars. The first to be founded in Paris in 1880 was the Société des Études Juives, which published the triannual *Revue des études juives* (1880–), designed to accomplish two ends: by casting its net over the entire field of Jewish studies, the *Revue* served to challenge the German hegemony embodied in Breslau's *Monatsschrift für die Geschichte und Wissenschaft des Judentums* (1851–1939), a policy that accorded with the rancor sown by the Franco-Prussian War; at the same time, the *Revue* placed at the heart of its agenda the twofold intent of encouraging the study of Jews in the history of France and of French Jews in the history of medieval Judaism. By 1897 the new subfield could boast of a volume of universal Jewish import. In *Gallia Judaica* (1897) Henri Gross, Hungarian-born as were so many of the *Wissenschaft* circle, produced a geographical dictionary that listed, along with ample historical information, all French localities in which Jews are known to have lived according to medieval Hebrew sources. In the twentieth century, this accomplishment became the model for the *Germania Judaica* (1917–) of the Gesellschaft zur Förderung der Wissenschaft des Judentums and the *Sefer ha-yishuv* (1939–) of the Palestine Historical and Ethnographical Society.

American Scholarship. In America too, Jewish scholarship was enlisted to stem the growth in anti-Semitism set off by the massive influx of eastern European Jews. Jewish notables exploited the occasion of the four-hundredth anniversary of Columbus's discovery of America in 1892 to create an American Jewish Historical Society, which would restrict its mission to assembling data on the role of Jews in "the discovery, settlement, and development of our land." Its president Oscar S. Straus, who had served as the American ambassador to Constantinople a few years before, invited and funded a noted European scholar of Spanish Jewish history, Meyer Kayserling of Budapest, to write *Christopher Columbus and the Participation of the Jews in the Spanish and Portuguese Discoveries* (1894) to "bring to light the extent to which our race had direct part and share with Columbus in the discovery of our continent." Straus hoped that the historical confirmation of "this fact would be an answer for all time to come to anti-Semitic tendencies in this country."

Far more important than Kayserling's careful study of 1894 was the publication in 1901–1906 of the twelve-volume *Jewish Encyclopedia,* edited by Isidore Singer and Cyrus Adler, by the non-Jewish firm of Funk and Wagnalls. Produced in a land on the fringes of the *Wissenschaft* movement with no scholarly tradition of its own, this first Jewish encyclopedia represented a collective venture of huge proportions and astonishingly high quality, a magnificent summation of nearly a century of Jewish scholarship, and, above all, the transplantation of *Wissenschaft des Judentums* to America. But the level of scholarly attainment should not obscure the pragmatic concerns of its genesis. The preface alluded to the anxieties of the moment: ". . . the world's interest in Jews is perhaps keener than ever before. Recent events, to which more direct reference need not be made, have aroused the world's curiosity as to the history and condition of a people which has been able to accomplish so much under such adverse conditions." Accordingly, the editors were eager to present a balanced picture of Jews as both integrated and parochial, as both cosmopolitans and cultivators of their own traditions.

Anglo-Jewish Scholarship. The founding of *The Jewish Quarterly Review* in 1888 and the Jewish Historical Society of England in 1893 certainly suggests a similar set of circumstances for Anglo-Jewry. The fact that Lucien Wolf launched the research program of the society in 1901 with his splendid edition of *Menasseh ben Israel's Mission to Oliver Cromwell* reflects the same need as felt in America for a "foundation myth" that intersects at a decisive juncture with the history of the nation. In one sense both Wolf's texts and the very idea of the society owed their patrimony to Henrich Graetz, who in his address to the immensely successful Anglo-Jewish Historical Exhibition of 1887 had called for an organized scholarly effort to study local history. *The Jewish Quarterly Review,* on the other hand, became the academic organ for a talented cluster of English scholars who had gathered around the charismatic figure of Solomon Schechter. For two decades it not only encompassed the full panoply of Jewish studies, but also often protested the jaundiced scholarship on ancient Judaism coming out of Germany.

Russian Scholarship. Under the guidance of Simon Dubnow, the small and ever more beleaguered liberal sector of Russian Jewry also began to display an interest in the study of local history to firm up its sense of belonging and distinctiveness. Fully aware of the social role of Jewish scholarship in the West, the young Dubnow transformed his own religious alienation into a lifelong program for the cultivation of historical consciousness. In 1891 to 1892, he issued appeals in Russian and Hebrew to set up a Jewish historical society that would coordinate a nationwide effort to collect the diverse sources, fast disappearing, related to the nine-hundred-year history of Jews in Poland and Russia. He pointed with envy to what had been accomplished in the West and berated Russian Jews for failing to realize the cohesive power of historical consciousness. However, his own conception of Jewish history had already begun to diverge from that of his *Wissenschaft* mentors. While he too stressed the greater importance of the internal Jewish sources, he articulated for the first time a vision of Jewish political history in the Diaspora that went far beyond the passive endurance of persecution. In the institution of the *gahal,* Diaspora Jews, wherever they settled, had created a unique instrument of national self-government that preserved a large measure of political initiative. The still-unemancipated status and traditional character of Russian Jewry had sensitized Dubnow to the medieval political expression of Jewish nationhood, and he pleaded for the sources to study its history. In his *History of the Jews in Russia and Poland* (3 vols., Eng. ed., 1916–1920) and *Weltgeschichte des jüdischen Volkes* (10 vols., 1925–1929), Dubnow not only combined his many preliminary studies into a coherent narrative of a millennium of Jewish history in Poland and Russia, but also fully formulated and espoused his theory of Diaspora nationalism.

Dubnow's original proposal finally bore fruit in 1908 in Saint Petersburg with the founding of the Russian Jewish Historical Ethnographic Society by Maxim Vinaver and David Günzberg. Also at Saint Petersburg that same year, the scholarly, artistocratic Günzberg opened at his own expense an academy of Jewish studies in which Dubnow delivered public lectures on Jewish history and conducted seminars for advanced students, whose rank included some of the leading Zionist historians of the next generation. Most important of all, Dubnow's call to collect and record had become part of the credo of the nationalist Jewish renaissance emanating from Saint Petersburg. In the last three years before the war, the writer Solomon Anski led an ambitious ethnographic expedition sponsored by the society into the Jewish hinterland of the Ukraine to plumb its rich deposits of folklore and iconography, bringing back thousands of photographs, tales, folkways, manuscripts, and artifacts. In 1915, Issachar Ryback, a young art student, financed his own study of the wooden synagogues of White Russia, and in 1916 the society sent him and fellow artist El Lissitzky back to the Ukraine to do the same for its synagogues. In a far more somber vein, Anski in *Khurbm Galitsye* (1921) documented the agony of Galician Jewry inflicted by war in a monumental memoir of his heroic relief mission, and Elias Tcherikower, entirely in the spirit of Dubnow, organized and administered at great personal risk during the years 1918 to 1920 an archive to record the unparalleled slaughter of as many as seventy-five thousand Ukrainian Jews amidst the chaos of civil war.

Folklore. The wholesale consumption of Jewish folklore in Russian exuded all the enthusiasm of the populist fervor unleashed by the socialist and Zionist rebellions at the turn of the century. But as an academic field, its origins lie in Germany, and as such it marked a sharp departure from the preoccupation with high culture that absorbed the founders of *jüdische Wissenschaft.* With fewer acknowledged luminaries than in the Sefardic world to distract them, the early students of Ashkenazic Judaism were forced to look at popular expressions of religious culture. The skein of development runs from the midcentury writers of ghetto novellas about central European Jewish life at the threshold of emancipation through the often overlooked collection of Judeo-German proverbs and expressions, *Sprichwörter und Redensarten deutsch-jüdischer Vorzeit* (1860) by Abraham Tendlau, the pioneering social histories of medieval Ashkenazic Jewry in Abraham Berliner's *Aus dem inneren Leben der deutschen Juden im Mittelalter* (1871), and Moritz Güdemann's *Geschichte des Erziehungswesens und der Cultur der abendländischen Juden während des Mittelalters und der neueren Zeit* (3 vols., 1880–1888), to Max Grunwald's work at the end of the century. A graduate of Breslau and at the same time rabbi in Hamburg, Grunwald delivered a manifesto in 1896 urging creation of a society, museum, and journal of Jewish folklore, and two years later he began publishing the first number of the *Mitteilungen der jüdischen Volkskunde* (1898–1929), which he was to edit singlehandedly in different formats for thirty volumes. That the first chair in Jewish folklore established at the Hebrew University in 1973 bears the name of this polymath is resounding testimony to his decisive role in launching the field.

The fascination with folklore signaled a broadly felt need to reconnect with the irrational, to reinvigorate an excessively cerebral tradition with the life-giving forces of imagination. Rabbinic Judaism as codified in the East or spiritualized in the West did not exhaust the record of Jewish lore and legend begun in the first decade of the twentieth century by scholars as diverse as Martin Buber, Ḥayyim Bialik and Yehoshuʿa Ravnitzki, Louis Ginzberg, and Micha Josef Berdyczewski. Ginzberg's monumental *The Legends of the Jews* (7 vols., 1909–1938), elegantly designed for scholar and layman alike, not only revealed the popular wellsprings of rabbinic religion, but also demonstrated the extent to which Jewish legends preserved and mediated the folklore of antiquity.

Art. Jewish art, as cultural expression and scholarly discipline, was similarly invigorated by the discoveries of folklore. In no area of contemporary Jewish life did creativity require quite as urgently the validation and inspiration of a historical tradition. Jewish artists and historians faced the same deep-seated stereotype, shared by friend and foe alike, that Jews by virtue of religion and race were singularly bereft of any aesthetic sensibility. But dramatic historical evidence to the contrary began to mount: the exhibition of the Isaac Strauss collection in Paris in 1878, the publication of the Sarajevo Haggadah in 1898 along with the recovery of a Jewish tradition of manuscript illumination, the formation of Jewish art societies and collections, the publication in 1916 of *Antike Synagogen in Galilaea* by Heinrich Kohl and Carl Watzinger of the first study of Galilean synagogues, and, above all, the plethora of folk art unearthed in the wooden synagogues of Russia. For artists projecting a secular Jewish culture, historians were supplying the resources of an indigenous past. In the beautiful pages of *Rimon,* a lavish magazine of Jewish arts and letters published in Berlin after the war in both a Hebrew and Yiddish edition, the artistic and historical dimensions converged symbiotically.

Sociology. From Jewish folklore to sociology was but a small step, for the interest remained primarily nonelitist. The impetus for this expansion of Jewish scholarship came directly from the nascent Zionist movement. Although Zunz had clearly foreshadowed the sociological study of the Jews in a programmatic essay in 1823, *Grundlinien zu einen künftigen Statistik der Juden,* it took the Zionist indictment of assimilation with all its putatively alarming consequences for Jewish survival to effect a scholarly shift to the present. At the fifth Zionist Congress in 1901, Max Nordau, who annually treated the delegates to a foreboding assessment of the Jewish situation, called for the systematic assemblage of data to confirm the Zionist consensus. The proposal took institutional form three years later in Berlin in the Bureau für Jüdische Statistik, manned by a small staff of unpaid Zionists, which for the next eighteen years would publish an invaluable journal for Jewish demography and statistics. Its first editor, till he went to Israel in 1908 to head the Palestine Office of the Zionist Organization, was Arthur Ruppin, who in 1904 had produced in his *Die Juden der Gegenwart* the first work of Jewish sociology. Not surprisingly, the first generation of scholars was drawn largely from the ranks of Zionists. By 1930 Ruppin's own research had grown into a sweeping two-volume *Soziologie der Juden* (1930–1931), and in 1938 he was the natural candidate for the Hebrew University's first professor of Jewish sociology.

Early Twentieth-Century Scholarship. The first century of Jewish studies ends where it began, in Berlin, with the formation of another association of young scholars still in rebellion against rabbinic ascendancy. In 1919 Eugen Täubler, this time with substantial Jewish backing, founded the Akademie für die Wissenschaft des Judentums. The idea was the outgrowth of a *cri du coeur* in 1917 by Franz Rosenzweig to German Jewry to revitalize its scholarly forces against the onslaught on ancient Judaism by the ever more confident scholarship of liberal Protestantism. Judaism's exclusion from the university remained unaltered, its incorporation into German society riddled with problems, and its laity unequipped for adversity. In final form, the academy, stripped of any polemical or educational intent, came to represent German Jewry's last attempt to bring *Wissenschaft des Judentums* out of its academic isolation and thereby to set its course for the twentieth century. In Täubler the academy had a classicist trained by Theodor Mommsen yet fully conversant with Jewish sources, a historical thinker of great conceptual power, and a proven administrator, who some years before had organized a national Jewish archive as the central repository for Jewish communal records.

As enunciated by Täubler, the mission of the academy was to end *jüdische Wissenschaft*'s obsession with anti-Semitism and reliance on practicing rabbis and to reunite it with the highest standards of modern scholarship. This meant specialization, systematic use of non-Jewish archival sources, philological analysis broadly conceived, and contextual and comparative research. Talmudic research in particular still suffered from the absence of a firm philological basis. Täubler dreamed of creating eventually a library of critical editions of all Jewish texts prior to the eighteenth century. In the meantime, he divided the field of Jewish studies into nine distinct specialities, delineated the nature of ancillary instruments of resources, and funded the research of young scholars like Chanokh Albeck, Yitzhak Baer, David H. Baneth, Arthur Spanier, and Selma Stern.

Three years after Täubler died in 1950 in Cincinnati, he was eulogized in Jerusalem by Baer, Moshe Schwabe, and Benzion Dinur, three men whose lives he touched deeply. But the tribute signified more than personal indebtedness. The very conceptualization, ethos, and instruments of Jewish studies as they came to be embodied in the Hebrew University after 1924 were conceived by Täubler in Berlin. The professionalization of Jewish scholarship was under way, though communal concerns would continue to influence research agendas.

ISMAR SCHORSCH

Jewish Studies since 1919

In the years following World War I, Jewish studies grew slowly but steadily as research institutions and organizations were established where previously there had been none. Those institutions established in Germany and Austria before the war continued to flourish despite the adverse economic conditions brought about by the worldwide economic depression. Indeed, it was precisely this economic situation that led to Berlin's becoming a major center of Hebrew and Yiddish printing and publication of a remarkably high quality during the 1920s.

The Gesellschaft zur Förderung der Wissenschaft des Judentums (established 1902) achieved its peak membership of over seventeen hundred members in 1920. Open to both institutions and individuals, the Gesellschaft sponsored the continued publication of the *Monatsschrift für die Geschichte und Wissenschaft des Judentums* (1851–1939) as well as a number of significant monographs.

Two noteworthy encyclopedias appeared in Germany during the 1920s. The *Jüdisches Lexikon* (1927–1930) was a popular work, although less scholarly than the *Jewish Encyclopedia* (1901–1906), concentrating more on contemporary personalities and events. The purpose of the *Encyclopaedia Judaica* (1928–1934) was to update the *Jewish Encyclopedia* and to include areas and material not treated in the earlier work. The rise of the Nazi regime, however, put an end to this project. Although incomplete, not going beyond the entry "Lyra," the encyclopedia is of such a remarkably and consistently high level that it is still an indispensable and authoritative reference work.

To the east, in the newly reconstituted Polish republic, where there was the greatest concentration of Jewish population, Jewish studies took root. In Vilna (Vilnius), the Yidishe Visinshaftlikhe Institut (YIVO) was established in 1925, with subsidiaries in Berlin, New York, Warsaw, and later, Buenos Aires. Its emphasis was largely on the Jewish experience in eastern Europe, especially the Yiddish-speaking world, and it continued the lines of research begun earlier by S. Anski and Simon Dubnow. YIVO's singleminded adherence to the Yiddish language was part of its desire to raise the intellectual level of eastern European Jewry and to make Yiddish a fully developed and modern national Jewish language.

Aside from publishing a number of scholarly monographs on history, language, literature, and music, YIVO established a journal, *YIVO Bleter* (1931–1939; since 1940 in New York). In 1940 New York became the center of its activities, and at the end of the war the Vilna library, which miraculously survived intact, was transferred to the United States. To meet the challenge of the new environment a second journal was issued, *YIVO Annual of Jewish Social Science* (1946–). In 1953 YIVO was the moving force that established the Yiddish Dictionary Committee, and in 1961 there appeared the first volume of the *Groyser Verterbukh fun der Yidisher Shprakh* (1961–1980).

In Warsaw the Instytut Nauk Judaistycznych, established in 1928, continued the earlier *Wissenschaft* tradition, for its major scholars, including Majer Bałaban, Mojżesz Schorr, and Ignacy Schiper, were products of Austrian Galicia. In addition to scholarly activity and publication, the institution was intended to train rabbis with university educations, teachers, and communal workers.

In Great Britain, Jewish studies were on a slightly stronger footing within the local academic setting because universities such as Oxford and Cambridge were noted centers of Hebraic learning. Among the notable scholars there were Israel Abrahams, H. M. J. Loewe, and Cecil Roth. The Soncino Press of London undertook a major translation project, bringing out the first complete English-language editions of the Babylonian Talmud (1935–1948), Midrash Rabbah (1939), and the *Zohar* (1931–1934).

The United States until 1939. In the United States, the field of Jewish studies as a separate discipline was still in its infancy. While Hebrew was offered in many universities, most professors were interested solely in Old Testament times. Notable exceptions were Richard Gottheil of Columbia University, William Popper of the University of California, and Isaac Husik of the University of Pennsylvania. Before World War II, however, positions were established at two major institutions: Harry A. Wolfson was the Littauer Professor of Jewish Literature and Philosophy at Harvard from 1925 until 1974, and Salo W. Baron occupied the Miller Chair for Jewish History at Columbia from 1930 until 1968. Otherwise, Jewish studies were largely restricted to the rabbinical seminaries—Hebrew Union College, the Jewish Institute of Religion, the Jewish Theological Seminary of America, and Yeshiva University—and to one secular institution, Dropsie College.

To support and encourage Jewish studies, the American Academy for Jewish Research was organized in 1920 and incorporated in 1929. Since 1930, its *Proceedings* have been published annually. Similarly, the Conference on Jewish Relations, whose purpose was to study modern Jewry, was founded in 1933 and incorporated in 1936. Its journal, *Jewish Social Studies*, has appeared since 1939.

Other periodical publications appearing in America during this time were the *Jewish Quarterly Review (New Series)* (1910–), *Hebrew Union College Annual* (1924–), and *Historica Judaica* (1938–1961). An encyclopedia project, the *Universal Jewish Encyclopedia* (1939–1943), had two basic aims: to provide detailed coverage of American Jewish life and to demonstrate the contributions of Jews to American life. This was the traditional *Wissenschaft* attitude, that Jewish scholarship should show the gentile world that the Jew was worthy of equality and civil rights.

Europe since 1945. With the end of any sizable Jewish community in Germany, Jewish studies after the war were limited largely to biblical studies. During the 1970s, however, there developed rather rapidly a group of institutions concerning themselves with postbiblical Judaism and Judaica. In Frankfurt, the Gesellschaft zur Förderung Judaistische Studien was established; it published a monographic series, *Frankfurter Judaistische Studien* (1971–1979), and a regular serial, *Frankfurter Judaistische Beiträge* (1973–). In 1975 the Institutum Judaicum of Tübingen University undertook the publication of a German translation, with critical notes, of the Jerusalem Talmud. Other centers include one for the study of German Jewish history at Hamburg and the Hochschule für Jüdische Studien at Heidelberg, as well as chairs at the Johann Wolfgang Goethe Universität and the University of Cologne.

The touchstone of Jewish studies in England since World War II has been the *Journal of Jewish Studies*. Begun in 1948 in Cambridge, its publication was taken over in 1951 by the London weekly *Jewish Chronicle*, which continued to publish it until 1976. Beginning in 1955 the journal was sponsored by the Institute of Jewish Studies in Manchester and the Society for Jewish Study in London. In 1971 editorship passed to Géza Vermès, of the Oriental Institute at Oxford, and in 1976 the Oxford Centre for Postgraduate Hebrew Studies took over publication.

While Jewish studies continue to thrive at the major universities, the Oxford Centre for Postgraduate Hebrew Studies has, since the early 1980s, been the focal point of activity. Although under the academic aegis of Oxford University, the Centre is financially independent and administrated by its own board. The Oxford Centre is also copublisher (along with the International Association of Jewish Lawyers and Jurists) of the *Jewish Law Annual* (1978–).

Postwar Jewish studies in France were dominated by Georges Vajda (1908–1981), who was instrumental in the creation of positions in Jewish studies in Paris, Strasbourg, Lyons, and Nancy. Aside from a monumental output of articles, monographs, and reviews in Jewish-Islamic studies, especially in medieval philosophy, he almost single-handedly revived the *Revue des études juives* (1880–), when, at the end of the war, it was the only scholarly Judaica journal remaining in Europe.

United States after 1945. During the twenty years after the war, a growing need was felt in the Jewish community for degree-granting programs in Jewish studies. To fill this need, many of the colleges of Jewish studies that had been established before the war (in such cities as Boston, Baltimore, Cleveland, Chicago, and Philadelphia) to train religious-school teachers and communal workers established such programs. In 1955 the Leo Baeck Institute was established in New York, with branches in London and Tel Aviv. This research institution concentrates on the Jewish experience in the German-speaking countries, emphasizing the modern period. The Institute publishes an annual on German Jewish history, the *Leo Baeck Year Book* (1956–), as well as a monographic series.

A number of noteworthy works of scholarship were produced in the United States during this time. An English translation of Moses Maimonides' *Code of Law* was undertaken by Yale University Press (1949–). Salo W. Baron's magisterial work *A Social and Religious History of the Jews* (1952–) is perhaps the single most ambitious project in Jewish history in modern times; its first eighteen volumes cover from antiquity to 1650. Saul Lieberman produced a critical edition of the Tosefta as well as a commentary, *Tosefta' ki-feshuṭah* (both 1955–1973). Israel Davidson compiled *Otsar Ha-shirah ve-ha-piyyuṭ*, a four-volume thesaurus of medieval Hebrew poetry (1924–1933).

Since 1967, a proliferation of ethnic studies has contributed to the rapid growth of Jewish-studies programs (with new support and involvement from outside the campus), as has a pool of experienced academics who, although they may not previously have been involved in Jewish studies, were available to create programs and fill openings.

A number of outstanding scholars of European background encouraged this process, including Alexander Altmann, Nahum N. Glatzer, and S. D. Goitein. This in turn has led to the emergence of a generation of American-born and educated Judaica specialists.

Indicative of the growth of Jewish studies is the parallel trend in the world of book publishing. Prior to World War II trade publishers had little if any interest in the publication of popular, let alone scholarly, Judaica; such works were handled by small Jewish publishing houses, often vanity presses. Since the late 1960s, however, the number of books issued by the major trade and university presses has increased dramatically.

Another indication of growth is the number of new professional organizations: the Association for Jewish Studies (1969), which publishes the *AJS Review;* the Association for the Sociological Study of Jewry (1971); and the Jewish Law Association (1980). In the field of librarianship there are two complementary organizations, the Association of Jewish Libraries (1965) and the Council of Archives and Research Libraries in Jewish Studies (1973).

Israel. Jewish studies constitute a significant part of the study and teaching of the humanities in Israel. Each of the five universities—Hebrew University (est. 1923), Bar-Ilan (1955), Tel Aviv (1956), Ben-Gurion University of the Negev (1970), and Haifa (1970)—has a major program in Jewish studies; even the Technion, an engineering institution, has a nondegree program in Jewish studies in its Department of General Studies. As a result, the impact of Israeli scholars is great. Individuals such as Chanoch Albeck, Yitzhak Baer, Jacob N. Epstein, Gershom G. Scholem, E. E. Urbach, and others have set a high standard for their colleagues in the Diaspora.

The number of journals, many of them highly specialized, carrying articles in Jewish studies is great. The two oldest and most prestigious are *Taarbiz* (1929–), published by the Institute of Jewish Studies, Hebrew University; and *Zion* (1930–), a publication of the Historical Society of Israel. The Jewish National and University Library publishes two bibliographic periodicals: *Kiryat Sefer* (1924–) and *Index to Articles in Jewish Studies* (1969–).

In 1947 the first World Congress of Jewish Studies was convened in Jerusalem. Since 1957 the congress has been held quadrennially and has become a major event attracting scholars from the world over. The proceedings of the sessions are published in several volumes covering all areas, from biblical archaeology to modern Jewish thought.

Conclusion. Since World War II an interesting trend has developed in Jewish studies, especially in the United States. Previously, a Judaica scholar had an educational background that was well grounded in classical Jewish texts; those who attended a European *Gymnasium* received further training in Latin and Greek. In many respects, methodology available to scholarship in general was limited, as it was still in its formative stages. Consequently, much of the scholarship produced by these earlier generations of scholars, concerned as it was with the preparation and publication of texts, is perceived by present-day scholars as mechanical and the product of deductive reasoning.

Present-day scholars are products of a different educational system, few of them having had intensive exposure to classical texts at a young age. Rather, they are more broadly educated, especially in the social sciences, and they come to the texts at a relatively late time. With this as their background, their scholarship can be seen a product of inductive reasoning.

These two approaches are not in competition. Indeed,

the later research is highly dependent upon the basic textual work done by scholars who were truly pioneers. Moreover, there are many areas in which much work in texts remains to be done where today's scholars must stand on the shoulders of their teachers.

PHILIP E. MILLER

JEWISH THOUGHT AND PHILOSOPHY.

[*This entry consists of three articles:*

Premodern Philosophy
Modern Thought
Jewish Ethical Literature

The first article discusses the thought of the major medieval Jewish philosophers, from Sa'adyah to Mendelssohn, and the second presents modern Jewish thought from Mendelssohn to the present. The third article treats major medieval and modern ethical writings and writers.]

Premodern Philosophy

Usually the term *medieval* designates a historical period falling "between" ancient and modern times. In the history of philosophy, then, the medieval period would occur between the last of the ancient Greek and Roman philosophers and Descartes. However, following H. A. Wolfson (1947), one may construe "medieval" philosophy as a style of thinking that, although prevalent during the Middle Ages, need not be temporally restricted. It is a style of philosophy that attempts to make use of two radically different sources of information for the establishment of a general worldview and way of life. These sources are human reason, particularly philosophy, and divine revelation, especially some sacred text. A medieval philosopher is someone whose intellectual outlook and language are shaped by both philosophy and prophecy.

Beginnings of Medieval Philosophy. Speaking from a strict historical perspective, one would have to say with Wolfson that the first medieval philosopher was Philo Judaeus (d. 45–50 CE). Most of Philo's many books are commentaries on various biblical narratives or legal codes, commentaries in which philosophical, especially Platonic, concepts are used to formulate and explain the text. In reading the Bible in this way, Philo introduced not only a new period in philosophy but also a novel style of philosophy, which we shall henceforth call "medieval." In general, Philo saw no fundamental cleavage between reason and revelation and optimistically sought to make "the sons of Japheth dwell in the tents of Shem." The subsequent story of medieval philosophy is in a sense a long and still ongoing drama on this Philonic theme. Nevertheless, a history of medieval Jewish philosophy cannot begin with Philo, who had little or no influence upon Jewish thought. Instead, it begins nine centuries later with Sa'adyah.

Sa'adyah Gaon. Originally an Egyptian, Sa'adyah ben Yosef (882–942), known as Sa'adyah Gaon, became the dean of the rabbinic academy in Baghdad, the most important in the Jewish world. Unlike Philo, Sa'adyah did influence subsequent Jewish thinkers who read his main philosophical work, *The Book of Beliefs and Opinions.* By Sa'adyah's time, the intellectual world had changed: whereas Philo had to contend with a dying paganism and several warring philosophical schools, Sa'adyah confronted the rival monotheistic religions of Christianity and Islam, Jewish sectarian movements, and the rejuvenated Greek philosophical traditions, now formulated in Arabic with a Muslim accent. Although *The Book of Beliefs and Opinions* is clearly a theological polemical treatise designed to vindicate rabbinic Judaism against its opponents, its method and language are philosophical. Sa'adyah makes use of the philosophical sources available to him through the Muslim theological tradition of *kalām,* the earliest philosophical school in Islam. The *mutakallimūn,* or Muslim theologians, attempted to defend Islam against its religious and philosophical rivals by using arguments and theories gleaned from Greek philosophy. Although *kalām* was initially polemical, rather than purely philosophical, in intention and method, it eventually evolved into a distinct philosophical style or school. Sa'adyah was in this sense a representative of Jewish *kalām.*

Since the only common ground among the various rivals in this religious-philosophical debate was reason, Sa'adyah begins *The Book of Beliefs and Opinions* with a defense of reason against the skeptics and fundamentalists who would disparage it on either philosophical or religious grounds. For Sa'adyah there are three main sources of truth, of which two belong to man's native powers: intellect and sense perception. In addition to these human capacities there is a prophetic tradition, which includes the original revelation to the prophets and the reliable, continuous transmission of their communications throughout a religious community, in particular the Jewish people. Sa'adyah clearly indicates that although prophetic tradition corroborates the two cognitive sources, it is ultimately based upon the senses and grounded in reason. It is based upon the senses since in a prophetic vision one *hears* God speaking or *sees* certain things. It is grounded in reason since the content of the revelation will be for the most part rational, or at least it will not be irrational. This epistemic foundation for revelation has an important prac-

[illegible]ence: a scriptural passage is to be understood according to its literal meaning *unless* it violates sense perception, reason, reliable tradition, or another passage whose meaning is clear. Thus the cognitive faculties serve as criteria for religious doctrine. A corollary of this "rationalistic bias" is that miraculous deeds performed by someone do not by themselves constitute proof of his prophetic authenticity if what he says violates reason.

Firmly convinced of the potency of reason, Sa'adyah offers his readers a rationalistic reconstruction of the Jewish faith, the goals of which are (1) to clarify the main dogmas of Judaism and to prove them where possible, and (2) to refute the opponents, internal and external, of Judaism. Sa'adyah's philosophical theology has, then, as its main purpose the transformation of our unreflective inherited opinions into rationally grounded beliefs. The "true believer" is thus someone who not only has true beliefs but in addition knows that they are true and why. Those who undertake this kind of inquiry will achieve something important and valuable—religious knowledge. Those who do not, but rather follow reliable tradition, will still merit divine favor so long as they willingly obey God's commandments. Sa'adyah's rationalism is thus not a religion of the intellectual alone.

Having laid these epistemological foundations, Sa'adyah next undertakes to prove basic principles of the Jewish faith, such as creation of the universe, the existence and nature of God, and man's free will. In general his argumentation follows the lines drawn up by the *kalām* on these topics, although it deviates considerably from the *kalām* on the subject of freedom. Like his *kalām* predecessors, Sa'adyah believed that the fundamental dogma of divine religion is creation *ex nihilo*. Once this principle has been demonstrated, he thought, it is easy to prove God's existence and to discover some information about his nature. Of the four proofs Sa'adyah gives for the creation of the universe, the first and fourth were to have considerable impact upon subsequent Jewish thought. The first argument asserts that if the universe is, as Aristotle admitted, finite in size, then it must have only finite energy. But a body of finite energy must ultimately decay and eventually disintegrate. However, if it disintegrates, then it must have had a beginning; for, as Aristotle argued, everything that is generated is corruptible, and the converse (Aristotle, *On the Heavens* 1.12). In this argument Sa'adyah cleverly uses Aristotle's physics to show that the Aristotelian claim that the universe is eternal is inconsistent with this physics. The fourth argument claims to show that on the hypothesis of infinite past time there would be an infinite series of moments and events prior to any chosen moment. But such an infinite series, *ex hypothesi*, can never be traversed such that the chosen moment is ever reached. But if this moment is never reached, then it never comes into being, which is *contra hypothesim*. Hence, past time is not infinite. A version of this argument appears in Kant's *Critique of Pure Reason* ("First Antinomy of Reason," B 454).

Convinced that these arguments are valid, Sa'adyah then proceeds to show that creation is out of nothing, which doctrine had become orthodox in Judaism, Christianity, and Islam by the tenth century. Of the various arguments in behalf of this dogma, one is especially significant: if there were some eternal matter out of which God fashioned the universe, as Plato had suggested in the *Timaeus*, this matter would be *co*-eternal with God and hence independent of him. But an independent entity may very well not want to be fashioned into anything! So God would in this view be beholden to matter if he were to create or not create at all.

Sa'adyah's defense of creation *ex nihilo* leads him to develop a theology that stresses God's creativity. First, the proof that the world has been created *ex nihilo* is proof also of God's existence, for a created world needs a creator. Second, Sa'adyah claims that it is the very nature of God to be creative: "In the beginning God created . . ." All the major divine attributes—power, wisdom, life, love—are different facets of God's essential creativity. Every other attribute is a corollary of this divine primal productivity. Hence corporeal characteristics cannot be applied to God, for such qualities can be true only of creatures, entities made by God out of nothing. To ascribe such features to God is to transform the creator into a creature. Sa'adyah is so convinced of the complete incorporeality of God that in his Arabic translation of the Bible he "cleanses" scripture of many anthropomorphic expressions. For example, "the hand of God" becomes "God's power." This conception of God also leads him to criticize the Christian doctrines of the Trinity and incarnation as contaminations of pure monotheism.

No matter how "pure" this monotheistic God may be, he is still a power that reveals himself to man. All the scriptural religions agree that God speaks to prophets and sends them to communicate God's will to man, usually in the form of divine law. Nevertheless, the question whether the Jewish law is a good and rational law or whether it has been superseded by another divine law revealed to a prophet other than Moses was controversial in Sa'adyah's day, as it is now. Sa'adyah's aim is to show (1) that a good God provides the means for his creatures to find their happiness and to receive divine reward; (2) that Mosaic law is based upon reason;

and (3) that this law is still valid and cannot be abrogated.

For Sa'adyah it is rationally obligatory for a person to worship God, the creator, just as it is required that we respect and honor our parents. But it is also reasonable that God give us the means whereby we worship him and thereby obtain human perfection and reward. Unlike Paul and the religious antinomians, Sa'adyah sees divine grace as merited by good works; otherwise, the giving and receiving of grace would be arbitrary and undeserved. The Torah and its many commandments are therefore neither incitements to sin, as Paul claimed, nor a punishment of Israel, as Muḥammad believed. Just the contrary, they are expressions of God's love. But if this is so, the laws themselves cannot be capricious or irrational; otherwise, God would be a despotic tyrant, not a loving father and king. Accordingly, following the lead of both the earlier rabbis and the *kalām*, Sa'adyah initially distinguishes between those divine commands that obviously have some reason or purpose and those that do not readily exhibit such a rationale. The former he calls rational commands, the latter revelational commands. As examples of the former he gives the injunctions to abandon the worship of idols and to love our neighbor as ourselves; as examples of the latter he gives the festival laws and the laws concerning incest. Whereas the rational precepts are or can be derived from certain fundamental truths of reason, the revelational commands are neither dictated nor prohibited by reason.

However, as he proceeds to develop his account of law, it is clear that Sa'adyah virtually abandons this distinction and claims that on closer examination even the revelational commands are found to have some reasonable explanation and justification. For example, the selection of the Sabbath and other holy days may seem at first to be arbitrary. After all, neither the Greeks and Romans nor the Muslims have a complete day of rest on one specified day of the week. Yet, Sa'adyah argues, if we remember that "reason requires" (one of his favorite phrases) that we worship God, we have to worship him at some time, in some place, and in a certain way; otherwise, the initial rational precept to worship our creator is empty. Accordingly, our reasonable creator specifies for us through his prophet Moses the time, place, and manner of worship. If there were no uniform code of regulations, people would worship God at diverse times and in different ways. No community could survive such religious anarchy. Moreover, on practical grounds a Sabbath is quite beneficial: it affords not only physical rest but also mental relaxation and the opportunity to study Torah, to reflect, and to converse on spiritual matters. Although Sa'adyah does not, as did Philo, undertake to "rationalize" the whole body of Jewish law, he does suggest in outline how such an enterprise could and should be done. In this sketch he establishes the precedent for future medieval philosophers of Jewish law, such as Maimonides and Levi ben Gershom (Gersonides).

Of greater polemical urgency, however, is Sa'adyah's defense against the twin charges of falsification and abrogation in the Jewish law. The whole Jewish-Muslim-Christian debate in the medieval period turned on these issues. In reply to the Muslim accusation that the Bible in general, and Jewish law in particular, do not represent the pristine and true revelation, Sa'adyah appeals to the notion of reliable tradition, one of the original sources of truth referred to earlier. What is it that makes a religious text and tradition worthy of credence, Sa'adyah asks. Consider a tradition not based upon reliable evidence: it would be full of contradictions and discord. The Jewish tradition, at least as it existed prior to the nineteenth century, is unique in that it contains not only a text that one of its main rivals (i.e., Christianity) accepts as true and correct, but also a body of law that was almost universally accepted by its adherents. Were this tradition unreliable, such unanimity would be inconceivable.

But suppose one were to contend that the Torah is a true revelation but claim that it has been superseded by a more perfect divine law, such as the New Testament or Qur'ān. Sa'adyah counters this argument with several replies, some based upon reason, others on scripture, which, after all, the Christians accept as true. On purely rational grounds, the notion of a divine law being superseded by a totally different and in some cases contrary divine law is inconceivable, for two reasons. First, why would a perfect and immutable God give an imperfect law in the first place and then, only a few centuries later, replace it with a better but very different code? Wouldn't it have been more sensible to have revealed the better code at the outset? Moreover, does God really change his mind, as we do? Second, suppose the New Testament is more perfect than the Torah. But the Muslims claim that the Qur'ān is more perfect than both and hence supersedes them. Yet why stop at this point? Perhaps tomorrow God will reveal another law that abrogates the Qur'ān, and so on *ad infinitum*. To stop the regress at one point is just bias. So why concede a regress at all? Finally—and this argument is primarily directed against the Christians—the Torah, which the Christians accept in principle, testifies to its own eternal validity (*Jer.* 31, *Dt.* 33). The Christians, Sa'adyah implies, cannot have it both ways: either they should accept the whole Torah, especially if they see it as the basis for the messianic claim and role of Jesus, or they should drop it altogether and admit that their religion has no relationship at all to Judaism.

A rational and perfect law revealed by a reasonable and perfect lawgiver must, by logical implication, be such that its recipients are able to obey it, and in obeying it receive an appropriate reward. Man has to be a free agent in order to be a subject of the divine commandments and must have the conviction that his obedience to the law will have beneficial consequences for him. Otherwise the lawgiver would be arbitrary and the law unreasonable. At this point in his inquiry, Sa'adyah grapples with one of the most thorny problems in classical theology, the alleged dilemma between divine omnipotence and omniscience and human free will, a problem that was especially vexing to the *kalam*. Sa'adyah unambiguously defends humanity against any divine encroachment: we are completely free agents, capable of assuming full responsibility for our actions despite God's omnipotence and omniscience. Unlike some Muslim theologians, Sa'adyah does not believe that God's infinite power would be curtailed if man had some power of his own; nor is it the case that whenever we do some deed God is the co-agent, as some other Muslim theologians claim. God is not so niggardly or envious that he would deprive human beings of any power to act from their own will, and the notion of one action with two co-agents is both implausible and unnecessary. To be an agent is *ex hypothesi* to be able to perform a deed. If I cannot do it myself, then I am not an agent! Nor is God's omniscience an impediment to my free action, as Cicero thought. Although God knows what I shall do tomorrow, he does not cause that action, just as my knowing what day it will be tomorrow does not bring about that day.

Sa'adyah maintains that each human soul is originally a pure and superior substance that is created by God to direct the body in their joint earthly undertaking. The soul needs the body to perform its mission as much as the body requires the soul for its guidance. No Platonic dualism, with its subsequent Christian overlay of original sin, infects Sa'adyah's optimistic religious psychology. The soul and body together act and bear jointly the responsibility for these actions. Upon death, the human soul will be separated from its body because it is a finer substance than the body, and it will reside in some supernal realm until the day of its eventual return to its original body, which will ultimately be resurrected with the soul. Sa'adyah recognizes two stages of resurrection: the first involves the righteous of Israel alone and is associated with the coming of the Messiah in this present world of human history; the second involves the resurrection of all mankind for ultimate judgment and initiates the world to come with its everlasting reward or punishment. These eschatological predictions are ultimately not the teachings of the philosophers but the promises of scripture, which, however, do not violate reason. Indeed, if God is able to create the world ex nihilo, why can he not resurrect the dead, not just once, but twice? With the establishment of these eschatological doctrines on both scriptural and rational grounds, Sa'adyah has completed his philosophical reconstruction and defense of Judaism.

Spanish Jewish Philosophers. Whereas the beginnings of both Islamic and Jewish philosophy were in the East, the second major phase in Jewish philosophy occurred in Muslim Spain, which became the philosophical-scientific center for the Jews for nearly the remainder of the Middle Ages. In Spain the philosophical tradition that molded the Jewish mind was the "Neoplatonic" philosophy developed by the Muslim *falasifah* al-Farabi and Ibn Sina as a synthesis of Aristotelian and Plotinian themes. For about two centuries both Muslim and Jewish philosophy developed within the metaphysical framework provided by Aristotle and Plotinus, as interpreted by Porphyry and Proclus. During this period Jewish cultural life in Spain flourished in virtually every domain, but especially in philosophy and poetry. Indeed, two of three leading thinkers in this epoch were poets as well as philosophers: Shelomoh ibn Gabirol and Yehudah ha-Levi.

Shelomoh ibn Gabirol. The philosophical fate of Shelomoh ibn Gabirol (c. 1021–c. 1058) is especially interesting. His major philosophical work, *The Fountain of Life*, was written in Arabic, as were most Jewish philosophical books until the fourteenth century; but the original Arabic text was lost and survives only in a Latin translation as *Fons vitae*. Its impact upon Jewish thought was minimal, and this is evidenced by the fact that no medieval Hebrew translation of the work was ever made; only a thirteenth-century Hebrew summary survives. The reason for this neglect in Judaism is that *Fons vitae* contains not one biblical or rabbinic reference. It is a pure philosophical treatise, having no obvious connection with the traditional theological problems that had preoccupied Sa'adyah and other Jewish thinkers. So it was soon forgotten by the Jews, although preserved by the Christians, who believed its author to be a certain Avicebrol, a Muslim, or perhaps a Christian Arab. It was not until 1846 that Solomon Munk proved that the author of *Fons vitae*, Avicebrol, was the famous Jewish poet Shelomoh ibn Gabirol.

Since Ibn Gabirol's *Fountain of Life* had no significant influence upon Jewish philosophy, we shall not discuss it here. Instead, we shall examine his poetry, and for two reasons. First, several of his poems are philosophical. Second, his poetry, including some of the philosophical poems, was popular among Spanish Jewry. One work in particular is deserving of study in this context: the forty-stanza philosophical poem *The Crown of Royalty (Keter malkhut)*. This poem is part of the liturgy of Spanish Jewry and is recited on the holiest of the holy days, Yom Kippur.

Consistent with the hierarchical mode of thinking characteristic of the Middle Ages, and especially of Neoplatonic philosophy, the philosophical schema of *The Crown of Royalty* begins "on top," with an account of the divine attributes, expressing the apparently contradictory themes of Plotinian divine transcendence and ineffability and the biblical awareness of God in created nature. Then Ibn Gabirol proceeds down the "scale of being" to the mundane world of the four terrestrial elements, the home of man. Finally, he ascends the scale step by step through all the celestial spheres until the divine domain is reached. The *terminus a quo* turns out to be identical with the *terminus ad quem*. By beginning with God, Ibn Gabirol is telling us that the whole universe derives from and depends upon God, who is its creator and sustainer. Among all the standard attributes usually applied to God, it is the divine will that is, for Ibn Gabirol, most important, for God's will is responsible for creating the universe *ex nihilo*. God's will is of course "guided" by wisdom, which is for Ibn Gabirol "the source of life." Creation, then, is the very essence and purpose of reality.

As Ibn Gabirol ascends the ladder of being and reaches the sphere of the angels, or the supernal intellects, he indicates that man's true domicile is not the terrestrial domain of the four basic elements but the world of the intellect. It is here that the human soul has its origin, and it is here that the truly religious person will turn his attention. Committed to a current philosophical theory of immortality according to which man's ultimate reward (to use Alexander Altmann's phrase) consists in intellectual contact with some supernal intellect, Ibn Gabirol interprets the traditional Jewish idea of the world to come in these philosophical terms. The righteous will go beyond their original home of the sphere of the angels, or cosmic intellects, and reach the "seat of glory," a traditional Jewish metaphor referring to the divine domain itself. There the souls of the righteous are "bound up in the bundle of life," for they have reached the "source of life." But, Ibn Gabirol insists, this ascent is accomplished through a life of intellectual and moral discipline, in which philosophy plays a central role. For the soul is in its very nature and origin an intellect, and it is by virtue of intellectual perfection through philosophy that the soul attains immortality.

Baḥye ibn Paquda. The second representative of the Spanish school of Jewish philosophy was not a poet but a professional judge—Baḥye ibn Paquda (1080–1120). Baḥye's *Duties of the Heart* is perhaps the most widely read book of medieval Jewish philosophical literature. Not only was it studied and commented upon by scholars, but it has been read by ordinary Jews, who have regarded the book as a guide to religious and moral improvement. Its success lies in the emphasis it gives to the notion of personal piety, focusing upon both the individual's intellectual and emotional development and his progress toward the goal of complete love of God. Showing the external influences of both *kalām* and Neoplatonism on the philosophical side, and the Islamic mystical school of Sufism on the religious side, Baḥye wove these elements into the inherited fabric of the Bible and Talmud to produce a remarkably unified book of Jewish philosophical pietism, or "rationalistic mysticism." Contrary to the "duties of the limbs," which are concerned only with our external actions, such as what we eat, where we pray, and so on, the "duties of the heart" demand a specific mode of mental and emotional discipline whose ultimate purpose is to free us from the world of materiality and allow us to devote our whole being to God. This *methodos*, like Ibn Gabirol's ascent, stresses the primary and prior intellectual duty to reflect upon God and his created world in order to arrive at the most adequate understanding of God available to man. This duty leads Baḥye to embark upon a rigorous demonstration of God's existence and unity and his creation of the universe. Baḥye's arguments are an amalgam of *kalām* and Aristotelian and Plotinian elements, with the last's emphasis upon unity. For Baḥye, God is virtually identical with the One of Plotinus, so much so that all the traditional biblical and rabbinic divine attributes are regarded as only concessions to the exigencies of human language. The only true attribute of God is unity, which expresses God's essence.

Once it is understood that God is the ultimate One from which everything else is derived, it is clear that we have another "duty of the heart": to devote our whole lives to the worship of this absolute unity upon whose existence everything depends. Most of Baḥye's treatise lays out a graded manual of emotional discipline whereby the reader is progressively prepared to serve and love his creator. Throughout these "purificatory" chapters concerning such topics as trust in God, humility, and self-examination, Baḥye proposes a form of asceticism that seems to be borrowed from the Muslim mystics but that is tempered by the Jewish insistence upon the duty to be a co-creator with God. Yet, it is evident that for Baḥye this world is not only a "ves-

losopher but the pagan king of the Khazars, a medieval Asiatic people living near the Black Sea who converted to Judaism in the middle of the eighth century. According to legend, the king decided to abandon paganism and summoned representatives of Judaism, Christianity (Greek and Roman), and Islam to prove in a debate which is the true religion. At the end of the debate the king was convinced by Judaism and hence converted. Ha-Levi uses this legend but modifies it in several ways. First, and most significant, he introduces a philosopher into the debate; indeed, it will turn out that philosophy is for ha-Levi the main intellectual rival of Judaism. Second, initially the king, despising the Jews as an inferior and persecuted people, resists inviting a Jew to the debate. It is only after both the Christian and the Muslim confess that their own religions presuppose the truth of Judaism for their own validity that the king invites a Jew to the discussion. Ha-Levi's book, usually referred to as the *Kuzari,* has as its complete title *The Kuzari, a Book of Proof and Argument: An Apology for a Despised Religion.* Like the books previously discussed, it was written in Arabic but soon translated into Hebrew, by Yehudah ibn Tibbon (1120–1190), the same translator who had rendered Saʿadyah's and Baḥye's works.

The opening paragraph of the book establishes the ground plan of the whole debate. The king receives a divine communication via an angel in a dream in which he is told that although his religious intentions are

The king now turns to a Christian theologian and then to a Muslim scholar, both of whom begin their speeches with a recital of theological dogma, supporting these beliefs by appealing to the Israelites and their Torah. Without Judaism there is no Christianity and no Islam. At this point the king realizes that he needs to summon a Jewish scholar, whose opening speech, unlike those of the Christian and the Muslim, is not a theological credo but a recitation of historical facts. Against the king's criticism that such facts have no significance to a non-Jew and hence Judaism is a "particularistic" religion, the Jew replies that the very historical facts are precisely the advantage of Judaism, especially over the philosopher. The last point intrigues the king, for he has already dismissed the philosopher precisely because of the latter's cavalier attitude to the facts. So now the king warms up to the Jewish scholar, who follows with a diatribe against philosophy, not so much for any specific philosophical theory as for its method. Since by definition philosophy is the *human* search for wisdom through *reason,* it is necessarily limited and subject to error. The clearest proof of this is the notorious inability of philosophers to agree on anything. This point is especially interesting to the king, who now listens avidly to the Jewish scholar. Later this epistemological skepticism is buttressed by another argument of a quasi-skeptical nature drawn from ethics: a purely philosophical morality, which the philosopher claimed was sufficient for man, is at best no better than a system of prudential maxims that may be broken at any time to suit one's convenience. Such a "morality" is insufficient to bind a society together or even to guide the individual in the complexities of moral action. Divine revelation alone can supply this required information.

And thus we are back to prophecy. Judaism, the scholar insists, rests upon the historical fact that God does speak to man. This belief is accepted by the Christian and the Muslim as well. Against the testimonies of sense experience, even if it is prophetic experience, logic is impotent, especially if the experience in question is attested to by over six hundred thousand people and unanimously reported. Here ha-Levi enunciates a philosophy of religious empiricism that emphasizes the role of experience over reason, prophecy over logic. When the king objects that experience is always subjective and particularistic, no matter how many people may be involved, the rabbi concedes the point but tries to turn it to his own advantage. Yes, prophecy is a special sense faculty that is found only in some people. After all, if everyone were a prophet, who would listen to any prophet? And again, even if prophecy is restricted to Israel, as ha-Levi somewhat excessively and heterodoxly insists, this is not so embarrassing, for again the Christian admits that the Israelites are God's chosen people, and the Muslim concedes that only Moses spoke to God directly. If the philosopher has trouble with this fact, so much the worse for him! After all, ha-Levi reminds us, the philosopher is really tone-deaf to prophecy. So why listen to him?

Convinced of both the irrelevancy of philosophy to his religious search and the derivative status of Christianity and Islam, the king converts to Judaism. The rabbi then instructs him in the basic teachings and practices of Judaism, of which one is especially pertinent to philosophy. Instead of giving the standard rabbinic distinction that *Yahveh*, God's proper name, expresses the divine attribute of love or mercy, whereas the name *Elohim* expresses the attribute of justice, ha-Levi distinguishes between two radically different ways of knowing, thinking, and talking about God. A philosopher—Aristotle, for example—arrives at his conception of the divine through a process of observation and logical inference. The outcome of this ratiocination is a first cause that serves as an explanatory hypothesis or entity. If Aristotle's theory is true, then its theological statements give an accurate description of reality, just as, if his astronomy is true, the astronomical statements correctly describe the heavens. But one does not pray to such a god! Ha-Levi's philosopher in book 1 of the *Kuzari* is right: the philosopher's god isn't interested in our world. But if this is so, how can we be interested in this god? "The God of Abraham, Isaac, and Jacob is not the god of the philosophers!" the rabbi insists. Through philosophy we may reach God; but this power is not the person who spoke to Abraham and Moses. This person is referred to in Hebrew by the tetragrammaton *(YHVH)*, a name so holy that only the high priest pronounced it. This person is not known indirectly through inference but directly through prophecy. Here ha-Levi anticipates both Pascal's rejection of philosophical theology and Russell's distinction between knowledge by description and knowledge by acquaintance. The prophet "sees" and "tastes" the Lord (*Ps.* 34:9) with whom Moses at least spoke as friend to friend; the philosopher knows God as a hypothesis that, as the French mathematician Pierre La Place once said, may very well be superfluous. The former we may have to die for; the latter we can ignore with impunity.

Maimonides. The next major figure in medieval Jewish philosophy, Moses Maimonides (Mosheh ben Maimon, 1135/8–1204), was also a native of Spain; but unlike his Spanish predecessors he was heir to a different philosophical tradition, in which Aristotle was "the Philosopher." Maimonides' mastery of this new intellectual outlook altered the whole philosophical scene in the medieval Jewish world. This renascent Aristotle is a "purer," more authentic Aristotle than the one who was encountered in the Neoplatonic-Aristotelian synthesis of Ibn Sīnā or Ibn Gabirol. Henceforth, until Spinoza, Jewish philosophers will have to cope with this Aristotle. Moreover, the power and style of Maimonides' own philosophical personality was such that his successors had to deal with him as well. This overwhelming influence is to be attributed to the character of Maimonides' chief philosophical work, *The Guide of the Perplexed*, translated from Arabic into Hebrew by Shemu'el ibn Tibbon (1150–1230).

Maimonides states at the outset that the *Guide* is no ordinary philosophical book. Although he indicates the goals of the book and his motives for writing it, he warns his readers that besides some stringent intellectual qualifications that they must possess before reading the *Guide*, they should not expect that the way out of their perplexities will be easily understood, clearly visible, or unambiguously stated. Indeed, it is one of the great ironies of this book that although one of its purposes is to discuss and clarify the various ambiguities in the Bible, and religious language in general, it is itself highly ambiguous, giving rise to all kinds of difficulties to its interpreters, both medieval and modern. Maimonides tells us that philosophical truth, especially in metaphysics, the divine science, cannot by its very nature be divulged and expressed in a public and discursive manner. In the first place, very few are fit to study and appreciate its problems. Second, by its very nature, metaphysical truth is not apprehended in a systematic, discursive, continuous manner; on the contrary, like lightning it comes suddenly, quickly, and discontinuously to those who do attain it. Rarely does a person reach a level of metaphysical knowledge that would enable him to set out its truths in a popularly accessible way. Do not expect, then, Maimonides tells us, that the *Guide* will be an easy book, since the book that it attempts to decipher—the Bible—contains the highest truths in science and philosophy formulated in language that is perplexing. In short, Moses was the greatest metaphysician, who via prophecy was charged with the assignment of disseminating these truths in a book containing many levels of meaning. Maimonides, on the other hand, set himself the task of uncovering some of these layers to the select few, whose philosophical-religious perplexities had reached such a pitch that a guide was needed.

Two basic methodological principles are laid down at the outset. First, the Bible cannot be read literally; otherwise it would be full of worthless doctrines and downright errors. Second, human reason has limits, especially in metaphysics, where the philosopher, in spite of his keen and deep desire for truth, must recognize the limited scope of his intellectual reach. The first of these rules is familiar, going back to both rabbinic and earlier philosophical sources, such as Philo and Saʿadyah. That the Torah "speaks the language of men" is a well-known Jewish hermeneutical principle. Thus, we must learn how to read the Bible, which for Maimonides is a philosophical book that has to be read philosophically. One consequence of this exegetical method is that we shall have to begin our new study of the Bible by applying a philosophical filter to purify the text of its anthropomorphic dross. Virtually all of part 1 of the *Guide* is devoted to this task. Maimonides philosophically translates many of the "offending" words and phrases; for example, the expression "face" in "my face shall not be seen" (*Ex.* 33:23) connotes God's essence, not any physical organ. The core of Maimonides' conception of God is a radical defense of the *via negativa:* the most accurate and appropriate way to speak of God is to say what he is not. Human language is essentially incapable of describing the nature of God.

In spite of this apparent theological agnosticism, Maimonides still holds that several of the basic beliefs of Judaism can be soundly proved by means of true philosophical principles, which have been established by Aristotle. To this extent a philosophical theology is possible, for we can demonstrate God's existence, unity, incorporeality, and simplicity philosophically. These "theological theorems" are as solid as the theorems of geometry or physics. Thus our "belief in God" is for Maimonides knowledge, not just "blind fa[illegible] have to remember that there are limits to re[illegible] theological questions will remain recalcitran[illegible] reason: we shall not be able to resolve them [illegible] This is essentially so in the issue of creation [illegible] verse, a problem that becomes increasingly ve[illegible] the spread of Aristotle's physics, one of who[illegible] rems" was the eternity of the universe. This [illegible] was regarded as crucial, since if the world is et[illegible] would seem that divine providence would be [illegible] nonexistent, and hence miracles would be imp[illegible] Saadyah believed that he could prove creation *ex* [illegible] the Muslim *falāsifah* claimed that they could pro[illegible] eternity of the universe. Here we have one of the ea[illegible] appearances of a metaphysical antinomy, two con[illegible] theses with seemingly persuasive arguments. Like K[illegible] seven centuries later, Maimonides attempts to sh[illegible] that none of the arguments pro or con are valid, t[illegible] the question is not "decidable" for human reason.

Of course, Maimonides has a theological ax to grin[illegible] he wants to defend Moses against Aristotle; but he pro[illegible]ceeds in manner quite different from the *kalām.* He firs[illegible] shows that with one exception all the *kalām* arguments are either invalid or rest upon false premises. The only argument that he finds acceptable is, however, inductive and thus does not constitute a decisive proof against Aristotle, since inductive arguments are falsifiable. Having removed the *kalām* from consideration, Maimonides then examines the Aristotelian arguments for the eternity hypothesis. These proofs divide into two classes: scientific and metaphysical. The first group rests, he claims, upon the assumption that the laws of physics are unrestrictedly applicable to every moment in the past including the first instant of time, which in the theory of creation begins the history of the world. Given this assumption, Aristotle argues that the hypothesis of a first instant is incompatible with the laws of physics; hence, such a hypothesis must be false (Aristotle, *Physics* 8.1). Maimonides claims, however, that this assumption is arbitrary, indeed a *petitio principii.* Must we say that at the very moment when the universe was created the laws of mechanics were true? Since for the creationist there is no history of the universe prior to or at the first instant of time, there is nothing that such laws would be true of. Maimonides believes that these laws are true after there is a universe, but not before or when it comes into being. Nor are the metaphysical arguments for eternity any less arbitrary; for they, too, assume that certain metaphysical principles are true of God such that creation would be precluded. But why say God is subject to such principles? After all, part 1 of the *Guide* has shown us how *different* God is from us!

From the inadequacy of the arguments both for creation and for eternity Maimonides infers that the question can be decided only by choosing one or the other hypothesis; neither has been proved true. Believers in the Bible will of course opt for creation, since it is this belief that makes their religion possible. For without creation there would be no miracles, and revelation is a miracle. But Maimonides does not leave the matter just to choice and religious pressure; he believes there is an inductive argument, drawn from the *kalām,* that renders the creation hypothesis more plausible than the eternity theory. The latter, Maimonides maintains, fails to explain certain specific natural phenomena; for example, why does the planet Venus emit a bluish color whereas Mars looks red, especially since both planets have, Aristotle claims, the same chemical structure? In eluding the reach of Aristotle's physics, these "accidental facts" are evidence for, but do not decisively prove, the creation theory. For in the latter theory these facts are explained by appealing to God's creative will. Finally, although Maimonides offers no philosophical argument for creation *ex nihilo,* as Saʿadyah did, he dismisses its rival Platonic model of creation from eternal matter as unproved. Accordingly, the way is open to accept the traditional belief in creation *ex nihilo.*

Since the ultimate purpose of Maimonides' defense of creation is to vindicate the possibility of miracles, Maimonides now proceeds to discuss a phenomenon that the religious believe to be the greatest miracle besides creation itself—prophecy. Given, on the one hand, the competing Islamic claim that Muḥammad was the last and most authoritative prophet and, on the other hand, the theory of the *falāsifah* that prophecy is a purely naturalistic phenomenon that requires no supernatural intervention for its occurrence, Maimonides was constrained to defend both the superiority of Moses against Muḥammad and the role of God in the granting of prophecy. Yet he was too committed to a scientific outlook indebted to Aristotle and al-Fārābī to dismiss altogether their explanation of prophecy as a necessary emanation from God through the Agent Intellect, or angel responsible for human intellection, to a properly prepared and qualified individual, in whom both the intellect and imagination have been perfected. His problem was to find an opening for divine intervention within this deterministic-naturalistic theory of prophecy. He discovered this opening by making two modifications in this theory. First, even though a person has satisfied the requisite conditions for prophecy, God can withhold the emanation. In this sense prophecy is "up to God." Second, in Moses' case the divine emanation reached his intellect free from any admixture of the imagination and without the mediation of the Agent Intellect. Thus, the Bible says of Moses, "he spoke to God face to face" (*Nm.* 12:8). This too, like creation, occurs outside the normal, natural course of events.

The third part of the *Guide* is devoted to the solution of several theological problems that were becoming increasingly vexing in the Aristotelian atmosphere surrounding Maimonides. Does God know particular events, especially the deeds of men? Is God's providence concerned with particular humans or just with the human race in general? Finally, are the commandments rational or just the whims of an arbitrary divine despot? The first two questions are treated together since they are different facets of the general question of how God relates himself to man. Contrary to both the philosophers' belief that God is so beyond man that he cannot know individual human deeds, especially their future actions, since such knowledge would mean that God would enter time and the events themselves would be necessitated, Maimonides claimed that the philosophers' fear again rests upon an illicit analogy drawn between divine and human cognition. Just as God's nature eludes our grasp, so too his way of knowing escapes our finite understanding. God does know particular human actions, and he knows them without their being necessitated. "Everything is foreseen; yet freedom is given" (*Avot* 3.15). The way out from this apparent dilemma lies in the realization that God's knowledge is not subject to the logic that our own knowledge obeys. Once it is admitted that God does know particular events, the question about divine providence is easily answered. If God can know particular men, he exercises his care over them as particulars; for man, unlike any other species, is directly linked to God by possessing reason. This link makes possible divine providence over individual human beings. Since these individuals will differ in their level of intellectual perfection, individual providence will vary; but this is only what one would expect.

The concluding chapters of the *Guide* focus on the question of the rationality of the divine commandments, which for the Jew are the supreme expression of God's care for man and for Israel in particular. Like Saʿadyah, Maimonides is committed to the general principle that the Mosaic legislation is a body of law based upon reason. God desires that human beings attain moral and intellectual perfection. Obviously, then, the laws must lead to these goals and hence cannot be without sense, as some of the *kalām* theologians had argued with respect to Muslim law. Unlike Saʿadyah, however, Maimonides proceeds to give a systematic and detailed analysis of Jewish law, showing that there is hardly anything in this whole legal corpus that cannot be understood. Take dietary laws, for example. Some of them are just good hygiene. (Remember that Maimonides was a practicing physician.) Others were designed to prevent assimilation with pagan nations. In general, Jewish law, for Maimonides, is a divinely revealed system of rational laws.

Jewish Averroism and Gersonides. By the beginning of the thirteenth century, Aristotle had overwhelmed the medieval intellectual world. Besides Maimonides, he had another ally, one who was even more influential: he was the Muslim philosopher Ibn Rushd (1126–1198), known in the West as Averroës. Like Maimonides, Ibn Rushd was born in Cordova, but unlike his Jewish colleague he remained there most of his life. The two never met, and Maimonides knew of Ibn Rushd's writings only after he had written the *Guide*. Had he known the Muslim's philosophy before the writing of the *Guide*, a much different book would have been written, for Ibn Rushd represents a less adulterated Aristotle, one virtually stripped of its Plotinian-Avicennian accretions. Nevertheless, this confrontation between Ibn Rushd and Maimonides does take place, but after their death and throughout almost all post-Maimonidean Jewish medieval philosophy. Indeed, the story of Jewish philosophy after Maimonides and prior to Spinoza is a drama whose main protagonists are Aristotle as interpreted by Ibn Rushd and Maimonides, although these roles are played by characters bearing different names.

Through his commentaries on Aristotle as well as by virtue of his own independent treatises, Ibn Rushd exerted an enormous influence upon Jewish thinkers, ultimately resulting in a "school" of philosophers who could be dubbed "Jewish Averroists." This circle included such figures as Yitsḥaq Albalag of northern Spain or southern France (fl. 1250–1280), Yosef Kaspi of Provence (1279–1340), and Mosheh Narboni of Provence (died c. 1360). One immediate consequence of this confluence of Ibn Rushd and Maimonides was that these Jewish Averroists read Maimonides from the perspective of Ibn Rushd's thought and arrived at an interpretation of their Jewish teacher that distinguished the exoteric teaching of the *Guide* from its esoteric meaning.

One Averroist thesis that is advocated by these three Jewish thinkers as part of Maimonides' esoteric message is the doctrine of eternal creation. This seeming cosmological oxymoron was advocated by Ibn Sīnā and explicitly rejected by Maimonides; but Ibn Rushd had reformulated it in terms of his new reading of Aristotle. In its new garb the theory asserts that the physical universe is a continuous emanation from God, who eternally sustains, and hence "creates," the world, his eternal product. In Narboni the relationship between God and the universe becomes so intimate that it almost results in pantheism. Another important Averroist thesis concerns human "eternity," or immortality, a topic on which the *Guide* is virtually silent. Ibn Rushd advanced the view that human immortality consists in a special "conjunction," or union, between man's intellect and the Agent Intellect, the cosmic power responsible for human intellection, prophecy, and terrestrial generation. Four features of this theory are especially important. First, immortality is literally intellectual, since it is of the intellect and attained through philosophical perfection. Second, in Ibn Rushd's psychology there is really only one human intellect, which is somehow "shared" by or exemplified in many individuals; this one intellect is, however, identical with the Agent Intellect, although only potentially so. Third, at death, or "decorporealization," a person's mind becomes actualized by being departicularized, that is, by "returning" to the Agent Intellect. Finally, in the Agent Intellect all previously particularized minds are now one and hence no longer individuated. Immortality is then for the Averroist literally *impersonal*. In this doctrine we have a kind of religiosity that several modern scholars have called "rationalistic mysticism."

Jewish Averroism did not go unchallenged, and its first important critic was thoroughly immersed in the literature of Ibn Rushd. Levi ben Gershom (Gersonides, 1288–1344) of Provence was an original, versatile, and prolific author whose writings encompass mathematics, astronomy, and biblical exegesis as well as philosophy. Although enamored of both Maimonides and Ibn Rushd, he took a critical stance toward both when he felt they were wrong; and they were wrong, he believed, on several important issues. To the elucidation and solution of these problems, Gersonides wrote in Hebrew *The Wars of the Lord*, which covers virtually all the main topics in medieval metaphysics, natural philosophy, and psychology, especially as they impinge upon religion. The common theme throughout the book is Gersonides' commitment to the power of human reason. Gersonides rejects ha-Levi's epistemological skepticism and Maimonides' moderate rationalism, and he expresses instead a robust confidence in man's intellectual powers. To use Kant's phrase, we can say that Gersonides attempted to bring "religion within the limits of reason alone."

The first major question discussed in *The Wars of the Lord* is human immortality, especially the doctrine of conjunction with the Agent Intellect. Although he retains the vocabulary and some of the principles of the psychology employed by the Muslim *falāsifah*, including Ibn Rushd, Gersonides rejects the possibility of construing human perfection in terms of such a conjunction. First, he criticizes the Averroist thesis that all human intellects are temporary manifestations of the one intellect, which in reality is the Agent Intellect. All of us, Gersonides maintains, have our own intellect, which persists after death and is different from all other human intellects. Its persistence and differentiation result from the cognitive capital that the individual intellect has accumulated throughout life. This knowledge is permanent but varies from person to person. Human immortality is then defined in terms of the knowledge possessed by each individual. The Agent Intellect helps us acquire knowledge but is identical neither with this knowledge nor with our intellects. Like God, the Agent Intellect is a transcendent power that continually influences us but eludes our grasp. No union with it is possible for man.

The next main issue Gersonides grapples with involves him in a struggle with both Maimonides and Ibn Rushd. On the question of whether God can know particulars, both of the earlier thinkers had appealed to the *via negativa* to solve all the apparent difficulties such a knowledge seemed to entail. Gersonides, however, rejects the *via negativa,* in general and especially in the case of God's cognition. He maintains that if God's knowledge or any other attribute is radically different from our knowledge, then we can know nothing about God, not even that he exists. After all, how could we justify an inference from our experience to God, if God is so different from any human attribute? Now turning to cognition in particular, Gersonides argues that God's knowledge is admittedly not like ours in every respect, but it is sufficiently like human cognition to apply to it certain basic epistemological and logical conditions. First, since it is required for our cognition of a spatiotemporal fact that we possess sense perception, God cannot know such facts, for since he has no sense organs, he has no sense perception. Second, God's knowing a future event is incompatible with its being contingent and free. Now we are back to the dilemma that Sa'adyah thought he had dissolved. Unlike most Jewish medieval philosophers, Gersonides is prepared to sacrifice God's knowledge of particulars, especially human actions, and to retain human freedom. Accordingly, he redefines divine omniscience as God's knowledge of all that is knowable. Future contingent events, however, are not knowable, as Aristotle pointed out, for if they were, they would not be contingent. Hence it is not an imperfection in God not to know them.

Another equally striking set of conclusions reached by Gersonides concerns his cosmology. Again he differs from both Maimonides and Ibn Rushd, not accepting the former's acceptance of creation *ex nihilo* and disbelief in a decisive proof on this topic and rejecting the latter's belief in the eternity of the universe. Gersonides shows Maimonides that it is possible to demonstrate the createdness of the world by giving several such proofs. One of these proofs goes like this: anything that exhibits teleological features must be made (for example, light); hence, the universe is made. Another proof, of which there are several varieties, shows that the Aristotelian hypothesis of a universe enduring for infinite time in the past is incompatible with Aristotle's physics and hence is false. For example, Aristotelian physics excludes an actual infinite, a magnitude all of whose infinite parts or members coexist. But if past time is infinite, Gersonides argues, we would have an actual infinite, since the past is in some sense actual insofar as all past events were real and have consequences. Infinite past time would be like a book so chock-full of facts that prior to any given page there are an infinite number of pages. Who could read such a book? Thus the universe is created at a definite moment, the first instant of time.

But how was it created? Sa'adyah, Ibn Gabirol, ha-Levi, and Maimonides all maintain *ex nihilo* creation, although only Sa'adyah undertook to prove it. Gersonides rejects this by-now orthodox doctrine and defends the Platonic view that the world was fashioned by God out of some formless preexistent matter. Here as before, his arguments are entirely philosophical. For example, if the world were created from nothing, then the matter that now constitutes the world would be preexisted by a vacuum, which it now partly fills. But a vacuum is impossible, as Aristotle had proved. Finally, unlike Sa'adyah but like Maimonides, Gersonides holds that the universe is everlasting. However, whereas Maimonides maintained this position on the basis of his interpretation of several biblical and rabbinic passages, Gersonides attempts to prove philosophically that the universe cannot be destroyed, not even by God. After all, what reason could he have for doing so? Spite, anger, regret, admission of a bad original job? Surely none of these human motives can be attributed to a perfect and immutable craftsman.

Crescas. Gersonides' thoroughgoing rationalism was to be most controversial; hardly any of his successors accepted its radical conclusions in cosmology or about divine cognition. His critics either reverted to some version of Maimonides' moderate rationalism or rejected completely the whole Aristotelian edifice upon which both Maimonides and Gersonides erected their philosophical reconstructions of Judaism. The best representative of the latter approach is Ḥasdai Crescas (1340–1410) of Spain, whose *Or Adonai* (Light of the Lord) consists both of a radical critique of Aristotle's natural philosophy and a redefinition of Jewish dogmatics on a different basis. Writing at the beginning of what would be the end of Spanish Judaism, Crescas claims that Maimonides committed a serious and fundamental mistake in attempting to establish Judaism upon Aristotelian foundations. One consequence of this error was Gersonides and the Jewish Averroists. So Crescas starts all over by first showing that Aristotle's natural philosophy is either false or weak, and that the natural theology based upon this "weak reed" is even more shaky. Crescas then proceeds to offer a new system of Jewish belief. The main thrust of his critique is his willingness to admit the twin Aristotelian horrors of the actual infinite and the void. After demonstrating the invalidity of the arguments against both these notions, Crescas seriously entertains the hypothesis that there may be an infinite vacuum surrounding our world, thus allowing for the possibility of a plurality of universes. Crescas was one of the earliest representatives of the modern theory of the "open universe."

The admittance of both an actual infinite and the void undermines, however, the arguments for several important theorems in medieval natural theology, such as the existence and unity of God and, in Gersonides' view, the impossibility of creation *ex nihilo*. Crescas is not unhappy with this conclusion and proceeds to draw out the theological implications of his new infinitist outlook. He does this by restructuring the Jewish creed, scrapping Maimonides' by-then famous Thirteen Articles and replacing them with his own "axiomatic reconstruction" of Jewish dogma. Arguing that Maimonides' list fails to exhibit the logical relationships among the various dogmas and omits any justification of why some of these articles are essential to Judaism, Crescas rearranges the creed into four categories: (1) the roots of religion, (2) the foundations of the Torah, (3) obligatory beliefs of Judaism, and (4) optional beliefs. Group 1 consists of the basic postulates of any monotheistic religion, such as the existence, unity, and incorporeality of God. Group 2 consists of the logical presuppositions of a revealed law, such as the Torah; among such postulates are divine cognition, prophecy, and omnipotence and human choice. Group 3 contains those beliefs taught in Judaism but not logically entailed by the fact of revelation; these ideas are contingent upon revelation but not essential to it. They include such beliefs as creation of the world, immortality of the soul, and resurrection of the dead. Finally, group 4, optional beliefs, includes opinions about a variety of topics, such as the plurality of universes or the truth of astrology, about which authoritative Judaism takes no definitive stand. On these matters Jews may believe as they wish.

Consider the existence of God—a root belief of any monotheistic religion. Since all the "classical" proofs have been undermined by his critique of their Aristotelian foundations, how does Crescas philosophically justify such a root belief? In the first place, for Crescas religious beliefs in general do not require a philosophical justification; the acceptance of religious authority, rather than the demonstration of logical proof, is decisive. Second, if philosophical argument is introduced into religion, say for explanatory or polemical purposes, it must be sound philosophy. And so Crescas provides a "new" argument for the existence of God, one which does not presuppose Aristotle's rejection of an actually infinite series of essential causes and effects. Crescas's proof purports to show that whether the causal series is infinite or finite, it is a series of contingent causes and effects and hence requires some necessary and eternal substance to bring it forth, for what is contingent is by its very nature a mere possible existent. As to God's unity and incorporeality, however, Crescas is doubtful whether philosophy is competent to prove such root beliefs; hence revelation must be the guide. On this latter point Crescas is close to the Christian Scholastic William of Ockham.

Crescas is most original and even radical in his treatment of the two closely related foundational beliefs of Judaism—divine cognition and human choice. Here he provides a deterministic solution to the classic dilemma between divine omniscience and human freedom. Rejecting Gersonides' equally radical indeterminist denial of divine cognition of future contingencies, Crescas claims that God's knowledge of some future event—say, Abraham's binding of Isaac—does fix the truth status of that event before its actual occurrence. True, Abraham's binding of Isaac takes place in time, but in God's "eternal vision" this event is eternally true and thus necessary. Abraham's freedom is, Crescas believes, ensured by virtue of the fact that from an abstract logical perspective, his binding of Isaac is a logically contingent state of affairs: in some other world it is possible that he would not bind Isaac. Here Crescas advances a view that, although novel in Judaism, is virtually identical with the doctrine of Boethius and Thomas Aquinas, but perhaps more pronounced in its deterministic flavor. Crescas's deterministic position is also reflected in his account of human choice. On purely psychological grounds he claims that human decisions, actions, and belief commitments are caused by a variety of factors. But if our choices, acts, and beliefs are all determined, are they free? Yes, so long as we have the correct understanding of what a free act, choice, or belief is. If we have not been compelled by an external cause to choose or act in a certain way and we feel no such compulsion, then we are free. As Hobbes and Hume were to say a few centuries later, as long as I can get up, move my legs, and walk, I am "at liberty" to walk, even though I have been conditioned to walk out of my office every time I hear the lunch bell. All of this, Crescas claims, is consistent with divine or human praise or blame, reward or punishment; for just as smoke naturally follows the kindling of a fire, so, too, does punishment follow the performance of an evil act. There is a divinely ordered moral plan in the universe whereby sins or crimes cause punishments and virtue brings about reward.

Crescas's account of creation is also original. Whereas almost all his predecessors and successors claimed that creation is either a "root" or a "foundation," Crescas contends that, although it is a belief taught by Judaism, it need not have been taught. If the Bible had begun with "From all eternity there was God and the universe," there could still have been a Jewish religion. After disposing of both Maimonides' and Gersonides' criticisms of the eternity cosmology, Crescas offers a "soft" defense of the eternal creation hypothesis, a doctrine that had been rejected by both Maimonides and Gersonides as internally incoherent. Crescas's presentation of this model is "soft" in the sense that he does not definitely commit himself to it. He allows for the view, occasionally expressed in rabbinic literature, that God has successively created a series of finitely enduring worlds, a series that may continue *ad infinitum.* On either of these models, Crescas claims, the universe is created, eternally or temporally, *ex nihilo,* since the universe is only a contingent being, whereas God is a necessary being, and as contingent, it depends upon God. This causal-ontological dependency means that it is created *ex nihilo.*

The Italian Renaissance. Crescas's radical critique of Aristotelianism and his own interpretation of some Jewish beliefs did not satisfy most of his successors in Spanish-Jewish philosophy. His pupil Yosef Albo, for example, rejected his determinism. For the most part, fifteenth- and sixteenth-century Spanish-Jewish philosophy reverts to some form of Maimonidean moderate rationalism. The new developments in Jewish philosophy take place on a different soil: Italy. With the emergence of Renaissance Platonism and the new physics of Galileo, different philosophic themes are sounded by several Italian-Jewish philosophical voices. The first of these "newer sounds" is of Spanish origin, Judah Abravanel (Leo Ebreo, c. 1460–1521), the son of the famous Spanish financier, biblical exegete, and philosopher Isaac Abravanel, who found asylum in Italy after the expulsion of the Jews from Spain in 1492. In Italy, especially in Florence, a "newer" Plato was discovered, who in many respects is closer to the historical Plato. Reading Plato directly either in the original Greek or from Latin translations of the Greek, Italian philosophers like Marsilio Ficino attempted to strip away the Aristotelian accretions to Plato that had accumulated during the Middle Ages, just as Ibn Rushd had tried to get at the real Aristotle. Judah Abravanel shows signs of this Platonic revival, even in the literary form of his philosophical work *Dialoghi d'amore,* which is a philosophical dialogue between two characters on the matter of love, both divine and human. This very topic betrays the new Renaissance spirit; for no previous medieval philosophical text, whether Jewish, Muslim, or Christian, made the Greek notion of *erōs* its central problem. But for a Platonic academy in Florence this was the problem *par excellence:* Plato's *Symposium* and *Phaedrus* had replaced the *Timaeus* and *Republic.*

Abravanel's *Dialoghi,* written most likely in Italian or perhaps in Spanish, represents an attempt to fit Plato's philosophy of *erōs* into a Jewish framework, even though there are in it citations drawn from classical mythology and even the New Testament. However, the Judaic orientation is clear. Not only are the Bible and rabbinic literature cited, but Maimonides and Ibn Gabirol are also referred to. Here Platonic *erōs* is legitimized by redefining it in terms of the Maimonidean motif that man loves God through his devotion to the life of the intellect. But man's intellectual love of God is reciprocated and complemented by God's love for man, indeed for the whole universe, which God creates freely out of love from preexistent matter. (Only Plato is cited on this point, not Gersonides.) Accordingly, the unifying and pervading power in the universe is *erōs,* redefined as man's intellectual love of God and God's creative love for man.

A very different tone is heard in the philosophical writings of another Italian-Jewish philosopher, Yosef Shelomoh Delmedigo (1591–1659), who, although born in the Venetian colony of Crete, studied in Padua under Galileo and absorbed some of the latter's new ideas in astronomy and physics. He was the first Jewish philosopher or astronomer to adopt the Copernican-Galilean system, rejecting the Aristotelian theory of the celestial spheres with their "separate movers," which were identified with the biblical doctrine of angels. The angels, for Delmedigo, are natural forces or powers, primarily human faculties, an idea that was also suggested by Maimonides. Delmedigo also advocated Crescas's eternal-creation cosmology: after all, a God who is eternally active cannot not create; hence, the universe must be eternal. The denial of the world's eternity would be tantamount to the thesis that God's creative power is finite. This explicit espousal of eternal creation leads him in the direction of pantheism, which, however, he expresses tentatively.

The End of Medieval Jewish Philosophy. Despite Delmedigo's enthusiasm for the new science of Galileo, he still retained some medieval Aristotelian ideas and had an ambivalent attitude toward Jewish mysticism, which he criticized yet occasionally adopted. It is not without significance that he spent a few years in Amsterdam, the locale of the last act in our philosophical drama. Befriended by Menasseh ben Israel, one of the local rabbis, a philosopher and a publisher of Hebrew books, Delmedigo was able to get his major philosophical-scientific work published there shortly before he left for Frankfurt in 1630. Two years later the man who was to reject medieval philosophy completely was born in Amsterdam, and studied in the very same school in which Delmedigo had taught a few years earlier—Barukh Spinoza (1632–1676). Several scholars have claimed that the Delmedigo–Spinoza connection is not fortuitous, that features of the latter's formalistic philosophy either exhibit elements of or express explicitly doctrines of the former's more diffuse and ambiguous writings. Whether or not this is so, Spinoza clearly and definitively cuts the tie that linked philosophy with religion and advocates the new science with no reservations or fond reminiscences of Aristotle or Maimonides. Spinoza is the first modern philosopher, the first thinker who no longer sees philosophy either as theology's handmaiden or as fertilized by prophetic seeds. Philosophy is for Spinoza not only autonomous, as Descartes maintained, but self-sufficient as well, a thesis that Descartes was unwilling to admit, at least in public.

Spinoza's emancipation of philosophy from theology, based upon both philosophical and biblical-critical grounds, permits him to erect a naturalistic philosophical system in which metaphysics, logic, psychology, political theory, and moral philosophy are all comprehended. The pantheistic suggestions of Delmedigo are explicitly expressed in Spinoza's equation *Deus, sive Natura* ("God, or Nature"). No longer is there a hiatus between a transcendent, incorporeal, infinite God and a corporeal, finite universe. As both thought and extension, Spinoza's God is not divorced from man and the universe; as infinite and eternal, the physical world is inseparable from its cause. Crescas's eternal creation model is stripped of its medieval garb and shown for what it really is: a picture of an eternal, dynamic universe displaying infinite divine attributes. Moreover, nature is for Spinoza a thoroughly deterministic system in which scientific law reigns supreme. The laws of nature are for Spinoza God's decrees. Again, Spinoza pushes Crescas a step further: the latter's deterministic psychology becomes the universal rule of all nature. Such a system, however, allows for no miracles, especially divine prophecies. The wardens of the Amsterdam Jewish community in 1656 had considerable justification in viewing Spinoza as no longer of the Jewish faith. Indeed, he was no longer a medieval man. Medieval philosophy, and medieval Jewish philosophy in particular, had with Spinoza been terminated, and a new philosophical epoch had begun.

[*See also the biographies of the major figures discussed herein.*]

BIBLIOGRAPHY

General. The best general philosophical study of Jewish philosophy is given by Julius Guttmann in his *Philosophies of Judaism,* translated by David W. Silverman (New York, 1964). Although a comprehensive historical survey beginning with the Bible and ending with Franz Rosenzweig, it contains five perceptive chapters on medieval thinkers. It has an excellent bibliography. Isaac Husik's *A History of Medieval Jewish Philosophy* (1916; reprint, New York, 1969) focuses upon individual thinkers. It is more detailed, but less analytical, than Guttmann's treatment. Harry A. Wolfson's *Philo: Foundations of Religious Philosophy in Judaism, Christianity and Islam,* 2 vols. (Cambridge, Mass., 1947), is the most comprehensive English study on Philo and establishes the conceptual framework adopted in this essay.

Sa'adyah and the Kalām. The most recent and comprehensive study of *kalām* is Wolfson's *The Philosophy of the Kalam* (Cambridge, Mass., 1976). The influence of *kalām* upon Jewish philosophy is discussed by Wolfson in his posthumously published *The Repercussions of the Kalam in Jewish Philosophy* (Cambridge, Mass., 1979).

Sa'adyah's *The Book of Beliefs and Opinions* was translated by Samuel Rosenblatt as the first volume in the now extensive "Yale Judaica Series" (New Haven, 1948). The best biography and general survey of Sa'adyah's literary career is still Henry Malter's *Saadia Gaon: His Life and Works* (1921; reprint, Philadelphia, 1978).

Jewish Philosophy in Spain: The Neoplatonic Tradition. No complete English translation of Shelomoh ibn Gabirol's *Fons vitae* has appeared. A few excerpts were translated from the Latin into English by Arthur Hyman in the anthology *Philosophy in the Middle Ages,* edited by Arthur Hyman and James J. Walsh (New York, 1967), pp. 347–357. The most accessible introduction to the *Fons vitae* is still Solomon Munk's French translation of Shem Ṭov ibn Falaquera's medieval epitome, which is included in Munk's *Mélanges de philosophie juive et arabe* (1859; reprint, Paris, 1927). Ibn Gabirol's *Crown of Royalty* was translated by Israel Zangwill and annotated by Israel Davidson, and is included in Davidson's anthology *Selected Religious Poems of Solomon ibn Gabirol* (New York, 1973). Baḥye ibn Paquda's treatise has recently been translated from the Arabic by Menahem Mansoor as *The Book of Direction to the Duties of the Heart* (London, 1973). It has a full introduction.

Yehudah ha-Levi has fared better with respect to secondary literature but worse in translation. The only full English translation of the *Kuzari,* by Hartwig Hirschfeld (1905; reprint, New York, 1964), is inaccurate. Fortunately, the scholarly literature in English is excellent. Wolfson's essays should be consulted, especially the following: "Halevi and Maimonides on Design, Chance and Necessity" and "Halevi and Maimonides on Prophecy," both reprinted in his *Studies in the History of Philosophy and Religion*, edited by Isadore Twersky and George H. Williams, vol. 2 (Cambridge, Mass., 1977).

Maimonides. The most accurate English translation of *The Guide of the Perplexed* is that of Shlomo Pines (Chicago, 1963). Besides Pines's own fine introduction it contains a stimulating, although debatable, introductory essay by Leo Strauss. Surprisingly, there is no comprehensive English monograph on Maimonides' philosophy, although studies on separate facets of his thought abound. Leo Strauss's "The Literary Character of the *Guide for the Perplexed*," reprinted in his *Persecution and the Art of Writing* (1952; reprint, Westport, Conn., 1973), will introduce the reader into the "esoteric" interpretation of Maimonides. A more traditional but perceptive introduction is Simon Rawidowicz's "Knowledge of God: A Study of Maimonides' Philosophy of Religion," in *Studies in Jewish Thought*, edited by Nahum N. Glatzer (Philadelphia, 1974). Wolfson's more specialized studies have been reprinted in both volumes of his *Studies in the History of Philosophy and Religion* (cited above).

Gersonides and Crescas. A complete English translation of Gersonides' *Wars of the Lord* is being prepared by Seymour Feldman; volume 1, *Immortality of the Soul*, containing the translation of book 1 of *The Wars* as well as an introductory monograph on Gersonides' literary career and general philosophical perspective, was published (Philadelphia, 1984); volume 2, containing the translations of books 2, 3, and 4, is forthcoming. A superb comprehensive study of Gersonides is Charles Touati's *La pensée philosophique et théologique de Gersonide* (Paris, 1973). For Jewish Averroism consult Alfred L. Ivry's "Moses of Narbonne's Treatise on the Perfection of the Soul," *Jewish Quarterly Review*, n.s. 57 (April 1967): 271–297.

No complete translation of Crescas's *Or Adonai* has been made. Wolfson translated most of book 1 in his masterful *Crescas' Critique of Aristotle: Problems of Aristotle's Physics in Jewish and Arabic Philosophy* (Cambridge, Mass., 1929). On Crescas's cosmology see Seymour Feldman's "The Theory of Eternal Creation in Hasdai Crescas and Some of His Predecessors," *Viator* 11 (1980): 289–320.

Jewish Philosophy in the Renaissance: Spinoza. A good descriptive survey of Italian-Jewish intellectual life, including philosophy, is given by Israel Zinberg in volume 4 of his *A History of Jewish Literature*, translated by Bernard Martin (New York, 1974). He discusses Judah Abravanel in chapter 1 and Yosef Shelomoh del Medigo in chapter 6. Isaac E. Barzilay has provided a good comprehensive study of Delmedigo in his *Yoseph Shlomo Delmedigo: His Life, Works and Times* (Leiden, 1974). Judah Abravanel's *Dialoghi d'amore* was translated into English by F. Friedberg-Seeley and Jean H. Barnes as *The Philosophy of Love* (London, 1937).

The literature on Spinoza is of course voluminous. A new translation of his *Ethics* was done by Samuel Shirley and edited by Seymour Feldman, *Ethics and Selected Letters* (Indianapolis, 1982). His *Theological-Political Treatise* was translated by R. H. M. Elwes (New York, 1951). Wolfson's *The Philosophy of Spinoza*, 2 vols. (Cambridge, Mass., 1934), and Leo Strauss's *Spinoza's Critique of Religion*, translated by E. M. Sinclair (1965; New York, 1982), are most helpful in relating Spinoza to the Jewish context.

SEYMOUR FELDMAN

Modern Thought

Modern Jewish religious thought is not simply a chronological category designating Jewish reflections that occur in the modern world. Rather, it is a category that denotes meditations by Jews about Judaism and Jewish destiny that take place within—or at least seek to take into account—the cognitive process distinctive of the modern world. Heir to the biblical image of knowledge, which is grounded in the concepts of divine creation, revelation, and redemption, modern Jewish thought seeks to come to terms with modern sensibilities and conceptions of truth. In this respect, of course, it is basically similar to modern religious thought in general. There are, however, specifics of the Jewish experience in the modern world that determine the agenda and peculiar inflections of modern Jewish thought.

It should therefore be recalled that Jews first truly encountered the modern world during the protracted struggle for emancipation in the eighteenth and nineteenth centuries. This struggle was not merely a legal process but engaged Europe in an intense and wide-ranging debate reviewing Jewry's eligibility to participate in the modern world. In the course of this century-long debate, Jews became exceedingly sensitive to the prevailing image of Judaism in European culture. Not surprisingly, modern Jewish thought was often guided by an apologetic motive. This defensive posture was also prompted by the rise of modern political and racial anti-Semitism, which was not confined to the mob but gained vocal support from more than a few intellectuals. The integration of the Jews into the modern state and culture that was achieved despite persistent opposition led to a profound restructuring of Jewish life, both organizationally and culturally. The Jews were no longer under the obligatory rule of the rabbis and the Torah. In acquiring the political identity and culture of the "non-Jewish" society in which they lived, the Jews tended to lose much of their venerable culture, for example, knowledge of both Hebrew and the sacred texts of the tradition. Moreover, for many, Israel's convenantal relationship to God as a chosen people presently in exile but piously awaiting God's Messiah and restoration to the Promised Land was no longer self-evident and unambiguous.

Modern Jewish thought was thus charged not only

with the task of explaining Judaism to both non-Jews and Jews estranged from the sources of their tradition but also with that of rethinking some of the fundamental concepts of the tradition that bear on the nature of the Jews as a people—covenant, election, exile, the Messiah, and the promise of national redemption—and in general the meaning of Jewish community, history, and destiny. These questions gained a unique urgency in the mid-twentieth century because of the Holocaust and the establishment of the state of Israel.

Thus whereas medieval Jewish philosophy was primarily concerned with the relatively circumscribed issue of reconciling faith and reason, modern Jewish thought is broader and by necessity more protean, addressing the multiple dilemmas of the Jew in the modern world.

The beginnings of modern Jewish thought may be traced, paradoxically, to the heterodox sixteenth-century Dutch philosopher, Barukh Spinoza (1632–1677). This renegade Jew was to leave the Jewish community without taking the "perfidious" step of converting to another religion, a revolutionary precedent that opened the possibility of a secular, cosmopolitan Jew who in discarding all primordial particularities found a home in the religiously and ethnically "neutral" world of reason and common humanity. Universally adored by all votaries of the modern spirit, this iconoclastic but estimable figure has been an abiding challenge to the Jews of modernity to shed their ancestral faith for more "noble," secular affiliations. Furthermore, Spinoza's harsh critique of Judaism as a religion has weighed heavily on modern Jews, not in the least because it has decisively influenced the negative image of Judaism in modern philosophy. Hence, despite his excommunication by the Jewish community of his native Amsterdam, Spinoza has remained preeminent in modern Jewish consciousness.

The First Modern Jew. In contrast to Spinoza, the eighteenth-century Berlin savant Moses Mendelssohn (1729–1786) represents the possibility that the Jew's creative participation in modern, secular culture need not negate a commitment to Judaism. Hailed by the Enlightenment as the German Socrates, he remained a proud and pious Jew. As a philosopher, he gained prominence for his disquisitions on aesthetics, epistemology, metaphysics, and psychology. Significantly, he based his arguments on reason alone; and although he made use of the metaphysical presuppositions of natural religion, his interest was strictly "secular." He scrupulously refrained from introducing scriptural proof texts and certainly never referred to his Judaism. As such, he was not a "Jewish" philosopher. In fact, implicit in his writings is the assumption that his Judaism is irrelevant to his philosophical endeavor, and is strictly incidental and a private affiar.

Nonetheless, and to his great chagrin, he was repeatedly challenged to defend his continued devotion to his ancestral faith, a fidelity that many of his contemporaries found flagrantly inconsistent with his adherence to enlightened, philosophical culture. Confrontation on these matters is what Mendelssohn sought to avoid, and at first he chose to make a vigorous appeal to the principle of tolerance. But this proved insufficient to quiet his traducers, and finally he penned his famous defense of his "dual allegiance" to the Englightenment and Judaism: *Jerusalem oder über religiöse Macht und Judentum* (1783). Framing his argument in a careful explication of the principle of religious liberty, Mendelssohn holds that philosophical rationalism, which is grounded in the deistic assumption that the "eternal verities" and "human felicity" may be acquired without divine revelation, poses no special problem for Judaism. For the faith of Israel, as he declares, is "not a revealed religion but a revealed legislation." In contrast to Christianity, Judaism is founded not upon doctrinal opinions and saving truths but rather upon "laws, commandments, ordinances, rules of life, instructions in the will of God" (*Jerusalem,* translated by Allan Arkush, 1983, p. 89f.). Mendelssohn suggests that these commandments, particularly the most enduring ceremonial laws, serve as symbolic acts that alert one to the eternal truths of reason, thus preventing the Jews from succumbing to the idolatry of false ideas. Herein lies the extensive meaning of Israel's election. The Jews "were chosen by Providence to be a priestly nation . . . a nation which . . . was continually to call attention to sound and unadulterated ideas of God and his attributes. It was incessantly to teach, to proclaim and to endeavor to preserve these ideas among the nations, by means of its mere existence, as it were."

Mendelssohn thus reduced Judaism to a body of ceremonial laws while expanding it into a universal religion of reason. His effort in this respect characterizes much of modern Jewish thought: unlike medieval Jewish philosophers, their modern descendents would no longer seek to reconcile revelation with reason as two distinct but homologous bodies of truth but would endeavor to demonstrate the significance of Judaism within the general framework of human reason and culture. Mendelssohn also anticipated another characteristic thrust of modern Jewish thought with his conception of Israel's "mission" to the nations, a notion that provided a universalistic justification of Judaism's continued particularity.

Mendelssohn's Legacy. Mendelssohn's definition of Judaism, however, was not unproblematic. His delineation of the distinctive essence of Judaism as "revealed legislation" exposed the religion to the charge—first developed by Mendelssohn's contemporary Immanuel Kant (1721–1804)—that Judaism is "heteronomous" religion of law that finds expression chiefly in religious ritual and ceremonies. In his *Religion within the Limits of Reason Alone* Kant regarded genuine religion to be the cultivation of moral autonomy; he correspondingly deemed ritual and ceremony to be "pseudoservice to God" and accordingly depicted Judaism as a "religious illusion." Kant's indictment of Judaism, based largely on his reading of Mendelssohn and Spinoza, was repeated by many modern thinkers and has according by troubled many modern Jews, especially those who shared Kant's philosophical presuppositions. Moreover, Mendelssohn's definition of Judaism satisfied few Jews. The traditional Jew felt he ignored the unique creedal core of Judaism; the liberal Jew was unhappy (and not only because of Kant's critique) with his emphasis on the ceremonial laws. Nonetheless, Mendelssohn's *Jerusalem* still stands as a monument to a Jew who sought to secure the integrity of Judaism while actively pursuing modern culture.

Eager to accommodate Judaism to the modern spirit, Jews of varying theological tendencies claimed Mendelssohn as their spiritual progenitor. For Jewish opponents of the modern world, Mendelssohn became associated with the new order, as a symbol, however, of betrayal. The *spiritus rector* of Jewish Orthodoxy as a self-conscious movement to guard the integrity of classical Judaism while fending off the putatively corrosive effects of the modern world, Mosheh Sofer (1762–1839), popularly known as Ḥatam Sofer, regarded Mendelssohn as the source of the contemporary Jew's beguiling infatuation with "alien culture." In his spiritual last will and testament, he cautioned all God-fearing Jews "not to turn to evil and never engage in corruptible partnership with those fond of innovations, who, as a penalty for our sins, have strayed from the Almighty and His law! Do not touch the books of Rabbi Moses [Mendelssohn] of Dessau, and your foot will never slip!" (Mendes-Flohr and Reinharz, 1980, p. 156). The document, written some fifty years after Mendelssohn's death, is still immensely popular among some Orthodox Jews (sometimes called "ultra-Orthodox," opposed to the Modern Orthodox who eventually did seek some accommodation with the modern world).

The militant antimodernism of these ultra-Orthodox Jews, who embraced much of the traditional Jewish community in the nineteenth century, especially in eastern Europe, is distinguished by a deliberate self-enclosure. Although not totally ignorant of the modern world, they failed to acknowledge its most significant epistemological presuppositions and social and political values. It would be erroneous, however, to assume that ultra-Orthodoxy was moribund or spiritually stagnant; on the contrary, in its own terms the movement was (and is) dynamic and creative. The nineteenth century witnessed a renaissance of rabbinic learning; new *yeshivot* (talmudic academies) were established, and new methods and approaches to learning and piety were advocated. *Yeshivot* were established by Ḥatam Sofer in Pressburg, Hungary, (modern-day Bratislava, Czechoslovakia), and by Ḥayyim ben Yitsḥaq (1749–1821) in Volozhin, Lithuania. [*See* Yeshivah.] Also notable is the pietistic movement founded by another Lithuanian rabbi, Yisra'el (Lipkin) Salanter (1810–1883), known as Musar (moral instruction). [*See* Musar Movement.] Hasidism, the movement of popular mystical piety, flourished in the nineteenth century. [*See* Hasidism.]

The opposition of the ultra-Orthodox to modernism is not as much epistemological as it is axiological. They view the modern world, given its sociological and cultural implications, with profound suspicion, for it leads, in their judgment, to religious laxity and even defection. Even Ḥatam Sofer did not oppose secular studies per se as long as they did not undermine the preeminence of Torah and Jewish tradition. With few exceptions, Orthodoxy has been indifferent to the epistemological (and ontological) issues raised by modern science and technology; its sole criterion for adjudging the developments in science has been to protect Torah observance.

Neither is science a salient issue for Jewish modernists. They have been principally exercised by the need to find a place for the Jews and Judaism in the modern world. Philosophically and theologically this objective necessitated a delineation of Judaism's relevance to the historical unfolding of a universal, human culture. Within the orbit of nineteenth-century discourse, the principal vectors of this effort were provided by Kant, Friedrich Schelling, and G. W. F. Hegel.

Judaism and Modern Historical Consciousness. Proponents of religious reform of Judaism were particularly drawn to the historiosophical teachings of Schelling and Hegel. Solomon Formstecher (1808–1889) and Samuel Hirsch (1815–1889), prominent rabbinical leaders of the nascent Reform movement in Germany (which was later divided between a radical fringe and the "liberal" majority favoring moderate reform), each in his own distinctive fashion recast the doctrines in support of religious reform and Jewish integration into modern society and culture. Because it viewed spiritual truths as developing and maturing dynamically in history, the philosophical idealism of Schelling and Hegel provided these advocates of religious reform with the conceptual perspectives justifying ritual and doctrinal change in Judaism: to be true to the spiritual truths with which it is entrusted, Judaism must be dynamic and evolutionary. The proposition of philosophical idealism that the historical unfolding of these truths leads to the progressive unification of human culture and sensibility also lent support to the Reformers' call for Jewish participation in general culture. But their affirmation of a universal culture, in turn, posed a severe challenge to account for the enduring identity, and thus particularity, of Judaism, which they, like all Reform leaders, clearly upheld.

Formstecher and Hirsch reflected their generation's characteristic interest in history as a dynamic process fraught with cultural and spiritual significance. The historical imagination, especially with its critical, "scientific" bent, first had its impact in Jewish circles with the founding in Berlin in 1819 of a society promoting the "scientific study of Judaism" *(Wissenschaft des Judentums)*. The primary motive of this society, many of whose members were to be associated with religious reform, was to correct the calumnious opinions about Judaism and illuminate the varied, ongoing contribution of Judaism to the shaping of European civilization. It was hoped that the objective, scholarly study of Judaism would irrefutably demonstrate that the Jews seek to participate in modern European culture not as "Asiatic" interlopers but by right of this contribution; culturally and spiritually the Jews are as much European as any other people.

This proposition was compatible with the presuppositions of Reform Judaism, which also shared the assumption that Judaism had made a decisive contribution to the historically unfolding "spirit of Europe." [*See* Reform Judaism.] The proponents of religious reform naturally supported *Wissenschaft des Judentums*. One of the founding proponents of Reform Judaism in Germany, Abraham Geiger (1810–1874), was also one of the most outstanding pioneers of *Wissenschaft des Judentums*. Critical historical scholarship, he maintained, would help identify the immanent forces in Jewish tradition sanctifying the change and renewal of Judaism that were deemed necessary by the advocates of reform. Implicitly adopting the Hegelian principle that history is the progressive revelation of the divine truth, Geiger presented the study of history as an alternative to *talmud Torah* ("study of Torah") as the Jew's mode of reflecting on God's will.

Orthodox leaders, even those who supported to some degree the Jew's entry into the modern world, objected strenuously to what they perceived to be the historicist bias of *Wissenschaft des Judentums*. The founder of Neo-Orthodoxy in Germany, Samson Raphael Hirsch (1808–1888) bitterly remarked that the tendency of *Wissenschaft des Judentums* to compare Judaism to other historical phenomena—"Moses and Hesiod, David and Sappho—in effect reduces Judaism to a "human and transitory [fact] of a by-gone age" (ibid., p. 208). Similarly, the Italian Jewish religious philosopher Samuel David Luzzatto (1800–1865) plaintively observed with reference to the the votaries of *Wissenschaft des Judentums*, "they study ancient Israel the way the other scholars study ancient Egypt, Assyria, Babylon and Persia" (ibid., p. 209). Luzzatto, although Orthodox, was a prolific author of scholarly studies of Judaism; nonetheless, he held that *Wissenschaft des Judentums* "must be grounded in faith"—as such it will "seek to understand the Torah and the prophets as the Word of God, [and] comprehend how, throughout our history, the spirit of God, which is our nation's inheritance, warred with the human spirit."

Luzzatto's indictment of *Wissenschaft des Judentums* for its historicist bias may have been somewhat overstated, for we now know that the early scholars of *Wissenschaft des Judentums* were not utterly devoid of the existential religious commitment that he called for. Nonetheless, the thrust of *Wissenschaft des Judentums* was largely philological and antiquarian, and its methodological assumptions unequivocally conformed to a historicist mold (which in the twentieth century, Jewish studies would seek to break). Naḥman Krochmal (1785–1840), for one, regarded the intellectual and spiritual dilemmas engendered by the historicism implicit in *Wissenschaft des Judentums* as the most exigent issue facing his generation. Krochmal, who lived in the politically and socially conservative Austrian provience of Galicia where emancipation and religious reform were remote prospects, published a monumental treatise in Hebrew on the challenge posed to Judaism by critical historical research. This work, published posthumously in 1851, was indicatively entitled *Moreh nevukhei ha-zeman* (Guide of the Perplexed of Our Time). The title alludes to Maimonides' famous *Guide of the Perplexed* (1190), and like the great Spanish rabbi in his day, Krochmal sought to offer guidance to the perplexed of his generation. The reference in the title to the perplexed "of our (lit., "the") time" may be understood as both "of our time" and "by time," that is, by the category of time, by historical time.

Krochmal begins his treatise with the observation that Jewish youths are genuinely perplexed by the results of critical scholarship that cast doubt on the traditional view of events and, particularly, on the traditional view of the sacred texts, their composition, and, ergo, authority. An observant Jew, Krochmal noted that the faith of these youths will surely not be fortified by an obscurantist response; the enjoining of dogma in the face of the fruits of scholarship would only exacerbate the estrangement of these youths. Faith, as Maimonides in his day indicated, must be allied with reason; in our day, Krochmal argues, faith must also be grounded in a proper philosophical understanding of history. This is what Krochmal's *Guide* sought to provide, hence its subtitle, *She'arei emunah tsurafah (Gates to a Purified Faith).*

Judaism and Moral Theology. With a few notable exceptions (e.g., Samuel David Luzzatto), virtually all Jewish religious thinkers in the nineteenth century who sought to accommodate Judaism to the modern sensibility were beholden to Kant's conception of ethical piety as the ultimate form of service to God. Even among those thinkers whose primary concern was to develop à la Hegel and Schelling a philosophy of Jewish history, one discerns an attempt to come to terms with Kant's critique of Judaism as a heteronomous pseudoreligion. Nineteenth-century thinkers associated with every tendency in modern Judaism from Reform to Neo-Orthodoxy shared a conviction that the faith of Israel properly understood actually promotes ethical piety. Even Luzzatto, a staunch traditionalist who expressly rejected the very premises of Kant's ethical rationalism, argued that Judaism is fundamentally a religion of moral sentiment. Samson Raphael Hirsch developed an elaborate exegesis of the traditional precepts of Judaism, the *mitsvot* ("commandments"), demonstrating how each in its distinctive manner fosters the development of "moral consciousness."

Moritz Lazarus (1824–1903), a professor at the University of Berlin from 1873 and prominent lay leader of Liberal Judaism in Germany, devoted numerous essays and a two-volume study, *Die Ethik des Judentums* (The Ethics of Judaism; 1898–1911), to a systematic demonstration of Judaism's inherent compatibility with Kant's conception of morality. In developing his thesis, Lazarus drew upon the principles he had formulated in founding the discipline of *Völkerpsychologie,* the comparative psychology of peoples. With respect to the "psychological" study of Judaism, he proposed an examination of the literary sources of classical Judaism as they most faithfully record the "will, intent and way of life" of the Jews. By insisting that only on the basis of such a study could Judaism be properly characterized, Lazarus abjured the speculative approach of Formstecher and Samuel Hirsch. He introduced Kantian categories not as speculative presuppositions of his study but merely as heuristic principles that to his mind best organize and elucidate the "empirical" structure of Judaism and help illuminate the objective unity of its "ethical cosmos."

Lazarus maintained that such a study demonstrates that Judaism in effect is a system of autonomous ethics; specifically, the rites and values of Judaism foster the development of what Kant celebrated as moral consciousness. The ethical piety engendered by Judaism may be best characterized as "holiness"—a quality of life that bespeaks neither a numinous nor a transcendent reality but, rather, the indomitable conviction that a moral life is the ultimate meaning and purpose of existence.

To his profound disappointment, Lazarus's *Ethics of Judaism* was severely criticized by the generation's foremost Kantian philosopher, Hermann Cohen (1842–1918), the founder of the Marburg school of Neo-Kantianism. Cohen faulted Lazarus for locating the source of Judaism's ethical teachings in the Jewish "folk-soul." To Cohen such a concept, grounded as it is in psychology and history, undermines the reliability and certitude required by a genuine ethical system. Ethics must derive its validity from rational, universal concepts. What renders Jewish ethics interesting, Cohen contends, is its distinctive dependence on the concept of a universal, unique God—and not just as a phantasm of the Jewish folk-soul but as a rationally defensible concept.

Like Lazarus, Cohen was prominently associated with Liberal Judaism, especially in his latter years, and he also sought to demonstrate the fundamental compatibility of Judaism with Kant's ethical idealism. Interpreting the master's teachings in a somewhat novel fashion, Cohen understands ethics not as primarily addressing the individual but in its fullest sense as summoning society to the "task" of molding the "future" according to the principle of a rationally determined, *a priori* "ought." According to Cohen's most mature conception of faith and ritual, however, religion, in contradistinction to ethics, does not address the individual merely as representative of rational humanity; rather, it appertains to the individual as such, especially through the notion of "sin," which Cohen understands as the individual's anguished realization of his own moral failings. This consciousness of sin, Cohen observes, bears the danger that the individual will despair of his own moral worth and abandon all subsequent moral effort. The self-estrangement attendant to sin requires the concept of a forbearing God who by the act of forgiveness serves to reintegrate the individual into an ethically committed humanity. The atonement of sin is not effected by God's grace but by the individual, who in acknowledging God's forgiveness dedicates himself anew to the moral task.

Religion is thus preeminently a series of acts of atonement—rites and prayers expressing remorse and repentance and focused on the belief in a merciful, forgiving God. To Cohen the reconciliation between God and man thus achieved in turn requires that God be conceived not as an idea but as a being who relates to the finite, ever-changing world of becoming, of which man is a part. Despite the fundamental ontological distinction separating them, being and becoming are interrelated through what Cohen calls "correlation." God and man are correlated when the individual cognizant of God's mercy—his love and concern—rededicates himself to emulating in his actions these divine qualities. Cohen speaks of correlation as a shared holiness in which God and man are "co-workers in the work of creation."

Cohen set forth these views in his posthumously published volume, *Religion aus den Quellen des Judentums* (Religion of Reason out of the Sources of Judaism; 1919, 1929). In it he expounds his new conception of religion through a selective exegesis of the sources of classical Judaism in the Bible, the Midrash, liturgy, and medieval Jewish philosophy. These traditional expressions of Jewish piety, Cohen avers, exemplify the most refined conception of religion. The emerging portrait of Judaism as a faith of deep, personal significance has suggested to many commentators that Cohen anticipated the existentialist theology characteristic of much of twentieth-century Jewish thought, with its emphasis on the dialogic relation of the individual with a living, personal God. Cohen, however, continues to speak of the "religion of reason," and his God remains the "rational" God of ethics. And although in a striking revision of his Kantian premises he accords religion *qua* prayer and ritual intrinsic significance, he still does not quite regard it as an utterly independent reality enjoying a unique ontological and epistemological status. While not entirely absorbed into ethics, the "religion of reason" is for Cohen ultimately ancillary to ethics. Religion, and Judaism in particular, is conceived as an instrument for enhancing moral consciousness (i.e., moral reason) and commitment; it facilitates the acceptance of "the kingdom of God."

Judaism and Religious Existentialism. Despite the fact that Cohen's concept of correlation does indeed adumbrate some important features of twentieth-century religious existentialism, his overarching moral theology renders him more a son of the previous century. Moral reason for Cohen is the heart of religion, and thus not surprisingly he identifies it with revelation: "Revelation is the creation of Reason" (*Religion of Reason*, 1972, p. 72). This identification of reason and revelation was typical of nineteenth-century philosophical idealism. Yet for religious existentialists the point of departure was revelation understood as a metarational category pointing to God's spontaneous and gracious address to finite man. In this respect, the transitional figure from nineteenth- to twentieth-century Jewish thought is not Cohen but the little-known lay scholar Solomon Ludwig Steinheim (1789–1866). A physician by profession, Steinheim was not affiliated with any ideological camp within the Jewish community in his native Germany; indeed, he spent the last twenty years of his life mostly in Rome, isolated from organized Jewish life. It was said by Hans Joachim Schoeps in his *Vom Bleibenden und Vergänglichen im Judentum* that Steinheim was "the first [truly] Jewish theologism of the modern age. . . . He was twenty years too late, and one hundred years too early" (Berlin, 1935, p. 81). If one views Jewish thought from Mendelssohn to Cohen as a sustained effort to interpret Judaism as a religion of reason *par excellence*, then Steinheim stands alone in the nineteenth century.

In his monumental study, *Offenbarung nach dem Lehrbegriff der Synagoge* (Revelation according to the Doctrine of the Synagogue; 4 vols., 1835–1865), Steinheim seeks to remove religion from the tutelage of reason, maintaining that religious truths are the "gift" of supernatural revelation. In a manner recalling Søren Kierkegaard's critique of Hegel, he holds that the truths disclosed by revelation are incompatible with and irreducible to reason. Furthermore, he notes that the concept of supernatural revelation posits God as the creator who, unbounded by necessity, creates the world freely and out of nothing. As such, revelation confirms the irrefragable human experience of freedom that freedom burdened by the principle of universal necessity perforce denies. Accordingly reason must acknowledge the primacy of revelation.

In that God is the logical presupposition of revelation, Steinheim observes, the affirmation of the possibility of revelation implicitly reestablishes the dignity and authority of God: "Our task is to present revelation [such that] we are constrained . . . to accept God. Therefore, it is for us to make a declaration the exact opposite of Mendelssohn's and to prove the Old Testament was given not to reveal law but the living God" (*Revelation according to the Doctrine of the Synagogue*, vol. 2, p. 38). Revelation is thus not an object of faith but a definite cognitive phenomenon, and its content corresponds to the postulates of Kant's moral reason: God, freedom, and immortality. It also follows for Steinheim that not only are these postulates granted in revelation; in addition, the categorical imperatives of morality derive their authority from God and his revelation. Judaism, he holds, represents the ideal religion of revelation, for its ritual laws are secondary to its moral code, which is commanded by the living God. The conclusions of

Steinheim regarding Judaism are hence not unlike those of other nineteenth-century Jewish thinkers; the crucial difference is that for him Judaism is a fact of supernatural revelation.

Significantly, the philosophy of Franz Rosenzweig (1886–1929) whose path to Judaism from the midst of assimilation has become emblematic of much of twentieth-century Jewish religious thought, is grounded in his adoption of what he calls *Offenbarungsglaube,* a belief in revelation as a historical and existential reality. Such a belief must be the fulcrum of any genuine theology; otherwise, as Rosenzweig observes in his first essay on religious matters, "Atheistic Theology," one arrives at the strange anthropocentric brew concocted by the nineteenth century, which in placing religion within the realm of human sensibility alone—be it called "spiritual experience," "moral consciousness," or "national soul"—is in effect godless (*Kleinere Schriften,* 1935, pp. 278–293). Theology, he contended, must proceed from the "theocentric" fact of divine revelation, the fact of God's address to man. Rosenzweig developed his understanding of this address on the basis of a radical critique of philosophical idealism, with its quest for universal, timeless, abstract truths. In contrast to the ratiocination of the philosophers, revelation is in time; it is an occurrence whereby God establishes a relation with specific time-bound individuals. Phenomenologically this relation is what is celebrated in biblical tradition as love: the divine sounding of "Thou" to the temporally contingent "I" of the individual. God addresses the individual in his finite existence, calling him, as it were, by his "first and last name," which distinguishes him existentially from all others. In revelation the contingent existence of the individual is thus confirmed in love and blessed with the kiss of eternity.

Occurring in time, revelation is hence inaccessible to a reason that considers only timeless essences. Yet this conception does not contradict reason but merely delimits its sphere of validity. Properly understood, philosophical reason and faith are complementary. This affirmation of revelation allowed Rosenzweig to discern in Judaism what many of his generation of assimilated German Jews had denied, that is, that Judaism was a theocentric faith of enduring existential significance. He elaborated his conception of faith and Judaism in *Stern der Elosung* (Star of Redemption, 1921).

Later Rosenzweig sought to incorporate into his life and thought more and more extraliturgical aspects of traditional Judaism, from the commandment of keeping a kosher kitchen to that of Torah study. His approach to the *mitsvot* however, was distinctive. Unlike Orthodox Jews, he could accept the *mitsvot* on the basis of rabbinic authority, for, as he once remarked, "religion based on authority is equal to unbelief" (cited in *Judaism despite Christianity,* ed. E. Rosenstock-Huessy, New York, 1971, p. 166). His approach to "the Law," as he explained in an open letter, now famous, to Martin Buber, was to encourage each individual Jew to explore the sacramental and existential possibilities of the *mitsvot,* so as to determine which of these precepts he personally feels called upon to fulfill. In an article entitled "The Builders: Concerning the Law," Rosenzweig further elaborated his position to Buber with reference to a rabbinic commentary to *Isaiah* 54:13: we are not only "Your" (God's) obedient "children" *(banayikh),* but also "Your builders" *(bonayikh):* every generation has the opportunity, indeed, the task, to recreate for itself the Law (in *On Jewish Learning,* ed. Nahum N. Glatzer, New York, 1965, pp. 72–92).

Rosenzweig's nondogmatic brand of traditionalism was, and continues to serve as, a guide to many who seek to reappropriate traditional forms of Jewish piety and to affirm Judaism as a relation to a living God. Furthermore, Rosenzweig signally inspired the serious, nonapologetic theological reflection characteristic of much Jewish religious thought in the twentieth century. Among those he most decisively inspired was his friend Martin Buber, who emerged as a genuine religious thinker only with the publication of *I and Thou* (1922). Buber's previous writings on spiritual matters, Jewish and otherwise, belonged to a genre of Romantic mysticism that Rosenzweig had in mind when he wrote "Atheistic Theology"; these writings were virtually devoid of any reference to the God of revelation. With his treatise on I–Thou, or dialogic, relations Buber affirmed faith as grounded in the revealed word of God and in so doing developed a novel conception of revelation.

For Buber revelation is homologous with what he calls dialogue. God, the Eternal Thou, addresses one through the varied life experiences—from the seemingly ephemeral and trivial to the grand and momentous—that demand a dialogic response, or a confirmation of the Thou, the unique presence, of the "other" who stands before one. In uttering "Thou" (the actual act of speech is superfluous), the self, or I, in turn finds its own presence confirmed. As a response to the continuously renewing presence and address of another, dialogue must be born ever anew. The I–Thou response thus requires spontaneity and cannot be determined by fixed expressions, gestures, and formulations. It also follows that God's address as being refracted (i.e., revealed) through the addressing presence of the Thou who stands before one likewise requires such spontaneity. Buber further contends that authentic service to God is found only in such spontaneous response to the Eternal Thou, who turns to man through the flux of life's ever-changing circumstances. Although not utterly dismissing prayer and ritual as bearing the possibility of spontaneous and hence authentic relation to God, Buber does not regard them as paradigmatic forms of religious service.

Clearly such a conception of divine revelation conflicts radically with the classical Jewish conception of a historical revelation (viz., the Torah) enjoying preeminence and enduring authority. Furthermore, Buber's antagonism toward liturgical prayer and the *mitsvot* as the proper form of divine service conflicts not only with tradition but also with all expressions of institutional Jewish religious life.

Acknowledging his anomalous position within Jewish religious thought, Buber insisted that he was not in a formal sense a theologian. He claimed he sought neither to justify revealed propositions about God nor to defend revealed scriptures and doctrine. He simply pointed to dialogue as a metaethical principle determining the life responses of an individual, ensuring that these responses will be informed by love and justice and crowned with existential meaning (i.e., the confirmation of the Thou). He taught that this principle is at the heart of all great spiritual traditions, but particularly that of Judaism. The concept of dialogue can thus be employed as a hermeneutical principle by which to read the Hebrew Bible and other formative religious texts in the Jewish tradition, such as those of Hasidism.

As a particular "community of faith," Judaism is for Buber distinguished by its millennial and clarion witness to the dialogic principle both in its collective memory (enshrined in its central myths and sacred texts) and, ideally, in its current institutions. In fact, as a Zionist, Buber held that Jewish religious life in the Diaspora had been falsely restricted to the synagogue and the home, thus losing hold of the founding dialogic principle of Judaism and its comprehensive purview of divine service. By restoring to the Jews the sociological conditions of a full communal life, Zionism allows for the possibility that the Jews' public life, guided by the principle of dialogue, will once again become the essential realm of their relation to God. The reappropriation of the public sphere as the "dialogic" responsibility of the community of faith is consonant with the supreme injunction of the prophets of Israel and thus constitutes the renewal of what Buber calls Hebrew, or biblical, humanism.

Buber's religious anarchism and often radical politics alienated him from many Jews committed to traditional forms of worship and conventional positions. Yet his philosophy of dialogue has manifestly inspired others, especially those eager for extrasynagogal expressions of Jewish spirituality. Furthermore, his—and Rosenzweig's—conception of dialogue as a way of reading sacred texts (viz., recognizing the divine voice in a text without necessarily accepting the written word uncritically) has had a seminal effect on contemporary Jewish studies and hermeneutical attitudes. Critical historical scholarship therefore need not be bound to an antiquarian bias or lead inevitably to a barren relativism. Critical historiography and philology may be employed to bare anew the "inner," eternal truth of Judaism. The dean of Jewish studies in the twentieth century, Gershom Scholem (1897–1982), for example, regarded *Wissenschaft des Judentums* as a means of uncovering dimensions and expressions of Jewish spirituality that may have been suppressed by Orthodoxy and, later in the nineteenth century, by apologetics in defense of specific conceptions of "normative" Judaism. Precisely because of its objective, nonprescriptive mode of inquiry, *Wissenschaft des Judentums* is capable of covering the full canvas of Jewish spiritual options in order to inspire religious renewal. To this end Scholem devoted his prodigious scholarship, researching the surprisingly ramified and hitherto little-known or misperceived Jewish mystical tradition, Qabbalah.

Zionism and Religious Renewal. Like Buber, Scholem was a Zionist, or, more precisely, a follower of Asher Ginzberg (also known as Aḥad ha-ʿAm, lit., "one of the people," 1856–1927) and his vision of Zionism as effecting the reconstruction of Judaism as a secular, spiritually revitalized national culture. Having abandoned the religious Orthodoxy of his Hasidic upbringing in Russia, Aḥad ha-ʿAm was acutely aware of the "spiritual crisis" afflicting his generation of Jews, whose fidelity Judaism as a religious faith had ceased to engage. In ever-increasing numbers young Jews were being drawn to the secular-humanist culture of the West—a culture, in Aḥad ha-ʿAm's judgment, whose intellectual, ethical, and aesthetic power one could not deny. In that the secular humanism of the contemporary world was sponsored by non-Jewish languages and national communities, the adoption of this new culture by its nature entailed a weakening of one's ties to the Jewish people and culture. To stem the consequent tide of assimilation, Aḥad ha-ʿAm taught, Judaism must be reformulated as a secular culture grounded in the autochthonous humanist values of Judaism (e.g., the ethical teachings of the Bible and the prophets) and in Hebrew as the "national" language of the Jewish people. In Zion a culturally autonomous, Hebrew-speaking community would arise and, by force of the example of its spiritually vital and creative culture, inspire the Jews of the Diaspora to adjust Judaism to the new secular reality and at the same time maintain a firm Jewish national consciousness. For Aḥad ha-ʿAm the prevailing secularism implied an irrevocable eclipse of religious faith and culture; for Buber, Scholem, and other cultural Zionists, secularism was but a necessary historical stage that does not preclude the possible renewal of Judaism as a meaningful religious faith.

The idea of Zionism as a framework for the development of a Jewish religious humanism also inspired the teachings of Aaron David Gordon (1856–1922). One of the most remarkable figures in modern Jewish religious thought, he discerned unique religious possibilities in Zionism, particularly in the ethos of the idealistic "pioneers" *(ḥalutsim),* the select band of youths who, beginning in the 1890s, had gone to Palestine to "prepare" the Land of Israel for the "ingathering of the exiles." At nearly the age of fifty, Gordon reliquished the comforts of affluence and bourgeois eminence in his native Russia and joined the youthful *ḥalutsim* in the labor of draining the swamps and tilling the soil. Working tirelessly by day, this Jewish Tolstoy would write at night, exploring the religious significance of the pioneering endeavor. With a weave of qabbalistic and Hasidic doctrine and Russian populist ideas about the pristine dignity of the peasantry and a life rooted in nature, Gordon developed a mystical pantheism in which he celebrates agricultural labor as a supreme act of personal, national, and cosmic redemption. Toil on the land, he taught, integrates one into the "organic rhythms" of nature and the universe. The resulting experience of the "unity and purpose of the cosmos" is the core religious experience—an experience that, he believed, had been largely denied to the Jews of the Diaspora. This "cosmic" experience ultimately leads one to God, regardless of one's intellectual attitude. For Gordon an authentic relation to God has nothing to do with formal religious beliefs and ritual practices. In noting that God or the hidden mystery of the cosmos is approached through physical labor, he is quick to point out that biblical Hebrew employs the same word (viz., *'avodah*) to designate both "work" and "divine worship." (See Gordon's writings in *The Zionist Idea,* ed. Arthur Hertzberg, New York, 1969, pp. 368–386.)

Orthodox Jews have also seen Zionism as bearing extensive religious significance. The first chief rabbi of Palestine, Avraham Yitsḥaq Kook (1865–1935), was also profoundly inspired by the *ḥalutsim,* whom, despite their often demonstrative irreligiosity, he regarded as instruments of God's *Heilsplan* ("plan of salvation"). Judging history from the perspective of the qabbalistic teaching that external events are but symbols of a deeper, hidden reality, he interpreted the secular actions of the *ḥalutsim* on behalf of the Jewish people's restoration to Zion as symbolically reflecting a divinely appointed cosmic process of restoring a fragmented world to its primal harmony. Kook in general saw the heightened "secular" movement of the modern world toward social and scientific progress as part of a providential design to quicken the eschatological conclusion of history with the return of the Jews to their ancient domicile as but the most glorious symbol of the eschaton.

Not all Orthodox support for Zionism was motivated by eschatological considerations. The principal theological motive prompting the founding of Mizraḥi, the movement of religious Zionists found in 1902 by Yitsḥaq Ya'aqov Reines (1839–1915) was a decidedly mundane endorsement of Theodor Herzl's program of Jewish political sovereignty as a solution to anti-Semitism. Furthermore, Mizraḥi welcomed the normalization of Jewish political and social life envisioned by Zionism as encouraging *halakhah* (Jewish religious law) to expand beyond the lamentably circumscribed scope allowed it by the conditions prevailing in the Diaspora. The prophetic vigor of the Torah would thus be restored as the comprehensive matrix of a holy and just life for the Jewish people.

The establishment of the state of Israel in 1948 generated special theological problems for Orthodox Jewish supporters of Zionism, foremost with respect to the messianic significance of the restoration of Jewish patrimony to the Land of Israel. Many regard this as a "miraculous" event pointing to the imminent advent of the Messiah and divine redemption. [*See* Messianism, *article on* Jewish Messianism.] In the flush of messianic euphoria, the chief rabbis of the nascent state took the rare step of introducing a new prayer into the traditional liturgy, blessing God for causing "the beginning of redemption to flower." To be sure, a significant minority of Orthodox opinion continues to oppose Zionism, precisely because of what it deems to be the movement's messianic pretensions and its "arrogant" attempt to preempt God's judgment and redemptive deeds. On the other hand, Orthodox Jews who support Zionism and yet are unwilling to view its political achievements in eschatological terms are obliged to reckon with the absence of traditional theological categories in order to comprehend the anomalous situation posed by the reestablishment of Jewish political sovereignty in Zion as a process that is not the work of the divinely appointed Messiah.

Since the early 1940s these issues have acquired a sharp focus and popular attention through the sustained and invariably controversial efforts of Yeshayahu Leibowitz (b. 1903), professor emeritus in biological chemistry at the Hebrew University of Jerusalem. A religiously observant and learned Jew, Leibowitz has, since his emigration to Palestine in 1935 from his native

Latvia, been a proponent of an approach to Zionist and religious questions that is rigorously rational and free from what he regards as platitudes and sentimental pieties. For Leibowitz Zionism and the state of Israel have no messianic import; he regards messianism as fundamentally a folkloristic accretion to Judaism that is best ignored by serious, God-fearing Jews. He is particularly fond of citing Maimonides' admonition that one ought not preoccupy oneself with messianic speculations, for "they lead neither to fear [of God] nor to love [of Him]" (*Mishneh Torah,* Kings and Laws 12.2).

Furthermore, Leibowitz argues, those who ascribe religious or any other intrinsic value to the state are committing the cardinal sin of "idolatry" (*ʿavodah zarah,* i.e., the worship of false gods). Leibowitz thus refuses to regard Zionism as a religious phenomenon but views it simply as a movement for the political liberation of the Jewish people. He calls upon religious Jews to rejoice in this fact and greet the Zionist state as providing the framework for a fuller expression of *halakhah* and the Jewish people's religious vocation. He conceives of this vocation in strictly theocentric terms. By accepting the "yoke of the Torah and its commandments," Jews are foremost God's servants, and not vice versa. Service to God must be for its own sake, without regard for spiritual, moral, or material enhancement. Judaism is not meant to render the Jews happier, more noble, or more prosperous. Even the perfection of society and history are extraneous to Judaism. (While Leibowitz does not object to humanistic and progressive political endeavors, he insists these are in the realm of humans and their fallible judgment and thus are not to be theologically sanctified.) Although he recurrently appeals to the authority of Maimonides, Leibowitz's theological position also betrays the decisive influence of Kant, Kierkegaard, and Karl Barth. His sevère, almost priestly view of Judaism has evoked considerable, seminal discussion within both religious and secular circles of contemporary Israel.

Judaism and the American Experience. The reentry of the Jews into history as a sovereign nation has profoundly affected Jewish self-perception everywhere. In North America, Jewish thought is most strikingly distinguished by the effort to accommodate the new understanding of Jewish peoplehood, correlating it with the unique experience of life in an unambiguously free and pluralistic society. Mordecai Kaplan (1881–1983) developed a conception of Judaism that boldly articulates these apparently contrasting poles of the contemporary American Jewish reality. Regarding himself as a follower of Aḥad ha-ʿAm's cultural Zionism, Kaplan affirmed the centrality of the Land of Israel in Jewish life while upholding the creative and social viability of the Diaspora. In light of the secular definition of Jewish peoplehood legitimated by Zionism, Kaplan redefined Judaism as a "civilization," a designation that allowed him to conceive of Judaism in the broadest social and cultural terms. As a civilization, Judaism is thus not in the first instance a system of religious beliefs and practices but the life of the Jewish people. The civilization of Judaism is "religious" in that it is set in a distinctive "religious" universe of discourse with a body of shared symbolic gestures and rituals.

Kaplan's understanding of religion and God, however, is neither traditional nor theistic. Indebted to the philosophical pragmatism of the American educator John Dewey (1859–1952), Kaplan views God as a functional concept pointing to a nonpersonal and nonmetaphysical "power" or "process" in the universe that bespeaks order, justice, and goodness and upon which man must rely in order "to fulfill his destiny as a human being." This "Godhood of the cosmos" is a transnaturalistic principle: it is not a supernatural entity, nor is it to be understood simply as a metaphorical reification of human possibilities; it is, rather, an ontological concept that is continually being refined as human civilization advances on all fronts of knowledge, in the physical and normative sciences and in the imaginative arts. Religion and God thus have for Kaplan an ever-evolving pragmatic function of enhancing human well-being and dignity by "orienting us to life and eliciting from us the best of which we are capable."

Religion also has the more specifically sociological function of articulating and reenacting through certain ritualized practices (not necessarily liturgical or devotional) the collective self-consciousness and memory of its constituent community. As such, religion serves to foster the community's sense of historical continuity and shared values. Judaism so understood is unabashedly anthropocentric and humanistic. Moreover, as a religion that exists for the Jewish people and not vice versa (cf. Leibowitz), Judaism is not to be construed as a heteronomous discipline of ritual and codes, nor are its beliefs to be amplified catechistically.

Lest Judaism fail the contemporary Jew, Kaplan avers, it must respect his democratic and this-worldly temperament. Judaism therefore must be projected as an ongoing discourse that eschews all anachronistic, supernatural constructs of traditional religion and allows for diversity of opinion, especially with respect to questions of ultimate existential significance, such as the meaning of suffering, death, and evil. The specific "theological" function of Judaism, however, is to give focus to the needs and mutual responsibilities of the Jews as a people. While the movement associated with Kaplan's conception of Judaism, Reconstructionism, has remained relatively small, it has been observed that Kaplan gave expression to the emerging "folk religion of American Jewry," irrespective of formal denominational affiliation (Charles S. Liebman, "Reconstructionism in American Jewish Life," *American Jewish Year Book,* 71, 1970, p. 91). [*See* Reconstructionist Judaism.]

While the ideology of Kaplan's Reconstructionism may have given expression to the regnant naturalism and ethnic orientation of American Jewry, the same community has paradoxically demanded of its "religious elite," its rabbinical leadership, a theology that articulates, with due modifications, the theocentric, supernatural convictions that have classically defined Judaism. The image of Judaism even for the most theologically "naturalistic" would seem to require a supernatural definition, and herein lies the explanation of why Reconstructionism, despite its fidelity to the folk religion of American Jewry, has remained numerically insignificant; and hence also the receptivity of American Jews to the theocentric teachings of Buber and Rosenzweig.

European-educated religious thinkers, anchored in traditional Judaism and theological conviction, have also found in America a supportive environment. Emigrating to the United States in 1940, Abraham Joshua Heschel (1907–1972), a Polish-born scion of great Hasidic masters, developed for an appreciative American audience a lyrical theology that is more a persuasive personal witness than a conceptual argument. He presents a phenomenological explication of his own experience and "prophetic consciousness." Blending Hasidic spirituality, which he held as resonating the innermost truths of traditional Jewish faith, with nuanced Western learning, Heschel sought to elaborate a conception of piety relevant to the contemporary Jew. Noting that the aptitude for faith of Western man has been dulled by technological, bourgeois civilization, in his writings Heschel endeavors to reawaken the *sensus numinus*—the *a priori* sense of wonder and awe evoked by the mystery of life, which he, with Rudolf Otto (1869–1937), regards as the font of faith—by introducing his readers to the Hasidic-qabbalistic teaching that all reality refracts the divine presence.

The life of traditional Jewish piety governed by *halakhah,* according to Heschel, creates an inner, "holy" reality that heightens one's sense of the divine presence. As a system of deeds, *halakhah* has also ritualized the prophetic teaching that faith is ultimately a "leap of action": we respond to God's presence by making his work our own. Indeed, the convenantal relation between God and Israel implies an intimate partnership between man and God. The prophets, Heschel emphasizes, were particularly conscious of the intimate, passionate relation between man and God: our sins anger and sadden God, and in fearing and loving him we resolve to bring him joy by sharing in his work to crown creation with justice and compassion.

Despite his conviction that the "prophetic consciousness" captured the heart of traditional Judaism, Heschel's thought found its primary resonance not among the adherents of *halakhah* but among those Jews in need of an interpretation of Judaism that would authenticate their participation as Jews in the humane causes of their generation. Heschel's message of prophetic concern and responsibility spoke to a generation of American Jews in the 1960s and 1970s who felt themselves called upon as Jews to join the struggle on behalf of civil rights for black Americans and to oppose the Vietnam War, which they regarded as unjust.

American-educated Orthodox Jews who are sensitive to the philosophical and religious questions raised by the contemporary West have found their voice in Joseph Ber Soloveitchik, a descendant of renowned Lithuanian rabbis. Emigrating to the United States in 1932, he became one of the twentieth century's most esteemed Talmudists; he has spoken with rare authority within the Orthodox community, pondering from the perspective of one firmly and unapologetically grounded in *halakhah* those questions generated by what he regards as the ambiguous position of "the man of faith" in a technological, pragmatic civilization shaped by pronouncedly secular bias. Assuming the self-evident validity of Judaism and religious faith, Soloveitchik does not challenge the premises of technological civilization but, rather, chooses to defend within the context of that civilization the integrity of "the halakhic man." He achieves this by a phenomenological description of the religious consciousness of the halakhic man, elaborating his exposition with insights garnered from a subtle reading of modern philosophy, especially Neo-Kantianism and existentialism. He concludes that halakhic man is not antagonistic to the moral and cognitive concerns of technological man; but whereas the latter requires a social and gregarious personality, halakhic man accepts the individual's existential loneliness, overcoming the attendant isolation and anxiety through a "redemptive" love of God and Torah. The congregation of Jews forged by the Torah is a "covenantal community" that respects the solitary, existential reality of each of its members, who are joined to God and each other in a common covenantal relation sacrally objectified by the *halakhah.*

The European Jewish intellectual heritage has also inspired a generation of American-born Jewish religious thinkers, including Eugene B. Borowitz (b. 1924), Arthur A. Cohen (b. 1928), Will Herberg (1902–1977), David Hartman (b. 1931), Jacob J. Petuchowski (b.

1925), Richard L. Rubenstein (b. 1924), and Milton Steinberg (1903–1950). Characteristically, the writings of these individuals have been largely interpretative commentaries on the thought of their European predecessors. This dependence may be indicative not only of a pervasive sense of being the indebted heirs of the European intellectual tradition but also of a portentous feeling of being their survivors. The tragic, catastrophic end of European Jewry has created, in the words of Arthur Cohen, a profound "caesura" in Jewish collective and personal existence, engendering a sense of inconsolable mourning and obligation.

In reflecting upon the tragedy of the Nazi era and its theological implications for the "surviving remnant" of Jewry, American Jews have been at their most original and probing. The resulting "theology of the Holocaust" may in many respects be viewed as a theology of survival—a theology that seeks to affirm the obligations of the remnant of Jewry to survive somehow as Jews. Auschwitz, in the words of Emil L. Fackenheim (b. 1916 in Germany) issues "a commandment" to Jews to endure and to ensure the survival of Judaism. This commandment has also inspired the slow but impressive reconstruction of European Jewry, which has likewise witnessed the renewal of Jewish religious thought, most notably represented by Louis Jacobs (b. 1920) in England and Emmanuel Levinas in France.

Emmanuel Levinas (b. 1905), one of the most esteemed philosophers of post–World War II France, represents a continuation of the existentialist thought pioneered by Rosenzweig and Buber. Employing the metaphysical phenomenology he developed as a critique of Edmund Husserl's and Martin Heidegger's concept of "the other," Levinas has sought to illuminate the religious meaning of Judaism. Our moral experience of the other, borne by a compelling sense of responsibility toward him, is the only genuine knowledge we have of him. Levinas contrasts the antihumanistic tendency of Western culture, which masquerades as liberty but which is in fact bereft of responsibility for the other, with the biblical concept, especially as elaborated by the rabbis, of "a difficult liberty" (the title of his most important collection of essays on Judaism, *Difficile Liberté*). The Jew obtains transcendence and thus liberty by paradoxically living under God's law, which requires of him ethical and social responsibility for the other. Biblical man, Levinas observes with oblique reference to Heidegger, "discovers" his fellow man before "he discovers landscapes." As the custodian of biblical humanism, Levinas avers, Judaism defiantly proclaims to the contemporary world that liberty entails responsibility and obligation.

For all Jewish thinkers who regard themselves as living in the shadow of Auschwitz, the state of Israel, born on the morrow of the Nazi nightmare, is the overarching symbol of Jewish survival and resolve to endure. Survival is affirmed, however, not simply in defiance of Satan and his zealous agents but, rather, as an existential commitment to the God of Israel. Despite his horror and anguish, it is held, the Jew must affirm God as the author of a purposeful and good universe. Fackenheim cites the Psalmist: "I shall not die but live, and declare the works of God" (*Ps.* 18:17).

[*Aspects of modern Jewish thought are also discussed in* Holocaust, The, *article on* Jewish Theological Responses, *and* Zionism. *See also* Jewish Studies, *which comprises two articles that survey modern Jewish scholarship, and the independent entries on the major thinkers mentioned herein.*]

BIBLIOGRAPHY

An admirably lucid introduction to the major figures and themes of modern Jewish thought is provided in Robert M. Seltzer's *Jewish People, Jewish Thought: The Jewish Experience in History* (New York, 1980), chaps. 12, 13, 15, and 16. A nuanced weave of intellectual and social history, this volume illuminatingly places the development of Jewish thought within its cultural and historical context. A more strictly philosophical survey of the major protagonists of modern Jewish thought is *Jewish Philosophers*, edited by Steven T. Katz (New York, 1975). This volume is a useful compilation of articles on Jewish philosophers from the ancient period to the present that originally appeared in the *Encyclopaedia Judaica* (1971). The editor concludes the volume with a concise review of Jewish thought since 1945, dealing extensively with Heschel, Soloveitchik, post-Holocaust theologians, and other "contemporary voices."

For authoritative, scholarly analyses, which the general reader might find occasionally arcane, see Julius Guttmann's *Philosophies of Judaism: The History of Jewish Philosophy from Biblical Times to Franz Rosenzweig*, translated by David W. Silverman, with an introduction by R. J. Zwi Werblowsky (New York, 1964), and Nathan Rotenstreich's *Jewish Philosophy in Modern Times: From Mendelssohn to Rosenzweig* (New York, 1968). With somewhat less attention to philosophical detail, Heinz M. Graupe's *The Rise of Modern Judaism: An Intellectual History of German Jewry*, translated by John Robinson (Huntington, N.Y., 1978), provides an excellent and thorough discussion of "the cultural history of Jewish thought in Germany from Mendelssohn to Rosenzweig." Graupe has also provided an excellent bibliography of the relevant German-language literature.

The best biography of Mendelssohn is Alexander Altmann's magisterial *Moses Mendelssohn: A Biographical Study* (University, Ala., 1973). Altmann has also written a most instructive introduction and commentary to Mendelssohn's *Jerusalem*, translated by Allan Arkush (Hanover, 1983).

The impact of Kant, Schelling, and Hegel is subtly traced by Nathan Rotenstreich in *Jews and German Philosophy: the Polemics of Emancipation* (New York, 1984). Fundamental documents with commentary of the *Wissenschaft des Judentums* may be found in Paul R. Mendes-Flohr and Jehuda Reinharz's *The Jew in the Modern World: A Documentary History* (Oxford, 1980), chap. 5. Ideological issues surrounding the founding of modern Jewish scholarship are discussed at length in Michael A. Meyer's *The Origin of the Modern Jew: Jewish Identity and European Culture in Germany, 1749–1824* (Detroit, 1967), chap. 6. The problems posed to Jewish thought by *Wissenschaft des Judentums* and historicism are considered both historically and analytically in Rotenstreich's *Tradition and Reality: The Impact of History on Modern Jewish Thought* (New York, 1972), chaps. 2–4. Historical memory and the modern Jewish imagination are sensitively discussed in Yosef Hayim Yerushalmi's *Zakhor: Jewish History and Jewish Memory* (Seattle, 1982), chap. 4. The relation between Jewish historiography and philosophies of Jewish history is the subject of Lionel Kochan's *The Jew and His History* (New York, 1977).

Hermann Cohen's basic Jewish writings are available in *Religion of Reason out of the Sources of Judaism* (1919), translated and with an introduction by Simon Kaplan (New York, 1972), and *Reason and Hope: Selections from the Jewish Writings of Hermann Cohen,* translated and edited by Eva Jospe (New York, 1971).

Although the writings of Ludwig Steinheim are unfortunately not available in English, each of the above-mentioned general surveys of modern Jewish thought provides an overview of his thought. For a detailed and critical examination of Steinheim's unique theological position, see Graupe's *The Rise of Modern Judaism*, pp. 231ff., and Joshua O. Haberman's "Solomon Ludwig Steinheim's Doctrine of Revelation," *Judaism* 17 (Winter 1968): 22–41. One should also consult the remarkable collection of essays in *Salomon Ludwig Steinheim zum Gedenken,* edited by Hans Joachim Schoeps et al. (Leiden, 1966).

The best introduction to Rosenzweig remains *Franz Rosenzweig: His Life and Thought,* 2d rev. ed., edited by Nahum N. Glatzer (New York, 1961). The most sustained and careful analysis of Rosenzweig's thought is Stéphane Mosès' *Système et révélation: La philosophie de Franz Rosenzweig* (Paris, 1982), which also includes a comprehensive bibliography of Rosenzweig's works in translation as well as the scholarly secondary literature.

Buber's writings are widely available in English, and commentaries on his thought constitute a veritable library. Two excellent bibliographical guides to this literature are of immeasurable value: Margot Cohn and Rafael Buber's *Martin Buber: A Bibliography of His Writings, 1897–1978* (Jerusalem and New York, 1980) and Willard Moonon's *Martin Buber and His Critics: An Annotated Bibliography of Writings in English through 1978* (New York, 1981). For a synoptic view of Buber's thought, see Maurice Friedman's *Martin Buber's Life and Thought*, 3 vols. (New York, 1981–1984).

Levinas has gathered his essays on Jewish themes in his *Difficile Liberté*, 2d ed. (Paris, 1976). The most comprehensive discussion of his thought including his views on Judaism is Stephan Strasser's *Jenseits von Sein und Zeit: Eine Einführung in Emmanuel Lévinas' Philosophie* (Leiden, 1978).

For a concise but judicious introduction to the issues of twentieth-century Jewish thought, with specific focus on Hermann Cohen, Franz Rosenzweig, Martin Buber, A. D. Gordon, and Rav Kook, see Samuel H. Bergman's *Faith and Reason: An Introduction to Modern Jewish Thought,* translated and edited by Alfred Jospe (Washington, D.C., 1961). A comprehensive and nuanced analysis of the abiding issues and unresolved tensions of modern Jewish religious thought is given in Gershom Scholem's "Reflections on Jewish Thought," in his *On Jews and Judaism in Crisis,* edited by Werner J. Dannhauser (New York, 1976), pp. 261–297.

PAUL R. MENDES-FLOHR

Jewish Ethical Literature

The Hebrew term *sifrut ha-musar* ("ethical literature") can be defined either very explicitly or in a general way. In a more proscribed sense it is a well-defined literary genre; the works belonging to it are easily recognizable because each chapter in these books deals with a specific religious and theological subject—belief in the unity of God, trust in God, repentance, fear and love of God, and so forth. The classical examples of books in this genre begin with Baḥye ibn Paquda's *Ḥovot ha-levavot* (The Duties of the Heart) in the eleventh century and include Mosheh Ḥayyim Luzzatto's *Mesillat yesharim* (The Path of the Righteous) in the eighteenth century. In addition to the few dozen books written in this manner are some other minor genres, namely, *sifrut ha-tsavva'ot* ("ethical wills") and various monographs on subjects such as repentance.

In its broader meaning, the term *sifrut ha-musar* includes other religious literary genres, especially the vast literature of Hebrew homiletics, of which thousands of volumes were written between the twelfth and nineteenth centuries, as well as other popular works intended for the religious instruction of the masses. Hence, in general terms, "ethical literature" includes many literary genres; indeed, it refers to almost everything written for religious instruction except works of Jewish law *(halakhah)* or theology (philosophy or mysticism, i.e., Qabbalah).

Jewish ethical literature, in both its narrower and broader meanings, is not primarily intended to instruct the Jewish reader how to behave in certain circumstances. Practical instruction is reserved mainly for the literature of the *halakhah,* since Jewish law does not distinguish between religious and ethical commandments. Everything demanded by the Torah and the Talmud is included in the law, even subjects like the giving of *tsedaqah,* donations to the poor, or the proper behavior at a funeral. The main purpose of ethical literature is to explain to the Jew why it is necessary to follow the strict demands of Jewish law and ethical commandments. Thus, *sifrut ha-musar* is the literary genre that teaches the observant and devout Jew how to feel and how to organize his desires and intentions in order to be able to concentrate all his spiritual powers on the performance of the commandments that were enumerated by God in the ancient sources. The following brief description focuses on the development of Jewish ethical literature in its stricter sense, though reference will be made where possible to the broader field as well.

Beginnings in the Middle Ages. The first stage of the development of Jewish ethical literature in the Middle Ages signified a complete deviation from Jewish ethical works in the ancient period. While biblical and postbiblical Jewish literature included books dedicated specifically to the teaching of ethical values (*Proverbs, Ben Sira,* etc.), during the Talmudic period in late antiquity ethics was incorporated within the vast treasury of Midrashic homiletics and lost its standing as a separate literary genre. Rabbinic sayings dealing with ethical problems appear in Talmudic and Midrashic literature side by side, without any literary differentiation, with sayings dealing with astronomy, history, or medicine. The new insights and concepts in the field of ethics, which abound in this literature, were not expressed in a systematic way.

When Greek philosophy began to influence Jewish thinkers in the late geonic period (tenth and eleventh centuries), ethical problems began to be treated in a special literary form and in a systematic way. The first Jewish philosophers who developed such systems in the tenth to the twelfth century saw themselves, with some justification, as innovators, formulating their concepts as if there were no previous Jewish ethical system. They were right in the sense that in previous Jewish literature it is impossible to find a systematic explanation of why a Jew should follow the divine commandments and how to educate oneself to accept and perform them.

One of the clearest examples of this approach is Sa'adyah Gaon's treatment of ethics in the first half of the tenth century. The tenth and last chapter of his great philosophical work, *Sefer emunot ve-de'ot* (The Book of Beliefs and Opinions), is devoted to this subject. This chapter, which was probably written as a separate treatise, deals systematically with the main values of Jewish ethical behavior. According to Sa'adyah (882–942), God created man's psyche with thirteen different impulses or drives, each of which tends to impel him to fulfill it alone and thereby clashes with the others. Sa'adyah included in this list drives like sex, laziness, revenge, and craving for food together with the urge to study the Torah and worship God. None of these, according to Sa'adyah, is either "right" or "wrong," "good" or "evil." Each of these drives is right and good if used in moderation, according to one's needs, and wrong and evil if it becomes one's sole or main preoccupation. Most of the chapter is dedicated to demonstrating the negative results of concentrating one's energies on the fulfillment of one drive alone, be it revenge or worship, eating or studying. Sa'adyah's arguments against such extreme behavior are mainly hedonistic: complete submission to one drive turns even pleasure into pain and brings on suffering and ill health, while moderation and harmonic use of all of them together brings happiness, health, and long life. Sa'adyah uses some biblical and rabbinic references to strengthen his arguments, but his main thesis does not rely on Jewish sources; he is expressing, in fact, a secular conception of ethics.

A completely different approach was adopted by Baḥye ibn Paquda in Spain in the eleventh century. Like Sa'adyah, he wrote his ethical-philosophical treatise in Arabic, but his major work, *Ḥovot ha-levavot,* is the first book-length medieval Jewish work dedicated to the subject of ethics. In the introduction Baḥye complained that previous Jewish writers devoted all their works to the physical and material demands of Jewish religious life, neglecting completely the spiritual ones. His book was written in order to present the other, spiritual and ethical, side of the Jewish religion, which is, according to Baḥye, the most important and essential.

Baḥye's distinction between the physical and spiritual religious precepts was a major innovation in Jewish ethical thought. According to his system, prayer and religious studies cannot be included among the spiritual values because man's body and senses participate in their performance. Spiritual precepts, Baḥye explained, are those that are carried out completely "within the heart," that is, without any reliance or mediation of the limbs or the senses, and only the completely spiritual precepts have religious meaning and can be regarded as worship. The physical deeds, which include all the legal Jewish *mitsvot,* do not have any impact on one's religious life. A physical deed can have a religious meaning only if it is accompanied by spiritual concentration and intention—*kavvanah*—and even then its value is dependent on the spiritual intention and not on the deed itself. Thus Baḥye presented a completely spiritualized and internalized conception of Jewish religious life, which is a radical departure from the teachings of previous thinkers, who always insisted—as does Jewish law—that the physical performance of the *mitsvot,* both ritualistic and ethical ones, is the basis of Jewish worship.

Another new variation in the field of ethics in that period was introduced by Shelomoh ibn Gabirol (c. 1021–c. 1058), the great poet and philosopher, author of *Meqor ḥayyim,* which was known in Latin under the title *Fons vitae.* Ibn Gabirol wrote a short ethical treatise in Arabic, known in Hebrew as *Tiqqun middot ha-nefesh* (The Correction of Ethical Attitudes). Ibn Gabirol's approach to ethics in this work is a physical-anthropological one. Man's characteristic attitudes, he asserted, are dependent on the individual's complexion and physical harmony. Ibn Gabirol maintained that each of the twenty basic ethical attitudes is closely related to a certain combination of the four elements and the four liquids that constitute the human body according to medieval physiology. Using homiletical methods, Ibn Gabirol analyzed the ethical attitudes and arranged them in ten binary opposites (pride and humility, etc.), as an expression of man's physical constitution. Two such pairs are connected to each of the five senses. Ibn Gabirol's treatise is an attempt to give a scientific, secular, and physical basis to man's ethical behavior and to correct every flaw in the same way that physical ailments are corrected.

The greatest Jewish philosopher of the Middle Ages, Moses Maimonides (Mosheh ben Maimon, 1135/8–1204), dedicated important discussions to ethical problems in several of his major works but did not write a special work on ethics. His philosophical works, commentaries, and legal works contain chapters and portions dealing with ethics. When writing in Arabic, he, like Sa'adyah Gaon and Ibn Gabirol, established Jewish ethics on scientific concepts, derived from psychological and anthropological analysis. The works of Aristotle and the Arab philosophers who followed him served as sources for Maimonides' own formulations. When writing in Hebrew, however, especially in *Sefer ha-madda'* (The Book of Knowledge), the first book in his fourteen-book magnum opus of Jewish law, the *Mishneh Torah,* he very often based his ethical demands on old rabbinic ethical sayings.

Maimonides confronted the basic problems resulting from the meeting between rabbinic ethics and medieval philosophy and science in a profound way, taking pains to preserve the practical demands of ancient traditions while reconciling them with contemporary conceptions of spiritualized religious behavior. He contributed to the popularization in Hebrew literature of Aristotelian concepts like "the golden rule" of the "good" middle between two "evil" extremes, although their impact outside the immediate school of his followers was minimal. Even Maimonides, when dealing with the subject of ethics, saw himself not as a thinker who continued the deliberations of a long line of Jewish traditional teachers of ethics but as a philosopher who created a new system, relying mainly on non-Jewish scientific and philosophical sources and only assisted by biblical and Talmudic traditions.

Early Hebrew Works and Qabbalah. While Sa'adyah, Baḥye, Ibn Gabirol, and Maimonides wrote mainly in Arabic and addressed themselves to Jewish intellectuals in the communities under Arab rule who were familiar with Arabic philosophy based on the Greek, almost no works were written in Hebrew and intended for a larger Jewish public. Only in the twelfth century do we find the beginnings of Hebrew medieval ethical literature written by Jewish thinkers in a contemporary manner. The first among these was Avraham bar Ḥiyya', who contributed to ethics his collection of four homilies, called *Hegyon ha-nefesh ha-'atsuvah* (The Sad Soul's Deliberations), which was based on Neoplatonic philosophy. That same philosophy also influenced Avraham ibn 'Ezra', the great commentator on the Bible, who dedicated to ethics a brief treatise called *Yesod mora'* (The Foundation of the Fear of God). It is typical that these two works were written in the first half and middle of the twelfth century by philosophers from Spain who traveled and visited Jewish communities in Christian Europe, where Arabic was not understood, and were aware of the need for such material.

The first school of writers of Hebrew ethical works in medieval Europe did not emerge in the areas influenced by Arabic culture but in the small town of Gerona in northern Spain ruled by the Christians in the first half of the thirteenth century. The four important writers of this school were Moses Nahmanides (Mosheh ben Naḥman), Ya'aqov ben Sheshet Gerondi, Yonah ben Avraham Gerondi, and Asher ben David. All four belonged to the school of qabbalists that flourished in Gerona early in the thirteenth century. The mystical element in their ethical works is not dominant, and in the case of the best-known ethical writer among them, Yonah Gerondi, it is completely absent. If it were not for a letter written by Yitsḥaq the Blind, the great mystic of Provence, to the qabbalists in Gerona, naming Yonah Gerondi among them, it would never have been known for certain that he was indeed a qabbalist.

The most important innovation of the ethical works of this school of qabbalists is the revival of rabbinic ethics, almost completely neglected by their predecessors. Many parts of their works can be read as anthologies of Talmudic and Midrashic sayings concerning various ethical problems. It is clear that these writers intended to show, in contrast to the Jewish philosophers, that Judaism has an authentic ethical tradition which can answer every contemporary problem without relying on medieval philosophy and science. They tried to revive and reestablish the dominance of the traditional Jewish sources of antiquity as the normative guide to religious behavior. In this, their qabbalistic beliefs could have contributed to the spiritual depth and the pathos of their adherence to the traditional sources, but their works are not dependent on mystical symbolism.

The Gerona qabbalists viewed their concerted effort in the field of ethical works as a response to the threat that Jewish philosophy presented to Judaism. Extreme spiritualization on the one hand and profane, scientific systems of ethics on the other endangered the traditional conceptions of the primacy of ethical deeds and the observance of the practical precepts. Yonah Gerondi was one of the first Jewish thinkers to criticize Maimonides publicly and participated actively in the great controversy concerning Maimonides' works in 1232–1235. His ethical works, and especially his monograph on repentance, *Sha'arei teshuvah,* are intended to offer a traditional alternative to philosophical ethics. Nahmanides' ethical homilies include direct criticism of Aristotelian philosophy and indirect polemics against Maimonides.

Other writers of this period adopted the same attitude and created traditionalistic systems of ethics based on ancient sources as an alternative to the works of the philosophers. Prominent among them was Yeḥi'el ben Yequti'el of Rome, in the middle of the thirteenth century, whose ethical work *Ma'alot ha-middot* (The Ascending Ladder of Ethical Values) is an anthology of rabbinic paragraphs with some antiphilosophical undertones. Yeḥi'el was not a qabbalist, and his work proves that the return to the ancient sources in the realm of ethics was not motivated by mystical reasons alone.

Later in the thirteenth century another qabbalist, Baḥya ben Asher ibn Halawa, wrote one of the most influential works of Jewish ethics in a homiletical form, *Kad ha-qemaḥ* (A Bowl of Flour). In this work the author discusses ethical values, arranged in alphabetical order, dedicating a sermon to each. He seldom used qabbalistic symbolism, and the work is one of the most important books in medieval rabbinic ethics.

At the same time, Jewish philosophers continued to publish Hebrew books on philosophical ethics. The most prominent among them were Ya'aqov Anatoli in his collection of sermons, *Malmad ha-talmidim,* and Shem Ṭov ben Yosef Falaquera, who wrote several ethical treatises. Like other philosophers of the thirteenth century, these two relied heavily on the teachings of Maimonides, though very often their attitudes were more radical than those of their teachers.

In the thirteenth century in Spain, southern France, and Italy the two major schools of Hebrew ethical literature thus took shape, the philosophers, mostly Maimonidean, on the one hand, and the traditionalists, creators of rabbinic ethics, many of them qabbalists, on the other hand. New literary forms emerged in the two antagonistic schools, such as the ethical monographs, ethical homiletical literature, and ethical "wills," which summarize in a brief treatise a complete ethical system. From the thirteenth to the fifteenth century, Hebrew ethical literature is clearly divided along these basic ideological lines.

Ethics of the Ashkenazic Ḥasidim. While controversy raged in Spain, Italy, and southern France, an independent school of ethical thought was established in western Germany by the German-Jewish pietists, adherents of the esoteric, and often mystical, theology of Ashkenazic Hasidism. The main work of this school, which had a profound impact on Jewish ethical thought for many centuries, is the *Sefer Ḥasidim* (Book of the Pietists), written by Yehudah ben Shemu'el "the Pious" of Regensburg (d. 1217).

Sefer Ḥasidim is different from previous Hebrew ethical works in its concern with everyday behavior in minute details, relating to the performance of the religious precepts. Besides homilies that expound the theoretical basis of ethical ideas, the book, which is divided into brief, independent paragraphs, deals with specific ethical issues: how to choose a dwelling place; relationships with parents, teachers, neighbors, and the non-Jewish society; how to conduct business relations; attitude toward rabbis; and so forth.

The instructions of this book are based on a strict, radical ethical theory. The Ashkenazic Ḥasidim believed that God's presence in the world is evident only in the unusual and the miraculous. Natural and social laws are not a reflection of divine benevolence but are rather trials put before pietists by God in order to distinguish between the righteous and the wicked by testing their ability to obey God's commandments. Man's life, according to the pietists, is a continuous struggle to prove one's devotion to God by overcoming all the obstacles that God himself put on the path of his believers. Ethical behavior, in this system, is choosing the most difficult and painful alternative. The pietist must always concentrate on the performance of that deed which most people around him neglect; by so doing he proves that this is the most difficult path, and following it gives him the maximum religious reward. This worldview is the complete reversal of the hedonistic tendencies found in the ethical works of Jewish philosophers of the Middle Ages such as Sa'adyah and Yeḥi'el ben Yequti'el.

Ashkenazic Hasidism both reflected and served as an ideological response to the massacres and persecutions that German Jewry suffered during the period of the Crusades. *Qiddush ha-shem* ("sanctifying the Holy Name") was regarded by the Ḥasidim as the supreme religious and ethical achievement, because it was the most total and difficult expression of devotion to God in spite of terrible hardships. If the sacrifice of one's life is the final goal, everyday life should reflect the same attitude and be conducted as if every religious and ethical deed had an element of sacrifice in it—the larger the sacrifice, the more meaningful the deed. Anything that negates the demands of the body has religious value, while every deed that satisfies physical needs signifies ethical surrender.

Ashkenazic Hasidic ethics are closely related to the esoteric theology of the teachers of Ashkenazic Hasidism. Whereas the theology did not continue to develop but was absorbed by qabbalistic mysticism, which spread in central Europe during the late thirteenth and the fourteenth century, the ethical teachings of the Ḥasidim survived for many centuries. Numerous ethical treatises written in Germany in the thirteenth to the fifteenth century are based on *Sefer Ḥasidim*, many of them dealing with the concept of repentance in Ashkenazic Hasidic ethics. Their teachings served as a basis for later Jewish ethical literature, even when Qabbalah began to develop its own specific mystical ethical literature.

Sixteenth- and Seventeenth-Century Qabbalistic Ethics. In the sixteenth century the study of Qabbalah became more and more popular among Jewish intellectuals, after being confined, during the thirteenth to fifteenth centuries, mainly to small circles of esoteric mystics. Since the sixteenth century, and especially in the seventeenth and eighteenth centuries, Qabbalah spread very rapidly and eventually became the dominant ideology in Judaism. This change was, to some extent, the result of the destruction of the great Jewish center in Spain in the expulsion of 1492 and of the rapid decline of Jewish philosophy at that time. The dissemination of Qabbalah among the Jewish masses was assisted mainly by the fact that in the sixteenth century qabbalists began to write and publish popular ethical works based on qabbalistic symbolism, which made Qabbalah easily accessible—and religiously relevant—to the Jewish masses.

Qabbalistic ethical literature appeared in sixteenth-century Safad, a small town in the Upper Galilee that served, after the expulsion from Spain, as a center for many Jewish halakhists, preachers, thinkers, and mystics. In this town Qabbalah became a way of life, so that ethical treatises explaining the close interdependence of human social and religious behavior and mystical occurrences in the divine world were relevant and meaningful. Mosheh Cordovero (1522–1570), the great qabbalist who wrote systematic works of Qabbalah that were very influential in the sixteenth century, wrote a brief ethical treatise, *Tomer Devorah* (The Palm Tree of Deborah), wherein he pointed out the ways by which the earthly ethical behavior of the righteous influenced the mystical processes in the divine world, the realm of the mystical *sefirot*, the divine hypostases central in qabbalistic symbolism. A disciple of Cordovero's, Eliyyahu de Vidas, followed suit by writing a major book on ethics, *Re'shit ḥokhmah* (The Beginning of Wisdom), in which he interpreted many sections of ancient qabbalistic works, mainly the *Zohar*, as explaining the central values of Jewish ethics. Ḥayyim Vital (Klippers), the great disciple of Isaac Luria, wrote a short ethical work, *Sha'arei qedushah* (The Gates of Holiness), describing man's spiritual ascension from involvement in secular life and sin up to the immersion of his soul in the divine world. One of the great followers of Luria's mysticism, Yesha'yah Horowitz, wrote the largest ethical work of that time, *Shenei luḥot ha-berit* (The Two Tablets of the Covenant), which remains to this day one of the most influential works of Jewish ethics ever written.

The new impact of Qabbalah on Jewish ethics was based to a large extent on the revolutionary mystical views introduced by Isaac Luria (1534–1572). Whereas previous qabbalistic systems were characterized by withdrawal from the contemporary world, Luria's Qabbalah was intensely messianic. According to his mythical symbolism, the world was created in order to serve as a battleground between the divine powers of good and evil, where good will ultimately be victorious. The historical orientation of this philosophy demands action from its followers. By righteousness and religious and ethical activity, man assists God in the struggle against the powers of evil that resided within God and that now, following an upheaval in the divine world, rule all on earth but the souls of the righteous.

Luria's theology brought a new intensity and a renewed, profound meaning to all religious and ethical demands. In his system, every word of every prayer, every humble ritualistic act, and all ethical human deeds become either messianic acts that facilitate the redemption or evil deeds that support the satanic powers in their struggle against God. There are no neutral acts; everything done or left undone carries enormous spiritual significance and may help decide the fate of all creation.

Following Luria, countless works of ethics and ethical homiletics were written by Jews in the East and the West during the seventeenth and eighteenth centuries. This period is undoubtedly the peak of the influence that Hebrew ethical literature had on Jewish life, social behavior, and historical activity. The spread of Lurianic theology served as a basis for the messianic theology of the Shabbatean movement beginning in 1665, and quite a few authors of ethical works were Shabbatean believers, like Eliyyahu ha-Kohen of Smyrna and Yonatan Eibeschutz of Prague. Some authors were influenced by Shabbateanism even though they themselves did not belong to the movement, among them Mosheh Ḥayyim Luzzatto, the Italian author of the popular *Mesillat yesharim.* The fusion between mysticism and ethics was complete in the eighteenth century.

Hasidism and Modern Trends. Hasidic ethics are, on the one hand, a continuation of the process of applying Lurianic mysticism to the field of ethics and, on the other hand, a response to the ideological crisis brought about by the Shabbatean messianic movement. The Hasidic *rebeyim*—who perpetuated the preachings of the movement's founder, the Besht (Yisra'el ben Eli'ezer, 1700–1760), and his disciples, Ya'aqov Yosef of Polonnoye and Dov Ber of Mezhirich (now Międzyrzecz, Poland)—based their ethical homiletics on qabbalistic terminology and the Lurianic myth. They had, however, to contend with a reality which the messianic theology of Natan of Gaza, the "prophet" of the messiah Shabbetai Tsevi, had greatly influenced, and with the deep disappointment that ensued when the movement engendered the antinomian heresy of the Frankist movement in the eighteenth century. Among the disciples of Dov Ber, especially in the works of Elimelekh of Lizhensk (now Lezajsk, Poland), a new theology emerged, attributing to the figure of the *tsaddiq,* the leader of a Hasidic community, powers to assist a sinner in obtaining forgiveness from God and influence in the divine realm over the affairs of every Hasidic adherent. The concept of the *tsaddiq* as an intermediary between the righteous and God (originally derived from Shabbatean theology) became one of the most important elements in the Hasidic movement, together with a new emphasis on mystical communion with God *(devequt)* and devotion to ethical behavior at the expense of intensive study of the Torah.

The *mitnaggdim,* the main "opponents" of Hasidism, developed ethical thinking, especially in the Musar ("ethics") movement, founded by Yisra'el Salanter in the middle of the nineteenth century. This movement carried great weight in rabbinic academies *(yeshivot)* throughout eastern Europe in the second half of that century and the beginning of the twentieth. Yisra'el Salanter did not use qabbalistic terminology, preferring instead a modern way of preaching, though at times it seems that the content of his ideas was still under the influence of Lurianism. The same can be said about the ethical works of the modern rabbi Avraham Yitsḥaq Kook (1865–1935), one of the most profound modern Jewish thinkers, whose thought is still influencing Jewish Orthodox movements in Israel today. He placed repentance in the center of his mystical theology as a way toward redemption, and his modern language sometimes hides Lurianic symbolism.

[*For discussion of other forms of Jewish literature, see* Midrash and Aggadah *and* Halakhhah. *See also* Qabbalah; Hasidism, *overview article;* Ashkenazic Hasidism; *and the biographies of the principal figures mentioned herein.*]

BIBLIOGRAPHY

Works in Hebrew

Dan, Joseph. *Sifrut ha-musar ve-ha-derush* (Ethical and Homiletical Literature). Jerusalem, 1975. Includes a detailed bibliography.

Heinemann, Isaak. *Ta'amei ha-mitsvot be-sifrut Yisra'el.* Jerusalem, 1956–1959.

Tishby, Isaiah. *Mishnat ha-Zohar* (The Wisdom of the *Zohar*), vol. 2. Jerusalem, 1961.

Tishby, Isaiah, and Joseph Dan. *Mivkhar sifrut ha-Musar* (Hebrew Ethical Literature: Selected Texts). Jerusalem, 1970.

Works in English

Barzilay, Isaac E. *Between Reason and Faith: Anti-Rationalism in Italian Jewish Thought, 1250–1650.* Paris, 1967.

Bettan, Israel. *Studies in Jewish Preaching: Middle Ages.* Cincinnati, 1939.

Bokser, Ben Zion. *From the World of the Cabbalah: The Philosophy of Rabbi Judah Loew of Prague.* New York, 1954.

Bokser, Ben Zion, trans. *Abraham Isaac Kook.* New York, 1978.

Cronbach, Abraham. "Social Thinking in the *Sefer Ḥasidim.*" *Hebrew Union College Annual* 22 (1949): 1–147.

Ginzberg, Louis. *Students, Scholars and Saints.* New York, 1928.

Ginzburg, Simon. *The Life and Works of Moses Hayyim Luzzatto.* Philadelphia, 1931.

Glenn, Mendel G. *Israel Salanter.* New York, 1953.

Husik, Isaac. *A History of Mediaeval Jewish Philosophy* (1916). New York, 1969.

Lazaroff, Allan. "Bahyā's Asceticism against Its Rabbinic and Islamic Background." *Journal of Jewish Studies* 21 (1970): 11–38.

Marcus, Ivan G. *Piety and Society: The Jewish Pietists of Medieval Germany.* Leiden, 1981.

Rosin, David. "The Ethics of Solomon Ibn Gabirol." *Jewish Quarterly Review* 3 (January 1891): 159–181.

Scholem, Gershom. *Major Trends in Jewish Mysticism* (1941). New York, 1961.

Werblowsky, R. J. Zwi. *Joseph Karo: Lawyer and Mystic.* London, 1962.

Werblowsky, R. J. Zwi. "Faith, Hope and Trust: A Study in the Concept of Biṭṭahon." *Papers of the Institute of Jewish Studies* 1 (1964): 95–139.

JOSEPH DAN

JIEN (1155–1225), Japanese Buddhist leader and renowned poet. Jien was a highly influential figure at a critical time in the political, social, and religious life of Japan. Appointed abbot of the Tendai sect four times, he enjoyed close family ties with emperors and regents, composed poems that made him a leading poet of the day, and wrote Japan's first known interpretive history, the *Gukanshō*.

At the age of eleven, Jien was entrusted to the Enryakuji, a Buddhist temple, for training under a monk who was the seventh son of Retired Emperor Toba. Early poems by Jien, as well as entries in the diary of his distinguished brother Kanezane (1149–1207), indicate that he was a lonely child who was soon attracted to Buddhist teachings on transience and impermanence. A biography (the *Jichin kashōden*) states that when he was about twenty-five and was fasting at a temple on the Katsura River, he had a miraculous vision of the Buddhist deity Fudō Myō-ō.

Jien was ordained as a Buddhist monk, appointed to the headship of several important temples, and selected as personal priest to the emperor Go-Toba (r. 1183–1198) before reaching the age of thirty. When he was thirty-one, his elder brother Kanezane was designated regent, an appointment that further enhanced Jien's influence within Buddhist centers and at the imperial court. At the age of thirty-seven he received his first appointment as Abbot of Tendai. During the four years that he held the post, he devoted considerable time to the conduct of Buddhist rites in high places. He built new temples and promoted the practice and study of Buddhism in diverse ways.

In 1196 Jien and other members of his house (the Kujō) were ousted from office. Until his death nearly thirty years later, neither he nor his house ever again reached the dizzy heights attained during the Kanezane regency. For a time, Jien continued to be a favorite at court, largely because of his fame as a poet and his personal relationship with Go-Toba, but gradually the latter (who was now attempting to control state affairs as a retired emperor) moved to establish independence from *bakufu* control, rather than adopt the compromises favored by Jien and the Kujō house.

In the years immediately preceding the outbreak of civil war in 1221—a time of intense political rivalry within the court and between the court and the Kamakura *bakufu*—Jien turned frequently to written prayers, rituals, dreams, letters, and finally history in trying to convince Go-Toba and his advisers that drastic steps against the *bakufu* should be avoided. What Jien wrote in those troubled years suggests that he was especially interested in signs and revelations of what the native *kami* (gods) desired or had ordered.

Jien's history (the *Gukanshō*), written a year or so before the outbreak of war in 1221, was meant to show how national events had taken, and would continue to take, an up-and-down course in the direction of a political arrangement that would end the current crisis, an arrangement in which the Kujō house would figure prominently. He tried to show how a complex interplay of divine principles *(dōri)* was propelling events along that course: some Buddhist principles were forcing it downward to destruction, and some *kami*-created (Shintō) principles were pulling it upward toward a state of temporary improvement.

Since Jien was primarily interested in *kami*-created *dōri* that would bring improvement, scholars have concluded that native Shintō belief was stronger than imported Buddhist ideas in his interpretive scheme, although the Buddhist flavor was strong. As the outbreak of civil war in 1221 attests, Go-Toba did not ultimately adopt the compromises that Jien favored and that the *Gukanshō* predicted as inevitable. But Jien remained convinced, to the end, that he had charted the "single course" of Japanese history correctly.

[*See also* Tendaishū.]

BIBLIOGRAPHY

For a Jien biography, see Taga Munehaya's *Jien* (Tokyo, 1959), vol. 15 of "Jinbutsu Sōsho." His study of Japanese history has been translated by Delmer M. Brown and Ishida Ichirō in *The Future and the Past: A Translation and Study of the Gukanshō, an Interpretative History of Japan Written in 1219* (Berkeley, 1979).

DELMER M. BROWN

JIHĀD is the verbal noun of the Arabic verb *jāhada*, meaning "to endeavor, to strive, to struggle." It is generally used to denote an effort toward a commendable aim. In religious contexts it can mean the struggle against one's evil inclinations or efforts toward the moral uplift of society or toward the spread of Islam. This last undertaking can be peaceful ("*jihād* of the tongue" or "*jihād* of the pen"), in accordance with surah 16:125 of the Qur'ān ("Call thou to the way of the Lord with wisdom and admonition, and dispute with them in the better way"), or involve the use of force ("*jihād* of the sword") as mentioned in surah 2:193 ("Fight them until there is no persecution and the religion is God's; then if they give over, there shall be no enmity save for evildoers"). In pious and mystical circles spiritual and moral *jihād* is emphasized. This they call "greater jihād" on the strength of the following tradition *(ḥadīth)* of the prophet Muḥammad: "Once, having returned from one of his campaigns, the Prophet said: 'We have now returned from the lesser *jihād* [i.e., fighting] to the greater *jihād.*'"

In view of the wide semantic spectrum of the word *jihād,* it is not correct to equate it with the notion of "holy war." And in those instances where the word *jihād* does refer to armed struggle, we have to bear in mind that Islam does not distinguish between holy and secular wars. All wars between Muslims and unbelievers and even wars between different Muslim groups would be labeled *jihād,* even if fought—as was mostly the case—for perfectly secular reasons. The religious aspect, then, is reduced to the certainty of the individual warriors that if they are killed they will enter paradise.

Jihād in the Qur'ān and the Ḥadīth. In about two-thirds of the instances where the verb *jāhada* or its derivatives occur in the Qur'ān, it denotes warfare. Its distribution—and that of the verb *qātala* ("combat," "fight") for that matter—reflects the history of the nascent Islamic community. Both words are hardly used in the Meccan parts of the Qur'ān, revealed during the period when the Muslims were enjoined to bear patiently the aggressive behavior of the unbelievers, but abound in the Medinese chapters, sent down after the fighting between the Muslims and their Meccan adversaries had broken out. They are often linked with the phrase "in the way of God" *(fī sabīl Allāh)* to underscore the religious character of the struggle. And in order to indicate that warfare against the Meccans ought to be the concern of the whole community and not only of the direct participants in warfare, the words "with their goods and lives" *(bi-amwālihim wa-anfusihim)* are frequently added to these verbs.

Traditionally surah 22:39 ("Leave is given to those who fight because they were wronged—surely God is able to help them—who were expelled from their habitations without right, except that they say 'Our lord is God'"), revealed shortly after Muḥammad's Emigration (Hijrah) from Mecca to Medina in 622 CE, is regarded as marking the turning point in the relations between the Muslims and the unbelievers. Many later verses on *jihād* order the believers to take part in warfare, promise heavenly reward to those who do, and threaten those who do not with severe punishment in the hereafter. Some verses deal with practical matters such as exemption from military service (9:91, 48:17), fighting during the holy months (2:217) and in the holy territory of Mecca (2:191), the fate of prisoners of war (47:4), safe conduct (9:6), and truce (8:61).

Careful reading of the Qur'anic passages on *jihād* suggests that Muḥammed regarded the command to fight the unbelievers not as absolute, but as conditional upon provocation from them, for in many places this command is justified by aggression or perfidy on the part of the non-Muslims: "And fight in the way of God with those who fight with you, but aggress not: God loves not the aggressors" (2:190) and "But if they break their oaths after their covenant and thrust at your religion, then fight the leaders of unbelief" (9:13). Authoritative Muslim opinion, however, went in a different direction. Noticing that the Qur'anic verses on the relationship between Muslims and non-Muslims give evidence of a clear evolution from peacefulness to enmity and warfare, Muslim scholars have argued that this evolution culminated in an unconditional command to fight the unbelievers, as embodied in verses such as 5:9 ("Then, when the sacred months are drawn away, slay the idolaters wherever you find them, and take them, and confine them, and lie in wait for them at every place of ambush"). These "sword verses" are considered to have repealed all other verses concerning the intercourse with non-Muslims.

There is an abundant body of *ḥadīth* on *jihād.* Owing to their practical importance many of them were already recorded in special collections during the second century AH, before the compilation of the authoritative collections. The *ḥadīths* deal with the same topics as the Qur'ān but place more emphasis on the excellence of *jihād* as a pious act, on the rewards of martyrdom, and on practical and ethical matters of warfare. A typical *ḥadīth* from the last category is: "Whensoever the Prophet sent out a raiding party, he used to say, 'Raid in the name of God and in the way of God. Fight those who do not believe in God. Raid, do not embezzle spoils, do not act treacherously, do not mutilate, and do not kill children.'"

Jihād in Islamic Law. The prescriptions found in the Qur'ān and *ḥadīth,* together with the practice of the early caliphs and army commanders, were, from the latter half of the second century AH on, cast in the mold of a legal doctrine to which a separate chapter in the handbooks on Islamic law was devoted. The central part of this doctrine is that the Muslim community as a whole has the duty to expand the territory and rule of Islam. Consequently, *jihād* is a collective duty of all Muslims, which means that if a sufficient number take part in it, the whole community has fulfilled its obligation. If, on the other hand, the number of participants is inadequate, the sin rests on all Muslims. After the period of conquests the jurists stipulated that the Muslim ruler, in order to keep the idea of *jihād* alive, ought to organize an expedition into enemy territory once a year. If the enemy attacks Muslim territory, *jihād* becomes an individual duty for all able-bodied inhabitants of the region under attack. Those killed in *jihād* are called martyrs (*shuhadā'*; sg., *shahīd*). Their sins are forgiven and they go straight to paradise.

Shīʿī legal theory on *jihād* is very similar to Sunnī doctrine, with one important exception, however: the existence of the *jihād* duty depends on the manifest presence of a Shīʿī imam. Since the last of these went into concealment *(ghaybah)* in AH 260 (874 CE), the *jihād* doctrine should have lost its practical importance for the Shīʿah. However, in an attempt to strengthen their position vis-à-vis the state, Shīʿī scholars have claimed to represent collectively the Hidden Imam and, therefore, to be entitled to proclaim *jihād.* This explains why, during the last centuries, many wars between Iran and its neighbors have been waged under the banner of *jihād.*

The ultimate aim of *jihād* is "the subjection of the unbelievers" and "the extirpation of unbelief." This is understood, however, in a purely political way as the extension of Islamic rule over the remaining parts of the earth. The peoples thus conquered are not forced to embrace Islam: with payment of a special poll tax *(jizyah)* they can acquire the status of protected minorities and become non-Muslim subjects of the Islamic state (*dhimmīs*). In theory certain categories of non-Muslims are barred from this privilege: some scholars exclude Arab idolaters—a class of mere academic interest after the islamization of the Arabian Peninsula; others hold that only Christians, Jews, and fire worshipers *(majūs)* qualify. In practice, however, the definition of fire worshiper could be stretched to include all kinds of pagan tribes.

Before the final aim—Muslim domination of the whole world—has been achieved, the situation of war prevails between the Islamic state and the surrounding regions. This situation can be temporarily suspended by a truce, to be concluded by the head of state whenever he deems it in the interest of the Muslims. Most scholars stipulate that a truce may not last longer than ten years, the duration of the Treaty of al-Ḥudaybīyah, concluded in AH 6 (628 CE) between Muḥammad and his Meccan adversaries.

The *jihād* chapters in the legal handbooks contain many practical rules. Warfare must start with the summons in which the enemies are asked to embrace Islam or accept the status of non-Muslim subjects. Only if they refuse may they be attacked. Other prescriptions concern, for example, the protection of the lives of noncombatants, the treatment of prisoners of war, and the division of the spoils.

Jihād in History. Throughout Islamic history the doctrine of *jihād* has been invoked to justify wars between Muslim and non-Muslim states and even to legitimate wars between Muslims themselves. In the latter case the adversaries would be branded as heretics or rebels to warrant the application of the *jihād* doctrine. In the eighteenth and nineteenth centuries there arose movements all over the Muslim world for whom *jihād* was so central to their teachings and actions that they are often referred to as *jihād* movements. Despite their wide geographical range—from West Africa to Southeast Asia—and the different social, economic, and political causes from which they sprang, they employed the same notions from the Islamic repertoire. *Jihād* for them meant the struggle within an only nominally Islamic society for the purification of religion and the establishment of a genuine Islamic community.

In combination with the *jihād* doctrine the obligation of *hijrah,* the duty of Muslims to emigrate from areas controlled by non-Muslims, was frequently appealed to. Often the notion of a Mahdi played a role, either because the leader proclaimed himself as such, or because he was regarded as a minister appointed to prepare the Mahdi's advent. The organizational framework of these movements was usually that of a Ṣūfī order. Although their main struggle was within their own society, many of these movements developed into formidable adversaries of the colonial powers once they collided with their expansionist policies.

Examples of *jihād* movements are the Wahhābīyah in Arabia, founded by Muḥammad ibn ʿAbd al-Wahhāb (1703–1787), the Fulbe *jihād* in northern Nigeria led by Usuman dan Fodio (1754–1817), the Padri movement in Sumatra (1803–1832), the West African *jihād* movement of ʿUmar Tāl (1794–1864), the *ṭarīqah-i muḥammadī* ("Muhammadan way") in northern India founded by Aḥmad Barēlī (1786–1831), the Algerian resistance against French colonization, headed by ʿAbd al-Qādir (1808–1883), the Sanūsīyah in Libya and the Sahara, founded by Muḥammad ibn ʿAlī al-Sanūsī, and the Mahdist movement of Muḥammad Aḥmad in the Sudan (1881–1898). In the twentieth century the *jihād* doctrine lost much of its importance as a mobilizing ideology in the struggle against colonialism; its place was taken by secular nationalism. [*See also* Wahhābīyah *and the biographies of Ibn ʿAbd al-Wahhāb, Dan Fodio, ʿUmar Tāl, and Muḥammad Aḥmad.*]

The Contemporary Significance of the Jihād Doctrine. Since the nineteenth century attempts have been made to reinterpret the prevailing doctrine of *jihād.* One of the first thinkers to do so was the Indian reformer Sayyid Ahmad Khan (1817–1898). Believing that the interests of the Indian Muslims would be served best by close cooperation with the British colonizers, he sought to improve relations between both groups. Especially after the 1857 revolt (the so-called Mutiny), the British, who had laid the blame solely on the Muslims despite massive Hindu participation, had favored the latter on the grounds that collaboration with Muslims would pose a security risk because of their allegiance to the doctrine of *jihād*. By offering a new interpretation of the *jihād* duty, Sayyid Ahmad Khan wanted to refute these views and prove that Muslims could be loyal subjects of the British Crown. He rejected the theory that the "sword verses" had repealed all other verses concerning the relations with non-Muslims. On the basis of a new reading of the Qur'ān he asserted that *jihād* was obligatory only in the case of "positive oppression or obstruction in the exercise of their faith, impairing the foundation of some of the pillars of Islam." Since the British, in his view, did not interfere with the Islamic cult, *jihād* against them was not allowed.

In India this extremely limited interpretation of the *jihād* doctrine found some support. In the Middle East, however, reformers such as Muḥammad ʿAbduh (1849–1905) and Muḥammad Rashīd Riḍā (1865–1935) did not go so far. Yet their opinions differed considerably from the classical doctrine. They contended that peaceful coexistence is the normal relationship beween Islamic and non-Islamic territory and that *jihād* must be understood as defensive warfare, regardless, however, of whether the aggression on the part of the non-Muslims is directed against religion or not. In their view, then, *jihād* could indeed be proclaimed against Western colonial rule in the Islamic world. A recent development in modernist *jihād* literature is the presentation of an adapted and reinterpreted version of the *jihād* doctrine as Islamic international law, equating the notion of *jihād* with *bellum justum*. [*See also the biographies of Ahmad Khan and Muḥammad ʿAbduh.*]

Although modernist opinion is nowadays widespread, one ought not forget that there are also other schools of thought with regard to *jihād*. Apart from the conservative trend that contents itself with repeating the classical legal texts, there is the fundamentalist or revivalist tendency, whose adherents want to change the world according to Islamic principles. They view their struggle for the islamization of state and society as *jihād*, explained by them as "the permanent revolution of Islam." They follow the classical doctrine and reject the modernist interpretation of *jihād* as defensive warfare. The most radical groups among them advocate the use of violence against their fellow Muslims, who, in their opinion, are so corrupt that they must be regarded as heathens. To this trend belonged the Tanẓīm al-Jihād ("*jihād* organization"), which was responsible for the assassination of the Egyptian president Sadat in 1981.

BIBLIOGRAPHY

The most extensive and reliable survey of the classical doctrine of *jihād* is Majid Khadduri's *War and Peace in the Law of Islam* (Baltimore, 1955). The same author has translated the oldest legal handbook on *jihād*, written by Muḥammad al-Shaybānī (749–805) and published under the title *The Islamic Law of Nations: Shaybani's Siyar* (Baltimore, 1966). Muhammad Hamidullah's *Muslim Conduct of State*, 6th rev. ed. (Lahore, 1973), is based on an extensive reading of the classical sources but is somewhat marred by the author's apologetic approach. In my *Jihad in Mediaeval and Modern Islam* (Leiden, 1977), I have translated and annotated a classical legal text and a modernist text on *jihād;* also included is a comprehensive bibliography of translations into Western languages of primary sources on *jihād*. Albrecht Noth's *Heiliger Krieg und heiliger Kampf in Islam und Christentum* (Bonn, 1966) and Emmanuel Sivan's *L'Islam et la Croisade: Idéologie et propagande dans les réactions musulmanes aux Croisades* (Paris, 1968) both deal with the *jihād* doctrine in the historical setting of the Crusades. In addition, Noth compares *jihād* with similar notions in Christianity. Hilmar Krüger's study *Fetwa und Siyar: Zur international rechtlichen Gutachtenpraxis der osmanischen Şeyh ül-Islâm vom 17. bis 19. Jahrhundert unter besonderer Berücksichtigung des "Behcet ül-Fetâvâ* (Wiesbaden, 1978) examines the role of the *jihād* doctrine in Ottoman international relations from the seventeenth to the nineteenth century. Mohammad Talaat Al Ghunaimi's *The Muslim Conception of International Law and the Western Approach* (The Hague, 1968) attempts to apply the notions of modern international law to the *jihād* doctrine and asserts that islamic law, thus recast, could nowadays be applied in international relations. The political role and the interpretation of the *jihād* doctrine in the nineteenth and twentieth centuries are the main themes of my *Islam and Colonialism: The Doctrine of Jihad in Modern History* (The Hague, 1979). On the Egyptian *jihād* organization see Johannes J. G. Jansen's *The Neglected Duty* (New York, 1986).

RUDOLPH PETERS

JIMMU, the first emperor of Japan, direct descendant of Amaterasu, the supreme deity, and generally regarded as the ancestor of the present Japanese emperor. Amaterasu's offspring, Ame no Oshiho-mimi, begot Ho no Ninigi, who descended from Heaven to earth. His offspring, Hiko-hohodemi, begot Ugaya-fukiaezu, whose offspring was Jimmu.

Jimmu is a Chinese-style name given to this emperor much later; his original name was Kamu-yamato-iwarehiko. *Kamu* means "divine," and *Yamato* is the name of the location of the ancient capital. The semantically significant portion of this name is *iwarehiko*. *Iwa* means "rock," and *are* means "to emerge." Since *hiko* means "a respectable person," Jimmu's original name, *Iwarehiko*, suggests "a respectable person who emerged (or was born) from a rock."

According to the early chronicles, Jimmu was born in the province of Himuka on the island of Kyushu in western Japan. He led a successful expedition to conquer the east and ascended the throne in Yamato in 660 BCE. Historians, however, reject this date because at that time the Japanese still lived in scattered tribal communities. It was only in the second century CE that a unified political organization emerged in western Japan. There is no significant archaeological evidence that a kingdom in Himuka dominated western Japan or that a Himuka army invaded Yamato. Judging from the analysis of his name, Jimmu is most likely a legendary figure. Whether or not he was also a historical figure who actually established the Yamato state has not yet been demonstrated.

[*See also* Amaterasu Ōmikami *and* Japanese Religion, *article on* Mythic Themes.]

BIBLIOGRAPHY

Aston, W. G., trans. *Nihongi: Chronicles of Japan from the Earliest Times to A.D. 697* (1896). Reprint, 2 vols. in 1, Tokyo, 1972.

Chamberlain, Basil Hall, trans. *Kojiki: Records of Ancient Matters* (1882). 2d ed. With annotations by W. G. Aston. Tokyo, 1932; reprint, Rutland, Vt., and Tokyo, 1982.

Philippi, Donald L., trans. *Kojiki*. Princeton, 1969.

Tsuda Sōkichi. *Nihon koten no kenkyū*, pt. 1, vol. 1 of *Tsuda Sōkichi zenshū*. Tokyo, 1963.

KAKUBAYASHI FUMIO

JINGŌ (169–269?), legendary Japanese empress, mother of Ōjin, Japan's first emperor, and symbol of Japanese female shamanism. Jingō is one of fifteen imperial figures fabricated by the authors of the oldest Japanese chronicles (the *Kojiki* and *Nihonshoki*, both seventh century) in order to fill the gap between the real beginning of Japanese history in the fourth century and its fictitious start in 660 BCE. Jingō, therefore, is not historical, but rather symbolic. She stands for the establishment of Japanese relations with the Asian mainland (Korea and China) and is representative of the important role of female shamans in early Japanese history and mythology.

The details of Jingō's legendary history are to be found only in the *Nihonshoki*, which records that she was born in the year 169, the daughter of Prince Okinaga no Sukune and Princess Takanuka of Katsuraki. Immediately after her death she was renamed Okinaga Tarashi hime no Mikoto ("The very witty and well-footed princess"). Almost three centuries later she was given a much shorter, Chinese-style honorary title, Jingō, still in use today. This title, literally "merit of the gods" or "divine merit," implies that she was either divine herself or served to convey divine commands. In this latter capacity she carried out Amaterasu's instructions to have temples erected to her throughout Japan.

In 194 Jingō married the emperor Chūai. In 201 she joined a campaign to subjugate the barbarous tribes of the Kumasō ("land spiders") in Kyushu. During this unsuccessful expedition, she lost her husband, who was probably hit by a Kumasō arrow. After his death, Jingō continued his reign for nearly seventy years.

Upon withdrawing from the campaign in Kyushu, Jingō was advised by the gods to conquer the three Korean states of Bakan, Benkan, and Shinkan, then known as Paekche, Silla, and Koguryŏ, respectively. Clad in male attire like an emperor, Jingō crossed the straits between Japan and Korea with an enormous army. Upon her arrival in Korea, she established on its south coast the protectorate of Mimana, the Japanese bridgehead from which for centuries to come Korean and Chinese religions and civilizations would spread to Japan. Within two months she had subdued the kingdom of Silla. After this, the kings of Paekche and Koguryŏ voluntarily agreed to continue yearly tribute to Japan.

Immediately after her return from Korea, Jingō gave birth to a boy, the future emperor Ōjin, whom she named Homuda or Honda. The chronicles of the thirty-ninth year of her reign quote the Chinese chronicles of Wei (composed in 445), in which the Japanese queen Himiko of Wa (in Kyushu) is reported to have paid tribute to the Chinese emperor. It is rather doubtful, however, whether Himiko (the real name of Jingō?) was the same person as Jingō, for the two resided in different regions of Japan. The *Nihonshoki* reports that Jingō died in the palace called Wakazakura (Fresh Cherries) at the age of one hundred.

[*See also* Japanese Religion, *article on* Mythic Themes.]

BIBLIOGRAPHY

Aston, W. G., trans. *Nihongi: Chronicles of Japan from the Earliest Times to A.D. 697* (1896). 2 vols. in 1. Reprint, Tokyo, 1972.

Florenz, Karl. *Die historischen Quellen der Shinto-Religion aus dem Altjapanischen und Chinesischen übersetzt und erklärt.* Leipzig, 1919.

Kamstra, J. H. *Encounter or Syncretism: The Initial Growth of Japanese Buddhism*. Leiden, 1967.

J. H. KAMSTRA

JĪVA. *See* Soul, *article on* Indian Concepts; *see also* Jīvanmukti.

JĪVANMUKTI. The Sanskrit term *jīvanmukti* means "liberation as a living being." A person who has attained liberation in his lifetime is called *jīvanmukta*. Although these precise terms seem to have been popularized only by followers of Śaṅkara, late in the first millennium CE, the concept of a liberated person had become a commonplace of Indian religious thought many centuries earlier. This article will concentrate on the concept.

The final goal of every Hindu is to attain release *(mukti)* from *saṃsāra,* the endless cycle of death and rebirth that all living beings—gods, human beings, animals, and lower spirits—undergo. The cause of rebirth is *karman,* or intentional action. All intentional action originates from "passion" *(rāga),* or emotional involvement with the world. As *mukti* is release from *saṃsāra,* it is thus release from *karman* and its results; and this abandonment of *karman* is to be attained by cultivating "dispassion" *(vairāgya),* emotional disengagement from the world.

In those forms of Hinduism that see devotion to God as the means to salvation, such detachment from the world, and hence *mukti,* is to be attained only at death. However, in the religions that dominated Indian culture from about 500 BCE to late in the first millennium CE, salvation is due to a liberating insight, or gnosis. It is a corollary of all gnostic religion that liberation can be attained in this life. (In India this possibility is explicitly restricted to human beings.) Thus, there can be human beings who are already saved, who are devoid of passion and of the kind of intentionality that will cause them to be reborn: in such cases, at the death of the body, the sequence of cause and effect set in motion by the individual's *karman* will cease.

Although the content of this gnosis varies in detail from school to school, for all Hindus it involves the realization that one's essential nature is pure spirit, immortal and immutable. Whatever is not pure spirit is impermanent and liable to change; it is utterly other than one's essential nature. The Western distinction between mind and matter is a misleading analogy, for most of what Western thought assigns to mind Indian thought categorizes as nonspiritual. The only apparently "mental" characteristic allowed by all Hindus to the spirit is pure consciousness. All schools agree that the gnostic who has successfully discriminated between his purely conscious spirit and the transient phenomena that comprise the rest of his apparent empirical personality is thereby freed from suffering *(duḥkha);* most go further and characterize this state as bliss *(ānanda).*

The earliest texts containing this kind of gnostic religion are the early Upaniṣads (c. seventh century BCE). Buddhism and Jainism are religions of this gnostic type; but the metaphysics of both are, in separate ways, different from those of Hinduism; and as the term *jīvanmukti* is never applied, even retrospectively, to Buddhist or Jain saints, we here deal only with Hindu formulations of the concept.

The Hindu gnostic sees through the unreality of changing phenomena, in particularly their duality; he rises above pleasure and pain, good and evil. The enlightened person is thus beyond moral categories; but as he is free from all emotional attachments, he will never do evil. The person seeking this gnosis will tend to renounce worldly life since it involves types of activity—sexual, economic—that cannot be carried on without attachment. Although the early Upaniṣads stress the intellectual pursuit of gnosis, in most schools it was pursued through the practice of yoga. On whether the liberated person continues to perform ritual, opinions differ sharply.

All later Hindu sects were influenced by the metaphysics of Sāṃkhya, an atheistic path to salvation. The spirit *(puruṣa/ātman)* is considered here as utterly other than nature/matter *(prakṛti),* which is one, though diversified. Spirits are many and are inactive and transcendent, mere conscious witnesses of the activity of *prakṛti,* the material cause of the phenomenal world, including all mental functions and intelligence. Involvement with the world and suffering arise from a failure of discrimination *(viveka).* Once one has dissociated one's spirit from mind and ego, one stands sheer and alone *(kevalin),* untouched by emotion. This isolation *(kaivalya)* of the spirit ensures that at death one is never reborn. The *kevalin* lives on after attaining gnosis because his *karman,* which had begun to bear fruit, must exhaust its momentum, like the potter's wheel after the potter has stopped spinning it. The *Bhagavadgītā* describes such a man as *sthitaprajña,* "of serene wisdom."

The Advaita Vedānta school established by Śaṅkara virtually accepted the Sāṃkhya view of the *kevalin,* despite a different metaphysical basis. In the tradition of the early Upaniṣads, the Vedāntins regarded the plurality of individual souls *(ātman)* as an illusion: there is only one reality, *brahman,* with which all souls must realize their unity. *Prakṛti* is not only other than spirit; it is in fact nonexistent. Our entire view of a plural world is just a mistake. He who has undone this mistake is *jīvanmukta.*

Hindu Tantric sects hold a different view of *mukti.* For these monotheistic gnostics, salvation is achieved through God's grace, which is then instantiated in the successful efforts of the practitioner, who aims to change his impure body into the pure substance of *śākti,* God's energy, the source of all things. If he succeeds, he becomes a *siddha* ("successful one"). The idea occurs in the Śaiva Tantras, in the Vajrayāna Tantras, and in *haṭhayoga.* The pure body of a *siddha* was conceived by some to be immortal, so that *jīvanmukti* amounted to apotheosis. Specialists in alchemy *(rasaśāstra)* hoped to achieve immortality by ingesting mercury, the essence of Śiva, and some Tantrics continue to believe that breathing exercises can render them immortal, or at least ensure them very long life.

[*See also* Indian Philosophies *and* Tantrism, *article on* Hindu Tantrism.]

BIBLIOGRAPHY

Brunner, Hélène. "Un chapître du *Sarvadarśanasaṃgraha:* Le Śaivadarśana." In *Tantric and Taoist Studies in Honour of R. A. Stein,* edited by Michel Strickmann, vol. 20 of *Mélanges chinois et bouddhiques,* pp. 96–140. Brussels, 1983.

Dasgupta, Surendranath. *A History of Indian Philosophy,* vols. 1 & 2. Cambridge, 1922–1932. A traditional treatment of the views of Śaṅkara and his followers, including a lucid discussion of the gnostic view of salvation. See especially pages 207, 268, and 291–292 in volume 1 and pages 245–252 in volume 2.

Eliade, Mircea. *Yoga: Immortality and Freedom.* 2d ed. Princeton, 1969. Still the best work on the yogic path of release.

Hiriyanna, Mysore. *The Essentials of Indian Philosophy.* London, 1949. A concise historical introduction. See especially pages 31–56 and 129–174.

Kaw, R. K. *Pratyabhijñā Kārikā of Utpaladeva: Basic Text on Pratyabhijñā Philosophy (The Doctrine of Recognition).* Sharada Peetha Indological Research Series, vol. 12. Srinagar, 1975. Includes a clear description of the Śaiva Tantra path of salvation.

SANJUKTA GUPTA

JIVAROAN RELIGION. *See* Quechua Religions, *article on* Amazonian Cultures.

JIZŌ. *See* Kṣitigarbha.

JÑĀNA. The Sanskrit root *jñā* is cognate with the Old English *knawan.* Hence on etymological consideration one normally translates *jñāna* as "knowledge." Although this translation seems harmless in many contexts, in a philosophical text that deals with epistemology, or *pramāṇa-śāstra,* it will often be wrong and misleading. In fact, in nontechnical Sanskrit *jñāna* often means knowledge. But when it is contrasted with *pramā* ("knowledge, knowledge-episode"), it means simply a cognition or awareness, and it is meant in an episodic sense. A cognition is an episode that happens in a subject, and when such a cognitive episode becomes true it becomes knowledge, as in *pramā.* Thus, we must say, only some cognitions are knowledge; others may be cases of doubt, misperception, error, false judgment, opinion, and so forth.

In epistemology, the problem is formulated as follows: what is it that makes a *jñāna* or a cognitive event a piece of knowledge, *pramā*? The general answer is that if the causal factors are faultless and no opposing or counteracting factor *(pratibandhaka)* intervenes, the result would be a true cognitive event, a piece of knowledge. The Nyāya school uses *jñāna* in the more comprehensive sense. For according to Nyāya, to be conscious means to be conscious of something, there being no such thing as "pure consciousness," and this again means to cognize or to be aware of something, that is, to have a *jñāna* of something. The conscious subject, or self, is analyzed as the subjunct that *has* cognition or *jñāna,* the obvious conclusion being that a *jñāna* or a particular cognitive event is a quality *(guṇa)* or a qualifier *(dharma)* of the self. The Buddhists, however, analyze the person or the self into five aggregates, of which the awareness series, or the awareness aggregate, is the main constituent. The self is therefore only an awareness series in this view where in each moment an awareness arises, conditioned by the preceding one, along with a number of attending factors. Feelings such as pleasure, pain, and anger are part of the awareness event, according to the Buddhists. But Nyāya wishes to introduce a distinction between the pleasure-event or pain-event and our cognitive awareness *(jñāna)* of such events.

The Sāṃkhya view of *jñāna* is different. In this view the intellect *(buddhi)* and ego-sense or I-consciousness *(ahaṃkāra)* are all evolutes (*vikāra*s) of matter. The spiritual substance is called *puruṣa* ("man"). Consciousness is the essential attribute of *puruṣa,* the spiritual reality. But since the intellect (a material evolute) is extremely transparent and mirrorlike by nature (Vācaspati's view), it reflects the consciousness of the *puruṣa,* that is, it becomes tinged with awareness, and thus an awareness-event arises. It is called a *vṛtti* ("modification") or transformation *(pariṇāma)* of the intellect. It is therefore the spiritual illumination of the mental form, that is, *buddhi* transformed into the form of an object, which makes *jñāna* possible. In Advaita Vedānta, a special manifestation of consciousness (the self-consciousness) is *jñāna* in the primary sense. But the *vṛtti* that the *buddhi* ("intellect") obtains is also called *jñāna* in a secondary sense. Of the two components, the *vṛtti* grasps the form of the object and destroys our veil of ignorance or the state of "unknowing" *(avidyā),* but the particular manifestation of consciousness is what actually *reveals* the object.

Jñāna has soteriological significance. It is almost unanimously claimed (except by the Cārvāka) that some sort of *jñāna,* or *tattva-jñāna* ("knowledge of the reality as it is") is instrumental in bringing about the final release from our bondage. Here, of course, *jñāna* stands for "knowledge." Knowledge is what liberates us from human bondage. Even the *Nyāya Sūtra* states that the ultimate good *(niḥśreyasa)* springs from our knowledge *(tattva-jñāna)* of different realities. It is commonplace to say in Advaita Vedānta that *brahmajñāna* ("knowledge of the *brahman*") is the ultimate means for liberation: it is that which establishes the essential identity of the individual self with the ultimate Self or universal Self, *brahman*. Our congenital misconception *(avidyā)* creates a false disunity between the individual and the *brahman*, but *jñāna* establishes their ultimate union. In some Buddhist texts (cf. Vasubandhu, *Triṃśikā*) a distinction is made between *jñāna* and *vi-jñāna* where the latter is subdivided into *ālaya-vijñāna* and *pravṛtti-vijñāna*. The *pravṛtti-vijñāna* stands for all the ordinary cognitive events of life, cognition of blue for example; while the *ālaya* is said to be the seed *(bīja)* or the subterranean current that causes the "waves" of other cognitive experiences and in turn is fed back by such experiences to continue the process of *saṃsāra* ("the round of births and deaths"). But when the saint acquires *jñāna*, there is a complete reversal *(parāvṛtti)* of the base *(ālaya-āśraya)* in him. There is pure *jñāna*, which is also called *bodha* and which eliminates the *vijñāna* series. For there cannot be any *grāhaka* or *vijñāna* or apprehension when there is no *grāhya*, no apprehensible object. This is called the *dharmakāya* of the Buddha.

In certain religious or philosophical texts that promote syncretism, such as the *Bhagavadgītā*, three principal ways of attaining the final goal of salvation are mentioned. They are *karmayoga* (the path of action), *jñānayoga* (the path of knowledge), and *bhaktiyoga* (the path of devotion). The path of knowledge means that ultimate knowledge, or comprehension of the ultimate truth, is sufficient to bring about liberation. But sometimes this path is combined with the path of action, which means that religious and moral duties are performed with a completely unattached disposition *(niṣkāma karma)*. Our actions with motivation to obtain results create bondage, but if we are unattached to the result our actions cannot bind us. Hence knowledge of the Ultimate, when it is combined with such "unattached" action, opens the door to liberation. *Bhakti*, devotional attachment and complete surrender to the deity, is another way. Sometimes a situation is recognized as *jñāna-karma-samuccaya-vāda*, that is, it is claimed that *jñāna* and *karma* are like the two wings of a bird: it cannot fly with just one of them.

[*For discussions of* jñāna *within the context of the six systems of orthodox Hindu philosophy, see* Nyāya; Vaiśeṣika; Sāmkhya; Yoga; Mīmāṃsā; *and* Vedānta. *See also* Ālaya-vijñāna.]

BIBLIOGRAPHY

For *jñāna* in Nyāya-Vaiśeṣika, see chapter 2 of my *The Navya-nyāya Doctrine of Negation* (Cambridge, Mass., 1968). For the views of other schools, see Kalidas Bhattacharya's "The Indian Concept of Knowledge and Self," *Our Heritage* (Calcutta) 2–4 (1954–1956). For *jñāna-yoga*, one may consult Surendranath Dasgupta's *A History of Indian Philosophy*, vol. 2 (London, 1932), chap. 14. Editions and translations of the *Bhagavadgītā* are too numerous to be mentioned here.

Bimal Krishna Matilal

JOACHIM OF FIORE (c. 1135–1202), Italian monk and biblical exegete. Joachim was born in Calabria, and after a pilgrimage to Palestine he returned to southern Italy, where he became successively abbot of the Benedictine, later Cistercian, monastery at Curazzo and founder of his own Florensian congregation at San Giovanni in Fiore. The Mediterranean was then a crossroads of history, with pilgrims and Crusaders coming and going and rumors of "the infidel" rife. Joachim was acutely aware of living in the end time and sought an interpretation of history through biblical exegesis illumined by spiritual understanding, a view elaborated upon in works such as *Liber Concordie Novi ac Veteris Testamenti* (1519), *Expositio in Apocalypsim* (1527), and *Psalterium decem chordarum* (1527).

Joachim recorded two experiences of mystical illumination (and hints of a third) in which the trinitarian understanding of history was revealed to him. He developed his theology of history through investigations into biblical concords, or sequences. The first sequence arises from the relation of the old and new dispensations. The second sequence, the procession of the Holy Spirit from both Father and Son, exemplifies his famous "pattern of threes": the first stage *(status)*, that of the law, belongs to the Father and lasts until the incarnation of Jesus Christ; the second, that of grace, belongs to the Son and lasts until a near future point; the third, that of the Spirit, proceeding from the first two and characterized by love and liberty, runs until the second advent of Christ. Joachim found the clues for his scheme of history in particular biblical sequences, for instance, in the references to the twelve patriarchs, the twelve apostles, and the twelve expected future leaders, and in references to Noah's sending forth of a raven and a dove paralleling the mission of Paul and Barnabas, which he took as evidence for the future founding of two orders of spiritual people.

Joachim's originality lay in the concept of a third stage still to come, whereas in the standard threefold pattern (before the law, under the law, and under grace) the church had already entered the third stage. Joachim believed that the transition to the third *status* must be made only through the tribulation of the greatest Antichrist (the seventh dragon's head), who was imminent. This age to come, the age of the Spirit (equated with the seventh, or sabbath, age), was part of history and should be distinguished from the eighth day of eternity.

Joachim was recognized as a prophet in his lifetime. Richard I of England, leading the Third Crusade, interviewed him at Messina. In the thirteenth century his concept of the coming of two orders of spiritual people achieved a "prophetic scoop" when the Dominicans ("ravens") and Franciscans ("doves") were founded. In both orders, especially the Franciscan, some friars claimed the role outlined by Joachim, which successively fired the imagination not only of heretical groups—the Apostolic Brethren, Fraticelli, Provençal Beguines, and others—but also of some Augustinian hermits and Jesuits. Pseudo-Joachimist works spread the prophecies, and Joachimist influence is traceable as late as the seventeenth century in the myths of the Angelic Pope and the Last World Emperor. In 1254 occurred the "scandal of the eternal evangel," when a Franciscan proclaimed Joachim's works to be the new gospel, replacing the Old and New Testaments. This was widely documented and later referred to by Lessing, the eighteenth-century German philosopher whose *Education of the Human Race* was widely influential in promoting an optimistic view of the future age. Consequently, the nineteenth century saw a revival of interest in Joachim's third *status* among visionaries such as Jules Michelet, Edgar Quinet, Pierre Leroux, and George Sand who were antiecclesiastical but looked for a new gospel. Some scholars claim Joachim as the source of all later threefold patterns of history, but this is questionable.

BIBLIOGRAPHY

Bloomfield, Morton. "Joachim of Flora: A Critical Survey of His Canon, Teachings, Sources, Biography, and Influence." *Traditio* 13 (1957): 249–311. The best bibliographical survey, now updated in "Recent Scholarship on Joachim of Fiore and His Influence," in *Prophecy and Millenarianism,* edited by Ann Williams (London, 1980), pp. 23–52.

McGinn, Bernard. *The Calabrian Abbot.* New York, 1985. An account of Joachim's place in the history of Western thought.

Reeves, Marjorie E. *The Influence of Prophecy in the Later Middle Ages.* Oxford, 1969. Deals with Joachim's life and thought and traces his influence down to the seventeenth century.

Reeves, Marjorie E. *Joachim of Fiore and the Prophetic Future.* London, 1976. A brief account summarizing material in the preceding and the following book and incorporating some new material.

Reeves, Marjorie E., and Beatrice Hirsch-Reich. *The Figurae of Joachim of Fiore.* Oxford, 1972. A study of Joachim's use of symbolism, especially in his *Liber figurarum.*

West, Delno C., ed. *Joachim of Fiore in Christian Thought: Essays on the Influence of the Calabrian Prophet.* 2 vols. New York, 1975. Reprints essays from various journals, dating from 1930 to 1971.

MARJORIE E. REEVES

JOAN OF ARC (c. 1412–1431), French visionary; also known as the Maid of Orléans. Joan, who called herself Jeanne La Pucelle, used her claims to mystical experience to influence the course of French history in the fifteenth century. Led by her visions, she inspired the French army to turn the tide of the Hundred Years' War. Born around 1412 in Domrémy-la-Pucelle, a village on the border between Lorraine and France, Joan was a peasant who, in her own words, did not "know A from B." As she grew up she heard the magical lore and local saints' legends of Lorraine and reports of continuing French defeats at the hands of the English.

At age thirteen Joan began to hear a voice from God instructing her to go to the dauphin Charles, the uncrowned Valois king. Believing that she was called to drive the English out of France, Joan privately took a vow of virginity and prepared herself for the role of prophetic adviser to the king, a type of female mystic familiar in the late medieval period. At some point in these troubled years the voice became three voices, whom she later identified as the saints Catherine of Alexandria and Margaret of Antioch, both known for their heroic virginity, and the archangel Michael, protector of the French royal family.

Joan established her authority through her urgent sincerity, by identifying herself with prophecies about a virgin who would save France, and by accurately announcing a French defeat on the day it took place 150 miles away. No longer able to ignore her, the garrison captain at the nearby town of Vaucouleurs refused to endorse her mission to save France until she was exorcised, raising the issue that would haunt her mission henceforth: Did her powers come from God or from the devil? Not fully assured, the captain nonetheless gave her arms and an escort. Cutting her hair short and donning male clothing, Joan and her companions made their way through enemy territory, reaching the dauphin's court at Chinon in late February 1429.

Joan's indomitable belief that only she could save France impressed Charles, his astronomer, and some of the nobles. But they too moved carefully, requiring an examination for heresy by theologians at Poitiers, who declared her a good Christian, and a physical examination by three matrons, who certified that she was indeed a virgin. For a woman about to attempt the "miracle" of defeating the English, virginity added an aura of almost magical power.

Given the desperate nature of Charles's position, he had little to lose in allowing Joan to join the army marching to the relief of Orléans, which had been besieged by the English. Her presence attracted volunteers and raised morale. Charging into the midst of battle, Joan was wounded and became the hero of the day. With Orléans secured, Joan impatiently counseled the army to move on. Town after town along the Loire fell, others offered their loyalty without battle. By late July, the dauphin could be crowned King Charles VII at Reims with Joan by his side.

But Joan's days of glory were brief. Driven by her voices, she disobeyed the king and continued to fight. Her attack on Paris failed, and several other ventures ended inconclusively. In May 1430, Joan was captured in a skirmish outside Compiègne. Neither Charles nor any of his court made an attempt to rescue or ransom her.

Determined to discredit Joan as a heretic and a witch, the English turned her over to an inquisitional court. Manned by over one hundred French clerics in the pay of the English, Joan's trial in Rouen lasted from 21 February to 28 May 1431. Under inquisitional procedure she could not have counsel or call witnesses. As a layperson she had no religious order to speak for her, nor had she ever enlisted the support of a priest. Yet although she had spent months in military prisons, in chains and guarded constantly by men, Joan began with a strong defense. Reminding her interrogators that she was sent by God, she warned that they would condemn her at great risk. The charges came down to the question of ultimate authority: the judges insisted that she submit to the church's interpretation that her visions were evil, but Joan held to her claim that they came from God. Perhaps without intending it, Joan thus advocated the right of individual experience over the church's authority.

After weeks of unrelenting questioning, Joan began to break. Threatened with death by fire, she finally denied her voices and agreed to wear women's dress. We do not know precisely what happened next, but three days later she was found wearing male clothing again. She claimed that she had repented of betraying her voices; there are indications that her guards may have tried to rape her. Whatever her motivation, her actions sealed her fate. Declared a relapsed heretic on 31 May 1431, Joan was burned at the stake.

In 1450, because he was uneasy that he owed his crown to a convicted heretic, Charles instigated an inquiry into the trial, which led to a thorough papal investigation. Although the verdict of 1431 was revoked in 1456, the main charges against Joan were not cleared. Despite this ambiguity, Joan's memory received continuous attention from the French people through the centuries. It is ironic that in 1920 she was declared a saint, because none of the church's proceedings has acknowledged her right to interpret her divine messages, leaving the main issue for which she was condemned unaddressed.

BIBLIOGRAPHY

The basic materials relative to the trial are found in Jules Quicherat's five-volume *Procès de condamnation et de réhabilitation de Jeanne d'Arc* (Paris, 1841–1849; New York, 1960). For an updated edition of the trial in French and Latin, see *Procès de condamnation de Jeanne d'Arc*, 3 vols., edited by Pierre Tisset and Yvonne Lanhers (Paris, 1960–1971), and of the retrial, see *Procès en nullité de la condamnation de Jeanne d'Arc*, 3 vols., edited by Pierre Duparc (Paris, 1979–1983). An abridged English translation of the trial can be found in Wilfred P. Barrett's *The Trial of Jeanne d'Arc* (London, 1932), and of the retrial, in Régine Pernoud's *The Retrial of Joan of Arc*, translated by J. M. Cohen (London, 1955).

Of the vast secondary literature, the following biographies are good places to begin: Frances Gies's *Joan of Arc: The Legend and the Reality* (New York, 1981), Lucien Fabre's *Joan of Arc* (New York, 1954), and Victoria Sackville-West's *St. Joan of Arc* (London, 1936; New York, 1984). See also my study *Joan of Arc: Heretic, Mystic, Shaman* (Lewiston, N.Y., 1985) and Régine Pernoud's *Joan of Arc by Herself and Her Witnesses*, translated by Edward Hyams (London, 1964).

ANNE LLEWELLYN BARSTOW

JOB. The biblical *Book of Job*, called in Hebrew *Iyyov*, is classed among the Writings (Ketuvim) of the Hebrew Bible and among the Poetic Books of the Old Testament. Its hero, Job, is ordinarily presented as a model of patience (see *Jas.* 5:11), although he is presented in the biblical poem as a rebel.

The Man from Uz. The Hebrew word *iyyov* may have meant "enemy," while its Arabic cognate meant "the penitent." A certain prince in the land of Bashan (northeast of Galilee) was known in Akkadian texts of the fourteenth century BCE as A-ya-ab. The land of Uz has been identified either with Bashan (where the supposed tomb of Job was shown to medieval pilgrims) or with Edom (*Jer.* 25:19ff., *Lam.* 4:21), a country reputed for wisdom. The site of Kirbet el ʿIts, about 89 kilometers south-southeast of the Dead Sea, may well have been that of the town of Uz, in Edom.

The Folk Tale and the Poem. Interpreters have long observed profound discrepancies of style, language, and ideas between the prose prologue and epilogue on the one hand (*Jb.* 1:1–2:13, 42:7–17) and the poetic discussion on the other (*Jb.* 3:1–42:6). The hero of the folk tale is a seminomadic sheik, pious, virtuous, and prosperous, suddenly stricken with the loss of his children, his health, and his wealth. To Job, his wife, and his three friends (Eliphaz, Bildad, and Zophar), this uncommon misfortune is inexplicable, but the audience is permitted to learn, through a vista into the heavenly council, that Job is being tested, with the acquiescence of God (whom Job calls Yahveh), by the prosecuting attorney of the celestial court, called "the *saṭan*" (not a proper name), one of "the sons of Elohim [a name for God]." Job refuses to curse the deity for his unfair treatment. After the visit of the three friends, "who had not spoken the truth about [God]" (*Jb.* 42:7), the hero receives again his health and his wealth along with a new set of sons and daughters. Like the Hebrew patriarchs, this model foreigner dies at an advanced age. The poem provides an entirely different picture.

The prose prologue and epilogue are separated by a complex sequence of poems, two soliloquies, the discourses of the three friends with the hero's rebuttals, a hymn, an oath of innocence, the speeches of a younger friend (Elihu), and, finally, God's intervention with a long series of questions spoken from the whirlwind, with Job's responses.

Composition and date. Various features of the folk tale suggest that it was in oral form among the seminomads of the second millennium BCE. Several of its rhetorical devices present affinities with those of the early tradition depicting the rise of the monarchy under Samuel and Saul (*1 Sm.* 9:1–12:25). Only in archaic times would a storyteller place in the mouth of Job—a Syrian or an Edomite—the covenant name of Yahveh. Several centuries after this folk tale had become a treasure of Hebraic oral traditions, it may have been used by an anonymous poet who wished to comfort his fellow deportees in Mesopotamia by raising the question of undeserved suffering. The sapiential genius who composed the poetic discussion was probably a disciple of the prophet Jeremiah, whose curse of existence (*Jer.* 20:14–18) was a model for Job's opening soliloquy (*Jb.* 3:1–26). At the beginning of the Babylonian exile (sixth century BCE), the prophet Ezekiel mentioned Job among the righteous men of the distant past (*Ez.* 14:14). The dialogue between the suffering man and his friends is probably to be dated between the prophetic activity of *Ezekiel* (c. 592–580) and "Second Isaiah" (c. 549–545). Those critics who propose a postexilic date ignore the many signs of thematic as well as stylistic influences of the poem upon Second Isaiah's description of Israel as the suffering servant of Yahveh (*Is.* 41:8ff. et al.). Most likely, however, the poem remained in an oral form for several generations. It was a member of the Jobian school who introduced the speeches of Elihu (*Jb.* 32:1–37:24), while another rearranged some of the third cycle of discussion (*Jb.* 22:1–27:23) in order to tone down some of the extreme statements of the man in revolt. The hymn on the inaccessibility of wisdom (*Jb.* 28:1–28) was probably sung as a chorus during the chanted presentations of this masque of pure religion. Postexilic scribes finally wrote out the poem and included the traditional ending of the folk tale, which reaffirms beliefs in punishment and reward.

Occasion of the poem. According to an attractive conjecture, the poet was a sage of the prophetic tradition who produced a piece of "liturgical entertainment" for an early celebration of the New Year festival (Ro'sh ha-Shanah). Unknown in early days, this feast eventually came to precede the Day of Atonement (Yom Kippur) and Tabernacles (Sukkot) as the Jewish adaptation of the earlier Middle Eastern autumn festival, in some forms of which the king or other ruler was ritually slain and raised from the dead. Such ceremonies were held either at the vernal equinox, when vegetation was about to dry up from summer heat, or at the autumnal equinox, when vegetation was renewed by seasonal thunderstorms and rains. The poem of *Job* contains allusions to a royal figure, tortured unto death and waiting for a resurrection. The cycle of seasons appears especially in the discourses of Elihu which anticipate the advent of the Lord of the whirlwind (*Jb.* 38:1–38). The poet displaced the myth-and-ritual environment of the old fertility cults and made of the New Year festival a celebration of trust in the Lord of creation, victor not only over chaos in nature (Leviathan and Behemoth) but also over oppression in history. He will not abandon his people now prostrate.

Literary Genre and Oriental Parallels. Taken in its final composite form as a unit, the book defies literary classification. It combines parabolic narrative, lament, hymn, diatribe, proverb, judiciary procedure, sapiential discussion, theophany, prophetic vision, and introspective meditation. The dialogue genre became well known in Greece, but its Hellenic form differed markedly from the Jobian exchanges. In Plato's philosophic dialogues, conversation moves back and forth with lively interruptions and quick repartee, whereas in *Job,* each character speaks at length. The discourses of the friends, the hero, and God present strophic structures and stately developments appropriate for chanting in a cultic environment. The hero's short answers to Yahveh's questioning constitute an exception on account of their climactic impact (*Jb.* 40:1–5, 42:1–6). In form and general themes, the Jobian poem is closely similar to the wisdom writings of Mesopotamia, the Akkadian *Poem of the Righteous Sufferer* (fourteenth century BCE) and the *Acrostic Dialogue on Theodicy* (ninth century BCE). It even recalls the Egyptian *Dialogue of the Man Weary of Life and His Soul.* The poet of *Job* may have borrowed the genre, but his ideas were strikingly original.

The Triumph of Faith over Moralism. The Jobian poet did not attempt to solve the problem of the existence of evil. He used the scandal of undeserved suffering as a starting point for an exploration of the nature of faith. The antique folk tale offered him the clue for positing the problem. "Is it for nothing that Job fears God?" (*Jb.* 1:9). The folk tale argued against the idea of a religion in which moral achievement is always rewarded. Virtue and devotion do not always find their recompense. Nevertheless, the end of the story superficially upheld the dogma of retribution outlined in *Deuteronomy* 12–26 (promulgated by Josiah in 621 BCE), but it may well have been originally a parable of divine grace. Realities of history had dashed the hopes of the poet's audience. Deprived of land, Temple, and monarch, they doubted the power of their God. Some of them asked, "How shall we live?"

The poet of *Job* presents a man of unassailable piety who has lost everything. In his agony, the hero comes close to blasphemy. He accuses the deity of injustice, capriciousness, and even sadism. He compares God to some brute who elbows him into the refuse-filled ditch or to a soldier who kills for pleasure. He knows that the prayers of the dying and the cries of infants remain unanswered. He does not beg for the healing of his disease, the restoration of his wealth, or the gift of posterity. His sole plea is for the divine recognition of his innocence and the renewal of his honor in the midst of his community.

The poet also portrays Job as an exemplar of hubris. Job's trust in divine omnipotence is so unshakable that he feels himself to be the special target of divine enmity, just as the sea serpent is (*Jb.* 7:12). The intensity of pain causes in him a spiritual deterioration that Eliphaz recognizes when he queries, "Are you Adam, the first man? Were you brought forth before the hills?" (*Jb.* 15:7).

The characters of the three friends remain static throughout the three cycles. Dogmatic and doctrinaire, they are sure that Job is guilty of a secret crime. On the contrary, the character of the sufferer slowly develops, with moments of progress and regress, from despair to some form of obscure hope. First, he says, with a touch of dark humor, that his divine murderer will miss him after he has ceased "to be" (*Jb.* 7:21). Second, he wishes, but only for an instant, that a go-between might bring God and him together for a meeting face to face (*Jb.* 9:33). Third, he expects that after his death a heavenly witness will testify on his behalf (*Jb.* 16:19). Fourth, he passes from expectation to certainty when he affirms that his redeemer or avenger *(go'ali)*—a heavenly intermediary?—will stand over the dust of his grave and that "within [his] flesh" he will at last see God (*Jb.* 19:25–26). This controversial passage in Jerome's Latin translation was understood as a prediction of the resurrection of the dead. The poet merely used the metaphor of "flesh" to indicate that after his death Job was assured of being a fully responsible person, claiming direct access to the divine presence.

From Pride to Self-Gift. It has often been said that the questions hurled at Job by Yahveh from the whirlwind amount to a cruel display of omnipotence. This charge would be legitimate had Job in the poem remained the humble and patient man of the prologue. The man in revolt, however, seeks to condemn God in order to force an acquittal and obtain the recognition of his righteousness (*Jb.* 40:8). He renounces his claims only after he is permitted to discern that the Sovereign of nature had his own problems with the forces of cosmic evil. He does not "repent" *(shuv)* of crimes he has not committed (as the traditional translators erroneously put it), but he utterly grieves (*niḥamti; Jb.* 42:6). Job's guilt is that of a titanic arrogance. He erected himself the judge of deity. The poet intended to disengage the freedom of God from human manipulation, either by cultic rite or moral rectitude. For him, religion is not a technique for happiness but the offering of the self to the faithful Creator.

Job in the Jewish and Christian Traditions. The figure of the righteous sufferer is found elsewhere in the biblical literature but with significant differences. In *Psalms,* lamenters passionately plead for deliverance but are not specifically concerned with their honor, as Job is. In Second Isaiah, the suffering servant of Yahveh stands for the remnant of Israel atoning for the sins of the nations.

The chief Greek version of *Job* (in the Septuagint) paraphrases, softens, and considerably shortens the Hebrew original. In spite of the clear teaching of the poem, rabbis and church fathers have presented Job as a paragon of humble endurance under stress. The frescoes of the Roman catacombs picture him as a prototype of Jesus. The *Moralia* of Gregory I (sixth century) represents him as a paradigm of piety. The Middle Ages were hardly acquainted with the biblical book but read widely an apocryphal *Testament of Job* that is filled with fanciful adventures and portrays the hero as a king of Egypt. After the Crusades, Job became the favorite protector of lepers. In the sixteenth century, "Monsignor Job" was the intercessor for syphilitics. In Flanders, he appeared on many altars as the patron saint of musical guilds. Contemporary secularism hails him as a type of defiance in a meaningless universe. Jewish and Christian thinkers salute him as a theological fighter and a nonconformist seeker of truth.

[*For further discussion of Jewish and Christian approaches to the theological issues raised in* Job, *see* Suffering. *See also* Wisdom Literature, *article on* Biblical Books.]

BIBLIOGRAPHY

Hundreds of books and articles on *Job* have appeared in the twentieth century alone. The following list suggests contemporary trends.

Crenshaw, James L., ed. *Theodicy in the Old Testament.* Philadelphia, 1983. An incisive treatment of the problem of evil in Israelite and early Jewish wisdom literature.

Gammie, John G. "Behemoth and Leviathan: On the Didactic and Theological Significance of Job 40:15–41:26." In *Israelite Wisdom,* edited by John G. Gammie et al., pp. 217–231. Missoula, Mont., 1978. A valuable and original contribution.

Gordis, Robert. *The Book of God and Man.* Chicago, 1965. A study of *Job.*

Gordis, Robert. *The Book of Job: A Commentary, New Translation and Special Studies.* New York, 1981. Elucidation of many obscure passages on the basis of conjectural emendations.

Pope, Marvin H. *Job: Introduction, Translation, and Notes.* Anchor Bible, vol. 15. Rev. ed. Garden City, N.Y., 1973.

Rad, Gerhard von. *Weisheit in Israel.* Neukirchen-Vluyn, 1970. Translated by James D. Martin as *Wisdom in Israel* (Nashville, 1972); see pages 206–226.

Sarna, Nahum M. "Epic Substratum in the Prose of Job." *Journal of Biblical Literature* 76 (1957); 13–25. Analysis of the folk tale.

Terrien, Samuel. "Job: Introduction and Exegesis." In *The Interpreter's Bible,* vol. 3, pp. 877–1198. New York, 1954.

Terrien, Samuel. *Job: Poet of Existence.* New York, 1958. A popular treatment of Job and modern literature.

Terrien, Samuel. *Job: Commentaire de l'Ancient Testament.* Neuchâtel, 1963. A new French translation with strophic structure.

Terrien, Samuel. "Le poème de Job: Drame para-rituel du Nouvel-An?" *Supplement to Vetus Testamentum* 17 (1968): 220–235. An attempt to discover the historical occasion of the poem.

Tsevat, Matitiahu. *The Meaning of Job and Other Biblical Studies: Essays on the Literature and Religion of the Hebrew Bible.* New York, 1981.

Westermann, Claus. *Der Aufbau des Buches Hiob.* Stuttgart, 1977. Translated by Charles A. Muenchow as *The Structure of the Book of Job: A Form-Critical Analysis* (Philadelphia, 1981).

SAMUEL TERRIEN

JŌDO SHINSHŪ.

The Jōdo Shinshū, or True Pure Land Sect, is a school of Japanese Buddhism that takes as its central religious message the assurance of salvation granted to all beings by the Buddha Amida (Skt., Amitābha). Its founder, Shinran (1173–1262), a disciple of the eminent Japanese monk Hōnen (1133–1212), founder of the Jōdoshū (Pure Land Sect), stands in a line of Buddhist thinkers who emphasize faith in the salvific power of Amitābha and the hope of rebirth in his Pure Land, a paradisical realm created out of the boundless religious merit generated by Amitābha's fulfillment of a series of vows taken eons ago while still the *bodhisattva* Dharmākara. Jōdo Shinshū, or Shinshū as it is often called, is but one of a number of "Pure Land" traditions in East Asia, and is today the largest of the denominations of Japanese Buddhism.

Pure Land devotionalism is a perennial element in both Chinese and Japanese Buddhism. Beginning nominally with the visualization cult of Amitābha inaugurated in the year 403 by the Chinese monk Hui-yüan, Pure Land practices have served as adjuncts to the teachings of a variety of East Asian Buddhist traditions and, from the sixth century, as the foundation of several religious movements devoted more or less exclusively to the worship of Amitābha. [*See the biography of Hui-yüan.*] These movements combine faith in the power of Amitābha with the practice of the Nembutsu, which various schools interpret in differing ways but that in general consists now of the formulaic recitation of the name of Amitābha. Although standing firmly within the Pure Land tradition of its Chinese and Japanese antecedents, Jōdo Shinshū is conspicuous in the interpretation it gives to Nembutsu practice and to the assurances of salvation found in the vows of Amitābha.

Texts. Like all Pure Land traditions, the core texts of the Shinshū are a cycle of scriptures originating in northwest India and, perhaps, Buddhist Central Asia, that detail the spiritual career of Amitābha, the glories of Sukhāvatī ("land of ease," i.e., the Pure Land) created by him, the vows he has undertaken for the salvation of all beings, or certain meditative techniques that the devotee can undertake in order to visualize Amitābha and his Pure Land. Although the texts of the so-called "triple Pure Land scripture" began as individual works (the visualization scripture appears of widely different provenance than the other two), the three Pure Land *sūtras* are considered by the Japanese to preach a wholly consistent religious message. These texts are the *Larger Sukhāvatīvyūha Sūtra* (Jpn., *Muryōjukyō;* T.D. no. 363), the *Smaller Sukhāvatīvyūha Sūtra* (Jpn., *Amidakyō;* T.D. no. 366), and a text no longer extant in Sanskrit, known in Japanese as the *Kanmuryōjukyō* (T.D. no. 365). The first and second contain elements of the mythic cycle of Amitābha; the third is a meditation scripture. Also important to Shinshū thought is the work of one of the patriarchal figures of Chinese Pure Land Buddhism, the *Wang-sheng lun-chu* (Jpn., *Ōjōronchū;* T.D. no. 1819) of T'an-luan (476–542). This text was held in great esteem by Shinran, who relied upon it in the composition of the founding document of the Jōdo Shinshū, the *Kyōgyōshinshō* (Teaching, Practice, Faith, and Enlightenment). [*See the biography of T'an-luan.*]

Shinran. At the age of nine Shinran began his formal Buddhist training at the Tendai center on Mount Hiei. He remained there as a monk in the Jōgyōzammaidō for almost twenty years. At the age of twenty-nine, unable to attain peace of mind, Shinran decided to leave Hiei for Kyoto, where he became a disciple of Hōnen (1201). Despite, or perhaps owing to, the popularity of Nembutsu practices among the common people, monks from the established, traditional Buddhist sects began to denounce and censure Hōnen's Jōdoshū doctrines. This, coupled with certain improprieties of several of Hōnen's disciples, led to the official prohibition of Nembutsu Buddhism and the banishment of Hōnen and his main disciples from Kyoto. Shinran was defrocked and exiled to Echigo (in present-day Niigata Prefecture) in 1207. During his years in exile Shinran lived as a layman—he took the humble name Gutoku ("old fool"), married, and raised a family. It was this experience that led Shinran to realize that enlightenment and rebirth in the Pure Land were not contingent on adherence to the monastic precepts, the study of scriptures and doctrine, or the severance of worldly ties. Shinran used his own experience as a model for the religious life, holding that salvation could be attained in this world and this life in the midst of one's common, daily activities. In this way, Shinran extended Hōnen's notions of universal salvation and completed Pure Land's transformation of Buddhism from a "religion of renunciation" to a "household religion." [*See the biography of Hōnen.*]

The year 1211 saw Shinran officially pardoned. Thereafter, he lived with his family in the Kantō region, where he began proselytizing his new understanding of Pure Land doctrines. He attracted large numbers of followers—some estimate ten thousand—some of whom were instrumental in establishing and maintaining Shinshū centers after Shinran's death. During the period between 1235, when he returned to Kyoto, and his death Shinran was most prolific. It was during this period that he completed and revised the *Kyōgyōshinshō,* his most important work on Jōdo Shinshū doctrine. In this work Shinran traced the tradition of Pure Land teachings by collecting passages from scriptures and earlier commentaries, to which he added his own interpretations. The *Kyōgyōshinshō* represents an attempt by Shinran to lend legitimacy and orthodoxy to Shinshū teachings by establishing its affiliation with traditionally accepted authorities, an attempt necessitated by the virulent criticisms of the Jōdoshū by the monks of other Buddhist sects. Other of his works written during this period were intended to systematize his teachings for the guidance of his disciples and to settle the numerous small feuds among his followers in the Kantō region.

True Pure Land Doctrine. In his religious thought Shinran was influenced by Hōnen's division of Buddhist practices into two paths leading to enlightenment: the *shōdōmon* ("path of sages"), that is, the difficult path wherein enlightenment is dependent on the individual's "own power" *(jiriki)* and capability to adhere to the monastic precepts and to engage in arduous meditative practices and study; and the *jōdomon* ("path of Pure Land"), or the easy path in which one depends on "other power" *(tariki),* namely, the salvific power of Amida. Like Hōnen, Shinran held that during *mappō* (the "latter days of the Law"; i.e., an age of widespread degeneration and decadence) traditional Buddhist practices were all but useless for the attainment of enlightenment. In such an age, he claimed, faith in Amida and in the truth of his "original vow" *(hongan)* to save all sentient beings was the only path to salvation and rebirth in the Pure Land. As opposed to earlier forms of Buddhist practice, which uphold the path of wisdom *(prajñā),* meditation *(dhyāna),* and disciplined austerities *(śīla),* and are based on unlimited self-reliance, Pure Land practices provide a way to salvation in the face of the ineffectiveness of self-effort.

Struck by the very limitations of human capabilities and the inherent sinfulness of human nature, Shinran took Hōnen's advocacy of faith in Amida to an even greater degree. While Hōnen held that the individual must "choose" to have faith in Amida and that this choice must be continually reaffirmed through repeated invocations of the Nembutsu, Shinran argued that it was Amida who chose to save all humans. According to Shinran, what effectuates Amida's salvific power is the power of his Original Vow to save all beings as embodied in the Nembutsu. By participating in and allowing oneself to be permeated by this power, one transcends the world of causal necessity *(karman).* Implicit in the Pure Land teachings concerning the power of the Original Vow is the belief that, even if the escape from this world of *saṃsāra* (the round of birth and death of unenlightened existence) is possible through inspired insight alone, the ground of the possibility of that insight depends in turn on something higher or deeper than mere human insight: the divine power (Skt., *adhiṣṭhāna)* of the Buddha. This divine power of the Buddha does not lie merely within his human career and character; it transcends his individual personhood, breaking through the limited framework of time and space to embrace all living beings eternally and without limitation. This interpretation of faith led Shinran to reevaluate Hōnen's use of Nembutsu invocation. Like Hōnen, Shinran believed that the only means to apprehend Amida and to participate in his Original Vow was to invoke his name. By intoning the Nembutsu ("Namu Amida Butsu," or "Adoration be to Amida Buddha"), one accumulates boundless stores of merit and virtue. The necessary requisite is, of course, faith. Hōnen held that repeated invocations of the Nembutsu were necessary to build faith and to ensure rebirth in the Pure Land. Shinran, however, argued that one's practice must *begin* with faith. In any single invocation the devotee must direct his thoughts to the origins of that practice, that is, to faith in Amida's Original Vow. As such, the invocation of the Nembutsu is an expression of gratitude to Amida for being allowed to participate in the salvation promised by his vows. Yet Shinran did not deny the value of repeated invocations, for, although not leading directly to faith, the repeated invocation has the valuable function of awakening one's heart to Amida's existence. In this way, Nembutsu practice and faith come to be two sides of the same coin, with Shinshū emphasizing the moment of salvation and Jōdoshū stressing the process of arriving there. [*See the biography of Shinran.*]

Institutionalization and Subsequent History. After Shinran's death his tomb became the center of his movement's religious activities. Ten years later his youngest daughter, Kakushinni, built a mausoleum in the Higashiyama Ōtani area east of Kyoto in which she enshrined an image of Shinran and his ashes. In presenting the mausoleum and its grounds to her father's disciples, Kakushinni stipulated that the maintenance of the temple and the direction of the religious services held there were to be provided by Kakushinni and her descendants in perpetuity. While this marked the origin of the unique Jōdo Shinshū practice of hereditary succession, at the time it was not interpreted by Shinran's disciples as a move toward increasing authoritarian control over the movement. During this period the movement had still not been formally organized into a sect with a central temple under a single leader. Shinran himself had preferred to establish small, informal meeting places *(dōjō)* in the homes of his disciples, around which communities of followers *(monto)* could gather. Indeed, Shinran had no intention of becoming the founder of a new sect or religion. He considered himself the true successor to Hōnen's teaching and continued to think of his movement as part of the Jōdoshū. For this reason, there was a time when the disciples of Hōnen and those of Shinran, both claiming to represent the "true" Pure Land teachings, quarreled over the right to use the name Jōdo Shinshū. It was only in relatively recent times—in 1872—that this conflict was at last resolved and the name Jōdo Shinshū reserved for the groups stemming from Shinran. (Naturally, Shinshū adherents regard Hōnen as a patriarchal figure in his own right in the lineage of Pure Land teachers.) Prior to that date, Jōdo Shinshū was more commonly known as the Ikkōshū or the Montoshū. In the Kantō region, the *monto* evolved into large local organizations headed by the most powerful of Shinran's disciples. These groups took their names from the territories in which they were located and, for the most part, remained organizationally unrelated to other such groups.

After Kakushinni's death her son Kakunyo succeeded to the directorship of Shinran's mausoleum. His greatest wish was to consolidate and organize the various regional groups into a unified sect centered around the mausoleum. Toward this end, he transformed the mausoleum into a temple, naming it the Honganji (Original Vow Temple) and attempted to draw the local *monto* into the organization as branch temples. Kakunyo's efforts mark the establishment of the Jōdo Shinshū as a single, centralized organization. In 1332 the Honganji received official recognition as the central temple of the Shinshū movement. The government, however, still considered it an affiliate of the Tendai school. Kakunyo's plans met with resistance from the various local groups and movements, particularly in the Kantō. Many leaders began to erect temples and establish their own regionally based sects. As a result, numerous subsects of Jōdo Shinshū were founded throughout the country.

Although the Honganji continued to thrive, it was not without its problems. In 1456 the Honganji complex was burned to the ground by Tendai monks from Mount Hiei. This was not too serious a setback, for the Honganji had numerous affiliated congregations and temples throughout the country. However, the eighth successor to the head of the temple, Rennyo (1415–1499), was forced to move and ultimately established Shinshū headquarters in the Yamashina district of Kyoto. In the interim, Rennyo's determination to sever all ties with Tendai—he destroyed Tendai scriptures, scrolls, and images in his temples—and his plans to expand and strengthen the Shinshū organization aroused the anger of various Buddhist sects and local feudal lords *(daimyō)*. The numerous attacks suffered by Rennyo and his followers at the hands of these detractors, led them to form an alliance with local peasants and samurai. During the Ōnin war such groups led armed uprisings known as *ikkō ikki* in an effort to protect their land holdings from the powerful daimyo. It was during this period that Jōdo Shinshū gained widespread acceptance and popularity among the masses. The success of his armed uprisings acquired for Rennyo the title "saint of the restoration of the Honganji." [*See the biography of Rennyo.*]

The attacks against Shinshū followers continued throughout the Muromachi period. When the Honganji was again burned, this time by Nichiren monks, the tenth successor, Shōnyō, rebuilt the temple in the Ishiyama district of Osaka. It was under Shōnyō's leadership that membership in Shinshū began to spread beyond the peasant masses. The daimyo, recognizing both the potential of the armed peasant uprisings and the power of their affiliation with Shinshū, began to join the sect. When the eleventh successor to the Honganji, Kennyo, became the abbot of the temple, the sect was politically and militarily as powerful as any of the major aristocratic and military families in Japan. Shinshū's strength posed a serious threat to several of the contending military rulers, and in 1570 the powerful daimyo Oda Nobunaga attacked the Honganji. The temple, supported by peasant groups, samurai, and local daimyo, was able to ward off Nobunaga's troops for ten years. In 1580 the Honganji was forced to surrender, and Kennyo fled to Kii Province. This siege marks both the height of Shinshū's power and the beginning of its decline. It also marks the end of the sect's involvement in armed peasant uprisings.

After Kennyo's death a dispute over succession divided and further weakened the Honganji. Two branches were formed: the Western Honganji (Honpa Honganji), led by Kennyo's second son, Junnyo, and the Eastern Honganji (Ōtani Honganji), led by his eldest son, Kyōnyo. Both established their temple headquarters in Kyoto. It should be noted that the establishment of sects within the Jōdo Shinshū, from the earliest divisions during Kakunyo's leadership until the schism between Kennyo's sons, were all the result of factional, political, and succession disputes, and personality differences. Thus, there are few discernible differences in doctrine and practice among the various sects.

The major sects of today's Jōdo Shinshū religion were established between the latter part of the Kamakura period and the beginning of the Tokugawa. Today there are ten sects, of which the Eastern and Western Honganji sects are the most influential, each outnumbering the combined membership of all the smaller sects. These smaller sects include the Takada, Bukkōji, Sanmonto, Kibe, Yamamoto, Koshōji, Joshoji, and Izumoji groups. The practice of handing down the leadership of temples through family lines is upheld by all sects. The leaders of the Honganji sects claim descent from Shinran, and the leaders of the other sects trace descent to Shinran's direct disciples. In the post–World War II era the Honganji sects have undertaken foreign missionary activity, opening temples in Hawaii, North and South America, and elsewhere in countries with large Japanese populations. In 1983 the Shinshū movement claimed over thirteen million adherents, forty thousand priests, and twenty-one thousand temples throughout the world.

[*For an overview of Amida pietism, including a précis of Amida's spiritual career, see* Amitābha. *The* mappō *eschatology is discussed in* Mappō. *For a survey of the antecedents of Shinshū thought, see* Ching-t'u *and* Jōdoshū. *Pure Land devotional practices are discussed in* Nien-fo *as well as in* Worship and Cultic Life, *article on* Buddhist Cultic Life in East Asia. *See also* Pure and Impure Lands.]

BIBLIOGRAPHY

The most accessible works in English describing the history and thought of the Shinshū are D. T. Suzuki's *Collected Writings on Shin Buddhism* (Kyoto, 1973) and his *Shin Buddhism* (New York, 1970). Shinshū ideas presented in these works are skewed somewhat by Suzuki's own idiosyncratic interpretation of Pure Land doctrine. His earlier work in Japanese, *Jōdokei shisōron* (Kyoto, 1948), presents an easily understandable account of Jōdo Shinshū thought within the larger Pure Land tradition. English translations of Shinshū scriptures and texts are available in *The Shinshū Seiten*, 2d rev. ed., edited by Kōshō Yamamoto (San Francisco, 1978); in *The Kyō Gyō Shin Shō*, translated by Hisao Inagaki, Kōshō Yukawa, and Thomas R. Okano (Kyoto, 1966); and in the *Shin Buddhism Translation Series* (Kyoto, 1978–).

Many more sources on the Shinshū are published in Japanese. For example, good accounts of Shinshū history can be found in Inoue Toshio's *Honganji* (Tokyo, 1962); in *Shinshūshi gaisetsu*, edited by Akamatsu Toshihide and Kasahara Kazuo (Kyoto, 1963); and in *Honganjishi*, 3 vols., edited by the Honganji Shiryō Kenkyūjo (Kyoto, 1961–1969). A good treatment of the historical evolution of Jōdo Shinshū can be found in Akamatsu Toshihide's *Kamakura bukkyō no kenkyū* (Kyoto, 1957). *Shinshū nempyō*, edited by Ōtani Daigaku (Kyoto, 1973), provides a convenient one-volume chronology of Shinshū history. Hayashima Kyōsei's *Ningen no negai: Muryōjukyō* (Tokyo, 1955) presents a straightforward commentary on the central scripture of Pure Land Buddhism, the *Daimuryōjukyō*.

The most widely cited collection of Shinshū scriptures and texts is *Shinshū shōgyō zensho*, 5 vols., 2d rev. ed., edited by the Shinshū Shōgyō Zensho Hensanjo (Kyoto, 1981–1984). Particularly useful commentaries on Shinran's central work, the *Kyōgyōshinshō*, include Yamabe Shūkaku and Akanuma Chizen's *Kyōgyōshinshō kōgi* (Kyoto, 1928); Takeuchi Yoshinori's *Kyōgyōshinshō no tetsugaku* (Tokyo, 1931); and Kaneko Taiei's *Kyōgyōshinshō sōsetsu* (Kyoto, 1959). Soga Ryōjin's *Tannishō chōki* (Kyoto, 1961) is an outstanding exposition on the *Tannishō*. General outlines of Shinshū doctrine are available in Fu-gen Daien's *Shinshū gairon* (Kyoto, 1950) and in *Shinshū gaiyō,* edited by the Kyōka Kenkyūjo (Kyoto, 1953). More extensive discussions of Shinshū thought and development are found in Ishida Mitsuyuki's *Shinran kyōgaku no kisoteki kenkyū,* 2 vols. (Kyoto, 1970–1977). Concerning the religious organization of Jōdo Shinshū, see Uehara Senroku and Matsugi Nobuhiko's *Honganji kyōdan* (Tokyo, 1971). The most detailed reference work on Jōdo Shinshū is *Shinshū daijiten,* 3 vols., edited by Okamura Shūsatsu (Kyoto, 1935–1937).

HASE SHŌTŌ
Translated from Japanese by Carl Becker

JŌDOSHŪ. The Jōdoshū, or Pure Land Sect, is a school of Japanese Buddhism founded in the twelfth century by the monk Hōnen (1133–1212), who took as the centerpiece of his religious teaching sole reliance on the power of the Buddha Amida (Skt., Amitābha) to save all beings. The Jōdoshū was the first of a series of independent Pure Land traditions to flourish in Japan, and continues to this day as a major force in the religion and culture of the nation.

In both China and Japan, Pure Land (Chin., *ching-t'u;* Jpn., *jōdo*) practices and doctrines existed both as adjuncts to the teachings of most Buddhist sects and as independent traditions in their own right. Pure Land devotion emphasized faith in the salvific power of Amida, the desirability of attaining rebirth in his Pure Land, Sukhāvatī ("land of bliss"), and the efficacy of *nembutsu* practices (i.e., the recitation of the name of, or meditation on, Amida Buddha) for attaining salvation. For the precursors of the Jōdoshū, including Eikū, Ryōnin, and Genshin (942–1017), *nembutsu* meditation (Jpn., *nembutsu zammai*) involved the invocation of Amida's name while visualizing his body and circumambulating his image. Some, like Genshin, also advocated the practice of invoking Amida's name while engaging in the accompanying meditative exercise. [*See the biography of Genshin.*] While *nembutsu* meditation and invocation (although the latter was considered an inferior practice) were practiced by many monks of the Tendai sect, they were regarded at best as complements to other established practices. It was not until the Kamakura period (1192–1336), when Hōnen founded the Jōdoshū, that the invocation of the Nembutsu (here conceived as the formulaic recitation of the name of Amida) became the sole practice advocated by a sect as the superior method of attaining salvation.

Basic Texts. Pure Land practices are founded upon a cycle of texts that emphasize either a technique of visualizing Amitābha and his Pure Land or that outline Amitābha's spiritual career, his vows to create a haven for suffering sentient beings, and the methods for winning rebirth there. A scripture of the first type, the *Pratyutpannasamādhi Sūtra,* was translated into Chinese as early as 179 CE and became the basis for the early Chinese worship of Amitābha on Mount Lu under the direction of the famous literatus-monk Hui-yüan (334–416). [*See the biography of Hui-yüan.*] By the fifth century another "meditation" scripture, the *Kuan wu-liang-shou-fo ching* (Skt., *Amitāyurdhyāna Sūtra**; T.D. no. 365) was also available in Chinese. Unlike the aforementioned *Pratyutpanna Sūtra,* which has as its aim the bringing into one's presence in meditation the "Buddhas of the ten directions," this text was devoted exclusively to meditation on Amitābha and his Pure Land. Techniques advocated in both of these texts were introduced to Japan principally through the T'ien-t'ai (Jpn., Tendai) system of meditation formulated by the Chinese monk Chih-i (538–597). [*See* Meditation, *article on* Buddhist Meditation, *and the biography of Chih-i.*] The scriptures of the latter type, those having to do with Amitābha's spiritual career and the glories of Pure Land, are two in number: the "larger" *Sukhāvatīvyūha Sūtra,* translated as many as five times into Chinese but known best to the Pure Land schools through Buddhabhadra's fifth century translation (traditionally attributed to Saṃghavarman), the *Wu-liang-shou ching* (T.D. no. 363), and the "shorter" *Sukhāvatīvyūha Sūtra,* first translated into Chinese as the *O-mi-t'o-fo ching* (T.D. no. 366) by Kumārajīva (343–413). The *Kuan-ching,* known in Japanese as the *Kanmuryōjukyō,* and the *Larger* and *Smaller Sukhāvatīvyūha Sūtras,* known as the *Muryōjukyō* and the *Amidakyō,* respectively, together constitute the "triple Pure Land scripture," the core *sūtra* literature of the Chinese and Japanese Pure Land traditions.

The teachings of the Jōdo sect (and of its sister school, the Jōdo Shinshū) also draw their inspiration from the *Sukhāvatīvyūhopadeśa** (Chin., *Wu-liang-shou ching yu-p'o-t'i-che yüan-sheng chi;* T.D. no. 1524), a collection of hymns *(gāthā),* with autocommentary, on Pure Land topics by the eminent Indian *ācārya* Vasubandhu. The *Ōjōron,* as this text was known in Japan, was usually read in conjunction with the *Wang-sheng lun-chu* (Jpn., *Ōjōronchū;* T.D. no. 1819), a commentary on Vasubandhu's work by the Chinese Pure Land thinker T'an-luan (476–542). [*See the biography of T'an-luan.*] T'an-luan's commentary opens with reference to an "easy path to salvation" (Jpn., *igyōdō*) suitable to an era of the "five corruptions." This doctrine of an "easy path," worship of the Buddha rather than the more traditional practices of mental cultivation, T'an-luan attributes to Nāgārjuna, the Mādhyamika thinker and alleged author of a treatise on Pure Land. [*See the biography of Nāgārjuna.*]

The Life and Thought of Hōnen. Hōnen began his formal Buddhist training at the Tendai center on Mount Hiei, where he was ordained at the age of fourteen. Three years later, discouraged by the decadent and somewhat militaristic behavior of his fellow monks, Hōnen went to Kurodani to study under Eikū, a charismatic proponent of Pure Land devotion. For the next twenty-five years Hōnen studied Pure Land texts and practiced *nembutsu zammai* as advocated by Eikū, in accordance with Genshin's *Ōjōyōshū* (Essentials of Pure Land Rebirth). During this period Hōnen also studied the doctrines, scriptures, and practices of the six Buddhist sects of the Nara period, Shingon (Vajrayāna), and Zen. Hōnen became convinced that Japan had entered the age, foretold in scripture, of *mappō* (the "latter days of the Law"), a period when Buddhist teachings had so degenerated that the attainment of salvation by one's own efforts was deemed all but impossible. In 1175, while reading the great Chinese Pure Land master Shan-tao's commentary on the *Kanmuryōjukyō,* Hōnen had a realization that the only path to salvation was to declare one's absolute faith in Amida's vow to save all sentient beings and to engage in "single-practice *nembutsu" (senju nembutsu),* which for Hōnen meant placing sole reliance on the invocation of Amida Buddha's name as a means to salvation. [*See the biography of Shan-tao.*] That year Hōnen left Kurodani for Kyoto, where he began to disseminate his teachings. This move marks the founding of Jōdoshū.

In 1197 at the request of the prime minister, Kujō Kanezane (1149–1207), Hōnen wrote his influential *Senchaku hongan nembutsushū* (Collection of Passages on the Original Vow of Amida in Which Nembutsu Is Chosen above All). This work establishes Hōnen's essential teachings as the foundation of the Jōdo sect. Following Tao-ch'o (542–645), another Chinese Pure Land master, Hōnen divided Buddhist teachings into two paths, the *shōdōmon* ("gate of the sages") and the *jōdomon* ("gate of Pure Land"). Because it advocates reliance on one's own power and capabilities *(jiriki)* to attain salvation, Hōnen characterized the *shōdōmon* as the more difficult path. He argued that during *mappō* few people were able to attain rebirth in the Pure Land through the arduous practices of traditional Buddhism (e.g., adherence to the Vinaya, meditation, and study). Instead, he considered the *jōdomon* as the easy path to salvation. Owing to its complete reliance on "other power" (*tariki;* i.e., dependence on Amida's saving grace), the *jōdomon* is open to all people, masses and aristocracy alike. Hōnen argued that to be saved one need only make the "choice" *(senchaku)* to place absolute faith and trust in Amida's vow. In discussing Other Power and Self Power Hōnen agreed with T'an-luan, who asserted that during this degenerate era reliance on Other Power is the easy but nevertheless superior path to salvation. However, he disagreed with T'an-luan's characterization of diverse Buddhist practices as reliance on Other Power. For Hōnen, the only practice representing faith in Amida's grace was the invocation of Amida's name.

In addition to outlining these larger doctrinal issues, Hōnen discussed the need to repeat the invocation over a prolonged period of time. Constant repetition of the Nembutsu, he held, ensures the continual purification of one's mind and body and the dissolution of doubt. Moreover, it leads to a moment of awakening *(satori)* in this lifetime and, eventually, to rebirth in the Pure Land. To those detractors who argued that repeated recitations signified reliance on Self Power Hōnen answered that the necessary requisite of each invocation was the proper concentration and sincerity of the mind that comes only from absolute faith in Amida's salvific power. However, he never fully explicated the relation between faith, the Nembutsu, and Other Power.

Because of its appeal to members of all social classes, Hōnen's school soon gained widespread popularity. The monks of the established Buddhist sects, threatened by this popularity, sent a petition to the government charging the monks of the Jōdo sect with breaking the Vinaya precepts. In 1204 Hōnen, along with his main disciples, was compelled to compose and sign a seven-article pledge that would act as a guideline for his conduct. This quieted his enemies until 1205, when another petition was presented to the retired emperor, Go Toba, calling for the prohibition of *senju nembutsu.* In 1206 the situation was further aggravated when two of Hōnen's disciples were accused of attracting the attention of two court ladies while the emperor was absent from Kyoto. The Emperor thereupon banned the teachings of the Jōdo sect and exiled Hōnen and most of his main disciples. Five years later Hōnen was pardoned and returned to Kyoto, where he died in 1212. [*See the biography of Hōnen.*]

Early Schisms. After Hōnen's death his disciples were unanimous in calling for faith in Amida's vow and in promoting the invocation of the Nembutsu as a valuable practice for attaining rebirth in the Pure Land. However, they were left to grapple with many of the doctrinal and methodological issues that remained ambiguous in Hōnen's writings and in his way of life. As the debate over the correct interpretation of Self Power heightened, Hōnen's disciples became divided into two groups: those who moved toward the purest form of *senju nembutsu,* some of whom held that *ichinen* ("a single invocation") was sufficient for salvation, and those who compromised with other Buddhist sects, advocating the use of a variety of practices in conjunction with the Nembutsu. Benchō (1162–1238), considered the most orthodox of Hōnen's disciples, and Shōkū (1177–1247), who had helped compile the *Senchaku hongan nembutsushū*, both stressed the importance of repeated invocations of the Nembutsu, but disagreed on the value they accorded of other practices. The subsect founded by Benchō, the Chinzei-ha, advocated *senju nembutsu* and became the main school of Pure Land. Today, the Chinzei-ha is synonymous with Jōdoshū. Shōkū, on the other hand, in incorporating elements of Tendai and Esoteric Buddhism into his practice, argued that he was merely following the example of Hōnen, who engaged in meditative and ceremonial practices throughout his life. Because Shōkū was not an advocate of *senju nembutsu*, his sect, the Seizan-ha, was instrumental in gaining acceptance of Pure Land doctrines among other Buddhist schools. [*See the biographies of Shōkū and Benchō.*]

The debate among the second group of disciples centered on the question of the relative value of one invocation of the Nembutsu, performed with absolute faith and sincerity, over and against repeated and continual recitation. Ryūkan (1148–1227), founder of the Chōrakuji subsect, argued that prolonged recitation was required as a prelude to salvation, which was attained only at the time of death. During the fifteenth century his sect was absorbed into the Jishū. Kōsai (1163–1247), founder of the Ichinengi sect, was perhaps the most controversial of Hōnen's disciples. Kōsai held that the continual invocation of the Nembutsu was futile since salvation was attained in one moment only, that is, that rebirth in the Pure Land was assured at any moment that the Nembutsu was chanted. Because many of Kōsai's followers were accused of excessively amoral conduct the sect did not enjoy the favor of other Buddhist sects. After Kōsai's death the school declined and many of his followers became members of Shinran's Jōdo Shinshū (True Pure Land sect).

Another form of Pure Land devotion to develop during the Kamakura period is best exemplified by Ippen (1239–1289), founder of the Jishū (Time Sect). Ippen began his Pure Land training at the age of fourteen when he went to Daizaifu to study under the Seizan-ha teacher Shōtatsu. According to legend, while visiting the Kumano shrine in 1276 Ippen had a divine revelation in which a *kami* told him that it is Amida's enlightenment that determines mankind's salvation and that an individual's faith was, therefore, inconsequential. Thereafter, Ippen traveled through the country, handing out *nembutsu* tablets and performing *nembutsu* dances, obtaining for himself the name Yugyō Shōnin ("wandering sage"). Believing that Amida existed everywhere, Ippen's disciples did not associate themselves with a particular temple but rather followed Ippen's example by wandering through the countryside. For Ippen, the name Jishū implied that the practice (i.e., the Nembutsu) accorded with the age (the "time"), that is, that the Nembutsu was the only appropriate practice in an age of *mappō;* for his followers, however, it came to mean that Nembutsu was to be chanted at all time and in all places. [*See also the biography of Ippen.*] From its inception, the Jishū was an independent tradition, doctrinally related to, but unaffiliated with, the Seizan-ha.

Brief mention should be made of Shinran (1173–1262), founder of the Jōdo Shinshū, who considered himself the true successor to Hōnen's teachings. Shinran, however, rejected the Vinaya precepts (the code of monastic discipline), which the Jōdo sect had retained. Declaring himself "neither monk nor layman" he set an example for his disciples by marrying, eating meat, and otherwise living as a layman. While Shinran held that faith in Amida was an essential requisite for salvation, he also argued that such faith could not be ascribed to the individual's will but was entirely a result of Amida's grace as demonstrated by his vow to save all sentient beings. Unlike Hōnen, who claimed that one must make the "choice" to believe in Amida, Shinran was emphatic in stating that it is Amida who "chooses" all beings to be saved. Today, the Jōdo Shinshū is the largest Buddhist sect in Japan. [*See the biography of Shinran.*]

The Tokugawa, Meiji, and Modern Eras. During the Tokugawa period (1600–1867) Buddhism was particularly favored by the shoguns, who wished to minimize the influence of Christian missionaries. The Tokugawa rulers made Buddhism an integral part of the government organization, lavishly supporting the monks and temples of the established Buddhist sects. But the government also controlled ordinations, temple administration, and other activities, and prohibited sectarianism and factionalism. Thus, despite government patronage, Buddhism became spiritually stagnant. Within this context, the Jōdoshū was the personal favorite of the shoguns; the first shogun, Tokugawa Ieyasu, was a devotee of Jōdoshū, and his successors followed his example. The monks of the sect, however, indulged in this patronage and gradually became more corrupt and devoid of spiritual depth. Among the few who attempted to infuse new life into the Jōdoshū was Suzuki Shōsan (1579–1655), a practitioner of both Nembutsu and Zen. He combined Pure Land devotion and Zen notions of the value of work, teaching farmers that by reciting the Nembutsu while working in their fields they could sever their ties to earthly passions and ensure their attainment of the final awakening. Suzuki firmly believed that only by practicing in one's workplace could one attain salvation. [*See the biography of Suzuki Shōsan.*]

The Meiji era (1868–1912) saw a reversal in the government's attitude toward Buddhism. Shintō was adopted as the state religion, and Neo-Confucianism continued to hold strong influence over the state ideology. Without the revitalization and modernization of its doctrines and practices, the very survival of Buddhism was threatened. Two trends that developed in the Jōdo sect during the Meiji period still continue to exert an influence on Pure Land practice today. The first stressed the attainment of salvation through the personal religious experience of Nembutsu practice. A representative of this position was Yamazaki Bennei (1859–1920), founder of the Kōmyōkai, who advocated intensive recitation of Nembutsu to attain an awakening in this very life. The members of his sect gather to invoke the Nembutsu continually for a few days at a time. Owing to its promise of salvation in this world and during this lifetime, Kōmyōkai practices became popular among adherents of Jōdoshū. However, because it demanded that members devote extended periods of time to their practice, the movement proved ultimately not suited to the lives of most lay people. The second trend emphasized that salvation is attained through social action. Shiio Benkyō (1876–1971), founder of Kyōseikai and a leading scholar of Buddhism, advocated purification and salvation of the entire world rather than the individual's rebirth in the Pure Land. The members of this movement place little emphasis on personal religious experience and instead participate in social work and welfare activities.

In the 1980s the total number of Jōdoshū temples and nuneries is approximately seven thousand. The Jōdoshū supports two Buddhist universities, many women's colleges and high schools, and has established numerous houses for the aged and orphaned.

[*For an overview of Amida pietism, including a précis of Amida's spiritual career, see* Amitābha. *The* mappō *eschatology is discussed* in Mappō. *For a survey of the Chinese antecedents of Japanese Pure Land Buddhism, see* Ching-t'u. *Pure Land devotional practices are discussed in* Nien-fo *and* Worship and Cultic Life, *article on* Buddhist Cultic Life in East Asia. *See also* Jōdo Shinshū *and* Pure and Impure Lands.]

BIBLIOGRAPHY

Works in Japanese

Chionin Jōdo Shūgaku Kenkyūjo, eds. *Hōnen bukkyō no kenkyū.* Tokyo, 1975.

Chionin Jōdo Shūgaku Kenkyūjo, eds. *Jōdoshū no oshie: rekishi, shisō, kadai.* Tokyo, 1974.

Fujiyoshi Jikai, ed. *Jōdokyō ni okeru shūkyō taiken.* Kyoto, 1979.

Fujiyoshi Jikai. *Jōdokyō shisō no kenkyū.* Kyoto, 1983.

Hattori Eijun. *Jōdokyō shisōron.* Tokyo, 1974.

Katsuki Jōkō. *Hōnen jōdokyō no shisō to rekishi.* Tokyo, 1974.

Katsuki Jōkō, ed. *Jōdoshū kaisoku no kenkyū.* Kyoto, 1970.

Takahashi Kōji. *Hōnen jōdokyō no shomondai.* Tokyo, 1978.

Tamura Enchō. *Hōnen Shōnin den no kenkyū.* Kyoto, 1972.

Tōdō Kyōshun. *Hōnen Shōnin kenkyū.* Tokyo, 1983.

Tsuboi Shunei. *Hōnen jōdokyō no kenkyū.* Tokyo, 1982.

Works in English

Coates, Harper H., and Ishizuka Ryūgaku. *Hōnen, the Buddhist Saint.* 5 vols. Kyoto, 1949. An introduction to Hōnen's life and thought.

E. B. Cowell, et al., eds. *Buddhist Mahâyâna Texts* (1894). Sacred Books of the East, vol. 49. Reprint, New York, 1969. Includes English translations of the Pure Land scriptures.

Fujiyoshi Jikai

JOHANAN BAR NAPPAḤA. *See under* Yoḥanan bar Nappaḥa'.

JOHANAN BEN ZAKKAI. *See under* Yoḥanan ben Zakk'ai.

JOHN XXIII (Angelo Giuseppe Roncalli, 1881–1963), pope of the Roman Catholic church (1958–1963). Born in Sotto il Monte, near Bergamo in northern Italy, on 25 November 1881 to a family of sharecroppers, Roncalli attended the local grammar school, was taught Latin by the parish priest, and entered the minor seminary at age eleven. Given a scholarship to the Roman seminary (the Apollinare), he was ordained a priest on 10 August 1904, after completing a year of military service. The following year he obtained a doctorate in theology (with Don Eugenio Pacelli, the future pope Pius XII, on his examining board) and became secretary to the bishop of Bergamo, Giacomo Radini-Tedeschi, an ecclesiastical activist in the social, economic, and political movements of the area. Roncalli accompanied the bishop on his visitations in the diocese and on frequent visits to France, Milan, and Rome, and so became acquainted with influential ecclesiastics, including Archbishop Giacomo della Chiesa (the future Benedict XV) and Monsignor Achille Ratti (the future Pius XI). Despite these contacts, both the bishop and his secretary came under suspicion during the heresy hunt that was occasioned by Pope Pius X's condemnation of modernism in 1907. Gravely affected by the accusation, as pope Roncalli corrected the record of the incident in the Vatican archives. His own attitudes were revealed in his granting of total freedom of theological expression to the Second Vatican Council.

At the outbreak of World War I, Roncalli was inducted into the Italian army as a sergeant in the medical corps and served on the front at Piave and as a chaplain in the nearby military hospitals. On his return to Bergamo he was engaged in diocesan education until 1921, when he was called to Rome by Pope Benedict XV and instructed to coordinate the activities of the Society for the Propagation of the Faith, a funding organ for foreign missions. After visiting the dioceses of Italy, he was persuaded to transfer the organization's headquarters from Lyons, France, to Rome.

Consecrated a titular archbishop of Aeropolis, Palestine, in March 1925, Roncalli was sent to Bulgaria as apostolic visitor to confront the problems of the Latin and other Eastern Christian Catholics in conflict with the Orthodox church and the local government. Settling in Sofia, he visited Catholic centers, brought relief to political and religious refugees from Thrace and Macedonia, organized a congress of Bulgarian Catholics in Yambol in 1928, and in 1930 arranged the canonical dispensation for the marriage of King Boris of Bulgaria, an Eastern Orthodox, to Princess Giovanna of Savoy, a Roman Catholic. Despite guarantees to the contrary, the marriage was repeated in the Orthodox cathedral in Sofia and so put the papal envoy "in a most difficult position." Nevertheless, in 1931 he regularized his position as apostolic delegate, encouraged the use of Bulgarian in the Catholic schools and liturgy, and became a welcome guest at cultural, social, and political events in the nation's capital.

In 1934, as titular archbishop of Mesembria (Thrace), Roncalli was appointed apostolic delegate to Turkey and Greece with residence in Istanbul, a difficult assignment. He had to contend with the secularization policies of the Turkish president Kemal Atatürk (1923–1938), adopting civilian garb in public, and with the anti-Catholicism of the Orthodox clergy in Greece. While serving as parish priest for the small Catholic community in the Turkish metropolis, he visited the minute clusters of Catholics scattered throughout the country, called on the Orthodox patriarch Benjamin in the Phanar, the patriarchal residence in Istanbul, and introduced the use of Turkish in church publications and liturgy.

With the outbreak of World War II, Turkey became a center of political intrigue, and Roncalli, an intimate of the German ambassador Franz von Papen as well as of other diplomats, found himself a frequently consulted confidant, dispatching intelligence information to the Vatican. Aiding countless Jews and others fleeing persecution in central and eastern Europe, he established a unit of the Holy See's bureau for tracing missing persons, refugees, and prisoners of war. In 1942 he flew to Rome to urge Pius XII to persuade the British government to modify the blockade of Greece by allowing the import of food and medical supplies.

In December 1944 Roncalli was dispatched to France to replace Archbishop Valerio Valeri, the papal nuncio. On New Year's Day, as dean (ex officio) of the corps of ambassadors, he presented the ambassadorial body to the new French government of Charles de Gaulle. Together with reconciling the Catholic factions split by the resistance movement, he helped prevent the deposition of six or seven bishops accused of collaborating with the Pétain regime and initiated a renewal of the French episcopate, supporting Cardinal Suhard of Paris in his attempt to rechristianize the country with his Mission de France. He inaugurated a seminary for training German prisoners of war for the priesthood and did his best to mitigate the Vatican's condemnation of the worker-priest movement. Through Monsignor Giovanni Battista Montini in the Vatican, Roncalli persuaded the Holy See to establish a permanent observer to the United Nations Educational, Scientific, and Cultural Organization (UNESCO). He smoothed over the displacements caused by the publication of Pius XII's encyclical *Humani generis* (Of the Human Race; 1950), which was used to censure such theologians as Yves Congar, Jean Daniélou, M.-J. Chenu, and Henri de Lubac, all of whom, as pope, John was to welcome as experts to the Second Vatican Council. [*See also* Vatican Councils, *article on* Vatican II.]

Roncalli was created a cardinal in January 1953 and, following an ancient custom, received the red hat from the ruler of France, the Socialist president Vincent Auriol, before taking possession of the See of Venice as its patriarch. On his arrival in the City of the Doges, he assured the faithful that he had always wanted to function as a parish priest and would end his days among them. Visiting the parishes of the archdiocese, he frequently wrote exhortatory letters in support of the vigorous religious, social, and labor movements then in vogue. He downgraded the left-wing faction of the Christian Democratic party and its weekly publication, *Il popolo Veneto,* and in an episcopal letter of 1955 he opposed the party's policy of "opening to the left." Changing precedents set by his predecessor, however, he accepted the Biennial Arts Festival of 1956 and welcomed the Italian Socialist party's congress in 1957. That same year he had organized a diocesan synod and was correcting the proofs of its ordinances when he was called to Rome on 9 October 1958 upon the death of Pius XII.

On 28 October, the third day of the conclave, he was elected pope and supreme pastor of the Roman Catholic church. On accepting the election, he said that he would be called John XXIII and intended to imitate John the

Baptist in making straight the path of the Lord. Within a month he created twenty-three cardinals, including Archbishop Montini of Milan and Monsignor Domenico Tardini; the latter he appointed his secretary of state. In January, to the consternation of the cardinals of the papal Curia, he announced plans for convening an ecumenical council aimed at updating the church's image and achieving Christian unity. By way of preparation he held a synod in Rome in 1960 and appointed a commission for the revision of canon law and a committee to deal with the moral aspects of birth control.

In outlining plans for the ecumenical council, John declared that it would be the work of the bishops and would not be under the control of the Curia. Nevertheless he appointed Cardinal Tardini as coordinator of the preparatory commissions and allowed Cardinal Alfredo Ottaviani of the Holy Office to dominate their activities. Under their aegis, prelates and professors from the Roman ecclesiastical institutions prepared seventy-two *schemata*, or topics for discussion, bulging with textbook theology as an agenda for an assembly of over two thousand prelates that was to meet for one or two months. While saddened by the opposition of his curial advisers, John pushed ahead and in so doing gained the support of cardinals and prelates from the outside world, who at the council's start had reduced the number of *schemata* to seventeen.

In his opening address to the Second Vatican Council, on 11 October 1962, the pope said that the council had not been called to discuss the basic doctrines of the church; those were well known and defined. Instead, the assembly was aimed at restoring unity, first among Christians and then in the world. To do this the church would have to take a leap ahead *(balzo in avanti)* in penetrating the consciousness of contemporary men and women. While in the past, he asserted, the church had used severity in confronting error, now it was called upon to apply the medicine of mercy. Dismissing his opposition as "prophets of doom," John said that they knew no history. He insisted that "the truths of the deposit of faith are one thing; how they are expressed is another," and he said that the church had to restate its teaching in a medium that would employ the tools of modern scholarship and technology. Many of the prelatial listeners felt that the pope was close to heresy.

The council quickly took on a Johannine contour as it concentrated on updating the liturgy by introducing the vernacular languages for the celebration of the Mass and the sacraments; discussed the relationship between the Bible and tradition in formulating the church's teachings; and discussed the structure of the church itself and the way priests, the laity, nuns, and prelates were to conduct themselves in the contemporary world. Listening to the discussions on closed-circuit television, John seldom intervened, and then did so only to resolve a knotty impasse.

In preparing for the council, John invited Orthodox and Protestant churches to send observers. He presented these observers with the documents relating to the council, gave them permission to attend the debates, and provided informal settings where prelates, theologians, and observers got to know one another intimately. While concerned with the organized opposition to his liberalizing aims by a group of 250 prelates, John felt, as the first session drew to a close on 8 December, that the intended updating *(aggiornamento)* had been initiated. Expressing his satisfaction that the "opening of the church's window" had been accomplished, he announced that the council's second session would begin in September 1963.

By early November suspicions were aroused regarding the pope's fatal cancer. John nevertheless continued his busy schedule, visiting parishes, receiving diplomats, and giving general audiences to pilgrims and visitors. During the Cuban missile crisis, he made a radio broadcast in which he admonished President Kennedy and Chairman Khrushchev to achieve a peaceful solution, thus enabling the two leaders to back off gracefully. On receiving telegrams of recognition for his efforts, he decided to leave the world a legacy in his noted encyclical *Pacem in terris* (Peace on Earth), which was honored by a symposium at the United Nations in New York. His previous encyclical, *Mater et magistra* (Mother and Teacher), dealing with the world's social and economic needs, had caused some problems for conservative Catholics. And when the pope received the son-in-law of Nikita Khrushchev, Aleksei Adzhubei, in a private audience, there was talk of papal indiscretion. These incidents were compounded by John's reception of the Balzan Peace Prize, awarded by an international committee that included four Soviet members, in the spring of 1963, which was his last public appearance.

Throughout his career John proved a facile writer. As a young priest he produced a noted essay on the seventeenth-century church historian Cardinal Baronius. He also wrote a history of the practice of public charity in the diocese of Bergamo as well as a biography of Bishop Radini-Tedeschi. During the course of his diplomatic career he edited a five-volume, documented history of the effects of the Council of Trent on the diocese of Bergamo as it was administered by Cardinal Carlo Borromeo, one of John's favorite saints. From the journal of his seminary days he produced *Journal of a Soul* (New York, 1965), a spiritual diary that is the key to understanding his intimate relation with God and the placidity with which he accepted the ups and downs of everyday life, in keeping with his heraldic motto, "Peace and Obedience."

In the course of his pontificate, John named fifty-five cardinals; he did not hesitate to break with the tradition of holding the college of cardinals to seventy members. He canonized ten saints and beatified five holy men and women, including Elizabeth Seton of Baltimore. Labeled a transitional pope on his election at age seventy-seven, John accepted the designation as a challenge and, as the most innovative pontiff in over five centuries, proceeded to revolutionize the church. When John died on 3 June 1963, he was mourned by the whole world; one newspaper carried the headline "A Death in the Family of Mankind."

BIBLIOGRAPHY

Aradi, Zsolt, et al. *Pope John XXIII: An Authoritative Biography.* New York, 1959.

Fesquet, Henri, ed. *Wit and Wisdom of Good Pope John.* Translated by Salvator Attanasio. New York, 1964.

Hales, E. E. Y. *Pope John and His Revolution.* Garden City, N.Y., 1956.

Hebblethwaite, Peter. *John XXIII, Pope of the Council.* New York, 1985.

John XXIII. *Scritti e discorsi, 1953–1958.* 4 vols. Rome, 1959–1964.

John XXIII. *Discorsi, messagi, colloqui del Santo Padre Giovanni XXIII.* 5 vols. Vatican City, 1961–1964.

John XXIII. *Souvenirs d'un nonce: Cahiers de France, 1944–1953.* Rome, 1963.

John XXIII. *Journal of a Soul.* Translated by Dorothy White. New York, 1965.

Murphy, Francis X. *Pope John XXIII Comes to the Vatican.* New York, 1959.

Murphy, Francis X. *The Papacy Today.* New York, 1981.

Trisco, Robert. "John XXIII, Pope." In *New Catholic Encyclopedia,* vol. 7. New York, 1967.

Zizola, Giancarlo. *The Utopia of Pope John XXIII.* Translated by Helen Barolini. Maryknoll, N.Y., 1978.

FRANCIS X. MURPHY

JOHN OF DAMASCUS, also known as John Damascene; eighth-century Christian saint, church father, monastic, theologian, author, and poet. Little is known with certitude about John's life. The dates of both his birth and his death are disputed, as are the number of years that he lived. A conservative assessment of the evidence indicates that he was probably born about 679 and died at the age of seventy in 749. It is generally accepted that he was born into a Greek-speaking Syrian family of Damascus, known as Mansour ("victorious," or, "redeemed"). His father, Sergius, held the high position of *logothetēs* in the Muslim caliphate at the end of the seventh century. John enjoyed a full course of instruction as a youth, including mathematics, geometry, music, astronomy, rhetoric, logic, philosophy (Plato and Aristotle), and theology.

Following the death of his father, John assumed an economic administrative position *(protosumboulos)* in the government of Caliph Walid (r. 705–715). He left public service just before, or shortly after, the outbreak of the Iconoclastic Controversy to become a monk in the famous Monastery of Saint Sava outside Jerusalem. He was ordained a priest by John V, patriarch of Jerusalem (r. 706–735). John Damascene left a rich legacy of writings reflecting the theology and religious tradition of Eastern Christianity and the spiritual tradition of the Greek fathers.

John was a prolific writer, who, though completely faithful to the Eastern church and its theological tradition, also evinced significant theological creativity. Several of his earlier writings were revised and enlarged after their original publication. John's works reflect his broad educational background and cover numerous areas of concern.

He wrote a number of exegetical works on the Old and New Testaments. Among the better known of these are a shortened version of Chrysostom's commentaries on the letters of Paul, to which he added some of his own observations. In the same manner he published an epitome of the sermons on the *Hexaemeron* attributed to Chrysostom but written by Severian of Gabala (c. 400).

John's major theological production was in the area of doctrinal writings: his most important work is *Pēgē gnōseōs* (Fount of Knowledge). This work has been translated into many languages and is the foundation of his reputation as a theologian and dogmatician. The work, divided into three parts, appears to have been revised several times, which explains why at least two dates for its composition are recorded, 728 and 743. Each of the parts is found in three versions, of differing length, indicating that they were written independently and at different times, revised, and subsequently gathered together into the unified work.

The first part of *Fount of Knowledge* consists of a treatment of general knowledge (the philosophical and physical sciences of his day) as an introduction to theology. Based primarily on Aristotle, this portion of the work is theologically important because of its holistic perspective. The method used is definitional, by which major terms are defined in brief sections or chapters, in two areas: theoretical (theology, physics, and mathematics), and practical (ethics, economics, and politics).

The second part of *Fount of Knowledge* deals with heresies, or various false teachings, from the perspective of orthodox Christianity. In large part it is a compilation and elucidation of other antiheretical writings, but the three chapters on Islam, Iconoclasm, and the *aposchistai* (wandering monks who rejected all sacraments), were written as new material by John. Additional chapters were added subsequently by others.

The most important part of this work is the third, an outline of orthodox theology *(Ekthesis orthodoxou pisteōs)* consisting of 100 short chapters. In chapters 1–14 the doctrine of God is discussed; cosmology follows in chapters 15–44 dealing with angelology, demonology, good and evil, the created world, and anthropology; Christology and soteriology are discussed in chapters 45–73; and the last chapters deal with a variety of topics including Mariology, icons, self-determination *(autexousion)*, faith, and the saints. The theological tenor of this work is basically Cappadocian, with perspectives from other theological streams of thought such as those derived from Dionysius the Areopagite, Chrysostom, Athanasius, and Maximos the Confessor.

A number of John's polemical works are doctrinal in character. Among these are *Concerning Faith against the Nestorians*, several works against monophysitism, *Against the Jacobites*, and a work concerning the Trisagion Hymn, in which he opposes a purely christological reference to this popular and liturgical hymn. In his works *Concerning the Two Wills and Energies in Christ*, and *Against Monophysites and Monothelites*, John deals with the Monothelite Controversy. Between 726 and 731 he wrote three different studies entitled *Concerning the Icons*, reflecting various early stages of the Iconoclastic Controversy. He also concerned himself with treating other religious traditions from an Eastern Orthodox perspective, including Judaism, Manichaeism, and Islam. John also dealt with ethical topics in a three-part work entitled *Sacra Parallela*: *Concerning the Holy Fasts*, *The Eight Spirits of Evil*, and *Concerning Virtues and Vices*.

It has been difficult to determine which of the many sermons attributed to John of Damascus are genuine. Among those whose authenticity is in doubt are three sermons on the Dormition of the *theotokos*, one of two on the Annunciation, sermons on the Transfiguration of Christ, the Fig Tree, the Birth of Christ, and Christ's presentation in the Temple. In addition there are a number of sermons on saints attributed to him.

Although disputed, it is now generally accepted that John also wrote a Christian version of an ancient Buddhist tale under the title *Barlaam and Joasaph*. It is essentially a story of the conversion to monastic Christianity of a young profligate through the hearing of a striking parable.

John of Damascus is highly regarded as a hymnodist. He is well known for the fourteen published collections of hymns known as canons. In addition, approximately ninety canons are attributed to him in the manuscript tradition. John is primarily responsible for the hymnology of the basic weekly cycle of Eastern Orthodox services found in the liturgical book the *Oktoēchos* (Eight Tones). The hymns are characterized by theological exactness coupled with poetic warmth and power.

Tradition attributes to John of Damascus the epithet Chrusorroas ("golden-flowing"). His memory is commemorated by the Eastern Orthodox church on 4 December, the date of his death, and by the Roman Catholic church on 27 March. He is considered an authoritative voice for contemporary Orthodox theology. His writings were also an important source for Peter Lombard and Thomas Aquinas. Pope Leo XIII declared him a doctor of the Roman Catholic church in 1890.

BIBLIOGRAPHY

Texts and Translations

Barlaam and Iosaph. Edited by Harold Mattingly; translated by G. R. Woodward. Loeb Classical Library, vol. 34. Cambridge, Mass., 1937.

Homélies sur la Nativité et la Dormition. Introduction, French translation, and notes by Pierre Voulet. Paris, 1961.

On the Divine Images: Three Apologies against Those Who Attack the Holy Images. Translated by David Anderson. Crestwood, N.Y., 1980. A readable translation.

Opera omnia quae exstant. Edited by Michel Lequien. Paris, 1712. Reproduced in *Patrologia Graeca*, edited by J.-P. Migne, vol. 94. Paris, 1860. The standard received text.

Die Schriften des Johannes von Damaskos. 4 vols. Edited by P. Bonifatius Kotter. Berlin, 1969–1981. These definitive critical texts have extensive documentation and textual critical material.

Hē Theotokos: Tesseres Theomētorikes Homilies. Edited by Athanasius Gievtits. Athens, 1970. Contains the text, with an introduction and commentary by the editor. Each of the four homilies has been rendered into modern Greek by a different translator.

Writings. Translated by Frederic H. Chase, Jr. Fathers of the Church, vol. 37. Washington, D.C., 1958. Includes only *Fount of Knowledge*. The best existing English translation. Contains an introduction by the translator that deals with many of the unresolved historical questions.

Studies

Barnard, Leslie W. "Use of the Bible in the Byzantine Iconoclastic Controversy, 726 to 843 A.D." *Theologische Zeitschrift* 31 (March-April 1975): 78–83. John's use of scripture is discussed as it relates to the Iconoclastic Controversy.

Chevalier, Celestin M. B. *La Mariologie de saint Jean Damascène*. Rome, 1936. A literary and theological examination of John of Damascus's teaching concerning the *theotokos*.

Sahas, Daniel J. *John of Damascus on Islam: The "Heresy of the Ishmaelites."* Leiden, 1972. A revision of a doctoral dissertation. The best detailed biographical treatment in English. It includes a careful treatment of the major problems regarding John of Damascus's teaching concerning Islam.

STANLEY SAMUEL HARAKAS

JOHN OF KRONSTADT. *See* Ioann of Kronstadt.

JOHN OF THE CROSS (1542–1591), mystic, saint, and doctor of the church. John was born Juan de Yepes y Alvarez in Fontiveros, Spain, the youngest of three sons. His father's untimely death left the family in poverty. Nevertheless, young John received an excellent education in the humanities at the Jesuit college in Medina del Campo, and in 1563 he entered the Carmelite order at the Monastery of Santa Ana. That same year he received the habit of the order and the religious name Juan de Santo Matía. He completed further studies at Salamanca and in 1567 was ordained to the priesthood.

Shortly after ordination the young monk returned to Medina del Campo, where he met the great Carmelite reformer Teresa of Ávila. Teresa, fifty-two years old at the time, recognized in the twenty-five-year-old John the intelligence and holiness that would make him her spiritual and mystical compatriot and her collaborator in the reform movement, he doing in the masculine branch of the order what she was already accomplishing in the feminine branch. On 28 November 1568, after Teresa, as his spiritual mentor, had judged him ready, Juan professed the Primitive Rule and took the name John of the Cross.

Captured by enemies of the reform movement and imprisoned in the calced (mitigated, or unreformed) monastery at Toledo, John spent nine months in a tiny cell. He was deprived of adequate food and was regularly scourged; yet his established holiness manifested itself in patient acceptance of these hardships and while in prison he began to write the exquisite religious poetry that was to place him among the greatest of the Spanish poets and form the kernel of his great mystical legacy.

In 1578 he escaped from prison and began a twelve-year period of administration within the reformed branch of the order. He was a remarkably able superior and as spiritual director was much sought after by religious and laity alike. In 1590 John again became the object of persecution, this time by jealous confreres within the reform movement. An effort to have him expelled from the movement was frustrated by his death. John died at Ubeda on 13 December 1591 at the age of forty-nine.

John of the Cross was beatified in 1675 and canonized in 1726. In 1926 Pius XI declared him a doctor of the church under the title "Mystical Doctor." Besides a few letters, various maxims and counsels, and a number of extraordinarily beautiful poems, John left only four major works, and these have become the instruments of his remarkable influence on the history of Christian spirituality. All four were written from the vantage point of the full maturity of John's own mystical experience, and they reflect the wisdom of accomplished holiness well served by biblical and theological scholarship. Each consists of a poem followed by a long spiritual commentary.

The Ascent of Mount Carmel (1579–1585) and *The Dark Night* (poem, 1579–1581; commentary, 1582–1585) together form a treatise on the double purification (of the sensory and of the spiritual dimensions of the person) that leads to full mystical union. *The Spiritual Canticle* (1578, 1582–1585, 1586–1591) is the longest of John's poems, a rapturous overflowing of what he called "mystical wisdom" as he himself had experienced it. It describes four stages of the mystical journey, but the commentary sets forth the whole of that journey from its ascetical beginnings to total transformation in the mystical marriage, the last stage of the spiritual life. *The Living Flame of Love* (poem, 1582–1585; commentary in two redactions, 1585–1591) treats the most perfect experience of love within the highest mystical state of transforming union. The commentary frequently digresses from the poem's subject matter to treat various important aspects of the spiritual life as a whole.

Through the example of his sublime personal holiness and his wonderfully fruitful and very human friendship with Teresa of Ávila, his establishment of the Discalced Carmelites, and, especially, his unsurpassed poetic and doctrinal writings on mystical theology, John of the Cross continues to exercise an influence in Western Christian spirituality probably unequaled by anyone except Thomas, Augustine, Dionysius, and Teresa herself.

BIBLIOGRAPHY

The Collected Works of Saint John of the Cross. Translated by Kieran Kavanaugh and Otilio Rodriguez. Washington, D.C., 1979.

The Complete Works of Saint John of the Cross, Doctor of the Church. 3 vols. Translated by E. Allison Peers. London, 1953. Contains an extensive international bibliography useful for any study of John of the Cross.

Crisógono de Jesús. *The Life of Saint John of the Cross.* Translated by Kathlene Pond. New York, 1958.

SANDRA M. SCHNEIDERS

JOHN THE BAPTIST. Born of a poor priestly family in the hill country of Judea, John renounced the priesthood and entered upon an ascetic existence in the wilderness surrounding the Jordan River. There he inaugurated a baptism rite so unprecedented that he was named for it. His contemporary Jesus unhesitatingly ascribed the impetus for John's baptism to divine revelation (*Mk.* 11:30), and even though priestly lustrations in the Temple, the daily baths at Qumran, or even proselyte baptism (first attested in the second century CE) may provide certain parallels, they are wholly inadequate to account for John's demand that Jews submit to a once-only immersion in anticipation of an imminent divine judgment by fire. Rejecting all claims to salvation by virtue of Jewish blood or the "merits of Abraham," John demanded of each person works that would reflect a personal act of repentance. The examples preserved in *Luke* 3:10–14 indicate that John stood squarely in the line of the prophets, siding with the poor ("He who has two coats, let him share with him who has none; and he who has food, let him do likewise"). He demanded that toll collectors and soldiers desist from extorting unjust exactions from travelers and pilgrims. His dress was the homespun of the nomad, his diet the subsistence rations of the poorest of the poor (locusts and wild honey, *Mk.* 1:6). He even described the eschatological judge, whose near advent he proclaimed, in terms of a peasant or a man of the soil (chopping down trees, separating wheat from chaff).

Through baptism, John provided a means by which common people and other "sinners" (tax collectors and harlots, *Mt.* 21:32) could be regenerated apart from meticulous observance of the Jewish law. His influence on Jesus in this and other respects was profound. Jesus and his disciples were baptized by John. But whereas John demanded that people come out to him in the wilderness, Jesus went to the people in their towns and villages, rejecting an ascetic life (*Mt.* 11:18–19), and began to regard the future kingdom as an already dawning reality (*Mt.* 11:2–6). Despite these differences, Jesus continued to speak of John in terms of highest respect (*Mt.* 11:7–9, 11a).

John's execution by Herod Antipas was provoked by John's criticism of Herod for divorcing the daughter of the Nabatean king Aretas IV and entering upon an incestuous remarriage with Herodias, his half-brother's wife. John's attacks on Herod took place in Perea, a region controlled by Herod but bordered by Nabatean territory, an area inhabited by Arabs and infiltrated in winter by nomads. Herod's divorce provoked guerrilla warfare, and ultimately Aretas avenged his daughter's shame by a shattering defeat of Herod's army—a defeat that Josephus directly ascribes to divine punishment for Herod's execution of John (*Jewish Antiquities* 18.116–119). John's preaching must also have contributed substantially to popular disaffection from Herod.

Following the publication of the Dead Sea Scrolls, some scholars suggested that John might at one time have been an Essene. It is true that he preached but eight miles from Qumran, that he shared with the Essenes an imminent eschatological hope, and that he lived out (perhaps deliberately) the prophecy of *Isaiah* 40:3 and sought to prepare the way in the wilderness. Both John and the Essenes warned of a coming purgative fire associated with the Holy Spirit and with washing; both issued a radical call to repentance; both employed immersion in water as a religious rite; both believed that only an elect would be saved, and called the rest vipers; both condemned the priesthood and other authorities; both renounced society and abstained from strong drink.

These similarities, however, can in large part be accounted for: both John and the Essenes belonged to the larger phenomenon of Jewish wilderness sectarianism. Their differences, in any case, are more decisive than all their similarities. John was a solitary. He established no settled community, moved around in the Jordan wastes, was inclusive rather that separatist, public rather than reclusive, addressing the whole nation rather than withdrawing into an isolated life. His baptism was granted once and for all, not daily, and for a forgiveness of sins on which eternal salvation hung, not for physical purity. His dress was camel's hair, not white linen. He did not require a long novitiate for his converts, nor did he organize them under rigid requirements. Almost all the other similarities with Qumran can be traced to common dependence on the prophet Isaiah. Indeed, if John had ever been connected with Qumran, his break was so radical that it scarcely seems necessary to posit any original connection at all. When he steps upon the stage of history, his message and mission are altogether his own.

All four evangelists treat John as "the beginning of the gospel." This reflects both the historical fact and the theological conviction that through John, Jesus perceived the nearness of the kingdom of God and his own relation to its coming. The church continued to treat John as the perpetual preparer for the coming of Christ, calling out for people to repent and let the shift of the aeons take place in their own lives, to "make ready the way of the Lord" (*Mk.* 1:2).

BIBLIOGRAPHY

Kraeling, Carl H. *John the Baptist.* New York, 1951. Despite more recent publications, this work remains definitive. Historical sleuthing at its best.

Scobie, Charles H. H. *John the Baptist.* London, 1964. Adds some interesting conjectures on the Samaritans.

Wink, Walter. *John the Baptist in the Gospel Tradition.* Cambridge, 1968. A critical study of the use made of the Baptist traditions by the evangelists.

WALTER WINK

JOHN THE EVANGELIST, according to ancient Christian tradition one of the Twelve chosen by Jesus; the son of Zebedee, brother of James, and author of the Fourth Gospel, the Johannine letters, and the *Book of Revelation*. Called by Jesus from his vocation as a fisherman, John is mentioned frequently in the synoptic Gospels, where with James and Peter he forms the inner circle of disciples. He appears in all four lists of the Twelve in the New Testament (*Mt.* 10:2, *Mk.* 3:17, *Lk.* 6:14, *Acts* 1:13). Usually he is mentioned after his brother James, which suggests that he is the younger, but in the *Acts of the Apostles* his name stands second, after Peter's. Moreover, he appears along with Peter in several of the Jerusalem scenes in the early chapters of *Acts* (e.g., 3:1, 3:4, 3:11, 8:14). Interestingly enough, the episodes in which John figures in the synoptic Gospels (e.g., the raising of Jairus's daughter, the Transfiguration) are missing from John's gospel, and the sons of Zebedee are mentioned only once, in the final chapter (*Jn.* 21:2).

Although, like the other Gospels, *John* is anonymous, it is ascribed to an unnamed beloved disciple (*Jn.* 21:24), who figures prominently in the passion and resurrection narrative of this gospel only. He always appears with Peter, except at the cross. Christian tradition has identified this disciple with John, although the gospel itself does not. In the late second century both Irenaeus and Polycrates ascribe the Fourth Gospel to John, and from that time on it becomes a commonplace that John wrote his gospel in Ephesus after the others had been composed.

Irenaeus traces the Johannine tradition to Papias and Polycarp, bishops during the first half of the second century (Eusebius, *Church History* 3.39.1–7, 4.14.3–8). This testimony is not without problems, however, as Eusebius recognized in reporting Irenaeus's statements about Papias. John's gospel was known in some circles throughout most of the second century; it was popular among Christians who were later condemned as heretics (the Gnostics) and was rejected by others, such as Gaius of Rome and the Alogoi, who objected to its departures from the synoptic Gospels. Such a reception raises questions about the status or recognition of the Fourth Gospel as an apostolic work during this period.

Nevertheless, when after several centuries the gospel, the letters, and *Revelation* had gained universal acceptance as Christian scripture, they were all regarded as the work of John the son of Zebedee. As early as the third century, however, Bishop Dionysius of Alexandria pointed out the stylistic and theological difficulty of regarding *Revelation* as the work of the author of the Fourth Gospel and the letters. Only *Revelation* is expressly the work of someone named John (*Rv.* 1:2), and this John makes no claim to being an apostle (cf. *Rv.* 18:20, 21:14). Both *2 John* and *3 John* are from "the elder," while *1 John* is anonymous. Modern scholars are inclined to see three or more authors represented in the Johannine corpus.

Evidence against the traditional view that John lived to an old age in Ephesus is provided by the silence of Ignatius, who wrote to the Ephesian church (c. 115) mentioning Paul's role at Ephesus prominently but John not at all. There is a strain of evidence, perhaps supported by Jesus' prediction in *Mark* 10:39, that John was martyred with James in Jerusalem during the 40s (*Acts* 12:2). However that may be, manifold difficulties stand in the way of tracing church tradition about John the Evangelist back through the second century.

Despite these difficulties, the *Gospel of John* and *1 John* clearly claim to be based on eyewitness testimony. The validity of that claim does not necessarily stand or fall with the traditional attribution of authorship, which reconciles John's gospel with synoptic and other data about Jesus' disciples. In Christian symbolism dating back to the second century, the fourth evangelist is appropriately represented by the eagle, for the Fourth Gospel goes its own way, apparently independent of the other Gospels and their traditions. John's feast is celebrated on 27 December.

BIBLIOGRAPHY

Aside from the New Testament the most important primary source is Eusebius's *Church History*, which brings together earlier testimony of Christian writers on the origin and authorship of the Gospels. The most convenient edition is the two-volume "Loeb Classical Library" text and translation of Kirsopp Lake, J. E. L. Oulton, and Hugh J. Lawlor (Cambridge, Mass., 1926).

Werner G. Kümmel's *Introduction to the New Testament*, rev. ed. (Nashville, 1975), pp. 234–246, succinctly states the modern, critical case against the tradition of Johannine authorship. Robert Kysar's *The Fourth Evangelist and His Gospel: An Examination of Contemporary Scholarship* (Minneapolis, 1975), pp. 86–101, gives a balanced summary and appraisal of scholarship on this question. A constructive effort to understand the evangelist and his milieu is Raymond E. Brown's *The Community of the Beloved Disciple* (New York, 1979). Ronald Brownrigg's *The Twelve Apostles* (New York, 1974), pp. 85–122, is a popular treatment that takes into account critical perspectives. Note also F. F. Bruce's "St. John at Ephesus," *Bulletin of the John Rylands University Library* (Manchester) 60 (1978): 339–361; and J. J. Gunther's "Early Identifications of Authorship of the Johannine Writers," *Journal of Ecclesiastical History* 31 (1980): 407–427.

D. MOODY SMITH

JONAH, or, in Hebrew, Yonah; an Israelite prophet in the Bible who, as told in the book preserved in his name, was divinely commissioned to announce a prophecy of imminent doom to the Assyrian people of Nineveh (*Jon.* 1:1–2). Fleeing his task, Jonah hopped aboard a commercial vessel bound for Tarshish, in the west (*Jon.* 1:3). Subsequently, a violent storm broke out that was recognized through divination by lots to be due to a sin of Jonah's. The storm was quelled when Jonah was cast into the sea (*Jon.* 1:4–10). However, the Lord arranged for a great fish to swallow the prophet, who presumably repented his folly in attempting to flee divine destiny (*Jon.* 2:8). In any event, he was regurgitated upon the dry land and traveled to Nineveh, where he first announced doom to the city and its inhabitants and then witnessed the pagans' repentances and God's forgiveness (*Jon.* 3). Grieved at this expression of divine mercy, Jonah wished to die, but, in the parable of chapter 4, was given instruction and reproof by God in the form of a recinus plant that sprouted to shade him in the heat of the day but then as quickly withered. Jonah regretted its loss, although he had done nothing to care for it. How much more (he is asked rhetorically) should God have compassion for people like the Ninevites and their cattle—his creatures?

Both language and theology, as well as the inaccurate depiction of Nineveh, suggest that the *Book of Jonah* is a relatively late postexilic composition, from about the fourth century BCE (it is first cited in *Tobit*). The book is artistically organized and integrated: chapters 1 and 3 deal with penitent pagans and their salvation from the wrath of Israel's God; chapters 2 and 4 deal with the Israelite prophet and his theological lessons in and by miraculous circumstances. But the concern of the text has, since antiquity, perplexed its readers.

In ancient Jewish Midrashic and aggadic literature, commentators have drawn out various lessons from the story of Jonah. In the failure of Jonah's flight they saw proof that a prophet could not escape his destiny. In his refusal to prophesy they detected a noble desire not to insult Israel, who—unlike the pagans—did not repent. In God's final response to the Ninevites, the rabbis underscored the power of repentance to affect the divine will. (Since antiquity the *Book of Jonah* has been the prophetic lection for the afternoon service of Yom Kippur, the Day of Atonement; see B.T., *Meg.* 31a.) Finally, in Jonah's refusal to utter a prophetic oracle of doom in the name of a merciful God, many interpreters have seen his fear of being killed as a false prophet. The church fathers, in contrast to the rabbis, argued that Jonah wanted by his prophecy to the Ninevites to teach a lesson to the stubborn Jews, and thus found in *Jonah* precedent and support for missions to the gentiles.

Divine mercy, false prophecy, and repentance combined are the core of the prophetic meditation reflected in this book: initially concerned that divine mercy would limit the dignity of prophecy and so make the divine oracular word conditional upon human behavior, Jonah rejected his office only to realize finally that repentance has no independent, magical effect, since divine mercy is an attribute of an utterly transcendent and free God. The asymmetry between the parable at the story's end, the prophet's situation, and the lesson derived from it, has often been regarded as support for this theological point. God will have mercy in the end upon whomsoever he chooses.

At another level, the ingestion and regurgitation of Jonah by a fish is a motif that dramatizes the inner transformation and spiritual rebirth of the prophet. Typologically, moreover, the three days spent by Jonah in the belly of the fish were seen in early Christian tradition as prefiguring the three days spent by Jesus "in the heart of the earth" (*Mt.* 12:40). The fish and salvation motifs are found frequently in the Roman catacombs and on the sarcophagi and were used extensively in Byzantine manuscripts and in medieval miracle plays. In Jewish Neoplatonic texts, the themes of the story of Jonah were understood allegorically in terms of the fate of the human soul in the world.

BIBLIOGRAPHY

Bickerman, Elias J. *Four Strange Books of the Bible: Jonah, Daniel, Koheleth, Esther.* New York, 1967.

Cohn, Gabriël H. *Das Buch Jona.* Assen, 1969.

Ginzberg, Louis. *The Legends of the Jews* (1909–1938). 7 vols. Translated by Henrietta Szold et al. Reprint, Philadelphia, 1937–1966. See the index, s.v. *Jonah.*

Goitein, S. D. "Some Observations on Jonah." *Journal of the Palestine Oriental Society* 17 (1937): 63–77.

Scholem, Gershom, ed. *Zohar, the Book of Splendor* (1949), vol. 6. Reprint, New York, 1963.

Urbach, E. E. "The Repentance of the People of Nineveh and the Discussions between Jews and Christians" (in Hebrew). *Tarbiz* 20 (1949): 118–122.

MICHAEL FISHBANE

JOSEPH, or, in Hebrew, Yosef; the firstborn son of Jacob's favorite wife, Rachel. The account of Joseph's life, which the Qur'ān calls "the most beautiful of stories" (12:3), is described in a uniquely detailed and sustained biblical narrative.

As Rachel's son, Joseph was treasured by his father. Resentful of Joseph's resulting conceit, his brothers sold him to a group of passing traders, who took him to Egypt where he was purchased by one of Pharaoh's officers. When Joseph, who is described as "attractive and good-looking" (*Gn.* 39:6), rejected the advances of the officer's wife, she accused him of attempted rape and had him imprisoned. In jail, he demonstrated his ability to interpret dreams and was therefore brought to Pharaoh, whose dreams could not be otherwise understood. Joseph recognized them as warning that a period of abundance would be followed by famine. Elevated to high office in order to prepare Egypt for the coming threat, Joseph was given both an Egyptian name (Zaphenath-paneah) and wife (Asenath).

When difficult times did arrive, Egypt was ready and served as a resource for surrounding peoples. Joseph's brothers came from Canaan to purchase grain; he recognized and tested them before revealing himself and bringing the entire family to settle in the eastern Nile Delta. Joseph died at the age of 110; his bones were brought to Canaan by the Israelites during the Exodus.

Joseph's special status is attested by the ascription to him of two biblical tribes, named after his sons Ephraim and Manasseh. Ephraim was to dominate the northern kingdom of Israel, which therefore is also called the House of Joseph. Joseph's childhood dreams were thus fulfilled by his descendants as much as during his own lifetime.

The story of Joseph is remarkable for its numerous human touches, which lead to the apparent absence of divine intervention so common elsewhere in *Genesis*. In fact, however, God is very much present, if not always visible, acting through human behavior (*Gn.* 45:5, 50:20). The narrative incorporates many elements found in other biblical tales, most strikingly in the stories of Daniel and Esther, which also describe an Israelite's rise in a foreign court.

The historicity of the Joseph story has been defended on the basis of its incorporation of Egyptian vocabulary, customs, and narrative motifs. Historians since the first-century Josephus Flavius (*Against Apion* 1.103) have linked Joseph with the Hyksos, a West Semitic people who dominated Egypt toward the end of the Middle Bronze Age. Their expulsion in the sixteenth century might then explain the Bible's statement that "there arose a new king over Egypt who did not know of Joseph" (*Ex.* 1:8). Actually, none of these factors is sufficient historical proof. The land of Canaan was long under Egyptian control, and several cases of apparently Semitic figures holding high positions in the Egyptian bureaucracy are attested over a long period of time. Finally, the author's accurate knowledge of Egyptian culture hardly proves the story's historicity; indeed, there are several different periods in which such knowledge could have been acquired.

BIBLIOGRAPHY

An overview of modern scholarship relating to the entire patriarchal period is contained in Nahum M. Sarna's *Understanding Genesis* (New York, 1972). This must now, however, be read in conjunction with the historical information contained in Roland de Vaux's *The Early History of Israel*, translated by David Smith (Philadelphia, 1978). A detailed examination of the Joseph story, including both its literary characteristics and its Egyptian coloration, can be found in Donald B. Redford's *A Study of the Biblical Story of Joseph (Genesis 37–50)* (Leiden, 1970). Louis Ginzberg's *The Legends of the Jews*, 7 vols. (Philadelphia, 1909–1938), contains an exhaustive collection of rabbinic lore relating to biblical stories.

FREDERICK E. GREENSPAHN

JOSEPH OF VOLOKOLAMSK (1439–1515), born Ivan Sanin; Russian Orthodox monastic saint. Joseph succeeded his spiritual father, Pafnutii, as abbot of the Borovsk monastery in 1477. But the reforms toward a stricter form of communal life that he sought there did not find favor with his community, and Joseph undertook an extensive tour of Russian monasteries in search of alternative models. Ultimately Joseph established an entirely new monastery at Volok or Volokolamsk (1479), where he remained for the rest of his life.

Since his early years at Volok, Joseph had been involved in politics, campaigning against the widespread reformationist heresy of the so-called Judaizers, the Novgorodian-Muscovite opponents of church order and trinitarian teaching. Joseph was to urge consistently (and in 1504 finally attain) the physical elimination of the leading heretics at the hands of the state. In his view, even professions of repentance should not allow heretics to be spared. Joseph's zeal in this regard was expressed in his *Prosvetitel'* (*The Enlightener*, c. 1502–1503; expanded version, c. 1511), a compilation of antiheretical writings. In 1507 Joseph transferred the allegiance of his now influential monastery to the Muscovite grand prince, a serious breach of ecclesiastical discipline, resulting in alienation from the Novgorodian archbishop.

More positive and more lasting than his work against heretics was Joseph's contribution to the shaping of Russian monastic discipline and piety. He composed two rules, the second (and longer) of which dates from his final years. The aim of each was to ensure sobriety and discipline in liturgy and daily life. Poverty was enjoined on the individual monk. Yet the community as a whole was expected to flourish for the service of society at large, especially at times of dearth or distress. As many as seven thousand people would be fed daily during a famine; an orphanage for fifty children was regularly maintained. The orderly and dutiful expression of Christian philanthropy was Joseph's dominant concern and principal contribution to Russian Orthodox tradition.

Joseph was the foremost proponent of the Possessors' school of thought; he insisted that monastics should own land and he effectively countered the contrary claim of certain Orthodox ascetics and of Ivan III (1440–1504). The Moscow church council of 1503 heeded Joseph and decided the question in favor of the Possessors. Had it been otherwise, Joseph might have felt impelled to act in accordance with the daring principle that obedience to a ruler was conditional on the ruler's righteousness, which he had enunciated earlier. An unjust ruler is "no tsar, but a tyrant." In the words of Georges Florovsky (1893–1979), Joseph bordered here on "justification of regicide." In fact, Joseph was to become ever more dependable a collaborator of the state.

It was Joseph's hope that his monastery would attract well-born postulants and that these would provide the bishops of the future. His expectations were fulfilled in the course of the sixteenth century. By the end of it his posthumous reputation was firmly established, and his local canonization (1578) was followed by the proclamation of his sanctity by the Russian Orthodox church as a whole in 1591.

BIBLIOGRAPHY

Joseph's *Prosvetitel'* was edited (anonymously) by Ivan I. Porfir'ev as *Prosvetitel' ili oblichenie eresi zhidovstvuiushchikh: Tvorenie prepodobnago ottsa nashego Iosifa, igumena Volotskago* (Kazan, 1857); while his prolific correspondence appeared more recently as *Poslaniia Iosifa Volotskogo*, edited by Aleksandr A. Zimin and Iakov S. Lur'e (Leningrad, 1959). Only one of Joseph's major writings has been translated into English: *The Monastic Rule of Joseph of Volokolamsk*, translated and edited by David Goldfrank (Kalamazoo, Mich., 1983). His spiritual counsels and regulations are surveyed in an orderly manner in Thomas Špidlík's *Joseph de Volokolamsk: Un chapitre de la spiritualité russe*, "Orientalia Christiana Analecta," no. 146 (Rome, 1956).

SERGEI HACKEL

JOSEPHUS FLAVIUS (37/8–c. 100 CE), born Yosef ben Mattityahu; Jewish general, historian, and apologist. Josephus was perhaps the most prolific, significant, and controversial of Jewish writers in Judaea during the Hellenistic-Roman era. Born in Jerusalem, he traced his paternal lineage from the priesthood and his maternal descent to the Hasmonean dynasty, and he claimed to have been educated not only within the priestly circles but also among the various Judaic sectarian movements of his day. In 64 he went to Rome and obtained the release of imprisoned Jewish priests, returning to Judaea on the eve of the Great Revolt, a Jewish uprising against Rome. Although he was a moderate, he was appointed to command the Galilean forces, and upon their defeat by Vespasian in 67 he surrendered after his comrades committed suicide. Josephus claims that while in captivity he predicted the accession of Vespasian to emperor, and two years later he was freed by the newly acclaimed ruler of Rome. Josephus accompanied Vespasian's son Titus during the siege and destruction of Jerusalem and the Temple. After the war, Josephus lived under imperial patronage in Rome, where he wrote four major works that survive thanks to their preservation by the Christian church.

Less than a decade after Jerusalem fell in 70, Josephus completed *The Jewish War*, a seven-book narrative of Judean history from the accession of the Seleucid king Antiochus IV (175 BCE) to the fall of Masada in 74 CE. This work was written first in Aramaic and later translated into Greek in order that readers in both the Parthian kingdom and the Roman empire would learn why the revolt occurred and how it failed. With Flavian approval, Josephus portrayed a Jewish nation tragically swept by a small band of fanatics into a war that could only demonstrate Rome's invincibility.

Jewish Antiquities, published in 93/4, recounts in twenty books the Jewish experience from earliest times until 66 CE. Josephus drew heavily from biblical and later Jewish and non-Jewish sources, which he carefully reworked and edited into a treatise modeled on the *Roman Antiquities* of Dionysius of Halicarnassus. The result is a highly creative *apologia* that within its Greek historiographic form emphasizes the antiquity and philanthropy of the Jews and Judaism even as it underscores biblical concepts of divine justice and providence. Josephus subsequently made these apologetic arguments more explicit in the two books collectively titled *Against Apion*, which quote and refute many anti-Semitic works from the Hellenistic age.

Finally, Josephus appended to *Jewish Antiquities* an autobiographical book that is almost entirely devoted to defending his conduct of the Galilean campaign. While in *The Jewish War* he portrayed himself as a committed, efficient general, in his autobiographical work, *The Life*, he emphasizes that he went to Galilee as a moderate who unsuccessfully attempted to restrain his countrymen.

Josephus and his works are no less controversial in modern scholarship than they were in their day. The literature is without equal in breadth and detail; therefore, paradoxically, questions about its reliability often cannot be resolved. Principal foci of contemporary analysis of Josephus include: (1) modes of hellenization within Palestinian Judaism; (2) the nature of the Pharisaic, Sadducean, and Essene movements, among others; (3) Jewish and Roman political dynamics prior to and in the aftermath of the revolt; (4) Josephus's own motives and conduct, particularly during the revolt and then in light of his Flavian patronage; and (5) the brief, but extraordinary, passage in *Jewish Antiquities* that refers to Jesus but generally has been judged to be at least in part a forgery.

In sum, Josephus emerges as a crucial source for the reconstruction of Judaism and Jewish history in late antiquity. Many contemporary scholars eschew Jerome's claim that Josephus was the "Greek Livy," yet few would deny his contribution to our understanding of his era or his skill and passion in explaining and defending his people to their neighbors.

BIBLIOGRAPHY

The standard text and translation of Josephus's complete works is that of the "Loeb Classical Library," edited by Henry St. John Thackeray, Ralph Marcus, Allen Wikgren, and Louis H. Feldman in ten volumes (Cambridge, Mass., 1926–1965). A classic introduction is *Josephus: The Man and the Historian* by Henry St. John Thackeray (New York, 1929), republished with a new introduction (New York, 1967); and a fine, more recent overview is Tessa Rajak's *Josephus: The Historian and His Society* (London, 1983). The most complete annotated bibliography is Louis H. Feldman's *Josephus and Modern Scholarship, 1937–1980* (Hawthorne, N.Y., 1984).

DAVID ALTSHULER

JOSHUA, or, in Hebrew, Yehoshu'a; Israelite leader who flourished, according to tradition, in the thirteenth century BCE. The *Book of Joshua* tells how its namesake led the twelve tribes of Israel in a concerted military invasion and conquest of the land of Canaan, whose territory was divided among the tribes. Joshua attributes the success of the campaign to the direct action of YHVH, Israel's God (see *Jos.* 10:14, 23:3, 23:10)—a claim underscored by the miraculous nature of the defeats of the cities of Jericho (whose wall was toppled by the shouts of the Israelites) and Gibeon (where the sun stood still until the Israelites were victorious). After the victory, Joshua assembles the Israelites at Shechem to renew the covenant with YHVH made in the preceding generation through the mediation of Moses. He exhorts the people to remain devoted to YHVH and to keep his law.

Joshua's role as leader of the conquest is anticipated in the biblical narrative by his introduction as the field commander in the battle against Amalek (*Ex.* 17:8–13) and as a spy sent by Moses to reconnoiter Canaan (*Nm.* 13). Moses elevates his status by changing his name from *Hoshe'a* to *Yehoshu'a* ("YHVH is salvation") and by appointing him as his successor. Indeed, the *Book of Joshua* frequently refers to Moses' tutelage of Joshua and shapes many aspects of Joshua's career to parallel similar aspects of the career of Moses. For example, Joshua's splitting of the Jordan River recalls Moses' splitting of the Sea of Reeds; Joshua's theophany (*Jos.* 5:13–15) specifically evokes that of Moses at the burning bush (*Ex.* 3–4); the image of Joshua holding out his spear until the city of Ai is taken (*Jos.* 8:26) recalls the image of Moses extending his arms until the Amalekites are routed (*Ex.* 17:12); and Joshua, like Moses, dispatches spies ahead of his army (*Jos.* 2).

Because most of Joshua's military activities took place in what became the tribal territory of Benjamin and Ephraim, modern scholars tend to believe that the historical Joshua was not a leader of the entire Israelite group, but of the north-central (Ephraimite) Israelites only. He is said to have received an Ephraimite estate in Timnath-serah (*Jos.* 19:50) and to have been buried there. When the compilers of the *Book of Joshua* combined traditions of the Exodus with traditions of the conquest, they cast Joshua as the lieutenant and successor of Moses, thus forging these once-disparate traditions into a unified narrative.

BIBLIOGRAPHY

Summaries and discussions of the scholarly debate over the nature of the Israelite occupation of Canaan and Joshua's role in it are found in Manfred Weippert's *The Settlement of the Israelite Tribes in Palestine*, translated by James D. Martin (Naperville, Ill., 1971), and in Roland de Vaux's *The Early History of Israel*, translated by David Smith (Philadelphia, 1978). For the view that Joshua founded a northern Israelite confederacy, see Theophile J. Meek's *Hebrew Origins* (1936; reprint, New York, 1960) pp. 18–48. A close literary reading of the *Book of Joshua* is Robert Polzin's *Moses and the Deuteronomist: A Literary Study of the Deuteronomic History* (New York, 1980), pp. 73–145.

EDWARD L. GREENSTEIN

JOSHUA BEN HANANIAH. *See* Yehoshu'a ben Ḥananyah.

JOSHUA BEN LEVI. *See* Yehoshu'a ben Levi.

JOSIAH, or, in Hebrew, Yo'shiyyahu; a king of Judah (c. 640–609 BCE). Josiah came to the throne at eight years of age upon the assassination of his father, Amon.

The account of his reign in *2 Kings* 22–23 is almost entirely taken up with a presentation of his cultic reform program in the eighteenth year. The parallel account in the much later history of *2 Chronicles* 34–35, which divides this reform activity between the twelfth and eighteenth years, probably has no independent validity and so should not be used in the reconstruction of the events of his reign.

The version in *Kings* states that during the course of the renovations of the Temple a "book of the law" *(sefer ha-torah)* was found. Its contents raised great consternation in the royal court and led to a large-scale reform program to purify the cult in Jerusalem. This last act meant the obliteration of other cult places throughout Judah and as far north as the region of Bethel, with the unemployed Levitical priests of "the high places" becoming wards of the state.

Because of the close match between the nature of the cultic reform program, especially the centralization of worship, and these same concerns in *Deuteronomy*, scholars have long identified "the book of the law" with this part of the Pentateuch. The time of Josiah is thus understood as a period of nationalistic and religious fervor resulting from the decline of Assyrian domination and influence in the west. It was within the context of these events that the framers of *Deuteronomy* were able to promulgate their reform program.

It must be kept in mind that the presentation of events in *2 Kings* 22–23 is shaped by a historian whose outlook is strongly influenced by *Deuteronomy*. It is possible, however, that both purification and centralization of the cult did not become firmly established until the Second Temple period, and even then there were exceptions. Some scholars have sought to offer archaeological evidence for the destruction of Judean sanctuaries at Arad and Beersheba in the late seventh century BCE, but the evidence is ambiguous and must be treated with caution.

Josiah is also credited with a brief revival of the Judean state and some expansion into the former Israelite kingdom to the north. About this, however, the Bible says little except for its reference to Josiah's destruction of the altar at Bethel. The archaeological evidence for Josiah's territorial control consists mostly of royal seal impressions on jar handles, which would limit his sphere of activity within the borders of Judah.

Apart from its description of the cultic reform, *Kings* contains only a few enigmatic remarks about Josiah's death at the hands of Pharaoh Necho at Megiddo while Necho was on his way to aid the Assyrians at Carchemish (*2 Kgs.* 23:29–30). The subsequent Babylonian hegemony led to the end of *de facto* Judean independence for the next four centuries.

The author of *Kings* rates Josiah highest of all the kings of Judah after David because of his religious reforms, and there is some further reflection of this esteem in *Jeremiah* 22:15–16.

BIBLIOGRAPHY

Treatments of the history can be found in John Bright's *A History of Israel*, 3d ed. (Philadelphia, 1981), and in the contributions by Hanoch Reviv, Yohanan Aharoni, and Yigael Yadin to *The World History of the Jewish People*, vol. 4, *The Age of the Monarchies*, edited by Abraham Malamat (Jerusalem, 1979), pt. 1, chaps. 9, 14; pt. 2, chap. 8. On the relationship of *Deuteronomy* to the reforms of Josiah, see E. W. Nicholson's *Deuteronomy and Tradition* (Philadelphia, 1967), Moshe Weinfeld's *Deuteronomy and the Deuteronomic School* (Oxford, 1972), and Hans-Detlef Hoffmann's *Reform und Reformen* (Zurich, 1980).

JOHN VAN SETERS

JǪTNAR ("giants"), also known as *troll, þursar,* and *risar,* represent a superhuman race in northern Germanic mythology that engages in endless battles with the gods. *Jǫtnar* play a central role in the myths of the creation and the destruction of the world. Life itself originated in the primeval *jǫtunn,* Ymir, who quickened in the melting ice. The world was later created from Ymir's body; ultimately the world will perish in the fire kindled by another giant, Surtr.

Though the gods and *jǫtnar* are implacable in their mutual hostility, there is much intercourse between the two groups. The gods trace their descent from the giantess Bestla. Gods sometimes wished to marry the daughters of *jǫtnar* (as in the case of Gerðr, wooed by Freyr); gods also seek to obtain from *jǫtnar* their important possessions (as Óðinn gained mead) or important knowledge (as Óðinn learned magic chants). A god's journey to Jǫtunheimr ("giantland") forms the central theme of mythic narrative poetry. *Jǫtnar,* then, were seen to possess great wealth and wisdom.

In prose narratives, *jǫtnar* are invariably depicted as living in caves and are always related to the local landscape. A sojourn in a *jǫtunn*'s cave and a love relationship with a *jǫtunn* maiden became standard features in the lives of young warrior heroes. *Jǫtnar* also appear as hostile, man-eating monsters. Their land is often described as lying in the north, in the midst of the snow and ice.

Jǫtnar have been viewed variously as ancestors and primeval spirits; as an older generation of gods; as forces of untamed nature, of chaos and destruction, or of death and infertility; and as the evil powers of wintertime. Scholars generally overlook the *jǫtnar*'s strong generative powers, the many benefits rendered by them to gods and men, and their lasting presence—as ogres or as friends—in folk belief and tradition.

BIBLIOGRAPHY

In spite of their prominence in Norse mythology and folk beliefs, the *jǫtnar* are not the subject of many scholarly studies. The classic work on folkloric giants and their counterparts in northern myth is Carl Wilhelm von Sydow's "Jätterna i mytologi och folktro," *Folkminnen och folktankar* 6 (1919): 52–96. His views are contested in my study "Giants in Folklore and Mythology: A New Approach," *Folklore* 93 (1982): 70–84. The benevolent, educational aspects of the giant are emphasized in Hilda R. Ellis Davidson's "Fostering by Giants in Old Norse Sagas," *Medium Aevum* 10 (1941): 70–85. Still timely is Jacob Grimm's description of West and North Germanic giants in *Teutonic Mythology*, 4 vols., translated by James Steven Stallybrass (1882–1883; reprint, Gloucester, Mass., 1976).

LOTTE MOTZ

JOURNALISM AND RELIGION.

[*This entry discusses reporting on religious topics in the daily print and broadcast media in the United States.*]

Alexis de Tocqueville devoted a chapter of his *Democracy in America* (1835), "Of the Relation between Public Associations and the Newspapers," to the interdependence of communications media and other institutions in a democratic society. Tocqueville highlights this interdependence in the following observation:

> There is a necessary connection between public associations and newspapers; newspapers make associations, and associations make newspapers. . . . A newspaper can survive only on the condition of publishing sentiments or principles common to a large number of men. A newspaper, therefore, always represents an association that is composed of its habitual readers. This association may be more or less defined, more or less restricted, more or less numerous; but the fact that a newspaper keeps alive is proof that at least the germ of such an association exists in the minds of its readers.
>
> (Tocqueville, ed. Bradley, 1960, vol. 2, pp. 120, 122)

The Creation of the News. Tocqueville's view ties newspapers and other media closely to their own associations of readers and viewers, and, at the same time, gives newspapers and other media a representative function. The representative function is actually twofold. First, the media represent the associations that make up their readerships and regular listeners, those in whose minds the germs of such associations exist. Second, the media, while being associations themselves, also represent other associations. They are both lamp and mirror in a society in which many groups seek to keep their own torches bright, thereby creating a need among the citizens for mirrors in which to perceive what is going on among the diversity of associations, each with its own self-interested agenda. In their preoccupation with matters of personal and neighborhood interest, the citizens "require a journal to bring to them every day, in the midst of their own minor concerns, some intelligence of the state of their public weal" (Tocqueville, p. 120).

In their interdependence the media and the associations they serve are among the central institutions in American society. Media shape and are shaped by the dynamic consensus of advocacy and counteradvocacy among the associations. To read a newspaper, listen to radio, or view television is to participate, whatever the attenuations, in a communion with the central institutions and ethos of the society, an act more powerful for being in large part symbolic and hence less obvious. The media, then, are a part of the consensus-making and consensus-reflecting exchanges that create a public out of a diverse and scattered population, encompassing even peoples of the globe, many of whom depend on American media for their news of the world.

Without an understanding of media as symbolic matrix, there can be no helpful understanding of "the news," much less the news of religion. The publication of the news is little noticed in its symbolic aspect, and the news becomes more powerful than it should be in a democratic society because the media through which news is mediated are disregarded. Why, then, are citizens not more critical of the media—not as institutions with their own affiliations, self-interests, and eccentricities, but rather in their symbolic function? Citizens are in fact critical of the media because of "bias" (writing and broadcast that takes words and images "out of context," or that touts a standard party line). Rarely, however, does criticism of the media touch on the means by which they make news out of persons, issues, movements, and events in the world. Why is this so? It is not possible to proceed to an examination of the way religion is reported in the media in the absence of some field against which to assess the ways in which aspects of various religions and religious practices become, and do not become, news. The "news" must be understood first.

News is not fact, but the mediation of facts through symbolic media, through conventions of writing and editing, and through inclusions and exclusions created in the practice of such conventions. This is not generally understood because the creators of the news and its readers and viewers are in common agreement on a key theory about what constitutes knowledge, particularly that form of knowledge called "news." News is not self-evident, since it is the creation of the media, but it is assumed to be self-evident because it is understood to be identical with "facts." Both reporter/editor and reader/viewer typically share a theory of knowledge that tacitly teaches them that news gets its status solely by reference to facts. What is published are matters of fact, a set of signs whose primary reason for being is to refer, copy, or imitate brute facts (the person who spoke, the event that occurred) or actions that happened beyond the pages and film, in the real world. On this view, news is reference; it is what is reported or photographed. The news-as-reference theory leaves unnoticed the nature of the media as symbolic matrices through which "facts" become "news."

Conventions of Storytelling. The Princeton historian Robert Darnton, for an article in which he reflects upon his days as a reporter for papers in New Jersey and New York City, took as his epigraph a graffito he found in 1964 on the wall of the press room of the Manhattan police headquarters: "All the news that fits we print." Darnton called his article, which appeared in *Daedalus* in 1975, "Writing News and Telling Stories"; in it he tells how the reporting of facts becomes news through the repertory of conventions for writing stories. While the facts that can be reported are without limit, the conventions into which facts are translated are limited, though they may vary from medium to medium, from one journalistic tradition to another.

Conventions of writing include the type of story an event or set of facts is judged to be, the stereotypes and rhetorical modes common to reporters, and editors' norms of judgment. Darnton makes clear that reporters are not rote writers; they are enterprising in seeking new twists on old ways of telling stories, but they typically do so within an approved genre of storytelling. Facts may be observed, recorded, and quoted, but before the reader or viewer sees the results, the reporter, under supervision of editors, writes the news. This sequence is as true of television reporting as it is of radio and print media (one may note, for example, the beginning and ending sentences of every television report from "the scene").

These conventions of story writing compose the symbolic matrix through which the media translate facts into news. Thus the graffito "All the news that fits we print" captures in an aphoristic formulation the "neatness of fit that produces the sense of satisfaction like the comfort that follows the struggle to force one's foot into a tight boot. The trick will not work if the writer deviates too far from the conceptual repertory that he shares with his public and from the techniques of tapping it that he has learned from his predecessors" (Darnton, 1975, p. 190).

"Conceptual repertory" comes in the form of rhetorical conventions, descriptive types, and formulaic devices, and not in the form of explicitly held taxonomies of types of stories. The tacit sharing of these conventions of writing and reading (or viewing) stories is the underlayment that supports the public status of the media, that is, the means for publicity based on publicly shared symbolic forms. Even though they may be biased on specific issues, the media in this understanding are representative and consensual.

As a good historian of his own abandoned career as a reporter, Darnton recounts that the first move a reporter makes upon being given an assignment is to go to "the morgue" in search of relevant sheets, a cluster of examples that inscribe an exemplary way of telling the story. "The dead hand of the past therefore shapes his perception of the present" (ibid., p. 189). This is how journalistic traditions of writing are maintained. This practice demonstrates in important if little-noticed ways that news is old. "There is an epistemology of the *fait divers*" (ibid.). And this epistemology of tradition is displayed not as a theory of knowledge but as a set of slowly changing styles of writing, and through the rhetorical conventions of the trade.

Darnton reinterprets Tocqueville, or rather extends Tocqueville's observations by particularizing them. One important meaning of *association* is the communion between habitual readers and the newspapers, the sharing of "sentiments and principles" of which Tocqueville wrote; Darnton particularizes the devices of this sharing in arguing that an essential dimension of the media is their symbolic matrix. Many historians and critics of American journalism have neglected or overlooked what Darnton calls "the long term cultural determinants of the news," in part because they have neglected to consider the enduring styles of storytelling through which news is mediated to various publics. Darnton writes:

> Of course, we did not suspect that cultural determinants were shaping the way we wrote about crimes in Newark, but we did not sit down at our typewriters with our minds a *tabula rasa*. Because of our tendency to see immediate events rather than long term processes, we were blind to the archaic element in journalism. But our very conception of "news" resulted from ancient ways of telling stories.
>
> (ibid., p. 191)

The reason that newspapers and other media are consensus-making and consensus-made institutions is that stories fit a range of cultural preconceptions of news. These cultural preconceptions are expressed, not as such, but rather in the "fit" of the facts, the fit of a new story into available conventions for writing that story. To study the way the media report religion is to study some of the constitutive rules that govern the display of stories in the media, rules that are never stated as such but that are presented through the conventions of news writing.

Treatments of the news and how it becomes so are also examinations into the epistemology of power through the analysis of rhetorical forms and conventions that translate facts. The philosopher John Searle, drawing on earlier work by J. L. Austin and G. E. M. Anscombe, summarizes the hierarchical relations that obtain among facts, institutions, or associations, and those constitutive rules that order both: "The description of the brute facts can only be explained in terms of institutional facts. But the institutional facts can only be explained in terms of the constitutive rules which underlie them" (Searle, 1969, p. 52).

To understand how rules operate as norms and mediating symbols and to comprehend how they are refigured, historically, as they confront novel situations, requires an inquiry that can be usefully assisted by the work of historians of religion such as Jonathan Z. Smith. Especially helpful are two of Smith's essays, "Sacred Persistence: Toward a Redescription of Canon," and "The Bare Facts of Ritual," from his collection *Imagining Religion* (1982). Studies of revision in the canonical status of taxonomies that function as constitutive rules for the governance of facts through sanctioning of particular forms of storytelling would find many useful analogies from similar studies of canonical and ritual change occasioned by time and circumstance.

Media is an overlapping of associations: the association as institution, association as representing other associations, association between the media and habitual readers and viewers, and association as symbolic matrix. Through these complicated connections the news is made.

Media and Religion. With the larger context of the multiple meanings of media established, it is possible to move to the question of the media and religion. How do the media represent religion? It is necessary that the preceding discussion be joined to this key question at many points, since the long-term cultural determinants that decisively affect the play of the news in general affect the ways the media represent religion in particular. The discussion is focused on daily national media in the United States, not on local, state, or ethnic media, nor on the vast array of media owned by various religious organizations, nor on the weekly and monthly periodical press and television programs. The defining pressures of daily and hourly deadlines impose their "fits" on the representation of religion in the national media. This is the most illuminating case for understanding how the central associations in the society transmit and receive news about religion.

In the preceding paragraph I have borrowed Darnton's term "cultural determinant" to refer to a catalog of conventions relied upon by reporters to write their stories. Yet one of the problems attending the effort to write with critical consciousness about religion is precisely that the available typologies and formulaic devices used to report on politics, war, sports, and other areas are used to write on religion.

Another sort of cultural determinant involves prevalent ideas among people working in the media about what religion is. Thus notions about religion in the American context determine not only how the news of religion is reported in this society, but also how religious leaders, movements, and traditions abroad are interpreted. Consensus about religion in this country, therefore, involves the ways that religions beyond this country are reported.

The ways the media represent religion through the mediations of their various conventions are different from the ways members of religious groups view their own and other religions, and different also from the ways scholars study religion. These differences account for many misunderstandings and criticisms. The representations of religion in the media are the combined results of both kinds of cultural determinations: the predetermination of story schema and the ideas held by writers and editors about religion, and the repertory of conventions and the conceptual repertories of ideas and images about religion. It is the interplay of these two sets of cultural determinations that make the constitutive rules that govern representations of religion in the media.

The first set requires that a story have a "hook" or "lead" that organizes its telling. The favorite convention or model for organization is some form of drama. Usually a type of conflict, this drama is something that can be grasped in a sharply delineated "take" that arrests the attention and woos the eye to read further. The dramatic, or conflict, scheme may come in cameo or in large-scale settings.

Those aspects of religious life that lend themselves to this prefiguration—namely, highly condensed, dramatic actions—are more likely to appear as stories: controversy, charge and countercharge, conversions, schisms, deviations of many sorts, novel conjunctions of tradition and modern style. Of special importance is the time sense required by this particular model or convention. This time sense is congruent with that that characterizes the entire world according to the media: a time sense made up of a series of discrete units, each more or less self-contained. Any religious practices that lend themselves to dramatic portrayal, that are of limited duration, and that are novel in appearance best meet these requirements. Of course, as has been noted, there is nothing in these requirements that is unique to religion. The way religion is reported must be regarded as essentially similar to the ways news of politics, economics, athletics, law, or military affairs is reported; there is no special category for "religious news" in contrast to "the news."

Formulaic pieces that report the visits of presidents and royalty, for example, work well for popes: the airport arrival, the crowds along the route of the motorcade, appearances in public places, presentations, brief speeches and testimonies, then departures—a series of sharp segments highly adaptable to the rhetorical inscription, transmission, and display requirements of the media. If drama, in one of its many variants, is the favored model, second in usefulness is the "personality" who dramatizes great conflicts in his or her gestures. Here two major genres for best coverage are those that focus on the spectacle or the personality. These genres, of course, are just as effective for athletic heroes, criminals, and political figures as they are useful in the portrayal of religious persons. Just as the presidential candidate's rally may have the form of a religious revival meeting, so papal visits have the form, according to the taxonomy relied upon by the media, of visits by heads of state. The substitutions of different events or personalities within the same format for writing or image making is a reminder of the power of the image types and story conventions that are used to schematize quite different situations in similar ways. "Facts" are not canonical for the media, but the forms within which they are organized have a canonical status worthy of the attention of scriptural scholars.

One idea that fits neatly with the conventions used to report religion is that religion is most authentically itself when it dramatizes itself, particularly in the lives of interesting human beings. Religion as ordinary living or as tradition, as a symbolic complex regularly reenacted, or as a complicated set of ideas with long histories (even with revolutionary consequences) does not attract the attention of the daily media. It is striking that the same features in religion—its symbolism, use of conventions, dependence on repetitions in institutional life and personal behavior—turn up in the media's analyses and that members of the media pay about as much attention to these aspects of religion as they pay to similar aspects in their own modes of operation. Personal lives and institutional histories do not lend themselves to translation into the major news-reporting conventions. In fact, the category of pastness and the category of the ordinary, so characteristic of much religious life and practice, are alien categories in the prevailing modes and ideas. The ways symbols work in the living of lives and in the continuities of institutional life, of habits of mind and textures of sensibility, of forms of conviviality, and of matters of taste legitimated by religious belief are outside the typical scope of the media—unless they are caught in the portmanteau category of "features," a prime location for worthy efforts that deviate from the prevailing norms and conventions.

The cultural historian will be intrigued by the hypothesis that the disposition to favor the drama of religion over the prose of religion is not original with the media, even though it happens that forms of storytelling most favored by the media conform to this dramatic idea of religion. My hypothesis is that one particular strand, a long and dominant strand, in Protestantism's religious practice has become thoroughly part of the media's ideas about religion: the media's dramatic model for religion is in fact derived from the conversion rituals so typical of evangelical Protestantism in particular and of a variety of conversion-oriented religions in general. Conversion and its opposite, deconversion, are metaphors that support the dramatic model for writing news about religion. Manifestly all dramatic stories about religion are not conversion stories, but the metaphor of conversion may serve as the tacit root for a variety of conflict models for use in the coverage of religion.

To write about the slow pace of institutional life and the erosions of change over time; to write about the variety of ways religious identity and sensibility affect other associations and expressions in society, the arts, manners, styles of living, family life; to describe ways of thinking about and imagining sexuality, work, leisure, competition, cooperation, war; and to analyze inside/outside group relations appear staggering tasks within the idioms and notions about religion that prevail in the media.

When necessary the media can do a competent job in reporting formal properties present in the collective life of religious groups, particularly when some of the properties—sexual ethics, for example—generate conflict within individual persons and families. But the distance is vast between the common forms and ideas about religion in the media and the remote but powerful ways religious symbols and behavior affect political and economic actions, for example.

When an understanding of religion moves beyond the personal and specifically institutional and goes in the direction of the less formal and more implicit ways religious belief and sensibility work themselves out in a variety of associations, such indeterminate but no less important aspects of religion place impossible strains on the media's conceptual framework, not to speak of the framework of its writing conventions. These elusive but important aspects of religion are rarely noticed in these idioms, and for good reasons, because they cannot be categorized within the prevailing forms of classification presupposed by reporters' assignments; by story types; by the specialized competences of reporters in politics, law, science, economics, sports; and, not least, by the departmentalization of media into corresponding sections on politics, law, science, economics, sports, and style. There is another set of reasons for large areas of religion's impact on society being dropped from notice by the media; it has to do with a set of intellectual traditions about religion that powerfully affect the outlooks of reporters, producers, editors, and columnists alike.

Some Specific Cases. Mary Catherine Bateson, an anthropologist, used the occasion of the Islamic Revolution to call to the attention of the editors and readers of the *New York Times* the consequences of the intellectual attitude toward religion that is held today by many experts upon whom the media wait for authoritative deliverances about such events as the mass suicide at Jonestown, Guyana, in 1978, and the Islamic Revolution of the late 1970s and early 1980s. She points to the failure of the media and of policymakers in the United States government, as others had pointed to the failure of the American CIA, to grasp the revolutionary forces at work in Iran. Such failures were extended in the systematic misrepresentations of the Ayatollah Khomeini by the American media, misrepresentations of a kind that will continue unless "there is a fundamental reappraisal of the role of religion in the world today" (letter to the *New York Times*, 20 February 1979).

What needs reappraising are notions about religion resident in large portions of the professions and among policymakers, as well as in the media. These ideas comprise an unsteady mixture of the Enlightenment idea that religion is at root superstition and liberalism's teaching that religious beliefs are primarily of interest in the private lives of persons. Neither attitude helps those who hold it to gain advanced notice of a crisis, much less write about many aspects of religion, until there is a dramatic crisis like a revolution, something that is of course political and economic, not merely "religious"; this is particularly so since such a revolution would be unimaginable in America. Consensus reporting does not prepare the media to view religion as having the power to redirect the history of a nation, let alone affect the life of many other nations. Bateson notes that a new understanding of religion is necessary that will "transcend the fashionable tendency to see religion either as fanaticism or as a cloak for other interests; it must be premised on a recognition that for vast numbers of the world's people the symbols of religion sum up their highest aspirations."

When the media seek expert consultants on religious matters, they frequently call in members of the psychological profession, who are often disposed to see religion as a form of pathology, or other social scientists who see religion as a "cloak," or an ideology covering a variety of other interests, whether ethnic, economic, or political. Neither media notions of religion, derived from Enlightenment critique, nor courtship of the social sciences for authoritative enlightenment about unusual religious phenomena such as Jonestown, prepares the media to understand the power of symbols to inspire group visions other than those of progress and economic growth. The frequency of use of the term "medieval" in describing the forces led in Iran by Ayatollah Khomeini discloses much of the media's own misunderstanding of religion. The irony is that it was precisely this misunderstanding that led so many intellectuals in America to be surprised by the Islamic Revolution.

The media, then, work with conventions and ideas that reinforce each other in determining the ways religion is represented. In addition, the American press, used to the consensual reporting of religion in this country, is ill prepared to report on religion in other cultures where the manners of pluralism do not obtain and where religious power is often disintegrative of the existing social order instead of communing with it.

Just as there are working models in the media for what is authentically religious, so there is at work a pattern for the typical relationship between religion and the central social order. Nowhere is this model so clearly disclosed as when the media attempt to report minority or fundamentally different forms of religious practice, different ways of being religious than those practiced in the mainline associations and in the major religious traditions. Again, the ways the media report minority religious practices in American society indicate how foreign religions will be reported, or not reported.

On Sunday, 8 June 1980, the *New York Times* ran a story headlined "Police Seize Animals Prepared for Sacrifice by Cult in the Bronx," accompanied by a two-column picture of an officer of the American Society for the Prevention of Cruelty to Animals holding a lamb with the caption "Lamb Saved from Slaughter." The lead on this story was as follows: "Police officers and agents of an animal protection society raided a garage in the

Southview section of the Bronx early yesterday and confiscated 62 animals that they said were apparently being held for sacrifice by a religious cult." The raid, following one that had occurred three weeks previously, was termed in the second lead paragraph "the first major successful raid on secret cults practicing animal sacrifice." The final sentence of the ten-paragraph story read "The animals used in the cultic rituals are usually killed by having their throats slit, according to Mr. Langdon," the officer pictured holding the saved lamb. The drama of the raid, as reported, was followed by lists and numbers of animals confiscated. Officer Langdon was the major source for the story, and apparently the quoted authority on the meaning and history of the cult. "People will give one of the sect's priests $100 to perform a sacrifice so that good things will happen, so they will get money, or become healthy," he said. Not until the seventh paragraph were any words attributed to a member of the group raided, and no leaders were quoted. There was no reference to scholarship on this form of religious practice. Not until the penultimate paragraph was any background information supplied about this group and its affiliations. Again, Officer Langdon was the informant quoted: "Mr. Langdon said that the people in the house belonged to a sect closely related to Santería, which, he said, was derived from a Nigerian religion called Yoruba that was brought to Cuba by slaves in the 18th century and which once practiced infanticide as well as animal sacrifice."

A generous critic of this story may doubt if many adherents of Santería were assumed to be included in the *Times*'s readers that Sunday morning. All the key terms of the story—"raid," "sacrifice," "religious cult," "slaughter," "cruelty to animals," "sect," "a Nigerian religion called Yoruba," "slaves," "infanticide as well as animal sacrifice"—along with the quoted final sentence, combine to project a consistent image of the exotic. No reporter would describe a mainline religious group as "an American religion called X that was brought to this country in the seventeenth century by visionaries, refugees, indentured servants, and fortune seekers."

True to form, the story angles on a dramatic event, a police raid, followed by confiscation of the animals. But not so true to form is the hybrid mixture of conventions tugging at each other in the story. The alleged violations of city laws on the treatment of animals and on harboring farm animals in the city are in tension with the story of the religious rite interrupted by the raid, and nowhere is the issue of freedom to practice religion hinted at as an issue. The mixture of types struggling with each other here—the police raid; the exotic practices of a minority religion; the motivation for such practices as involving exchange of money with priests of the cult (a constant, formulaic consideration in reporting of religion); the sentimental story involving officers rescuing animals from danger (no pictures provided of goats or guinea hens, which were also saved)—disclose a clash of genre and, perhaps unwittingly, reveal the problematics of conventional treatments of the exotic for an intended majority readership. All information supplied about the minority religious group only highlights the alien, if not pathological and illegal, status of such groups and their practices.

The loosely braided character of the several story conventions at work demonstrates what happens when news that does not neatly fit gets published. Perhaps here was a telltale occasion when "All the news that's fit to print" prevailed over "All the news that fits we print." The misfits here illuminate the standard fits that prevail in most reporting of religion. The heterogeneity of the "brute facts" on which this story was based may have placed too much pressure on the ruling conventions for them to operate effectively.

The repetition of key words in the story shows how the alien and the minority is encoded for the familiar and majority. Terms such as "cult," "secret sacrifice," "infanticide," "slaughter," and the like had echoed through the media during the previous eighteen months, following the reporting of events at Jonestown, Guyana, in November 1978; at that time, other terms—"fanatical," "paranoid," and "bizarre"—were added to the code to alert readers and viewers to the alien and "other" status of such religious practices and leaders. These signals of differentness serve to reaffirm readers' and viewers' tacit association and to reassert the normative and "normal" status of the familiar and dominant. "Charismatic preacher" may work as a term of approval, but "cult leaders" become "self-proclaimed messiahs," while their believers become "victims."

The mix of conventions used to report the practice of Santería in the Bronx bear close relations to similar encodings in the reporting of Jonestown and its leader Jim Jones and of the revolution in Iran and Ayatollah Khomeini, who was constantly referred to as a "madman," and whose country was classified as backward, if not primitive, by being called "medieval." The visual image of the shouting mob became the set for television reporting from Iran, recalling a scene type that goes back to the crowd imagery used by those writers hostile to the French Revolution.

Generalizations about the media as a consensual association enforcing what Tocqueville called "principles and sentiments" are routinely inscribed in the particulars of ordinary stories like the *Times* story discussed above. The ways that particular "facts" are represented contribute to the consensus while embodying many of the consensus's assumptions. Such representations not only define themselves and their constituents affirmatively toward their conception of the normal but also negatively toward the alien, the exotic, the criminal, the pathological, the animal, the medieval, the primitive, and so on. These terms of exclusion and their encoded idioms within the rhetorical commonplaces of news writing carry power to refamiliarize the normal by distancing the alien. Thus the rhetoric of the media bears close analogies to rituals of inclusion and of exorcism. In these ways the media make their contribution to the manners of discourse and good taste in a society that has shown a decided disposition to view religion as private, lest the plurality of prescriptive and assertive religions within its borders cease observing good form. This equivocal achievement is sustained by a studied absence of attention to the power of symbols, those of religion and those of the media, to affect the lives of the unreported many, who take the former with much more seriousness than the latter.

[*For related discussion, see* Law and Religion, *article on* Religion and the Constitution of the United States, *and* Religious Broadcasting.]

BIBLIOGRAPHY

Anscombe, G. E. M. "On Brute Facts." *Analysis* 18 (1958): 69–72. A brief and influential article setting forth elementary distinctions among different kinds of facts and their relations. See Searle (1969), cited below.

Bensman, Joseph, and Robert Lilienfeld. *Craft and Consciousness: Occupational Technique and the Development of World Images.* New York, 1973. Journalists and intellectuals are among the occupational groups treated in this work in the sociology of knowledge. Alert to the power of images arising out of occupations, it is, in effect, a theoretical expansion of Kenneth Burke's dictum, "occupations engender pre-occupations."

Cuddihy, John Murry. *No Offense: Civil Religion and Protestant Taste.* New York, 1978. While not directly about media in American society, this work offers a provocative and controversial thesis about the function of discourses of civility and taste in a pluralistic society. Cuddihy's multiplication of examples from a variety of sources is a persuasive exercise in the hermeneutics of unmasking.

Darnton, Robert. "Writing News and Telling Stories." *Daedalus* 104 (Spring 1975): 175–194. Darnton shows himself to be a master of two conventions here, making the personal memoir serve the larger purposes of an historical and rhetorical analysis of the ways the news is prefigured. An exemplary approach suggesting literary and cultural analyses can be usefully combined with historical study of the media. Included is a selective and critical annotated bibliography.

Gans, Herbert J. *Deciding What's News: A Study of CBS Evening News, NBC Nightly News, Newsweek, and Time.* New York, 1979. Gans's analysis focuses on decision making. This is a standard approach in work on the media. The identification of sets of image traditions, however, such as the pastoral, makes his an important contribution to the symbolic analysis of the media.

Goethals, Gregor T. *The TV Ritual: Workship at the Video Altar.* Boston, 1981. While not strong on the history of the images employed on television, this art historian offers a novel thesis about the religious functions of television images in their various formats. An effort to suggest a ritual analysis of television image sequences.

Hughes, Helen MacGill. *News and the Human Interest Story.* Chicago, 1940. This is one of the earliest of the few works that stress the long-term cultural determinants at work in the conventions of news reporting. Like Darnton's memoir, it sets a good precedent for further work on the sociocultural determinants of news writing.

Innis, Harold A. *Empire and Communications* (1950). Reprint, Toronto, 1972.

Innis, Harold A. *The Bias of Communication.* Toronto, 1951. These two undervalued works have inspired more famous treatments of media, none of which have equaled Innis's cross-cultural scope and empirical incisiveness. Historians and anthropologists of religion can benefit from Innis's treatment of the role of intellectuals in various media in a variety of cultures, ancient and modern. Innis is particularly helpful in outlining, through comparative study, different time senses in various societies and within various strata of society.

Lippmann, Walter. *Public Opinion.* New York, 1922. Few subsequent works have approached the comprehensiveness of sweep and the use of telling detail of Lippmann's pioneering study. It is an extensive elaboration of many of Tocqueville's intuitions and notes. Most of interest to the student of religion is Lippmann's fine treatment of censorship and privacy, stereotypes (all of the third section of the book), the role of interests, and the recurrent attention to the function of rhetorical forms in media in a democratic society. A classic work meriting a new edition.

Rockefeller Foundation. *The Religion Beat: The Reporting of Religion in the Media.* New York, 1981. Papers by journalists and academic specialists in religious studies, followed by excerpts from a day's consultation, sponsored by the Rockefeller Foundation, Humanities Division, in the aftermath of Jonestown and the Islamic Revolution. A good collection of occasional pieces, many with bibliographical reference, for beginning an inquiry into the representation of religion in the news. Of particular note is the stress in several parts of the consultation on the interplay between the coverage of religion in America and the coverage of religion in other countries.

Schudson, Michael. *Discovering the News: A Social History of American Newspapers.* New York, 1978. A quality work clearly represented by its title. In the tradition of the Hughes book noted above.

Schudson, Michael. "Why News Is the Way It Is." *Raritan* 2 (Winter 1983): 109–125. Other than the Darnton article cited above, the single most useful article on the subject. Schudson is not held captive by any one theory but is deft in relating the reigning theories about the news to each other and in using them to criticize each other. The result, particularly since one of the theories he treats is the semiotic, is a minor classic of synthesis.

Searle, John. *Speech Acts: An Essay in the Philosophy of Language.* London, 1969. Drawing on the work of J. L. Austin and G. E. M. Anscombe, Searle is important for his placement of a philosophy of language in conjunction with questions of factuality, on the one hand, and institutional contexts, on the other, and he dialectically weaves the relations among them. An analysis that is useful to applied work in religion or in the media, or both.

Shils, Edward. "Center and Periphery." In *Center and Periphery: Essays in Macrosociology,* vol. 2, *Selected Papers,* pp. 3–16. Chicago, 1975. Shils offers a dialectic in the understanding of the central institutional system in a society, with dissensual forces imaged as "periphery." The bias toward the center is clear, though the delicacy of the analysis, if used to think about the functional and symbolic roles of media, is helpful. Should be supplemented by Shils's chapter on consensus in the same volume.

Smith, Jonathan Z. *Imagining Religion: From Babylon to Jonestown.* Chicago, 1982. Smith provides the only available treatment of Jonestown by a historian of religion. In addition, his essays "Sacred Persistence: Toward a Redescription of Canon" and "The Bare Facts of Ritual," included in this volume, not only illuminate problems in the history and anthropology of religion but are also helpful in understanding media as a canonical symbolic matrix and in exploring the problems attending changes in that canon.

Strauss, Leo. *Persecution and the Art of Writing* (1952). Westport, Conn., 1973. Strauss offers a hermeneutic for understanding writing performed under particular repressions, especially the threat of official censorship. The work's relevance ranges far beyond issues of writing and censorship if censorship is broadened to include a variety of forms of cultural suppression or exclusion.

Tocqueville, Alexis de. *Democracy in America.* Edited by Phillips Bradley. 2 vols. New York, 1960. This work is included because, in addition to the observations on newspapers in a democratic society, Tocqueville's chapters on language and speech in America are early instances that can now be seen to be a part of social semiotics.

RUEL W. TYSON, JR.

JOURNEY. *See* Ascension; Descent into the Underworld; Flight; Pilgrimage; *and* Quest.

JUDAH. *For Jewish figures whose given names are commonly rendered as Judah, see* Yehudah.

JUDAISM. [*This entry consists of an overview of the origins and development of the Jewish religious tradition and seven historical surveys of Judaism in the major regions of the Diaspora:*

In addition to the related articles referred to in this entry, see also the biographies of the principal figures mentioned herein.]

An Overview

Neither of the sacred Jewish classics, the Bible or the Talmud, speaks of "Judaism." Hellenistic Jews created this Greek word to describe their uncommon way of serving God (*2 Mc.* 2:21, 8:1, 14:38; *Gal.* 1:13–14). All such mediating terms, because they utilize alien categories as the means of self-representation, necessarily distort as much as they explain. Thus, while the Jews of the first century CE integrated their ethnicity and their religion, Paul, writing *Galatians* for gentile readers, must sunder faith from folk in order to communicate.

Contemporary Jewish thinkers radically disagree as to the nature of Judaism and even the advisability of employing the term. Interpretations of Judaism today range from steadfast traditionalism to radical universalism. The traditionalists themselves differ strongly on accommodation to modernity. The right-wing Orthodox resist accommodation, while the Modern Orthodox accept any cultural good not forbidden by God's revelation. Debates over the role of mysticism add further diversity. Other contemporary Jews have rejected Orthodoxy because they deem it incompatible with the practice of democracy and the findings of the natural and social sciences, especially critical history.

Among nonreligious Jews, some are humanists who assimilate their Jewishness to contemporary culture, especially ethics. Others identify Judaism with Jewish folk culture. Zionism and the state of Israel represent the secularization of Judaism at its fullest.

Among liberal—that is, non-Orthodox—religious Jews, four differing emphases occur. (1) Jews who have an ethnic attachment to Judaism often find that it ac-

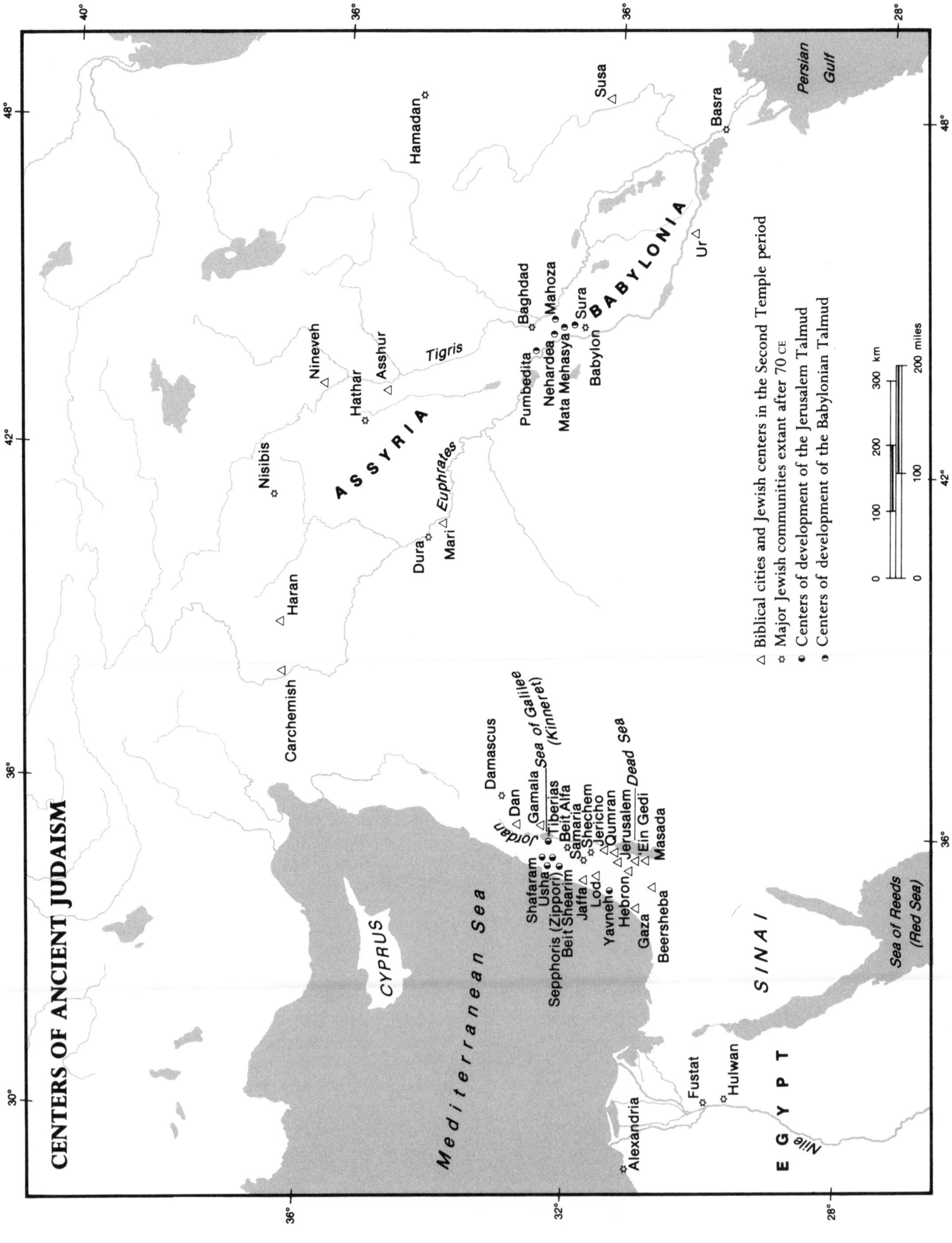
CENTERS OF ANCIENT JUDAISM
Persian Gulf
Susa
Basra
Hamadan
Ur
BABYLONIA
Baghdad
Mahoza
Sura
Babylon
Pumbedita
Nehardea
Mata Mehasya
Nineveh
Asshur
Hathar
Tigris
ASSYRIA
Nisibis
Euphrates
Dura
Mari
Haran
Carchemish
Damascus
Sea of Galilee (Kinneret)
Dan
Gamala
Jordan
Tiberias
Beit Alfa
Samaria
Shechem
Jericho
Qumran
Jerusalem
Dead Sea
Ein Gedi
Masada
Shafaram
Usha
Sepphoris (Zippori)
Beit Shearim
Jaffa
Lod
Yavneh
Hebron
Gaza
Beersheba
Mediterranean Sea
CYPRUS
SINAI
Sea of Reeds (Red Sea)
Fustat
Hulwan
Alexandria
EGYPT
Nile
Biblical cities and Jewish centers in the Second Temple period
Major Jewish communities extant after 70 CE
Centers of development of the Jerusalem Talmud
Centers of development of the Babylonian Talmud
0 100 200 300 km
0 100 200 miles
30°
36°
42°
48°
28°
32°
40°

quires a core of universal spirituality that, in turn, revitalizes their attachment. (2) Jews seeking a more disciplined Jewish religiosity direct their ethnic life through Jewish law, dynamically interpreted, as a historically evolving structure. (3) Jews concerned with the demands of rationality assert that Judaism uniquely comprehends the idea of ethical monotheism, a universal truth that is reinforced by their sense of ethnicity. (4) Jews who adopt a personalist approach conceptualize Judaism as a relationship, a covenant mutually created by God and the Jewish people and re-created in every generation. This article describes postbiblical Judaism in terms of the evolving expression of the Jewish people's covenant with God, understood in liberal religious terms.

From the Bible to Rabbinic Judaism

We have little hard data by which to trace the progress from biblical to rabbinic Judaism, despite some help from the biblical *Book of Daniel.* From Ezra and Nehemiah (Hebrew leaders of the mid-fifth century BCE) to the earliest rabbis (the authorities mentioned in the Talmud) in the first half of the first century CE, the sources in Jewish tradition that are considered authoritative provide little reliable historical information. Learned conjectures can fill this gap, but as their validity rests on hermeneutic foundations that often shift, all such speculations are best left to historians. [*See* Rabbinic Judaism in Late Antiquity.]

The rabbis themselves affirmed an unbroken transmission of authoritative tradition, of Torah in the broad sense, from Moses to Joshua to the elders, the prophets, and thence to the immediate predecessors of the rabbis (*Avot* 1.1). By this they meant that along with the written Torah (the first five books of the Bible, also known as the Pentateuch or Law) Moses also delivered the oral Torah, or oral law, which contained substantive teaching (legal and nonlegal) as well as the proper methods for the further development of the Torah tradition. As inheritors and students of the oral (and written) law, the rabbis knew themselves to be the authoritative developers of Judaism.

Modern critical scholarship universally rejects this view. For one thing, the Bible makes no mention of oral law. Then, too, it is reasonable to think of Torah as undergoing historical development. When, over the centuries, Judaism grew and changed, later generations validated this unconscious process by introducing, retroactively, the doctrine of the oral law.

We may see rabbinic Judaism's mix of continuity and creativity more clearly if we briefly note these same features in their late biblical predecessors. Ezra and Nehemiah believe that God and the Jewish people have an ancient pact, and they seek to be faithful to it by their lives. Though they acknowledge that God rules the whole world, they and their fellow Babylonian Jews manifest a deep loyalty to a geographic center returning from an apparently more prosperous land to resettle Jerusalem and restore God's Temple there. They are ethnic separatists, rejecting offers of help from the Samaritans and requiring Jewish males to give up their gentile wives. They carefully restore the Temple cult and insist on observance of the Sabbath. But their Judaism involves sensibility as well as statute. When Nehemiah discovers people collecting debts in a time of hardship, he denounces such hard-heartedness as incompatible with covenant loyalty, and they desist.

Ezra and Nehemiah also evidence a new religious concern: acting in accordance with "the book of God's Torah" (*Neh.* 9:3). In a great public ceremony, the book is read to all the people, men, women, and children, and explained to them in detail. By the mid-fifth century BCE, then, a written tradition has taken the place formerly occupied by divination, prophecy, and priestly teaching. [*See* Israelite Religion.]

Nearly three centuries later, *Daniel* gives us another glimpse of late biblical Judaism. Daniel, the paradigmatic Jew, lives outside the Land of Israel, among idolaters. He perseveres in the prescribed Jewish patterns of eating, drinking, and praying, despite the threat of severe punishment. A heavy eschatological focus distinguishes this book, as do its bizarre visions and their cryptic interpretations. After calamitous persecutions of the holy people, including wars against them by foreign powers, God intervenes, sending one who defeats their foes and establishes their kingdom forever. A time of cosmic judgment follows that dooms the wicked to eternal reprobation while the righteous live on forever. The biblical prophets' expectations of an ideal king, descended from King David, who would one day establish worldwide justice, compassion, and recognition of God have here been radically extended.

The Judaism of the Rabbis

Rabbinic Judaism appears as a mature development in its earliest datable document, the Mishnah, a compilation of Jewish traditions redacted about 200 CE. [*See* Mishnah and Tosefta.] We can flesh out its sparely written text by consulting the more extensive classic works of rabbinism, the Talmud and the Midrash. The Talmud—essentially a collection of rabbinic discussions on the Mishnah—exists in two forms: the Jerusalem Talmud *(Yerushalmi)*, redacted about 400 CE, and the Babylonian Talmud *(Bavli)*, redacted about 500 CE and considered the more authoritative of the two. [*See* Talmud.] The Midrash is a body of homiletic and other exegeses of the Bible, of which the earliest compilations date from the third to the sixth centuries CE. The rabbis proceed on the assumption that the Temple, destroyed by the Romans in 70 CE, will be rebuilt only in "the days of the Messiah." They refer to the Temple cult mainly as the stuff of memory and hope and as material for study. Their Judaism centers about the Torah, particularly the oral Torah. To the critical eye, the distinctive features of rabbinic Judaism reflect creative development as much as reverent continuity with the past.

A structural innovation of the rabbis provides a convenient entry into their Judaism. They utilize parallel, mutually reinforcing modes of instruction, *halakhah* ("the way," the law, the required pattern of living) and *aggadah* (all else, including lore, preachment, speculation, and theology). Both are considered Torah, which literally means God's own instruction. In rabbinic texts they are often found organically intertwined, but they carry different degrees of authority. When dealing with *halakhah*, the rabbis, for all their disagreement and debate, seek to attain coherence and to decide what constitutes lawful practice. (The rabbis' courts can inflict severe penalties on transgressors.) By contrast, the realm of the *aggadah* is unregulated. The rabbis appear to delight in finding ingenious ways to amaze their colleagues with their imaginative exegeses and dicta. In all their contradiction and contrariety, these teachings too are part of the oral law. [*See* Midrash and Aggadah.]

Way of the Rabbis. For the rabbis, the covenant entails the adoption of a way of life faithful to God more than acquiescence to a specific doctrine. All later varieties of Judaism—including, despite radical differences, the modern ones—have echoed these spiritual priorities. A description of Judaism, therefore, should begin with some highlights of the rabbinic way. What follows represents the norms stated in authoritative rabbinic texts much more than it does the realities of community practice of the rabbinic era, about which we have no direct independent data.

Responsibility of the individual. The bulk of rabbinic literature concentrates on how the ordinary Jewish man ought to conduct himself so as to sanctify his life. Feminists have correctly pointed out that the rabbis take men to be the primary focus of God's instruction, with women essentially considered to be their adjuncts. Thus, men make all the halakhic decisions about women's duties, and though any man might qualify to render such decisions, traditionally no woman can. The rabbis did assign women a comparatively high personal and communal status. Nonetheless, by egalitarian standards, the differentiation of women's duties from those of men, which are viewed as the norm, imposes on women a loss of dignity and worth.

The troubling issue of sexism aside, rabbinic Judaism is remarkably democratic. It calls all Jews to the same attainable virtues: righteousness in deed, piety of heart, and education of the mind. It may derogate the wicked and the ignorant, but it never denies they might change and attain the highest sanctity. The sacred elite, the rabbinate, remains open to any man and recognizes no substantial barriers between rabbis and other Jews.

With the Temple destroyed, rabbinic Judaism made the ordinary Jew a "priest" by transforming many rituals once connected with the Temple cult so that they became a way of sanctifying one's everyday life at home or in the marketplace. Before eating or after excreting, one was to wash one's hands ritually and recite an appropriate blessing. Each morning and afternoon—the times of the Temple sacrifices—men worshiped in a prescribed liturgical structure. (An evening service was added later.) In the morning, men said their prayers wearing head and arm phylacteries (Heb., *tefillin*), small leather boxes that contain biblical citations. (The very pious wore them all day.) The doorpost of a Jewish home bore its own small container, the *mezuzah*, which contained Torah texts. A special fringe on the corner of a man's garment served as a reminder of his responsibility to God.

The Jew's table became an altar. What came to it had to be ritually acceptable, *kasher*. The list of foods proscribed by the Torah was amplified by rabbinic interpretation. Animals had to be slaughtered in a religiously acceptable, humane manner, and their carcasses had to be examined for diseases. Rabbinic law extended the biblical prohibition against boiling a kid in its mother's milk to prohibit mixing any meat with any milk product. [*See* Kashrut.] It also mandated various blessings to be recited prior to eating bread, fruit, grain, vegetables, and other foods. After a meal, a longer, preferably communal grace was to be said.

The recitation of blessings was a constant part of the Jew's day. Hearing good news or bad news; seeing the sea, or a flowering tree, or an odd-looking person, or a meteor; smelling spices; acquiring something new; passing a place where a miracle had been done—all such occasions, and many more, required brief words of prayer.

The conduct of business also exhibited this intermingling of the commonplace with the transcendent. The rabbis spelled out in detail their religious equivalent of what Western civilization calls civil law. The covenant embraced such issues of justice as the proper treatment by employers of workers and the responsibilities of workers to their employers; the definition of reasonable inducements to customers and of illegitimate restriction of trade; the extent of a fair profit and a seller's responsibility in the face of changing prices; the duty to testify in the rabbinic court and the form in which contracts were to be written. Disputes between Jews on any of these matters were to be taken to the rabbinic court, which had detailed standards for administering justice.

The rabbis made daily study—for its own sake and as a ritual observance—a religious responsibility of the highest significance. The minimum requirement could be satisfied by studying selected biblical verses and rabbinic passages, but even the liturgy included numerous study texts and regular Torah readings. Besides, the acquisition of knowledge was a source of community esteem, a typical example of social custom strengthening rabbinic ideals. The rabbis endowed Jewish religiosity with its bookish cast, and their argumentative, analytic form of study made Jewish life uncommonly verbal and cerebral.

Because much that the rabbis valued could not usefully be made law, they surrounded their precepts with their individual opinions about what constitutes the good person and the ideal community. Like the Bible's authors, they abominate lying, stealing, sexual immorality, violence, and bloodshed. They decry gossip, slander, faithlessness, injustice, hard-heartedness, arrogance, and pride. They glorify industry, honesty, compassion, charity, trustworthiness, humility, forgiveness, piety, and the fear of God. Believing in the Jewish community's good sense, they urge individuals to acquire a "good name."

They do not underestimate the difficulties involved in striving to be a good Jew—yet they never doubt that, with God's help, one can be more righteous than wicked. They picture humans as being in perpetual conflict between their *yetser ha-ra'* ("urge to do evil") and their *yetser ṭov* ("urge to do good"). The former they describe as a relentless, wily, indefatigable foe that seeks to dominate human consciousness and easily infects human sexuality and that can be defeated only momentarily. Realists that they were, the rabbis acknowledge that the evil urge often leads to good. Its driving energy causes people to marry, build homes, engage in useful commerce, and the like. Though one ought never to underestimate its destructiveness or one's own vulnerability, human beings can harness some of its strength for their own good and to do God's work.

One can best fight off or sublimate the "urge to do evil" by studying, remaining pious, keeping good companions, and above all by observing the Torah. However, nothing guarantees its defeat, and self-righteousness practically invites its victory. Death alone terminates the struggle, and only at the "end of days" will the "urge to do evil" be destroyed. Until then, Jews continually beseech God's help, confident that, as the Bible teaches and the rabbis continually reiterate, God will aid them in their striving for purity.

The rabbis do not expect anyone to remain sinless. (Even Moses, their model, was not sinless.) Having sinned, one should do *teshuvah*, "turning" or "repentance." Elaborating on a biblical theme, the rabbis specify the stages by which sinners right their relationship with God. One begins by becoming conscious of having sinned and feeling remorse. That should lead to a confession of one's sin before God and thus to confrontation with one's guilt. But morbidity leaves no energy for sanctification. Instead, guilt should motivate one to recompense those one has wronged and ask their forgiveness. Having firmly resolved never to repeat the iniquity, one may then beseech God's mercy with confidence, for God loves this effort of the human will and graciously accepts each sincere initiative, granting atonement.

One need not be Jewish to do *teshuvah*, and the rabbis directed that the *Book of Jonah* be read on the annual Day of Atonement to remind Jews that even the wicked Ninevites had once done so. Even for Jews *teshuvah* involves no special rites or sanctified personnel. Rather, each day's dynamic of striving but often failing to fulfill the Torah involves the individual in practicing *teshuvah*. (On Yom Kippur, the Day of Atonement, the Jewish people, in a unique sequence of four worship services, carries out a corporate *teshuvah*.) [*See* Atonement, *article on* Jewish Concepts.]

Family in rabbinic Judaism. The rabbis usually think of individuals not as isolated entities but as organically connected to their families and their people. For the rabbis the Jewish way primarily involves an ethnic group's unique covenant with God and its consequences for the lives of the individuals who constitute the group. The Jewish family replicates in miniature the greater covenant community.

The rabbis consider marriage a cardinal religious obligation, though they tolerate some exceptions. Through marriage one carries out the biblical command to have children. Because marriages were arranged in their era, the rabbis provide much counsel about this important process. They strongly urge that men marry early and that they take a wife from a good family who has a pleasant personality. They favor monogamy but do not require it (it was finally made obligatory by the medieval sages). They subordinate good looks, love, sexual pleasure, and even fecundity—in all of which they delight—to their goal of family well-being, *shalom*, which comes from a couple's mutual dedication to the Torah.

The rabbis hope that a deep love will arise between the spouses, on whom they enjoin sexual fidelity. (Talmudic law defines such fidelity in terms of the wife's behavior; medieval writers tend to apply similar standards to husbands.) They expect male dominance in the household, but counsel the temperate use of power by husbands and fathers. They also display a canny sense of the critical, even decisive, role the wife/mother plays in family affairs.

Despite this exaltation of marriage in their sacred way of living, the rabbis provided for the possibility of divorce. Though they decried the breakup of a family, they did not make divorce administratively impractical. Divorced men and women often remarried.

From biblical times, Jews experienced infertility as grievous suffering. If Jews have no offspring, the covenant expires. Through future generations all prior Jewish devotion hopes to reach completion. Children—particularly sons, in the rabbinic view—therefore come as a great blessing, and if they grow up to be good people, respected in the community, their parents enjoy inestimable fulfillment. Should they be wicked, their parents consider it a major judgment on themselves. Some rabbis identify suffering caused by one's children as the worst of divine visitations.

Only occasionally do the rabbis discuss parents' obligations to their children, perhaps because they believed that natural sentiment, guided by Jewish folkways, would adequately direct them. By contrast, they say much about children's duties toward their parents. The rabbis' amplification of the Fifth Commandment—"Honor your father and mother"—not only reflects their regard for wisdom and experience but testifies to the covenant between the generations that revivifies the covenant between God and Israel. Jewish personal names add to this intimacy, for one is called the "son (or daughter) of so-and-so" and thus carries one's parent in one's personhood all one's life.

These relationships functioned within the Jewish home, the primary scene of ongoing Jewish observance. Particularly since it might also be one's place of business, the home brought the diverse aspects of Jewish life together in mutually strengthening integrity. [*See* Domestic Observances, *article on* Jewish Practices.]

Jewish community and Jewish people. In rabbinic times most Jews lived away from the Land of Israel, in the Diaspora, and from about the fifth to the tenth century CE, Babylonian Jewry exercised preeminent religious authority. To carry on their faith, the Jews who were scattered across the Parthian and Roman empires found it helpful to live near other Jews. The experience of anti-Semitism also brought Jews together. As always, the social and the sacred interpenetrated.

The responsibility of the Jewish community to uphold the covenant received its most visible expression in the liturgy of the daily worship services at which communal prayer was offered. (Obligatory individual prayer derives from this corporate duty.) A quorum of at least ten adult males, representing the entire Jewish people, was required to be present. At the morning service on Mondays, Thursdays, Sabbaths, and festivals, and on Sabbath afternoons, the group read a portion of the Torah scroll, often followed by a selection from the prophetic books. If a particularly learned man were in the congregation, he might give a sermon.

Any man with the requisite knowledge could lead the service or read from the scroll. Various religious functionaries enhanced the community's life, but a rabbi was not a requirement. Both a ritual slaughterer (so there could be kosher meat) and a teacher for the children took priority. Devoted volunteers attended and buried the dead and took care of other such communal duties.

Rabbis in the Talmudic period were not employed by the Jewish community but, like other Jews, worked at some ordinary occupation. When the community did have a rabbi, he functioned as both scholar and judge. He exemplified the Jewish duty to study and he answered questions about Jewish law, when necessary convening a rabbinical court *(beit din)*. Decisions of the *beit din* were considered part of the oral law and hence carried divine authority, yet they could be appealed by writing to a greater scholar elsewhere who might, by the authority of his knowledge and piety, indicate that the ruling was faulty.

Corporate life turned about several institutions. One, the synagogue, which may have predated the earliest generations of rabbis, was recognized by them as a surrogate for the destroyed Temple, with prayer as a fully adequate substitute for sacrifice and laymen in the place of priests. The rabbis also made it possible for a synagogue to function anywhere a quorum met, including a private home. A populous settlement might have many congregations. A prosperous community would erect an appropriate building to house synagogue activities. [*See* Synagogue.]

Another institution was the study house, where those devoted to learning would find a place to study and to meet with other students of Torah. Often this was a room in the synagogue.

The rabbinical court, which was composed of three learned men, did more than hear significant cases. It bore responsibility for the community's spiritual wellbeing. In special situations, its executive power had few limits, and it could enact decrees that were binding on the community.

The community's rabbinical authorities shared power with its lay leadership. Jewish communities in the Diaspora often possessed considerable legal independence, and their gentile rulers expected the community leaders to collect taxes, regulate the markets, and generally supervise Jewish internal affairs. All these matters were handled by applying the Torah's teaching to the immediate social and political realities.

Community leaders, carrying out a prime Jewish obligation, collected and disbursed charity (the Hebrew term, *tsedaqah,* literally means "justice"). Every Jew had obligations toward every other Jew, particularly those who needed help. Gathering and distributing the funds were among the most honored community tasks. Many communities so esteemed *tsedaqah* that even its recipients gave to others.

Geography and cultural differences produced variations in Jewish practice between the two leading centers of Jewry, one in the Land of Israel (under Roman rule) and the other in Babylonia (under Parthian and, after 226 CE, Sasanid rule). No single agency existed to enforce uniformity in practice or theory. Instead, a relatively loose pattern of authority emerged. From time to time, certain institutions or individuals arose whose scholarship and piety commanded the respect of many Jews. In time, their teachings established precedents for later Jewry.

Despite the open texture of the Judaism of this era, the rabbis exhibited a clear-cut sense of the unity and identity of the Jewish people, who were the sole recipients of God's law and thus bore unique witness to God. They detested the idolatry and immorality they saw all about them. Hence they consciously sought to distinguish and separate Jews from the nations. But most rabbis happily accepted sincere converts. The isolation of the Jews made hospitality to strangers critical: Jews on a journey could always expect to find a welcome in other Jewish communities, which, despite variations in custom, clearly followed the same Torah in the same basic way. [*For further discussion, see* Jewish People.]

Three rhythms of Jewish time. Jews live in three interrelated dimensions of time: the personal, the annual-historical, and the eschatological. The critical passages of each individual's life are marked by sacred rites. On the eighth day after his birth, a newborn boy receives the physical sign of the covenant in the ceremony of circumcision. At thirteen he assumes personal responsibility for performing the commandments, becoming *bar mitsvah.* Should he complete the study of a classic text, he marks the occasion with a small celebration. Marriage is preceded by formal betrothal. The wedding itself is as elaborate as the family's means and the community's standards will allow. The birth of children, the experience of bereavement and mourning, the dissolution of marriage in divorce are all social acts that involve community participation; many of them are also sanctified by prayer and ritual. [*See* Rites of Passage, *article on* Jewish Rites.]

Prayer and ritual similarly mark the great moments of each year. The six workdays climax in the rest, worship, study, and feasting of the Sabbath. On Friday eve (in the Jewish calendar, the day begins at sundown) it is traditional that women light the Sabbath candles and say a blessing over them. Before the special Sabbath meal is eaten, a prayer of sanctification is recited over a cup of wine. When the Sabbath has ended, its "holy time" is demarcated from the "profane time" of the weekday by the recitation of blessings over wine, spices, and a multi-wicked flame in a ritual called Havdalah ("separation"). [*See* Shabbat.]

The year begins in the autumn during the period of the High Holy Days. The solemn synagogal rites of Ro'sh ha-Shanah celebrate God's sovereignty, justice, and mercy. The ensuing ten days of penitence are climaxed by the all-day fast and worship service of Yom Kippur, the Day of Atonement, in which the congregation beseeches God's promised forgiveness. In the course of the year there are three "pilgrimage" festivals, Passover, Shavu'ot (Weeks or Pentecost), and Sukkot (Tabernacles; Feast of Booths). Originally these were agricultural festivals during which all Jews came on pilgrimage to the Temple in Jerusalem, but they were transformed by the rabbis into historical symbols: Passover celebrates the Exodus from slavery in Egypt, Shavu'ot the giving of the Torah, and Sukkot God's providential care of the Israelites in the wilderness. Thus, the undeviating cycle of the year becomes a reminder and renewal of the Jewish people's unique historical experience.

Rabbinic creativity likewise embellished the minor festivals of the year. The rabbis established a ceremony of special psalms, prayers, and a reading from the Torah scroll to greet the beginning of each lunar month. For the fast day of Tish'ah be-Av, commemorating the destruction of the Temple, they enjoined a reading of the *Book of Lamentations.* They memorialized other tragic events with lesser fasts. The salvation of ancient Persian Jewry, recounted in the *Book of Esther,* is remembered on the feast of Purim. The Maccabees' rededication of the Temple in 164 BCE, after its desecration by the Hellenistic ruler of Syria, Antiochus IV, is celebrated as Ḥanukkah at about the time of the winter solstice with a ritual that includes the kindling of lights in the home over the course of eight nights. [*See also entries for each holiday and* Jewish Religious Year.]

The number of each Jewish year indicates the time since creation, according to rabbinic calculation, even as the rhythm of the year directs attention toward history's promised climax, God's manifest rule on earth. A messianic hopefulness infuses all Jewish observance, for the end might begin at any moment; yet the Jews' heartbreaking experience with premature messiahs—particularly Bar Kokhba in the rebellion against Rome of 132–135 CE—indicated that the Messiah would come only at the "end of days."

We can surmise something of the tone and quality of the rabbis' Judaism from what their traditions tell us about the way they lived. Their teachings show that they can be wildly playful, though they are usually highly serious; exuberant in celebration, yet careful of minutiae; free in opinion, yet obedient to discipline; guilt-stricken at sinning, yet confident of forgiveness; desirous of intention in the performance of *mitsvot* (the commandments), yet content with the deed itself; highly individualistic, yet absorbed in community; concerned with the practical, yet oriented toward the eschatological. They were simultaneously mystic and rationalistic, emotionally demonstrative and devoted to order, foolish sinners and pious martyrs. They were ordinary people who might be one's neighbors, yet they were saintly, endowing their spirituality with intellect and a communal and personal activism. And the communities that were guided by their teachings seem much like them, human and holy at once.

Above all, the rabbis have a passion for this mundane life, despite the finer one to come. They delight in its opportunities to serve God through the routines specified by Torah. Yet they insist that in order to save a life, all the laws of the Torah could—indeed, must—be broken (except the prohibitions against idolatry, murder, and sexual sin). Similarly, when the survival of the Jewish people seems to be at risk, the rabbis find ways to accommodate reality, but not by compromising principle. For they believe, above all, that the world was created for the sanctification of life, and that only through holy Jewish living can it hope to endure and reach completion.

Beliefs of the Rabbis. It is characteristic of the rabbis that their faith is inseparable from their way of life. Their test for heresy was behavioral, not creedal. Their explicit statements of belief are generally more poetic than precise, more fragmentary than general, and they exhibit little interest in systemic coherence.

While acknowledging the notorious elusiveness of what they call rabbinic theology, some modern scholars have yet found it possible to explicate some of its major themes. The rabbis' theological creativity operates mainly in their reshaping of the multitudinous ideas and images of biblical belief. In this process they continue the millennial Jewish experience of reinterpreting the covenant as times change and as their own intellectuality and religious sensitivity demand.

The primacy of continuity in rabbinic belief helps explain what modern readers often consider the rabbis' surprisingly modest response to the Temple's destruction. Though they were deeply traumatized, the rabbis did not see the loss of the Temple as a disaster requiring major theological reconstruction; rather, they found it a confirmation of the Bible's teaching. God had done what God had promised to do and had done once before (in 587/6 BCE). Sin eventually begets punishment, even to the destruction of God's Temple and the exile of God's people. But the punishment has a covenant purpose, to bring the people back to God's service. In due course, the rabbis believed, God would again restore the holy people and their Temple. Continuing the faith of the Bible as they understood it, the rabbis indomitably transcended profane history.

God. Monotheism anchors the rabbis' faith, just as it anchors the later biblical writings. The rabbis abominate idolatry and passionately oppose the notion that there are "two powers" in heaven. That does not prevent their speaking of God's heavenly retinue, the subordinates by whom God's governance of the universe usually proceeds. Similarly, they exhibit no inhibition about using metaphors to describe God. These may be abstract names, such as "the Place," "the Power," "the Holy," or images drawn from human life, such as references to God's phylacteries, or daily schedule, or emotions.

Another typical rabbinic dialectic moves between the utter greatness and the immediate availability of God. The ineffably glorious Sovereign of all universes attends and responds to a human whisper or fleeting meditation.

Rabbinic theology often pivots about God's justice and mercy. The declaration "There is no Judge and no justice" seems to be the rabbinic equivalent of atheism, but the rabbis give elaborate validations of the reliability of God's justice. They believe that the world could not survive if God were absolutely just: human fallibility and willfulness make such stringency impractical. For people freely to come to righteousness, God must also be merciful and compassionate. But if there were mercy without justice, this same rebellious humankind would never become responsible for its own actions. Undaunted by the paradoxes, the rabbis affirm that the one and only God is both just and merciful, demanding and forgiving, the ultimate idealist and realist in one.

Much of what other people might take to be evil the rabbis steadfastly consider the subtle working-out of God's justice. They do not deny that unmerited suffering occurs. Sometimes they explain this as "chastisements of love," torment given to the pious in this world so that rewards will await them in the afterlife. Sometimes they merely ascribe it to God's inexplicable will, God's "harsh decree." (Parallel reasons are offered by the rabbis for the gift of God's unmerited blessing—that is, it comes because of the "merit of the patriarchs," or simply because God loves or chooses to bless the recipient.) Less frequently, the rabbis will picture God, as it were, as somehow unable to prevent a tragedy or as lamenting its occurrence. With reason or without, they hold God to be the ultimate source of evil as well as good and so call for the recitation of a blessing upon hearing evil tidings. They devoutly trust God, whom they know they cannot hope to understand despite all their study and piety. [*See* Attributes of God, *article on* Jewish Concepts, *and* God, *article on* God in Postbiblical Judaism.]

Perhaps they evince such confidence because they have a strong, full belief in life after death. Several stages of the afterlife may be identified in rabbinic traditions. At death, the soul is taken from the body for preliminary judgment and purification and stays with God until the general bodily resurrection that will take place at the "end of days." Then the soul, rejoined to its purified body, receives judgment. The wicked are utterly destroyed, and the less culpable receive a limited term of expiatory punishment. Finally, the individual enters the "future to come," the blissful but indescribable reward God has promised the righteous. [*See* Soul, *article on* Jewish Concepts.]

Humankind and human destiny. The rabbis' conception of humankind stands behind their Jewish self-understanding. Human beings literally constitute a family since God created them from one pair of progenitors. And God made and maintains a covenant with all the descendants of Noah. Under it, God promised that there would be no more annihilatory floods and commanded all people to obey seven laws: six negative—not to blaspheme God, or worship idols, or steal, or murder, or commit sexual offenses, or eat the limb of a living animal—and one positive—to set up courts of justice.

Human nature being so torn between its evil and good urges, people regularly transgress these simple laws. So God brought a special nation into being, the Jews, to serve God devotedly by accepting a covenant of 613 commandments. In the rabbinic sociology of religion, people are either Jews, faithful servants of the only God, or part of "the nations," idolaters and therefore sinners. The Jews' experience of anti-Semitism reinforced this view and strengthened the Jewish commitment to separatism for God's sake.

The customary strife between the nations and the people of Israel will greatly intensify as the "end of days" nears. But God will send the Messiah, a human, Davidic king descended from King David, to lead God's people to victory. Once again, the rabbinic accounts grow hazy and irreconcilable. Some see the nations converting to Judaism; others see them accepting Jewish leadership. There is little elaboration of the biblical poems that prophesy a time of universal justice, peace, contentment, and lack of fear. However, the rabbis anticipate that at the final judgment the nations will be found guilty of wickedness and denied entry to the "future to come." Some rabbis mitigate this attitude by teaching that individuals who are "pious among the nations of the world have a share in the world to come."

Of course, any sinner might become righteous by repenting. The rabbis tell—occasionally with considerable envy—of a number of gentiles and Jews who by a heartfelt act of *teshuvah* immediately gained the life of the world to come.

Most of these matters became part of rabbinic law concerning non-Jews. Hence this doctrine, in general, may be said to be authoritative rabbinic teaching.

Rabbinic theory of Torah. Radical theological creativity appears starkly in the rabbis' doctrine of the oral law. Unlike some of their other distinctive ideas, such as repentance, the Messiah, and resurrection, the notion of the oral law has no explicit biblical foundation. Since it undergirds all of rabbinic Judaism, it may be said to be the rabbis' most characteristic doctrine. To reiterate what has been said above, the rabbis taught that God gave Moses not only the first five books of the Bible (and, by implication, the rest of it) but also unrecorded verbal instructions, including specific duties and the methods for educing further oral law.

The rabbis also delimit the content of the written law in its broader sense of holy scripture, that is, the Hebrew scriptures. They apparently inherited fixed versions of the five books of the Torah and of the Prophets (including *Joshua, Judges, Samuel,* and *Kings*) and they determined what would be included in the Writings, admitting *Ecclesiastes,* for example, but rejecting *Ben Sira.* With these three divisions (Torah, Prophets, Writings; abbreviated in Hebrew as *Tanakh*) they closed the canon, for they believed that revelation ended with *Haggai, Zechariah,* and *Malachi* and that the books of the Writings had preceded these prophetical books. Though the rabbis occasionally hear a "heavenly echo" concerning matters under discussion, they may disregard it. Effectively, therefore, postbiblical Judaism derives from the rabbis' delimitation of the written law and their continuing explication of the oral law.

God excepted, no aspect of Jewish belief arouses the rabbis' awe as does Torah. They describe it as existing before creation, as God's guide to creation, and as God's most treasured possession, one so precious the angels tried to keep it from being taken to earth. The people of

Israel, by virtue of having been given and having accepted the Torah, have become infinitely precious to God and central to human history. The rabbis acknowledge that wisdom may be found among the nations, but for them Torah contains God's fullest truth for humankind, making it the arbiter of all wisdom.

The rabbis do not detail the correct means or institutional structure for amplifying the oral law. Rather, the living practice of the master (*rabbi* means "my master") sets the model for his disciples. From time to time various institutions have emerged that temporarily exercised some general authority, but none lasted or created a form that later generations utilized. We have no way of gauging the extent to which Jews accepted the rabbis' leadership even in their own time. It seems paradoxical to seek control and integrity with such lack of structure and tolerance of diversity, but the arrangement has persisted to the present day.

With God's teaching available in verbal form, learning became a major Jewish religious activity. On a simple level, study motivated Jewish duty and specified its content. On a more advanced level, pondering God's instructions—even those of only theoretical relevance, like the rules for the Temple service—enabled one to have intellectual communion, as it were, with God. Gifted men sought to become rabbis, perhaps even to have their teachings cited by others, but always to set a living example for other Jews. Often reports of a master's deeds themselves became part of the oral law.

This heavy intellectual emphasis should not be divorced from its religious context. The intellectually keenest rabbis are also depicted as deeply pious, passionate in prayer, caring and virtuous in their dealings with people, intimately involved in the ordinary activities of life. Many also were mystics, though we have only hints about their esoteric spirituality.

The rabbinic doctrine of Torah brought fresh dynamism to Judaism. By authorizing new and open forms of authority and practice it enabled the Jewish people to keep the covenant vital, no matter what changes were brought by time and dispersion. With Judaism now centered on the individual and communal practice of Torah rather than on the Temple cult in Jerusalem, one could live as a faithful Jew anywhere. And as life created new problems, one only needed to find or become a learned Jew to determine what God wanted now, God's continuing command, and hence feel God's continuing care and concern. This oversimplifies a highly sophisticated process, but also conveys its providential gist. [*For further discussion, see* Torah.]

The Jews as God's treasured people. The people of Israel uniquely serve the one God of the universe by living by God's teachings. Whatever superiority the people of Israel might claim over the gentiles derives from their faithfulness in living according to the covenant. Having the Torah does not exempt the Jews from God's demand for righteousness; if anything, because they have more commandments to fulfill they bear more responsibility before God. At the same time, God has a special love for the people of the covenant. When the people of Israel sin, God patiently waits for them to repent and helps them do so, sometimes by punishing them to remind them of their responsibilities.

The rabbis directly applied these beliefs to their situation, with the Temple destroyed and Jewish life in the Land of Israel degenerating. They lamented the calamities of their time: their inability to fulfill the commandments regarding God's cult and the material and spiritual distress brought on by dispersion and Roman rule. But their faith did not waver. They held that this people had been justly punished for its sins, though they often pictured God as pained at having had to execute so dire a sentence. To the rabbis, this new exile came because of the covenant and not as its negation; God had fulfilled what the covenant called for in response to egregious iniquity.

The Jews' political and social insignificance in the Roman empire did not negate their faith in their continuing spiritual uniqueness. Rather, the idolatry and immorality of the Romans proved them unworthy of Jewish admiration and God's esteem. To keep their service of God uncontaminated, the Jews set a distance between themselves and the nations. They also lived in the hope that their stubborn loyalty to God would one day be vindicated before all humankind. The eschatological savior described in the *Book of Daniel* had become an important figure in rabbinic Judaism, the King Messiah. One day—perhaps today—God would send him to restore the holy people to its land, defeat its enemies, reestablish its throne, rebuild its Temple and reconstitute its cult, institute a world order of justice and compassion, and usher in a time when all the promise of creation and the covenant would be fulfilled.

This was a human and historical expectation. As a consequence, some Jews would, from time to time, declare one or another figure of their day to be the anticipated Son of David, in the hope that the Jewish people had so lived up to its covenant responsibilities that God had sent the Messiah. Even if the folk did not merit him, it was understood that God would, in God's own time, send redemption. In either case, the rabbis could only fantasize as to what God would then do to transform and perfect creation. They imagined nature pacified and responsive, the nations admiring of the Torah or even converted to Judaism. Diverse as these conceptions were, all the rabbis agreed that this glorious time will be succeeded by the resurrection of the dead, the final judgment, and the climactic but indescribable "future to come."

The rabbis taught the people of Israel to remain confident of God's rule and favor and to await in history and beyond it God's sure deliverance and blessing—a faith that carried them through history until modern times. [*See also* Messianism, *article on* Jewish Messianism.]

From Talmudic to Modern Times

After the editing of the Talmud, countless variations of the rabbis' way appeared as Jews lived in diverse countries, cultures, social orders, and historical circumstances. Mostly they added observances; some of these became generally accepted, such as the holiday of Simḥat Torah (Joy of Torah), which became the ninth day of the festival of Sukkot, and the *yohrtsayt,* the later Ashkenazic practice of memorializing a close relative's day of death. A selective factor also operated, as in the abandonment of the triennial cycle of reading the Torah scroll during worship services in favor of an annual cycle. The range of this cultural creativity was greatly extended by the folk or ethnic nature of the Jews.

Two major cultural streams emerged. The Sefardic tradition (from the medieval Hebrew word *Sefarad* for the Iberian Peninsula) chiefly embraced the Jews of the Mediterranean Basin, many of whom were descended from families exiled from Spain in 1492, as well as those in Arab countries. The Ashkenazic tradition (from the medieval word *Ashkenaz* for northern France and Germany) encompassed the Jews of northern and eastern Europe, from whom most Jews in North America descend. Sefardic rabbis led Jewry throughout the Diaspora from the eleventh through the sixteenth century; meanwhile, the Ashkenazic sages created a halakhic scholarship that eventually brought them to the fore in Jewish life.

Each cultural style encompassed diverse national and local ways of living that changed over the centuries. Sefardic spokesmen have often taken pride in their community's urbanity, its respect for form and decorum, its devotion to liturgy, and its esteem of clear intellectuality. Similarly, Ashkenazic leaders have proudly noted their group's passionate energy, its fierce individuality, its dedication to study, and its love of Talmudic erudition.

Developing the Rabbinic Way. We know little about the actual practices of Jews for much of this period, though we know much about what rabbis said ought to be done. But the quasi-institutional means that evolved to control the development of Jewish life so evidences the spirit of Judaism that it deserves description. In their far-flung Diaspora, Jews recognized no institution or group as universally authoritative. Yet despite the slowness of communication, or lack of it, among the Jewish communities, and the immense diversity in local practice, the Jews remained and recognized one another as one covenant people.

Persecution intensified this sense of identity. With the rise of Islam early in the seventh century, Jews, living mostly in Islamic lands, became a group tolerated, but given second-class social and legal status. Among Christians, the occasional anti-Jewish outbreaks of the early centuries gave way after the First Crusade (1096 CE) to nearly seven centuries of harassment, including economic limitations, forced conversions, pogroms and riots, and communal expulsions, culminating about 1500 CE in the formal creation of the ghetto, the walled-in Jewish quarter of European cities. This pariah status strongly affected Jewish practices and attitudes and helped give rise to an elemental spiritual resistance founded on the certainty of possessing God's revelation and favor. The immediate contrast between their way of life and that of their oppressors empowered Jews to live and die steadfast in their faith. [*See* Anti-Semitism.]

Jewish communities vested authority in those whose learning and piety evoked it. Early on, the geonim, leaders of the Babylonian academies *(yeshivot)* that produced the Babylonian Talmud, began responding to questions addressed to them by distant Jews. This pattern of questions and answers, *she'elot u-teshuvot,* established itself as a way to get and give authoritative guidance. To this day, *teshuvot,* also known as *responsa,* remain the preeminent device for Jewish legal development. The power of a *teshuvah* derives entirely from the prestige and scholarship of its author. Many *teshuvot* became academic additions to the body of Jewish "case law." Others became widely authoritative, like one of Rav Amram, gaon of the *yeshivah* in Sura, Babylonia, from 856 to 874 CE. His lengthy answer to a question from Spanish Jews about liturgical practice established the prototype for Jewish prayer books.

The geonim and other sages sometimes wrote commentaries to portions of the Talmud or composed treatises on an aspect of the law. Eventually, the growing accretion of law led some teachers to compile codes. Each code became the subject of critical commentaries, some of which are printed alongside the code text in modern editions. The *Shulḥan 'arukh* of Yosef Karo (1488–1575), a Sefardic master, published in 1565 CE, became generally accepted among Ashkenazic Jews as well after Mosheh Isserles (c. 1525–1572) wrote glosses to it that reflected Ashkenazic practice. To this day, the *Shulḥan 'arukh* remains the authoritative code of Jewish law, though scholars continue to rework some of its sections. [*For a discussion of the development of Jewish law, see* Halakhah.]

Only one serious internal challenge to rabbinic Judaism emerged in the medieval period: the Karaite (biblicist) movement, which rejected the authority of the oral law and created a pattern of practice based on the Bible alone. Beginning in the eighth century CE in the Middle East, it reached the peak of its appeal and literary productivity in the eleventh and twelfth centuries. By then rabbinic authorities had declared Karaism heretical and prohibited intermarriage with Karaites. Some few thousand Karaites still exist, largely in the state of Israel. [*See* Karaites.]

In many other fields, as well as law, the range of Jewish study continually expanded. Biblical exegesis, homilies, poetry, mystical accounts, chronicles, polemics, explorations of piety, handbooks for good conduct, philosophy—every period produced its books and the students to ponder them. The invention of printing added further impetus to Jewish learning.

New Ideas and Their Effect on Practice. Four particularly significant, if not always distinguishable, intellectual currents moved through much of the Jewish world during the Middle Ages: pietism, mysticism, philosophy, and polemic. It will help to consider pietism, the most popular, first, though mysticism, an elitist enterprise, predates it.

Medieval pietism. The Talmud and Midrash devote much attention to the virtues a Jew should manifest, but do so only in passing. About the eleventh century, a popular, specifically pietistic literature known as *musar* began to appear. Well into modern times, large numbers of Jews read and sought to live by the high spiritual standards its authors advocated.

The title of the early, exemplary *musar* book, *Duties of the Heart,* written in Arabic by Baḥye ibn Paquda in the late eleventh century, epitomizes the movement's aims. While the Talmud focused on the good Jew's acts, Baḥye stressed the inner life as the basis for action. He and other pietists called attention to the need for intimacy between the individual and God, stressing the humility of the one and the greatness of the other. Consciousness of this relationship, they said, should strongly motivate one to cultivate personal holiness, particularly through loving behavior to others—an emphasis so pronounced that the pietists' writings are often called "ethical" books. [*See* Jewish Thought and Philosophy, *article on* Jewish Ethical Literature.]

Two concerns of *musar* teachers gradually became common in most medieval Jewish writing. First, the pietists strongly contrast the purity of the soul with the grossness of the body. This duality, alluded to in both the Bible and the Talmud, became central and intense in *musar* piety. With corporeality the soul's antagonist, the pietists commend a measure of asceticism and social withdrawal. Yet they do not go so far as to become full-fledged dualists, for they believe that God created the body and ordained social life.

Second, the pietists express great anxiety about sinning and cultivate the fear of incurring guilt. How can anyone who is intensely aware of God's greatness not find the idea of defying God utterly reprehensible? One of the most common *musar* strategies for avoiding or surmounting temptation is to remember the punishment awaiting the wicked in the next world. The *musar* writers therefore urge heartfelt remorse and repentance for every sin, even suggesting compensatory atonements one might undertake. In no small measure, the conflict between the values of modern life and the values of premodern Judaism arose from disagreement over these matters.

Maturation of Jewish mysticism. Whereas pietism reached out to ordinary Jews, mysticism limited itself to select individuals who were initiated into an esoteric doctrine by masters who often concealed as much as they revealed.

The Jewish mystical writings describe and exhibit phenomena that are associated with mysticism in many cultures: stringent spiritual discipline, bizarre language and exalted spiritual expression, techniques for gaining mystical experience, visions of the heavenly realm, physical images of God coupled with assertions of God's utter ineffability, longing for religious consummation and ways of hastening it—all these and more appear refracted in perplexing and fascinating fashion through sensitive temperaments affected by highly diverse situations.

The main tradition of Jewish mysticism is known as Qabbalah. Developed in response to God's revelation of a holy way of life, it has a highly cognitive content that is concerned with cosmogony and theosophy. Its most significant document, the *Zohar* (Book of Splendor), written primarily in Aramaic in late thirteenth-century Spain, is a commentary on the Torah that elaborates a mystical doctrine of God's complex nature. Ultimately, God is Ein Sof, "without limit," hence the one about whom nothing at all can be said. Yet God is also intimately known, contemplated, and related to through interacting loci of divine energy, the *sefirot* (lit., "spheres" or "numbers"; in qabbalistic terminology, emanations from God's inner being). The mystics speak of the *sefirot* with a freedom of metaphor that is almost limitless, not even excluding sexual anthropomorphisms. Feminine metaphors for God, rare in the Bible and occasional in the Talmud, now come into full use alongside masculine metaphors in explications of God's nature.

The Jewish mystics, for all the immediacy of their relationship with God, believe that Torah—the written and oral law—remains primary to Judaism. They therefore eschew antinomianism—the idea that faith, not law, is sufficient—and cultivate meticulous observance. By ascribing supernal significance to commandments and customs that reason cannot explain, they easily provide absolute justification for them.

Two late developments in Jewish mysticism have had continuing repercussions. The first was the qabbalistic thought of Isaac Luria (1534–1572). According to his cosmogonic explanation of evil, creation began with an act of divine self-contraction that produced an outflow of generative light. God projected this light into the vessels, or material forms, that had been prepared for it. These vessels proved too fragile and shattered, leaving unsanctified shards or husks that contain only sparks of God's creative, transformative light. By observing God's commandments, people can free the heavenly sparks from their husks and mend the broken vessels, thus restoring the world and rescuing it from evil. God appears passive in this process, as it is human action that brings the Messiah—a striking anticipation of modern liberalism. [*See also* Qabbalah *and the biography of Isaac Luria.*]

In the eighteenth century, in southern Poland and the Ukraine, the Hasidic movement transformed qabbalistic tradition through a radical appropriation of God's accessibility (prompting charges by their opponents that the Ḥasidim were pantheists). To the Ḥasidim, God's nearness implied that life should be lived with joy and enthusiasm. For cleaving to God, one need not be a spiritual virtuoso but only give God one's heart. This attitude encouraged new practices and fervent observance, though its opponents claimed that its emphasis on spontaneity and inner experience led to laxity in ritual.

Hasidism became a mass movement that carried a dialectical tension. On the one hand, the humblest person could live the mystical life. The Hasidic leaders encouraged this egalitarianism by putting many of their teachings in exoteric form, as tales, stories, and popular preaching, and by promoting a close community life. On the other hand, Hasidism established a religious elite. Each community was led by a *tsaddiq,* or *rebe.* The *tsaddiqim* represent Hasidism's esoteric side, privately practicing an exalted mysticism and serving as the intermediary between their followers and heaven. Their followers believed that the *tsaddiqim* could work wonders and thus beseeched their intercession on every personal problem. Since each community thought its own *tsaddiq* the most powerful, some Hasidic communities isolated themselves even from other Ḥasidim.

Later, Hasidism became institutionalized around dynasties and antagonistic to modernity. The groups that managed to survive the Holocaust have had a resurgence in the state of Israel and the United States. They have gained recruits from Jews who, disillusioned with secular culture, seek out the intensity of immersion in a separatist Jewish esoteric community.

The encounter with philosophy. The Talmud knows nothing of Philo Judaeus of Alexandria (fl. first century CE) or any other Hellenistic Jewish philosopher. Certain that they possessed God's revelation, the rabbis spurned formal Greek philosophy, which they associated with idolatry. In the ninth century CE, Jews encountered Muslim philosophy, which claimed that it taught the purest monotheism because its doctrine of God had been refined through rational argument. For the next seven centuries—that is, as long as cultural involvement with the Muslims persisted—a tiny Jewish intellectual aristocracy created Jewish philosophy. Their work had little direct impact on Jewish life, though some of their ideas—for example, Moses Maimonides' excoriation of anthropomorphism—became widely influential.

The early philosophical thinkers, such as Sa'adyah Gaon (882–942), adduced proofs for God's creation of the world, from which they deduced God's unity and sovereign power. On this basis they sought to give rational justification to such problems as miracles, providence, evil, and why Judaism was the true revelation. The rational defense of certain inexplicable commands of the Torah evoked considerable philosophic ingenuity.

In the course of time, most medieval Jewish philosophical thought came to employ Aristotelian categories. The occasional Neoplatonic voice found little philosophic resonance, though the mystics found the Neoplatonic concept of emanation congenial to their notion of levels of being. Sometimes, as in the case of Yehudah ha-Levi (c. 1075–1141), a thinker became critical of philosophy and subordinated reason to revelation, rather than making it an equal or senior partner.

Modern thought rejects the medieval concept of causality, and the philosophy based on it remains of interest mainly to academic specialists. However, the contemporary clash between reason and faith seems prefigured in the writings of Moses Maimonides (Mosheh ben Maimon, 1135/8–1204), the preeminent Jewish philosopher. The author of the first great code of Jewish law, the *Mishneh Torah* (lit., "Second Torah"), he gained incomparable stature among Jews. He faced an intellectual crisis: the resolution of the Torah's teachings with the views of Aristotle, who had denied the idea of creation and affirmed the eternity of the universe. Maimonides refused to repudiate the demands either of reason or of faith, and his masterful effort to harmonize Judaism with a scientific view of reality became the model for all later rationalist validations of religious faith. But when, at the end of the fifteenth century, the Jews were expelled from Spain and Portugal, where philosophy was an important part of the culture, this fruitful intellectual enterprise came largely to an end.

The intellectual defense of Judaism took a more popular form in the polemics against Christianity that circulated from the twelfth century on. The Talmud contains remnants of earlier polemics, but not until major Jewish centers suffered under Christian religious oppression did Jewish books criticizing Christianity appear. (Fewer polemical works were directed against Islam, whose treatment of Jews as inferiors was based on sociopolitical stratification rather than harassment and was often mitigated by pragmatic considerations. Relatively quiescent relations existed between Muslims and Jews after the early centuries of Muslim conquest.)

Jewish teachers could elaborate their faith without reference to Christianity or Islam, though the Bible and Talmud are replete with attacks on idolatry. Besides, the Christian claim that Jesus of Nazareth was the Messiah seemed, to the Jews, self-refuting, as the world remained radically unredeemed. But as the church increasingly attacked Jewish belief, Jewish leaders found it necessary to refute the church's claims and invalidate its doctrines.

Jewish polemics sought to demonstrate Christian misinterpretation of biblical texts by citing the original Hebrew texts and the traditional Jewish understanding of them. Christian converts from Judaism countered these arguments by citing Talmudic and Midrashic passages that were alleged to prove Jesus' messiahship. The Jewish disputants attacked the credibility of the conflicting gospel accounts of Jesus' life and the evangelists' ignorance of Talmudic law (which they assumed to have been operative in Jesus' time). They also caustically exposed the irrationality of such Christian doctrines as the virgin birth, the incarnation, and the Eucharist. By contrast, they contended, Judaism was a religion a rational man could accept. It was a theme that Jews would continue to find persuasive into modern times. [*For further discussion, see* Polemics, *articles on* Muslim-Jewish Polemics *and* Jewish-Christian Polemics.]

Modernity: Opportunity and Peril

Emancipation, the fitful process by which the segregation and oppression of European Jewry was encouraged to end, began in earnest with the French Revolution. Gradually, as nationality was severed from membership in an official Christian faith, Jews and other minority denominations received equal political rights and social opportunity. As a result, most modern Jews, despite their religious heritage, have avidly supported keeping government and civil society neutral with regard to religion. Because their politics and religion are closely intermixed, the Islamic nations that granted Jews complete equality were among the last states to do so.

After some fifteen hundred years of degradation and centuries of grinding oppression, most European Jews enthusiastically welcomed equality. To those raised in the ghettoes or in the *shṭeṭls* (Yi., "villages") of eastern Europe, every new freedom, no matter how hedged by limitations or by secularized forms of anti-Semitism, came as a near fulfillment of messianic hopes. A politicized, humanistic hope now became the dominant tone of Jewish existence.

But the price of equality was conformity to the larger culture. European society did not allow for much cultural diversity, and although the accepted social conventions were ostensibly secular, they often reflected their Christian origins.

As emancipation proceeded, the consequences for rabbinic Judaism were devastating. One group of Jews rejected modernization altogether, another group rejected the major doctrines of Judaism. Most Jews found these reactions too extreme, preferring a middle way.

A small minority of traditionalists, rather than surrender anything that they felt God asked of them, spurned modernization. Many pious eastern European Jews long refused to immigrate to America with the hundreds of thousands of Jews who began to do so in the last decades of the nineteenth century. This produced a social situation unique in Jewish history. Elsewhere, long established Orthodox institutions formed the basis of community life. The non-Orthodox movements that arose with the coming of modernity were reactions to them. In the United States, non-Orthodox institutions became well established in the late nineteenth and early twentieth centuries, and only after World War I did Orthodox institutions slowly come to prominence.

Most Jews rejected this strategy of separatism for pragmatic and intuitive reasons. Practically, emancipation offered Jews a dignity they had known only sporadically for two thousand years. Hence their embrace of modernity can be understood as an existentially transformed way of keeping the covenant, arising from the intuition that Western civilization, as evidenced by its movement toward liberation, contained a considerable measure of the universal truth of Judaism.

Some Jews carried this appreciation to the point of

urging Jews to assimilate fully and allow their "parochial" faith to die so that they might participate in humankind's emerging universal culture. Again, most Jews demurred. Given their passion for modernity, their insistence on also remaining Jewish has been difficult to explain, especially since no single philosophy of modern Jewish living has ever become widely accepted. Anti-Semitism has kept some Jews Jewish—yet its continuing virulence seems more a reason to defect than to stay. Moreover, even in the absence of overt hatred of Jews, many Jews have refused to assimilate. Modernist believers see this as an act of persistent loyalty to the covenant: Jews remain personally faithful to their ancient pact even if uncertain about how to live it, while God, in some inexplicable but familiar way, does not let them go.

Postemancipation Jewry has chosen to be both modern and Jewish, thus fixing its continuing agenda: first, establishing a less separatistic, more adaptive way of living; and second, validating the authenticity of that way in Jewish and modern terms.

Sundering the Unity of the Way. Modernity made religion a private affair and defined religious groups in terms derived from Christianity—that is, as communities united by common faith and ritual practice. Nationality was dissociated from religion and subordinated to the nation-state, an arrangement that can still cause social unrest in multinational countries. On both counts, Judaism could not maintain itself as a religio-ethnic entity (the hybrid designation modernity has forced upon students of Judaism). As a result, an unprecedented dichotomy came into Jewish life: one group of Jews defined their Judaism as "religious," while another group defined theirs in secular terms, as an ethnicity.

Religious ways of liberal Jews. Faced with the unacceptable options of either staying Jewish but in an isolated manner—as though still within ghetto walls—or joining modern society by converting to Christianity, some early nineteenth-century German Jewish laymen began experimenting with a Judaism adapted to European modes of religiosity. In that spirit, they reformed synagogue worship. Essentially, they adorned it with a new aesthetic, eliminating liturgical repetitions and poetic embellishments and introducing solemn group decorum, vernacular prayers, sermons, and contemporary musical styles (including the use of a pipe organ and female as well as male singers). They also abolished the halakhic requirement of the separation of the sexes at services, allowing families to sit together in worship. [*For an overview of the traditional mode, see* Worship and Cultic Life, *article on* Jewish Worship.]

This early version of Reform Judaism paved the way for subsequent non-Orthodox Jewish movements. The early reformers justified their form of Judaism with the notion, derived from contemporary German culture, that eternal essences take on transient forms. The essence of Judaism, in their view, is ethical monotheism, which its rituals and customs serve to transmit and strengthen. When times change and old forms no longer function well, they should be altered or abandoned and new forms created.

Most modern Jews have accepted moral duty as the core of Jewish obligation. Many believe that the Jewish people have a mission to teach humankind the religious primacy of universal ethics. In any case, modern Jews often reduce the teachings of the Torah to ethics and, though allowing much else in rabbinic Judaism to atrophy, devote themselves to the moral transformation of society. This universalized sense of covenant responsibility accounts for the astonishing record of modern Jewish contributions to the improvement of human welfare.

In the latter part of the nineteenth century, a new movement emerged: Conservative Judaism. Many eastern European immigrants to America found that their sense of Jewish modernity was not satisfied by the adaptive tone and the essentially ethical content of Reform Judaism, which had been brought over by earlier immigrants from Germany. While seeking to be modern, these Russian and Polish Jews also wanted to preserve a considerable measure of particular Jewish practice. Devotion to the Jewish people as the dynamic creator of Jewish law was their counterpoise to the Reform concentration on ethics. Over the decades, smaller movements have also arisen, positioning themselves essentially in relation to these central communal groups. The most significant of these is Reconstructionism, a movement which derives from the theory of Mordecai Kaplan (1881–1983) that the Jewish community, acting in democratic fashion, ought to be authoritative with regard to Jewish practice.

By the 1970s, the denominational lines had become blurred. Most American Jews, regardless of affiliation, now follow one of several patterns of liberal Jewish living. These vary in their loyalty to classic observance and spirituality, but show considerable similarity in the cultural activities they integrate into their Judaism—especially participation in higher education, civic affairs, and the arts, music, and literature. But the interplay between Judaism and modernity can best be illustrated by the devotion of Jews to interpersonal relationships. American Jews today express the longstanding rabbinic commitment to family and community by their disproportionate involvement in the helping professions (such as teaching, social work, and psychotherapy) and their intense concern for family relationships. In these areas they demonstrate a dedication lacking in their observance of the halakhic dietary laws and laws governing sexual relations between spouses. They seem to believe that sanctifying life, their covenant goal, now requires giving these general human activities priority in Jewish duty.

Despite this heavy cultural borrowing, American Jews manifest a significant measure of particular Jewish action. Even at the humanist end of the religious spectrum, the concern with ethics and other universal issues is reinforced by an attachment to the Jewish folk. Such Jews invest energy and self in Jewish charity, organized defense against anti-Semitism, support of the state of Israel, and occasional ritual acts, most notably those associated with life-cycle events, High Holy Day services, and the home Seder, the Passover meal. In this group one sees clearly a problem that continues to bedevil all liberal Jews: the freedom not to be Orthodox is often taken as a license to do and care little about Judaism altogether.

At the other end of the liberal religious spectrum stands a small minority of Jews whose lives are substantially guided by Jewish tradition, interpreted through a modern ethical and cultural sensibility. They exhibit the rabbinic devotion to self, family, people, and God, seeking to live by rabbinic law wherever they can. They constitute the spiritual heart of non-Orthodox Judaism, whose viability depends upon its acceptance of their leadership in combining modernity and tradition.

The outstanding achievements of liberal Judaism derive from its pursuit of a mediating spirituality. It has radically enlarged the horizon of Jewish duty by its dedication to ethics and democracy. It has revolutionized the study of Judaism by its insistence upon the adoption of modern scholarly methods. Above all, it has convinced most of the Jewish community that modernity and Judaism can successfully be integrated. What many in a prior generation passionately feared and fought, most Jews now consider of great benefit to Judaism.

Nothing so well illustrates the continuing promise and problem of liberal Judaism as its response to feminism. Early in the nineteenth century, the German reformers recognized an ethical imperative to break with the Jewish laws and customs that discriminate against women. But it took more than a century for Reform congregations to elect women officers and until 1972 for the first American woman to be ordained a rabbi; women cantors followed quickly. Since then, the Reconstructionist and Conservative movements have accepted both innovations.

Much of the community has welcomed this development, but it is not clear how far it will tolerate alteration of the old patterns—for example, removing the sexist language of the prayer book, or allowing the genuine sharing of power between men and women. If liberal Jewish daring in this matter eventually becomes part of the accepted covenant way, then its experimentation will again have taught Jews a new way of sanctifying Jewish existence. Orthodox critics rejoin that in breaking with the traditional rabbinic understanding of the Torah which defines separate roles for the sexes, the liberals are more likely to dilute Judaism than to win its future.

Religious ways of Orthodox Jews. As a self-conscious movement, Jewish Orthodoxy arose in response to liberal Judaism with the purpose of correctly delineating Jewish authenticity. Traditional Judaism knows only one standard of faithfulness to God: loyalty to God's law as expounded in the Torah, especially the oral law in its continuing development by contemporary sages. The Torah has absolute primacy. Modernity can come into Judaism only as the Torah allows. Hence the lives of believing Orthodox Jews display religious continuity more than religious change. Variations in observance among Orthodox Jews derive from local custom, from the differences between Ashkenazim and Sefardim, Ḥasidim and other Orthodox Jews, and from the variety of opinion passed down by various sages.

The major forms of Orthodoxy can be distinguished by the degree to which they are open to modernity. They stand united, however, in defense of the Torah against what they consider the faithlessness of most other Jews. Even innovations permissible under Jewish law are often resisted lest they give credence to other Jews' radical departures from tradition.

Orthodox attitudes toward the acceptance of modernity range from antagonistic to embracing. The Hasidic sects visibly project their hostility to modernity and their distance from the gentile world (and other Jews) by their distinctive dress, hair, and body language. Several Orthodox groups also seek to reconstitute the cultural isolation of eastern European Jewry, but in less separatistic ways—a goal more easily accomplished in the state of Israel than elsewhere. The continued use of Yiddish, the Judeo-German vernacular of eastern European Jewry, characterizes this entire wing of Orthodoxy. Its antagonism to modernity does not prevent the pious from utilizing technological advances that enhance observance of the commandments or from having contacts with gentiles when necessary, as in commerce. Some groups have marginal affiliates who live in more modern fashion but maintain their ties to the group by keeping some of its special customs, visiting its communities, and giving financial support.

Another wing, known as Modern Orthodoxy, contends that Jewish law allows, and many sages exemplify, the virtue of embracing any cultural good that enhances human existence as the Torah delineates it. The Modern Orthodox have been most innovative in creating two new instruments for Jewish education, the Jewish university and day school, which feature the sciences and sports, both once considered un-Jewish. They generally speak the vernacular (English in America, Hebrew in Israel), not Yiddish, and their only distinguishing visual sign is the small, often knitted skullcap (Yi., *yarmulke;* Heb., *kippah*) worn by males. But their disciplined loyalty to the Torah appears in such matters as prayer, diet, study, and Sabbath and festival observance.

Orthodoxy has enjoyed a significant resurgence as the twentieth century moves toward its end. Some Jews have lost their once great confidence in Western civilization and have withdrawn from it somewhat by adopting a more distinctive practice of Judaism. A minority have joined the separatistic Jewish sects. Most Orthodox Jews have rejected self-ghettoization, choosing to live a dedicated Jewish life as part of an observant community so as to differentiate themselves from an ofttimes pagan society. Their approach to living the life of Torah has nonetheless carried a modern overlay their Orthodox great-grandparents would probably have opposed; even so, the movement to greater Jewish authenticity has debilitated Modern Orthodoxy's innovative zeal.

The large number of Jews who are only nominally Orthodox testifies to the continuing influence of modernity. Despite their affiliation, these Jews are only sporadically observant and their faith fluctuates or is inconsistent. They often consider their private preferences in Jewish law to be genuine Judaism, a heresy in the eyes of Orthodox sages.

Orthodoxy has notable accomplishments to its credit. Despite dire predictions of its death from the effects of modernity, it has created a cadre of Jews whose personal piety and communal life demonstrate the continuing religious power of rabbinic Judaism. It has kept alive and advanced eastern European Jewry's exalted standards of the study of Jewish law. Particularly in the field of bioethics, but in other areas as well, it has shown the continuing vitality of the oral law.

As with liberal Judaism, the issue of feminism best clarifies the continuing promise and problems of Orthodox Judaism. In refusing to grant women substantial legal equality, contemporary sages have defended the integrity of God's law as they received and understand it. Considering how modernity has shattered family life, they do not deem it to possess a wisdom superior to that of Torah. Rather, every genuine faith demands some sacrifice, and Judaism, abandoned by so many and in such worldwide peril, deserves the obedient dedication of all who wish it to remain true to itself and God.

Many Orthodox authorities have long acknowledged that some laws regarding women create suffering—for example, the woman who, because she cannot meet certain technical criteria, is barred from receiving a Jewish divorce. Liberal Jews perceive the inability of contemporary Orthodox sages to institute legal remedies for this situation as a telling indication that, good will notwithstanding, the laws' inequities are still operative. Feminists cannot believe that, with most Orthodox Jews committed to the general self-fulfillment of women, Orthodox women will long be content with sex-segregated duties and roles. However, Orthodox Judaism has shown no significant loss of membership from its defense of classic Judaism in this matter.

Culture as "Torah" of secular Jews. In late nineteenth-century Europe and mid-twentieth-century America, as Jews became university educated and urban dwelling, they secularized. They believed that modernization meant the acceptance of the idea that there is no God and the end of practices that differentiated Jews from their neighbors. Yet, as they became thoroughly secularized, they generally did not do so to the point of assimilation. Large numbers retained a connection with the Jewish people, if only by discovering that many of the humanitarians they enjoyed associating with were also secularized Jews. Two interrelated major patterns of secular Jewish living arose from this process, one cultural, the other political.

The early foes of emancipation argued that the Jews could not modernize because they had no capacity for high culture. Liberal Jews sought to refute them by aestheticizing Jewish worship. Secular Jews did the same by devoting their lives to literature and the arts, often achieving uncommon success in these areas. Existentially, secular Jews made high culture their "Torah," bringing to it the intense dedication they had once given to faith, for it now validated their existence.

To keep the Jewish people alive, some European Jewish secularists suggested that Jews participate in universal culture through the development of a secular Jewish literature, initially in Hebrew, but later in Yiddish as well. This movement toward Haskalah (Enlightenment) revived the Hebrew language, which had long been used only for traditional scholarship and religious purposes. The long-range hopes of the leaders of Haskalah did not survive the realities of anti-Semitism, acculturation, and migration. Only in the state of Israel, where Jews have created a national culture, has the Hebrew language successfully been used as a means for the modernization of Jewish life. In the Diaspora, few

Jews now maintain their Jewishness by utilizing Hebrew or Yiddish to pursue humanism. Yet Diaspora Jews and those of the state of Israel commonly consider a positive attitude to culture an integral part of their Jewishness.

Jewish secularity also directed itself to ethical politics, that is, redeeming the world through the achievement of social justice. Jews became advocates of the rights of labor and the virtues of socialism, seeing in the struggles for civil rights and civil liberties their own cause as it affected other minorities. Prayer and piety no longer seemed effective responses to social injustice. Being politically informed and involved therefore became for Jews the modern equivalent of a commandment.

This movement's effects have been felt both in general society and in the Jewish community. Jewish politicians and Jewish activists have been a significant influence in humanizing modern society. Simultaneously, the notion of pluralistic democracy has reshaped Jewish life in America. The American Jewish community now operates on a fully voluntary basis and features a broad inclusiveness, diverse organizations, and a dynamism undaunted by emergency or changing times. It has raised more money for Jewish charity than any other voluntary philanthropic effort in history. In the midst of secularization, the lineaments of the covenant appear.

Nationalism: Zionism and the State of Israel. The cultural and political drives in Jewish secularization climaxed in Zionism, the movement that reinterpreted Judaism as Jewish nationalism. Organized on a worldwide basis by Theodor Herzl (1860–1904) in 1897, the Zionists began a crusade to liberate Jews on two levels. First, they sought freedom from persecution by acquiring a land where the Jewish masses might find economic opportunity and political security. Second, they wanted to create a genuinely Jewish culture that would express, in an untrammeled way, the Jewish people's spirit.

Many liberal and Orthodox Jews initially opposed Zionism for religious reasons. The former found its secularism Jewishly aberrant and its nationalism a threat to Jewish emancipation in the Diaspora. The latter objected to its notion of a Jewish state independent of the Torah and found its nationalistic activism a usurpation of God's role in bringing the Messiah. Vestiges of these anti-Zionist attitudes still exist, but most religious Jews now ardently support the state of Israel.

Before the founding of the state of Israel in 1948, Zionism generated a new form of Jewish living in the Diaspora, one built on political activity, immigration and the preparation for it, and participation in the renewal of Hebrew culture. The barbarity of Nazi Germany and the callousness of the rest of the world toward the Jews in the 1930s and 1940s gave Zionism an additional concern: acquiring one place in the world to which Jews could immigrate without restriction.

With the birth and growth of Israel, Jews could return to a way of living they had not known for nearly two millennia: as a Jewish community living on the Jewish homeland in Jewish self-determination. Israel is a secular state—though Orthodox Judaism retains special rights in it—and its ethos is democratic and welfare-oriented. Its extraordinary effort, amid the most trying political circumstances, to hold itself to ethical standards higher than those pursued by most other nations has won it the admiration and identification of world Jewry. Nothing in postemancipation Jewish life has remotely approached its ability to arouse Jewish devotion and action.

Israeli Jews, the great majority of whom consider themselves nonreligious (that is, non-Orthodox), live by the rhythm of the Jewish calendar and draw their ideals from the Bible, the great national saga. Their everyday language is Hebrew and their culture increasingly reflects the concerns of individuals and a society facing the awesome dilemmas of modern existence. In every human dimension, Jews living in the state of Israel are, even without thinking about it, living Jewishly. And for those who carry on Orthodox Judaism or the tiny minority who are Reform or Conservative Jews, the reconstituted Jewish society provides an incomparable context for religious existence.

Outside the state of Israel, Zionism as a total way of life has virtually disappeared. Most Diaspora Jews do not carry on a Jewish cultural life in Hebrew or plan to immigrate to Israel. They may be deeply emotionally attached to Israel, but it does not provide the essential content of their Jewish lives. Zionism has had an incomparable triumph in the high human and Jewish accomplishment of the state of Israel. Yet Zionism's thorough secularization of the covenant has apparently rendered it incapable of guiding Diaspora Jewish life. [*For further discussion, see* Zionism.]

Philosophic Grounds of Modern Jewish Life. Judaism makes its claims upon the Jew in the name of God and the Jewish people's corporate experience—but modernity radically individualizes authority. A modern philosophy of Judaism must mediate between autonomy and tradition and do justice to each of them.

Contemporary Orthodoxy does not wait for each individual to make a decision about what constitutes Jewish duty. Orthodoxy begins with faith and has felt no pressing need for theoretical expositions of its beliefs. It has therefore largely left to liberal Jews the task of constructing systematic Jewish theologies. Five distinctive intellectual statements have gained continuing attention—six, if Zionist ideology can be considered an equivalent system.

Two rationalist interpretations. Rationalism had an irresistible appeal to nineteenth-century Jewish modernizers. It compellingly distinguished between the lastingly valuable essence of Judaism, ethical monotheism, and its transient historical expression in ceremony and ritual. This early liberal criterion of continuity and change first attained sophisticated statement in the work of Hermann Cohen (1842–1918), the famed Marburg Neo-Kantian philosopher.

In rigorous academic works, Cohen delineated the religion a rational person could accept. Cohen sought to demonstrate that rationality requires a philosophical idea of God to integrate its disparate scientific, ethical, and aesthetic modes of thinking. His system was dominated by ethics and he argued that this ethical monotheism appeared for the first time in history in the work of the biblical prophets. As the earliest and purest proponent of ethical monotheism, the Jewish people had a mission to humankind: to teach the universal truth of rational religion. Messianism could no longer be the miraculous advent of God's regent, but became humankind's task of ethically perfecting itself. (This view led Cohen to oppose Zionism as a constriction of the Jewish ethical horizon.) All customs that strengthened Jewish ethical sensitivity or kept Jews faithful to their mission ought to be maintained; those that thwarted them ought to be abandoned. In greatly diluted fashion, Cohen's ethical reworking of Judaism became the accepted ideology of modern Jews. [*See also the biography of Cohen.*]

Leo Baeck (1873–1956), the German thinker who remained closest to Cohen's Judaism of reason, felt the need to supplement reason with the experience of mystery, even though that meant sacrificing Cohen's logical rigor. Baeck pointed to religious consciousness as the deepest foundation of ethical monotheism. He evocatively described the sense human beings have of being creations yet also ethical creators, of being utterly transient yet linked in spirit with that which is eternal.

However, Baeck's rationalism remained sovereign. Fearing the dangers of romanticism, he insisted that religious consciousness should lead to action only as ethics permitted. Thus, while authorizing some nonrational commandments, he ruled out anything that smacked of superstition and bigotry. He also conducted a vigorous polemic against Christianity and Buddhism, finding both of them deficient in their ethics and monotheism. He so closely identified Judaism with a universal rational faith that he alone among modern Jewish thinkers urged Jews to seek converts.

Baeck called for a broad horizon of Jewish obligation. He believed the Jewish people to be so historically identified with the idea of ethical monotheism that should Judaism die, ethical monotheism would also die. The Jewish people, therefore, must survive. To keep it alive, the Jewish people continually create group practices that strengthen and protect the people from the perils it encounters in history. [*See also the biography of Baeck.*]

Rational validations for the primacy of peoplehood. Zionist ideologists proclaimed the Jews a nation, not a religion, and looked forward to a renewal of Judaism as the communal life of the Jewish folk resettled on its ancient soil. They demythologized the biblical interpretation of exile—which Jewish mystics had applied metaphorically even to God—and made it a purely sociopolitical concept. Redemption would not come by a Messiah but with geographic relocation, cultural self-expression, and political reconstitution.

One early Zionist debate still roils the community: is modern Jewish nationalism rigorously secular, and thus free of religious and ethnic values, or is it distinctively Jewish? No one raised this issue more penetratingly than the essayist Aḥad ha-ʿAm ("one of the people," pseudonym of Asher Ginzberg, 1856–1927).

Aḥad ha-ʿAm's Zionism drew on the ninteenth-century concepts of folk psychology and cultural nationalism to assert that Jews, like other peoples, had a folk "character" to which they needed to be true. The Jewish national soul exhibited a talent for ethics and high culture with a devotion to absolute justice as the central theme of great literature and other arts, as the Bible indicates. Jewish nationalism, therefore, had to work for the re-creation of an ethically and aesthetically elevated Jewish culture. A renascent Jewish state could serve as its worldwide spiritual center, and Diaspora Jewish communities would survive spiritually by participating in its cultural life.

Most Zionist ideologists simply assumed that Zionism mandated humanistic values and rarely sought to explicate them. Besides, crises in Jewish life followed so hard upon one another in the twentieth century that arguing such abstractions seemed frivolous. But various events in the life of the state of Israel have kept the issue alive. Its very persistence testifies to its unusual combination of secularity and religiosity. The Israeli courts, in rulings on the legal definition of Jewishness and other issues, have refused to sever the connection between Jewish nationalism and Jewish religion. Some thinkers therefore insist that, for all its putative secularity, the state of Israel can best be understood as an eccentric development of classic Jewish ethnic religiosity.

An American thinker, Mordecai M. Kaplan (1881–1983), created another distinctive Jewish rationalism in terms of philosophic naturalism. Basing his thinking on ideas derived from the recently developed science of sociology, Kaplan held that for Jewish life today to be meaningful, it must reflect the scientific worldview and democratic commitment of modernity. Kaplan therefore carried on a vigorous polemic against supernaturalism in Judaism. He inverted the central idea of traditional Judaism: that God gave the Torah to the Jewish people (thus giving it its distinctive character). Kaplan now claimed, arguing from the perspective of sociology, that the Jewish people had created Judaism, which he defined as an ethnic civilization, based on a land, a language, a history, a calendar, heroes, institutions, arts, values, and much else, with religion at its core. Through its concept of God, Jewish civilization expressed its highest values. The Jewish people's health could be restored only by fully reconstructing its folk life; hence Kaplan called his movement Reconstructionism. The involvement of American Jews in Jewish art, music, and other cultural forms owes much to Kaplan. Kaplan also called for the Jewish community to reorganize itself institutionally so that the community, not a given religious movement or synagogue, would be the focus of Jewish affiliation. Though pluralistic, it could then democratically seek to legislate for its members and meet the full range of religious, political, cultural, and social needs of a healthy ethnic group. But no Jewish community has yet so reconstituted itself.

Kaplan proposed a daring definition of God as the power (or process) that makes for "salvation," by which he meant "human fulfillment." Speaking of God in impersonal, naturalistic terms indicates the purely symbolic status of folk anthropomorphisms and the modern rejection of miracles, verbal revelation, and the idea of the chosen people. Equally important, defining God in finite terms—as that aspect of nature that abets human self-development—solves the theological problem of evil. Kaplan's God does not bring evil, only good. We can now maturely see evil as caused by nature and take it as a challenge to our moral creativity.

Kaplan's bold recasting of Judaism won him a small but enthusiastic following. However, his equation of modernity with scientific rationality lost its appeal in the Jewish community as the interest in nonrationalist Jewish thinkers heightened. [*See also the biography of Kaplan.*]

Nonrationalist Jewish thinkers. After World War I, Franz Rosenzweig (1886–1929), the youthful German author of a magisterial work on Hegel, pioneered Jewish existentialism with his effort to situate Judaism in selfhood rather than in acts or ideas. Rosenzweig connected being Jewish with acting Jewishly—that is, observing the law insofar as one was existentially able to acknowledge it as possessing the quality of commandment. He thus specified, but never fully clarified, a greatly appealing balance between duty and freedom, bequeathing to later liberal Jewish thought one of its central issues.

Martin Buber (1878–1965), an older contemporary and sometime collaborator of Rosenzweig's, created a more extensive system. He suggested that human existence is dynamically relational, occurring either in an objectifying mode he called I–It, or a value-conferring mode of personal openness and mutuality he called I–Thou, which he carefully differentiated from romanticism and mysticism. Romanticism involves an I–It of emotion or experience; mysticism, a loss of self in the One. Buber had in mind something as subtle yet much more common.

Like all significant personal involvements, an I–Thou relationship with God (the "Eternal Thou") evokes responsive action—it "commands." Transgression of such duty involves guilt and the need to atone. All this has a corporate dimension, for whenever two persons truly meet, God is present as well. Consequently, the I–Thou experience directs us to create true human community, a society of Thou's.

Religions arise when relationships with God take on social forms. In time, this process of institutionalization, instead of expediting living contact with God, obstructs it. Institutionalized faiths may designate one sphere of life as holy, leaving the rest to be profane. But the I–Thou relationship knows no limits, and all life should be lived on its terms. Hence Buber opposed all "religion."

According to Buber, the Hebrew Bible recounts the I–Thou experiences of the Jewish people with God, which, over centuries, created an indissoluble relationship between them—the covenant. No other ethnic group has ever so identified its corporate existence with loyalty to God. Because of its covenant, the Jewish folk undertook the messianic task of creating community among its members and thus, eventually, among humankind. While Jews sometimes lost sight of this task, it could never be completely lost, as indicated by early Hasidism and by Zionism. During Buber's decades of residence in Israel, his public insistence that the state should live up to his ideal of the covenant made him a figure of considerable controversy there. [*See also the biographies of Rosenzweig and Buber.*]

Another great system-builder, Abraham Joshua Heschel (1907–1972), integrated much of twentieth-century Jewish experience in his own life. The scion of a Polish Hasidic dynasty, he took a doctorate in Berlin, escaped World War II by going to the United States to teach at the Reform rabbinical school (Hebrew Union College) in Cincinnati. He later taught a near-Orthodox theology at the Conservative seminary in New York.

Heschel faulted the existentialists for defining religion as the movement of people toward God. Modern Jewry's very skepticism, he said, should make it awestruck at the power Someone has given humankind. When such "radical amazement" opens people to the reality of the giver, it becomes apparent, as the Bible indicates, that God pursues humankind, forcing upon it God's self-revelation, and that the biblical prophets accurately transmit God's message.

The meaning of the prophets, Heschel said, is clear: God is a God of pathos, one who suffers when people transgress and who rejoices when they achieve holiness. To argue that God would be more perfect if God had no feelings reflects a Stoic, that is, a Roman point of view, not that of the Bible. Revelation proceeds by "sympathos," by uncommonly gifted individuals coming to feel what God feels. They may verbalize this understanding in different ways, but they do not interpose themselves between God and humankind. The commandments transmitted by Moses and the sages accurately reflect God's injunctions. They are the divinely sanctioned media for meeting God by doing God's will.

Two themes in Heschel's thought mitigate his absolute acceptance of Jewish tradition. First, he emphasized the paucity of revelation compared with the subsequent plethora of interpretation, thereby suggesting the virtue of continuing development. Second, he carefully documented the prophets' intense ethical devotion, implying, perhaps, that human considerations should predominate in interpreting the Torah. He nobly exemplified this in his participation in the civil rights and antiwar struggles of the 1960s. But he never indicated whether he would advocate changes in Jewish law for these or other reasons. [*See also the biography of Heschel.*]

Since the articulation of these six positions, much theological writing and discussion has gone on, but no distinctive new pattern has won substantial acceptance.

Confronting the Holocaust. For reasons still debated, not until the mid-1960s did Jewish thinkers confront the theoretical implications of the Nazi murder of six million Jews. With the emergence of the short-lived "death of God" movement, some Jewish philosophers demanded that a Jewish theology be created that would focus on the reality revealed at Auschwitz, the most notorious of the Nazi death camps and the symbol of the Holocaust. Where the revelation at Sinai spoke of God's rule, God's justice, and God's help to the people of Israel, Auschwitz now spoke of God's absence, of the world's injustice, and of the terrible abandonment of the Jewish people. But it was in the creation of the state of Israel that the Jewish people had given its deepest response to Nazi destructiveness: it was the expression of an intense determination to survive with high human dignity. The Arab-Israeli Six-Day War of 1967 which threatened Israel's (and therefore Jewish) existence catalyzed Jewry worldwide to identify even more intensely with the state of Israel. Israel, therefore, for all its secularity, took on a numinous quality for those who strove to maintain the covenant.

The survival of the Jewish people now became a central preoccupation of Diaspora Jews and a major motive for individuals to assume or extend their Jewish responsibilities. Associated with this was a reassessment of the values of the emancipation. Because of the messianic hope that emancipation had awakened, Jews had surrendered much of their traditional way of life. Now, even as Western civilization began to lose its ultimate confidence in science, technology, education, and culture—in utter human capability—so Jews started to approach their tradition with new receptivity. For some, this partial withdrawal from universal concerns led back to Orthodoxy. Most Jews found that though their social activism could no longer take on redemptive guise, they still could not spurn the ethical lessons of the emancipation, especially with regard to feminism. The critical challenge now facing such chastened liberal Jews is the delineation of their duty and the creation of communities to live it, a concern giving rise to considerable experimentation.

The theoretical response to the Holocaust had an ironic outcome. Experience made substituting Auschwitz for Sinai was unacceptable to most Jews. Despite the mass depravity that continues to plague the twentieth century, the revelation of God's absence and of humanity's depravity in the Holocaust does not constitute the norm of human or Jewish existence. Sanctifying the routine without forgetting the extraordinary remains the Jew's fundamental responsibility, as the revelation at Sinai taught. The primary response to the Holocaust, Jews agree, must be an intensification of human responsibility.

Some Orthodox leaders, like the *rebe* of the Lubavitch Hasidic sect, say, in the tradition of the *Book of Deuter-*

onomy, that in the Holocaust God grievously punished a sinful generation. Most Jews find it impossible to view the Holocaust as an act of divine justice. Alternatively, rationalist teachers assert that God has only finite power and was incapable of preventing the Holocaust, so humankind must actively help God bring the Messiah. Others have come to a Job-like stance. They remain stunned that God can entrust humans with the freedom to become as heartless as the Nazis did. They admit they do not understand God's ways. Nonetheless, they accept God's sovereignty and seek to build their lives on it. [*For further discussion, see* Holocaust, The, *article on* Jewish Theological Responses.]

All these views of evil circulated in the Jewish community well before the Holocaust, leading some to suggest that what truly died in the Holocaust was the Enlightenment's surrogate god, the infinitely competent human spirit. As a result of the loss of absolute faith in humankind, a small minority of modern Jews have sought answers in Jewish mysticism. [*See* Qabbalah.] For others, Orthodoxy has gained fresh appeal. For most Jews, the emancipation has only been qualified, not negated. Mediating between Judaism and modernity continues to be the central spiritual concern of the people who believe themselves to stand in covenant with God, working and waiting for the realization of God's rule on earth.

[*For further discussion of the mainstream movements in contemporary Judaism, see* Reform Judaism; Orthodox Judaism; Conservative Judaism; Reconstructionist Judaism; *and* Hasidism. *Aspects of Judaism that are not rabbinic in origin are discussed in* Folk Religion, *article on* Folk Judaism. *Jewish religious thought is discussed in* Jewish Thought and Philosophy.]

BIBLIOGRAPHY

The *Encyclopaedia Judaica*, 16 vols. (Jerusalem, 1971), encapsulates contemporary scholarship on Judaism, not altogether replacing the first magisterial survey, *The Jewish Encyclopedia*, 12 vols. (1901–1906; reprint, New York, 1964). Louis Jacobs's *A Jewish Theology* (New York, 1973) provides erudite historical accounts of major Jewish ideas from a believing but nonfundamentalist viewpoint. Robert M. Seltzer's comprehensive survey *Jewish People, Jewish Thought* (New York, 1980) adroitly balances history and religious ideas. The finest recent account of the Jewish religious sensibility of the Bible is Jon D. Levenson's *Sinai and Zion* (New York, 1985).

Reliable, if not altogether comprehensible, English translations of the central rabbinic texts exist: *The Mishnah*, translated by Herbert Danby (Oxford, 1933); *The Babylonian Talmud*, 35 vols. (1935–1948; reprint in 18 vols., London, 1961); and *Midrash Rabbah*, 10 vols., translated by Harry Freedman et al. (London, 1939). An English rendering of the Jerusalem Talmud by Jacob Neusner is under way as *The Talmud of the Land of Israel* (Chicago, 1982–); thirty-five volumes are projected. Current scholarship has raised so many questions about rabbinic Judaism that great care must be exercised in utilizing any single source. A well-rounded overview can be gained from the revised (but not the original) edition of Emil Schürer's *The History of the Jewish People in the Age of Jesus Christ*, 2 vols., edited and revised by Géza Vermès and Fergus Millar and translated by T. A. Burkill et al. (Edinburgh, 1973–1979).

No history of the development of Jewish practice exists. Valuable insights may still be gained from the dated work of Hayyim Schauss, *The Jewish Festivals*, translated by Samuel Jaffe (Cincinnati, 1938), and *The Lifetime of a Jew* (New York, 1950). Menachem Elon treats some central themes of Jewish law in *The Principles of Jewish Law* (Jerusalem, 1975), and an invaluable guide to more specific themes is the presently incomplete *Entsiqlopedeyah Talmudit*, edited by S. Y. Zevin and Meir Bar-Ilan (Jerusalem, 1947–).

The *aggadah*, because of its human appeal, is more readily accessible. Two good anthologies available in English are Louis Ginzberg's *The Legends of the Jews*, 7 vols., translated by Henrietta Szold et al. (Philadelphia, 1909–1938), which follows the organization of the Bible, and C. G. Montefiore and Herbert Loewe's *A Rabbinic Anthology* (1938; reprint, Philadelphia, 1960), which is thematically organized. The most comprehensive anthology, however, is in Hebrew: H. N. Bialik and Y. H. Ravnitzky's *Sefer ha-aggadah*, 3 vols. (Cracow, 1907–1911), often reprinted.

Three valuable, if problematic, introductions to rabbinic thought are Solomon Schechter's *Some Aspects of Rabbinic Theology* (New York, 1909), and George Foot Moore's *Judaism*, 3 vols. in 2 (1927–1930; reprint, Cambridge, Mass., 1970), both of which show apologetic tendencies, and E. E. Urbach's *Ḥazal* (Jerusalem, 1969), translated by Israel Abrahams as *The Sages*, 2 vols. (Jerusalem, 1975), which unconvincingly seeks to resolve rabbinic inconsistencies by applying a historical hermeneutic. Jacob Neusner's continuing researches in this literature deserve careful attention. For his demonstration of how ahistorical (by Western academic standards) rabbinic "theology" was, see his *Judaism in Society* (Chicago, 1984).

Most of the great Jewish legal works of the Middle Ages await reliable translation according to the standard set by *The Code of Maimonides*, 15 vols. to date (New Haven, 1949–), the now nearly complete translation of Maimonides' *Mishneh Torah*. The burgeoning scholarship on mysticism builds on the paradigmatic researches of Gershom Scholem, whose synoptic statement is *Major Trends in Jewish Mysticism* (1941; reprint, New York, 1961). Many major works of medieval Jewish philosophy have been translated. The older, still useful survey of the field is Isaac Husik's *A History of Mediaeval Jewish Philosophy* (New York, 1916). Its modern successor is Julius Guttmann's *Philosophies of Judaism*, translated by David W. Silverman (New York, 1964).

The documents of the emancipation and its aftermath are bountifully supplied and valuably annotated in Paul R. Mendes-Flohr and Jehuda Reinharz's *The Jew in the Modern World* (Oxford, 1980). Some sense of the reality of modern Jewish life as it is lived in North America can be gained from the ideals projected in the works of some of its leading guides (respectively, Modern Orthodox, far-right-wing Conservative, tradition-seeking independent, and Reform): Hayim Halevy Donin's *To Be a Jew* (New York, 1972); Isaac Klein's *A Guide to Jewish Religious Practice* (New York, 1979); *The Jewish Catalog*, edited by Richard Siegel, Michael Strassfeld, and Sharon Strassfeld (Philadelphia, 1973); and *Gates of Mitzvah*, edited by Simeon J. Maslin (New York, 1979), and *Gates of the Seasons*, edited by Peter Knobel (New York, 1983).

Developments in Jewish law are difficult to track even for seasoned experts, but since its founding, *The Jewish Law Annual*, edited by Bernard S. Jackson (Leiden, 1978–), has been a most valuable guide. Reliable introductions to current Jewish theologies are William E. Kaufman's *Contemporary Jewish Philosophies* (New York, 1976) and my own *Choices in Modern Jewish Thought* (New York, 1983).

For the Holocaust, the early works of Elie Wiesel, fiction and nonfiction, uniquely limn the paradoxes of trying to live and write about the ineffable. Two focal statements about the Holocaust are Richard L. Rubenstein's *After Auschwitz* (Indianapolis, 1966) and Emil L. Fackenheim's *To Mend the World* (New York, 1982).

Modern Orthodoxy is surveyed in Reuven P. Bulka's *Dimensions of Orthodox Judaism* (New York, 1983), but the ideas of its preeminent theoretician, Joseph B. Soloveitchik, are most available in his early, searching essay *Halakhic Man*, translated by Lawrence Kaplan (Philadelphia, 1983). My book *Liberal Judaism* (New York, 1984) explicates the religious positions of much of American non-Orthodox Judaism.

EUGENE B. BOROWITZ

Judaism in the Middle East and North Africa to 1492

Judaism is indigenous to the Middle East. There in antiquity the Israelite people formed its unique identity. There the Bible came into being, and there by late antiquity Israelite religion was transformed into normative rabbinic Judaism. The basic texts of rabbinic Judaism—the halakhic *midrashim*, the Mishnah (compiled c. 200 CE), the two Talmuds, that of Palestine and that of Babylonia (compiled in the fifth and sixth centuries), and the first compilations of rabbinic lore *(aggadah)*—were all written in the Middle East. In the formative period of rabbinic Judaism, sectarian groups such as the religious communities of Qumran (the Dead Sea sects) manifested other varieties of Judaism. An esoteric mystical trend within rabbinic Judaism itself also grew in the Middle East of late antiquity. In Egypt in the first century CE, the Greek writings of Philo Judaeus of Alexandria gave voice to a hellenized philosophical trend within Judaism.

Jews carried their religion to North Africa in late antiquity, where some form of Judaism penetrated the native Berber population, and to Arabia, where, in the seventh century, Judaism had some influence on the formation of the new religion of Islam. After the Middle East and North Africa were brought under the dominion of Islam, following the Arab conquests, and the centuries-old separation of Jewry into two branches, one living under Sasanid-Zoroastrian rule, and the other living under a Roman-Christian regime, was brought to an end, Judaism underwent further change. Under Islam, rabbinic Judaism, faced with the unification of North African and Middle Eastern Jewry under one empire, became consolidated. In addition, as Jews adopted Arabic in place of Aramaic as both their written and spoken language, the intellectual culture of their host society became accessible to all layers of Jewish society for the first time in history. Responding to the challenge of dynamic Islamic civilization, perceived with unmediated intensity by Arabic-speaking Jewry, Judaism also experienced new developments in sectarianism, philosophy, and mysticism. These characteristic developments in Judaism between the Muslim conquests and the end of the fifteenth century will form the focus of this article.

The Babylonian Center. In the middle of the eighth century the capital of the Muslim caliphate was moved from Syria (where it had been located since 661 CE) to Baghdad. Under the Abbasid dynasty, Iraq became the center from which power and scholarly creativity radiated to the rest of the Islamic world. In this setting, the institutions of Babylonian Judaism were able to consolidate their own authority and religious leadership over the Jews living within the orbit of Islam. Successive waves of Jewish (as well as Muslim) migration from the eastern Islamic lands, long subject to the religious guidance of the Babylonian Talmud, to the Mediterranean and other western provinces of the caliphate, contributed substantially to this process.

The main instrument of this consolidation was the *yeshivah*. Though usually translated "academy," the *yeshivah* then was actually more than a center of learning. It was, as well, a seat of supreme judicial authority and a source of religious legislation. In pre-Islamic times there were already three *yeshivot*, one in Palestine, headed by the patriarch (the *nasi'*), and two in Babylonia, named Sura and Pumbedita. The Palestinian (or Jerusalem) and Babylonian Talmuds were redacted, respectively, in the Palestinian and Babylonian *yeshivot*. [*See* Yeshivah.]

After the middle of the eighth century the Babylonian *yeshivot* began to outshine their counterparts in Palestine. The heads of the *yeshivot* (first of Sura, later of Pumbedita, too) acquired a lofty title, "gaon" (short for *ro'sh yeshivat ge'on Ya'aqov*, "head of the *yeshivah* of the pride of Jacob," see *Psalms* 47:5). In an effort to as-

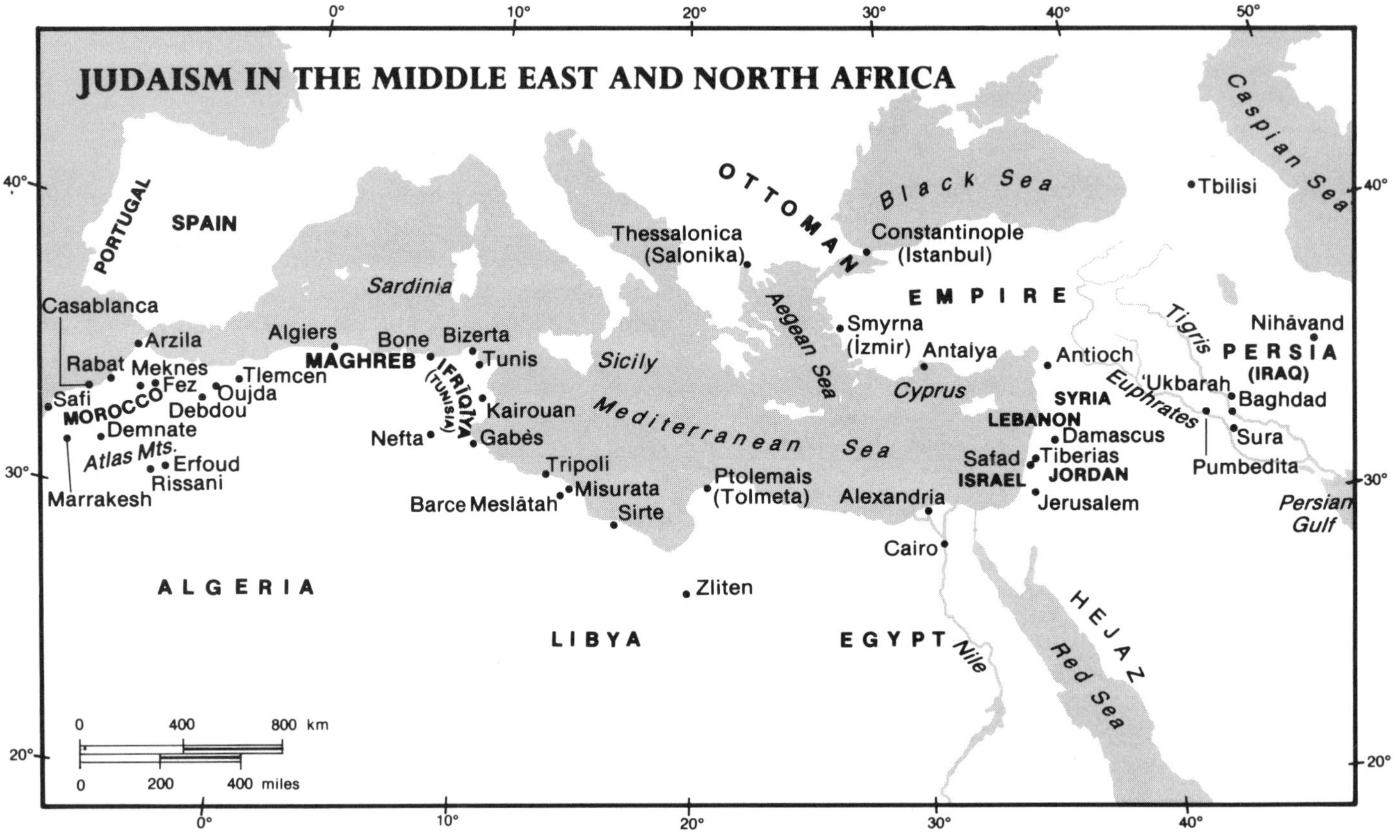

JUDAISM IN THE MIDDLE EAST AND NORTH AFRICA

sert the authority of Babylonian Judaism throughout the caliphate, the geonim developed many types of halakhic (legal) literature. They were undoubtedly influenced by the intense efforts to consolidate Muslim legal traditions that were going on at the same time in Iraq. However, owing to the centrality of *halakhah* in Jewish life the consolidation of legal authority in the hands of the Babylonian geonim also served the political purpose of endowing the Babylonian gaonate with administrative hegemony over Islamic Jewry.

One of the most important literary vehicles used to this end was the system of questions and answers *(responsa).* Like its analogue in Roman and in Islamic law, a *responsum* (Heb., *teshuvah*) is an answer to a legal question. It can be issued only by a scholar of recognized authority. Something like the *responsa* seems to have existed in pre-Islamic Palestine, but the Babylonian geonim developed the legal custom into a major enterprise for the extension of their spiritual and political domination over the communities of the Islamic empire. Queries dispatched to Babylonia were accompanied by donations, which constituted one of the chief means of support for the *yeshivot* there.

A large number of *responsa* are extant from the mid-eighth century onward. They were sent to places as far away as North Africa and Spain and were transmitted mainly by Jewish merchants. In communities along the trade routes through which they passed, copies of the geonic rulings were often made. In Old Cairo, for instance, a major commercial crossroads of the Islamic Middle Ages, many such *responsa* were discovered in the famous Cairo Genizah, where they had lain undisturbed for centuries owing to the Jewish custom of burying, rather than physically destroying, pages of sacred writings. Once a *responsum* reached the community that had sent the question, it was read aloud in the synagogue, a procedure that strengthened local reverence for the spiritual as well as the political authority of the geonim.

The two geonim from whom we have the largest number of *responsa* are Sherira' and his son H'ai, whose consecutive reigns as gaon of the *yeshivah* of Pumbedita spanned the years 968–1038. The fact that very few *responsa* emanating from their rivals, the Palestinian geonim, are known is a further measure of the success of the Babylonian *responsa* enterprise in creating a strong Babylonian orientation among the Jews of the Islamic world.

Another device employed by the Babylonian geonim to universalize Babylonian Judaism was the *taqqanah* (legislative ordinance). These *taqqanot* were new laws, or modifications of existing laws, designed to adapt Talmudic law to realities not foreseen by the rabbis of the Mishnah and the *gemara'*. For instance, with the large-scale abandonment of agriculture by Jews and their increasing involvement in commerce, the issue of collection of debts by proxy became problematic. The Talmud permitted this only in conjunction with transfer of land. The Babylonian geonim, conscious of the deagrarianization of Jewish life, promulgated a *taqqanah* stipulating that debt transfer could be effected even by the nonlanded by employing the legal fiction that every Jew owns four cubits of real property in the Land of Israel.

To further their ecumenical authority the geonim also wrote commentaries on the Mishnah and Talmud. These originated as answers to questions about unclear passages in the Talmud that were posed by Jews living far from the center of living Talmud study in Babylonia. In their commentaries, the geonim gave pride of place to halakhic sections, owing to the juridical priorities of the *yeshivot* and to the practical needs of the Jews. The geonim also sought to make the Babylonian Talmud more accessible to those lacking training at the *yeshivah* itself. To this end they wrote introductions to that literature, explaining the methods, rules, and terminology of rabbinic jurisprudence. One type of introduction consisted of a chronological survey of Mishnaic and Talmudic teachers. This established their historical relationship and linked the rabbinic authority of the geonim with the divine source of Jewish law at Mount Sinai. The most famous work of this type, which in form was actually a *responsum* sent to a North African questioner, is the "Epistle" *(Iggeret)* of Sherira' Gaon, which forms our best single source for the history of geonic rule.

The geonim also compiled the first post-Mishnaic codes of Jewish law. The *Halakhot pesuqot* of Yehudai Gaon (in office 757–761 CE) is an abridged paraphrase of the Babylonian Talmud in Aramaic. A practical book, it omits nearly all of the *aggadah* (non-legal literature) and the agricultural and sacrificial laws and concentrates on such practical subjects as precepts regarding festivals, commercial law, family law, and synagogue and other ritual observances. A more comprehensive work of this type was the *Halakhot gedolot* of Shim'on of Basra (c. 825), a student at the *yeshivah* of Sura.

Like the Muslim legists, the geonim composed specialized codes, extracting for handy reference Talmudic laws of inheritance, of deposit, of buying and selling, and of juridical procedure.

The first written prayer books in Jewish history were actually geonic codes of liturgical procedure. The one by the ninth century gaon Amram was sent in response to a request from a community in Spain for guidance in these matters. Sa'adyah Gaon (882–942) also wrote a prayer book, one which, for the first time, used Arabic for the explanatory sections.

It was, however, not only by way of these various literary endeavors that the Babylonian geonim imposed their authority on most of the Arabic-speaking Jewish world and universalized their form of Judaism; they further consolidated their spiritual and political sovereignty by training and licensing judges and by teaching Talmud to Jews who came from afar to hear lectures at the *yeshivah's* semiannual conclaves *(kallot)*. By the beginning of the eleventh century the process had been successfully completed. The Palestinian gaon Shelomoh ben Yehudah (in office 1026–1051) had to send his own son to the Baghdad *yeshivah* to complete his Talmudic education. Shelomoh's successor as gaon in Jerusalem, Daniyye'l ben 'Azaryah, was a Babylonian scholar and a member of the family of the Babylonian exarchs, the descendants of the Davidic royal house who were living in Babylonian exile and were recognized by the caliph, as they had been by the pre-Islamic rulers of Persia, as "heads of the Diaspora." Ben 'Azaryah, who died in 1062, brought Babylonian learning for a brief time to the *yeshivah* of Jerusalem.

New Centers in North Africa and Egypt. In the course of time, the very universalization of Babylonian Judaism and the dispersal of Babylonian-trained judges and scholars throughout the Diaspora in Islamic lands created a foundation upon which new independent centers of religious learning and authority could be built. This happened in North Africa in the tenth and eleventh centuries and in Egypt somewhat later.

Kairouan. In the ninth and tenth centuries, the Jews of Kairouan, the capital of Muslim Ifrīqiyā (modern Tunisia), were firmly within the camp of the Babylonian geonim. Indeed, most of the Jewish settlers in Kairouan had originated in Iraq and Iran, the heartland of geonic authority. But in these two centuries, Muslim Kairouan achieved considerable prosperity and became a major center of Islamic legal studies. Against this background, the local Jewish community began to create its own center of Talmudic scholarship. The first mention of a formal house of study in Kairouan—the term used was *midrash* rather than *yeshivah*—occurs at the end of the century. Led by Ya'aqov bar Nissim ibn Shahin, who belonged to a family whose origins lay in the East (probably Iran) and who was a loyal adherent of Babylonian Judaism, this *midrash* was not yet a rival institution to the Babylonian *yeshivot.* Detachment from Babylonian religious sovereignty became pronounced a generation later, following the arrival in Kairouan of a scholar, believed to have hailed from Italy, named Ḥushi'el. Italian Jewry had been influenced more by Palestinian than by Babylonian traditions, so when Ḥushi'el opened a second *midrash* in Kairouan, some Palestinian traditions were taught alongside Babylonian Talmudic scholarship.

In the first half of the eleventh century two of Ḥushi'el's students placed native North African religious scholarship on a firm literary footing: his son, Ḥanan'el ben Ḥushi'el, and Nissim, the son of Ya'aqov bar Nissim (who had died in 1006/7). Ḥanan'el wrote *responsa,* commentaries on the Torah, on *Ezekiel,* on the dietary laws, and, most importantly, a comprehensive commentary on the Babylonian Talmud. In innovative fashion, this last-mentioned work employed material from the Palestinian Talmud to explain passages in the text, though, like the commentaries of the Babylonian geonim, its primary focus was juridical.

Nissim (d. 1062) maintained his father's loyalty to the Babylonian geonim. However, like his contemporary Ḥanan'el, he too wrote a fresh commentary on the Talmud utilizing material from the Palestinian text. Duplicating Babylonian geonic efforts to disseminate knowledge of the Talmud, Nissim composed in Arabic his own "Introduction" entitled *The Book of the Key to the Locks of the Talmud.* Other religious writing of his include a chain of transmission of rabbinic tradition reminiscent of Sherira' Gaon's "Epistle," *responsa* (of which many are extant), and a "Secret Scroll" *(Megillat setarim),* written in Arabic, that consisted of a potpourri of miscellaneous ritual laws. None of Nissim's rabbinic works has been preserved in its entirety and its original form; they are known of only from fragments or through quotations in the works of others.

Ḥushi'el's disciples completed the process of fashioning an independent center of religious creativity in North Africa. Their period of activity coincided with the decline of the Babylonian gaonate following the death of H'ai Gaon in 1038. However, the budding new center of rabbinic Judaism in North Africa was cut off abruptly in 1057 when Kairouan was destroyed by bedouin tribes sent by the Fatimid ruler of Egypt to punish his disloyal vassals, the Zirids, in that city.

Fez. Another creative center of Judaism in North Africa developed in Fez (present-day Morocco). *Responsa* addressed to Fez by the geonim of Sura and Pumbedita testify to the presence of learned scholars in that distant North African city. The most famous rabbinic master from Fez, Yitsḥaq ben Ya'aqov Alfasi (c. 1013–1103), wrote an abridged version of the Talmud that later became part of the apparatus of the standard printed Talmud text. He also wrote many *responsa.*

Egypt. In Egypt a local school of advanced religious study (a *midrash*) was established at the end of the tenth century by Shemaryah ben Elḥanan, a scholar educated at one of the Babylonian *yeshivot.* Egyptian Jewry at that time was subject to the political authority of the gaon of the Palestinian *yeshivah,* who was recognized by the Fatimid caliph in Cairo as head of the Jews in his empire (Egypt and Palestine). When Shemaryah's son and successor Elḥanan began to expand the activities of the Egyptian *midrash* by soliciting donations even from Palestine and by assuming some of the religious and political prerogatives of the Palestinian gaon, he was excommunicated by the Jerusalem *yeshivah.* This put a temporary halt to the growth of native Egyptian religious scholarship until, in the latter part of the eleventh century, several distinguished scholars settled in Egypt.

As in the case of Nissim ben Ya'aqov of Kairouan, the writings of these scholars are known from fragments, from quotations in later works, and medieval book lists. One notable author was Yehudah ha-Kohen ben Yosef, who wrote commentaries on the Bible and on portions of the Talmud, a code of regulations concerning ritual slaughtering, liturgical poems, and a commentary on the mystical *Sefer yetsirah* (Book of Creation). Another was a scholar from Spain named Yitsḥaq ben Shemu'el, who wrote an Arabic commentary on some if not all of the Former Prophets, a commentary on at least one Talmudic tractate, *responsa,* and liturgical poems. Though neither of these scholars opened an academy of learning, they gave Egyptian Jewry a renewed sense of independence from the traditional sources of religious leadership in Babylonia and from the political dominion of the *yeshivah* in Palestine.

Related to the activity of these respected rabbinic scholars in Egypt toward the end of the eleventh century was the emergence there of a new Jewish institution of central leadership. This was the office of "head of the Jews" (Arab., *ra'īs al-yahūd),* more commonly known in Hebrew as the office of the *nagid.* The scholarly family of court physicians headed by the brothers Yehudah and Mevorakh ben Sa'adyah was the first to hold this position of dignity. The office of head of the Jews, inheriting the sovereignty formerly reserved for the Palestinian gaon, was invested with supreme religious as well as political authority over the Jews in the Fatimid empire.

In the third decade of the twelfth century the Palestinian *yeshivah,* which had been located outside the borders of Palestine since the Seljuk conquest of Jerusalem around 1071, transferred its own headquarters to the capital of Egypt. With this move the office of head of the Jews temporarily passed into the hands of the newly arrived Palestinian gaon, Matsliaḥ ha-Kohen ben Shelomoh. How much teaching went on in the relocated Palestinian yeshivah we do not know. However, the arrival of Moses Maimonides (Mosheh ben Maimon) in Egypt around 1165 established Egypt as a respectable center of Jewish religious scholarship. Maimonides attracted a circle of students and substituted the study of his own code of Jewish law, the *Mishneh Torah,* for the study of the Babylonian Talmud in the curriculum of Jewish higher education. The Babylonian gaonate voiced opposition to Maimonides, who was seen as a threat to its efforts to reassert its former supremacy over world Jewry. Nevertheless, the Maimonidean tradition of learning in Egypt, modified by a distinctive mystical bent, was continued by his son Avraham and by a succession of Maimonidean descendants until the beginning of the fifteenth century.

Yemen. A center of Jewish learning much influenced by Moses Maimonides was to be found in Yemen. Already in late antiquity there was a small Jewish presence in South Arabia, as we know from the evidence of Hebrew inscriptions and from stories about the conversion to Judaism of rulers of the South Arabian kingdom of Ḥimyar (the last of these Jewish kings of Ḥimyar, who was also the last Ḥimyarite ruler, died in 525 CE). In the Islamic period the Jewish settlement was considerably strengthened by the migration of Jews from Babylonia and Persia. Naturally, from the outset the Yemenite community maintained loyalty to the Babylonian geonim and the Babylonian exilarch, supported the Babylonian *yeshivah* financially, and adhered to the Babylonian interpretation of rabbinic Judaism.

In the eleventh and twelfth centuries, however, Yemen and Yemenite Jews became closely connected with Egypt as a result of general political and economic developments. Thus, they identified in the twelfth century with the *yeshivah* of Matsliaḥ ha-Kohen in Cairo and especially with Maimonides after his arrival in Egypt. In the later Middle Ages a considerable indigenous religious literature developed among the Yemenite Jews, much of it consisting in commentaries on various works of Maimonides. In Yemen, moreover, Maimonides' *Mishneh Torah* became the principal code of Jewish practice. Among Yemenite works from the later Middle Ages that cite passages from Maimonides' oeuvre is the voluminous anthology of homiletic and legal *midrashim* on the five books of the Torah compiled in the thirteenth century by David ben ʿAmram of the Yemenite port city of Aden, entitled *Midrash ha-gadol.*

Karaism. Not long after the Muslim conquest, the most important religious schism in medieval Judaism, known as Karaism, occurred in the Middle East. The Karaites rejected the jurisdiction of the Talmud and of rabbinic Judaism in general, claiming exclusive reliance on the Bible. Some scholars believe that Karaism actualized a latent anti-Talmudism that had existed beneath the surface since the time of the Sadducees, who centuries earlier had denied the validity of the oral Law. Others identify in Karaism affinities with the religion of the Dead Sea sects, notably the asceticism shared by these two religious movements.

It is difficult to prove the influence of one sect on another separated from it in time by so many centuries. What is certain, however, in terms of immediate causes is that Karaism arose in opposition to the extension of the authority of rabbinic Judaism by the Babylonian geonim in the early Islamic period and out of resentment towards the power wielded by the Jewish aristocracy of Iraq through the Davidic exilarchate.

The Iranian Plateau, fertile ground for sectarian rebellion in early Islam, spawned several antirabbinic Jewish revolts prior to the crystallization of a cohesive Karaite movement. One example was the sect of Abū ʿĪsā al-Isfahānī, whose period of activity is variously given as 685–705, during the reign of the Umayyad caliph ʿAbd al-Malik ibn Manṣūr, or at the time of the transition from Umayyad to Abbasid rule, between 744 and 775. His ascetic, anti-Talmudic program included the prohibition of divorce and a change in the daily liturgical cycle from three to seven prayers. Abū ʿĪsā was also driven by his belief in the imminent coming of the Messiah to take up arms against the Muslim government.

Abū ʿĪsā's sect was but one of many groups whose antirabbinic halakhic practices were collected together in the eighth century by ʿAnan ben David, an important link in the chain leading to the consolidation of Karaism in the ninth and tenth centuries. ʿAnan may have hailed from the Iranian Plateau, but he operated in the center of geonic-exilarchal territory in Babylonia. He was, in fact, said to have been a member of the exilarchal family. A biased Rabbinite account of his sectarian rebellion ascribes his motives to personal disappointment after being passed over for appointment to the office of exilarch.

ʿAnan's principal achievement was to assemble scattered bits of sectarian *halakhah* into a code called *Sefer ha-mitsvot* (Book of Commandments). In this book, he employed Talmudic methodology for his own end: his biblical exegesis served to lend credibility and respectability to the deviant practices that he codified. This use of rabbinic methods and language to establish the legitimacy of nonrabbinic Judaism constituted a serious challenge to the authority of the geonim.

ʿAnan seems to have envisaged the creation of separatist communities of nonrabbinic Jews living in various locales within the Diaspora. One scholar has even proposed that he wished to gain government recognition for a second legitimate school of law within Judaism, coexisting with the school of the Babylonian geonim much like the different *madhhabs* (schools of jurisprudence) in Islam.

Later Karaites attributed to ʿAnan the formulation of a principle, expressed as an apothegm: "Search thoroughly in the Torah and do not rely upon my opinion." This legitimated, in theory at least, the exclusive reliance on the Bible that distinguished Karaism from rabbinism and sounded the call for individualistic exegesis in place of slavish adherence to rabbinic tradition. It also justified a proliferation of non-ʿAnanite sects in the ninth and tenth centuries, such as the sect of Ismāʿīl al-ʿUkbarī (from ʿUkbara, near Baghdad), the sect of Mishawayh al-ʿUkbarī, the sect of Abū ʿImrān al-Tiflisī (from present-day Tbilisi, U.S.S.R.), and the sect of Malik al-Ramlī (from Ramleh, Palestine). Much of our information about these groups comes from the law code, *Kitāb al-anwār wa-al-marāqib* (Book of Lights and Watchtowers), by the tenth-century Karaite thinker Yaʿqūb al-Qirqisānī, which contains an introduction on the history of sects in Judaism. Not surprisingly, for Qirqisānī it is the Rabbinites, beginning with the Pharisees, rather than the Karaites, who were the real religious deviants. ʿAnan ben David's role as reformer was to rediscover the long-suppressed true path.

The first to employ the term *Karaites* (*Benei Miqra'*, "children of scripture") was the ninth-century Binyamin al-Nahāwandī (of Nihāvand, Iran). He was known for his tolerance of observance of rabbinic laws, especially where biblical legislation failed to answer practical questions of everyday life. This liberalism with respect to Talmudic law was matched by an insistence on the right of every individual to interpret scripture as he saw fit. Troubled by the rationalist critique of biblical anthropomorphisms, Binyamin taught that the world was called into being by an angel created by God, and that all anthropomorphic expressions in the Bible were to be ascribed to that angel. A judge by profession, Binyamin wrote a *Sefer mitsvot* (Book of Commandments) and a *Sefer dinim* (Book of Laws). He also wrote biblical commentaries.

Daniyye'l al-Qūmisī, another Karaite thinker of the end of the ninth century, was a messianist who settled in Jerusalem in order to mourn for Zion (the group he headed was called Avelei-Tsiyyon, "Mourners for Zion") and to pray for redemption. In his approach to the Bible he rejected the liberal individualism of Binyamin al-Nahāwandī and the latter's theology of the creator angel. However, in his own exegesis, he was, according to some sources, a rationalist.

By the tenth century Karaism was sufficiently consolidated to pose an active threat to the Babylonian geonim. Saʿadyah Gaon took up the cudgels of defense on their behalf, writing a refutation of ʿAnan *(Kitāb al-radd ʿalā ʿAnan)* and opposing Karaite views in others of his writings. Saʿadyah's hostility inspired a Karaite counterattack. Indeed, he was the polemical object of much of the rich Karaite literature of the "golden age" of the tenth and eleventh centuries.

Several important figures of this Karaite golden age bear mention here. Yaʿqūb al-Qiriqisānī (tenth century) composed, in addition to the code of law, the *Book of Lights and Watchtowers,* commentaries on several books of the Bible, a refutation of Muḥammad's claim to prophecy, and a treatise on God's unity. Salmon ben Yeroḥam (tenth century) wrote a poetical tract against the Rabbinites, *The Book of the Wars of the Lord,* that bristles with polemic against Saʿadyah, and among other works, biblical commentaries on *Psalms* and the *Song of Songs.* Yefet ben ʿEli wrote commentaries in Arabic on the entire Hebrew Bible, accompanied by translations of Hebrew text into Arabic. Sahl ben Matsliaḥ composed a *Book of Commandments,* only partly extant, and a letter to a Rabbinite disputant in Egypt extolling Karaism at the expense of rabbinism. Yūsuf al-Baṣīr (Yosef ha-Ro'eh, from Basra) wrote a *Book of Commandments* and important *responsa,* and initiated a liberalization of Karaite marriage laws which, on the basis of literal interpretation of the Bible, had multiplied the number of incestuous (and therefore forbidden) marriage combinations, thus threatening the biological continuity of the sect. Like al-Baṣīr, Yeshuʿah ben Yehudah composed a treatise refuting the Karaite laws of incestuous marriage. He also penned commentaries on books of the Bible. [*For further discussion, see* Karaites.]

Revival of Jewish Religious Philosophy. Several factors converged to bring about a revival of Jewish religious philosophy, dormant since Philo, among the Jews of the Muslim world, Rabbinites and Karaites alike. Most important were the new availability of Hellenistic philosophy in Arabic translation; Jewish awareness of the application of rationalist inquiry to theological questions in Islam; the critique of biblical anthropomorphism; the attack on the Bible by Jewish skeptics like Ḥiwi al-Balkhī; and the desire to prove that Judaism embraced the same universalistic truths as Islam. The lion's share of Jewish religious philosophy was written in Spain. However, the founder of Judeo-Arabic philosophy, Saʿadyah Gaon, and the most important philosopher of them all, Maimonides, wrote in the Middle East.

The earliest venture by Arabic-speaking Jews into rationalism followed the lead of the Muslim science of *kalām. Kalām* means "speech" and refers specifically to discussion of theological problems. The most rationalistic trend in the *kalām* was that of the Muʿtazilah, which originated in Iraq in the cities of Basra and Baghdad, and it was from this doctrine that Saʿadyah, who lived in Baghdad, drew the inspiration for his pioneering work of Jewish religious philosophy, *Kitāb al-amanāt wa-al-iʿtiqādāt* (The Book of Beliefs and Convictions). Like the Muʿtazilah, he began his treatise with an epistemological discourse establishing the indispensability of reason as a source of religious knowledge. To this he added the category of reliable transmitted knowledge—doubtless in response to skeptics and Karaites who discredited the reliability of biblical stories and laws. The idea that reason and revelation lead to the same religious truths remained a cornerstone of all medieval Jewish religious philosophy after Saʿadyah. Like the Muʿtazilah, Saʿadyah placed the discussion of the creation of the world out of nothing *(creatio ex nihilo)* at the head of his treatise, since from the premise of creation flowed the belief in the existence of God and hence all other religious convictions.

The Muʿtazilah struggled with two major challenges to rationalism: scriptural anthropomorphisms that seemingly denied God's unity, and the question of the existence of evil in this world that appeared to contradict God's justice. [*See* Muʿtazilah.] Like the Muslim Muʿtazilah, Saʿadyah devoted separate chapters to these two subjects in his philosophical treatise. Divine unity was defended by invoking the principle that the Torah uses metaphor to describe God in terms understandable to human minds. The problem of divine justice was resolved with the Muʿtazilī solution of claiming freedom of the human will. Saʿadyah took other leads from the Muʿtazilah, for instance, in drawing a distinction between laws knowable through reason and laws knowable only through revelation, as well as in his treatment of retribution. In addition, he addressed Jewish eschatology in his chapters on resurrection and redemption.

The Muslim *kalām* influenced other Jewish writers in the Middle East. Before the time of Saʿadyah, David ben Marwān al-Muqammiṣ (ninth century) combined Muʿtazilī views with Greek philosophical notions. So did the Babylonian gaon Shemuʾel ben Ḥofni (d. 1013) in his commentary on the Bible. Nissim ben Yaʿaqov of Kairouan showed familiarity with Muʿtazilī teaching in his commentary on the Talmud. Finally, the Karaites, liberated from the commitment to tradition as a valid source of religious knowledge, adopted Muʿtazilī rationalism with even less reserve than its Rabbinite exponents. Prominent among the Karaite rationalists were the above-mentioned Yaʿqūb al-Qirqisānī, Yūsuf al-Baṣīr (eleventh century), and Yeshuʿah ben Yehudah (mid-eleventh century).

These Karaites went beyond the principle of the equivalence of reason and revelation and gave primacy to the former. It was, in fact, among the Karaites of Byzantium alone that Muʿtazilī *kalām* continued to have influence on Judaism after the eleventh century. In contrast, among the Rabbinites, Neoplatonism and especially Aristotelianism took over the role that Muʿtazilī thought had played during the pioneering phase of Jewish religious philosophy in the Islamic world.

Neoplatonism and Aristotelianism flourished mainly among the Jews of Spain. However, the first Jewish Neoplatonist, Yitshaq Yisraʾeli (c. 850–950), was born in Egypt and composed philosophical works in Arabic while serving as court physician to the Muslim governor in Kairouan. Of his works the *Book of Definition* and the *Book on the Elements* (extant only in Hebrew and Latin translations) and a commentary on *Sefer yetsirah* (Book of Creation), revised by his students, show how he tried to incorporate the Neoplatonic doctrine of emanation into Judaism. Though he did not abandon the biblical premise of divinely willed creation out of nothing for a pure Neoplatonic cosmogony, he adopted the Neoplatonic conception of progressive emanation of spiritual substances in the supraterrestrial world. As with the Islamic Neoplatonists, some aspects of Yisraʾeli's philosophy of religion show the influence of Aristotelian ideas. For instance, his concept of reward for ethical conduct is based on the ascent of the human soul toward its final reunification with the upper soul. The phenomenon of prophecy, a problem for Muslim religious philosophers, similarly occupied Yitsḥaq Yisraʾeli; his theory employs the naturalistic explanation offered by the Islamic Aristotelians but leaves a place for divine will in connection with the form of the vision accorded prophets.

The most important full-fledged Jewish Aristotelian was Maimonides. Born in Spain, where in the twelfth century Aristotelianism replaced Neoplatonism as the preferred philosophy, Maimonides did most of his writing, including his philosophic magnum opus, the *Guide of the Perplexed,* in Egypt, where he lived out most of his life as a refugee from Almohade persecution in Spain and North Africa. Maimonides sought to achieve a workable synthesis between Judaism and Aristotelianism without glossing over the uncontestably incompatible elements in each of those systems. Writing for the initiated few in the *Guide,* he took up troublesome theological questions. He argued for the existence of God, which he demonstrated, not in the by-then-unsatisfactory manner of the old *kalām,* but by exploiting scientifically and logically more credible Aristotelian philosophical concepts. He upheld the unity of God, not by accepting the identity of God's attributes with his essence, as *kalām* would have it, but by combining the metaphoric interpretation of scriptural anthropomorphisms with the doctrine of negative attributes, which leaves the fact of God's existence as the sole bit of positive knowledge of divinity available to believers. He even addressed the problem of the creation of the world, which forced him to suspend Aristotle's doctrine of the eternity of the world in favor of the biblical account of the miraculous creation by the will of God.

Maimonides also attempted to bring an Aristotelian conception of Judaism within the reach of the philosophically uninitiated. This he did with a philosophical introduction to, and other occasional rationalistic comments in, his *Mishneh Torah* (Code of Jewish Law); with an Aristotelian ethical introduction to the Mishnah tractate *Avot;* and by formulating a philosophic creed for Jews in his commentary on the Mishnah.

Pietism and Jewish Sufism. A new religious development in Judaism began in the Middle East in the twelfth and thirteenth centuries. Individual Jews began to be attracted to the pious asceticism of the Muslim Ṣūfīs. In his introduction to the Mishnah tractate *Avot,* called "The Eight Chapters," Maimonides chastises such people for engaging in extreme self-abnegation, thereby straying from the more moderate path advocated by Judaism.

In the thirteenth century in Egypt, some representatives of the Jewish upper classes (physicians, government secretaries, judges, and scholars) joined together in pietistic brotherhoods akin to the Ṣūfī orders that were then flourishing in Egypt under the patronage of the Ayyubid dynasty of Muslim rulers founded by Salaḥ al-Dīn (Saladin). These Jews called themselves *ḥasidim,* using the regular Talmudic word for the pious. They fasted frequently, practiced nightly prayer vigils, and recited additional prayers accompanied by bowings and prostrations more typical of Islam than of Judaism. Rather than exhibiting their pietism in public they maintained a private place of worship where they followed their special path. Rather than wearing wool outer clothing like the Muslim Ṣūfīs, they designated as the symbol of their asceticism the turban that they all wore (Arab., *baqyār* or *buqyār*). [*For comparison see* Sufism.]

The most illustrious member of this circle of *ḥasidim* was the *nagid* (head of the Jewish community) Avraham, the son of Moses Maimonides. He wrote a long code of Jewish law entitled *Kifāyat al-'ābidīn* (The Complete Guide for the Servants of God), which, in its fourth and final book, contains a program of mystical piety for the Jewish elite based on the ethical tenets of Sufism.

The *ḥasidim* in Avraham Maimonides' brotherhood made attempts to influence the general Jewish public to adopt some aspects of their pietism. Earlier, Moses Maimonides himself had introduced reforms in the Egyptian synagogue service aimed at imitating the more decorous environment of the mosque. Driven by pietistic zeal, his son went further. He tried to introduce the kneeling posture of Islamic prayer into the synagogue; he insisted that worshipers face the direction of prayer even while seated; and he required people to stand in straight rows during the Eighteen Benedictions, in imitation of the orderly, symmetrical pattern of the mosque. These and other pietistic reforms aroused much opposition, and some Jews actually denounced Avraham to the Muslim authorities for attempting to introduce unlawful innovations into Judaism. In response, Avraham wrote a vigorous defense of pietism, which has been found in the Cairo Genizah.

Avraham Maimonides' son 'Ovadyah wrote his own Ṣūfī-like book. Called *Al-maqālah al-ḥawḍīyah* (The Treatise of the Pool), it attempted to impart intellectual respectability to Jewish Sufism. In the later Middle Ages, some Jews in Egypt imitated the style of life of the Ṣūfī convents in the hills surrounding Cairo. In Egypt, too, Jewish thinkers, outstanding among them the descendants of Maimonides, continued to compose treatises in the Ṣūfī vein. This turn towards mystical piety in the Jewish world, at just about the time when Jewish religious philosophy reached its climactic stage in the Middle East in the writings of Maimonides, recalls the replacement of philosophy by Sufism as the dominant religious mode in Islam in the later medieval period. Possibly Jewish interest in Sufism similarly reflects a dissatisfaction with the answers given in the past by Jewish rationalism to religious questions. Only when the study of Jewish Sufism, still in its infancy, has progressed further will it be possible to gain a clear sense of its place in the history of Judaism in the Islamic world and of the influence it might have had on the Lurianic Qabbalah that sprouted in Muslim Palestine after the expulsion of Jews from Spain in 1492.

[*See, for context and comparison,* Islam, *overview article and article on* Islam in Spain. *Further discussion on the earliest period covered by this article can be found in* Rabbinic Judaism in Late Antiquity. *Related articles include* Jewish Thought and Philosophy, *article on* Premodern Philosophy, *and* Polemics, *article on* Muslim-Jewish Polemics. *See also the independent entries on important figures mentioned herein.*]

BIBLIOGRAPHY

The most thorough general work on Jewish history and religion is Salo W. Baron's *A Social and Religious History of the*

Jews, 2d ed., rev. & enl., 18 vols. (New York, 1952–1980). A good introduction to Jewish life under Islam is to be found in *The Jews of Arab Lands: A History and Source Book,* compiled and introduced by Norman A. Stillman. An older but still valuable book on Jewish history and literature under early Islam is Simḥa Assaf's *Tequfat ha-ge'onim ve-sifrutah* (Jerusalem, 1955).

Regional studies include Jacob Mann's *The Jews in Egypt and in Palestine under the Fāṭimid Caliphs,* 2 vols. in 1 (1920–1922; reprint, New York, 1970); my *Jewish Self-Government in Medieval Egypt: The Origins of the Office of the Head of the Jews, ca. 1065–1126* (Princeton, 1980); Eliyahu Ashtor's *Toledot ha-Yehudim be-Mitsrayim ve-Suryah taḥat shilṭon ha-Mamlukim,* 3 vols. (Jerusalem, 1944–1970), which concerns the Jews of Egypt and Syria; his *The Jews of Moslem Spain,* translated by Aaron Klein and Jenny Machlowitz Klein, 3 vols. (Philadelphia, 1973–1984); and H. Z. Hirschberg's *A History of the Jews in North Africa,* 2d rev. ed., 2 vols. (Leiden, 1974–1981). On the Yemenite Jews see S. D. Goitein's *Ha-Teimanim* (Jerusalem, 1983) and David R. Blumenthal's edition and annotated translation of *The Commentary of R. Ḥōṭer ben Shelōmō to the Thirteen Principles of Maimonides* (Leiden, 1974). Goitein's magisterial work, *A Mediterranean Society,* 5 vols. (Berkeley, 1967–1983), presents a detailed portrait of Jewish life, in both its worldly and religious aspects, in the Mediterranean Arab world of the High Middle Ages. On Karaism, see *Karaite Anthology,* edited and translated by Leon Nemoy (New Haven, 1952), and the introduction to Zvi Ankori's *Karaites in Byzantium* (New York, 1959). Julius Guttmann's *Philosophies of Judaism,* translated by David W. Silverman (New York, 1964), and Georges Vajda's *Introduction à la pensée juive au Moyen Age* (Paris, 1947) offer excellent introductions to the subject of the revival of religious philosophy in medieval Judaism in the Islamic world. The major Jewish philosophical works mentioned in this article exist in partial or complete English translation, such as the selection of Yitsḥaq Yisra'eli's philosophical writings translated into English in *Isaac Israeli: A Neoplatonic Philosopher of the Early Tenth Century* by Alexander Altmann and Samuel M. Stern (Oxford, 1958); *Saadia Gaon: The Book of Beliefs and Opinions,* translated by Samuel Rosenblatt (New Haven, 1948); and Maimonides' *Guide of the Perplexed,* translated by Shlomo Pines and introduced by Leo Strauss (Chicago, 1963). On pietism and Jewish Sufism, see the introduction to Paul Fenton's translation of Obadiah Maimonides' *Treatise of the Pool* (London, 1981) and Gerson D. Cohen's "The Soteriology of R. Abraham Maimuni," *Proceedings of the American Academy for Jewish Research,* 35 (1967): 75–98 and 36 (1968): 33–56.

For additional bibliography on the general subject of Jewish life and culture in the medieval Islamic world, consult the *Bibliographical Essays in Medieval Jewish Studies,* edited by Yosef H. Yerushalmi (New York, 1976), especially my chapter, "The Jews under Medieval Islam: From Rise of Islam to Sabbatai Zevi," reprinted with a supplement for the years 1973–1980 as "Princeton Near East Paper," no. 32 (Princeton, 1981); and that by Lawrence Berman, "Medieval Jewish Religious Philosophy."

MARK R. COHEN

Judaism in the Middle East and North Africa since 1492

The year 1492 marks a turning point in the history of the Jewish people. The expulsion of the Jews from Spain closes a brilliant and complex chapter in Jewish history, releasing a massive group of talented and despondent refugees upon the shores of the Mediterranean. They were soon followed by other waves of Jewish émigrés from Portugal, France, Provence, and the various Italian states as a result of the forced conversions or expulsions in those countries in the late-fifteenth through mid-sixteenth centuries. Even within the tragic annals of the Jews, rarely had the contemporary scene appeared so bleak. With most of the gates of Europe closed, the refugees of western Europe fled to the world of Islam, injecting new life and much controversy into the Jewish communities there that had been living in a state of decline for at least two centuries. The emergent period was marked by fervent yearnings for redemption, painful attempts at evaluating why the Spanish Jewish experience had ended in such ignominy, a brief but brilliant renaissance of Jewish life in Turkey, the outburst of antinomianism in seventeenth-century Ottoman Jewry and a final period of increasing intellectual stagnation of Jews in Muslim lands. Beginning in the nineteenth century, winds of change swept the Near East, propelled by the influence of the European powers. Jews were especially receptive to the attempts of western Jews to reform the eastern Jews and their situation, unleashing a chain of events and attempts at modernization whose effects are still being felt.

Jewish Legal Status in Muslim Lands. From its inception, Islam exhibited an ambivalent attitude toward non-Muslims. The prophet Muḥammad had clearly enunciated his indebtedness to the faith of his monotheistic predecessors in the Qur'ān, tolerating their continued existence with certain provisos. Jews and Christians were to be recognized as possessors of scripture, *ahl al-kitāb* ("people of the Book"), were not to be forcibly converted, and were to be afforded a modicum of protection. Implied in the status of protection, *dhimmah,* or of protected peoples—*dhimmīs*—was the right of the Jews to exercise their Judaism provided they accepted a position of subordination.

Over the centuries Muslim jurists worked out elaborate codes of what constituted subordination and "signs of humiliation." Typically, Jewish and Christian houses of worship were to be inconspicuous, Jews and Christians were to wear distinguishing garments, such as special headgear or footwear and clothing of designated colors. They were prohibited from riding horses or engaging in occupations that would place them in a position of authority over Muslims. In addition, they were required to pay special discriminatory taxes on produce of the land and a special head tax *(jizyah)*.

Implementation of the discriminatory decrees was never uniform; the earlier Middle Ages exhibited a far greater degree of tolerance than the later Middle Ages. On the peripheries of the Muslim empire, moreover, in Morocco, Persia, and Yemen, the Muslim regimes tended to enforce discriminatory codes much more rigorously than in the heartland. By the nineteenth century, the entire system of carefully balanced toleration tempered by discrimination had broken down and Jews increasingly turned to the European powers for protection. In general, however, Middle East society was marked by public displays of religiosity, which found particular expression in the family or clan unit. Judaism, too, was a family and communal tradition strengthened by generations of relative economic, social, and political isolation in Muslim lands. Known in Turkish as a *millet* ("nation") in the Ottoman realm (from the mid-fifteenth century), Jews and Judaism enjoyed a relatively self-contained and protected position in the lands of Islam.

Jewish Demography in Muslim Lands: Pre- and Post-1492. Population estimates of Jews in Muslim lands are extremely risky, since even at the height of the Muslim state its records of tax collection are partial and incomplete at best. It is generally accepted by historians that between 85 and 90 percent of world Jewry lived in the Muslim world in the period from the eighth through the tenth century. As that world became increasingly anarchic in the twelfth century, and as a result of the pogroms unleashed by the Almohads after 1147, Jewish population migrations to Christian lands increased. By the mid-seventeenth century, there were approximately three-quarters of a million Jews in the world, half of whom lived in the Muslim realm and half in Christian Europe (primarily Poland and Lithuania). During the sixteenth century acme of population growth in the Ottoman empire, the Jewish population in Istanbul alone reached forty thousand. At least as many Jews resided in contemporary Salonika. Perhaps as many as ten thousand Jews resided in Fez in Morocco, fifteen thousand in Iraq, and as many as fifteen thousand in the city of Safad (in Palestine) in the sixteenth century.

The Jewish population in the Ottoman empire began to decline dramatically in the seventeenth century as a result of fires, earthquakes, infant mortality, and increasing political insecurity. By the eve of World War II, Jews from Muslim lands numbered approximately one million out of the global Jewish population of approximately eighteen million. Since the Holocaust, Sefardic Jews (of Spanish origin) and Oriental Jews (of Middle Eastern and North African origin) have increased in demographic importance, both absolutely and relatively, since they constitute a majority of the Jewish population of Israel and France, the second and third largest Jewish communities in the free world. (The term *Sefardic Jews* hereafter may include Oriental Jews, when their distinction is not necessary.)

The Exiles from Spain to the Maghreb. Jewish flight from Spain began as a mass movement, not in 1492, but in 1391. In that year, waves of violence inundated the Jews of Spain and the Balearic Islands, and while many Jews were martyred, others converted, and still others fled. One of the most important places of refuge of Spanish and Majorcan Jewry in 1391 was Algeria. Sefardic Jews met a mixed reception from the fearful indigenous Jews but quickly assumed leadership positions in the community, providing a new élan to North African Jewish life. The scholar refugee leaders Yitsḥaq ben Sheshet Perfet (1326–1408) and Shim'on ben Tsemaḥ Duran (1361–1444) have left a voluminous collection of rabbinic decisions and correspondence *(responsa)* revealing that Sefardic Jewry was troubled, not simply by the arduous task of communal reconstruction following flight, but also by very difficult questions of ritual and law as a result of the large-scale apostasy that had accompanied the waves of persecution. Questions of marital, ritual, and dietary law could not easily be resolved as demands for compassion clashed with real issues of communal continuity and Jewish identity.

The wave of refugees rose, and the question of secret Jews and forced converts (Marranos and *conversos*) grew more complex after 1492, as over 150,000 left Spain in haste. [*See* Marranos.] One of the favored refuges was Morocco, where Jews found asylum in the kingdom of Fez after a journey made perilous by unscrupulous captains and pirates. Chroniclers such as Avraham ben Shelomoh of Ardutiel, Avraham Zacuto, and Shelomoh ibn Verga dramatized the hazards of the flight from Spain. In Fez, Meknes, Marrakesh, Safi, Arzila, and smaller towns the Sefardic refugees injected new leadership and frequent controversy into the midst of small indigenous communities. In the coastal regions they exploited their connections with the Iberian Peninsula, serving as commercial agents for the Spanish and Portuguese.

Wherever the Spanish refugees came, they brought with them great pride, loyalty, and nostalgia for their cities of origin. Many of their customs were unfamiliar to the local Jews, particularly the halakhic leniencies that they had devised in response to the religious persecution they had endured. But they considered their customs to be sacrosanct, and controversy raged among the Spanish Jews and between the Spaniards (known as *megorashim,* "expelled ones") and the indigenous Jews (known as *toshavim).* In Morocco, these communal divisions were reflected in a duplication of many communal institutions and a protracted communal debate in Fez that required Muslim intercession.

In Tunisia, divisions between the refugees and the indigenous population were also institutionalized. They were aggravated by the influx of Jews from Livorno, Italy, who reinforced the separatism of the Spaniards. Two communities were established and the divisions between the newcomers (known as the *grana*) and the natives *(touansa)* persisted until the twentieth century. (This internecine struggle enabled local Turkish governors to exploit the Jews more easily.)

Jewish life in the Maghreb bore a number of distinctive features in the period following the advent of the Jews from Spain. On the one hand, most communities were torn by division as Sefardim attempted to impose their customs upon the local Jews. Given their large numbers, superior educational level, and self-confidence, Spanish Jewry assumed the helms of power in most of the Maghreb. New Jewish intellectual centers emerged in Fez (Morocco) and Tlemcen (Algeria), and the ordinances *(taqqanot)* of the Jews of Castile soon became the guide for natives as well as newcomers. In matters of personal status as well as questions of communal leadership, inheritance, and ritual slaughtering, the Sefardic way became the standard mode of behavior for most Maghrebi Jews.

North Africa was not, however, a mere replica of pre-1492 Spain. Local customs, such as worship at the tombs of saints, the special celebration at the end of the festival of Passover known as the Mimuniah, and belief in the efficacy of amulets and talismans became part and parcel of Maghrebi Jewry as a whole. [*See* Pilgrimage, *article on* Jewish Pilgrimage.] The special role of the emissary from Palestine, the *ḥakham kolel,* in the intellectual life of the Maghreb was already discernible by the fifteenth century. Through the *ḥakham kolel* the mystical movements of sixteenth-century Palestine spread rapidly in North Africa. North African Judaism was characterized by a melding of the study of Talmud with that of Qabbalah or mysticism, and this blending lent a special flavor to the scholarship that emerged there in a long line of teachers, jurists, judges, and mystics.

The Aftermath of 1492: The Ottoman East. Even before the expulsion of 1492, Jews in the West began to hear that the Ottoman empire was welcoming Jewish immigration. Yitsḥaq Tsarfati reportedly addressed the Jews of northern Europe under the reign of Murad II (1421–1451):

> Brothers and teachers, friends and acquaintances! I, Isaac Sarfati, though I spring from French stock, yet I was born in Germany, and sat there at the feet of my esteemed teachers. I proclaim to you that Turkey is a land where nothing is lacking and where, if you will, all shall yet be well with you. The way to the Holy Land lies open to you through Turkey.

Indeed, Ottoman might appeared to be invincible for over one hundred years. By the reign of Süleyman I ("the Magnificent," 1520–1566) the Ottoman borders extended from Morocco in the west to Iran in the east, from Hungary in the north to Yemen in the south.

Throughout the sixteenth century, while the empire was reaching its acme, successive boats brought Jewish refugees ashore in the eastern Mediterranean, particularly to its fairest port on the Aegean, Salonika. Some of the refugees came directly from the Iberian Peninsula while others arrived after an initial stop in Italy or North Africa where many succeeded in recouping their assets. They were eagerly welcomed by the sultan Bayezid II (1481–1512), especially since many were reputed to be skilled munitions-makers who would undoubtedly be helpful allies in the repeated wars against the Habsburgs.

The newcomers to the Ottoman empire displayed a degree of separatism and individualism that surpassed that of their Sefardic coreligionists in the Maghreb. They tended to divide along geographic lines so much so that before long there were more than forty congregations in Istanbul and Salonika each. The very names of the congregations—Catalan, Castile, Aragon, Barcelona, Portugal, Calabria—evoked identification with their origins. Distinctive identities were reinforced by the separate formations of self-help societies of all sorts. The very mixture of Jews, not only various groups of Sefardim, but also Ashkenazim from Germany and Hungary, Greek-speaking Jews from the Balkans (known as Romaniots), and Italian Jews created strains and tensions. It was not long before the preponderance of Sefardim overwhelmed the smaller native communities and the Castilian language, with an admixture of Hebrew, Turkish, and Slavic words known as *Ladino,* became the primary language of Ottoman Jewry and it remained such until the twentieth century.

The city of Salonika emerged as the preeminent Jewish community of the sixteenth century. The fame of its Talmud Torah (a rabbinic academy) spread far and wide, as did the rabbinic decisions of its rabbis Shemu'el de Medina (1505–1589) and his contemporary Yosef Taitasaq. The sixteenth-century Jewish historian

Samuel Usque called Salonika in 1545 "a true mother in Judaism." Salonika's preeminence as a city of Sefardic culture remained down to its last days when, in 1943, the community was destroyed by the Nazis, its vast library sacked, and its four-hundred-year-old cemetery desecrated and dismantled.

One of the salient characteristics of the generation of exile was its melancholy brooding on the meaning of the tragic history of Israel, and especially of its Sefardic standard-bearers. A series of historians emerged among the Jewish people to record and comment upon the recent events. In his *Consolations for the Tribulations of Israel,* Samuel Usque, writing in Portuguese, adumbrated a lachrymose view of Jewish existence. His contemporary, Yosef ha-Kohen (d. 1578) in his *'Emeq habakhah* compared Jewish history to a journey through a "valley of tears." A third sixteenth-century Sefardic commentator, Shelomoh ibn Verga, also sought to decipher the reasons for Jewish suffering in his *Shevet̩ Yehudah* (Scepter of Judah). It has been suggested that this unparalleled outpouring of Jewish historical writing during the sixteenth century not only represented an intense intellectual attempt to understand what had happened but was also perceived by the very writers themselves as a *novum* in Jewish history. Jews were now seeking for the first time to understand the ways of oppressive nations, not only the ways of God. The chronicle *Seder Eliyyahu zut̩a'* by Eliyyahu Capsali of Crete is devoted in large part to discussions of Ottoman history. The events of the time also called forth two more enduring reactions in the mystical and messianic meanings ascribed to the Spanish Jewish tragedy.

Spanish Jews brought not only their contentiousness and tragic vision but also their critical intellectual and technological skills to the Ottoman realm. Among the most important of the technological skills was the fine art of printing. Soon after the expulsion, a Hebrew press appeared in Fez, and it was followed soon thereafter by Hebrew printing presses in Salonika (1500), Constantinople (1503), Safad (1563), and Smyrna (1764). Hebrew printing spread from there to Baghdad, Calcutta, and Poona and eventually to Jerba, Sousse, Algiers, and Oran. (Not until more than two hundred years after the establishment of the first Hebrew printing press in Turkey was the first Ottoman Turkish press established.) A large number of the works printed by the Jewish presses were tracts dealing with practical Qabbalah or mysticism. Indeed, the rapid spread of mysticism from sixteenth-century Safad throughout the Mediterranean world, as well as the *Zohar*'s dissemination as a popular Sefardic text, can be attributed to the introduction of Hebrew printing in the Ottoman empire. [*See* Qabbalah.]

United under the umbrella of one dynamic and expansive empire, the Jews of Muslim lands enjoyed a cultural renaissance and an era of prosperity in the sixteenth century. Jewish physicians emerged in the royal courts of Constantinople to reassert their special role as courtiers and diplomats. Mosheh Hamon (1490–1554), the personal physician to Süleyman I, managed to outlast the intrigues of the harem to excel as a physician, medical scholar, bibliophile, and protector of Jews against the blood libel (false accusation that Jews have committed a ritual murder). Rabbis Mosheh Capsali (1453–1497), Eliyyahu Mizraḥi (1498–1526), and Yosef ben Mosheh di Trani (1604–1639) held considerable sway over the Ottoman Jews through their reputation as scholars rather than through any official position.

Two personalities of sixteenth-century Ottoman Jewish history embody many of the qualities of the Sefardim in this generation. Graćia Nasi' (d. 1568?), a Portuguese Marrano (whose *converso* name was Beatrice Mendès), Jewish banker, entrepreneur, and patron of scholars and schools, arrived in Constantinople amid great splendor. Her many activities in the Ottoman empire included the rescue of Marranos from the Inquisition, the restoration of Jewish learning through enormous charitable donations, and the judicious use of diplomatic levers to assist foreign Jews in distress. Graćia was assisted in her spectacular business undertakings by her nephew Yosef Nasi' (1514–1579; that is, Joseph Mendès). Yosef was also adviser to Selim II, the sultan who awarded him a dukedom over the island of Naxos and a permit to recolonize the city of Tiberias. The awards were apparently made in recognition of the astuteness of Yosef's advice, particularly concerning the conquest of Cyprus in 1571.

Jewish life in the Arab provinces of the Ottoman empire also began to quicken as a result of the Ottoman conquests in the first quarter of the sixteenth century. Egypt produced David ibn Abi Zimra (1479–1573), one of the most prolific *responsa* writers of his day. Despite the Ottoman conquest of 1526, Iraq did not succumb to Ottoman control until the seventeenth century. Its small Jewish community, however, emerged from isolation and resumed contact with the outside Jewish world, turning, for example to the rabbis of Aleppo, Syria, for religious guidance. The Ottoman conquest of Arab provinces did not necessarily improve the lot of the Jews. For the Jews of Yemen, Ottoman incursions and conquest in 1546 destabilized an already precarious situation. Caught between warring Muslim forces, the Jews of Sanaa were subjected to severe discriminatory legislation, culminating in the destruction of synagogues and expulsions in the seventeenth century. Literarily, the community underwent a period of cultural flowering, despite these hardships, during the career of the Yemenite poet Shalom Shabbazi (1617–1680?).

Safad as a Center of Sefardic Search and Jewish Mysticism. The Sefardic refugees of the sixteenth century were a melancholy and restless generation, torn by guilty memories of community apostasy, perplexed by their continuing suffering and exile, and fevered by expectations of imminent salvation. Messianism ran deep in the community, easily aroused by flamboyant pretenders such as David Reubeni who went to Clement VII and other Christian leaders with the offer of raising Jewish armies to help them recapture Palestine from the Ottomans. One of his most illustrious followers, a Portuguese secret Jew, Shelomoh Molkho (1501–1532), heeded Reubeni's call, circumcised himself, and set out for Italy preaching the advent of the Messiah. Ultimately he fell into the hands of the Inquisition and was burned at the stake in Mantua in 1532. His influence, however, spread as far as the settlement of Safad in Palestine.

After the Ottoman conquest of Palestine in 1516, Jewish migration to the Holy Land increased. Soon a remarkable galaxy of scholars and mystics emerged in Safad. Three generations of extraordinary mystics engaged collectively and individually in ascertaining practical means of hastening the redemption of the Jewish people while providing mythic formulations for comprehending the Sefardic catastrophe. These mystics were not recluses but were, rather, legal scholars actively engaged in history. One of their giants, Ya'aqov Berab (d. 1546), arrived in Safad after wanderings in North Africa and Egypt. Believing the time ripe for the messianic redemption of the Jewish people, Berab set out to restore the ancient rite of rabbinical ordination *(semikhah)* in 1538 as a prerequisite for the reestablishment of the Sanhedrin which was, in turn, prerequisite to the proper repentance of the Jewish people that would bring redemption. While his disciples eagerly accepted the new charge placed upon them, Berab's movement was ultimately thwarted by the forceful opposition of Levi ibn Habib of Jerusalem.

Another towering intellectual figure of that generation who eventually found his way to Safad after many years of wandering was Yosef Karo (1488–1575). Karo's halakhic authority was established by his major work *Beit Yosef.* He is remembered by posterity, however, through the utility of his comprehensive legal handbook *Shulḥan arukh.* In the *Shulḥan arukh* Karo presented numerous Sefardic as well as Ashkenazic practices in a readily accessible fashion, rendering his work one of the most useful codes for subsequent generations of Jews. Karo also possessed a mystical bent that emerges in his work *Maggid mesharim,* a mystical diary of angelic revelations, and he served as mentor to the remarkable cluster of mystics and pietists in sixteenth century Safad. [*See the biography of Yosef Karo.*]

With the arrival of Isaac Luria at Safad in the 1560s, Jewish mysticism reached its greatest heights. A charismatic personality with a stirring effect on his followers, Luria decisively influenced the development of Jewish mysticism in the following generations. Lurianic Qabbalah, with its doctrines of a cataclysmic scattering of divine sparks at creation and the unique role of Israel in liberating and reunifying these sparks, together with a belief in metempsychosis and new mystical modes of prayer, deepened the expectation of messianic redemption and altered the way many Jews thought about themselves for at least a century and a half. [*See the biography of Isaac Luria.*]

The mystics of Safad delved into the vast corpus of Jewish literature, frequently using the *Zohar* as their point of departure. Many unusual personalities in this group were characterized by their frequent walks in the Galilee and fervent embellishment of the Sabbath and daily ritual actions. One of the participants was the poet Shelomoh Alkabets. He is best remembered for the poem *Lekhah dodi,* a Sabbath invocation welcoming the Sabbath as bride and queen that has been included in the Friday evening Sabbath services in all Jewish communities.

After Luria's death in 1572, his disciple Ḥayyim Vital (1543–1620) began to disseminate a version of the teachings of the Lurianic school of Safad. The prominence of the city itself did not last much longer. In 1576 the Ottoman sultan ordered the deportation of one thousand Jews from Safad to repopulate the newly conquered island of Cyprus. The order was rescinded soon thereafter, but many Jews had already left the city. The vitality of Safad's Jewish community was further sapped by the corruption of Ottoman provincial governors, the impact of devastating earthquakes, and the periodic depredations of local Arabs. In the seventeenth century Safad reverted to its former role as an inconspicuous settlement in a backwater province while the qabbalistic ideas that had emerged there spread rapidly throughout the Diaspora.

Influence of Shabbetai Tsevi. The decline of the Jewish communities in Muslim lands was a slow process caused by a number of external factors. An especially prominent symptom of this decline is the bizarre and tragic career of Shabbetai Tsevi. Shabbetai Tsevi was born in the city of Smyrna in 1625, began to engage in mysticial studies in 1648, and fell under the spell of Natan of Gaza in 1665, pronouncing himself the Messiah in that year. An anarchic outburst of antinomian activity and frenzy ensued as news of Shabbetai's bizarre behavior spread. Even his conversion to Islam in 1666 did not discredit the movement, but rather accelerated the tendency of that generation to perceive the Spanish experience as one with messianic overtones. The fact that Tsevi converted shook Marrano circles everywhere. Scholars in Italy and Amsterdam were agitated; poets in Kurdistan wrote poems on Shabbetean themes; Jewish followers of Tsevi, known as *Donmeh,* converted to Islam and continued to believe in Tsevi as the Messiah for generations after his death. The energy, confusion, guilt, and false hopes with which the Shabbatean movement had tried to break out of the mold of Jewish suffering left a hyperagitated Jewry deeply depressed. [*For further discussion of this major event, see the biography of Shabbetai Tsevi.*]

Ultimately the messianic storm subsided, rabbis, especially in the Ottoman empire, began to destroy books with references to Shabbetai Tsevi, and concerted efforts were made once again to integrate mystical studies into rabbinics. Ultimately, Near Eastern Jewry repressed Shabbeteanism while retaining traces of it in its particular fondness for an integration of Judaism with such practices as saint worship and visiting holy sites *(ziyārah),* and a strengthened belief in the efficacy of practical Qabbalah such as the casting of lots or the interpretation of dreams.

Ottoman Jewish decline accelerated after the debacle of Tsevi. It was temporarily halted in 1730 when the first volume of the multivolume encyclopedia *Me'am lo'ez* appeared. This popular compendium of Oriental Sefardic lore by Ya'aqov ben Mahir Culi instructed while entertaining the masses with a vast array of legends, anecdotes, customs, and laws. Compositions in Ladino as well as Hebrew continued to be recited in the salons of Salonika, but the once vibrant Jewry of Ottoman lands found itself enfeebled by a series of natural catastrophies and by the mounting hostility of Ottoman Christians as well as Muslims. While some of this hostility was the product of economic rivalry, some of it can also be traced to the influx of anti-Semitic notions from the West alongside the growing influence of Western, particularly French, power among the Christians.

Near Eastern Jewry on the Eve of the Modern Era. Jewish life in the easternmost part of the Ottoman empire did not share in the renaissance of sixteenth-century Ottoman Jewry. Persian Jews were particularly endangered by the campaign of forced conversion that the Shīʿī Safavid dynasty (1501–1732) undertook in the seventeenth century. Isolated from Ottoman Jewry, the forty thousand Jews of Persia were subjected to an especially harsh code of discriminatory legislation, known as the Jami Abbasi, which was operative until 1925. Even the increasing influence of the European powers couldn't spare the Jews of Mashhad from a forced conversion during the nineteenth century.

Ottoman rule in Yemen (1546–1629) was succeeded by a harsh succession of independent imams of the Zaydī sect. Despite the frequent expulsions from villages and towns and the implementation of the policy of kidnapping Jewish orphans to raise them within Islam, Yemenite Jews continued to produce a significant poetic and qabbalistic tradition during this period. Males were largely literate, the printed prayer books of the period attesting to the spread of Lurianic Qabbalah into the remote corners of the Hejaz. By the nineteenth century, even some of the tenets of Haskalah, European Jewish Enlightenment, had reached such communities as Sanaa. Change brought with it conflict and the Jews of Yemen were internally split. It was the worsening status of the Jews in Yemen, however, and not the ideological conflicts, that precipitated their mass migration from Yemen to Palestine in the 1880s. By the early twentieth century, Yemenite Jews formed a significant community in the city of Jerusalem.

Jews in the East had never ceased their close contact with other Jews even in the age of Ottoman military and political decline. Jews in the Ottoman realm (especially Sefardic Jews) continued to serve as merchants, diplomats, commercial agents, and interpreters throughout the period of Ottoman ascendancy and decline, reinforcing their ties with coreligionists. But by the nineteenth century, the Jewish position in Arab and Turkish lands was one of abject poverty, extreme vulnerability, humiliation, and insecurity. Pressures on the Ottomans to reform were brought to bear by the European powers, not so much to assist the Jews as primarily to assist the Ottoman Christians. Under these pressures the Ottoman reform movement, Tanẓīmāt, ended special discriminatory taxation, agreed to protect the legal rights of non-Muslims, and granted civil equality to them. Reforming legislation, however, could not restore the Ottoman empire to good health. Jewish well-being came increasingly to depend upon the intervention of Western powers and Western Jews. No incident highlighted this vulnerability and dependency more clearly than the Damascus blood libel in 1840. When the Jews of Damascus were falsely accused of murdering a Christian for ritual purposes, the community of Damascus, as well as other Syrian communities, faced grave danger. Through the intervention of Moses Montefiore of London and Adolphe Crémieux of Paris, the Jews of Damascus were rescued and the Sublime Porte was forced to publicly repudiate the blood libel accusation. Despite this intervention, Near Eastern Jewry was subjected to a host of unfortunate blood libel accusations at the hands of the Greeks, Arabs, and Armenians in the nineteenth century. More than once the indefatigable Montefiore went to the Near East and the Maghreb to intercede personally on behalf of Jews. [*For discussion of the blood libel and other false accusations, see* Anti-Semitism.]

In 1860 the Alliance Israélite Universelle was founded in France. Among its guiding principles was the goal of protecting the Jewish communities of Muslim lands and modernizing and uplifting them from their abject state of poverty and ignorance. The altruistic goals of French Jewry dovetailed well with the political and imperial goals of the French government. The Jews of France set out with almost missionary zeal to transform the face of Near Eastern Jewry and to forge a community that would embody some of the cherished ideals of the French Revolution. Beginning with the establishment of their first school in Morocco in 1860, the Alliance Israélite Universelle proceeded to introduce modern, secular notions and technical skills to a new generation of Jews throughout the Near East. By World War I, over one hundred Alliance schools teaching the French language and secular subjects had been set up in Morocco, Algeria, Tunisia, Libya, Egypt, Iran, Turkey, and the Balkans. The Alliance schools succeeded in undercutting poverty and Jewish female illiteracy and, introducing secular studies to all Jews, prepared a new generation of Jews for entry into modernity.

The introduction of Western-style education among Near Eastern Jews did not result in a parallel movement of religious reformulation and the building of a new, modern Jewish identity there. This was partially because Near Eastern Jews, unlike the Jews of Europe, were not presented with the option of entering their majority society provided they refashioned themselves since religion remained a fundamental basis of social and political organization in the Middle East. Many Jewish autonomous institutions ceased to exist as a direct result of European colonial legislation. For example, early in their administration, the French authorities in Algeria abolished the independent Jewish system of courts. While Jews were granted French citizenship in Algeria in 1870, elsewhere they adopted European culture without attaining the benefits of European citizenship. Their cultural identity with the European powers, especially in North Africa, ushered in a period of confusion when Arab nationalism began to flower. In some parts of the Arab world, such as Iraq, the Jewish minority became one of the segments of the population most active in creating modern Arabic literature. Yet, at the same time that they pioneered in the language, press, and modernization of the economy of the Arab states, Jews were increasingly isolated from the pan-Arab and pan-Islamic culture then capturing the hearts of the masses. For Middle Eastern Jews, however, the modern period of Western encroachment did not result in indigenous Jewish attempts to form new self-identifying modes of expression. Even the Zionist movement of national self-determination, a late nineteenth-century European Jewish response to emancipation and modernity, echoed only faintly in Muslim lands.

Jewish life in Muslim lands came almost to a complete end in the wake of the creation of the state of Israel and the emergence of Arab nationalist states in the post–World War II period. Fewer than 10 percent of the Near Eastern Jews living in Muslim countries in 1948 still reside in those countries in 1986. Only 17,000 of the former 250,000 Moroccan Jews remain in Morocco. All other Jewish communities have virtually disappeared except the communities of Turkey and Iran. The Judaism of the more than one million Jews who fled their ancestral homes for Israel or the West is a Judaism still in flux. Middle Eastern Jewish religiosity was always anchored in familial and communal action, especially in the post-1492 period. In the Muslim world, people had stayed in their communities for generations, passing on hereditary communal offices from father to son. Although these lines of tradition have been irrevocably cut with the great migration to Western, technological, modern societies, the Judaism of the Middle Eastern Jew has retained some remnants of former times. Among those remnants must be included the fervent love of the land of Israel with its messianic and mystical overtones, the expression of religiosity within a familial context, and the special pride and quality imparted by a specific link with the Sefardic tradition.

Just as 1789 set in motion a crucial reorientation of Jewish identities and Judaism in western Europe, and just as 1881 set in motion a process of change that eventually led to a permanent transformation in the structure of Jewish politics among Ashkenazim, especially in eastern Europe, so too, one suspects, 1948 will be found to have marked a transforming date in the lives of Middle Eastern Jews. With the end of living on the fringes of Muslim society, the Jewish communities from the world of Islam have embarked upon a new path in Jewish history.

[*For further discussion of the religious beliefs and customs of the Jews of North Africa and the Middle East, see* Folk Religion, *article on* Folk Judaism. *For various messianic movements mentioned, see* Messianism, *article on* Jewish Messianism. *For a discussion of Judaism in the state of Israel and the history of Jewish immigration there, see* Zionism. *One dimension of the historic relationship between Jews and Muslims is explored in* Polemics, *article on* Muslim-Jewish Polemics.]

BIBLIOGRAPHY

The best introductory volume on the subject is S. D. Goitein's survey *Jews and Arabs: Their Contacts through the Ages,* 3d rev. ed. (New York, 1974). Norman A. Stillman's *The Jews of Arab Lands: A History and Source Book* (Philadelphia, 1979) provides a fine introductory essay and a large collection of documents translated from Arabic and Hebrew and a variety of Western languages. More recently, Bernard Lewis's *The Jews of Islam* (Princeton, 1984) has offered a fresh interpretation of the broad sweep of Middle Eastern Jewish history. André N. Chouraqui's *Between East and West: A History of the Jews of North Africa,* translated by Michael M. Bernet (Philadelphia, 1968), gives a balanced survey of the Jews of the Maghreb and is particularly informative for the modern period. For a more detailed examination of the Maghreb, see H. Z. Hirschberg's *Toledot ha-Yehudim be-Afriqah ha-Tsefonit,* 2 vols. (Jerusalem, 1965), translated by M. Eichelberg as *A History of the Jews in North Africa,* vol. 1, *From Antiquity to the Sixteenth Century* (Leiden, 1974) and vol. 2, *From the Ottoman Conquests to the Present Time* (Leiden, 1981). Hirschberg analyzes the political history of the Jews in Arab lands and the Maghreb extensively in his article "The Oriental Jewish Communities,"in *Religion in the Middle East: Three Religions in Concord and Conflict,* edited by A. J. Arberry (Cambridge, 1969), pp. 119–225.

Older multivolume studies of Ottoman Jewry such as Solomon A. Rosanes' *Divrei yemei Yisra'el be-Togarma,* 6 vols. (Jerusalem, 1930–1945) and Moïse Franco's *Essai sur l'histoire des Israelites de l'Empire Ottoman depuis les origines jusqu'à nos jours* (Paris, 1897) still contain valuable material culled from rabbinic sources. Volume 18 of Salo W. Baron's exceptionally important *A Social and Religious History of the Jews,* 2d ed., rev. & enl. (New York, 1983), updates these earlier studies, extending the geographic scope to include the Jews of Persia, China, India and Ethiopia as well as the Ottoman empire. Especially useful is Baron's discussion of demography.

The problem of the general question of the legal status of the Jews under Islam has been treated by A. S. Tritton in *The Caliphs and Their Non-Muslim Subjects* (London, 1930). While Tritton is still the standard reference work on Muslim theories regarding the *dhimmīs*, a methodical discussion can be found in Antoine Fattal's *Le statut légal des non-Musulmans en pays d'Islam* (Beirut, 1958).

Four monographs of varying value treat the specific problems of individual Jewries based on rabbinic *responsa.* These studies are sill useful as the sole English source on significant rabbinic figures and their age. Isidore Epstein's *The Responsa of Rabbi Simon B. Zemah Duran as a Source of the History of the Jews in North Africa* (1930; reprint New York, 1968), Israel Goldman's *The Life and Times of Rabbi David Ibn Abi Zimra* (New York, 1970), Morris S. Goodblatt's *Jewish Life in Turkey in the Sixteenth Century as Reflected in the Legal Writings of Samuel de Medina* (New York, 1952), and Abraham M. Hershman's *Rabbi Isaac ben Sheshet Perfet and His Times* (New York, 1943) each explores the major problems of an age of transition and the response of a leading rabbinic luminary.

A delightful account of the city of Safad and its Qabbalistic circles is Solomon Schechter's essay "Safad in the Sixteenth Century," which can be found in his *Studies in Judaism* (1908; reprint, Cleveland, 1958) and in *The Jewish Expression,* edited by Judah Goldin (New York, 1970). The Qabbalistic movement of Safad also can be seen in the excellent biography *Joseph Karo: Lawyer and Mystic* by R. J. Zwi Werblowsky (London, 1962). For an exhaustive and monumental treatment of the life and times of Shabbetai Tsevi, see Gershom Scholem's *Sabbatai Sevi: The Mystical Messiah, 1626–1676* (Princeton, 1973).

Hayyim Cohen's *The Jews of the Middle East, 1860–1972* (New York, 1973) is one of the few books in English on recent trends among the Jews in the Arab world. Michael Laskier's exhaustive study *The Alliance Israélite Universelle and the Jewish Communities of Morocco, 1862–1962* (Albany, 1983) is a thorough monographic consideration of the educational role of the alliance.

The latest studies on Jews in the Middle East can be found in such Israeli publications as *Sefunot* (Jerusalem, 1956–1966), *Pe'amin* (Jerusalem, 1979–), and *Mizraḥ u-ma'arav* (Jerusalem, 1919–1932). Interdisciplinary approaches can be fruitfully employed in this field, and the works of contemporary anthropologists such as Moshe Shokeid, Harvey Goldberg, Shlomo Deshen, and Walter Zenner have been especially illuminating in analyzing Middle Eastern Jewish communities in Israel. These studies frequently begin with considerations of individual Near Eastern Jewish communities in their traditional milieu and historical structure.

JANE S. GERBER

Judaism in Asia and Northeast Africa

From its origin in the Middle East, in western Asia, Judaism spread to neighboring regions of Africa, Europe, and Asia, eventually reaching far corners of these continents. This article deals with the peripheral Jewish communities of Inner Asia, Ethiopia, India, and China.

Inner Asia. The most important Jewish communities in the area that today forms part of the Soviet Union to the east of the Caspian Sea were those of Bukhara and Samarkand. In contrast to the other Jewish communities discussed in this article, the Bukharan and Samarkand Jews never lost contact with the main Jewish centers. According to their legends, Habor (*2 Kgs.* 17:6), where the ten tribes of Israel were exiled, was the old name of Bukhara. Reliable information about the origin of the Bukharan Jews is sparse. Some scholars hold that they came from Khiva (today Khorezm, an oblast in the northwest of the Uzbek S.S.R.). More probably, they came from Iran, as indicated by the Tajiki (Iranian) dialect they spoke. East of Bukhara, in Samarkand (capi-

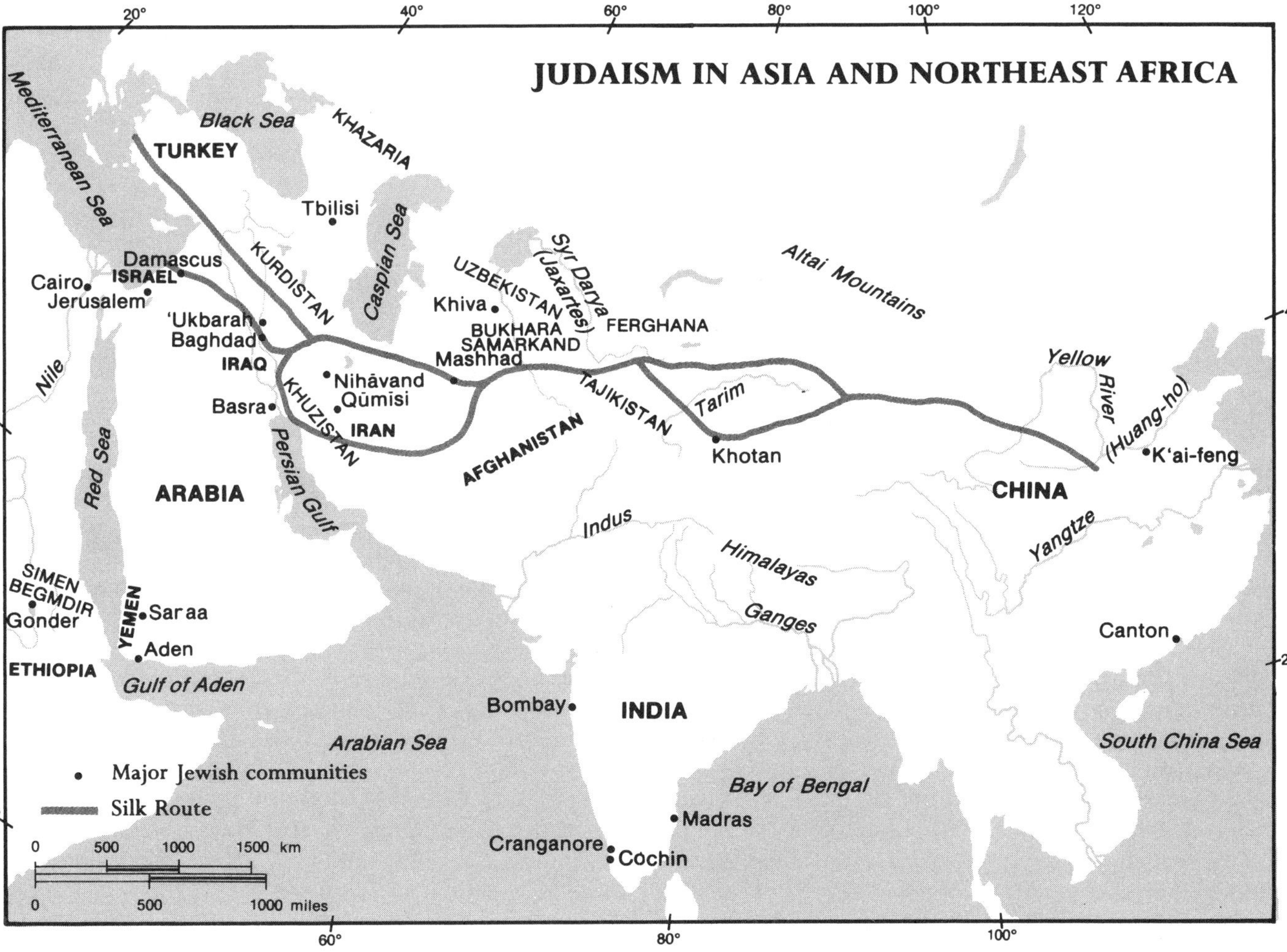

tal of the Samarkand oblast, Uzbek S.S.R.), if one can rely on a report by the twelfth-century Jewish traveler Binyamin of Tudela, there were 50,000 Jews in his time. As against these rumors, historical data attest to Jewish presence in Samarkand only from the first half of the nineteenth century, when the Jews asked for, and were given, a tract of land on which to build a quarter of their own. In the 1880s there were fewer than 400 Jews in Samarkand, most of them having come from Bukhara. In the 1960s, their number was estimated at 15,000, part of the increase having come from Ashkenazi Jewish migration during World War II. The religious customs of the Jews in Samarkand did not differ from those of the Bukharan Jews.

Bukhara itself is not mentioned by Binyamin of Tudela, but there is some evidence that by the thirteenth century Jews lived in Bukhara and that they suffered under the Tatar-Mongolian rulers in the fourteenth. Bukharan Jewish tradition has it that prior to the sixtenth century, when Samarkand was destroyed and its Jews fled to Bukhara, there was only a very small Jewish community in Bukhara. From the sixteenth to the nineteenth century the Bukharan Jews suffered from persecutions and forced conversion to Islam.

With the second half of the nineteenth century the Russian conquests of the area began, and the Jews started to migrate from the principalities of Khiva and Bukhara, and also from Afghanistan, to the Russian-held territories, where somewhat better conditions awaited them. In 1920 the whole of Bukhara was conquered by the Russians and became a People's Soviet Republic. Immigration of Bukharan Jews to Palestine began in 1868, and by 1900 there were about 1,000 Bukharan Jews in Jerusalem; in 1936 there were 2,500. In the Uzbek S.S.R. there were in 1959 about 23,000 Jews, concentrated in Samarkand, Bukhara, and the urban centers of the Ferghana Valley. Another 5,000 lived in the Tajik S.S.R.

In the eighteenth century, despite the emergence of a few poets who wrote in Judeo-Persian, the cultural level of the Bukharan Jews was very low. In 1793 an emissary from Safad, Palestine, brought about a revival in their spiritual and religious life, which was intensified with the arrival after 1839 of Jewish refugees from Mashhad, Iran, where Jews had been forced to convert to Islam. By the midcentury the old synagogue of Bukhara was renovated, and subsequently a network of *khomlas*, Hebrew religious primary schools, was established, and also several higher schools for the study of the Bible and the Talmud. Those Bukharan Jews who settled in Jerusalem produced numerous prayer books, books of customs, works on the Qabbalah, *midrashim*, commentaries, and other religious literature.

In the twentieth century the religious life of the Bukharan Jews differed little from that of the neighboring Persian and Afghan Jewish communities. That is to say, in contrast to the Falashas of Ethiopia and the native Jews of India, whose Judaism was based almost exclusively on the Bible, the Bukharan Jews were well versed in, and observed, the *halakhah*, the Jewish ritual law as it developed in Talmudic and post-Talmudic times. They had trained ritual slaughterers, and observed the full complement of Jewish feasts, fasts, family celebrations, and rites.

Ethiopian Jewry. The Black Jews of Ethiopia are called Falashas ("exiles") in Amharic, the national language of Ethiopia. The name is derived from the root *fälläsä*, which in Geez (the old literary language of Ethiopia) means "emigrate" or "wander." The Falashas call themselves Beta Israel ("House of Israel").

Falasha legend has it that when the queen of Sheba returned from her visit to King Solomon with their son Menelik, several notables from Jerusalem accompanied her and settled in Ethiopia, where they became the ancestors of the Falashas. Scholars consider the Falashas to be the descendants of Agau tribes. This group of tribes of Hamitic (Cushitic) origin had lived in Ethiopia prior to the arrival of the Semitic tribes from southern Arabia. Judaism could have reached them either from southern Arabia or from Egypt, or may have spread from Jews already living in Ethiopia prior to the fourth century, when the Aksum dynasty converted to Christianity. Their numbers were augmented in 525 when Negus Kaleb brought Jews back from southern Arabia after his campaign against the Jewish king of Himyar, Joseph Dhu Nuwas.

The Falashas took part in the internal struggles between the Zagau and the Aksum dynasty, revolted a number of times, and were repeatedly defeated and massacred or forced to adopt Christianity. Still, they retained a measure of independence, had their own kings, and fought either on the side of the Muslims or on that of the Christian negus. The worst massacre of the Falashas was perpetrated by Negus Susenyos (r. 1607–1632), who put to death all the Falashas who refused to accept Christianity, including the Falasha king, Gideon. Despite these reversals, the Falashas preserved their distinctiveness, and some time later were allowed to return to Judaism. In the nineteenth century they resisted the Protestant missionaries, and from 1904 on, when Jacques Faitlovitch organized the Pro-Falasha Committee, their situation improved. Schools were established for Falasha children, and some educated Falashas obtained government positions. During the Italian occupation (1936–1941) they proved their loyalty to the emperor.

Following the independence of Israel (1948) and the adoption of the Law of Return (giving the right to every Jew to immigrate to Israel), the Israeli rabbinate had to face the question of whether the Falashas were to be considered Jews and therefore allowed, perhaps even helped, to come to Israel. In 1975 the question was decided in the affirmative, and the authorities responsible for immigration, who formerly had been disinclined to bring Falashas to the country, took a positive attitude toward them. In November 1981 it was reported that about 1,400 Falashas had reached Israel "by circuitous routes." In 1984–1985 the Israeli government operated an airlift from Sudan to Israel that brought about 10,000 Falashas to Israel. In 1986 their total number in Israel was estimated at 12,000. An unofficial census in Ethiopia, carried out in 1976, found 28,000 Falashas scattered in 490 settlements. In 1986 their number was estimated at 20,000.

Racially the Falashas represent an intermingling of Hamitic and Semitic strains, which manifests itself in a variety of physical types ranging among those of the Amara, the Agau, and the Asian Jews. Their typical traditional settlements are small hilltop villages near rivers. One of their huts serves as the synagogue, called *mäsgid* (from the Arabic *masjid*). Some of the synagogues consist of two rooms, in which case the inner part, called *qĕddĕstä qĕdusan* (Geez, "Holy of Holies"; cf. Heb., *qodesh ha-qodashim*), can be entered only by a *kahen* ("priest"; Heb., *kohen*) and a deacon. In it are kept the Torah (written in Geez), and the ceremonial clothes of the priests. Of the women, only the unmarried and the old are allowed to enter the synagogue.

In addition to agriculture, which is their main occupation and which they practice as tenant farmers (since they are not allowed to own land), the Falashas also engage in various crafts, such as pottery, basketry, spinning, and weaving. Some are blacksmiths and goldsmiths, others work in the construction trades in the towns. Those Falashas who live in central Ethiopia speak Amharic, the national language; in the north they speak Tigrinya, while in the mountains of Simen, the northern part of Begemdir, some of them still speak Agau dialects. However, all their literature is in Geez, a Southeast Semitic language closely akin to certain South Arabian dialects, which is sufficiently different from the current Ethiopian colloquials, such as Amharic, to require translation.

The Judaism of the Falashas differs considerably from the halakhic observance of the traditional Jewish communities. Their religion is based entirely on the Bible, which they do not have in the original Hebrew but possess in the same old Geez translation that is used also by the Ethiopian church, and which includes, in addition to the canonical books, several books of the Apocrypha. Ignorant of the postbiblical (Talmudic) development of Judaism, they retained numerous rites that had long become obsolete in mainstream Judaism, some of which resemble Samaritan and Karaite observances. They offer up Passover and other sacrifices on a stone altar in the synagogue courtyard and observe the biblical laws of clean (edible) and unclean (forbidden) animals, the rite of slaughtering, of washing the hands before eating, and the laws of female sexual impurity, including ritual segregation in confinement huts of menstruating women and of mothers for forty days after the birth of a boy and for eighty after that of a girl (cf. *Leviticus* 12). In general, there is among them a greater emphasis on ritual purity and ablutions than is found in the Bible. Their villages must be situated near a river, since water is essential for compliance with their religious precepts, which demand frequent washing. Thus, purification by washing the body and the clothes is required of a woman in her menses and after childbirth, of the person performing male or female circumcision, of those who touch a corpse, grave, dead animal, or any unclean person or thing, of those who come in contact with a non-Falasha, and of a priest and his wife after intercourse. All unclean individuals must live outside the village for a number of days and then perform the ablutions. Every Friday at noon all purify themselves by immersion, and then put on their special Sabbath clothes.

In addition to the usual Sabbath observances, they also abstain from sexual intercourse on the Sabbath, and the men emphasize the special importance of the Sabbath by spending most of the day in prayers (in the Geez language) in the synagogue, with breaks only for communal meals. Two of the best-known original Falasha literary works deal with the Sabbath. They are the *Tĕʾĕzāza Sanbat* (Precepts of the Sabbath), a collection of Sabbath laws and legends in which the Sabbath is described as a heavenly queen and which is attributed to Abba Zabra, a fifteenth-century monk; and *Abba Elias* (Father Elijah), date unknown, which deals with the Sabbath, the Ten Commandments, and the vanity of all pleasures.

Several of the Falasha religious observances are non-Jewish in origin. The Falashas practice, in addition to the circumcision of boys on the eighth day after birth as prescribed in the Bible, also female circumcision, which is an African rite that has spread into the Arab world. (Female circumcision is performed by a woman, and has no fixed date on which it is performed.) They have monks and nuns who live either in monasteries or in seclusion outside the villages, practice abstinence, and consecrate their lives to serving God—an institution that seems to be of old Christian origin. They believe in the *zār*, a spirit that can take possession of a person (usually a woman) and can be exorcised with the performance of specific ceremonies—another African ritual and belief complex that penetrated Arab countries as well. They share with the Ethiopians the belief in and use of various amulets, charms, incantations, and magic prayers and procedures in which many divine, angelic, and demonic names are invoked. They diagnose and make prognoses of ailments with the help of the patient's star, using methods of number-letter arithmetic. [*Falasha practices do, however, have parallels within other Jewish folk traditions. See* Folk Religion, *article on* Folk Judaism.]

The Falashas believe in the only God, who has chosen Israel to be his people and who will send the Messiah to lead them back to their Holy Land. This belief gave rise to prophets who announced the coming of the Messiah and triggered messianic movements. One such movement, in 1862, resulted in the death of many Falashas who had set out to reach the Land of Israel on foot. The Falashas believe in angels, the World to Come, rewards and punishments after death, the resurrection of the dead, and the Last Judgment. Some of them retained the tradition of Aaronic descent and function as priests, although any Falasha who is well versed in the Bible and the prayers can be a priest. One of the priests in every region is elected as high priest, who becomes the leader of the community. The high priest or the priest recites the prayers in the synagogue, prays for the sick, and blesses the circumcised child, the woman who leaves the "hut of the blood," the newly married couple, and those who put on new clothes. He slaughters the animal sacrifices, blesses the Sabbath and festival offerings, and commemorates the dead. He is the confessor to whom sinners confess their sins whenever they feel in need of absolution (another feature foreign to rabbinic Judaism); he is a counselor and spiritual authority in the community. For his function the priest receives remuneration: money, the firstborn of animals, a bar of salt, a measure of cereal, and so on.

Undoubtedly under Christian Ethiopian influence, the monk (*mänokse;* a word of Greek origin) plays an important role in Falasha life. According to Falasha tradition the son of the Ethiopian king Zar'a Ya'qob (r. 1434–1468) converted to Judaism, compiled prayers, and instituted monasteries for the Falashas. Where no monastery exists, the monks live on the outskirts of the village, in huts enclosed by a low stone wall. Anybody can become a monk if he is inclined to renounce the world and live in celibacy. For monks, contact with other Falashas is defiling: after working with other men they wash their clothes. Some monks, who go to live in deserted places, receive divine inspiration, and then return to preach, are considered saints. An older monk has the title *abba* ("father"); the most highly venerated among them have the title *abbew abba.*

The Falashas observe a considerably larger number of festivals and fasts than prescribed by rabbinic *halakhah.* They have monthly festivals that serve as reminders of the main annual feasts and fasts. On the tenth of every moon there is a celebration in remembrance of the Day of Atonement; on the twelfth, one in remembrance of the Festival of Harvest (which they celebrate on the twelfth of the third month); on the fifteenth, one in remembrance of Passover and of Tabernacles (Sukkot). The third Sabbath of the fifth moon is celebrated as the "Sabbath of Sabbaths" with special prayers and readings. On the eighteenth of the sixth moon they commemorate the deaths of Abraham, Isaac, and Jacob. On the twelfth of the ninth moon another Festival of Harvest is celebrated as a reminder of the Harvest Festival of the twelfth of the third moon.

Parallel to these festivals run weekly, monthly, and annual fast days on which no food or drink is taken until the sunset. The weekly Fast of Thursday, in remembrance of Ezra's exhortation of the exiled Israelites (see *Ezra* 8:21), is kept only by the priests and older people. On the twenty-ninth of every lunar month a fast is observed. The Fast of Passover is on 14 Nisan. The Fast of Tomos (Heb., *Tammuz*) is observed from 1 Tammuz to 10 Tammuz, by the priests and older people, and the Fast of Av from 1 Av to 17 Av in remembrance of the destruction of Jerusalem. (In halakhic Judaism there is only one fast day on 17 Tammuz, and one on 9 Av, Tish'ah be-Av.) On 10 Elul (the sixth moon) a fast is observed as a reminder of the Day of Atonement. On 29 Heshvan (the eighth moon) is the Fast of Supplication. The Fast of Esther is observed twice: from the eleventh to the thirteenth of the eleventh moon, and from the thirteenth to the fourteenth of the third moon.

In conclusion it can be stated that the Falashas are a community in whose life religion has played a central role, and whose religion is composed of a form of biblical Judaism with the addition of some traditional African and Christian Ethiopian elements.

India: Cochin and the Bene Israel. Legends still heard among the Jews of India have it that their earliest ancestors arrived in the subcontinent after the destruction of the Second Temple of Jerusalem (70 CE), or even a thousand years earlier, in the time of King Solomon. Reliable historical data, however, are available only from about 1000 CE, from which time documents found in the Cairo Genizah contain references to commercial relations between Jews of southern Europe, North Africa, Egypt, and Aden, and the west coast of India.

The Jews of Cochin. Also from about 1000 CE date the famous inscribed copper tablets, still in the hands of the Jews of Cochin, which state that the Hindu ruler of Malabar, Bhaskara Ravi Varma, granted certain privileges to Yosef Rabban, including the village of Anjuvannam, on the outskirts of Cochin, as a hereditary estate. About 1170 the Jewish traveler Binyamin of Tudela reports the presence of a thousand Black Jews on the Malabar Coast who, he says, "are good men, observe the Law, possess the Torah of Moses, the Prophets, and have some knowledge of the Talmud and the halakhah." From the twelfth to the fourteenth centuries, scattered references by Arab and Christian travelers and geographers (including Qazwini, Marco Polo, and Ibn Battuta) attest to the presence of Jews on the Malabar Coast, and according to an inscription dated 1245, the Kachangadi synagogue of Cochin was rebuilt in that year.

From the fifteenth century on historical sources flow more abundantly. In 1524 the Portuguese destroyed the Jewish settlement of Cranganore (north of Cochin), which had been so impressive that it gave rise to the notion that the Jews had an independent kingdom there. Jewish refugees from Cranganore, as well as Jewish immigrants from Spain and Portugal, and later some from Aleppo, and even Holland and Germany, were welcomed by the raja of Cochin, who granted them land near his palace (the section known to this day as "Jew Town"), and religious, cultural, and internal administrative autonomy under their own hereditary chief, known in Tamil as the *mudaliar.* The Paradesi ("foreigners") synagogue in Jew Town was built in 1568.

In the course of the Portuguese-Dutch struggle for Cochin (1662/3) the Portuguese plundered and burned the synagogues and Jewish homes, and massacred the Jews. The defeat of the Portuguese by the Dutch signaled an era of prosperity and freedom of religion. The

Dutch Jews took an interest in the remote and exotic Jewish community of Cochin, and in 1686 dispatched a delegation headed by Moses Pereira de Paiva, bringing the most precious of gifts—Hebrew books. From de Paiva's book *Notisias dos Judeos de Cochim* (Amsterdam, 1687), we learn that there were nine synagogues with a total membership of 465 households who are called White Jews, who, he says, had come to Cochin from Cranganore, Castile, Algiers, Jerusalem, Safad, Damascus, Aleppo, Baghdad, and Germany. It is probable that among these white immigrant Jews there were refugees who had been expelled from Spain in 1492, or their descendants. In the seventeenth century, prayer and hymn books were printed in Amsterdam for the Cochin Jews by Athias and Proops, and the Bible and other holy books of the Cochin Jews destroyed by the Portuguese were replaced by the Sefardic community of Amsterdam. These books reached Cochin on 15 Av, which day thereafter became a local quasi-holiday.

While the Near Eastern and European origin of the White Jews is thus clear enough, that of the Black Jews remains questionable. Since Benjamin of Tudela refers in the twelfth century to the Jews of the Malabar Coast as "Blacks" (Heb., *Sheḥorim;* he does not mention "White Jews"), one must assume that for some generations prior to his time an intermingling was taking place between Jewish immigrants, who were mostly male, and local "black" Indian women, with the addition of those native slaves and servants who converted to Judaism.

The religious beliefs and observances of the Cochin Jews in the last three centuries developed under the influence of contacts with the Jewish world to the west of India. In the seventeenth and eighteenth centuries (that is, after de Paiva's visit), Jewish immigrants from the West continued to arrive, to attain leading positions in the community (as well as in the country), and to impose their own religious customs and beliefs on both the White and the Black Jews of Cochin. An important role in this respect was had by the Rahabi family, whose ancestor David Rahabi (d. 1726) had come from Aleppo to Cochin in 1664, and who, in 1686, gave a splendid banquet in honor of de Paiva. David Rahabi taught the Jews of Cochin the religious tenets held and rites practiced in the ancient Jewish community of Aleppo. His son Yeḥezqe'l David and his grandson, also called David (d. 1790), continued this internal missionary activity as a result of which, by the end of the eighteenth century, the religious life of the Jews of Cochin conformed, by and large, to that of the Syrian Jews, including the study of the Talmud. David Rahabi the younger wrote several Hebrew religious works including one that contains a comparison of the Jewish and Muslim calendars. Together with his brother Elias he translated parts of the Bible and the prayer book into the vernacular, Malayalam.

Among the White Jews of Cochin there were several Hebrew poets, scholars, translators, scribes, and copyists, most of whose works were published in Amsterdam. In 1840/41 they introduced Hebrew printing into India, and printed in Bombay and in Calcutta numerous Hebrew halakhic, literary, and liturgical works for their own community, as well as for the Bene Israel. The teacher Joseph Daniel Kohen established in 1877 a Hebrew and Malayalam printing press in Cochin itself. As the name *Kohen* indicates, there were *kohanim* (men who claim priestly descent) among the White Jews of Cochin. There were no *kohanim* among the Black Jews. In their liturgical compositions a strong messianic spirit is evident, and from the eighteenth century on emissaries from the Land of Israel fostered their interest in and devotion to the Holy Land. A subgroup called Meshuararim (a distortion of the Hebrew *meshuḥrarim,* "liberated ones") comprises both White and Black Jews. The Meshuararim were the descendants of either White or Black Jewish men and their black slave concubines, and also the emancipated slaves of either of the two groups.

The Indian caste system has inevitably left its mark on the Cochin Jews. To all intents and purposes, the White Jews constituted a caste with strict endogamy, which enabled it to preserve its separate identity for several centuries. Their synagogues, as far as one can gather from the available information, have been strictly segregated. Black Jews did not count in the *minyan* (quorum of ten adult men) of White Jews, and vice versa. In the sixteenth, and again in the seventeenth and nineteenth centuries, the White Jews of Cochin addressed questions to famous rabbinical authorities in Cairo, Alexandria, and Jerusalem about the permissibility of marriage unions between them and the Black Jews. These questions were answered to the effect that if the Black Jews underwent ritual conversion, which for women required only *ṭevilah* (immersion), then White Jews could enter marriage with them according to the *halakhah.* However, despite these repeated rabbinical decisions, the White Jews did not lower the barriers of caste, and the Black Jews maintained their opposition to intermarriage with White Jews. The Black Jews persisted in their claim that they were pure Jews whose skin color darkened as a result of centuries of exposure to the tropical sun. However, the absence of *kohanim* among them militates against this contention and rather speaks for conversion as their origin.

The segregation in religious functions went so far that the *kohanim* of the White Jews would not perform the

Pidyon ha-Ben (Redemption of the Firstborn Son) ceremony for the Black Jews, who had to wait until the fortuitous visit of an outsider *kohen* who then performed the rite for all unredeemed firstborn Black Jews. Although in recent years there has been some easing up of the Black-White segregation in religious life, in general the two communities continued relatively self-contained with parallel and separate facilities and functions. An anthropologist, David G. Mandelbaum (1939), who studied the Jews of Cochin in 1937, observed that the lives of the Black Jews were "even more synagogue-centered" than those of the White Jews, that they adhered more closely to old customs, and that they were more learned in the Talmud than the White Jews.

The synagogue architecture of the Cochin Jews has certain unique features. Of them the most conspicuous is a stairway leading from the back of the main hall up to a platform on which there is a reading desk. Behind the stairway, and level with it, is the women's gallery, separated from it by a lattice wall. The reading of the Torah and the other important parts of the service take place on this elevated platform. This, despite the fact that there is also an *almemar* (platform) in the middle of the synagogue.

In 1948 there were 2,500 Black and 100 White Cochin Jews in India. Within a few years thereafter, all the Black Jews emigrated to Israel, while most of the White Jews remained, because they were unwilling to leave behind their assets, which Indian government regulations did not allow them to take out of the country. In 1968 there were 4,000 Cochin Jews in Israel. In 1983 the total number of Cochin Jews in India, including all the old and new elements, was estimated at 4,500.

Bene Israel. The largest Jewish group in India is that of the Bene Israel. Their origin, like that of the Cochin Jews, is wrapped in legend. They explain their name, which means "Children of Israel" (Heb., *benei Yisra'el*), as referring to the ten tribes of Israel that seceded from Rehoboam, the son of Solomon. Various other, later, dates of their arrival in India are also mooted—all these legends having in common the story of a shipwreck off the Konkan coast, and the drowning of all the passengers except seven Hebrew couples who were cast ashore and settled in the village of Nawgaon, some 26 miles south of present-day Bombay. Because of their isolation in the village they forgot much of their religion and of the Hebrew language, and adopted instead the language (Marathi), customs, garb, and names of their Hindu neighbors. But they clung tenaciously to some rudiments of Judaism, observing circumcision, dietary laws, the Sabbath, and some festivals. They never forgot the Shema' prayer. Because they earned their livelihood by producing oil, their neighbors called them Shanwar Telis, "Sabbath-keeping oilmen." Oil pressing was a very humble occupation, and hence the Teli caste, to which the Bene Israel were assigned, was a low one: members of higher caste were defiled by contact with them.

Whatever the actual time of their arrival in India, until the eighteenth century there was little or no contact between the Bene Israel and other Jews. According to Bene Israel tradition the man who saved them from total assimilation and reestablished Judaism among them was David Rahabi, who was a brother of Moses Maimonides (Mosheh ben Maimon, 1135/8–1204). Actually, this man was none other than the David Rahabi whom we have already met in connection with his educational and religious role among the Jews of Cochin. However, it was not he himself but his son Ezekiel David Rahabi (1694–1771) who, in the course of his travels in the service of the Dutch East India Company, became acquainted with, and interested in, the Bene Israel. Appalled by their ignorance of Judaism, he taught them Hebrew and prayers and selected his three most outstanding pupils to serve as teachers and preachers, with the title *kaji* (from the Arabic *qāḍī*, "religious judge"), which was confirmed by the local rulers. By that time the Bene Israel were dispersed in dozens of villages, and the *kaji*s traveled from place to place to attend circumcisions, weddings, and other religious ceremonies, and to settle disputes. Their office (and title) became hereditary, but by the second half of the nineteenth century their authority had dwindled, owing to their ignorance in both religious and secular matters.

By the mid-eighteenth century the Bene Israel began to leave their villages and settle in Bombay, attracted by the employment opportunities offered by the big city, where they could serve as skilled laborers and clerks, and in the regiments of the East India Company. Their first synagogue in Bombay was built in 1796, and by 1833 about two thousand of them (one-third of their total number) lived in Bombay.

Probably some centuries before Rahabi contacted them, the Bene Israel had become divided, like their Cochin coreligionists, into Gora ("white") and Kala ("black") subcastes. The Gora were believed to be the pure descendants of the original seven couples, while the Kala were held to be the offspring of unions between Bene Israel men and non–Bene Israel (native) women. The Gora were recognized as superior by the Kala, kept themselves aloof and apart from the latter, and did neither intermarry nor eat with them.

As the religious and secular education of the Kala progressed, so did their dissatisfaction grow over being relegated to what amounted to a lower-caste position in relation to the Gora. Following Rahabi, other teachers and preachers came to them from Cochin, and wealthy Baghdad Jews, who had arrived in Bombay in the early nineteenth century, established a school for them. American and other Protestant missions opened Hebrew schools, and from 1819 on a Marathi translation of the Bible began to appear in installments. A Hebrew grammar in Marathi was published by John Wilson of the Scottish Presbyterian Mission. While these missionary efforts resulted in very few conversions of Bene Israel, they spread the knowledge of the Bible, of Hebrew, and of Jewish religion among them. The English the Bene Israel learned from the missionaries enabled them not only to find jobs in the civil service as clerks, but also to read Jewish publications from England and America.

Just as the Gora discriminated against the Kala, so did the Baghdad Jews against the Gora. They excluded their native coreligionists from their synagogues, and tried to exclude them even from the use of beds reserved for Jews in the largest hospital in Bombay. The Baghdad Jews attempted to build a wall around a separate part of the Jewish cemetery to serve only them. The resentment of the Bene Israel over their treatment at the hand of the Baghdad Jews grew in the nineteenth century parallel with that of the Kala against the Gora. However, in neither case did it come to concerted action, nor go beyond occasional, half-hearted protests. The situation underwent a change with India's independence in 1947, when the caste system was officially abolished. The Jews too were caught up in the general movement toward eliminating caste discrimination. Nevertheless, intermarriage between Gora and Kala, or between them and Baghdad Jews, has remained rare.

One of the most interesting aspects of the religious life of the Bene Israel is their attitude to Hindu religion. The Jews of India are the only Jewish community in modern times (if we disregard the handful of Chinese Jews) to live in a polytheistic environment. Ever since biblical times, nothing has been so abhorrent to Jewish religious sentiment as polytheism, in which it has seen nothing but idolatry, the fountainhead of immorality and inhumanity, the source of all vice and sin. No traces of this ancient, ingrained antiheathen attitude could be found among the Bene Israel. The influence of the Hindu environment, over the centuries, produced in the Bene Israel an appreciative understanding, even a positive attitude, toward Hinduism, its beliefs and values. A factor in this development seems to have been the absence of hostility, persecution, and oppression, and the multiple-caste system that allotted the Jews their special niche in which they could live in peace. In this sociocultural environment, which was historically a totally exceptional experience for the Jews, the religion upon which such a social relationship was based had to appear in the eyes of the Bene Israel as having redeeming values and possessing features not incompatible with their own faith. Thus, in the Bene Israel view, the polytheistic character of Hinduism could be disregarded, or at least relegated into the background, and its moralistic features, its teachings of kindness, of nonviolence, of the sanctity of all life, whether human or animal, could be emphasized, appreciated, and upheld. In fact, until quite recently, the Bene Israel believed that the eating of beef was prohibited in the Bible, and they considered the remarriage of widows impermissible—both views in conformity with Hinduism.

China. Fragmentary documents testify to the presence of Jews in Khotan, Chinese Turkistan (later Sinkiang province), in 718 CE. During a rebellion in the southern port city of Canton in 878/9, some 120,000 Muslims, Jews, Christians, and other foreigners are said to have been massacred. Unverifiable reports speak of the presence in the ninth century of Jews in the Fukien and Chekiang provinces. In the ninth or tenth century a group of some one thousand Jews, including women and children, settled in K'ai-feng, the capital of Honan Province, at the invitation of an emperor of the Sung dynasty. They came either from Persia or from India, and were Persian-speaking. They were specialists in the manufacture, dyeing, and pattern-printing of cotton fabrics, which industry was developed in China at the time to meet the acute silk shortage. The first synagogue in K'ai-feng was built in 1163. Marco Polo (1254–1324) reported that Jews, Muslims, and Christians were disputing the merits of their respective religions before the Mongol conqueror and his court—a procedure duplicating that reported from the Khazar court in the eighth century. In the fourteenth century the Mongol rulers issued decrees pertaining to the taxation of Jews, prohibiting levirate marriage, and summoning wealthy Jews to the capital to join the army. In 1653 the Jewish mandarin Chao Ying-ch'en restored the K'ai-feng synagogue and its sacred Torah scrolls, but thereafter, as a result of its complete isolation from other Jewish centers, the community fell into decay. Several outstanding K'ai-feng Jews became officials and military officers. Gradually, the Jewish families adopted Chinese names and customs. In the eighteenth century a Jesuit missionary still witnessed and described the reading of the Torah in Hebrew in the K'ai-feng synagogue, but soon thereafter both the knowledge of Hebrew and the memory of the ancestral faith disappeared, and the last remnants of the Chinese Jews ceased to exist. At the end of World War II some two hundred persons in K'ai-feng were still able to trace their descent to Jewish ancestry.

BIBLIOGRAPHY

The literature on the Jews of Bukhara is extremely meager. Useful articles by D. Iofan, I. M. Babkhanov, and Rudolf Loewenthal are found in *Central Asian Collectanea* 1 (1958):5–8; 9–13 and 8 (1961):1–13. Also, see Walter J. Fischel's "Israel in Iran: A Survey of Judeo-Persian Literature," in *The Jews*, edited by Louis Finkelstein (New York, 1960). A few more articles are listed in the bibliography to the article "Bukhara," in *Encyclopaedia Judaica* (Jerusalem, 1971).

The Falashas have fared better. Their literature and customs are described in Wolf Landau's *Falasha Anthology* (New Haven, 1951), Simon D. Messing's *The Story of the Falashas* (Brooklyn, N.Y., 1982), David Kessler's *The Falashas: The Forgotten Jews of Ethiopia* (New York, 1982), and Tudor Parfitt's *Operation Moses: The Untold Story of the Secret Exodus of the Falasha Jews from Ethiopia* (New York, 1985).

The Jews of Cochin are discussed in David G. Mandelbaum's "The Jewish Way of Life in Cochin," *Jewish Social Studies* 1 (October 1939): 423–460, and in Schifra Strizower's *Exotic Jewish Communities* (New York, 1962), pp. 88–124.

The Bene Israel of India are the subject of Haeem S. Kehimkar's *The History of the Bene Israel of India* (Tel Aviv, 1937), Schifra Strizower's *The Bene Israel of Bombay* (New York, 1971), and Ezekiel Barber's *The Bene-Israel of India: Images and Reality* (Washington, D.C., 1981); see also Isaac S. Abraham's *Origin and History of the Calcutta Jews* (Calcutta, 1969). On the Jews of India in general, see my own *The Vanished Worlds of Jewry* (New York, 1981), pp. 173–185.

On the Chinese Jews there is the three-volume compilation by William Charles White, *Chinese Jews* (New York, 1966). Additional material is supplied by Daniel Leslie in his "The Chinese-Hebrew Memorial Book of the Jewish Community of K'ai-feng," *Abr-Nahrain* 4 (1963–1964): 19–49, 5 (1964–1965): 1–28, 6 (1965–1966): 1–52, and 8 (1968–1969): 1–35. Herman Dicker's *Wanderers and Settlers in the Far East* (New York, 1962) deals only with the recent Jewish immigrants in China and Japan.

See also, on each of the communities discussed, my book *Tents of Jacob* (Englewood Cliffs, N.J., 1971), pp. 255–258, 415–426.

RAPHAEL PATAI

Judaism in Southern Europe

Despite a differential development, Judaism in southern Europe's many communities has been united geographically by the Mediterranean Sea and historically by a common heritage. The heritage has informed its creativity, while the sea has fostered its communication. As with other areas, the sources on Judaism in southern Europe tend to portray Judaism as conceived by leadership rather than as practiced by laity. Within this region, with its wide variations of time, place, and circumstance, popular Judaism ran the gamut from paradigmatic devotion to listless ignorance, exhibiting also elements of syncretistic blending with indigenous folklore, superstitition, and magic. Jewish sources from Renaissance Italy, for example, document the use of amulets, charms, fortune-telling, witchcraft, and prayers to repel evil spirits. Such often widespread practices are deprecatorily recorded by rabbis, heads of *yeshivot*, and other religious leaders in sermons, *responsa*, and ethical treatises.

The Judaism of all these communities thus reveals two strata: (1) a continuing complex of practices and beliefs, diversely syncretized with alien elements and followed by the majority, and (2) the idealized religion of the intellectual leadership, expressed in a variety of approaches often in conflict with one another, always reflective of the surrounding environment and ultimately influencing the tone of Judaism in the society as a whole. A description of Judaism in all these communities must necessarily focus on the creativity of its leadership, with the caveat that the individuals directly involved were more significant tonally than numerically. One must also bear in mind that the religious creativity of these areas varied greatly from time to time and place to place.

The history of Judaism in southern Europe embraces the experience of Jews on the Iberian Peninsula, in southern France, in Italy, and in the Greek territories. It is divisible into four occasionally overlapping chronological eras: the origin of Jewish settlement until approximately 700 CE; the medieval world (700–c. 1500); the Renaissance and Enlightenment (c. 1300–c. 1850); and the modern and contemporary world (beginning about 1800). The great period of Jewish productivity in the Greek territories, which occurred under Ottoman rule, is outside the scope of this study.

Origins. Legends locate Jews in early biblical times in places as remote from the Land of Israel as the Iberian Peninsula, but the inscriptions that constitute the earliest Jewish records of southern European Jewry do not antedate the third century BCE for Greece, the second for Italy, and the first for Iberia and southern France. During this time, Greece and Italy enjoyed thriving Jewish cultures; the Greek regions had the greatest Jewish population, with communities in places like Cyprus, Rhodes, Crete, Kos, and Sparta already established during the Hasmonean period (*1 Mc.* 15:23). Probably from Rome comes the *Collatio legum Mosaicarum et Romanarum*, a work compiled at the end of the third or the beginning of the fourth century CE that contains a comparison between biblical and Roman law.

Little is known about the Jew's religious life in the early centuries of their settlement. Prior to the Hasmonean Revolt (168–165 BCE), Jews most likely brought

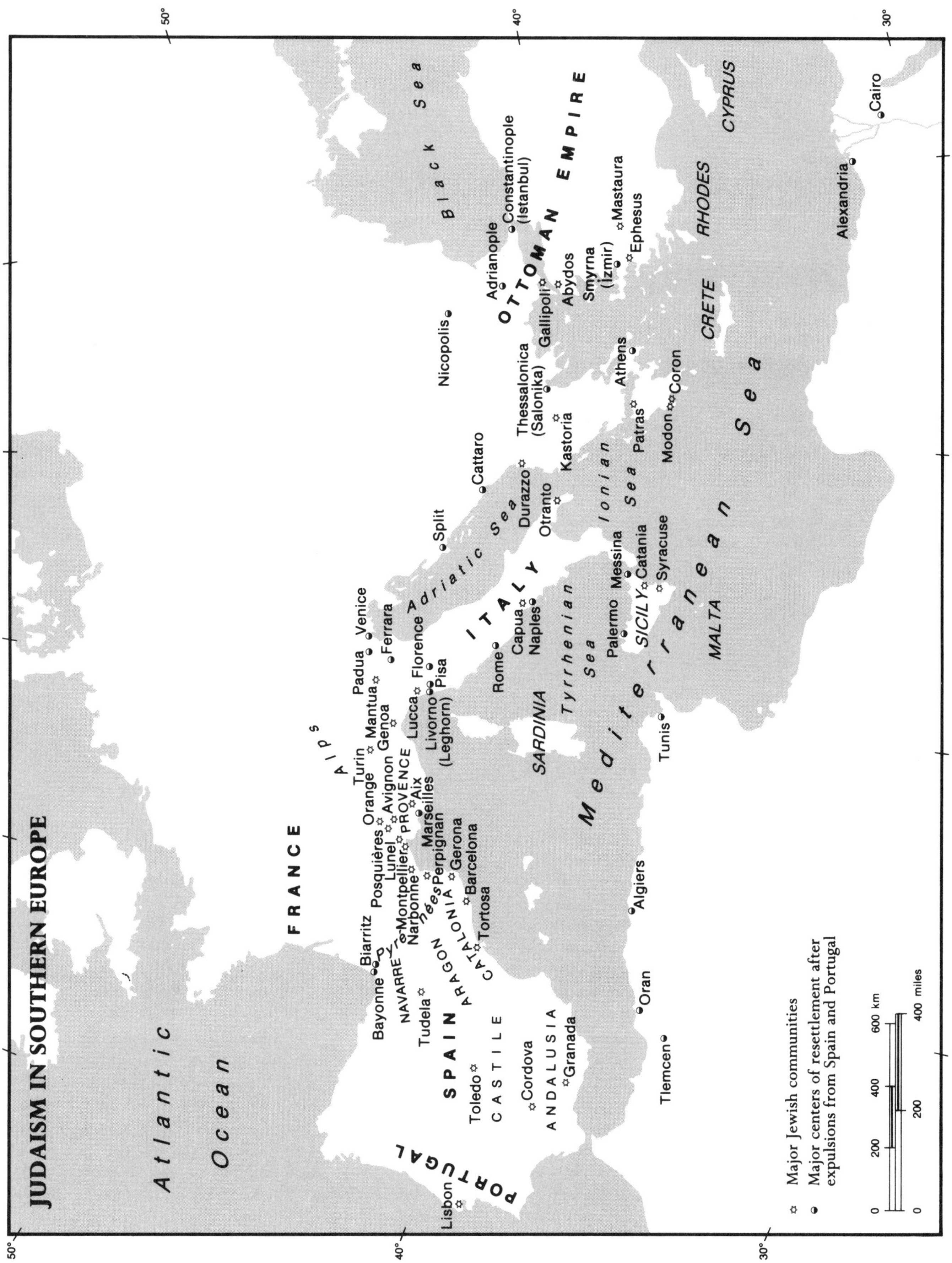
JUDAISM IN SOUTHERN EUROPE
Atlantic Ocean
FRANCE
Alps
SPAIN
PORTUGAL
Lisbon
CASTILE
ANDALUSIA
Toledo
Cordova
Granada
NAVARRE
Tudela
ARAGON
CATALONIA
Tortosa
Barcelona
Gerona
Perpignan
Pyrenees
Bayonne
Biarritz
Narbonne
Montpellier
Lunel
Posquières
PROVENCE
Orange
Avignon
Aix
Marseilles
Turin
Genoa
Mantua
Padua
Venice
Ferrara
Lucca
Florence
Livorno (Leghorn)
Pisa
Rome
Capua
Naples
ITALY
SARDINIA
Tyrrhenian Sea
Palermo
Messina
Catania
Syracuse
SICILY
MALTA
Tunis
Algiers
Oran
Tlemcen
Mediterranean Sea
Adriatic Sea
Split
Cattaro
Durazzo
Otranto
Ionian Sea
Kastoria
Thessalonica (Salonika)
Patras
Modon
Coron
Athens
Nicopolis
Adrianople
Gallipoli
Abydos
Constantinople (Istanbul)
OTTOMAN EMPIRE
Smyrna (Izmir)
Ephesus
Mastaura
Black Sea
CRETE
RHODES
CYPRUS
Alexandria
Cairo
Major Jewish communities
Major centers of resettlement after expulsions from Spain and Portugal
0 200 400 600 km
0 200 400 miles
50°
40°
30°
20°
10°
0°
10°

with them only a form of Pentateuchal Judaism, while later arrivals were likely influenced by proto-rabbinic institutions. In addition to its diplomatic tasks, the patriarch Gamli'el of Yavneh's embassy to Rome (95–96 CE) may have intended to reorganize the substantial Jewish population there under closer rabbinical control. The account of an academy established in Rome by Matya' ben Ḥeresh (early second century) appears historical (B.T., *Me'il* 17a), as does the purported guidance offered him by the sages Shim'on bar Yoḥ'ai and El'azar ben Yose on their visit to Rome.

Prior to the advent of modern secular states, Jews in southern Europe lived with quasi-automony under Jewish law *(halakhah)*, which in turn was subject to the laws of the host society. These societies generated harsh legislation against the Jews, from *ad hoc* decrees to major compilations of law such as the Theodosian Code (438) and the *Siete Partidas* (Seven Sections) of the Castilian king Alfonso X (r. 1252–1284). This legislation, however, was often overlooked or minimally implemented in those societies where such actions suited the rulers' needs. Within the bounds of this legislation, the range of Jewish autonomy varied; at times it included even the right to inflict capital punishment. Accordingly, Jewish communities maintained their own separate legal and communal institutions; foremost among them were the local court *(beit din)*, synagogues (often there were separate synogogues for practitioners of a particular craft or members of a certain guild), and cemeteries. Though it followed traditional Jewish models, the Jewish community was often formally influenced by the structure of the surrounding society: its officers often bore Hebrew titles that directly translated the titles of comparable positions in the general society or utilized the language of the society, as in the case of the ancient Greek communities, where we find the titles of *archisynagogos* for the community head, *gerousiarch* as head of the synagogue council, and *presbyter* for elder.

Evidence of numerous synagogues exists for the early centuries CE, particularly for Rome and Greece; the one at Delos (dating to before 69 BCE) is among the earliest discovered. Various sources, from the New Testament and rabbinic literature to the canons of the Council of Elvira (c. 305), attest to a continuing interest in, and conversion to, Judaism by non-Jews. The official recognition of Christianity as Rome's imperial religion in the early fourth century spurred efforts at the wholesale conversion of Jews. If authentic, Bishop Severus's letter on the forced conversion of Minorca's Jews in 418 constitutes the earliest record of mass conversions, which were in any case definitely ordered by several Merovingian and Visigothic kings in the sixth and seventh centuries. Continuous reports on Jewish religious life begin in the mid-tenth century in two centers: Iberia and Italy.

Islamic Iberia (Spain and Portugal). Iberia, conquered by the Muslims between 711 and 715, stood at the beginning of the medieval period on the threshold of a golden age. Iberia's Jewish community of approximately 250,000, the largest at the time, shared this development. Organized politically under the *nasi'* ("prince") Ḥasdai (or Ḥisdai) ibn Shaprut (c. 915–c. 970) and constitutionally under Talmudic law, the Jews inaugurated a golden age that continued long after Islamic Iberia splintered into some thirty polities in the early eleventh century.

Pervading the high culture of Jewry under Islam was a broadly rationalistic tone. Rationalism encouraged the centralization of *halakhah*, a process signified by the *Sefer halakhot* (Book of Laws) composed by Yitsḥaq ben Ya'aqov Alfasi (1013–1103) in Fez and brought by him to Lucena. It led ultimately to the magisterial *Mishneh Torah* (Repetition of the Torah, or Code of Law) in 1180 by Moses Maimonides (Mosheh ben Maimon), though this work also was composed outside of the peninsula, in Egypt. The rational spirit also helped produce scientific studies of the Hebrew language, by Menaḥem ibn Saruq (mid-tenth century), compiler of the first Hebrew dictionary; his rival, Dunash ibn Labrat, who projected a Hebrew grammar; their contemporary, Yehudah ibn Hayyuj, who discovered the triliteral nature of Hebrew roots; and the prolific Yonah ibn Janaḥ (early eleventh century), whose *Kitāb al-tanqīḥ* (Book of Minute Research) is the oldest extant complete work on Jewish philology.

The same spirit also facilitated the ingress of Greek thought, especially Neoplatonism and Aristotelianism, into Judaism. These philosophies challenged critical doctrines of the revealed tradition—those concerning revelation, creation, providence, prophecy, miracles, immortality, resurrection, and God's attributes. In response, some Iberian thinkers rejected philosophy and others, revelation. Still others created syntheses, the foremost among them given in *Keter malkhut* (The Crown of Royalty), by the Neoplatonist Shelomoh ibn Gabirol (mid-eleventh century); *Kitāb al-hidāyah ilā farā'iḍ al-qulūb* (The Duties of the Heart), by the Neoplatonist Baḥye ibn Paquda (second half of the eleventh century); the *Kitāb al-radd wa-al-dalīl fī al-dīn al-dhalīl* (Book of Refutation and in Defense of the Despised Faith), commonly called in Hebrew the *Kuzari*, by Yehudah ha-Levi (eleventh to twelfth century), who combines elements of Neoplatonism and Aristotelianism; and in *Al-'aqīdah al-rafīyah* (The Exalted Faith), by Avraham ibn Daud of Toledo (twelfth century) and Maimonides' *Dalālat al-ḥā'irīn* (Guide of the Perplexed), both of which draw on medieval Aristotelianism. Except for Ibn Gabirol's work in Hebrew, these were all composed in Arabic with Hebrew characters. Though differing by school and bent, these philosophers all rationalized belief innovatively and at times controversially. For them, God was neither anthropomorphic nor anthropopathic, and the contrarational was tempered by rational explanations. For the Neoplatonists, the soul's ultimate aim was union with the upper world, while for the Aristotelians it was the rational faculty's approximation to the Active Intellect that was of ultimate value. Unlike most of these philosophers, who focused primarily on the individual, ha-Levi dwelt on corporative Israel, its election and receipt of God's revelation.

The rational-philosophical atmosphere also pervaded other religious creativity, including the biblical commentaries of Mosheh ibn 'Ezra' (c. 1055–after 1135) and Avraham ibn 'Ezra' (c. 1089–c. 1164) and the religious poem, or *piyyuṭ*, written especially for the Sabbath and holiday liturgy. Born in Talmudic times, the *piyyuṭ* had developed with the fixing of the liturgy. Iberian Jewry played an important role in this process. Responding to a question from the Lucena community, Naṭron'ai, the gaon of the Babylonian academy of Sura from 853 to 858, listed the one hundred daily blessings prescribed in the Talmud. To another query, apparently from Barcelona, Naṭron'ai's successor, 'Amram bar Sheshna (known as 'Amram Gaon, d. 875), sent a complete order of prayers, along with corresponding *halakhah* for the entire year. *Seder 'Amram* ('Amram's Order), the oldest in Judaism, spurred liturgical creativity through the *piyyuṭ*.

Iberian poets, like Ibn Gabirol, Mosheh ibn 'Ezra', ha-Levi, Yosef ibn Abitur (tenth to eleventh century), and Yitsḥaq ibn Ghayyat (1038–1089), further developed the conventional categories, emphasizing the penitential poems, and conceived new ones for Havdalah, the Sabbath table, and other private occasions, as well as *reshuyyot* ("introductory poems") for public recitation. Their *piyyuṭim* are distinguished by lucid style, biblical vocabulary, and a special meter of their own creation, though at times they employ Arabic meter and rhyme. Their themes are manifold: God's nature and creation; the human soul and life's meaning; sin, repentance, redemption, and the Messiah; ethical virtues; the Torah and its saintly teachers; and the longing for God's proximity and favor. Noteworthy are ha-Levi's poems on his migration to Zion (especially the *Ode to Zion*), and Ibn Gabirol's philosophical-religious paean to God, the *Crown of Royalty*, which is still recited by Sefardic Jews on the eve of Yom Kippur.

The same themes inform the sermons of this era, which, while no longer extant, can be reconstructed from biblical commentaries like those of David Kimḥi (c. 1160–c. 1235), Avraham ibn 'Ezra'; from philosophical works, notably Ibn Paquda's *Duties of the Heart* and ha-Levi's *Kuzari;* and from ethical treatises, like Maimonides' introduction to the Mishnaic tractate *Avot*, known as the *Shemoneh Peraqim* (Eight Chapters). These works evince an intensive religious life, a flourishing synagogue, and a passion for sermonic instruction. Maimonides even recommended a resident preacher for each community (before local rabbis were the rule), while his son Avraham compiled a treatise on traditional rabbinical sermons.

No synagogues remain standing from communities under Muslim rule during this period, but those constructed contemporaneously in the Christian sectors of the peninsula, as in Toledo, for example, unmistakably reveal the influence of Islamic architecture. Equally impressive was the effect of Islamic music upon the Iberian synagogue chant.

Medieval Christian Europe. The second center of Jewry was the medieval Christian world. Here, despite chronic disabilities, many Jewish communities were religiously creative. Jewish learning was regularly accompanied by secular knowledge: Talmudists were physicians and scientists conversant with Latin, Greek, Arabic, and their local vernaculars. Their creativity began in tenth-century Italy, in theology with Shabbetai Donnolo (913–c. 982), in history with the anonymous author of the *Yosippon* (Pseudo-Josephus), and in lexicography with Natan ben Yeḥi'el (1035–c. 1110). Donnolo was a physician and theologian acquainted with Hebrew, Greek, and Latin literature as well as colloquial Italian, and he was the first person in Christian Europe to write on medicine in Hebrew. He sought scientific explanations for creation and asserted that man was created not in God's image but in the image of God's creation. The author of *Yosippon* wove a Latin version of the writings of Josephus Flavius and other works, including the apocrythpal and Talmudic literature, into an imaginative and historiographically perceptive narrative. Natan's *'Arukh,* a lexicon of Talmudic and Midrashic literature, became influential because of the quality of its readings, etymologies, and explanations.

By the thirteenth century, religious culture flourished in southern France, especially Provence, and in the expanding Christian sector of the Iberian Peninsula, the kingdoms of Castile, Aragon, and Navarre. There the rationalist philosophical tendencies that had developed in Islamic Iberia clashed with the traditional view of Judaism regnant in Christian feudal Europe. According to the traditional view, God, usually conceived anthropomorphically and anthropopathically, repeatedly interrupted the processes of nature to reward and punish and to make possible revelation, resurrection, prophecy and other miracles.

The most dramatic ideological battles between the two worldviews revolved around Maimonides' *Guide of the Perplexed.* Maimonideans, such as Shem Ṭov ibn Yosef Falaquera (c. 1225–1295), Yosef ibn Kaspi (1279–1340), and Moses of Narbonne (Mosheh Narboni, d. after 1360), upheld Maimonides' reconciliation of philosophy and faith and even defended the eternity of matter. In 1305 these controversies culminated in a ban by Shelomoh ben Avraham (c. 1235–c. 1310), rabbi of Barcelona, against the study of Greek philosophy by any Jews under twenty-five years of age. Anti-Maimonideans, like Avraham ben David (c. 1125–1198) of Posquières and Shelomoh of Montepellier (thirteenth century), attacked the *Guide.* Like the courtier physician Yehudah ibn Alfakhar (d. 1235) and the polymath Moses Nahmanides (Mosheh ben Naḥman), who defended Judaism at the disputation of Barcelona (1263), the anti-Maimonideans accepted biblical literalism, divine anthropomorphism, and miracles.

Stemming from the traditional Jewish worldview were the luxuriant developments in Jewish mysticism in Provence and Iberia. By the middle of the twelfth century, the study and practice of Qabbalah flourished in Provence. From this period comes *Sefer ha-bahir,* the earliest work, properly speaking, of qabbalistic literature. Appearing in southern France at the end of the century, *Sefer ha-bahir,* written in Hebrew, reveals recent Iberian influence but may be a composite work harking back to the geonic period. Its ideas are couched in short statements discussing or explaining biblical verses. The most eminent early practitioner of Qabbalah was Yitsḥaq, son of Avraham ben David, known as Isaac the Blind (d. about 1235), who inspired numerous followers in both Provence and Catalonia. The renowned qabbalistic circle bearing his influence developed in the northern Iberian town of Gerona; the sages of Gerona, dating from the beginning of the thirteenth century, include, among distinguished others, the great Nahmanides. An eminent disseminator of the qabbalistic thought of this period was Baḥye ben Asher, a popular author whose commentary on the Pentateuch and whose *Kad ha-qemaḥ,* an alphabetically organized work on faith and ethics, enjoyed wide circulation.

Due in no small measure to the prevalence of philosophical learning, Iberian Qabbalah possessed a philosophical orientation, an awareness of the Neoplatonists, Aristotle, and, among earlier Iberian Jews, the writings of Ibn Gabirol, ha-Levi, Avraham ibn 'Ezra', and Maimonides. The philosophical bent is patent, for example, in the writings of Yitsḥaq ben Avraham ibn Latif (c. 1210–c. 1280), who follows Neoplatonism in his identification of God with the primoridal will of Aristotelianism in his concepts of form and matter. The more colorful qabbalist Avraham ben Shemu'el Abulafia (c. 1240–after 1291), who once tried to convert Pope Nicholas III to Judaism, conceived of both philosophy and Qabbalah as propaedeutics to the attainment of a "prophetic Qabbalah."

From this period also is the most important work of Qabbalah, the *Zohar,* composed in Aramaic with many Hebraisms and unusual foreign terms. The *Zohar* is a commentary on the weekly sections of the Torah (preponderantly on *Genesis* and *Exodus*), interrupted by a number of small connected treatises. Though attributed to the second-century sage Shim'on bar Yoḥ'ai, who appears as its chief teacher, the *Zohar* was actually compiled in the main by the Iberian Moses (Mosheh ben Shem Ṭov) de León (c. 1240–1305).

Rationalist and antirationalist philosophizing also continued, throughout the Middle Ages, apart from any overt disputation between the views. Hillel ben Shemu'el (d. 1295), an early Jewish philosopher in the Italian Peninsula, learned in Aristotelianism, Neoplatonism, and Christian Scholasticism, wrote a commentary on the twenty-six Aristotelian propositions in Maimonides' *Guide.* Subsequent Jewish philosophers shared Hillel ben Shemu'el's interest in the soul, and some in the fourteenth century, like Narboni, shared his interest in the related question of freedom of the will. Second only to Maimonides as an exponent of Aristotelianism was the philosopher, scientist, and biblical commentator Levi ben Gershom (Gersonides, 1288–1344), author of *Milḥamot Adonais* (Wars of the Lord). On the other hand, in *Or Adonai* (Light of the Lord), Ḥasdai Crescas (d. 1410) presented a critique of Aristotle and offered positive attributes for God. Crescas's pupil Yosef Albo (fifteenth century), who represented Iberian Jewry in the disputations of Tortosa and San Mateo (1413–1414), attained considerable vogue with his *Sefer ha-'iqqarim* (Book of Theological Dogmas).

Concern for the strengthening of tradition also informed authors of *responsa* (Heb., *teshuvot*), exemplarily Ibn Adret, who was also versed in Roman and Aragonese law, and Asher ben Yeḥi'el (known as the Ro'sh), (c. 1250–1327), a German Talmudist who became rabbi in Toledo in 1305. Asher's traditionalism also appears in his compilation of Jewish law, *Pisqei ha-Ro'sh* (Decisions of the Ro'sh), which follows Yitsḥaq ben Ya'aqov Alfasi's model and offers an alternative to the *Mishneh Torah,* and in Shemu'el Sardi's *Sefer ha-terumot,* (1225), the first comprehensive systematization of civil law following the order of the Talmud. Sardi in turn influenced the epoch's principal code, the *Arba'ah ṭurim* (Four Columns), known simply as the *Ṭur,* written by Asher's son Ya'aqov (c. 1270–1343).

Jewish religious experience in this epoch is often reflected in great detail in its sermons, *responsa,* and ethical and other literature. These include the deftly crafted collection of Hebrew homilies *Malmad ha-talmidim* by Ya'aqov Anatoli of Provence (thirteenth century), a rabbi schooled in Plato, Aristotle, Maimonides, and Michael Scot (whom he met in Naples at the court of Emperor Frederick II); ethical works, like *Higgayon ha-nefesh ha-'atsuvah* (Meditation of the Sad Soul) by the Barcelonese Avraham bar Ḥiyya' (d. about 1136); works of social criticism, like the *Iggeret musar* (Epistle on Morality) composed in Portugal by Shelomoh Alami (c. 1370–1420); and even halakhic codes, like the *Tseidah la-derekh* (Provision for the Way) by Menaḥem ibn Zeraḥ of Navarre (c. 1310–1385). Similarly, *'Aqeidat Yitsḥaq* (Binding of Isaac), a compendium of one hundred and five consummately artistic sermons by Yitsḥaq Arama (1420–1499), reveals interest in philosophy, polemics, and history. Its many editions attest to its popularity. Prevailing religious customs, especially prayer and other synagogal activities, are also to be found in descriptions by travelers, beginning with the *Universal Guide* by Avraham ben Natan of Lunel (c. 1155–1215), which describes Iberian Jewry, and the *Sefer minhagim* (Book of Customs) by Asher ben Sha'ul of Lunel (early thirteenth century), an account of travels in Narbonne and Lunel. Such sources reveal increasing communal and regional deviations in liturgical practice within the two major rites—the Palestinian, dominant in Greece and Corfu (the Romaniot rite) and in Italy (the Roman, or Italian, rite) until subordinated by the Sefardic (Spanish-Portuguese) rite in the sixteenth century; and the Babylonian rite followed with distinctive nuances in Catalonia, Provence, and, except for an identical daily service, Aragon and Castile. Responding to this variety, *Sefer Abudarham,* written in 1340 by David Abudarham of Castile, comments on prayers and rituals and includes treatises on various subjects, like the Passover Haggadah, the *halakhah* regarding various benedictions, and the weekly Pentateuchal and Prophetic readings, as well as astronomical and calendrical tables. In addition to the Talmud, *responsa,* and the works of Avraham ben Nathan of Lunel and Asher ben Sha'ul, Abudarham cites much Ashkenazic, French, Provençal, and Iberian material that he was apparently the last author to consult.

The centuries of relative security for Jewish communities and good relations with the Christian rulers came to an end with persecutions and the expulsion of the Jews from nearly all of France (in 1306 and 1394) and Spain (in 1492) and the forced conversion of those in Portugal (in 1497). The synagogues, where not destroyed, were often converted into churches, including the two great sanctuaries of Toledo: the first, dating from around 1200, became Santa María la Blanca; the other, constructed around 1357 by the financier Shemu'el ha-Levi Abulafia, became Nuestra Señora del Tránsito, or simply El Tránsito.

Though officially proscribed, Judaism continued clandestinely among some of the New Christians, as Jewish converts to Christianity and, at least theoretically, all their descendants, were called. Isolated from authentic Jews (though some transient Jews were permitted on the peninsula) and Hebrew learning, the New Christian judaizers, often called Marranos, developed a distinctive Judaism out of some surviving rabbinic traditions and the Vulgate translation of the Hebrew Bible that was read in church and studied in seminaries. Traces of Marrano practice persist to this day among some Catholics of Spanish and Portuguese descent. [*See* Marranos.]

Subject to persecution for judaizing, many New Christians fled in the sixteenth century to three havens in southern Europe: southern France, where they could not live openly as Jews until the eighteenth century; the Ottoman empire, where they could not live as Christians; and the Italian states, where they could choose their identity. In Italy and the Ottoman empire, they found established Jewish communities, augmented by refugees from the expulsion of the Jews from Spain in 1492. At the end of the century, Amsterdam too became an important refuge.

Renaissance and Early Modern Italy. The Renaissance influence on Jewish culture and religion is divisible into three periods. The first, from the early fourteenth century to the mid-sixteenth, was one of considerable freedom and manifold interaction with non-Jewish intellectuals. The second, after the burning of the Talmud in 1553 and the creation by the city-states of the ghetto in 1555 and for at least a century thereafter, was characterized by chronic insecurity and sporadic oppression; in this period, varied Jewish creativity nevertheless continued. The third, from approximately 1650 to the middle of the nineteenth century, witnesses an increasing inwardness of Jewish life and thought.

In Italy the refugees from the Iberian Peninsula entered a native community proud of its ancient Italian roots and already augmented by Ashkenazi newcomers from northern Europe in the previous century. Italy became a religious microcosm of western European Jewish life, with each language group retaining its distinctive customs and synagogue rituals. By the middle of the sixteenth century Rome had nine synagogues, including separate congregations of French, Castilian, Catalonian, and Barcelonese Jews. The most notable of all the recent Sefardic immigrants was Isaac ben Judah Abravanel (1437–1508), ethicist, exegete, philosopher, historian, mystic, and diplomat and unsurpassed in his Jewish devotion. By example and philosophy, Abravanel sought to stimulate faith in Judaism and its future. In this he was joined by others notably the grande dame, the former New Christian Doña Gracia Mendes Nasi. Perhaps her most dramatic effort in this regard was her support of the so-called Marrano press at Ferrara. Established by the former New Christian Yom Ṭov ben Levi Athias (also known as Jerońimo de Vargas), it was continued by his associate, Avraham Usque. Following Athias's plan, Usque between 1552 and 1555 published works of religious interest in Hebrew, like Menaḥem ben Zeraḥ's spiritual vade mecum; in Spanish, like the Ferrara Bible; and in Portuguese, like Samuel Usque's classic of Jewish historiography, Jewish apologetics, and Portuguese prose, the *Consolation for the Tribulations of Israel* (1552).

Jews played a significant role in the early capitalist economy of the various Italian states. Numerous Jewish savants were humanists at home in the classics and in the vernacular cultures. Exemplary were Eliyyahu Delmedigo (c. 1460–c. 1497), head of Padua's rabbinical academy and lecturer on philosophy to general audiences; Yehudah Moscato (c. 1530–c. 1593), rabbi at Mantua, whose knowledge of Platonism, Neoplatonism, Arabic philosophy, the sciences, astronomy, and rhetoric adorns his influential commentary on the *Kuzari;* Leone da Modena (1571–1648), rabbi in Venice, musician, polemicist, scholar, and author of works in Hebrew and Italian; ʿAzaryah dei Rossi (c. 1511–c. 1578), an outstanding classicist and the era's greatest Hebraist, whose empirical investigations and utilization of non-Jewish sources revolutionized Jewish scholarship; Simone Luzzatto (1583–1663), Modena's rabbinical successor in Venice and author of a treatise in Italian pleading for Jewish rights, a work later translated into English by John Toland; and Mosheh Ḥayyim Luzzatto (1707–1747), who was steeped in classical, Italian, and Jewish culture and whose *Mesillat yesherim* (Path of the Upright) remains one of the most influential works in Judaism's ethical literature.

Renaissance humanism stimulated the fourteenth-century philosopher and translator Yehudah Romano to compare the prophet Isaiah to Cicero. It affected biblical commentaries, like those of ʿOvadyah Sforno (c. 1470–c. 1515) and the classical Mishnah commentary of ʿOvadyah ben Avraham yareh of Bertinoro (c. 1450–1515). It touched the Hebrew poetry of Devorah Ascarelli (c. 1600), Yeshaʿyah Bassani (d. 1739), and Bassani's son Yisra'el (d. 1790). It spurred translations of classics, like Delmedigo's of Ibn Rushd (Averroës) into Latin and that of *Ecclesiastes* into Italian by David de' Pomis (1525–1593), who also prepared a Hebrew-Latin-Italian lexicon. It led to efforts by Yehudah Romano to acquaint Jews with non-Jewish thought and to Delmedigo's defense of philosophical study in his *Beḥinat ha-daʿat* (Examination of Religion; 1496). It fostered philosophy in biblical commentaries, like those of Eliyyahu, "the Philosopher," of Crete (fifteenth century), and, among others, the *Ets ha-daʿat* (Tree of Knowledge) by Shimshon Marpurgo (1681–1740), rabbi, halakhist, and humanitarian physician. It linked Christian and Jewish savants in intellectual pursuits, with Christian humanists being influenced by Jewish scholars, like Cardinal Domenico Grimani by the grammarian Avraham Balmes (c. 1440–1523) and the famed Cardinal Egidio di Viterbo by the grammarian Eliyyahu ben Asher Levita (1469–1549), who lived in the cardinal's home for thirteen years. Other Christian humanists were influenced by Jewish qabbalists. Yehudah Romano was reported to have guided the king of Naples, Robert II of Anjou (r. 1309–1343), in his studies of the Bible in Hebrew.

Italian humanism provided models for Jewish belles lettres, as in the *Moḥbarot* (Notebooks) of ʿImmanu'el ben Shelomoh of Rome (c. 1260–1328?) and *Miqdash meʿaṭ* (The Small Sanctuary) by Mosheh of Rieti (1388–1460?), both at least in part inspired by Dante's *Commedia.* Numerous Renaissance dialogues also show humanist influence, including David de' Pomis's *Discourse on Human Suffering and How to Escape It* in Italian; the Neoplatonic classic *Dialogues of Love* by Judah Abravanel (known as Leo Ebreo, c. 1460–after 1521); and Simone Luzzatto's *Socrates,* or *Concerning Human Reason* (1651). The Renaissance stimulated sixteenth-century apologetic histories by Samuel Usque, Yehudah ibn Verga *Shevet Yehudah* (Scepter of Yehudah; 1553), Yosef ha-Kohen *ʿEmeq ha-bakhah* (The Vale of Tears), and Gedalyah ibn Yaḥya *Shelshelet ha-qabbalah* (The Chain of Tradition). Though diversely oriented, the secular learning and the historical concerns of their time inform the works of these writers.

In addition to the poetry of the synagogue's liturgy, the Renaissance also inspired its architecture, which was especially distinguished in the Baroque period. Salomone Rossi (1570?–1630?), the most renowned of many Jewish court musicians, composed settings such as his *Ha-shirim asher li-Shelomoh* (Songs of Solomon; 1622/3) for sacred services; his polyphonic choral works show the influence of Palestrina and Gabrieli. The Renaissance also promoted the homiletical virtuosity of brilliant preachers Yehudah Moscato, ʿAzaryah Picho (also known as Figo, 1579–1647), rabbi of Pisa, and Simone Luzzatto. Their sermons, along with ethical texts like *Degel ahavah* (Banner of Love) by Samuel Archivolti (1515–1611) or the *Path of the Upright* and a panoply of *responsa*, especially those of Me'ir ben Yisra'el Katzenellenbogen of Padua (1473–1565), provide insight into the life of the individual and the community—the divergences in belief and practice, the zeal for faith and quiet devotion on the one hand and the flaunting of wealth and flouting of morality on the other—and into a range of community issues, including the redemption of Jewish captives, integration of former New Christians, individual as against community rights, and the permissibility of a polyphonic chorale and a community theater, swaying during prayer, and playing ball or riding in a gondola on the Sabbath.

The conclusion of this era witnessed the publication of two towering works: *Yad Malakhi*, a systematic compilation of Talmudic methodology, codifiers, and laws, by Malakhi ha-Kohen (d. 1785/90) and *Paḥad Yitsḥaq*, the fullest and most renowned encyclopedia of *halakhah* ever composed, by Yitsḥaq Lampronti (d. 1756), a rabbi, physician, and educator who strongly advocated an education in the humanities as well as Torah.

Modern Italy. In Italy the way to Jewish emancipation was paved dramatically by two brief French occupations (1796–1798 and 1800–1815), and thereafter desultorily and differentially in the various Italian states. On the one hand, emancipation stimulated the modern study of Jewish tradition by such scholars as Graziadio Coen (1751–1834), pioneer in the study of the sources of Mishnaic Hebrew and especially Hebrew poetry; Isacco Samuele Reggio (1784–1855), translator into Italian of biblical books and the Mishnaic tractate *Avot* (Ethics of the Fathers), and Samuel David Luzzatto (1800–1865), a disciple of Moses Mendelssohn, philosopher, commentator on the Bible, translator of the liturgy into Italian, and staunch champion of traditional beliefs. Luzzatto served as the first rector of the modern, yet traditional, seminary, the Collegio Rabbinico Italiano, founded in Padua in 1829. Scientific journals appeared, like *Il Vessillo Israelitico,* founded in Turin 1874 as successor to the *Educatore Israelita,* and the strongly Zionist *Rassegna Mensile di Israel,* edited from 1922 to his death by Dante Lattes (1875–1965), distinguished biblical commentator, educator, and journalist.

On the other hand, as elsewhere, emancipation led to the dissolution of Jewish corporative life, the diminution of religious study and observance, and accelerated assimilation. The blandishments of new opportunities also contributed to the demographic and religious desiccation of many rural communities. The construction of beautiful urban synagogues did not stem the tide of apathy and defection. An impressive if limited revival of Jewish identification and education initiated by Samuel Hirsch Margulies (1858–1922), rabbi of Florence from 1890, and his disciples was curtailed by the Nazis.

From the Enlightenment on, the Italian synagogues have been at least nominally orthodox. The Reform movement from across the Alps, particularly Germany, made few inroads in the peninsula because of Italy's conservative Catholic environment and the suppleness of Italian Judaism, which permitted variation without prescribing change. Internal tendencies toward liberalism at least as strong as elsewhere hark back to the Renaissance and beyond and include the nineteenth-century figures Reggio, Samuel David Luzzatto, and Marco Mortara (1815–1894), who in 1866 proposed a convention of Italian rabbis to effect reforms in Jewish practices.

Contemporary Jewish Life in Southern Europe. After World War II, Jewish life returned to all of southern Europe. In Greece the reconstituted community of some ten thousand has experienced increasing religious apathy and intermarriage. Italy, with its thirty thousand Jews augmented by nearly as many refugees, experiences similar erosions. But it has also demonstrated a strong affirmation of Jewish life, especially in its larger communities like Rome and Milan. This affirmation may be seen in support for seminaries, like the Collegio Rabbinico Italiano, located in Rome since 1934 (though closed for part of the Fascist period), and the Samuel Hirsch Margulies Seminary in Turin; in the creation of umbrella organizations with religious dimensions, notably the Union of Italian Jewish communities; in the continuance of Jewish day schools, attended by some 60 percent of Italian Jewish children; and in strong communal ties with the state of Israel. Among the dramatic chapters of Jewish religious life in modern Italy was the conversion to Judaism by most of the Apulian village of San Nicandro between 1930 and 1944, during the Fascist regime. Led by a winegrower named Donato Menduzio, the group displayed distinctive customs, including hymns utilizing the local dialect and local melodies. After Menduzio's death in 1948 many of these Jews moved to Israel.

Spain has witnessed the establishment of the first Jewish community since 1492. From the late nineteenth century on, Jews had been tolerated only as individuals. Many Jewish refugees had passed through Spain during World War II, and many abroad with Spanish citizenship had been protected by Spain. A statute promulgated in December 1966 guaranteed Jews equal rights with all other citizens, including the right of their own corporative institutions. Two years later, the Spanish government formally repealed its 475-year-old Edict of Expulsion. In 1985 Spain had some nine thousand Jews, over 80 percent Serfardic, a dozen synagogue communities, five synagogue buildings, and five active rabbis. Since 1940 Spain has evinced an intense interest in its Jewish heritage, as witnessed by the erection of statues to native sons, like that of Binyamin of Tudela (twelfth century), rabbi and world traveler, in his native city and that of Maimonides in Cordova, and by burgeoning scholarship, exemplified by the creation of various chairs in Judaica at universities, a Sefardic center in Toledo, the Arias Montano Institute of Jewish and Near Eastern Studies in Madrid and its organ, *Sefarad,* a distinguished quarterly in Judaica.

Portugal, too, had allowed Jews to settle by the beginning of the nineteenth century, but not until 1892 were they recognized as a community and permitted to hold religious services. Their numbers were small and by the beginning of World War II barely reached one thousand, of whom 650 were refugees. During the war, Portugal protected its Jewish nationals, aided Hungarian Jews, and initiated a liberal immigration policy. Since World War II, the Portuguese Jewish community has numbered approximately 650, with now two traditional synagogues and one rabbi.

After World War I, a military officer of New Christian descent, Artur Carlos de Barros Basto (1887–1961), inaugurated a revival of the Jewish identity among New Christian families when he became a Jew, built a synagogue at Oporto, organized a community, and established a journal to promote Judaism among the Marranos. (His efforts, though short-lived, attracted attention to the history of Iberian Jews and their manifold contributions to Western civilization.)

[*Many of the figures and topics mentioned herein are the subjects of independent entries. For further discussion of the literature and religious trends described here, see* Jewish Thought and Philosophy, *article on* Premodern Philosophy.]

BIBLIOGRAPHY

Adler, Israël. *La pratique musicale savante dans quelques communautes juives.* 2 vols. Paris, 1966.

Adler, Israël. *Hebrew Writings concerning Music, in Manuscripts and Printed Books.* Munich, 1975.

Ashtor, Eliyahu. *The Jews of Moslem Spain.* 3 vols. Translated by Aaron Klein and Jenny Machlowitz Klein. Philadelphia, 1973–1984.

Ashtor, Eliyahu. *Levant Trade in the Later Middle Ages.* Princeton, 1983.

Avni, Haim. *Spain, the Jews and Franco.* Translated by Emanuel Shimoni. Philadelphia, 1982.

Baer, Yitzhak. *A History of the Jews in Christian Spain.* 2 vols. Philadelphia, 1961–1966.

Dozy, Reinhart. *Spanish Islam.* Translated by Francis G. Stokes. London, 1913.

Hilberg, Raul. *The Destruction of the European Jews.* Chicago, 1961.

Marcus, Jacob R. *The Jew in the Medieval World: A Source Book, 315–1791.* Cincinnati, 1938.

Milano, Attilio. *Storia degli Ebrei italiani nel Levante.* Florence, 1949.

Milano, Attilio. *Storia degli Ebrei in Italia.* Turin, 1963.

Molho, Michael, and Joseph Nehama, eds. *In Memoriam: Hommage aux victimes juives des Nazis en Grèce.* 2d ed. 3 vols. Thessaloniki, 1973.

Netanyahu, Benzion. *Don Isaac Abravanel, Statesman and Philosopher.* Philadelphia, 1953.

Netanyahu, Benzion. *The Marranos of Spain from the Late Fourteenth to the Early Sixteenth Century.* New York, 1966.

Parkes, James. *The Conflict of the Church and the Synagogue* (1934). Reprint, New York, 1969.

Reitlinger, Gerald. *The Final Solution: The Attempt to Exterminate the Jews of Europe.* London, 1953.

Roth, Cecil. *The History of the Jews of Italy.* Philadelphia, 1946.

Roth, Cecil. *The Jews in the Renaissance.* Philadelphia, 1959.

Starr, Joshua. *The Jews in the Byzantine Empire, 641–1204.* Athens, 1939.

Usque, Samuel. *Consolation for the Tribulations of Israel.* Translated by Martin A. Cohen. Philadelphia, 1965.

MARTIN A. COHEN

Judaism in Northern and Eastern Europe to 1500

Although Jews lived in the northern European provinces of the ancient Roman empire, long-lasting communal settlements began only in the tenth century, when Christian monarchs promoted the economic vitality of their domains by inviting Jewish merchants into the newly developing towns.

Settlement and Early Institutions. A pattern of early royal support followed by royal opposition and instability characterized Jewish political life first in western Europe and then later in the East. The earliest royal policy toward the Jews in northern Europe dates from Charlemagne and, especially, from his son, Louis the Pious, who issued three private charters *(privilegia)* to individual Jewish merchants in about 825. These texts indicate that Jews were among the international merchants doing business in the Carolingian empire and were granted protection of their lives, exemption from tolls, and guarantees of religious freedom. This Carolingian policy toward Jewish merchants was also pursued by subsequent rulers of the German empire, and it encouraged the Jewish immigration that became a factor in the demographic and urban expansion of early medieval Europe.

The first communities developed gradually in the

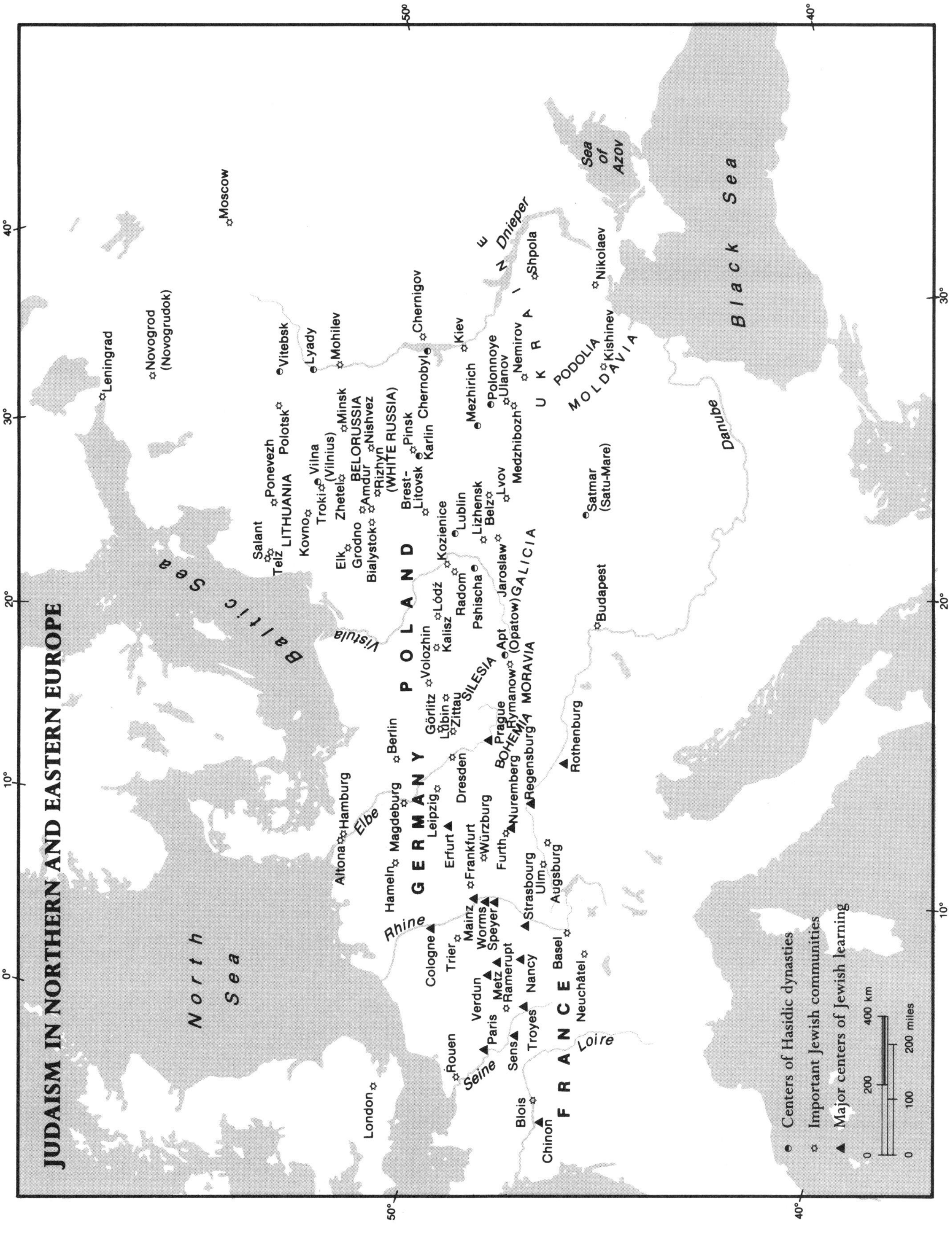
JUDAISM IN NORTHERN AND EASTERN EUROPE
North Sea
Baltic Sea
Black Sea
Sea of Azov
Vistula
Elbe
Rhine
Seine
Loire
Danube
Dnieper
FRANCE
GERMANY
POLAND
LITHUANIA
BELORUSSIA (WHITE RUSSIA)
UKRAINE
PODOLIA
MOLDAVIA
GALICIA
SILESIA
BOHEMIA
MORAVIA
London
Leningrad
Novogrod (Novogrudok)
Moscow
Vitebsk
Lyady
Mohilev
Chernigov
Kiev
Chernobyl
Polotsk
Minsk
Nishvez
Pinsk
Karlin
Ponevezh
Vilna (Vilnius)
Troki
Kovno
Salant
Telz
Zhetel
Amdur
Rizhyn
Brest-Litovsk
Grodno
Elk
Bialystok
Mezhirich
Polonnoye
Ulanov
Nemirov
Medzhibozh
Kishinev
Nikolaev
Shpola
Lublin
Lizhensk
Belz
Lvov
Jaroslaw
Kozienice
Radom
Pshischa
Apt (Opatow)
Satmar (Satu-Mare)
Budapest
Volozhin
Lódź
Kalisz
Görlitz
Lubin
Zittau
Rymanow
Prague
Berlin
Hamburg
Altona
Magdeburg
Hameln
Leipzig
Dresden
Erfurt
Frankfurt
Würzburg
Nuremberg
Regensburg
Rothenburg
Furth
Augsburg
Ulm
Strasbourg
Mainz
Worms
Speyer
Cologne
Trier
Ramerupt
Metz
Verdun
Nancy
Basel
Neuchâtel
Paris
Rouen
Troyes
Sens
Blois
Chinon
● Centers of Hasidic dynasties
✡ Important Jewish communities
▲ Major centers of Jewish learning
0 200 400 km
0 100 200 miles
50°
40°
30°
20°
10°
0°

Rhineland towns, where various family groups settled and intermarried. Of special significance were the Qalonimos family from Lucca, Italy; the descendants of Abun, a rabbi from Le Mans in northern France; and other families from France, which became the nucleus of the Mainz Jewish elite. Cut off from the Jewish political and religious authorities in Palestine and Babylonia, as well as Spain, the leaders of the Mainz community had considerable room to improvise and experiment with new patterns of autonomous local governance.

From the beginning, communal leadership assumed two overlapping but distinct forms. On the one hand, legal decisions were rendered by religious judges or rabbis who acquired expertise in the Talmud. On the other hand, communal control over nonlegal public affairs devolved upon the "elders," whose authority derived from their age, wealth, family lineage, and other personal qualities. They maintained public order, collected taxes for the Christian authorities and for support of Jewish social services, and were the liaison between the community and the gentile rulers.

In the period of first settlement the rabbis were merchants, like the rest of the community, and were among the elders who decided public policy. As communities grew in size and complexity, communal roles became more differentiated. A paid rabbinate gradually developed only in the thirteenth century.

The location of the early northern Jewish communities on a frontier prompted religious leaders and elders alike to be innovative. We see this in the legal decisions of Gershom ben Yehudah (d. 1028), the first major rabbinical figure in Mainz. Gershom functioned as an appeals judge on matters of Jewish law, and his legal opinions rarely mention the decisions and precedents of the Babylonian geonim. Rather, he answered questions by interpreting Talmudic or even biblical passages, thereby imitating rather than following the geonim. His ordinances against polygyny and a woman's involuntary divorce became binding precedents.

We also find signs of improvisation in the actions of the early community board *(qahal)* and communal leaders *(parnasim)* contemporary with Gershom, who undertook to maintain law and order, supervise the weights and measures in the market, and provide for the indigent. The institution of *ma'arufyah,* an individual Jewish merchant's trade monopoly with a specific Christian client, was widespread in the Rhineland, and boards adopted measures to protect it. As the Jewish population grew in the eleventh century, local community boards placed a ban on new settlement *(ḥerem ha-yishuv)* to prevent excessive economic competition.

By the middle of the eleventh century, questions about the limits of local autonomy had arisen in newer areas of settlement, like the duchy of Champagne. Yehudah ha-Kohen, Gershom's successor, decided that in the area of general public welfare and security each local Jewish community was completely autonomous, but if a community violated religious law, another community or outside religious authority could hold it accountable.

An additional sign of new communal development occurred in 1084, when some of the Mainz Jews moved to Speyer, where they were welcomed by Bishop Rüdiger, who issued them a formal charter. Modeled on the early Carolingian *privilegia,* this charter extended to the new community guarantees of life, religious protection, and exemption from tolls. Confirmed by the German emperor Henry IV in 1090, this continued the Carolingian policy of royal or imperial legal protection of European Jews until the late thirteenth century. The patterns of royal protection and local Jewish self-rule that had first developed in the German towns became the model for local Jewish communities in the regions of royal France, England, and central Europe.

Developments in the High Middle Ages. The late eleventh and twelfth centuries were a time of social and cultural consolidation in northern Europe. New religious orders were founded; the popes renewed the claims of canon law to establish the primacy of the church over the empire in spiritual and even temporal affairs; and in Paris the university attracted students who eagerly came from all over Europe to sit at the feet of popular scholars like Peter Abelard. It is possible that the Christian Schoolmen were in part motivated to restate Christian doctrine in a clear and logically consistent way because Jews were raising doubts about Christianity in the minds of Christian townsmen. In return, an awareness of Christian religious innovation and ferment stimulated reappraisals of Judaism.

The First Crusade precipitated the first major crisis of Jewish cultural identity in northern Europe. Urban II's call for an armed pilgrimage to Jerusalem in the spring of 1095 led local German peasants and petty knights on their way to the Holy Land to riot in the towns of Mainz, Worms, Cologne, and Speyer. According to the Latin and Hebrew chronicles that recount what happened on this Peasants' Crusade, just before and during the Jewish holiday of Shavu'ot in the spring of 1096, the righteous Jews of Mainz and Worms ritually slaughtered their families and themselves in order to prevent the Christian rioters from forcibly baptizing or killing them. The victims included leaders of the rabbinical elites of Mainz and Worms as well as hundreds of innocent men, women, and children.

Many Jews escaped or were subjected to baptism by

force, but the survivors' guilt only heightened the loss of the saintly martyrs, whose memory now cast a shadow over the following generations of German Jews. Among the liturgical memorials they instituted in Europe was the earlier geonic prohibition of celebrating Jewish weddings between Passover and Shavu'ot, still observed as an annual period of collective mourning. New prayers were written to recall the righteousness of the slain and to invoke God's vengeance on the guilty Christians. Each spring the martyrs' names were recited in the Rhenish synagogues in order to keep alive the memory of the sacrificed dead and to invoke their merit as a form of vicarious atonement for the living.

Two other important northern Jewish ideals emerged in the twelfth century; the first of these was the *ḥasid,* or pietist. By the second half of the twelfth century, an ascetic, pietistic movement emerged in Speyer, the one Jewish community that did not suffer major losses in 1096. It was led by descendants of the branch of the Qalonimos family that survived the riots of 1096. The pietists placed special emphasis not only on punctilious observance of Jewish law but also on certain spiritual exercises including concentrated prayer, physical self-denial, and the mystical and magical manipulations of Hebrew letter combinations that represent the secret names of God. One of the mottos of Shemu'el ben Qalonimos the Elder (fl. mid-twelfth century) is "be resourceful in the fear of God," a Talmudic dictum (B.T., *Ber.* 17a) that he reinterpreted to mean that the pietist, or truly God-fearing Jew, must search scripture resourcefully in order to infer additional prohibitions and higher degrees of self-discipline.

In *Sefer ḥasidim* (Book of the Pietists), written by Shemu'el's son Yehudah the Pietist (d. 1217), we find a sectarian fellowship of pietists, led by their own sages, who are constantly challenged and tested by their inner passions and by the harmful presence of nonpietistic Jews, whom the author calls "the wicked." Among Yehudah's innovations is the requirement that pietists who sin should confess their sins to a sage and receive penances proportional to the sinful act and to the pleasure experienced while sinning. [*For further discussion of the pietists, see* Ashkenazic Hasidism.]

This new Jewish pietistic ideal, incorporating ancient Jewish mystical and ascetic practices, began as a regimen for religious virtuosos but became a commonplace of European Jewish spirituality after the late twelfth century and continued to define the dominant style of Jewish piety in eastern Europe even after it was challenged by the eighteenth-century revival movement of Hasidism.

The second new mode of Jewish spirituality that developed in the twelfth century in northern France was the Talmud scholar who excelled in intellectual prowess by discovering new interpretations of difficult passages. At the very time that Christian Schoolmen were reconciling the logical inconsistencies in authoritative theological texts and scholars of canon and Roman law were resolving contradictions by making new distinctions, rabbinical scholars began to study systematically the entire Talmudic corpus and apply canons of logical consistency to it. This activity developed in northern France and not in the Rhineland for two reasons. On the negative side, the older academies of Mainz and Worms suffered a loss of leadership in the riots of 1096. On the positive side, the newer schools in Champagne were able to build on the foundations in Hebrew Bible and Talmud interpretation established by the late-eleventh-century rabbinic master Rashi (Shelomoh ben Yitsḥaq, 1042–1105).

In the duchy of Champagne, another Jewish frontier, the master of Troyes taught generations of students who were geographically and culturally removed from the living oral culture of rabbinic studies in Mainz and Worms. For them Rashi produced the first comprehensive running commentary on almost the entire Hebrew Bible and the Babylonian Talmud, the canon of the Ashkenazic curriculum. Because of his extraordinary sensitivity to the biblical usage of language and his knowledge of the Talmudic corpus, he succeeded in providing the one gloss to both the Hebrew Bible and the Babylonian Talmud that has remained standard for all students of those texts to this day.

The next generation's scholars, who glossed Rashi's commentary *(ba'alei ha-tosafot),* introduced a synoptic method of dialectical study designed to discover and resolve potential contradictions among different parts of the Talmud and between the Talmud and Jewish life in Christian Europe. [*See* Tosafot.] The shift from the piecemeal to the synoptic study of the Talmud resulted in an expansion of the scope and detail of Jewish law. The new distinctions that resolved contradictions between divergent traditions added conceptual subtlety to categories of law that had been created for a Mediterranean society. Adjustments were also made to accommodate the Talmudic traditions, a product of ancient pagan and medieval Muslim societies, to the actual practices of the Jews living in Latin Christendom.

The Judaism that resulted from these encounters with Christian Europe in the twelfth century was more complex than the relatively homogeneous religious culture of the eleventh. The righteous self-image, the reverence of the dead martyrs, German Hasidism, and the scholasticism of the tosafists were part of a twelfth-century transformation of classical Judaism into a "traditional" Ashkenazic Judaism. Paralleling these developments were the creative philosophical synthesis of Moses Maimonides (d. 1204) in Egypt and the writing down for the first time of qabbalistic mystical traditions in southern France. [*See* Qabbalah.]

Expulsion and Resettlement in the Later Middle Ages. The pattern of royal support in return for Jewish economic usefulness appears in England in the twelfth century. Henry I (r. 1100–1135) issued a charter, no longer extant, similar to the continental ones, offering the Jews protection of life and toll exemptions backed by royal justice. Henry II (r. 1154–1189) extended Jewish privileges to include self-government under Jewish law. By this time, sizable Jewish communities existed not only in London but also in Norwich, Lincoln, and Oxford.

In addition to obtaining funds on demand from the community, the English kings turned to especially wealthy Jews, such as Aharon of Lincoln, for major loans. When Aharon died, in 1185, he had outstanding loans of fifteen thousand pounds, three quarters of the annual receipts of the royal exchequer. To protect the safety of these financial records, Jewish and Christian officials were appointed to see to it that duplicate copies of loans were drawn up and deposited in chests *(archae)*. By 1200 the office of exchequer of the Jews was filled entirely by Christians, called the justices of the Jews. Another centralized official of the end of the twelfth century was the *presbyter Judaeorum*, not a chief rabbi but a wealthy Jew appointed by the king to serve as the liaison between the court and the Jewish community.

Jewish money lending at immoderate interest, or usury, became a major factor in the decline of the Jewish communities in England and France in the thirteenth century. Although papal policy condoned Jewish lending at moderate rates of interest, canon lawyers opposed it absolutely, and in the late thirteenth century the English and French kings implemented policies based on the stricter position. These measures against usury were neither economically nor politically motivated; rather, they were successful royal efforts at spiritual reform undertaken at a time of waning papal authority.

In royal France, money lending with interest was made illegal in 1230. To support his crusade, Louis IX (r. 1226–1270) confiscated Jewish loans, as provided by the Council of Lyon (1245), expelled only Jewish usurers from France in 1248/9, and confiscated their property. In England, Edward I (r. 1272–1307) issued his Statute on the Jews (1275), which outlawed Jewish lending completely, and in 1290 the Jews were expelled from his kingdom. Philip the Fair (r. 1285–1314) expelled the Jews of royal France in 1306.

Whereas royal policy toward the Jews shifted from support in the period of settlement to antagonism in the late thirteenth century, papal policy remained relatively constant and supportive. But when heretical movements posed a threat to the church itself, measures adopted to fight heresy sometimes were directed against the Jewish infidel as well. Thus papal approval of the new urban reforming orders of the Franciscans and, especially, the Dominicans as disciplinary arms of the church in the early thirteenth century created a source of new pressure against Jewish distinctiveness. Individual friars, sometimes zealous apostates from Judaism, actively sought to persuade Jews to convert.

At the same time that the Jewish communities were eliminated in England and royal France in the late thirteenth and fourteenth centuries, organized Jewish life in the north shifted increasingly eastward to the politically fragmented German empire, the central European territories of Bohemia, Moravia, and Hungary, and Poland and Lithuania. The thirteenth and early fourteenth centuries were a time of continuous demographic expansion in Europe, and the Jewish communities in central and eastern Europe were augmented by natural increase and new immigration from the West.

The major turning point for central European Jewry was the Black Death of 1349, a trauma that reduced the population of some areas of Europe by as much as 50 percent. Unable to explain a catastrophe of such magnitude, the popular mind personalized the agents of destruction by blaming the Jews for poisoning the wells of Europe. Aside from being subject now to unpredictable waves of violence, whole Jewish communities were routinely expelled. The theme of death began to play an increased liturgical role in the religious sensibilities of Ashkenazic Judaism. In particular, the annual anniversary of a parent's death (Yi., *yahrzeit*) is first attested at the end of the fourteenth century. The regular recitation by mourners of the Qaddish prayer also seems to have begun around the fourteenth century, in this period of increased Jewish martyrdom and random violence.

As a gradual demographic and economic recovery slowly began, Jews were readmitted for specified periods into towns of early settlement, like Speyer, and into newer Jewish communities in Austria and Bohemia. The decline of imperial authority over and protection of the Jews is reflected in the growing influence of the Christian burghers, who reserved the right to expel "their" Jews at will. The elimination of effective royal protection added to the Jewish communities' increased political vulnerability in the later Middle Ages in the West.

In the late fourteenth and fifteenth centuries, Jewish legal authorities generally lost prestige and control in their communities. No intercommunal councils were established in the German empire after 1350, and local rabbis complained that the wealthy members of the community ignored them. To be sure, masters like Mosheh Mintz and Yisra'el Isserlein of Austria continued in the fifteenth century to exert their authority as great sages of the age, as had Gershom in the late tenth, but the influence of local rabbis declined after 1350.

Politically the proliferation of independent principalities and cities in the German empire constituted a safety valve for the Jews there. Whenever residents of one particular community were expelled, they could find refuge in another until the edict was rescinded. But as economic instability reduced the demand for Jewish money lending in the towns, some Jews began to settle in villages and on rural estates. Gradually they entered new occupations as agricultural merchants and middlemen. The decline in economic opportunities in the empire also led many Jews to join the eastward emigration of German Christian burghers attracted by new opportunities in Poland and Lithuania, still another frontier.

Although Jews had been settling gradually in the duchies of Poland and Lithuania for some time, official recognition of their communities appeared only in the thirteenth century. In 1264, Prince Bolesław granted the Jews of Great Poland a charter modeled on those issued by Frederick II, duke of Austria, in 1244; Béla IV, king of Hungary, in 1251; and Otakar II, king of Bohemia and Moravia, in 1254. Unlike the Carolingian-type charters issued to Jewish merchants from the ninth through twelfth centuries, these were designed for Jews whose primary occupation was money lending. But like the earlier ones, the Polish charters provided for Jewish self-government and royal protection. In 1364, Casimir III (r. 1133–1170) issued a confirmation of these regional charters that was valid in the unified kingdom of Poland. Some Jews served the kings or dukes as money lenders and bankers; others managed estates forfeited to them for bad debts, lived in towns that the nobles founded, or farmed tolls. Jews were also prominent in the export trade of agricultural products to the German empire and the Crimea.

The Jews who migrated to Poland from Germany, Austria, and Bohemia brought along their familiar forms of communal government. The frontier model applies to Poland as it had before to the first settlements in western Europe, but with one important difference. The eastern immigrants could rely on support and spiritual guidance from their former homeland in the German empire.

The arrival of Ya'aqov Polak in Cracow, where he opened his innovative Talmudic academy, marks the beginning of advanced Jewish religious study in Poland and with it the first condition for cultural independence from the West. In 1503, Alexander I (r. 1501–1506) appointed him rabbi of Jewry there. Symbolically, a new era of centralized Jewish self-government and cultural ferment was about to begin.

[*Major developments in European Judaism of this period are discussed further in* Halakhah; Rabbinate; Polemics, *article on* Jewish-Christian Polemics; *and* Jewish Thought and Philosophy, *article on* Premodern Philosophy. *See also the biographies of the major historical figures mentioned herein.*]

BIBLIOGRAPHY

Detailed critical discussions of the rich bibliography on this period can be found in my "The Jews in Western Europe: Fourth to Sixteenth Century" and Kenneth R. Stow's "The Church and the Jews: From St. Paul to Paul IV," both in *Bibliographical Essays in Medieval Jewish Studies* (New York, 1976).

Despite its tendency to emphasize Jewish persecution in the Diaspora, parts of chapters 25–41 in *A History of the Jewish People*, edited by H. H. Ben-Sasson (Cambridge, Mass., 1969), contain important discussions of medieval Jewish communal life and also refer to many of the primary sources. On the Jewish communities of England, one still must turn to Cecil Roth's *A History of the Jews in England*, 3d ed. (Oxford, 1964), chaps. 1–5, and the more solid study by H. G. Richardson, *The English Jewry under Angevin Kings* (London, 1960). On northern France, Louis Rabinowitz's *The Social Life of the Jews of Northern France in the Twelfth to Fourteenth Centuries*, 2d ed. (New York, 1972), and Robert Chazan's *Medieval Jewry in Northern France* (Baltimore, 1973) should be supplemented by the pertinent studies of Gavin Langmuir, such as "'Judei Nostri' and the Beginnings of Capetian Legislation," *Traditio* 19 (1963): 183–244, and William Chester Jordan, such as "Jews on Top," *Journal of Jewish Studies* 29 (Spring 1978): 39–56. A synthetic scholarly treatment of German Jewry still does not exist but readers may consult with profit Guido Kisch's *The Jews in Medieval Germany*, 2d ed. (New York, 1970). Important trends in the early years of the European Jewish community are discussed by Avraham Grossman in "On 'The Early Sages of Ashkenaz'," *Immanuel* 15 (Winter 1982–1983): 73–81, a summary of his book *Ḥakhmei Ashkenaz ha-ri'shonim* (Jerusalem, 1981).

The history and institutions of the medieval Jewish community are treated in depth in Salo W. Baron's *The Jewish Community*, 3 vols. (1942; reprint, Westport, Conn., 1972), which is out of date in some areas. On the major intellectual and religious trends discussed above, see Haym Soloveitchik's "Three Themes in the *Sefer Hasidim*," *AJS Review* 1 (1976): 311–357, especially on the influence of the Tosafists, and my book *Piety and Society: The Jewish Pietists of Medieval Germany* (Leiden, 1981) on German (Ashkenazic) Hasidism.

Two important studies on the deterioration of Jewish life in the thirteenth century are Kenneth R. Stow's "Papal and Royal Attitudes toward Jewish Lending in the Thirteenth Century,"

AJS Review 6 (1981): 161–184, and Jeremy Cohen's *The Friars and the Jews* (Ithaca, N.Y., 1982).

For Jewish life in central Europe during the late Middle Ages, see Shlomo Eidelberg's *Jewish Life in Austria in the Fifteenth Century* (Philadelphia, 1962) and Eric Zimmer's *Harmony and Discord* (New York, 1970). A basic work on eastern European Jewry that deals with the early period is Bernard D. Weinryb's *The Jews of Poland* (Philadelphia, 1972).

Ivan G. Marcus

Judaism in Northern and Eastern Europe since 1500

As a result of a series of Jewish expulsions and of Poland's increasing economic attractiveness, in the sixteenth-century Ashkenazic world Poland was widely recognized as the most promising of the European communities.

Poland and Lithuania. The expulsion of Jews from numerous German cities and secular principalities and from much of Bohemia and Moravia, coupled with the final division of Hungary (previously relatively hospitable to Jews) into Habsburg, Ottoman, and Transylvanian sections, encouraged Jews to look eastward. Poland's rapid commercial expansion, the relative weakness until the late sixteenth century of its craft and trade guilds, and the religious toleration that characterized crown policy reinforced these migratory trends. Jewish adjustment to the new surroundings was eased because of German influences in the cities, which (despite the rapid polonization of the German immigrants) may have encouraged the retention by Jews of Yiddish. Greater occupational diversity was possible here than in Germany. Most Polish Jews worked in domestic trade, moneylending, and artisanry but some Jews also captured important roles in the trade between Constantinople and western and central Europe and in the export of Polish textiles, grains, and cattle. Others acquired the leases over minting and other crucial fiscal and administrative functions.

The increasing impact and militancy of the Roman Catholic church in the wake of the Counter-Reformation and the rising antagonism of burghers toward Jews led to the partial expulsion of Jews from about fifty Polish cities by the end of the sixteenth century. Rarely were they completely barred; most often they were forced to move to suburban enclaves or to the *jurydyki* within the municipal boundaries but under the jurisdiction of the nobility. Jews continued to live in the same neighborhoods with Catholics in the cities where they were freely permitted to reside. However, the introduction of clauses permitting *non tolerandis Judaeis* and the effective unification of Poland and Lithuania with the Union of Lublin in 1569 encouraged Jewish migration to the southeastern Ukrainian expanses of Lithuania.

The *pacta conventa* of 1573, which confirmed the gentry's accumulation of considerable power at the expense of the crown, cemented close relations between the upper *szlachta* ("the magnates") and the Jews. The magnates frequently favored Jews as their commercial agents and lessees. Commerce, artisanry, and, in the southeastern regions, leaseholding (often tied to trade in agricultural goods) became the most common Jewish occupations. By the middle of the seventeenth century—when the Jewish community of Poland and Lithuania numbered, according to varying estimates, somewhere between 250,000 and 450,000—nearly 40 percent of the Jews lived, according to Samuel Ettinger, in the Ukrainian area.

Jewish participation in the Polish nobility's colonization of the Ukraine involved Jews in a system of pledges where Jewish lenders received a part of the income from estates pending the repayment of loans. What evolved was a more direct system of leaseholding, called the *arenda,* in which Jews leased agricultural properties from the nobility, generally for a period of three years, at a designated price. Profits would be extracted from taxes and fees on the local peasantry. The acquisition of a lease frequently constituted the beginning of a new Jewish community, since lessees would encourage other Jews to settle with them to run inns, flour mills, and so forth. Poland's rapidly growing population required ever-increasing supplies of agricultural and meat products, and the colonization of the Ukraine—in which Jews played an important and visible role—ensured a steady supply to domestic (and foreign) markets.

Jewish communal autonomy in Poland. A highly ramified system of Polish-Jewish autonomy with a centralized consultative council was created as Jews settled in Poland in large numbers. It was the product of several factors, including the Jewish community's wide geographic dispersion, the example of Jewish communal institutions in Bohemia and Moravia, pressures from the crown for a centralized Jewish leadership, and the diminishing power of the king, which motivated many sectors of Polish society to claim a measure of self-government. On the bottom tier of Jewry's system were the *qehalim,* or Jewish communal councils, which functioned alongside and were structured similar to the municipal councils of Polish cities. Above them were the district councils composed of representatives from the *qehalim.* At the uppermost tier were the super-councils, which met, beginning in 1569 and perhaps even earlier, at the fairs of Lublin and less frequently at Jaroslaw. Representatives from all parts of Poland and Lithuania participated in these meetings of the Council of the Lands of Poland (until a separate Lithuanian council was established, for fiscal reasons, in 1623), where *taqqanot* ("regulations") were issued, individual and communal grievances were aired, and protests against *qehalim* were reviewed. The Council deliberated on halakhic matters and, perhaps most important, intervened on behalf of the community before the authorities. From the vantage point of the state, the Polish Council was a tax-farming body but even the state recognized, at least tacitly, the Council's more extensive functions.

Talmudic study in Poland and Lithuania. At the same time, the challenge posed by the distinguished Talmudist Mosheh Isserles of Cracow (1520–1572) in numerous works, particularly his *Darkhei Mosheh* to the Sefardic codification of Jewish law, the *Beit Yosef* of Yosef Karo, consolidated Poland's standing as the preeminent center of Ashkenazic learning. Isserles promoted the legitimacy of Polish-Jewish customs along with a rationalist-mystical understanding of *mitsvot.* The rich rabbinical literature of the period—which, in addition to Isserles, was represented by Shelomoh Luria, Yom Ṭov Lippman Heller, and many other Talmudic masters—was efficiently disseminated by the rapid expansion of printing in the sixteenth century.

Pilpul, a casuistic method based, in Poland, on the application of principles of logical differentiation to reconcile apparent Talmudic contradictions, was the focus of much of the *yeshivah* curriculum. This method was increasingly criticized beginning in the fifteenth century for its alleged obfuscation of the plain meaning of the texts. But it only declined in importance and was supplanted by an alternative pedagogical system in the early nineteenth century. Polish Jewry's wealth helped promote the spread of *yeshivah* study, but Polish-Jewish moralists, preeminently the late-sixteenth-century preacher Efrayim Luntshitz, argued that wealth was a certain sign of corruption and hypocrisy. By the seventeenth century the study of Torah was widely disseminated in Poland and Lithuania—though the Ukraine still provided fewer opportunities for serious study than more settled regions of eastern Europe. [*See* Yeshivah.]

The Khmel'nitskii uprising. Religious, economic, and ethnic tensions in the Ukraine erupted in 1648, and for the next twelve years the Polish state was faced with a series of Cossack uprisings (initially with Tartar support) and with invasions from Sweden and Muscovy. The Cossacks, led by Bogdan Khmel'nitskii, massacred rural and urban Jewish communities on both sides of the Dnieper river. Hatred of Jews—which had little influence in sparking the Deluge (as both Polish and Jewish accounts refer to it)—resulted nonetheless in the killing of large numbers of Ukrainian Jews and in the evacuation of nearly all the remainder. The Jews of Ukraine quickly rebuilt their communities after the uprising was put down, but it left its mark on the increasingly deleterious fiscal standing of the *qehalim* and the councils.

Movement Westward. A westward trend in Jewish migratory patterns was now apparent. In particular, Jews from areas of Poland devastated by the Swedish invasion moved in large numbers to Silesia, Moravia, and elsewhere in central Europe. (To be sure, Germany had retained Jewish communities in the intervening period, despite the widespread expulsions, particularly in areas under imperial and ecclesiastical protection and in the central and southern parts of the Holy Roman Empire.) Small numbers of Polish Jews also found their way in this period to Amsterdam and London. Some joined the growing ranks of the central European *Betteljuden* or *Schnorrjuden* (Jewish beggars), but most were absorbed, if only marginally, into the economic life of the Empire, which offered greater opportunities for Jews after the Thirty Years' War.

The skill of Jewish agents and contractors during the war and the rise of absolutist and mercantilist tendencies in government policy helped improve the economic and even the social standing of German Jewry. Jews moved into new localities (especially noteworthy were the Sefardic settlement in Hamburg and the Ashkenazic enclave in suburban Altona) and, with the support of rulers, were permitted to participate in an increasingly wide range of occupations, particularly commerce. German princes, concerned about competition from Atlantic ports better able to trade with the New World, saw wealthy Jews as useful commercial allies. Central European armies had benefited from Jewish contacts with Poland during the Thirty Years' War, and the experience (and wealth) gained by some Jews in this period helped contribute to the eventual emergence of court Jews who served local princes.

Humanist appreciation for Hebrew and the gradual laicization of European culture that accompanied the appearance of humanism in the fifteenth and sixteenth centuries set the stage for some cultural collaboration between Jews and Christians. In the Ashkenazic world, the influence of humanist trends was most clearly reflected in a moderation of anti-Jewish sentiment in certain small but influential intellectual circles. In Johannes Reuchlin's (1455–1522) defense of the Jews against the anti-Talmudic charges of Johannes Pfefferkorn, for instance, he referred to Jews and Christians as "fellow citizens of the same Roman Empire [who] live on the basis of the same law of citizenship and internal peace." The religious wars, which culminated in treaties which acknowledged that religious toleration—at least toward other Christians—was essential if only to save Europe from ceaseless strife, led to arguments for tolerance. More important in this regard, however, were the Protestant sects, most of them marginal, which began to question the connection between religious truth and political rule and showed an often intense interest in the biblical constitution and an attachment to the people and language of the Bible. Such trends were most apparent in Cromwellian England, where the impact of the Judaizers, the growing appreciation for Hebrew, the spread of millenarianist sentiment, and the renewed search for the Ten Lost Tribes with the discovery of the New World created a suitable cultural climate for a receptiveness to Menasseh ben Israel's mission to promote Jewish readmission to England.

Around the time of the Whitehall conference of 1655, which considered the readmission of Jews to England but left the matter undecided, small numbers of New Christians as well as Ashkenazic Jews settled in England, mostly in London. This small community came from Amsterdam, where an increasingly sizable and economically prominent Jewish community had lived since the unification of the northern provinces of the Netherlands and their declaration that the new state would be free from religious persecution.

Within the Ashkenazic sphere, Jewish thought remained largely indifferent to indications (however uneven and contradictory) of changes in Christian attitudes toward Jews. Indeed, a renewed sense of cultural segregation, as Jacob Katz (1961) has characterized it, was apparent in the sixteenth and seventeenth centuries, as reflected in a complete lack of Jewish interest in anti-Christian polemics and in the formation of a set of Jewish attitudes toward non-Jews that saw differences between the two as inherent rather than doctrinal. This case was argued most coherently by Yehudah Löw ben Betsal'el (c. 1525–1609). Yet the same period saw the promulgation of important halakhic decisions that permitted Jews to trade in gentile wine and even in rosaries (in contrast to earlier rabbinic prohibitions against such trade) on the grounds that the Talmudic prohibitions against trade with idol worshipers were not relevant to Christians, who, at least for practical purposes, did not fall under this category.

A stratum of well-placed Jews had, since the religious wars, played a significant role in the centralizing administrations of the absolutist German states. Jewish moneylenders, minters, and agents were selected to perform important administrative, fiscal, and even diplomatic functions because their loyalty to the princes was unaffected by guild attachments or local enmities. Close links were forged between Polish-Jewish agricultural exporters and wealthy Jewish importers in Leipzig, Frankfurt, and Hamburg. Court Jews, as some of these magnates were called, emerged as a group relatively free from Jewish communal and rabbinical control and with independent access to the gentile authorities.

The wealth of the court Jews, their relatively easy access to the Christian elite, and the example of the acculturated Sefardim of Hamburg and elsewhere in central and western Europe encouraged some Ashkenazim to imitate Sefardic and even non-Jewish social patterns. In certain well-to-do German-Jewish circles in the early eighteenth century, dance lessons, the study of French, and even the cutting of beards was common. In the same circles, Polish Jews were frequently characterized as superstitious and culturally inferior.

However, until the late eighteenth century and the spread of the Enlightenment and emancipatory movements, distinctions between German and Polish Jews remained fluid. This essential fluidity was reflected, for instance, in the careers of Ya'aqov Emden and Yonatan Eibschutz, the eminent rabbinic figures at the center of the most vociferous Jewish polemical battle of the eighteenth century, which spanned the major Jewish communities of eastern and central Europe. Cultural unity was also apparent in the response of Ashkenazic Jewry in the 1660s to the news of Shabbetai Tsevi, whose claim to be the Messiah was received with the greatest enthusiasm by Sefardim but who was supported, according to Gershom Scholem, by most of European Jewry. [*See* Shabbetai Tsevi.]

Shabbetai Tsevi's conversion to Islam in 1666 led to the disintegration of the movement and to its rebirth, on a much smaller scale, as a secret network of sects. In Podolia, where the Frankist movement arose out of this Shabbatean network in the second half of the eighteenth century, it attracted the support of only small numbers of Jews, and its leader, Ya'aqov Frank (1726–1791), along with about six hundred followers, eventually converted under some duress to Catholicism. The teachings of Ya'aqov Frank, which combined an eclectic reliance on Qabbalah and an intense fascination with worldly power, had a limited impact outside Poland when Frank moved to Brno, Offenbach, and elsewhere in central Europe in the last years of his life. The sect served as a syncretistic pathway for some poor as well as rich Jews to a less insular, larger world.

Hasidism. In contrast to Frankism, the Hasidic movement, which also arose in Podolia, gradually spread beyond the Ukraine after the death of its founder Yisra'el ben Eli'ezer (1700–1760), known as the Besht, and won widespread support in Poland, Belorussia, and, to a more limited extent, Lithuania. Completely devoid of the Christological tendencies that would attract some acculturated Jews to Frankism, Hasidism embraced qabbalistic concepts and built on Jewish spiritual yearnings stirred by the heretical mystical movements. At the same time, it effectively neutralized the potentially subversive elements of Lurianic Qabbalah.

The concept of *devequt* (cleaving to God), for instance, was shorn by Hasidism of its cosmic and elitist features and placed within a mundane framework. Hasidism promoted a strategy whereby Jews might focus on the prosaic and even the patently profane in order to transform and elevate them. Cosmic elements in Lurianic Qabbalah were transformed into individualized landmarks in the psychology of faith and repentance.

Hasidism's moderation helped it eventually gain the acceptance of rabbis sympathetic to mysticism. Its halakhic innovations were minor: the introduction of a sharper knife for ritual slaughter (perhaps to capture Hasidic control over a crucial communal sphere) and some liturgical changes, such as use of the Lurianic liturgy and a less punctilious attitude toward the traditionally designated times for prayer. Moreover, though Hasidism has come to represent for some modern interpreters a democratized form of Judaism, it promoted no concrete social program and, indeed, did not attract the support of the urban artisans who constituted at the time the severest critics of Jewish communal authority. Among its most ardent and earliest supporters were rural Jews, particularly arendators, who were unhappy with the inability of the *qehalim* to defend their traditional right of *ḥazaqah* (protection from competition) and whose interests were frequently protected by the Ḥasidim. In this respect communal decline helped to fuel the movement, and it is unlikely that it would have spread as quickly or widely—by 1800 close to one half of the Jews of east Europe flocked to its banner—had the Polish and Lithuanian councils not been abolished by the state in 1764. When challenged, for instance, by a charismatic spokesman of the communal elite, as in Lithuania by Eliyyahu ben Shelomoh Zalman, known as the Gaon of Vilna (1720–1797), Hasidism's momentum was temporarily checked.

Rather than introducing a new egalitarian note into Jewish religious life, Hasidism's most influential innovation was the promotion of a new elite that differed from both the traditional rabbinic scholars and the qabbalistic ascetics. The Hasidic *tsaddiq* forged a link between the qabbalistic master and the Jewish masses by emphasizing his communal responsibilities (in contradistinction to the asceticism of the qabbalist). The eighteenth century witnessed a marked decline in rabbinical stature. Jewish popular sentiment, rather than feeling alienated from the rabbis because of their self-imposed scholastic isolation, criticized them for their inability to live up to their own austere and still widely accepted standards.

Haskalah. The German-speaking lands produced at the same time a westernized, acculturated elite. It was shaped by the emphasis of enlightened absolutists on the state as a secular rather than a Christian polity; the compulsory education system introduced (briefly) into Austria; the Enlightenment's vision of a neutral society where religious distinctions were rendered irrelevant or, at least, subordinate to other considerations; and the French Revolution, which emancipated the Jews of France in 1791. Most central European Jews, particularly after the Polish partitions (1772–1795) when Galicia was absorbed by Austria and east Poznań was added to Prussia, were Yiddish-speaking and religiously traditional and remained so until the mid-nineteenth century. But the self-consciously "enlightened" elite that emerged emphasized the sensualist rather than the divine source of knowledge, the ultimate importance of earthly existence, and a revised understanding of the relationship between religion and state. As the leading German-Jewish Enlightenment figure, Moses Mendelssohn (1729–1786) argued that Judaism was able (better than Christianity) to fit into a new order constructed on the basis of natural truth, rationalism, and a clear distinction between the functions and tools of church and state.

Russian Jewry. The Prussian state did not repudiate Jewish autonomy as anticipated by Mendelssohn, but in Austria, France, and even, if somewhat ambiguously, in Russia, the unity of Jewish society had to be maintained despite the lack of support and even the hostility of the government. Russia had prohibited Jewish settlement before the Polish partitions but it absorbed in the late eighteenth century approximately eight hundred thousand Jews. The regime was unwilling, and perhaps unable, to integrate Jews into the existing estates, disinclined to believe that Jewish assimilation was possible, and suspicious of the potentially deleterious impact that the Jews might have on the Russian peasantry. The result was the creation of a large area in which Jews were permitted to live, called the Pale of Settlement, in the fifteen provinces of Lithuania, Belorussia, the Ukraine, and so-called New Russia (on the northern littoral of the Black and Azov seas). Jews were also allowed to live in the ten provinces of central Poland, although these were formally excluded from the Pale. Jews constitued an average of 12 percent of the total population in this area of west and southwestern Russia (and often the majority of the urban population) by the late nineteenth century. The classification of Jews as *inorodtsy* (in 1835), the legal category created for the semi-autonomous primitive and nomadic tribes at the periphery of the empire, highlighted their essentially anomalous status in Russian law, since the regime abolished the *qehalim* soon afterward, in 1844. Indeed, despite intermittent governmental attempts to assimilate Russia's Jews, the regime continued to share an abiding preoccupation (sometimes more and sometimes less acute) with their irredeemable separateness.

There was little intervention by the Russian state into the communal life of the Jews until the 1840s. Even after the *qahal* was abolished, a separate Jewish judiciary continued to function and many of the duties of the *qahal* were subsumed by other representative Jewish bodies (though Jewish autonomy was now checked by municipal supervision). The Russian Jewish community grew rapidly over the course of the century and by 1880 numbered four million; it increased in size to more than five million in 1897 despite the mass migration to the west in the same period. Rapid demographic increase, the legal discrimination suffered by Russian Jewry, and the sluggishness of those sectors of the Russian economy in which most Jews were employed contributed to the eventual politicization of the community and to its migratory trends in the late nineteenth and early twentieth centuries. At the turn of the twentieth century, more than 40 percent of the world's fourteen million Jews lived in the Russian empire; 7.5 million Jews lived in eastern Europe as a whole, including Galicia and east Prussia.

Rapid urbanization and economic change in the nineteenth century challenged the foundations of Russian Jewish social and economic life. Repeated expulsions from villages, moves against rural Jewish innkeepers, and the concentration of the liquor trade (which employed about 30 percent of prepartition Polish Jewry) in the hands of a small number of wealthy contractors contributed to the community's urbanization. Petty trade, on the other hand, was undermined by the decline of fairs, the rise of permanent markets, and the government's war on smuggling. Eventually the construction of railway lines destabilized previously crucial commercial and banking centers which were bypassed by the railroad. The decline of the commercial sector led to an overcrowding in others, such as artisanry, where Jews tended to concentrate in the garment trade and in shoemaking.

At the same time, improved transportation, renewed efforts at the exploitation of the agriculturally rich Ukrainian steppe, and the construction of major grain exporting ports (the most important being Odessa) where Jews played prominent economic roles all produced a stratum of successful Jewish entrepreneurs and merchants. Jews made substantial contributions to industrial manufacturing (particularly in Bialystok and Łódź), to the sugar trade (where Jews revolutionized marketing techniques), and the construction of railways. By 1851, 20 percent of the members of Russia's wealthiest merchant guild were Jews, though they constituted only about two or three percent of the total Russian population.

Jewish communal authority. In the absence of a state-recognized body that represented Russian Jewry (except for the infrequent, government-convened delegations of Jewish deputies and later the tepid rabbinical commissions), considerable pressure and responsibility was placed in the hands of *qehalim* and private associations. The authority of the *qehalim* was undermined by the 1827 statute which instituted the conscription of Jews and which placed responsibility for the draft in the hands of local *qahal* officials. This led to widespread abuse: the exemption of the rich, the forced conscription of the poor, the drafting of boys of twelve and younger who were subjected, once they were drafted and handed over to the military, to intense pressure to convert to Russian Orthodoxy. Protests by Jews against the *qahal* oligarchy erupted in Podolia, Minsk, Mogilev, and elsewhere, and the rabbinical elite—whose *yeshivah* students were protected by communal officials from the draft—mostly remained silent in the face of these abuses, which further eroded their popular stature.

Russian Haskalah. Nineteenth-century Russian Jewry nonetheless retained a traditional profile. There was little scope in Russia for acculturation; the multiethnic character of the empire mitigated assimilation; and anti-Jewish sentiment remained pervasive among liberals and conservatives alike. Yet the introduction by the state in the 1840s and 1850s of a network of schools where secular as well as Jewish subjects were taught, the liberalization of government policy (and the emancipation of the serfs) under Alexander II (1855–1881) which excited Jewish hopes, and the example of an acculturating western and central European Jewry helped create a Russian Haskalah, or Jewish enlightenment movement. Haskalah stressed those aspects of Jewish life that non-Jews presumably considered positive: the purity of biblical Hebrew, the stability of Jewish family life, the Jews' financial aptitude, their agricultural past, and Judaism's philosophical legacy. On the other hand, the movement denounced aspects of contemporary Jewish life at variance with the beliefs of the larger society (and presumably with the true character of Judaism), such as mystical speculation, disdain for secular study, and ignorance of the vernacular.

In contrast to the exponents of the German-Jewish enlightenment in the decades after Moses Mendelssohn's death, Russian *maskilim* (Jews who subscribed to the goals of the Haskalah) hoped to see Jewry rendered acceptable to its neighbors without relinquishing its distinctive social or religious character. In their view, Judaism was to be purified but not entirely stripped of its idiosyncratic tendencies. The Haskalah movement gave rise to efforts to promote a secular Hebrew literature and periodical press and new types of philanthropic and self-help institutions, and it later had a decisive impact on Jewish nationalist and socialist movements. Its promotion of secular study also helped contribute (especially after the 1870s) to the precipitous rise in the number of Jews enrolled in Russian and secular Jewish schools.

Musar. The Musar movement was one response to modernizing trends within the traditional camp. It stressed self-discipline (an echo of the highly influential system of Eliyyahu ben Shelomoh Zalman, which saw the prodigious study of Torah as taking precedence even over the performance of *mitsvot*) but Musar's founder, Yisra'el Salanter (1810–1883), promoted a pedagogical system in which communal meditation and introspection were integrated into the traditional Talmudic curriculum. At the same time, a series of relatively well-funded and prestigious *yeshivot* were established in Lithuania to counter the inroads made by the Haskalah and secular education. Charismatic rabbinic figures, perhaps most prominently Yisra'el Me'ir Kagan (known as the Ḥafets Ḥayyim, 1838–1933), continued to represent the community's highest ideals in their personal piety, humility, and devotion to learning.

Integration and Emancipation. Nineteenth-century German and Austrian Jewry—with the major exception of the Jews of Galicia—eventually entered the middle class, discarded Yiddish for German, and produced ideologies of Reform and Neo-Orthodoxy which minimized or rejected aspects of Judaism considered as sacrosanct in the east. Joseph II's *Toleranzpatent* (1782) attempted to legislate against Jewish separatism while opening up new economic and educational options for some Jews. The long and contentious debate in Germany over the feasibility of Jewish emancipation made its small Jewish community (which constituted about 1.75 percent of the total population in 1871 when emancipation was finally granted) highly visible and particularly sensitive to the vagaries of public opinion. In Prussia, 58,000 of its 124,000 Jews were in fact emancipated by 1815; elsewhere in Germany restrictions on employment in the public and private sectors and limitations on Jewish residence were abolished, or at least substantially modified, by the 1850s. To be sure, the 1848 uprisings were followed by new restrictions in Austria and Bavaria, and they were also accompanied by a new anti-Semitic argument which identified Jews with the most disruptive and oppressive features of modern society.

In Galicia, where over 800,000 of Austria's 1.2 million Jews lived in 1900, 85 percent of the Jewish population, according to one report, subsisted at substandard conditions and worked as petty moneylenders, agents, and innkeepers. Yet the majority of Germany's Jews, who were concentrated until the mid-nineteenth century in petty trade, small retailing establishments, and artisanry had by 1871 entered the middle and upper-middle classes. The most telling indication of their social mobility was the disappearance of the *Betteljuden* (many of whom immigrated to the United States), who had, together with day laborers and domestic servants, made up 15 to 20 percent of the German-Jewish population in the late 1830s. German Jews continued to be concentrated in a cluster of occupations, but now these were wholesale trade, commerce, the money market, the professions, and journalism.

Emergence of reform. Attempts at integration by German Jews produced ideologies of religious reform that accepted the diminution of the national traits of Judaism as espoused by the larger society and emphasized those aspects of Judaism most conducive to cultural symbiosis. Abraham Geiger (1810–1874), Germany's major Reform exponent, saw Judaism as having evolved historically and asserted that every generation had to determine for itself what religious practices and concepts retained a contemporary relevance. Geiger identified monotheism and the teachings of the prophets as the quintessential message that had characterized Judaism throughout the ages and that constituted the basis for its ethical system. In a radical departure from the traditional understanding of *galut,* Geiger saw the Jewish dispersion as a positive condition, since it helped Jews promote the universalistic teachings of their faith. This emphasis on mission served to justify continued Jewish peculiarity and helped to reinforce, albeit within a substantially modified context, traditional assumptions of Jewish specialness and chosenness. The fundamental principles of Reform were elaborated in a series of rabbinical conferences held in the 1840s, and these assemblies constituted the culmination of a long period in which Reform promoted a substantially modified Jewish educational curriculum and alterations in synagogue service and decorum.

Emergence of Orthodoxy. The response of Pressburg's (modern Bratislava) influential Mosheh Sofer (Ḥatam Sofer, 1762–1839) to the emergence of Reform was summarized in his pithy "Ḥadash asur min ha-torah" ("everything new is forbidden by the Torah"), which denounced all change as undermining Judaism. The call for traditional Jews to segregate themselves from the increasingly Reform-dominated communities of Germany was promoted by many Orthodox rabbis, most prominently by Samson Raphael Hirsch (1808–1888), who argued for the universalizing of Judaism and, at the same time, for an uncompromising affirmation of its traditional commitment to *mitsvot.* Traditional Judaism in Germany, and elsewhere in Europe, began to employ the tools—and in Hirsch's case also the terminology—of the larger, secularizing world in order to combat Reform, and this led to the creation of Orthodox newspapers and political parties. The first such party was established in Hungary in 1867.

Acculturation and Responses to Anti-Semitism. European Jewry's acculturation led, to be sure, to a diminution of the importance that Jewish concerns played in the lives of many Jews, but it also provided an increasingly westernized Jewry with new and sophisticated tools with which to promote Jewish interests. Jewish liberals and a small number of political radicals played a prominent role in the 1848 revolutions, in contrast to the political passivity of the Jews of France in 1789; another indication of the tendency of westernized Jews to employ new and innovative means to promote Jewish causes was the creation of a highly diversified Jewish press mostly published in European languages.

Jewish assimilation, whose goal was the fusion of Jewry into the majority culture, was most feasible in settings were Jews formed a small percentage of the population in large urban areas; where acculturation was widespread but anti-Semitism prevalent, the promotion of social integration was thwarted. A precipitous rise in anti-Semitism in societies where Jews had experienced substantial acculturation often contributed to an increase in the incidence of conversion. On average, 145 Jews converted annually in Prussia between 1880 and 1884 while, in the wake of the anti-Semitic agitation of the last decade of the century, the number doubled to 349 between 1895 and 1899.

Of the smaller Jewish communities of western and northern Europe, about 35,000 Jews lived in England in the 1850s, 80,000 in France, about 52,000 in Holland (in the 1840s), 64,000 in Belgium, and fewer than 1,000 in Sweden. In France and England, Jews were concentrated in the largest cities (a process that had begun earlier in England than in France). In both societies, despite the emancipation of French Jewry more than half a century before the Jews of England were admitted into the House of Commons in 1858, acculturation preceded the complete abrogation of Jewish restrictions. An absence of denominationalism was another feature common to both English and French Jewish life, and in the two communities Reform tendencies were absorbed or neutralized by the dominant religious institutions and they did not precipitate the sectarianism characteristic of German Judaism. The absorption into the middle class of most English and French Jews by the late nineteenth century helped encourage a privatization of Jewish identity, which was eventually challenged by the east European migration. Between 1881 and 1914 the English Jewish population increased, mostly as a result of the immigration of Russian Jews, from sixty-five thousand to three hundred thousand. Thirty thousand immigrants settled in Paris in the same period (arriving in particularly large numbers after 1905), and they introduced into the western urban Jewish milieu an ethnic dimension previously unknown. Indeed, between 1881 and 1924, about 2.5 million east European Jews (mostly from Russia) migrated to the West; two-thirds of them left their homes between 1903 and 1914 and the vast majority of immigrants moved to the United States. About 10–15 percent settled in western and central Europe. Russian Jews in particular emigrated in large numbers because of the oppressive tsarist legislation of the 1880s and 1890s, shrinking economic prospects, and often exaggerated rumors of economic prospects in the West.

East European Jewish immigrants became a special focus of attack by the anti-Semitic movement that erupted in western and central Europe in the late nineteenth century. This movement was the product of a general anti-liberal reaction which promoted romantic conservatism over constitutionalism, a free market economy, and freedom of speech and assembly. Anti-Semitism (the term was coined in the 1870s) provided a seemingly plausible target for a wide range of social and economic frustrations. Its literature drew on secular (and often scientific) rather than religious terminology and sometimes, as in Edouard Adolphe Drumont's *La France juive* (1886), it drew on left-wing ideology in its case for the illegitimacy of Jewish wealth and position. Influential anti-Semitic parties appeared in Germany and Austria. Anti-Semitism became a cultural code, in Shulamit Volkov's characterization, for a wide range of groups that stressed militant nationalism, imperial expansion, racism, anticolonialism, antisocialism, and respect for authoritarian government.

The rise and resilience of the anti-Semitic movement compelled some European Jewish leaders to reassess their communal and political strategies. In Germany this gave birth in 1893 to the *Centralverein deutscher Staatsbürger jüdischen Glauben,* which departed from the classical Mendelssohnian stance both in its promotion of a conspicuously Jewish (as opposed to philo-Semitic, liberal, and gentile-led) response to anti-Semitism and in its insistence that the Jewish case be aired and vindicated in courts of law. In Russia, as in the West, before the 1880s Jewish politics was seen as predicated entirely on the goodwill of gentiles and its goal was the encouragement of Jewish emancipation. A new understanding took hold after the 1881–1882 pogroms, best encapsulated in the title of Odessa physician Leon Pinsker's *Auto-Emancipation* (1882), which called upon the Jews to cease their efforts to adapt themselves to the larger environment and to create instead a new one outside of Russia. A new type of Russian Jewish leader emerged in the same period: young, russianized (or partially so), who came to compete with the communal magnates of St. Petersburg and the rabbinical elite.

Zionism. Two major ideological currents emerged: Zionism and Jewish socialism. Zionism drew its constituency and vitality from eastern Europe but the Austrian journalist, Theodor Herzl (1860–1904), gave the small and Russian-based movement a measure of stature and international recognition in the 1890s and early twentieth century. Herzl's most important Zionist adversary was the Odessa intellectual Asher Ginsberg (better known as Aḥad ha-ʿAm, 1856–1927), who provided Zionism with influential ideological underpinnings very different from those of Herzl. From Herzl's perspective, the promotion by Zionism of a Jewish homeland would undercut the growth of anti-Semitism, restore Jewish economic productivity, and provide Jews throughout the world (as well as the threatened liberal order) with renewed stability. Ginsberg, on the other hand, saw Zionism as a framework that could allow Jewry to absorb Western values without having them submerge Jewish identity. He stressed the cultural benefits of the rebuilding of a Palestinian Jewish homeland and minimized its immediate economic impact.

Jewish socialism. A second Jewish political movement emphasized the need to transform Russia itself—a goal Russian Zionists also eventually adopted in their Helsinki platform of 1906—and the Jewish Socialist Labor Bund, established in 1897, charted a course between the two poles of nationalism and Marxism. Jewish socialism's following, not surprisingly, expanded in moments of revolutionary turmoil and contracted with rapidity in times of relative quiescence. But the heroism of the Jewish revolutionaries, their organization of self-defense groups during the pogroms, their participation in widespread philanthropic endeavors, and even their conspiratorial form of internal organization came to infuse them with an almost legendary respect in the Pale of Settlement.

World War I and Its Aftermath. The war seemed at first to present a singularly unfavorable scenario for Jewish political activity but was, ironically, followed by a series of outstanding victories for Jewish leaders in the diplomatic sphere and by a new and apparently more encouraging political order. The Russian Revolution of 1917 brought down the imperial regime and emancipated Russia's Jews; the Balfour Declaration, issued by the British the same year, was Zionism's first concrete diplomatic achievement and it would serve, until the state of Israel was established in 1948, as a central focus of the movement's strategy. Moreover, the adoption of international guarantees for the observance of national minority rights in the new states of east central Europe (along with prewar Romania) was largely the product of the maneuvering of British and American Jewish leaders. The mass evacuation of hundreds of thousands of Galician and Russian Jews in 1914–1915 (the Russian ones evacuated under particularly degrading conditions) lent Jews a special visibility, which was reinforced by the fact that much of the war was conducted in regions heavily populated by Jews. Misperceptions of the strength and dimensions of Jewish influence (suppositions which gained worldwide notoriety after World War I with the dissemination of the anti-Semitic tract *Protocols of the Elders of Zion*) helped Jews wrest major political concessions for themselves. The Balfour Declaration, in which the British declared sympathy for Zionist aspirations in Palestine, resulted partly from the Allies' belief that Russian (and American) Jewish support was crucial in bolstering the war effort. The Russian liberalization of Jewish residence restrictions in 1915 was the product of a misperception that Jewish-controlled Western loans would be denied to Russia if it continued to be seen as brutally anti-Semitic. Western support for national minority rights in east central Europe was given special impetus in the wake of the Ukrainian pogroms of 1918–1919 in which more than five hundred Jewish communities were attacked and about seventy thousand Jews were killed. The effort of the Bolsheviks—who in November 1917 had overthrown the liberal anti-tsarist government that had been in power in Russia since the fall of the Romanovs earlier that year—to put down the anti-Jewish disturbances and to pacify the Ukrainian separatist movement won widespread (if somewhat equivocal) support for them among Russia's Jews.

The new Soviet government associated anti-Semitism with tsarist reaction and fought it vigorously, but Bolshevism also denied Jewish demands for national recognition on the basis of its authoritative statement on minority nationalism, *Marxism and the National Question* (1913). Nonetheless, Jewry's distinctive cultural and, implicitly, also its national needs were acknowledged by the regime, which was interested in consolidating Jewish support. Secular cultural activity in Yiddish was encouraged; Hebrew was barred as bourgeois and religious institutions and functionaries were harassed. By the early 1930s even Yiddish-language publishing, research, and pedagogical activity were restricted. At the same time, the Soviet Jewish population as a whole—which numbered about three million in 1926—benefited from the expanding economy, became urbanized (it was eventually concentrated in Moscow, Leningrad, and a few other large cities), and was absorbed, despite the existence of a residual popular as well as institutional anti-Semitism, into the industrial working class, the bureaucracy, the professions, and the sciences.

The Jews of interwar Poland (who numbered just under 2.9 million in 1921, 10.5 percent of the total population) underwent a process of acculturation different from that of Soviet Jewry. Ravaged as Poland was by the war and separated from its natural markets and sources of energy by the boundaries of the new Polish state, its postwar economic development was sluggish before 1929 and singularly depressed in the 1930s. Poland's depressed economic state reinforced a widespread integral nationalism that persuaded many Poles that the Jews, as members of a faith inimical to Christianity, had no place in Poland. Particularly after 1936, nationalist xenophobia, church-sponsored anti-Semitism, and economic decline combined to persuade Poles of varied political persuasions that anti-Jewish policies were a necessary cruelty. About one-third of Poland's Jews retained a largely traditional religious profile and promoted Orthodox interests with tenacity and some sophistication. Jewish acculturation was also vividly reflected in the growth of secular Jewish culture and widely diversified socialist and Zionist political activities, which took on different forms in various regions of Poland, Galicia, central Poland, and Lithuania-Belorussia.

The Holocaust. The vast majority of Germany's approximately 600,000 Jews (constituting about one percent of the population in the early 1920s) were solidly based in the middle class, though one-fifth of the Jewish population were foreign-born and maintained a less prosperous occupational profile. Anti-Semitic sentiment—which reached ferocious levels in the immediate post-World War I period when wide segments of the population associated the sudden loss of the war with the treachery of the Jews—was marginalized during the economic prosperity of 1923–1929. Anti-Semitism regained a mass following with the onset of the worldwide depression. Once Hitler was appointed Chancellor in 1933, German Jewry was gradually segregated from the larger population, denied employment, and those who did not emigrate by 1939 were eventually deported and either worked to death or gassed in labor and death camps. Germany's invasion of Poland led to the effective segregation of its large Jewish community, and Jews elsewhere in Nazi-occupied or Nazi-dominated western and east central Europe were placed in ghettos where they too were starved, brutalized, and, in the end, sent to death camps. More than one million Soviet Jews were killed by Nazi mobile killing units during the German invasion of 1941; the introduction in 1942 of highly efficient means for mass extermination led to the construction of a series of death camps designed expressly for the extermination of European Jewry. Over the course of World War II during the Nazi Holocaust about 6 million Jews were killed: 4.5 million in Poland and the Soviet Union; 125,000 German Jews, 277,000 Czechs, 402,000 Hungarians, 24,000 Belgians, 102,000 Dutch, 40,000 Romanians, 60,000 Yugoslavs, 85,000 French, and tens of thousands in Greece and Italy.

Post-Holocaust Jewish Community. The resilience of postwar anti-Semitism in Poland encouraged most Holocaust survivors to emigrate, and the Polish Jewish community, numbering about 30,000 in the late 1950s, was further decimated following the migration of large numbers of Jews in the wake of the 1968 anti-Semitic governmental campaign. Germany's 25,000 Jews in the late 1960s experienced a high rate of intermarriage (72.5 percent among males in the years 1951–1958) and a death rate that far exceeded its birthrate. The most culturally vibrant Jewish community of east central Europe was Hungary, where between 80,000 and 90,000 Jews in the 1960s maintained, eventually with government support, a wide range of religious and philanthropic institutions, including a rabbinical seminary. The post-1967 resurgence of Jewish nationalist sentiment among Soviet Jews led to a revival of (largely clandestine) cultural activity and helped precipitate a large migration of Jews to Israel and the United States. The centers of European Jewish cultural life in the postwar period were England and France. The French Jewish community, in particular, has demonstrated a marked vitality, encouraged by the migration of North African Jews, primarily from Algeria, in the 1960s.

[*For further discussion of the historical movements and events discussed herein, see* Messianism, *article on* Jewish Messianism; Haskalah; Hasidism, *overview article;* Musar Movement; Agudat Yisra'el; Zionism; Orthodox Judaism; Reform Judaism; *and* Holocaust, The, *article on* History. *Many of the principal historical figures mentioned in this article are the subjects of independent entries.*]

BIBLIOGRAPHY

Early Modern Period. The most authoritative work in English on the Jews of Poland and Lithuania in the sixteenth and seventeenth centuries is volume 16 of Salo W. Baron's *A Social* *and Religious History of the Jews*, 2d ed., rev. and enl. (Philadelphia, 1976). For a sociological analysis of Jewish communal autonomy in eastern and central Europe, see Jacob Katz's *Tradition and Crisis* (New York, 1961). On Jews in the late medieval Germanic empire, see Selma Stern's *Josel of Rosheim* (Philadelphia, 1965). Useful methodological questions are raised in an article by Gershon David Hundert, "On the Jewish Community in Poland during the Seventeenth Century: Some Comparative Perspectives," *Revue des études juives* 142 (July–December 1983): 349–372. On the seventeenth century, there is interesting material in Jonathan I. Israel's "Central European Jewry during the Thirty Years' War," *Central European History* (March 1983): 3–30. The best treatment of Polish-Jewish cultural life in the same period is H. H. Ben-Sasson's *Hagut vehanhagah* (Jerusalem, 1959). Jewish migratory trends in the seventeenth and eighteenth centuries are studied in Moses A. Shulvass's *From East to West* (Detroit, 1971). On the readmission of English Jewry, see David S. Katz's *Philo-Semitism and the Readmission of the Jews to England, 1603–1655* (Oxford, 1982).

Modern Period. An incisive analysis of the social features of Hasidism may be found in Samuel Ettinger's "The Hassidic Movement: Reality and Ideals," in *Jewish Society through the Ages*, edited by H. H. Ben-Sasson and Samuel Ettinger (London, 1971), pp. 251–266. For a discussion of French Jewish identity, see Phyllis Cohen Albert's "Nonorthodox Attitudes in Nineteenth-Century French Judaism," in *Essays in Modern Jewish History: A Tribute to Ben Halpern*, edited by Frances Malino and Phyllis Cohen Albert (Rutherford, N.J., 1982), pp. 121–141. Michael Stanislawski's *Tsar Nicholas I and the Jews* (Philadelphia, 1983), and Hans Rogger's "Russian Ministers and the Jewish Question, 1881–1917," *California Slavic Studies* 8 (1975): 15–76, study imperial Jewish policy. The essays in *Revolution and Evolution: 1848 in German-Jewish History*, edited by Werner E. Mosse, Arnold Paucker, and Reinhard Rürup (Tübingen, 1981), examine nineteenth century German Jewry, with particular emphasis on the community's socioeconomic transformation. Todd M. Endelman's *The Jews of Georgian England, 1714–1830* (Philadelphia, 1979) is a skillful social history. The political responses of east European Jews are studied in Jonathan Frankel's *Prophecy and Politics: Socialism, Nationalism and the Russian Jews, 1862–1917* (Cambridge, 1981). Ezra Mendelsohn reviews the interwar period in *The Jews of East Central Europe between the World Wars* (Bloomington, Ind., 1983). The best study of Soviet Jewry is Zvi Y. Gitelman's *Jewish Nationality and Soviet Politics* (Princeton, 1972). A particularly insightful essay in Yehuda Bauer's *The Holocaust in Historical Perspective* (Seattle, 1978) is his "Against Mystification: The Holocaust as a Historical Phenomenon."

STEVEN J. ZIPPERSTEIN

Judaism in the Western Hemisphere

If the records of the Inquisition are to be believed, Jews were among the earliest settlers in the Western Hemisphere. They were Marranos, Spanish and Portuguese Jews who had been coerced to convert to Christianity, but continued to practice their religion secretly. While Jews had been expelled from Spain in 1492 and were, of course, forbidden to settle in the Spanish colonies, not until 1523 did a royal decree exclude even the New Christians, that is, recent converts to Christianity. The first auto-da-fé at which New Christians alleged to be Marranos were burned at the stake was held in Mexico City in 1528. [*See* Marranos *and* Inquisition.] Independent tribunals of the Holy Office of the Inquisition were established in Mexico City in 1571 and in Lima in 1572 and thereafter Inquisitorial trials and executions of "judaizers" *(judaizantes)* were held regularly. In the great auto-da-fé of Lima on 23 January 1639, sixty-two suspected heretics were convicted and twelve hundred unrepentant victims were burned at the stake. While it is impossible to know how many of the accused were in fact Jews and to ascertain the nature of their Jewish practices, it is clear that the continued existence of the Inquisition in Central and South America into the nineteenth century prevented the emergence of an openly Jewish community until the last decades of that century.

Jewish Settlement in the New World. The earliest Jewish community in the Western Hemisphere was established in Recife, Brazil, during the brief period of Dutch rule there between 1630 and 1654. Holland, following its independence from Spain in 1579, had become a center of commercial capitalism as well as of toleration. The combination of religious freedom and economic opportunity had attracted Sefardic Jews to Amsterdam, and in the late sixteenth century a thriving Jewish center arose there that played a significant role in trade with the New World.

In 1630 the Dutch captured the settlement at Recife and Jews arrived among the earliest settlers. As long as the Dutch retained control of the colony, the Jewish community there flourished. At the peak of its prosperity in 1645 the community is reported to have numbered 1,500—about 50 percent of the European civilian population. In 1654, the Portuguese recaptured the city, and Dutch and Jewish inhabitants were given three months in which to depart. Most returned to Amsterdam; others moved to islands in the West Indies where they joined existing groups of Jewish settlers. One band of twenty-three landed in New Amsterdam (present-day New York) in September 1654. The end of the first Jewish community in South America coincided with the establishment of the first such community in North America.

Settlement of North America. As may be seen from letters from the directors of the Dutch West India Company to Peter Stuyvesant, the presence of this group was grudgingly accepted by the local authorities on condition that "the poor among them shall not become a burden to the [Dutch West India] Company or to the community but be supported by their own nation." Subsequently the rights of Jews to settle, trade in real estate, and practice their religion "in all quietness within their homes" was granted (Max Kohler, "Beginnings of New York Jewish History," *Proceedings of the American Jewish Historical Society* 1, 1905, pp. 47–48). In 1656, a group of Jewish petitioners was granted a cemetery, the first institution signifying that a community of practicing Jews had been established. In 1644, English conquerors replaced the Dutch. They renamed the city New York and confirmed the atmosphere of toleration in what was already a mosaic of religious and ethnic diversity.

During the century that followed, a small but steady trickle of immigration led to the establishment of Jewish congregations along the eastern seaboard in Newport, Philadelphia, Charleston, and Savannah, as well as New York. All followed the Sefardic (Spanish-Portuguese) rite in their worship. Because of the small size and informal organizational pattern of the community, little information has survived concerning the details of institutional practice. During the colonial era, no ordained rabbi served in America; not a single Jewish journal of any kind was established, nor was there any other instrument for the exchange of ideas or information. Colonial American Jewry, sparse in numbers and weak in intellectual resources, left only a meager documentary record.

Despite the difficulties and shortcomings, Jewish religious life, conducted by devoted but often poorly educated laymen, sustained itself. In 1682, a Dutch cleric recorded that the Jews "hold their separate meetings in New York." That same year, the Jewish community purchased its second cemetery, a burying ground that exists in lower New York to this day and is one of the oldest historic sites in the city. In 1695, an English clergyman noted in his memoirs that the approximately 855 families in New York included 20 Jewish families. On a map of the city, he marked a site as "The Jews Synagogue." A subsequent real estate document describes a house on Mill Street as "commonly known by the name of Jews Synagogue." These references offer no information concerning the life of the community, but they do testify to the existence of a small congregation that had established its right to public worship, had rented a building for this purpose, and had made its presence palpable in the city. In 1728, the Jewish citizens of New York purchased a lot and undertook the erection of a building intended specifically for use as a synagogue.

Throughout the eighteenth century, Jewish immigrants were few in number. It is estimated that in 1790 no more than 2,000 to 2,500 Jews resided in the United States. The masses of Jews lived in east-central and eastern Europe and in the Near East in areas not yet awakened to the possibility of migration. An increasing percentage of those who did come were Ashkenazim—Jews of northern European origin. Despite the differences in Ashkenazic and Sefardic religious custom, without exception the Ashkenazim joined the established Sefardic congregations. Colonial American Jewry remained Sefardic in its formal religious practice.

Americanization of colonial Jewry. At the same time, the style of life in this small community underwent significant changes. Encouraged by the atmosphere of toleration and the openness of the society, colonial Jews became americanized and entered into general social life to a degree that would have been inconceivable in Europe. Although the ritual practices in the synagogue were preserved without change, Jewish knowledge and practice became increasingly attenuated. In the traditional community, an all-pervasive pattern of Jewish thought, action, outlook, and association had been punctuated by occasional excursions into the general society primarily in pursuit of economic ends. In the newly developing American Jewish mode, a distinctively American style of thought, action, outlook, and association was punctuated by occasional excursions to the synagogue for the performance of increasingly marginal ceremonial functions.

In 1761, the *ḥazzan* (cantor) of Shearith Israel congregation in New York, Isaac Pinto, published the first Jewish book to be printed in the Western Hemisphere. It was a translation of the Sabbath prayer book into English. In his introduction, Pinto explained that Hebrew was "imperfectly understood by many, by some not at all" and expressed the hope that an English translation would "tend to the improvement of many of my Brethren in their Devotion." A report from Philadelphia to Amsterdam in 1785 concludes that "most of the sons of this province are not devoted to Torah and do not understand our holy tongue [Hebrew]. Despite accounts clearly demonstrating that the American Jewry that emerged in the early decades of the nineteenth century was highly acculturated and substantially transformed, no account can deny the achievement of this isolated Jewish group in maintaining its identity at all.

When George Washington was inaugurated president in 1790, Gershom Mendes Seixas, the American-born *ḥazzan* of Shearith Israel congregation in New York, was recorded as one of the clergymen in attendance. Small as it was, the Jewish community was unable to agree on sending one letter of felicitations to the president, and three letters were dispatched. In a gracious response, Washington reciprocated the good wishes of the "children of the stock of Abraham" and expressed his confidence in their continued well-being in a society which "happily gives to bigotry no sanction, to persecution no assistance and requires only that they who live under its protection should demean themselves as good citizens" (Joseph L. Blau and Salo W. Baron, eds., *The Jews of the United States, 1790–1840: A Documentary History,* New York, 1964, vol. 1, p. 9). American Judaism was recognized as a component in the mosaic of American religious pluralism.

American Jewry in the Nineteenth Century. In the early years of the nineteenth century, revolution and war in Europe reduced immigration to a trickle. American Jewry, small in numbers and weak in intellectual resources, entered a phase of steady attrition. The new American version of Judaism was viable but it never succeeded in becoming vital. "Alas," wrote Rebecca Gratz of Philadelphia, the founder of the Sunday school movement for Jewish children, "it is thought among our degenerate sons and daughters of Israel that only its women and priests acknowledge the force of patriotism and zeal for Judaism" (ibid., vol. 8, p. 955).

Large-scale immigration to America resumed after 1815 when the return of peace restored normal transportation across the Atlantic. A large proportion of these immigrants originated in central European provinces, and among them were increasing numbers of Jews. In 1818, Mordecai Manuel Noah, New York journalist, playwright, and Jacksonian politician, estimated the Jewish population of the United States at three thousand. By 1826, Isaac Harby, a Charleston schoolmaster, put the number at six thousand. The presence of immigrants and the prospect of further immigration stirred signs of life in the near-moribund American Jewish community.

In 1823, the first Jewish periodical in North America appeared. It was a monthly called *The Jew* and devoted solely to reporting the conversionist polemics of Christian missionary societies, especially the so-called Society for Ameliorating the Condition of the Jews. In its two years of publication *The Jew* did not include a single reference to events in the Jewish community of its time. The circumscribed contents of the journal reflect the meagerness of Jewish life; however, the very existence of such a publication is a token of awakening enterprise and growing awareness of need and opportunity.

Grandiose schemes for encouraging immigration proliferated in America during these years. English, German, Swiss, and French groups attempted to establish semi-independent national settlements beyond the Appalachian mountains in what was then the "West." In 1825 Mordecai Noah proposed the establishment of a Jewish settlement on Grand Island in the Niagara River, proclaiming himself as "Judge and Governor of Israel." Nothing came of the proposal; it was dropped after a flurry of publicity without Noah ever having set foot on Grand Island. The significance of the scheme lies in its testimony to Noah's consciousness of the renewed Jewish immigration which had already begun and of the prospect of an increased flow in the future.

The growth in numbers and in diversity of background created strains within the Jewish community. Newcomers from northern Europe soon outnumbered the settlers of the prerevolutionary period. It was inevitable that they would establish their own synagogues. The first synagogue to follow the Ashkenazic (German) rite in worship had been established in Philadelphia possibly as early as 1795. The congregation, however, did not succeed in establishing itself on a sound footing until the late 1820s, when the influx of new immigrants reinforced its ranks. At the same time two new Ashkenazic congregations were established—one in Cincinnati and one in New York. In new areas of settlement, as well as in old established centers, immigrants were forming congregations in accord with their own mode of worship. In 1828, a third synagogue was established in New York.

The most common explanation for the proliferation of congregations was the increasing resistance of Ashkenazim to the Sefardic manner of conducting the ritual. In fact the motives were far more complex. Acculturated native American Jews found the newcomers alien, abrasive, and uncouth, while immigrants found their americanized fellow Jews lax in religious observance. Established citizens wanted an orderly and undemanding "Jewish church" that would affirm their respectability; insecure newcomers sought an environment of involvement and interaction reminiscent of the intimate village gathering place they had known, where they could pray in their accustomed way among sympathetic peers and find acceptance by God and men. The bewildered newcomers of one decade became the solid and settled bourgeoisie of the next. Each succeeding wave of immigration brought a repetition of the pattern.

By 1840, before the largest influx of immigrants had begun or a single rabbi had yet arrived, the number of congregations in New York had risen to six. The pace of institutional growth accelerated sharply in the 1840s with congregations organized in cities from Boston to San Francisco. In 1848, Isaac Leeser, editor of *The Occident and American Jewish Advocate* in Philadelphia, observed that "synagogues are springing up as if by magic. . . . From the newly gotten Santa Fe to the confines of New Brunswick and from the Atlantic to the shores of the Western sea, the wandering sons of Israel are seeking homes and freedom" *(The Occident and American Jewish Advocate* 4, 1848, pp. 317, 366). Before the end of the decade two or more congregations existed in cities with substantial Jewish populations, such as Albany, Baltimore, Cincinnati, New Orleans, Philadelphia, Richmond, and Saint Louis. New York had fifteen congregations, with more in the process of formation.

Beginnings of communal structure and leadership. The voluntarism and pluralism of America, the lack of a Jewish communal structure, and the absence of religious or intellectual leadership together combined to foster an atmosphere of chaos in American Jewish life. Well-intentioned but poorly educated laymen assumed leadership in seeking to establish the rudiments of community. However, they lacked the credentials to interpret Jewish law or to render decisions concerning modifications in religious practice in response to changed conditions. [*See* Rabbinate *and* Halakhah.] No one had the power to enforce traditional norms even within the synagogue. Every congregation and indeed every individual was free to act or refrain from acting according to his own inclination. Authority was absent and unity in dealing with common concerns seemed unattainable.

The earliest manifestations of national communal consciousness came in response to a perceived threat from the outside. In 1840, the ancient blood libel—the false accusation that Jews had murdered a Christian child for ritual purposes—was revived in Damascus. The specter of revived medieval bigotry even in faraway Damascus shook native-born as well as immigrant Jews. "If such calumny is not nipped in the bud, its effect will not be limited to any particular place but will be extended to every part of the globe," wrote Abraham Hart, president of the Sefardic Mikveh Israel congregation in Philadelphia. Disparate Jewish groups in major urban centers joined together with each other, with Jews in other American cities, and with communities in Europe in expressions of mutual concern. The response signified an awakening of group consciousness.

The quickening sense of mutual concern led to the first proposals for a permanent link between Jews in various cities and for an attempt to address the deficiencies and improve the quality of Jewish religious life. Impoverished immigrants struggling to make their way in a strange new land were eager to preserve their Jewish practices and to give their children a Jewish education. They established not only synagogues but also day schools in which Hebrew as well as English and sometimes German were taught. But individual congregations and communities lacked the financial and cultural resources to fulfill the aspirations of their constituents. In an attempt to overcome the inadequacies, Isaac Leeser, then *ḥazzan* of the Mikveh Israel congregation in Philadelphia, took the initiative and prepared a detailed plan for a national union of American Jewish congregations, which he circulated in July 1841. Leeser, himself of German Jewish background, had emigrated to the United States as a young man in the 1820s. His formal educational background was modest and in the European setting would have qualified him to be no more than an elementary-school teacher. However, he was bright, ambitious, and energetic, and was soon elected to serve as *ḥazzan* of the established old Sefardic congregation. The absence of religious functionaries with more impressive credentials enabled Leeser to assume a national-leadership role. His proposed "Union for the Sake of Judaism" projected the establishment of a "Central Religious Council" consisting of three "gentlemen of undoubted moral and religious character" to be elected by congregational representatives. The council was to "watch over the state of religion," certify the competence of ritual slaughterers and cantors, and oversee the quality of religious schools (for both sexes). The schools were to be established "in every town where Israelites reside" but were not to "interfere directly or indirectly in the internal affairs of the congregations." The proposal—modest as it was—did not elicit a single positive response. American voluntarism and Jewish congregational autonomy combined to subvert any attempt to achieve unity or to establish authority.

Leeser may have been disheartened, but he was not daunted and proceeded at once with other ventures. The following year he announced plans for publishing a monthly journal, and in April 1843 the English-language *Occident and American Jewish Advocate* appeared. Leeser proposed "to give circulation to everything which can be interesting to the Jewish inhabitants of the Western Hemisphere." American Jewry not only had a spokesman; it now had a forum for exchange of information and ideas.

In 1844, Leeser contributed an article entitled "The Jews and Their Religion" to *An Original History of the Denominations at Present Existing in the United States*, edited by Daniel I. Rupps (Philadelphia, 1844). Leeser is described in this volume as "pastor of the Hebrew Portuguese Congregation of Philadelphia" and as the "most prominent divine" among American Jews. In his essay, Leeser states:

> We have no ecclesiastical authorities in America other than the congregations themselves. Each congregation makes its own rules for its government, and elects its own minister, who is appointed without any ordination, induction in office being made through his election. (p. 368)

Within American Judaism, as experienced and explained by Leeser, the traditional scholar-rabbi was marginal, at best.

At the time Leeser wrote, the first ordained rabbis

had arrived in America, but they had not yet found a recognized place or function for themselves in the new environment. Abraham Rice, who arrived in 1840 and served for a time as rabbi of the Baltimore Hebrew Congregation, wrote to his teacher in Germany: "I dwell in complete darkness, without a teacher or a companion. . . . The religious life in this land is on the lowest level. I wonder whether it is even permissible for a Jew to live in this land." Rice's gloom was not shared by Isaac Leeser, who wrote:

> In America, where the constitution secures to every person the enjoyment of life, liberty, and the pursuit of happiness without anyone having the right to question him concerning his religious opinion or acts, the Children of Jacob have received a new home.

Leeser proceeded in 1845 to establish an American Jewish Publication Society to publish material on Jewish subjects in English and to make it possible "to obtain a knowledge of the faith and to defend it against the assaults of the proselytemakers [sic] on the one side and of infidels on the other." Among its first publications was an edition of the Pentateuch with an English translation printed parallel to the Hebrew text.

That same year, Max Lilienthal arrived in America. Lilienthal was the first rabbi with unquestioned credentials and prior reputation to settle in America. In his earliest endeavors he sought to introduce traditional Jewish practices and to promote "decorum" in worship. Lilienthal further undertook to organize a *beit din*, a rabbinical court, that would render, in his words, "beneficial service to the Jewish congregations of America" (David Philipson, *Max Lilienthal, American Rabbi: His Life and Writings*, New York, 1915, p. 55). In deference to the autonomy of American congregations, Lilienthal stipulated that the *beit din* would not assume any "hierarchical authority" but would act "only in an advisory capacity." The effort was unsuccessful, and Lilienthal soon withdrew from congregational life and established a Jewish day school, which he operated for a number of years with considerable success.

A year after Lilienthal settled in America, another rabbi arrived who was to assume a significant leadership role. He was Isaac Mayer Wise. Wise, who had served as a rabbi in a provincial town in Bohemia, lacked reputation or credentials, but he was energetic, ambitious, and ideologically flexible. He was also an effective orator and a competent organizer. He secured a position in Albany and began at once to project himself onto the national scene and to establish himself as an aspirant to leadership.

In December 1848, Wise published a call for a union of congregations addressed "To Ministers and Other Israelites" in the *Occident*. Although both Leeser and Lilienthal associated themselves with this call and nine congregations responded favorably, no meeting was held. Wise was not discouraged. Five years later he was elected rabbi of a synagogue in Cincinnati, and promptly set about convening a conference to organize a "Union of American Israel" whose aim would be to establish a "regular synod consisting of delegates chosen by congregations and societies." At the same time Wise began publication of an English-language newspaper, *The Israelite*, and in Cincinnati established "the first Hebrew college in the United States and England," which he called Zion College.

The college closed after one year. The newspaper, however, flourished, and the conference did take place, in Cleveland in October 1855. A series of resolutions were adopted that straddled ideological issues and attempted to bridge the growing conflict between traditionalist and reformist factions. Unfortunately, personal rivalries, sectional antagonism between the Eastern "elite" and Midwestern "yokeldom," and residual hostility between the older native "aristocracy" and newer immigrant "upstarts" proved more intractable and less amenable to compromise than did ideology. A second conference was scheduled but never convened.

The Reform movement. During the early decades of the central European immigration there was little evidence of the struggle over religious reform that was stirring German Jewry during these years. Of the scores of synagogues established between 1825 and 1860, only three were founded with the avowed intention of introducing "reforms," and actual changes introduced even in these congregations were relatively modest. On the contrary, most immigrants, in the period immediately following their arrival, seemed more interested in preserving the synagogue unchanged as a refuge from the compromises with observance in their private lives often dictated by economic necessity. In Europe, the Jewish religious Reform movement had radical overtones and consequences. It was linked to the struggle for political emancipation and for the elimination of feudal disabilities. It therefore came to be regarded as a challenge not only to the traditional Jewish communal structure but to the established social and political order as well.

In America, precisely the opposite dynamics were at work. When Jewish reformism emerged, it reflected a desire not to change the established social and political order but to join it. Jewish religious Reform in nineteenth-century America began with a series of modest ritual changes and shifts in emphasis that were primarily concerned with appearances and social conformity. Ideology in the European sense played a minimal role and a predetermined program was virtually absent. In Germany, Reform was viewed as a precursor of acculturation and integration. In America acculturation and integration proved to be precursors of Reform.

The earliest reformist attempt had been made in 1825 in Charleston, South Carolina, by a native-born, thoroughly americanized group. Their proposal stressed decorum and intelligibility to worshipers who no longer understood Hebrew or German rather than substantive revisions of either faith or practice. The effort expired after a few years and exercised no influence on subsequent developments. When "Reform" emerged again as an issue in the 1850s, it was once more primarily concerned with issues of decorum and the use of English rather than with principles. The group most interested in Reform were upwardly mobile immigrants whose economic advance and americanization were rapidly progressing.

In 1855 David Einhorn arrived in America and took up a rabbinical post in Baltimore at the Reform Har Sinai congregation. Einhorn had been a leader of the radical faction at the German rabbinical conferences of the 1840s. In his pulpit and in *Sinai*, the German-language monthly magazine that he established in America, Einhorn espoused intellectually consistent Reform and ridiculed piecemeal efforts to achieve decorum. He denounced both Wise and Leeser and expressed his contempt for the level of intellectual life in America, which he called "a land of humbug." Einhorn was never at home in America. His continued stress on the use of the German language (which he called the "carrying case of Reform") was disregarded by his eagerly americanizing congregants. Ultimately many of Einhorn's ideas were accepted but they did not derive from the intellectually rigorous reform he had espoused. Rather, they provided an *ex post facto* justification for a patchwork of practices that had been accepted for pragmatic reasons.

As the decade of the 1850s drew to a close, American Jewry was gaining in vigor and self-confidence. Without a formal change in ideology, ritual practice, or institutional structure, a basic transformation of image and outlook had taken place. As Isaac M. Wise wrote in 1859: "We are Jews in the synagogue and Americans everywhere." Formal commitment to Reform was still minimal. I. J. Benjamin, the German Jewish traveler who completed his tour of America in 1861, reported that "in a land that numbers more than two hundred Orthodox congregations, the reform congregations number eight." A decade later, there were few congregations in which substantial reforms had *not* been introduced.

The Civil War experience accelerated the americanization of all immigrant groups, and economic growth stimulated upward mobility. American Jewry was moving from margin to mainstream; Isaac M. Wise became a member of the board of directors of the Free Religious Association alongside Ralph Waldo Emerson. Sumptuous new edifices arose in all the major cities of the land to house affluent congregations now eager for an elegant, decorous style of worship compatible with the new setting.

In 1869, David Einhorn convened a conference of rabbis in Philadelphia to formulate a statement of principles that would serve as a platform for the reformation of Judaism in America. Twelve rabbis, most of them recently arrived in America, participated. The brief credo which was adopted disavowed the hope for the restoration of Zion or for a personal Messiah, stressing Israel's "universal mission" and the goal of a messianic age that would "realize the unity of all rational creatures and their call to moral sanctification." The statement was issued in German; not surprisingly, it had little discernible impact.

Four years later, in 1873, Wise succeeded in organizing a "Union of American Hebrew Congregations" in Cincinnati with thirty-four congregations participating. In 1875, this Union became the sponsoring organization of the Hebrew Union College, the Reform seminary that has ever since trained and ordained rabbis.

With the exception of the old-line Sefardic synagogues, most of the well-established congregations in the country had become affiliates of the Union by the end of the decade. Reform had carried the day. Without any formal action or specific reformulation, Jewish doctrine had been redefined to conform to the presumed dictates of reason. Jewish ritual practice had been modified to reflect the tastes of an increasingly acculturated constituency in search of "respectability." For a brief period it seemed as though an increasingly homogeneous American Jewry of 250,000 had achieved what it regarded as a generally accepted "American Jewish" pattern.

The formal platform of American Reform Judaism was adopted after the reformation had been achieved. In 1885, Kaufman Kohler, son-in-law and intellectual heir of David Einhorn, convened a conference of rabbis in Pittsburgh at which he proposed adoption of a platform "broad, compassionate, enlightened, and liberal enough to impress and win all hearts and also firm and positive enough to dispel agnostic tendencies or those discontinuing the historic thread of the past." An eight-point resolution was adopted by the seventeen rabbis who assembled. It hailed "the modern era of the universal culture of heart and intellect [and] the approach of the realization of Israel's great Messianic hope for the establishment of the kingdom of truth, justice, and peace among all men." All ceremonies regarded as "not adapted to the views and habits of modern civilization" were rejected. The traditional hope for national restoration was repudiated: "We consider ourselves no longer a nation but a religious community." Judaism emerged, in the words of the resolution, as a "progressive religion ever striving to be in accord with the postulates of reason."

The Impact of the New Immigration. By the time this platform was adopted the situation of American Jewry was being radically altered by the influx of eastern European Jewish immigrants. Beginning in 1881, a flood of immigrants virtually inundated the existing community. By 1900 more than a half million had arrived and between 1900 and 1914 another million and a quarter. Reform was reduced to a marginal position representing only a fraction of American Jews of an upper social and economic level.

The new immigrants were poor, spoke Yiddish (derided as "jargon" by Jewish speakers of "pure" German and English), and, in large part, traditional in their religious practices, though few of them were highly educated or sophisticated in their religious training. They were mostly simple people from towns and villages whose folk religion and natural piety were not easily transplanted to the turbulent industrial urban environment of America. The surviving representatives of traditional Judaism in the established American Jewish community attempted to respond to the new constituency and in 1885 organized the Jewish Theological Seminary of America in New York to train rabbis. The gap between the decorous, acculturated, English-speaking Orthodoxy and the new immigrants was too great to permit communication, and the seminary failed to gain a following among the new immigrants until it was reorganized in 1901.

An attempt was made by the immigrants to transplant their European religious pattern to the New World. In 1888 a group of eastern European synagogues in New York joined together to bring Jacob Joseph, a well-known scholar from Vilna, to New York to serve as "chief rabbi." But the effort was undermined by the indifference of the majority of Orthodox congregations, which were not involved in the project, by opposition from Reform rabbis and the americanized Orthodox, and by the antagonism of secular and radical immigrants. Jacob Joseph, confused and disheartened, was never able to assert rabbinical authority in the fragmented and increasingly heterogeneous American Jewish community.

Traditional Judaism remained weak and disorganized in the years before and after the turn of the century. The few attempts to raise the level of religious study, to maintain standards of observance, and to exercise authority met with little success. The Rabbi Isaac Elchanan Theological Seminary—the first *yeshivah* to be established in America—was founded in 1897. Decades later it became the basis for the development of Yeshiva University, but at the time, it remained small and exercised little influence. In 1898, Henry Pereira Mendes, the rabbi of the Sefardic Shearith Israel Congregation in New York, organized a Union of Orthodox Jewish Congregations, and in 1902, a Union of Orthodox Rabbis was formed. Both remained marginal and their influence at the time was negligible. No institution emerged to serve as a center for the religious life of eastern European Jewry. An impoverished immigrant community, struggling to establish itself and to deal with problems of poverty, social dislocation, and linguistic adjustments, could not yet deal with the challenge of a new and radically different religious environment.

In response to the circumstances and opportunities of American life, new institutions emerged that in part fulfilled the vacuum created by religious inadequacy. *Landsmannschaften*—fraternal organizations of Jews from the same European town or province—flourished. To the extent of their ability they addressed problems of mutual aid and provided support in the face of illness and death. Jewish trade unions assumed functions not only in conducting labor negotiations but also in providing cultural and educational opportunities for workers. A vigorous Yiddish press provided a forum for disseminating ideas and giving circulation to literature. The flourishing Yiddish theater served as a vehicle for the expression and release of shared emotions and experiences. Political organizations of all shades and hues competed for the allegiance and support of the Jewish masses. In the midst of poverty and struggle one irrepressible characteristic flourished: vitality.

After the turn of the century, leaders of the americanized and largely native-born community took increasingly effective measures to deal with the problems of the immigrant element. Jacob Schiff and Louis Marshall were two who exercised leadership in organizing communal agencies that dealt with social welfare and civil rights. Among their endeavors was the reorganization of the Jewish Theological Seminary of America (JTSA) in 1901 to serve as a center for the creation of an American version of traditional Judaism. Their financial support made it possible to bring Solomon Schechter from England to serve as president of the seminary.

Schecter was a distinguished scholar who had both eastern European rabbinic training and a German university education. In addition he served as reader in rabbinics at Cambridge University in England. Schechter created a seminary in which traditional Jewish learning was combined with critical scholarship and use of the English language. Like the pragmatic reformers fifty years earlier, he emphasized decorum and dignity in religious worship.

Schechter and his associates accepted the idea that Judaism would change in response to modern conditions but believed that the necessary changes must be made within the framework of the Jewish legal tradition. The type of modified americanized traditionalism espoused at the Jewish Theological Seminary came to be known as Conservative Judaism—a position between Reform and Orthodoxy. In 1909, a Teachers Institute was established at the seminary. By 1913, Schechter was able to form the United Synagogue of America with sixteen congregations identified as Conservative and with the participation of the association of Conservative rabbis called the Rabbinical Assembly.

When the eastern European immigration grew enormously in the 1890s, an effort was organized by the Jewish Colonization Association to divert a portion of the immigrant stream to Argentina. The Jewish population of Argentina was then 6,085. By 1914, it was estimated as 100,000–117,000. The Jewish settlers who went to Argentina were predominantly secular in their outlook, and religious life remained at a low level. Not until 1910 were Jews there able to acquire their own cemetery. Not until the late 1930s did religious institutions of significance emerge in Argentina.

Changes after World War I. The outbreak of World War I interrupted the mass immigration to the United States. After the war it was briefly resumed and then was permanently reduced by Congress's adoption of stringent immigration quotas in 1921 and 1924. The process of americanization was accelerated as Jews moved out of immigrant ghettoes into second areas of settlement and up into the middle class. By the mid-1920s, the Jewish population of the United States was estimated at about four million.

The increase in affluence and acculturation resulted in a rash of synagogue building, especially in areas of new settlement. New structures were often elaborate and contained classrooms, auditoriums, and occasionally gymnasiums. Mordecai Kaplan (1881–1983), a Conservative rabbi and dean of the Teachers Institute of the Jewish Theological Seminary, developed the idea of a "synagogue-center" and established such an institution in New York.

The United Synagogue grew rapidly during the 1920s and 1930s. Conservative Judaism provided a combination of traditional ambience with English-language readings and sermons that appealed to the acculturated immigrant and the second-generation Jewish citizen for whom Reform was too cold and old-fashioned Orthodoxy too chaotic. Men and women sat together, the prayers were slightly abbreviated, and individuals whose attachment was more directed to the Jewish people than to religion could feel at home.

The Reform movement during this decade was at a virtual standstill. Its institutions were located in Cincinnati, now far from the centers of Jewish life, and its mode of worship attracted few of eastern European origin. Moreover, the prevailing anti-Zionism of the movement antagonized secularists with Zionist sentiments. To counter this trend, Stephen S. Wise, a Reform rabbi and leading Zionist, established the Jewish Institute of Religion in New York in 1922. In 1947, the institute was united with the Hebrew Union College and maintained as the New York branch of the combined Reform seminary.

The state of Orthodoxy in the 1920s is less clearly defined. On the one hand, americanized immigrants and their children were becoming less and less observant and many were abandoning religious practice and affiliation altogether. At the same time, small but significant steps were taken to develop an American form of Orthodoxy that might confront the challenge. In 1915 in New York, Bernard Revel became head of the Rabbi Isaac Elchanan Theological Seminary, which merged with Yeshivat Etz Chaim. Secular studies were introduced, and in 1928 Yeshiva College was established as the first general (nonrabbinic) institution of higher education under Jewish sponsorship. In 1923, the Rabbinical Council of America, in which alumni of American *yeshivot* predominated, was formed.

The restriction of immigration to the United States in the 1920s diverted a significant number of immigrants to Canada. Prior to 1900, the Jewish population of Canada numbered less than 16,000 and most of these were recent immigrants. By 1930, the population had increased to 140,000. The predominance of eastern European Jews who were recent immigrants and the multilingual nature of Canadian society resulted in a stronghold of Yiddish language and Jewish secular culture. The progress of the Reform movement there was slow whereas the Conservative movement made rapid strides. Both Conservative and Reform congregations and their rabbis are affiliated with the movements in the United States.

In the 1930s the rise of Hitler and the resurgence of anti-Semitism brought a radical change in the outlook and orientation of American Jewry. The Reform movement reassessed its attitude toward Jewish peoplehood, Zionism, and traditional practices. In 1937, the Reform Central Conference of American Rabbis (CCAR) adopted a new platform embracing these changes which stressed the "group-loyalty of Jews" and affirmed "the obligation of all Jews to aid in the rebuilding [of Palestine] as a Jewish homeland by endeavors to make it not only a haven for the oppressed but also a center of Jewish culture and spiritual life." The Union of American Hebrew Congregations (UAHC) unanimously passed a resolution urging restoration of traditional symbols and customs. In 1940, a revised version of the Reform movement's Union Prayer Book appeared; it restored some ceremonies and moved closer to the traditional prayer book.

The Conservative movement was energized by the ideas of Mordecai Kaplan, who described Judaism as a "religious civilization," and who stressed "peoplehood" and the totality of Jewish culture. In 1935, Kaplan founded the Reconstructionist movement as an ideological tendency within American Jewry in general and within the Conservative movement in particular. His theological emphasis on religious naturalism was less influential than his sociological emphasis on Jewish communality.

Orthodoxy in America was strengthened by the arrival of distinguished European scholars and rabbinic leaders at the end of the 1930s. Joseph Soloveitchik (1903–) became the leading rabbinical figure among the "enlightened Orthodox" associated with Yeshiva College and the religious Zionists. Moshe Feinstein (1895–1986), one of the leading rabbinical authorities in *halakhah* (Jewish law), became an outstanding figure in right-wing Orthodoxy and in the Agudat Yisra'el movement. The presence of these and other rabbinical leaders together with numbers of refugee *yeshivah* students paved the way for a revival of Orthodoxy in the postwar period.

The flow of refugees in the 1930s, seeking admission to any haven in which they could find respite, led to the strengthening of small Jewish communities in Central and South America. Immigration restrictions everywhere in the Western Hemisphere held the number of immigrants to a minimum, and religious life south of the border remained diffuse and disorganized. However, communal organizations stressing mutual aid and defense against anti-Semitism did emerge in countries such as Mexico, Brazil, and Chile. In 1982 the Jewish population of Latin America was estimated as 464,700. Of this total, 233,000 resided in Argentina, 100,000 in Brazil, 35,000 in Mexico, and 20,000 in Chile (*American Jewish Yearbook*, vol. 85, 1985, p. 55).

American Judaism since World War II. As a consequence of the destruction of European Jewry during World War II, the center of gravity of Jewish life shifted to the United States and to the newly founded state of Israel. The catastrophe in Europe and the struggle for the establishment of Israel had drawn hundreds of thousands of Jews into Jewish fund-raising and rescue activity. The heightened sense of Jewishness, combined with rapid suburbanization and the stimulus of the general religious revival in America, resulted in an unprecedented growth in Jewish religious institutions. The Reform movement, which claimed 290 temples and 50,000 families in 1937, reported 520 congregations and 255,000 families in 1956. The Conservative movement, with 250 synagogues and 75,000 member families in 1937, claimed over 500 congregations and 200,000 families in 1956. Both Reform and Conservative seminaries opened branches in the Los Angeles area. Synagogue affiliation—if not personal observance—had become a central element of Jewish identification in America.

New influences exerted themselves on Jewish religious life. Rabbis like Joshua Loth Liebman (1907–1948) led the way in reconciling religion with psychology. Will Herberg, sociologist and philosopher, and himself a returnee from Marxism to Judaism, led the way in redefining Judaism in terms of religious existentialism. Herberg also proposed a revision of the "melting pot" theory of American pluralism in which the three major religious traditions—Catholic, Protestant, and Jewish—would become the vehicle for preserving diversity in American society in what he described as a "triple melting pot." Abraham Joshua Heschel (1907–1972), a refugee rabbi and scholar from eastern Europe who became an influential member of the faculty of the Jewish Theological Seminary, espoused a Neo-Orthodox, neo-mystical approach to Judaism that proved to be extremely appealing to rabbis and laity alike.

Orthodoxy, which suffered numerical losses in the large-scale move from city to suburbs, nonetheless showed remarkable vigor. In 1945, Yeshiva College became Yeshiva University, and in subsequent years expanded to include Stern College for Women, Revel Graduate School, and Einstein Medical College. Jewish all-day schools on both the elementary and high school levels proliferated, primarily under Orthodox auspices.

Post–World War II immigration greatly strengthened the ultra-Orthodox segment of American Jewry, especially its Hasidic branch. Survivors of Hasidic Jewish communities, uprooted by Hitler, emigrated together with their rabbinic leaders *(rebeyim)* and settled in enclaves primarily in New York City and its vicinity. The branch of Hasidism known as Habad (Lubavitch) established a network of schools and centers and adopted a policy of outreach to secular and non-Hasidic Jews. In contrast, the extremist Satmar Hasidic sect maintained its isolation and its vigorous opposition to Zionism and the state of Israel on the grounds that the re-creation of a Jewish commonwealth must await the coming of a supernatural messiah sent by God. [*See* Hasidism.]

From the left wing of Reform to the most extreme right wing of Orthodoxy, Judaism in the United States and Canada grew in institutional strength and in vitality.

The Jewish religious revival of the 1950s seemed to wane in the early 1960s when the Jewish community, like the general society, was swept up in a wave of social action. While the "God is dead" movement never exercised significant influence within Judaism, there was a palpable diminution of involvement in religious institutions and a loss of influence by religious leaders. This tendency was sharply reversed in the late 1960s. The changing mood of the general community fueled a revival of ethnicity that strengthened Jewish identity and motivated increased Jewish communal involvement. At the same time, the threat to Israel's existence prior to the Six Day War in 1967 evoked strong emotions of commitment and solidarity among American Jews. The energies that were generated led to new initiatives within all religious movements in Judaism, especially on the part of young adults.

Among the results of this revival was a significant increase in the number and quality of Jewish day schools under Conservative and Reform, as well as Orthodox, auspices. A new form of religious fellowship called the *ḥavurah* emerged as a significant factor. These self-generated, intimate groups of intensely committed Jews were sometimes independent and sometimes to be found within large synagogues. In either case, they generally functioned without rabbinical supervision. Despite the informal structure and the absence of rigid institutional or ideological affiliation, *ḥavurah* groups grew sufficiently to form a network of their own and in 1979 established a National Havurah Committee which serves as a vehicle for exchange of ideas and experiences. In 1985, this committee estimated that between fifteen hundred and two thousand *ḥavurot* functioned regularly with membership ranging from twenty to eighty participants. Approximately 30 percent of these were affiliated with synagogues.

At the same time, the study of Judaism and Jewish subjects on the college campus expanded rapidly, often stimulated by student interest and by communal support. Together with these formal developments, a movement of *ba'alei teshuvah*—"penitent returners," who might be characterized as "born-again" Jews—gained strength. The returnees were to be found in all of the movements, but most visibly among the Orthodox.

While the general tendency in all branches of Judaism in recent years has been toward increased observance, the gap between the Orthodox and non-Orthodox has been widened by the conflict over women's rights. The Orthodox have resisted demands for changes in status in Jewish law by women in their own ranks and have maintained the traditional role of women as mothers and homemakers. The Reform and Reconstructionist movements have ordained women as rabbis and as cantors. The Conservative movement engaged in a lengthy struggle on this issue that was resolved only in 1984. The movement decided by a split vote to begin the ordination of women. Despite ongoing opposition by a "traditionalist" minority, the decision is being implemented.

Perhaps the most serious challenge faced by the community as a whole is the growing rate of intermarriage and the low birthrate. This tendency has been even more pronounced in the relatively small Jewish communities of Central and South America. Demographic projections envision a substantial reduction in the size of the Jewish community of the Western Hemisphere unless these tendencies can be reversed or at least contained. The Reform movement has reacted to this problem by initiating a program for converting non-Jewish spouses and integrating them into the community. It has also modified the traditional Jewish law that maintains that the child of a Jewish mother is a born Jew while the child of a Jewish father and a non-Jewish mother is not. Such changes have widened the gap between the movements and threaten to produce a schism within the Jewish community over the question "Who is a Jew?"

The prognosis for the future of American Jewry is subject to widely differing assessments. Optimists point to the increase in observance among significant numbers of American Jews; pessimists point to the large and growing number who are not affiliated with a synagogue or with any Jewish communal organization. Optimists point to the growth of Jewish day schools and their emergence in the Conservative and Reform branches of American Jewry; pessimists decry the decline in numbers and quality of supplementary afternoon and weekend schools and the sharp decline in enrollment. Optimists point to the development of programs of Jewish studies in universities, to developments in Jewish ritual art and cultural programs, and to innovative experiments in liturgy, music, and drama; pessimists view the increase in intermarriage and the low birthrate among Jews as symptoms of a decrease in numbers and vitality. Given the complexity and uncertainty of conditions in the last decades of the twentieth century, both points of view are plausible. American Jewry in 1986 remains a vigorous, densely organized, diverse community of 6.2 million, 45 percent of whom are affiliated with more than three thousand synagogues that encompass a wide variety of institutional and ideological options.

[*For further discussion of the four main movements in America, see the independent entries on* Orthodox Judaism; Reform Judaism; Conservative Judaism; *and* Reconstructionist Judaism. *See also the biographies of the leading figures mentioned herein.*]

BIBLIOGRAPHY

Blau, Joseph L. *Judaism in America.* Chicago, 1976.

Eisen, Arnold. *The Chosen People in America: A Study in Jewish Religious Ideology.* Bloomington, Ind., 1983.

Glazer, Nathan. *American Judaism.* Chicago, 1972.

Halpern, Ben. *The American Jew: A Zionist Analysis.* New York, 1956.

Jick, Leon A. *The Americanization of the Synagogue, 1820–1870.* Hanover, N.H., 1976.

Koltun, Elizabeth. *The Jewish Woman in America.* New York, 1976.

Korn, Bertram Wallace. *American Jewry and the Civil War.* New York, 1970.

Liebman, Charles S. *The Ambivalent American Jew: Politics, Religion and Family in American Jewish Life.* Philadelphia, 1973.

Marcus, Jacob R. *The Colonial American Jew, 1492–1776.* 3 vols. Detroit, 1970.

Marcus, Jacob R. *The American Jewish Woman, 1654–1980: A Documentary History.* New York, 1981.

Sherman, Charles Bezalel. *The Jews within American Society: A Study in Ethnic Individuality.* Detroit, 1961.

Sidorsky, David, ed. *The Future of the Jewish Community in America.* New York, 1973.

Sklare, Marshall. *America's Jews.* New York, 1971.

Sklare, Marshall. *Conservative Judaism: An American Religious Movement.* New York, 1972.

Teller, Judd L. *Strangers and Natives: The Evolution of the Jew from 1921 to the Present.* New York, 1968.

LEON A. JICK

JUDGMENT OF THE DEAD.

In religions where a differentiation is made between the righteous and sinners in the hereafter, the decision to which category to assign each individual can be thought to take place in different ways. Sometimes it is an automatic process, as in the Indian doctrine of *karman*; each individual's deeds in this life determine his status in his next existence. In other cases, it is believed that the deceased has to pass over a narrow bridge; if he is good there is no difficulty, but if he is evil he is thrown down. This idea is found in ancient Iranian religion, and similar beliefs exist among the Algonquin Indians, the Mari (Cheremis) in Russia, and the Bojnang of the island of Sulawesi. Here no god or personal being seems to be involved in the decision. In other cases, however, a court scene is presupposed, with divine or semidivine judges passing on each individual.

Ancient Near East. The evidence from ancient Mesopotamia is scanty. One Assyrian text tells the story of a crown prince descending into the netherworld and appearing before its king, Nergal, who decides that he is to return to life. It seems likely that this text presents the mythical background of an incantation rite, and thus refers only to a decision in the netherworld whether a sick person should die or recover. It does not refer to a regular judgment of the dead. Texts from the sixth century BCE, found at Susa in southwestern Iran, mention some sort of judgment that gives the good some advantage over the wicked, but they hardly represent genuine Babylonian belief; possibly they were influenced by Iranian ideas.

Ancient Egyptian religion is especially known for its concern about life in the hereafter. However, in the Pyramid Texts, the oldest funerary texts at our disposal, there is no reference to a judgment of the dead. Though we find the idea that the king still carries out his earthly function as a judge, he is not said to judge the dead in general. Several tomb inscriptions from the Old Kingdom warn that anyone who violates the tomb will be "judged by the Great God at the place of judgment." But that again is no judgment of the dead. On the other hand, autobiographical texts from the same period express the wish that the author's name "may be good before the Great God." This seems to imply some kind of judgment in the hereafter. The same is true of inscriptions in which the dead person promises to defend anyone who respects his tomb "in the judgment hall of the Great God." But in the *Instruction for Merikare* (early Middle Kingdom) there is a clear passage referring to "the judges who judge the sinner" in the hereafter as not being lenient. Therefore man should remember that he must die, and that after his death his sins will be laid beside him in a heap. Anyone who lives unmindful of the judgment in the hereafter is foolish, but anyone who has not sinned will be like a god in eternal freedom.

A different outlook is reflected in the Coffin Texts. Here magical spells are used to secure various privileges for the deceased in the hereafter. There is also reference to a court of judgment presided over by the earth god Geb, who issues decrees to the benefit of the deceased in the same way as an earthly court might. Gradually it becomes customary to add to the name of the deceased person the epithet *maa kheru*, which denotes him as cleared by the court of an accusation. This title was also given to Osiris, when he had been declared righteous in the court of Geb and had been reinstated in his royal rights (though he was now in the netherworld). As it became customary to identify every dead person with Osiris, he was also certain of being *maa kheru*.

The final result of this development appears in the well-known judgment scene in the *Book of Going Forth by Day*. Chapter 125 describes how the deceased appears before Osiris, the divine judge of the netherworld, who is assisted by forty-two assessors, one for each of the provinces of Egypt. It seems that we are here confronted with two different sets of ideas. According to the text, the deceased addresses the assessors, asserting that he has not committed forty-two specific sins; this is often referred to as the "negative confession." The scene depicted, on the other hand, shows the deceased being led before the judges by Horus; in front of Osiris there is a balance, attended by the god Anubis. On one scale is put the heart of the dead man, on the other a feather, the symbol of the goddess Maat ("truth"). The wise god Thoth takes down the result of the weighing on his scribe's palette. The illustrations always present the scales in perfect equilibrium, indicating that the dead man's life has been in accordance with *maat*, the principle of order and truth. If such is the case, the deceased is declared to be *maa kheru*, "true of voice," that is, acquitted in the court of Osiris. If not, he will be eaten by the "devourer of the dead."

All this seems to imply high moral standards. But in fact this chapter of the *Book of Going Forth by Day* is hardly more than another magic spell, intended to protect the deceased from the perils of the other world. The negative confession is rather an expression of acceptance of the validity of certain moral principles (in the last count, of *maat*) than a real declaration that one is not guilty. In addition, there are also spells to prevent the heart from "standing up against" the deceased (*Book of Going Forth by Day*, chap. 30). Thus there is a tension between moral obligations on the one hand and recourse to magical spells on the other.

India and China. Ancient Indian religion seems to know King Yama as the judge of the other world. A late Vedic text (*Taittirīya Āraṇyaka* 6.5.13) states that before Yama those who have been faithful to truth and those who have spoken lies will part company. There is no explicit reference to a judgment, but it may be implied. The weighing of good and wicked deeds is referred to in the Brahmanic texts.

This same Yama appears again in the pantheon of Mahāyāna Buddhism. In China he is called Yen-lo or Yen-lo Wang. Together with nine others of Chinese origin ("the Ten Kings") he is believed to be the administrator of the punishments of Hell. It is believed that all men are to meet him after death and be judged with the strictest impartiality. It is supposed that he fixes the hour of dissolution, and that once the decision is made, nothing can alter or postpone it. In Japanese Buddhism he is called Enma-ō.

Ancient Greece and Rome. In ancient Greece, we find, in Homer and Hesiod, for example, the idea of a shadowy and dreary realm of the dead, called Hades, to which the "souls" of all dead come; but there are also at times the ideas of a miry place where the wicked are punished and of the Elysian Fields, where a few righteous are allowed to enter. But we are not told how it is decided who is going where. Homer says that Minos gives laws to the dead but does not act as judge (*Odyssey* 11.567ff.).

Gradually, however, under the influence of the mystery cults and of the Orphic and Pythagorean movements, the ideas of judgment and retribution were developed. Pythagoras taught a judgment of souls (according to the biography of Iamblichus), and the Orphic judgment is depicted on a vase that shows Aiakos, Triptolemos, and Rhadamanthos as judges.

The ideas of the Orphics and Pythagoreans are reproduced by Pindar and by Plato in some of his dialogues (*Gorgias*, *Apology*, the *Republic*). Usually, the judges are three, Minos, Rhadamanthos, and Aiakos; in the *Apology* Plato adds Triptolemos. They give judgment in a meadow, at the parting of the ways, one of which leads to the Abode of the Blessed, the other to Tartaros.

In *Gorgias* Plato says that in the beginning the dead were sent to the Island of the Blessed or to the punishment in Tartaros; the judgment was pronounced on the day of death, but apparently it was sometimes influenced by the outer appearance of the person in question. Therefore Zeus decreed that souls should be judged naked, without their earthly frame. Punishment could serve for purification and improvement; but there are some evildoers who cannot be saved. Here, in part, Plato is using traditional ideas, possibly Orphic and other; but he may have created the eschatological myth he presents here to illustrate his philosophical ideas.

Such beliefs were probably widespread among the Greeks, as is shown by numerous references to judgment and the fate of souls in Lucian's satires, and by the caricatures of Aristophanes. The classical dramatists rarely mention a judgment of the dead, but there are a few references in Aeschylus, and it figures sporadically in other authors and in grave inscriptions. In Vergil's picture of the underworld, Minos judges certain crimes, and Rhadamanthos is judge in Tartaros (*Aeneid* 6.426ff., 540ff.).

Judaism. The writings of intertestamental Judaism contain occasional references to a judgment of the dead. The scene in the seventh chapter of the *Book of Daniel*, where the Ancient of Days opens the books and passes judgment, is not concerned with individuals, but with the kingdoms of the earth, and it is Israel that stands acquitted. But in chapter 50 of the Ethiopic *Apocalypse of Enoch* there is an explicit mention of judgment, in which the Lord of the Spirits will show himself righteous, sinners will be punished, and the righteous will be saved. Chapter 51 then speaks of the resurrection of the dead, and says that the Chosen One will sit on God's throne, probably as judge. The same idea is found in *2 Esdras* (chapter 7): the earth will give up those who are asleep in it, and the Most High will appear on the seat of judgment. The emphasis here, however, is not on the scene of judgment but on the resurrection, and on the destiny of the righteous and the wicked.

There are occasional references in these scriptures to books in which the deeds of men are recorded, and according to which they will be judged (Ethiopic *Apocalypse of Enoch* 47:3, 90:20), but the context does not mention a final judgment in connection with the resurrection. Thus, the weighing of men's works on a balance is referred to (ibid. 41:1, 61:8) without mentioning the judgment.

Christianity. Jesus tells the parable of the last judgment in chapter 25 of the *Gospel of Matthew*. The Son of man is to come and sit on his glorious throne, and all nations will gather before him; he will "separate them as a shepherd separates the sheep from the goats." Those who have acted in love for their neighbors will receive eternal life; those who have not will be sent away into eternal punishment.

Though this description of a final judgment is found only in the *Gospel of Matthew*, it is obvious from other occasional references in the New Testament that the idea was essential in early Christian preaching. Thus, in *Acts* 17:31, "God has fixed a day on which he will judge the world in righteousness by a man whom he has appointed [i.e., Jesus Christ]." In *Acts* 10:42, Christ "is the one ordained by God to be judge of the living and the dead"; in *2 Corinthians* 5:10, "we must all appear before the judgment seat of Christ [or, in *Romans* 14:10, of God], so that each one may receive good or evil, according to what he has done in the body." The last judgment is thus connected with the Parousia, or second coming of Christ.

In the *Gospel of John*, the idea of the judgment has been transformed in a peculiar way. Though it is stated that God the Father "has given all judgment to the Son" (5:22), we learn that one who believes "has eternal life" (here and now) "and does not come into judgment, but has passed from death to life" (5:24). In other words, the outcome of Christ's judgment is decided here and now, according to the belief or unbelief of each one; this should leave no room for a final judgment at the end of time.

The Christian church has placed considerable emphasis on the idea of the final judgment (that is, rather than on the judgment here and now). Both the Apostles' Creed and the Nicene Creed state that Christ "will come again (in glory) to judge the living and the dead."

Islam. In the preaching of Muḥammad the imminent day of judgment (*yawm al-dīn*) has a prominent place. Since many of the accompanying motifs correspond to Jewish and Christian ideas (not the least to the preaching of the Syriac church), it seems obvious that he has taken over the idea of judgment from these sources. The day is also referred to as the day of resurrection, the day of decision (Qur'ān, surah 77:13), the day of gathering (64:9), the day of eternity (50:34), and so forth. It is a day of great catastrophes that cause fear and terror on the earth. The judgment is individual. On that day "no soul will be able to help another, for the decision belongs to God" (82:19). Each soul must defend itself (16:112) and cannot bear the load of another (17:15, cf. 16:25); no soul will be able to give satisfaction or to make intercession for another (2:48); no ransom will be accepted (5:36). The works of each man will be documented in an irrefutable way. Books will be produced, in which "everything that they have done, great and small, is recorded" (54:52ff.). "The book will be put (before them), and you will see the sinners fearful at what is in it. . . . It leaves nothing behind, small or great, but it has numbered it. And they shall find all they did present, and your Lord shall not wrong anyone" (18:49). Every man shall find a book wide open: "Read your book! Today you are yourself a reckoner against yourself" (17:13ff.). The idea of books that are opened is found in the Hebrew Bible (*Dn.* 7:10) and in other Jewish literature (see above) in connection with a judgment scene. In addition, it may be that Muḥammad, as a merchant, was familiar with the keeping of accounts.

There is also in the Qur'ān the idea of weighing man's deeds. "We shall set up the just balances . . . so that not one soul shall be wronged anything; even if it be the weight of one grain of mustard-seed we shall produce it; and we know how to reckon" (21:49). "The weighing that day is true; he whose scales are heavy—they are the prosperous, and he whose scales are light—they have lost their souls" (7:8ff.; cf. 23:102 and 101:5ff.). There is here hardly any connection with the Egyptian ideas discussed above; the ideas of Muḥammad seem rather closer to those of the Jewish texts.

In the case of Islam, those who stand the trial will enter Paradise, and those who fail will be thrown into Hell. However, no one belief concerning the fate following judgment of the dead is common to all religious traditions. That fate is determined according to each tradition's conception of what happens after death. Just as the judgment of the dead is conceived in different ways within the different traditions, so too is the ultimate fate of the person who is judged.

[*See also* Afterlife.]

BIBLIOGRAPHY

A cross-cultural collection of sources on this topic is *Le jugement des morts: Égypte ancienne, Assour, Babylone, Israël, Iran, Islam, Inde, Chine, Japon*, "Sources orientales," no. 4 (Paris, 1961). For a treatment of the beliefs about the judgment of the dead in Egyptian religion, see *Die Idee vom Totengericht in der ägyptischen Religion* (Hamburg, 1935) by Joachim Spiegel. See also *The Dawn of Conscience* (New York, 1933), pp. 250ff., by James Henry Breasted. See my *Religions of the Ancient Near East*, translated by John Sturdy (Philadelphia, 1973), pp. 122ff., for a brief treatment of Mesopotamian ideas on the judgment of the dead. Volume 1 of H. C. C. Cavallin's *Life after Death*: *Paul's Argument for the Resurrection of the Dead* (Lund, 1974) treats the topic as it relates to Judaism. Two discussions of Christian beliefs about the judgment of the dead are John A. T. Robinson's *Jesus and His Coming* (New York, 1957) and his article "The Parable of the Sheep and Goats," *New Testament Studies* 2 (May 1956): 225–237. The only monograph on Greek ideas about judgment is in Latin: *De mortuorum iudicio* (Giessen, 1903) by Ludwig Ruhl. See also Fritz Graf's *Eleusis und die orphische Dichtung Athens in vorhellenistischer Zeit* (Berlin, 1974), pp. 79–150, and Franz Cumont's *After Life in Roman Paganism* (1922; reprint, New York, 1959). On Plato's treatment of the topic, see *Les mythes de Platon* (Paris, 1930) by Perceval Frutiger. Two studies of the Iranian view are *The Zoroastrian Doctrine of a Future Life* (New York, 1926) by J. D. C. Pavry, and R. C. Zaehner's *The Teachings of the Magi* (New York, 1956), pp. 131ff. Arthur Berriedale Keith's *Indian Mythology* (Boston, 1917), pp. 159ff., and Bimala Churn Law's *Heaven and Hell in Buddhist Perspective* (1925; reprint, Varanasi, 1973), pp. 96ff., present Indian and Buddhist ideas of judgment.

HELMER RINGGREN

JULIAN OF HALICARNASSUS (d. after 518), Christian bishop and theologian. The place and date of birth of this prominent fifth- and early sixth-century churchman are unknown. Of his early life we know that as bishop of Halicarnassus in Asia Minor he had sojourned in Constantinople around 510, perhaps between 508 and 511. There he participated in the discussions as to whether the decisions of the Council of Chalcedon (451) ought to be abrogated in order to achieve church unity.

As bishop of Halicarnassus, Julian had been a protagonist of the monophysites, who maintained that Christ had only a divine nature, denying the reality of his humanity. At first Julian followed the moderate views of his friend Severus of Antioch, one of the leading critics of the Chalcedonian formula, according to which Christ is "one hypostasis [essence, entity] in two natures."

Julian's significance lies in the fact that he parted with the moderate monophysites. Deposed from his see in 518, he fled to Egypt, where he promulgated his theory known as aphthartodocetism (incorruptibility). Julian taught that, from the moment of its conception, the human nature of Christ was incorruptible, impassible, immortal, and free from all physical burdens such as hunger, thirst, and pain. Thus Christ's human sufferings were apparent rather than real, a theory similar to docetism. His followers in Alexandria established their own community and became known as Aphthartodocitae and Phantasiastai.

Not only the Orthodox Chalcedonians but also Julian's former friend Severus of Antioch attacked his teachings. Julian wrote a treatise entitled *Peri aphtharsias* (About Incorruptibility), directed against Severus, and an *Apologia* defending his own teachings. Of his writings only two letters and fragments of his theological works, in the original Greek and in Syriac translation, have survived.

BIBLIOGRAPHY

The sources for Julian's writings are *Spicilegium Romanum*, vol. 10, *Synodus cpolitana*, edited by Angelo Mai (Rome, 1844), pp. 206–211, and *Anecdota Syriaca*, vol. 3, edited by J. P. N. Land (Leiden, 1870), pp. 263–271. Studies of Julian include René Draguet's *Julien d'Halicarnasse et sa controverse avec Sévère d'Antioche sur l'incorruptibilité du corps du Christ* (Louvain, 1924) and "Pièces de polémique antijulianiste," *Le Muséon* 44 (1931): 255–317; Martin Jugie's "Julien d'Halicarnasse et Sévère d'Antioche," *Échos d'Orient* 24 (1925): 129–162, 257–285; and Robert P. Casey's "Julian of Alicarnassus," *Harvard Theological Review* 19 (1926): 206–213.

DEMETRIOS J. CONSTANTELOS

JULIAN OF NORWICH (1342–1416?), known as Lady Julian, Dame Julian, and Mother Julian; English mystic and Christian theologian. Julian lived in the century in which Europe was ravaged by the Black Death, and England and France were torn by the Hundred Years War. Against a background of war, plague, social turmoil, and religious unrest she shared in a flowering of English mysticism along with Walter Hilton, Richard Rolle, Margery Kempe, and the anonymous author of *The Cloud of Unknowing*.

Highly literate—despite a polite disclaimer in her book *Revelations* [or *Showings*] *of Divine Love*—and demonstrating a knowledge of the Vulgate rare for a layperson of her day, she was the first woman to compose a literary work in English. Although scholars have traced many general theological influences in Julian's book, specific influences are hard to identify, so thoroughly assimilated are they into a theology that is at once deeply traditional and highly original. She was probably familiar with the writings of William of Saint Thierry (d. 1148) and Meister Eckhart (d. around 1327), but the only two writers whom she mentions by name are Dionysius the Areopagite (c. 500) and Gregory I (d. 604), from whose *Life of Saint Benedict* she quotes.

Little is known about Julian's life. In May 1373, when Julian was thirty years old, she became severely ill. At what seemed the point of death, she revived and received what she described as fifteen "showings of God's love"; on the following day she had a sixteenth such experience. Her mother, her parish priest, and possibly others were with her at these times. Some time later Julian wrote a description of these showings that is now referred to as the "short text" or "short version." Twenty years later, after profound meditation, she felt she had come to a fuller understanding of the showings, and she wrote a much longer version, concluding: "So I was taught that love is our Lord's meaning. And I saw very certainly in this and in everything that before God made us he loved us, which love was never abated and never will be" (Colledge and Walsh, *Showings*, p. 342).

At some time in her life Julian became an anchoress, living in a cell attached to the church of Saint Julian in King Street. It was probably from this saint that she took the name by which she is known.

The all-encompassing theme of Julian's *Revelations* is the compassionate love of God as universally manifested throughout the process of creation and as focused in the passion of Jesus, whose delight was to suffer for his beloved humankind. One aspect of Christ stressed by Julian is his "motherhood." Many earlier writers, including Anselm, had written of Christ's motherhood, but Julian wrote more extensively on this theme.

Julian's theology is eschatologically orientated. The resolution of the problem of evil (a problem over which she agonizes at length) will come through a "great deed ordained by our Lord God from without beginning, treasured and hidden in his blessed breast, known only to himself, through which deed he will make all things well" (Colledge and Walsh, *Showings*, pp. 232–233). This aspect of Julian's theology proved particularly interesting to T. S. Eliot, who quotes from her book and alludes to her thought in his mystical poem *Four Quartets*.

The enduring contemporary interest in Julian was expressed in an ecumenical celebration in Norwich in May 1973, the six-hundredth anniversary of her *Revelations*. Her influence continues at the Julian shrine in Norwich, where prayer and spiritual counsel continue in a chapel built where her cell once stood.

BIBLIOGRAPHY

Basic information on Julian herself and on the six-hundredth-anniversary ecumenical celebration of *Revelations* is conveniently given in *Julian and Her Norwich: Commemorative Essays and Handbook to the Exhibition "Revelations of Divine Love,"* edited by Frank D. Sayer (Norwich, England, 1973). This book includes a useful bibliography of Julian publications prior to 1973: five manuscripts, twenty-six printed editions (in German, French, and Italian as well as English), and fifty-six books and articles about Julian and her thought. For works published since 1973, the *Fourteenth-Century English Mystics Newsletter* (Iowa City), published quarterly since 1974, is indispensable. Renamed *Mystics Quarterly* in 1984, this journal contains articles, book reviews, descriptions of scholarly studies in progress, and bibliographies of the many books and articles on Julian, including a Swedish translation and two French translations of *Revelations*. Among the post-1973 works, one of the most significant is the definitive edition of the original text prepared by Edmund Colledge and James Walsh, *Juliana, anchoret, 1343–1443: A Book of Showings to the Anchoress Julian of Norwich*, 2 vols. (Toronto, 1978). From this critical text Colledge and Walsh have made a modern translation, *Julian of Norwich: Showings*, "The Classics of Western Spirituality," vol. 1 (New York, 1978). Another significant English translation published since 1973 is *Revelations of Divine Love by Juliana of Norwich*, translated with a particularly good introduction by M. L. Del Mastro (Garden City, N.Y., 1977). The chaplain of the Julian shrine in Norwich, England, Robert Llewelyn, has written *With Pity, Not with Blame: Reflections on the Writings of Julian of Norwich and on The Cloud of Unknowing* (London, 1982). Many Julian publications are available at the shrine. In addition, the Norwich Public Library has a sizable collection of printed material on Julian.

Barbara Bishop

JUNAYD, AL- (AH 210?–298?/825?–910? CE), more fully Abū al-Qāsim al-Junayd; Ṣūfī master associated with the sober trend in Islamic mysticism. Born into a Baghdad family of merchants who originally came from Iran, he was brought up under the care and guidance of his uncle, Sarī al-Saqaṭī (d. 867?), who may be considered the founder of the Baghdad school of Sufism. Al-Junayd himself turned to Sufism after studying *sharī'ah* (law), *ḥadīth* (tradition), and *kalām* (theology). The most important of his Ṣūfī teachers were al-Saqaṭī and Ḥārith al-Muḥāsibī (d. 857?); he was also influenced by Abū Yazīd al-Bisṭāmī (d. 848), whose teaching he probably came to know through Yaḥyā al-Rāzī (d. 872). Among his friends, associates, and pupils were Abū Sa'īd al-Kharrāz (d. 890), Abū Bakr al-Shiblī (d. 848), and Abū al-Ḥasan al-Nūrī (d. 907). It is interesting to note that al-Junayd refused to accept al-Ḥusayn ibn Manṣūr al-Ḥallāj (d. 922) as a pupil.

The central point of al-Junayd's teaching is the doctrine of *tawḥīd* (unification), which he defines as "the isolation of the eternal [*al-qadīm*] from the contingent [*al-muḥdath*]." According to al-Junayd, the soul, shorn of its attachments to the world, returns to the state in which it existed prior to entering the physical body. This is the state in which the soul made a covenant *(mīthāq)* with God by answering "yes" to his question "Am I not your Lord?" (surah 7:171). Thus, in a state of unification, the pristine soul is reunited with the divine. The last state of the Ṣūfī becomes the first.

Al-Junayd's teaching manifests a well-structured body of thought. He classified men of *tawḥīd* into three categories: ordinary Muslims, theologians, and Ṣūfīs. Ordinary Muslims affirm God's oneness as expressed in the formula "Lā ilāha illā Allāh" ("There is no god but God"). The theologians possess reason and understanding in addition to affirming God's oneness. These additional qualities enable them to understand God's essence and attributes and distinguish between right and wrong. Finally, the Ṣūfīs not only possess the qualities of the other two groups but also verify in their own experience the truth of God's oneness. Thus the men of *tawḥīd* represent varying degrees of truth; for al-Junayd, all Muslims, including theologians and Ṣūfīs, are on the right path.

Corresponding to the three degrees of truth are three degrees of knowledge. The knowledge of ordinary Muslims is based on mere faith, while that of the theologians is based on faith and reason. The Ṣūfīs have both faith and reason, but in addition they have *ma'rifah,* which is God's knowledge of himself bestowed on the select.

A significant aspect of al-Junayd's teaching is the doctrine of *ṣaḥw* ("sobriety"), according to which the Ṣūfī who has reached the state of unification must become involved in the everyday world and serve as a guide to the community. This doctrine shows al-Junayd's respect for the *sharī'ah* and concern for the community.

Whereas the Ṣūfīs of the early period were primarily concerned with actual mystical experience and the practical methods of attaining it, al-Junayd served as a bridge to the period that saw the emergence of Ṣūfī theorists. He also may be credited with bringing about a synthesis of *sharī'ah* Islam and Sufism. In his assertion that Sufism is bound up with the tradition of the Prophet he brought Sufism within the framework of orthodoxy and in this respect was a precursor of Abū Ḥāmid al-Ghazālī two centuries later.

BIBLIOGRAPHY

An important source of information on al-Junayd is provided by the letters *(Rasā'il)* that he wrote to his fellow Ṣūfīs, although the language was made deliberately obscure for non-Ṣūfīs because of the hostility of the religious establishment at the time. These letters have been preserved in Istanbul (Shehit Ali MS 1374).

Further information about his life and thought is available in the *Kitāb al-luma'* of al-Sarrāj (d. 988), the *Qūt al-qulūb* of al-Makkī (d. 996), and the *Ta'arruf* of al-Kalābādhī (d. 995).

For modern studies, see Ali Hassan Abdel-Kader, *The Life, Personality and Writings of al-Junayd* (London, 1976), which includes the Arabic text of the *Rasā'il* and an English translation that is not altogether satisfactory. See also my "Al-Junayd's Doctrine of Tawḥīd: An Analysis of His Understanding of Islāmic Monotheism" (M.A. thesis, McGill University, 1967).

MUHAMMAD ABDUR RABB

JUNG, C. G. (1875–1961), originator of analytical psychology: a theory of individual psychotherapy, of religion, and of Western culture. Until recently, accounts of the life and work of Carl Gustav Jung have emphasized the great influence of Sigmund Freud and have portrayed Jung as first an obedient follower of Freud and then a rebellious dissident. While it is true that Jung's personality and his ideas were to a great extent shaped by his contact with Freud, it is just as important to recognize Jung's independence and originality. In at least three major respects, his person and thought stand apart from Freud's influence: his Christian background, his mature conviction that psychoanalysis or depth psychology is inseparable from a religious appreciation of the world, and his commitment to the religious humanism of the Western university. These inform in one way or another Jung's life and all his works, his psychology of religion and his appeal to scholars of religion. For Jung exercised greater influence upon humanistic religious scholarship than did Freud, whose psychology has been taken up more by the social sciences.

Life and Principal Works. Jung was born in the village of Kesswil, Switzerland, the son of a Protestant minister. When he was four, the family moved to Basel, on Lake Constance, where Jung spent his childhood and youth, taking a medical degree from the University of Basel in 1902. Believing that psychiatry would allow him to combine his scientific and humanistic interests, he joined the staff of the Burghölzli, the psychiatric clinic of the University of Zurich, where he worked under Eugen Bleuler, its highly regarded director. In 1903, he married Emma Rauschenbach and moved to Küsnacht, a small village near Zurich, on the shore of Lake Zurich, where he lived for the rest of his life.

Shortly after the beginning of his psychiatric career, Jung's life became active and eventful. In 1900, Sigmund Freud published what came to be his most famous book, *The Interpretation of Dreams,* and began to attract a talented following. Among the most gifted was Carl Jung. A correspondence developed, and the two men met in 1906. For the next seven years, Jung's life was shaped almost entirely by his relationship to Freud. The two men became intimate friends and their correspondence became lengthy. Jung concluded that Freud's theories of the unconscious, dreams, childhood conflict, and psychological illnesses (the neuroses) were essentially correct, and he adopted them in his own psychiatric work. He wrote various papers, which he delivered to scientific societies, explaining and advancing Freud's ideas. During this period, Freud considered Jung to be his most promising colleague.

For many reasons, however, this close and spirited collaboration did not last. Each man began to misunderstand the other, and strong, heated resentments made their appearance. There were important differences regarding the nature of psychological theory: Freud insisted upon the sexual roots of neurosis, whereas Jung advanced a nonsexual approach. Also significant was the fact that, as both men began to apply psychoanalysis to religion, they evolved different assessments of the psychological significance of religion. Jung believed he could discern a religious dimension in psychoanalysis, whereas Freud insisted upon an entirely scientific understanding of it. As a result, the two broke off their personal correspondence and abandoned all professional collaboration in 1913. From this time forward, their personal lives, careers, psychological theories, and theories of religion went down divergent paths, and neither ever forgot the bitterness that brought this period of Jung's life to an end.

Freud survived his disappointment with Jung by turning his energies to his other followers and to the increased recognition his own ideas were receiving from the world, but Jung had far less upon which to fall back. He found it necessary to isolate himself. In 1913, he resigned the teaching post at the University of Zurich that he had held since 1905, and he withdrew from the International Psychoanalytic Association. He had left the Burghölzli in 1909. Having made these breaks, Jung entered a period of intense inner psychological stress, during which he found himself beset by disturbing fantasies, visions, and dreams. For the next several years he occupied himself with the products of his own mind, analyzing them and devising theories for interpreting them.

In 1918, Jung was able to look back upon this turbulent period and to understand it in retrospect as the most creative time of his entire life. At its close, he wrote what have become his two most important works; they contain all the major ideas of what became, taking its form from these books, analytical psychology. In *Two Essays on Analytical Psychology* (both essays were revised several times during his life), Jung set forth his understanding of the psychological process of individuation, and in *Psychological Types* he created a long and complex set of definitions for the various concepts that were unique to his system of thought. These books established Jung's reputation as the founder of the school of analytical psychology.

For the remainder of his life, Jung practiced his particular approach to psychotherapy, wrote voluminously, and lectured and traveled widely. In addition to psychotherapy, two subjects were of special interest to him, Western religion and the moral failures of modern society. His best-known books on these are *Answer to Job* (1952) and *The Undiscovered Self* (1957). Late in his life Jung dictated an autobiographical memoir, *Memories, Dreams, Reflections* (1963), in which he reviewed and explained his own personal psychological history, his major works, and his philosophical and religious values.

Analytical Psychology of Religion. Although Jung began his professional career as a psychiatrist, he was always deeply interested in religion. Unlike Freud, who applied psychoanalysis to religion, Jung thought that religion was an essential dimension of the psychotherapeutic process as well as of life. His analytical psychology of the mind was therefore also a religious psychology. Furthermore, he in effect situated his psychological theory of psychotherapy and of religion in the flow of Western religious and scientific traditions, creating a sweeping understanding of the modern world.

Unlike Freud, who highly valued enhanced social adaptation for his patients, Jung set forth individuation as the goal of his therapy. By this he meant a process of psychological transformation in which the patient gradually abandoned the stereotyped expectations of conventional society, which Jung called the *persona,* or mask, in order to discover his or her hidden, unique, and true self. Individuation does not proceed by conscious willing and thinking, but by making the unconscious conscious, and this in turn can occur only through the analysis of dream symbols. Dream interpretation integrates the contents of the unconscious into conscious mental life. Jung distinguished between fantasies and dreams deriving from personal development and those that he thought were universal or common to all historical periods and civilizational contexts. He named the latter "archetypes" and linked them to a universally shared unconscious, the collective unconscious. Thus Jung spoke of the archetype of the mother, or of the father, or of the child. So understood, the process of individuation refers not only to the psychology of the immediate psychotherapeutic situation but also to the lifelong process of growth. [*See* Archetypes.]

Jung's psychology of individuation cannot be completely understood without explicit reference to religion and to the concept of God. Jung discovered that, as his patients neared the end of their treatment, their archetypal imaginings usually portrayed an awesome authority figure who resembled a powerful father, and he named this figure a "god-imago." The word *imago* refers to the inner psychological experience of God and not necessarily to his objective reality. Thus Jung espoused psychological functionalism, in effect confessing that he was more interested in people's experiences of God than in the theological problem of the existence or nonexistence of God. Once the god-imago or god archetype had been created, projected, experienced consciously, and finally understood or interpreted, the individuation process was well-nigh complete.

While Jung thought that this version of the individuation process was valid for most of his patients, whose Christian heritage contained a shared imago of the one transcendent god of the Western traditions, his psychology of archetypes was broader still. It was really a psychology of all religious myths—and Jung did not hesitate to refer to the Christian "myth." He believed that all religious myths in all civilizational contexts were the product of archetypal experiences. Borrowing a concept from the Protestant theologian Rudolf Otto, and universalizing it, Jung declared that myths, or archetypal products, exercised "numinous" or awe-inspiring effects, which derived from the unconscious. Following this insight, Jung was able to write psychological commentaries on Eastern religions as well as on Western traditions.

A good deal of scholarly discussion of Jung's psychological theories of religion state that he found in Eastern religion a solution or cure for the spiritual ills or meaninglessness of the modern West. But most of Jung's work on religion in fact focused on Western traditions, and in particular on Christianity. This was due in part to his own Christian upbringing, against which he vigorously rebelled as a youth, but which also continued to influence him, and in part to his deep love of the humanistic traditions of the West, inspired as these were by Christian values and ideals. In fact, Jung sought to situate his new psychology of the unconscious, and Freud's as well, in the religious traditions of the West. In doing so, he evolved his own psychology of Western religion and science.

Jung proposed that Western culture had developed in three stages—first religious, then scientific, and finally psychological—and that each stage was in effect a different response to the universal reality of the unconscious. The Middle Ages, he said, were almost entirely religious. In that period the unconscious was experienced by all in the form of religious images: God (the father archetype), the church and the Virgin Mary (the mother archetype), and Christ (the archetype of the self). In the Renaissance and the Enlightenment, science and reason became dominant, and these repressed, through the development of the ego, the collective unconscious and religious reality. Finally, in the modern period, characterized by the discovery of the unconscious, religion and science became realigned. Jung believed that his psychology—and Freud's as well—were sciences; but they were sciences of the unconscious, of the deep psychological forces that had created religion. Therefore analytical psychology brought religion and science into a new synthesis. In this way, Jung was able to offer his psychology to modern men and women as a means of being both modern or scientific and religious or traditional, without compromising one or the other.

Contribution to the Study of Religion. That Jung's psychological theories have exercised more influence on humanistic studies of religion than have Freud's is due at least in part to Jung's own view that religion is an enduring dimension in human life, a view that does not reduce religion to either psychological-developmental or sociological factors. But there are other reasons. Humanistic scholars of religion are principally concerned with figures, symbols, myths, interpretation, and meaning. Jung's psychological theory of unconscious, archetypal dream symbols facilitates the scholar's task of relating the imagination of readers and audiences directly and immediately to the symbols in literary and religious texts. And because archetypes are a kind of universal language of symbols, an analysis of texts can be made without taking into account the historical and sociological contexts in which they were created.

Many excellent and widely acclaimed studies of religious myths have been created that utilize Jung's psychology. Of these, the best known are the works of Joseph Campbell, in particular *The Hero with a Thousand Faces.* Campbell combines an extensive knowledge of the mythologies of the world's religions with his profound grasp of Jung's psychological theories, and incorporates as well many of Freud's insights. Campbell's method is that of psychological interpretation. He attempts to reconstruct a single pattern of meaning that threads itself throughout the otherwise diverse contents of various myths; this he calls the "monomyth." This single or privileged theme is the story of the journey of the hero, an archetypal figure. It takes place in three stages: departure of the hero from the community; mysterious and threatening adventures that lead to the wresting of a boon or prize from powerful authorities; and return with the prize or boon, which the hero presents to the community. The myths of various cultures and civilizations, otherwise so diverse, tell and retell this story. Although the details of each version seem unique, the psychological meaning remains constant in all because the archetypal contents of the collective unconscious are the same the world over.

The eminent historian of religions Mircea Eliade has made a very different use of Jung's psychology. Like Campbell, Eliade believes that myth is the key to understanding all religions. But whereas Campbell employed Jung's method of the psychological interpretation of myths, Eliade draws upon the more philosophical values and ideals espoused by Jung in his analytical psychology. Eliade often applauds Jung's theory of Western religion and science, his threefold conviction that human life retains a religious dimension, that the forces of modernity—such as science and empirical historiography—have eroded this dimension, and that a depth-psychological perspective on the religions of humankind can restore this dimension. Eliade has found valuable Jung's idea that the human mind is essentially religious, especially when religiosity is expressed in myths that are grounded in psychological depth or in the unconscious. Eliade has therefore often referred to, and sometimes adopted for himself, such concepts as archetype, collective unconscious, and the human psyche.

A fresh and more recent approach to religious myth, also deeply influenced by Jung, is the work of Wendy Doniger O'Flaherty. It differs from that of Campbell and Eliade in several ways. Both Campbell and Eliade have used Jung to evolve a universal theory of religious myths, whereas O'Flaherty focuses her attention on the textual details of the myths, uses several interpretive tools in addition to psychology, and emphasizes the historical and cultural contexts of the myths she analyzes. For example, in *Women, Androgynes, and Other Mythical Beasts,* O'Flaherty discusses myths in which mares are central figures. In order to achieve a maximum of concreteness and vividness, she cites exact portions of various texts that describe the mare, its actions, and the figures to which it is related. Then she acknowledges that the myth of the mare has multiple sources or levels: it symbolizes the psychological conflicts of family life, it represents political tension, and it is also a statement about the nature of divinity. But O'Flaherty also attempts to describe the cycles of myths in which mares predominate, locating them in their particular historical, geographic, and civilizational contexts. The influence of Jung can be seen in O'Flaherty's attempts to give the religious image all the concreteness and immediacy of an individual fantasy, while at the same time linking this image to other texts around the world. Her work could be described as a "multiple perspectives" approach to the mythologies of all religions. As such, it promises to extend the uses of Jung's psychology for understanding religious symbols first made by Campbell and Eliade.

BIBLIOGRAPHY

Jung's writings are available to the English-speaking scholar in *The Collected Works of C. G. Jung,* 20 vols., translated from German by R. F. C. Hull and edited by Gerhard Adler, Michael Fordham, and Herbert Read (Princeton, 1953–1979). Because the range of Jung's works is so wide and because these volumes contain only the briefest editorial information, the general reader is strongly advised to consult Anthony Storr's excellent and thorough selection of Jung's writings: *The Essential Jung* (Princeton, 1983). This includes excerpts from Jung's autobiographical memoir, *Memories, Dreams, Reflections,* edited by Aniela Jaffé and translated from German by Richard Winston and Clara Winston (New York, 1963), which provides the personal circumstances of Jung's intellectual pilgrimage.

A sympathetic and appreciative—though unofficial—intellectual biography by a former patient of Jung, who later became a Jungian analyst, is Barbara Hannah's *Jung: His Life and Work* (New York, 1976). Many of Jung's distinctive clinical-psychological insights are developed in an introductory fashion by John R. Staude in *The Adult Development of C. G. Jung* (London, 1981). Henri F. Ellenberger's comprehensive and somewhat encyclopedic review of the rise of depth psychology, *The Discovery of the Unconscious: The History and Evolution of Dynamic Psychiatry* (New York, 1970), contains informative chapters on Jung's life, thought, and times. Although it has been widely criticized for its lack of historical detail, the best single application of Jung's analytical psychology to the study of world religions remains Joseph Campbell's *The Hero with a Thousand Faces,* rev. ed. (Princeton, 1968).

PETER HOMANS

JUNO. The name *Iuno* is a derivative of *iun-* and the ending *-on-*. It is very likely a shortened form of *iuven-*, as found in *iunix* ("heifer") and the comparative *iunior* ("younger"). The derivative *Iunius (mensis)*, or "month of June," was linked by the ancients sometimes to *iunior* (Varro, *De lingua Latina* 6.33) and sometimes to *Iūno* (Servius, *Ad Georgica* 1.43). *Uni,* the name of an Etruscan goddess, is borrowed from the Latin *Iuno,* just as *Ani,* the name of an Etruscan god, comes from *Ianus.*

The goddess personifies creative youth. She oversees birth, both on a human and on a heavenly level. Upon beginning labor, women call upon Juno Lucina ("she who brings into light"), who is honored at the Matronalia of 1 March (cf. Plautus, *Aulularia* 692; Terence, *Adelphoe* 487). Juno Covella is the patroness, along with Janus, of each month's calends in order to further the labor of the young moon from the calends until the nones.

Several other ancient cults of Juno fall on the first of the month: 1 February (Juno Sospita); 1 June (Juno Moneta); 1 September (Juno Regina of the Aventine); 1 October (Juno Sororia). Exceptions to this rule are the cults of Juno that lost their autonomy. Thus Juno Caprotina is honored on 7 July, the nones, in a ceremony "intended to strengthen the light of night" (Dumézil, 1975) and connected with the cult rendered to Jupiter in the Poplifugia of 5 July. Similarly, Juno Regina of the Capitol is venerated, along with Jupiter, on 13 September, the ides, in the left chapel of the Capitoline temple, the anniversary of which falls on that date (Livy, 7.3.5).

In Roman history Juno intervened in several instances. In 396 BCE the dictator M. Furius Camillus obtained the consent of Uni, the Etruscan homologue of Juno and the protectress of the hostile town of Veii, to be transferred from her besieged town to the Aventine in Rome. Thus a second Juno Regina, this one of foreign origin, was established in the capital (Livy, 5.21.3, 22.4–6). In 390 BCE the Capitol was saved from the Gauls by the honking of geese, birds sacred to Juno (Livy, 5.47.3–4). Was this an intervention of Juno Moneta ("the warner"; see Cicero, *De divinatione* 1.101)? In 344 BCE a temple was dedicated to her by the dictator L. Furius Camillus, the son of the aforementioned Marcus (Livy, 7.28.4). The establishment of a mint near this sanctuary to Moneta (*Ad Monetae;* Livy, 6.20.13) gave to the word *moneta* the meaning of "money."

Syncretism had little effect upon Juno. In the *lectisternium* of 217 BCE she was simply paired with Jupiter after the example of the Greek couple Zeus and Hera.

BIBLIOGRAPHY

Dumézil, Georges. *La religion romaine archaïque.* 2d ed. Paris, 1974. See page 299 on the etymology and pages 303–310 on the Italic Junoes. This work has been translated from the first edition by Philip Krapp as *Archaic Roman Religion,* 2 vols. (Chicago, 1970).

Dumézil, Georges. *Fêtes romaines d'été et d'automne.* Paris, 1975. See pages 271–283 on Juno Caprotina, written in partnership with Paul Drossart.

Schilling, Robert. *Rites, cultes, dieux de Rome.* Paris, 1979. See pages 233–239 on Juno Covella and pages 239–244 on Juno Sororia.

Wissowa, Georg. *Religion und Kultus der Römer.* 2d ed. Munich, 1912. See pages 181–191 for a general treatment.

Robert Schilling
Translated from French by Paul C. Duggan

JUPITER. The name *Iuppiter* is made up of two elements: the first, *Iou-*, stems from Indo-European **dyeu-* (the same root serves for *dies,* "day"); while the second, *pater,* absorbed a stress on its initial consonant, *p,* and an apophony of its first vowel, *a. Iuppiter,* originally a vocative, identifies the "god of heavenly light" (a rarer nominative, *Diespiter,* appears in Plautus, *Poenulus* 739). The ancients were aware of this meaning, for the epithet *Lucetius,* referring to the god, is thus explained by Paulus-Festus (ed. Lindsay, 1913, p. 102 L.): "Lucetium Iovem appellabant quod eum lucis esse causam credebant" ("Jupiter was called Lucetius since he was believed to be the author of light"). This epithet is also documented among the Oscans (Servius, *Ad Aeneidem* 9.567). The name *Iuppiter* belongs to the Indo-European domain: it is semantically related to the Greek *Zeus,* which stems from **dyeus.*

Jupiter was recognized by all Italians as their god in common, particularly by the Latins, who honored him under the title of Jupiter Latiaris during the Feriae Latinae. This feast was celebrated each year under the auspices of Alba Longa on the summit of the Alban Hills. It was continued in the same place as a movable feast *(feriae conceptivae)* after Rome replaced Alba in the direction of this federal ceremony.

In Rome, Jupiter was ever honored as the supreme god. This preeminence was never called into question, not even when syncretism brought in the *ritus Graecus* ("Greek rite"): in the *lectisternium* of 217 BCE, Jupiter, paired with Juno, held the highest rank. Jupiter served as the keystone in the ancient triad along with Mars and Quirinus, as well as later in the Capitoline triad that gave him Juno and Minerva as companions. The Jupiter of the archaic epoch, specified as *Feretrius*—an epithet that the ancients traced to either *ferre* ("to bear, carry") or *ferire* ("to slay, strike"; Paulus-Festus, op. cit., p. 81 L.)—was venerated in a chapel located on the summit of the Capitoline (Aedes Iovis Feretri; cf. ibid., p. 204 L.) that Romulus was thought to have founded (Dionysius of Halicarnassus, 2.34.4). It was there that the first king of Rome consecrated to the god the first *spolia opima* (spoils seized from a slain enemy commander; Livy, 1.10.6–7). The sanctuary of Jupiter Feretrius contained "sceptrum per quod iurarent et lapidem silicem quo foedus ferirent" ("a sword for swearing oaths and a flintstone for concluding treaties"; Paulus-Festus, op. cit., p. 81 L.). The Roman Fetialis, the college of priestly officials responsible for ritual declarations of war or peace, concluded a treaty in the name of the Roman people with the Alban people (Livy, 1.24.7–8); they prayed precisely to Jupiter Feretrius to smite *(ferire)* the Roman people if they should deviate from the treaty, just as he himself struck the sacrificial pig with the flintstone. Near the sanctuary of Jupiter Feretrius the Ludi Capitolini ("Capitoline games") were celebrated each year on the ides of October (Plutarch, *Romulus* 25); they consisted of hand combat and foot races.

Being god of heaven, Jupiter was protector of all the ides, or "days of full light," so called because the day was then prolonged by a full moon (the thirteenth of most months, but the fifteenth in March, May, July, and October). On these days the god was offered a sacrificial lamb *(ovis Idulis).* His cult was maintained by the *flamen Dialis,* who was "in the god's permanent service," and was "celebrated every day" (*cotidie feriatus;* Aulus Gellius, *Noctes Atticae* 10.15–16). His principal feast was celebrated on the Vinalia, which were divided into the Vinalia Rustica (19 August), marked by the consecration of grapes, and the Vinalia Priora (23 April), marked by the offering of wine. Together with Venus, he was venerated as the sovereign god, protector of the Romans-Aeneades, following the "Trojan" interpretation.

Many other epithets illustrate different aspects of the god. Some correspond to atmospheric manifestations: Jupiter Tonans ("the thunderer"), Jupiter Fulgur ("he who throws lightning"). Others refer to magical or juridical interventions: Jupiter Stator ("he who immobilizes"; Livy, 1.12.4–6), Jupiter Fidius ("loyalty warranter"). However, during the historical epoch his principal title was officially Jupiter Optimus Maximus. The anniversary of his temple on the Capitoline fell on the ides of September and was followed by the Ludi Romani ("Roman games"). On the calends of January the new consuls would go there, accompanied by senators, magistrates, priests, and common people. It was there that the consul named for a military expedition would pronounce the *vota,* prayers and promises for gaining a victory. Upon his return he would go to give thanks to the sovereign god, if he had won as the conquering general.

BIBLIOGRAPHY

Dumézil, Georges. *La religion romaine archaïque.* 2d ed. Paris, 1974. Translated from the first edition by Philip Krapp as *Archaic Roman Religion,* 2 vols. (Chicago, 1970).

Schilling, Robert. *Rites, cultes, dieux de Rome.* Paris, 1979. See pages 354ff. on Jupiter Optimus Maximus and pages 358ff. on Jupiter Fulgur.

Schilling, Robert. *La religion romaine de Vénus.* 2d ed. Paris, 1982. See pages 131–148 on the Vinalia.

Wissowa, Georg. *Religion und Kultus der Römer.* 2d ed. Munich, 1912. See pages 113–129.

ROBERT SCHILLING

Translated from French by Paul C. Duggan

JUSTICE. *See* Cosmology; Dharma; Eschatology; Fate; Judgment of the Dead; Law and Religion; *and* Theodicy.

JUSTIFICATION. [*This entry examines Christian doctrines concerning justification as the subjective aspect of salvation. For further discussion of Christian views of salvation, see* Atonement, *article on* Christian Concepts; Free Will and Predestination, *article on* Christian Concepts; Grace; *and* Merit, *article on* Christian Concepts. *For discussion of salvation in broad religious perspective, see* Incarnation; Redemption; *and* Soteriology, *overview article.*]

Redemption, as Christianity understands it, is objective. It is an event, the act of redemption, with a result: the objective fact of being redeemed. This event is ontologically prior to the justification and sanctification of the human being (subjective redemption) and is consequently to be distinguished from them. This distinction is often denied in a modern Christian existentialist anthropology for which redemption as such takes place solely in the occurrence of faith; this anthropology does not bear on an objective event of history prior to the act of faith. The basis for the distinction between prior event and act consists in the fact that created finite freedom, even in working out its salvation, presupposes a situation that is not identical with the necessary essence or nature of the human being and his freedom but is a concrete temporal situation that constitutes the real nature of freedom as it is in fact exercised. Objective redemption, therefore, means the constitution by God of that concrete historical situation of freedom in which the will of God to forgive and save is exercised and manifested as an offer made to human freedom—historically and in eschatological irreversibility. It constitutes the situation on the basis of which and in which alone the human being can accept in freedom the proffered forgiveness.

Justification as Subjective Redemption. *Justification* is the word used by the apostle Paul that has come to refer, especially in Western theology since Augustine, to the subjective side of the process of redemption and, as a result of the stormy discussions at the time of the Reformation, has become the all-embracing central concept associated with redemption. The Roman Catholic understanding of faith, along with the Reformation understanding, holds that confession of the unique, justifying grace of God is a basic truth of the Christian faith. However, it is critical to the interpretation of this message that it be protected from individualistic narrowness and that the gracious deed of God toward humanity, which opens humanity up toward God, be understood from the outset as the founding of true, genuine, human community.

What we call "salvation" or "justification" comes to the human being, as creature and as sinner, only through the free, unearned grace of God, that is, through that which cannot be humanly laid claim to, the free self-opening of God in Jesus Christ, the crucified and resurrected one. The relationship of human beings to God, which constitutes their salvation, cannot be established or maintained by the human being himself through his own autonomously powered initiative. It originates instead through the sovereign act of God. There are no "works" by which the human being can first make himself favorable to God out of human power and goodness, no initiative that would have a human beginning. All the human work of salvation has only a responsive character, and even this response, in the capacity for it and as a real act, is still enabled by God, who in his action toward us also allows that we, accepting it, can and actually do respond to it.

The gracious act of God toward us must be accepted by us in freedom. But the freedom that in faith accepts God's grace is a freedom liberated by God's grace from creaturely finitude and sinful egoism. Therefore, even the Roman Catholic doctrine of justification confesses no semi-Pelagian synergism according to which salvation would be divided into God's act of grace and a human act of freedom independent of it. Rather, the free human act in response to God is itself still a gift of the grace of God.

This gift of God, in which God shares himself with sinful humanity, is an "event" (not simply an ever-existing dialectical condition) in which the sinner becomes a justified person, in which the grace of God really comes to the human being, sanctifies him, and makes him a true heir of eternal life, someone who he previously was not and now truly is. This declaration, referring to the individual human being, does not autocratically and absolutely fix the moment of arrival of this event. It is instead experienced by each individual person for himself and with reference to himself in the act of faith and hope itself, not in the reflection upon a simply empirically given state of affairs. It is not an act of self-absolution, but a hopeful and appreciative reception of God's merciful judgment upon us.

The event that happens to us through God and is accepted in hopeful faith, although now truly transforming us, is by its entire essence oriented toward the final judgment of God's mercy where it will first come to fulfillment. It is thus the event of promise that is now present only in hopeful faith but never becomes a possession at our autonomous disposal.

In harmony with the scriptures, one may legitimately articulate this grace-given event—in its aspects and possible phases in the human being who develops in history and time—as faith, hope, and love. However, one can also, with Paul, simply call the entirety of this event faith, and then it can be said that we are justified through faith and faith alone.

If even the justifying act of grace by God upon the human being is such that it truly encounters and changes the human being, and if it is also embraced with unconditional, hopeful faith, the event of justification is still not somehow simply effected by means of the free act of God. It remains constantly dependent upon God's sovereign grace. It is inaccessible to theorizing reflection, which relinquishes the hope of faith and leaves the human being under the threat of the power of sin in the world. Moreover, the human being can never, in absolving himself, decide with certainty whether his daily sinfulness, which he must acknowledge even if he hopes it does not exclude him from the kingdom of God, is not after all a symptom, manifestation, and disguise for a secret and radical "no" to God. In this sense, one can and must (even as a Catholic) absolutely speak of being *"simul iustus et peccator"* (just and sinner at once). It must be said that the human being is only justified in that he flees again and again away from himself, in faithful hope, to the saving grace of God. The basis of his justification is the real possibility, constantly permitted by God's salvific will, of again and again going away from himself in the hope of God's mercy.

This justifying grace of God, in its bestowal, frees humans from the enslaving powers of death, of the merely external demands of the law, and of the world. It gives ability and deed to the children of God. It gives a mission and assigns a task and claims an obligation, the one command—however much it must be interpreted for the varied dimensions of the human being—that is founded upon the love given by God. From then on the human being must do the "work" of responsive love to bring forth the fruit of the Holy Spirit that is given to him. This work of responsive love is valuable in itself because it is—in both the ability to love and the act of loving—the work of God, because it "is worked in God" (*Jn.* 3:21). But exactly in this way this work of responsive love is not what the human being can lay claim to with regard to God, for it is itself a gift of God to humanity, and it only *is* when it is done in love and when the human being sees God and not himself. All praise for the objective dignity of this work of the justified may be understood only as glorifying the genuinely creative grace of God, which truly gives life and thus, however, only "crowns its own work," that is, truly says "yes" to what it does itself as our liberated freedom.

History of the Concept. The various heretical positions in the general doctrine of redemption and grace in early Christian theology affect the formulation of the church's doctrine of justification: the pharisaical work ethic of Jewish Christianity, pagan-Christian antinomianism and libertinism, gnosticism (and also Manichaeism), with its theory of spiritual-intellectual self-redemption, and finally Messalianism, against which the graciousness of the mystical as well as the necessity of the sacramental must be emphasized. At the time these positions were conceived, sin and grace had not yet been theologically understood as the actual structural moments of a Christian statement about the human being.

It was Augustine—and Western theology follows from him—who brought the doctrine of justification into a new perspective. His struggle with Manichaeism as well as with Pelagianism enabled the new Christian understanding of existence, in its personally free and grace-given components, to become an actual problem for him. The basic givens of the biblical order of salvation—creation and freedom, the world that suffers under the effects of sin but stands in the grace of redemption, Jesus Christ and his efficacious sacrament in the church, the human being as creature and graced sinner—all these data are brought together theologically as constitutive moments of justification.

Augustine's theology of justification experienced enlargements and differentiations in medieval Scholasticism. The Augustinian *conversio*, conversion and turning toward God, underwent in monastic theology an elaboration in the doctrine of penance *(poenitentia)*, the turning away from sin. Under the influence of the Germanic and Irish ideological world, the penitential view then reoriented itself more strongly toward the idea of justice and the notions of merit connected with it. As a result, there arose later the problem of the necessary preparation for justification and that of the meaning of the grace of justification for meritorious work. In the framework of the late medieval discussion of the doctrine of merit, there is a mixture of views that show the danger of a Pelagian misunderstanding. Also, the pious practice of this time—we point only to the institution of indulgences and pilgrimages—sometimes obscures the central theological view of the gratuitousness of all justification.

Here Luther's critique begins. With Luther, the concept of justification becomes the key concept in becoming a Christian and being a Christian. His specific doctrine of justification must first be read and understood within the context of his theological thought before it is set over against the doctrine of the church.

At the start of the Reformation, the connection between redemption and justification was at first so strongly emphasized on the basis of the tropological method that there was little distinction between objective redemption and subjective acceptance of justification through Christ. Further development, building upon foundations laid by Melanchthon, worked out this distinction more clearly. Lutheran orthodoxy was characterized by recourse to the satisfaction and redemption theory. Pietism understood conversion and sanctification as the objectification of redemption. Enlightenment theology destroyed the connection between Christology and the doctrine of redemption, along with the metaphysical and theological presuppositions of Christology, so that soteriology could be derived only from anthropology. More recent Protestant theology (for example, that of Paul Althaus, Gerhard Ebeling, and Eberhard Jüngel) again has recourse to the starting point of the early reformers.

In the view of redemption given in the theology of the Eastern Orthodox churches, the idea of divinization *(theōsis)* as classically formulated by Athanasius, remains prevalent along with the recapitulation theory of Irenaeus. Redemption is a process in which the believer has a share: through the assumption of a human body by the Logos in the incarnation, through the suffering and death of Christ, and through the resurrection and second coming of the God-man. In spite of original sin, the human person remains free and acts in the process of salvation that encompasses the entire cosmos. The transformation of humanity begins with the incarnation because at that point humanity is integrated into this process in faith, hope, and love. Through their own actions human beings show themselves worthy of the grace of God. Universal redemption resulting from the human reality taken on by the God-man is a residual problem for this theology.

Church Teachings. Human beings are justified before God, and hence freed from original sin and from grave personal (habitual) sin (if not necessarily always from every remnant of the punishment of sin), and are put into a position of friendship and peace with God (1) through baptism (as an infant), (2) through faith, hope, and love, (3) through repentance along with baptism, or (4) through the sacrament of penance. Faith is the foundation and root of justification, but it is not simply identical with it or with the process of justification, even if we understand by faith not the fiducial faith required for justification but confessional faith. Whoever, therefore, is morally accountable before God must prepare himself for justification (with the help of anticipatory grace). This free preparation does not mean a pharisaical or Pelagian self-justification or an actual meriting *(de condigno)* of the justification, but it is an occurrence that signifies a true change in the state of salvation of the person.

Justification does not consist in a mere leaving behind of sin but rather in the "infusion" of sanctifying grace, of the theological virtues, and of the gifts of the Holy Spirit as habitual qualifications for supernatural just action toward God. As the concept is used in the official doctrine of the church, it is identical with the inner sanctification (which includes holiness and justification) and supernatural elevation of the human being and may not be conceived of as the purely forensic imputation of justification or as double justification. This sanctification as the habitual possession of sanctifying grace signifies an inner rebirth, a renewal, being a child of God, a claim to eternal salvation, and the indwelling of God. As a capacity of the human being (created grace), sanctification differs from divine capacities. The effective cause of justification (God in God's mercy) and the meritorious cause (Christ), on the one hand, and the formal cause of justification (grace), on the other hand, cannot simply be identified with each other. This is so even if in the creaturely realm human beings are thought of both as the prerequisite and effect of the self-communication of God (uncreated grace) and even if God's own self appears there as quasi-formal cause of justification.

Justification can be lost. It is canceled not only through the refusal of faith but also through every serious sin, even if the general capacity for supernatural, moral, religious behavior (love) is not destroyed along with it. There is normally no certainty about one's state of justification. However, justification must be accepted with absolutely firm hope by the one who tries to believe and to love and yet is always tempted, in spite of the "habitual" character of justification. Justification must be constantly newly acquired in faithful, active love, so that one can grow in the grace of justification and, although always remaining a sinner, be liberated to fulfill the commandments of God through this grace of justification.

Transmission of Justification. As a result of the redemptive act of Christ, human beings undoubtedly are already other than they would be on their own as simple sinners, and this is so not merely in the intentions of God. Current theology has no name for this "subjective" condition that is given through "objective redemption." (There is a name for its opposite: original sin.) Of itself, however, this condition could certainly already be called "justification" (corresponding to a usage of speech to be found, for example, in Paul's letters) as long as the reality and necessity of justification as inner sanctification are not obscured by the believing-hoping-loving acceptance of the grace of justification and by the sacrament of baptism. Only by means of a terminological clarification of this "justification" could the essence of original sin be made adequately clear in the present Christian order of salvation, which is not determined solely by Adam. Only with this clarification can the efficaciousness of God's will for universal salvation be grasped and understood: that redemption is not merely the gift of a chance for salvation but is itself already salvation.

It remains to be asked whether this purely objective justification of the universal salvific will of God in Christ, which already determines every human subject, may be identified with the supernatural grace of justification to the extent that it is "merely" but also "constantly and really" offered. That the process of justification is a "process" from anticipatory ("actual") grace does not contradict such an assumption. For Thomas Aquinas also, the process of justification proceeds from the grace of justification (in order to make that comprehensible, he distinguished between *gratiae infusio* and *gratiae consecutio*), and it can be thought of as the existentially gradual acceptance of this grace through its own power. Faith would then be completely comprehensible simultaneously as the *means* (of the acceptance) and the *fruit* of the grace of justification in mutual causality. "Actual," supernaturally elevating grace can be seen as the "arrival" or the "working out" of the grace of justification.

The grace of justification in the traditional sense appears then directly as the grace *accepted* through the *free* act of faith, which is "offered" to every human being in every "justification" that as such has already taken place through redemption. The justification given only through the sacrament of infant baptism appears then as a sacramental-historical form of "justification" (sacramental character) that in its possession by the human being may not be thought of as identical with the grace of justification of the Christian adult (the actual believer). It is different from this not only because of a different causation external to it but also because it is possessed only in the form of a gift in anticipation of freedom (like "nature") and not yet in the form of personal appropriation, even if this possession through baptism must always be distinguished in every individual from the continuous offering of the grace of justification.

How and to what extent justification, which is mediated through faith, can and must also be thought of as likewise mediated through baptism (and necessary for salvation) is a problem of sacramental theology in general whose solution cannot be correctly sought on the model of infant baptism. The sacrament can be an efficacious, historical, and ecclesiological manifestation of the first (or existentially deeply accepted) process of justification in faith and love, because salvation is fulfilled principally "in the flesh," even already where the sacrament, strictly speaking, has not yet been given. The sign and the signified therefore have a mutually conditioning, growing unity that can even shift historically. Thus the progressively deepening justification remains accompanied by a sacramental embodiment (from confirmation to anointing of the sick). To the extent that grace is the life of the church and its sacramental embodiment is a moment of the visibility of the church itself, and is not only administered "by" it, every process of justification is also a moment of the internal and external essence of the church.

The habitual grace of justification is accepted only in a spiritual, still-continuing process of historically self-fulfilling freedom. It is possessed in temptation, uncertainty of salvation, and "mere" hope and is preserved only through the always unearned and never simply "possessed" efficacious grace given by God for the fulfillment of the commandments. Thus it is not acquired by the human being even in the sense of an actual synergism. For these reasons the already present justification is always oriented toward the justification that occurs only at the judgment of God (that is, with death), so that the latter justification does not simply signify the manifestation of the former.

Justification really and fully occurs only through that sanctification which, on the part of God, is God's unfathomable love and, on the part of the human being, is also love, the love that constantly is made present as the "infused" habit of love. Justification exists, therefore, as the interaction of God and the human being in an act that has always surpassed "justice" as "law," in that love in whose higher essence all justice is subsumed and thus preserved. Only the one who in love forgets himself over God and hence even forgets God's justice (without prejudice to an authentic creaturely pluralism of virtues and the exercise of them) is justified before God. From this there would emerge the equality and mutuality of an ontic statement about justification, as in the Council of Trent (justification as prepared change and as a condition of "law" and merit before God), and of an existential statement (justification as "merely" believed, ever newly to be grasped, eschatologically future), even if the latter statement was often heretically isolated in Old Protestantism. Likewise, the Roman Catholic "yes" and "no" to the formula "simul iustus et peccator" could be deepened and clarified: justification, which transforms the human being from a sinner into a justified person, is a real change of condition *and* still in process and therefore is determined by the beginning and the end points.

Since an absolutely certain knowledge of his state of grace is closed to the human being, so also is the completion of the process of justification really not adequately observable. Its description is therefore rather the naming and structuring of the moments that are implied in acceptance of the justification given by God. This is especially so because the acts of preparation for justification can be thought of as proceeding from the offered grace of justification and must be distinguished from each another only to the extent that they are acts of the acceptance of the grace of justification that are of existentially different depth and extent.

BIBLIOGRAPHY

For the history of the problem of soteriology, see, in addition to manuals of dogmatic history, the summaries by Basil Studer, "Soteriologie in der Schrift und Patristik," in *Handbuch der Dogmengeschichte,* vol. 3, fasc. 2a (Freiburg, 1978), and Boniface Willems, "Soteriologie von der Reformation bis zur Gegenwart," in *Handbuch der Dogmengeschichte,* vol. 3, fasc. 2c (Freiburg, 1972). Systematic presentation is found in the classic work of Jean Rivière, *Le dogme de la rédemption,* 2d ed. (Paris, 1931), Peter Fransen's *The New Life of Grace* (London, 1969), and Otto H. Pesch's *Gottes Gnadenhandeln als Rechtfertigung und Heiligung des Menschen,* "Mysterium Salutis," vol. 4.2 (Einsiedeln, 1975), pp. 831–913.

The richest discussion of justification in Catholic religious philosophy is provided by Bernhard Welte in *Heilsverständnis* (Freiburg, 1966), in which see especially parts 2 and 3. Paradigmatic for the evangelical (Lutheran) perspective is Paul Althaus's *Die christliche Wahrheit,* 8th ed. (Gütersloh, 1969), pp. 228–238, 596–654. In connection with the interfaith and ecumenical discussion, see the important works by Hans Küng, especially *Justification* (Zurich, 1964); Otto H. Pesch's *Theologie der Rechtfertigung bei Martin Luther und Thomas von Aquin* (Mainz, 1967); Ulrich Kühn and Otto H. Pesch's *Rechtfertigung im Gespräch zwischen Thomas und Luther* (Berlin, 1967); and, finally, the instructive and substantial study by August B. Hasler, *Luther in der katholischen Dogmatik: Darstellung seiner Rechtfertigungslehre in den katholischen Dogmatikbüchern,* "Beiträge zur ökumenischen Theologie," no. 2 (Munich, 1968).

KARL RAHNER and ADOLF DARLAP
Translated from German by Charlotte Prather

JUSTINIAN I (482–565), Roman emperor. Justinian was born in or near Skopje in Macedonia, a city where the local aristocracy spoke Latin. The trusted minister of his uncle, Justin I, from 518, Justinian was made his co-emperor and succeeded him in 527. Justinian worked for the liberation of the Latin West from armies of occupation: Ostrogoths in Italy and Illyricum, Vandals in Africa and Sicily, Visigoths in Spain. To this end it was necessary to repair the breach between the court and church of Constantinople, and the church and city of Rome, which had been caused by concessions made in the East to those who held that the Council of Chalcedon (451) had pressed the distinction between the divine and human natures of Christ too far in a direction that could be called Nestorian.

Before the reign of Justinian, Chalcedonians in the East were a party opposed to anything that might obscure the distinction between the natures of Christ. During his reign, some Chalcedonians in the East came to stress what is common to the letters of Cyril of Alexandria, who wrote of a union of two natures in the incarnate Word, and of Leo of Rome, who wrote of one person in two natures. Both Cyril and Leo affirm that the manhood of Christ is the same as our own and subject to suffering. John Mayentius and a group of Scythian monks from the Dobruja, who said that "one of the Trinity suffered in the flesh," had a cool reception in Rome in 519. But Justinian used their language in edicts in 529 and 533, which were included with a letter of approval from Pope John II (received in 534) in the definitive edition of his collection of Roman law, the *Corpus juris civilis* (535). So the suffering and death as well as the birth of the Son of God became part of the vocabulary of church and state in East and West.

The *Corpus juris* became the standard textbook of Roman law in the West, at Bologna and elsewhere, but Justinian did not succeed in restoring imperial government. In Africa the Vandals were eliminated, but the mountain tribes were not subdued. In Italy the Ostrogoths were defeated, but they fought on as guerrillas, preferred by the peasants to rent collectors and tax gatherers. Pope Agapetus I came from Rome to Constantinople in 536 in search of a diplomatic solution. He insisted on a purge of those whom he considered disloyal to the Council of Chalcedon and pressed the emperor to introduce a Chalcedonian patriarch into Alexandria. But when he died suddenly his successor at Rome was elected while the Ostrogoths were still in possession. Pope Silverius, deposed and exiled as soon as the imperial armies arrived, obtained a review of his case from Justinian, but he was deposed again and died in prison.

Vigilius, who replaced Silverius, was regarded as an intruder, an agent of Theodora, Justinian's empress, who patronized the monophysite opponents of the Council of Chalcedon. In 543–544 Justinian issued the "Three Chapters" edict against the person and writings of Theodore of Mopsuestia, who, though the master of Nestorius, died in 428 before the Nestorian controversy broke out; and against criticisms of Cyril of Alexandria by Theodoret of Cyrrhus and Ibas of Edessa, who at Chalcedon were received as orthodox. In a revised form (551), which has been preserved, this edict contained a series of directions for the use of terms in appropriate contexts, for instance for the proper use of *in* and *of two natures*. Vigilius did not criticize these, but he kept up criticism of the "Three Chapters" before and after he was brought to Constantinople in 548 and during the Second Council of Constantinople (553), where a final version of the edict was approved.

The war in Italy continued until 553. After it was over, Vigilius consented to confirm the council, but he died on the way home. His successor at Rome, Pope Pelagius I, succeeded in limiting schism to a few places in northern Italy around Aquileia, but by this time the monophysites in Syria had acquired their own hierarchy. There and in Egypt, where they kept control, their leaders were not extreme, but they feared to lose their followers if they accepted the orthodoxy of the Council of Chalcedon, as Vigilius feared to lose support in the West if he admitted their orthodoxy. Justinian continued to strive for a balance that can be seen in the architecture of the great churches built in his reign in Constantinople and Ravenna. He kept the West open to Eastern influence but failed to restore the unity of the East.

BIBLIOGRAPHY

A review of the political background can be found in George Ostrogorsky's *History of the Byzantine State,* rev. ed. (New Brunswick, N.J., 1969), pp. 68–79. For the history of theology, see Jaroslav Pelikan's *Christian Tradition,* vol. 1, *The Emergence of the Catholic Tradition, 100–600* (Chicago, 1971), pp. 267–279, and John Meyendorff's *Christ in Eastern Christian Thought* (Crestwood, N.Y., 1975), pp. 29–89.

GEORGE EVERY

JUSTIN MARTYR (c. 100–163/5), Christian apologist. Justin is generally regarded as the most significant apologist of the second century. With him Christianity moved from competition with the popular Hellenistic mystery cults, which attracted chiefly persons of limited education and culture, to competition with philosophies that appealed to persons of higher education and culture. In his apologies he presented Christianity as "the true philosophy" uniting the wisdom of both Jews and gentiles.

Life. Although born at Flavia Neapolis (modern Nablus) in Palestine, the site of ancient Shechem in Samaria, Justin claimed neither Jewish nor Samaritan ancestry. His grandfather was named Bacchius (a Greek name), his father Priscus (a Latin name), and, according to his own statements, he was uncircumcised, reared according to gentile customs, and educated in the Greek fashion. His writings, however, reveal considerable familiarity with Jewish customs and thought, particularly in handling the scriptures.

From his youth, Justin possessed a serious religious and philosophical interest. In quest of truth (God) he studied successively with Stoic, Peripatetic (Aristotelian), Pythagorean, and Platonist teachers. The Stoic, Justin reports, disappointed him; the teacher failed to help him further his knowledge of God. The Peripatetic evinced greater interest in collecting fees than in education. The Pythagorean, a philosopher of some note, rejected Justin when he found the latter had no acquaintance with music, astronomy, and geometry. Downcast but not despairing, Justin turned to Platonists, whose emphasis on the spiritual and on contemplation caused his spirit to soar.

Like many others after him, Justin crossed the Platonist bridge to Christianity. Witnessing the fearlessness of Christians in the face of death, he was convinced that they could not be living in wickedness and pleasure as their detractors charged. Further, he was influenced by an unidentified elderly Christian "philosopher," perhaps in his native Palestine or in Ephesus, where he went as a young man. Although some scholars have characterized Justin's account of his conversion to Christianity as an idealization, most have defended it as authentic, if somewhat stylized. The conversion itself entailed less a substantive shift than a change of commitment from Greek (Socrates and Plato) to Hebrew (the prophets and Jesus) truth. Justin opted for Christianity, he explained, "not because the teachings of Plato are different from those of Christ, but because they are not in all respects similar, as neither are those of the others, Stoics, and poets, and historians."

This philosopher-evangelist taught in Rome during the reign of Antoninus Pius (138–161). His students included Tatian (fl. 160–175), the brilliant Assyrian founder of the Encratites, and Irenaeus (c. 130–c. 200), bishop of Lyons and noted antiheretical writer. Justin suffered martyrdom early in the reign of Marcus Aurelius (161–180); he was betrayed by a Cynic philosopher named Crescens, whom he had bested in an argument. Summoned before the Roman prefect Rusticus, according to a reliable early martyrology, Justin and several companions who were apprehended at the same time refused to offer the sacrifices required by law, saying, "No right-thinking person falls away from piety to impiety." By command of the prefect they were scourged and beheaded. The date of his death is uncertain, but traditionally it has been commemorated in the Roman calendar on 13 and 14 April.

Writings. Although Justin was the first prolific Christian author, only three of his writings are extant in complete form. Works that have perished include the following treatises: *Against Marcion* (Marcion, d. 160?, was the founder of a heretical anti-Jewish sect); *Against All Heresies;* two entitled *Against the Greeks; On the Sovereignty of God; Psaltes;* and *On the Soul.* The works that survive in their entirety are *1 Apology, 2 Apology,* and *Dialogue with Trypho, a Jew.* The second *Apology* is often characterized as an appendix to the first, but it seems to have been occasioned by different circumstances and probably was written several years later.

In *1 Apology,* addressed around AD 150 to the emperor Antoninus Pius, Justin weaves together a refutation of stock pagan charges against Christians and a positive case for Christianity as the true religion. He calls for a halt to punishment of Christians for the name alone and demands an impartial investigation of the common charges of atheism, immorality, treason, social aloofness, and theological absurdity. Justin holds that pagan sources reveal ample analogies to Christian teachings on the Resurrection, the virgin birth, the life and death of Jesus, and Christ's Sonship. Thus while pagans have not been excluded from the truth, they have obtained this truth by imitation of the prophets or the Word, which became incarnate in Jesus, and they have mixed the truth with falsehood. Christianity alone expounds pure truth. Before Christ, the Word was in the world so that whoever lived reasonably, that is, according to the teaching of the Logos, the divine Word, or universal reason, such as Socrates or Heraclitus, was a Christian. Concluding *1 Apology* with an explanation of Christian baptism, the Eucharist, and the Sunday liturgy, Justin then appends the rescript of Hadrian.

In *2 Apology,* a very brief work addressed to the Roman Senate, Justin enters a plea for three Christians condemned to death by the prefect Urbicus at the urging of an irate husband whose wife divorced him for infidelity after she converted to Christianity. Confessing that he expects a similar fate because of the hatred of the Cynic Crescens for him, he offers to debate Crescens before the Senate itself. Why do not all Christians simply commit suicide if they love death so much? Because, replies Justin, the death of all Christians would mean the end of those instructed in divine doctrines and perhaps even the end of the human race, for God delays his final judgment for the sake of Christians. Christians do not differ from others in whom the Logos dwells, for all of these have suffered persecution inspired by demons. They differ only in the fact that they possess the whole truth because Christ "became the whole rational being, both body, and reason, and soul." Thus they do not fear death; rather, by dying, they prove the validity of their faith.

In *Dialogue with Trypho* Justin ostensibly reports a debate in Ephesus between himself and a Jew named Trypho, a recent refugee from Palestine during the Bar Kokhba Revolt (132–135). Some scholars have identified Trypho as Rabbi Ṭarfon, but this is improbable. Although the work could reflect an actual dialogue, in its present form it cannot be dated earlier than *1 Apology,* from which it quotes. Since Rabbi Ṭarfon remembered the Temple, destroyed in 70 CE, he most likely would not have been alive at the date required for the debate. Some scholars, moreover, have argued that the *Dialogue,* in which Justin makes skillful use of Jewish arguments based on scripture, was not an apology to Judaism per se but rather was addressed to gentiles who cited Jewish objections to Christian claims (as did Celsus in his *True Discourse,* c. 175). It has also been argued that the *Dialogue* was designed as a treatise to prop up the faith of wavering Christians.

The longest of Justin's extant writings, the *Dialogue* consists of four major parts. After narrating at length the story of his conversion (chaps. 1–10), Justin proceeds to explain why Christians no longer keep the whole Mosaic law (11–31). Christianity, he claims, is the true Israel under a new covenant. The new covenant, requiring religion of the heart, has supplanted the old one, which required sacrifices, observance of the Sabbath, fasts, observance of dietary laws, and circumcision. Christians still keep the eternal (moral) law, but not the ritual law prescribed to Israel because of its hardness of heart and transgressions. In the longest section (32–114) Justin replies to Jewish objections to Christian claims concerning Jesus as fulfiller of Jewish messianic hopes and as Lord. He bases his argument wholly on the citing of Old Testament texts and types. In the final section (115–142) he makes a case for the conversion of the gentiles by citing Old Testament texts. The rather one-sided "dialogue" ends with an appeal to Trypho but not with a conversion.

Thought. Justin was not a theological giant. As his rejection by his Pythagorean teacher indicates, Justin lacked cultural depth. In his apologies, moreover, he wavered back and forth, relying now on citation of authorities and now on logical argument. As one of the first to grapple seriously with questions posed by more cultured gentiles, he wobbled and tottered, very uncertain of his footing.

Nevertheless, because he tried, Justin established a permanent niche in Christian history. As a philosophical evangelist, he dared to undertake the difficult task of reinterpreting the biblical message in the idiom of what most scholars now recognize as Middle Platonism. Unlike other Christians of his day, even his own pupil Tatian, he acknowledged the truths found in Greek philosophical thought, especially Platonism. Although he sometimes ascribed such insights to borrowing from Moses and the prophets, he developed the more credible theory of illumination or inspiration by the preexistent Logos. Thus Socrates and Heraclitus, in advance of Jesus' advent, merited the title of "Christian." Whereas they, however, grasped truth partially, in Jesus the whole Logos dwelt bodily, thus vouchsafing to Christians the whole of truth.

The significant place that Christians ascribed to Jesus both in worship and in doctrine posed for Justin and other apologists an urgent theological problem: how to preserve belief in one God while recognizing Jesus as God. The eventual solution was the doctrine of the Trinity, but Justin's thinking did not reach that far. In his doctrine of God he wedded the Platonist idea of God as unknowable and transcendent, the unmoved first cause, nameless and unutterable, and the biblical conception of a living creator, the compassionate Father who has come near in Jesus Christ. Often the former idea dominated. For his understanding of the Logos he appropriated and developed elements of earlier Christian tradition in relation to either Stoic or Middle Platonist concepts. The Logos is God's personal reason—not only in name but numerically distinct from the Father—in which all partake but which in Jesus Christ became a man. Lest this dualism that he posits of God land him in ditheism, however, Justin emphasized the unity of the Father and the Logos prior to creation. The Logos is not eternal, as in later thought, but a product of the Father's will from the beginning, thus subordinate to the Father in person and function. His universal activity, Justin liked to say, is that of the *Logos spermatikos,* or Seminal Logos. Justin did not clearly differentiate the activity of the Holy Spirit from that of the Logos, though he evidently did believe in a personal Holy Spirit. The Spirit's chief office is prophetic inspiration.

Justin turned to Christian philosophy for the same reason that most people turned to one of the philosophies current in his time—as a means of salvation. Here he sounded two notes: truth and victory over demons. In line with his Platonist philosophical assumptions, he emphasized human freedom. In each person dwells a spirit or a part of the Seminal Logos. Thus each person has power of choice morally. None inherits sin or guilt; that comes from actual sin, which is the result of letting demons lead one into sin. Christianity offers two things to remedy this situation. One is the teaching and example of the Incarnate Logos, who was both divine and fully human. To live by his teaching is to avoid sin. The other is the power to overcome demons, the demons that Justin, like his contemporaries, believed to be everywhere in fearsome power. Through his death and resurrection Christ has triumphed. Demons, frequently exorcised in his name, are now subject to him.

Justin did not elaborate on his understanding of the church and the ministry, but he did supply some of the earliest extant evidence on Roman baptismal and liturgical practice in the second century, including the earliest liturgy. A period of instruction, the length of which is not indicated, preceded baptism. Prayer and fasting came immediately before. Baptism itself was in the name of the Trinity and accompanied by a confession, but Justin did not mention laying on the hands after baptism. The Eucharist was celebrated following baptism. The weekly liturgy combined a service of the word and a eucharistic service. Held on the "day of the sun," a designation Justin employed with some reservation, it consisted of reading "as long as time permits" the "memoirs" of the apostles or the writings of the prophets, exposition by the person presiding (presumably the elder or bishop), prayers said in a standing position, presentation of the bread and wine mixed with water, prayers and thanksgivings by the one presiding "to the best of his ability," distribution and reception of the bread and wine by those present, dispatch by the deacons of remaining portions to those absent, and a collection of alms for orphans, widows, the sick, visitors, and other needy persons.

Justin ascribed considerable significance to both baptism and the eucharistic meal. In baptism the Holy Spirit brings new birth (as promised in *John* 3:3–4). Baptism is "illumination" *(photismos)* by the Logos, which empowers one to live a truly moral life, thus achieving the goal of the philosopher. In the eucharistic meal the divine Logos unites with the bread and wine in such a way that they become the body and blood of the incarnate Jesus. This food, consecrated "by the word of prayer which comes from him," and thus no longer ordinary and common, fortifies the recipient with the mind and power of the Logos to live the Christian life. Although Justin uses the word *change* to describe the effect of consecration on the elements, his understanding should not be confused with the later doctrine of transubstantiation.

Suspended between two worlds, Greek and Hebrew, Justin sometimes did not know which way to lean. When in doubt, he opted for the biblical, as his eschatology (doctrine of "last things") indicates. In support of Christian messianic convictions he held tenaciously to his belief in the second coming of Christ, though he seems not to have worried about its delay. The first advent of Christ, he contended, was in lowliness; the second one will be in glory. The delay of the second coming, according to Justin, is a sign of God's patience with a recalcitrant humanity for the sake of Christians. Justin also sided with biblical authors on resurrection and the millennium. He was not wholly consistent here; in the *Dialogue* he envisioned the millennium inaugurated by a resurrection of the righteous and concluded by a general resurrection and judgment, as in the *Revelation to John*. He cited the judgment as a major part of his argument against persecution of Christians. Both human beings and angels would be judged according to their use or abuse of free will, and the wicked would be condemned to eternal fire. In his apologies Justin also spoke of a world conflagration, but his attention to this Stoic idea seems to have been more an accommodation to gentile thinking than a contradiction of his belief in an eternal Jerusalem.

[*See also* Apologetics.]

BIBLIOGRAPHY

The standard critical edition of the text of Justin's writings is that by J. C. T. S. Otto, *Justini philosophi et martyris opera*, 3d ed. (Jena, 1875–1881). Reliable English translations of the three authentic works of Justin can be found in volume 1 of *The Ante-Nicene Fathers*, edited and translated by Alexander Roberts and James Donaldson (1867; reprint, Grand Rapids, Mich., 1975). A more up-to-date translation of the *Dialogue* is A. L. Williams's *Justin Martyr: The Dialogue with Trypho* (London, 1930). Excellent introductions to the life and thought of Justin are L. W. Barnard's *Justin Martyr: His Life and Thought* (Cambridge, 1967) and E. F. Osborn's *Justin Martyr* (Tübingen, 1973), which revise and correct Erwin R. Goodenough's one-sided judgments in *The Theology of Justin Martyr* (1923; reprint, Amsterdam, 1968). Willis A. Shotwell's *The Biblical Exegesis of Justin Martyr* (London, 1965) supplies useful information about Justin's knowledge of Judaism.

E. GLENN HINSON

K

KA'BAH. The Ka'bah (lit., "cube"), the House of Allāh, is located in Mecca. It is the principal Islamic shrine, the *qiblah,* or specific point faced by Muslims when performing the daily ritual prayers *(ṣalāt)* anywhere in the world. Located at the center of the great open Ḥaram Mosque, it is the geographical and religious center of the Islamic world, the lifetime goal of Muslims who respond to the Qur'anic obligation to make at least one pilgrimage there. Muslim tradition also locates it directly below the heavenly Ka'bah.

The Ka'bah is constructed of Meccan granite and, as its name indicates, is a cubelike building, measuring more than sixteen meters high, thirteen meters long, and eleven meters wide. Its single door (there are no windows) is located on the northeast side, about two meters above the pavement of the open mosque. On the infrequent occasions when the Ka'bah is opened, mobile stairs give access to its interior. Inside are gold and silver lamps suspended from the ceiling. Three wooden pillars, recently replaced, support the ceiling.

It is, however, the building as a whole, not its contents, that is sacred to Muslims, and the most important object at the Ka'bah is located on the exterior: this is the Black Stone *(al-ḥajar al-aswad)* embedded in the eastern corner. Actually dark red-brown, and now encased in a massive silver band, the Black Stone is of unknown pre-Islamic origin, possibly meteoric. Myths affirm that it fell from heaven or that it was brought forth by the angels as a white stone to provide the cornerstone for the original Ka'bah; darkened by the touch of humans across the millennia, it serves as a register of human degradation. Muslims commonly refer to it as the "cornerstone of the House" and the "right hand of God on earth," but they are at pains to insist that it is not an idol and not to be worshiped: prayers here are addressed to God, not to the Black Stone. When beginning the rite of circumambulation *(ṭawāf)* of the Ka'bah, which during the pilgrimage season forms part of the pilgrimage performance, Muslims kiss or touch the Black Stone, as Muḥammad is reported to have done. The *ṭawāf* is performed in the immediate vicinity of the Ka'bah on a broad pavement of polished granite called the *maṭāf,* the place of circumambulation.

Between the Black Stone and the raised door is a section of exterior wall known as the *multazam,* where worshipers press their bodies at the conclusion of the circumambulations in order to receive the *barakah* ("blessing, power") associated with the holy house.

The Ka'bah is usually covered by the *kiswah* ("robe"), a thick black and gold embroidered cloth fabricated each year by Meccan artisans. Prior to 1927 it was provided annually by the Egyptians and was brought to Mecca in the pilgrimage caravan from Cairo. The *kiswah* contains wide bands of Arabic calligraphy, mostly verses from the Qur'ān.

Near the Ka'bah stands a gilded glass cage (replacing an earlier simple wooden framework) that contains a stone marking the Station of Ibrāhīm (Abraham). This stone is said to have miraculously preserved the footprint of Ibrāhīm, who stood on it in order to complete the construction of an earlier Ka'bah: it is, as it were, the builder's mark.

Opposite the corner of the Black Stone is a small building housing the sacred well of Zamzam, from which pilgrims drink water at the conclusion of their circumambulations and prayers. Its origin is mythically associated with Hājar (Hagar) and Ismāʿīl (Ishmael), for whom God provided water in this desert place after commanding Ibrāhīm to abandon mother and child and promising to care for them in his place.

The historical origin of the Kaʿbah is uncertain, but it had undoubtedly existed for several centuries before the birth of Muḥammad (c. 570 CE). By his time it was the principal religious shrine of central Arabia and, located at the center of a sacred territory *(ḥaram)*, had the characteristics of a Semitic sanctuary. [*See* Ḥaram and Ḥawṭah.] Islam incorporated it as part of its monotheistic cultus, a process begun by Muḥammad, who, upon capturing the Kaʿbah, cleansed it of the idols (and perhaps icons) it contained.

The Kaʿbah has been severely damaged by fire, flood, earthquake, and attack during its long history. The current building dates from the seventeenth century but contains stones from earlier buildings. As recently as 1958 the Saudi government repaired its walls and roof. Two years earlier it began a remodeling and enlargement of the Ḥaram Mosque that added over 6,000 square meters to its area; the mosque now has a total area of 16,326 square meters and can accommodate 300,000 persons.

[*See also* Pilgrimage, *article on* Muslim Pilgrimage.]

BIBLIOGRAPHY

Descriptions of the Kaʿbah are included in studies and accounts of the *ḥajj*. The classic studies are Christian Snouck Hurgronje's *Het Mekkaansche Feest* (Leiden, 1880) and Maurice Gaudefroy-Demombynes's *Le pèlerinage à la Mekke* (Paris, 1923). A recent study is David E. Long's *The Hajj Today: A Survey of the Contemporary Makkah Pilgrimage* (Albany, N.Y., 1979). See also Snouck Hurgronje's *Mekka*, 2 vols. (The Hague, 1888–1889), and Eldon Rutter's *The Holy Cities of Arabia*, 2 vols. (London, 1928), for descriptions of the holy places, including the Kaʿbah. Accounts of the *ḥajj* include John L. Burckhardt's *Travels in Arabia* (1829; reprint, London, 1968) and Richard F. Burton's *Personal Narrative of a Pilgrimage to Al-Madinah and Meccah*, 2 vols., edited by Isabel Burton (London, 1893), as well as Saleh Soubhy's *Pèlerinage à la Mecque et à Médine* (Cairo, 1894) and Ahmad Kamal's *The Sacred Journey* (New York, 1961).

HARRY B. PARTIN

KABALLAH. *See* Qabbalah.

KABĪR (fifteenth century CE), one of the most famous saints and mystics in the Indian tradition. Kabīr is unique in that he is revered by Hindus and Muslims alike, yet his personality and his biography remain shrouded in mystery. The only certain fact about him is that he was born a Julāhā, a low-caste Muslim weaver, in or near the city of Banaras toward the middle of the fifteenth century CE, at a time when North India was under the rule of the Lodi dynasty. The Julāhās were probably recent converts to Islam, and it is not certain that Kabīr himself was circumcised. He refers to the Muslims as "Turks."

The legendary biography of Kabīr includes his alleged persecution by the Muslim ruler Sikander Lodi and his initiation (presumably in the Rāmāite faith) by a rather mysterious Hindu saint known as Rāmānand. The most famous story about Kabīr, however, concerns the saint's death and burial-cremation at Magahar, a small town of ill repute in northeastern Uttar Pradesh, near Gorakhpur. As Kabīr was about to die, two armed parties of his followers allegedly converged on Magahar, ready to fight in order to secure possession of the saint's body. Kabīr retired into a small tent to die, and immediately after his death his body disappeared. Nothing was found but a heap of flowers, which was divided between the two parties: the Muslims buried their share of the flowers on the spot and erected a cenotaph over it; the Hindus cremated their share and later built a *samādhi* (memorial tomb) over it, although most sectarian devotees of Kabīr believe the flowers were cremated at the important Kabīr Chaurā Maṭh in Banaras itself. In later times, Kabīr's fame continued to grow among Hindus. In an attempt to "hinduize" the saint, devotees told of his having been born miraculously of a brahman virgin widow; she committed the child to the Ganges, but he was saved and reared by Julāhās.

There is no fully authoritative version of the *Kabīr-vāṇīs*, the "words of Kabīr." The poet was probably illiterate, and it is certain that he himself never committed anything to writing. His utterances took the form of the popular couplets known as *dohā*s, or the equally popular form of short songs *(padas)* set to a refrain. His language was a nondescript form of Old Hindi, which may have served as a sort of lingua franca for the wandering holy men of his time. So great was his eloquence, however, that his "words" spread like fire over a large area of Hindustan, at least from Bihar in the east to the Panjab and Rajasthan in the west. Immensely popular, the *Kabīrvāṇīs* were largely imitated and interpolated even before they could be written down. The oldest dated written record is found in the *Guru Granth* of the Sikhs, compiled by Guru Arjun in the Panjab around 1604. In the *Granth*, Kabīr's utterances are recorded as the words of the foremost among the *bhagats* (devotees or saints) who were the predecessors of Guru Nānak, the founder of the Sikh Panth ("path" or "way"). [*See* Ādi Granth.] Two more undated recensions of Kabīr's "words" are known: one in Rajasthan, preserved in the

Pāñcavāṇīs compiled by the Dādūpanthīs of Rajasthan (c. 1600) and known as *Kabīr Granthāvalī*, and the other, known as the *Bījak*, popularized, if not compiled, in Bihar by putative disciples of Kabīr who called themselves Kabīrpanthīs, although Kabīr himself never founded a sect. The *Bījak* represents the eastern recension of Kabīr's words. A fair idea of Kabīr's teachings, however, can be inferred only from a comparison of the three main recensions.

Some Muslims in the past tended to view Kabīr as a Ṣūfī, since many of his "words" are somewhat similar to those of the most liberal and unorthodox Indian Ṣūfīs. Modern Hindus and Muslims tend to see him as the champion of Hindu-Muslim unity, although Kabīr himself expressed outright rejection of the "two religions" and bitterly castigated their official representatives: pandits and *pāṇḍes* on the one side, *mullas* and *kāzis* on the other. For Kabīr, there could be no revealed religion at all—no Veda, no Qur'ān. All scriptural authority he emphatically denied, and he warned people against searching for truth in "holy books": "Reading, reading, the whole world died—and no one ever became learned!"

There is a tendency in modern times, especially among Hindu scholars with Vaiṣṇava leanings, to view Kabīr as a "liberal" Vaiṣṇava, one opposed—as indeed he was—to caste distinctions as well as to "idol worship," but a Vaiṣṇava all the same, since he made use of several Vaiṣṇava names to speak of God. Actually, Kabīr's notion of God seems to go beyond the notion of a personal god, despite the fact that he may call on Rām or Khudā. If he often mentions Hari, Rām, or the "name of Rām," the context most often suggests that these are just names for the all-pervading Reality—a reality beyond words, "beyond the beyond," that is frequently identified with *śūnya* ("the void") or the ineffable state that he calls *sahaj*. In the same way, though Kabīr often speaks of the *satguru* (the "perfect guru") it is clear that he is not alluding to Rāmānand, his putative guru, nor to any human guru. For Kabīr, the *satguru* is the One who speaks within the soul itself. Although he often borrows the language of Tantric yoga and its paradoxical style to suggest the "ineffable word," Kabīr held all yogic exercises to be absurd contortions and the yogis' pretention to immortality as utter nonsense.

Kabīr's view of the world is a tragic one. Life is but a fleeting moment between two deaths in the world of transmigration. Family ties are insignificant and rest on self-interest. Woman is "a pit of hell." Death encompasses all: living beings are compared to "the parched grain of Death, some in his mouth, the rest in his lap." There is no hope, no escape for man but in his own innermost heart. Man must search within himself, get rid of pride and egoism, dive within for the "diamond" that is hidden within his own soul. Then only may the mysterious, ineffable stage be achieved within the body itself—a mystery that Kabīr suggests in terms of fusion:

> When I was, Hari was not.
> Now Hari is and I am no more.

For one who has found the hidden "diamond," for one who has passed "the unreachable pass," eternity is achieved. Mortal life seems to linger, though in truth nothing remains but a fragile appearance. In Kabīr's own words:

> The yogin who was there has disappeared:
> Ashes alone keep the posture.

In its rugged, terse, fulgurant brilliance, Kabīr's style is unique. His striking metaphors and powerful rhythms capture the heart of the listener. His scathing attacks on brahmans and the "holy men" of his time have never been forgotten by the downtrodden people of India. Probably no greater voice had been heard on Indian soil since the time of the Buddha, whom Kabīr resembles in more ways than one. His pessimistic view of worldly life, his contempt for holy books and human gurus, his insistent call to inwardness have not been forgotten. His own brand of mysticism may appear godless if one takes "God" as a divine personality. In one sense, Kabīr is not only an iconoclast, he may even be called irreligious—and yet he appears as a master of the "interior religion."

[*For an overview of devotional poetry in the Indian tradition, see* Poetry, *article on* Indian Religious Poetry. *For further specific discussion of Kabīr within the context of North Indian religious traditions, see* Hindi Religious Traditions.]

BIBLIOGRAPHY

For the *Kabīr Granthāvalī*, see the editions prepared by Shyam Sundar Das (Banaras, 1928); by Mata Prasad Gupta (Allahabad, 1969), which includes a modern Hindi paraphrase; and by Parasnath Tiwari (Allahabad, 1965), which is a critical edition. The *Kabīr Bījak* has been edited a number of times. The standard edition is by S. Shastri and M. Prasad (Barabanki, 1950), and has been partially translated into English by Linda Hess and Shukdev Singh as *The Bījak of Kabīr* (San Francisco, 1983). Kabīr's words in the *Guru Granth* have been collected and edited by S. K. Varma in *Sant Kabīr* (Allahabad, 1947); this edition includes a paraphrase in modern Hindi.

For a translation of Kabīr's *dohās* in the Western recensions, see my *Kabīr* (Oxford, 1974) and my *Kabīr-vāni; The Words of Kabīr in the Western Tradition* (Pondicherry, 1983). See also my "Kabīr and the Interior Religion," *History of Religions* 3 (1964).

CHARLOTTE VAUDEVILLE

KAGAN, YISRA'EL ME'IR (c. 1838–1933), also known as Ḥafets Ḥayyim; rabbi, ethical writer, and Talmudist. Born in Zhetel, Poland, Yisra'el Me'ir Kagan (or ha-Kohen) revealed his scholarly abilities at an early age, and his father decided to devote his life to developing the talents of his son. He took the ten-year-old Yisra'el to Vilna; there the boy studied Talmud and came under the influence of the Musar movement, which sought the revitalization of the ethical life within the framework of traditional Judaism. [*See* Musar Movement.] After his marriage at the age of seventeen (which was normal for his circle), he moved to Radun, the hometown of his wife. At first he devoted himself to study while being supported by his wife, who ran a grocery store. For a short time afterward he served as the town rabbi, but he left the position when he found himself unsuited for it.

At the age of twenty-six, Kagan took a position as a Talmud teacher in Minsk, and in 1869 he returned to Radun and opened a *yeshivah* there. A few years later he published his first book, *Ḥafets ḥayyim* (Seeker of Life), the title of which is the epithet by which he became best known. It is an impressive work on the seriousness of the sins of gossip and talebearing as violations of Jewish law. His concern with morality attracted many students to him and gave him a position of leadership in the developing Jewish Orthodoxy of eastern Europe.

His messianic beliefs led Kagan to set up a program in his *yeshivah* in which students descended from the priestly clan studied intensively the laws of the Temple so that they would be prepared upon its rebuilding. He also published a compilation of laws and texts dealing with the Temple service. At the end of the century he began to publish a commentary on the parts of the *Shulḥan 'arukh* (a standard code of Jewish law) that deal with rituals, ceremonies, and holidays. This commentary, known as the *Mishnah berurah* (Clear Teaching), incorporated the views of the later legal decisors and became the authoritative commentary.

After spending the years of World War I in Russia, Kagan returned in 1921 to newly independent Poland, where he reestablished his *yeshivah.* In his later years he was active in Agudat Yisra'el (the world Orthodox organization), and during the interwar period he was probably the most influential rabbi in Poland. His influence was due not so much to his intellect as to his absolute honesty, his modesty, and his energy.

BIBLIOGRAPHY

The first full-scale biography, which still has value and charm, though it is clearly hagiographical, is Moses M. Yoshor's *Saint and Sage* (New York, 1937). A more recent treatment, with an academic apparatus, though still somewhat hagiographical, is Lester S. Eckman's *Revered by All* (New York, 1974). At least one of Kagan's works has been translated into English: see Leonard Oschry's translation *Ahavath Chesed: The Love of Kindness as Required by G-D*, 2d rev. ed. (New York, 1976).

SHAUL STAMPFER

KAGAWA TOYOHIKO (1888–1960), Japanese Christian novelist, social worker, statesman, and evangelist. He alerted a whole generation of Japanese to the need for a practical expression of Christian ethics and symbolized to non-Japanese the power of faith in action.

Both of Kagawa's parents died before the boy entered school. As a middle-school student he was befriended by American missionaries who converted him to Christianity and treated him like a son. Extremely gifted mentally but weak physically, he spent four months in the hospital and then nine months alone in a hut recuperating shortly after he had entered a theological seminary. His close encounter with death became the basis of his later novel *Shisen o koete* (translated as both *Across the Death Line* and *Before the Dawn*). For the rest of his life, glaucoma and tuberculosis threatened his many activities.

Back in the seminary, Kagawa concurrently started social work in the Kobe slums. After ordination into the Japanese Presbyterian church and marriage, he traveled to the United States to study at Princeton University and Princeton Theological Seminary. This experience abroad began a pattern that developed into frequent lecture trips to many parts of the world. To the West he brought a message of hope based on his experience; in Japan he threw himself into social reform. He supported his slum work by royalties from his writing. He also organized both urban workers and farmers to improve their livelihoods.

In the late twenties Kagawa moved to Tokyo, which became his headquarters. There he helped found consumer cooperatives and led pacifist movements. On a 1941 trip to the United States, he vigorously opposed militarism. Back in Japan, police incarcerated him several times; his foreign friends made him suspect. Then, when the war ended, he was made a member of the cabinet formed to proffer Japan's surrender. In the liberal postwar climate after 1945, Kagawa helped form the Socialist party and worked to return Japan to the world community under the United Nations. In 1955 he was nominated for the Nobel Peace Prize. Until his death, he served as the pastor of a Tokyo congregation.

Kagawa's thought reflected the accomplishments born of his great energy. Quick to analyze a problem, he would form an organization to remedy it, assign it to trusted associates, and move on, giving his friends the sense that he considered the problem solved. Those who questioned problems more deeply found his expression of faith facile. Nevertheless, they could not disagree with his postmillenarian conviction that work in service of the Social Gospel would help realize his aims. His writings all reflected this combination of faith and the need for hard work. The novel *Mugi no hitotsubo* (A Grain of Wheat) showed how an individual could change the moral climate of a whole village through his dedication to reform. Kagawa's nonfiction works included analyses of economics that showed how cooperation serves the interests of the community better than competition.

Kagawa's tireless writing and other activities drew attention to the very practical aspects of the Christian gospel. He used royalties from the sixteen printings of *Shisen o koete* to help start the Japanese labor movement. He led and assisted groups that worked to alleviate various social wrongs and thereby gained the respect of many individuals who otherwise had little interest in Christianity. He had the highest profile among Japanese Christian leaders. In contrast to most of them, Kagawa also showed respect to foreign missionaries, a number of whom translated his writings for publication in their homelands and arranged speaking tours for him. With over a dozen titles in English, he remains one of the most translated Japanese writers. During the thirties his message of faithful economic improvement brought hope to North American communities whose self-confidence had been severely eroded by the Great Depression. His name, along with those of other world figures such as Mahatma Gandhi and Chiang Kai-shek, became a household word as an example of the fruits of Christian mission.

Events near the end of World War II tarnished Kagawa's saintly image. He broadcast over the Japanese national radio network, invoking Lincoln's second inaugural address (1865) as he urged American troops to lay down their arms. Other Japanese, themselves concerned with war responsibility, felt that this cooperation with the government, however well intentioned, had compromised Kagawa's pacifism. Yet only four decades later his countrymen began to reassess his true worth. More than any other Japanese Christian of his generation, Kagawa tried to implement the Christian gospel in everyday life and formed a bond with Christians throughout the world.

BIBLIOGRAPHY

The works of Kagawa Toyohiko are collected in *Kagawa Toyohiko zenshū*, 24 vols. (Tokyo, 1962–1964), which forms the basis for all further studies. *Kagawa Toyohiko den* (Tokyo, 1959), by Haruichi Yokoyama, is considered the standard biography. Charley May Simon's *A Seed Shall Serve: The Story of Toyohiko Kagawa, Spiritual Leader of Modern Japan* (New York, 1958) presents a summary Western view of the man and his work. George Bikle, Jr.'s *The New Jerusalem: Aspects of Utopianism in the Thought of Kagawa Toyohiko* (Tucson, 1976) deals with Kagawa's ideas. Yuzo Ota's "Kagawa Toyohiko: A Pacifist?" in *Pacifism in Japan: The Christian and Socialist Tradition*, edited by Nobuya Bamba and me (Kyoto, 1978), discusses the quite differing attitudes in Japan and abroad toward Kagawa's work.

JOHN F. HOWES

KAIBARA EKKEN (1630–1714), Japanese Neo-Confucian scholar. Ekken was born in Fukuoka on the island of Kyushu in southern Japan. Although he was the son of a samurai family, he had early contacts with townspeople and farmers of the province. This no doubt influenced his later decision to write in simplified Japanese in order to make Confucian teachings available to a wide audience. His father taught him medicine and nutrition, awakening a lifelong interest in matters of health that would culminate in the composition of his well-known book *Yōjōkun* (Precepts for Health Care), completed in 1713. It was his older brother Sonzai, however, who urged Ekken to abandon his early interest in Buddhism and to immerse himself in the Confucian classics. Under Sonzai's tutelage, Ekken became well versed in the classics and in the Neo-Confucian writings of Chu Hsi. During a seven-year stay in Kyoto under the patronage of the lord of the Kuroda domain, he came into contact with the leading Confucian scholars of his time, including Nakamura Tekisai, Kinoshita Jun'an, the botanist Mukai Gensho, and the agronomist Miyazaki Yasusada. These contacts continued throughout his life by virtue of Ekken's numerous trips to Kyoto and Edō. Ekken's tasks as a Confucian scholar included lecturing to the lord of the Kuroda domain and tutoring his heir. In addition, he was commissioned to produce lineage of the Kuroda family that required some sixteen years of research and writing. He also recorded the topography of Chikuzen Province, in a work that is still considered a model of its kind. Ekken's other major research project, entitled *Yamato honzō*, consisted of a classification and description of the various types of plants in Japan. It has been praised by Japanese and Western scholars alike as a seminal work in the history of botany in Japan.

Ekken's enduring interest, however, was the popularization of Confucian ethics and methods of self-cultivation for a wide audience. Accordingly, he wrote a number of *kunmono*, instructional treatises for various groups such as the samurai, the lord, the family, women, and children. His work *Onna Daigaku* (Learning for Women) is especially well known. In addition, he wrote on methods of study, on literature, on writing, on precepts for daily life, and on the five Confucian virtues. Although a devoted follower of Chu Hsi, toward the end of his life he wrote *Taigiroku,* a work that records his "great doubts" about Chu's dualism of Principle *(li)* and material force *(ch'i).* Ekken's ideas were influenced by the thought of the Ming scholar Lo Ch'inshun (1416–1547), who had articulated a monistic theory of *ch'i.* Ekken felt that the dynamic quality of Confucianism had been lost by certain Sung and Ming thinkers, and he hoped through the monist theory of *ch'i* to reformulate a naturalism and vitalism that he, like Lo, viewed as essential to Confucian thought. Consequently, Ekken was concerned to articulate the vital impulse of the material force that suffused all reality. His thought can thus be described as a naturalist religiosity rooted in profound reverence and gratitude toward Heaven as the source of life and earth as the sustainer of life. He felt that by recognizing one's debt to these "great parents," human beings activated a cosmic filiality toward all living things. This idea of filiality implied that one should preserve nature, not destroy it. The highest form of filiality was humaneness *(jin),* through which humans formed an identity with all things. Ekken, then, was a reformed Chu Hsi scholar whose broad interests, voluminous writings, and naturalist religiosity mark a high point in Japanese Neo-Confucian thought.

[*See also* Confucianism in Japan.]

BIBLIOGRAPHY

Kaibara Ekken's works are collected in *Ekken zenshū,* 8 vols. (Tokyo, 1910–1911) and *Kaibara Ekken, Muro Kyūsō,* "Nihon shisō taikei," vol. 34, edited by Araki Kengo and Inoue Tadashi (Tokyo, 1970). Works on Ekken include Inoue Tadashi's *Kaibara Ekken* (Tokyo, 1963); *Kaibara Ekken,* "Nihon no meicho," vol. 14, edited by Matsuda Michio (Tokyo, 1969); and Okada Takehiko's *Kaibara Ekken* (Tokyo, forthcoming).

MARY EVELYN TUCKER

KALĀBĀDHĪ, AL- (d. AH 380/5, 990/5 CE), more fully Abū Bakr Muḥammad ibn Isḥāq ibn Ibrāhīm al-Kalābādhī; author of a famous treatise on early Sufism. As his name indicates, he was a native of the Kalābādh district of Bukhara. Details of his biography are lacking, but he is stated to have been a pupil of the Ṣūfī Abū al-Ḥusayn al-Fārisī and a Ḥanafī jurist with pro-Māturīdī views who studied jurisprudence *(fiqh)* under Muḥammad ibn Faḍl.

Of the works attributed to al-Kalābādhī, two are extant. The *Ma'ānī al-akhbār,* also known as *Baḥr al-fawā'id* and by other titles, was compiled in 985 and remains as yet unpublished. It consists of a brief ethical commentary, Ṣūfī in coloring, on 222 selected traditions of the Prophet and includes parallel passages cited in al-Kalābādhī's principal work, the *Kitāb al-ta'arruf li-madhhab ahl al-taṣawwuf.* This masterpiece has been edited several times, most reliably by A. J. Arberry (Cairo, 1933), who also translated it into English with a detailed introduction as *The Doctrine of the Sufis.*

The work is a principal source for the development of early Sufism (second/eighth to fourth/tenth centuries). It is divided into seventy-five chapters that fall into two parts. Beginning with a sketchy introductory survey of important early Ṣūfīs, the first part sets out the tenets of Islam as accepted by the Ṣūfīs; these can be traced back to the articles of faith elaborated in the creed known as *Al-fiqh al-akbar II* (The Greater Understanding II), which, it seems, al-Kalābādhī quotes directly. The second part discusses the ascetic endeavors, spiritual experiences, technical terms, and miraculous phenomena of the Ṣūfīs, based on their sayings and verses.

Throughout the work it is al-Kalābādhī's stated purpose to stave off the decay of Sufism and to prove that Sufism lies within the boundaries of Islamic orthodoxy. As a primary source for the history of early Sufism, al-Kalābādhī's *Ta'arruf* may rank with the works of al-Sarrāj (d. 988), Abū Ṭālib al-Makkī (d. 996), and al-Sulamī (d. 1021).

The *Ta'arruf* reflects the Ṣūfī tradition that became current in Transoxiana during Samanid times. It soon achieved the status of an authoritative treatise on Sufism, and commentaries were written on it. The most important of these is the Persian *Nūr al-murīdīn wa-faḍīhat al-mudda'īn,* also known as *Sharḥ-i Ta'arruf* (Commentary on the *Ta'arruf*), of Abū Ibrāhīm Ismā'īl ibn Muḥammad ibn 'Abd Allāh al-Mustamlī (d. 1042), a Ṣūfī of Bukhara. The work is the oldest surviving Ṣūfī treatise in Persian prose and is extant in several manuscripts, one of them copied in 1081. The value of this voluminous source for the development of Sufism in Transoxiana lies in its copious comments on each Ṣūfī statement quoted in the *Ta'arruf,* and in the fact that it was compiled with apparently no motive other than the instruction of Ṣūfī disciples. From the point of view of the Persian language, the work gives testimony to dialectal forms of tenth-century Persian, with an extraordinarily frequent occurrence of Arabic words.

The commentary on the *Ta'arruf* ascribed to 'Abd Allāh ibn Muḥammad al-Anṣārī (d. 1089) appears to be lost, while the *Ḥusn Al-ta'arruf,* an Arabic commentary on the work written by the Shāfi'ī judge 'Alā' al-Dīn 'Alī ibn Ismāʿīl al-Qūnawī (d. 1327 or 1329), is extant in manuscript. There is also an anonymous Arabic commentary that is erroneously ascribed to Yaḥyā Suhrawardī (d. 1191), who nonetheless summed up the importance of the *Taʿarruf* in the watchword: "But for the *Taʿarruf* we should not have known of Sufism."

BIBLIOGRAPHY

Anawati, Georges C., and Louis Gardet. *Mystique musulmane.* 3d ed. Paris, 1976.

Arberry, A. J. *The Doctrine of the Sufis.* Cambridge, 1935.

Lazard, Gilbert. *La langue des plus anciens monuments de la prose persane.* Paris, 1963. See pages 67–71.

Nwyia, Paul. "Al-Kalābā<u>dh</u>ī." In *The Encyclopaedia of Islam,* new ed., vol. 4. Leiden, 1978.

GERHARD BÖWERING

KALĀM. In common usage *kalām* signifies speech, language, sentence, proposition, words, but in the field of Muslim religious thought it has two particular meanings: the word of God *(kalām Allāh)* and the science of *kalām (ʿilm al-kalām),* which may be understood as dogmatic theology or more precisely the defensive apologetics of Islam. Apart from a few preliminary remarks on *kalām* as the word of God, the present article is devoted to *kalām* in the latter sense. [*For further discussion of* kalām Allāh, *see* Qur'ān.]

Etymology and Definitions

Kalām Allāh is mentioned several times in the Qur'ān (for example, surahs 2:75, 9:6, 48:15). God spoke to the Prophets (2:253). He "spoke clearly to Moses" (4:164, 7:143, and elsewhere). However, one finds neither *kalām* nor *mutakallim* (speaking) in the list of the most beautiful names of God *(asmā' Allāh al-ḥusnā).* Rather, it was the theologians who, on the basis of Qur'anic evidence, ascribed the attribute of *kalām* to God and designated the Qur'ān as *kalām Allāh.* From this development arose the very controversial problem of the relationship of the Qur'ān to the Word as a divine attribute. Here we may mention in passing that during the European Middle Ages, Thomas Aquinas described the *mutakallimūn* (whose occasionalism and negation of causality he refuted) as "loquentes in lege maurorum" ("those who speak on behalf of Islam").

As for the science of *kalām,* this term came to mean Muslim dogmatic theology. In his effort to determine the origin of the usage, Harry A. Wolfson suggests that the word *kalām* was used to translate into Arabic the different meanings of the Greek term *logos* as "word," "reason," "argument." It was also used to signify the act of expounding or discussing a specific science, and the *mutakallimūn* became those who deal with this science, for example *al-kalām al-ṭabīʿī, peri phuseos logoi.* The "physicians" *(phusikoi, phusiologoi)* are sometimes called *al-mutakallimūn fī al-ṭabīʿīyāt,* those who deal with questions of physics. The Greek term *theologoi* is translated by *aṣḥāb al-kalām al-ilāhī* or *al-mutakallimūn fī ilāhīyāt* (i.e., those who deal with the divine). Gradually, the term came to signify the specific, perfectly defined science that is the object of the present study.

In his renowned *Muqaddimah,* Ibn Khaldūn gives the following definition of *ʿilm al-kalām:* "The science of *kalām* is a science that involves arguing with logical proofs in defense of the articles of faith and refuting innovators who deviate in their dogmas from the early Muslims and Muslim orthodoxy. The real core *(sirr)* of the articles of faith is the oneness of God" (Cairo, n.d., p. 321; trans. Rosenthal, New York, 1958, vol. 3, p. 34).

This role of defensive apologia and of apologetics attributed to the science of *kalām* has remained standard in Islam. The modernist shaykh Muḥammad ʿAbduh wrote that the purpose of *kalām* was the "fixing of religious beliefs for the aim of working to conserve and consolidate religion" (*Risālat al-tawḥīd,* p. 5; trans., p. 5).

Al-Ījī (d. 1355), commented on at length and intelligently by al-Jurjānī (d. 1413), initially defines the function of *kalām* as seeking "to guarantee the proof (of the existence) of the Creator and of his unicity" (*Mawāqif,* vol. 1, p. 26). Later in the same work he explains that "*kalām* is the science that bears the responsibility of solidly establishing religious beliefs by giving proofs and dispelling doubts" (pp. 34–35). He goes on to state explicitly the purpose, the usefulness, the degree of excellence, the questions treated, and the explanation of the chosen term.

Finally, to cite a nineteenth-century popular manual, al-Bājūrī's gloss on the *Jawharat al-tawḥīd, kalām* or *tawḥīd* is defined as "the science that enables one to establish clearly religious beliefs, based on definite proofs of these beliefs" (*Ḥāshiyah ʿalā Jawharat al-tawḥīd,* p. 8). For al-Bājūrī this definition is the first of the ten "foundations" that converge to form each branch of knowledge. The second element is the subject: God, the envoys and the prophets, the contingent being insofar as he serves to give existence to his Maker, and the *samʿīyāt,* or traditionally accepted truths. The third element is its utility: the knowledge of God supported by decisive proofs and the acquiring of "eternal happiness." The fourth is the degree of excellence, and the fifth, the relationship of this science to the other disciplines. The people of *kalām* consider their science to be the most noble of all because of its subject and see it as the basis of all other fields of knowledge. The sixth element specifies the founders of the science: for orthodox *kalām*, al-Ash'arī (d. 935) and al-Māturīdī (d. 956), who "coordinated the writings related to this science and refuted the specious ambiguities introduced by the Mu'tazilah." The seventh element is the name: *tawḥīd* or *kalām*. The eighth is the means used, namely rational and traditional arguments. The ninth is its legal category, since the study of *kalām* is considered obligatory by its adherents. Finally, the tenth includes the questions treated, which deal with what is necessary and impossible to attribute to God and to the prophets.

Origins and Sources of the Science of Kalām

Among the influences that can be detected in the science of *kalām*, direct sources include the Qur'ān, *ḥadīth*, consensus of the community, and reason, while indirect sources can be traced to the pre-Islamic religions of the Byzantine and Sasanid empires and Greek philosophy as well as political dissensions of the early Islamic period.

The Qur'ān. This is the primary element on which the science of *kalām* is built. Islam is first of all the religion of the Book: it is a surrender to a God who, in the eyes of the believers, reveals himself in the book *par excellence*, the Qur'ān, his uncreated word. The Qur'ān is neither a history of the people of God nor a life of Muḥammad; it is rather a "discourse" that God holds with humanity in the first person.

The Qur'ān presents itself in effect as an absolute beginning of revelation. The earlier revelations (Jewish and Christian) have not been preserved in the authentic versions and thus cannot serve a "given." Consequently Muslim theology finds itself before an all-encompassing document, transmitted by a single man and corresponding to a very limited period of time. There is no progressive revelation, no *preparatio coranica* according to a divine plan, no development comparable to that of the Old Testament in relation to the New, or that within the New Testament itself. All the dogma is explicitly given in the Qur'anic text.

This Qur'anic core, the starting point of the science of *kalām*, is not systematic. It is essentially a collection of "revelations" stretched out over approximately twenty years, in which the Prophet informs his followers of the orders of God according to the circumstances, some of which are political.

A person knowledgeable in *kalām* finds four elements in the Qur'ān. First there is a theodicy: the existence of God, his unity, his eternal self, his omnipotence, the source of life and death, his fixity, his omniscience, and his mercy. God is endowed with speech and with will. He is the Creator. Second comes an anthropology: God created man from dust. He breathed his spirit into him *(wa-nafakha fīhi min rūḥihi)*. The human intelligence is superior to that of the angels. Adam disobeyed God, but his sin is not passed down to his descendants; thus, there is no original sin in Islam. The human being is the vicegerent of God *(khalīfat Allāh)* on earth, the ruler of the created world, which must be submitted to God's will. Third there is an eschatology: the judgment of the individual, heaven, hell, and the Last Judgment; God is the master of death. Finally there is morality: personal, familial, social; the rights of God.

Although the Qur'ān presents itself as a divine revelation, it nonetheless communicates no mysteries that are truly supernatural. There is the global mystery of the divine being *(al-ghayb)*, which is transcendent and entirely inaccessible in itself to human intelligence, but no mystery of the Trinity nor of the incarnation, nor of the redemption, and therefore no mystery of the church or of the sacraments. Quite the contrary, the very idea of the incarnation is vigorously rejected. Thus the theologians, those knowledgeable in *kalām*, have only to organize the elements of a natural theodicy in their attempt at synthesis. If we disregard the pejorative connotation that the word *rationalism* has acquired in Western Christian milieus since the eighteenth century, we can say that Muslim theology is basically rationalist: in practice it denies the possibility of access to an order of supernatural mysteries. For its clearest representatives who are not necessarily always the most religious, Muslim theology is essentially a superior metaphysical system to which are added, in an incidental manner, a few positive notions relating to matters of cult, which are revealed by God in the Qur'ān.

Finally, the Qur'ān was revealed in Arabic. For Muslim theologians this fact indicates an essential link between the religious notion and the nature of God. The Arabic Qur'ān is the very word of God himself. Consequently the Arabic language is seen as itself revealed, or at least as the one that best expresses the word of God. This explains the primary role played by language in the elaboration of Muslim theology and the importance of the schools of grammar in the interpretation of the sacred texts.

Ḥadīth. This term refers to the corpus of words and actions of the Prophet, the "perfect model" whose least word assumes normative value. In dogmatic and moral authority, the canonical collections of these *ḥadīth* are second only to the Qur'ān, at least according to traditional Muslim thinkers.

The Consensus of the Community (Ijmā'). This consensus of the community as represented by its doctors is an internal factor of regulation. According to Henri Lammens, it is a kind of instinct of the people, who when faced with certain innovations react according to the spirit of Islam. The Prophet had said, "My community will never agree on an error," and from this his disciples concluded that the community is infallible as far as its beliefs and religious practices are concerned.

The idea of *ijmāʿ*, although quite complex in theory, showed itself to be effective in practice to maintain a traditional line of orientation through the stirrings caused by new conditions. Since Islam has neither an official ministry nor an advisory body, the *ijmāʿ* exercises more or less tacitly the role of regulator within the Muslim community. Qualified reformers aroused by God could legitimately undertake to reestablish the Muslim community in the purity of its original line or could propose solutions to the demands of the modern world in conformity with the religious law.

Reason. For a certain number of narrow traditionists, especially in the early period, the only acceptable attitude from the religious point of view was an exclusive loyalty to the Qur'ān and the *ḥadīth* with no rational elaboration. Nevertheless, for traditional theology reason became an essential factor in the problem of faith. It is necessary for every adult, who should not be satisfied with a blind acceptance of tradition *(taqlīd)* but must be able to demonstrate rationally the existence of God and the truth of the Muslim religion. The theologians themselves use reason to establish the authenticity of their historical notions, to criticize evidence, to defend dogmas, and to refute objections. This tendency went so far that in certain treatises on theology the major part is devoted to *ʿaqlīyāt,* those truths that reason can reach on its own, with the Qur'ān serving as a confirmation. A certain number of positive notions, the *samʿīyāt,* are known only by revelation; these are concerned with eschatology, prophetology, the caliphate, and similar matters. The degree to which reason is used also varies with the schools: some restrict its use to logic as instrument; others apply an untiring dialectical zeal to the smallest theological problems.

Christianity. The influence of Christianity was felt either in an informal way, notably through the Bible itself or through contacts that Muslims had with Christians living in Muslim lands, or formally via discussions with Christian theologians, especially in Damascus and Baghdad. Among these theologians were the Nestorians concentrated in Hira, the Jacobites (monophysites), and finally the Melkites, including John of Damascus and his disciple Abū Qurrah, as well as several dissident sects that were more or less Christian. As they attempted to defend the dogma of Islam in discussions with these groups, Muslim theologians were led to address certain problematic issues such as free will and predestination, the divine attributes, and the uncreated Qur'ān. (In the Qur'ān Jesus is considered to be the word of God.)

Greek Philosophy. In the eyes of Muslim thinkers, Greek philosophy was perceived as a single body of knowledge within which Plato and Aristotle, far from being in opposition, played complementary roles in relation to each other. Apocryphal Neoplatonic writings such as *De causis* and the *Pseudo-Theology of Aristotle* served to reinforce this conviction. These Greek teachings, known directly or via the commentators, exercised an influence in two directions. Certain Muslim thinkers adopted an orientation that was straightforwardly rational in the eighteenth-century French sense of the term. They denied all revelation, maintaining only a vague notion of a distant philosophical God. This was especially true of Abū Bakr al-Rāzī, the Rhazes of the Latins.

Other thinkers, loyal to their faith, took on the task of defending the principal dogmas of their religion with this instrument newly placed between their hands—Greek thought. These were the Muʿtazilah, the first theologians of Islam. They soon split into two main groups. The dissidents among them, such as al-Ashʿarī, wished to retain only the minimum of philosophy indispensable for theological elaboration and stressed more the properly religious core of the Qur'ān. The other group, the *falāsifah,* including hellenizing philosophers such as al-Kindī, al-Fārābī, Ibn Sīnā, Ibn Rushd, and others, were more philosophers than Muslims; for them religious ideas were only a superstructure or a pretext for philosophizing. The *ijmāʿ* came to favor the first trend, and the ideas of the Ashʿarīyah became the shared philosophy of Islam, while the second tendency was met with great reticence, and its doctrine was hardly tolerated.

Manichaeism and Mazdakism. The invasion of Iran brought the Muslims in contact with a very rich and complex cultural climate, where the Armenian and Syrian Christians in particular were already engaged in controversies with the Mazdaeans and the Magians. The ardent monotheism of Islam, which for fear of taking anything away from God's omnipotence made God the creator of evil as well as good, offered a new battlefield for Mazdaean apologists, as is demonstrated by the *Shkand gumānīk vichār,* a ninth-century Mazdaean apologetic treatise. The theologians responded by elaborating treatises against the dualists.

As for the Manichaeans, their survival in the tenth-century East, attested by Ibn al-Nadīm's *Fihrist,* leads one to believe that with the fall of their Mazdaean persecutors and the period of calm that followed the Muslim conquest, their doctrine was able to find a new lease on life.

Political Dissensions. The political struggles among Muslims mark the starting point for the elaboration of theological problems. Given that traditional Islam is inseparably *dīn wa-dawlah,* "religion and state," it is normal that everything concerning the polity, the transmission of power, legitimacy, and the struggle for public authority should express itself in religious terms and provoke violent conflicts among the partisans of opposing opinions. It was in this way that the problems of the nature of faith, of its relationship to works, of the possibility for faith to increase or decrease, of the status of the unrepentant sinner who is nevertheless a believer, of the caliphate, and like questions developed among the Muslims.

The Principal Schools and Major Themes

Here I shall pursue a mainly chronological order that will permit me to trace the emergence and development of the problem.

The Early Creeds. The earliest surviving documents that give an official expression of doctrine are the first creeds, some of which have been studied by A. J. Wensinck in *The Muslim Creed.* From what we have observed concerning the fragmentary nature of the Qur'ān, it is not surprising to find no systematic resumé of doctrine there. What Muḥammad affirms above all are the divine transcendence and unity, the declaration in fiery terms of the horrors of the judgment, and the prophetic character of his message. [*See* Creeds, *article on* Islamic Creeds.]

But a few decades after Muḥammad's death, the expansion of the new religion and the political and social questions that arose led the heads of the community to express the essential traits of Islam and to condense them into a formula that was easy to recite and easy to remember. We find some of these formulas in the *ḥadīth* collections. For example, Muḥammad is asked, "What is Islam?" and he answers, "It is to associate nothing with God, to perform the ritual prayer, to give the prescribed alms, and to fast during Ramaḍān." When he is asked, "And what is faith?" he answers, "It is to believe in God, his angels, his book, his meeting [with believers in Paradise], and his Prophet, to believe in the resurrection and the final destiny."

The development of Islam, the struggle with the tribes in revolt, and the conquests slowly necessitated a distinction between *islām* ("submission") and *īmān* ("faith"). [*See* Īmān and Islām.] It is possible to be Muslim in different ways, and external posture is not necessarily a sign of inner faith. It was at this point that the "five pillars of Islam" were defined. These are usually expressed in the following terms: "Islam is built on five pillars: faith, ritual prayer *(ṣalāt),* the tithe *(zakāt),* the fast of Ramaḍān, and the pilgrimage." Thus Islam presents itself in its entirety as faith and acts. The holy war is not yet mentioned.

However, conversion to Islam prompted the development of a simple formula expressing in a few words the essential message of the new religion: the *shahādah* ("witnessing") served this function. By reciting it, the new converts entered the Muslim community; it was their profession of faith: "There is no god but God, and Muḥammad is the messenger of God."

A profession of faith reduced to its simplest expression, the *shahādah* would be sufficient as long as internal discussions did not pit the disciples of the same master against one another. But once dissension arose, there was inevitably an orthodox party that sought to set down its position in precise terms and heaped anathema on those who did not accept it in its entirety. It was in this context that the first creeds would appear.

The Fiqh al-akbar. One of the principal creeds to come down to us is the *Fiqh al-akbar*. Although we are tempted to see it as nothing more than the simple development of the formula of the profession of faith, such is not the case. The *shahādah* is a formula of adherence to the Muslim community; the creed is the profession of faith of the community itself, which wishes to state its position in relation to the dissenting sects. This particular profession mentions neither the unity of God nor the mission of Muḥammad, since neither is called into question. It states the following articles:

1. We consider no one (of those who profess Islam) to be an unbeliever on account of his faith, nor do we deny his faith.
2. We command the good and forbid the evil.
3. What reaches you could not have missed you, and what misses you could not have reached you.
4. We do not disavow any of the companions of the Apostle of God, nor do we adhere to any one of them in particular.
5. We leave to God the question of ʿUthmān and ʿAlī. He alone knows the secret and hidden matters.
6. Knowledge in matters of religion is better than knowledge in matters of the law.
7. The difference of opinions in the community is a blessing of God.
8. Whoever believes what should be believed but says, "I do not know if Moses and Jesus are prophets or not," is an unbeliever.
9. Whoever affirms that he does not know if God is in heaven or in hell is an unbeliever.
10. Whoever says he does not know the punishment in the tomb belongs to the sect of the Jahmīyah, which is condemned to perdition.

The Waṣīyah. It is with the *Waṣīyah* (Testament) of Abū Ḥanīfah (d. 767) that the major problems begin to emerge; it is true that these are not yet classified in homogenous groups, but one feels that the work of collecting has started. We can separate the twenty-seven articles of this creed into the following themes.

1. *The problem of faith.* The text affirms that faith resides in witnessing with the tongue, believing with the mind, and knowing with the heart. It does not increase or decrease (art. 2). The believer and unbeliever really are such (art. 3). Muslim sinners do not cease to be Muslim (art. 4). Works are distinct from faith (art. 5). Finally, faith allows people to be classified in three categories: believers with pure intentions, unbelievers who recognize their lack of belief, and hypocrites (art. 14).

2. *Predestination.* This problem is treated throughout the *Waṣīyah.* First of all it is affirmed against the dualists and the Qadarīyah that God alone controls good and evil (art. 6), that mortal acts are created by God (art. 11) since human beings have no natural power (art. 12), and that God creates the faculty at the same time as the act (art. 15). Finally it is God who orders the (celestial) pen to write (art. 17); that is to say, he determines all things.

The theme of human actions is very closely associated with that of predestination, since these actions are totally dependent on divine will. The relationship between these two forms the crucial problem of speculative moral philosophy. Along with predestination, the distinction of three kinds of actions is affirmed: these are the obligatory, the optional, and the reprehensible. About ten affirmations follow to detail the eschatological beliefs: the punishment of the tomb (art. 18), questioning in the tomb (art. 19), heaven and hell (art. 20 and 27), the scale (art. 21), the reading of the book (art. 22), the resurrection (art. 23), God's meeting with the inhabitants of Paradise (art. 24), the intercession of the Prophet (art. 25), and God's sitting on the throne (art. 8). In addition there are affirmations concerning the uncreated or created nature of the Qur'ān (art. 9), the order of precedence of the first caliphs (art. 10), the precedence of ʿĀ'ishah (art. 26), and the validity of ablutions performed on shoes (art. 16).

Fiqh al-akbar II. The *Fiqh al-akbar* II leads us onto much more defined ground, for debate had obliged the religious leaders to clarify beliefs, to reject anything that could threaten the transcendence of God, and to specify the role of the prophets and the value of their message.

From the very first affirmation, the global content of the faith reveals itself: God, the angels, his envoys, the resurrection, the decree concerning good and evil, the calculation of sins, the scale, heaven and hell. The entire theological base to date is thus set out: theology already possesses all the material it will have to systematize. The different articles of the creed, about forty in all, take up each point in turn and develop them slightly without, however, following the order proposed at the start.

Muʿtazilī Problematic and Theses. The Muʿtazilah, "the first thinkers of Islam," gave the science of *kalām* a systematic form. The great Muʿtazilah lived either in Basra (Abū al-Hudhayl al-ʿAllāf, d. 849; al-Naẓẓām, d. 846; al-Jāḥiẓ, d. 872) or in Baghdad (Bishr ibn al-Muʿtamir, d. 825; Abū Mūsā al-Mirdar, d. 841; Thumāmah ibn al-Ashras, d. 828).

Although they did not teach the same doctrine on all matters, they nonetheless shared a common spirit. Historians and heresiographers have not been wrong in summarizing the characteristics of their doctrine in five affirmations called *al-uṣūl al-khamsah:* the unity of God *(al-tawḥīd),* his justice *(al-ʿadl),* the promise and the threat *(al-waʿd wa-al-waʿīd),* the "neutral" position in relation to the sinner *(al-manzilah bayn al-manzilatayn),* and finally the "commanding of good and forbidding of evil" *(al-amr bi-al-maʿrūf wa-al-nahy ʿan al-munkar).*

First thesis: tawḥīd. Concerned with avoiding the slightest anthropomorphism in the question of divine attributes, the Muʿtazilah applied in all its vigor the *via remotionis,* God's transcendence *(tanzīh).* The anthropomorphic verses should be "interpreted" symbolically, and in some cases even rejected. Similarly, contradictory *ḥadīth*s were set aside. Against the "people of *ḥadīth*" and the ʿAlids, the Muʿtazilah could affirm their agnosticism on the matter of the nature of God. Without going as far as the Jahmīyah, who completely denied the attributes of God, they affirmed that all these attributes are identical with God's essence and that they have no real existence. Against the Dahrīyah (materialists) they affirmed a personal creator God. If God is completely spiritual, he cannot be seen by the senses, from which came their rejection of the "vision of God" in the future life, the *ru'yah* of the traditionists. The absolute transcendence of God in relation to the world led them to distinguish rigorously between the preeternal and the *muḥdath* (that which has begun to be) and made them reject energetically any notion of *ḥulūl* (the infusion of the divine into the created).

The Muʿtazilah accepted a "contingent" or "created" divine knowledge of free intentions and of possibilities in general. They studied the object and the limits of divine power, analyzed human control over their actions, and affirmed that they created such actions by "generation" *(tawallin).*

With the same concern to eliminate any suspicion of associationism, they affirmed the created character of the Qur'ān, the word of God. In the history of the Muʿtazilah, this position attracted the most attention because of its political repercussions. The Qur'ān, they held, is a "genus" of words, created by God. It is called the "word of God" since, in contrast to our own words, the Qur'ān was created directly.

Second thesis: the justice of God. In conjunction with *tawḥīd,* this belief served to describe the Muʿtazilah, or rather, they proudly described themselves as the "people of justice and unity." By analyzing the notion of human justice and extending it to God, they drew two conclusions.

1. As an intelligent and wise being, God must necessarily act according to a purpose, with a view to a determined plan. There is a chosen, objective order in the universe, and thus intermediary purposes, themselves related to an ultimate purpose. Consequently there are an objective good and evil prior to the determination brought by religious law. God is obliged always to do the best, *al-aṣlaḥ;* he can wish only the good.

2. God does not want evil. He does not order it since his wish *(irādah)* and his commandment *(amr)* are identical. Evil is created by humans, as is good for that matter, since people create all their actions, good or evil. They have in effect received from God a "power" *(qudrah),* that allows them to act freely. For this reason they will inevitably receive a reward for their good actions and a punishment for their evil ones.

Third thesis: the promise and the threat. This concerns the fate of the believer *(mu'min),* the sinner *(fāsiq),* and the unbeliever *(kāfir)* in the hereafter. The term "the names and the statutes" *(al-asmā' wa-al-aḥkām)* is also used, referring to the juridical statutes that determine the fate of each group. The basic problem is that of faith and disbelief. For the Muʿtazilah, to have faith is not merely to assent in the heart and to make the verbal profession *(shahādah)* but also to avoid the "major sins" *(kabā'ir).* The unbelievers and the unrepentant Muslim sinners are condemned to hell.

Fourth thesis: the "intermediate position" between faith and disbelief. This is a corollary to the Muʿtazilī concept of divine justice and faith and is easily assimilated to the preceding thesis. The position of the Muslim sinner *(fāsiq)* is intermediate between that of the believer and that of the unbeliever. Although condemned in the hereafter to eternal damnation (albeit one less rigorous than that of the *kāfir*), he remains nonetheless a member of the Muslim community while on earth.

Fifth thesis: "commanding the good." In contrast to those who saw internal criticism as sufficient, the Muʿtazilah favored direct action. Order must be reestablished "by the sword." If there is a hope of defeating adversaries one must overthrow the guilty leaders, even kill them if necessary, and force them, on pain of death, to accept the true doctrine.

This is not the place to discuss the history of the Muʿtazilah, their temporary triumph and final defeat. [*See* Muʿtazilah.] History books recount different stages of the *miḥnah* (inquisition), which represents the final struggle of the upholders of rational doctrines against the narrowly traditionalist thinkers. The rationalists were defeated and the "people of *ḥadīth*" triumphed decisively. The fact remains nevertheless that the Muʿtazilah represent a turning point in the history of Muslim thought and they left a definitive mark, even if by reaction, on the problematic of *kalām.*

It was one of the deserters from the Muʿtazilah, Abū al-Ḥasan al-Ashʿarī, who succeeded in finding the conciliatory *via media* between their rationalism and the literalism of the traditionists. A longtime disciple of al-Jubbā'ī, the head of the Muʿtazilah of Basra, he broke publicly with his teacher and turned violently against his former companions. At first he attempted to win over the literalists by expressing his admiration for Ibn Ḥanbal, as can be seen at the start of his *Ibānah,* or "elucidation" of the principles of religion.

However, his real theological work would consist of attempting to reconcile the different schools. By his conversion he intended to rediscover the meaning of traditional doctrine, to "return" to the Qur'ān and to the teaching of the first Muslims. In the field of exegesis he energetically rejected the overly drastic *tanzīh* of the Muʿtazilah as this led to *ta'ṭīl,* a complete dissection of the notion of God. He wished to maintain a literal interpretation of the text and in this respect appeared to present himself as a faithful disciple of Ibn Ḥanbal. This was a literalism peculiar to al-Ashʿarī, however, since the later Ashʿarīyah would distance themselves considerably from the rigid literalism of their founder and thus would provoke the anger of Ibn Ḥazm and the Ḥanābilah themselves (Laoust, *Ibn Taymiyya,* pp. 81–82). Likewise on the question of the "vision of God" and of the anthropomorphic terms and the attributes (*Ibānah,* p. 47), he presented positions to which Ibn Ḥanbal would have ascribed without hesitation.

Such was the al-Ashʿarī of our direct sources. But for al-Juwaynī (d. 1085), who became al-Ghazālī's master, al-Ashʿarī was not a theologian following the opinions of Ibn Ḥanbal but rather a conciliator of two extreme positions. In his *Tabyīn* (pp. 149ff.) Ibn ʿAsākir shows us how his master, when dealing with the principal questions, followed a middle course between the exaggerations of the Muʿtazilah and those of the *ḥashwīyah* who, it is true, were recruited among the extremist Hanābilah. Table 1 summarizes the principal Ashʿarī positions in comparison with those of the extremists. All later *kalām* would see al-Ashʿarī as its founder.

Al-Māturīdī (d. 956) was a follower and contemporary of al-Ashʿarī. His disagreements with al-Ashʿarī

TABLE 1. *The Conciliating Position of al-Ash'arī, according to the Qāḍī Abū al-Ma'ālī ibn 'Abd al-Malik (al-Juwaynī) as Reported by Ibn 'Asākir, Tabyīn (pp. 149ff.)*

EXTREME BY DEFAULT	AL-ASH'ARĪ	EXTREME BY EXCESS
1. The attributes		
Denied *(ta'ṭīl, ibṭāl)* by the Mu'tazilah, Jabarīyah, Rāfiḍah.	They are real, but not like human attributes.	They are like human attributes *(ḥashwīyah).*
2. Human acts		
People have a power *(qudrah).* They are susceptible to *kasb* (Qadarīyah, Mu'tazilah).	No power. God creates the acts of human beings, who are endowed with *kasb* (attribution, juridical charge).	Neither power nor *kasb* (Jabarīyah).
3. The vision of God		
Denied by the Mu'tazilah, Jahmīyah, and Najjārīyah.	God will be seen (by the eyes) but without *ḥulūl,* without terms, without modes, as he sees us.	God will be seen like things of the senses (*ḥashwīyah*).
4. Omnipresence of God		
God is everywhere without *ḥulūl* or direction (Mu'tazilah).	God existed before there was place. He created the throne and the seat. He has no need of place. The creation of place has in no way changed his nature.	God is "infused" *(ḥulūl)* in the throne. He is seated on the throne which is his place (*ḥashwīyah*).
5. Ta'wīl (interpretation)		
Hand = power and grace; face of God = his existence; descent of God = descent of certain verses, or of his angels; sitting on the throne = domination (Mu'tazilah).	The hand and face are real attributes like hearing and sight . . . = attribute . . . = attribute. . . .	The hand is a real limb, the face is a face with human form. The descent is real, as is sitting on the throne (*ḥashwīyah*).
6. The Qur'ān		
It is the created word of God (Mu'tazilah).	The [eternal] Qur'ān is the uncreated word of God, eternal, unchangeable. The individual letters, the ink with which it is written are created.	All is uncreated (*ḥashwīyah*).
7. Faith		
It is created (Mu'tazilah, Jahmīyah, Najjārīyah).	Faith is of two kinds: that of God, uncreated; that of the believers, created.	Faith is absolutely uncreated (*ḥashwīyah*).
8. The eternal punishment		
The Muslim who commits a grave sin is eternally damned (Khārijīs, Mu'tazilah).	The Muslim sinner is given up to divine goodwill. God can accept that person immediately into Paradise or mete out punishment in a temporary Hell.	The fate of the Muslim sinner will be debated only on the Day of Judgment (Murji'ah).
9. Intercession		
The Prophet does not have the power of intercession (Mu'tazilah).	Intercession of the Prophet on behalf of believing sinners with the permission of God.	Muḥammad and 'Alī can intercede without God's order or permission, even for unbelievers (Rāfiḍah).
10. The caliphate		
Mu'āwīyah, Ṭalḥah, Zubayr, and 'Ā'ishah are guilty. Their testimony is not accepted (Mu'tazilah). They are not guilty (Umayyads).	Every *mujtahid* achieves a result. There is general agreement on this principle.	All these people are unbelievers (Rāfiḍah).

SOURCE: Gardet and Anawati (1948), pp. 58–59.

stemmed above all from the fact that they followed different legal rites. Al-Ashʿarī was probably a disciple of al-Shāfiʿī. Al-Māturīdī was by contrast a clear disciple of Abū Ḥanīfah, a Persian like himself. He favored liberal, rational solutions, staying as close as possible to the Muʿtazilah while remaining within the limits of orthodoxy. We see an example of this approach in his attitude toward the problem of liberty and *kasb*. Al-Māturīdī's solution attempted to respect the intervention of the human being, to whom he attributes the "qualification" of acts. Similarly al-Māturīdī affirms that the believer can say, "I am a believer in truth," whereas al-Ashʿarī required the restriction, "if God wishes it." (This is the problem of the *istithnā'*.) For the Māturīdīyah it was inconceivable that God would punish those who had obeyed him, while the Ashʿarīyah accepted the possibility, at least in theory. For the Māturīdīyah, often called "shameful Muʿtazilah," reason, even without the religious law, would have taught us that there is an obligation to know God; for the Ashʿarīyah, this awareness comes exclusively from revelation. The different points of divergence, which number about fifty, remain secondary and in no way prevent the Ashʿarīyah and Māturīdīyah from being considered without distinction as "people of tradition and *ḥadīth*," the former in the western part of the empire (Syria, Iraq, Egypt), and the latter in the eastern part.

The Ashʿarīyah spread into Persia under the Seljuks, then into Syria and Egypt under the Ayyubids and the Mamluk sultans, and finally into the Maghreb under the Almohad dynasty led by Ibn Tūmart (d. 1130?). This triumph was characterized by ongoing development of the doctrine, with the names of the *qāḍī* al-Bāqillānī, al-Juwaynī (Imām al-Ḥaramayn), and finally al-Ghazālī serving to demarcate the principal stages. [*See* Ashʿarīyah.]

From the Via Antiqua to the Via Moderna. In his famous *Muqaddimah*, Ibn Khaldūn (d. 1406) presents the time of al-Ghazālī (d. 1111) as a watershed in the evolution of *kalām*. The *via antiqua*, characterized by a dialectic inspired primarily by the logic of the doctors of the law, gave way to the *via nova*, which relied on the Aristotelian syllogism. This break should not be overemphasized, however: at least from the point of view of the subjects discussed, influences must have been felt earlier via the Muʿtazilah, some of whom had read Aristotle. This tendency can already be seen in the writings of al-Bāqillānī (d. 1013), himself an untiring opponent of the Muʿtazilah, and even more strongly in those of his disciple al-Juwaynī (d. 1085). The latter was indeed an ancient in his dialectic, but an ancient who foretold the victory of the new method, which would triumph through his disciple al-Ghazālī and come even closer to the *falāsifah* with later theologians.

I shall now trace this evolution in the *Tamhīd* of al-Bāqillānī, the *Irshād* of al-Juwaynī, and the *Iqtiṣād* of al-Ghazālī. I shall finish with the treatises in which the new tendency takes full shape.

The Tamhīd of al-Bāqillānī. In his *Tamhīd*, al-Bāqillānī, who has not yet broken away from his apologetic preoccupations, mixes his presentation of beliefs with long discussions against non-Muslim sects and dissident Muslims themselves. The following is the schema of his presentation:

Preliminary. Science; nature; foundations.

I. *De Deo Uno*. (1) Existence of God: (a) division of known objects; (b) accidents; (c) created nature of the word and proof of the existence of God. (2) His attributes: he is one, living, knowing, hearing, seeing, speaking, willing; he has no appetite. (3) Divine action: neither motive *(gharaḍ)* nor cause *(ʿillah);* he acts freely.

II. *Apologetic Section*. Refutation of the astrologers, dualists, Magians, Christians, Brahmans (Hindus), Jews, and corporalists *(mujassimah*, i.e., those who maintain a literal interpretation of the anthropomorphic verses of the Qur'ān).

III. *The Caliphate*. (1) Principles of methodology and nature of the caliphate. (2) Qualities required of the caliph. (3) The first four caliphs. (4) Validity of their caliphate. (See also Gardet and Anawati, 1948, pp. 154–156.)

The Irshād of al-Juwaynī. Al-Ghazālī's master, also called Imām al-Ḥaramayn ("imam of the two holy places"), presents the principles of his classification more than once in his *Irshād*. At some points he divides his treatise between what exists necessarily in God and what is possible, that is to say, between what God can and cannot accomplish. At others he distinguishes between matters accessible to reason and those attainable only through the traditional path. Although it is not easy to find one's way through the *Irshād*, its plan can be drawn up in the following manner:

Introduction. The character of reason; the nature of science.

I. *The Existence of God*. (1) Contingency of the world (its beginning in time). (2) Proofs of the existence of God (*a novitate mundi*).

II. *What Necessarily Exists in God*. (1) Attributes of the essence: the unity of God. (2) Attributes of qualification: (a) knowledge of the attributes; (b) knowledge of the attributes themselves (the word; the divine names; other attributes).

III. *What God Can and Cannot Accomplish.* (1) Visibility of God: the creation of human acts. (2) The promise and the threat. (3) Prophetology. (4) The "traditional" questions *(samʿīyāt):* (a) sundry aspects: terms assigned to things, subsistence for maintaining life, censure of human actions; (b) eschatology; (c) names and the juridical qualifications; (d) the caliphate.

The Iqtiṣād of al-Ghazālī. The author of the *Iḥyāʾ* discussed *ex professo* and with precision the science of *kalām* in a compendium entitled *Al-iqtiṣād fī al-iʿtiqād* (The Just Mean in Belief). He intended to remain loyal to Ashʿarī orthodoxy, simplifying to the extreme the dialectical debates and eliminating the philosophical investigations that his master al-Juwaynī had integrated into his treatises.

Al-Ghazālī devotes four chapters to a general introduction on *kalām.* The first underlines the importance of this science: it allows us to know God, his attributes, and the work of his messengers. However, he takes pains to tell us in the second chapter that this concerns only a certain number of people, since, with relation to the truths of faith and the doubts that can arise, one must distinguish different categories of people who are not equally able to devote themselves to this science. *Kalām* is safely used only to resolve certain doubts of the believers and to try to convince intelligent unbelievers. Finally, the fourth chapter analyzes the sources.

Next al-Ghazālī divides all the questions considered into four large sections, each precisely articulated. Since God is the object of *kalām,* we must first study him in his essence; this is the aim of the first section. The second section deals with the attributes; the third, with the action of God and his personal acts; and the fourth, with his envoys. The following is a general outline of the whole work:

Preliminaries. The nature of *kalām;* its importance; its methodology.

I. *The Divine Essence.* (1) God exists. (2) He is eternal. (3) He is permanent. (4) He is insubstantial. (5) He is incorporeal. (6) He is nonaccidental. (7) He is undefined. (8) He is not localized. (9) He is visible and knowable. (10) He is one.

II. *The Attributes of God.* (1) The attributes in themselves: life, knowledge, power, will, hearing, sight, speech. (2) The "status" of the attributes: (a) they are not the essence; (b) they are in the essence; (c) they are eternal; (d) the divine names.

III. *The Acts of God* (what God can or cannot do). (1) God can choose (is free) to impose no obligation on his creatures. (2) Or he can choose to impose on them what they cannot do. (3) God does nothing in vain. (4) He can make innocent animals suffer. (5) He can fail to reward one who obeys him. (6) The obligation of knowing God comes from revelation alone. (7) The sending of prophets is possible.

IV. *The Envoys of God.* (1) Muḥammad. (2) Eschatology (and faith). (3) The caliphate. (4) The sects.

Evolution of the Via Moderna. Elsewhere (Gardet and Anawati, 1948) I have shown the evolution of the *via moderna* with the progressive introduction of philosophy through an examination of *kalām* treatises such as the *Nihāyat al-aqdām* of al-Shahrastānī (d. 1153), the *Muḥaṣṣal* of Fakhr al-Dīn al-Rāzī (d. 1209), and the *Ṭawāliʿ al-anwār* of al-Bayḍāwī (d. 1286). Here I shall give the end result of this evolution as it is crystallized in the *Mawāqif* of al-Ījī (d. 1355) with the commentary of al-Jurjānī (d. 1413). With this work we reach the high point of the science of *kalām* in Sunnī Islam. Ījī/Jurjānī, with the glosses of other commentators, represent the largest (four volumes of more than five hundred pages each) and most systematic work of orthodox Muslim speculative thought. The work supplied material for years of specialization in the great Muslim universities, and one is obliged to recognize, especially by comparison with previous works, that its fame is well deserved. Even if the truly traditional parts, and the theology strictly speaking, are treated soberly, the philosophical part with its long critical introduction receives ample development. Consisting of six treatises and an appendix, the work is divided and subdivided with care:

I. *Preliminaries.* (1) The presuppositions of *kalām* and all knowledge. (2) Science (or knowledge) *in genere.* (3) The division of knowledge (the first two operations of the spirit). (4) The existence of sciences or necessary knowledges. (5) Reasoning. (6) The different forms of reasoning.

II. *General Principles.* (1) Being and nonbeing. (2) Essence. (3) The necessary and the possible. (4) The one and the many. (5) Cause and effect.

III. *The Accidents.* (1) *In genere.* (2) Quantity. (3) Quality. (4) The relations *(nisab):* local relations, space, movement. (5) Relationship *(iḍāfah).*

IV. *Substance.* (1) The body. (2) Accidents of bodies. (3) The separate soul. (4) The intellect.

V. *"Rational" Theology (Ilāhīyāt).* (1) The divine essence. (2) The transcendence of God (the *via remotionis*). (3) His unity. (4) The positive attributes. (5)

"Possible" attributes: visibility, knowability. (6) The acts of God (problem of human acts). (7) The divine names.

VI. *The Traditional Questions (Sam'īyāt).* (1) Prophethood. (2) Eschatology. (3) Statutes and names. (4) The caliphate.
Appendix. The sects.

Rigid Ash'arīyah. The so-called way of the "modernists" was in effect the most original line of thought in the fully evolved Ash'arī *kalām.* We can note among the most characteristic representatives al-Shahrastānī, Fakhr al-Dīn al-Rāzī, and al-Isfahānī (d. 1348). Al-Rāzī, although he called himself an Ash'arī, did not hesitate to adopt Māturīdī theses, or even Mu'tazilī influences.

Other modernists, possibly less daring, nonetheless did not hesitate to borrow in their turn from *falsafah* various ideas on logic, nature philosophy, or metaphysics. This was the most orthodox of the tendencies that issued from the thought of al-Ījī, including al-Jurjānī, who called himself an Ash'arī. Very close to him in methodology was his adversary al-Taftāzānī (d. 1389), who attempted to oppose the conclusions of *falsafah* while still placing himself on the same plane as philosophy.

The glosses, commentaries, and discussions multiplied, often with a great richness of argumentation and certain original views. But this did not serve the elaboration of *kalām* as a theological science: the clearest result of such studies was to throw the teaching of *kalām* by reaction into the constraints of "rigid conservatism."

Kalām would soon ossify under the Ash'arī writ, and, losing the freshness of its early years, it would become frozen in the stereotyped forms of "manuals" endlessly commented and recommented. If we compare the nineteenth-century *Jawharat al-tawḥīd* of al-Bājūrī with the *Muḥaṣṣal* of al-Rāzī, we find the same major divisions, the same responses, the same "intemporality." The manuals of that age are often a compendium of all the past, but framed and codified by the most rigid solutions of the school.

An enumeration of these manuals and their authors would be lengthy indeed; suffice it to mention the two writers who are situated at the beginning and the end of this long period, and who had and still have an important place in official teaching. One is al-Sanūsī, from the fifteenth century, famous for his *kalām* treatises set out according to the three cycles of teaching *(Umm al-barāhīn)* called *Al-ṣughrā* (The Small), or the *Sanūsīyah,* then *Al-wusṭā* (The Median) and *Al-kubrā* (The Great). The other is Ibrāhīm al-Bājūrī, (d. 1860), rector of al-Azhar, who wrote commentaries on his predecessors, al-Sanūsī himself, al-Laqānī, and his own master, al-Faḍālī. The differences are minimal between al-Sanūsī and al-Bājūrī. One of those who would attempt to arouse theology from its sleep, Shaykh Muḥammad 'Abduh (d. 1905), would write of this period, "Whoever studies the works of this era will find only discussions on words, studies on methodology. And he will find these in only a small number of works chosen by weakness and consecrated by impotence."

Reformist Period. It was precisely Muḥammad 'Abduh, the disciple of the reformer Jamāl al-Dīn al-Afghānī (d. 1897), who would try to renew the problematic of *kalām* within the scope of the general renaissance of the Middle East. His originality in this field was his religious rationalism. He believed deeply in Islam, but he wanted a thoroughly interpreted religion that could respond intellectually to the demands of criticism, socially to the desire of the humble to live a decent life, and politically to the ardent passion among the people for liberty.

Against the traditional Ash'arī ideas that crushed the believer under the weight of a fatalist predestination, he would state the existence of human liberty as the basis of all action and responsibility. He did not want to concern himself with what he considered metaphysical subtleties and turned instead to a somewhat agnostic pragmatism. It was practice that interested him above all. Thus divine law, reason, conscience, and common sense affirm human responsibility and therefore human freedom. It was useless to go over the old discussions again on the bases and nature of this freedom. It was enough to recognize that it did not contradict God's omnipotence, since, as he said, "God is the cause to the extent that people act, and people are the cause to the extent that God acts." Here we are far from the Ash'arī *kasb* ("acquisition") that denies any real power to human beings.

He added to this clear attitude toward human freedom an affirmation of natural law, which once again suggests the influence of the Mu'tazilah. Like the latter he recognized that there are things objectively good or evil, naturally beautiful or ugly, and concludes that a "natural law" is possible. Religious law does not differ essentially from natural morality. "The law came simply to show what exists *(al-wāqi').* It is not the law that makes it good" (*Risālah,* p. 80, trans., p. 56).

In his discussion of prophecy, he shows similarly rationalist tendencies. While keeping the orthodox position, he stresses the psychological and social aspects of prophecy (ibid., p. 127/86).

In discussing *kalām* he insists above all on the political factor in the formation and differentiation of the schools. He recognizes that foreign elements integrated into the community prompted the first dogmatic discussions (ibid., intro., p. 55). The rational character of the science of *kalām* is affirmed forcefully: it is reason that is called upon to examine the proofs of the beliefs and rules of conduct imposed by religion in order to show that they truly come from God (ibid., p. 129/88). In response to Hanotaux he does not hesitate to write, "In the case of a conflict between reason and tradition, it is reason that must decide. This is a position that would only be opposed by a few people, from among those whose views cannot be taken into consideration" (Gardet and Anawati, 1948, p. 86, n. 3).

In his *Risālat al-tawḥīd,* Shaykh ʿAbduh spends little time on the metaphysical introductions so common in traditional manuals. After stating the usual definitions of the impossible, the contingent, and the necessary, he establishes the classic proof of the existence of God and his attributes. To be necessary, endowed with life, knowledge, and will, to be all-powerful, free, one—these are all attributes that reason can discover on its own. He is very circumspect on the question of the relationship of the attributes with the essence of God: he advises [the believer] to have the wisdom to "stop at the limit that our reason can reach" (*Risālah,* p. 52/37).

The "new theology" of the Egyptian grand mufti also shows itself in his attitude toward the origins of faith: he contests the authority of the juridical schools resting on the consensus of the community *(ijmāʿ)* and rejects servile traditional imitation *(taqlīd).* Only the Qurʾān and authentic *sunnah* should serve as the base of *ijtihād,* this effort of personal elaboration of religious positions by qualified theologians. The same concern for adaptation is shown in his commentary on the Qurʾān, which he wished to be pragmatic and oriented essentially toward "moral direction" *(hidāyah);* it was to be in accord with modern civilization and encourage activity, energy, and personal labor. The anthropomorphic passages should be interpreted by using reason *(taʾwīl ʿaqlī)* in the manner of Ibn Rushd. God's transcendence *(tanzīh)* must be ensured at all costs.

Muḥammad ʿAbduh was able to inspire the best of his disciples with a spirit of openmindedness and renewal. Especially worthy of mention is Shaykh Muṣṭafā ʿAbd al-Rāziq, who was appointed rector of al-Azhar in 1945.

Parallel to this reformist movement in Egypt and the Near East a no less sustained effort for renewal, *sui generis,* occurred in British India. This was particularly due to the work of Sayyid Ahmad Khan (d. 1898), whose *Tabyīn al-kalām* (Commentary on the Holy Bible) dates from 1862 to 1865; Syed Ameer Ali (d. 1928), author of *The Spirit of Islam* (London, 1922), and Muhammad Iqbal, whose *Six Lectures on the Reconstruction of Religious Thought in Islam* was published in 1934.

Two Final Remarks. A complete presentation of *kalām* in Islam should also take into consideration Shīʿī *kalām,* in particular the disciples and successors of Mullā Ṣadrā (d. 1640) in the nineteenth and twentieth centuries. These include among others Ḥājī Mullā Hādī Sabziwārī, Ashtiyānī, Ṭabāṭabāʾī, Rāfiʿī Qazwīnī, and Muhammad Amūlī (see Seyyed Hossein Nasr's articles on the school of Isfahan and Mullā Ṣadra in M. M. Sharif's *A History of Muslim Philosophy,* vol. 2, Wiesbaden, 1966).

Among contemporary Muslim writers a certain number outside the traditional framework of theology have tried to speak of God and Muslim doctrines in a way adapted to the modern world, including Kāmil Ḥusayn, Sayyid Quṭb, Tawfīq al-Ḥakīm, ʿAbbās Maḥmūd al-ʿAqqād, and Muṣṭafā Maḥmūd. The historian of *kalām* should not overlook their contributions.

[*See also the biographies of the principal scholars mentioned herein.*]

BIBLIOGRAPHY

General Works. The best works on *kalām* for the general reader are Harry A. Wolfson's overview, *The Philosophy of the Kalam* (Cambridge, Mass., 1976); D. B. Macdonald's article "Kalām" in the first edition of *The Encyclopaedia of Islam* (Leiden, 1934); and Louis Gardet's "ʿIlm al-Kalām" and "Kalām" in the new edition of *The Encyclopaedia of Islam* (Leiden, 1960–). Louis Gardet's and my *Introduction à la théologie musulmane* (1948; 2d ed., Paris, 1970) and W. Montgomery Watt's *Islamic Philosophy and Theology,* 2d rev. ed. (Edinburgh, 1984), are useful surveys. J. Windrow Sweetman's *Islam and Christian Theology,* 2 vols. (London, 1942–1947), and A. S. Tritton's *Muslim Theology* (1947; reprint, Westport, Conn., 1981) should also be consulted.

Sources in Translation. The works of al-Ashʿarī have been translated by several scholars. *Al-ibānah ʿan uṣūl al-diyānah* has been translated and edited by Walter C. Klein as *The Elucidation of Islam's Foundation* (New Haven, 1940); *The Theology of al-Ashʿarī,* edited and translated by Richard J. McCarthy (Beirut, 1953), contains translations of two creeds by al-Ashʿarī; and D. B. Macdonald's *Development of Muslim Theology, Jurisprudence and Constitutional Theory* (1903; reprint, New York, 1965) contains translations of creeds by al-Ashʿarī as well as al-Ghazālī, Abū Ḥafṣ al-Nasafī, and al-Faḍālī. Ibn Qudāmah's *Taḥrīm al-naẓar fī kutub ahl al-kalām* has been edited and translated by George Makdisi as *Censure of Speculative Theology* (London, 1962). Al-Shahrastānī's *Kitāb nihāyat iqdām fī ʿilm al-kalām* has been edited and translated by Alfred Guillaume as *The Summa Philosophiae of al-Shahrastānī* (Oxford, 1934). Al-Taftāzānī's *Sharḥ al-ʿaqāʾid al-nasafīyah* has been edited and translated by E. E. Elder as *A Commentary on the Creed of Islam* (New York, 1950).

Critical Studies. An excellent study is A. J. Wensinck's *The Muslim Creed: Its Genesis and Historical Development* (1932; reprint, New York, 1965), which contains translations of three Ḥanafī creeds. Michel Allard's *Le problème des attributs divins dans la doctrine d'al-Ašʿarī et de ses premiers grands disciples* (Beirut, 1965) is a detailed study of the works and teachings of al-Bāqillānī, al-Baghdādī, al-Bayhaqī, and al-Juwaynī. Also useful are Max Horten's *Die philosophischen Systeme der spekulativen Theologen im Islam* (Bonn, 1912) and my article, with R. Caspar and M. El-Khodeiri, "Une somme inédite de théologie mo'tazilite: le *Moghnī* du qādī 'Abd al-Jabbār," in *Mélanges de l'Institut Dominicain d'Études Orientales* 4 (1957): 281–316.

For modern developments in India and Pakistan, see Aziz Ahmad's *Islamic Modernism in India and Pakistan 1857–1964* (London, 1967); Syed Ameer Ali's *The Spirit of Isla.* · rev. ed. (London, 1922); A. A. Fyzee's *A Modern Approach to Islam* (Bombay, 1963); Wilfred Cantwell Smith's *Modern Islām in India*, rev. ed. (London, 1972); and Christian Troll's *Sayyid Ahmad Khan: A Reinterpretation of Muslim Theology* (New Delhi, 1978).

GEORGES C. ANAWATI
Translated from French by Richard J. Scott

KALEVALA. *For discussion of the compilation and structure of the* Kalevala, *see the biography of Lönnrot; see also* Finnic Religions.

KĀLĪ. *See* Goddess Worship, *article on* The Hindu Goddess.

KALISCHER, TSEVI HIRSCH (1795–1874), rabbi, messianic theorist, and activist. Kalischer spent his entire life in the Posen district of Prussia. He received an intensive education in Talmudic literature and independently studied Jewish philosophy. With his wife's financial support, he pursued a life of community service and scholarship. His works include commentaries on Jewish law, exegeses of the Bible and Passover Haggadah, and philosophical studies reconciling religion and reason. In his messianic writings he argued that Judaism encouraged efforts to accelerate the arrival of the messianic age. Historically, this opinion was accepted by only a few religious authorities; the dominant rabbinic tradition regarded messianic activism as a rebellion against God.

Starting with the rationalist assumption that God steers the course of history toward the messianic age without abrogating natural laws, Kalischer asserted that human participation in the redemptive process was essential. He contended that biblical prophecies, when interpreted through the ideology of messianic activism, indicated that the messianic age would arrive in gradual stages. A nonmiraculous stage, in which the Holy Land would be repopulated and made agriculturally productive by Jews, would be followed by a miraculous stage consisting of the other features described in biblical prophecies. The miraculous stage would be ushered in when the Jews reestablished their intimate connection with God by offering sacrifices on the rebuilt altar in Jerusalem.

In 1836, encouraged by European interest in the Jews' return to Zion and the Orthodox rabbinate's insistence on retaining in the liturgy prayers for the restoration of sacrificial worship, Kalischer wrote to Anschel Mayer Rothschild and several influential rabbis about acquiring the Temple Mount and studying the possibility of restoring sacrificial worship. Most Jewish leaders withheld their support when they realized that to Kalischer the sacrifice renewal was not academic and was actually part of a messianic plan. By 1860 he realized that focusing only on the agricultural development of Palestine would receive wider support; he still believed that the sacrifice renewal and other messianic events would flow naturally from that. This tactical change has led some historians to the mistake of describing Kalischer as a Zionist rather than a messianist.

Kalischer's writings and activities eventually helped legitimize messianic activism, and religious Jews who regard the state of Israel as a step toward the messianic age have adopted his formulation of this ideology.

BIBLIOGRAPHY

The only comprehensive examination of Kalischer's messianic ideology is my "Seeking Zion: The Messianic Ideology of Ẓevi Hirsch Kalischer, 1795–1874" (Ph.D. diss., University of California, 1985). A complete bibliography of Kalischer's writings and secondary literature is included. A critical edition of Kalischer's major work, *Derishat Tsiyyon* (Lyck, 1862), and most of his messianic writings are collected in *Ha-ketavim ha-tsiyyonim shel ha-Rav Tsevi Hirsch Kalischer*, edited and with an introduction by Israel Klausner (Jerusalem, 1947).

JODY ELIZABETH MYERS

KAMALAŚĪLA (eighth century CE), also Ācārya Kamalaśīla; Indian monk-scholar, author, chief disciple of Śāntirakṣita, and early propagator of Buddhism in Tibet. Not much is known about Kamalaśīla's early career. He is said to have been, prior to his summons to Tibet, an *upādhyāya* (teacher/abbot) of Nālandā. The Tibetan accounts (our only sources for his life) begin with his studentship under Śāntirakṣita at Nālandā and then proceed quickly to his main achievement in Tibet: his triumphant victory over the rival Chinese Buddhist faction in the famed debate at Bsam-yas (c. 792–794).

There is little doubt that intellectually Kamalaśīla followed in his teacher's footsteps. Both Śāntirakṣita and Kamalaśīla deftly propounded the philosophical viewpoint of the Yogācāra-Mādhyamika-Svātantrika (a view that follows one influential line of development stemming originally from the great Buddhist logician Dharmakīrti). Śāntirakṣita composed a mammoth treatise, the *Tattvasaṃgraha,* which employed this type of logical reasoning to refute one by one (i.e., *svatantra*) all opposing views, whether Buddhist or non-Buddhist, and covered some three hundred years of previous philosophical activity in India. Kamalaśīla thereafter composed a well-known commentary on that text called the *Tattvasaṃgraha-pañjikā.* He composed many other texts as well; in fact, the Tibetan Bstan-'gyur attributes some eighteen separate works to him. In addition to the *Pañjikā,* his major composition was the *Bhāvanākrama* (Stages of Meditation; Tib., *Sgom rim rnam gsum*), which is arranged in three sections: (1) *Pūrva-bhāvanā-krama,* (2) *Madhyma-bhāvanā-krama,* and (3) *Uttara-bhāvanā-krama.* Bu-ston's *Chos-'byuṅ* (History of Buddhism) lists this text among those of the "intermediate period" of scripture, in which the theoretical and practical sides of the Doctrine are expounded jointly.

In the latter half of the eighth century CE, great impetus had been given to "establishing" Buddhism in Tibet under the auspices of King Khri-sroṅ-lde-btsan. Padmasambhava and Śāntirakṣita had planned and seen through to completion the construction of the first Buddhist monastery in the country, called Bsam-yas. Śāntirakṣita had trained and later ordained the first seven indigenous Tibetan monks at Bsam-yas, where he had also begun a mammoth project of assembling and translating Indian Buddhist scriptures. Chinese Buddhists also gathered there, and for a time there was a spirit of cooperation. Near the end of Śāntirakṣita's life, however, frictions began to surface and the issue of which teachings should hold sway—Indian or Chinese—became a pressing one.

The king finally arranged for a great debate to be held at Bsam-yas to settle the issue, and following Śāntirakṣita's advice, he sent for Kamalaśīla to represent the Indian side. The Chinese faction was led by a monk called Hwa-śaṅ Mahāyāna. Kamalaśīla's great prowess in debate resulted in victory for the Indian side, and the Chinese Buddhists were expelled from the country. As David Snellgrove points out in *A Cultural History of Tibet* (Boulder, 1980, p. 79), "perhaps political considerations also weighed in this result, for at this time Tibet was openly at war with China." It is for his victory at Bsam-yas that Kamalaśīla is lauded in the annals of Tibetan religious history. Little is said there about the tragic personal consequences for him. However, Bu-ston's *History* records that following the conclusion of the debate, four assassins, sent by the Chinese faction, killed Kamalaśīla by "squeezing his kidneys."

[*See also* Tibetan Religions, *overview article;* Buddhism, *article on* Buddhism in Tibet; *and* Buddhism, Schools of, *article on* Tibetan Buddhism.]

BIBLIOGRAPHY

Demiéville, Paul. *Le Concile de Lhasa.* Paris, 1952. A detailed study focusing specifically on the Bsam-yas debate.

Obermiller, Eugene, trans. *History of Buddhism.* 2 vols. Heidelberg, 1931–1932. A translation of Bu-ston's *Chos-'byuṅ.*

Obermiller, Eugene. "A Sanskrit Manuscript from Tibet: Kamalaśīla's Bhāvanā-krama." *Journal of the Greater India Society* 2 (January 1935): 1–11.

Tucci, Giuseppe. ed. *The Contents of the first Bhāvanākrama; Sanskrit and Tibetan Texts with Introduction and English Summary.* Minor Buddhist Texts, part 2. Rome, 1958.

Tucci, Giuseppe. ed. *Third Bhāvanākrama.* Minor Buddhist Texts, part 3. Rome, 1971.

JANICE D. WILLIS

KAMI. The Japanese term *kami,* often translated as "gods," or "divine forces," denotes the focus of Shintō worship. Since the eighteenth century many attempts have been made to clarify its etymology. One popular theory claims that it means "upper" or "above," also pronounced *kami* in Japanese. Such a theory was derided, however, as early as the late eighteenth century by Motoori Norinaga (1730–1801), who pointed out that the Chinese characters used to write the two words are entirely different and were never confused in the text of the *Man'yōshū,* the oldest collection of poems in Japan. Norinaga himself spurned etymological study in favor of careful research of the *Kojiki,* the oldest Japanese chronicle. As a result, he defined *kami* as "any entity with an unusually powerful spiritual function that imparts a feeling of awe." No better definition has ever been formulated.

In the *Kojiki* (Records of Ancient Matters), compiled in 712 CE, and the *Nihonshoki* (Chronicles of Japan), compiled in 720 CE, there are two types of *kami. Kami* of the first and most important type figure anthropomorphically in the early myths. For example, the first three *kami* were said to have revealed themselves in the High Celestial Plain (according to the *Kojiki*) or among marsh reeds between heaven and earth (according to the *Nihonshoki*). *Kami* of the second type appear as offspring of earlier *kami.* Most "nature" *kami,* stones, mountains, rivers, and trees, and the ancestral *kami* as well, belong to this second category. Entities in nature, including human beings, are individually considered to be *kami. Kami,* therefore, can be regarded as the spiritual nature of each individual existence. The number of *kami* is infinite, although only a finite number of them are actually enshrined. The Japanese emperor, believed to be the direct descendant of both the sun goddess Amaterasu and the "high life-giving *kami,*" Takamimusubi, has been especially venerated.

Numerous attempts have been made to establish categories of *kami* from a phenomenological point of view. Some scholars, for instance, speak of nature and ancestral *kami,* while others divide them into family, local, and tutelary *kami.* Most of these categories are not helpful in understanding the nature and function of *kami,* however, as most *kami* do not fit exclusively into a single category. For example, most *kami* of nature are also conceived of as ancestral, family, or tutelary *kami,* and are the object of clan cults. One useful division distinguishes among heavenly *kami,* earthly *kami,* and *kami* of foreign descent, and assigns highest status to the heavenly *kami.*

After Buddhism came to Japan in the sixth century, a gradual change took place in the understanding of *kami.* At first, the Buddha was accepted as a foreign *kami,* but with the support of the imperial household the Buddha attained an independent status politically and socially equal to that of the traditional *kami.* From the ninth century on the syncretization of Buddhism and Shintō was promoted by the Buddhist clergy. Subsequently, *kami* were treated as guardians of the Buddha and were sometimes given the title *bodhisattva.* As a result, Buddhist *sūtras* were commonly recited in Shintō shrines for the salvation of *kami.* Moreover, although Shintō originally produced no iconic representations of *kami,* statues of *kami* began to appear during the thirteenth century at some shrines in imitation of Buddhism. In the Kamakura period (late twelfth through early fourteenth century), the Esoteric sects of Buddhism taught that Mahāvairocana (in the Shingon tradition) and Śākyamuni (in the Tendai tradition) were the central manifestations of the Buddha, and that the *kami* were manifestations of one or the other of these Buddhas, depending on the sectarian affiliation of the claimant. In response to these trends, the priests of the outer shrine of Ise Grand Shrine began to teach that the *kami* of the outer shrine was both Ame no Minakanushi, the Eternal Center of Heaven (in the *Kojiki*) and Kunitokodachi, the Eternal Center of the Country (in the *Nihonshoki*), the supreme original *kami* who existed before the creation of the universe. This tendency to exalt one particular *kami* as the ultimate being was continued by later schools of Shintō, including those of Yoshida, Yoshikawa, Suiga, and even the school of National Learning (Kokugaku). Hirata Atsutane (1776–1843), after studying the works of the Jesuits in Ming China, regarded Ame no Minakanushi as the creator, similar to the Christian God. After the Meiji restoration in 1868 some sectarian and ideological groups extended this line of teaching even though the government mandated the separation of Shintō and Buddhism. Today, the Association of Shintō Shrines rejects any monotheistic interpretation that could detract from the independent dignity of individual *kami* in the Shintō pantheon. Shintō is a polytheistic religion, permitting worship of many *kami* at the same time, although Amaterasu retains the central and highest position.

[*See also* Shintō.]

BIBLIOGRAPHY

The proceedings of the Second International Conference on Shinto, published by Kokugakuin University as *Jizoku to henka* (Tokyo, 1968) contains much valuable information on the nature and development of the term *kami;* see especially "Kami kannen," pp. 15–38. Other important references include Kōno Seizō's "Kami," in *Shintō yōgoshū, shūkyō hen,* vol. 1 (Tokyo, 1977), pp. 102–112, and my own "Shintō, sonzaironteki rikai e no kokoromi," in *Tozai shii keitai no hikaku kenkyū,* edited by Mineshima Akio (Tokyo, 1977), pp 278–298. For a discussion of the concept of *kami* in relation to folk belief, see *Kami kannen to minzoku,* vol. 3 of *Nihon no minzoku shūkyō,* edited by Miyata Noboru et al. (Tokyo, 1982). *Amaterasu Ōmikami, kenkyū hen,* vol. 1 (Tokyo, 1982), offers a comprehensive treatment of the figure. Readers of English may want to consult Allan G. Grapard's article "Kami" in the *Encyclopedia of Japan* (Tokyo, 1982).

UEDA KENJI

KAMO NO MABUCHI (1697–1769), Japanese scholar of classical studies in the Tokugawa period (1603–1868); he wrote classical poetry under the pen names Shōjyō, Moryō, Iyō, and Agatai.

Mabuchi was born on 4 March 1697 into the Okabe family, descendants of the overseers of Kamo Shrine in Kyoto, at Iba, Ōmi Province (modern Shizuoka Prefecture). Mabuchi's father was a Shintō priest and part-time farmer who encouraged his son to write poetry. At the age of ten (eleven by Japanese count) Mabuchi, who received initial instruction from the poet Kada Masako and then from her renowned husband, Sugiura Kuniakira, began taking active part in poetry tournaments.

At the age of twenty-five, Mabuchi made the acquaintance of Kada Azumamaro (1668–1736), scholar of classical studies and headmaster of the school of National Learning (Kokugaku) in Kyoto. Through his association with Watanabe Myōan, a scholar of Ogyū Sorai's school of Ancient Rhetoric (Kobunjigaku), Mabuchi met the Confucian Dazai Shundai, who introduced him to the study of classics in the manner developed by Sorai. Later, as he turned away from Chinese influences to embrace things Japanese, Mabuchi repudiated the scholarship of the members of the Sorai school as the work of eccentrics.

In 1734, after enrolling in Kada Azumamaro's school, Mabuchi began work on the eighth-century collection of poetry known as the *Man'yōshū*. Following Kada's death in 1736, Mabuchi moved to the capital at Edo (modern Tokyo), but returned frequently to Iba, for he believed it was possible to see the reality of human existence in the naiveté of the rural people. Thus he developed his concept of society based on an agricultural economic model combined with the Taoist principle of natural life. At the same time, he composed poetry and participated in poetry competitions. In 1742, he joined the service of Lord Tayasu, a member of the Tokugawa family, as a teacher of classical studies.

Opposing the tradition that saw the right of succession in schools of scholarship passed down through families, Mabuchi considered himself the successor to the Kada school. The number of his followers increased to almost three hundred fifty, and three subschools emerged. In 1763, when Mabuchi was returning from a trip to the Yamato area (modern Nara), he met Motoori Norinaga (1730–1801), his future successor and a leading figure in the National Learning school.

It was Mabuchi's aim to understand the terminology and ideology of ancient (pre-Nara) times. He advocated adherence to Shintō doctrine and a return to the "natural" concepts of the ancient period as a means of discovering the supreme and correct *kokoro* ("soul, spirit") of the Japanese people. Influences from China and Confucian ideology were, in his interpretation, unnatural. In opposition to the principles set down by Confucians and Buddhists, Mabuchi stressed the philosophy of nonaction, or naturalness, by which it would be possible to unite one's *kokoro* with the spirit of the universe. He maintained that "artificial" knowledge, such as that propounded by Confucians and Buddhists, would only harm the spirit of the people. Therefore, since Japan's ancient period was based on what was pure and natural, it was essential that there be a return to the things of the past. In adoration of such an ideal concept, he attempted to revive the spirit of the classical times not only through the doctrines he propounded, but also in his style of clothing and the furnishings of his home. He studied ancient poetry and literature as a means of practicing the principles of old, thereby setting a high value on the myths of Japan's ancestral gods, the emperor, and the elements of nature.

Mabuchi pointed to the virtuous character of a bright, naive, and pure *kokoro,* a soul that was brave, honest, and gentle. This type of spirit would only manifest itself in a subject who was courageous and loyal to the emperor. Yet he did not regard the Tokugawa regime as suppressive of the interests of the emporor but rather praised its founding ruler, Tokugawa Ieyasu (1542–1616), for establishing a government with Shintō as its base.

[*See also* Kokugaku.]

BIBLIOGRAPHY

One may find useful the details concerning the poetry of Kamo no Mabuchi in the book by Tamura Yoshinobu entitled *Kamo no Mabuchi wakashū no kenkyū* (Tokyo, 1966). The following biographical accounts are recommended for their detail: Koyama Tadashi's *Kamo no Mabuchi den* (Tokyo, 1938) and Terada Yasumasa's *Kamo no Mabuchi shōgai to gyōseki* (Hamamatsu, 1979). Descriptions of Mabuchi's religious philosophy can be found in Ōishi Arata's *Kamo Mabuchi* (Tokyo, 1942) and in Araki Yoshio's *Kamo no Mabuchi no hito to shisō* (Tokyo, 1943). On the scholarship of Mabuchi, see Inoue Minoru's *Kamo no Mabuchi no gakumon* (Tokyo, 1943). For Inoue's evaluation of the accomplishments of Mabuchi and his successors, see his *Kamo no Mabuchi no gyōseki to monryū* (Tokyo, 1966). The part that the interest in agriculture played in forming his philosophy is taken up by Saegusa Yasutaka in *Kamo no Mabuchi, jimbutsu sōsho* (Tokyo, 1962).

HAGA NOBORU
Translated from Japanese by Irene M. Kunii

KAMUY. When used alone, the Ainu term *kamuy* may refer to the generalized notion of the divine, that is, to the deities collectively, or it may refer to the bear, the supreme deity in the Ainu pantheon. *Kamuy* may also refer to a multitude of beings and objects when it is used in combination with other words. It is used in expressions referring to the soul, nondeified animals, humans, afterbirth, deities other than the bear, and various other objects. Even demons may be referred to as "demon deities" or "night deities," a usage that stems from the belief that demons may not exercise their negative power when treated with respect.

Conceptually, however, the bona fide deities are distinguished from others. The most important characteristic of these deities is their power over humans (*ainu* or *aynu* means "human being"). As such, the deities can exercise benevolent power, providing food and welfare if humans behave respectfully toward them. Although the deities do not directly combat demons, they can extend aid to humans in the efforts of the latter to contend with demons. If humans are disrespectful toward them, however, the deities can act like demons and punish the humans by sending them natural disasters, illnesses, and other calamities.

The terms most frequently used to describe divine qualities are *nupuru* ("holy") and *pirika* ("beautiful"). *Nupuru* is used in describing the mountains, for example, which as the residence of the mountain deity are considered as sacred space. *Pirika* may be synonymous with *nupuru,* although it may refer to any desirable quality; for example, *pirika* may be used to describe a plant that is well developed. In short, holiness and beauty are considered attributes of deities, who are the most desirable beings of the universe; consequently the terms *holy* and *beautiful* are used to refer to desirable qualities of other beings.

[*See also* Ainu Religion.]

BIBLIOGRAPHY

Chiri Mashio. *Bunrui Ainugo jiten.* 3 vols. Tokyo, 1953–1962. See especially volume 3, pages 187, 243–244. Chiri maintains (volume 1, page 119) that the term *kamuy* originally referred to demons.

Munro, Neil G. *Ainu Creed and Cult.* New York, 1963. See pages 9–10.

Ohnuki-Tierney, Emiko. *The Ainu of the Northwest Coast of Southern Sakhalin* (1974). Reprint, Prospect Heights, Ill., 1984. See pages 89–107.

EMIKO OHNUKI-TIERNEY

K'ANG YU-WEI (1858–1927), political reformer and Confucian thinker of modern China. K'ang Yu-wei first attained national prominence as leader of the political reform movement that ended in the defeat of the Hundred Days Reform of 1898. Although primarily political, the movement also had a spiritual and moral dimension. K'ang called not only for the "protection of the nation" but also for the "preservation of the faith," by which he meant the spiritual revitalization of Confucianism and the promotion of its teachings as the state religion. This position was partly a response to the cultural and political crises that China was undergoing at the time. By revitalizing Confucianism, K'ang hoped to strengthen China's self-esteem and national solidarity. But his call for the "preservation of the faith" must not be seen solely in this practical light; it was also the culmination of a moral and spiritual quest that had started in his early youth.

K'ang Yu-wei was born to a family of scholars and officials in Nan-hai County, Kwangtung Province. His father died while K'ang was still a child, and thereafter his grandfather, a devoted Neo-Confucian scholar, personally took charge of the boy's education. Shortly before the age of twenty, K'ang entered a period of spiritual restlessness, triggered by the sudden death of his grandfather and by the beginning of his subsequent apprenticeship under an inspiring Confucian teacher. He rebelled against his conventional Confucian education and temporarily withdrew from society altogether. Plunging into a frantic intellectual search, he fell under the influence of various non-Confucian persuasions, especially Mahāyāna Buddhism, philosophical Taoism, and "Western learning."

K'ang's intellectual quest finally culminated in the formation of a moral and historical worldview that he expressed in a series of writings published in the decade from the early 1890s to the early 1900s. Based on a bold and comprehensive reinterpretation of Confucianism that centered on the pivotal Confucian ideal of *jen* (human-heartedness), this view also reflected, in its redefinition of *jen,* K'ang's interest in non-Confucian thought. *Jen* provided K'ang with a worldview that saw the essential and ultimate state of the cosmos as a selfless all-encompassing whole. K'ang also retained the Confucian belief central to *jen* that the intrinsic goal of human existence is the moral perfection of individual and society. But his definition of moral perfection bears the profound influence of non-Confucian thought, for his vision of the ideal society, the "great unity" *(ta-t'ung),* was that of a universal moral community where egalitarianism, libertarianism, and hedonism would prevail. Since his conception of hedonism resulted from the impact of the materialistic doctrines of Western industrial society, his ideal society offered the radical combination of moral perfection, technological development, and material abundance.

The radical tendencies in K'ang's conception of *jen* were tempered by his historical interpretation of that ideal. In his view, the full realization of the ideal can be attained only through the gradual course of human history. Borrowing a scheme from an ancient commentary on the Confucian classic *Ch'un-ch'iu,* K'ang took the view that human history evolves through three stages, from "the age of chaos," which lay in the past, through an intermediate age of "emerging peace," to the final stage of "universal peace," or "great unity," to be realized in the future. K'ang insisted that it was for this latter age alone that his radical reevaluation of *jen* was appropriate. He believed that, meanwhile, in the era preceding the "age of great unity," many of the conventional values of Confucianism remained relevant. These were the tenets of the moral-historical worldview that lay at the core of his efforts to have Confucianism accepted as a state religion.

K'ang's reform movement culminated in 1898, when, under his guidance, the Kuang-hsü emperor attempted to put into practice a wide-ranging program of political reform. The intervention of the dowager empress Tz'u-hsi, who moved to imprison the emperor and nullify the imperial edicts little more than three months after they were issued, brought K'ang's reforms to an abortive end. Together with his student Liang Ch'i-ch'ao, K'ang fled China and began an exile that lasted until 1913. During this period he continued his reformist efforts abroad and traveled extensively, deepening his understanding of the social and political forces that were shaping the modern world.

Upon his return to China, K'ang resumed his efforts to implement the promotion of Confucianism as a state religion. Convinced that the revolution of 1911, in which the traditional monarchy had been replaced by a republican form of government, had only served to impede the historical evolution of the ideal society, he joined the warlord Chang Hsün in an ill-fated attempt to restore Manchu rule in 1917. In the writings of his later years, K'ang remained faithful to the interpretation of Confucianism that he had formulated in the 1890s, but, because the intellectual climate of China had changed, his views never regained their former influence.

[*See also* Confucian Thought, *article on* Neo-Confucianism.]

BIBLIOGRAPHY

Hsiao Kung-chuan. *A Modern China and a New World: K'ang Yu-wei, Reformer and Utopian, 1858–1927.* Seattle, 1975.

Lo Jung-pang, ed. and trans. *K'ang Yu-wei: A Biography and a Symposium.* Tucson, 1967.

Thompson, Laurence G., trans. *Ta T'ung Shu: The One-World Philosophy of K'ang Yu-wei.* London, 1958.

HAO CHANG

KANNON. *See* Avalokiteśvara.

KANT, IMMANUEL (1724–1804), German philosopher. Kant was born in Königsberg, a provincial town in East Prussia. He grew up in a religious family of relatively low social status. His father was a saddler, and both his parents were dedicated members of the Pietist movement, which stressed the interior devotion of the heart in opposition to the prevailing Lutheran practice of external observances. The spirit of Pietism pervaded not only Kant's family but also the Collegium Fridericianum, a local school, where he received his early education from 1732 to 1740. [*See* Pietism.]

In 1740 Kant entered the University of Königsberg, where he studied science and philosophy for six years. After graduation, he earned his living as a private tutor for a number of East Prussian families. During this period he kept up his studies and earned his master's degree at the university in 1755, which allowed him to teach as a privatdocent, a private lecturer accepted as a member of the faculty without compensation from the university. He occupied this financially precarious and academically undistinguished position for fifteen years. In 1770 he was appointed professor of logic and metaphysics.

While holding this position, Kant produced a stream of masterpieces. His best-known works are his three critiques: the *Critique of Pure Reason* (1781), the *Critique of Practical Reason* (1788), and the *Critique of Judgment* (1790). These three volumes expound Kant's critical idealism, or critical philosophy, which has also been known as Kantianism. Kantianism was the first phase of German Idealism, which gained fuller development in the writings of Johann Fichte (1762–1814), Friedrich Schelling (1775–1854), and G. W. F. Hegel (1770–1831). Kant's religious ideas not only constitute essential features of his critical philosophy but also play a pivotal role in the transition from his critical idealism to the absolute idealism of his intellectual successors.

Kantianism as a Worldview. Kantianism was an attempt to reconcile British empiricism and continental rationalism. British empiricism had been developed by a succession of British and Scottish philosophers, namely, Thomas Hobbes (1588–1679), John Locke (1632–1704), George Berkeley (1685–1753), and David Hume (1711–1776). Continental rationalism had been advocated by René Descartes (1596–1650), Gottfried Leibniz (1646–1716), and Christian Wolff (1679–1754). During his formative years, Kant learned his philosophy from Leibnizians and Wolffians, but he later came to appreciate the importance of empiricism, especially Hume's theory of ideas. [*See* Empiricism.]

The central point of the dispute between rationalists and empiricists was the theory of ideas. Since all our ideas are derived from sensation, the empiricists maintained, the objects of sensation are the only proper objects of knowledge. In opposition to this view, the rationalists argued that some of our ideas are not derived from sensation but are innate to reason. They further claimed that these innate ideas give us a knowledge of supersensible reality such as God. The idea of a supersensible reality, although espoused by some early empiricists, became unpopular with the later empiricists, because they considered it incompatible with empiricism. This later tendency of empiricism amounted to recognizing sensible reality, or the physical world, as the only reality. Thus the dispute that had begun with the epistemological issue concerning the origin of ideas came to have the ontological implication of admitting or not admitting any reality beyond the domain of sensation.

Kant's *Critique of Pure Reason* is a critical assessment of these two contending views. He holds that there are two kinds of ideas: those derived from sense and those innate to reason. The latter are the *a priori* elements of cognition; the former are its *a posteriori* elements. These two are equally indispensable for human knowledge. Kant is emphatic on the mutual dependence of sensibility and understanding: "Percepts without concepts are blind; concepts without percepts are empty." Although the domain of knowledge is limited to the domain of sensation, as the empiricists claimed, the use of *a priori* concepts, Kant argues, is indispensable for knowledge of sense objects.

This epistemological compromise between rationalism and empiricism has the following ontological consequence: Kant maintains that the objects of sensation are not reality itself (things-in-themselves) but its appearance. He bases this claim largely on his argument that space and time are not objective entities but subjective forms of intuition, that is, the manner in which human beings are given objects of sensation. Since all objects of sensation are given through space and time, Kant holds, they cannot be objective realities. They are only appearances to us. Kant calls these appearances "phenomena" and the things-in-themselves "noumena."

Unlike phenomena, noumena are not located in space and time; nor are they given as objects of sensation. They are the supersensible realities. That the domain of knowledge is limited to the world of phenomena means that we can never know the true reality but only its appearances. That we can have no knowledge of noumena, however, does not mean that we have no ideas about them. Kant maintains that we have *a priori* ideas about the supersensible reality. But to have these ideas is not to know the world of noumena, because there is no way of proving their truth or falsity.

In Kant's view, knowledge is inseparable from the power of demonstrating the truth or falsity of an idea, and that power is inexorably limited to the domain of sensibility. For this reason, knowledge is limited to the world of phenomena. The rationalists have assumed that the truths of *a priori* ideas can be demonstrated by rational arguments alone, that is, without appealing to sensibility. But rationalist arguments divorced from the constraint of sensibility can produce only sophistical illusions and confusions, according to Kant. He gives the name "transcendental dialectic" to the pseudoscience constituted by those sophistical arguments, because they are dialectical arguments transcending the domain of sensibility.

Kant recognizes three branches of transcendental dialectic: transcendental psychology, transcendental cosmology, and transcendental theology. These three are supposed to prove the immortality of the soul, the freedom of the will, and the existence of God. In the *Critique of Pure Reason,* Kant provides a systematic examination of their arguments and exposes their common error, namely, the error of employing *a priori* concepts beyond the domain of sensibility. [*See* Immortality; Free Will and Predestination; *and* Proofs for the Existence of God.]

The immortality of the soul, the freedom of will, and the existence of God are three of the central dogmas in many religions. That none of them can be proved, however, should not be mistaken to mean that they can be disproved. Kant is emphatic on this point. A transcendental assertion can neither be proved nor be disproved, because sensibility is essential not only for proofs but also for disproofs. Hence the three religious dogmas can still be regarded as possible truths of the supersensible reality. As such, they can be accepted in faith.

Kant demarcates matters of faith from matters of fact. The latter are the objects of knowledge; the former are the objects of belief. The objects of knowledge are situated in the world of phenomena; the objects of faith belong to the world of noumena. The objects of faith transcend the domain of sensibility, while the objects of knowledge are immanent in it. Although theoretical reason cannot settle the question of accepting or rejecting the objects of faith, Kant says, practical reason has a way of ruling over their admissibility.

Kantianism as a Moral View. Practical reason is the rational faculty concerned with human conduct, and a critical examination of this faculty is given in his second critique, the *Critique of Practical Reason.* Kant recognizes two mainsprings for human conduct: the will and the inclination. The inclination is the working of our desires and feelings, which are subject to the causal laws of the phenomenal world. The will is the rational faculty for moral actions. Unless the freedom of this faculty is presupposed, Kant says, it makes no sense to talk of the moral worth of human conduct. Since freedom is impossible in the phenomenal world of causal necessity, it can be accepted only as an entity belonging to the noumenal world. Kant calls the noumenal world the domain of freedom and the phenomenal world the domain of necessity. Thus he installs the noumenal world as the practical ground for morality and the freedom of the will as the first postulate (presupposition) of practical reason.

Besides the postulate of freedom, Kant says, two other postulates are demanded by morality: the existence of God and the immortality of the soul. The immortality of the soul is required for moral perfection. Our inclination has the natural propensity to go against the moral dictates of pure reason, and our moral perfection can be achieved by transforming this natural propensity into the willing obedience to the moral law. Since this moral transformation of the soul is infinitely time-consuming, it can be accomplished only if the soul continues to live after the death of its body. For this reason, Kant says, the postulate of the immortality of the soul is dictated by the practical ideal of moral perfection.

In Kant's ethics, the ideal of moral perfection is inseparably connected with another practical ideal, the notion of the complete good *(summum bonum)*. Kant defines it as the harmony of moral perfection and happiness (natural good). He regards moral perfection as the absolutely necessary condition for rendering human beings worthy of happiness. In this world, however, happiness can be denied to a person morally worthy of it, while it can be given to a person morally unworthy of it. The dispensation of happiness in proportion to each person's moral worth is their harmony, that is, the ideal of the complete good. This ideal can, Kant maintains, be fulfilled only by God in the other world. This is the third and the final postulate of practical reason.

Kant's third postulate has sometimes been known as the moral proof for the existence of God, and as such it has been the object of many disputes and misunderstandings. But to call it a proof is highly misleading; a "proof" for the existence of God generally means the demonstration or assurance of his existence. In Kantianism, as we have already seen, demonstration or assurance can be given only for the objects of the phenomenal world. Therefore the reasons Kant gives for the existence of God cannot constitute a proof. It is only a postulate. Whereas a proof can give certainty or assurance, a postulate can give only possibility, a supersensible ground for hope.

Kant's notion of rational postulates is inseparable from his ideal of practical rationality. To regard the harmony of moral and natural goods as an ideal of practical reason means that the world in which this ideal is fulfilled is a rational one and, conversely, that the world in which it is not fulfilled is an irrational one. It is impossible to find out whether our world is ultimately rational or irrational in this regard. As rational beings, however, we can, for practical purposes, opt and hope for the possibility that our world is ultimately rational. If this possibility is to be true, Kant argues, there must be a God who assures the harmony of moral and natural goods for every moral being. This is all that is meant by this and other postulates of practical reason.

The unique feature of Kant's ethics is that it has to be supported by a set of postulates that have formed the central dogmas of traditional religion. That may give the impression that Kant's ethics is not autonomous and requires religious sanctions. Nothing could be farther from the truth. The autonomy of ethical subjects and values is the most essential feature of Kant's ethics. The religious framework introduced by the postulates of practical reason only serves the function of supporting and supplementing the moral framework. Religion is the continuation and completion of morality. Hence Kant regards religion as an inseparable feature of ethics.

Kant's Conception of God and the Religious. In Kant's philosophy, God does not stand as a power that has its own laws and commands different from the moral law and its dictates. What God demands from ethical subjects is none other than what is dictated by moral reason. To do the will of God is to perform the duties of the moral imperative. There is no way to please God other than to be morally perfect. To be religious is to be moral; to be moral is to be religious. As far as human behavior is concerned, morality and religion are functionally identical, and their functional identity is expressed in Kant's statement that religion and God are internal to morality.

Kant's internalism, as he admits, goes against the traditional view that assumes an external relation between morality and religion. In general, the traditional religions portray God as a powerful being, whose will is independent of our will, whose commands can override even our moral dictates, and whose favor can be sought by special rituals and devotions. In short, the traditional religions stand on the existence of powers and values external to the powers and values of morality. Kant rejects such externalism because it is incompatible with the autonomy of practical reason.

In Kant's view, externalism is the anthropomorphic misconception of God and his relation to us, that is, the error of understanding God as someone like a powerful human being who demands our service and devotion. This misconception lies behind the religions of what Kant calls *"cultus externus."* These religions impose on their devotees a set of obligations or observances that consists of prayers, rituals, services, and various prohibitions. Furthermore, the gods of these religions are assumed to be pleased or displeased by the performance or nonperformance of these religious duties. Most of these religions have specially ordained experts called priests, ministers, or shamans, who have the power of officiating and facilitating the performance of religious duties.

Cultus externus, Kant insists, makes no sense to anyone who correctly understands the nature of God as the most perfect being, that is, omniscient, omnipotent, and, above all, morally perfect. It makes no sense to render any service to such a being, because he is in need of nothing and can derive no benefit from our services. Even the praise of his perfection cannot add anything to his perfection any more than flattery can to his honor. God does not need our prayers to find out what we need. Nor can he be moved by our supplication, because his mind is governed only by moral dictates. The *cultus externus* can fulfill none of the religious functions that it has been assumed to fulfill.

Kant uses the label "natural religion" to designate his view of religion, because it can be fully comprehended by the natural power of human reason, that is, without the aid of supernatural revelation. Kant's idea of natural religion may appear to reduce religion to morality. But he insists that natural religion retains all the essential features of traditional religions. In his view, those features are the moral attributes and functions of the supreme being, as the holy lawgiver, the benevolent ruler, and the just judge. Any other attributes of God such as omniscience, omnipotence, and omnipresence are only supplementary to his moral attributes; they are the requisite conditions for discharging his moral functions.

Kant argues that Christianity is the only moral religion, while the others are servile religions. The central function of servile religions is to curry favor from the supernatural powers; they place human beings in a servile relation to those powers. This servile relation has, Kant holds, been transformed into a moral one by Jesus of Nazareth. Jesus transformed the "old" law of Moses, the rules for external observance, into the "new" law, the rules for internal disposition. Kant finds Jesus' moral interpretation of religious life most conspicuously in his Sermon on the Mount, and he reads its concluding remark—"Therefore be perfect, as your heavenly father is!"—as an exhortation for moral perfection.

In *Religion within the Limits of Reason Alone* (1793), Kant offers his moral interpretation of Christian dogmas. The dogma of original sin concerns our innate propensity to do evil, which is to flout the maxims of duty and to succumb to the maxims of inclination. Kant regards it as a superstition to believe that this propensity was generated by Adam's fall from grace and then passed on to his posterity. On the contrary, Kant holds that the innate propensity to go against the moral law is in the very nature of man. No doubt, original human nature is said to be good. This original goodness, however, is not incompatible with the innate propensity to do evil. The original goodness of man means the freedom to obey the moral law by disciplining and mastering inclinations. Hence, original goodness and the innate propensity to evil are two essential features of every human being.

Kant interprets the incarnation of God in Christ not as a miracle of the supernatural order but as the manifestation of a moral ideal. As moral agents, he says, all of us have the ideal of a morally perfect human being. Such an ideal, if ever realized in this world, can be called an incarnate God, because the ideal in question belongs to pure practical reason, whose dictates are one with the dictates of God. Kant calls the ideal of moral perfection the archetype of moral life. But this archetype, he insists, cannot be identified with Jesus Christ himself. For he is only an instance or example, while the archetype belongs to all of us as agents of practical reason.

The relation of archetype and example, Kant says, is misrepresented in the traditional dogma of the incarnation, which exalts Jesus as a member of the Holy Trinity. He regards the dogma of the Trinity as theoretically incomprehensible and practically unserviceable. If the Son of God is so exalted as to stand above all human temptations and struggles, he is too remote from our existence to serve as a useful model. The value of the Son of God as our practical model lies in his essential identity with all human beings, and every human being who strives to achieve moral perfection can be called a son of God, a man well-pleasing to God.

Kant interprets the kingdom of God as an ethical commonwealth, a community of moral agents each of whom treats the other as an end-in-itself by obeying the moral law. He distinguishes the ethical commonwealth from the political commonwealth by virtue of the former's freedom from coercion. Whereas the power of coercion is indispensable for the maintenance of a political commonwealth, the freedom of the will is sufficient for the administration of an ethical commonwealth. The constitution of such a harmonious community, Kant says, becomes possible only through the moral rebirth of its members, which involves the radical transformation of their hearts from the propensity to follow inclination into the willing obedience to the moral law, that is, through conversion. The same moral transformation is required for the admission to the ethical commonwealth.

Kant shows special caution in handling the claims of supernatural revelation. He rejects the claim that revelation has the authority of discovering and authenticating the supernatural truths inaccessible to human intelligence. He also rejects the view that revelation is totally gratuitous with respect to the discovery of religious truths. Although the truths of natural religion can be discovered by natural reason, revelation makes easier their discovery and propagation. Since he recognizes only the practical value of expedition, he rejects the traditional distinction between natural and revealed religion. As in Christianity, he says, a natural religion can be a revealed one.

Since natural religion belongs to the pure practical reason, Kant asserts the unity of all religions. There is only one true religion, he says, although there can be many different faiths. He distinguishes the particular ecclesiastical faiths from pure religious faith. Whereas pure faith consists of the ideals of practical reason, the particular faiths are the manifestations of those ideals through the historically instituted churches. Since the formation and development of those institutions have been influenced by historical contingencies, Kant holds, the ecclesiastical faiths are bound to show their differences. Nevertheless, he is confident that they can still display the unity of pure religious faith insofar as they are faithful to their original ideals.

Kant's Critics and His Influence. Kant's idea of natural religion provoked the charge among his contemporaries that he was a Deist. Deism was the view, prevalent among the scientific-minded intellectuals of the eighteenth century, that God does not intervene in the running of the universe because it has been placed under the working of immutable laws since its creation. Kant categorically denied the charge of being a Deist and attributed it to the misrepresentation of his position. [*See* Deism.]

The misrepresentation in question was largely due to Kant's skeptical attitude toward miracles, God's interventions *par excellence* in the running of the world. Because miracles contravene the laws of nature, they cannot be reconciled with the use of reason. Both in theoretical and practical functions, human reason appears crippled in the presence of miracles. Furthermore, he says, miracles are not essential for the functions of true religion, because these functions can stand securely on moral beliefs alone. In fact, any demand for miracles as the authentication of religious beliefs betrays the lack of firm faith in the authority of moral commands, which are engraved upon the heart of man through reason. Because of this, Kant says, Christ rebuked the miracle-seekers: "Unless you see signs and wonders, you will not believe" (*Jn.* 4:48). In spite of these reservations about miracles, Kant categorically refused to impugn their possibility or reality.

Another charge against Kant was that he compromised his doctrine of moral autonomy by retaining the traditional doctrine of grace. Grace, for Kant, means God's help; it presupposes man's weakness, dependence, and heteronomy. The Pietists under whose influence Kant had grown up stressed the indispensability of grace and tended to take a passive attitude toward life. Kant rejects this passive attitude and praises the positive value of active efforts in moral life. Nevertheless, he admits the possibility that even our best efforts may fail to secure moral perfection. In that event, he says, we can hope that God will, in his wisdom and goodness, make up for our shortcomings.

His critics have pointed out that man is not a truly autonomous moral agent if even his best moral efforts are not enough to secure his moral perfection. They have further argued that Kant's notion of moral autonomy is also incompatible with his notion of the complete good. In their view, the intimate connection between worthiness and happiness makes morality too dependent on the idea of happiness, which is admittedly outside the control of a moral agent. Kant had guarded himself against this charge by stressing that the connection in question was a matter of belief rather than knowledge. Even if it is only a belief, his critics have maintained, it compromises the notion of moral autonomy as long as it is acted upon in the practical world.

Perhaps the most serious charge against Kant was addressed to his demarcation between phenomena and noumena. At the time he was concluding his second critique, the *Critique of Practical Reason,* he was not terribly disturbed by this criticism. So he confidently singled out the starry heavens above and the moral law within as two objects of awe and admiration, respectively representing the world of phenomena and the world of noumena. This observation was intended to mark the end not only of the second critique but of his entire critical enterprise. For he believed that his two critiques had fulfilled his ambition of critically assessing the two worlds of phenomena and noumena.

Shortly thereafter, however, Kant became preoccupied with the question of transition and mediation between the two worlds. Although moral precepts belong to the noumenal world, they can be realized in the phenomenal world. Kant found it difficult to explain the transition from the world of precepts to the world of practice, because one was supposed to be governed by necessity and the other by freedom.

In order to resolve this problem of transition, Kant wrote his third critique, the *Critique of Judgment,* and introduced reflective judgment as the faculty of mediation between the two worlds. But his theory of mediation was far from convincing, and most of his intellectual heirs resolved his problem by collapsing his two worlds into one. This post-Kantian development in German idealism made it impossible to retain Kant's postulates of immortality and the other world, because there was only one world left.

The fusion of Kant's two worlds into one was the climax of the progressive secularization that had begun in the Renaissance. Kant played a pivotal role in this development. His demarcation between phenomena and noumena was a modification and retention of the medieval demarcation between the natural and the supernatural orders. Unlike the medieval demarcation, however, Kant's did not completely coincide with the demarcation between this world and the other world. Kant made the transcendent noumenal world functionally immanent for moral life, thereby initiating the descent of the transcendent reality to the immanent level. The post-Kantians completed this process of descent and converted Kant's theism into pantheism. Kant's transcendent God became their immanent force in history.

The resulting pantheism also resolved the tension in Kant's notion of human autonomy. Although he claimed autonomy and independence for moral life, he acknowledged heteronomy and dependence for happiness. He stressed this admixture of dependence and independence in his notion of the complete good and the postulate for the existence of God. But this admixture was unacceptable to his successors, because they insisted on the total autonomy of human reason. The totally autonomous human reason became indistinguishable from the immanent God, and the two-in-one came to be called the "Absolute Spirit" by Hegel. With Kant, religion and morality became functionally identical; with Hegel, God and man were given their ontological identity.

BIBLIOGRAPHY

Kant's Works in English Translation

Critique of Judgement. Translated by J. C. Meredith. 1928; reprint, London, 1973.

Critique of Practical Reason. Translated by Lewis White Beck. Chicago, 1949. Kant's preliminary view of this subject is given in his *Foundations of the Metaphysics of Morals,* translated by Lewis White Beck (Chicago, 1949).

Critique of Pure Reason. Translated by Norman Kemp Smith. New York, 1929. An abridged version is available in Kant's *Prolegomena to Any Future Metaphysics,* edited by Lewis White Beck (Indianapolis, 1950).

Lectures on Ethics. Translated by Louis Infield. London, 1979. These lectures are not from Kant's own writings but from his students' notes.

Religion within the Limits of Reason Alone. Translated by Theodore M. Greene and Hoyt H. Hudson. LaSalle, Ill., 1960. This translation contains two fine introductory essays by Theodore M. Greene and John R. Silber.

Works on Kant's View of Morality and Religion

Beck, Lewis White. *A Commentary on Kant's Critique of Practical Reason.* Chicago, 1960.

Cassirer, Ernst. *Kant's Life and Thought.* Translated by James Haden. New Haven, 1981. This is perhaps the most comprehensive introduction available in English to Kant's life and philosophy. A shorter general introduction to his philosophy can be found in Stephan Körner's *Kant* (1955; reprint, New Haven, 1982) and in Ralph C. S. Walker's *Kant* (Boston, 1978).

Collins, James D. *The Emergence of Philosophy of Religion.* New Haven, 1967. This volume provides a good account not only of Kant's conception of religion but also of what comes before and after Kant's conception, especially Hume's and Hegel's ideas on the issue.

England, F. E. *Kant's Conception of God.* New York, 1929.

Kroner, Richard. *Kant's Weltanschauung* (1914). Chicago, 1956. This book is limited to Kant's ethical outlook.

Paton, Herbert J. *The Categorical Imperative: A Study in Kant's Moral Philosophy.* Chicago, 1948.

Silber, John R. "Kant's Conception of the Highest Good as Immanent and Transcendent." *Philosophical Review* 68 (1959): 469–492.

Silber, John R. "The Moral Good and the Natural Good in Kant's Ethics." *Review of Metaphysics* 36 (December 1982): 397–437.

Webb, Clement C. *Kant's Philosophy of Religion.* Oxford, 1926.

Wood, Allen W. *Kant's Moral Religion.* Ithaca, N.Y., 1970.

T. K. SEUNG

KAPLAN, MORDECAI (1881–1983), American rabbi, author, and religious leader; creator of the theory of Reconstructionist Judaism and founder of the Reconstructionist movement. The son of Rabbi Israel Kaplan, a Talmudic scholar, Mordecai Menachem Kaplan was born in Švenčionys, Lithuania, on 11 June 1881. The family left eastern Europe in 1888 and reached the United States in July 1889. Kaplan was instructed in traditional Jewish subjects by private tutors while attending public schools in New York City. He received degrees from the City College of New York and Columbia University, and rabbinic ordination from the Jewish Theological Seminary of America. In 1909, following a tenure as minister and rabbi of Kehillath Jeshurun, an Orthodox congregation, Kaplan returned to the Jewish Theological Seminary, where he served for more than fifty years: as principal (later dean) of the recently established Teachers Institute until 1945, and as professor of homiletics and philosophies of religion until his formal retirement in 1963.

Beyond his roles as a leader within the Conservative rabbinate and the Zionist movement and as an important contributor within the field of Jewish education, Kaplan's major achievement remains his formulation of Reconstructionism, which he presented to the public through a series of lectures and publications, chief among which was *Judaism as a Civilization* (1934; Philadelphia, 1981). Kaplan developed his theories in response to his own loss of faith in the traditional concept of revelation (*Torah mi-Sinai,* "the Law from Sinai"), one result of his studies with the iconoclastic Bible scholar Arnold Ehrlich. Attempting to rebuild a personal cosmology, Kaplan drew from Western philosophers and social scientists as well as Jewish sources, using the sociological findings of Émile Durkheim, the pragmatic philosophy of John Dewey and William James, and the theological insights of Matthew Arnold in combination with the spiritual Zionism of Aḥad ha-ʿAm (pen name of Asher Ginsberg). This synthesis of materials made Kaplan unique among twentieth-century Jewish thinkers as a redactor who sought to combine modern science with an affirmation of Judaism.

At the heart of Kaplan's thought is his definition of Judaism as an "evolving religious civilization." Opposing those who sought the maintenance of Jewish life solely through preservation of the religion, he argued that a Jewish civilization that included within it a land, language and literature, mores, laws and folkways, arts, and a social structure transcended religion. Kaplan also presented a radical change in the God-idea. Preferring to use the term *divinity,* he rejected notions of an anthropomorphic and personal God active in human history, favoring instead a functional understanding of God as the creative source within the universe, the Power that engenders a salvation to which the Jewish people have long been particularly responsive. These conceptual shifts infuriated Orthodox Jewry, creating a division exacerbated further by Kaplan's efforts to transfer the center of concern and authority from divinely revealed text to the Jewish people itself, as well as by his justification of the transcendence of Jewish law *(halakhah)* and custom *(minhag)* when those sources no longer met the needs of the Jewish people. Kaplan differed from his Conservative colleagues in his use of extratraditional resources; his approach remained distinct from that of Reform Judaism through his efforts to retain traditional forms while providing new content.

Kaplan also sought to modernize Jewish organizational structure. Realizing the superior strength of the Diaspora cultures, he argued that emancipated Jews lived within two civilizations and that, on most occasions, the general (gentile) culture exerted the primary hold upon the individual. In an effort to counterbalance the impetus toward total assimilation, Kaplan called for maximal development of opportunities for the individual to function within a Jewish environment. The locus of those activities was to be the synagogue, which Kaplan sought to transform from a simple prayer room to a modern institution, the focus for worship, study, and recreation. Attracting supporters for these theories, Kaplan supervised the creation of the first such community and synagogue center, The Jewish Center on Manhattan's West Side, in 1918. The commitment of the lay leadership to Orthodox Jewish practice, as well as Kaplan's own temper, soon led to difficulties, however, resulting in his resignation from the Center in 1922. Kaplan next established the Society for the Advancement of Judaism, which served thereafter as the living laboratory for his experiments with Jewish worship, such as the inclusion of women within the *minyan* (prayer quorum) and the creation of *bat mitsvah* as a young woman's rite of passage equivalent to the *bar mitsvah.*

When editing the *Sabbath Prayer Book* (1942), Kaplan retained the traditional service structure, but replaced statements regarding resurrection of the dead with declarations that God remembered the living. In a similar manner, prayers for restoration of the Temple and the coming of the Messiah were removed in favor of recollections of the faith of those who had worshiped within the Temple and prayers for a messianic age, to be achieved through human efforts. Perhaps most controversial, because it was most readily apparent, was Kaplan's replacement of the phrase "who has chosen us from all the nations" in the benediction prior to reading of the Torah with "who has brought us near in His service." Copies of the prayer book were burned at a rally of Orthodox Jews in New York City in 1945, and a ban *(issur)* was pronounced against Kaplan.

Kaplan's followers included Conservative rabbis Eugene Kohn, Ira Eisenstein, and Milton Steinberg, as well as laypeople throughout the country. Kaplan resisted their desire to establish Reconstructionism as a fourth movement within American Judaism, and Reconstructionism thus remained identified as the "left wing" of Conservative Judaism until the 1960s. Only upon his retirement from the Seminary did Kaplan devote himself to the establishment of a distinct Reconstructionist movement; by then, many of his concepts and practices had diffused and become accepted within Reform and Conservative Judaism. As a result, although the influence of Kaplan's ideas has been broad, the Reconstructionist movement has remained small.

[*See also* Reconstructionist Judaism.]

BIBLIOGRAPHY

Works by Kaplan not mentioned above include *The Future of the American Jew* (1948; New York, 1967), which examines the needs of Jews and Judaism following the creation of the state of Israel. For an examination of religion and the concept of God as it functions within the Jewish civilization, there is *The Meaning of God in Modern Jewish Religion* (1936; New York, 1975); *The Greater Judaism in the Making* (1960; New York, 1967) studies the modern evolution of Judaism; and *The Religion of Ethical Nationhood* (New York, 1970) is an advocacy of the idea of ethical nationhood as the only means of avoiding world disaster.

For works on Kaplan, see my own *Mordecai M. Kaplan and the Development of Reconstructionism* (Toronto, 1983), an intellectual biography drawing upon Kaplan's personal papers. For a treatment of Kaplan's place in the Reconstructionist movement, see Gilbert Rosenthal's *Four Paths to One God* (New York, 1976).

RICHARD LIBOWITZ

KARAITES. The Karaites (Heb., Qara'im; Arab., Qarā'īyūn) are a Jewish sect that recognizes only the Hebrew scriptures as the source of divinely inspired legislation, and denies the authority of the postbiblical Jewish tradition (the oral law) as recorded in the Talmud and in later rabbinic literature. The term is believed to appear first in a ninth-century Karaite work by Binyamin al-Nahāwandī. According to a twelfth-century Karaite author, Eliyyahu ben Avraham, the name was first coined by rabbinic Jews (called Rabbinites) and was appropriated by the Karaites; how true this explanation is remains unclear. The term is variously interpreted as "scripturaries, champions of scripture" (from the Hebrew *qara'*, "to read," particularly "to read scripture") and as "callers," that is to say, those who call for a return to the original biblical religion (from the alternate meaning of *qara'*, "to call, to summon"). It is the only Jewish sect (excluding the Samaritans) that has survived for more than twelve hundred years, is still in existence, and has produced an extensive scholarly literature, much of which has been preserved.

The Rise of Karaism. Sectarian dissent in Judaism goes back at least as far as the pre-Talmudic period, when it was represented by the Sadducees, the Essenes, the Qumran community (whose literary archives are known as the Dead Sea Scrolls), and possibly other movements, whose literary remains are hopelessly lost or may yet be discovered. The growth and eventual codification of the postbiblical rabbinic tradition in turn gave rise to further dissent, so that Karaism represents not a new phenomenon but another link in the long line of groups insisting that the Hebrew scriptures are the sole genuine depository of God's word, and that no subsequent traditional law may modify or supplement them.

The traditional Rabbinite account of the origin of Karaism, cited by Eliyyahu ben Avraham, ascribes it to the disappointment of an aristocratic Babylonian (Iraqi) Rabbinite scholar named ʿAnan ben David, who was next in line for election as exilarch (secular leader) of the Iraqi Jewish community in the second half of the eighth century but was voted down on suspicion of heretical leanings and was replaced by his younger brother. He thereupon declared himself head of the dissident group of Ananites, who formed the nucleus of what later became the Karaite sect.

This simplistic account suffers from a number of historical and psychological difficulties. Already in the late seventh and early eighth centuries the antitraditional leaders, Abu ʿĪsā and Yudghan, had been active in the vicinity of Iraq. In the ninth and early tenth centuries other such leaders, as Ismāʿīl and Mīshawayh in ʿUkbarā (Iraq), Binyamin al-Nahāwandī in Iran, Mūsā al-Zaʿfarānī in Iraq and subsequently in Armenia, and Malik al-Ramlī in Palestine, presided over their own sectarian followings. All of these separate dissident groups developed their own heterogeneous teachings, although they seem to have vaguely regarded themselves as members of the larger community of antirabbinic sectarians.

Theological disagreement seems to have been only one of several causes of this new flowering of schisms; others were political, social, and economic. The large autonomous Jewish community in Iraq was administered by a bureaucracy serving the exilarch and the presidents (called the geonim) of the academies, who codified, interpreted, and developed the rabbinic tradition and acted as supreme courts of appeal; this bureaucracy was maintained by internal taxation that added to the heavy taxes already paid by non-Muslims to the Muslim state. The poorer classes of the Jewish community—and they formed the great majority—thus had ample reason for dissatisfaction with their lot. At the same time, the extension and consolidation of the Muslim empire in the seventh and eighth centuries enabled such discontented elements in the Iraqi community to emigrate to the sparsely settled and less regulated mountainous provinces of the east and north, where they observed the conquered Persian population, united under the banner of Shiism, seething with resentment and resistance against their Arab masters. Finally, the meteoric speed and astounding ease of the Arab conquests of the Byzantine and Persian dominions must have aroused anew in the local Jewish population the expectation of an impending end of exile, the restoration of Zion, and the ingathering of the exiles in the Holy Land under their own government. This hope was, however, quickly shattered: the new Muslim masters, like their Christian and Zoroastrian predecessors, had not the slightest interest in Jewish national aspirations and dreams. All these factors probably contributed to discontent with the status quo, particularly among the disadvantaged elements of the Iraqi Jewish community.

By the beginning of the tenth century the schism had expanded from its Iranian-Iraqi birthplace into Palestine (Jerusalem), Syria (Damascus), and Egypt (Cairo). The individual quarreling groups, including the Ananites, gradually went out of existence by merging into the general community of Karaites. Zealous Karaite missionaries traveled far and wide to the Jewish settlements in the Near East, preaching to both Karaite and Rabbinite audiences—not to Muslim ones, since Muslim law forbids non-Muslim missionary activity among Muslims—but apparently with not much success, at least among the better-educated elements, since ʿAnan himself is the only early Karaite scholar known to have been converted from rabbinism. So far the relationship between the new sect and the Rabbinite majority seems to have remained, if not amicable, at least indifferent. But about the second quarter of the tenth century a radical change set in. Saʿadyah al-Fayyumī (d. 942), an accomplished and encyclopedic Egyptian Jewish scholar who ultimately became president of the rabbinic academy at Sura, in Iraq, published several polemical works against Karaism, condemning it as outright heresy and branding its adherents as complete seceders from the Mother Synagogue. Saʿadyah's prestige and forceful scholarly argumentation effected a decisive break between the two camps that has never been healed. [*See the biography of Saʿadyah.*]

The consequences of this break were far-reaching. Karaite missionary activity among Rabbinites became more difficult and even less productive of converts than before, and the sect's hope of eventually persuading all their Rabbinite brethren to return to the pure Mosaic—that is, Karaite—faith was extinguished. At the same time, Saʿadyah's devastating attack and the urgent need to reply to it gave impetus to what became the golden age of Karaite literary activity (tenth–eleventh centuries) in the fields of theology, philosophy, biblical exegesis, and Hebrew philology, with which the Karaites endeavored to meet Saʿadyah's criticisms on an equal level of serious and competent scholarship. A Karaite academy flourished in Jerusalem during the eleventh century and gave advanced training to students from Karaite settlements as far-flung as Muslim Spain.

The onset of the First Crusade in 1099 put a stop to all Jewish activity—Rabbinite and Karaite alike—in Palestine. New Karaite settlements were established in the Balkans (then under Byzantine rule), Cyprus, the Crimea, Lithuania, and Poland. Some Karaite activity continued in the ancient community of Cairo, but on a greatly reduced scale.

Karaite history from the twelfth to the nineteenth century, and indeed down to the middle of the twentieth century, is marked by the characteristic tendency of the Karaites, a small minority of Jewry, to seek safety and strength in withdrawing as far as possible from the world—rabbinic, Christian, or Muslim—that surrounded them. Unlike their Rabbinite brethren, they did not seek to participate actively in the intellectual and material civilization of the Christians and Muslims around them, nor did they play a substantial part in government service, the medical profession, or the higher echelons of local and international commerce. Their innate conservatism and their dislike and fear of innovations and outside influence precluded any substantial changes in their beliefs or mode of life. Karaite history from about 1200 to about 1900 is thus almost a blank page. Rabbinite travelers, such as the twelfth-century Binyamin of Tudela and Petaḥyah of Ratisbon (Regensburg), mention in their accounts the Karaite communities in Byzantium and in southern Russia (Crimea), but have little more to say about them. Relations between Karaite and Rabbinite communities in neighboring city districts remained distant but peaceful and never (except perhaps once) reached a point of physical violence. Scholars on both sides polemicized against one another, sometimes in rather sharp terms, but this action remained a mere war of words. Mixed marriages between Karaite and Rabbinite parties, especially in Egypt in the earlier centuries of this period, seem to have been limited to the wealthy aristocracy; conversions from one group to the other were also apparently rather rare, so that the anti-Karaite tenor of some of the Rabbinite polemics is probably merely theoretical and is not based on actual fear that Karaite missionaries might seduce too many Rabbinites to abandon their forefathers' faith. Maimonides, the greatest Rabbinite mind of the medieval period, summed up the Rabbinite attitude by advising reserved but helpful behavior toward Karaites as fellow Jews, albeit wayward ones, so long as they desisted from hostile attacks on Rabbinite dogma and practice. The Christian and Muslim authorities usually did not differentiate between the two groups and regarded them as two variations of Jews, so that occasionally Karaites had to endure the same indignities and persecutions as did the Rabbinites. Karaite history during this long period is thus mainly the record of Karaite scholars and their works.

The Karaite community in Constantinople, the capital of Byzantium, developed into a substantial scholarly center and continued as such after the Ottoman conquest in 1453, when the city was renamed Istanbul. But with the steady decline of Turkish power in the seventeenth and eighteenth centuries, the Karaite communities in the Crimea, Lithuania, and Poland assumed the leading role. Soon thereafter these communities came under Russian rule, and their leadership succeeded in obtaining from the tsarist government full citizenship rights for Karaites; thus they were set even further apart from the Rabbinite majority in Russia, which continued to bear the full weight of the oppressive and discriminatory anti-Jewish laws.

World War I affected the Russian Karaites only where they found themselves directly in the way of military operations. During World War II the Karaites in the occupied territories of Poland and western Russia were generally not molested by the German authorities, on the ground (generously supported by Rabbinite representatives consulted by the Germans) that they were ethnically not Jewish but rather were descended from the ancient Turkic nation of the Khazars, converts to Judaism who once ruled southern Russia. These Karaites were therefore not subject to wholesale extermination, as were their Rabbinite brethren. After 1945 the Arab-Israeli conflict had a serious effect on the Karaite communities in the neighboring Arab states. Owing to emigration, the ancient community of Hit, in Iraq, ceased to exist, and the equally ancient community in Cairo was vastly reduced when most of its members moved to Israel, Europe, and the Americas. Statistics of the Karaite population in the world at the present time are unreliable, and the usually cited figures of twelve thousand to thirteen thousand are probably far too low.

Karaite Literature and Its Reproduction. If any of the pre-Ananite sectarian leaders did actually commit their teachings to writing, these works are yet to be discovered. The earliest Karaite work available, and then only in fragments, is ʿAnan's code of law, known under the Hebrew title of *Sefer ha-mitsvot* (Book of Precepts) but written in Aramaic, the language of a large part of the Talmud. ʿAnan's successors, Binyamin al-Nahāwandī and Daniyye'l al-Qūmisī, wrote in Hebrew, while later Karaite scholars in the Muslim dominions, up to the fifteenth century, wrote in Arabic. In the Balkans and in Lithuania, Poland, and western Russia, Karaite scholars wrote in Hebrew. In recent times the Russo-Polish Karaites wrote in part also in the spoken Karaite-Tatar dialect, brought by their ancestors from the Crimea.

The first major scholar of the golden age of Karaite literature was Yaʿqūb al-Qirqisānī (second quarter of the tenth century), whose *magnum opus* is a two-part Arabic commentary on the Pentateuch. The first part, entitled *Kitāb al-anwār wa-al-marāqib* (Book of Lighthouses and Watchtowers), comments on the legal parts of the Pentateuch and forms not only a detailed code of Karaite law but also a veritable encyclopedia of early Karaite lore. The second part, *Kitāb al-riyāḍ wa-al-ḥadā'iq* (Book of Gardens and Parks), deals with the nonlegal portions of the Pentateuch. Al-Qirqisānī also wrote an extensive commentary on *Genesis* that seems as well to have dealt in detail with the various philosophical problems involved, such as the nature of the deity and of matter, creation *ex nihilo*, and good and evil. Of all his works, including several equally important minor ones, only the *Kitāb al-anwār* has been published. In the tenth and eleventh centuries, Karaite scholars, some connected with the Karaite academy in Jerusalem, produced a number of important works, mostly in Arabic, in the areas of exegesis, theology, philosophy, law, philology, apologetics, and polemics. Their authors included Yefet ben ʿEli (the premier early Karaite Bible commentator), Salmon ben Yeroḥam and Sahl ben Maṣliaḥ (zealous Karaite apologists and missionaries), David al-Fāsī (a lexicographer), Yosef ben Noaḥ (president of the Jerusalem academy), Aharon ben Yeshuʿah (a grammarian and exegete), Yosef ha-Ro'eh (an eminent philosopher better known under his Arabic name, Yūsuf al-Baṣīr), and Yeshuʿah ben Yehudah (the reformer of the Karaite law of consanguinity).

With the transfer of most Karaite literary activity to the Greek-speaking Balkans after the First Crusade, there was a need to translate the Karaite Arabic classics into Hebrew, since the Byzantine (and later on, the Lithuanian-Polish-Russian) Karaites were not fluent in Arabic. A series of translators, headed by Ṭoviyyah ben Mosheh and Yaʿaqov ben Shimʿon, provided such translations, often heavily larded with Greek loanwords and rather clumsy Hebrew constructions. A more fluent Hebrew style appears in an extensive encyclopedia of Karaite scholarship begun in 1148 by Yehudah Hadassi of Edessa and entitled *Eshkol ha-kofer* (Cluster of Henna), and in Yaʿaqov ben Re'uven's commentary on the Bible. In Egypt, where Arabic continued as the Karaite literary vehicle, Karaism produced its most eminent Hebrew poet of the period, Mosheh Darʿī (of Darʿah, in Morocco, but born in Alexandria, Egypt; lived probably in the twelfth century). In the fifteenth century Sama'al al-Maghribī wrote the last known Arabic code of Karaite law, and David ibn al-Hītī composed a brief but important chronicle of Arabic scholars from Anan down to his own time. Another poet, Mosheh ben Shemu'el, produced a corpus of Hebrew poetry, including an epic account of his tribulations in the service of the emir of Damascus, who in 1354 forced the poet to become a Muslim and to accompany his princely master on a pilgrimage to Mecca. He finally escaped to Egypt, where he seems to have returned to his ancestral faith.

In the Balkans there was a literary revival during the thirteenth to fifteenth centuries. Aharon (the Elder) ben Yosef (fl. late thirteenth century) wrote a philosophical commentary on the Pentateuch, but is best known as the redactor of the official Karaite liturgy. Another Aharon (the Younger), ben Eliyyahu (d. 1369), composed a complete summa of Karaite theology, in three volumes: philosophical (*'Ets ḥayyim*, Tree of Life), legal (*Gan 'Eden*, Garden of Eden), and exegetical (*Keter Torah*, Crown of the Torah). Eliyyahu Bashyatchi (d. 1490) left an unfinished code of law, *Adderet Eliyyahu* (Mantle of Eliyyahu), which was edited by his brother-in-law Kaleb Afendopolo (d. after 1522), a many-sided scholar in both theology and the secular sciences, and became the most esteemed legal manual among most modern Karaites.

As the Ottoman empire progressively declined, the center of Karaite literary activity again shifted northward, to the Crimea, Lithuania, and Poland. The Karaite community of Troki (near Vilnius, in Lithuania) counted as one of its most illustrious sons Yitsḥaq ben Avraham Troki (d. 1594, or perhaps 1586), the author of a critical tract against Christianity entitled *Ḥizzuq emunah* (Fortification of the Faith), who was later admired by no less an expert in polemics than Voltaire. In the seventeenth and eighteenth centuries a group of Protestant theologians (Rittangel, Peringer, Puffendorf, Warner, Trigland), seeing a parallel between the Karaite secession from the Rabbinite synagogue and the Protestant secession from the Church of Rome, encouraged the composition of several works by their Polish Karaite informants, including Shelomoh ben Aharon of Troki (d. 1745) and Mordekhai ben Nisan of Kukizów (near Lvov, in Polish Galicia, now part of the U.S.S.R.), setting forth their view of Karaite history, dogma, and ritual. The community of Lutsk (in Volhynia, southwest Russia) produced the first Karaite literary historian and bibliographer, Simḥah Yitsḥaq ben Mosheh (d. 1766).

In the nineteenth century the outstanding Karaite man of letters was Avraham Firkovitch (1785–1874), who during his travels in the Crimea, the Caucasus, Syria, Palestine, and Egypt amassed a large collection of Karaite manuscripts, one of the richest on this subject in the world, now in the Leningrad Public Library. He was also a prolific writer, although the authenticity of the historical data he cited from the colophons of manuscripts and from tombstones has been questioned by scholars. An older contemporary of his, Mordechai Sultansky (d. 1862), wrote several works, among them a history of Karaism, *Zekher tsaddiqim* (Memorial of the Righteous), valuable mainly as an exposition of the modern official version, authorized by the leading circles of the Russian-Polish-Lithuanian community.

No significant scholarly works have been produced by twentieth-century Karaite authors, but there is some reason to hope that the large new Karaite community in Israel may eventually develop a cadre of scholars trained to produce modern critical research, especially for the urgently needed publication of critical editions of early Karaite literary documents that are still in manuscript or that have not yet been discovered and identified.

The invention of printing with movable type was eagerly seized upon by Rabbinite bookmen and was used to produce an abundant flow of printed religious and lay literature from the 1470s down to the present day. On the Karaite side the picture is quite different. No Karaite incunabula were printed, and only four Karaite books (the first, an edition of the Karaite liturgy, published by the Christian bookmaker Daniel Bomberg in Venice in 1528–1529) appeared in the sixteenth century, all set in type and run off the press by Rabbinite compositors and pressmen. Only one Karaite book came out in the seventeenth century, printed in 1643 at the Amsterdam press of Menasseh ben Israel, a Rabbinite scholar and publisher known also for his negotiations with Lord Protector Oliver Cromwell on the readmission of Jews into England. The earliest Karaite presses were those of the brothers Afdah (or Afidah) and Shabbetai Yeraqa in Istanbul, (1733) and in Chufut-Kale, in the Crimea, (1734–1741); and another press, also in Chufut-Kale (1804–1806). They were short-lived and succeeded in publishing only a few books. The first more or less successful Karaite press was established in 1833 in Yevpatoriya (called Gozlow, its Tatar name, by the local Karaites), in the Crimea, and published several important old texts.

One can only guess at the reason for the typographical backwardness of the modern Karaites. One factor was very likely their historical dislike of innovative change. Their limited number and the comparative paucity of prospective purchasers and interested readers among them probably also made printing unprofitable unless supported from time to time by a wealthy patron from their own midst.

Dogma and Practice. As far as dogmatic theology is concerned, except for the disavowal of the postbiblical (Talmudic and rabbinic) tradition, there is no conflict between Karaism and rabbinism. The most authoritative Karaite creed, formulated by Eliyyahu Bashyatchi in ten articles (to correspond to the Ten Mosaic Commandments), postulates the existence and oneness of God, creator of all the world, the genuine inspiration of Moses and the subsequent Hebrew prophets, the divine authority of the legislation set forth in the Torah and the duty of studying it, the certainty of the resurrection of the dead and of final judgment, the responsibility of each individual for his own actions, and the eventual advent of the Messiah. Even the rejection of the rabbinic tradition has turned out to be not quite absolute, for with the passage of time, changing conditions have forced the formation of a native Karaite tradition in order to cope with new situations and problems that were not foreseen and provided for by Moses the lawgiver. Hence the development of the three pillars of Karaite legislation: (1) the scriptural text (Heb., *katuv;* Arab., *naṣṣ*); (2) analogy (Heb., *heqqesh;* Arab., *qiyās*) based on scripture; and, in cases where the first two pillars are of no help, (3) the consensus of scholarly opinion (Hebrew *qibbuts* or *ʿedah*, "community," the latter term possibly influenced by the Arabic *ʿādah*, "customary practice, common law"; Arabic *ijmāʿ*, "agreement"; later termed in Hebrew *sevel ha-yerushah*, "burden of inheritance").

Where Karaism and rabbinism go different ways is in religious practice, and here the differences are substantial and fundamental. For the Jewish calendar, which governs the fixing of the dates of holy days, Karaism rejected the rabbinic mathematical reckoning and depended solely on the observation of the phases of the moon; only comparatively recently was limited reckoning admitted locally. In dietary law, the scriptural interdict against seething a kid's flesh in its mother's milk was not broadened (as it was in rabbinic law) to cover all "fleshy" and all "milky" eatables. In the law of consanguinity, Karaism originally followed the so-called catenary (chain) theory (Heb., *rikku;* Arab., *tarkīb*), which permitted piling analogy upon analogy to deduce further forbidden marriages from those explicitly listed in scripture. The social consequences of this practice finally became so threatening to the physical survival of the Karaite community that Yeshuʿah ben Yehudah was successful in modifying it, although the Karaite definition of consanguinity is still much more extensive than the Rabbinite one. This remains, however, the only instance of a major reform in Karaite law. The scriptural prohibition of kindling fire on the Sabbath day is interpreted literally to mean the total absence of all fire, even if kindled before the onset of the Sabbath and left to continue burning, as permitted by rabbinic law. The modest relaxation of this rule in the Russo-Polish-Lithuanian communities, where the absence of light and heat throughout the cold and sunless winters inflicted unbearable hardship, was the subject of strong opposition. Other differences relate to ritual cleanness, particularly rigorous for Karaite women, inheritance (the Karaite husband has no claim upon his deceased wife's estate), and other matters. Polygyny is not officially prohibited—as it was by a medieval European rabbinical enactment recently extended to eastern Jewries as well—but it seems to have been quite uncommon even in Muslim countries, probably for social and economic reasons; in Western countries it was of course outlawed and was recognized as such by Jewish law. The Karaite liturgy, originally limited to selected biblical psalms and prose passages, was eventually developed into a large corpus of both prose and verse (some written by Rabbinite poets) quite distinct from the Rabbinite one.

The connection between Karaism and Sadduceeism, suggested by some early Rabbinite polemicists, or between Karaism and the recently discovered Qumran sect, as advanced by some modern scholars, is too hypothetical to be taken seriously, at least until more direct and more reliable documentary evidence is discovered. Similarities in some observances are merely earmarks of the age-old continuous chain of dissent in Judaism (the outstanding example, the rule that Shavuʿot must always fall on a Sunday, seems to be one of the oldest points in Jewish dissent). The chief stumbling block here is the hiatus of some five hundred years between the Sadducees and the Qumranites on the one hand, and the earliest known representatives of primitive Karaism on the other. The most that can safely be said at present is that the primitive Karaites may possibly have had access to some Sadducee or Qumranite literary documents now no longer extant. Whether they have been influenced by them, and if so, to what extent, cannot yet be determined.

BIBLIOGRAPHY

Modern critical study of Karaism is barely a century and a half old, and scholars who have devoted their full attention to it are few. Much of the early and extremely important Karaite literature is still in manuscript, awaiting scholarly publication and use. Some of it has undoubtedly been lost; some may yet be discovered or recognized. Certain aspects of Karaite history—for example, the role of social and economic factors, at least in medieval and early modern times—have not yet been examined at all. Some basic modern works, while very good as far as they went in their time, are in urgent need of being brought up to date. Even such an important work as the bio-bibliographical dictionary of Karaites left in manuscript by Samuel Poznański (d. 1921) is still unrevised and unpublished. Moreover, the Firkovitch collection of Karaite manuscripts in Leningrad and similar collections elsewhere in Russia have not yet been properly catalogued, and access to them by Western scholars is fraught with almost insurmountable difficulties, while Russian scholars seem (whether willingly or unwillingly, one cannot tell) uninterested in this field of study.

It is therefore not surprising that the two general works on Karaism—Julius Fürst's *Geschichte des Karäerthums*, 3 vols. (Leipzig, 1862–1869), and W. H. Rule's *History of the Karaite Jews* (London, 1870)—should be used with great caution. Zvi Cahn's *The Rise of the Karaite Sect* (New York, 1937) is a compilation of minimal value. Simḥah Pinsker's *Liqquṭei qadmoniyyot* (Vienna, 1860) retains much of its value by virtue of the original documents published in it for the first time. A similar but far more reliable work is Jacob Mann's *Texts and Studies in Jewish History and Literature*, vol. 2, *Ḳaraitica* (Philadelphia, 1935), a veritable treasure trove of original documents and excellent studies, dealing mainly with the modern period after 1500. A thought-provoking but tendentious work is Raphael

Mahler's *Karaimer* (Karaites; New York, 1947; in Yiddish), which regards Karaism as a phenomenon of political and socioeconomic liberation rather than as a theological schism, albeit with social and economic overtones. Moritz Steinschneider's *Die arabische Literature der Juden* (Frankfurt, 1902), which also surveys the Arabic literature of the Karaites, was supplemented by Samuel Poznański in 1904—his additions first appeared in three issues of *Orientalistische Literatur-Zeitung* 7 (July–September 1904) and were later collected in *Zur jüdischearabischen Literatur* (Berlin, 1904)—but a revised and updated edition is one of the major desiderata in this field. Poznański's *The Karaite Literary Opponents of Saadiah Gaon* (London, 1908) surveys the Karaite polemics against Sa'adyah from the tenth to the nineteenth century. Bernard Revel's *The Karaite Halakah*, pt. 1 (Philadelphia, 1913), surveys Karaite law but is somewhat antiquated. A selection of extracts, in English translation with explanatory notes, from the early (before 1500) Karaite literature, forms my own *Karaite Anthology* (New Haven, 1952). The early Karaite philosophical literature is treated expertly by Isaac Husik in *A History of Mediaeval Jewish Philosophy* (New York, 1916). A useful but imperfect guide to Karaite liturgy is P. S. Goldberg's *Karaite Liturgy and Its Relation to Synagogue Worship* (Manchester, 1957), which should be supplemented by my own "Studies in the History of the Early Karaite Liturgy: The Liturgy of al-Qirqisānī," in *Studies in Jewish Bibliography, History and Literature, in Honor of I. Edward Kiev*, edited by Charles Berlin (New York, 1971), pp. 305–332.

See also Salo W. Baron's study *A Social and Religious History of the Jews*, vol 5, *High Middle Ages, 500–1200*, 2d ed., rev. & enl. (New York, 1957), pp. 209–285, 388–416 (for further references to Karaism, see the index to volumes 1–8, New York, 1960); Zvi Ankori's *Karaites in Byzantium: The Formative Years, 970–1100* (New York, 1959); Naphtali Wieder's *The Judean Scrolls and Karaism* (London, 1962); André Paul's *Écrits de Qumran et sectes juives aux premiers siècles de l'Islam: Recherches sur l'origine du Qaraïsme* (Paris, 1969); and Samuel Poznański's "Karäische Drucke und Druckereien," *Zeitschrift für hebraeische Bibliographie* 20, 21, 23 (1917, 1918, 1920).

LEON NEMOY

KARDECISM is the name given the system of spiritist doctrines and practices codified by the French spiritist Allan Kardec. Kardec's religio-philosophical principles and therapeutic techniques have been especially influential in the development of spiritism among the urban middle classes in Brazil from the mid-nineteenth century until the present.

Kardec's Life and Work. Allan Kardec was born Hypolyte Léon Denizard Rivail on 3 October 1804 in Lyons, France. The son of Justice Jean-Baptiste Antoine Rivail and Jeanne Duhamel, Rivail received a thorough education. Descended on his father's side from a family of magistrates, and on his mother's side from a family of theologians, writers, and mathematicians, Rivail was sent as a boy to Switzerland, to study under the famous pedagogue Henri Pestalozzi. He distinguished himself with his intelligence and precocity: at fourteen, Rivail had a command of several languages and was conversant in Greek and Latin.

Having received training as a teacher, he returned to Paris, and earned a bachelor's degree in sciences and letters. According to some of his biographers, Rivail concluded the course in medicine at twenty-four years of age. During his studies, he taught French, mathematics, and sciences. Having failed at his attempt to create a teaching institution after Pestalozzi's model, he survived by doing translations and teaching courses at schools and institutes. Notwithstanding his medical studies, the eight books written from 1824 to 1849 deal with mathematics, grammar, and the physical sciences in general, in which his pedagogical concerns prevail. He joined several professional, pedagogical, and scientific associations.

In short, Rivail was a typical European scholar of his time, with a classical training in letters, positivist beliefs, an interest in the theoretical and applied development of science, and a professional specialization in teaching. But Rivail was not an orthodox positivist. Imbued with a great curiosity about phenomena unheeded and even shunned by official science, he belonged to the French Society of Magnetists. Hypnotism, sleepwalking, clairvoyance, and similar phenomena strongly attracted him. He studied them as physical phenomena resulting from unknown causes, an approach resulting from his being a follower of the theory of animal magnetism, called Mesmerism, expounded by Franz Anton Mesmer (1734–1815).

Magnetism brought Rivail in contact with spiritism. He was by then fifty-one years old and had consolidated his scientific background. In the years 1854 and 1855, the so-called turning table and talking table invaded Europe from the United States and created an intense curiosity. Several people would sit around a table, hand in hand, in a state of mental concentration; after a certain lapse of time, the table would begin to rotate, to produce noises, and even to answer, in code, questions proposed by the participants. This practice became quite a fad, especially in the more elegant circles. Rivail was introduced by magnetist friends to such sessions, which were already accepted by their promoters as demonstrations of spiritual phenomena. He was initially skeptical about their authenticity but was soon to revise his opinion. Under his supervision, the sessions were no longer dedicated to frivolous consultations and guessing games but became serious study sessions.

Rivail considered such phenomena both relevant and natural, though invisible, and believed one should adopt a "positivist and not an idealist" attitude toward them. If the conditions in which such phenomena manifested themselves hindered the use of common scientific instrumentation, he believed that one should at least employ the scientific method of "observation, comparison, and evaluation."

Inspired by his own experiences, stimulated by illustrious spiritists who supplied him with fifty notebooks containing messages from the souls of deceased persons, and guided by the spirits that conferred on him the role of codifier of spiritism, Rivail became Allan Kardec; he adopted this pen name under the inspiration of one of his guiding spirits, who revealed that it had been his name in a former incarnation, in which he had been a druid in ancient Gaul. In 1857 he published his fundamental work, *Le livre des esprits,* which contained 501 questions answered by the spirits themselves. By the time of its twenty-second and definitive edition, the number of questions had grown to 1,019.

Thereafter followed his other works: *Qu'est-ce-que le spiritisme?* (1859); *Le livre des médiums* (1861); *Refutation aux critiques au spiritisme* (1862); *L'évangile selon le spiritisme* (1864); *Le ciel et l'enfer, ou La justice divine selon le spiritisme* (1865); and *La genèse, les miracles et les predictions* (1868). The literature further includes his *Œuvres posthumes,* published in 1890, and an incalculable number of articles published over a period of eleven years in the *Spiritist Journal,* issued by the Parisian Society for Spiritist Studies that had been founded by Kardec in 1858 and of which he was the chairman to his death in 1869.

Kardecism, as codified by Kardec, defines the spiritist doctrine in this way: there are souls, or spirits, of deceased persons that are capable of communication with the living through mediumistic phenomena. They belong to an invisible but natural world; there is no discussion of magic, miracles, and the supernatural in Kardecism. This invisible and nonmaterial world is, as part of the natural world, susceptible to experimentation, but, unlike the natural world, it is eternal and preexistent and is identified with goodness, purity, and wisdom. There is a spiritual hierarchy ranging from that most closely identified with the material plane (and hence with evil, impurity, and ignorance) up to that of spiritual fullness.

God is the primary cause that generates the material and the spiritual; the spirits are engendered by him, and although they receive a mission and submit to the law of constant progress, they are endowed with free will. Spirits continually progress toward perfection, and they fulfill their missions through successive reincarnations, not only on earth (considered a planet of atonement) but also on other worlds. The law of cause and effect explains human happiness or misfortune as consequences of good or evil practiced in previous incarnations. Christian charity is the supreme virtue (Christ is considered the most elevated spirit that has ever incarnated) that makes spiritual evolution possible; it is closely followed in importance by the virtue of wisdom. As the locus of the activity of the developing but morally free spirits and as the product of evolution, the social world, even with its injustices and inequalities, is seen as ultimately just, and the search for perfection is ruled by individualistic ethics.

It is a rather curious fact that Kardec remained practically unknown for a long time outside French spiritist circles. Approximately sixty years after his death, Arthur Conan Doyle, as chairman of the London Spiritist League and honorary chairman of the International Spiritist Federation, only devoted a few scanty pages to Kardec in one of the twenty-five chapters of his comprehensive *History of Spiritualism* (1926). There seem to be two related reasons for this obscurity: British spiritism did not accept the idea of reincarnation, and, except in France, Kardec's claim to be the true codifier of spiritism by virtue of a mission entrusted to him by the spirits was not readily accepted. Although this role currently tends to be universally accepted by spiritists, the name of Kardec (or Rivail) is not mentioned in the main European encyclopedias, and he remains known only within spiritist circles.

Kardecism in Brazil. Originally introduced in Brazil in the middle of the nineteenth century in the form of "talking tables," spiritism mainly attracted teachers, lawyers, physicians, and other intellectuals. One of the reasons for its appeal was the pseudoscientific character of Kardecism. Kardecist groups were soon organized, first in Bahia (1865), and later in Rio de Janeiro (1873, where the Brazilian Spiritist Federation was created in the following year), São Paulo (1883), and gradually throughout the entire country. Kardecism was already attracting large sectors of the urban middle class.

Although Kardec did not consider spiritism a religion (but rather a philosophy of science with religious implications), Kardecism in Brazil was soon to take on a religious character, centering on the idea of charity, which led to therapeutical practices such as the "pass." Kardecism followed the same pattern of evolution as positivism, which had already become a religion in Brazil, with an organized church and cult.

The 1940 and 1950 censuses in Brazil showed an intense expansion of spiritism: though its adherents did not exceed 2 percent of the population in 1950, it was growing at a much more rapid pace than any other religion, including Catholicism, the unofficial but dominant creed (then adhered to by about 90 percent of Brazil's people). For this reason, the Catholic Church initiated an antispiritist campaign during the fifties.

A distinguishing feature of Brazilian spiritism is the

fact that it is an almost exclusively urban phenomenon. In these regions, however, Kardecism is not the only spiritist current that manifests itself. Another trend is that of Umbanda spiritism, a syncretic product of Afro-Brazilian religions under the influence of Kardecism. [*See* Afro-Brazilian Cults.] While Kardecism proper tends to be a religion of those of the urban middle classes who have been city-dwellers for several generations, drawing people who have a certain level of secular education and who are disposed to accept its pseudoscientific discourse, Umbanda remains a religion of the unschooled lower classes of more recent urbanization. Unlike Kardecism, Umbanda is still linked to a magical conception of the universe.

Currently, Kardecism and Umbanda encompass significant population groups in Brazil. The censuses, however, do not register their extension, since both Kardecists and Umbandists often also declare themselves to be Catholics, especially for social purposes such as christenings, marriages, funerals, and statements given in official forms. In spite of the evident importance of spiritism in Brazil—an importance that is easily verified by other indicators (e.g., the medium Chico Xavier's book sales are exceeded only by those of the novelist Jorge Amado)—the census still reports the number of spiritists as approximately 2 percent.

Despite census data to the contrary, it seems fairly certain that Umbandists outnumber Kardecists in Brazil. Though until the forties Kardecism was predominant, in the sixties the situation was utterly reversed in favor of Umbanda. It should be noted, however, that the fifties mark the stage of the greatest penetration of Umbanda by Kardecism. Up to that time, Umbanda subsisted as a semiclandestine cult under severe and tyrannical police control. From 1953, many Kardecists, disenchanted with the prevailing intellectualism of their spiritist centers, turned to Umbanda. Under their leadership, federations were organized that grouped Umbanda adherents into units called "yards" and "tents," and these disenchanted Kardecists took over, in a less repressive and more persuasive fashion, the control that formerly had been exercised by the police. The price Umbanda had to pay for this protection was its adjustment to a rationalization and moralization of the cult—processes that were based on Kardecist models. One may therefore conclude that although Umbanda has grown much more rapidly than Kardecism over the last few decades, the influence of Kardecism in the context of Brazilian spiritism continues to remain strong.

BIBLIOGRAPHY

Sociological, anthropological, and historical studies on Kardecism are scarce. With respect to the historical aspects, one will search in vain for a single work by any specialist in the field; the only texts available are biographies of Kardec written by spiritist intellectuals. Among these the best are José Herculano Pires's *O espírito e o tempo: Introdução histórica ao espiritismo* (São Paulo, 1964), a scholarly and interesting work, and the voluminous book by Zeus Wantuil and Francisco Thiesen, *Allan Kardec, pesquisa bibliográfica e ensaios de interpretação*, 3 vols. (Rio de Janeiro, 1979–1980), which offers a comprehensive analysis and represents the official view of Brazilian Kardecism on the life and work of its inspirer.

Among sociological and anthropological studies, the following are worth mentioning: Cândido Procópio Ferreira de Camargo's *Kardecismo e Umbanda: Una interpretação sociológica* (São Paulo, 1961); Roger Bastide's article "Le spiritisme au Brésil," *Archives de sociologie des religions* 12 (1967): 3–16; and Maria Viveiros de Castro Cavalcanti's work, *O mundo invisiuel: Cosmologia, sistema ritual e noçao de tempo no espiritismo* (Rio de Janeiro, 1968). The first two are solid sociological analyses of Kardecism in Brazil, with Umbanda as a counterpoint; studies solely dedicated to Kardecism, such as Cavalcanti's interesting and lucid book on Kardecist cosmogony, are few and far between.

Finally, one can mention the doctoral dissertation of J. Parke Ronshaw, "Sociological Analysis of Spiritism in Brazil" (University of Florida, 1969), which contains historical data and analyses, and Donald Warren, Jr.'s articles "The Portuguese Roots of Brazilian Spiritism," *Luso-Brazilian Review* 5 (December 1968): 3–33, and "Spiritism in Brazil" in *Journal of Inter-American Studies* 10 (1968): 393–405.

Lísias Nogueira Negrão

KAREN RELIGION. *See* Southeast Asian Religions, *article on* Mainland Cultures.

KARMAN. [*This entry consists of two articles.* Hindu and Jain Concepts *introduces the concept and discusses its development in Vedic, Brahmanic, Hindu, and Jain thought.* Buddhist Concepts *highlights the particular analysis of the term in the Buddhist tradition.*]

Hindu and Jain Concepts

As diverse as the culture of India may be, one common assumption undergirds virtually all major systems of South Asian religious thought and practice: a person's behavior leads irrevocably to an appropriate reward or punishment commensurate with that behavior. This, briefly stated, is the law of *karman*.

The importance of the idea of *karman* is not limited to the religions of the subcontinent. It is likely that no other notion from the sacred traditions of India has had more influence on the worldviews assumed by non-Indian cultures than that of *karman*, for in it lie the foundations of a wealth of astute ethical, psychological, metaphysical, and sacerdotal doctrines. Translations of the word (Pali, *kamma*; Tib., *las*; Chin., *yeh* or *yin-kuo*; Jpn., *gō* or *inga*) have for centuries been a key part of the religious lexica of the various canonical languages of Asia. Furthermore, the word *karma* (the nominative form of the Sanskrit *karman*) has in the last few generations also entered the vocabulary of European languages, appearing first in technical Indological works and more recently in popular or colloquial use as well.

The term is based on the Sanskrit verbal root *kṛ*, meaning "act, do, bring about," the idea being that one makes something by doing something; one creates by acting. It may be of interest to note that some linguists see the Indo-European root of the word *karman* (namely, **kwer*, "act") in the English word *ceremony*, which can mean either a combination of sacred acts performed according to prescribed norms or a system of proper behavior that keeps the world running smoothly. The same meanings hold, in part, for *karman*. Originally referring to properly performed ritual activity, the notion was ethicized to include the larger meaning of any correct activity in general. Granting this view, the religious, social, and medical philosophers of India, particularly those intrigued by the doctrines of rebirth and of the origins of suffering (but also of the related problems of the source of personality and the justification of social status), expanded the meaning of the term. Under this new understanding, *karman* came to denote the impersonal and transethical system under which one's current situation in the world is regarded as the fruit of seeds planted by one's behavior and dispositions in the past, and the view that in all of one's present actions lie similar seeds that will have continuing and determinative effect on one's life as they bear fruit in the future.

The language here ("fruit," Skt., *phala*; "seed," *bīja*; etc.) is remarkably consistent throughout the long history of Indian religions. Some scholars have seen in it evidence of an agricultural ecology and value system that knows that a well-planted field yields good crops; that the land will give birth repeatedly if healthy seeds find in it a place to take hold and grow; that the apparent death of a plant in the fall is merely the process by which that plant assures its own renewal in the spring; and that life, therefore, is a periodic cycle of death and then rebirth determined by the healthy or unhealthy conditions of former births.

Possibly originating, therefore, in the agrarian experience of aboriginal India, the notion of an impersonal law of cause and effect subsequently pervaded the (often decidedly un-agricultural) ideology of Vedic ritualism, Yoga, the Vedānta, Ayurvedic medicine, and sectarian theism, and it stands as a central theme in the lessons recorded in the scriptures of Jainism and Buddhism. This is not to say that all of these traditions share the same teachings regarding the nature of action, the desirability of the result, and the effective mechanism that links the two. On the contrary, views vary widely in this regard. This means that there is no single South Asian notion of *karman*.

Early Ritual Notions. The poets who composed the sacred hymns of the Vedic Mantrasaṃhitās in the twelfth century BCE sang praises to the gods in reverential, supplicatory, and sometimes cajoling tones. Deities were powerful beings who held control over the lives of the people on earth but who nevertheless could be propitiated and pleased with sacrificial gifts and who enjoyed staged battles, chariot racing, gambling, and riddles. The Vedic Brāhmaṇas (900 BCE and the following few centuries) present images of elaborate priestly actions performed in order to offer these gifts and entertainment to the gods, to the advantage—wealth, prestige, immortality, and so on—of the person who paid for the expert services of the priests and their assistants. This sacerdotal performance was known as *karman*, the "action" of the ritual undertaken to gain a particular end. The rites were often quite expensive and the rewards not always immediately realized, so the patrons were reassured that their support of the ceremony would benefit them sometime in the future.

Arguments in defense of this notion that the reward for one's present ritual action is reaped in the future laid part of the foundation for later doctrines of rebirth and transmigration. This development can be seen in the use of synonyms or near-synomyms for the word *karman*. For instance, the term *iṣṭāpūrta* ("the fulfillment of that which is desired") refers to a kind of package, as it were, that holds all of one's deeds and that precedes a person to the world to come, where it establishes a place for him (see *Ṛgveda* 10.14.8). The Brāhmaṇas also describe the rewards as events that will happen in the future and describe the sacrifice as *apūrva-karman*, "action the results of which have not yet been seen."

Evidence suggests that in the early Brahmanic period the gods were generally free to accept or reject the gifts and therefore were not bound to respond in kind. Over time, though, the Pūrva Mīmāṃsā philosophers came to view the ritual in magical terms: if the priest performed the prescribed actions correctly, he controlled the gods, who were forced by the devices of the ritual to respond in the way the priest desired. Conversely, the priest's improper performance of the ceremony led to the certain ruin of him or his patron. *Karman* for these thinkers therefore did not involve divine will; it was part of an impersonal metaphysical system of cause and effect in which action brought an automatic manipulated response. The Brahmanic notion of *karman* thus centers on the view that a person is born into a world he has made for himself (see *Kauṣītakī Brāhmaṇa* 26.3, for example). This meant that every action in the ritual was important and that every action brought a result of one kind or another, and did so irrevocably.

Renunciant Notions. The renunciant tradition provided two principal contexts for the elaboration of the notion of *karman.* The Upaniṣads speculate, among other topics, on human action and its consequences in this and in subsequent lives; the Yoga literature provides a more systematic and pragmatic approach to liberation from the consequences of action.

Karman in Upaniṣadic thought. The composers of the major Upaniṣads (eighth to fifth century BCE) generally saw two paths open to the deceased at the time of death. The lower path, one on which the person eventually returns to earth in a subsequent birth, is described as the "way of the fathers" *(pitṛyāna)* and is traveled by those who perform the rituals in hopes of material gain. The higher path, the way of the gods (*devayāna*), is one that does not lead to rebirth on earth and is taken by those who have renounced worldly ends and practice austerities in the forest. *Bṛhadāraṇyaka Upaniṣad* 4.4.4 describes the process with the doctrine that, as a goldsmith forms a new and more beautiful form out of a rough nugget, the soul leaves the body at death and fashions for itself a new and fairer body. Human happiness is said to be a fraction of the bliss known by a celestial man-spirit *(manuṣya-gandharva)*, which in turn is meagre compared to that of a *karma-deva*, a human who has become a god by his actions (see *Taittirīya Upaniṣad* 2.8 and *Bṛhadāraṇyaka Upaniṣad* 4.3.33).

Seeking to understand the Brahmanic notion of the ritual in anthropological rather than sacerdotal terms, the Upaniṣadic sages taught that all physical and mental activity was an internal reflection of cosmic processes. Accordingly, they held that *every* action, not only those performed in the public ritual, leads to an end. One's behavior in the past has determined one's situation in the present, and the totality of one's actions in the present construct the conditions of one's future. Thus, the *Bṛhadāraṇyaka Upaniṣad*'s assertion that "truly, one becomes good through good action, bad by bad" (3.2.13) represents the encompassing Upaniṣadic scope of *karman.* From this notion arises the idea that one's worldly situation and personality are determined by one's desire: that is, one's desire affects one's will; one's will leads one to act in certain ways; and, finally, one's actions bring proportionate and appropriate results.

For the most part the composers of the major Upaniṣads disdained actions performed for the resulting enjoyment of worldly pleasures, for such material pursuit necessarily leads from one birth to another in an endless cycle characterized by dissatisfaction and, thus, to unhappiness. "The tortuous passage from one birth to another [*sāmparāya*] does not shine out to who is childish, careless and deluded by the glimmer of wealth," the Lord of the Dead tells Naciketas. "Thinking 'this is the world, there is no other,' he falls again and again under my power" (*Kaṭha Upaniṣad* 2.6).

The only way to break this turning wheel of life and death *(saṃsāra)* was to free oneself of the structures and processes of *karman.* The composers of the Upaniṣads understood this liberation to take place through the practice of *yoga* or through the intervention of a personal supreme deity who lived beyond the karmic realm. [*See also* Upaniṣads.]

Karman in classical Yoga. The practioners and philosophers of classical Yoga agreed with the Upaniṣadic idea that one's circumstances are determined by one's actions. Like some of those sages they, too, understood *karman* to involve what might be called a substance that leads the soul from one body to another as it moves from birth to birth. Patañjali's *Yoga Sūtra* (the pertinent passages of which were composed in the second century BCE) analyzes the ways in which such transfer takes place. Any act *(karman)* performed as a result of desire creates what is known as *karmāśaya*, the "accumulation for receptacle of *karman*" that is either beneficial or harmful depending on the quality of the act itself. *Karmāśaya* can be understood as a kind of seed that will mature either in one's present life or, if not fully ripened, in another lifetime *(adṛṣṭajanman)*. That seed includes one's personal dispositions *(saṃskāra)*, including those themes or memories imprinted at the unconscious levels of one's mind *(vāsanā)* and that serve as the source of the five habitual personal "afflictions" *(kleśa)* of ignorance, ego, hatred, and the will to live (see *Yoga Sūtra* 2.3). The *kleśa*s tend to reinforce the ignorant notion that activity directed to some end is desirable, and in so doing are the main reason that people stay trapped in the wheel of life and death. If a person dies before all of his accumulated *karmāśaya* is gone, that karmic residue joins with his unfulfilled thoughts, desires, and feelings in search of a new body whose nature is receptive to his pertinent dispositions, which it then enters (*āpūra*, literally, "making full") and through which the unripened seeds can come to fruit. A person with a passion for food thus may be reborn as a hog. One eventually gets what one wants, even though it may take more than one lifetime to do so. That's the problem. For in order to get what one wants one needs a body, and in order to have a body one needs to be born. Birth leads to death, death leads to birth. Unless the cycle is broken it never stops.

Without values directed towards the attainment of worldly goals a person will cease to behave according to one's desire, and without that desire no karmic residue, no unmatured seeds, can accumulate. Classical Yoga, as represented by Patañjali, presents the *yogin* with a set of practices by which that person can be free of the karmic process. In these exercises the meditator reduces the power of the *kleśa*s by performing actions that are opposed to their fulfillment. Traditionally this meant the practice of ascetic renunciation of physical pleasures. Thorough renunciation makes it impossible for new *kleśa*s to arise, and through more and more subtle meditations the *kleśa*s that remain from the past are diluted so much that they no longer produce any *karmāśaya*s. At this point the person *(puruṣa)* within the *yogin* no longer needs a body because it no longer has any unripened *karmāśaya,* and at the death of the present body the person no longer migrates to another life. The *puruṣa* is liberated from the entrapping demands of habitual afflictions and experiences *kaivalya,* "autonomy." [*See also* Yoga.]

Ontological or Materialistic Notions. The terms *bīja* (seed), *karmāśaya* (karmic residue), *vāsanā* (pychological traces) and others suggest a general South Asian notion that some "thing" is created and left behind by one's actions. At times the Upaniṣads describe *karman* almost as a substance that not only influences one's subsequent births but can also be passed from one person to another, especially from father to son. The *Kauṣītakī Brāhmaṇa Upaniṣad*, for example, tells a dying father to transfer his *karman* to his son, saying "let me place my deeds in you" (2.15). The son is then able to perform atoning actions such that the father is free of the consequences of his own improper behavior (see *Bṛhadāraṇyaka Upaniṣad* 1.5.17).

Ritual practices in which one either supplements or attenuates the *karman* acquired by one's ancestors take place in various Vedic *śrauta* and Hindu *pūjā* ceremonies that have been practiced from the time of the Brāhmaṇas and Dharmaśāstras. They appear, for example, in the postclassical *sāpiṇḍīkaraṇa* and *bali* rites in which balls of rice and other foods that are said to contain an ancestor's *karman* are ceremonially offered to the deceased.

Indian medical texts of the Āyurveda traditions agree that *karman* is a material entity of sorts that can be passed from one generation to the next. The *Caraka Saṃhitā* (first century CE), for example, maintains that *karman* resides in substance *(dravya)* and is one of the causes of physical health and disease. Accordingly, *karman* is seen as an important factor in medical etiologies and in techniques of fertility in which a father and mother perform certain actions so that the embryo (*garbha*, sometimes called the "seed") can acquire the most desirable or auspicious karmic elements and thus be born a strong person with admirable character.

By far the most assertive thinkers concerning the material nature of *karman*, however, are the Jains, who since the sixth century BCE have followed the teachings and traditions surrounding the founder of Jainism, Mahāvīra Vardhamāna. Central to Jain doctrine in general is the notion that the living entity (*jīva*, "life") within a person is by nature blissful and intelligent. Traditional teachings sometimes describe the *jīva* as a pure, colorless, and transparent energy and maintain that all of the infinite creatures in the universe—including animals, plants, and rocks as well as human beings—possess such an ethereal crystalline life within them. But, also according to Jain thought, the spatial world occupied by the *jīva*s is permeated with a kind of subtle dust or stained liquid that has existed since time immemorial and that "sticks," as it were, to each *jīva*, soiling and infecting its original nature with a color *(leśya)*, the hue and intensity of which corresponds to the amount of desire, hatred, and love with which that being performs any given action. This glutinous blurry stuff is *karman*. Virtuous and selfless action attracts to the *jīva* the lighter and less cloudy colors, which hardly obscure the *jīva*'s nature at all, compared to the dark and muddy colors brought together by acts engendered in self-concern. The amount and color of the *karman* that adheres to any given *jīva* determines the conditions and circumstances of its subsequent rebirth. Competitive, violent, self-infatuated people carry the heavy weight of *karman* and will sink downwards through their many lifetimes as demons or as animals who live by eating others; gentle, caring, and compassionate beings gradually cleanse their *jīva* of its encumbering *karman* and rise through rebirth towards enlightenment.

Even unintentional violence, however, burdens the *jīva* with the stain of *karman*. Thus, Jain tradition demands absolute *ahiṃsā*, a complete unwillingness to kill or injure any and all living beings. Jains, therefore, are absolute vegetarians, some of whom in their attempts to sustain themselves with food in which no living creature has met a violent death refuse even to pick the living fruit from a tree, waiting instead until it falls of its own (ripened) accord.

A *jīva* finds release from the bonds of rebirth only when it stops accumulating new *karman* and removes that *karman* already there. This is described as a long and arduous task, one that takes many lifetimes to complete. Although the necessary discipline can be practiced by lay members of the community, traditionally only renunciate Jains can undergo the physical austerities and rigorous mental concentration that are needed to remove the *karman* from their *jīvas*. One who through many ascetic lifetimes has completely removed the cloud of *karman* from his *jīva* is known as a *siddha* (one who has "succeeded") or a *kevalin*, an omniscient and enlightened being. The paradigmatic ascetic here is Mahāvīra Vardhamāna, who, according to Digambara tradition, wandered naked and homeless as he practiced nonviolence, truthfulness, honesty, renunciation of possessions, and sexual abstinence. [*See also* Jainism *and the biography of Mahāvīra*.]

A Theistic Notion: Karman in the Bhagavadgītā. Some thinkers in ancient India found practical problems in the renunciate attitude towards *karman*. For example, if all actions, including good actions, bring consequences, don't all actions, including good actions, lead inevitably to rebirth? Does this mean that one must renounce all actions, even good ones? Isn't renunciation itself an act, and therefore constitutive of karmic residue; isn't the desire for liberation still a desire? Doesn't the final end of renunciation of all action result in willful death, since one must actively eat and breathe in order to live; yet isn't suicide itself considered an evil and thus entrapping action?

The author or authors of the *Bhagavadgītā* (c. first century BCE) seem to have been aware of these problems. Generally supportive of the value of disciplined meditation (see *Bhagavadgītā* 6.10–6.13), those philosophers nevertheless saw the impossibility of complete inaction, for "even the maintenance of your physical body requires activity" (3.8).

Noting that one cannot remain inactive, and aligning themselves with the social philosophy presented in the Dharmaśāstras and related Hindu orthodox literatures on law outlining specific responsibilities incumbent on people in various occupations and stages of life, the authors of the *Bhagavadgītā* present the idea that one should perform those actions that are obligatory *(niyata)* to one's position in society *(svadharma)*, and the better one performs those actions the purer their result (*Bhagavadgītā* 18.23, 2.31). Personal preference should have nothing to do with one's duties. In fact, to perform someone else's responsibilities well is worse than performing one's own badly (3.35, 18.45–48).

The *Bhagavadgītā* justifies its teaching with a theological argument: social responsibilities arise from divine law (*Bhagavadgītā* 3.15a). Therefore, priests should perform rituals, soldiers should fight battles, and merchants should conduct the affairs of business (18.41–44) not because they want to but because it is ordained by God to do so. If done properly, such action cannot be considered evil and therefore does not lead to rebirth.

But if action itself does not lead to rebirth, then what does? The authors of the *Bhagavadgītā* supported the general South Asian notion that karmic action arises from desire; from this idea they developed the doctrine that it is the desire for certain results, and not the action itself, that gives rise to the mechanism of karmic processes. For these sages, freedom from the bonds of *karman* comes not when one ceases acting but when one acts without desire, when one renounces the attachment one has for the fruits of one's actions (*Bhagavadgītā* 4.19–23).

According to the *Bhagavadgītā* and similar devotional texts, this renunciation of desire for specific ends can be obtained only through *bhakti-yoga*, the loving surrender to God's will. Ritual actions properly performed are meritorious, and ascetic meditation leads to release. But these two modes of action either require wealth or are difficult to perfect. Purportedly quoting Kṛṣṇa (that is, God) himself, the *Bhagavadgītā* offers a theological response to these difficulties: "Those who dedicate all of their actions [*karman*] to Me, intent on Me, with unwavering discipline, meditating on Me; those who revere Me—for those I am the Savior from the sea of the cycle of deaths" (12.6–12.7b); those who see their actions as God's actions and the results as God's will "are also liberated from the traps of *karman*" (*mucyanti te'pi karmabhiḥ*, 3.31d).

[*Theistic notions of* karman *are further discussed in* Bhagavadgītā *and* Bhakti. *For treatment of the complementary roles of* karman *and* dharma, *see* Dharma, *article on* Hindu Dharma.]

BIBLIOGRAPHY

Bhattacharyya, Haridas. "The Doctrine of Karma," *Visva-Bharati Quarterly* 3 (1925–1926): 257–258.

Bhattacharyya, Haridas. "The Brahmanical Concept of Karma." In *A. R. Wadia; Essays in Philosophy Presented in His Honor*, edited by Sarvepalli Radhakrishnan et al., pp. 29–49. Madras, 1954.

Bhattacharyya, Kalidas. "The Status of the Individual in Indian Metaphysics." In *The Status of the Individual East and West*, edited by Charles A. Moore, pp. 29–49. Honolulu, 1968.

Dilger, D. *Der indischer Seelungswanderungsglaube*. Basel, 1910.

Falke, Robert. *Die Seelenwanderung*. Berlin, 1913.

Farquhar, J. N. "Karma: Its Value as a Doctrine of Life," *Hibbert Journal* 20 (1921–1922): 20–34.

Glasenapp, Helmuth von. *The Doctrine of Karman in Jain Philosophy*. Translated by G. Barry Gifford. Bombay, 1942.

Hall, Rodney. *The Law of Karma*. (Canberra, 1968).

Henseler, Éric de. *L'âme et le dogme de la transmigration dans les livres sacrés de l'Inde ancienne*. Paris, 1928.

Kalghatgi, T. G. *Karma and Rebirth*. Ahmadabad, 1972.

Keyes, Charles F. and E. Valentine Daniel, eds. *Karma: An Anthropological Inquiry*. Berkeley, 1983.

O'Flaherty, Wendy Doniger, ed. *Karma and Rebirth in Classical Indian Traditions*. Berkeley, 1980.

Silburn, Lilian. *Instant et cause: Le discontinu dans la pensée philosophique de l'Inde*. Paris, 1955.

Steiner, Rudolf. *Die Offenbarungen des Karma: Ein Zyklus von elf Vorträgen* Dornach, 1956.

William K. Mahony

Buddhist Concepts

As noted in the previous article, South Asian religious traditions have held a variety of positions regarding the notion that one's behavior and thoughts determine one's destiny. Buddhist texts recorded in Pali in the centuries following the death of the historical Buddha, which occurred about 480 BCE according to the most common dating, imply that Buddhist thinkers of that time were aware of five general and contending philosophical views regarding the cause of a person's fate, pleasant or unpleasant, in this world. The doctrine of no causality (Pali, *adhiccasamuppanna-vāda*) held that a person's good or bad fortune has no relation to direct or indirect causes or conditions; all fates, whether fortunate or unfortunate, take place accidentally. This doctrine recommended the appreciation of casual good fortune and the enjoyment of its momentary pleasure, an epicurian position that was advocated by the materialists. [*See also* Cārvāka.] The doctrine of the combination of bodily elements *(sangatibhāva-hetu-vāda)*, also based on materialism, maintained that the good or bad combination of the physical elements of earth, water, fire, and wind in a human being's body decides one's fortune throughout one's life. (In some ways this idea resembles the temperament theory in ancient Greece.) The doctrine of cause through lineage *(abhijāti-hetu-vāda)* argued that a person's fortune has been predetermined by the caste into which he or she was born. The doctrine of divine intention *(issaranimmāna-hetu-vāda)* centered on the idea that a person's happiness or unhappiness is determined by the gods or by a supreme deity who created and controls the universe and all human lives. Those who held this notion did not recognize the possibility for human freedom in the realm of cause and effect. Finally, the doctrine of fatalism *(pubbekata-hetu-vāda)* stated that a person's happiness or unhappiness in the present life is determined by one's good or bad actions in a previous life and that accordingly, a person should be resigned to the circumstances of his present life. Those who argued for this position, like those who held the doctrine of divine intention, did not allow for the possibilities of one's intentions in performing an act. [*See also* Pratītya-samutpāda.]

The composers of the Upaniṣads, the earliest of which predate the time of the historical Buddha, accepted and rejected various elements of these five doctrines. They taught that the fate of an individual is brought about by one's own behavior and intentions. Such physical or mental "action," which determines one's fate, was known as *karman*. One's deeds, either good or bad, were known as one's "deed *karman*"; one's motivations and thoughts were described as "mental *karman*."

Early Buddhist thinkers aligned their teachings on *karman* to some degree with these Upaniṣadic ideas. The Buddhist doctrines of the causal efficacy of action *(karma-vāda)*, behavior *(kiriya-vāda)*, and of effort *(viriya-vāda)* advocate the freedom of a human being's intentions and his diligence and effort in reaching the Buddhist ideal. However, whereas the Upaniṣadic philosophers were primarily interested in the karmic source of specific states of being, early Buddhists emphasized the retribution *(vipāka)* or fruit *(phala)* of those actions and intentions. According to early Buddhist thinkers, the more good *karman* a person accumulates, the happier he or she will become and the better the recompense he will receive. Similarly, the more bad *karman* a person accumulates, the unhappier he will be and the worse the influence he will receive.

According to Buddhist doctrine appearing in various Sanskrit (Abhidharma) sources, *karman* is dependent upon three elements: *cetanā* (volition) refers to the intention or purpose a person has when he or she begins to act; *samudācāra* (actual behavior) or *vijñapti karman* ("expressed" action) comprises the physical actions, both good and bad, that are performed by one's body or through one's speech; *vāsanā* (impression or residual effect) and *saṃskāra* (habit or disposition) are the effects or traces in one's life of those good and bad deeds one has previously performed with one's body and speech. In this last sense, *karman* is also known as "unexpressed" *(avijñapti)*, since the effect is not apparent to others. Early schools of Buddhist philosophy held that it is the accumulation of this third element that shapes one's character, constitution, and general personality, for it is through *avijñapti-karman* that good habits *(śīla)* and bad habits *(anuśaya)* are created. Hīnayāna schools viewed *avijñapti-karman* in both moral and physical terms and described it as a "seed," or germ *(bīja)*, or as an accumulation *(upacaya)* of characteristics that determine one's present and future situation.

Varieties of Karman. Buddhist philosophers, especially those teaching in the context of Abhidharma thought, recognized several varieties of *karman*.

The most inclusive category of *karman* is defined in terms of its moral value. Thus, there are said to be ten forms of good or meritorious activity *(kuśala-karman)*. These are characterized as (a) refraining from all forms of taking life; (b) refraining from taking what is not given; (c) refraining from sexual misconduct; (d) refraining from lying; (e) refraining from slandering; (f) refraining from abusive language; (g) refraining from gossip; (h) refraining from covetousness; (i) refraining from ill will; and (j) generally maintaining healthy views. The ten bad or abominable forms of activity *(akuśala-karman)* are described as the opposite of the ten forms of meritorious actions: taking life; theft; sexual transgression; lying; and so on. Buddhist scholiasts also see a type of action that is neither good nor bad *(avyākṛta-karman).*

Another variety of *karman* is distinguished by the specific mechanism of action. That is, of those actions listed above, the first three pertain to the physical body *(kāya-karman);* the next four, to speech *(vacī-karman);* and the final three, to thought *(mano-karman).*

A third distinction is made in terms of the value of "tainted" *karman (sāsrava-karman),* which is acquired in the phenomenal or profane world, and "pure" *karman (anāsrava-karman),* sublime or sacred action that extinguishes tainted *karman.* Types of tainted *karmas* include nonmeritorious action *(apuṇya-karman),* meritorious action *(puṇya-karman),* and steady or firm *karman (aniñjya-karman).* This last is the good *karman* acquired through the proper practice of meditation.

Buddhist thinkers understood a fourth variety of *karman* in terms of an action's good or bad results. The worst *karmas,* called the *pañca ānantarya karmāṇi* ("five *karmas* of immediate retribution") were *mātṛghata* ("matricide"), *pitṛghata* ("patricide"), *arhadvadha* ("killing an *arhat*"), *saṃghabheda* ("causing a schism in the *saṃgha*"), and *rudhirotpādana* ("causing blood to flow from the body of a Buddha"). "Black" (that is, bad) *karman,* which engenders miserable (black) results, is known as *kṛṣṇa kṛṣṇa-vipāka karman.* "White" (good) *karman* engenders happy (white) results, or *śukla śukla-vipāka karman.* "Both black and white" *karman,* which gives rise to both miserable and good results, is *kṛṣṇa-sukla kṛṣṇasukla-vipāka karman.* "Neither black nor white" *karman* engenders no results, although it leads to the extinguishing of the preceding three types of *karman,* and is known as *akṛṣna-aśukla avipāka karma karmakṣayāya saṃvartate.* This last type is the pure *karman* of the saints, which is referred to above.

Buddhist philosophers distinguished a fifth variety of *karman* according to whether its results or fruits will be experienced in this present life *(dṛṣṭadharma-vedanīya-karman),* in the next life *(upapadya-vedanīya-karman),* in the lives following the next life *(aparya-paryāya-vedanīya-karman),* or in an undetermined life *(aniyata-vedanīya-karman).*

A final variety of *karman* relates to the communal scope of action and causation. Most of the *karman* described thus far relates to the individual and may therefore be called *asādhāraṇa-karman* (specific or idiosyncratic *karman.*) However, all of the categories may be applied to one's family, lineage, ethnic tradition, region, and nation, since any individual's behavior and thoughts are also bound to other people's actions and ideas. This "communal" or "common" *karman* is known as *sādhāraṇa-karman.*

Inevitability and Changeability of Karman. The mechanism of *karman* is generally believed to assure inevitable results gained through one's actions and thoughts. Accordingly, Buddhist philosophers hold, for the most part, that a person's present circumstances in life are determined by one's past actions, the fruits of which are inevitably experienced until that person "uses up" all of his acquired *karman* and the law of causation has run its course.

It is believed, however, that a person's *karman* may be altered in three ways. First, by repenting of previous misdeeds and making a habit of leading a good life, one performs good deeds, which themselves become good *karman* and reduce or exterminate the power of bad *karman.* Second, if an individual's close relative, a monk, or a nun chants sacred verses or holds a religious service for him, then such assistance—in addition to his own good deeds—lightens or destroys his own bad *karman.* Third, if a relative or religious specialist chants sacred verses after a person's death, such actions, themselves meritorious, will help alleviate the dead person's accumulated *karman.*

The assumption behind the idea of these corrective actions is that good *karman* can commute or wipe out bad *karman.* Such an idea, however, does not in any way deny the doctrine of *karman*—the law of cause and effect—as a whole. It does, however, bear upon the general question as to whether the merit from wholesome actions can be transferred to others. On this point, the tradition abets a variety of views. [*See also* Merit, *article on* Buddhist Concepts.]

Karman and Transmigration. To some Buddhist philosophers, the theory of *karman* appeared to violate in some way the central Buddhist teaching that there is no immortal soul, that nothing in any realm is stationary or unchanging. According to Buddhist doctrine, all phenomena in the world appear and disappear in a continually changing flux resulting from the ongoing causal chain known as *pratītya-samutpāda,* or "dependent co-origination." But does not the doctrine of causal reward and punishment for actions committed in a previous life presume the existence of a soul to which karmic residue accrues?

The general Buddhist response to such criticism is to

assert the reality of the *process* of rebirth but to deny that this process is supported by an underlying substance, or "soul." Rebirth is likened in some texts to the process of a flame being transmitted from one source to the next: the second flame is neither identical with nor totally different from its source. In terms of the process of rebirth, the karmic legacy of past actions gives rise to ever new psychophysical formations in accordance with the workings of *pratītya-samutpāda*. Seen in this way, sentient beings are but a collocation of karmically determined factors. But what is it that accounts for the continuity of the flux that we experience as the person?

Buddhist thinkers formulated a variety of responses to this question, among which two in particular deserve special mention. According to the Abhidharma speculations of the Sarvāstivādins, a special *dharma* (constituent of reality) called *prāpti* ("acquisition") continually remanifests itself in the stream of the elements and serves to unite the particular karmic stream as a seemingly discrete and coherent entity. The Sautrāntikas rejected this theory but asserted the existence of a latent or subtle consciousness that is a repository of past experiences. This notion, possibly an adumbration of the "storehouse consciousness" *(ālaya-vijñāna)* of the Yogācāra thinkers, was believed to preserve the karmic seeds *(bīja)* of actions until they "ripen" into new elements in the series. As such, this consciousness constitutes the continuity of the series as a whole. In later, Mahāyāna thought, the continuity of the individual was supported by recourse to a variety of similar notions.

[*See also* Buddhist Philosophy; Sarvāstivāda; Sautrāntika; *and* Dharma, *article on* Buddhist Dharma and Dharmas.]

BIBLIOGRAPHY

Pali sources on *karman* are conveniently abstracted in Henry Clarke Warren's *Buddhism in Translation* (1896; reprint, New York, 1976) and E. J. Thomas's *The History of Buddhist Thought*, 2d ed. (1933; New York, 1963). For a canonical account, see the various passages in the *Kathāvattu*, translated by Shwe Zan Aung and C. A. F. Rhys Davids as *Kathāvattu: Points of Controversy* (London, 1915). A more technical introduction to the theories of *karman* indigenous to other Buddhist schools, including Mahāyāna traditions, is Étienne Lamotte's "Le traité de l'acte de Vasubandhu: *Karmasiddhiprakaraṇa*," in *Mélanges chinois et bouddhiques* 4 (1934–1936): 151–288, with a useful summary by this eminent Buddhologist. Recent Japanese studies include two volumes devoted to articles on the topic: *Nihon bukkyōgakkai nenpō* 25 (March 1980) and *Gō shisō no kenkyū*, a special issue of *Bukkyōgaku seminaa* 20 (October 1974).

MIZUNO KŌGEN

KARO, YOSEF (1488–1575), Talmudic scholar, codifier of rabbinic law, and qabbalist. Yosef Karo (or Caro) grew up and lived in the century following the expulsion of the Jews from the Iberian Peninsula (first from Spain in 1492 by the Catholic rulers Ferdinand and Isabella, then from Portugal in 1497). It was a period of turmoil, major demographic shifts, messianic longings, and mystical revival. Karo was the scion of a family of illustrious scholars. Whether he was born in Toledo or whether his family had already left Spain for Turkey (either directly or via Portugal) before the expulsion is uncertain. His father and first teacher, Efrayim, died when Yosef was still very young, and his place was taken by Yosef's uncle, Yitsḥaq Karo, to whom he frequently and respectfully refers in his writings as "my uncle and master."

We do not know exactly at which schools Yosef Karo studied, but most of the first half of his life was spent in the Balkan provinces of the Ottoman empire (Salonika, but mainly Adrianople and Nikopol). The influx of Iberian Jewish (Sefardic) refugees had turned Ottoman Turkey into one of the most important centers of sixteenth-century Jewry, and Jewish communities and academies of learning were flourishing. In Salonika Karo also met Yosef Taytazak, one of the leading Talmudic scholars and qabbalistic charismatics of his generation, as well as the young ex-Marrano enthusiast and visionary Shelomoh Molkho. The latter's death at the stake in 1532, after his ill-fated mission to the pope, left a deep impression on Karo and no doubt inspired his unfulfilled desire to die a martyr's death. (In fact he died in Safad at the ripe age of eighty-seven.)

In addition to the academies of rabbinic learning, circles of qabbalistic and mystical pietists also flourished in the various Jewish centers of the Ottoman empire, especially in the Balkans, and Karo and his friend and disciple Shelomoh Alkabets were among their most prominent figures. These circles undoubtedly were the seedbed of the great mystical, and subsequently messianic, revival that took place in Safad in Galilee and from there swept over world Jewry. Because of the deaths of his wives, Karo married at least three times and had several children, of whom three survived him.

The dates of Karo's biography and literary activity have to be pieced together from incidental references in his writings. By 1522 he was settled in Nikopol and already enjoyed a reputation as one of the foremost rabbinic scholars. In that year he began work on his monumental commentary on the code of the great Talmudist Ya'aqov ben Asher (1270–1343). He finished this work, the *Beit Yosef*, twenty years later in Safad. Whereas the classic and most complete code, that of

Moses Maimonides (Mosheh ben Maimon, 1135/8–1204), simply and clearly set forth the law without argument or discussion, Ya'aqov ben Asher's *Arba'ah ṭurim* (Four Rows, i.e., four main parts) also reviewed the opinions of earlier authorities. Such review may have been the reason why Karo chose this code as the basis of his commentary, which is, in fact, a complete digest of the whole relevant halakhic literature. Ya'aqov ben Asher's code, however, unlike that of Maimonides, omits all subjects not applicable in exile and after the destruction of the Temple (e.g., laws concerning the Temple, its priesthood, ritual, and sacrificial cult; legislation concerning kingship, the Sanhedrin, the Jubilee year, and so on). On the basis of his *Beit Yosef,* Karo subsequently produced the *Shulḥan 'arukh* (Set Table, or Short Book, as he himself called it). This précis and synopsis soon established itself as the standard code of Jewish law and practice, especially after Mosheh Isserles of Cracow (d. 1572) had added glosses incorporating the sometimes divergent customs of Ashkenazic Jewry. Since then Karo's code has served as the revered or, alternatively, reviled symbol of orthodox rabbinic Judaism. Karo also wrote a commentary, *Kesef mishneh,* on the code of Maimonides, supplementing the earlier commentary *Maggid mishneh* by the fourteenth-century Spanish scholar Vidal of Tolosa.

Many *responsa* of Karo are also extant. Although of less historical influence than the aforementioned works, they throw much light on the social history of the period, in addition to illustrating Karo's standing as a leading Talmudic authority.

In Safad an attempt was also made—probably inspired by the messianic temper of the age—by one of the foremost Talmudic authorities, Ya'aqov Berab, to renew full rabbinical ordination, which had lapsed in the first centuries of the common era. Karo was one of the four scholars ordained by Berab, but the initiative proved abortive, mainly because of the opposition of the scholars in Jerusalem.

It was probably mystical and messianic ideology that prompted many qabbalists and devout scholars to move from the Diaspora to the Holy Land. Around 1536 Karo, too, realized his long-standing intention and settled in Safad in upper Galilee, which soon became a center of intense mystical and devotional life. The leading qabbalists of the time had converged there, among them Mosheh Cordovero (who belonged to Karo's intimate circle) and Isaac Luria. Karo, like most rabbis of his generation, was also a qabbalistic scholar but, in addition, led a somewhat unusual (though by no means unique) charismatic life. According to various reports, Karo was visited every night by a heavenly mentor who, in the form of what psychology would describe as "automatic speech," revealed to him qabbalistic mysteries, exhortations to ascetic practice, and other matters related to his personal life and to his Talmudic studies. Afterward Karo wrote down the communications received from his celestial *maggid* ("speaker"), who identified himself (or perhaps herself) as the heavenly archetype of the Mishnah. Among Karo's writings there is, therefore, a "mystical diary," printed later in edited form under the title *Maggid mesharim.* Unconvincing attempts have been made to deny the authenticity of the diary, probably because scholarly rationalism, especially in the nineteenth century, could not come to terms with the idea that the great Talmudist, legal scholar, and codifier Yosef Karo was also an ascetic qabbalist and mystical enthusiast, subject to paranormal experiences. While as a qabbalist Karo was less outstanding than many of his Safad contemporaries, the existence of the *Maggid mesharim,* in the shadow, as it were, of the *Beit Yosef* and the *Shulḥan 'arukh,* is indicative of the complexities of rabbinic Judaism and of the role that Qabbalah played in it, especially in the sixteenth century.

BIBLIOGRAPHY

Twersky, Isadore. "The *Shulḥan 'Aruk:* Enduring Code of Jewish Law." In *The Jewish Expression,* edited by Judah Goldin, pp. 322–343. New York, 1970.

Werblowsky, R. J. Zwi. "Caro, Joseph ben Ephraim." In *Encyclopaedia Judaica.* Jerusalem, 1971.

Werblowsky, R. J. Zwi. *Joseph Karo: Lawyer and Mystic.* 2d ed. Philadelphia, 1980.

R. J. Zwi Werblowsky

KARUṆĀ, normally translated as "compassion," is a term central to the entire Buddhist tradition. When linked with *prajñā* ("wisdom") it constitutes one of the two pillars of Buddhism. *Karuṇā* is frequently described as the love for all beings, as exemplified by a mother's love for a child. However, *karuṇā* is quite unlike conventional "love" (Skt., *priya, kāma, tṛṣṇā*), which is rooted in dichotomous thinking *(vijñāna, vikalpa)* and centered on self-concern. Love in this latter sense is egoistic, possessive, clouded by ignorance *(avidyā),* and easily subject to its opposite passion, hate.

In contrast, *karuṇā* is manifested in the non-dichotomous mode of *prajñā* that has broken through the self-other discrimination. Thus freed of self-centeredness, *karuṇā* is concerned only with the welfare of the other. The root meaning of *karuṇā* is said to be the anguished cry of deep sorrow that elicits compassion. Love in the conventional sense and compassion in its Buddhist sense may be loosely equated to *eros* and *agape,* respectively.

The life of Śākyamuni Buddha, especially his missionary work of forty-five years, is a manifestation *par excellence* of compassion. The cruciality of compassionate deeds for the attainment of supreme enlightenment is evident in the Jātakas, a collection of fables recounting the previous lives of the Buddha. The evolution of Buddhism in Asia and its spread throughout the world are, from a Buddhist point of view, none other than the unfolding of *karuṇā* in history.

In Buddhist doctrine, *karuṇā* is most commonly found as the second of the Four Immeasurable Attitudes *(catvāri apramāṇāni)* that are to be cultivated in meditative practice: *maitrī* ("friendliness"), *karuṇā* ("compassion"), *muditā* ("sympathetic joy"), and *upekṣā* ("equanimity"). Friendliness is said to give pleasure and happiness to others, compassion uproots pain and suffering, and sympathetic joy refers to one's joy for the happiness of others. Finally, equanimity frees one from attachment to these attitudes so that one may go forth to practice them in the service of all those in need.

The Mahāyāna scriptures, in spite of their diversity and differences, reveal the multifaceted dimensions of *karuṇā.* Central to all Mahāyāna texts is the *bodhisattva* vow, which puts the deliverance of all beings from *saṃsāra* (i.e., the cycle of births and deaths) before one's own deliverance. To put it in a more personal way, the vow states, "As long as there is one unhappy person in the world, my happiness is incomplete." The vow acknowledges the absolute equality of self and other *(parātmasamatā)* and the interchangeability of self and other *(parātmaparivartana),* such that one willingly takes on the suffering of others.

Philosophically, the justification of compassion is rooted in the notion of *śūnyatā* ("emptiness"), which sweeps away all divisions and discriminations—self and other, good and bad, like and dislike, and so forth—that are created by the arbitrary conceptions of the subjective mind. This clearing away of all forms of discursive thinking, originating from the fictive self, is none other than the working of *prajñā,* which is inseparable from *karuṇā.* Wisdom and compassion are said to be like two wheels of a cart or two wings of a bird.

Another important dimension of compassion that figures in Mahāyāna Buddhism is *mahākaruṇā* ("great compassion"). The adjective "great" connotes the transcendent nature of the compassion that is an essential quality of Buddhahood. All Buddhas—whether Śākyamuni, Vairocana, Bhaiṣajyaguru, Amitābha, Akṣobhya, and others—manifest great compassion. Amitābha (Jpn., Amida) Buddha, for example, reveals great compassion in his "primal vow" (Jpn., *hongan*), which states that his attainment of supreme Buddhahood was contingent upon the guarantee of the selfsame enlightenment for all beings who have faith in him. The practitioner of the Mahāyāna path, then, becomes a recipient of great compassion. In fact, it is said that the *bodhisattva* progresses on the path to enlightenment by virtue not of his own powers but of the powers of great compassion.

Historically, however, *karuṇā* is also manifested in such practical expressions as acts of generosity or charity *(dāna).* Among the *puṇyakṣetra* ("merit-fields", i.e., sources for creating religious merit) available to the devotee are compassion, wherein those in need, helpless beasts, and even insects are the objects of care and concern; gratitude, where parents, all sentient beings, rulers, and the Three Treasures (Buddha, Dharma, Sangha) are revered; the poor, where the destitute are fed, clothed, and housed; and animals, which are to be released from human enslavement. In premodern times, *karuṇā* was also understood and appreciated in much more concrete forms: planting fruit orchards and trees, digging bathing ponds, dispensing medicine, building bridges, digging wells along highways, making public toilets, establishing clinics and orphanages, teaching sericulture, farming methods and irrigation, building dikes and canals, and countless other welfare activities.

[*See also* Prajñā.]

BIBLIOGRAPHY

There is no single monograph on *karuṇā* in any Western language. Since it permeates Buddhist literature, it is best to go to the original sources. A good sampling may be found in Edwin A. Burtt's *The Teachings of the Compassionate Buddha* (New York, 1955). For the relationship between *śūnyatā* and compassion, see *The Holy Teaching of Vimalakīrti,* translated by Robert A. F. Thurman (University Park, Pa., 1976); for the working of wisdom, compassion, and *upāya* (liberative technique), see *The Threefold Lotus Sutra,* translated by Bunnō Katō and others (New York, 1975); and for the Primal Vow of compassion, see "The Larger Sukhāvatī-vyūha," in *Buddhist Mahāyāna Texts,* edited by E. B. Cowell, in "Sacred Books of the East," vol. 49 (1894; reprint, New York, 1969).

TAITETSU UNNO

KASHMIR ŚAIVISM. *See under* Śaivism.

KASHRUT, from the Hebrew word *kasher* (Eng., kosher), meaning "acceptable" (see *Est.* 8:15), denotes anything permitted by Jewish law for use. More specifically, it connotes the Jewish dietary laws. *Kashrut* pertains directly to (1) permitted and forbidden animals, (2) forbidden parts of otherwise permitted animals, (3) the method of slaughtering and preparing permitted animals, (4) forbidden food mixtures, and (5) proportions of food mixtures prohibited *ab initio* but permitted *ex post facto*. The rules of *kashrut* are derived from biblical statute, rabbinic interpretation, rabbinic legislation, and custom, as outlined below.

Biblical Law. According to the Bible, animals permitted for Jewish consumption must have fully cloven hooves and chew the cud (*Lv.* 11:3). Forbidden fowl are listed (*Lv.* 11:13–19, *Dt.* 14:11–18), as are forbidden insects (*Lv.* 11: 21–22, *Dt.* 14:20), but no characteristics are presented for determining their forbidden status. Fish must have fins and scales (*Lv.* 11:9, *Dt.* 14:9). Both Jews and gentiles are forbidden to eat flesh torn from a living animal (*Gn.* 9:3). Jews are not to consume the blood of permitted animals or the fat that covers their inner organs (*Lv.* 3:17, 7:23), that is, tallow or suet. Both this blood and this fat were to be offered on the altar of the Temple in the case of animals fit for sacrifice (e.g., *Lv.* 1:11–12). In the case of an animal permitted for ordinary consumption but not for sacrifice, the blood is to be poured on the ground and covered (*Lv.* 17:13, *Dt.* 12:16). The same is the case with the blood of fowl slaughtered for ordinary use. Animals that died of internal causes or that were killed by other animals are not to be consumed (*Ex.* 22:30). Also, the sciatic nerve of slaughtered animals is not to be eaten (*Gn.* 32:32). Finally, a kid is not to be cooked in the milk of its own mother (*Ex.* 23:29, 34:26; *Dt.* 14:21).

Rabbinic Interpretation. The rabbinic sources present a number of important and wide-reaching interpretations of these biblical laws which are seen as being themselves "oral Mosaic traditions" (*halakhah le-Mosheh mi-Sinai*). Thus, the rabbis determined that all birds of prey are forbidden for Jewish consumption (*Ḥul.* 5.6). The requirement that fish have fins and scales was qualified to include any fish that had scales at any point in its development even if they subsequently fell off (B.T., *Ḥul.* 66a-b). Milk from nonkosher animals was forbidden because it was judged as having the status of its source (*Bekh.* 1.2). An important exception to this rule is the honey of bees, which the rabbis determined does not have anything from the bee's body in it (see B.T., *Bekh.* 7b). The Babylonian Talmud presents criteria for distinguishing between permitted and forbidden fat (B.T., *Ḥul.* 49b). The blood drained from permitted animals and fowl after slaughter is covered with soil or ashes (*Ḥul.* 6.7).

Sheḥiṭah. The method of slaughtering permitted animals and fowl, known as *sheḥiṭah,* is not explicated in scripture but is seen as the prime example of a law commanded orally by Moses, to whom it was divinely revealed (B.T., *Ḥul.* 28a). The throat of the animal or bird must be slit with a perfectly smooth blade by a highly trained and supervised slaughterer (*shoḥeṭ*), who recites a blessing before cutting across the gullet and windpipe, severing the jugular. Detailed regulations govern the process; internal irregularities found in the lungs and other organs render even properly slaughtered animals unfit for consumption by Jews (*ṭerefah, Ḥul.* 3.1ff.). Various procedures are presented for draining the blood from the slaughtered animal, such as opening the arteries and veins, soaking and salting the meat, and broiling the meat over a flame. The laws that required Jews to eat meat slaughtered by a trained *shoḥeṭ* often determined where Jews could and could not live, and the presence of a kosher butcher has, in modern Jewish history, often symbolized the existence of an observant Jewish community.

Milk and meat. In the area of mixing milk and meat, rabbinic interpretation considerably expanded the biblical prohibition of simply not "cooking a kid in its mother's milk." The rabbis extended this law from animals fit to be offered on the altar (i.e., the lamb) to all animals and fowl in order to avoid any possible confusion (B.T., *Ḥul.* 104a). The Talmud interprets the threefold mention of this prohibition in the Pentateuch as entailing three distinct prohibitions: (1) eating, (2) cooking, and (3) deriving any monetary benefit from such a mixture of meat and milk. These prohibitions were elaborated by requirements for the use of separate dishes and utensils for meat foods and milk foods.

Rabbinical Legislation. In addition to the interpretations presented as ultimately Mosaic, the rabbis legislated additional rules in connection with those seen as biblical or traditional. All insects were forbidden because it was assumed that there was no longer to be found the necessary expertise to distinguish between those permitted and those forbidden. (*Ṭaz* [David ben Shemu'el ha-Levi] on *Shulḥan 'arukh, Yoreh de'ah* 85.1). Because of concern that gentiles might mix milk from nonkosher sources in the milk they sell to Jews, and that cheese from gentiles might contain nonkosher rennet, the precaution arose that milk and cheese must be prepared under Jewish supervision (*'A.Z.* 2.6). When this was not a likely possibility, however, this precaution was relaxed (*Responsa Tashbatz,* 4.1.32). The rabbis ruled that whereas one may follow a milk meal with a meat meal (except when hard cheese was eaten), after washing the hands and rinsing the mouth, one must wait a period of time before consuming a milk meal after a meat meal.

Because at times meat foods and milk foods are accidentally mixed, the rabbis developed a number of rules to determine whether or not the mixture could be used *ex post facto.* Generally, if the ratio is 60 to 1 or more, then the smaller substance is considered absorbed *(baṭel)* in the larger substance (B.T., *Ḥul.* 97b), provided the smaller substance neither changes the flavor of the larger substance, or gives the larger substance its actual form, and provided the smaller substance is not still found intact.

In order to discourage social contact between Jews and gentiles which might lead to intermarriage and assimilation (B.T., *'A.Z.* 36b; J.T., *Shab.* 3c), and because non-Jewish wine might have been produced for idolatrous purposes, the rabbis forbade Jews to drink wine or wine products made by non-Jews (B.T., *'A.Z.* 29b). However, because certain non-Jews were no longer considered idolators, and for other reasons, a number of authorities relaxed some (but not all) of these prohibitions. (See, for example, Maimonides' *Mishneh Torah,* Forbidden Foods 11.7; Mosheh Isserles's *Responsa,* no. 124.)

Custom. Custom determines a number of *kashrut* regulations, often being divergent in different communities. If certain fowl is not customarily eaten in a particular community, then this custom has the force of law there for no other reason. Although the hindquarters of permitted mammals may be eaten after the sciatic nerve has been totally removed, because of the great amount of energy and time required by this procedure, and because of the greater availability of meat in modern times, it has become the custom in Western Europe and America (but not in Israel) for the hindquarters of slaughtered animals to be sold to non-Jews as a regular practice rather than their being eaten by Jews.

Because of the rabbinic requirement for the internal examination of slaughtered animals *(bediqah)* to determine whether or not any abnormalities were present before slaughtering, elaborate methods of certification have evolved to guard against error or fraud. Often there are today competing rabbinical groups giving approval to different sources of kosher meat inasmuch as demands for reliability vary. Also, advances in food technology have led to the requirement that most processed foods be rabbinically certified *(hekhsher)* as not containing any forbidden substances.

Because of the custom in many Hungarian communities not to consume meat with certain irregularities nevertheless permitted by rabbinical legislation, the practice of certifying meat as *glaṭ kosher* (Yi., "smooth," without blemish) arose. In America, since the immigration of many Hungarian Orthodox Jews after World War II, *glaṭ kosher* has become a connotation of a stricter and more reliable level of *kashrut.*

Custom varies as to how long one is to wait after consuming meat before consuming milk. Moses Maimonides (1135/8–1204), followed by most other authorities, required a six-hour interval (*Mishneh Torah,* Forbidden Foods 9.28). Other authorities require a much shorter interval (B.T., *Ḥul.* 105a; Tos., s.v. *le-se'udata*). Customarily, eastern European Jews and Sefardic Jews and their descendants follow Maimonides; German Jews and their descendants wait three hours; and some Dutch Jews of Sefardic origin wait as little as slightly over one hour.

Orthodox and Conservative Judaism generally follow the same standards of *kashrut,* based on biblical, rabbinic, and customary rules. Conservative Judaism, however, tends to follow more lenient options within the law itself, such as not requiring cheeses manufactured in the United States to be certified kosher. Reform Judaism, because it does not regard *halakhah* in toto as authoritative, does not, therefore, regard *kashrut* as binding. Some Reform Jews as an individual option do follow *kashrut* completely, and others follow at least those rules that are biblically explicit.

Theological Interpretation. Although scholars have long recognized similarities between the biblical laws and other ancient Near Eastern customs, the laws of *kashrut* are traditionally considered to be *ḥuqqim,* that is, laws about which "Satan and the gentiles raise objections" (B.T., *Yoma'* 67b), namely laws without apparent reasons. Nevertheless, Jewish theologians have attempted to penetrate their deeper meaning to discover hidden reasons for them.

Because of the frequent biblical mention of holiness (*qedushah*) in connection with these laws (e.g., *Lv.* 11:44–45), a number of the rabbis emphasized that their very unintelligibility is a test of one's full acceptance of the authority of God's law (e.g., *Gn. Rab.* 44.1). However, even here the general reason of holiness is taken to mean separation of Jews from gentiles (*Lv.* 20:26). The importance of this general motif is seen in texts from the Maccabean period (c. 150 BCE), when the forced assimilation of Jews usually began with making them eat forbidden foods (*Dn.* 1:8, *2 Mc.* 7:1ff., *4 Mc.* 5:1ff.). In rabbinic law one is required to die as a martyr rather than violate *kashrut,* when the violation is clearly symbolic of general apostasy (B.T., *San.* 74a).

Some of the earliest and latest rationales for *kashrut* have emphasized the moral intent of having Jews refrain from foods that are either taken from cruel animals (*Letter of Aristeas,* 2nd ed., trans. Isidor Grunfeld, London, 1962, 2.314 ff.), or, also, symbolize bad moral traits (S. R. Hirsch, *Horeb,* Altona, 1837, chap. 68). Interestingly, early Christian criticism of Judaism argued that Jewish preoccupation with these laws actually leads to the neglect of morality (*Mk.* 7:14–23).

Maimonides saw the reasons for these laws as being based on both considerations of safe and healthy diet and the avoidance of some ancient idolatrous practices

(*Guide of the Perplexed,* ed. Shlomo Pines, Chicago, 1963, 3.48; cf. *Ḥinukh,* no. 92). This emphasis on physiological reasons is followed by other Jewish scholars, such as Shemu'el ben Me'ir in the twelfth century (e.g., on *Lv.* 11:30 in B.T., *Shab.* 86b) and Moses Nahmanides in the thirteenth century (e.g., on *Lv.* 11:9 in his *Commentary on the Torah*). Others, however, reject this whole approach as unduly secular (e.g., Avraham ben David of Posquières on *Sifra: Qedoshim,* ed. I.H. Weiss, 93d; *Zohar* 3:221a–b). The qabbalists, based on their view that every mundane act is a microcosm of the macrocosm of divine emanations *(sefirot),* worked out elaborate symbolic explanations of how the laws of *kashrut* reflect the cosmic economy and of their spiritual effect on human life. Among these mystics were, in the fourteenth century, Menaḥem Recanati, author of *Ṭa'amei ha-mitsvot* and, in the fifteenth century, Yitsḥaq Arama, author of *'Aqedat Yitsḥaq.* In these classic qabbalistic treatments of *kashrut,* forbidden foods were seen as imparting the cosmic impurity of the demonic forces that work against the godhead.

[*For discussion of specific laws of kashrut for Passover, see* Passover. *For a broad discussion of cross-cultural religious attitudes toward food, see* Food.]

BIBLIOGRAPHY

The literature on *kashrut* is enormous, in both English and Hebrew. The following English works are particularly useful: J. J. Berman's *Shehitah: A Study in the Cultural and Social Life of the Jewish People* (New York, 1941); Samuel H. Dresner and Seymour Siegel's *The Jewish Dietary Laws,* 2d rev. ed. (New York, 1966); Isidor Grunfeld's work by the same name, especially volume 1, *Dietary Laws with Particular Reference to Meat and Meat Products* (New York, 1972); Isaac Klein's *A Guide to Jewish Religious Practice* (New York, 1979); and my *Law and Theology in Judaism,* vol. 2 (New York, 1976). Two very different approaches to understanding the relationship between dietary and other purity laws can be found in Jacob Neusner's *The Idea of Purity in Ancient Judaism* (Leiden, 1973) and Mary Douglas's *Purity and Danger* (London, 1966), and in Douglas's "Critique and Commentary" on Neusner in his volume, pp. 137–142.

DAVID NOVAK

KĀŚI. *See* Banaras.

KATHENOTHEISM. *See* Henotheism.

KAUFMANN, YEḤEZKEL (1889–1963), Israeli Bible scholar and philosopher of Jewish history. Born in the Ukraine, Kaufmann was educated in Bible, Talmud, and Jewish history and received a doctorate in philosophy from the University of Bern in 1918. From 1914 to 1928 he lived in Germany, writing on Jewish nationalism. Immigrating to Israel (then Palestine) in 1928, he published a four-volume historical-sociological interpretation of Jewish history, *Golah ve-nekhar* (Exile and Alienage; 1928–1932). His eight-volume *Toldot ha-emunah ha-Yisre'elit* (A History of the Religion of Israel; (1937–1956) is the most comprehensive study of biblical religion by a modern Jewish scholar. From 1949 until 1957 he was professor of Bible at the Hebrew University of Jerusalem.

Kaufmann's major writings, historical and ideological, are distinguished by philosophical sophistication, methodological reflectiveness, and detailed textual analysis. In *Toldot,* a comprehensive, detailed analysis of the Bible and biblical religion, he argues (1) that the idea of one God ruling over nature was the unique creation of the nation of Israel, (2) that monotheism arose during the early stages of the nation's history, and (3) that, far from being influenced by genuine paganism, Israel was virtually ignorant of it. This work, which criticized prevalent ideas of modern biblical scholarship regarding the dating of the Torah texts, Israelite monotheism, and the impact of paganism on Israelite religion, had a decisive influence on an entire generation of Jewish Bible scholars.

In *Golah ve-nekhar,* Kaufmann employs historical-sociological arguments to demonstrate (1) that Israel's commitment to the monotheistic idea was the decisive factor ensuring the nation's survival in exile and (2) that in the modern era of secularization and nationalism, only a Jewish homeland could ensure the people Israel's survival. Like his biblical studies, this work is distinguished from other works on Jewish history both by its scope and by its mode of argumentation.

BIBLIOGRAPHY

Works by Kaufmann. Kaufmann's major works remain untranslated. An abridged translation of *Toldot ha-emunah ha-Yisre'elit,* containing Kaufmann's major arguments, is *The Religion of Israel from Its Beginnings to the Babylonian Exile,* translated and abridged by Moshe Greenberg (Chicago, 1960). An English essay, "The Biblical Age," in *Great Ages and Ideas of the Jewish People,* edited by Leo W. Schwarz (New York, 1956), covers the development of Israelite religion to the end of the Second Temple. A preliminary presentation of his Hebrew studies of *Joshua* and *Judges* is *The Biblical Account of the Conquest of Palestine,* translated by M. Dagut (Jerusalem, 1953).

Works about Kaufmann. A critical discussion of Kaufmann's basic arguments regarding biblical Israel is Moshe Greenberg's "Kaufmann on the Bible: An Appreciation," *Judaism* 13 (Winter 1964): 77–89. For Kaufmann's interpretation of Jewish history, see my own "Religion, Ethnicity and Jewish History: The Contribution of Yehezkel Kaufmann," *Journal of the American Academy of Religion* 42 (September 1974): 516–531. Kaufmann's historical-sociological method is discussed critically in my "Historical Sociology and Ideology: A Prolegomenon to Yehezkel Kaufmann's *Golah v'Nekhar*," in *Essays in Modern Jewish History: A Tribute to Ben Halpern*, edited by Frances Malino and Phyllis Cohen Albert (East Brunswick, N.J., 1982), pp. 173–195.

LAURENCE J. SILBERSTEIN

KAZAKH RELIGION. *See* Inner Asian Religions.

KEIZAN (1268–1325), more fully Keizan Jōkin; a fourth-generation master of the Sōtō school of Zen established in Japan by Dōgen, and the first abbot of the Sōjiji monastery. Born in Echizen Province, not far from Dōgen's Eiheiji monastery, Keizan at thirteen years of age became a monk under Ejō, the devoted disciple of Dōgen and the second abbot of Eiheiji. After Ejō's death, he sought instruction from Jakuen, the Chinese disciple of Dōgen at Hōkyōji, as well as from the masters of the Rinzai school of Zen. In 1295, Keizan received the Dharma Seal from Tettsū Gikai, Ejō's Dharma heir and by then abbot of Daijōji in Kaga Province. Although he was chosen abbot of Daijōji in 1302, after Tettsū's death, and served in that capacity until 1313 under the patronage of Jino Nobunao and his wife, Keizan founded numerous new Sōtō Zen monasteries in the north-central region of the main island of Honshū, notably Yōkōji and Sōjiji, both in Noto Province. Out of his respect for Keizan, Emperor Go-Daigo designated Sōjiji an imperial monastery.

While Ejō and some of his followers, including Jakuen, sought to preserve intact the purity of Dōgen's teaching and the severity of his discipline, Tettsū considered it of greater importance to reach out to the masses and popularize the school. Keizan devoted himself to Tettsū's cause, and his foresight contributed to the eventual development of the Sōtō school into one of the largest and the most powerful ecclesiastical establishments in Japan. Eminent among his disciples are Myōhō Sotetsu and Gasan Jōseki, abbots of Yōkōji and Sōjiji, respectively. Today, Sōjiji, relocated in 1910 in the metropolitan Tokyo area, is one of the two major centers, along with Eiheiji, of Sōtō Zen. The two centers continue in the distinct traditions that originally separated the school in the thirteenth century. Keizan was decorated posthumously with three imperial titles; he was designated Zen Master Butsuji by Go-Murakami, National Master Kōtoku Emmyō by Go-Hanazono, and, in modern times, Grand Master Josai by the Meiji emperor.

Keizan's success in expanding Sōtō Zen would not have been possible without its appealing to institutions and sentiments that had hitherto played an important role in the religious life of the Japanese. Notable is Keizan's interest in and connection with Esoteric Buddhism, particularly that of the Tendai school. The masters of Rinzai Zen under whom he studied, Hakuun Egyō and Muhon Kakushin, are known to have been influenced by Tendai esotericism. Tettsū's Daijōji and Keizan's Sōjiji had once been Tendai temples. Yōkōji had once enshrined Kannon Bosatsu (Bodhisattva Avalokiteśvara) as the chief deity of the temple before it was converted to a Zen monastery. Keizan's Dharma heir at Sōjiji, Gasan, had been ordained a Tendai monk before he turned to Zen. His renaming of Shogakuji to Sōjiji on the occasion of its change from Shingon to Zen suggests his abiding respect for the Esoteric Buddhist prayers known as *sōji* (Skt., *dhāraṇī*), which were designed to generate extraordinary capacity to retain memory. It is also known that Keizan inherited his mother's unswerving devotion to Kannon, the goddess of mercy, which is at the heart of the Mahāyāna Buddhist teaching so popular in Japan.

Among his writings are *Denkōroku* (Record of Transmission of the Light), a compendium of biographies and teachings from Śākyamuni Buddha to Ejō, and *Keizan shingi* (Monastic Rules according to Keizan).

[*See also* Zen.]

BIBLIOGRAPHY

Imaeda Aishin. *Zenshū no rekishi.* Tokyo, 1966.
Imaeda Aishin. *Chūsei Zenshūshi no kenkyū.* Tokyo, 1970.
Imaeda Aishin. *Dōgen to sono deshi.* Tokyo, 1972.
Kagamishima Genryū. *Dōgen zen*, vol. 1, *Den to jimbutsu.* Tokyo, 1960.
Ōkubo Dōshū. *Dōgen zenji den no kenkyū.* Rev. ed. Tokyo, 1966.

T. JAMES KODERA

KEMPE, MARGERY (c. 1373–c.1440), English pilgrim, autobiographer, and professional holy woman. Kempe was the daughter of a prosperous merchant of King's Lynn, England. Although happily married, she tended to have hysterical fits during which God spoke to her. At about the age of forty, having had fourteen children, she persuaded her husband that God wished them to take a vow of chastity. By this time the Deity was conversing agreeably with her nearly every day. Her meditations tended to concentrate on the Passion and to bring on wild lamentations, uncontrollable floods of tears, and rollings on the ground. These were widely acceptable signs of grace in the Middle Ages, but there were always some who declared her a fraud. Such charges were dangerous, as they several times led to her arrest as a heretic and a narrow escape from burning. For about twenty-five years, Kempe was a perpetual pilgrim, visiting not only every shrine in England but also the Holy Land, Rome, Santiago de Compostela in Spain, and various northern German centers, gradually establishing a reputation as a prophetess and seer among the less learned.

Kempe's importance for history lies in her autobiography, the first in English, a book intended for the edification of nuns. Although full of moralizing and sermons, it has a saving shrewdness and interest in the world. In the course of her travels, Kempe had numerous alarming encounters and met a host of people, from the archbishops of Canterbury and York, the holy Julian of Norwich, and innumerable friars to a wide range of fellow pilgrims and lesser government officials. It was her wish to write a mystical treatise, such as the famous *Cloud of Unknowing*, but what she did, in her autobiography, was to lay the fifteenth-century world before us in all its violence and piety; its blend of the spiritual and the venal, ignorance and learning, feudalism, democracy, and petty officialdom; its magnificence and utter filth. Here is the authentic background to Chaucer's *Canterbury Tales*. No other medieval document enables us so clearly to realize what it was actually like for a humble pilgrim to live and to travel in fifteenth-century Europe.

BIBLIOGRAPHY

The Book of Margery Kempe, edited by Hope E. Allen and Sanford B. Meech (London, 1940), is the text dictated by Kempe to a priest about 1438, in the original spelling and fully annotated. The narrative is confused in many places, and the reader will be greatly assisted by the only modern study, *Memoirs of a Medieval Woman: The Life and Times of Margery Kempe*, by Louise Collis (New York, 1964), also published under the title *The Apprentice Saint* (London, 1964). This biography places Kempe's adventures in their proper historical perspective, relating them to the wider political, social, and religious issues of the day.

LOUISE COLLIS

KEPLER, JOHANNES (1571–1630), discoverer of the laws of planetary motion named after him. He was born at Württemberg, Germany. Owing to his family's poverty, the young Kepler had to leave school to work in the fields, but his physique was too frail for such labor. In 1584, therefore, he decided to train for the priesthood. His brilliant academic record earned him acceptance at the University of Tübingen, where he was introduced to the ideas of Copernicus. In 1594 he was appointed to the professorship of astronomy at Graz. There, in addition to preparing astrological almanacs, he devoted himself to studying the solar system. His publication of *Mysterium cosmographicum* (1595) attracted the attention of the great Danish astronomer Tycho Brahe, who invited him to Prague and whom he succeeded as imperial astronomer to the emperor Rudolf II, in 1601. Kepler published some optical discoveries in 1604 and, in 1609, found that the orbit of Mars was elliptical in shape. In the latter year he also explained the cause of tides. In his *Dioptrice* (1611), Kepler developed the principle of the astronomical (or inverting) telescope. Deeply anguished by the untimely death of his favorite child and, soon after, that of his wife, Kepler sought release by plunging into his studies of the heavenly bodies. By 1619 he had discovered the last of his three famous laws, which he published in *De harmonice mundi*. It should be remarked that "Kepler's laws of motion" were scattered amid many other conjectures and planetary relationships postulated by Kepler and that he himself did not attach particularly great importance to them (as opposed to other relationships that did not prove so fruitful for later science).

Kepler's work is permeated with his conviction that the book of nature is written in mathematical symbols and that reality can be grasped only through mathematics. "Just as the eye was made to see colors, and the ear to hear sounds," he said, "so the human mind was made to understand, not whatever you please, but quantity." Kepler seems never to have shown any opposition to or disrespect for theology, although he regarded the realms of the theologians and the natural philosophers as quite different. He insisted that the Bible, when it refers to natural objects and events, should not be taken literally.

Kepler took his religion, in which he displayed an unyielding individualism, seriously. He was expelled from his home and from his position at Graz for refusing to embrace Roman Catholicism, and he was excluded from communion in the Lutheran church in Linz both for his refusal to give a written statement of conformity with the Lutheran doctrine and also on suspicion of being a secret Calvinist. He wanted to find a genuine harmony among these three factions: "It hurts my heart that the three factions have miserably torn the truth to pieces between them, that I must collect the bits wherever I can find them, and put them together again."

In his astronomical work—discovering laws and harmonies of the solar system and the music of the spheres, to which he assigned specific musical notes—Kepler regarded himself as priest of God in the temple of nature. Having insisted in his *Astronomia nova* (1609) that the biblical references to nature are not natural philosophy, he goes on to say:

> And I urge my reader also not to be forgetful of the divine goodness imparted to men, when the Psalmist invites him particularly to contemplate this, when having returned from the temple, he has again entered the school of astronomy. Let him join with me in praising and celebrating the wisdom and greatness of the Creator which I disclose to him from the deeper explanations of the form of the universe, from the enquiry into its causes, from the detection of errors of appearance. Thus not only let him recognize the well-being of living things throughout nature, in the firmness and stability of the world so that he reveres God's handiwork, but also let him recognize the wisdom of the Creator in its motion which is as mysterious as it is worthy of all admiration.

BIBLIOGRAPHY

The definitive biography of Kepler is Max Casper's *Johannes Kepler* (Stuttgart, 1950), which has been translated and edited by C. Doris Hellman as *Kepler* (New York, 1959). A popular and very readable account is Arthur Koestler's *The Watershed: A Biography of Johannes Kepler* (New York, 1960). Books 4 and 5 of Kepler's *The Epitome of Copernican Astronomy* and book 5 of his *Harmonies of the World* can be found in the series "The Great Books of the Western World," vol. 16 (Chicago, 1952).

RAVI RAVINDRA

KERÉNYI, KÁROLY (1897–1973), Hungarian-born scholar of classical philology, the history of religions, and mythology. He was born in the southeastern corner of the Austro-Hungarian empire, in the town of Temesvár (now Timişoara, Romania). Growing up in a Roman Catholic family of small landowners, Kerényi learned Latin and was drawn to the study of languages. Classical philology was his major subject at the University of Budapest; his doctoral dissertation (1919) was entitled "Plato and Longinus: Investigations in Classical Literary and Aesthetic History." He spent several years as a secondary-school teacher, traveled in Greece and Italy, and undertook postdoctoral studies at the universities of Greifswald, Heidelberg, and Berlin, under Diels, Wilamowitz-Moellendorff, Eduard Norden, Eduard Meyer, and Franz Boll. To Boll he dedicated his first book, *Die griechisch-orientalische Romanliteratur in religionsgeschichtlicher Beleuchtung* (1927), the scholarly reception of which led to Kerényi's appointment as privatdocent in the history of religions at the University of Budapest. He became professor of classical philology and ancient history at Pécs in 1934 and at Szeged in 1941, while retaining his docentship at Budapest.

During a visit to Greece in 1929, Kerényi met Walter F. Otto, whose approach to the history of religions influenced him profoundly. He resolved now to combine the "historical" and the "theological" method and to go beyond the limits of academic philology. His first works in the new direction were the essay collection *Apollon* (1937), and *Die antike Religion* (1940).

Two significant influences from outside his field came to bear on Kerényi in the 1930s. In 1934 he began a correspondence with Thomas Mann that, except for a wartime hiatus, lasted until Mann's death in 1955. In the late 1930s Kerényi came into contact with C. G. Jung, and their joint publications on mythology appeared first in 1941. Jung encouraged Kerényi's move to Switzerland in 1942, first as a cultural attaché charged with maintaining contact with the Allies in spite of Nazi domination of Hungary; the following year, when the Germans occupied his homeland, Kerényi chose permanent exile. In 1962 he and his family became Swiss citizens. They lived near or in Ascona, in the Italian-speaking canton of Ticino, where he led the life of an independent humanist, though he taught occasionally in Basel, Bonn, and Zurich. He was a cofounder of the C. G. Jung Institute in Zurich, where he also lectured. In the course of his work with Jung, Kerényi conceived a plan of serial studies on the Greek gods, toward developing a view of the Greek pantheon that modern man could encompass; to this end he took the findings of psychology into consideration, while maintaining that he followed a path separate from that of Jungian psychology. As he saw it, every view of mythology is a view of human culture. Thus every "theology" is at the same time an "anthropology." Kerényi's method was to test the "authenticity" of mythological tradition by examining stylistic traits. The essence of his work, Kerényi thought, consisted in establishing a science of ancient religion and mythology based not merely on a detailed knowledge of the literature and archaeology but also on a reciprocal sympathy between the interpreter and his material; this would broaden the field of learning already opened by the traditional historical methods.

In exile, Kerényi's reputation as a mythologist prospered both among scholars and as a popular interpreter of myths. His honors included membership in the Norwegian Royal Academy of Sciences, an honorary doctorate from the University of Uppsala, the Humboldt Society gold medal, and the Prickheimer Ring of Nuremberg; he was a Bollingen Foundation fellow from 1947 until his death in 1973. Between 1941 and 1963 he lectured frequently at the annual Eranos conferences in Ascona.

In Geo Widengren's words, "As very few others in our time, Kerényi was seriously concerned with the great central problems of research in the history of religions.

He spoke of them with the authority of a scholar who dominates his field. And in philology too—for Kerényi was a brilliant philologist, without the pedantic overload that most academic philologists like to show off. He gave no more than what was required to support the interpretation. *Esse, non videri* was his axiom" (*Numen* 14, 1967, pp. 163–164).

BIBLIOGRAPHY

Kerényi (Károly, Karl, Charles, or Carlo, according to the language in which his work appeared) produced 295 separate original works, in Hungarian, German (chiefly), and Italian. With different versions and translations, the total number of his publications is more than 500: some 470 appeared during his lifetime and some 40 were issued posthumously. His collected works, including monographs on philology, mythology, and literature, as well as diaries and travel journals, are in course of publication as a *Werke in Einzelausgaben* (Darmstadt, 1966–) under the editorship of Magda Kerényi. Twelve volumes are projected.

Kerényi's best-known works in English, intended for the general reader, are *The Gods of the Greeks*, translated by Norman Cameron (1951), *The Heroes of the Greeks*, translated by H. J. Rose (1959), and *The Religion of the Greeks and Romans*, translated by Christopher Holme (1962). All have appeared in subsequent editions and in other translations.

Other works in English include five monographs in the Bollingen Series, under the title "Archetypal Images in Greek Religion": *Asklepios* (1959), *Prometheus* (1963), *Eleusis* (1967), *Dionysos* (1976), all translated by Ralph Manheim, and *Zeus and Hera* (1975), translated by Christopher Holme. Two works written in collaboration with C. G. Jung are *Essays on a Science of Mythology* (1949) and *The Trickster* (1956), in which Paul Radin also collaborated; both were translared by R. F. C. Hull. Three volumes of "Papers from the Eranos Yearbooks" (part of the Bollingen Series), edited by Joseph Campbell and translated by Ralph Manheim, contain essays by Kerényi: volumes 1, *Spirit and Nature* (1954); 2, *The Mysteries* (1956); and 4, *Spiritual Disciplines* (1960).

Monographs translated by various hands include *Hermes, Guide of Souls* (1976), *Athene, Virgin and Mother* (1978), *Goddesses of Sun and Moon* (1979), and *Apollo* (1983). Kerényi's correspondence with Thomas Mann appears in *Mythology and Humanism*, translated by Alexander Gelley (1975).

All works in English cited herein are published by both British and American publishers.

WILLIAM MCGUIRE

KEROULARIOS, MICHAEL. *See* Cerularios, Michael.

KESHAB CHANDRA SEN. *See* Sen, Keshab Chandra.

KEYS. Doors held shut with bars, and bars and bolts, were common long before locks and keys became prevalent. Some of the oldest myths reflect this. In Babylonian mythology, for example, Marduk makes gates to the heavens and secures them with bolts. Many later divinities in the ancient world were both guardians of closed doors and bearers of keys.

The possession of keys usually signified power over regions guarded by the locks that the keys could open or close. The regions in question were often the underworld or places of the afterlife—for example, the realm of Hades, the Abyss in the *Book of Revelation*, and the Mandaean "dark worlds" that had locks and keys different from all others. The keeper of keys was charged not only with guarding the passage as human beings went from this world to the next but also with keeping the dead where they belonged. A Babylonian funerary chant entreats the gatekeeper of the underworld to keep close watch over the dead, lest they return.

The locked realm can also be this earth, the seas, or even the cosmos itself. In Greek mythology Cybele holds the key to Earth, shutting her up in winter and opening her again in the spring. Similarly, Janus opens the door of the sky and releases the dawn. In Mesopotamian myth, Ninib guards the lock of heaven and earth and opens the deep, while Ea unlocks fountains. The Egyptian Serapis has keys to the earth and sea. In Breton folklore menhirs are the keys to the sea and also the keys to hell; if they were turned in their locks and the locks should open, the sea would rush in.

Since in the ancient world, many divinities were key bearers, their priestesses bore keys signifying that the divine powers belonged to them as well, or that they were guardians of the sanctuaries of the gods. Priestesses were represented carrying on their shoulders large rectangular keys. A key pictured on a gravestone indicated the burial place of a priestess.

There is a morphological relationship between the key and the *nem ankh* sign, where the anserated cross of the Egyptian gods is carried by its top as if it were a key, especially in ceremonies for the dead. Here the cross, playing the role of the key, opens the gates of death onto immortality. [*See* Cross.]

Keys also symbolize a task to be performed and the means of performing it. In the Hebrew scriptures the accession to kingly power occurred through "laying the key of the House of David upon [his] shoulders" (*Is.* 22:22). For ancient Jewish and some non-Jewish royalty, the passing on of keys was a natural symbol for the transfer of the monarch's task and the power to accomplish it.

The key symbolizes initiation into the mysteries of the cult. In Mithraic rites the lion-headed figure who is central to the ceremony holds in his hands two keys. It is possible that they function in the same way as the two "keys of the kingdom" held by Saint Peter in Christianity: one represents excommunication whereby the door is locked against the unworthy soul, while the other represents absolution whereby the door is opened and the initiate achieves salvation.

BIBLIOGRAPHY

Information about the symbolism of keys can be found in primary sources of various kinds. J. A. MacCulloch's "Locks and Keys," in the *Encyclopaedia of Religion and Ethics,* edited by James Hastings, vol. 8 (Edinburgh, 1915), contains material about the development of locks, locks and bolts, and keys as mechanical contrivances as well as symbols. Franz Cumont in *The Mysteries of Mithra,* 2d ed., translated by Thomas J. McCormack (New York, 1910), and Robert C. Zaehner in *Zurvan: A Zoroastrian Dilemma* (Oxford, 1955) both discuss at length the initiation rites of Mithraism and speculate about the keys of the lion-headed god.

ELAINE MAGALIS

KHAN, SAYYID AHMAD. *See under* Ahmad Khan, Sayyid.

KHĀNAGĀH is a Persian word for the lodge or hospice where Ṣūfī masters (*mashā'ikh*) reside, teaching disciples (who sometimes are also residents), conversing with visitors, welcoming travelers, and feeding the poor. The word is functionally interchangeable with equivalent technical terms of Ṣūfī vocabulary, such as *ribāṭ, tekke, takīyah, zāwiyah, dā'irah,* and *dargāh,* though each has a distinct, region-specific connotation.

Mystics must live in the world. Literature by or about mystics frequently emphasizes the importance of escaping not only involvement in the world but, by extension, concern with all material needs and desires. *Khānagāh,* together with its lexical equivalents, inverts that emphasis, riveting attention to the physical spaces which Ṣūfīs inhabit, interacting with others and relying on instruments from the very world which they seek to escape.

Usage of the word *khānagāh* dates back to the tenth century, although its actual origin remains obscure. The modern attempt to relate it to *khān,* the widely used term for commercial way-stations, has been dismissed by those who argue that the Ṣūfī concept of a hospice bears no relation to the mercantile institution of *khān.* But the distinction seems specious since both *khān* and *khānagāh* were clearly places for Muslim wayfarers, whether they sought rest on a trade route or guidance on a spiritual path.

The *khānagāh* itself is embedded in a pre-Muslim, pre-Ṣūfī history from which it was never fully disentangled. It derives from Manichaean antecedents as well as pre-Ṣūfī ascetic communities (the Karrāmiyah of Khorasan in eastern Iran). One of the earliest Ṣūfī masters to establish a *khānagāh,* Shaykh Abū Sa'īd ibn Abī al-Khayr (d. 1049), also laid down rules that were to apply to its inmates: he is extolled in a posthumous family biography for the firm but moderate spiritual discipline he imparted to the residents of his *khānagāh.* Later Ṣūfī masters were less collegial and more autocratic, but they, like Abū Sa'īd, utilized a *khānagāh* or similar facility for engaging in a variety of communal relations.

It was also in the late eleventh century, beginning with the Seljuk rulers of Egypt and Syria and continuing under their successors, that the establishment of *khānagāhs* and their equivalents became widespread. The most renowned hospices were clustered in places which were also the commercial and political capitals of major Muslim dynasties—Cairo, Baghdad, Mosul, Lahore, and Delhi. Their persistence is suggested by the fact that *ribāṭ*s founded in Baghdad in the eleventh and twelfth centuries were replicated, at least in their broad outlines, by *zāwiyah*s built in North Africa during the nineteenth century.

Although one would expect to find accounts detailing *khānagāh* architectural design and physical layout, few exist from the medieval period. One of the most graphic relates to the foremost saint of pre-Mughal North Indian Sufism, Shaykh Niẓām al-Dīn Awliyā' of Delhi (d. 1325). His *khānagāh* was a huge building, consisting of a main hall *(jamā'at khānah),* courtyard, veranda, gate-room, and kitchen. It accommodated several senior disciples in lower rooms, but its crowning structure was also the least imposing: an isolated, small room on the roof where the shaykh passed his late evening and early afternoon hours in prayer, meditation, and (rarely) sleep. The plan seems to have been repeated, with adaptations to local taste, in many regions of Central and South Asia.

The appeal of the *khānagāh*s as the most visible expression of institutional Sufism was multiple. To the outer circle of disciples, including Muslims and non-Muslims of mixed social background who came to visit at irregular intervals, it housed at once a saintly presence deemed to be magical and a public kitchen dispensing free food. Closer to the shaykh were disciples who pursued mystical studies and began meditative exercises at his behest; they would frequent the *khānagāh* on a regular basis and occasionally take up residence there. The most intimate circle of disciples were the permanent residents designated as successors (*khalīfah*s) to the shaykh: not only did he entrust them with his deepest insights, but he also allowed them to initiate others into the tradition of his order *(ṭarīqah;* pl., *ṭuruq).*

Despite the continuous and widespread association of the *khānagāh* with Ṣūfī orders and their masters, the nonmystical dimension of *khānagāhs* was never fully excised. Throughout the medieval and early modern periods, there is ample evidence of non-Ṣūfī hospices and also non-mystical Muslims in charge of Ṣūfī hospices. The reason is evident: the source of support for every *khānagāh* was lay: it derived from the income, earned or not, of those who dwelled outside its walls. Even in those not-so-rare instances of rural hospices where inmates engaged in agricultural pursuits, their continued existence depended on contributions from the wider lay circle of the shaykh's followers and admirers. Not all sources of income were acceptable to all Ṣūfīs, however. For the Chishtī and Naqshbandī masters, it was normative (despite major exceptions) that they reject all governmental assistance, while for the Suhrawardī and Qādirī communities, any benefactor from the wealthy mercantile and ruling classes was usually welcome to make occasional offerings or even to set up permanent charitable endowments *(awqāf;* sg., *waqf)* supporting the *khānagāh* and its operations. Those saints who attempted to refuse governmental offers of assistance were often overruled and compelled to yield: such was the power of the medieval state that few Ṣūfī masters or their successors could resist a headstrong ruler who wished to use the spiritual power of a *khānagāh* and its saintly denizens to undergird his own legitimacy.

That the *khānagāh* continued for centuries to be the mainstay of institutional Sufism has never been questioned, but its vitality has. Some chart a decline in the major orders from the time that the *khānagāh* ceased to house a fraternal group of like-minded Ṣūfīs and became instead a tomb complex. This institution may have retained the name of *khānagāh,* but in fact it perpetuated the memory of a dead shaykh through greedy relatives who ignored his legacy yet lived off his spiritual capital by accepting all forms of public and private subsidy. Indeed, as early as the fourteenth century, the *khānagāh* was commonly linked to a tomb, as well as to an adjacent mosque and *madrasah.* [*See* Madrasah.] Most Muslims, however, accepted this extension of the public profile of Ṣūfī agencies, since they acknowledged the *mashā'ikh* as exemplars of the prophetic standard *(sunnah)* and boons for their own local communities.

Nonetheless, and no matter how one evaluates the *khānagāh* and institutional Sufism, the theory of diachronic decline and charismatic sclerosis is weakened, if not refuted, by the emergence of North African reformist orders, especially the Sanūsīyah, during the nineteenth century. Even that most extreme of puritanical groups, the Wahhābīyah, tacitly acknowledged the benefits which accrued to all Muslims from the extension of Sanūsī influence. The instrument for that extension was a network of hospices (*zāwiyahs*), deliberately located in areas that would maximize support for the Sanūsī armed resistance to Italian colonial administration.

Nor was the Sanūsī movement the death rattle of institutional Sufism or the last dramatic staging of fraternal lodges. Their continued influence in modern Egypt and Algeria has been well chronicled, and for many Muslims the physical abode of saints, by whatever name it is denoted, continues to embody the cosmic quality attributed to it by the thirteenth-century Kubrawī saint Najm al-Dīn al-Rāzī: "The world is in truth like a hospice where God is the shaykh and the Prophet, upon whom be peace, is the steward or servant" (Hamid Algar, trans., *The Path of God's Bondsmen from Origin to Return,* New York, 1982, p. 485).

BIBLIOGRAPHY

There is no single book to consult on the *khānagāh* or its equivalent terms. For an appreciation of its origin and medieval development, the best starting points are the two articles by Jacqueline Chabbi, "*Khānḳāh,*" in *The Encyclopaedia of Islam,* new ed. (Leiden, 1960–), and "La fonction du ribāṭ à Bagdad du cinquième siècle au début du septième siècle," *Revue des études islamiques* 42 (1974): 101–121. On the contribution of Abū Sa'īd, there is the incomparable study by Fritz Meier, *Abū Sa'īd-i Abū L-Ḫayr* (Leiden, 1976), especially pages 296–336. The South Asian evidence is set forth in a number of articles and monographs, the best being K. A. Nizami's "Some Aspects of Khanqah Life in Medieval India," *Studia Islamica* 8 (1957): 51–69; Fritz Lehmann's "Muslim Monasteries in Mughal India," unpublished paper delivered to the Canadian Historical Association, Kingston, 8 June 1973; and Richard Maxwell Eaton's *Sufis of Bijapur, 1300–1700: Social Roles of Sufis in Medieval India* (Princeton, 1978), especially pages 165–242.

To understand the Sanūsīyah in their North African setting, one can do no better than consult the comprehensive analysis of Bradford G. Martin, *Muslim Brotherhoods in Nineteenth Century Africa* (Cambridge, 1976), chap. 4. Also indicative of the persistent role of the *zāwiyahs* in another vital context are two monographs on Egyptian Sufism: F. de Jong's *Turuq and Turuq-Linked Institutions in Nineteenth Century Egypt* (Leiden, 1978) and Michael Gilsenan's *Saint and Sufi in Modern Egypt* (Oxford, 1973). J. Spencer Trimingham's *The Sufi Orders in Islam* (New York, 1971), despite its seeming comprehensiveness, is unfortunately limited by pseudotypological explanations and an Arab puritan bias.

BRUCE B. LAWRENCE

KHANTY AND MANSI RELIGION. Together with Hungarian, the Mansi (Vogul) and Khanty (Ostiak) languages form the Ugric branch of the Finno-Ugric (and, ultimately, the Uralic) language family. During the first millennium BCE, the proto-Ob-Ugrians withdrew along the Ob River northward from the forested steppe region of southwest Siberia, simultaneously assimilating the autochthonous population and losing their own Iron Age culture and equiculture. The Ob-Ugrians (Khanty and Mansi) thus became secondarily primitivized, emerging as a fishing, hunting, and reindeer-breeding sub-Arctic people. Between the twelfth and sixteenth centuries the Ob-Ugrians split into quasi-tribal or clan-based "chiefdoms," a system that disintegrated as a consequence of sixteenth-century Russian colonization. The Eastern Orthodox church began conversion of the Ob-Ugrians in the eighteenth century, but the character of this conversion was formal and thus did not essentially influence the original religion.

The Mansi number 7,700, the Khanty, 21,000; of these, respectively 49 and 68 percent speak their ancestral language. The ethnographic macrogroups correspond to dialect groupings. Yet, while the culture and language of the various macrogroups is divergent enough to justify their classification as distinct peoples, the Mansi and Khanty *within* the same microgroup differ from one another only in language and in their consciousness of identity. The ethnographic subgroups (i.e., dialects) subdivide according to fluvial regions. The religion of the Mansi and Khanty is identical: within one and the same macrogroup the same supernatural beings are revered regardless of which people's territory they are affiliated with. Mansi and Khanty folklore, too, is uniform on a nearly word for word basis. A few general nature deities are known to all groups; key figures of mythology are associated with the northwest region, although these same figures may appear in the religion of the other groups under different names. The Northern macrogroup, for instance, is familiar both with a high-ranking spirit from the Eastern Mansi and with another high-ranking spirit from the Western Mansi. On the other hand, Eastern Khanty spirits are completely unknown to them. From the perspective of both system and cult, the religion of the Vasjugan Khanty is the most complex. Ob-Ugric culture as a whole is of a marginal West Siberian type, distinct in quite a few traits. Its study is complicated by the factor of secondary primitivization.

The following is a description of the best documented macrogroup, the Northern. Characteristic of this society are a dual moiety system (*moś* and *por:* the former relatively positive, the latter relatively negative in connotation) and the loose agglomeration of patriarchal consanguineous groups that trace their origins to spirit ancestors conceptualized as simultaneously anthropo- and zoomorphic. This description, however, must unavoidably portray a more archaic form of social organization than is actually the case today. When technical terms are referred to, they derive from either the Sosva Mansi (Man.) or the Kazim Khanty (Kh.).

Anthropomorphy is dominant in Ob-Ugrian religion today, but a latent zoomorphic character can be demonstrated for many categories of supernatural beings. The cult of spirits that arise from the shadow souls of the dead is a productive element in many forms, supporting (1) the ancestor cult in general; (2) the cult of hegemonic personalities, of which the earlier (chiefdom period) variant is a hero cult, and the later variant is the cult of shamans and other worthies; and (3) the cult of those who have died extraordinary deaths. It is a peculiarity of the northern groups that they have incorporated both the major mythological personalities and various individuals of the unindividuated classes into a system of guardian spirits tied to concrete places and societal units. This category, which may be termed "warlord guardian spirits," became primary in both the religious system and cultic life.

Roughly speaking, the following categories may be distinguished according to the degree of the cult:

1. The true individual cult beings. These have their own prescriptions and prohibitions and their own regular festivals and sacrifices; in folklore they have their own summoning songs and prayers. The terms *pupigh* (Man.) and *łungx* (Kh.) refer to their most general class (which may be represented in idol form as well).
2. The higher-level belief beings. Relations with these beings are well regulated, and their benevolence may be won with the practice of hospitality or, in unusual cases, by means of more serious sacrifice. A lower level of belief being is also acknowledged. It is connected only with prohibitive and preventative practices. The lesser forms of word magic (incantation, short prayer) are addressed to the belief beings, who are portrayed in plays at the bear festival. Certain belief beings have no cult whatsoever. Folklore beings play no role in either belief or cult.

Conceptions of the Universe

Ob-Ugric cosmology was originally vertical and tripartite: upper (sky), middle (earth), and lower (underworld). A conception of these worlds as seven-layered is known, but not concretely elaborated. In the lower sphere of the sky dwell the Wind Old Men, named after the cardinal points. In the various upper layers of the sky revolves Sun Woman, with her team of horses, or Moon Old Man with his arctoid dog sled. Later, this worldview became contaminated with a horizontal system: Upper-Ob (southern), Middle-Ob, and Lower-Ob (northern). Accordingly, the productive region is located in the South, which sends migratory birds and which is the home of the world tree and the fountain-of-youth lake. Conversely, at the mouth of the Ob, on the Arctic Ocean, lies the dark land of the dead. At present, syncretistic twofold conceptualizations predominate.

The earth, brought up as a chunk by two bird representatives of the netherworld (a little and a big loon), is spread out over the primeval sea; it is disk-shaped: a fish or a fantastic animal holds it up. In the present-day version, the son of the mythic ancestral pair (identified either with the Pelim god or with World-Overseeing Man, both warlord guardian spirits) plays a salient part. With the collaboration of the chief god's counterpart, the folklore figure Kuĺ, he created man; he then decimated his progeny with a fiery flood and scattered them over the world. Before the present-day Mansi and Khanty, the myth alleges, there were many other periods: in folklore the most richly depicted are the period of the moiety ancestors and the heroic time of the origin of the warlord guardian spirits.

General Mythological Personalities. In the vertical system, the upper sphere is embodied by the positive-functioning chief god, Upper Sky Father (Man., Num Torem Aś; Kh., Nŭm Turem Aśi). Symbolized by the vault of heaven, he has the form of an old man and is active in climatic changes connected with the change of seasons, passive in regard to humans. He may be approached only through the intervention of high-ranking spirits, having scarcely any cult. [*See* Num-Tūrem.] His wife is (Lower) Earth Mother (Man., [Joli-]Mā Angkw). His counterpart is the lord of the netherworld. Admixture with the horizontal worldview and the localization of cults to particular places produced syncretistic personality trinities. Above Sky Father there appeared two ancestors (Man., Kośar Tōrem and Kores Tōrem, both folklore figures), or there appeared alongside him two other personifications (the Khanty folklore figures Nŭm Sĭwes and Nŭm Kŭres). His wife was reinterpreted as belonging to the same category, with the name Sky Mother (folklore figure). Elsewhere she was identified with the warlord guardian spirit goddess Kalteś. This same female fertility principle is repeated in the trinity South Woman, Kalteś, Gold Woman. Concrete incarnations of the lord of the netherworld include the warlord guardian spirits Sickness Lord and Lower-Earth Old Man, and "Devil," the fictive master of the harmful spirits called *kuĺ*.

Warlord Guardian Spirits. These are nature deities tied to societal units of a higher level (moieties, perhaps at one time tribes). Their antiquity is evidenced by the fact that their *attributa* often preserve features of the equiculture of the steppe rim. Their most representative group is now indigenous to the Middle-Ob territory of the Mansi and Khanty, the once-famous region of the Koda principality. The members of this group, listed here with corresponding zoomorphy, associated moiety, and cult center, are as follows:

1. Kalteś, popularly, Mother (Man., Śāń; Kh., Ăngki; female wild goose, swan, hare; *mość* moiety; village of Kaltisjan). Originally a sky goddess, Kalteś is the only equestrian female warlord guardian spirit. It is she who decides the number, sex, and longevity of children; she also aids in childbirth. Her persona is interpreted variously as wife, sister, or daughter of the sky god. Among her properties there is a negative one: infidelity or stubbornness.
2. World-Overseeing Man (Man., Mir Susne Xum; Kh., Mĭr Šawijti Xu; wild goose, crane; *mość* moiety; village of Belogorje). His other names include Golden Lord, Horseman, and Upriver Man. He is the youngest son of the sky god, the central figure of Ob-Ugric religion, and functions as a mythic hero in the creation of the world order. Married to the daughters of persons symbolizing nature, he excels in providing humans with their needs. His sphere of activity ranges through all three worlds. His is the highest position of honor among his brothers: the overseeing of the world and of humans. He accomplishes this by circling the world on his winged horse. In early formulations he is a solar god; later formulations preserve traces of the shamanistic mediator: he is the chief communicator with Sky God.
3. Holy City Old Man (Man., Jalp-ūs Ōjka; Kh., Jem Woš Ĭki), also known as Clawed Old Man (Man., Konsing Ōjka; Kh., Kŭnšeng Ĭki; bear, mouse; *por* moiety; village of Vežakar). In the region of his cult center he is held to be a son of the sky god. Functionally, he is the counterpart of World-Overseeing Man: in the shape of a mouse he goes under the earth and regains the shadow souls of sick people from underworld spirits who have stolen them. He is a totem ancestor of the *por* moiety.

Sickness Lord (Man., Xuĺ Ōter; Kh., Xĭń Wurt; big loon, village of Sumutnyol) and Lower-Earth Old Man (Kh., Ĭł Mŭw Ĭki; little loon; Sumutnyol) are two incarnations of the lord of the netherworld. The former steals souls; the latter either rules over them or eats them. In their empire they have a family and teeming army of servants consisting of illness spirits. They are also the source of unpleasant insects and vermin. Some versions interpret the lord of the netherworld as the son of the sky god; in any case, he functions as the subordinate of the sky god in the vertical system and the subordinate of Kalteś in the horizontal system. Under the name Downriver Man he also constitutes a complement to World-Overseeing Man.

Models of the Middle World. Beliefs concerning the middle world reveal a general but not extensive symbolization of natural elements. The most significant is Fire Mother, but Earth Mother and Water Mother enjoy lesser cults.

The land-water opposition. Such an opposition is clearly represented by the forest and aquatic variants of the positive-functioning *łungx*-type spirits; these oversee the natural resources of a particular territory. In eastern and southern areas they are important cult beings; in the north, they have been overshadowed by local warlord guardian spirits and the cult of the *mis* people. Closely connected with their cult is that of the more individualized *łungx*-type spirits associated with particular natural objects (high places, boulders, trees, whirlpools). Their negative counterparts are the forest and aquatic *kuł*, beings that represent the netherworld.

The forest sphere. In the animal world-model there is no notion of lord over the individual animal types. In addition to the totemistic animal cult, the greatest veneration surrounds the larger aquatic birds (symbols of fertility), the elk (because of its celestial references), and the bear. Around the bear, merged with the totem ancestor of the *por* moiety, developed a highly characteristic feature of Ob-Ugrian culture: a bear cult that is one of the most elaborate in the world.

The bear cult. The fusion of conceptualizations from various periods has conferred upon the bear the character of universal mediator. His origins tie him to the upper world; his dwelling place and connections with human society tie him to the middle world; his mouse-shaped soul ties him to the netherworld. Child of the sky god, he acquired knowledge of the middle world despite paternal prohibition and conceived a desire to descend there. His father permitted the descent but prescribed the most harmless manner of acquiring food. (At the same time he makes the bear the judge of societal norms, the guardian of the bear oath.) But the bear violates the prohibitions, thus becoming fair game for humans.

The slain bear is a divine guest who, after the ritual consumption of his flesh, transfers into the heavens the sacrifices dedicated to him and the cultic folklore performed for his benefit, thereby ensuring his own rebirth and that of the natural order. A separate taboo language exists in connection with the bear and the bear hunt, and the activities therein are highly ritualistic.

What follows is a description of the bear festival in its most characteristic (northern) variant. After purifying ceremonies, the bear (i.e., the bear hide, placed on a stand) is regaled for three to seven nights (depending on the bear's age and sex) with performances of a hospitable, educational, and amusing nature. Only men may participate as performers. The diurnal repertoire begins with a didactic section in which the offense of murder (of the bear) is brushed aside and epic songs are sung about the origin of the bear, the first bagging of a bear by a mythical personage, the bear's function as judge, and the death of the particular bear present at the ceremony. Thereafter follows a section punctuated by danced interludes, intended as entertainment for the bear, although its function for humans is didactic. Players in birchbark masks perform brief plays with song and pantomime. The plays are only a few minutes in duration, but they may number in the hundreds. These reflect the key motifs of nature and society and supranormal and everyday categories and their interdependence. Their aesthetic quality ranges from the comic to the sublime. Separate genres are represented by songs and games that depict the proliferation, way of life, and capture of various animal species, and by songs and games performed by a mythical being or clown figure who draws the spectators into the action.

In the most sacred section of the festival the warlord guardian spirits are summoned. Portrayed by costumed performers, they perform a dance that ensures the well-being of the community. When the bear meat is consumed, it is consumed under the illusion that birds are feasting. After this, the bear is instructed on the manner of returning to the heavens. Meanwhile, the bear's skull and the festival paraphernalia are taken to a special place where cult objects are stored.

The mirroring of social structure in the forest sphere. Two types of anthropomorphic forest beings pursue daily activities similar to those of the human community and may even intermarry with humans. The *mis* people are outstanding hunters; their benevolence provides humans with a good hunt. The *mis* take as their mates those people who disappear in the forest without a trace. The *mengk* people are supposed to be simple-minded malevolent giants. Northern Mansi associate the *mis* people with the *mos̀* moiety and the *mengk* people with the *por* moiety. The origins of certain warlord guardian spirits is derived—with the mediation of the cult of the dead—from these beings.

The aquatic sphere. While the dominant being of the forest is the bear, the lord of the waters, Water King (Man., Wit Xōn; Kh., Jĭngk Xon, Jĭngk Wurt) is similar to a high-ranking warlord guardian spirit. Water King is not tied to a societal unit, but each group thinks it knows of his dwelling place, which in each case is the stream from which fish migrate (e.g., northern groups place it in the mouth of the Ob, southern groups in the mouth of the Irtysh). Water King has a family and is the superior of water sprites and other beings. The chief function of Water King is the direction of the migration of fish; warlord guardian spirits that dwell at the outlets of tributaries supply a redistribution network.

The forest-settlement opposition. The sylvan pantheon is much richer than its aquatic counterpart. This is explained, in part, by the fact that the forest participates in the opposition of forest and settlement. The proper place of *łungx*-type spirits is indicated by the location of their sacred place; certain lower-ranked beings (e.g., the Eastern Khanty ghostlike *potčak*) are subdivided into explicitly forest or village variants. Other figures may lack pertinent counterparts but may nevertheless be construed in terms of this opposition. Examples include the birchbark-rucksack woman, identified with the (folkloristic) figure of the anthropophagous *por* woman, the elf called Village-Square Being, Trash-Heap Woman, Bathhouse Woman, Sinew-String-Making Woman, and others.

The Human Sphere

The warlord guardian spirit that is tied to a concrete place is not only the sole form representing the community but also the central category of all of cultic life. The primary functions of the warlord guardian spirit are to ward off harmful (especially disease-causing) spirits, to provide succor in situations of peril, and to ensure good fortune in hunting and fishing. The warlord guardian spirit appears in two forms: as a human, generally in the form of a luxuriantly ornamented woman or a warrior in sword and armor, or as an animal, in the form of a specific species of wild beast, which is then taboo for the pertinent social unit. These may be portrayed by wooden images in the form of a human (or, more rarely, an animal), sometimes with the addition of metal disks, or made entirely of metal. The appurtenances of the image are a sacred spot outside the settlement and the items stored there: the idol and/or its *attributa*, a small chamber built on stilts for preserving offerings, a sacrificial table, poles or trees called *tir*, and a sacred tree. The warlord guardian spirit addresses his kindred group as his "little ones" or "children"; as a projection of the actual relations within the group, he enjoys spirit kinship both ascendant and descendant, agnate and cognate. Characteristic features of the cult are a special idol guardian or shaman and prescriptions concerning both cyclical communal ceremonies and sacrificial animals and objects.

Although tied to a concrete place, a warlord guardian spirit may appear anywhere and at anyone's summons. Its connection with the individual is manifested by the fact that it selects a protegé. Every human has a warlord guardian spirit "master of his head." Higher-ranked spirits can select anyone as protegé; lower-ranked spirits are restricted to members of their own community. Ob-Ugrians oriented themselves with one another in terms of the relations obtaining among their warlord guardian spirits; they identified the spirits according to the village held to be the center of a given cult.

Hierarchy of Warlord Guardian Spirits. The community associated with a spirit can be of various levels in the social hierarchy—upper (moiety, base clan), middle (roughly, units corresponding to a clan and its branches), or lower (smaller, local groups). The rank of a spirit is determined by this hierarchy and by the "power" and functions attributed to it, which are generally in direct proportion to the antiquity of the spirit and the complexity of its typological profile. Roughly speaking, the Ob-Ugrians distinguish three hierarchical categories of spirits. Spirits belonging to the high (and upper middle) rank are qualified as "powerful" (Man., *ńangra;* Kh., *tarem*). Among these, the children of the sky god are set apart as a separate group. To this rank belong, besides mythological personae in general, Old Man of the Middle Sosva, the Lozva Water Spirit, the Tegi Village Old Man, and the Kazim Lady. The middle category, which is the chief locus of the hero cult, is subdivided in terms of the opposition between indigenous and immigrant groups. The spirits of immigrant groups are called "land-acquiring" spirits. Among the lower-ranked spirits, those of local character are sometimes distinguished by the terms "master of the village" or "master of the region." The superior of the spirits is the chief deity.

The warlord guardian spirits, like the social groupings associated with their cults, do not form a clearly structured system. The interpretation of their rank and kinship varies from one fluvial region to another. Genealogical, local, or functional subsystems, however, can develop in particular regions. The basis of the genealogical order resides in the fact that migrating groups either bring a copy of their original spirit with them or declare the indigenous spirit of their new home to be their original spirit's offspring. The range of the cults of higher-ranked spirits roughly corresponds to dialect areas. Their descendants may appear with names differing from those of their parents, and may even appear in animal form. The children of middle-ranked spirits are often—at least with regard to name and form—exact copies of one another. For example, spirits named Winged Old Man or Old Man with the Knife, in eagle and firefly form, respectively, crop up in villages at far remove from one another. In local subsystems, the high-ranked spirits are the superiors of all other spirits in their cult sphere.

The development of these spirits was determined along two lines: diverse nature cults and multiple intertwinings of cults of the dead. Both lines of development contain zoomorphic and anthropomorphic elements that are reflected in the diploid form of the spirits. The animal symbology of natural forces is zoomorphic. The oldest layers of this symbology (e.g., the cult of aquatic birds) date to at least the Finno-Ugric period. The other zoomorphic component is totemistic in character; its earlier layer may be Ugric, while its more recent layer is arctoid and may bear the influence of the religion of assimilated autochthonous Siberian populations. The oldest demonstrable layer of the anthropomorphic component is a group of nature deities that preserves traces of southern equiculture. Similarly anthropomorphic are the ancestor cult and hero cult, which are the source of the dominant mark of warlord guardian spirits. To the cult of warlord guardian spirits was juxtaposed the cult of those persons whose decease is in some way extraordinary. A further component is the cult of proprietary spirits of natural places and objects.

Family Guardian Spirits. Termed "house spirits" (Man., *kol puping;* Kh., *xot łungx*), these anthropomorphic spirits are difficult to differentiate from the lower-ranked warlord guardian spirits. They are variously conceived as descendants of a warlord guardian spirit or its spirit assistant, as the spirit of a deceased relative, or as the proprietary spirit of an object that is interesting in some way (e.g., an archaeological find made of metal). Its votaries approach them through dream or the instructions of a person with cult functions. Such spirits serve to protect and to ensure success in hunting and fishing. Successful execution of this latter office may occasion a widening of its circle of devotees; in case of failure, on the other hand, its idol representations suffer mistreatment or even complete destruction as punishment. The idol, its *attributa,* and ceremonies associated with the family guardian spirit are miniature duplicates of those of the warlord guardian spirits; its folklore, however, is on the wane. Individual protective spirits have similar typological profiles.

Mediator Spirits. Documentation for the individual shaman spirit assistant—known as a "living spirit" (Man., *liling puping;* Kh., *łileng łungx*) or, when functioning purely as an acquirer of information, a "talking spirit" (Man., *potertan puping*)—is extremely poor. Typologically, such a being is similar to family and individual spirits and probably serves merely as a messenger in the interactions of shaman and warlord guardian spirits.

Conceptions of the Soul. Conceptions of the soul are syncretistic and not always clear even to the Ob-Ugrians. Originally, they were twofold: breath spirits (Man., *lili;* Kh., *łił*) and shadow spirits (Man., Kh., *is*).

The breath spirit—roughly, a symbol of the individual personality—has the form of a small bird; its seat is the hair or crown of the head. Characters in heroic epics could send birds that lived on the crown of their heads or caps to fetch information; they also practiced scalping, by which they were able to take possession of any enemy's soul. The soul called *is* may have been regarded as a posthumous variation of the breath spirit (in men, it consists of five parts, in women, three; it is reborn in consanguineous progeny).

The shadow souls—symbols of emotional and vegetative functionings—have the form of humans or birds. One subtype may leave the body during sleep or in case of fear or fainting; it may also fall prey to illness spirits. After death it remains for a certain time in the vicinity of the house, then departs, northward, for the land of the dead. The other subtype has a more material character; its properties are roughly those of shadows. After death it lives a quasimundane life in the cemetery until the body fades away. The free soul is a type of sleep soul living in the form of a grouse; its destruction results in sleeplessness, then death. Under unfavorable circumstances shadow souls turn into ghosts.

Conceptions of the Hereafter. The hereafter is a mirrorlike inversion of the real world, lacking, however, the celestial bodies. The soul lives the same life, in the same form, as its owner did on earth, but backwards. Once returned to the time of birth it reappears in the real world as an insect or spider. Differentiation is minimal, but separation and punishment of the souls of suicides is known. Atonement for moral offenses seems to be the result of nonindigenous influence.

The soul of a dead person can have three material representations. It was obligatory to make for the reincarnating soul a doll of wood, cloth, or hair (Man., *iterma;* Kh., *šungŏt;* literally, "suffering one"; *upet akań,* "hair baby"). Long ago, this figure was so identified with the deceased that widows fed it regularly and slept with it. Among certain groups, the doll was passed from generation to generation; among others it was eventually placed in the grave or burned. A special wooden figure was carved for the souls of outstanding individuals. Through time, the worship of such a figure made it possible for these souls to achieve the status of family guardian spirits. Finally, for those whose remains were inaccessible, in some regions a figure was made and kept in a separate storing place after a symbolic burial ceremony.

Mediators. The Ob-Ugrians belong to the marginal zone of Siberian shamanism. The figure of the shaman is relatively unimportant, the shaman's significance being somewhat overshadowed by mediators who function without deep ecstatic trance. Overall, the study of Ob-Ugrian shamanism is hampered by extraordinarily imprecise documentation.

If as a hypothesis we limit true shamanism to the practice of drum-accompanied deep ecstatic trance, we are left with two types of people who fall outside this strict delimitation. The first group, the "one-sided interaction type," includes those who transmit from the human sphere to the spirits, but who cannot perceive the spirits' reactions. To this class belong the idol guardian in the role of master of ceremony, the "praying man," and epic singers, whose activity is not of a healing nature. The second group, the "two-sided interaction type," consists of those capable of obtaining information from the spirits, and who—to a certain degree—can set them into motion. They can perform these feats in sleep, however, or in a light trance. The only categories known among the Eastern Khanty are those who mediate through singing accompanied by string instruments, dreams, or the summoning of the spirits of forest animals. To the north, a possible equivalent is the Mansi *potertan pupgheng xum* ("talking spirit-man"), who summons his prophetic spirits by means of a stringed instrument.

Terminologically, the Ob-Ugrians make little distinction between the activity of shamans and that of persons who mediate by means of iron objects (axe, knife) and light trance: the noun "magic" (Man., *pēnigh;* Kh., *śărt*) and its verbal derivate "perform magic" (Man., *pēnghungkwe;* Kh., *śărtti*) can refer, in both languages, to the activity of either practitioner. The Mansi consider the "magic(-performing) person" who operates without the use of a drum (Man., *pēnghen xum*) to belong to a lower degree of the shaman category; they do, however, distinguish terminologically between this degree and the full-fledged drum shaman.

Destructive magic, which moves the spirits to negative ends, is used by the "spell-casting one" (Man., *sēpan;* Kh., *šepan(eng) xu;* the latter term is also used to refer to the shaman) and by the Mansi "destructive person" *(śurkeng xum)* or "spell-knowing person" *(mutrang xum).* These persons are capable of spoiling luck in hunting; they can also cause sickness and death. While terminologically distinct, they stand in an unclear relation to the shaman.

Shaman. Shamanism among the Ob-Ugrians is apparently a rather developed variant of a Paleo-Asiatic type that lacked the shamanistic journey. Exceptionally, and owing to foreign influence, there exists among the Eastern Khanty a more elaborated system of journeying and assistant spirits. No special folklore is associated with the shaman. Similarly, the figure of the female shaman who prophesizes by means of a gyratory dance appears conspicuously late, in a more recent type of heroic song. There is no specific evidence of the influence of neighboring peoples on Ob-Ugrian shamanism; although in peripheral regions certain features have been adopted from every possible donor, none of the various influences can be called dominant.

The shaman can provide any cultic service. His chief task is the defense of one's shadow soul against disease spirits. The shaman also fills an extremely important role as acquirer and interpreter of information (given that at least a dozen different supernatural causes may give rise to unfavorable events). His functions also include prophesy, the finding of lost objects, inquiry after the souls of the dead, and the steering of a sacrificial animal's soul to the spirits. The number of functional elements that may be demanded of the shaman varies from region to region. The shaman's participation in rites of passage, the bear festival, and lesser sacrificial ceremonies is not typical. There is no evidence of the shaman possessing the role of conductor of souls. The shaman acquires the greatest significance in situations of peril that affect the community.

There are no explicit categories of shamans among the Ob-Ugrians. The shaman's strength depends on the nature and number of his spirit assistants, or on the warlord guardian spirits, which are susceptible to influence. Stronger and weaker shamans are distinguished, but without special terminology. There are no reliable data for a distinction between "black" and "white" shamans. In fact, the activity of the shaman is ambiguous, since he may, to redeem the sick person's soul, offer up the soul of another; at times of rivalry he endangers the life of himself and his family.

The shaman, like all other mediative persons, is in principle at everyone's disposal. His activity, whether unreciprocated or remunerated with minor gifts and/or hospitality, is insufficient for independent subsistance. The shaman can increase his income only as the preserver of high-ranked warlord guardian spirits. Both men and women can be shamans, but in general the former have higher status.

There are no reliable data for special shamanic attire or accoutrements; the cap and the headband, however, are documented as headgear. The primary type of drum is oval, with a frame both decorative and resonating; its Y-shaped handle is sometimes embellished with representations of a spirit's face. The skin is unadorned; the position of the pendants (made of metal) varies. The drum may be replaced by a stringed instrument. Fly agaric is the usual narcotic.

Selection and recruitment of apprentice shamans is passive; it is generally attributed to the will of the chief deity, or World-Overseeing Man. Sensitivity, deviant behavior, and musical proclivities are required; somatic marks, illness, and inheritance are also documented but not universal. The candidate rehearses his repertoire as an assistant without benefit of initiation, only gradually assuming his role.

The shamanic séance takes place in a darkened house, where the shaman communicates—with drum-accompanied song, then with gyratory dance—with the warlord guardian spirits appropriate to the occasion. Metal objects (such as arrows) set out for the purpose announce by their rattling that the spirits have arrived (through the roof). When contact is established, the shaman is overcome by a warm breeze. Thereafter a protracted, dramatized debate takes place on the following subjects: (1) determining the cause of the problem; (2) summoning the spirit responsible or contacting it through an assistant spirit; (3) probing the cause of the problem and the nature of the sacrifice needed for its termination; and (4) ensuring the benevolence of the spirits. The role of the shaman is limited to setting events in motion; the actions themselves (i.e., journey, recovery of the sick person's soul) are carried out by the spirits, who, should they resist, can torment the shaman severely. The shaman ends his state of trance and announces the result; he may also take part in the offering of a sacrificial animal.

Other Features of the Cultic Life

Characteristic of the entire region are the restrictions on religious practice for women considered impure. If invested with any kind of special significance or cultic character, an object, living creature (especially the horse), place, or ceremony carried a list of prohibitions for such women. They were not allowed to visit the sacred locales of warlord guardian spirits. At the bear festival they could participate only in the interlude dances. Customs connected with birth and death were in the hands of the old women. Women sometimes had a separate sacred place near the village and a separate cult rendered to Kalteś. Among males, those who had assumed the care of the family idols after their parents' death were most fully esteemed.

In the cult of warlord guardian spirits there were presumably differences of ceremony according to moiety (especially with regard to the bear cult) and according to consanguineous group. Accordingly, at joint ceremonies the proprietors of the cult being played active roles, while newcomers or guests played relatively passive roles.

Periodic communal holidays were important in the maintenance of social relations. The most inclusive and involved such holiday was the festival organized by the *por* moiety in the village of Vežakar. Held every seven years, it lasted three months and followed the pattern of the bear festival. Several hundred participants were attracted to this event from northern regions. Periodic visits to warlord guardian spirits were sometimes prescribed, during the course of which the devotees made joint sacrifices. Regularly intermarrying groups invited one another to the larger festivals, which could be linked with cultic competitions, prophetic practice, the singing of epics (for the entertainment of the spirits), plays, and amusements. Generally prescribed pilgrimages to high-ranking warlord guardian spirits brought about more extensive relations, as did various alms-collecting tours undertaken in the interest of maintaining the cults of such spirits.

Sacrificial Ceremonies. There are two kinds of sacrifices. (1) In bloodless sacrifice (Man., *pūri;* Kh., *por*) the spirits absorb the vapors (or "strength") of the food and alcoholic beverages that have been set out for them; later, the humans present eat it. (2) In blood sacrifice (Man., Kh., *jir*) the spirits receive a portion of the animal's soul-bearing body parts (the blood, certain organs, the head, the entire skin) and thus take possession of the animal's shadow soul. The most precious sacrificial animal is the horse, which was sacrificed to high-ranking mythological personalities (especially World-Overseeing Man) throughout the entire region irrespective of the presence or absence of an equestrian culture. In addition, reindeer (in the north) and horned cattle and roosters (in the south) were usual sacrificial animals. Spirits of the upper sphere were said to favor light-colored animals; those of the nether sphere favor dark-colored animals. In a typical northern sacrifice, the animal is either strangled or dealt a blow to the head with the back of an axe; simultaneously, the spirit is summoned by shouts. The animal is then stabbed in the heart with a knife and its blood is let. The blood and entrails are consumed raw on the spot; there are separate prescriptions concerning the cooking and distribution of the flesh. In addition to animals, fur, cloth, and coins may serve as objects of sacrifice. Among metals, silver has the highest value.

Periodic sacrifices may be classified into two types, annual and macroperiodic (every three or seven years). Required communal sacrifices are tied to the economy of the seasons; so, for example, in spring (fishing season) and autumn (hunting season) sacrifices carried out to ensure a good catch and bountiful quarry were frequent at the beginning of the season, while thanksgiving sacrifices were general at the end of the season. For animal sacrifices autumn was the most propitious season. During important communal sacrifices the shaman would take part, and men in a light ecstatic trance would perform sword dances in commemoration of the ancient heroic deeds of certain warlord guardian spirits.

It should also be mentioned that the idol-like representation of spirits among the Ob-Ugrians is not fetishistic in character and is thus not absolutely obligatory. It is of importance only as an exterior representation or as a dwelling-place for the spirit; if necessary, the image can be replaced with a new representation.

Nonindigenous Influences. The most archaic (but far from the oldest) exterior influence may be found in the cultural elements derived from assimilated sub-Arctic populations. These elements are evident in magic related to production, in certain elements of totemism, and in the bear cult. If we accept the hypothesis that the *por* moiety is connected with this unknown sub-Arctic people, the number of such elements grows larger. Iranian speaking and Turkic speaking peoples influenced the proto-Ob-Ugrians in several phases from the Finno-Ugric period (fourth millennium BCE) through the Ugric period (until circa 500 BCE). These peoples played an important role in the development of equiculture among the Ob-Ugrians. Traces of steppe culture are preserved in the dominant role of the horse as a sacrificial animal and divine *attributa,* in the representation of mythological persons from the upper sphere dressed in open, wide-sleeved garb, and in the symbology of images found on hitching posts. Contact with Turkic peoples also brought, most recently, elements of Islam (from the Siberian Tatars), as can be seen in the book of destiny that occurs as an *attributum* and in elements of relatively differentiated conceptions of the netherworld. A surprisingly large number of religious terms were borrowed from or through the Komi (Zyrians), especially in connection with conceptions of the soul and the goddess of fertility. Such Komi influence may have been enhanced when the Komi fled into Siberia to escape conversion to Christianity by Stephen of Perm (fourteenth century).

The first intention of Eastern Orthodox efforts at conversion (which began in the eighteenth century) was the annihilation of the most important idols. This external threat had two consequences: heightened solicitude for cultic objects and a disassociation of spirits from their representations. Within a century, a network of church-centered villages had developed, displacing, wherever possible, the cult centers of ranking warlord guardian spirits. At times, the clergy exploited the possibilities of identifying the personalities of the two religions; formulas of correspondence thus quickly gained ground; the sky god was equated with God the Father, Kalteś with the Virgin Mary, World-Overseeing Man with Jesus, Pelim with Saint Nicholas. Ob-Ugrians understood the new religion entirely in terms of their own categories. Thus, a church was the idol chamber of the Russian god, the icon was the idol itself (before which even animals were sacrificed), the cross worn about the neck was an amulet for warding off harmful forest beings, and so on. The Christian worldview brought little change other than a gradual increase in the significance of the sky god. Qualitative change arose in step with russification, especially for southern groups. At present, in consequence of the spread of civilization and atheism, Ob-Ugrian young people are ill-informed about religious matters, and their attitude toward their religious heritage is inconstant.

[*See also* Finno-Ugric Religions; Shamanism, *article on* Siberian and Inner Asian Shamanism; *and* Bears.]

BIBLIOGRAPHY

Folklore Collections

Avdeev, I. I. *Pesni naroda mansi.* Omsk, 1936.

Chernetsov, V. N. *Vogul'skie skazki.* Leningrad, 1935.

Kálmán, B. *Manysi (vogul) népköltési gyüjtemény.* Budapest, 1952.

Kannisto, Artturi. *Wogulische Volksdichtung.* 4 vols. Helsinki, 1951–1963.

Kulemzin, V. M., and N. V. Lukina. *Legendy i skazki khantov.* Tomsk, 1973.

Munkácsi, B. *Vogul népköltési gyüjtemény.* 4 vols. Budapest, 1892–1921.

Pápay, J. *Osztják népköltési gyüjtemény.* Budapest and Leipzig, 1905.

Patkanov, S. *Die Irtyschostjaken und ihre Volkspoesie.* 2d ed. Saint Petersburg, 1900.

Reguly, A., and J. Pápay. *Osztják hősénekek.* Budapest, 1944.

Reguly, A., and J. Pápay. *Osztják (changi) hősénekek.* Budapest, 1951.

Steinitz, W. *Ostjakische Volksdichtung und Erzählungen,* vol. 1. Budapest, 1975.

Steinitz, W. *Beiträge zur Sprachwissenschaft und Ethnologie.* 4th ed. Budapest, 1980.

Vértes, E. *K. F. Karjalainens südostjakische Textsammlungen,* vol. 1. Helsinki, 1975.

Secondary Sources

Chernetsov, V. N. "Fratrial'noe ustroistvo obsko-ugorskogo obshchestva." *Sovetskaia etnografiia* 2 (1939): 20–42.

Chernetsov, V. N. "K istorii rodovogo stroia u obskikh ugrov." *Sovetskaia etnografiia* 6–7 (1947): 159–183.

Chernetsov, V. N. "Concepts of the Soul among the Ob-Ugrians." In *Studies in Siberian Shamanism,* edited by Henry N. Michael. Toronto, 1963.

Gondatti, N. L. *Sledy iazychestva u inorodtsev Zapadnoi Sibiri.* Moscow, 1888.

Hoppál, Mihály. "Folk Beliefs and Shamanism among the Uralic Peoples." In *Ancient Cultures of the Uralic Peoples,* edited by Péter Hajdú, pp. 215–242. Budapest, 1976.

Karjalainen, K. F. *Die Religion der Jugra-Völker.* 3 vols. Helsinki, 1921–1927.

Kulemzin, V. M. "Shamanstvo vas''iugansko-vakhovskikh

khantov." In *Iz istorii shamanstva*, pp. 3–155. Tomsk, 1976.
Kulemzin, V. M. *Chelovek i priroda v verovaniiakh khantov.* Tomsk, 1984.
Sokolova, Z. P. *Sotsial'naia organizatsiia khantov i mansov v XVIII–XIX vekakh.* Moscow, 1983.
Toporov, V. N. "On the Typological similarity of Mythological Structures among the Ket and Neighbouring Peoples." *Semiotica* 10 (1974): 19–42.
Tschernejtzow, V. N. "Bärenfest bei den Ob-Ugrien." *Acta Ethnographica* (Budapest) 23 (1975): 285–319.

Bibliographies

Nikol'skii, N. P. "Obzor literatury po etnografii, istorii, fol'kloru i iazyku khantov i mansov." *Sovetskaia etnografiia* 2 (1939): 182–207.
Novitskii, G. "Kratkoe opisanie o narode ostiatskom" (1715). Reissued in Hungarian in "Studia Uralo-Altaica," no. 3. Szeged, 1973.

Eva Schmidt
Translated from Hungarian by Daniel Abondolo

KHĀRIJĪS are the "third party" in Islam, who anathematize both the majority Sunnīs and the Shī'ī partisans of 'Alī. Although few in number today, the Khārijīs played a role of great importance in the history of Muslim theology and political theory.

Their origins lie in the agreement between the fourth caliph, 'Alī, and his challenger, Mu'āwiyah, kinsman and avenger of the murdered third caliph, 'Uthmān, to submit their quarrel to arbitration, following the Battle of Ṣiffīn (AH 37/657 CE). A group of 'Alī's followers, at first mostly from the Arab tribe of Tamīm, held that 'Alī had, by agreeing to treat with rebels, committed a great sin and could no longer be considered a Muslim. They made an exodus *(khurūj)* from his camp and collected at Ḥarūrā' near 'Alī's capital of Kufa in Iraq: hence Khārijīs ("those who went out") are sometimes referred to as Ḥarūrīyah. From the beginning they insisted on the equality of all Muslims regardless of race or tribe, "even if he be a black slave," and they found an important following among the non-Arab converts.

Despite all efforts, 'Alī was unable to conciliate them. In the end he was forced by their raids and provocations to attack their headquarters on the Nahrawān canal (17 July 658). This attack became more of a massacre than a battle, and it aroused sympathy for the Khārijīs. Within three years 'Alī was murdered at the door of his mosque in Kufa by Ibn Muljam al-Murādī, a Khārijī seeking revenge for the slain of Nahrawān.

The intellectual center of Khārijī doctrine for the next century was the great Iraqi port of Basra, but then moved to North Africa. There Khārijī doctrine struck a responsive chord among the Berber tribes, and North Africa became the Scotland of these Muslim Puritans. Khārijī revolts making effective use of guerrilla tactics helped to weaken Mu'āwiyah's Umayyad dynasty before it was overthrown by the Abbasid revolution in 750. Their revolts continued under the early Abbasids, and the appellation *khārijī* came to mean "rebel."

Being from the first people who could not compromise, the Khārijīs quickly separated into sects: Muslim heresiographers list over twenty. Each sect usually elected an imam, a "commander of the faithful," and regarded itself as the only true Islamic community. Basic to Khārijī doctrine are the tenets that a Muslim who commits a major sin has apostatized, and the shedding of his blood is lawful; that any pious Muslim is eligible to become an imam; and that if he sins or fails to be just, he may be deposed. Non-Khārijī Muslims were regarded as either polytheists or infidels. Jews or Christians who accepted Khārijī rule were, however, scrupulously protected. Khārijīs who sought death in *jihād* (religious war) against other Muslims were considered *shurāt*, or "vendors" (of this world for paradise).

The principal sects were the Azāriqah, the Ṣufrīyah, and the Ibāḍīyah. The Azāriqah probably took their name from Nāfi' ibn al-Azraq, son of a former Greek slave and blacksmith. They excluded from Islam all those who were content to coexist peacefully with non-Khārijī Muslims or who believed in *taqīyah*, dissimulation of their true beliefs, and all who would not make the *hijrah*, or emigration, to join them. They practiced *isti'rāḍ*, or "review" of the beliefs of their opponents, putting to death those who failed to pass their catechism, often including women and children, and held that infants of "polytheists" went to hell with their parents. They maintained that even a prophet was not immune from sin, and hence from final infidelity; that menstruating women should still pray and fast; that a thief's "hand" should be cut off at the shoulder; and that it was not lawful to stone adulterers, because this punishment is not prescribed in the Qur'ān. They broke with the other Khārijīs of Basra in 684 and left the city to conduct a terrible civil war in the southern provinces of Iraq and Iran. This was led by Zubayr ibn Māhūz until 688, then by Qatarī ibn Fujā'ah until their final defeat in 699. Qatarī was one of a series of gifted Arab Khārijī poets.

The Ṣufrīyah are said to have originated among the followers of 'Abd Allāh ibn Ṣaffār al-Tamīmī. They believed that peaceful coexistence with other Muslims was legally permissible; unlike the Azāriqah they did not practice *isti'rāḍ*, and unlike the Ibāḍīyah they held that non-Khārijī Muslims were polytheists rather than merely infidels. They emerged as an active sect in 695 and found an enthusiastic following among the Arab tribes of the upper Euphrates Valley. Under a series of fierce leaders they made their own bid for supreme power in the troubled events at the close of the Umayyad caliphate. From 745 to 751 they fought in Iraq, then Fārs, then Kishm Island, and finally in Oman, where their imam was slain by an Ibāḍī imam. The sect's activities then moved chiefly to North Africa, where it had found Berber adherents after 735. Berber Ṣufrīyah captured the important caravan city of Sijilmāsah in southern Morocco in 770 under an imam named Abū Qurrah. Like many other Khārijīs they were active traders. They maintained an imamate for about a century but at last seem to have been converted to the Ibāḍīyah and to Sunnism.

The Ibāḍīyah are the only surviving division of the Khārijīs, and because they have preserved their writings, they are also the best known. Numbering probably fewer than a million, they are found in the oases of the Mzab and Wargla in Algeria, on the island of Jerba off Tunisia, in Jabal Nafūsah and Zuwāghah in Libyan Tripolitania, in Zanzibar, and in Oman, where the ruling family is Ibāḍī. The merchants of the Mzab, Jerba, and Oman present a good example of closed religious trading communities similar to the Jews, the Parsis, or the Ismā'īlī Muslims. Practicing Ibāḍīyah do not tolerate tobacco, music, games, luxury, or celibacy, and must eschew anger. Concubinage can be practiced only with the consent of wives, and marriages with other Muslims are heavily frowned upon. They disapprove of Sufism, although they have a cult of the saintly dead. Sinners in the community are ostracized until they have performed public admission of guilt and penance.

The sect was first mentioned about 680, in Basra. It took its name from 'Abd Allāh ibn Ibāḍ, who broke with the Azāriqah in 684 and continued to live in Basra, where he presided over a secret council called the Jamā'at al-Muslimīn (Collectivity of the Muslims). His work was continued under Jābir ibn Zayd, an eminent scholar and traditionist. The earliest *mutakallimūn*, or theologians, of Islam were Ibāḍīyah who debated with the circle of Ḥasan of Basra. Jābir was from the Omani tribe of Azd and did much to organize the sect. It had close contacts with the Basran Mu'tazilah and, like them, held that the Qur'ān was created, that man has power over his own acts, and that there will be no beatific vision. [*See* Mu'tazilah.] The Ibāḍīyah have also been called the Wāṣilīyah, after Wāṣil ibn 'Aṭā', an early Mu'tazilī.

After Jābir, the Basra collectivity was headed by Abū 'Ubaydah Muslim al-Tamīmī. He retained the Basra headquarters as a teaching and training center and prepared teams of teachers (*ḥamalat al-'ilm*) to go and spread the doctrine in remote Muslim provinces. When the time was ripe, these teams were to set up imams: like the Zaydī Shī'īah and many Mu'tazilah, the Ibāḍīyah hold that there can be more than one imam if communities of widely separated believers need them. At other times, when circumstances dictate, Ibāḍī communities may legally dispense with the imamate, to be ruled by councils of learned elders.

Ibāḍī imamates rose and fell in Yemen, Oman, and Tripolitania in the eighth century. Omani traders carried the doctrine to East Africa in the ninth century. The greatest Ibāḍī imamate was that of Tāhart, founded in central Algeria around 760, which became hereditary in a family of Persian origin, the Rustamīs. During the latter part of the eighth century and the first half of the ninth century, the imams of Tāhart were recognized by Berber tribes from Morocco to Tripolitania, as well as by the Ibāḍīyah of Basra, Iran, and Oman. Their traders were early missionaries of Islam in sub-Saharan Africa. In the latter half of the ninth century, this state was weakened by a series of religious schisms and by external enemies, and many of its Berber supporters converted to Sunnism. The remains of the state were destroyed in 909 by the rise of the Fatimid caliphate, based in Kairouan. The last imam fled to Sadrātah in the oasis of Wargla. The descendants of the fugitives of Tāhart live today in the oases of the Mzab, deep in the Sahara.

Twelve subsects of the North African Ibāḍīyah are mentioned by historians of the sect. Three of these, the Nukkārīyah, the Nafāthīyah, and the Khalafīyah, have survived to modern times in small numbers, chiefly in Tripolitania.

[*See also* Caliphate; Imamate; *and* Ummah.]

BIBLIOGRAPHY

The best sources on the Khārijīs are, of course, in Arabic, with others in French, German, and Italian. Most of these will be found listed after three excellent articles in *The Encyclopaedia of Islam*, new ed. (Leiden 1960–): G. Levi Della Vida's "K͟hārid͟jites," Tadeusz Lewicki's "Ibāḍiyya," and R. Rubinacci's "Azāriḳa." Two classic Sunnī heresiographies have been translated into English, however, and are valuable reading, though written from a distinctly hostile stance. These are 'Abd al-Qāhir al-Baghdādī's *Moslem Schisms and Sects (Al-Farḳ Bain al-Firaḳ)*, translated by Kate Chambers Seelye (New York, 1919–1935), pp. 74–115, and A. K. Kazi and J. G. Flynn's "Shahrastānī: Kitāb al-Milal wa'l Niḥal (The Khārijites and the Murji'ites)," *Abr-Nahrain* 10 (1970/71): 49–75. A valuable article by a leading scholar of the Ibāḍīyah is Tadeusz Lewicki's "The Ibádites in Arabia and Africa," parts 1 and 2, *Cahiers d'histoire mondiale* 13 (1971): 51–130. An older but still useful introduction is William Thomson's "Khārijitism and the Khārijites," in *The Macdonald Presentation Volume: A Tribute to Duncan Black Macdonald* (1933; reprint, Freeport, N.Y., 1968).

JOHN ALDEN WILLIAMS

KHILĀFAH. *See* Caliphate.

KHMER RELIGION. The Khmer, who constitute the dominant ethnic population of Cambodia (also known as Kampuchea), have a complex and syncretic religio-cosmological system composed of Theravāda Buddhism, indigenous folk traditions, and elements historically derived from other regions such as China and especially India. The prehistoric origin of the Khmer is unclear, but various polities emerged in the general area of what is now Cambodia from about the first century CE, and Khmer civilization reached notable heights of power and magnificence during the Angkor period (802–1431 CE). Some rulers of the ancient kingdoms adopted Mahāyāna Buddhism or Hinduism (Śiva and/or Viṣṇu cults) as the state religion, while others maintained syncretic practices. But when Theravāda Buddhism of the Sinhala form entered Cambodia in the thirteenth century, it gradually displaced Hinduism and Mahāyāna and was adopted by both the ruling elite and the general populace. Theravāda remained the state religion throughout Cambodia's succeeding history, including the era of French colonialism and subsequent achievement of independence in 1954, until the communist revolution in the 1970s. Democratic Kampuchea under Pol Pot (r. 1975–78) attempted to crush religion as an "exploitative" institution; the *sangha* (Buddhist priesthood) was abolished and many temples were destroyed or desecrated. In 1979, following Vietnamese occupation, the new regime (People's Republic of Kampuchea) permitted religion to be revived. Theravāda is no longer a state religion, however, and there are fewer monks and temples than in the precommunist period.

The Khmer can be characterized as Buddhist insofar as Theravāda was Cambodia's official national religion for some six centuries (although minority populations were permitted to practice their own religions). However, it is critical to recognize that Khmer culture has woven strands of Buddhism, animistic folk beliefs, and elements of Hindu and Chinese practices into a distinctive Cambodian fabric. Scholars might identify particular traits as deriving from one or another religious tradition, but the Khmer themselves, especially peasant villagers who make up the bulk of the population, do not generally think of their beliefs and practices as constituting separate religions, and it can be argued that they have a single, syncretic religious system. Moreover, Khmer religion is not a realm separate unto itself, but pervades daily life and various spheres of culture. In both historic and modern Cambodia, religion has been intimately connected to the political system, subsistence activities, social organization, literature, music, dance, drama, architecture, and the visual arts. For purposes of clarity this discussion will treat the Buddhist and folk components of Khmer religion separately, but it must be remembered that such compartmentalization rarely occurs in the thoughts and behavior of most Khmer.

Khmer Buddhism is divided into two orders: the Mahānikāy, "the great congregation," and the Dhammayutt (Thommayut), "those who are attached to the doctrine." The former is older and larger: in prerevolutionary Cambodia, over 90 percent of all temples and monks were Mahānikāy. The Dhammayutt order was brought to Cambodia in 1864 by a Khmer monk who had studied in Thailand, where it originated, and it acquired prestige by being adopted by royalty and other elite, although there were also adherents among the common people. [*See also* Thai Religion *and the biography of Mongkut.*] Monks of both orders are given the highest respect as living embodiments and spiritual teachers of Buddhism; the *vatt (wat)*—with its temple, meeting hall, shrines, school, and shelters for monks and laypeople—serves as a moral, social, and educational center for its congregants. The widespread distribution of temples and monks brings the populace into close and constant contact with Theravāda.

The average layperson, enjoying little hope of achieving *nirvāṇa,* strives principally to acquire merit *(piṇḍ)* and to avoid wrongdoing in order to bring about an advantageous rebirth. One can gain merit in various ways:

1. The Five Precepts *(sīl pram̥*—to refrain from killing living creatures, stealing, lying, drinking intoxicants, and pre- and extramarital sexual relations—are considered major moral norms for virtuous behavior. Additional injunctions comprising the Eight or Ten Precepts are usually observed only by the most devout laypeople or on the Buddhist holy days *(thṅai sīl)* that fall on the eighth and fifteenth days of the waxing and waning moons.
2. Donations of food, money, goods, and services to the temple and monks are another principal means of gaining merit. Monks receive daily food alms as well as offerings on Buddhist holidays and other occasions, and donations are made for *vatt* construction projects, organization of ceremonies, and domestic services for monks.

3. Merit is also earned by prayer, meditation, listening to sermons, and recitation of scriptures. Such devotions may be performed at home (every house has a Buddhist altar), at temple services on holy days, in the annual cycle of Theravāda ceremonies, and at other events such as fund-raising festivals. Devout elderly persons sometimes go into retreat at the *vatt* to meditate and serve the monks.
4. For males, a primary way to achieve merit is to become a monk or novice. In prerevolutionary Cambodia, many men entered the *sangha* at some point in their lives, usually for a temporary period ranging from a few months to a few years, although some remained monks for their entire lives.

Khmer culture also includes conceptions that people's lives are affected by various factors, forces, and entities. For example, the Khmer use the Chinese twelve-year cycle in which each year is associated with a particular creature (year of the dog, cock, etc.). A person's birth year is vital to horoscopic calculations that determine diverse aspects of life, such as auspicious and inauspicious days, the choice of a compatible marriage partner, and diagnosis of illness. An individual also has "vital spirits" *(bralỳṅ)* that are capable of leaving the body (e.g., during dreams). Their absence causes misfortue or sickness, and ritual procedures are used to recapture or retain these spirits. Particular days of the week, months, phases of the moon, and cardinal directions also have auspicious or inauspicious qualities.

Of major importance in Khmer religion are beliefs that the world is populated with diverse nonhuman beings, some relatively benign and others frightening. Most are capable of causing misfortune, although some can be helpful if properly propitiated. The precise nature of these entities is not always clear. The term *qnak tā* ("old or ancestral people") is applied to a complex host of beings that include guardian spirits of localities (e.g., villages, districts, mountains); animistic nature spirits (living in trees, rice paddies, forests, etc.); spirits of known and unknown deceased persons; and spirits sometimes identified with Hindu deities. They can bring adversities such as sickness or drought if treated disrespectfully, but they can also be appeased or asked for aid in times of trouble through offerings and supplication. There are several kinds of ghosts of the dead (e.g., *khmoc laṅ, brāy)*, especially those who suffered unfortunate deaths (e.g., murder victims, suicides, and women who died in childbirth). Ghosts are greatly feared, and some are capable of causing illness. Somewhat different are spirits of the dead known as *qārakkh*, sometimes identified by human names, that can be mischievous but also protective toward those who give them offerings. *Me ba* are spirits of ancestors and deceased relatives who watch over living members of the family and may punish misdeeds or quarrels among kinsmen by causing some innocent member of the family to fall ill. *Mreñ gaṅvāl* are guardian spirits of certain wild and domestic animals who bring misfortune to anyone who mistreats these beasts.

The folk realm has its own specialists who mediate with the spirits or possess special skills. The *grū* is a shamanlike practitioner who has the knowledge and talent to perform any of a variety of procedures, such as curing illness through rituals for spirits, using folk medicines, or "blowing" on the afflicted part of the body. He may also be skilled in finding lost objects, practicing love magic, and making amulets to protect against misfortune or to confer invulnerability. The *rup qārakkh* are spirit mediums who, in a special ceremony once a year, become possessed by and speak for various *qārakkh* that wish to convey grievances and messages to the living. The *qācār* has expertise in the proper conduct of life cycle and other domestic ceremonies at which he officiates; he may also have other abilities such as curing. Quite rare, but feared, is the *dhmáp*, a sorcerer who, using various procedures, can cause a person to sicken and die unless treated by a *grū*.

There is generally little conflict between Theravāda and folk beliefs: shrines for *qnak tā* are sometimes found on Buddhist temple grounds, and most Khmer combine obeisance both to Buddhism and to the spirit world. The two are complementary because Theravāda deals with transcendental questions such as the general nature of existence, while folk beliefs and practices offer explanations for, and means to cope with, more immediate problems such as illness, drought, and unrequited love.

The Khmer have a rich ceremonial life. The annual cycle is punctuated by a succession of Buddhist observances: the New Year; the anniversary of the birth, enlightenment, and death of the Buddha; the entry of monks into rainy season retreat; the Bhjuṃ Piṇḍ, a festival for the dead; the monks' departure from retreat; the *kathin* ceremony to present new clothing and other gifts to the monks; and the anniversary of the Buddha's last sermon. In Cambodia before 1975 other calendrical observances included a national celebration called Guṃ Duuk, with boat races held in Phnom Penh, and court ceremonies such as the Plowing of the First Furrow that symbolically marked the beginning of the rice-growing season. At the local level there are life cycle observances associated with birth, marriage, death, and (in former times) a girl's first menses; there are also ordination ceremonies, agricultural rites, seasonal celebrations, and observances for occasions such as the erection of a new house. Ritual procedures, paraphernalia, and symbolism are quite complex and, like the Khmer religious system as a whole, a ceremony combines features from diverse sources into a single totality.

[*See also* Southeast Asian Religions, *article on* Mainland Cultures; Buddhism, *article on* Buddhism in Southeast Asia; *and* Theravāda. *For a discussion of the interrelation of popular and elite traditions in local Buddhist cultures, see* Folk Religion, *article on* Folk Buddhism. *Other pertinent discussions can be found in* Kingship, *article on* Kingship in Southeast Asia, *and* Saṃgha, *article on* Saṃgha and Society.]

BIBLIOGRAPHY

David P. Chandler's *History of Cambodia* (Boulder, 1983) offers a sophisticated study of Cambodian history from prehistoric to modern times that incorporates recent scholarship, places religion in its sociopolitical context, and provides annotated references to important literature. No detailed study of Cambodian Buddhism exists. A brief but useful account of its nature and organization is François Martini's "Le bonze cambodgien" and "Organisation du clergé bouddhique au Cambodge," *France-Asie* 12 (November–December 1955) 409–425. The major study of Cambodian ceremonialism is Eveline Porée-Maspero's *Étude sur les rites agraires des cambodgiens*, 3 vols. (Paris, 1962–1969). While some points in this work are debatable (including the author's thesis regarding certain cultural influences from early Chinese culture), it is a detailed compendium of Khmer rituals and beliefs going beyond agricultural rites. Ethnographic accounts of religious beliefs and practices among Khmer villagers are few and are limited primarily to chapters in Gabrielle Martel's *Lovea, village des environs d'Anqkor* (Paris, 1975) and to my own "Svay, a Khmer Village in Cambodia" (Ph.D. diss., Columbia University, 1968) and "Interrelations between Buddhism and Social Systems in Cambodian Peasant Culture," in *Anthropological Studies in Theravāda Buddhism*, edited by Manning Nash et al. (New Haven, 1966).

MAY EBIHARA

KHOI AND SAN RELIGION. The Khoi and San are the aboriginal peoples of southern Africa. The appellations formerly applied to them (*Hottentot* and *Bushmen*, respectively) have gone out of use because of their derogatory connotations. Properly, the terms *Khoi* and *San* refer to groups of related languages characterized by click consonants and to speakers of these languages, but they are frequently applied in a cultural sense to distinguish between pastoralists (Khoi) and foragers (San). In historical time (essentially, within the past 250 years in this region), these people were found widely distributed below the Cunene, Okavango, and Zambezi river systems, that is, in the modern states of Namibia, Botswana, Zimbabwe, and South Africa. Smaller numbers were, and are, to be found in southern Angola and Zambia. The once large population of San in South Africa has been completely eliminated; perhaps 20 percent of contemporary Khoi still live in that country. Accurate censuses of these people are available only for Botswana, where today about half the estimated forty thousand San live. The fifty thousand Khoi (except as noted above) are concentrated in Namibia.

Archaeological and historical evidence document the coexistence in these areas of herding and foraging economies for at least the past fifteen centuries. Bantu-speaking as well as Khoi and San agropastoralists have been in the region along with foragers during this entire span of time. The first ethnographies were compiled by German ethnologists in the last decade of the nineteenth century; a few accounts by missionaries, travelers, and traders are available for the preceding one hundred years.

All of these herders and foragers were seasonally migratory, circulating within group-controlled land tenures in response to seasonal distributions of pastures and plant and animal foods. The basic residential group was an extended family often with close collateral extensions; it seldom exceeded fifty persons in size. Two or more of these units, or segments thereof, came together for social, economic, and ritual reasons at specified times, and contact among adjacent groups was maintained by frequent visiting. Descent among the San is bilateral. Patrilineal clans are attributed to the Khoi. Neither social system contains hierarchical strata at present, although there is evidence for them in the past.

On the surface, Khoisan cosmological concepts are not uniformly coherent. The apparent ad hoc and sometimes ambivalent quality of explanations about natural phenomena has led anthropologists to treat these concepts in a descriptive, folkloristic manner. Yet there is an underlying order of shared symbolic categories that represents an inclusive process of cultural management. In its broad outlines, this system is common to all Khoisan groups, even though there is variation in content and emphasis from one group to another.

The key to understanding Khoisan cosmology lies in its creation myths. In the beginning of time all species were conflated. Body parts were distributed in a haphazard, capricious manner by the creator and were intermixed among the different animals. These beings moved through mythical time, eating and mating with each other and being reincarnated in different forms. In the process, each species assumed the identity suggested by its name and thereafter lived in the surroundings and ate the food appropriate to it. As order was achieved, the creator played an ever smaller active role in events; now he lives in the sky, relatively remote from earthly affairs. Generally positive values are attributed to him. Another being has the role of administrator; he is responsible for and is the cause of everything that occurs on earth. He is said to be stupid because he continues to make mistakes. One of the principal mistakes is that people continue to die when, in the logic of creation, they should not be mortal. He also capriciously sends or withholds rain, interferes in the conception and birth of children, and dictates success or failure in food production.

There is, accordingly, a dual conception of death. The death of animals is properly a part of their being; they are food. Human death is rationalized as the caprice of the administrator and justified on the grounds that he eats the dead, whose spirits then remain with him. These spirits have an incorporating interest in death because "their hearts cry for their living kin," and they wish to perpetuate the social order from which they came. The dead are thus agents of the administrator and a danger to the living, especially during dark nights away from camp.

This duality is pervasive in Khoisan cosmological thought. Aside from the obvious oppositions between life and death, earth and sky, that are found among so many peoples, a deeper configuration of a dialectical nature is present. Comparative data is scarce; however, a good deal is known about the Žu/hõasi San (!Kung) of Namibia and Botswana; these people are by far the most numerous living San. This, plus the fact that they share some specific details with Nama Khoi, is suggestive ground for using the data obtained from them for a paradigm case. The Žu/hõasi creator, !xo, and the administrator, //angwa, may be seen—and are sometimes described by informants—as a contrasting pair. Some of their respective attributes may be listed:

!XO	//ANGWA
Creative	Destructive
Passive	Active
Cool	Hot
Clean	Dirty
Hairless	Hirsute
Bees/Honey	Flies/Feces
Cattle/Sheep	Horses/Goats
The color blue	The color red
Cultural order	Natural order

In other words, !xo is a completed proper being, as is a Žu/õa person. (The name *Žu/hõasi* means "completed people": *žu* means "person," */hõa* "finished" or "complete," and *si* is a plural suffix.) //angwa is incomplete, chaotic, "without sense." !xo's attributes are desirable, //angwa's despicable. The one gives life, the other takes it away. Some Žu/hõasi think of them as alternative aspects of the same person. That this division, and by implication the cosmological system of which it is a part, may have considerable time depth is suggested by the attribution of cattle and sheep to the cultural order of !xo, while horses and goats are assigned to the unfinished domain of //angwa. Archaeological evidence places both cattle and sheep firmly within the first millennium CE in southern Africa; horses are much more recent. Linguistically, cattle and sheep are derived from a single native stem in most Khoisan languages; horses and goats, on the other hand, are called by a term borrowed from Setswana or—in the case of horses—by extensions of the local word for zebra.

Among the Nama, the creator (rendered Tsui //goab by Schapera) has functions identical to those of !xo and, like his Žu/hõasi counterpart, had an earthly trickster manifestation during the time of creation. It was this trickster (≠gaun!a among Žu/hõasi; Heitsi Eibib among the Nama) who carried out the actual acts of creation. Khoi, in the past, had annual rain ceremonies in which several groups joined. Pregnant cattle and sheep were slaughtered on these occasions and their flesh consumed; their milk, blood, and the water in which they were boiled were used to douse the fire on which they had been cooked. Prayers for rain were offered to Tsui //goab as this was done. The Nama counterpart of //angwa is //gaunab, derived from *//gau,* "to destroy." Their administrative roles are parallel. Earlier writers claim that southern Khoi and southern San worshiped the moon, but as Schapera notes, these reports are inadequate and unsystematic; it is, therefore, difficult to give full credit to such claims. Contemporary San use the moon as a quite specific and accurate timepiece. When referring to the time of occurrence of an event, they will point to a position of the moon in the sky or state that the moon's return to a position will coincide with some event. Women mark their menstrual cycles and the durations of their pregnancies in like manner, but they do so strictly for calendric purposes. It is possible Europeans interpreted these actions as "moon worship."

Although the mythological past is not thought to be active in the present natural world, many of its elements are very much involved in the control of this world. The administrator eats not only humans but also flies, which he attracts by smearing honey around his mouth. This reversal of propriety and the fact that he is covered with long hair (Khoisan have little body hair) is taken as further proof of the confused incompleteness that situates him in residual mythological time. Shamans enter this time while in trance to confront the administrator.

Žu/hõasi shamans go in disembodied flight to the sky and wrestle with //angwa in an attempt to force him to correct some error—an illness, a social disfunction, or an uncertainty about events. In entering this state, shamans take on some of its attributes; they sprout body hair or feathers, become partly or wholly animal, and fly. To be able to participate in this realm they must partake of it. They eat the bile of a lion, the musk gland of a skunklike weasel, the fat from an eland and a porcupine, and the roots of the three plants that grow in the supernatural world. Bitterness (of bile and gland) and fat are the dual sources of strength, as are the roots of extrasensory vision. These elements—eaten once during the course of learning to be a shaman—empower ordinary men to challenge the strength of the supernatural and, by overcoming it, to restore order to the social and natural universe.

The ritual context in which these activities take place involves the entire kin-based community. Only a few people who are directly affected may participate in minor cases, but, small or large, the form of both divinatory and curing rituals is the same. Both involve trance as the essential visionary condition in which the shaman is enabled to exercise his or her power. Women and girls sit in close physical contact, forming a circle facing a fire; they sing and clap songs that are associated with specific natural elements, usually animals but also plants or their products. Men and boys dance closely around the circle, chanting a counterpoint to the songs. Certain dancers are identified with particular animals and their songs; they are more likely to enter trance during performances of these songs. As a dancer feels the trance state approaching, he or she intensifies his or her movements and vocalizations, uttering piercing cries and calling for help, which is signified by heightening the intensity of the music. It is said that in the mythological past, the actual animal being danced (an eland, for example) was attracted to the performance, but now only its spirit attends.

During divinatory trances, Žu/hõasi shamans shout descriptions of their encounter with //angwa in which the cause of the social or physical illness under investigation is revealed. This cause is almost invariably some transgression on the part of either the patient or a close kinsman, usually involving the violation of rights to property (especially the products of land) or personal rights (infractions of obligations, sometimes extending to ancestors). But this direct cause is always expressed indirectly as having disrupted the cosmological order through some mediating agency; for example, the offender may have eaten (or only have killed) a forbidden animal. During the curing trance, the shaman rubs the patient and everyone else present with his hands and arms, thereby transferring healing energy through the mediating agent—sweat.

Thus the myths and their reenactment constitute the conceptual dimensions of Khoisan reality. They integrate subjective experience with the larger structural context through a repertoire of causal principles that, though not expressly verbalized in ordinary discourse, are based on an underlying symbolic order. Trance rituals mediate between these realms. Although couched in causal metaphors, responsibility is normally allocated to living individuals (through their having transgressed the cosmological order) and almost always involves a consensus solution to current social disruptions. The act of divination translates the cosmological constructs in terms of the specific instance at hand. The random, amoral, impersonal forces of nature—which have an order of their own, personified by the administrator and his domain—are temporarily neutralized by this dialectic between culture and society. In the process, although the internal logic remains intact, both are transformed.

There is abundant evidence that these contemporary systems of thought are derived through transformations of more ancient systems. Many rock paintings throughout southern Africa depict persons in postures identical to those assumed during trance today. Therianthropic and theriomorphic figures comparable with those of current creation myths abound among these paintings. The basic structure of these myths and many specific referents (rain bulls whose blood brings rain; water snakes that have hair, horns, limbs, and ears; beings that partake of the mythic past in the present) are shared by many Khoisan and southern Bantu-speaking peoples, suggesting a long history of associated cosmological construction. There is also evidence for comparatively recent change from more active totemic association with natural elements, especially animals, prominent today in trance. The colonial era and its aftermath disrupted the political and economic lives of Khoisan as well as Bantu-speaking peoples; in this process, it is possible but not yet certain that destructive, uncontrollable elements of the cosmological system became emphasized over the constructive forces of creation, and that today the administrator (//angwa of Žu/hõasi) has disproportionate power when compared historically with the role that the creator (!xo) has played.

BIBLIOGRAPHY

Biesele, Megan. "Sapience and Scarce Resources." *Social Science Information* 17 (1978): 921–947.

Lee, Richard B. *The !Kung San: Men, Women, and Work in a Foraging Society.* New York, 1979. The first comprehensive view of the San. Although it falls prey to many traditional faults of evolutionary theory in anthropology, it is much more systematic than its predecessors.

Lewis-Williams, David. *Believing and Seeing: Symbolic Meanings in Southern San Rock Paintings.* London, 1981. Excellent integration of prehistoric and historical rock art with contemporary and archival stories. Points the way toward further fruitful research.

Marshall, Lorna. "!Kung Bushman Religious Beliefs." *Africa* 32 (1962): 221–252. Narrative and descriptive account containing useful information but no comprehensive analysis.

Schapera, Isaac. *The Khoisan Peoples of South Africa.* London, 1930. Based on accounts of missionaries and travelers. Valuable information but outdated synthesis.

Silberbauer, George B. *Hunter and Habitat in the Central Kalahari Desert.* Cambridge, Mass., 1981. Primarily an ecological, evolutionary study, but also includes information on the religious system of the G/wi San.

Wilmsen, Edwin N. "Of Paintings and Painters, in Terms of Žu/hõasi Interpretations." In *Contemporary Studies on Khoisan in Honour of Oswin Köhler on the Occasion of His Seventy-fifth Birthday,* edited by Rainer Vossen and Klaus Keuthmann. Hamburg, 1986. An economic and political analysis of prehistoric and contemporary San paintings.

EDWIN N. WILMSEN

KHOMIAKOV, ALEKSEI (1804–1860), Russian Orthodox lay theologian. Khomiakov was influential in determining the character of the Russian intelligentsia in the 1840s and 1850s; the emergence of one of its principal schools of thought, Slavophilism, is closely linked with his name. He was a member of the landed gentry and a participant in the salons of Moscow. His skills as a dialectician and debater were respected even by those (such as Herzen) who shared few of his views. Khomiakov's skills as a writer were less evident in his own milieu as the result of censorship or at least the anticipation of censorship. Virtually all his writings on religion were published abroad and in French. Most of these were published posthumously in their country of origin; few were available in Russian before 1879.

Khomiakov graduated from the University of Moscow as a mathematician but never received any formal instruction in theology. In view of the limitations under which Russian academic theology labored at this time, this was probably an advantage. It allowed him to probe church life for the essentials of the Orthodox faith and to delineate them in a remarkably succinct and forceful fashion. Most notable among his theological compositions was the essay *The Church Is One* (c. 1850).

In this essay Khomiakov adumbrated his celebrated teaching on *sobornost'*, the cornerstone of his theology. The term—a Russian neologism—defies translation, and Khomiakov invariably preferred to transliterate rather than translate it. He himself objected to the French translation, *conciliarité*. In modern times no one word has been found as an acceptable, equally comprehensive, alternative.

Khomiakov derived *sobornost'* from the ninth-century (and subsequently standard) Church Slavonic translation of the Nicene creed, where the term *catholic (katholikos)* had been rendered as *sobornaia*. For him, the word denoted more than mere universality. It spoke rather of a church in which free and complete unanimity prevailed. Such freedom could admit of no constraint. Papal authoritarianism was indicative of a profound malaise in Western Christendom, and Khomiakov campaigned vigorously against it. Indeed, for Khomiakov, any kind of authoritarianism contradicted the very nature of the church. His intuition on this subject was to receive confirmation in 1848 when the Eastern patriarchs and bishops replied to the papal encyclical of that year. Their reply was enthusiastically echoed by Khomiakov (1850) in his correspondence with William Palmer: "The unvarying constancy and the unerring truth of the Christian dogma does not depend upon any Hierarchical Order: it is guarded by the totality, by the whole *people* of the church, which is the Body of Christ" (Birbeck, 1895, p. 94). By the same token, the individualism of the Protestant world was to be rejected. In 1851 he declared that it is in the Orthodox church that "a unity is to be found more authoritative than the despotism of the Vatican, *for it is based on the strength of mutual love*. There [also] a liberty is to be found more free than the license of Protestantism, for it is *regulated by the humility of mutual love*" (Birbeck, 1895, p. 102).

In the teaching of the Slavophiles, as of Khomiakov himself, a social expression of such mutuality was to be found in the Russian peasant commune, the *obshchina*. That the principles of *obshchinnost'* ("communality") and of *sobornost'* were interrelated, if not interdependent, was emphasized by Khomiakov's use of the one term *obshchina* ("commune") to designate both the ecclesiastical community (*koinonia*) and the peasant commune proper. But with the increasing disrepute and ultimate disappearance of the latter, this strand of Khomiakov's thought was itself to be obscured in later years. By contrast, his teaching on *sobornost'* was to capture the imagination of Russian religious thinkers throughout succeeding decades and to play its part also in the ecumenical debates of the century to come.

BIBLIOGRAPHY

Birbeck, William J., ed. *Russia and the English Church during the Last Fifty Years: Containing a Correspondence between Mr. William Palmer Fellow of Magdalen College, Oxford and M. Khomiakoff, in the Years 1844-1854* (1895). Reprint, Farnborough, 1969. Includes also the invaluable *The Church Is One.*

Bol'shakov, Sergius. *The Doctrine of the Unity of the Church in the Works of Khomyakov and Moehler*. London, 1946. Originally a doctoral dissertation which juxtaposes Khomiakov's thought with that of his Roman Catholic contemporary J. A. Möhler. The latter's *Die Einheit in der Kirche* (1825) provides important parallels for Khomiakov's work, even if it cannot be considered as its source.

Christoff, Peter K. *An Introduction to Nineteenth-Century Russian Slavophilism: A Study in Ideas*, vol. 1, *A. S. Xomjakov*. The Hague, 1961. A wide-ranging study of Khomiakov's work as a whole; the only such study in English to date.

SERGEI HACKEL

KHUSRAW, AMĪR (AH 651?–725?/1254?–1325? CE), distinguished Indo-Persian poet, musician, and panegyrist. His father, Sayf al-Dīn Shamsī, was most probably a slave-officer in the court of the Delhi sultan Iltutmish (r. 1211–1236). Orphaned at an early age, Khusraw was brought up in the household of his maternal grandfather, ʿImād al-Mulk, another high-ranking nobleman and a former Hindu rajput who must have converted to Islam following the establishment of Turkish rule in India in the early thirteenth century.

Almost every aspect of Khusraw's life and work has been mythologized to the point where it is difficult to separate the true historical personage from his current popular image. He is today hailed as a great patriot and is counted among the foremost Ṣūfīs of India. Credited with the composition of many lyrics used for *qawwālīs*, a genre of Ṣūfī devotional music, as well as numerous works in Hindi, he is also renowned as a creator of ragas and inventor of musical instruments, including the sitar. Popularly referred to as Ḥaẓrat Amīr Khusraw, he is accorded an honorific title raising him to the stature of a saint. His *ʿurs* (lit., "wedding," the anniversary of a saint's death) is celebrated with tremendous enthusiasm and devotion. He is also known as Turk Allāh ("God's Turk") and Tutī-yi Hind ("the parrot of India").

Khusraw displayed his precocious poetic talents at an early age. Seeking his livelihood in the only way open to poets of his time, in the service of rich patrons, he finally found a position at the royal court and had no scruples about flattering a series of royal masters, one of whom had acquired the throne after murdering his former benefactors. Khusraw was first employed by Sultan Kayqubād (1287–1290), at whose request he wrote a long poem, *Qirān al-saʿdayn* (The Conjunction of the Two Auspicious Stars). He continued in the service of the next ruler, Jalāl al-Dīn Khiljī (1290–1296), whose achievements he lauded in his *Miftāḥ al-futūḥ* (The Key to Victories). The reign of ʿAlāʾ al-Dīn Khiljī (1296–1316) saw Khusraw at his most prolific, with *Khazāʾin al-futūḥ* (The Treasury of Victories) and *ʿĀshiqah* (the love story of Khiḍr Khān and Dewal Rani). He also paid eloquent poetic tributes to the next ruler, Mubārak Shāh Khiljī (1316–1320), who was by all accounts vain and debauched, in *Nuh sipihr* (The Nine Skies). When the Tughlaqs replaced the Khiljīs, Khusraw continued in the service of Ghiyāth al-Dīn Tughlaq (1320–1325), the history of whose reign he encapsulated in the *Tughlaq-nāmah*.

Khusraw was the first poet in India to compose war and court epics in Persian. As a prose writer he was remarkably eloquent; as a poet he was the master of all forms of verse: *rubāʿīs* ("quatrains"), *qaṣīdahs* ("odes"), and *ghazals* ("lyrics"). A superb lyricist, Khusraw confidently mixed Persian and Hindi metaphors with striking results.

But it was his association with Shaykh Niẓām al-Dīn Awliyāʾ (d. 1325), a saint of the Chishtī order, that is responsible for Khusraw's present stature. The Chishtīyah, a Ṣūfī order that flourished only in India, were at the height of their popularity during the spiritual reign of Shaykh Niẓām al-Dīn. As liberal interpreters of Islam, they provided an effective counterpoint to the orthodox version of Islam as propounded by the court-associated *ʿulamāʾ*. The liberalism of this order was reflected not only in their attitude toward non-Muslims but also in their patronage of cultural activities. As firm believers in the power of music and dance to induce mystical ecstasy, for which they were constantly attacked by the orthodox, they naturally attracted poets and musicians to their hospices (*khāngāhs*). In fact, almost all literary activity among the Muslims of this period was influenced by the ideology of the Chishtīyah. Among notable contemporaries of Khusraw also associated with the Chishtī *khāngāh* were Amīr Ḥasan Sijzī, the great poet and mystic, and Ẓiyā al-Dīn Baranī, the courtier and historian.

Khusraw came into contact with Shaykh Niẓām al-Dīn in 1272, and though he was never initiated into the mystic order, his wit and poetical and musical talents endeared him to the saint. Remarks attributed to the shaykh indicate the special fondness that he had for Khusraw.

The atmosphere of Shaykh Niẓām al-Dīn's *khāngāh* was particularly conducive to Khusraw's sensibilities. As a crucible where a composite culture was evolving from the interaction between Islamic and Indic elements, it suited the genius of Khusraw, who was by birth the product of a similar fusion. As a poet he thrived on mystic themes and imagery; as a gifted musician he moved the audiences at sessions of devotional music (*samāʿ*) to ecstasy, and with his special ear for languages he contributed greatly to the evolution of a lingua franca that made communication possible among the various groups. In brief, Khusraw came to represent almost every aspect of the Ṣūfī tradition in India.

Khusraw also embodies the contradictions arising from his situation. As a courtier dependent on the political survival of the Muslim rulers, he vocalizes an intense and often crude hatred for the Hindus, identifying in them the main threat to his class. But as a poet inspired by the ideology of the Chishtīyah, he displays a touching sensitivity and respect for the religion and culture of India. For this reason Khusraw represents a fine example of the evolving synthesis between the Islamic and the indigenous cultures of the Indian subcontinent.

BIBLIOGRAPHY

Although there are many studies on Amīr Khusraw, most of them unfortunately lack critical analysis of the man or his writings. The most adequate work on Khusraw in English continues to be Mohammad Wahid Mirza's *The Life and Works of Amir Khusrau* (1935; reprint, Lahore, 1962). See *Amir Khusrau: Memorial Volume* (New Delhi, 1975) for a collection of some erudite articles by experts on various facets of his personality. Mohammad Habib's *Hazrat Amir Khusraw of Delhi* (Bombay, 1927), also included in *Politics and Society during the Early Medieval Period: Collected Works of Professor Mohammad Habib*, edited by K. A. Nizami (New Delhi, 1974), is a historical analysis of Khusraw by a leading scholar of medieval Indian history. For a list of Khusraw's works, see C. A. Storey's *Persian Literature: A Bio-Bibliographical Survey*, vol. 2, part 3 (London, 1939).

SALEEM KIDWAI

KHVARENAH is the Avestan term for "splendor" (OPers, *farnah;* MPers, Pahl., *khwarr;* NPers, *khurrah* or *farr*), designating one of the most characteristic notions of ancient Iranian religion. It is often associated with the aureole of royalty and of royal fortune, thanks to its identification in the Hellenistic period with Greek *tuchē* and Aramaic *gad,* "fortune" (*gd* is also the ideogram with which *khwarr* is written in Pahlavi), but its meanings go beyond the sphere of royalty, and its influence transcends the confines of the Iranian world. Aspects of the concept of *khvarenah* are found in Manichaeism and Buddhism and are interwoven with similar concepts characteristic of other cultures, as in the Turkish notion of *qut* and the Armenian *p'aṙk'*. In the Avesta and in Zoroastrian tradition in general, *khvarenah* is also personified as a *yazata* or a being "worthy of worship."

Fundamental to the concept of *khvarenah* are its connections with light and fire, attested in the root from which it is derived, *khvar* ("to shine, to illuminate"), which is—despite the opposing opinion of H. W. Bailey, author of an important essay on the question (1943, pp. 1–77)—the same root as *hvar,* "sun" (Duchesne-Guillemin, 1963, pp. 19–31). This explains why *khvarenah* is sometimes translated in Greek as *doxa* ("glory") and in Arabic-Persian as *nūr* ("light").

The *khvarenah* is a luminous and radiant force, a fiery and solar fluid that is found, mythologically, in water, in *haoma,* and, according to Zoroastrian anthropogony, in semen. It is an attribute characteristic of Mithra, of royalty, of divine and heroic figures in the national and religious tradition, of Yima, the first king, of Zarathushtra, and of the three Saoshyants, who perform their tasks (Pahl., *khwēshkārīh*) on earth thanks to the *khwarr* that they possess. It has the power to illuminate the mind and to open the eye of the soul to spiritual vision, enabling those who possess it to penetrate the mysteries of the otherworld.

Recently the winged disk in Achaemenid reliefs has been interpreted as the *khvarenah* (Shahbazi, 1980, pp. 119–147). Deified Khvarenah (Pharro) is depicted on coins from the Kushan empire as a standing man with flames rising from his back.

BIBLIOGRAPHY

Bachhofer, Ludwig. "Pancika und Harītī, *Pharo* und *Ardochro.*" *Ostasiaatische Zeitschrift,* n.s. 23 (1937): 6–15.

Bailey, H. W. *Zoroastrian Problems in the Ninth-Century Books* (1943). Oxford, 1971.

Bombaci, Alessio. "Qutlug Bolsun!" *Ural-Altaische Jahrbücher* 36 (1965): 284–291 and 38 (1966): 13–44.

Boyce, Mary. *A History of Zoroastrianism,* vol. 2. Leiden, 1982.

Bussagli, Mario. "Cusanica et Serica." *Rivista degli studi orientali* 37 (1962): 79–103.

Corbin, Henry. *Terre céleste et corps de résurrection.* Paris, 1961.

Cumont, Franz. *Textes et monuments figurés relatifs aux mystères de Mithra.* 2 vols. Brussels, 1896–1899.

Duchesne-Guillemin, Jacques. "Le 'Xărenah.' " *Annali dell'Istituto Universitario Orientale di Napoli,* Sezione Linguistica, 5 (1963): 19–31.

Eliade, Mircea. "Spirit, Light, and Seed." *History of Religions* 11 (1971): 1–30.

Gnoli, Gherardo. "Un particolare aspetto del simbolismo della luce nel Mazdeismo e nel Manicheismo." *Annali dell'Istituto Universitario Orientale di Napoli,* n.s. 12 (1962): 95–128.

Hertel, Johannes, ed. and trans. *Die awestischen Herrschafts- und Siegesfeuer.* Leipzig, 1931.

Itō, Gikyō. "Gathica." *Orient* 11 (1975): 1–10.

Litvinskii, B. A. "Das K'ang-chü-Sarmatische Farnan." *Central Asiatic Journal* 16 (1972): 241–289.

Shahbazi, A. S. "An Achaemenid Symbol." *Archaeologische Mitteilungen aus Iran,* n.s. 13 (1980): 119–147.

GHERARDO GNOLI
Translated from Italian by Roger DeGaris

KIERKEGAARD, SØREN (1813–1855), the most outstanding writer in the history of Danish letters and one of the leading religious philosophers of the nineteenth century. Kierkegaard's novel interpretation of the structure and dynamics of individual selfhood formed the basis of his radical critique of European cultural Protestantism and its philosophical counterpart, Hegelianism. His innovative ideas have remained extremely influential throughout the twentieth century.

Life. Søren Aabye Kierkegaard was a person of unusual complexity whose outward life was relatively uneventful. Having received a substantial inheritance, he never needed to secure a regular professional position. He devoted most of his short life to the production of an immense body of philosophical and religious literature. The formative events in Kierkegaard's life centered around two individuals: his father, Michael Pedersen Kierkegaard, and his one-time fiancée, Regine Olsen; and two public conflicts: the *Corsair* affair, and his celebrated attack upon the Danish church.

Michael Pedersen Kierkegaard was a successful Copenhagen businessman who retired at an early age to pursue his theological interests. The elder Kierkegaard was a sober, brooding man who was possessed by a profound sense of personal guilt. In an effort to come to terms with his malaise, he became deeply involved in the Protestant pietism that was then sweeping Denmark. Michael subjected his favorite son, Søren, to a rigorous and austere religious upbringing. The psychological and intellectual complexity of the father-son relation left a lasting impression on Kierkegaard and indirectly informed much of his theological reflection.

The other personal relationship that was decisive for Kierkegaard was his brief engagement to Regine Olsen. Shortly after proposing marriage to Regine, Kierkegaard precipitated a break with her. The apparent reason for this unexpected reversal was twofold. In the first place, Kierkegaard discovered an unbridgeable gap between his own introspective, tormented personality and the seemingly innocent, inexperienced Regine. Second, Kierkegaard became convinced that his religious vocation precluded marriage and family life. Many of Kierkegaard's most important works focus on issues raised by his perplexing relation to Regine.

The two major public events in Kierkegaard's life involved him in bitter controversy. Late in 1845, Kierkegaard published a criticism of the *Corsair,* a sophisticated Danish scandal sheet, in which he exposed the association of several leading intellectuals with this notorious journal. The embarrassed authors and editors responded by unleashing an abusive personal attack on Kierkegaard in which he was held up to public ridicule. This episode marked a turning point in his life. After 1846, Kierkegaard's writings became more overtly Christian. The full implications of this shift emerged clearly in Kierkegaard's attack on the Danish church. Kierkegaard believed that God had chosen him to expose the scandal of a society that espoused Christian principles but in which citizens lived like "pagans." In a series of articles entitled *The Moment,* Kierkegaard argued that the Christianity preached in the established church of Denmark was actually the opposite of the religion practiced by Jesus. His penetrating criticisms of church and society created a public furor. In the midst of this controversy, Kierkegaard died (11 November 1855).

Works. Few authors have written as wide a variety of works as Kierkegaard. Most of his writings can be grouped in four major categories.

1. *Pseudonymous works.* Between 1841 and 1850, Kierkegaard wrote a series of works under different pseudonyms. These are his best-known books: *Either-Or* (1843), *Repetition* (1843), *Fear and Trembling* (1843), *Philosophical Fragments* (1844), *The Concept of Anxiety* (1844), *Stages on Life's Way* (1845), *Concluding Unscientific Postscript* (1846), *Crisis in a Life of an Actress and Other Essays on Drama* (1848), *The Sickness unto Death* (1849), and *Training in Christianity* (1850). Not until the last pages of *Concluding Unscientific Postscript* did Kierkegaard publicly claim responsibility for his pseudonymous writings.

2. *Edifying discourses.* It was Kierkegaard's custom to accompany each of the pseudonymous texts with one or more religious works published under his own name. He frequently complained that while his pseudonymous writings received considerable attention, his religious works were virtually ignored. Two kinds of works make up the edifying discourses: ethical discourses and Christian discourses. While the ethical discourses consistently exclude Christian categories, the Christian discourses explore religious life from the perspective of Christian faith. The former are more common before 1845 and the latter more numerous after that date. The most important Christian discourses are: *Works of Love* (1847), *Christian Discourses* (1848), *The Lilies of the Field and the Birds of the Air* (1849), *For Self-Examination* (1851), and *Judge for Yourself* (1851–1852).

3. *Polemical tracts.* Since he understood himself as a necessary "corrective" to "the present age," Kierkegaard remained an irrepressible polemicist. As was the custom in Denmark at that time, he presented his views on current intellectual and social matters in the public press and in pamphlets that were directed to a general audience. Kierkegaard's most important polemical writings appeared in a newspaper, *The Fatherland,* and his own publication, *The Moment.* These articles provide a glimpse of Kierkegaard's immediate impact on Danish society.

4. *Journals and papers.* Throughout his life, Kierkegaard kept a detailed journal, which he knew would be published after his death. The journal, which runs to twenty volumes, contains a wealth of information about Kierkegaard's personality, writings, and his views of other philosophers and theologians.

Two important books do not fall within this general grouping. *The Concept of Irony, with Constant Reference to Socrates* (1841) was Kierkegaard's dissertation for the master of arts degree. This work presents an early version of his critique of Hegel and leading nineteenth-century Romantics. In addition, the analysis of Socrates developed in this book forms the basis of Kierkegaard's understanding of his own role as an author. This becomes obvious in the final text that deserves mention: *The Point of View for My Work as an Author* (written in 1848 and published posthumously in 1859). In this short book, Kierkegaard insists that in spite of appearances to the contrary, his diverse writings form a coherent whole that is constantly guided by a religious purpose.

Thought. Kierkegaard's sense of religious mission informs all of his writings. The overriding goal of his work is nothing less than "the reintroduction of Christianity into Christendom." Since Kierkegaard believes that authentic human existence is decisively revealed in Christianity, he is convinced that the struggle to lead a Christian life involves the attempt to realize true selfhood. Kierkegaard's writings represent a sustained effort to provide the occasion for individuals to make the difficult movement of faith. The most important part of Kierkegaard's carefully conceived strategy is his intricate pseudonymous authorship. The pseudonymous writings can best be understood by considering three interrelated assumptions that they all share: the notion of indirect communication, the understanding of the structure of selfhood, and the theory of the stages of existence.

Kierkegaard's method of communicating indirectly through pseudonyms reflects his effort to address problems peculiar to nineteenth-century Denmark and expresses his general conception of the nature of religious truth. He repeatedly insists that most of his fellow Danes were simply deluding themselves when they claimed to be Christians. The established Lutheran church had so domesticated Christian faith that the spiritual tensions that characterized original Christianity had all but disappeared. In this situation, Kierkegaard views his task as inversely Socratic. Rather than engaging in a rational dialogue that is supposed to uncover the truth implicitly possessed by all human beings, Kierkegaard tries to bring individuals to the brink of decision by offering them the opportunity to discover the errors of their ways. Each pseudonym represents a different point of view that reflects a distinct form of life. Kierkegaard presents these works as mirrors in which people can see themselves reflected. The self-knowledge that results from this encounter with the text creates the possibility of decisions that redefine the self.

Kierkegaard's method of communication is also a function of his conviction that religious truth is subjectivity. In contrast to Hegel's speculative approach to Christianity, Kierkegaard maintains that religious truth cannot be conceptually grasped but must be existentially appropriated through the free activity of the individual agent. In matters of faith, there can be neither knowledge nor certainty. Human existence in general and religious belief in particular always involve absolute risk. Kierkegaard's aim is to serve as a "midwife" who can attend but not effect the birth of the authentic self.

This understanding of indirect communication presupposes a specific interpretation of the structure of human selfhood. In *The Sickness unto Death,* Kierkegaard ironically employs Hegelian language to formulate an account of selfhood that overturns Hegel's understanding of subjectivity. The self, Kierkegaard argues, is a structure of self-relation that is created and sustained by the wholly other God. Each human being is called upon to relate possibilities and actualities through the exercise of his or her free will. This view of the self forms the basis of Kierkegaard's penetrating psychological analyses. In *The Concept of Anxiety,* Kierkegaard defines anxiety in terms of the subject's recognition of the possibilities opened by its own freedom. Despair is the subject's failure or refusal to be itself. Anxiety and despair combine to disclose the self's responsibility for itself.

The analysis of the structure of selfhood forms the foundation of the theory of the stages of existence. Although each person is irreducibly individual, Kierkegaard maintains that it is possible to discern recurrent patterns amid the variety of human lives. He identifies three basic stages of existence: aesthetic, ethical, and religious. Each stage represents a distinct form of life that is governed by different assumptions and expectations. Taken together, the stages provide an outline of the entire pseudonymous authorship. While Kierkegaard examines aesthetic existence in the first part of both *Either-Or* and *Stages on Life's Way,* the second section of each of these works is devoted to a consideration of ethical experience. The analysis of the religious stage is more complex. In *Fear and Trembling, Philosophical Fragments,* and *Concluding Unscientific Postscript,*

Kierkegaard approaches questions and dilemmas posed by religion from the perspective of nonbelief. *The Sickness unto Death* and *Training in Christianity,* by contrast, are written from an avowedly Christian point of view. Finally, the third part of *Stages on Life's Way* is a tortuous account of the inner struggle of an individual who is caught between belief and unbelief.

These three stages of existence are not randomly selected and arbitrarily presented. Rather, the stages are carefully ordered in such a way that as one advances from the aesthetic through the ethical to the religious, there is a movement toward authentic selfhood. Generally conceived, this progression charts the subject's advance from undifferentiated identification with its environment, through increasing differentiation from otherness, to complete individuation, in which the self becomes a concrete individual, eternally responsible for itself. The aesthetic stage of existence is characterized by the absence of genuine decision. The lack of free resolution results from either unreflective immersion in sensuous inclination and social life or the dispassionate absorption in abstract reflection. From the ethical point of view, the self has an obligation to become itself through free activity. Deliberate decision marks an essential moment in the process of individuation and forms a crucial stage in the journey to selfhood. The ethicist, however, is insufficiently sensitive to the self's radical dependence on God. The ethical actor eventually realizes that he actually divinizes the social order by regarding moral obligation as divine commandment. The "infinite qualitative difference" between the divine and the human creates the possibility of a conflict between obligation to other people and obedience to God. Kierkegaard labels this collision a "teleological suspension of the ethical." This clash between religious and moral responsibility effectively overturns ethical life.

The religious stage of existence represents the full realization of authentic selfhood. Kierkegaard's analysis of the self culminates in the paradoxical coincidence of opposites created and sustained by the faithful individual's absolute decision. Faith is the free activity of self-relation in which the self becomes itself by simultaneously differentiating and synthesizing the opposites that make up its being. In this critical moment of decision, a person who is fully conscious of his responsibility for his life constitutes his unique individuality by decisively distinguishing himself from other selves and defining his eternal identity in the face of the wholly other God. The qualitative difference between God and self renders impossible any immanent relation between the divine and the human. Left to himself, the sinful individual cannot establish the absolute relation to the absolute upon which genuine selfhood depends. The possibility of the proper relation between God and self is opened by the incarnate Christ. The God-man is an absolute paradox that can never be rationally comprehended. This absolute paradox poses an irreconcilable either-or: *either* believe, *or* be offended. Faith is a radical venture, an unmediated leap in which the self transforms itself. By faithfully responding to the absolutely paradoxical divine presence, the self internalizes the truth of the God-man. In this moment of decision, truth becomes subjective and the subject becomes truthful. Such truthful subjectivity is the goal toward which Kierkegaard's complex authorship relentlessly leads the reader.

Influence. Largely ignored in his own day, Kierkegaard's writings emerged during the early decades of the twentieth century to become a dominant force in theology, philosophy, psychology, and literature. Kierkegaard's theological impact is evident in Protestant neoorthodoxy. Karl Barth and Rudolph Bultmann developed many of the themes that Kierkegaard had identified. In the thought of Martin Buber, Kierkegaard's influence extends into the domain of Jewish theology.

Kierkegaard's work also forms the foundation of one of the most important twentieth-century schools of philosophy: existentialism. Kierkegaard set the terms of debate for major Continental philosophers like Martin Heidegger, Karl Jaspers, and Jean-Paul Sartre. By underscoring the importance of the problems of individual selfhood, authenticity, transcendence, absurdity, temporality, death, desire, guilt, despair, anxiety, and hope, Kierkegaard's texts provided rich resources for an entire generation of philosophers. [*See* Existentialism.]

Less often recognized is Kierkegaard's role in modern psychology. His ground-breaking analyses of the psychic states of the individual self have been expanded and extended by psychologists like Ludwig Binswanger and R. D. Laing. The psychological theories that have arisen from the work of Kierkegaard tend to complement and correct currents in traditional Freudian analysis.

Finally, it is important to stress Kierkegaard's influence on twentieth-century literature. The hand of Kierkegaard can be seen in the works of creative authors as different as Albert Camus, Franz Kafka, John Updike, and Walker Percy.

This summary can only suggest the extraordinary importance of Kierkegaard's work. The insights of this lonely Dane pervade contemporary thought and shape the way many people now understand their lives.

BIBLIOGRAPHY

Primary Sources. The standard Danish editions of Kierkegaard's writings are *Søren Kierkegaards Papirer,* 11 vols., edited by P. A. Heiberg et al. (Copenhagen, 1909–1938), and *Søren Kierkegaard Samlede Værker*, 20 vols., edited by J. L. Heiberg et al. (Copenhagen, 1962–1964). The best English translations of these works are *Søren Kierkegaard's Journals and Papers*, 7 vols., edited and translated by Howard V. Hong and Edna H. Hong with Gregory Malantschuk (Bloomington, Ind., 1967–1978), and *Kierkegaard's Writings*, edited by Howard V. Hong (Princeton, 1977–).

Secondary Sources. There is an enormous body of secondary literature on Kierkegaard. Emanuel Hirsch's *Kierkegaard-Studien*, 2 vols. (Gütersloh, 1933), remains the most comprehensive intellectual biography of Kierkegaard. Gregor Malantschuk's *Kierkegaard's Thought* (Princeton, 1971) and Jean Wahl's *Études kierkegaardiennes* (Paris, 1938) are fine accounts of Kierkegaard's overall position. James D. Collins's *The Mind of Kierkegaard* (Chicago, 1953) provides a good introduction to Kierkegaard's thought. For a helpful examination of the importance of Kierkegaard's pseudonymous method, see Louis Mackey's *Kierkegaard: A Kind of Poet* (Philadelphia, 1971). Stephen Crites's *In the Twilight of Christendom: Hegel vs. Kierkegaard on Faith and History* (Chambersburg, Pa., 1972) and my own *Journeys to Selfhood: Hegel and Kierkegaard* (Berkeley, 1980) analyze the complex relationship between Kierkegaard and Hegel.

MARK C. TAYLOR

KIMBANGU, SIMON (1889–1951), African religious prophet and founder of the Church of Jesus Christ on Earth through the Prophet Simon Kimbangu. Kimbangu was born on 24 September 1889 in the village of N'Kamba, located in the Ngombe district of lower Zaire (the former Belgian Congo). In Kikongo, the word *kimbangu* means "one who reveals the hidden truth." Many legends surround Kimbangu's youth and early religious activities. Some accounts claim that both his mother and father were traditional Kongo healers and that his visionary activities were related to theirs. Only since the mid-1970s has much of the original missionary and government documentation on Kimbangu's early activities become available to scholars.

Kimbangu attended a Baptist Missionary Society school at Wathen, near his home village. He became a Christian as a young man and was baptized on 4 July 1915 along with his wife, Marie-Mwilu, in the Baptist mission at Ngombe-Luete. He was trained as a catechist and religious instructor by the Baptist Missionary Society but failed his examination to become a pastor. During the typhoid epidemic of 1918 and 1919, in which many residents of his area died, Kimbangu is reputed to have received a calling to heal the sick. He is alleged to have heard a voice that said, "I am Christ. My servants are unfaithful. I have chosen you to bear witness before your brethren and convert them. Tend my flock" (Martin, 1975, p. 44). Frightened, Kimbangu was unable to respond and fled to the capital city of Kinshasa (then Léopoldville), where he worked briefly as a migrant laborer at an oil refinery.

Upon returning to his village, Kimbangu again received the calling to heal. On 6 April 1921 he performed his first public act of faith healing. He is reported to have laid hands on a critically ill woman and healed her. This act marked the beginning of Kimbangu's healing revival and six months of intensive religious activity. N'Kamba, the seat of Kimbangu's healing ministry, became known as the "New Jerusalem," and over five thousand local converts are reported to have flocked to him.

As the healing movement spread in popularity, colonial officials and merchants began to perceive it as a revolutionary threat. Missionaries were skeptical of Kimbangu's new teachings, and merchants complained that he incited followers to abandon their work and neglect the payment of taxes. With a small cadre of leaders to assist him, Kimbangu continued to preach and perform inspired acts of healing. On 6 June 1921, Léon Morel, a Belgian official, attempted to arrest Kimbangu and four of his most loyal assistants. Kimbangu eluded colonial officials until, prompted by a divine vision, he voluntarily surrendered on 12 September.

On 3 October 1921 Kimbangu was sentenced to death by 120 strokes of the lash for sedition and hostility toward the colonial authorities. His court-martial was characterized by arbitrary proceedings and legal irregularities. In November, the death sentence was commuted to life imprisonment by King Albert, who was reportedly influenced by the pleas of Belgian missionaries to exercise some leniency. Kimbangu was transported to Lubumbashi (then Elisabethville) in Shaba province, where he was imprisoned until his death on 12 October 1951 in the "hospital for Congolese." There is some debate concerning whether Kimbangu, whose teachings resembled those of fundamentalist Protestantism, converted to Catholicism on his deathbed. This possibility has been vehemently denied by his family and followers.

Kimbangu's arrest augmented the aura of mystery surrounding him as a prophetic figure and increased the popular appeal of his charismatic movement. Between 1924 and 1930, Belgian colonial authorities continued overt attempts to suppress the movement. Kimbangu's principal followers were imprisoned at Lowa, and others were confined over the years in thirty detention centers spread throughout the country. The Kimbanguist church estimates that there were 37,000 exiles, of whom 34,000 died in prison between 1921 and 1956. Recent scholarship, however, has established that this figure resulted from a typographical error in a newspaper article; the official exile and imprisonment figure was closer to 2,148. Although Kimbanguist detainees were isolated and kept under martial surveillance, the policy of detention eventually led to the spread of the Kimbanguist movement in various regions of what is now Zaire.

The movement gained strength, forming itself into a group that became known as the Church of Jesus Christ on Earth through the Prophet Simon Kimbangu. Followers were called *ngunza* ("prophets" or "preachers"). Kimbanguist offshoots, such as Salutism and Mpadism, and other manifestations of Kimbangu's influence appeared throughout present-day Zaire, Congo, and Zambia among populations with whom Kimbangu never had direct contact.

Between 1955 and 1957, Kimbangu's movement experienced a renewal and continued to spread throughout the Belgian Congo. After the prophet's death, his youngest son, Kuntima (Joseph) Diangienda, assumed leadership of the church in accordance with Kimbangu's wishes. He formalized its doctrine, sacraments, and egalitarian organizational structure. In 1969, the Kimbanguist church was admitted to the World Council of Churches, and in 1971, it was proclaimed as one of the four officially recognized ecclesiastical bodies in Zaire. By the end of the 1980s there were nearly four million Kimbanguists in Zaire.

Simon Kimbangu's direct and indirect influence on African prophetic movements has been far-reaching. The Kimbanguist church is one of the most extensively documented African religious groups. It is possible to view the history and transformation of the Kimbanguist church as a prototype for many contemporary African religious groups that have made the transition from grass-roots movements to established churches.

BIBLIOGRAPHY

Andersson, Effraim. *Messianic Popular Movements in the Lower Congo.* Uppsala, 1958. A historical account of Kimbanguism and other prophetic movements in the Lower Kongo (Zaire); analyzes the history of religious protest in the area and describes Kimbanguism as a messianic movement in the context of offshoot and related groups arising between the 1930s and the 1950s.

Asch, Susan. *L'église du prophète Kimbangu: De ses origines à son rôle actual au Zaïre.* Paris, 1983. A comprehensive study of the growth and development of the Kimbanguist church. Contains a historical and sociological analysis of the transition of the group from a popular movement to a church, spanning the years 1921–1981. Includes discussions of the group's origin, changing organizational structure, distribution throughout Zaire, and relations with the colonial and postindependence governments.

Chomé, Jules. *La passion de Simon Kimbangu.* Brussels, 1959. An account of the life and trial of Kimbangu by a Belgian lawyer who studied the legal documents in detail. Parallels Kimbangu's arrest and sentencing to the passion of Jesus and outlines the legal irregularities of Kimbangu's trial.

MacGaffey, Wyatt. *Modern Kongo Prophets: Religion in a Plural Society.* Bloomington, Ind., 1983. An analysis of prophetism among the Kongo, including a detailed discussion of Kimbanguism and related offshoot movements in the context of local cultural history and traditions.

Martin, Marie-Louise. *Kirche ohne Weisse.* Basel, 1971. Translated by D. M. Moore as *Kimbangu: An African Prophet and His Church* (Oxford, 1975). A history of the Kimbanguist movement in central Africa from 1918 to 1960, with discussions of responses to colonial authority, doctrine and ritual of the movement, and political attitudes of the followers. Contains a comprehensive bibliography on the Kimbanguist movement up to 1970.

Sinda, Martial. *Le messianisme congolais et ses incidences politiques: Kimbanguisme, matsouaisme, autres mouvements.* Paris, 1972. This book presents a comparative analysis of Kongo messianic movements as forms of religious protest. The author raises many interesting questions concerning leadership in prophetic groups and the history and motivations of African prophets and religious leaders in the context of the colonial government.

BENNETTA JULES-ROSETTE

KIMḤI, DAVID (c. 1160–c. 1235), known by the acronym RaDaK (Rabbi David Kimḥi); biblical exegete. David was the son of Yosef Kimḥi and the brother of Mosheh Kimḥi, exiles from Almohad Spain to Narbonne, where David was born. Both Yosef and Mosheh, David's principal teacher, were grammarians and exegetes of note, heavily influenced by contemporary Hispano-Jewish rationalism. David was the best-known graduate of the school of exegetes that the elder Kimḥis founded in Narbonne, a city whose tradition of biblical studies had been established by the eleventh-century Mosheh the Preacher.

Kimḥi was the author of a masoretic guide, the *'Eṭ sofer* (Scribe's Pen); the *Sefer ha-shorashim* (Book of Roots), a dictionary of biblical Hebrew; and the *Mikhol* (Compendium), the most authoritative Hebrew grammar of the Middle Ages. However, he is chiefly known for his biblical commentaries, which include expositions on *Genesis,* the Former and Latter Prophets, *Psalms, Proverbs,* and *Chronicles.* He also wrote two allegorical commentaries, employing Maimonidean philosophical concepts, on the Hexaemeron (chapters 1 and 2 of *Genesis*) and the chariot vision of Ezekiel.

Kimḥi's commentaries evince great interest in masoretic questions, and he traveled considerable distances to consult reliable manuscripts such as the *Sefer Yerushalmi* in Saragossa and the *Sefer Hilleli* in Toledo. His avowed aim was to follow the twelfth-century Andalusian grammarian Avraham ibn 'Ezra' and his own father and brother in establishing a *peshaṭ* ("plain sense") based on philological and contextual analysis. His extensive knowledge of rabbinic Hebrew, Aramaic, and Provençal, as well as his acquaintance with Arabic, contributed to his explication of the text. Concern for internal syntax within verses and for the general sequence of the biblical narrative became the hallmark of his commentaries. Yet despite Kimḥi's emphasis on *peshaṭ,* he cited abundant *midrashim,* or rabbinic interpretations—some because he felt them useful in explicating the plain sense, some as a foil against which he could highlight the *peshaṭ,* and some to add interest and liveliness to his text. His rationalism frequently comes to the fore in brief digressions on the nature of providence, prophecy, epistemology, and the rationales for observance of the commandments. He generally explained miracles naturalistically. Although the influence of Sa'adyah Gaon, Avraham ibn 'Ezra', and Yehudah ha-Levi can clearly be felt, the dominant tone of his work was set by Maimonides.

Kimḥi demonstrated his loyalty to Maimonides when, in his seventies, he journeyed across Languedoc and Spain to defend Maimonides' *Guide of the Perplexed* when that work came under attack by traditionalist Jews during the so-called Maimonidean controversy. He engaged in external polemics as well, and a number of antichristological and anti-Christian remarks can be found in his writings. Many of these were censored and survive only in manuscript. Kimḥi's depiction of exile and redemption in terms of darkness and light—a theme he developed at length—was prompted by his sensitivity to the tribulations of Israel brought about by internal division and external oppression.

Because of its accessibility, Kimḥi's work left an indelible mark on that of the Hebraists and humanists of the Renaissance and Reformation, and its influence on the King James Version of the Bible is unmistakable.

BIBLIOGRAPHY

An intellectual biography and analysis of Kimḥi's exegesis is my *David Kimhi: The Man and the Commentaries* (Cambridge, Mass., 1975), which contains a complete bibliography up to the date of publication. His philological work is analyzed in *David Kimchi's Hebrew Grammar (Mikhlol),* translated and edited by William Chomsky (Philadelphia, 1952). Specific themes are treated in the following articles by me: "R. David Kimhi as Polemicist," *Hebrew Union College Annual* 38 (1967): 213–235; "David Kimhi and the Rationalist Tradition," *Hebrew Union College Annual* 39 (1968): 177–218; and "David Kimhi and the Rationalist Tradition: 2, Literary Sources," in *Studies in Jewish Bibliography, History, and Literature in Honor of I. Edward Kiev,* edited by Charles Berlin (New York, 1971), pp. 453–478. Much detailed data in tabular form can be found in Ezra Zion Melamed's *Mefarshei ha-miqra': Darkheihem ve-shiṭoteihem,* vol. 2 (Jerusalem, 1975), pp. 716–932.

FRANK TALMAGE

KING, MARTIN LUTHER, JR. (1929–1968), Baptist minister and civil rights leader. The son and grandson of Baptist preachers, Martin Luther King, Jr., was born into a middle-class black family in Atlanta, Georgia. As an adolescent, King grew concerned about racial and economic inequality in American society. Sociology classes at Morehouse College taught him to view racism and poverty as related aspects of social evil, and reading Henry David Thoreau's essay "Civil Disobedience" (1849) convinced him that resistance to an unjust system was a moral duty. At Morehouse, King decided to become a minister, and after graduation he enrolled at Crozier Theological Seminary to study divinity. There he acquired from Walter Rauschenbusch's *Christianity and the Social Crisis* (1907) the conviction that the Christian churches have an obligation to work for social justice. In Mohandas Gandhi's practice of nonviolent resistance he discovered a tactic for transforming Christian love from a merely personal to a social ethic.

King's interest in theology, philosophy, and social ethics led him to enter the graduate program at Boston University School of Theology, where he earned a Ph.D. degree and developed his own philosophical position based upon the tenet that "only personality—finite and infinite—is ultimately real." In Boston, he met and courted Coretta Scott, and in 1953 they were wed. A year later, King accepted a call to be pastor of Dexter Avenue Baptist Church in Montgomery, Alabama. Chosen by E. D. Nixon, president of the Montgomery National Association for the Advancement of Colored People, to lead a boycott of the city's segregated buses, he gained national recognition when the boycott resulted in a Supreme Court decision that declared laws requiring segregated seating on buses unconstitutional.

Following the Montgomery bus boycott, King founded the Southern Christian Leadership Conference (SCLC) to coordinate scattered civil rights activities and local organizations. Operating primarily through the black churches, the SCLC mounted successive attacks against segregation in the early 1960s. Public demonstrations, especially in the South, dramatized for the nation the violence of white segregationists in contrast to the nonviolence of black demonstrators. Although immediate gains at the local level were often minimal, King's strategy drew national attention to the racial problem, awakened moral concern in many, pressured the federal government to act, and helped gain passage of legislation protecting the rights of blacks to vote and desegregating public accommodations. As the most eloquent speaker of the movement, King moved thousands to commit themselves to civil rights as both a moral and a political issue. For his nonviolent activism, he received the Nobel Peace Prize in 1964.

Against the arguments of militants, King maintained that nonviolence was the only practical and moral means for Afro-Americans to achieve equality. Violence would bring only more violence; nonviolence might convert the racist's conscience. Linking the cause of Afro-Americans to the struggle for independence of colonized peoples worldwide, King opposed the Vietnam War and condemned international violence.

While organizing a "poor people's campaign" to persuade Congress to take action on poverty, King accepted an invitation to participate in marches for striking sanitation workers in Memphis, Tennessee. There, on 4 April 1968, he was assassinated. Considered a modern prophet by many, King ranks with Gandhi as a major ethical leader of the twentieth century.

BIBLIOGRAPHY

Works by King. The best introduction to King's own version of his goals and values is *Stride toward Freedom: The Montgomery Story* (New York, 1958), which contains a chapter explaining his intellectual development in the midst of an eyewitness description of the bus boycott. *Strength to Love* (New York, 1963) is a collection of sermons. *Why We Can't Wait* (New York, 1964) includes "Letter from Birmingham Jail," one of King's most cogent justifications of his philosophy of nonviolent direct action. *Where Do We Go From Here: Chaos or Community?* (New York, 1967) outlines his detailed program for social justice in the United States.

Works about King. Of the many biographical sketches, the best critical treatment is David L. Lewis's *King: A Biography*, 2d ed. (Urbana, Ill., 1978). Stephen B. Oates's biography, *Let the Trumpet Sound: The Life of Martin Luther King, Jr.* (New York, 1982), is factually more complete but lacks interpretive analysis. *Martin Luther King, Jr.: A Profile*, edited by C. Eric Lincoln (New York, 1970), is a collection of insightful evaluations of King and his role in the civil rights movement. John Ansbro's *Martin Luther King, Jr.: The Making of a Mind* (Maryknoll, N.Y., 1982) is a valuable explication of King's thought.

ALBERT J. RABOTEAU

KINGDOM OF GOD. Among the central concepts of the great religions, that of the kingdom of God may be the most hopeful, for while it recognizes the reality of death and injustice, it affirms that a just and living transcendent reality is entering history and transforming it. This article discusses the concept of the kingdom of God in postbiblical Judaism, the New Testament, and the history of the Christian church, together with its antecedents in the ancient Near East, Israel, and Greece.

Divine Kingship in the Ancient Near East, Israel, and Greece

Although the notion of divine kingship is defined in human political terms, it is not a mere projection of human kingship onto a divine realm. Rather, the successive phrases in which this notion occurs show that divine kingship was understood as transcending and rejecting human kingship. [*See* Kingship.]

"King of the Gods." This phrase implies sovereignty over the created order. In a pantheon, one god can emerge as supreme (1) through political shifts, as does, for example, Enlil, the tutelary god of Sumerian Nippur, who becomes "lord, god, king . . . the judge . . . of the universe" (J. B. Pritchard, ed., *Ancient Near Eastern Texts relating to the Old Testament*, 3d ed. with supp., Princeton, 1969, p. 575); (2) through syncretism in favor of a solar deity such as Shamash (Pritchard, p. 387) or the Egyptian deity Amun-Re, who is the chief, lord, and father of the gods as well as creator of life (Pritchard, pp. 365–366); or (3) through the acclamation of one god as king by the others for his victory over the powers of chaos. This final form of acquiring sovereignty springs from a widespread mythical pattern illustrated in the texts of four ancient societies.

Babylon. The creation epic *Enuma elish*, recited at the spring New Year festival, describes the victory of Marduk over the sea monster Tiamat, from whose body Marduk creates heaven and earth. Even before the contest the other gods proclaim, "We have granted you kingship [*sharruta*] over the universe entire" (4.14), and "Marduk is king!" (4.28). After the battle, the gods ratify these proclamations and give Marduk the chief of his fifty Sumerian titles, "king of the gods of heaven and the underworld" (5.112).

Ugarit (modern Ras Shamra, Syria). Although the god El is routinely addressed as king in this literature (Pritchard, pp. 133 and 140), Baal is elevated to kingship after his victory over Yam, "Prince Sea." The craftsman-god tells Baal, "Now you will cut off your adversary, you will take your eternal kingship [*mlk 'lmk*], your everlasting dominion" (Pritchard, p. 131); and goddesses tell El, "Baal is our king [*mlkn*], our judge, and there is none above him" (Pritchard, pp. 133 and 138).

Greece. In the Homeric poems, Zeus is called the "father of gods and men" and is once called the "highest and best of the gods" (*Odyssey* 19.303). In Hesiod's *Theogony* (700 BCE?), Zeus leads the Olympian gods in battle against the Titans, who include Chaos (v. 700) and the dragon Typhoeus. Hesiod recounts that after the battle, "the blessed gods, at the urging of Earth [Gaia], requested far-seeing Zeus to reign and rule over them" (i.e., as *basileus* and *anax,* vv. 881–885). It is from this victory over the Titans that Zeus acquires the title "king of the gods" (v. 886). Similarly, in Pindar's *Seventh Olympian Ode* (464 BCE), Zeus is called "great king of the gods" (v. 34).

Israel. In the face of Israel's ostensible monotheism, a group of other gods, called *benei Elim* (lit., "sons of gods"), is also acknowledged. These gods, however, are not like the one God (who in this context always has the name whose consonants are YHVH, conventionally transcribed "Yahveh," *Ps.* 89:5–8); they must ascribe glory to him (*Ps.* 29:1), for it was Yahveh who crushed the sea-monster of chaos, Rahab (*Ps.* 89:10), or Leviathan (*Ps.* 74:13–14). And in *Psalms* 95:3, Yahveh is given the same title that Pindar gives Zeus, "a great king above all gods."

"Yahveh Is King." This phrase implies sovereignty over the people of Israel. In the historical books of Israel, the kingship of Yahveh is cited solely to refute the claims of human kings (*1 Sm.* 8:7, 12:2; cf. *Jgs.* 8:23). The concept is most fully developed in the *Book of Psalms,* the dating of which is problematic; however, Isaiah's vision of Yahveh as king (*Is.* 6:5) shows that this was a living belief in 742 BCE. In a compact group of Psalms, Yahveh is called "king" *(melekh)* or is made the subject of the corresponding verb *malakh* (*Ps.* 93:1, 96:10, 97:1, 99:1). These Psalms display a unique cluster of motifs associated with Yahveh's kingship: (1) his theophany in lightning or earthquake over Lebanon (*Ps.* 29) and elsewhere (*Ps.* 97, 99); (2) his supremacy over other gods who bow down to him or are reduced to "idols" (*Ps.* 29, 95–97, 47:2 in some texts); (3) his entrance into his holy place (*Ps.* 24) or ascent to his throne (*Ps.* 47; cf. *Ps.* 93, 97); (4) his act of creation (*Ps.* 24, 95, 96), portrayed as a conquest of great waters (*Ps.* 29, 33), where the personified elements sing a new song (*Ps.* 96, 98) and the floods, now beneficent, "clap their hands" (*Ps.* 98:8); (5) his sovereignty over other nations or over all the earth (*Ps.* 47, 96, 98); and (6) his future coming to judge the earth (*Ps.* 96, 98) as he has previously come to Israel (*Ps.* 99:4).

Sigmund Mowinckel, in his *Psalmenstudien* (2 vols., Oslo, 1921–1924), searching for a liturgical occasion for these psalms in the Temple, boldly hypothesized a festival of Yahveh's enthronement, a *Thronbesteigungsfest,* which he assigned to the autumn feast of Tabernacles (Sukkot) on the basis of *1 Kings* 8:2 (cf. *Zec.* 14:16). This theory, much developed by Scandinavian and British scholars, assumed that the king dramatically enacted the role of Yahveh in conquering chaos and the nations, in the god's enthronement, and, perhaps, even in a mock death, resurrection, and sacred marriage. But Roland de Vaux, in his *Ancient Israel* (vol. 2, New York, 1965, pp. 502–506), finds no evidence for such a festival. And while the theme of Yahveh's entrance to the holy place or ascent to his throne suggests a Temple liturgy, *Psalms* 132:8 suggests that the god was represented in this liturgy by the Ark rather than by the king.

As the contrast between these affirmations of divine kingship and Israel's state of exile (587/6–538 BCE) became too great, the concept is split up between present and future. In the present, God's kingship is individualized and he becomes "my king" (*Ps.* 5:3ff.); in an indefinite future, Yahveh as king will regather dispersed Israel (*Ez.* 20:33) and reign in Jerusalem (*Is.* 24:23, *Mi.* 4:7; cf. *Is.* 52:7–10).

"Kingship from Heaven." This Babylonian phrase introduces various concepts of the divine sovereignty in the state. Hammurabi in the prologue to his laws (c. 1700 BCE) tells how Anu established for Marduk an "enduring sovereignty" over the world. At first, the Babylonian myth *Etana* states, "the people had not set up a king"; but later "kingship descended from heaven" (Pritchard, p. 114). Although the concept of kingship as bestowed from the divine realm served to legitimate the state in Mesopotamia, in Zoroastrianism it provided an alternative to the state. One of the aspects of Ahura Mazdā is Khshathra, who combines the ideas of divine and human "kingship." In *Yasna* 44.7, kingship is presented as his creation along with Ārmaiti ("piety"); *Yasna* 33.10 speaks of "kingship and justice [*asha*]" in parallel just as *Matthew* 6:33 does in the New Testament. But the prophetic Zoroastrian sense of kingship is coopted for political ends by Darius, who begins his Behistun inscription (520 BCE), "I am Darius, the Great King, King of Kings . . . Ahura Mazdā bestowed the kingship upon me" (cited in Roland G. Kent's *Old Persian: Grammar, Texts, Lexicon,* 2d ed., New Haven, 1953, p. 119).

There are hints of such a semi-autonomous kingship in Stoicism, as in Epictetus's notion of the "kingship" *(basileia)* of the philosopher (Arrian, *Epictetus* 3.22.76). But the principal inheritor in the West of the concept of a quasi-independent divine kingship was later biblical Judaism. *Psalms* 22.28 affirms that "kingship [*melukhah*] belongs to Yahveh." The editor who wrote *1 Chronicles* 28:5 replaced the kingship *(mamlekhet)* of David and Solomon, which he found in his source, *1 Kings* 9:5, by substituting the divine *malkhut.* Echoing an Ugaritic theme, *Psalms* 145:11–13 proclaims, "thy kingship is a kingship of all the ages." This theme is developed in *Daniel:* "The God of heaven will set up an everlasting kingdom" (*Dn.* 2:44; cf. *Dn.* 4:3), which is to be handed over to one who is "like a son of man" (*Dn.* 7:14f) or to "the people of the saints of the Most High" (*Dn.* 7:27).

Among the Covenanters of Qumran it was believed that the "covenant of the kingship" *(berit malkhut)* over God's people was given to David and his descendants for ever (Edmund Lohse, *Die Texte aus Qumran,* Munich, 1964, p. 247). The Old Testament Pseudepigrapha sometimes ascribe the kingship to a Messiah (which may, however, be a Christian interpolation); for example, the Syriac *Apocalypse of Baruch* affirms that the "anointed one" will sit "in eternal peace on the throne of his kingship" (73:1).

"King of Kings." This phrase indicates first human, then divine, sovereignty over earthly kingships. It was first applied to human rulers annexing vassal kingships. It was standard among Old Persian royal inscriptions (cf. *Ezra* 7:12), and it is ascribed to the Babylonian king Nebuchadrezzar by *Ezekiel* 26:7 and *Daniel* 2:37 (but not by cuneiform sources). The Romans knew it as a Parthian title. Plutarch writes that Pompey refused the title to the Parthian king (*Pompey* 38.2) and that Antony called his sons by Cleopatra "kings of kings" (*Antony* 54.4).

In Stoicism and the Judeo-Christian tradition, this title is transferred to the God who rules over all human kingship. Cleanthes, in his *Hymn to Zeus* (270 BCE), names the abstract god of Stoicism "Zeus" and calls him "highest king"; a later Stoic gave him the Persian title "great king of kings" (Dio Chrysostom 2.75). Yahveh is called "God of gods and Lord of lords" in *Deuteronomy* 10:17—conceivably a late enough text to be under Babylonian-Persian influence. Once in Greek Judaism God appears as "king of kings" (*2 Maccabees* 13:4). Rabbi ʿAqavya' (c. 60 CE) expanded the title to underline God's claim over the highest of earthly monarchies, teaching that men are to give account "before the King of the kings of kings" (Mishna *Avot* 3.1). These usages are combined in *Revelation* 19:16 and 17:14 where the victorious Christ is proclaimed "King of kings and Lord of lords." The title became the rallying point for simple Christians to reject the divine status of the Roman emperor; thus the African martyr Speratus (180 CE) before a Roman proconsul confessed "my Lord, the Emperor of kings and of all peoples" (*dominum meum, imperatorem regum et omnium gentium;* text in Herbert Musurillo, *The Acts of the Christian Martyrs,* Oxford, 1972, no. 6).

"Kingship of Heaven." In the rabbinic tradition this phrase expresses an understanding of the universal sovereignty of God, future and/or eternal. The rabbis saw *Exodus* 15:18 ("Yahveh will reign for ever and ever") as the recognition that established God's kingship on earth (*Exodus Rabbah* 23.1). As the sovereignty assigned to the God of Israel grew, his name was replaced by the term *heaven.* The obligation to recite the Shemaʿ twice daily is called "taking on the yoke of the kingship of heaven [*ʿol malkhut shamayim*]" (Mishna *Berakhoth* 2.2); Rabbi ʿAqiva' ben Yosef did so during his execution under Hadrian (135 CE, Babylonian Talmud *Berakhot* 61b). Eventually the recognition of the divine sovereignty by Jews alone seemed to the rabbis insufficient: thus the great universalistic prayer *ʿAlenu* of Ro'sh ha-Shanah has the petition that all the inhabitants of the world "should accept the yoke of thy kingdom; and do thou reign over them speedily and forever; for the kingship is thine, and forever wilt thou reign in glory."

One set of rabbinic texts partially identifies the divine kingship with Israel's political autonomy. Rabbi Ayyvu (c. 320 CE) said: "Formerly the kingship was vested in Israel, but when they sinned it was taken from them and given to the other nations. . . . But tomorrow when Israel repents, God will take it from the idolaters, and the kingship shall be to the Lord" *(Esther Rabbah).* The fortunes of Israel are seen by the rabbis as coloring universal history: thus the Midrash on Psalm 99 states, "As long as the children of Israel are in exile, the kingship of heaven is not at peace and the nations of the earth dwell unperturbed."

Another set of texts portrays the coming sovereignty of God as wholly universal. In the *Mekhilta' de-Rabbi Yishmaʿe'l* (Jacob Z. Lauterbach, trans., 3 vols., Philadelphia, 1933, vol. 2, p. 159) one reads: "At the time when idolatry shall be uprooted . . . and the Place [*Maqom,* "God"] shall be recognized throughout the world as the One, then will his kingship be established for the age of the ages of ages." The Aramaic Targums, which regularly translate "The Lord will reign" as "The kingship [*malkhut*] will be revealed" (e.g., *Is.* 24:23; *Ex.* 15:18), twice attribute the kingship to the Messiah: the Targum on *Micah* 4:7–8 states that "to you, O Messiah of Israel, hidden because of the sins of the congregation of Zion, the kingship is to come," and the Targum on *Isaiah* 53:10 affirms that God's people, after being purified from sin, "shall look upon the kingship of their Messiah."

The Kingdom of God in the Words of Jesus

"The kingdom [*basileia*] of God" is the sole general phrase expressing the object of Jesus' proclamation. (In *Matthew* it mostly appears as "kingdom of heaven," probably as an artificial restoration of the rabbinic usage.) His affirmations about this kingdom are the unifying thread on which all his other sayings are strung.

Jesus' contemporaries shared with the rabbinic tradition at least a political coloration of the concept: thus *Acts* 1:6 represents disciples asking the risen Jesus, "Will you at this time restore the kingdom to Israel?" But the gospel narratives that presuppose Jesus' most characteristic ideas already in the minds of others, such as John the Baptist (*Mt.* 3:2), Joseph of Arimathea (*Mk.* 15:43), the Pharisees (*Lk.* 17:20), or the disciples (*Mt.* 18:1, *Lk.* 14:15), are unsupported by the rabbinic texts and are probably the work of the evangelists.

In the sayings of Jesus, the "kingdom of God" replaces the state of affairs that he calls "this generation"; for they are given exactly parallel introductions. Over against the obdurate "men of this generation" (*Lk.* 7:31–34), the kingdom of God grows from its tiny hidden beginnings like a man's mustard seed or a woman's leaven (*Lk.* 13:18–21). Into the present "faithless" and "adulterous" generation (*Mk.* 9:19, *Mt.* 12:29) there has broken a new historical reality. Four types of sayings each illustrate one dimension of Jesus' vision: (1) the kingdom as subject of verbs of coming; (2) the kingdom as object of verbs of entering; (3) the kingdom as object of search or struggle; (4) "in the kingdom of God" in the context of a banquet. (But the extended parables of *Matthew* are mostly omitted here, since their introduction "The kingdom of heaven is like . . ." seems editorial rather than organic.)

"The Kingdom of God Is at Hand." Here is implied a preliminary but decisive victory over injustice and death. In the first group of sayings, the kingdom of God is presented as a quasi-autonomous reality whose arrival is being announced. In *Mark* 1:15 the expression "The kingdom of God is at hand" is placed, perhaps editorially, as a motto or summary over Jesus' entire work.

The Lord's Prayer. This prayer contains the petitions "Hallowed be thy name, thy kingdom come" (*Lk.* 11:2, *Mt.* 6:9). They echo the Qaddish, the oldest Aramaic part of the synagogue liturgy: "Magnified and sanctified be his great name in the world which he created according to his will. And may he establish his kingdom [*yamlikh malkhuteh*] during your life and during your days and during the life of the house of Israel, even speedily and at a near time." The Qaddish plainly includes a covert petition for the political independence of Israel. And both texts by implication are asking for an end to those crimes against persons that are described in the Hebrew Bible as a "profanation" of God's name: debt-slavery and prostitution (*Amos* 2:6–8), enslavement (*Jer.* 34:14–16), and murder (*Lev.* 18:21).

Victory over dark powers. In *Luke* 11:20 Jesus proclaims, "But if I by the finger of God cast out demons, then the kingdom of God has come upon you." What is asked for in the Lord's Prayer is here announced as already operative. Jesus instructed his missionaries to "heal those who are sick and say to them, 'The kingdom of God has drawn near you'" (*Lk.* 10:9). Proofs that the kingdom has broken into history are the healing of sickness, often of psychosomatic types of sickness, and victory over the destructive social forces called "demons," such as Legion, so named as a sign of military oppression (*Mk.* 5:9), and Mammon (*Lk.* 16:13). God's "finger" is the creative force by which the heavens were made (*Ps.* 8:3), oppressors overthrown (*Ex.* 8:19), and the Law given (*Ex.* 31:18). No less a power, Jesus implies, could do what has already been done through him; hence God's sovereignty has already broken into history.

"To Enter the Kingdom of God." A second group of sayings defines the condition for entering the kingdom: becoming like the poor. Jesus expresses the condition negatively: "It is easier for a camel to go through the eye of a needle than for a rich man to enter the kingdom of God" (*Mk.* 10:25). He also expresses it positively: "Allow the children to come to me and do not forbid them, for of such is the kingdom of God" (*Mk.* 10:14–15; cf. *Mt.* 18:13–14, *Jn.* 3:3–5). With far-reaching irony he says, "The tax collectors and harlots enter the kingdom of God before you" (*Mt.* 21:31). The kingdom of God is further reserved for the handicapped (*Mk.* 9:47), the persecuted (*Mt.* 5:10), and those in tribulation (*Acts* 14:22). The rabbinic background for these sayings is the concept of "the coming age" *(ha-'olam ha-ba'):* "Master, teach us the paths of life so that through them we may win the life of the coming age" (B.T., *Ber.* 28b).

The link among these groups is a deep structure of Jesus' thought underlying Luke's "Sermon on the Plain." The beatitude "Blessed are you poor, for yours is the kingdom of God" (*Lk.* 6:20) shows that possession of the kingdom is the coming reward for the poor, hungry, and mourning. The saying "Love your enemies . . . and your reward will be great" (*Lk.* 6:35) shows that the characteristic of this ideal poor is love of enemies, that is, nonretaliation to evil. Hence Gerd Theissen (*Sociology of Early Palestinian Christianity*, John Bowden, trans., Philadelphia, 1978, p. 99) concludes: "The best description of the functional outline of the Jesus movement for overcoming social tensions is an interpretation of it as a contribution towards containing and overcoming aggression." Later, Jesus' criterion is reformulated with increasing degrees of legalism: to enter the kingdom of God one must keep two great commandments (*Mk.* 12:34); show persistence (*Lk.* 9:62); do the will of God (*Mt.* 7:21); serve the Christ hidden in the poor (*Mt.* 25:34); have a higher righteousness (*Mt.* 5:20); and avoid certain listed sins (*1 Cor.* 6:9–10, *Gal.* 5:21).

The Kingdom of God as Object of Search or Struggle. A third group of sayings defines the kingdom of God as the highest object of desire. Although certain forces "lock up the kingdom of heaven" (*Mt.* 23:13), we are told "seek first God's kingdom and all these shall be added to you" (*Lk.* 21:31; cf. *Mt.* 6:33). The kingdom is symbolized by the "treasure hidden in a field" and the "pearl of great price" (*Mt.* 13:44–46). But the nature of the "mystery of the kingdom of God" is left unexplained at *Mark* 4:11; and Paul only vaguely suggests with the expression "fellow workers for the kingdom of God" (*Col.* 4:11) the modern idea that the kingdom can be promoted by human energy.

"In the Kingdom of God." This phrase in a fourth group of sayings is always used in connection with a banquet at the end of time. When Jesus affirms, "I shall no more drink of the fruit of the vine until that day when I drink it new in the kingdom of God" (*Mk.* 14:25), he implies that the kingdom can only come in through his suffering. The greatest and least in the kingdom are paradoxically reversed (*Mt.* 5:19, 18:4; *Lk.* 7:28 and *Mt.* 11:11) as in the parable of the banquet (*Mt.* 22:2–14, *Lk.* 14:16–24). The final event will be inaugurated by the apostles: to them Jesus says, "I bequeath you as my Father bequeathed me a kingdom, that you may eat and drink at my table in my kingdom and sit on thrones judging the twelve tribes of Israel" (*Lk.* 22:29–30; cf. *Mt.* 19:28).

At the inauguration of the banquet, Jesus says, there will be a final division of humanity "when you see Abraham . . . and all the prophets in the kingdom of God, but you yourselves cast out; and they shall come from the east and the west . . . and recline in the kingdom of God" (*Lk.* 13:28–29; cf. *Mt.* 8:11–12). Two themes are combined in this text: the pilgrimage of all peoples to Jerusalem (*Is.* 49:12, etc.) towards the "house of prayer for all peoples" (*Is.* 56:7); and the banquet described in *Isaiah* 25:6–9, which ends with the archaic Ugaritic motif of Yahveh swallowing up death forever.

The Kingdom of God in Christian Tradition

Luke in his gospel and in the *Acts* when writing narrative regularly speaks of "preaching the good news of the kingdom of God." Paul inherits the phrase "kingdom of God" in fixed phrases from the gospel tradition; the structural parallel that plays the same role as the kingdom in his thought is the "righteousness [*dikaiosunē*] of God." The remaining letters of the New Testament, where, as Rudolf Bultmann says, Jesus "the Proclaimer becomes the one proclaimed" by the church, mostly speak of the kingdom of Christ. In the writings of the Greek church fathers the notion of the kingdom of God loses any sociopolitical connotation and is seen as the state of immortality or the beatific vision as entered through baptism. But in his commentary on *Matthew* 14:7 (244 CE), Origen coins a word that contains much of the original sense: as Christ is "wisdom itself, righteousness itself and truth itself," so is he also "the kingdom itself" *(autobasileia)*.

The development of the concept of the kingdom of God occurred primarily in the church of the West. In the thought of the Latin theologians and the official Reformation, it served to legitimate the state through Augustine's doctrine of two cities and Luther's of two kingdoms. The Englightenment, while discovering the primacy of the kingdom of God in Jesus' thought, tried to accommodate it to rational categories. It was the radical Reformation that most fully recovered Jesus' original understanding, and that transmitted the most vital form of the concept to contemporary Christian believers today.

Two Cities, Two Kingdoms. These concepts served to accommodate the church to the state. In his *City of God* (413–426 CE), Augustine developed his grandiose contrast between the *civitas Dei,* with a biblical basis in *Psalms* 87:3 and 46:5, and the *civitas terrena,* the "earthly city," with no biblical antecedent. This work laid a basis for relations between church and state that was not decisively challenged until the resistance to Hitler by the German Confessing church.

Augustine's concept of the earthly city is especially ambiguous. Sometimes (e.g., *Sermons* 214.11) he identifies the city of God with the historical church and attributes to the earthly city aspects of the state; here he has a predecessor in the rabbinic parallelism of the "kingdom [*malkhut*] of the earth" and the "kingdom of the firmament" (B. T. *Ber.* 58a), and in one interpretation of Jesus' saying about the "things of Caesar" and "things of God" (*Mk.* 12:17). Elsewhere for Augustine the city of God is the society of the redeemed, and the earthly city is the society of the devil; here the good and evil principles of the Manichaeism that Augustine previously embraced resurface.

While Augustine's language about church and kingdom fluctuates, his underlying thought is consistent. His predecessor Cyprian saw both distinction and continuity between present church and future kingdom: "One who abandons the church which is to reign [*regnatura est*] cannot enter the kingdom [*regnum*]" (*On the Unity of the Church* 14). So Augustine distinguishes the temporary "inn" of the church from the permanent "home" of the kingdom (*Sermons* 131.6). Hence there are two ages of the church, now with a mixture of wheat and tares, in the future transformed into a kingdom without evil. Correspondingly Augustine distinguishes two periods of the kingdom: a present "kingdom of militancy" *(regnum militiae)*, and a future "peaceable kingdom," a *pacatissimum regnum* (*City of God* 20.9).

When he goes on then to say that "the church even now is the kingdom of Christ and the kingdom of heaven" he does not imply it is that already perfected.

Two kingdoms in Luther. In the High Middle Ages, Hugh of Saint Victor (1096–1141) crystallized Augustine's two cities unambiguously into the "spiritual power" of the church and the "secular power" of the state, with the church in theory superior and in practice subservient. Martin Luther restored the New Testament term "kingdom of God" *(Reich Gottes)* but placed over against it a "kingdom of the world" *(Reich der Welt)*. God's kingdom is one of grace and mercy; the world's kingdom, one of wrath and severity (Martin Luther, *Works*, ed. Jaroslav Pelikan, Saint Louis, 1955–1976, 46.69, 30.76). In Luther's *On Temporal Authority* (1523) the children of Adam are divided between the two kingdoms (*Works*, 45.88). The sayings "Render to Caesar what is Caesar's" (*Mk.* 12:17) and "The powers that be are ordained of God" (*Rom.* 13:1) carry great weight for Luther (*Works* 45.99)—in part because of his dependence on the German princes for protection against Rome. Only when a political leader gives false religious commands does Luther permit the stance expressed in *Acts* 5:29, "We must obey God rather than men" (*Works* 45.111).

In a sermon of 1544, Luther boldly defined the two kingdoms as distinct operations of the one God:

> The worldly government [*das weltlich Regiment*] also may be called God's kingdom. For he wills that it should remain and that we should enter it; but it is only the kingdom with his left hand [*nur des reych mit der lincken hand*]. But his right-hand kingdom [*rechtes reych*], where he himself rules, and is called neither . . . Kaiser nor king . . . but rather is himself, is that where the Gospel is preached to the poor.
> (*D. Martin Luthers Werke*, Weimar, 1883–, 52.26; cf. 36.385)

Luther calls these two operations of God his "alien" and "proper" work (*opus alienum, proprium;* cf. *Is.* 28:21 Vulgate). In an early sermon of 1516 he maintains, "since God could justify only those who are not just, he is forced before his proper work of justification to carry out an alien work in order to make sinners" (*Works* 51:19; cf. 33.140).

Sometimes Luther opposed to God's kingdom not the kingdom of the world but Satan's kingdom (*Works* 33.227). Unlike Augustine he closely integrates the devil's work with the work of God. On *Hebrews* 2:14, Luther comments: "God pierced the adversary with that one's weapon . . . and so completes his proper work with an alien work" (*Works* 29.135). While he protests that "God does not wish us like the Manichaeans to imagine two gods, one the source of good, the other of evil" (*On Psalms* 90:16, *Works* 13.135), Luther comes close to postulating a duality within God, with the devil as God's dark side. Thus he holds that on occasion "God wears the mask [*larva*] of the devil" (*On Galatians* 5:11, *Works* 27.43).

Only one kingdom. The doctrine of "only one kingdom" was the affirmation of the German Confessing church. Luther's scheme of two kingdoms was pushed to an extreme in the 1930s by German theologians such as Paul Althaus and Emanuel Hirsch, who favored National Socialism. In their *Zwei-Reiche-Lehre* ("doctrine of the two kingdoms") the state is autonomous over against the church. Opposition to this doctrine led to a rethinking of Luther's position. For example, Dietrich Bonhoeffer in his *Ethics* (trans. N. H. Smith, London, 1955, p. 62) condemns any thinking about God and the world "in terms of two spheres," especially when "in the pseudo-Lutheran scheme the autonomy of the orders of the world is proclaimed in opposition to the law of Christ."

During World War II, Karl Barth wrote that the "illusory paganism of the German people" had been confirmed rather than restrained by the "heritage of the greatest Christian of Germany, by Martin Luther's error on the relation between . . . the temporal and spiritual order" (*A Letter to Great Britain from Switzerland*, London, 1941, p. 36). On the one hand Barth uses Luther's language when he states that "nothingness" (i.e., evil) is "on the left hand of God as the object of his *opus alienum*" (*Church Dogmatics*, trans. G. T. Thomson et al., 5 vols. in 14, Edinburgh, 1936–1977, vol. 3, part 3, p. 361). But, contrary to Luther, he emphasizes the uniqueness of God's kingdom, insisting on the radical "antithesis of the kingdom of God to all human kingdoms" and also to the "sphere of Satan" (*Church Dogmatics* 4.2.177, 2.2.688). "There is no collateral rule [*Nebenregierung*] side by side with [God's] and no counter-rule opposed to it. He alone can rule, and ought to rule, and wills to rule; and he alone does so" (*Church Dogmatics* 3.3.157).

Barth's views were accepted in principle by the newly formed German Confessing church at the Synod of Barmen (31 May 1934) in opposition to the Nazi state church. The fifth thesis of Barmen, drafted by Barth and going beyond previous Lutheran or Reformed confessions, says that "the State has by divine appointment the task of providing for justice and peace. . . . The Church acknowledges the benefit of this appointment. . . . It calls to mind the Kingdom of God . . . and thereby the responsibility both of rulers and of the ruled." The document contains nothing about the nature of the state, much less its alleged status as a parallel kingdom; it refers only to the state's assigned task (Cochrane, 1962, pp. 192, 241).

The Legacy of the Enlightenment. Here the concept of the coming of the kingdom of God is accommodated to rational categories. Hermann Samuel Reimarus (1694–1768), in a posthumously published manuscript, was the first modern scholar to recognize that the coming of the kingdom of God was Jesus' central theme (*Reimarus: Fragments*, ed. C. H. Talbert, Philadelphia, 1970, pp. 136–138). Reimarus presumes that Jesus' contemporaries expected no other savior "than a worldly deliverer of Israel, who was to release them from bondage and build up a glorious worldly kingdom for them." When to announce his kingdom (*Mt.* 10:7) Jesus "chose for his messengers men who were themselves under the common impression," Reimarus concludes, he could have had "no other object than to rouse the Jews . . . who had so long been groaning under the Roman yoke." Thus he sees Jesus as simply a political revolutionary or Zealot.

From an opposite, but no less rationalistic, perspective, Immanuel Kant argued for a universal philosophic interpretation of the kingdom of God. He took the title of the third book of his *Religion within the Limits of Reason Alone* (1793) from the language of Jesus: "The victory of the good over the evil principle, and the founding of a kingdom of God on earth." He ends the work by citing the phrase from *Luke* 17:22 ("the kingdom of God is in your midst") in the translation "the kingdom of God is within you," thus giving the saying the "spiritual" interpretation that remains popular: "Here a kingdom of God is represented not according to a particular covenant (i.e., not messianic) but moral (knowable through unassisted reason)."

Most nineteenth-century German New Testament scholars interpreted the Gospels according to Kant's presuppositions. This accommodation, however, collapsed with the publication in 1892 of the first edition of Johannes Weiss's *Jesus' Proclamation of the Kingdom of God* (trans. R. H. Hiers, Philadelphia, 1971, p. 130). Weiss concluded that "although Jesus initially hoped to live to see the establishment of the kingdom of God, he gradually became certain" that he must die first, but that after his death he would "return upon the clouds of heaven at the establishment of the kingdom of God, . . . within the lifetime of the generation which rejected him." He frankly recognized that this historical reconstruction contradicted the "modern Protestant world-view" that he shared with his contemporaries, since he could not take the "eschatological attitude" that the world was passing away. Likewise, Albert Schweitzer conceived of Jesus as an eschatological visionary awaiting an imminent end of the world. In his *The Mystery of the Kingdom of God* (1901; trans. W. L. Lowrie, New York, 1950, p. 55), Schweitzer explained the radical demands of the Sermon on the Mount as an *Interimsethik*, too rigorous for normal life, in the brief period before the full establishment of the kingdom.

A number of twentieth-century scholars have defined Jesus' idea of the kingdom of God as basically completed in his own work. Charles Harold Dodd in his *The Parables of the Kingdom* (London, 1935) rejects Schweitzer's "thoroughgoing eschatology" and argues that Jesus regarded the kingdom of God as having already come. He interprets "the ministry of Jesus as 'realized eschatology,' that is, as the impact upon this world of the 'powers of the world to come'" (p. 151). Rudolf Bultmann in his *Jesus and the Word* (1926; trans. L. P. Smith et al., New York, 1934, pp. 52, 131), anticipating his later program of "demythologization," interprets the absolute certainty of the coming of the kingdom as a "crisis of decision" in which every hour is the last hour. He defines the kingdom as "an eschatological deliverance which ends everything earthly" by confronting the human being with a decision in crisis as in Kierkegaard's "Either/Or."

Schweitzer laid much weight on the saying in *Mark* 9:1, "There are some standing here who will not taste death before they see the kingdom of God coming with power." If this verse is both historically attributed to Jesus and understood literally, Jesus will seem to have been in error. There have been many efforts to account for the apparent error. In his *On Being a Christian* (New York, 1978, p. 220), Hans Küng argues that Jesus' "apocalyptic horizon," the expectation of an immediate end of the world, is "not so much an error as a time-conditioned . . . world-view which Jesus shared with his contemporaries." Erich Grässer, in his *Das Problem der Parusieverzögerung in den synoptischen Evangelien* (Berlin, 1960), sees the entire development of the early church as a response to the "delay of the *parousia* [i.e., 'expected coming']," citing especially *2 Peter* 3:4: "Where is the promise of his coming?" John G. Gager in his *Kingdom and Community: The Social World of Early Christianity* (Englewood Cliffs, N.J., 1975, p. 39) explains the whole original Christian mission by analogy to a contemporary millenarian sect which, after its prediction of an immediate end is disconfirmed, "may undertake zealous missionary activity as a response to its sense of cognitive dissonance." Other scholars, such as Werner G. Kümmel and Norman Perrin, have characterized the supposed error as springing from the adoption of a literalistic antithesis of present/future.

A Kingdom of Righteousness and Peace. This kingdom was the heritage of the radical Reformation. Both the centrality and the original meaning of Jesus' concept of the kingdom of God were grasped by the radical reformers, less through their scholarship than through the conformity of their lives to Jesus' pattern. Menno Simons (c. 1496–1561), rejecting the violence of the Peasants' Revolt of 1525 under Thomas Münzer but speaking from the same social situation, based his stand of nonretaliation on the Sermon on the Mount. He wrote, "Christ has not taken his kingdom with the sword, although he entered it with much suffering" (*The Complete Writings of Menno Simons,* trans. L. Verduin et al., Scottsdale, 1956, p. 49). And again, "We acknowledge . . . no other sword . . . in the kingdom or church of Christ than the sharp sword of the Spirit" (p. 300). While leaving "the civil sword to those to whom it is committed," Menno's only kingdoms are those of "the Prince of Peace and the prince of strife" (p. 554). Similarly, in his *Journal,* George Fox, recording his famous testimony of 21 November 1660 before Charles II, characterizes the kingdom of God as wholly pacific: "The Spirit of Christ, which leads us into all truth, will never move us to fight and war against any man with outward weapons, neither for the kingdom of Christ nor for the kingdoms of this world."

The visual arts. The church early developed pictorial versions of the human scenes of the Gospels. But an adequate symbol of the kingdom of God first appears in the nineteenth century in the many versions of *The Peaceable Kingdom* painted by the American Quaker primitive Edward Hicks (1780–1849). These paintings illustrate *Isaiah* 11:6–8: against a Delaware River landscape the wolf and lamb, leopard and kid lie down together, the cow and bear feed side by side, and the lion eats straw with the ox, one child leads them, another plays on the serpent's den. In a background vignette William Penn signs his peace treaty with the Indians.

Councils, Catholic and Protestant. Paul had defined the kingdom of God as "righteousness and peace and joy in the Holy Spirit" (*Rom.* 14:17). Those identifications are taken up in the documents of the Second Vatican Council (1963–1965): "To the extent that [earthly progress] can contribute to the better ordering of human society, it is of vital concern to the kingdom of God" (*Gaudium et Spes* 39, cf. *Lumen Gentium* 5). Similarly, the Sixth Assembly of the World Council of Churches (Vancouver, 1983) affirms "the identification of the churches with the poor in their witness to God's kingdom"; and in its statement rejecting nuclear weapons says that "as we witness to our genuine desire for peace with specific actions, the Spirit of God can use our feeble efforts for bringing the kingdoms of this world closer to the kingdom of God."

The theology of liberation. A unity of piety with political struggle marks a new life in the Latin American church. A key spokesman is the Peruvian Gustavo Gutiérrez, who writes: "The process of liberation will not have conquered the very roots of oppression . . . without the coming of the kingdom of God, which is above all a gift. . . . The historical, political liberating event *is* the growth of the kingdom . . . but it is not *the* coming of the kingdom" (*A Theology of Liberation: History, Politics and Salvation,* trans. Caridad Inda and J. Eagleson, Maryknoll, N.Y., 1973, p. 177). This theology is adapted to North American experience by James H. Cone, who in his *A Black Theology of Liberation* (Philadelphia, 1970, p. 220) writes: "The appearance of Jesus as the Black Christ also means that the Black Revolution is God's kingdom becoming a reality in America . . . . The kingdom of God is what happens to a person when his being is confronted with the reality of God's liberation."

The movement for justice and peace. Dom Helder Câmara of Recife has often said that our world faces twin threats: the actual "M-bomb" of misery and the potential holocaust of the A-bomb. In that situation, the most critical in history, many readers of the New Testament are finding that its apocalyptic images of the end of the world, far from being alien to our mentality, are merely literal. To many Christian believers in the movement for justice and peace the kingdom of God has become the primary name for what is at work in them. James W. Douglass, in his *Resistance and Contemplation: The Way of Liberation* (Garden City, 1972, p. 107), writes: "The way of revolution is the kingdom because the revolution is the people coming together in a new humanity, ignited by a divine symbol given through the man of truth—Jesus in the Temple and on the cross, Gandhi by the sea [on the salt march], the Berrigans at Catonsville [destroying draft files]." In the slums of São Paulo a French priest, Dominique Barbé, drawing on an indigenous Brazilian tradition of nonviolent resistance, writes (*La grâce et le pouvoir,* Paris, 1982, p. 206): "If I have been snatched out of the empire of darkness to enter into the kingdom, that is, into that part of reality where death has been eliminated, the only means of combat left me is the Cross and not the revolver." After Martin Luther King Jr., the disciple of Rauschenbusch and Gandhi, delivered his speech "I have a dream" at the Lincoln Memorial on 28 August 1963 (*A Testament of Hope,* ed. J. M. Washington, San Francisco, 1986, p. 217), Coretta King commented: "At that moment it seemed as if the Kingdom of God appeared." She added, "But it only lasted for a moment." Contemporary belief in the kingdom of God requires it to be reappropriated freshly by human beings at each historical turning-point.

[*See also* Christian Social Movements; Political Theology; *and* Theocracy.]

BIBLIOGRAPHY

No comprehensive study of the topic exists. For a well-documented source of texts from the ancient Near East and an extensive bibliography, see Thorkild Jacobsen's *The Treasures of Darkness: A History of Mesopotamian Religion* (New Haven, 1976). The Ugaritic data with relation to Hebrew are clearly presented by Werner H. Schmidt in *Königtum Gottes in Ugarit und Israel: Zur Herkunft der Königsprädikation Jahwes*, 2d ed. (Berlin, 1966). The most reliable surveys for the biblical material as a whole are Rudolf Schnackenburg's *God's Rule and Kingdom* (New York, 1963) and "Basileus" and related entries in the *Theological Dictionary of the New Testament* (Grand Rapids, Mich., 1964). For excellent surveys of Old Testament scholarship on Yahveh's kingship, see Joseph Coppens's contribution to the entry "Règne (ou Royaume) de Dieu," in the *Supplément au Dictionnaire de la Bible*, vol. 10 (Paris, 1981), and the article "Melek" by Helmer Ringgren et al. in the *Theologisches Wörterbuch zum Alten Testament*, vol. 4 (Stuttgart, 1984). Martin Buber's *Kingship of God*, translated from the third German edition (New York, 1967), is more theological than exegetical in its handling of the topic. John Gray restates the "enthronement-festival theory" uncritically but offers a thorough bibliography in *The Biblical Doctrine of the Reign of God* (Edinburgh, 1979).

The rabbinic sources were first analyzed by Gustaf H. Dalman in *The Words of Jesus Considered in the Light of Post-Biblical Jewish Writings and the Aramaic Language*, rev. Eng. ed. (Edinburgh, 1909); see especially pages 91–102 in volume 1 on the "kingship of heaven." Thousands of rabbinic texts in German translation are included in Hermann L. Strack and Paul Billerbeck's *Kommentar zum neuen Testament aus Talmud und Midrasch*, 6 vols. in 7 (Munich, 1922–1961); see especially the collection on "kingdom of God" in volume 1, pages 172–180. The use of the term *kingdom* in the Targum is analyzed by Bruce D. Chilton in "Regnum Dei Deus Est," *Scottish Journal of Theology* 31 (1978): 261–276.

For an introduction to the teachings of Jesus, see Hans Küng's *On Being a Christian* (Garden City, N.Y., 1976) and Günther Bornkamm's *Jesus of Nazareth* (New York, 1960). The "form-criticism" *(Formgeschichte)* of the gospel materials, important for assessing the historicity of the different sayings on the kingdom, was begun and almost ended with Rudolf Bultmann's *The History of the Synoptic Tradition*, 2d ed. (New York, 1968). On the Aramaic background of the sayings, consult Joachim Jeremias's *New Testament Theology: The Proclamation of Jesus* (New York, 1971). The case for making Jesus a political revolutionary has been restated by S. G. F. Brandon in *Jesus and the Zealots* (Manchester, 1967).

For a bibliography of the research on Jesus' sayings on the kingdom, together with scrupulous exegesis of key ones, see Jacques Schlosser's *Le règne de Dieu dans les dits de Jésus*, 2 vols. (Paris, 1980). Two articles on the subject of Jesus' sayings are especially useful: Hans Windisch's "Die Sprüche vom Eingehen in das Reich Gottes," *Zeitschrift für die neutestamentliche Wissenschaft* 27 (1928): 163–192, and Heinz Kruse's "The Return of the Prodigal: Fortunes of a Parable on Its Way to the Far East," *Orientalia* 47 (1978): 163–214.

Ernst Staehelin offers a very large annotated compilation of texts from the Christian church in *Die Verkündigung des Reiches Gottes in der Kirche Jesu Christi*, 7 vols. (Basel, 1951–1965). The early church fathers' treatment of the concept is indexed in "Basileia," in *A Patristic Greek Lexicon*, edited by G. W. H. Lampe (Oxford, 1961). A reliable guide to Augustine's thought is Étienne Gilson's *The Christian Philosophy of Saint Augustine* (New York, 1960), especially pp. 180–183. For a brief introduction to the thorny controversy surrounding Luther's doctrine, consult Heinrich Bornkamm's *Luther's Doctrine of the Two Kingdoms in the Context of His Theology* (Philadelphia, 1966). Arthur C. Cochrane narrates the struggle within the German church in *The Church's Confession under Hitler* (Philadelphia, 1962).

Read in sequence, three works provide the history of scholarly research into the meaning of the kingdom in Jesus' sayings: Christian Walther's *Typen des Reich-Gottes-Verständnisses: Studien zur Eschatologie und Ethik im 19. Jarhundert* (Munich, 1961) offers the perspective of nineteenth-century thinkers; Albert Schweitzer's *The Quest of the Historical Jesus: A Critical Study of Its Progress from Reimarus to Wrede*, 2d ed. (London, 1911), moves from Reimarus to Schweitzer himself; and Gösta Lundström's *The Kingdom of God in the Teaching of Jesus: A History of Interpretation from the Last Decades of the Nineteenth Century to the Present Day* (Edinburgh, 1963) moves forward to the 1960s. The most extensive contemporary work is the lifetime opus of Norman Perrin: *The Kingdom of God in the Teaching of Jesus* (Philadelphia, 1963), *Rediscovering the Teaching of Jesus* (New York, 1967), and *Jesus and the Language of the Kingdom: Symbol and Metaphor in New Testament Interpretation* (Philadelphia, 1976). Werner B. Kümmel's *Promise and Fulfilment: The Eschatological Message of Jesus* (Naperville, Ill., 1957) is also useful.

Numerous texts otherwise barely accessible are cited in H. Richard Niebuhr's *The Kingdom of God in America* (Chicago, 1937); his schematism is to be taken with reserve.

JOHN PAIRMAN BROWN

KINGSHIP. [*This entry presents numerous interpretations of the theory of sacred kingship. It consists of six articles:*

An Overview
Kingship in the Ancient Mediterranean World
Kingship in Sub-Saharan Africa
Kingship in Mesoamerica and South America
Kingship in East Asia
Kingship in Southeast Asia

The first article is a cross-cultural overview of the religious meanings of kingship, including discussion of sacred kings, legitimate rule, divine right of kings, and the role of kingship in the evolution of culture. The companion articles treat the phenomenon of sacred kingship in specific historical settings.]

An Overview

Kingship is the central institution of states ruled by or centered upon the person of one man, the king. (In a few cases one woman, ritually identified with and treated as a man, assumes the central role.) As an institution of state, kingship is thus distinct from other social institutions typical of some stateless societies, such as chiefdoms. Societies ruled as kingdoms are characterized by a complex and hierarchical internal structure and are often dividied into different social classes; they are based upon an agricultural and/or manufacturing economy that requires centralized direction. Such societies require a political as well as an economic pivot. Although the monarch's personal political power may vary (he may be anything from an absolute ruler to a mere symbol), he is important because he represents that center or pivot of power. Power over the state is held, if not by him directly, then by his immediate entourage.

Though one cannot label all kings "sacred kings," all kings are "sacred" in some way. Indeed, modern scholars have stressed the common religious traits of kingship. Throughout the world kingship is the most widespread and the most archaic state institution. The only societies that were never ruled by kings at some point in their known history have no state. Most societies that were or are today organized as states have experienced, and in many cases rejected, kingship. The great cultures of antiquity that arose at the time of the so-called urban revolution—Mesopotamia, Egypt, and China—were state societies ruled by "sacred kings." The Central and South American agricultural states of the Aztec and Inca were organized as "sacred" monarchies, and state societies throughout Africa, Europe, and Asia continued as kingships for millennia. To define the common traits of the various forms of kingship, however, requires considerable care. Very often all that results is a general framework of similarities dictated by similar social and economic situations. And always the framework of similarities is filled in by specific realities that are profoundly different.

The King as Pivot and Totality. The most important aspect of kingship, stressed by different cultures in different ways, is the king's centrality and his role as a symbol of totality. Monarchs are symbolically, and indeed actually, the center of the society organized as a state. They are considered mediators between both the various parts and interests that make up the social order and between the human and extra-human worlds. The king holds the social "cosmos" together. Thus his rule is, like that of the supreme being of many religious systems, a symbol of totality. Often his abode and his person are symbolically indicated as a microcosm or as the center of the cosmos. Six symbolic and ideological expressions of this aspect of kingship come to mind.

1. In the ancient Near East and in the late Roman empire, the hall that contained the kingly throne was constructed as a reproduction of the cosmos itself. In the Iranian tradition, it was topped by a revolving sky-like rotunda. The conception of the monarch as "king of the four quarters" that is found both in Aztec Mexico and in ancient Mesopotamia, where it dates back at least to the third millennium BCE; the ancient Near Eastern identification of the king as a "cosmic tree" flanked by guardian monsters; the use of the kingly umbrella, which originated in ancient Assyria in the first millennium BCE and spread thence to many parts of Africa, Asia, and Europe—all have a similar meaning. The solar symbolism of monarchy prevalent in ancient Egypt and the Inca state continued during the European Middle Ages with the consecration of the emperor by elevation on shields and reappeared in the propaganda of Louis XIV of France. Like the cosmic symbolism given above, the solar symbolism refers to the king as a cosmic giver of life.

2. The king's role in the centralized organization of production, and, by extension, the role of the palace or court was expressed ideologically as redistribution: the monarch was seen as a giver of goods and a giver of riches. In myths of the Near East and of ancient Europe, kings keep or obtain their power if they are generous providers who take care of the needy. Many official and festive institutions based upon the distribution of food, such as the distribution of cereal to the people of Rome by the Roman emperors, are a response to this conception. A further aspect of the centrality of kings is their quality as judges, a quality that is obviously connected to their role as righteous redistributors: the biblical Solomon became the prototype of the kingly judge in Christian tradition.

3. The role of the king as a mediator is stressed symbolically by his equally intense relationship with all parts and aspects of the society he is the center of. This is especially conspicuous in societies where the different classes or social functions are clearly distinguished and precisely characterized. Thus, in Indian and Celtic kingly rituals tripartite symbolism clearly connects the monarch with the priestly, military, and productive functions.

4. The role of the king as mediator between the superhuman powers and the society is especially clear in his magical and priestly function. Such a function is never the sole responsibility of the king, and often it is de-emphasized or denied when a strong priestly class exists. But when the king has a priestly function, he is responsible for the cultic relationships between the society and the supernatural sphere. For instance, he often plays the central role in national and yearly agrarian festivals, and through prayers and sacrifice offered on behalf of the people.

5. In some societies (especially in sub-Saharan Africa) the king may be ritually killed if he loses his vigor, and as the very symbol of the kingdom's well-being, he must be replaced. Some ancient mythologies present a mythical king as a sacrificial victim. In some Indo-European traditions a first king, who is often a "first man," is the victim of the first, cosmogonic sacrifice and the world is created from his dismembered body. In Northwest Semitic traditions, and possibly in ritual practice in the first millennium BCE, a king offered his own son and future successor as a sacrificial victim to the gods in a period of crisis.

6. Finally, kings play a central role in warfare and are consistently the leaders of the national army. This aspect of kingship has recently been stressed in general studies on kingship; but no matter how important warfare may have been in the rise of specific dynasties, the notion of kings as war leaders seems only one specific aspect of the general symbolic system described above. Moreover, official historiography or mythology (for instance, the kingly genealogy of the Rwanda in central Africa or the Hebrew scriptures) often emphasizes the equal importance of "warlike" and "peaceful" (often, ritual) aspects of kingship by presenting an alternation of the two types of king in genealogical succession.

The Powers of Kings. The "real" political power of kings is often difficult to distinguish from their "symbolic" ("magical" or "religious") power, for the ideologies of many societies firmly intertwine the two. Indeed, the very fact of becoming a king is often seen as a consequence of a previous power, whether this happens at the mythical beginnings of dynasties or within dynastic succession. The previous power is represented as a supernatural quality, as the possession of a symbolic object or of the favor of a deity.

As for the "symbolic" or "religious" power of the king himself, it is represented mainly by the connection between the king's person and the global welfare of the country, people, and state. This implies that the forces of nature were controlled through him by the society, and that his personal welfare and correct ritual and moral behavior affected the outcome of crops and the risk of calamities such as famine or epidemics. Sir James Frazer (1911–1915) considered this conception the central aspect of kingship in its most archaic phases of development. In modern times it appears in African and East Asian kingdoms, but there are traces of it in ancient Greek, Hebrew, and Celtic societies. This conception of kings as vessels of supernatural power implies the necessity for strict social control over their daily lives down to the minutest details, examples being the enormous number of prohibitions surrounding the person of the monarch and the extreme phenomenon mentioned above of killing the king once he gives signs of having lost his vigor. The prohibitions surrounding the person of the king are meant to protect both him from unnecessary risk and his subjects or the soil of the kingdom from contact with the monarch that would be dangerous for them.

Laura Makarius (1974) has sought the origin of this supernatural power detained (or better, "contained") by kings in their own impurity especially in Africa but elsewhere as well. She has argued that the king's violation of prohibitions, mainly of the blood and incest prohibitions, comprises an essential aspect of kingship, for the violation turns him into a receptacle for the ambiguous, magical power of blood, both polluting and sacred. No doubt, royal incest and the many blood ceremonies of kingship described by Laura Makarius characterize the power of kings in these terms and stress their special and "superior" status. But the very fact that in so many ideologies of kingship the welfare of the realm is believed to be upheld not only by the well-being of kings but also by their correct behavior, behavior often identified with the king's capacity for upholding justice and for defending cosmic truth (as in ancient Egypt or the Celtic tradition), shows that the sacred king is not by definition a breaker of rules, or even above all rules. His power frees him from some of the rules common to humans, but it makes him an enforcer of rules and submits him to different rules that are not valid for common people. Hence, in some African, Asiatic, and American kingdoms, the monarch could marry his mother or sister, but he was not allowed to travel on foot or to share a meal. Paradoxically, though the political and the magical or religious powers of kingship are connected, the prohibitions that rule the behavior of sacred kings and protect their magical or religious power may limit their actual political power. China presents the clearest example of such a situation. Until the fall of the Chinese monarchy in modern times, the emperor of unified China, the Son of Heaven, lived intangibly and powerlessly in his palace; the bureaucracy controlled his actions in fear of a breach in the moral and cosmic order and could deprive him of his "heavenly" mandate if he broke rules. In other cases, the kingly rule is similarly "controlled" not by a bureaucracy but by other functional groups who possess the technique for praising and blaming the ruling monarch, such as the bards in Irish Celtic traditions.

The magical or religious power of kings is less important in more complex societies, particularly in those that believe in a developed polytheistic pantheon or in a single, all-powerful god. Yet some magical powers survive, notably the king's power to heal. Only rarely attested in antiquity, this power became important in Europe during the Middle Ages and remained so until the great revolutions of modern times. Both the English and the French kings were believed capable of healing subjects afflicted by a skin disease called scrofula, also known as "king's evil."

Kings and Gods. The ruling and special powers of kings, their central and cosmic value, and their role as mediators between the human and the extra-human sphere place them not only at the summit of the hierarchical pyramid of the state but also in a special category of superior humans. This status often implies the belief in the special connection between the monarch and the superhuman or divine sphere and in different ways equates the monarch with a god or with some mythical being. Indeed, kings are often treated like superhuman beings or gods. This treatment is expressed by the similarities between the architecture and organization of palaces and sanctuaries; between royal and divine rights, images, symbols, and paraphernalia; and between worshipers' and subjects' ritual attitudes, postures, and behaviors in relationship to sacred symbols, gods, or kings. Yet the specific forms of similarity between mythical beings or deities and kings vary greatly from culture to culture. In some cases, as in ancient Egyptian and Aztec cultures, the king was directly equated with a god; in other cases, as among the Kotoko or the Ankole, the king was directly equated with sacred animals. Elsewhere, the kingly dynasty was believed to descend either from a mythical figure, god, or deified hero, as in many Hellenistic kingdoms of the eastern Mediterranean, or from a sacred animal, as, for example, of the kings of Dahomey in West Africa. In still other instances, the king was believed to be the spouse of a great goddess (as typified by the Sumerian kingship of the third millennium BCE) or the son of a god with whom his mother had lain (as typified by King Alexander of Macedonia in the fourth century BCE). But other ideologies of kingship insist upon divine election and choice of the king rather than upon the divine quality or descent of the monarch. Obviously, any identification or genealogical connection of kings with divine or mythical beings became impossible in the context of monotheistic belief in a transcendent god, which rendered such identification absurd. In such a context the relationship between the kingly and the divine sphere evolved into one of profound inequality; the ideology of divine election became the main source of the sacrality of kings.

Court and Dynasty: Successors and Substitutes. Although the person of the king is the pivot of the state and often lives in ritual isolation, he is not really isolated: neither synchronically, for he is surrounded by the royal family and by a court of people who take care of him as well as of the kingdom, nor diachronically, for he is but a link in the chain of the royal dynasty that reigns over the state. The royal family thus plays an important and complex role in the state: the family surrounds the king during his lifetime, performing essential political and ritual functions and assuring succession, most often transmitted by patrilineal descent.

One or more members of the royal family may play a specific role and accompany the king at times of ritual and public display of power; in the most extreme cases the system leads to a dyarchy. Such is the case among the Inca of Peru (dyarchy of king and king's son), the Aztec of Mexico (dyarchy of king and king's brother), and the Lozi, Benin, and Rwanda of Africa (dyarchy of king and queen mother). Elsewhere, as in the kingdom of Buganda (East Africa), a merely ritual wife accompanies the king, subject to the same avoidance rules and costumed in identical dress and insignia. However, in still numerous other cases the royal family is absent from the ritual life of kings.

Members of the royal family, notably the heir to the throne if designated in advance, often act as substitutes for the king, who refrains from appearing in public when his presence is not ritually necessary; but official substitutes may also be enrolled from among the court personnel or from the people. In the Yoruba kingdom of Ọyọ (in present-day Nigeria), the king was flanked by seven important dignitaries, who could force him to kill himself if he was unsuccessful or if his older son or his slaves misbehaved. The dignitaries had in reserve no less than three possible official substitutes, only one of whom, the *kakanfo,* was of royal blood. The *kakanfo* could not reside in the capital and was thus an "invisible" substitute; only in war did he appear, acting as a war leader and representing the king during battles.

Permanent substitutes (who sometimes followed the monarch to his grave) should not be confused with the substitutes who took the king's place to suffer and die in ritual contexts, thus averting disaster from the monarch. The most famous example is the Assyrian substitute king who was buried alive, according to texts of the early first millennium BCE.

As stated above, the continuity of the kingship is identified with that of the royal dynasty, and royal blood is an essential prerequisite for kingly power. Sometimes the choice of the royal successor is very strictly and precisely ordered; more often it is only loosely prescribed, so that among the eligible members of the royal lineage a competition may break out. The period that follows the death of a king is thus usually a period of social (and cosmic) chaos, both actually and symbolically. Several ways of preventing this are known: the choice of an official successor during the monarch's life (which may lead to a dyarchy) or the temporary enthronement of a mock or fictitious ruler (for instance, a court jester in the Ankole kingdom of Uganda in East Africa and a daughter of the dead king among the Mossi of Burkina Faso in West Africa).

Kings often have many secondary wives and official concubines in addition to their official wife or wives, as is the case in ancient Egypt and modern Africa. In some cases, the official wife of the king was his sister or mother or another woman connected to him by kingship ties that normally would involve a marriage prohibition. Modern scholars have interpreted incestuous marriage among royalty in ancient Egypt, Peru, Hawaii, Madagascar, and Burma in different ways. Traditionally, this practice was interpreted by scholars as intended to keep the royal blood pure and to maintain the kingly power within a restricted kinship group. Increasingly, an alternate interpretation insists on the exceptional quality of royal incest and on its role in defining the special nature and status of kings.

Rituals of Kingship. Though the entire lives of monarchs were often subject to special rules and highly ritualized, some particular rituals of kingship can be singled out as both widespread and especially important. The classic study of such rituals by A. M. Hocart (1927) recognizes three main types of kingship rituals: consecration, marriage, and funerary rites.

The consecration, often preceded by a period of initiation, transforms the royal heir into a king or, in Hocart's words, "the future king into a god." The chief elements of the ritual are: a contractual encounter between king and people, including admonitions and promises; the washing and anointing of the new king; a communal meal; the investing of the new monarch with regalia; and a procession. This ritual serves to underline the fact that although one can be born a possible heir to the kingly throne, one *becomes* a king. Becoming a king often involves problems and contradictions on the political as well as on the symbolic level, for it gives great power to those enabled to anoint the monarch, who often are priests.

The kingly funerary rites are also significant, for they stress the continuity of kingship, both in the sense that the dead king has special postmortem expectations (to the extent of being deified after his death) and in the sense that the successor plays a special role in the ritual. In some extreme cases in Africa possible successors fight for the control of the body of the dead king.

In contrast to these rituals that sanctify kingly succession and uphold the ideology of kingship are the rites that deal with critical aspects of kingship and enact an institutional crisis on the symbolic level in order to express, control, and avoid actual crises. Examples are the ritual humiliation of ancient Babylonian kings during the Akitu or New Year festival and the ritual attack on modern African kings during major festive occasions, classified by Max Gluckman as "rituals of rebellion."

The Divine Right of Kings. In polytheistic, and especially in monotheistic, contexts, as stated above, the sacred quality of kings took on a different aspect: kings were not divine per se, but they received their power from the divine. In Christian Europe, the authority of kings was believed to derive not just from their descent from royal lineage but also and especially from their investiture. In turn, investiture soon took the form of ritual anointment with holy oil administered by prelates. Hence investiture was potentially controlled by the church, and the origin and control of kingly authority became an important issue in the conflicts between the church, the Holy Roman Empire, and the national monarchies during the Middle Ages and the Renaissance.

However, the kings' right to rule was divine, even though they themselves were definitely not divine. This belief developed into an important, complex theory during the Middle Ages and retained its force until the revolutions of the seventeenth and eighteenth centuries. Although he was no god, the king was believed to be singled out to represent God's will on earth and thus somehow godlike. Moreover, he was the head of the body formed by the society, called by theoreticians the "body politic," in imitation of the Christian concept of the church headed by Christ, the "mystical body." Finally, the physical continuity of the dynasty was identified with the continuity of the head of the body politic and of the body politic itself, so that, although the king's personal body could die, as the head of the body politic he was considered immortal.

Such complex theories were developed by intellectuals, and in this form they were probably never popular. More popular in the Middle Ages were views of the king as a father of his people, a good provider, and a healer. The English and French revolutions, however, tried, condemned, and executed kings, and destroyed medieval and modern ideologies of holy kingship together with the "absolute" power that monarchies had gained through their struggle against the feudal lords during the later Middle Ages and in early modern times.

[*See* Theodosius; Constantine; *and* Charlemagne *for illustrations of the form taken by sacred kingship in Christian Europe.*]

BIBLIOGRAPHY

The authors who shaped the modern study of sacred kingship on a comparative basis are James G. Frazer and A. M. Hocart. See Frazer's *The Golden Bough: A Study in Magic and Religion,* 12 vols., 3d ed., rev. & enl. (London, 1911–1915), especially part 1, *The Magic Art and the Evolution of Kings* (2 vols.) and part 4, *Adonis, Attis, Osiris* (2 vols.); and Hocart's *Kingship* (1927; Oxford, 1969). A useful text on archaic state forms and on monarchy in that context is the volume edited by Henri J. M. Claessen and Peter Skalnik, *The Early State* (The Hague, 1978). *The Sacral Kingship* (Leiden, 1959), a collective work containing most of the papers presented to the 1955 International Congress of the International Association for the History of Religions, held in Rome and devoted to the problem of kingship on a wide comparative basis, offers valuable information on the subject. Comparative studies of sacred kingship by single authors are rare; Ernesta Cerulli's *Ma il re divino viaggiava da sola? Problemi e contraddizioni di un "complesso culturale" di diffusione quasi universale* (Genoa, 1979) is one of the most interesting and contains a good general bibliography. An innovative discussion of sacred kingship is found in Laura Makarius's *Le sacré et la violation des interdits* (Paris, 1974); see pages 143–214 for the theory that the power of kings is derived from their classification as polluted and thus magically powerful violators of the blood taboo. On the problem of kingly incest, see Luc de Heusch's important *Essais sur le symbolisme de l'inceste royal en Afrique* (Brussels, 1958). On kingship, and especially on the healing power of kings in medieval Europe, see Marc Bloch's *Les rois thaumaturges: Étude sur le caractère surnaturel attribué à la puissance royale particulièrement en France et en Angleterre* (Strasbourg, 1924). On the divine right of kings, consult John Neville Figgis's *The Divine Right of Kings,* 2d ed. (Cambridge, 1914) and Ernst H. Kantorowicz's *The King's Two Bodies: A Study in Medieval Political Theology* (Princeton, 1957). A study of the attitudes to kingship in the modern European revolutions can be found in the volume edited by Michael Walter, *Regicide and Revolution: Speeches at the Trial of Louis XVI* (New York, 1974).

CRISTIANO GROTTANELLI

Kingship in the Ancient Mediterranean World

Early Kingship in the Fertile Crescent. The most ancient state organizations arose in the Fertile Crescent—the lowlands between the basins of the Tigris and Euphrates and the valley of the Nile—toward the beginning of the third millennium BCE. In Egypt, the Nile with its yearly inundation provided fertile land, easily cultivated to produce cereals, while in Mesopotamia an intricate system of canals was gradually built, extending the water from the two great rivers to more distant areas. These two means of irrigation were the material basis for the growth of a larger population and of complex state organizations, and in turn such organizations were needed to guarantee the full control of the new economic reality. Moreover, a tendency toward the unification of large areas led Egypt to a rapid fusion of the northern and southern valleys at the very beginning of its life as a monarchic state. This tendency surfaced more slowly in Mesopotamia, where it culminated only in the empires of the Babylonians, Assyrians, and Persians in the course of the first millennium BCE.

In Egypt the new organization of the society as a state was probably from the very beginning a monarchic system, while in Mesopotamia some of the oldest political organizations were centered around sanctuaries; but in the latter case, the monarchic state soon became the main, and then the only, political system. In both instances the new political forms arose together with, and interacted with, religious systems of a polytheistic type, based on the orderly coexistence of hierarchically organized deities forming a pantheon. The relationship between the polytheistic religions and the ideology of the new states was one of identity, and the monarchs were seen as pivots of the economic administration, as good shepherds of their people, and as efficient war leaders. But they were seen especially as the main link between the human and the divine spheres, while the social order, guaranteed by the kings, was envisaged as an aspect of the cosmic order, upheld by the gods. The ancient kingship of Egypt and Mesopotamia was thus a sacral kingship, because the ruler's powers and functions were directly dependent on the monarch's relationship with the gods of the polytheistic pantheon.

Egypt. While consistently shown as a good shepherd, a leader in battle, and a pious worshiper of the gods, the Egyptian king or pharaoh was, from the earliest times to the Persian conquest of 525 BCE, presented by the texts as a god. This implied the divine nature of each individual king as such: the king was described even in the archaic Pyramid Texts as having neither a (human) father nor a (human) mother. But the king was also seen as a god in a more specific way. First, he was an image of the supreme sun god of the Egyptians, Re-Atum. He was the latest successor of that creator god, a beloved son of that deity, the champion of the static order established in mythical times by Re-Atum, and destined to join the sun god after death, when "his divine body coalesces with its sire."

This relationship of similarity, kinship, and ultimate

union after death was profoundly different from the relationship between the pharaoh and the god Horus. In each kingly succession there took place a reenactment of the mythical struggle between the god Osiris, son of Geb (the earth god) and Nut (the sky goddess)—first king, Nile god, god of cereals, and lord of the dead—and his brother and murderer, Seth, followed by the revenge taken on Seth by Osiris' son and successor, the young god Horus. The living and reigning pharaoh was thus identified with the god Horus, while his dead predecessor ruled in the netherworld as the god Osiris.

The kingly rituals that were a central aspect of Egyptian religiosity and were tightly interwoven with the agricultural economy were in large part based on the Osirian mythology. The Pyramid Texts show, however, that in view of the pharaoh's expectations of resurrection and celestial survival after death, the acknowledgment of the identity between the dead king and Osiris, whose fate was repeated death but not resurrection, was accompanied by a further motif. The monarch was the dying Osiris and thus the winnowed grain that was identified with that deity, but he also mounted to heaven in the clouds of chaff that rose during the winnowing. On the other hand, the "agrarian" nature of Osiris was only an aspect of that deity's complex personality, which centered around his kingly nature.

Kings, "souls," and ancestors. The superiority of the monarchs was not expressed only by their connection or identification with deities. The king was also superior to his subjects because his *ka* ("soul, vital force, luck, fortune") was different from that of commoners. The pharaoh's *ka* was shown on monuments in the shape of the monarch's identical twin; as the king's protector in death, it announced the arrival of the dead monarch to the gods in heaven; it was identified (Frankfort, 1948) with the placenta enwrapping the newborn king. One of the standards that accompanied the king during festivals and processions probably represented the royal placenta, and may have been the image of the king's *ka*.

Other standards accompanying the king represented his ancestral spirits, whose functions were to give life to the pharaoh, thus protecting the land, and, after his death, to prepare his ascent to the heavens. The standards thus played an important part in kingly rituals. The fact that they were classified in two subgroups, the "souls of Pe" and the "souls of Nekhen," may point to an early artificial combination of two series of kingly ancestors, from southern and northern Egypt, respectively.

Kingly rituals. The main rituals of the Egyptian state were kingly rituals sanctioning the various aspects of the royal succession, a delicate mechanism that ensured the continuity of the social order. The death of the old king was followed by a period during which the new pharaoh assumed power, visited sanctuaries throughout Egypt, and issued his protocols, while his father's body and funerary temple were prepared for the burial rites. During this period, "the *ka*s rested."

On the day of the royal funerary ritual, a series of litanies, spells, and incantations were probably recited, insisting on the identity of the dead pharaoh with Osiris and of his son with Horus, and on the dead monarch's glorious survival in heaven, where he was embraced by the god Atum or received by the souls of Pe and Nekhen. Thus the king was buried as an embalmed mummy in his funerary abode, and was symbolically located in the regions (the netherworld, the west, and the north near the circumpolar stars) where his life continued. While the dead king ruled as Osiris among the dead, his son ruled on earth as the previous pharaoh had done, in perfect continuity.

The day after the celebration of the dead king's heavenly survival, the coronation of the new pharaoh took place. It was usually made to coincide with the New Year day or with some other important beginning in nature's cycle. The ritual involved cultic practices in the dual shrines of the royal ancestral spirits of Pe and Nekhen, and it culminated in the placing of the two crowns of Upper and Lower Egypt on the pharaoh's head. This was accompanied by the singing of litanies exalting the power that resided in the crowns and by prayers addressed by the king to the crowns or by others to Atum in behalf of the new pharaoh. One text, treating the accession ritual of Senusert I, describes the threshing of barley, the erection of the sacred Djed pillar (symbolizing the resurrection of the king's predecessor), a distribution of bread by the pharaoh, and the offering of gifts to the new king, as well as the coronation proper.

A further important kingly ritual was that of the Sed festival, which took place once or several times during a pharaoh's reign. This renewal of the kingly power was held on the date when the coronation had taken place. It included a procession; the offering of gifts to the gods; pledges of loyalty by the king; visits to shrines; the dedication of a field to the gods by the pharaoh, who twice ran across it in the four directions of the compass, first as king of Upper, then of Lower Egypt; and the shooting of arrows by the king in these four directions, symbolically winning him control of the whole universe.

Mesopotamia. In the Sumerian and Semitic cultures of Mesopotamia, the kings, as the summit and the pivot of human societies, were entrusted in a special way with a typically human function, the caretaking of the gods. In this perspective, the construction of shrines, the celebration of rituals, and the offering of food to the deities were among a good king's most important duties, and one of the proofs of his righteousness and power. Moreover, the central role of divination stressed the limitations in the autonomy and power of kings, who could not act without consulting omens.

In spite of all this, kings were not devoid of divine traits. Thus, in some cases (as indicated, for example, by the Sumerian inscription of King Gudea of Lagash, who says to the deity Gatumdug: "I have no mother, I have no father, thou art my father") the king is shown as a "son" of a god or goddess. More frequently, he is seen as chosen by the gods while in the very womb of his mother, and thus destined to rule. In the Sumerian states, the king was often presented as the spouse of a goddess; the sacred marriage between the two was ritually enacted during important festivals, and possibly was considered to be the source of the ruler's power. In such rituals the king was often identified with the young "dying" god Dumuzi-Tammuz, spouse of the goddess Inanna-Ishtar, and with a mythical shepherd and king. The names of kings may appear as components of proper names in a position similar to that held by names of deities, and they sometimes bear the divine determinative—a cuneiform sign preceding the name and indicating that it is the name of a deity. Although we know of only one case in which a shrine was dedicated to a king during his lifetime, it is certain that royal statues were set up in temples and received offerings.

In general, however, although a relationship of similarity between kings and deities is often stressed in Mesopotamian texts, kings were probably considered "godlike" more often than "divine" in their own right. Similarly, they were often said to be responsible for the fertility and prosperity of their land; but the connection between the king's person and behavior and the natural rhythms of agriculture was mediated by the relationship between the ruler and the gods, so that abundance in the kingdom could be taken as a proof that the king had not disappointed the gods who elected him.

The royal dead. After the end of the third millennium BCE, and surely in connection with the rise of the new Amorite dynasties, a new interest in kingly ancestors (if not an actual cult of the royal dead) arose in many Mesopotamian states, involving the redaction of lists of these ancestors, some of them historical and some mythical. As for funerary rituals, although we know that in Neo-Assyrian times kings were publicly buried and mourning ceremonies took place, the texts tell us little about the death rites and afterlife expectations of kings. Some information may be gathered from archaeological finds, however. In the royal cemetery of Ur rich burials have been discovered that go back to the middle of the third millennium BCE, containing precious objects as well as a great quantity of dead surrounding the monarch—probably courtiers and servants ritually killed in order to accompany their master to his funerary abode.

Kingly rituals. Rituals of kingship are less well attested in Mesopotamia than in Egypt. Our main evidence for accession rituals is found in a text describing the coronation of a king of Uruk and in Neo-Assyrian texts of the ninth to seventh centuries BCE. In the Uruk text, the king-to-be is shown approaching the throne dais of the goddess Inanna-Ishtar in her temple, with the goddess "placing the bright scepter in his hand" and "fastening the golden crown on his head." At this point the king was probably given a new, "royal" name. In the Neo-Assyrian texts, the king is carried to the temple of the god Ashur on a portable throne borne on the shoulders of men while a priest going in front beats a drum, calling out "Ashur is king!" The king then worshiped Ashur and offered gifts to the god. He was thereupon probably anointed and crowned, and was given the scepter of kingship by the head priest.

The king played a central role in the New Year festival (Akitu). The Babylonian Akitu took place during the spring month of Nisan, lasted several days, and included processions, a ritual determination of destinies, and a banquet. On the fourth day of Nisan, the creation epic *Enuma elish* was recited in its entirety. It exalted the great victory of the main city god, Marduk, over the forces of chaos, and his promotion to cosmic kingship. [*See* Enuma Elish.] In later stages of the Akitu, specific aspects of the cosmogonic battle (especially Marduk's temporary defeat and disappearance, and his final triumph) were ritually enacted. Probably in connection with Marduk's initial defeat, on the fifth day of the festival the king was stripped of his royal insignia by a priest of Marduk. The king then knelt down to pronounce a declaration of innocence before the god, was given back his insignia, and was slapped in the face by the priest. This was a ritual of atonement, meant to cleanse the king and city and to renew the kingship. The king may also have played the part of the god Marduk in a ritual enactment of a sacred marriage with a goddess that took place toward the end of the festival.

A means of protecting the king as a pivot of order and stability was the ritual of the "substitute king" (Shar Puhi), best attested in Neo-Assyrian texts. The substitute king, a subject of the king of Assyria, was chosen and invested with kingly authority, probably by the presentation of a royal weapon. He "took upon himself all the portents of heaven and earth," and was then probably buried alive.

Syria and Palestine, Including Israel. As shown by the texts discovered at the ancient sites of Ebla (mid-third millennium BCE), Mari (early second millennium BCE), and Ugarit (late second millennium BCE), kingship was the central institution in Syria from the beginning of that area's history. The king's function in the cult was as important as that of the Mesopotamian monarchs, but the texts do not offer material comparable to the rich ideological and ritual literature of Egypt and Mesopotamia. In the Ugaritic texts, however, we have what could be a trace of a hierogamy between the king and the goddess of dew, one mention of the queen's role in a ritual taking place in the fields, and myths that insist on the connection between the fate of a young king's son and agricultural fertility and that tell how the storm god, Baal, defeated the forces of chaos and attained cosmic kingship.

An important trait of kingship ideology in Bronze Age Syria was the cult of dead kings, which apparently began at the time of the Amorite dynasties. In Ugarit the royal ancestors, called *rapium* ("healers, saviors"; cf. the biblical *refaʿim*), the most ancient of which were probably mythical, were worshiped with offerings and periodic rites.

In the first millennium BCE, traces of Phoenician and Aramean kingship ideology are attested by alphabetic inscriptions. The godlike qualities of monarchs were sometimes indicated, but the main aspects of kingship were seen as the ruler's upholding of justice and peace and his role as a servant of the gods. They repaid him by giving peace and abundance to his kingdom. One Aramaic inscription, however, seems to present the king as enjoying a special existence ("drinking" with the storm god) after his death.

The Israelite monarchy in the Bible was not devoid of such "sacral" traits, and specific ritual aspects, such as royal anointing and royal burial rites, are attested by the biblical texts with some precision. Yet the Bible presents the kings as mere servants of the heavenly king and only true god, Yahveh, and it denies them any superhuman power or destiny. Moreover, kingship is presented as a foreign institution adopted by the Israelites, and most Israelite kings are depicted as unfaithful to the national deity, whereas the prophets of Yahveh play an important role in condemning monarchs on behalf of their god, and sometimes in anointing new and more pious kings to replace them. In the exilic and postexilic texts, many aspects of the Near Eastern kingship ideology (but not the divine nature of monarchs) seem to have converged in the eschatological expectations of the Israelites, who had no kings of their own but awaited the return of a descendant of the Davidic dynasty. In this sense, the roots of Jewish and Christian messianism must be sought in the kingship ideology of the ancient Near East.

Hittite Kingship. The Hittites, who spoke an Indo-European language but inherited much of their pantheon and many rituals from the non-Indo-European inhabitants of Anatolia and neighboring regions, were organized as a powerful monarchic state during much of the second millennium BCE. Although they were indirectly assimilated to deities, and to the sun god and storm god in particular, the Hittite kings were not presented as gods during their lifetime. After their death a complex ritual based on the cremation of the king's body took place, and food was ritually offered to the dead monarchs. When the texts refer to a king's death, they speak of his "becoming a god."

We have only minimal and indirect evidence for the coronation rites, but the king's central role in festivals and rituals in various sanctuaries throughout the kingdom is attested. Great importance was also given to the correctness of the monarch's behavior in relation to the divine sphere, and to his protection from pollution and hostile magic. Royal inscriptions insist on the fact that the monarch's power was due to the favor of the gods, often of a specific deity with whom the ruler had a special relationship.

Iran. The Iranian kingdom took shape around the middle of the first millennium BCE, was destroyed by Alexander the Great in the fourth century BCE, and arose again in different forms, to survive until the Muslim conquest. In many ways the kingdom was an heir to the great empires of the Near East: the Neo-Assyrian and the Neo-Babylonian. But the royal dynasty and the ruling class of the empire spoke an Indo-European language and in culture and religion were foreign to Mesopotamian traditions. Thus, the kingship ideology of Iran, both in the Achaemenid period and later, when the national tradition was resurrected in reaction to the Hellenistic culture of the Seleucid kings, was fundamentally autonomous and original.

The king was not himself considered to be divine but to hold his power from the divine sphere, and in particular from the supreme deity, Ahura Mazdā, the central figure in the reformed Iranian religion that is commonly attributed to the prophet and innovator Zarathushtra (Zoroaster). A strong ethical element is present both in the kingship ideology of the Achaemenid inscriptions and in that of the later Iranian texts: the king is depicted as the upholder of truth and justice, a champion of the correct religious order against the forces of evil. The royal power is symbolically connected to a suprahuman entity, the *khvarenah,* which was represented as a glow or flame and should be interpreted as the king's fiery splendor, glory, fortune, or fate. If the king proved unworthy, the *khvarenah* (and thus the kingship) left him, as had happened in mythical times to King Yima (in later texts, Jamshīd), whose sin caused him to lose his power. The monarch's sacred moral mission pertained mainly to the military and judicial spheres, while a powerful priestly class was in charge of the intricacies of doctrine and ritual.

Greece and Hellenism. Little is known about kingship in Crete in Minoan times (c. 2500–c. 1500 BCE) and in Greece and Crete of Mycenean times (c. 1600–c. 1100 BCE), since the relevant texts are either not yet translated (the Minoan Linear A inscriptions) or they are mainly concerned with problems of administration (the Mycenaean Linear B texts, in a language that is an ancestor of ancient Greek). All one can say is that a polytheistic religion was firmly connected with a state system of a Near Eastern type, although on a smaller scale, and that the states were headed by kings (the Mycenaean title is *wanax*).

When this state system collapsed around 1100 BCE, many aspects of that cultural tradition, including writing, were lost. A profound social transformation led, after many centuries, to the birth of a new organization, the typically Greek *polis*, or city-state. While kingdoms survived in the periphery of the new Greek world, the *polis* was a structure that had no place for monarchies of the type discussed above, although some kingly functions were inherited by magistrates, and even restricted forms of kingship (e.g., the Spartan "dyarchy") are attested. The monarchical tendencies of some rulers *(turannoi)* of cities in the seventh to fourth century BCE were exceptional and short-lived, though they arose again and again, especially in the colonial world of Sicily and Asia Minor. It was only when the *polis* system in its turn declined and the peripheral Macedonian dynasty gained control over Greece and later conquered the Iranian empire that the Greek-speaking world had to come to terms with the power of the Macedonian kings *(basileis)*, while most cities maintained, at least formally, their traditional regimes.

After the death of Alexander the Great of Macedonia (323 BCE), his empire was divided among his successors. The Near East of the Hellenistic age became a series of monarchies headed by kings of Macedonian descent. These kingdoms were ruled, and profoundly influenced culturally, by an elite of Greek soldiers and administrators. Hellenistic kingship ideology, like Hellenistic culture in general, was a combination of Greek (Macedonian) and traditional Near Eastern traits. Kings were believed to be descendants of divine ancestors (through Alexander), godlike—in some cases, divine—in life, and surviving as gods after their death. The court etiquette and the rituals of kingship, so far as can be ascertained, were derived mainly from the Iranian, Egyptian, and other Near Eastern traditions.

Rome. Although the most ancient Roman state was surely organized as a monarchy, the traditions about the seven Roman kings, transmitted by ancient historians, are probably in large part mythical; from the sixth century BCE, Rome was a republic headed by an aristocracy of *senatores* and governed by elected magistrates. Indeed, the antimonarchic ideology of ancient Rome was such that when—after the Roman conquest of most of the Mediterranean world—the crisis of the republican state led to the rise of a new form of monarchy, the rulers did not take on the traditional title of Indo-European origin, *rex* (king), but were called *imperator,* a word denoting the triumphing war leader of republican times. The Roman empire lasted from the first century BCE to the late fifth century CE, and the ideology of rulership changed profoundly during its history. Its original traits included the cult of the emperor's *genius* (personality, double) and the deification of the dead emperor through a complex ritual involving cremation and the flight of his spirit to the heavens in the form of an eagle flying from the funeral pyre. But these soon gave way, in the eastern provinces first and then in the entire imperial territory, to other forms of ruler worship, such as the identification of the emperor with mythical figures or gods, often directly imported by monarchs from the local cultures of their provincial homelands.

The emperor Constantine's conversion to Christianity in the late fourth century was the starting point of a further profound transformation in the imperial ideology. Obviously, the new Christian rulers could not be considered divine, yet many aspects of the system of beliefs, rituals, and etiquette typical of the imperial monarchy were adapted to the new religious context. According to the *Triakontaeterikos,* a treatise on imperial power by the Christian writer Eusebius of Caesarea (fourth century), the whole cosmos is a monarchic state *(basileia, monarchia)* ruled by the Christian God, and it is the emperor's task to imitate the divine monarch. The final result of the process of ideological transformation that began with Constantine was the ideology of the Christian ruler. This was the basis of Byzantine kingship ideology, and it later joined with other (mainly Celtic and Germanic) traditions to form medieval theories of kingship.

BIBLIOGRAPHY

The bibliography on this subject is huge, and it is not always easy to select from it without omitting important contributions, especially since debate is still in progress. On the sacral kingship of the ancient Near East, one should see C. J. Gadd's

Ideas of Divine Rule in the Ancient Near East (Oxford, 1948), Henri Frankfort's *Kingship and the Gods: A Study of Ancient Near Eastern Religion as the Integration of Society and Nature* (1948; reprint, Chicago, 1978), Ivan Engnell's *Studies in Divine Kingship in the Ancient Near East*, 2d rev. ed. (Oxford, 1967), and *Le palais et la royauté*, edited by Paul Garelli (Paris, 1974), which deals especially with Mesopotamia. Engnell insists on the fundamental similarity of patterns of sacral kingship throughout the Near East from Egypt to Anatolia, and on the divine nature of kings, whereas Frankfort is more attentive to differences, especially between the Egyptian and the Mesopotamian kingship ideology.

On the Egyptian kingship, the old volume by Alexandre Moret, *Du caractère religieux de la royauté pharaonique* (Paris, 1902), is still often cited as the fundamental work. For Mesopotamia there are many new studies; among them, Ilse Seibert's *Hirt, Herde, König: Zur Herausbildung des Königtums in Mesopotamien* (Berlin, 1969) discusses the "pastoral" overtones of the Mesopotamian kingship, but also many other aspects. René Labat's *Le caractère religieux de la royauté assyro-babylonienne* (Paris, 1939) remains the classic study.

Most works on Israelite monarchic ideology are based more on learned reconstruction and hypotheses than on actual evidence. An example is Geo Widengren's *Sakrales Königtum im Alten Testament und im Judentum* (Stuttgart, 1955), which offers interesting contributions about later Judaic ideology. Jean de Fraine's *L'aspect religieux de la royauté israélite* (Rome, 1954) is the most cautious and useful attempt. Joseph Coppens's *Le messianisme royal* (Paris, 1968) is a helpful introduction to the connections between Near Eastern royal ideology and messianism.

Arthur Christensen's *Les types du premier homme et du premier roi dans l'histoire légendaire des Iraniens*, 2 vols. (Stockholm, 1917–1934), is an illuminating study of the mythical traditions about the origin of kingship, and thus of the kingship ideology, among the Iranians. On Hellenistic ruler cults, Wilhelm Schubart's *Die religiöse Haltung des frühen Hellenismus* (Leipzig, 1937) is fundamental. For the Roman imperial ideology and ruler cult, one should see the contributions by various authors in *Le culte des souverains dans l'Empire romain*, edited by Elias J. Bickermann, Willem de Boer, and others, "Entretiens sur l'antiquité classique," vol. 19 (Geneva, 1973), and should consult the volume's bibliography.

CRISTIANO GROTTANELLI

Kingship in Sub-Saharan Africa

Kingship is always ritualized to some extent. Since the beginning of the twentieth century scholars have sought unsuccessfully to define a particular type of cultic complex in Africa as "divine kingship." Many now prefer the looser term "sacred kingship." Two opposed arguments dominate this and other anthropological discussions of ritual. One, derived from the work of the English anthropologist James G. Frazer (1854–1941), dwells on a purportedly distinct set of ideas in which the personal, physical health of the king is responsible for the generosity of nature and the well-being of his people. The other, derived from the great French sociologist Émile Durkheim (1859–1917), treats such ideas as expressions of sociopolitical realities rather than as primary factors. The sociological view predominated in the 1940s, but in the 1960s anthropologists renewed their interest in Frazer's thesis.

Although many of Frazer's data were drawn from Africa, he thought of divine kingship as characteristic of a particular phase of cultural evolution, not of a particular continent, and he also drew upon European and Middle Eastern ethnography, to which his model may have been more appropriate. Frazer supposed that primitive societies preoccupied with agricultural problems put their faith in a king whose vitality magically ensured the abundance of the harvest and whose death at the hands of a stronger challenger corresponded efficaciously to the seedtime planting of the next crop. Early ethnographic reports concerning the Shilluk people of the Sudan seemed to provide a contemporary example of such ritual regicide.

Dwelling on the association between the king's health and natural fertility, Frazer explained the kingship but not the kingdom. In the first modern treatment of the subject, in 1948, E. E. Evans-Pritchard, relying on better ethnography and a wholly different theory, asserted that the spiritual role of the king expressed the political contradiction between the corporate unity of the Shilluk people and the lack of any central authority capable of subordinating factional interests. In the absence of real control, the king's identity with the moral values of the nation could only be expressed in spiritual terms. Evans-Pritchard found no hard evidence of ritual regicide and suggested that the tradition merely reflected the fact that many kings came to a violent end at the hands of princely challengers.

Meyer Fortes modified this sociological thesis, arguing that all offices were social realities distinct from the individuals who held them. The function of ritual was to make such offices visible and to effect the induction of the individual into his office; as it is said in some parts of Africa, in rituals of investiture the kingship "seizes" the king. Rituals were not simply passive or even imaginary reflexes of the social order but instruments that maintained it and convinced the participants of the reality of royal powers; after the ritual process, the king himself felt changed in his person and took credit for ensuing events (a fall of rain, mysterious deaths) that seemed to confirm the efficacy of the ritual. In this respect, however, kingship did not differ from other social roles such as that of a diviner or an adept in a healing cult.

Another kind of sociological explanation, the reverse of the first, was advanced by Max Gluckman with respect to the Swazi people (Swaziland). Gluckman suggested that the great Ncwala ceremonies provided the people with an annual opportunity to express their resentment of the king's rule and thus stabilized the political system. This "rituals of rebellion" thesis, though widely cited, seems to be based on a misreading of the hymns sung at the Ncwala; on this, more below.

Explanations of rituals in terms of their political functions fail to account for the elaborate content of the rituals, which often involve hundreds of titleholders, experts, courtiers, and lineage heads in rich textures of song, dance, eulogy, costume, taboo, and medication extending over many days and weeks of the year. Rereading the Swazi ethnography, T. O. Beidelman argued that the purpose of the Ncwala was to set the king apart so that he might take on the supernatural powers necessary to his office. He showed how such details as the black color of a sacrificial ox, the king's nudity during the ritual, and the emptiness of his right hand while he danced are consistent with Swazi cosmology and symbolic usage. The color of the ox refers to the powerful but disorderly forces of sexuality that the king must incorporate and master; the king's nudity expresses his liminal status as the "bull of his nation," mediating between the supernatural and the living.

Other writers pointed out that many kings, such as the *ọba* of Benin (Nigeria) or the *mwami* of Bunyoro (Uganda), were powerful rulers whose spiritual powers seemed to express their real authority rather than compensate for the lack of it. In other instances, the rituals of kingship and respect for the king's supernatural powers remained constant despite pronounced, long-term changes in his real political importance. The same ritual complex might or might not be associated with a hierarchical organization of important functions, so that among the Kongo people (Zaire), legends and rituals alone fail to make it clear whether the chief to whom they refer is a ruler of thousands or of dozens. Among the Nyakyusa (Tanzania) the divine king remained essentially a priest, whereas among the neighboring Ngonde, who share the same culture and traditions of origin, the king acquired real powers through his control of the trade in ivory and other goods. In Bunyoro, princes fought to succeed to the throne, whereas among the Rukuba (Nigeria) and Nyakyusa the chosen successor must be captured by the officiating priests lest he abscond.

These and other commentaries tended to place Frazer's thesis in doubt. The components of what Frazer thought was a single complex are now seen to vary independently of each other. Also, it has proved impossible to verify any tradition of regicide, although both the tradition and, apparently, the practice of not allowing kings to die a natural death are also associated with some ritual figures who are not kings. Other observances once thought to be specific to divine kings, such as prescribed incest and taboos against seeing the king eat or drink, are present in some instances but not in others. Chiefs among the Dime (Ethiopia) are regarded as having a spiritual power called *balth'u* that seems to meet Frazerian expectations since, if the power is "good," it is believed to make the crops grow and livestock multiply, whereas if the harvest is poor the people say, "We must get rid of him; the thoughts he has for the country don't work." A Dime chief is not required to be in good health, however, and eventually dies a natural death.

Africans themselves often speak of the powers vested in kings as independent entities with organic properties. The spiritual power known as *bwami* among the Lega of Zaire, for example, is thought to grow and forever renew itself, like a banana tree; this *bwami* may be vested in a king *(mwami)* (as among the eastern Lega) or in a graded association (as among the western Lega). From this point of view the purpose of ritual is to favor the growth of kingship as a public resource. Whether or not the king rules as well as reigns, his person is one of the instruments of the process necessary to maintain the kingship. Relics of dead kings are often part of the regalia of their successors or are used to make medicines conferring royal powers. The jawbone of a *kabaka* of Buganda (Uganda) was enshrined after his death; in Yorubaland, an *ọba* of Ọyọ (Nigeria) consumed the powdered heart of his predecessor. More generally, the body of a living king is itself a sacred object, modified and manipulated for ritual purposes; among these manipulations, the observances that set him apart from ordinary people often bear more onerously upon him than upon anyone else.

This African perspective is consistent with the sociological one of Fortes, and it is here, perhaps, that we may discover the secret of regicide. Kingship, itself a perpetual office, stands for the corporate unity and perpetuity of the kingdom. Time is therefore intrinsic to the idea of kingship. Time, in turn, has two components: transience and constant renewal. The continuity of the body politic, and of human life within it, may be symbolized by the agricultural cycle or other natural phenomena, by communal rites of passage and succession, or by similar rites in which the king's own life, death, and replacement are made to embody the life process of the community. In such instances, agricultural cycles, initiation cycles, and the succession of kings are not merely metaphors for the continuity and vitality of the social order but substantial constituents of it.

It is not surprising, therefore, among widely separated peoples, including the Lovedu (South Africa), the Nyakyusa, the Rukuba, and the Mundang (Chad), that the death of a ruler or of a surrogate is supposed to coincide with a phase in the cycle of initiations whereby the succession of generations is regulated, although in all these examples the real timing of the events is obscure. The Rukuba king is required to ingest, at his installation, material from the bodies both of his deceased predecessor and of an infant, specially killed for the purpose, whose status is such that he might have been chosen to be king had he lived; these and other Rukuba rituals, which clearly express the theme of renewal and continuity, are believed to cause a long and therefore successful reign. The king himself is not burdened with many taboos; he may be deposed if his "blood" is not strong enough to keep misfortunes from afflicting his people, but he is not himself killed.

During the 1970s anthropologists expressed increasing interest in the subjective perspective in kingship cults, in the content of ritual and its capacity to shape the cognitive experience of participants. The reductionist view that ritual merely expresses political realities seemed inconsistent with the quasi-organic character attributed to kingly powers and with the intense secrecy that in many cases surrounds complex and central cultic performances.

This revival of Frazer's intellectualism did not extend, however, to his evolutionary assumptions about primitive thought, and it emphasized the particularity of symbols whose meanings should be sought in their local context. For example, the skull of a dead Temne chief (Sierra Leone) is kept in a shrine at which daily sacrifices are performed for communal well-being, but that of a Mundang king serves only as a magical device to force his successor to commit the expected suicide. The hair and nails of a deceased *mwami* of Bunyoro are cut after his death, to be buried with him, whereas those of a *lwembe* of the Nyakyusa must be taken before he has drawn his last breath, "so that Lwembe might not go away with the food to the land of the shades, that the fertility of the soil might always remain above," and they are used in a powerful fertility medicine. There can be no universal dictionary of symbols, and even in one context a ritual element usually has several kinds and levels of significance, some better defined than others.

In her review of the subject, "Keeping the King Divine," Audrey I. Richards (1969) recommended that in future more attention should be paid to kingship in its relation to other elements of the society in which we find it; for example, other forms of ancestor worship, other kinds of control over nature, other political authorities. Or as an ethnographer of eastern Zaire put it, "chiefship is simply a variant of Bashu ideas about healers, sorcerers, and women." The cultural pattern of the Shilluk (shared by the Anuak, Dinka, and other Nilotic peoples) is very different from that of the Azande (southern Sudan), in which the cultic attributes of kingship are minimal, and from those of the Temne, Rukuba, or Dime, all of which are in turn strongly dissimilar.

In a pattern that is widespread in central, southern, and parts of West Africa, violent powers associated with chiefs and the activities of men in hunting and war were supposedly derived from ancestors. Ancestral cults were paired and contrasted with those of local or nature spirits, from whom powers were procured that were beneficial to the fertility of nature, the activities of women, and the well-being of local communities. During the eighteenth and nineteenth centuries, such local cults were merged with the institution of kingship during the process of state formation; the Swazi, Luba and Bushong (Zaire), and Benin kingdoms provide examples.

In this pattern, the symbolization of violence is often intentionally shocking. A Luba chief, after being anointed with the blood of a man killed for that purpose, put his foot on the victim's skull and drank his blood mixed with beer. Such acts showed that the king possessed superhumanly destructive powers, similar to witchcraft, with which he would be able to defend his people against the attacks of witches and criminals. The Ncwala confers similiar powers on the Swazi king; the hymns sung are a national expression not of rebellion but of sympathy for him in his lonely struggle against such enemies. As the Swazi themselves say, the Ncwala is intended to strengthen the kingship and "make stand the nation." In some kingdoms, designated groups engage in looting, rape, and other disorderly behavior to show that the power that should contain violence is temporarily in abeyance. Often, however, the ritual representation of the chief's violent powers was greatly disproportionate to the amount of real force he commanded; he had authority as the embodiment of the social order but little power.

In contrast, local cults devoted to community well-being emphasized growth and fertility, employing as ritual symbols the color black (associated with rain clouds) and farming implements such as hoes rather than the color red and various weapons associated with war. In other configurations, as among the Nyakyusa, life-giving and death-dealing powers are not segregated in this way. In yet others, such as the Mundang, whose king was as much bandit as sovereign, looting at home and abroad, there was no cult of violence.

Although kings are "made" by the rituals that enthrone them, their powers are maintained by daily observances. The unfortunate leader of the Dime, known as *zimu*, though he had real political and military responsibilities, was so restricted in his diet and personal contacts as to be virtually an outcast. Besides installation and funerary rites and daily observances, kingship cults include bodies of myth and the ritual organization of space. The plans of royal palaces and grave shrines, even the distribution of shrines in the country, organize rituals in space in conformity with cosmological models. The bodies of some kings, as among the Mundang, are casually thrown away, but for the Nyakyusa the graves of the original kings are among the most fearfully sacred of all shrines. The dynastic shrines of the Ganda are replicas of the royal court, with their own elaborate rituals and personnel centered on a queen sister.

Royal myths commonly refer to the founding of the state and its subsequent history, which the rituals of investiture and periodic festivals may reenact. Until the 1970s, scholars tended to take such myths literally, especially those that attributed the origin of a kingdom to immigrants. Paradoxically, the intellectualist reappraisal of ritual was accompanied by a new view of myths as narrative expressions of real, contemporary sociopolitical relations. The "stranger" status of the king expresses his difference from ordinary people or the separation of dynastic, chiefly functions from local, priestly ones, just as prescribed incest or murder marks the king's removal from his ordinary status and his accession to a new one.

Colonial rule abolished or profoundly modified all kingships and their rituals, appropriating many of their powers and banning some practices deemed essential by the people to create true kings. Central mysteries of surviving cults were and are known only to the participating experts. Consequently, we have few descriptions of the working of kingship in practice, and only one extensive set of ritual prescriptions, for the kingdom of Rwanda. Even much better information, however, would not render unambiguous the functions of kingship, which have always been responsive to changing circumstances, or reveal beyond doubt the relationship between ritual prescription and actual event. Kings as well as anthropologists debate whether regicide is a necessary practice or symbolic truth; in the mid-nineteenth century an *ọba* of Ọyọ refused to submit to regicide, and in 1969 the king of the Jukun (Nigeria) was reported in the press to be sleeping with a loaded revolver under his pillow. Part of the power and mystery of kingship is its refusal to be bound by rules and its centrality to the political process.

[*For further discussion of kingship, see* Bemba Religion; Southern African Religions, *article on* Southern Bantu Religions; *and* Swazi Religion.]

BIBLIOGRAPHY

James G. Frazer's ideas on divine kingship can be found in the various editions of *The Golden Bough;* his one-volume abridgment (New York, 1922) has been frequently reprinted. The modern revival of Frazer begins with Michael W. Young's article "The Divine Kingship of the Jukun: A Re-evaluation of Some Theories," *Africa* 36 (1966): 135–152, and includes Luc de Heusch's *Sacrifice in Africa* (Bloomington, Ind., 1985). Recent neo-Frazerian accounts of divine kingship include Alfred Adler's *La mort est le masque du roi: La royauté sacrée des Moundang du Tchad* (Paris, 1982), Jean-Claude Muller's *Le roi bouc-émissaire: Pouvoir et rituel chez les Rukuba du Nigéria* (Quebec, 1980), and Dave M. Todd's "Aspects of Chiefship in Dimam, South-West Ethiopia," *Cahiers d'études africaines* 18 (1978): 311–332.

E. E. Evans-Pritchard established the sociological approach in opposition to Frazer in his *The Divine Kingship of the Shilluk of the Nilotic Sudan* (Cambridge, 1948). Relevant essays by Meyer Fortes include "Of Installation Ceremonies," *Proceedings of the Royal Anthropological Institute for 1967* (London, 1968). Max Gluckman's "rituals of rebellion" thesis is to be found in his *Order and Rebellion in Tribal Africa* (London, 1963). Audrey I. Richard's review, "Keeping the King Divine," is in *Proceedings of the Royal Anthropological Institute for 1968* (London, 1969).

Classic ethnographic accounts of kingship cults include John Roscoe's *The Bakitara or Banyoro* (Cambridge, 1923), in which he gives, for Bunyoro, the best account of a king's daily observances. Hilda Kuper's *An African Aristocracy: Rank among the Swazi* (London, 1947) sets a vivid description of the Ncwala in an analysis of the political system; T. O. Beidelman interprets the symbolism in "Swazi Royal Ritual," *Africa* 36 (1966): 373–405). Monica Wilson's richly detailed *Communal Rituals of the Nyakyusa* (London, 1957) includes trancripts of interviews with senior participants in kingship and other cults. Ray E. Bradbury's illustrated article "Divine Kingship in Benin," *Nigeria* 62 (1959): 186–207, is a useful companion to the film *Benin Kingship Rituals,* made by Bradbury and Francis Speed. The only extensive published set of esoteric ritual prescriptions is *La royauté sacrée de l'ancien Rwanda* (Tervuren, Belgium, 1964), edited by Marcel d'Hertefelt and André Coupez.

Among recent historical accounts of the development of divine kingships are, on the Bashu, Randall Packard's *Chiefship and Cosmology* (Bloomington, Ind., 1981), which explains the relationship between chiefly power and control of natural forces; on the Luba, Thomas Q. Reefe's *The Rainbow and the Kings* (Berkeley, 1981); and, on the Kuba, Jan Vansina's *The Children of Woot* (Madison, Wis., 1978).

WYATT MACGAFFEY

Kingship in Mesoamerica and South America

Essentially important for the study of kingship in Mesoamerica and South America is the profound connection between supernatural authority and political power residing in an elite class of sacred kings, who directed the interaction of the natural environment, the human population, technology, and developments in social structure, from sacred precincts and ceremonial cities. In the Aztec and Inca patterns of sacred kingship we find two distinct versions of this connection.

Aztec Sacred Kingship. The supreme authority in Aztec Mexico was the *tlatoani* ("chief speaker"), who resided in the imperial capital of Tenochtitlán. During the later stages of Aztec history, the *tlatoani* governed with the assistance of the Council of Four, which included the second in command, who occupied an office called the *cihuacoatl* ("snake woman"). The occupant of the *cihuacoatl* office was always male. The elite status of the Council of Four is indicated by the fact that the members were chosen from the royal family and included the king's brothers, sons, and nephews. Under normal circumstances this group chose the successor to a dead king from one of its members. A primary qualification for the Aztec king was military leadership, and a truly great king was a victorious general who conquered many towns. In broad terms the Aztec *tlatoani* was responsible for agricultural fertility, order and success in warfare, the maintenance of the ceremonial order, the stability of bureaucratic systems, and above all the orderly parallelism between society and the cosmos.

By the beginning of the sixteenth century, the Aztec *tlatoani* Motecuhzoma Xocoyotzin (Moctezuma II, r. 1503–1520) was surrounded by an elaborate court dedicated to carrying out the expressions of authority and pomp of the monarch. According to Hernán Cortés's second letter to the king of Spain, Motecuhzoma changed clothes four times a day, never putting on garments that had been worn more than once. The formation of this privileged position came about as the result of two decisive transformations in the social and symbolic structures of Aztec life—the acquisition in 1370 of the sacred lineage of kingship associated with the Toltec kingdom, and second, the consolidation of authority and power in the office of the king and a warrior nobility known as the *pipiltin* during the war against the city-state of Atzcapotzalco in 1428.

When the Aztec precursors, the Chichimec (from *chich,* "dog," and *mecatl,* "rope, lineage"), migrated into the Valley of Mexico in the thirteenth century, they encountered an urbanized world of warring city-states. The basic settlement pattern in the valley was the *tlatocayotl,* a city-state that consisted of a small capital city surrounded by dependent communities that worked the agricultural lands, paid tribute, and performed services for the elite classes in the capital according to various ritual calendars and cosmological patterns. Within this world of political rivalries, the most valued legitimate authority resided in communities tracing their royal lineage to the great Toltec kingdom of Tollan (tenth through twelfth centuries CE), which was remembered as the greatest city in history, noted for agricultural abundance, technological excellence, and cosmological order. As the Aztec slowly but systematically integrated themselves into the more complex social world of *tlatocayotl*s, they sought a means to acquire access to the Toltec lineage. According to a number of sources, they turned to the city-state of Culhuacan, which held the most direct lineal access to the authority represented by the Toltec, and asked to be given a half-Aztec, half-Culhuacan lord by the name of Acamapichtli as their first *tlatoani,* or royal leader. The successful transfer of legitimate kingship to the Aztec resulted in an internal adjustment of Aztec society. The first several *tlatoani*s were forced to negotiate their authority with the traditional social unit of Aztec life, the *calpulli.* The *calpulli* was a type of conical clan in which members were interrelated by family ties but hierarchically stratified according to lines of descent from a sacred ancestor. This sharing of authority took an abrupt turn at the collapse of the Tepanec kingdom between 1426–1428 and the formation of a new political order known as the Triple Alliance. During the last half of the fourteenth century the Méxica (Aztec) were military vassals of the powerful Tepanec kingdom centered in the capital of Azcapotzalco. During their tutelage to the Tepanec, the Aztec became the most powerful military unit in the region and adapted their political and economic structure to the more urbanized systems of the valley. When the king of Azcapotzalco died in 1426, the Tepanec kingdom was ripped apart by a war of succession. The Aztec *tlatoani* Itzcoatl, with his nephews Motecuhzoma Ilhuicamina and Tlacaellel, formed a political alliance with two other city states and successfully took over the lands, tribute, and allegiances that formerly belonged to the Tepanec. In the process these three leaders restructured the Aztec government by concentrating power and authority in the *tlatoani,* the Council of Four, and to a lesser extent in the noble warrior class known as the *pipiltin.* The *calpulli* were incorporated into less powerful levels of decision making. This restructuring marked the beginning of the rise of Aztec kingship on a road to the status of god-king.

Subsequent Aztec kings—for example, Motecuhzoma Ilhuicamina (Moctezuma I)—issued decrees defining the different classes of nobles, traders, warriors, and commoners according to their privileges, manner of dress, ownership, and education. Beginning around 1440 the cosmological traditions undergirding Aztec society were reinterpreted to legitimate the rise of sacred kingship and the concentration of authority in the elites. As a sign of this cosmic and political authority each king following Itzcoatl took the responsibility of enlarging the Great Temple of the capital and acquiring large numbers of enemy warriors to be sacrificed to the imperial gods Tlaloc and Huitzilopochtli.

Interestingly, the symbolic sources for the legitimation of Aztec kingship come from two lines of descent. On the one hand, Aztec kings drew their legitimacy from the Toltec priest-king Topiltzin Quetzalcoatl, while on the other hand they drew their power from the "all-powerful, the invisible, the untouchable" Tezcatlipoca. [*See* Quetzalcoatl *and* Tezcatlipoca.] This combination demonstrates both the strength and, surprisingly, the vulnerability of Aztec kings. The most intimate inspiration for Aztec kings came from the twisting maneuvers of the principal god, Tezcatlipoca. While Quetzalcoatl was an ancient underpinning of Aztec kingship, Tezcatlipoca's influence on the legitimacy, power, and conduct of Aztec rulers is immediate and all-pervasive. Perhaps the most vivid example of Tezcatlipoca's influence appears in the prayers recited at the installation of a ruler and upon his death.

When a new king was installed in Tenochtitlán, Tezcatlipoca was invoked as the creator, animator, guide, and potential killer of the king. The ceremony, according to book 6 of Fray Bernardino de Sahagún's *Historia general de las cosas de la Nueva España* (compiled 1569–1582; also known as the Florentine Codex), begins at the moment when "the sun . . . hath come to appear." The particular phrasing of the description of the sunrise in the prayer reported by Sahagún is related to the story of the creation of the Sun in the official cosmogonies of the Aztec elites. The king's installation and Tezcatlipoca's presence are seen as cosmogonic acts that result in the dawning of a new day. As the ritual proceeds, Tezcatlipoca is called the "creator . . . and knower of men" who "causes the king's action, his character," even the odors of his body. This intimacy is best stated when Tezcatlipoca is asked to inspire the king: "Animate him . . . for this is thy flute, thy replacement, thy image." This intimacy is carried to a surprising turn when, later in the narrative, the prayer asks Tezcatlipoca to kill the king if he performs badly. This resonates with the tradition about Tollan, in which the king Quetzalcoatl broke his vows of chastity and was sent away by the sorcerer Tezcatlipoca. The omnipotence of Tezcatlipoca is also evidenced in the repeated statement that the new king, like all the other previous rulers, was merely borrowing the "reed mat" (symbolic of kingship) and "thy [i.e., Tezcatlipoca's] realm" during his kingship. The invocation to Tezcatlipoca ends when the god is asked to send the king "to be on the offensive" in the "center of the desert, to the field of battle." Kings in Aztec society were expected above all to be successful in warfare.

As our historical narrative has demonstrated, the Aztec sense of legitimacy was derived from their acquired connection to the ancient kingdom of Tollan. This connection profoundly influenced Aztec kingship and provided an ironic destiny for the last Aztec *tlatoani,* Motecuhzoma Xocoyotzin (Moctezuma II). In fact, the power and fragility of Aztec kingship is reflected in a series of episodes involving Motecuhzoma Xocoyotzin and Hernán Cortés, the leader of the conquering Spanish expedition (1519–1521). According to the account of the conquest of Tenochtitlán told in book 12 ("The Conquest") of Sahagún's work, when word reached the magisterial city of Tenochtitlán that "strangers in the east" were making their way toward the high plateau, "Moctezuma thought that this was Topiltzin Quetzalcoatl who had come to the land. . . . It was in their hearts that he would come . . . to land . . . to find his mat . . . his seat. . . . Moctezuma sent five emissaries to give him gifts."

This passage demonstrates how an Aztec king used an ancient mythological tradition of kingly abdication in a new situation for the purpose of interpreting a threatening development. According to this tradition, the kingdom of Tollan (centuries before the Aztec arrived in the central plateau of Mexico) was ruled by the brilliant priest-king Topiltzin Quetzalcoatl, but it collapsed when a socerer (Tezcatlipoca) from the outside tricked him into violating his kingly vows and abdicating his throne. Topiltzin Quetzalcoatl left his kingdom, promising to return one day and reclaim his throne. In the crisis of 1519, the last Aztec king applied to a series of reconnaissance reports the archaic mythologem of Quetzalcoatl's flight and promised return to regain his throne. Moctezuma sent jeweled costumes of Aztec deities, including the array of Quetzalcoatl, to Cortés and instructed his messengers to tell Cortés that the king acknowledged the presence of the god for whom he had been waiting to return and sit in the place of authority. As the Spaniards advanced, Moctezuma fell into an emotional crisis ("He was terror struck . . . his heart was anguished"), and he made two gestures of abdication. First, he moved out of his kingly residence into a palace of lesser authority, and, second, he sought escape in a magical cave where he believed he could pass into the supernatural world. When Cortés arrived at the capital, a series of encounters took place in which Moctezuma instructed his nobles to transfer their power to the returning king. In this situation a form of "imperial irony" appears in the tradition of Aztec kingship. On the one hand, the Aztec drew their legitimacy from the tradition that depicted Tollan as a city-state characterized by agricultural stability, artistic achievement, and religious genius. But in drawing their legitimacy as Toltec descendants, they were also heirs to a tradition of kingly abdication. Like Topiltzin Quetzalcoatl, who gave his kingdom to Tezcatlipoca, Moctezuma opened the royal door for Cortés to enter.

In the case of the last great civilization of Mesoamerica, sacred kingship was an urban institution acquired by the Aztec, who utilized borrowed and indigenous religious symbols to legitimate their imperial expansion and social character. It also appears that this symbolic attempt at consolidation contributed to the final collapse of the imperial order during the war with the Spanish. [*See also* Aztec Religion.]

Inca Sacred Kingship. When Spanish soldiers led by Francisco Pizarro arrived on the Pacific coast of South America in 1527, they encountered the Inca empire, called Tahuantinsuyu ("land of the four quarters"). At its height, the empire extended from the northern border of present-day Ecuador south for more than forty-three hundred kilometers to the Maule River in Chile. This kingdom contained more than twelve million people organized into a tightly knit series of local, regional, and imperial administrative units, with authority centered in the capital city of Cuzco. When subsequent researchers attempted to reconstruct the history of the Inca empire, they found two impressive facts. First, the Inca achieved a meteoric rise from a small village settlement in the valley of Cuzco to an imperial power in less than one hundred years. Second, the Inca recorded their own historic developments in terms of the lives and achievements of their kings and the care of dead kings by the royal mummy cult.

At its most basic social level, the world of these kings and their royal mummies was organized by *ayllu*s, which appear to have been composed of well-ordered endogamous kinship groups that traced their descent to a common ancestor. *Ayllu* members emphasized self-sufficiency by rigorously practicing certain traditions such as assisting one another in the construction of homes and public buildings, the farming of lands together, and the care of specific deities within local ceremonial centers. In fact, certain common plots of land were used to produce goods for sacrifices at the shrine of ancestral deities.

These *ayllu*s were organized into larger units such as villages and chiefdoms that were involved in intense raiding and small-scale warfare among themselves. The social setting of *ayllu*s and competing chiefdoms helped to produce the emergence of *sinchi*s, or war leaders, who possessed the additional capacity to organize groups of men into firm alliances. These leaders were chosen from the prominent adult male members of the *ayllu*s, and if one was particularly successful in warfare and conquest of new lands, he utilized his acquisitions to achieve more permanent positions of leadership.

It appears that the earliest Inca kings were particularly prominent *sinchi*s who achieved a semblance of permanent and legitimate authority by manifesting an intimacy with the Inca sun god Inti. The actual reconstruction of the process of the rise of sacred kingship in the Inca culture is difficult to discern. However, the standard Inca histories hold that all Inca kings descended from this great solar god. In different primary sources, we find a standard list of thirteen Inca kings dating back to mythical times, but serious historical reconstructions reveal that the expansion of Inca power beyond the chiefdom level and the consolidation of authority in kings takes place with the career of the ninth Inca king, Pachacuti.

The sacred histories of the Inca tell of a crucial turning point in the creation of their empire. In 1438, the fledgling Inca village of Cuzco was attacked by the aggressive army of the Chanca. A threatening siege of the settlement resulted in the flight of the Inca king Viracocha and his designated successor, his son Urcon, from the capital. Another son, Cusi Yupanqui, commanded the defense of Cuzco. Just before the expected final attack, the commander had a vision of a terrifying deity that identified itself as the Inca sky god; the sky god called Cusi Yupanqui "my son," and he told Cusi Yupanqui that if he followed the true religion he would become the Sapay ("great") Inca and conquer many nations. Driven by this powerful vision and supported by increased political alliances, the Inca leader drove the invaders away, which resulted, after factional intrigues against his father and brother, in his ascension to the throne. The new king then embarked on an intense series of conquests resulting in the expansion of Inca lands and the laying of the foundation for the Inca empire. He became known as Pachacuti, which means "cataclysm" or "he who remakes the world." This remarkable episode, which is recorded in a number of sources, combines two major patterns of Inca religion: the sacred legitimacy of Inca kinship and the responsibility of the king to acquire new territories through conquest and warfare.

While it is difficult to present a satisfactory outline of Inca religion, recent studies have identified three major components, each relating to the power and authority of Inca kings: the omnipotence and omniscience of the creator sky god Viracocha, the cult of ancestor worship and mummies, and the pervasive pattern of the veneration of *huacas*.

Inca kings derived their sanctification from what Arthur Andrew Demarest calls the "upper pantheon" of Inca religion. According to Demarest's useful formulation, the single Inca creator sky god manifested himself in at least three subcomplexes organized around Viracocha (the universal creator), Inti (the sun god), and Illapa (the thunder and weather god). Ritual cycles and ceremonial events associated with political, astronomical, and economic schedules revealed the many aspects and versions of this upper pantheon. At the center of the sacred schedule of activities stood the Sapay Inca, who was venerated as the manifestation of Viracocha, as the descendant of Inti, and, upon his death, as the power of Illapa.

The second aspect of Inca religion related to kingship is the fascinating cult of ancestor worship and mummies. A pan-Andean tradition of ancestor worship, in which the bodies of dead family members were venerated as sacred objects and ceremonially cared for by the living, permeated Inca existence. Central to this tradition was the practice of oracular communication with the dead. The ancestral remains, in the form of a mummy or simply a collection of bones, were called *mallquis*. Specific questions concerning all aspects of life were put to the *mallquis*, and specific answers resulted. Specialists known as the *mallquipvillac* ("they who speak with the *mallquis*") were influential in Inca life. The ancestral spirits also manifested themselves in hierophanies of stones and plants, and, most powerfully, in the sparks of fires. Specialists called the "consultors of the dead" communicated with the ancestors through fire.

The quintessential expression of this pattern of ancestor worship was the royal mummy cult of Cuzco. I have already noted that the king was considered a descendant of the sky god Inti or Viracocha. At the death of a Sapay Inca, the authority to govern, wage war, and collect taxes passed on to one of his sons, ideally a son born of a union with the king's sister. However, all possessions of the dead king, including his palaces, agricultural lands, and servants, remained the property of the mummy. These possessions were to be administered by his *panaqa*, a corporate social unit made up of all the descendants in the male line. While the *panaqa* lived off a small portion of these lands, the group's primary purpose was to function as the dead king's court and to maintain his mummy in private and public ceremonial events, relaying his wishes through oracular specialists and carrying out his will. The public display of these mummies was a major element in Inca ceremonial life. Processions of kingly mummies, arranged according to their seniority, traveled through the fields at rainmaking ceremonies and paraded through the streets of the capital to the ceremonial center of Cuzco, where they observed and participated in state rituals. They also visited one another to communicate through oracular specialists, and participated in the dances, revelries, and ceremonies in their honor. All kings, alive and dead, were considered the living spirit of Inti.

What is vital to understand is the degree of influence the cult of mummies had on the conduct and destiny of the living king. For instance, when the Spanish captured the Inca ruler Atahuallpa and condemned him to death, he was given a choice of remaining a pagan and being burned at the stake or converting to Christianity and being garroted. Atahuallpa chose conversion and garroting, not because he believed in Christianity but so that his body would not be destroyed. After receiving a Christian burial, some surviving Incas secretly disinterred his body, mummified it, and then hid the mummy, continuing to treat it in the traditional manner. More impressive perhaps is the political and military pressure placed on the living king by his mummified father. Powerful in privilege but much poorer in lands and riches, the new Inca was spurred on to carry out expansive conquests in order to acquire his own territorial lands and riches so he could live in the expected manner. This forced him to carry out his kingly responsibilities of establishing short- and long-distance trading routes, building agricultural projects to sustain himself and his growing kingdom, building temples to the sky god Viracocha throughout the new regions of the empire, and establishing the local and imperial administration units into which the kingdom was organized.

At the more popular level, Inca religion was organized by the veneration of *huacas*. *Huacas* were the endless hierophanies in stones, plants, or other objects that animated the entire Inca landscape. The countless *huacas* were objects of offerings, sacrifices, and oracular events. Even major family relationships expressed in the concept of *villca* ("ancestor, descendant") were examples of *huacas*. Ancestors were *huacas*, and in this way the Inca mummies were the most sacred of *huacas*.

The last great civilization of South America, the Inca developed their concept of sacred kingship by combining their practice of ancestor worship with the historical process of imperial expansion and warfare. As in Mesoamerica, sanctified legitimacy was derived from connection with ancient and contemporary hierophanies, deities, and their human representatives. [*See also* Inca Religion.]

BIBLIOGRAPHY

Adams, Robert M. *The Evolution of Urban Society: Early Mesopotamia and Prehistoric Mexico.* Chicago, 1966. This concise study of urban development in Mesopotamia describes the step-by-step process of the rise of intense social stratification. It includes insightful passages on the persistence of the sacred in periods of secular growth.

Brundage, Burr C. *Empire of the Inca.* Norman, Okla., 1963. Though dated in some respects, Brundage's study provides a useful description of the religious forces contributing to the integration of the Inca empire.

Carrasco, Davíd. *Quetzalcoatl and the Irony of Empire: Myths and Prophecies in the Aztec Tradition.* Chicago, 1982. This work discusses the ironic dimensions of Aztec kingship and the roots of sacred kingship in five Mesoamerican capitals.

Carrasco, Pedro. "Los linajes nobles del Mexico antiguo." In *Estratificación social en la Mesoamérica prehispánica,* edited by Pedro Carrasco, Johanna Broda, et al., pp. 19–36. Mexico City, 1976.

Cobo, Bernabé. *History of the Inca Empire: An Account of the Indians' Customs and Their Origin, Together with a Treatise on Inca Legends, History, and Social Institutions.* Austin, 1979. One of the valuable post-Conquest primary sources for the study of various aspects of Inca history and religion.

Demarest, Arthur Andrew, and Geoffrey W. Conrad. *Religion and Empire: The Dynamics of Aztec and Inca Expansionism.* Cambridge, 1984. This study makes a significant contribution to the comparative study of social dynamics, religion, and imperialism in the two regions of New World primary urban generation.

Katz, Friedrich. *The Ancient American Civilizations.* Chicago, 1972. The standard starting point for a comparative analysis of the material and social character of Aztec and Inca kingship.

Wheatley, Paul. *The Pivot of the Four Quarters: A Preliminary Enquiry into the Origins and Character of the Ancient Chinese City.* Chicago, 1971. Wheatley places Inca and Aztec social and symbolic structures within a broad comparative analysis of the rise of primary urban generation.

Zuidema, R. Tom. "The Lion in the City: Royal Symbols of Transition in Cuzco." *Journal of Latin American Lore* 9 (Summer 1983): 39–100. One of the many important articles by Zuidema explaining the myths and rituals associated with kingship and authority in Inca religion.

DAVÍD CARRASCO

Kingship in East Asia

The central focus of East Asian civilization until the beginning of the twentieth century remained the king. He was the center of the universe, whether it was in China, Korea, or Japan, and he was supremely responsible for the well-being and prosperity of the society over which he reigned. The king's political authority was ultimately based on the religious claim that he possessed the mandate of Heaven, whether temporarily or perpetually. Moreover, the heavenly origin of the king was acknowledged almost invariably in East Asia. His status was generally defined as (1) the earthly representative of heaven or heavenly will, (2) the descendant of a god, or (3) the god incarnate.

The earliest institution of kingship to emerge in East Asia developed on the mainland of China with the establishment of the Shang kingdom (c. 1500–1027 BCE). The Shang state centered around the king *(wang)* for, according to oracle-bone inscriptions, he was the "unique man" who could appeal to his ancestors for blessings or, if necessary, dissipate ancestral curses that affected the state. It was believed that determining and influencing the will of the ancestral spirits were possible through divination, prayer, and sacrifice. The king's ancestors interceded, in turn, with Ti or Shang-ti, the supreme being in heaven, who stood at the apex of the spiritual hierarchy of the Shang.

The question of whether or not the Shang people defined the status of their king as Shang-ti's "descendant" has not yet been settled. The Shang dynasty was founded by members of the Tzu clan, who were descendants of the clan's founder, Hsieh. According to the *Shih ching,* Hsieh was born miraculously; his mother became pregnant after swallowing an egg dropped by a dark bird in flight. This mythic story might be taken to suggest that the Shang people believed in a blood link between Shang-ti and the king. It may be noted, however, that no oracle-bone inscription has thus far pointed to the genealogical relationship. According to David N. Keightley, the doctrine of the "mandate of Heaven" *(t'ien-ming),* usually considered a creation of the Chou dynasty (1027–221 BCE), has deep roots in the theology of the Shang. Ti, the supreme god of the Shang, is most impersonal in character; that is, it was not generally thought that he could be "bribed" by the sacrifices offered by the members of the royal family. It was precisely this impersonality that made it possible for Ti to harm the dynasty by sponsoring the attack of the Chou, the dynasty that followed the Shang. [*See* Shang-ti.]

The state religion of the Chou times centered on sacrifice to T'ien (Heaven) and the gods of the soil *(she).* A vast ceremonial was elaborated in which the Chou king played the leading role and on which the well-being of his state was deemed to depend. Two kinds of sacrifices were offered to T'ien, the supreme god of the Chou: in the ancestral temple and in the open fields. The sacrifice in the open fields, called the "suburban sacrifice," was the religious act *par excellence* of a reigning king; a burnt offering of an unblemished calf was offered to T'ien at the winter solstice, on the round hillock in the southern suburbs of the royal city. [*See* T'ien.]

The *Shih ching* narrates the origin of the Chou people: a woman named Yüan stepped on the big toe of Shang-ti's footprint and then gave birth to Hou Chi (Prince Millet), the god of agriculture, who was considered the primordial ancestor of the Chou. This notion of divine descent probably helped to establish the Chou's claim to the royal throne, and it may also have contributed to the Chou conception of the king as "son of Heaven" (*t'ien-tzu*). [*See also* Chinese Religion, *article on* Mythic Themes.]

The Son of Heaven was one who received the mandate of Heaven. This mandate signified that imperial authority could not become a permanent possession of the ruler, that Heaven had the complete freedom to confer or withdraw its charisma or "gift of grace" from the ruler on earth. Whether or not the king was given the divine mandate was generally determined by his acceptance by the "people" (the ruling class and their clients, i.e., the literati and landowners). If the people recognized his rulership, it was an indication that the heavenly mandate remained with him, but if they deposed him or killed him, it was a clear sign that he had lost Heaven's moral support. Under these circumstances, the Chou conception of the Son of Heaven tended to lose in the course of time whatever genealogical implications it may have had in its beginnings.

The classical Chinese conception of sovereignty took shape in the Ch'in and Han periods (221 BCE–220 CE). While the sovereign adopted the title, connoting supreme power, of *huang-ti* (emperor), he was never considered divine, at least while he was alive, nor was he regarded as an incarnation of a divine being. Rather, he was a "unique man" representing Heaven's will on earth and serving as the link between Heaven and earth. The Chinese notion of the Son of Heaven in its classical form had nothing to do with the genealogical conception of kingship, such as in ancient Egypt or Japan, that the king was the descendant of a certain god or the god incarnate; the emperor was simply the earthly representative of Heaven or heavenly will. The essential function of the Chinese emperor, as formulated in the Han period, was to maintain the harmonious cosmic order by means of ceremonials. "The Sage-Kings did not institute the ceremonies of the suburban sacrifices casually," states the *Han shu* (chap. 25). "The sacrifice to Heaven is to be held at the southern suburb. Its purpose is to conform to the *yang* principle. The sacrifice to earth is to be held at the northern suburb. Its purpose is to symbolize the *yin* principle." In short, the emperor maintained the cosmic balance by assisting Heaven and earth in the regulation and harmonization of the *yin* and *yang* principles.

In the centuries that followed the fall of the Han empire, China was often threatened and invaded by the nomadic peoples of Central and Northeast Asia. Here, too, the king (*khagan, khan*) was considered a sacred person, deriving his sacredness and authority from Tengri (Heaven); he was heavenly in origin, received the mandate from Heaven, and was a supremely important spokesman of heavenly will, serving as Heaven's representative on earth. [*See* Tengri.]

Significantly, the sacred nature of the king in Central Asia was often conceived after the archaic model of the shaman. Among the T'u-chüeh, who dominated the Mongolian steppes from 552 to 744, a series of strange rituals was performed when a new king acceded to the throne (*Chou shu,* bk. 50): the high-ranking officials turned a felt carpet, on which the king was seated, nine times in the direction of the sun's movement, and after each turn they prostrated themselves, making obeisance to him. Then they throttled him with a piece of silken cloth to the point of strangulation and asked him how many years he was to rule. In an almost unconscious state, the king uttered his answer.

This ceremony is somewhat reminiscent of the shaman's rite of initiation in Central Asia in which the felt carpet played a role. Seated on a felt carpet, the shaman was carried nine times around nine birches in the direction of the sun's movement and made nine turns on each of them while climbing. Nine turns symbolize the shaman's ascent to nine heavens. According to the belief of the T'u-chüeh, the king in his accession makes a symbolic ascent to the highest heaven through the nine cosmic zones, starting his journey from the felt carpet on which he is seated; then, after reaching the top of heaven, he descends onto earth. In this sense, the king was heavenly in origin. It seems also certain that the number of reigning years he uttered in an unconscious state was accepted as an announcement from Tengri, the supreme being in heaven.

The use of the felt carpet was not confined to the T'u-chüeh. It was also used among the T'o-pa, the Turkic or Mongolian people also known as the Hsien-pei, who established the Northern Wei dynasty (386–535) in China. When the enthronement ceremony for T'o-pa Hsiu was celebrated in 528, seven dignitaries held up a carpet of black felt on which the new emperor, facing west, made obeisance to heaven (*Pei shih,* bk. 5). In the Khitan state of Liao (907–1125), the enthronement ceremony had as its essential scenario the elevation of the new emperor on a felt carpet (*Liao shih,* bk. 49). Chinggis Khan, the founder of the great Mongol empire, was also lifted in his accession on a carpet of black felt supported by seven chiefs.

In ancient Korea, several states competed with each other for political supremacy until 676, when they became united by the kingdom of Silla. The beginnings of these nations are inseparably interwoven with myths narrating the miraculous birth of the founders, which point almost invariably to the heavenly origin of sovereignty.

The myths can be classified into two major types, one of which may be illustrated by the myth of Puyŏ: Tongmyŏng, the founder of Puyŏ, was born of a woman who became pregnant by a mystical light descending from heaven. A similar story is also told of Chu Mong, who founded Koguryŏ. This type of foundation myth is associated, outside of Korea, with T'ai-wu-ti (r. 424–452), the third emperor of the Northern Wei dynasty; with A-pao-chi, who founded the Khitan state of Liao; and with Chinggis Khan. There is no doubt that this mythic theme was widespread among nomadic peoples such as the Manchus and the Mongolians.

The other type of myth is characterized by the story of how the founder of a nation or a dynasty descended from Heaven onto mountaintops, forests, and trees. According to the myth of ancient Chosŏn, Hwang-wung, a son of the celestial supreme being Hwang-in, descended from Heaven onto Mount Tehbaek to establish a nation. The supreme god in Heaven approved of Hwang-wung's heavenly descent and granted him three items of the sacred regalia. He descended, accompanied by the gods of the wind, rain, and clouds as well as three thousand people. Similar stories of heavenly descent are known of Pak Hyŏkkŏse and Kim Archi of Silla. Also noteworthy is the myth of Karak, a small state variously known as Kaya or Mimana: Suro, the founder of Karak, descends from Heaven onto the summit of Mount Kuji at the command of the heavenly god; a purple rope is seen coming down from Heaven, and at the end of the rope there is a box containing six golden eggs covered by a piece of crimson cloth. Suro is born of one of the eggs.

Significantly, the heavenly origin of sovereignty is also recognized by the pre-Buddhist tradition of ancient Tibet: Gñya'-khri Btsam-po, the first mythical king, descended from Heaven onto the sacred mountain of Yar-lha-šam-po in Yarlung, by means of a rope or a ladder. He agreed to descend on the condition that he be granted ten heavenly magical objects. According to Giuseppe Tucci, the Tibetan royal ideology owes much to the religious tradition of the pastoral Turco-Mongolians. [*See* Tibetan Religions, *overview article.*]

Japanese kingship emerged at the end of the fourth century CE. The ruler called himself the "king [*ō* in Japanese; *wang* in Chinese] of Wa" or "king of the land of Wa" when he addressed the court in China. These designations simply followed what had become customary between the Chinese suzerains and the Japanese local princes since the middle of the first century CE. However, these titles were never used within Japan; the sovereign was called *ō-kimi* (*ta-wang* in Chinese; "great king") by local nobles. It is not until the beginning of the seventh century that the Japanese sovereign began to employ such titles as *tenshi* ("son of Heaven") and *tennō* ("emperor") to refer to himself, both of which have been in use until modern times.

In 600 Empress Suiko sent an envoy to the Sui dynasty, the first Japanese mission to China since 502. The *Sui shu* reports of that mission: "The king of Wa, whose family name was Ame and personal name Tarishihiko, and who bore the title of Ō-kimi, sent an envoy to visit the court." Meaning "noble son of Heaven," *Ametarishihiko* (or *Ametarashihiko*) was roughly equivalent to the Chinese *t'ien-tzu,* although its implications could be different. "Son of Heaven" in the Japanese conception of sovereignty referred invariably to the ruler who claimed his direct genealogical descent from the sun goddess Amaterasu as well as his vertical descent from the heavenly world. The Japanese mission to China was followed by another one in 607: "The Son of Heaven in the land where the sun rises addresses a letter to the Son of Heaven in the land where the sun sets" *(Sui shu).* According to the *Nihongi* (compiled in 720), in 608 Suiko forwarded a letter to China with the greeting: "The Emperor of the East respectfully addresses the Emperor of the West."

The classical Japanese conception of sovereignty took shape in the second half of the seventh century. It was an era when, under the influence of the Chinese legal system, a highly centralized bureaucratic state was created. Significantly, the creation of this political structure was accompanied by the completion of the sacred-kingship ideology that had been developing in the previous centuries; not only was the state conceived as a liturgical community with its paradigm in heaven, but also the sovereign who ruled the state was explicitly called the *akitsumikami,* manifest *kami* (god), that is, the god who manifests himself in the phenomenal world.

The essential part of the sacred-kingship ideology was the belief in the emperor's heavenly origin, and this belief was clearly expressed in the myths of Ninigi, as narrated in the *Kojiki* (compiled in 712) and the *Nihongi*. [*See* Japanese Religion, *articles on* Mythic Themes *and* Religious Documents.] Genealogically, Ninigi is connected with both the god Takaki (Takamimusubi) and the sun goddess Amaterasu through the marriage of Takaki's daughter to Amaterasu's son, to whom Ninigi is born. [*See* Amaterasu.] He is born in the heavenly world and, at the command of either Takaki or Amaterasu or both, descends onto the summit of Mount Takachiho. When Ninigi is about to descend, accompanied by the five clan heads, Amaterasu gives him rice grains harvested in her celestial rice fields, after which he comes down in the form of a newborn baby covered by a piece of cloth called *matoko o fusuma*. Especially noteworthy is the fact that Ninigi is granted the sacred regalia as well as the mandate of Heaven guaranteeing his eternal sovereignty on earth. Ninigi's heavenly descent was reenacted by the emperor at the annual harvest festival in the fall as well as on the occasion of his enthronement festival.

BIBLIOGRAPHY

There is no single book dealing with the problem of sacred kingship in East Asia as a whole. On kingship in ancient China, there is a classic study in Marcel Granet's *La religion des Chinois* (Paris, 1922), translated with an introduction by Maurice Freedman as *The Religion of the Chinese People* (New York, 1975), pp. 57–96. Valuable information is also presented in D. Howard Smith's "Divine Kingship in Ancient China," *Numen* 4 (1957): 171–203. David N. Keightley has made an excellent analysis of the kingship ideology of Shang China in "The Religious Commitment: Shang Theology and the Genesis of Chinese Political Culture," *History of Religions* 17 (February–May 1978): 211–225. More recently, kingship in ancient China has been brilliantly discussed in Kwang-chih Chang's *Art, Myth, and Ritual: The Path to Political Authority in Ancient China* (Cambridge, Mass., 1983).

The conception of kingship among the nomadic peoples in Central Asia has been skillfully analyzed in Jean-Paul Roux's "L'origine céleste de la souveraineté dans les inscriptions paléo-turques de Mongolie et de Sibérie," in *La regalità sacra / The Sacral Kingship* (Leiden, 1959), pp. 231–241. I have examined the symbolism of the felt carpet with special reference to both shamanism and kingship in my article "Notes on Sacred Kingship in Central Asia," *Numen* 23 (November 1976): 179–190.

On the ancient Tibetan conception of kingship, see Giuseppe Tucci's study "The Sacred Characters of the Kings of Ancient Tibet," *East and West* 6 (October 1955): 197–205.

The Tibetan conception of kingship has been compared with that of ancient Korea and Japan in my "Symbolism of 'Descent' in Tibetan Sacred Kingship and Some East Asian Parallels," *Numen* 20 (April 1973): 60–78.

The formation of kingship and its ideology in ancient Japan is discussed in my "Sacred Kingship in Early Japan: A Historical Introduction," *History of Religions* 15 (May 1976): 319–342. See also my article "Conceptions of State and Kingship in Early Japan," *Zeitschrift für Religions- und Geistesgeschichte* 28 (1976): 97–112.

Manabu Waida

Kingship in Southeast Asia

A highly complex and varied part of the world, with ten different countries today and at least as many political and cultural centers in premodern times, Southeast Asia nevertheless has been treated in academic circles as one unit. Although material, historical, and ideological differences amongst and even within each country do not allow any generalization to be entirely correct, from before the beginning of the common era to perhaps the fifteenth century, Southeast Asian societies have shared certain profound experiences that allow us to speak of them collectively. Most important in this respect was the formation and development of a "classical" tradition in each of the region's political and economic centers. To one degree or another, in one historical "period" or another, each of these classical states felt the stimulating intellectual influence of either India or China (in some cases both), which enhanced, and in some instances fundamentally changed, selected indigenous institutions. As a result, there evolved shared and uniform features of state and society, built on or around the same or similar Indic, Sinitic, and Southeast Asian ingredients, most notably those concerning the conceptions, functions, and structure of kingship. Conceptions surrounding the king ranged from deifying him to insisting on his human status. Functions varied from making him a symbolic link between the world of gods and the world of men, to a lord who disciplines his subjects, to a father who takes care of his children. Structures made of him, at one end of the spectrum, a true sovereign with a regularized, centralized, and bureaucratized authority, and at the other, a chief, *primus inter pares*, whose decentralized power was based on and administered by patron-client ties and whose legitimacy was more often spontaneously rather than institutionally derived.

Conceptions of Kingship. Throughout Southeast Asia during the first and second millennia CE, Indra, Viṣṇu, and Śiva (and their many localized manifestations) were perhaps the models *par excellence* of "divine" kingship, expressed most often, although not without some ambiguity, by the term *devarāja* ("god-king" or some close equivalent). In hinduized Arakan the model was clearly Indra, but in Buddhist Burma it was Viṣṇu as well as Sakka, while in Angkor, the center of Khmer power, the king (or, it has been argued, his symbol) was called *devarāja*. It is not clear which deity inspired the term, although Śiva seems to have been the most likely candidate, at least until the twelfth century when Buddhism became the state's preferred ideology and the *bodhisattva* assumed that role. Sometimes, Southeast Asian kings simply harnessed the attributes of these deities (the ascetic, the warrior, the destroyer, the compassionate savior) or of their *avatāras*. [*See* Indra; Viṣṇu; *and* Śiva.] In the Theravāda states, kings further associated themselves with the figure of the *bodhisatta* Metteyya (Skt., Maitreya) and his messianic characteristics. Thus, the king in Burma suggested that he was the future Buddha, and used titles such as *alàunghpayà* or *hpayàlàung* ("embryo Buddha"), whose counterparts were employed by kings in Thailand and Cambodia as well. In those kingdoms in which Mahāyāna influence dominated, the choice was usually Avalokiteśvara or a manifestation of that deity. [*See* Maitreya *and* Avalokiteśvara.]

Along with these divine models, Southeast Asian kings used human and/or mythical exemplars of kingship for purposes of legitimation and justification of certain political behavior. In the Theravāda Buddhist states, the most important of these remained Aśoka. The deliberate invocation and manipulation of Aśokan symbolism allowed these Buddhist kings to claim that they were *dhammarājas* ("kings of *dhamma*") and *cakkavattīs* (world conquerors or universal monarchs). Powerful sources of legitimation in any Buddhist society, the concepts of *dhammarāja* and *cakkavattī* served to establish internal social order and to pursue external economic and political interests. The concept of *cakkavattī* was particularly important in the conquest of neighboring kingdoms, almost always justified as *dhammavijaya* ("righteous conquest"). In the sinicized state of Dai Viêt, the Chinese concept of the emperor as the "Son of Heaven" (Chin., *t'ien-tzu*), one who has received Heaven's mandate to rule, seemed to have been the overriding functional ideology. In insular Southeast Asia, Rāma and other figures on the one hand, and—after Islam's arrival—Alexander the Great as Iskandar (or some variation of the term) on the other, played a similar human/mythical role in kingship ideology. [*See* Rāma.]

To these more "internationally" established intellectual influences were added indigenous beliefs of hereditary and charismatic leadership that often reshaped the intent behind Indian and Chinese concepts until they were no longer recognizable as such (and thus characterized as technically incorrect by students of Indian and Chinese kingship). This indigenous element invariably incorporated elements of the supernatural, allowing the king to possess qualities more superhuman than human, more magical than religious, more emotional than intellectual, and more chthonic than uranic. Thus, in Burma, Metteyya, Aśoka, and the spirits of once powerful kings were fused in the charismatic *mìn làung* ("immanent king"), noted for his millenarian features, while in Cambodia the king and the *bodhisattva* Lokeśvara Samantamukha merged to become guardians of the capital and kingdom of Angkor, majestically depicted in stone on Angkor Thom's major monument, the Bayon. In Vietnam, Heaven's mandate was obtained when genealogical ties to local, not Chinese, heroes were established; when both Chinese and Vietnamese rituals, such as the propitiation of local ancestors and spirits, were performed; and when law and order, defined by an ideal Chinese model as well as according to Vietnamese concerns, was maintained. Until the arrival of Islam in Insular Southeast Asia around the fifteenth and sixteenth centuries—and in some instances (such as Bali) even after Islam's domination in the region for several centuries—this type of Hindu-Buddhist-indigenous syncretism of kingship ideology prevailed. Here Śiva, Rāma, and Arjuna were fused with folk heroes, legendary kings, and historical leaders of repute.

Since most of these notions of kingship were multidimensional and therefore easily interchangeable, selective extraction of politically advantageous characteristics was routine. This process invariably permitted legitimation to be determined *ex post facto* as well, both in sinicized Vietnam and in the more indianized states, because the fusing of the general notion of *kamma* (Skt., *karman*), the principle of the mandate of Heaven and indigenous charismatic leadership ideology, allowed the creation of what is analytically referred to in the discipline as the *kammarāja*, one whose *kamma* had rendered him preeminently fit to rule, ultimately confirmed by his success. The conceptions of kingship in classical Southeast Asia, in short, were drawn from a wide spectrum of beliefs that included Indian, Sinitic, and indigenous notions of divinity, the supernatural, and humanity.

The Functions of Southeast Asian Kingship. There were myriad ways in which Southeast Asian kings fulfilled their roles, although it is their symbolic function that is most often emphasized by our sources. As symbols, the monarchs were links between several often contradictory poles: they bonded the world of humans and the world of the divine (the terrestrial and the celestial); they fused the past and the present; they tied the top with the bottom, the center with the periphery; they oscillated between asceticism and materialism; and they confirmed moral order by maintaining social order. Perched on a throne that represented Mount

Meru, under a towering structure that reached to the heavens, surrounded by a walled city that duplicated the regional version of the world of the gods (thereby suggesting paradise on earth), the king was the only living human and terrestrial link to the celestial world and to divinity. Because they ascended to the world of the gods and/or ancestors once they died, kings, as future divinities, semidivinities, or at least, "national" ancestors, also served as the only bridge between past royalty (and therefore dynasties) and the current ruling house, particularly if the former's genealogy had been ambiguous or political opposition between the two houses existed.

By claiming kinship ties with both past and present ruling houses, the king's own legitimacy, as well as that of the state, was assured, for legitimacy in early Southeast Asia ultimately rested not on change but on continuity, not on "progress" as we know it, but on the "purity" of the past. In a world of patron-client relationships without a true landed nobility of consequence, the king, in addition, was more often than not sovereign; as such, he was virtually the only link between royalty, officialdom, and commoners—that is, between court and countryside, center and periphery. As kings derived their power from asceticism (as in twelfth century Java and the Buddhist kingdoms) as well as from material resources, they symbolized (and resolved) the contradiction between, to use Stanley Tambiah's phrase, being "world conqueror and world renouncer" at the same time. Finally, the king was perceived by society as guardian of social and moral order because he was custodian of civil law and promulgator of criminal law (the father "who wipes away the nasal mucus from the noses of his children," as one inscription noted), while at the same time acting as patron, purifier, and defender of the faith and hence moral law.

Yet all these symbolic functions could not be realized without the more concrete powers and paraphernalia of office: the court, the governors, the treasury, the "church," the temples and monasteries, the harem, the army, the fleet, the elephantry, the cavalry, the crown lands and cultivators, the toll stations and tax registers, and in some cases, the bureaucracy. These enabled the symbolic functions of kingship to be realized, thus confirming the region's assumption that the world of symbols and the world that those symbols represent were inseparable.

The Structure of Southeast Asian Kingship. Although the political structures of the agrarian states in early Southeast Asia—Pagan, Angkor, Sukhodaya, Dai Viêt, and Majapahit in Central Java—varied, in general, they seemed to have been (partially or fully) pyramidal, centralized, and bureaucratized. The predominantly agrarian character of their economic systems, based on *sawah* (wet-rice *padi* production), must have been a major factor responsible for determining the shape of their polities, compelling their leaders to manipulate as efficiently as possible the relatively dry environment in which they were located. At the top of the pyramid was the king and royal family, usually supported by past or current relatives who comprised the upper officialdom. They in turn had under them the lower officialdom—locally selected headmen and elders as well as crown appointees in some cases—under whom was a large commoner class comprised largely of cultivators. In most cases, there were laws (or at least traditions) of succession whereby a crown prince was recognized by virtue of birth and ability. The state was normally divided into provinces, governed, *in situ* or *in absentia*, by crown appointees, whose tenures were usually held "at the royal compassion," and whose services were rewarded by rights to revenues (human as well as produce) derived from the "fief." Patron-client ties as well as bureaucratic structures performed the critical functions of administration and taxation. These were enforced and stabilized by a military, as well as in most cases, by a codified system of civil and criminal laws. If in theory the king was "lord of land and water," with the power of life and death over his subjects, in practice, however, commoners were often protected by and owed allegiance to, totally or in part, other sectors of society such as the church (Pali, *sangha*, or its equivalent), which acted as a balance to absolute rule.

In the maritime states, such as Śrī Vijaya, Singhasāri, Langkasuka, and other smaller but similar centers located on coasts that were sometimes part of the agrarian kingdoms themselves, where market forces predominated and commerce was vital, the structure that supported kings and other leaders seems to have been less centralized and bureaucratized. The independent nature of buying and selling and the individualistic ethos of merchants and traders rendered largely unnecessary the type of centralized structure that one might find in an agrarian context. As a result, these states were far more loosely organized into smaller socioeconomic units where people worked around a village or district leader. Although most of the paraphernalia of formalized ideology was present, *bona fide* leadership in such a loosely organized context required criteria of a more personal and spontaneous kind. Thus, while formal hierarchies or even features of a bureaucracy probably existed, the bureaucratic model was not typical in the maritime states as it was in the agrarian kingdoms. In the same way, spontaneity, smaller socioeconomic units of leadership based on personal relationships, and individualistic values were not nonexistent in the agrarian kingdoms, but were simply less typical. To a large extent then, kingship in both areas was regularized by a variety of legitimizing rituals as well as by the more mundane requirements of administration—in other words, a "structure."

Because the kings and kingdoms of the maritime world in Southeast Asia lived and died by the sea routes and what they demanded or supplied, the trading world and its structure reacted much more sensitively to outside forces, market and other, than did the agrarian kingdoms and their structure. The kings in the former were in many respects leaders with "international" concerns, flexible enough to adjust to the sometimes rapidly changing economic and political forces of India and China, and more externally oriented than inwardly inclined. To the agrarian states and their leaders, however, trade and outward-looking views were important but certainly not vital. The differences in conceptions and institutions that surrounded kingship reflected these different realities. It was this contrast, this contradiction of structures, material environment, and ideologies between the agrarian and commercial states, that gave Southeast Asian history its dynamism and the Southeast Asian conceptual system, most notably its perceptions of leadership, its variety.

[*See also* Cakravartin; Saṃgha, *article on* Saṃgha and Society; Southeast Asian Religions; *and the biography of* *Aśoka.*]

BIBLIOGRAPHY

Andaya, Leonard Y. "Kingship-*Adat* Rivalry and the Role of Islam in South Sulawesi." *Journal of Southeast Asian Studies* 15 (March 1984): 22–42.

Aung-Thwin, Michael. "Divinity, Spirit, and Human: Conceptions of Classical Burmese Kingship." In *Centers, Symbols, and Hierarchies: Essays on the Classical States of Southeast Asia,* edited by Lorraine Gesick, pp. 45–86. New Haven, 1983.

Aung-Thwin, Michael. *Pagan: The Foundations of Modern Burma.* Honolulu, 1985. See chapters 3 and 7.

Briggs, Lawrence P. *The Ancient Khmer Empire.* Philadelphia, 1951.

Geertz, Clifford. *Negara: The Theatre State in Nineteenth-Century Bali.* Princeton, 1980.

Gesick, Lorraine, "The Rise and Fall of King Taksin: A Drama of Buddhist Kingship." In *Centers, Symbols, and Hierarchies: Essays on the Classical States of Southeast Asia,* edited by Lorraine Gesick, pp. 87–105. New Haven, 1983.

Gullick, J. M. *Indigenous Political Systems of Western Malaya,* London, 1956.

Heine-Geldern, Robert. "Conceptions of State and Kingship in Southeast Asia." *Far Eastern Quarterly* 2 (November 1942): 15–30.

Kasetsiri, Charnvit. *The Rise of Ayudhya: A History of Siam in the Fourteenth and Fifteenth Centuries.* Kuala Lumpur, 1976.

Kulke, Hermann. *The Devarāja Cult.* Translated by I. W. Mabbett. Cornell Southeast Asia Program Data Paper, no. 108. Ithaca, N.Y., 1978.

Lieberman, Victor B. *Burmese Administrative Cycles: Anarchy and Conquest, c. 1580–1760.* Princeton, 1984. See chapter 2.

Mabbett, I. W. "Devarāja." *Journal of Southeast Asian History* 10 (September 1969): 202–223.

Moertono, Soemarsaid. *State and Statecraft in Old Java: A Study of the Later Mataram Period, Sixteenth to the Nineteenth Century.* Ithaca, N.Y., 1968.

Reid, Anthony, and Lance Castles, eds. *Pre-Colonial State Systems in South East Asia: Malay Peninsula, Sumatra, Bali-Lombok, South Celebes.* Kuala-Lumpur, 1975.

Reynolds, Frank E., and Regina T. Clifford. "Sangha, Society and the Struggle for National Integration: Burma and Thailand." In *Transitions and Transformations in the History of Religions: Essays in Honor of Joseph M. Kitagawa,* edited by Frank E. Reynolds and Theodore M. Ludwig, pp. 56–88. Leiden, 1980.

Shorto, H. L. "The Thirty-two *Myos* in the Medieval Mon Kingdom." *Bulletin of the School of Oriental and African Studies* 26 (1963): 572–591.

Tambiah, Stanley J. *World Conqueror and World Renouncer: A Study of Buddhism and Polity in Thailand against a Historical Background.* Cambridge, 1976.

Taylor, Keith W. *The Birth of Vietnam.* Berkeley, 1983.

Taylor, Keith W. "The 'Twelve Lords' in Tenth-Century Vietnam." *Journal of Southeast Asian Studies* 14 (March 1983): 46–62.

Van Naerssen, Frits Herman. "Tribute to the God and Tribute to the King." In *Southeast Asian History and Historiography: Essays Presented to D. G. E. Hall,* edited by C. D. Cowan and O. W. Wolters, pp. 296–303. Ithaca, N.Y., 1976.

Wheatley, Paul. *Nāgara and Commandery: Origins of the Southeast Asian Urban Traditions.* Chicago, 1983. See chapter 7.

Wiseman Christie, Jan. "Rāja and Rāma: The Classical State in Early Java." In *Centers, Symbols, and Hierarchies: Essays on the Classical States of Southeast Asia,* edited by Lorraine Gesick, pp. 9–44. New Haven, 1983.

Wolters, O. W. "Khmer 'Hinduism' in the Seventh Century." In *Early South East Asia: Essays in Archaeology, History and Historical Geography,* edited by R. B. Smith and William Watson, pp. 427–442. Oxford, 1979.

A volume from the conference "Southeast Asia before 1400," held at Australian National University in May 1984, is forthcoming and will contain several articles bearing on Southeast Asian kingship.

MICHAEL AUNG-THWIN

KINJIKITILE (d. 1905), religious leader in southeastern Tanganyika (now Tanzania) who provided inspiration for the anticolonial struggles known as the Maji Maji Wars. In 1904, Kinjikitile became famous as a medium in a place called Ngarambe in Matumbi country, where the oppressions of the German colonial system were severe. He was possessed by Hongo, a deity subordinate to the supreme being, Bokero, whose primary ritual center was at Kibesa on the Rufiji River. At Ngarambe, Kinjikitile blended the spiritual authority of Bokero and Hongo with more local elements of ancestor veneration at a shrine center where he received offerings from pilgrims seeking intercession with the spiritual world and relief from the adversities they faced, both natural and political. In the later part of 1904 and early 1905, Kinjikitile advised the pilgrims to prepare themselves to resist the Germans and dispensed a medicine that he promised would turn the enemy's bullets into water when combat commenced. The rebellion broke out in late July 1905 without the order coming from Kinjikitile, but the ideological preparation provided by his message and the system of emissaries that spread the word and the medicine have been viewed as critical in the struggles called the Maji Maji Wars.

The Maji Maji Wars continued from July 1905 to August 1907, extending over more than 100,000 square miles and causing terrible loss of life, estimated officially at 75,000 by the Germans and at over 250,000 by modern scholars. Out of this struggle, Kinjikitile emerged as a figure of epic proportions; he is said to be a religious innovator who devised a spiritual appeal that transcended particularism and allowed the people to unite against German rule.

By 1904, resentment of colonial rule and the desire to overthrow it had become widespread in southeastern Tanganyika. The times were especially troubled in Matumbi country, which experienced a succession of adversities that went beyond the capacity of political agents to handle. In 1903 there was a severe drought, and from 1903 to 1905 the Germans increasingly insisted that the people of Matumbi engage in communal cotton growing, promising payment for the crop once it had been marketed and the administration's overhead covered. Much to the anger of the people, the payments did not materialize.

Of Kinjikitile the person very little is known. The most certain event in his biography was his death by hanging on 4 August 1905 when, together with an assistant, he became the first opposition leader to be summarily executed by the German military forces. He had lived in Ngarambe for some four years prior to this time and had emerged as an influential person; the recipient of many gifts, he had become an object of jealousy on the part of local political leaders.

Kinjikitile was a synthesizer of many religious elements. There had long been a territorial shrine to Bokero on the Rufiji to which the people had recourse in times of drought. The drought of 1903 had activated this shrine and extended its range of influence as pilgrims came from greater and greater distances. Kinjikitile's teachings drew upon this long-standing religious institution, joining the territorial authority of Bokero with local beliefs in divine possession. His use of *maji* as a new war medicine, which helped to convince people to join the rebellion, combined Bokero's preeminent association with water with traditional beliefs concerning the efficacy of sacred medicines in protecting hunters. At Ngarambe, he also built a huge *kijumbanungu* ("house of God") for the ancestors; drawing on a resurrectionist theme, he announced that the ancestors were all at Ngarambe, ready to help their descendants defeat the Germans and restore the earthly realm. Furthermore, Kinjikitile's teachings contained elements of witch cleansing, whereby the evil within society was to be eliminated and the community morally purified. By drawing upon these traditional beliefs and using them to create an innovative ideology, Kinjikitile provided a regional and polyethnic basis for the spread of his message of resistance.

Maji Maji warriors knew that their weapons were inferior to those of the colonial forces, but the German presence was not so strong as to overawe them. They hoped for a political restoration, not of indigenous rulers, but of the Sultan of Zanzibar, whose regime became idealized because of the relatively benign form of commercial hegemony with which it was associated. Hence there was room for the Germans to investigate the possibility that Islamic propaganda or belief had played a role in the mobilization of resistance. Their conclusions were negative. Indeed, although Kinjikitile wore the traditional garb of Muslims, a long white robe called the *kanzu*, his message and idiom were decidedly drawn from traditional sources. Whether he really forged a universalistic traditional religion, as the Tanzanian historian G. C. K. Gwassa has claimed, demands closer scrutiny. Certainly his career obliges students of religion to pay well-merited attention to the structures and functions of territorial cults, ancestor veneration, and concepts of personal spiritual power and charisma. The context of the Maji Maji Wars must also be carefully weighed to refine notions of thresholds of moral outrage, recourse to religious leaders, and willingness to subscribe to a common ideology of resistance.

BIBLIOGRAPHY

Gwassa, G. C. K. "The German Intervention and African Resistance in Tanzania." In *A History of Tanzania*, edited by Isaria N. Kimambo and A. J. Temu, pp. 85–122. Nairobi, 1969.

Gwassa, G. C. K. "Kinjikitile and the Ideology of Maji Maji." In *The Historical Study of African Religion*, edited by T. O.

Ranger and Isaria N. Kimambo, pp. 202–217. Berkeley, 1972.
Iliffe, John. *A Modern History of Tanganyika.* Cambridge, 1979.

MARCIA WRIGHT

KIREEVSKII, IVAN (1806–1856), Russian publicist and Slavophile. In his early years Kireevskii's literary criticism gained him the patronage of Vasilii Zhukovskii (1783–1852) and the approval of Aleksandr Pushkin (1799–1837). He founded and was briefly the editor of a promising journal, *Evropeets*, closed by the authorities in 1832. This event drove Kireevskii into semiretirement, from which he was to emerge only occasionally and with reluctance. Only in the last decade of his life was he to find a cause which helped to justify his withdrawal from society: collaboration with the monastic elders of the hermitage at Optino. This in its turn provided him with a theological diagnosis for what in 1853 he called "the disorder of my inner forces."

In his early years Kireevskii was a proponent of westernization. But by the late 1830s he insisted on the role of Russia as a lodestar for a western Europe in decline. Without any marked chauvinism or aggressiveness (in this he differed from several of his contemporaries and successors), he had become one of the founding fathers of the Slavophile movement.

For Kireevskii this undertaking had involved a conversion or at least a return to the Orthodox church. At the prompting of his wife, Natal'ia Arbeneva, Kireevskii had turned his attention from Friedrich Schelling (1775–1854) to the church fathers. His first guide in Orthodox church life was his wife's confessor, Filaret (d. 1842), a monk of the Novo-Spasskii monastery in Moscow. But in his search for guidance Kireevskii also visited the Optino community, which was in the forefront of a Russian hesychast revival. Here he found two profound and subtle guides—the elder Leonid (1768–1841) and his successor Makarii (1788–1860). Kireevskii's acceptance of their guidance presaged the reconciliation of the westernized gentry and (subsequently) intelligentsia with the church; and it anticipated what is so often termed the Russian "religious renaissance" of the early twentieth century.

At Optino Kireevskii committed himself to an ambitious, unprecedented program—the editing, translation, and publication of Greek patristic texts. The program attracted the patronage of Metropolitan Filaret of Moscow and proved to be a landmark in the history of Russian publishing. Among the authors made available were Isaac the Syrian (d. 700?), Maximos the Confessor (c. 580–662), John Climacus (c. 570–649), Symeon the New Theologian (949–1022), and, representative of Russian mystics, Nil Sorskii (1433–1508). The first volume issued (1847) was, appropriately enough, called *The Life and Writings of the Moldavian Starets Paisii Velichkovskii* (1722–1794). Paisii's influence had stimulated the resurgence of hesychast spirituality at the Optino community.

With all his concern for the traditional spiritual disciplines, Kireevskii had no intention of discarding reason. Nor did he see Orthodox tradition as something finite. He spoke of patristic teaching as "an embryo for the philosophy of the future." That future philosophy must not be the task of an isolated individual. Kireevskii's "integrality" of the soul was to be attained solely by "the common endeavor of all who believe and think." The concept of *sobornost'*, first formulated by Kireevskii's friend Aleksei Khomiakov (1804–1860), was equally congenial to Kireevskii himself. Each was eager to promote that sense of Orthodox community and organic fellowship to which *sobornost'* refers.

Several of Kireevskii's insights were to prove seminal for Russian thinkers of succeeding decades. He died an early death of cholera and was buried at Optino, his spiritual home. Despite the neglect of Kireevskii's reputation and depredations of Optino during the Soviet period, his tombstone has recently been recovered and restored.

BIBLIOGRAPHY

Kireevskii's complete works were edited by M. O. Gershenzon as *Polnoe sobranie sochinenii I. V. Kireevskago* in two volumes (1911; reprint, Farnborough, 1970). To these should be added the German translation of Kireevskii's diaries for 1852–1854 (the original remains unpublished): "Das Tagebuch Ivan Vasil'evič Kirejevskijs, 1852–1854," translated by Eberhard Müller, *Jahrbücher für Geschichte Osteuropas* 14 (1966): 167–194. Two monographs may be mentioned: Abbott Gleason's *European and Muscovite: Ivan Kireevsky and the Origins of Slavophilism* (Cambridge, Mass., 1972) and Peter K. Christoff's *An Introduction to Nineteenth-Century Russian Slavophilism: A Study in Ideas*, vol. 2, *I. V. Kireevskij* (The Hague, 1972).

SERGEI HACKEL

KISSING. *See* Postures and Gestures; Salutations; *and* Touching.

KNEES. The knees have long been closely associated with religious attitudes of penitence, prayer, surrender, and humility. In the Near East since ancient times kneeling has sometimes been connected with prostration; Islam developed full prostration as the climax of a cycle of postures that includes a combined sitting and kneeling position. In ancient Israel, people considered the knees to be associated with the generation of new life and with adoption; thus Bilhah, Rachel's maidservant, bore a child on Jacob's knees (*Gn.* 30:3), for a baby born on a man's knees in biblical times and places was considered legally to be his child. There may be a reflection or survival here of a prehistoric notion of an intimate relationship between the knees and the reproductive process (Onians, 1951, pp. 174–180).

In ancient Rome, adoration at sacred temples included falling to the knees as well as kneeling during supplication and prayer. Romans also knelt when presenting pleas before earthly authorities. In ancient Greece, only women and children knelt before deities. The early Christians practiced kneeling, according to accounts given in the New Testament, and the posture appears to have been inherited directly from earlier Jewish practice. In the Hebrew scriptures, Solomon, Ezra, and Daniel are reported to have knelt at prayer (*1 Kgs.* 8:54, *Ezr.* 9:5, *Dn.* 6:10). It is likely that the ancient Israelites adopted kneeling as a religious posture from other Near Eastern peoples. Buddhists also kneel, when paying respects at sacred sites, for example.

Kneeling is not the only prayer posture mentioned in the Bible. Standing in prayer is recorded as well (*1 Sm.* 1:26, *Mk.* 11:25, *Lk.* 22:41). In fact, only once in the Gospels is Christ reported to have knelt, namely, on the Mount of Olives before his arrest (*Lk.* 22:41). But the *Acts of the Apostles* depicts both Peter and Paul kneeling in prayer (9:40, 20:36, 21:5), and Paul's great kenotic christological passage in the *Letter to the Ephesians* ends with this declaration: "In honor of the name of Jesus all beings in heaven, and on earth, and in the world below will fall on their knees, and all will openly proclaim that Jesus Christ is Lord, to the glory of God the Father" (2:10–11). The penitential aspect of kneeling was noted in the fourth century by Ambrose: "The knee is made flexible by which the offence of the Lord is mitigated, wrath appeased, grace called forth" (*Hexaemeron* 6.9.74.287).

The early Christians appear to have practiced both standing and kneeling at prayer. Later the Roman Catholic church appears to have encouraged standing for prayer, especially in Sunday congregational worship, but recommended kneeling for penitential and private prayer. Protestantism has emphasized kneeling as the prayer posture above all others, whereas Catholicism has regulated the postures of worship and prayer fairly rigorously, for example prescribing standing on Sundays and festival days and in praise and thanksgiving at all times. During low mass, the worshipers kneel except during the reading of the gospel.

Popular Christianity employs a kneeling posture for both supererogatory prayer and adoration. These practices sometimes extend to rather arduous ascending of stairs of shrines on the knees while uttering pious formulas at each step, as at Saint Joseph's Oratory in Montreal, where many supplicants have been healed of crippling afflictions. Cured persons have long left their crutches at this shrine, displayed in the sanctuary like sacred relics. Within the precincts of the Shrine of the Virgin of Guadalupe in Mexico City many pilgrims can be seen approaching the sacred places on their knees. Similar practices can be observed at other Christian holy places in both the Old World and the New.

Kneeling has been practiced not only in the presence of God but also in the presence of royalty in many cultures. The early Roman rulers required the northern Europeans, the Egyptians, and Asian peoples to bend the knee in submission, whereas earlier still Alexander the Great required it of all, declaring himself to be divine. When making supplication, ancient Greeks and Romans are reported to have knelt while kissing the hand of the superior person, at the same time touching his left knee with the left hand. Modern British subjects curtsy and bend the knee when in the presence of their sovereign.

Extreme flexing of the knees was once entailed in the binding of corpses for burial in a fetal position, as has been reported in ethnographical accounts and in reports on prehistoric burials. The reasons are unclear, as it is not certain whether the bent knees were especially significant in themselves. Certainly the corpse's submissive incapacity can at least be conjectured from this position, whether in order to prevent the spirit of the deceased from wandering about and haunting the living or to prepare the deceased for initiation into the secrets of the afterlife, which might possibly have included a ritual symbolism of returning to the fetal position.

BIBLIOGRAPHY

A. E. Crawley's article entitled "Kneeling," in the *Encyclopaedia of Religion and Ethics*, edited by James Hastings, vol. 7 (Edinburgh, 1914), is a useful source for Near Eastern, biblical, and Christian kneeling practices; the evolutionary perspective from which the topic is addressed must be rejected, however. For a convenient reference work, consult Betty J. Bäuml and Franz H. Bäuml's *A Dictionary of Gestures* (Metuchen, N.J., 1975); here are found numerous documented reports about knee symbolism and kneeling in the ancient Near East and Mediterranean world as well as in later European history and literature. For stimulating insights and observations on the knees and other parts of the body, see Richard B. Onians's *The Origins of European Thought about the Body, the Mind, the Soul, the World, Time, and Fate* (Cambridge, 1951).

Frederick Mathewson Denny

KNOTS. The sacred value attributed to knots throughout human history, and amid the most diverse cultures, has interested historians of religions since the nineteenth century. As products of the activity of tying or binding, knots have usually been studied in the context of the more general phenomenon of sacred bonds. [*See* Binding.] It is not surprising, therefore, that research into the religious value of knots has followed the same general pattern that one finds in the study of binding. In particular, the problems have been formulated in similar terms, similar methods have been employed, and consequently the results obtained have also tended to coincide.

Thus the leading students of the religious significance of binding and bonds have also led the way in the study of knots. Scholars such as James G. Frazer, Isidor Scheftelowitz, Walter J. Dilling, Georges Dumézil, and Mircea Eliade have made important contributions in both areas. In general, these scholars have expended considerable effort on the collection of data that are then subjected to comparative-historical study. Closer examination shows, however, that several quite different methods have been employed. Some scholars have been content with a simple exposition of individual instances of knots in particular cultures (Frazer, Dilling). Others have defined their study in terms of a definite cultural area (Dumézil). Finally, there has been an attempt at a phenomenological analysis of knots aimed at the identification of an archetype of the bond (Eliade). The results obtained by these methods, from Frazer to Eliade, have generally been formulated in exclusively symbolic terms, for the most part in the context of magical beliefs and practices. What has not been adequately studied up to now is the symbolic value that knots may have in the context of everyday life and the wholly secular and functional importance of binding and knots in that context.

Beginning with the work of Frazer at the beginning of the present century, scholars have repeatedly affirmed that the sacred action of tying or untying a knot serves to establish or remove some restraint and that it has either a positive or a negative effect, depending upon the specific circumstances under which it is done and the motives of the person doing it. Countless examples of such symbolic action have been furnished, drawn from both primitive cultures and higher civilizations. Every imaginable type of bond has been analyzed, bonds both concrete (such as are made from string or rope, or again, rings and chains) and abstract. Instances have been provided of knots tied in both public and private rituals as well as in nonritual contexts. Knots are found to be tied by superhuman beings as well as by ordinary mortals, and in the latter case by those who are religiously inspired as well as by those who are not. In all of this description, however, the deeper motives behind such widespread forms of activity have not been sought.

It has long been known that the activity of binding in its various forms has the essential goal of permitting human beings to extend their control over reality. The most striking example consists of the knotted ropes used in many preliterate societies as a means of organizing and storing information. Knots tied into ropes, often of different colors, are used to represent numbers, objects, persons, situations, actions, and so forth. Such knotted ropes are useful in resolving specific problems of a practical nature, since they extend man's ability to count, inventory, register, list, and in general to organize and communicate information. The problems solved in this way are not exclusively secular problems, however. They can often have a decidedly religious aspect. The practical function of such knots, and in fact, of all types of bond, even those of a purely symbolic nature, does not preclude their having a sacred function as well. Indeed, these two functions may exist in a relation of strict complementarity.

In the specific context of the ritual confession of sins, Raffaele Pettazzoni has shown how certain knots combine a symbolic value with the quite concrete purpose of restraining or fixating the sin, so that the guilt associated with it may be more effectively confronted and neutralized. Thus, for example, in preparation for their ritual journey in search of the sacred *híkuri* (a cactus used in a festival), the Huichol of Mexico require that each person making the trip indicate the number of his lovers by tying the appropriate number of knots in a rope, which is then destroyed by fire. A similar operation is performed by the women who remain at home. The Zapotec symbolically knot up the sins of the year by tying blades of grass together two by two, soaking them in the blood of the penitent, and then offering them to a superhuman being. In ancient Babylonia, one finds the idea of sin as a knot that has to be undone by various divinities, such as Nergal, "lord of the untying." In Vedic India, it is the god Varuṇa who captures the guilty with his knotted lasso. In the Shintō purification ritual, a piece of paper *(katashiro)* is cut out by the penitent, bound in bundles of wicker, and thrown into the flames.

The calculation of sacred and profane time can also be managed through the use of knots tied into a rope at set intervals. A mere glance at such a rope is enough to allow a person to comprehend a situation and act appropriately. Martin P. Nilsson has shown how various primal cultures use such ropes for measuring the duration of menstrual impurity (for example, the Nauru of the Gilbert Islands), the period during which justice should be administered (the Gogo of Tanzania), the period during which intertribal dances should be prepared (the Miwok of California), or the days to be dedicated to the celebration of a great festival (the Melanesians of the Solomon Islands).

In all these cases, knots are used to control a reality that is itself abstract, fluctuating, evanescent. Guilt, time, or fate itself, by being concretized in a knot, comes under the control of the person who ties it and who thereby resolves a given situation. But it is not only determinate problems that can be resolved through the use of knots and the control they give. The complexities of an entire empire can be made manageable thanks to the use of knotted ropes. This was the case in pre-Columbian Peru, where the use of knotted ropes called *quipu* as instruments for keeping records was essential for the orderly functioning of the Inca empire. The use of the *quipu* made it possible for the *quipucamayoc* (keeper of the *quipu*) to manage the enormous mass of data collected by local officials and thereby keep tabs on the complex economic and military situation of the empire.

Moreover, in every period, in the most diverse types of civilization, technology strives not only to gain control over the world but also to enhance human creativity by providing man with new tools with which to confront life's difficulties. The fabrication of such implements, however, involves the binding, weaving, and knotting together of the most diverse materials. It is precisely the enormous importance of the technology of binding that stands behind the transposition of all its means and forms from the mundane to the sacred. Forms of transposition that are particularly widespread include the attribution of extraordinary value and power to knots in magical rites; the creation of the type of the "god who binds," armed with ropes, lassos, and nets; and above all, the development of the majestic conception of a universe created by means of the art of weaving.

In this regard, Eliade's concept of the woven cosmos requires further development. Eliade's study of the symbolism of knots went beyond the study of knots per se to investigate those cases in which the universal order is believed to be produced by various types of tying and weaving, in much the same way as one would produce a rope, a chain, or a net. Among the Babylonians, for example, the *markasu* (rope) was both the cosmic principle that unites all things and the divine power or law that provides the framework for the universe. Similarly, the Vedic *prāṅa* (breath) was believed to have woven human life (*Atharvaveda* 10.2.13), while *vāyu* (air) bound all beings to each other like a thread (*Bṛhadāraṇyaka Upaniṣad* 3.7.2). In China, the Tao, which was the ultimate principle of the universe, was described as the chain of all creation. Now it is precisely comparisons from the history of religions that teach us that a motif of this type, far from being the distillate of an extremely sophisticated philosophical thought, is in fact an image of great antiquity, sinking its roots beneath the higher civilizations into the traditional patrimony of primitive peoples.

Indeed, the conception of creation as a whole—both the cosmic order and man's place within it—as the product of some type of binding activity, whether of knotting, tying, twining, or weaving, is quite widespread. We find, for instance, in the origin myths of several primal cultures the conception of the creator as a spider who weaves the universe just as a normal spider weaves its web. Similarly, specific forms of ropes or bonds are sometimes assigned cosmic functions. The rainbow, for example, can be interpreted as the belt with which the supreme being fastens his robe, as among the western Galla. Among the Witóto of Colombia, the "thread of a dream" binds together a creation that is believed to emerge out of nothingness. The Maidu of south-central California believe that a superhuman being once descended beneath the waters to procure the soil needed for creation by means of a rope woven of feathers. The Nootka of Vancouver Island and the Polynesians of Hoa Island relate that the light of the sun, having taken on the form of a basket, is lowered down to the earth by means of a rope. In a similar vein, the cosmogonic myths of various peoples of California tell of how, in a primordial epoch, the sea was put into a wicker container (the Salina), the world was sewn together like a small, tarred reed basket (the Yuki), or the entire universe took shape through the patient work of weaving as though it were a knotted mat (the Wintu).

In this cosmos, structured and woven like fabric, the creator taught human beings to tie fibers to make ropes and lassos. In this way the wild and unruly clouds were captured and humans began to exert a degree of control over the climate (the Wintu). Similarly, bindings were used to control the sun at the time of origin of the universe, when it was either too hot or too cold, and therefore threatened men, animals, and plants. The sun, caught in a trap like a lynx (the Chipewyan), half-tied like a slipknot (the Montagnais-Naskapi, the Alonquian Cree, the Ciamba of Nigeria), and captured in snares of various types (the Pende of the Kongo and the natives of the Gazelle Peninsula, Oceania, and Melanesia, as well as others), was forced to diminish or strengthen its rays, change its course, and settle into what must henceforth be its proper path. Neither could the moon avoid being caught with a rope and receiving thereby the spots that would forever mark it (the Naskapi). As for the stars, they are so high because one day the vine woven between earth and sky was cut in two (the Boróro of the Mato Grosso).

In this universe, variously knotted, tied, and woven, the differentiation of animals and men likewise was the result of binding. When the rope that had permitted access to the celestial sphere was broken, the animals tumbled hopelessly to earth (the Boróro). And once on earth, their existence was determined by the activity of binding. The armadillo, for example, set about weaving the "shirt" that would belong to it, and it is because it hurried too much and tied stitches of unequal size, now small and thick, now large and broad, that it looks the way it does today (the Aymara of Bolivia). The trout, for its part, while still in the hands of its creator felt drawn to its own fate so that it lamented and despaired, crying out for a net in which it could make its first appearance on earth (the Athapascan-speaking Kato).

As for human beings, bonds characterize their very existence in the details of their own body and in the countless components of the human condition. The Pomo of north-central California relate that Marunda created the first men by weaving and knotting together his own hair, while among the Melanesians of the island of Mota this usage is associated with an archetypal woman named Ro Vilgale ("deceptive bond") who is created from twigs, branches, and leaves woven and knotted together, much like the masks of a Melanesian secret society in historical times. Alternatively, primordial man may descend to earth by means of a skein let down from the sky (the Toba Batak of Indonesia) or a rope (the Carisi of Brazil, the natives of Belau [Palau]). The breaking of this rope, sometimes due to the clumsiness of the person who wove it, brings about human mortality (the Keres of New Mexico, the natives of Belau), and the resulting fall causes the articulation of the human body into joints or knots (the Carisi). In order to cover man's nakedness, the superhuman beings who preside over weaving gave these first humans cotton and taught them to spin and to weave (the Caduveo of South America, the Ifugao of the Philippines). To provide them with various necessities, they also taught them the art of weaving wicker (the Pomo).

At a certain point, however, men themselves became capable of using bonds to improve their own economic condition by capturing superhuman beings and forcing them to yield to their demands. A myth from Namoluk Island (Micronesia) tells how certain spirits, captured with a net, taught the cultivation of taro to those who until then had lived exclusively on fish. Stories are also told among numerous cultures of humanity's rescue from various cataclysms by means of specific products of binding: the net of the spider (the Pomo), a basket (the Wiyot of Algonquian language), and so on.

From this brief survey, it should be clear that knots and other types of bonds need to be studied not only in historical perspective but also in relation to the technology of the culture in question. Behind the motif of knots we find the exaltation of *homo faber*, who redeems himself from the infinite miseries and multitudinous limitations of his existential condition precisely by means of his ability to bind things together. It is he who catches spirits in nets, weaves the rope that permits him to live on earth, sets snares and traps in order to capture the stars and fix them in their course, weaves the basket in which he saves himself from the flood—in short, spins and weaves the mortal condition. In his full appreciation of manual ability as a creative force, in his elevation of this creativity to the cosmogonic level, and in his sublimation of his own work by means of implements and tools capable of controlling reality, man proves himself capable of binding and loosening the entangling and knotty problems that fill his existence: he shows himself to be the uncontested artificer of his own fate.

[*See also* Labyrinth *and* Webs and Nets.]

BIBLIOGRAPHY

Three works discuss the theme of knots and the binding action central to it: James G. Frazer's *The Golden Bough*, 3d ed., rev. & enl., vol. 3, *Taboo and the Perils of the Soul* (London, 1911); Isidor Scheftelowitz's *Das Schlingen- und Netzmotiv im Glauben und Brauch der Völker* (Giessen, 1912); and Walter J. Dilling's "Knots," in the *Encyclopaedia of Religion and Ethics*, edited by James Hastings, vol. 7 (Edinburgh, 1914). More detailed approaches are taken by Georges Dumézil in *Ouranos-Varuna* (Paris, 1934) and *Mitra-Varuṇa* (Paris, 1940) and by Mircea Eliade in *Images and Symbols: Studies in Religious Symbolism* (New York, 1961).

Concerning the use of knotted ropes, the Peruvian *quipu* and art of weaving are the subject of P. Matthey's "Gli esordi della scienze" and Enrica Cerulli's "Industrie e techniche," both in *Ethnologica*, vol. 2, *Le opere dell'uomo*, edited by Vinigi L. Grottanelli (Milan, 1965). Martin P. Nilsson discusses the measurement of time with the aid of knotted ropes in *Primitive Time-Reckoning* (Lund, 1920), pp. 320ff. On the use of ropes in the confession of sins, see Raffaela Pettazzoni's *La confessione dei peccati*, vol. 1 (1929; reprint, Bologna, 1968), and on the use of knots in divination, see William A. Lessa's "Divining by Knots in the Carolines," *Journal of Polynesian Society* 68 (June 1959): 188–204. For a discussion of the metaphor of the universe as something woven, see Pettazzoni's well-documented study *Miti e leggende*, 4 vols. (Turin, 1948–1963).

GIULIA PICCALUGA
Translated from Italian by Roger DeGaris

KNOWLEDGE AND IGNORANCE. A cognitive element is essential to most religions and probably to all, but exactly what constitutes religious knowledge is problematic. Strong belief, for example, may be subjectively indistinguishable from knowledge. In a 1984 BBC interview, Billy Graham asserted that he *knows* there is to be a second coming of Christ. At a lecture, the Hindu scholar Swami Bon declared that "transmigration is not a dogma, it is a fact." This article will examine the various and conflicting conceptions of religious knowledge that have emerged in the major traditions through history.

Primal Peoples. "It appears," Dominique Zahan has written, "that every religion, however primitive, contains a cognitive element" ("Religions de l'Afrique noire," *Histoire des religions* 3, 1976, p. 609). In primal religions, according to Åke Hultkranz, religious knowledge rests on a fundamental division of experience: "A basic dichotomy between two levels of existence, one orderly or 'natural'—the world of daily experience—the other extraordinary or 'supernatural'—the world of belief—conditions man's religious cognition" (Hultkranz, 1983, pp. 231, 239). The world of belief is in turn divided into that of the sorcerer and that of the magician. "They are opposed to one another on the plane of knowledge and wisdom, as a tortuous, obscure knowledge full of contradictions and uncertainties, over against a clear knowledge, imbued with evidence and conforming to the logic of a thought at the service of the community" (ibid., p. 632).

More simply, though, the world of belief may be identified with the invisible. As the Kiowa Indian N. Scott Momaday has said, "We see the world as it appears to us, in one dimension of reality. But we also see it with the eye of the mind" (ibid., p. 248). A slightly different note is struck by an Eskimo woman: "You always want the supernatural things to make sense, but we do not bother about that. We are content not to understand" (ibid., p. 247).

India. In India a cognitive element is conspicuous in the whole tradition that sprang or claimed to spring from the Veda. The *Ṛgveda* already comprised some speculative hymns, and the Brāhmaṇas were essentially an interpretation of ritual by means of myth. Finally, in the Upaniṣads, ritual itself gives way to speculation: salvation is achieved through recognizing one's identity with the essence of the universe, the *brahman.*

In classical Brahmanism, philosophy is a mere rationalization of the Vedic revelation (Biardeau, 1964). Contrary to what happened in both Christianity and Islam owing to the clash of two different traditions, in Brahmanism no distinction was made between philosophy and theology. But in Hinduism there was always "a deep-seated tension between the ascetic ideal as personified in the holiness of the *śramaṇa* and the ideal or ritual propriety for the ordinary believer" (Bendix, 1960, p. 192). One of three or four approaches to this tension was *jñānayoga* ("the way of knowledge"), which held that even a good action, since it is connected with ignorance *(avidyā),* can only produce the fruit of all attachment to things and beings, namely, reincarnation. In the Nyāya ("logic") school, there is finally only one mode of knowledge, that of perception, but in certain circumstances contact with the external senses is not required: contact between *ātman* ("soul") and *manas* ("inner sense") is sufficient. Natural and revealed knowledge are on the same plane: "The gods, the men and the animals make use of the [revealed] means of right knowledge, and there is no other" *(Nyāyabhāṣya* 1.1.17).

Concepts of nondualism and *brahman* have long had precise meanings in India. Both refer to a mystical doctrine of salvation through knowledge: as the Veda is endowed with the ontological fecundity of the *brahman,* so the latter is, in turn, the spring of all knowledge. In the Sāṃkhya school the most fatal attitude is nescience, or nondiscrimination between *puruṣa* (spectator spirit) and *prakṛti* (creative energy): this failure to discriminate is *avidyā* ("ignorance"), which keeps one in the bonds of the cycle of transmigration. But if language speaks only of things in themselves, it cannot express becoming, or change, Bhartṛhari objects, and he finds a way out of this difficulty not by suppressing permanence, as did the Buddhists, but by allowing thought to transcend perception without relinquishing being. He eventually does away with the authority of perception and relies only on interior revelation, which is essentially religious and nonrational. Bhartṛhari does not mention *avidyā* or *māyā* ("illusion"), which will be the pivots of Vedantic thought. Vedantism—the further development of Brahmanism—cannot be understood without reference to Buddhism.

Buddhism. The teachings of the Buddha presupposed a high level of schooling among his disciples: there were systematic, dispassionate discussions in which appeal was made to the intellect, in contrast to the popular similes, ironical retorts, and emotional preaching of Jesus or the visionary messages of Muḥammad (Bendix, 1960, p. 192). Buddhism is based on an illumination *(bodhi)* experienced by Śākyamuni. Its object was expressed in the form of a chain of causes and effects (Skt., *pratītya-samutpāda;* Pali, *paṭicca-samuppāda).* The list given in the *Mahānidāna Sutta* comprises only nine links, ending in (or starting from) *viññāṇa* ("consciousness"), without ignorance being mentioned. Not so in the *Mahāvagga,* which counts twelve terms, starting from *avijjā* ("ignorance"), in the chain of psychic formations, a notion parallel to that in Brahmanism where, unlike the Buddhist understanding, pure being shrouds itself, out of ignorance, in psychic formations. Essentially the Buddhist message is this: living is suffering, suffering stems from desire, and desire from *avidyā.* In order to be delivered one should vanquish ignorance and obtain wisdom, mystical lucidity (Pali, *paññā;* Sanskrit, *prajñā),* also called *āryaprajñā* ("noble knowledge"), which produces extinction, *nirvāṇa.* But, contrary to what is taught in Brahmanism, this knowledge implies the negation of all permanence, of all substance, of *ātman* as well as of *brahman,* the two terms whose equation was the foundation of the Brahmanic doctrine. This is the view of Hīnayāna Buddhism.

Mahāyāna Buddhism refines this negative position. The perfection of wisdom, *prajñāpāramitā,* does not give omniscience by providing a foundation of knowledge: the very lack of such a foundation constitutes omniscience, which is the revelation of emptiness. Still, there are two degrees of this revelation. According to the Vijñānavādins, pure thought is an absolute to which all things are reduced, while the Mādhyamikas go one step further: for them the doctrine of emptiness is itself emptiness (Bugault, 1968, p. 48). The effort toward knowledge results in nonknowledge, nescience.

According to Asaṅga, *prajñā* is only obtained subsequent to *dhyāna* ("appeased, introverted concentration"; in Chinese *ch'an,* in Japanese *zen*) and is a sort of *noēsis* without *noēta* (ibid., p. 41). *Prajñā* and *dhyāna* are like the two sides of a coin. *Dhyāna* concentrates; *prajñā* liberates. Supreme knowledge, *bodhi,* is only the realization that there is nothing to comprehend. This kind of knowledge would seem to be tantamount to sheer ignorance, but it is not, for then "the deaf, the blind and the simpletons would be saints" (*Majjhima Nikāya* 3.498). We must remember that Buddhism arose amid ascetics who practiced control of the senses, of breath, even of blood circulation—and of thought. In Chinese Buddhism, the direct approach of Hui-neng (seventh to eighth century) to sudden awakening rejected all distinctions between enlightenment and ignorance.

Vedānta. The ruin of Brahmanic ontology under the assault of Hīnayāna Buddhism had resulted in Hīnayāna positivism, which led to the Mahāyāna doctrine of absolute emptiness. This in turn brought about in Brahmanism Vedantism, a return to ontology on the basis of *avidyā* ("nescience"), as formulated by its first major exponent, Śaṅkara, in the eleventh century. The idea of the ego is produced by nescience; so are, in their literal sense, the Vedic texts. Nescience is the cause of all error, of suffering and of evil. *Brahman* is the only true object of knowledge, to which the soul goes back by exercising nescience. By substituting the word *nirvāṇa* for the word *brahman* we would get a perfect formula of Buddhist orthodoxy. But Rāmānuja (twelfth century), the second important exponent of Vedantism, went one step further. He admits, not unlike Śaṅkara, that subject, object, and the act of knowledge are only arbitrary distinctions created by *avidyā,* that the chain of acts is only a trick of nescience, and that salvation consists in the cessation of nescience through knowledge of *brahman,* which is accessible in the Veda. But this is transcendent knowledge, an intuitive revelation only made possible in a mystical union with *brahman,* which is also conceived as the universal lord. "He who possessing knowledge untiringly strives and is devoted to me only, to him I am infinitely dear and he is dear to me (*Bhagavadgītā,* 7.17).

Rāmānuja also restored to the individual soul its reality and substantiality. Whereas in the Upaniṣads and the teachings of Śaṅkara the divinity was conceived as sheer consciousness, in medieval Hinduism, whether Vaiṣṇava or Śaiva, it becomes a force in action, a sovereign energy. And knowledge must be fulfilled in *bhakti,* that is, unrelenting love of God. Rāmānuja refutes the notion of *avidyā* Śaṅkara had inherited from the Buddhists. To assume that the *brahman* necessarily develops into illusory nescience and plurality is to admit that the *brahman* itself is illusory, that ultimate reality is error and lie. This is, he says, to fall into the error of Mādhyamika Buddhism, which is contradicted by the teachings of the Upaniṣads, the *Bhagavadgītā,* and the *Viṣṇu Purāṇa* (Grousset, 1931, p. 391).

Taoism. Chinese thought, on the whole, aims at culture, not at pure knowledge. In Taoism, man falls by acquiring knowledge. Whereas for the Confucians man learns to use and to improve on nature, for the Taoists this is a profanation of nature: "Banish wisdom, discard knowledge, and the people will be benefited a hundredfold, for it was only when the great Tao declined, when intelligence and knowledge appeared, that the great Artifice began. . . . In the days of old those who practiced Tao with success did not, by means of it, enlighten the people, but on the contrary sought to make them ignorant. The more knowledge people have, the harder they are to rule. Those who seek to rule by giving knowledge are like bandits preying on the land. Those who rule without giving knowledge bring a stock of good fortune to the land" *(Tao-te ching).* Taoism is the declared enemy of civilization. Civilization based on knowledge is to be replaced by another kind of knowledge, the intuitive knowledge of Tao, through which man becomes the Tao.

The Greeks. The notion of Logos in Heraclitus implies that the universe can be known. He was the first philosopher to pose the epistemological problem. Still, for him "questions of cognition are inseparable from questions of action and intention, of life and death. The blindness he denounces is that of men who do not know what they are doing" (Kahn, 1979, p. 100).

The Pythagoreans were divided into acousmatics and mathematicians, the former following the tradition of *fides ex auditu,* the latter following reason and *veritas ex intellectu,* thus already exemplifying, as Léon Brunschwicg noted, the contrast between theosophy and philosophy. With the emergence of philosophy a conflict was bound to arise between reason and religion, between *logos* and *muthos.* It tended to be resolved, for instance by Theagenes of Rhegium (fourth century BCE), through the allegorical interpretation of myths.

In the sixth century BCE Xenophanes ridiculed the anthropomorphism of the myths and emphasized God's spirituality and omniscience. A century later Socrates (according to Xenophon) rejected the study of the world machine, wrought and ruled by the gods, and instead recommended studying human affairs. He equated virtue with knowledge and vice with ignorance (Xenophon, *Memorabilia* 3.9, 4.a; Plato, *Protagoras, Meno,* etc.).

According to Plato, faith, mystical enthusiasm, is but a stage in the pathway to knowledge; the knowledge of God is the soul's marriage with her ideal. Above the Logos, or Reason, is the Nous, or Intellect, the faculty of perceiving the divine, the instrument of contemplation. But the supreme idea, the Good, was raised by Plato beyond both being and knowledge, as the principle of their unity.

Aristotle replaced Plato's *anamnēsis* by abstraction. Man is like a mortal god, for he possesses a divine reality, the intellect, capable of knowing God. God, the Unmoved Mover, is *noēsis noēseōs.* This still reflects the primacy of the intellect and implies superiority of contemplation over any other way of life.

The Cynics reacted against the almost unlimited confidence in education as a means to form and transform man that had prevailed in Athens since the time of the Sophists. Virtue, said Antisthenes, lies in action and has no need of many discourses or of science. But the saying attributed to him by Diogenes Laertius (6.103) that "if one were wise, one would not learn to read, lest one should be corrupted by other people," is probably an exaggeration of his position.

For the Stoics the human intellect is not only akin to God, it is part of the divine substance itself. They appealed to Heraclitus, but their Logos was not, like his, simply a principle of explanation. It probably owed much to the notion of the commanding word, *davar,* which in Hebrew expressed the divine will.

In the Platonic tradition, according to Philo Judaeus, the human intellect is the source of, on the one hand, perception, memory, and reaction to impulses; on the other hand, as *apospasma theion* ("divine fragment"), it makes possible suprarational intuition.

The Hebrews. To the Hebrews, knowing was less a logical, discursive process than a direct psychological experience, less the expression of objective truths than a personal engagement. (The Hebrew for "to know," *yada',* signifies sexual intercourse.) Knowledge of the law was the basis of the moral life. In the *Book of Genesis,* however, a negative appraisal of knowledge was reflected in the story of the Fall: evil and death entered the world through man's "knowledge of good and evil." The myth resembles the Taoist one in which the loss of happiness results from the acquisition of knowledge.

In Israel, however, this conception remained isolated and, perhaps, misunderstood, over against the more widespread feeling that knowledge is from God, who "teaches man knowledge" (*Ps.* 94:10) and, in the Qumran texts, is even called "God of knowledge," and "source of knowledge." Such a notion also prevails in Jewish apocalyptic literature (Gruenwald, 1973, p. 63). Finally, skepticism is not absent from the Bible; *Ecclesiastes* expresses skepticism but compensates for it by adherence to authority.

Early Christianity. The role of knowledge in the Christian faith has varied considerably. Its importance was already recognized by Paul the apostle, who considered it the supreme virtue: ". . . after I heard of your faith . . . and love . . . [I prayed] that . . . God . . . may give unto you the spirit of wisdom and revelation in the knowledge of him" (*Eph.* 1:15–18; cf. *Col.* 2:2), which agrees with the educational ideal of a Jewish doctor of the law and with the mystical aspiration of apocalyptic; however, the ultimate object of knowledge, the love of Christ, "passeth knowledge" (*Eph.* 3:19), and Paul conformed to the specific Christian ideal when, addressing the Corinthians, he put charity above everything: "and though I have the gift of prophecy, and understand all mysteries, and all knowledge; and though I have all faith, so that I could move mountains, and have no love, I am nothing" (*1 Cor.* 13:2); "knowledge puffeth up, love edifieth" (*1 Cor.* 8:1).

Only John attempts a synthesis of love and knowledge: "for love is of God, and every one that loveth is born of God, and knoweth God" (*1 Jn.* 4:7). And in the prologue of the Fourth Gospel he identifies Jesus himself with the Logos. Contact with paganism, however, had already brought about in Paul a completely different reaction: "But we preach Christ crucified, unto the Jews a stumbling block, and unto the Greeks foolishness" (*1 Cor.* 1:23). A conflict between natural wisdom and revealed truth thus developed in Christianity and later, parallel to it, in Islam. On the other hand, Justin Martyr, the first Christian apologist, headed a long series of authors for whom the Christian revelation was the culmination of a more ample one that would include the thought of the pagan philosophers, also Christian in its own way since it came from the Word (Logos), and Christ was the Word incarnate.

Gnōsis. In the second century, when Plutarch, with his Platonic use of myth, bore witness to philosophy's overture toward mysticism and to the challenge of the primacy of the Logos, people were seeking to attain through revelation a kind of knowledge allowing union with God. There ensued a heated dialogue between faith *(pistis)* and intellectual knowledge *(gnōsis)*, the latter already suspect to Paul (*1 Tim.* 6:20: *pseudōnumos gnōsis*). Thus arose two conceptions of the knowledge accessible to the Christian: the one *(gnōsis)* is to replace faith; the other submits to faith in order to fathom its mystery. Gnosticism "traces back the origin of the world to an act of ignorance, the removal of which through knowledge is the aim of the Gnostic doctrine of redemption" (Rudolph, 1983, p. 71). The element earth has been produced by horror, water by fear, air by pain; within those three elements there is fire, a vehicle of death and destruction, as within the three passions is hidden ignorance (Irenaeus, *Against Heresies* 1.5.4).

Jewish apocalyptic contributed to gnosticism by its new idea of knowledge as a religious ideal (Gruenwald, 1973, p. 104), but the gnostics, according to Celsus, called the god of the Jews the "accursed god" because he created the visible world and withheld knowledge from men (Rudolph, 1983, p. 73). According to various gnostic texts the "tree of knowledge" imparts to Adam his appropriate godlike status over against the lower creator god, who prohibited the enjoyment of this tree out of envy. The serpent functions at the behest of the highest god for Adam's instruction, and thus has a positive task (ibid., p. 94). According to Irenaeus, however, mundane knowledge is to be rejected (*Against Heresies* 2.32.2). And according to Hippolytus, God will extend the great ignorance to all the world, so that each creature will remain in its natural condition and no one will desire anything against nature.

Direct information about gnosticism is available thanks to the discovery in Upper Egypt of the Nag Hammadi Coptic manuscripts. *Gnōsis* is a hidden, esoteric knowledge. One of the tractates bears the significant title *The Interpretation of Knowledge.* We read in the *Gospel of Truth* that "ignorance of the Father brought about anguish and terror. And the anguish grew solid like a fog so that no one was able to see. For this reason error became powerful; it fashioned its own matter" (Robinson, 1977, p. 38). In the *Gospel of Thomas:* "The Pharisees and the scribes have taken the keys of knowledge and hidden them. They themselves have not entered" (ibid., p. 122). In the *Authoritative Teaching:* "Even the Pagans give charity, and they know that God exists . . . but they have not heard the word" (ibid., p. 282). The God of this world is evil and ignorant, according to *The Second Treatise of the Great Seth.* In contrast, the Logos "received the vision of all things, those which preexist and those which are now and those which will be" (ibid., p. 77). Further: "The invisible Spirit is a psychic and intellectual power, a knowledgeable one and a foreknower" (ibid., p. 383). The function or faculty by means of which *gnōsis* is brought about is personified: it is Epinoia, a transformation of Pronoia, or Providence *(Apocryphon of John).* The world, on the contrary, was created through the union of Ialdabaoth, the demiurge, with Aponoia, the negative counterpart of Ennoia and a symbol of his intellectual blindness.

Knowledge liberates: "The mind of those who have known him shall not perish" (ibid., p. 52); The "thought of Norea" is the knowledge necessary for salvation. The *Testimony of Truth* contrasts knowledge with empty hopes for martyrdom and a fleshly resurrection. The tractate *Marsanes* speaks of the rewards of knowledge. But knowledge is not sufficient: according to the *Apocryphon of John,* Christ is sent down to save humanity by reminding people of their heavenly origin. Only those who possess this knowledge and have lived ascetic lives can return to the realm of light. In fact, says the *Testimony of Truth,* "No one knows the God of truth except the man who will forsake all of the things of the world."

In sum, "Gnosis is not a 'theology of salvation by nature,' as the heresiologists caricature it; it is rather thoroughly conscious of the provisional situation of the redeemed up to the realization of redemption after death." (Rudolph, 1983, p. 117). Similarly, in Mandaean religion (Manda d-Hiia, literally "knowledge of life"), a gnostic sect that survives to the present day in Iraq, knowledge alone does not redeem: the cultic rites, primarily baptism and the "masses for the dead," are necessary for salvation.

But God, according to the gnostics, is the incomprehensible, inconceivable one, who is superior to every thought, "who is over the world," "the one who is ineffable," "the unknowable" (Robinson, 1977, pp. 209, 213, 411).

Greek Fathers. In the third century Clement of Alexandria, "with his conscious use of the concept *gnōsis* for the Christian knowledge of truth, attempts to overcome the breach between faith and knowledge in the Church and not to remain stuck in a mere denial of the claims of the 'false' gnosis" (Rudolph, 1983, p. 16). "Should one say," he writes in *Stromateis* 2.4, "that knowledge is founded on demonstration by a process of reasoning, let him hear that the first principles are incapable of demonstration. . . . Hence, it is thought that the first cause of the universe can be apprehended by faith alone." But Clement's God is as unknowable as that of Plato or Philo Judaeus, who placed him above being. This is also the position of Plotinus, a contemporary of Clement.

In the fourth century at Antioch John Chrysostom wrote on God's incomprehensibility. According to Gregory of Nazianzus God's existence can be inferred from the order of the world, but we cannot know what he is. The motto of Theodoret of Cyrrhus (fourth to fifth century) was "first believe, then understand."

The Desert Fathers, in their simplicity, sometimes resented the intrusion of more sophisticated views from Alexandria or, later, from Cappodocia. In contrast to the newly converted intellectuals who were bringing to Christianity the aristocratic tradition of the pagan teachers, monachism reaffirmed, as the Franciscans were to do in the thirteenth century, the primacy of the unsophisticated, one of the essential teachings of the Gospels. *Libido sciendi* and excessive pretension to wisdom were regarded as temptations of the devil just as were sensuality or ambition. (Brunschwicg, [1927] 1953, p. 107).

In the sixth century a gnostic tendency expressed already in the *Gospel of Philip* was developed by Dionysius the Areopagite, who applied to God all the names the scriptures give him (affirmative theology), but only in order to afterward deny them (negative or apophatic theology). God is beyond affirmation or negation; he is a superbeing (superlative theology). The world is a theophany, our only means of knowing its author. Universal illumination is an immense circulation of love. Knowledge is above every affirmation or negation. This is the mystical ignorance, the supreme degree of knowledge. The other kinds of knowledge are defective, this one is superabundant.

To Maximos the Confessor (seventh century), man in his progress toward God through knowledge only ascends back, in a movement opposite to his fall, toward the eternal idea of himself that, as his cause, has never ceased to exist in God.

Latin Fathers. Among the Latin church fathers in the second and third centuries Tertullian (like Tatian among the Greeks) radically opposed philosophy. He wrote that the desire for knowledge leads to faith. This is perhaps rather simple, but not quite the same as the motto often attributed to him: "Credo quia absurdem."

The Platonic tradition survived and in the fourth and fifth centuries produced the philosophy of Augustine of Hippo, who after hoping to proceed through Manichaeism from reason to faith, always maintained the necessity of the preparatory role of reason but held that reason had also another role to play, subsequent to faith. Thus: "Intellige ut credas, crede ut intelligas." All our knowledge stems from our sensations, which, however, do not teach us the truths. This is done by something in us which is purely intelligible, necessary, motionless, eternal: a divine illumination. To know oneself (as Socrates recommended) is to recognize an image of God, therefore to know God.

Islam. Muḥammad's message presents itself as knowledge, so much so that the times preceding his coming are called the Jāhilīyah ("state of ignorance"). The same idea is found in *Acts of the Apostles* 17:30: "And the times of this ignorance God winked at; but now commandeth all men everywhere to repent." Islam initiated the times of illumination and right knowledge. But when the Muslims encountered the Greek philosophical heritage through Syriac texts, the problem of the relationship between philosophy and the Qur'anic tradition was bound to arise. Some Muslims quoted the Prophet in support of their contention that speculation was one of the duties of the believers; others, on the contrary, maintained that faith should be obedience, not knowledge.

As we know from the Jewish philosopher Maimonides' *Guide for the Perplexed,* "when the Muhammadans began to translate the writings of the Greek philosophers from the Syriac into the Arabic, they likewise translated the criticisms of those philosophers by such Christians as John Philoponus, the commentator of Aristotle" (Gilson, 1937, p. 39). Al-Kindī (ninth century) seems to have found in Philoponus the germ of his notion of a harmony between Greek philosophy and Muslim faith. He suffered under the repression of all philosophical activity ordered by the Abbasid caliph al-Mutawakkil.

According to Abū Bakr al-Rāzī, a tenth-century physician, only philosophy, especially that of the Greek sages, could lead to happiness. For him, there was no possible reconciliation between philosophy and religion.

"Where the revealed truth is, by hypothesis, absolute truth," writes Étienne Gilson, "the only way to save philosophy is to show that its teaching is substantially the same as that of revealed religion" (1937, p. 37). This was the purpose of al-Asha'rī (Baghdad, tenth century), who inaugurated Muslim scholasticism *(kalām)* in the Sunnī tradition, but whose doctrine "is a remarkable instance of what happens to philosophy when it is handled by theologians, according to theological methods, for a theological end" (ibid., p. 39). His contemporary al-Fārābī was a typical representative of the main current in Muslim philosophy: we know everything through a cosmic agent, the Active Intellect, whose final aim is to enable us to know God. Al-Fārābī's tendency culminated in the teachings of the Iranian Ibn Sīnā (Avicenna). Abū Ḥāmid al-Ghazālī (Iran, eleventh century) turned Aristotle's own weapons against the Aristotelianism of al-Fārābī and Ibn Sīnā in order to establish religion—accessible only through mystical knowledge—on the ruins of philosophy.

Faith could, in principle, be based either on authority *(taqlīd)* or on knowledge *(ʿilm)* or on the intuition of the mystic *(aʿyān)*. Islamic mysticism seems to have originated in some form of gnosticism, and in the tenth century Neoplatonism was adapted. Twelver Shiism distinguishes, in its epistemology, two parallel series. On the side of external vision are eye, sight, perception, and sun; on the side of internal vision, heart, intelligence *(ʿaql)*, knowledge *(ʿilm)*, and active intelligence *(ʿaql faʿʿāl)*. This, so far, is the philosophical approach. The prophetic approach considers as its source the Holy Spirit, Gabriel, the angel of revelation, who is distinct from the Active Intellect. But the two modes of perception ultimately converge. This is due, according to the Twelver Shīʿī theoretician Mullā Ṣadrā Shirāzī (seventeenth century), to the existence and activity, half-way between pure sense perception and pure intellection, of a third faculty of knowledge: creative imagination. (Aside from his Aristotelian theory of passive imagination, Ibn Sīnā held another, "Oriental" one, of active imagination, which was to be developed in Suhrawardī's "philosophy of light").

But to return to al-Ghazālī's destruction of philosophy: "There was bound," writes Gilson, "to appear a philosopher who, on the contrary, endeavored to found philosophy on the ruins of religion" (ibid., p. 35). Such was the Andalusian philosopher Ibn Rushd (Averroës, twelfth century). He distinguished between knowledge accessible to the lower classes and interpretations reserved for the philosophical elite. Philosophy was supreme in attaining absolute science and truth; next came theology, the domain of dialectical interpretation and verisimilitude; at the lowest level, religion and faith were adequate for those who needed them. His adversaries accused him of professing the doctrine of double truth. This, according to Gilson, is inaccurate and unfair. Ibn Rushd maintained only that reason's conclusions are necessary *and* that he adhered to faith's opposite teaching. His Latin followers supported his view that philosophy, when given the liberty to follow its own methods, reaches necessary conclusions that are contradictory to the teachings of religion.

The Schoolmen. Scholasticism was largely an answer to the challenge of Ibn Rushd (Averroës); it might also be seen, however, as little more than an obstinate endeavor to solve one problem, the problem of universals. The answer was far from unanimous.

Peter Abelard (eleventh to twelfth centuries) always insisted on the continuity between ancient wisdom, based on the natural usage of reason, and Christian wisdom, which, far from destroying the previous, fulfills it. But he soon reached the conclusion that he had no universal ideas. God alone has. Scientific and philosophical skepticism is compensated for by a theological appeal to the grace of God. Anselm of Canterbury (eleventh century) had written, "For I do not seek to understand that I may believe, but I believe in order to understand. For this also I believe, that unless I believed, I should not understand." Hence his motto: "Fides quaerens intellectum."

Hugh of Saint-Victor (twelfth century) wrote that from the beginning God wished to be neither entirely manifest to human consciousness nor entirely hidden. "If He were entirely hidden, faith would indeed not be added unto knowledge, and lack of faith would be excused on the ground of ignorance. . . . It was necessary that He should conceal Himself, lest He be entirely manifest, so that there might be something which through being known would nourish the heart of man, and again something which through being hidden would stimulate it" (*De sacramentis* 1.3.2). Further: "Faith is a form of mental certitude about absent realities that is greater than opinion and less than knowledge" (ibid., 1.10.2).

The position of the Franciscan Bonaventure (thirteenth century), like that of Abelard, was destructive of natural knowledge. This was a difficulty another Franciscan, John Duns Scotus, endeavored to deal with, but his own doctrine was "the death warrant of early Franciscan epistemology" (Gilson, 1937, p. 59).

The Dominican Albertus Magnus and his disciple Thomas Aquinas (who was almost exactly contemporaneous with Bonaventure) vindicated Aristotle's "abstraction" as a way of knowing God against the "divine illumination" of Augustine, Anselm, and Bonaventure, as well as against the Active Intellect of Ibn Rushd. But in an irenic mood Thomas observed that since God is the ultimate cause, his illumination is implied in abstraction also. Faith differs from knowledge in being determined in part by the choice of the believer, and from opinion in being held without misgiving:

> Faith implies intellectual assent to that which is believed, but there are two ways in which the intellect gives its assent. In the first way, it is moved . . . by the object iself . . . as are conclusions which are known scientifically. In the second way, the intellect gives its assent not because it is convinced by the object itself, but by voluntarily preferring the one alternative to the other. (*Summa theologiae* 2.2.1.4)

Commenting on *James* 2:19 ("Even the demons believe—and shudder"), Thomas further writes:

> The demons are, in a way, compelled to believe by the evidence of signs and so their will deserves no praise for their belief as they are compelled to believe by their natural intellectual acumen. (ibid., 2.2.5.2)

Moreover, while philosophy only teaches about God what is known *per creaturas* (Paul, *Rom.* 1:19), theology also teaches, thanks to revelation, "quod notum est sibi soli" ("what only He himself knows"; ibid., 1.6). Thomas's position has been characterized as intellectualist, fideistic, and voluntarist by John Hick (1966), who attempts to refute it.

William of Ockham (fourteenth century), yet another Franciscan, discusses various philosophical problems as if any theological dogma, held by faith alone, could become the source of philosophical and purely rational conclusions. Intuitive knowledge is self-evident. Not so abstractive knowledge. William denies the existence of ideas representing the genera and the species, and this even in God (thus outstripping Abelard). The universal mystery is but a concrete expression of the supreme mystery of God, a position that anticipates Hume's skepticism.

According to Gregory Palamas (fourteenth century), who lived in Constantinople and was thus outside Latin Scholasticism, knowledge acquired through profane education is not only different from but contrary to veritable, spiritual knowledge (*Triads in Defense of the Holy Hesychasts* 1.1.10).

After the breakdown of medieval philosophy, there seemed to be two ways of saving the Christian faith: either to resort, with Petrarch, Erasmus, and others, to the gospel, the fathers of the church, and the pagan moralists, which might lead to the skepticism of Montaigne (who, nevertheless, practiced Catholicism, to the extent of making a pilgrimage to Our Lady of Loretta), or to resort to mysticism. A mystical tide swept over Europe during the fourteenth and fifteenth centuries. Johannes (Meister) Eckhart's God is not simply beyond the reach of human knowledge, but in a truly Neoplatonic manner escapes all knowledge, including his very own: even if it be true that God eternally expresses himself in an act of self-knowledge, his infinite essence is unfathomable even to himself, for he could not know himself without turning this infinite essence into a definite object of knowledge. "It is only when man reaches that silent wilderness where there is neither Father, nor Son, nor Holy Ghost, that his mystical flight comes to an end, for there lies the source of all that is: beyond God, in the fullness of Godhead" (Gavalda, 1973, p. 111).

An English mystic of the fourteenth century wrote a treatise under the title, inspired by Dionysius the Areopagite, of *The Cloud of Unknowing.* Nicholas of Cusa (fifteenth century) applied Eckhart's theological principles to philosophy. In his *De docta ignorantia,* God is described as the coincidence of opposites and therefore as above both the principle of identity and the principle of contradiction. In short, God is unthinkable. The world was in great danger of becoming as unthinkable as God himself. But, according to Tommaso Campanella, the author of the utopian treatise *The City of the Sun,* an internal sense or intuition always allows us to know things divine.

Copernicus had put an end to geocentrism, but an accommodation between a newer cosmology and an older theology was nevertheless to prevail for a long time to come: Kepler and others saw the Holy Trinity reflected in the solar system, with the sun as God the Father.

Protestantism. In reaction to accomodating tendencies within monachism and Scholasticism, Luther loathed philosophy and ancient culture: reason was "the devil's highest whore"; hence his polemic against Erasmus. Calvin thought that man cannot know God in himself, but only as the Lord revealing himself to men. A Calvinist (as noted by Max Weber), because of his particular view of the relationship between the creator and the creature and of his own "election," would live and work in a certain way: "Puritanism's ethic of trade, which applied to believers and nonbelievers alike, was related to both religious doctrine and pastoral practice. Intense religious education, together with the threat of social ostracism, provided powerful incentives and sanctions" (Reinhard Bendix, *Max Weber: An Intellectual Portrait,* Garden City, N.Y., 1960, p. 91).

To combat Protestantism, the Roman Catholic church took an obscurantist stance, forbidding the reading of the Bible in translation, while it also attempted to reinforce its doctrines by the institution of catechism. Ignorance could be considered culpable, and a person could, "like a diseased limb . . . [be] cut off and separated by his ignorance and sin" (Miguel de Cervantes, *Don Quixote,* chap. 40). But ignorance could also be an excuse if it be, in terms of Catholic theology, "invincible," that is, if the agent is wholly unaware of his obligations or of the implications of a specific act (see G. H. Joyce, "Invincible Ignorance," in *Encyclopaedia of Religion and Ethics,* edited by James Hastings, vol. 7, Edinburgh, 1914).

For Pascal, there is an order of the spirit above that of the flesh; but above the order of the spirit there is that of love: "Le coeur a des raisons que la raison ne connaît pas" ("The heart has its reasons, which reason does not know"). And: "It was not then right that [Christ] should appear in a manner manifestly divine, and completely capable of convincing all men [through reason] . . . and thus [He was] willing to appear openly to those who seek Him with all their heart" (*Pensées* 430).

Cartesianism. Descartes's doctrine was "a direct answer to Montaigne's scepticism" and "a recklessly conducted experiment to see what becomes of human knowledge when moulded into conformity with the pattern of mathematical evidence: he had the merit of realizing that two sciences—geometry and algebra—hitherto considered as distinct were but one: why not go at once to the limit and say that all sciences are one? Such was Descartes's final illumination" (Gilson, 1937, pp. 127, 133). After confessing in the *Discourse on Method* that one could not talk of things sacred without assistance from heaven, he showed in the *Meditations* "the way to attain knowledge of God with more ease and certainty than that of things of this world" (ibid., p. 137).

Leibniz, Spinoza, and Malebranche were Cartesians: from God proceeded the unknown force that linked mind to matter and matter to mind. According to Spinoza, the mysticism of literal faith belongs to a kind of inferior knowledge that dissolves in the light of intelligence. Above imagination there is reason, but above reason, intellectual intuition, which leads to the unique and absolute truth, God.

Malebranche, although holding that we know everything in God, still believed in the existence of a concrete and actually subsisting world of matter. Not so Berkeley. Finally, Hume said that if we have no adequate idea of "power" or "efficacy," no notion of causality that we can apply to matter, where could we get one that we would apply to God?

For Jakob Boehme, knowledge was a way of salvation. Under the influence of Boehme and Paracelsus, Christian esotericism tried more and more to unite faith and knowledge. [*See* Esotericism.] But in eighteenth-century Europe, particularly in France, Germany, and England, the pursuit of happiness tended to prevail over concern for salvation; besides, unhappiness was regarded as due to a lack of knowledge or to erroneous judgment, and it was consequently believed that the progress of reason would bring happiness. For Leibniz, evil results from ignorance. Locke entitled a book *The Reasonableness of Christianity* (1695).

None of the German *Aufklärer* was inclined toward atheism; each tried to fit God into a rational scheme of things. For Samuel Reimarus, whose work was published by G. E. Lessing, religion did not proceed from a letter, Bible, or Qur'ān, dictated by some God; God was the presence, in our soul, of universal, eternal reason.

It was thought that one should stop bothering about what cannot be known and that morality could be free of any transcendent element and based on nothing more than the self-knowledge of conscience. If all that seemed superstitious in the beliefs of the Roman church and reformed religion were purged, only the unknown supreme being would remain. Pierre Bayle paved the way for Holbach, Voltaire, Shaftesbury, Locke, Montesquieu, Rousseau, and, eventually, Kant.

While the Encyclopedists were trying to apply the methods of the sciences to the improvement of the practical arts and of social institutions, Rousseau's opposition exploded like a bomb: his philosophy was to dominate the period before the French Revolution and the years that followed its failure. God had created man not only innocent but ignorant, wishing thereby to "preserve him from knowledge just as a mother would wrench a dangerous weapon from the hands of her child" (*Discours sur les sciences et les arts,* quoted in Zaehner, 1970, p. 330). "Reason too often deceives us," says the Vicaire Savoyard, but "conscience never deceives" (*Émile,* quoted in Brunschwicg, 1927, p. 271). Conscience is the soul's divine instinct. Such was the religion of instinct, already advocated by Swiss pietists. Bolingbroke had written that we cannot know what God is, only that there is a God—which was, more or less, Hume's position.

Kant. What was Hume, after all, asks Gilson (1937, p. 223), but a sad Montaigne? Hume's voice was soon to be heard by Immanuel Kant. So long as our mind applies itself to the mere mental presentation of possible objects, it does not form concepts of things, but mere ideas; these do not constitute scientific knowledge, but that illusory speculation that we call metaphysics. If reason does not lead to God, if, given Hume's skepticism, reason is destructive of the very principles of philosophical knowledge and morality, Rousseau's passionate appeal to feeling and to moral conscience, against the natural blindness of reason, is to Kant the revelation of a wholly independent and self-contained order of morality. But to posit God as required by the fact of morality is not the same as to know that God exists.

Maine de Biran, when young, surmised that the origin of belief lay in the sense of smell, but in his old age he wrote that Augustine, when meditating on his relation to God, found or proved that there might be a subtler, more refined organization above the coarse one of our sense (Brunschwicg, 1927, p. 618).

Hegel was in very much the same situation as Nicholas of Cusa in the fifteenth century. There had to be contradiction everywhere in the universe for the contradictions of philosophy to give a true picture of reality: this was another form of learned ignorance. But finally Hegelianism, by confining reason to the sphere of pure science, enslaved philosophy to the blind tyranny of the will (Gilson, 1937, p. 252).

Comte. At a primary level of each social group there is, according to Comte, a definite state of intellectual knowledge; at a secondary level, determined by the first, is a specific form of government; finally, a third element flows from the first two: a specific form of civilization. "We have only to reverse this doctrine to get Marxism," remarks Gilson (1937, p. 257). In his synthesis of positivism with the Hegelian tradition, Marx made possible a sociology of knowledge (actually founded by Karl Mannheim), a science that tries to explain ideas (including religion) as the outcome of social conditions.

By driving metaphysics out of its final position, Comte had ensured the uniformity of human knowledge. But science had failed to provide mankind with a systematic view of the world. By making love the ultimate foundation of positivism Comte was repeating in his own way Kant's famous step of decreeing the primacy of practical reason. Condemnation of metaphysics in the name of science invariably culminates in the capitulation of science to some irrational element (Gilson, 1937, p. 298).

Eighteenth-century rationalism believed it could eliminate the religious tradition simply by determining its human conditions through historical and psychological observation. The nineteenth century, on the contrary, established a psychology and a sociology of religion that, far from eliminating their object, posited its objective reality through the very principles of their method. This reality is attained by intuition (Léon Brunschwicg, *Les étapes de la philosophie mathématique,* Paris, 1912, p. 432).

The Protestant Perspective. The problem of religious knowledge has been dealt with extensively from the Protestant point of view by Douglas Clyde Macintosh (1940). He distinguishes not only between realism and idealism but between dualism and monism: "The object consciously experienced and the object existing independently of experience are, according to dualism, two wholly different existences, and, according to monism, existentially one, at least in part and sufficiently for some knowledge of the independently existing reality to be humanly possible" (Macintosh, 1940, p. vii). After excluding from the sphere of knowledge mysticism, ecstasy, the love-dialogue with God, and whatever is redolent of monasticism as "extreme monistic realism," Macintosh proceeds to an examination of "monistic idealism in religion."

Monism. Under the rubric "Religious Psychologism" Macintosh deals with the views of Hegel and others. Hegel's definition of religion is "the Divine Spirit's knowledge of itself through the mediation of a finite spirit." For Feuerbach religion is man's earliest, indirect form of self-knowledge. For Édouard Leroy dogmas are concerned primarily with conduct rather than with pure reflective knowledge. Barukh Spinoza wrote in his *Tractatus Theologico-Politicus* that faith does not demand that dogmas shall be true, but that they shall be pious—such as will stir up the heart to obey. For Durkheim, science refuses to grant religion its right to dogmatize upon the nature of things. For Freud, insofar as religion conflicts with science or would offer a substitute for scientific investigation of the cause and cure of human ills, it is open to criticism. Macintosh would strongly maintain that any tenable religious worldview must do full justice to science, including whatever scientific knowledge there may be in the field of religion, but such a worldview has the right to supplement scientific knowledge through a reasonable formulation of religious faith based upon the tested value of spiritual life.

Under "Philosophical Antecedents of Humanism" Macintosh deals with John Dewey, whose functionalism implies a behaviorist theory of thinking and knowing, which crowds out of the definition of knowing all elements of mental contemplation and rules out as "nonempirical" not only the idea of a transcendent God but even that of a persisting metaphysical ego as the individual subject of experience.

Under "Theological Antecedents of Humanism" Macintosh cites the work of George Burman Foster, whose early thought inclined to a dualistic theory of religious knowledge according to which the independently real but theoretically unknowable religious object was made the subject matter of judgments of religious faith and feeling, an attitude obviously inspired by Kant's. But Foster came to feel that he must give up the dualistic supernaturalism of all doctrines of a purely transcendent God.

Under "Humanism, Ecclesiastical and Other" Macintosh cites, among others, William Brown, who wrote that the world's savior, God, is knowledge, that the Gods of all the supernaturalistic interpretations of religion are so many creations of the dominant master class, and that "my God, Nature, is a triune divinity—matter, form, and motion—an impersonal, unconscious, non-moral being." Brown was expelled from the Episcopal church for espousing these ideas.

Under "Logical Idealism" Macintosh ranks Georg Simmel, Wilhelm Windelband, George Santayana, Benedetto Croce, and Giovanni Gentile. While the religious man, wrote Simmel, must be assured that God is, even if he may be in doubt as to what God is, the typical modern man knows very well what God is, but is unable to say that God is. Similarly, to Dean Inge the important question is not whether God exists but what we mean when we speak of God—the value of values, the supreme value. One could add Léon Brunschwicg, for whom God is the formal ideal of knowledge (as well as the intentional value of actions). Such a philosophy of religion is common to Platonism and Christianity.

In Croce's fusion of logical with psychological idealism, to the extent that religion as cognition intuits what is beautiful or thinks what is true, it is nothing beyond aesthetics or logic: to the extent that it intuits as beautiful what is not, or thinks to be true what is not true, it is not valid, theoretically considered. Gentile's attitude, even more than Croce's, is absolute idealism without the Absolute.

Under "Critical Monistic Realism" Macintosh endorses a form of religious knowledge that includes adequate and adequately critical (i.e., logical) certitude of the validity of ideals and values considered as divine (i.e., as worthy of universal human devotion). He cites as predecessors Friedrich von Hügel, Henri Bergson, and a few others. Von Hügel was convinced that we have real experience and knowledge of objects and that in religion in its higher reaches there is real contact with superhuman reality. For Bergson, the true metaphysical method is an immediate intuition or vision of reality, and in religious mysticism there is such a thing. According to Macintosh, "Bergson carried the needed reaction against intellectualism and rationalism to an equally objectionable irrationalism and anti-conceptualism." (Macintosh, 1940, p. 181).

"Empirical Theology" is the title under which Macintosh presents his own program. Whereas scholastics, he writes, defined theology as the science of God, a deductive science proceeding from assured premises, some theologians have occasionally claimed to proceed by the inductive method. Macintosh meets such objections as that of Georg Wobbermin, who as a confirmed Kantian dualist cannot but feel that all such terms as "empirical theology" involve a contradiction in terms. Macintosh finally formulates thirteen laws of empirical theology. But he never gives an example of what he means by "a truly reasonable belief."

Dualism. According to dualism, the divine reality is never experienced immediately, never perceived directly. How then can there by any knowledge? There is reason to question the conclusiveness of the so-called proofs of God's existence, the ontological, cosmological, anthropological, theological arguments. These proofs will be replaced by argument from moral values (as in Kant) or religious values.

But this has in fact led to agnosticism (a term coined in 1870 by Thomas Huxley), notably with Charles Darwin, who wrote that "the whole subject is beyond the scope of man's intellect," and with Herbert Spencer, the prophet of agnostic religion. For the agnostic, only the inductive method and the positive results of the empirical sciences can serve as an adequate check upon the too easy dogmatizing of theology and the speculative vagaries of metaphysics.

Friedrich Schleiermacher, "the father of modern theology," oscillated between pantheism and dualistic epistemological agnosticism. Theology, he thought, can only be a description of subjective states of mind. Albert Ritschl was, along with Schleiermacher, the most influential Protestant theologian of the late nineteenth century, he reacted vigorously against intellectualism in favor of the autonomy of religious consciousness. He found Schleiermacher guilty of the old error of making the doctrine of God a natural, as distinct from a revealed, theology, but in both cases, "religious knowledge" is distinguished from science, philosophy, and theoretical knowledge generally. "But," Macintosh asks (1940, p. 247), "how can be justified the use of the term religious knowledge as applied to the God and Father of our Lord Jesus Christ?" It should be recognized that the intuition in question is not perceptual but imaginal, that so-called religious knowledge is not knowledge in the scientific sense of empirically verified judgments and so on.

Adolf Harnack agreed with Ritschl that Christianity is essentially ethico-religious and experiential rather than metaphysically speculative and intellectualistic. Ritschlians have much to say about revelation, but the concept is left vague from the epistemological point of view.

Wilhelm Herrmann was quite as suspicious of the influence of mysticism as of the encroachments of metaphysics. For Julius Kaftan, Kant is the philosopher of Protestantism, as Aristotle is the philosopher of Catholicism. The object of religious knowledge is not religion, but God; theology can never be a science of the objects of faith, however, only a science of faith itself. Religious knowledge, as opposed to knowledge in the theoretical sense, presupposes an authentic revelation of God.

Wobbermin agreed with Ritschl in excluding from theology all the mixed articles in which the faith-knowledge of God was combined with and modified by the now discredited "natural" knowledge of God. "But," Macintosh concludes (ibid., p. 278), "no consideration of the value of a belief can establish it as knowledge in the absence of any possibility of 'first-hand experience.'"

Under "Critical Rationalism" Macintosh lists the Religionsgeschichtliche Schule, which gave promise of liberating modern theology from its perpetual oscillation between helpless agnosticism and the sheer dogmatism of exclusive supernaturalism. The comparative historical study of religions shows that the uniqueness of Christianity consists not in the manner of its proof, as resting upon a supernatural revelation, but in its content: an inclusive supernaturalism would acknowledge revelation and miracle in all religions. (How is religious knowledge possible? A "fourth critique," after Kant, should investigate the *a priori* conditions of religious experience.)

Rudolf Otto assumed that besides *Glaube,* which apprehends the rationally necessary idea of an ultimate reality, there is also *Ahnung,* a non-rational foundation for religion in human nature, the instinctive sense of a mysterious reality *(das Heilige),* transcendent and wholly other.

Under "Religious Pragmatism" Macintosh ranks, of course, William James, but also his less well-known precursor A. J. Earl Balfour, who wrote that we assent to a creed merely because of a subjective need for it, and who predicted the advent of a critical science of religion whereby what valid religious knowledge there may be will be given the universal form of an empirical science.

Under "Reactionary Irrationalism" Macintosh analyzes Søren Kierkegaard, Miguel de Unamuno, and the theologians of crisis. This tendency began as a response to the monistic idealism of Hegel. Kierkegaard rebelled against Hegel's equation of actuality and the rational Idea. For Kierkegaard, Christian faith is always contrary to reason: "The absurd is the proper object of faith, and the only thing that lets itself be believed."

Similarly, for Unamuno, reason and faith are enemies, and reason is the enemy of life. His despair of finding any theoretical defense of the Roman Catholic system of dogma led him to underestimate the arguments vindicating a Christlike God and the immortality of the soul.

Karl Barth. The theology of crisis in Germany was a consequence of World War I. But Karl Barth was also heir to Kant, Schleiermacher, Troeltsch, Herrmann, Otto, Kierkegaard, and Feuerbach. He condemned modern liberalism for its emphasis upon divine immanence, for "except in His Word, God is never for us in the world." As Kierkegaard insisted, following *Ecclesiastes,* "God is in Heaven, and thou upon Earth." The image of God, Barth argued, has been wholly destroyed in man by sin. The Bible is to be read in the old way, namely, not to find what men thought about God, but to find what God says to us. "This is," writes Macintosh, "pretty much the old externally authoritarian, irrationalistic theology of the Evangelical Calvinism of two or three hundred years ago."

Barth, hearkening back to Luther as well as to Calvin, emphasizes the distinction between faith, which he embraces, and religion, which he almost identifies with Roman Catholicism and abhors. In an essay on Barth's theology, Brand Blanshard offers this critique ("Critical Reflections on Karl Barth," in *Faith and the Philosophers,* ed. John Hick, Ithaca, N.Y., 1957):

> Faith, according to Barth, is itself the highest knowledge; but this knowledge differs completely from anything else which man calls knowledge, not only in its content, but in its modes of origin and form as well. (p. 159)
>
> That revelation is to be considered a kind of knowledge is detected by his entitling one of his books *Knowledge of God.* But he holds, with Ayer and Carnap, that the attempt by rational thought to go beyond nature to the supernatural is inevitably defeated, though of course he draws a different conclusion from the defeat. He concludes that since we cannot reach a knowledge of God through radical means, we must do so through non-natural means; the positivists conclude from the same premises that the attempt itself is meaningless. (p. 170)
>
> In the face of all the projectionists who, like Freud and Feuerbach, would make religious "knowledge" an imaginative fulfilling of need, of all the pragmatists who, like Dewey, would make it merely a means to human betterment, of all the rationalists who, like Hegel, would make it philosophy half grown-up, of all the psychologists who, with Schleiermacher and Ritschl, would make it essentially a matter of feeling, Barth proclaimed a full-fledged return to the theology of the Reformation, in which God is set over against the world as 'wholly other,' known indeed to faith, but unknowable, unapproachable and unimaginable by any natural faculties. (p. 160)

Bultmann and Jaspers. Aside from Barth's (or Luther's) distinction between religion and faith, Rudolf Bultmann discerns within faith a core of message *(kērygma)* that is to be extracted from the letter of the Bible through *"Entmythologisierung."* The Bible failed to eliminate philosophy, which tends to make the *kērygma* a reality subject to reason's grasp. Our knowledge of God does not refer to his essence, but to his will. God is neither in nature nor in history and cannot be attained there. The biblical authors are not completely innocent of the sin of natural man; they sometimes understood God's word through a naive kind of rationalism, mythological rationalism, which is as sinful as scientific rationalism. Serious, cultivated believers reject that popular mythology. They can accept science and technology since they affirm that science and faith belong to two wholly different orders. But although they discard magic, spiritism, and all forms of pagan miracles, they nevertheless accept Christian mythology, except in its most objectionable instances. Contrary to Barth's contention, faith should not utilize any philosophy. All philosophies are human projections of God, of man, and of the world and are as such incompatible with faith. It was the mistake of the *philosophia perennis* to limit itself to the domain of knowledge and objectivity. The destruction of metaphysics that was attempted by Heidegger helped Bultmann to reject all *Selbstsicherung*.

Karl Jaspers's philosophy appears to be "the last word of irrationalism," the last stage in the great movement of reaction against *Aufklärung*. Remembering Kant's motto: "I must suppress knowledge in order to make room for faith," Jaspers finally yields to the prestige of the ineffable. However, he expresses his philosophical irritation about the theologians' claim that the Christian faith is something absolute. Christians should give up the idea that Jesus was the one incarnation of transcendence; they should accept the fact that dogmas are symbols, ciphers, lacking all objective value, and they should renounce their claim to the monopoly of truth.

Jaspers's position is extreme, and exceptional in Germany. The general difference in philosophy between Germany and France is clearly formulated by Raymond Aron:

> German philosophers, especially in the last century, often belonged to a milieu of civil servants, chiefly clerical. Even when turned miscreants, they retain a sense of religion as a supreme form of spiritual aspiration; tending to a non-dogmatic religiosity, they distinguish between science, objectively true, and religion, humanly valuable although not liable to demonstration or refutation. This godless religiosity implies acknowledging the role of feeling, irreducible to that of reason. In France, the direct rivalry of religion and philosophy prompts both of them to thorough and contradictory claims. Profane philosophy (at least in its most characteristic exponents) is anti-Christian, even anti-religious. It is rationalistic and scientistic. (Aron, 1983, p. 135)

The Roman Catholic Perspective. The Roman Catholic point of view, in its most conservative aspect, was put forward by Étienne Gilson in many admirable books, especially in *Réalisme thomiste et critique de la connaissance* (1939). Religion justifies philosophy, which in turn illuminates religion through intelligence. Gilson writes on Bergson in *La philosophie et la théologie* (Paris, 1960):

> Bergson had a clear idea of two types of knowledge, that of intelligence, of which the purest expression is science, and that of intuition, akin to instinct, which becomes explicitly conscious in metaphysics. If questioned about faith, he could not for one instant imagine that it was, properly speaking, knowledge. The word "faith" suggested to him primarily the notion of obedience. To accept a number of doctrinal positions as true although accessible neither to intelligence nor to intuition, out of sheer submission to an external authority, was all this philosopher would resign himself to. (p. 177)

Gilson sums up his own attitude as follows:

> There is on the one hand scientific progress, on the other hand Christian faith, incarnated in the Church and defined by tradition. To speak summarily but not inexactly, there arises from the contact between the two a third kind of knowledge, distinct from both but akin to both, whose data are provided by science but whose main object is to achieve as complete a comprehension as possible of the Christian revelation received by faith. (p. 233)

But Roman Catholics are far from unanimous. They never were. They disagreed in the Middle Ages, as we have seen, as to whether we know truth in the light of our own intelligence, or in a divine light added to that of the intellect. In our own times we have witnessed the painful controversies surrounding Maurice Blondel's obstinate attempt at deducing the supernatural from the natural and Teilhard de Chardin's fusion—or confusion—of cosmology with Christology, of evolution with revelation. Both incurred anathema. Ever since the Counter-Reformation the church has been trying to combat Protestantism, or to catch up with it, not only (as we saw) by instituting catechism, but also by encouraging biblical studies. It has also tried to counter Kant's influence by reviving Thomism; by condemning, in the ninteenth century, all forms of fideism; and by condemning modernism in the early twentieth century, only to yield to liberal tendencies at the Second Vatican Council.

Roman Catholicism, in its existentialist variety, is represented by Henry Duméry, who also owes much to Blondel—and to Spinoza and Plotinus. He distinguishes, in his *Philosophie de la religion* (Paris, 1957), different noetic levels; he speaks of "a specified intelligible plane, halfway between God and empirical consciousness"—perhaps what he calls "le troisième genre de connaissance"—and treats faith as "un object spécifique, irréductible à tout autre." He speaks of "mentalité projective," "intentionalité vécue," "visée de transcendance." Although recognizing that the philosophy of religion should apply to all known religions, he bases his own attempt exclusively on Christianity. One example may be quoted from his *Phénoménologie de la religion* (Paris, 1958): "It would be erroneous to objectify the typical existence of the Virgin Mary onto a profane—nay, profaning—plane of registry office" (p. 57). Duméry, a Roman Catholic priest, has been granted permission to relinquish priesthood.

In the Anglican church the situation is different, as

suggested by the appointment as bishop of Durham in 1984 of David Jenkins, who had declared that teachings concerning the virgin birth and the resurrection might be more symbolic than literal, and that a person could be a good Christian even while doubting the divinity of Christ.

Epistemology. In England, modern epistemology is represented by, among others, Bertrand Russell and A. J. Ayer. In *Mysticism and Logic* (London, 1918) Russell defines the mystical impulse in philosophers such as Heraclitus, Plato, Spinoza, and Hegel as the "belief in the possibility of a way of knowledge which may be called revelation or insight or intuition, as contrasted with sense, reason and analysis, which are regarded as blind guides leading to the morass of illusion" (p. 16). But he calmly remarks that what is knowledge is science, and what is not science is not knowledge. In *The Problem of Knowledge* (1956) Ayer simply ignores religion altogether, as does Rudolf Carnap in his work. Both Ayer and Carnap belong to the logical positivist movement, based on the analysis of language, which started in Vienna with Ludwig Wittgenstein, who later migrated to England and was in close contact with Russell. But Wittgenstein's attitude toward religion was far less simple than that of those he influenced. Admittedly, he thought that religious creeds, in contradistinction to scientific concepts, are not more or less probable hypotheses: never have propositions pertaining to religion expressed positive possibilities. Their whole significance stems from their place in human existence; science and religion are entirely separate; between them there can be no conflict or relation whatsoever. But he writes in his *Tractatus Logico-Philosophicus* (6.54): "He who understands me finally recognizes my propositions as senseless, when he has climbed out through them, on them, over them," a position uncannily reminiscent of Mahāyāna Buddhism. Finally, Wittgenstein writes: "Whereof one cannot speak, thereof one must be silent" (ibid., 7.0). However, we read in *Notebooks 1914–1916* that "to believe in God means understanding the question of life, means seeing that life makes sense" (11 June 1916), which amounts to what has been called Wittgensteinian fideism.

A brave attempt at overcoming positivism was made by Michael Polanyi, another scientist and philosopher, who migrated from central Europe (in his case, Hungary) to England. In his great book *Personal Knowledge* (London, 1958), he refutes the Laplacean ideal of objective knowledge and calls for a return to Augustine in order to restore the balance of our cognitive powers and to recognize belief once more as the source of all knowledge. He tries to define a form of knowledge neither purely objective nor purely subjective, namely, personal knowledge: "Into every act of knowing there enters a tacit and passionate contribution of the person knowing what is being known, and . . . this coefficient is no mere imperfection but a necessary component of all knowledge" (p. 312). Unfortunately, in the vast field of religion he only takes into account Christianity. Even more narrowly, he subscribes to the following statement by Paul Tillich: "Knowledge of revelation, although it is mediated primarily through historical events, does not imply factual assertion, and it is therefore not exposed to critical analysis by historical research. Its truth is to be judged by criteria which lie within the dimension of revelatory knowledge" (*Systematic Theology*, London, 1953, vol. 1, p. 144). The phrase "revelatory knowledge" begs the whole question of the nature of religious knowledge.

Yet another scientist and philosopher, Alfred North Whitehead, who migrated to the United States from England, dealt with the problem of religious knowledge, especially in his book *Religion in the Making* (1928) and again in his great *Process and Reality* (1929), in which we read: "Religion is the translation of general ideas into particular thoughts, emotions, and purposes; it is directed to the end of stretching individual interest beyond its delf-defeating particularity. Philosophy finds religion, and modifies it" (*Process and Reality*, New York, 1978, p. 15). On Christianity, his position is summed up as follows:

> The notion of God as the 'unmoved mover' is derived from Aristotle, at least as far as Western thought is concerned. The notion of God as 'eminently real' is a favourite doctrine of Christian theology. The combination of the two into the doctrine of an aboriginal, eminently real, transcendent creator, at whose fiat the world came into being, and whose imposed will it obeys, is the fallacy which has infused tragedy into the histories of Christianity and of Mahometanism. (ibid., p. 342.)

Whitehead's own ideas, albeit somewhat obscure, have produced process theology.

Research has recently been started to try to locate, in the brain, a specific area of the mythical function (Eugene G. d'Aquili and Charles D. Laughlin, Jr., "The Neurobiology of Myth and Ritual," in *The Spectrum of Ritual*, ed. Eugene d'Aquili et al., 1979); and the symbolic approach has brought forth a new discipline: theolinguistics (J. P. Van Noppen, *Theolinguistics*, Brussels, 1981). [*See* Neuroepistemology.]

In the fervent, adventurous notebooks of a modern gnostic, Simone Weil, published posthumously under the title *La connaissance surnaturelle* (Paris, 1950), we read: "Intelligence remains absolutely faithful to itself in recognizing the existence, in the soul, of a faculty superior to itself and leading thought above itself. This faculty is supernatural love" (p. 80). And: "Since evil is the root of mystery, suffering is the root of knowledge" (p. 43).

Two recent writers, Terence Penelhum and John Hick, have developed the idea of faith as a form of knowledge. "There is," writes the latter, "in cognition of every kind an unresolved mystery" (Hick, 1966, p. 118). "But," writes Basil Mitchell, "there is an important sense of 'know' in which even the 'great religious figures' cannot be said to know that there is a God (let alone the Christian doctrines) so long as it remains a genuine possibility that some non-theistic interpretation of their experience might turn out to be true" (Mitchell, 1973, p. 112). However, as Nicholas Lash writes: "The possibility of theological discourse constituting a mode of rational knowledge could only be excluded if religious faith could be shown to be in no sense experimental knowledge of its object" (Lash, in Peacocke, 1981, p. 304).

[*See also* Truth; Epistemology; *and* Philosophy, *article on* Philosophy and Religion. *For further discussion of the Western opposition of knowledge to faith, see* Faith.]

BIBLIOGRAPHY

Aron, Raymond. *Mémoires: Cinquante ans de réflexion politique.* Paris, 1983.

Bendix, Reinhard. *Max Weber: An Intellectual Portrait.* Garden City, N.Y., 1960.

Biardeau, Madeleine. *Théorie de la connaissance et philosophie de la parole dans la brahmanisme classique.* Paris, 1964.

Brunschwicg, Léon. *Le progrès de la conscience dans la philosophie occidentale* (1927). 2d ed. Paris, 1953.

Bugault, Guy. *La notion de 'prajña' ou de sapience selon les perspectives du 'mahāyāna.'* Paris, 1968.

Gavalda, Berthe. *Les grands textes de la pensée chrétienne.* Paris, 1973.

Gilson, Étienne. *The Unity of Philosophical Experience.* New York, 1937.

Gilson, Étienne. *La philosophie et la théologie.* Paris, 1960. Translated by Cécile Gilson as *The Philosopher and Theology* (New York, 1962).

Grousset, René. *Les philosophies indiennes.* 2 vols. Paris, 1931.

Gruenwald, Ithamar. "Knowledge and Vision." *Israel Oriental Studies* 3 (1973): 63ff.

Hick, John. *Faith and Knowledge.* 2d ed. Ithaca, N.Y., 1966.

Hultkrantz, Åke. "The Concept of the Supernatural in Primal Religion." *History of Religions* 22 (February 1983): 231–253.

Kahn, Charles H. *The Art and Thought of Heraclitus.* Cambridge, 1979.

Macintosh, Douglas C. *The Problem of Religious Knowledge.* London, 1940.

Mitchell, Basil. *The Justification of Religious Belief.* New York, 1973.

Peacocke, A. R., ed. *The Sciences and Theology in the Twentieth Century.* London, 1981.

Robinson, James M., ed. *The Nag Hammadi Library in English.* San Francisco, 1977.

Rudolph, Kurt. *Gnosis.* Translated by Robert M. Wilson. San Francisco, 1983.

Swinburne, Richard. *Faith and Reason.* Oxford, 1981.

Zaehner, R. C. *Concordant Discord.* Oxford, 1970.

JACQUES DUCHESNE-GUILLEMIN

KNOX, JOHN (c. 1514–1572), Protestant reformer of Scotland. Born in Haddington, Knox likely studied at Saint Andrews under the nominalist theologian John Majors. He was ordained to the priesthood at the age of twenty-five, held the post of apostolical notary, and served as a tutor to the children of gentlemen in East Lothian.

Knox was a rugged political fighter, but he was also, as his biographer Jasper Ridley writes, a person of "profound and sincere religious sensitivity." The source of this sensitivity was the Bible, which he apparently studied with devotion early in life. When dying, he asked his wife to "go read where I cast my first anchor" in the seventeenth chapter of *John.*

Knox, converted to Protestantism by the preaching of Thomas Gwilliam in Lothian, was confirmed in the Protestant movement by his association with George Wishart. After the burning of Wishart, Protestants took the castle at Saint Andrews and the life of Cardinal Beaton, Scotland's Catholic leader. Knox, under threat of persecution, moved from place to place, eventually taking refuge in the castle with his students. Protestant leaders urged him to "take up the public office and charge of preaching," a role that would identify him with Gwilliam, John Rough, and Wishart. He was reluctant to accept the vocation, as he emphasized in his *History,* but having done so, he filled it with remarkable skill and became a leading spokesman of the Protestant cause.

The castle fell to the French fleet in 1547, and Knox became a galley slave until his release was arranged by the English. For five years (1549–1554) he was active in the Puritan wing of the English Reformation movement. With the accession of Mary, Knox left England and was named the minister of the church of the English exiles in Frankfurt. The exiles soon divided over the use of *The Book of Common Prayer,* whether to revise it or to substitute a new liturgy. As a result of the controversy, Knox left Frankfurt for Geneva, where he became pastor of the English congregation. Knox's stay there was significant for the consolidation of his own theology, as he was impressed by Calvin's achievement in establishing the Reformed church in Geneva.

Knox visited Scotland briefly in the autumn of 1555 to encourage the Protestant leadership. When the religious and political struggle came to a crisis in 1559, Knox left Geneva to assume a leading role in the Protestant cause. His powerful preaching, political wisdom, and determination contributed significantly to the Scottish Parliament's action in 1560 abolishing the papal jurisdiction and approving a confession of faith as a basis for belief in Scotland.

In addition to his public leadership, Knox had a role in three major documents of the Scottish Reformation of 1560. The Confession of Faith was written in four days by John Knox and five others. It conveys the intensity of the moment and the personal quality of the confession of believers who were putting their lives at risk for their faith. It has been described as "the warm utterance of a people's heart." It states the Protestant faith in plain language and is more pictorial and historical than abstract in style.

The *First Book of Discipline* was written by Knox in collaboration with four others. It is notable not only for its reform of the church but also for its vision of universal compulsory education up to the university level and for its provisions for relief of the poor. The book was never adopted by Parliament because its members did not want the wealth of the church expended on Knox's "devout imaginings."

Knox's third contribution to the official documents of the church was *The Book of Common Order,* which Knox and his collaborators had written in Frankfurt and used in Geneva. It now became the worship book of the Church of Scotland.

Knox disavowed speculative theology, but his writings, filling six volumes, were as powerful as his preaching. "The First Blast of the Trumpet against the Monstrous Regiment of Women" (1558), although dealing with the situation in Scotland, caused him difficulty with Elizabeth I of England when he needed her support. Knox's *History of the Reformation of Religion within the Realm of Scotland* is a history of the man and the cause and a justification of both. Other notable writings include "Letter of Wholesome Counsel" and "Treatise on Predestination."

Knox was a remarkable human being. Scholars have debated whether or not he was a man of courage, perhaps because of his own misgivings. He took precautions, but he did "march toward the sound of guns." Scholars have accused him of demagoguery, but a supporter declared that he was able in one hour to do more for his contemporaries than five hundred trumpets continually blustering in their ears. He believed that he had been called by God, that through his life God's purposes were being fulfilled, and that the Reformation was God's cause and must triumph.

Knox's biographer, Jasper Ridley, points to the Church of Scotland as Knox's greatest achievement. Catholicism would probably have been overthrown without Knox, but it is due to Knox that the Church of Scotland was Calvinist rather than Anglican, and that after his death it became presbyterian rather than episcopal. Knox also contributed significantly to the struggle for human freedom. His emphasis on the responsibility not only of lower magistrates but of individuals to resist evil rulers, and the dramatic way he expressed this idea in his own life, especially in his encounters with Queen Mary, and in his sermons and writings cannot be overestimated. His Presbyterian and Puritan followers made these ideas part of the tradition of public and political life in the English-speaking world.

BIBLIOGRAPHY

Cheyne, Alec. Review of *The Scottish Reformation* by Gordon Donaldson. *Scottish Journal of Theology* 16 (March 1963): 78–88.

McEwen, James S. *The Faith of John Knox.* London, 1961.

Percy, Eustace. *John Knox.* London, 1937.

Ridley, Jasper. *John Knox.* New York, 1968.

Shaw, Duncan, ed. *John Knox: A Quartercentenary Reappraisal.* Edinburgh, 1975.

JOHN H. LEITH

KŌBEN (1173–1232), also known as Myoē Shōnin; an important figure in the Kamakura-period revival of Nara Buddhism. This revival consisted of criticism of the exclusivist doctrines of the Pure Land and Nichiren sects and a renewed interest in, and devotion to, the historic Buddha, Śākyamuni. As a prominent Kegon (Chin., Hua-yen) mentor, Kōben attempted to introduce Tantric elements into Kegon practice, as evidenced by his compilation of Kegon-Tantric *(gommitsu)* rituals and consecrations. He also worked for the revival of traditional Kegon learning, emphasizing the study of Fa-tsang's works rather than those of Ch'eng-kuan, whose doctrines were transmitted within the Shingon tradition, and the cultivation of Kegon visualization meditations. [*See the biography of Fa-tsang.*]

Kōben was born in the village of Yoshiwara, on the Ishigaki estate, in Arita-koori in the province of Kii (present-day Wakayama Prefecture). In the fall of 1181, following the death of his parents, the boy was sent to the Jingoji monastic complex, located on Mount Takao north of Kyoto, where he began his studies under the master Mongaku. Kōben subsequently studied Tantric doctrines (*mikkyō*) and Fa-tsang's *Wu-chiao chang.* At the age of fifteen (sixteen by Asian reckoning), Kōben became a novice and received the full monastic precepts (the *gusokukai*) at the Kaiden'in monastery of the Tōdaiji, in Nara. Following his ordination in Nara, Kōben began his study of the *Kusharon* (Vasubandhu's *Abhidharmakośabhāṣya,* a major Hīnayāna Abhidharma text). At the age of eighteen Kōben received the transmission of the dual *maṇḍalas* of the *jūhachidō* tradition from the *ācārya* Kōnen. Following this transmission, which centered around an eighteen-part Tantric *sādhana* to be undertaken by new initiates, Kōben began the cultivation of the *butsugen* ritual, a ritual centered on a visualization of the eyes of the Buddha, and his biography records that he experienced many miracles due to this practice.

In 1193, Kōben received an imperial order commanding him to work for the restoration of the Kegon tradition; thereafter, he took up residence as abbot in the Shōson'in of the Tōdaiji in Nara. Seeing the conflicts that racked the Buddhist world at this time, Kōben decided to retire from all worldly and ecclesiastical concerns. In 1195, Kōben left the Jingoji monasteries, and building himself a rude hut in the Kii mountains he retired, spending his time in the cultivation of *sādhana* rituals and in meditative visualizations. During this time he read the bulk of the commentaries and subcommentaries to the *Kegongyō* (Skt., *Avataṃsaka Sūtra*). This task, it is recorded, was also rewarded with many miracles and visions.

Later, returning to Mount Takao, Kōben began the teaching of the Kegon doctrines, lecturing on the *Kegon tangenki* (Chin., *Hua-yen t'an-hsüan chi*), a major Hua-yen commentary composed by Fa-tsang. It was here that Kōben initiated a series of lectures and debates on Kegon doctrine. In 1198 a number of disturbances between monastic factions on Mount Takao broke out, and Kōben, taking with him the chief image *(honzon)* of the monastery and its sacred texts, once more retired to his hermitage in the province of Kii. Here he constructed another hut with the aid of a local military leader and, as previously, he devoted himself to meditation, the recitation of scriptures, and writing.

In the eleventh month of 1206, the retired emperor Go-Toba presented Kōben with the Togano-o monastic complex in the hope that it would long be a center for the revival of the Kegon tradition. The monastic complex was given the new name of Kōzanji, and Kōben soon set to work repairing the buildings and reviving the tradition. Kōben was asked many times to administer the precepts to both the retired emperor Go-Toba and the Lady Kenreimon'in, his two most important patrons. After the death of her husband, Emperor Takakura, and her son, the infant emperor Antoku, Lady Kenreimon'in became a nun.

Kōben's fame came to the attention of the shogun in Kamakura, Hōjō Yasutoki, and on numerous occasions he would visit Kōben at his mountain monastery and receive his teachings. Subsequently, Yasutoki left the householder's life to become a monk under the guidance of Kōben.

After Kōben fell ill and died, at the age of fifty-nine, his many disciples continued their master's work toward the revival of the Kegon tradition. Modern scholars have attributed some forty-two works to Kōben. Included among them are essays on Kegon practice and doctrine, numerous ritual texts, literary works, and Japanese poems (*waka*), which are preserved in both the *Shinzoku kokinshū* and the *Shin shūishū.*

[*See also* Shingonshū *and* Hua-yen.]

BIBLIOGRAPHY

For a chronology of the life of Kōben and a complete list of his works see the article "Kōben," in *Bukkyō daijiten,* edited by Mochizuki Shinkō (Tokyo, 1933–1936), vol. 2, pp. 1083c–1084c. For a general overview of Kegon doctrine and its Japanese development, see Sakamoto Yukio's *Kegon kyōgaku no kenkyū* (Tokyo, 1976), Ishii Kyōdō's "Gommitsu no shisō Kōben," *Taishō Daigaku gakuhō* 3(1928):48–72, traces Kōben's attempt to establish purely Kegon Tantric rituals, thereby making the Kegon tradition of his day fully Tantric. On the orthodoxy of Kōben in the Kegon tradition, see Kamata Shigeo's "Nihon Kegon ni okeru seito to itan," *Shisō* (November 1973). A popular work on Kōben is Tanaka Hisao's *Myōe* (Tokyo, 1961). Like many other Buddhist monks of his day, Kōben kept a record of his dreams, *Yume no ki.* For a study of this work, see Yamada Shōzen's "Myōe no yume to *Yume no ki,*" in *Kanazawa Bunko kenkyū* (Tokyo, 1970). An English-language summary of Kōben's criticisms of Hōnen's doctrines is Bandō Shōjun's "Myōe's Criticism of Hōnen's Doctrine," *Eastern Buddhist,* n.s. 7 (May 1974): 37–54.

LEO M. PRUDEN

KOHANIM. *For discussion of priesthood in Israelite religion, see* Levites.

KOHELETH. *See* Ecclesiastes.

KOHLER, KAUFMANN (1843–1926), Reform rabbi, scholar, and theologian. Born in Fürth, Bavaria, into a pious Orthodox family of rabbinical ancestry, Kohler entered the *Gymnasium* in Frankfurt in 1862 and continued his earlier rabbinic training with Samson Raphael Hirsch, leader of German Neo-Orthodoxy, whose crucial religious impact on him Kohler frequently acknowledged. Gradually, however, with exposure to modern science and the critical studies of philology, the Bible, history, and comparative religion at the universities of Munich, Berlin, and Erlanger (where he received his Ph.D. in 1867), his faith in Orthodox Judaism was shattered.

Attracted to the religious orientation of Abraham Geiger, leader of German Reform Judaism, Kohler embraced Reform as an outlet for both his profound religious faith and his scholarly proclivities. When a rabbinical appointment in Germany was not forthcoming, he moved to the United States in 1869 and served congregations in Detroit and Chicago until, in 1879, he succeeded his father-in-law, David Einhorn, in one of the most prestigious Reform temples in the country, Beth El in New York City.

During the next decade, through his books and articles, Kohler became recognized as a preeminent advocate of classical Reform Judaism. Undaunted by controversy, he defended Reform against critics such as Felix Adler and Alexander Kohut; in the wake of his celebrated polemic with the latter, Kohler convened the Pittsburgh Rabbinical Conference in November 1885 and steered its eight-point statement of principles to reflect his own views; these corresponded to and articulated most Reformers' religious self-understanding for the next two generations. From 1903 to 1921, Kohler served as president of the Reform seminary at Hebrew Union College in Cincinnati.

Kohler's scholarship included works in theology, Semitics, Hellenistic studies, comparative religion, and intertestamental literature. These were consistently marked by the application of modern scientific analysis to Jewish literary sources, an approach reflecting the nineteenth-century *Wissenschaft des Judentums*. He assumed that this historicist reassessment of Judaism and its texts uncovered the essence of Judaism, which he identified with the central beliefs of Reform Judaism. His scholarship therefore was often an adjunct to his religious beliefs.

Recognized as a giant in his day, Kohler now has scant influence. His scholarship is generally dated, and his rationalist, anti-Zionist Reform orientation has long since been set aside by the mainstream of Reform Judaism. Nevertheless, he typified one of its most significant stages and expressed its major ideals in a bygone era.

BIBLIOGRAPHY

Kohler's most notable work, well reviewed in its day, is *Jewish Theology Systematically and Historically Considered* (1918; a revised edition of the 1910 German version); the current edition (New York, 1968) includes a fine introductory essay by Joseph L. Blau that combines biographical data with a critical assessment of Kohler's text. His other scholarly writings can be found in *Hebrew Union College and Other Addresses* (Cincinnati, 1910), *Heaven and Hell in Comparative Religion* (New York, 1923), and two posthumously published books, *The Origins of the Synagogue and the Church* (1929; New York, 1973) and *Studies, Addresses, and Personal Papers* (New York, 1931). The best retrospective on Kohler, written by an admirer and colleague, is H. G. Enelow's "Kaufmann Kohler," *American Jewish Year Book* 28 (1926–1927): 235–260.

BENNY KRAUT

KO HUNG (283–343), Chinese writer on alchemy and Taoism. Although a number of works have been attributed to Ko Hung, the only incontestable source for his thought is his *Pao-p'u-tzu* (The Master Who Embraces Simplicity). This consists today of twenty "inner chapters" on Taoist themes, fifty "outer chapters" on more Confucian topics, and an account of his own life. In both portions of his work Ko demonstrates an encyclopedic eclecticism that has caused later scholars a certain amount of difficulty in assessing his ideas.

To understand Ko Hung's intellectual orientation, it is necessary to know his cultural situation. Ko was a member of the old aristocracy that had lived in the lands south of the Yangtze since the Han dynasty and had served in the separatist kingdom of Wu that in 222 succeeded the Han in South China. The Wu state was conquered from the north by the Chin in 280, but the expulsion of the Chin court from North China by barbarian invasions in the early fourth century forced this new regime to transfer its capital to present-day Nanking. This demoralizing cultural invasion further accentuated the southern aristocrats' loss of independent political power, for the southerners saw themselves as the true heirs of Han civilization, unlike the northern immigrants, who had abandoned much of the Han heritage. Ko at first had some hopes of a political career under the Chin, but the premature death of his patron forced him to turn increasingly to a life of scholarship. As a consequence, his writings manifest an urge to collect the various strands of the old culture of pre-Chin times and make from them a compendium of southern intellectual conservatism. Dominant in this is a defense of local occult traditions against introduced religious and philosophical ideas.

To what degree Ko, the political outsider, managed to compensate for his disappointments by becoming a master of the occult is not clear. Recent scholarship has preferred to see him as an enthusiast who derived his knowledge from written sources more than from initiation into secret lore. But Ko used this knowledge to the full to defend his thesis that any man may become a genuine immortal. In arguing against those who interpreted immortality as a symbol of liberation from human limitations and against those who believed that immortals where born, not made, Ko provides a treasure trove of information on ancient techniques for achieving immortality. Ko's references to the alchemical preparation of elixirs of immortality have attracted the attention of modern historians of science, but he provides information on much else besides: sexual and other physiological practices, the use of talismans, herbal aids to longevity, lists of occult texts, and heterodox cults to be avoided. Since by the end of the fourth century, the religious situation in south China had been transformed totally by outside influences and internal developments, the *Pao-p'u-tzu* constitutes virtually our only source for this type of lore at an earlier period.

Although the exact date of the *Pao-p'u-tzu* is unknown, it would appear to have been substantially completed by 317. The Chin court bestowed on Ko honorary, politically powerless appointments in the following decade, but thereafter Ko seems to have sought to distance himself from court life in favor of alchemical pursuits. He managed eventually to obtain a posting to the far south (present-day North Vietnam) in order to search for the ingredients of the elixir of immortality. He was detained en route in present-day Kwangtung and remained there, on Mount Lo-fu, until his death. His contemporaries readily believed that this was a feigned death and that he had in fact reached his goal of immortality.

Despite the philosophical Taoist underpinnings that he provides for his repertory of techniques, Ko Hung's contributions to the development of Taoism were in a sense negligible. His approach to the beliefs that he recorded remained a purely individual one, and his writings, in all their contradictory richness, can in no way be taken as representative of the religion of any particular body of believers. Indeed, the group religious practices of his day seem to have fallen largely outside the scope of his research. Nonetheless he may be seen as the first of a number of southern aristocrats with similar concerns. Such later figures as Lu Hsiu-ching (406–477) and, especially, T'ao Hung-ching (456–536), though priests in the mainstream of Taoist belief, maintained Ko's emphasis on broad erudition and surpassed him in critical scholarship. But for Taoists and non-Taoists alike, the *Pao-p'u-tzu* remained one of the most widely cited apologies for the pursuit of immortality.

[*See also* Taoism, *article on* Taoist Literature, *and* Alchemy, *article on* Chinese Alchemy.]

BIBLIOGRAPHY

James R. Ware's *Alchemy, Medicine, and Religion in the China of A.D. 320: The Nei P'ien of Ko Hung* (Cambridge, Mass., 1967), provides a complete translation of the "inner chapters" of the *Pao-p'u-tzu* and of Ko's autobiography. Jay Sailey's *The Master Who Embraces Simplicity: A Study of the Philosopher Ko Hung, A.D. 283–343* (San Francisco, 1978) translates the autobiography, plus twenty more of the "outer chapters"; a lengthy study of Ko Hung and his thought is also appended. Neither volume is beyond criticism, but taken together they give a good picture of the diversity of Ko Hung's work.

T. H. Barrett

KOKUGAKU. The Japanese intellectual movement known as Kokugaku ("national learning") constitutes the Shintō revival that began in the middle of the Edo period (1600–1868). Inspired by the spirit of nationalism, Kokugaku thinkers deplored the lack of scholarship on Japanese history and literature and attacked the wholesale adoption of such foreign influences as Confucianism and Buddhism. According to Kokugaku thinkers, Japanese history can be divided into three periods: antiquity, during which time Japan's indigenous, original spirit emerged and was manifest in its purest form; the middle ages, when this spirit became "contaminated" and was suppressed by the introduction of Chinese culture, in particular Confucianism and Buddhism; and the modern ages, when Japan's ancient, original spirit was revived and rediscovered. Although the Kokugaku movement encompassed various fields of study, among them literature and philology, I shall limit my discussion to its concern with religion.

In the Genroku period (1688–1704), which marks the rise of the Kokugaku movement, the Buddhist priest Keichū (1640–1701) proposed that the poetic conventions popular during the middle ages in Japan be abolished so as to allow free composition of the Japanese *waka* poems. Keichū applied philological analysis to the *Man'yōshū*, but said only that Shintō differed from both Confucianism and Buddhism and that the *kami* were beyond the understanding of men. Kada Azumamaro (1669–1736), a Shintō priest at Inari Shrine in Kyoto, was active during the second period (i.e., Meiwa to Kansei period, 1764–1801) of Kokugaku history. Azumamaro was opposed to the synthesis of Confucianism and Shintō in which Confucian terms and concepts—for example, the principles of *yin* and *yang* and the Five

Elements *(wu-hsing)*—were used to interpret Shintō. Although he also advocated the founding of a college for "national learning" to combat the influence of Confucianism, he himself did not engage in the study of ancient Shintō.

The men considered the most representative thinkers of the movement—Kamo no Mabuchi (1697–1769) and Motoori Norinaga (1730–1801), among the second generation of Kokugaku scholars, and Hirata Atsutane (1776–1843) among the third generation—were also the most prominent of the advocates of National Learning to focus their attention on religious issues. Kamo no Mabuchi founded the school of Kogaku ("ancient learning") Shintō, which sought a reawakening of and a return to ancient Shintō. That is, he called for a revival of Shintō as expressed and practiced prior to the introduction of Buddhism and Confucianism. His main ideas are presented in his *Kokuiko* (On the Spirit of the Nation). Motoori Norinaga further clarified and developed Ancient Learning Shintō. He established the *Kojiki,* the earliest recorded Japanese history, as the scriptural authority for the movement and wrote a commentary on it, the *Kojikiden.* Other of his works include *Naobi no mitama* (Straightening Kami) and *Tamaboko hyakushu* (One Hundred Poems on the Way). Hirata Atsutane argued even further the religiosity of Ancient Learning Shintō, and asserted that Shintō was superior to other religions. His works include *Tama no mahashira* (The Pillar of the Soul), *Tamadasuki* (The Jeweled Sash), and *Honkyō gaihen* (Supplement to My Theory of Shintō).

While calling for an end to the influence of all foreign ideas and for a revival of Shintō in its original form, in reality these three men found certain foreign ideas conducive to the advancement of Kokugaku ideology. Both Mabuchi and Norinaga turned to the philosophy of Lao-tzu and Chuang-tzu, with Mabuchi borrowing from the former and Norinaga from the latter. Atsutane, however, made use of the teachings of Christianity, a religion that had been proscribed during the Tokugawa era. Their purpose in doing so was to eradicate the influence of Confucianism and Buddhism and to clarify the identity of Shintō and establish its supremacy. For example, believing that the teachings of the Buddhists and Confucians were "unnatural," that is, products of mere human artifice, Mabuchi used Lao-tzu's notion of *tzu-jan wu-wei* (Jpn., *shizen mui;* "spontaneity and nonactivity") to reject their interpretations of Shintō. He argued that Shintō, or the way of life of the ancient Japanese, was completely in accord with the nature of heaven and earth and thus did not give rise to the artificial systems found in China.

Accepting Mabuchi's basic thesis, Norinaga applied the knowledge gained through his research of the Japanese classics to criticize even more fervently than Mabuchi the precepts and doctrines of Neo-Confucianism. Norinaga borrowed Chuang-tzu's philosophy of nature (the philosophically exclusive principle of causality whereby there is no cause for an occurrence other than from the self) to reject the synthesis of Neo-Confucianism and Shintō that had been popular in the previous century. As a physician, Norinaga refused to accept the complex Neo-Confucian methodology that used the metaphysical theories of *yin* and *yang* and the Five Elements to determine the causes of diseases and their cures. He devoted himself to the task of reviving the ancient practices of medicine (*koihō*) that limited medicine to the sphere of empiricism. Accordingly, he asserted that all existence and phenomena arise from the self through divine will and that both the cause and reason for the occurrence of things cannot be fathomed by man; daring to inquire into such causes showed disrespect for the *kami.* Thus, Norinaga sought absolute obedience to the *kami.* He maintained that since the activities of the *kami* recorded in the *Kojiki* had actually been witnessed by the people of that early era, they should be accepted as fact and be studied with the same empiricist method as that used for *koihō.* According to the Mito scholar Aizawa Yasushi (1781–1863), Norinaga's concept of the creator and sovereign *kami* was influenced by Christianity. Norinaga did read Christian doctrine, but one can also see in his work an adaptation of the Neo-Confucian concept of *t'ai-chi* (Jpn., *taikyoku;* "ultimate principle" or "great ultimate").

Following the Shintō theories of Norinaga, Atsutane continued to develop Kokugaku Shintō, giving it a theological foundation. Although he showed it to no one, Atsutane's most important work is *Honkyō gaihen,* which he subtitled *Honkyō jibensaku* (Flagellation of My Theory of Shintō). All of his theologically important works were written after this. Muraoka Tsunetsugu (1884–1946) has verified that this work is composed of adaptations or selected translations of books on Christian doctrine that had been written by missionaries in Chinese during the Ming dynasty. Atsutane was impressed by such missionaries as Matteo Ricci, whose works presented arguments in support of Christianity, particularly in the face of Confucian opposition. Atsutane adapted these arguments to elevate Shintō over both Confucianism and Buddhism. He reasoned that the three *kami* Ame no Minakanushi, Takamimusubi, and Kamimusubi were a "Trinity;" which he identified as Musubi no Ōkami ("great creator *kami*"). He also advanced the notion that the human soul receives final judgment by Ōkuninushi no Mikoto in the netherworld, and that one's eternal happiness or hardship was based on one's deeds during life. Atsutane held that ancestor worship was central to Shintō practice. Unlike Chinese ancestor worship, which was limited to consanguineous relationships, Shintō ancestor worship especially revered the creator and sovereign *kami* as the ancestral *kami* of the entire nation, the head of which was the imperial family. Atsutane institutionalized the religious observances celebrating the ancestral *kami,* the writing of prayers, and promotion of Shintō practices.

The legacy of Atsutane's ideas lay in their political implications. In asserting that the imperial system, in which the emperor (*tennō*) was supreme ruler over all the people, was the original form of the Japanese polity, he held that system as the purest and most natural structure of governement. In his view, the (Tokugawa) shogunate was a later accretion that was not in accordance with Shintō and was thus disrespectful of the divine origins of the imperial family. Atsutane's criticisms provided a religious foundation for the nineteenth century policial movement that resulted in the Meiji Restoration of 1868.

[*See the biographies of Kamo no Mabuchi, Motoori Norinaga, and Hirata Atsutane.*]

BIBLIOGRAPHY

For a lucid introduction to the intellectual history of the Tokugawa era as a whole, see Maruyama Masao's *Studies in the Intellectual History of Tokugawa Japan*, translated by Mikiso Hane (Princeton, 1975). Selected writings of Kokugaku thinkers are provided in *Sources of the Japanese Tradition*, edited by Wm. Theodore de Bary et al., vol. 2 (New York, 1958), pp. 1-46. See also Muraoka Tsunetsugu's *Studies in Shintō Thought*, translated by Delmer M. Brown and James Araki (Tokyo, 1964), and my works *Shintō shisōshu* (Tokyo, 1970) and *Kami to Nihon bunka* (Tokyo, 1983).

ISHIDA ICHIRŌ
Translated from Japanese by Jenine Heaton

KONGO RELIGION. The Kikongo-speaking peoples of the Niger-Congo linguistic group represent a rich and diverse cultural heritage associated with the ancient kingdom of Kongo. Today, three to four million strong, they live in rural and urban areas of western Zaire, the Republic of Congo, Angola (and Cabinda), from 4° to 7° south latitude to 11° to 14° east longitude, as well as in several New World settings. Since the fourteenth century they have gained their livelihood primarily from the cultivation of various food crops (oil palm, yams, plantains, manioc, and so forth), and from hunting, fishing, and livestock tending. Smithing (of weapons, tools, jewelry, and ritual articles), weaving, tanning, sculpting, and carpentry, as well as trading in the famous Kongo markets, have been important commercial skills.

Increasingly from the late fifteenth century on, Kongo peoples were profoundly affected by contacts with European merchants, missionaries, and travelers, especially in connection with the great coastal trade, which included (from the eighteenth to late nineteenth centuries) massive slave traffic. Hardly had the slave trade ended in the 1860s when the Kongo region became the launching ground for colonial exploration and the establishment of the Congo Free State and the Belgian Congo. One indicator of the social dislocation and upheaval suffered by Kongo peoples is their gradual decline in population. From the fifteenth century to the early twentieth century it was reduced by half, despite a high birthrate. Only in 1930 did this population trend change to one of growth.

Life in Kongo society is characterized by a sense of unity of all aspects, articulated through numerous complementary oppositions. An individual is born, and remains, a juridical member of his mother's lineage and clan, yet the tie to the father and the father's kin is also strong and provides a source of spiritual identity. An individual's property relations lie inherently with the matrilineal estate, yet throughout life a "child" may enjoy rights to use the "father's" property. The collective children of a matrilineage's men constitute a continuing source of political consolidation of such a lineage. Alliances between lineages, often in reciprocal "father"-to-"child" marriages, reinforce existing bonds and create the basis of the social fabric.

Kongo religious beliefs and practices derive from these pervasive social realities. There are a number of basic Kongo religious concepts that have persisted amid the profound viscissitudes of Kongo history. Among them is the belief in a supreme being, known as Nzambi Kalunga or Nzambi Mpungu Tulendo, who is thought to be omnipotent. Although Nzambi Kalunga is the creator and the ultimate source of power, lesser spirits and ancestors mediate between humanity and the supreme being. Evil, disorder, and injustice are believed to be the result of such base human motives as greed, envy, or maliciousness. As constant sources of life and well-being, both the land and the matrilineal ancestors buried in it form the basis of the preoccupation in Kongo thought with fertility and the continuity of the community. Patrifilial relations and other alliances formed in the public sphere bring forth in Kongo religion a concern with the nature of power, its sources, applications, and the consequences of beneficent and malevolent uses of it.

Kongo Religious History. The range of diverse cults, movements, and beliefs in the religion of the Kikongo-speaking peoples may best be presented here in terms of a historical sketch. By 1500, the period when historical records were first kept, Kongo agrarian communities had been drawn into numerous kingdoms and large chiefdoms established centuries earlier; on the coast there were the Loango, Kakongo, and Ngoyo kingdoms; inland on the north bank of the Kongo (Zaire) River, there was Vungu and numerous other chiefdoms; on the south bank, Nsundi and Kongo. In all these polities, shrines and insignia of authority represented the complementarity of power: the autochthonous spirits of the land and the awesome, detached, acumen of conquering, alliance building, and conflict judging.

The Portuguese explorer Diogo Cão contacted the king at Mbanza Kongo, the capital, in the late fifteenth century, and later the Portuguese king and merchants entered into diplomatic, mercantile, and missionary relations with Kongo, unleashing significant forces of change. In a succession struggle between the traditional prince Mpanzu and Christian prince Afonso in 1510, the victory of the latter brought about the official endorsement of Catholicism, schools, and the europeanization of Kongo culture. A more centralized model of government prevailed, with Portuguese backing. At the same time, but against the king's wishes, the slave trade began to have serious repercussions in the kingdom. After Afonso's death in the mid-fifteenth century the kingdom began to disintegrate and, although usually supported by Portuguese militia and Catholic missionaries, it became increasingly subject to extended succession feuds between contending houses and lineages. During the centuries of the coastal trade, especially the slave era (eighteenth to late nineteenth century), all of the region's historical kingdoms gradually lost their control over tax levying, trade, and orderly administration. A variety of cults and renewal movements made their appearances.

Crisis cults and movements in Kongo history must be seen against the background of more long-term, focused, therapeutic rituals and life-cycle rituals, with which they share the underlying symbolic logic that will be described later. To a degree the crisis cults of Kongo history arise from the ground of routine rituals. Thus, initiation rites of Kimpasi (widespread south of the river) and Kinkhimba (north of the river), mentioned as early as the seventeenth century, are known to have had a periodicity of occurrence that intensified with droughts, political chaos, and rising perception of witchcraft activity. Both types of initiation were promoted by chiefs and sought to instruct youth and to legitimate political regimes.

As chiefdoms and kingdoms suffered loss of legitimacy in the trade or because of the decline of central states, new insignia and charms of power spread to enhance authority. As infertility and population decline became acute, especially in areas subjected to venereal disease and other epidemics, fertility and birthing medicine cults emerged, such as Pfemba, organized by midwives in the western north bank region. As the coastal trade increased in intensity and caravans moved from the coast to inland markets and trading points, challenging local polities and demanding provisions, medicine cult networks arose to buttress regional market and alliance structures and to protect those who were involved in the trade from the envy of their subordinates; Lemba, the great medicine of markets and government, is an important instance of this. Nkita, an ancient medicine of lineage structure, emerged wherever segmentary lineage fragments were beset by misfortune and sought to restore authority and ties to ancestors.

Kongo cultic history may be seen as a veritable tradition of renewal, either at the local lineage level, the national level, or in terms of a specific focus. Often the appeal is for restoration of public morality and order; individualized charms are commanded to be destroyed, the ancestors' tombs are restored, cemeteries purified, and group authority is renewed. Although often the originators of new cultic forms are unknown, some exceptional founding individuals are remembered and may be identified.

An especially severe and prolonged succession crisis in the Kongo kingdom in the eighteenth century brought to the fore a Kongo Joan of Arc, the prophetess Kimpa Vita, or Dona Béatrice, to reconcile the contending factions and restore authority to the capital. Her syncretic doctrine of national salvation combined royalist ideals of restoration of the capital with the call for fertility and the appeal to Christian love, subsumed under the banner of Saint Anthony, for whom the prophetess's followers were named Antonines. Kimpa Vita's work was cut short when she was charged with heresy by the Capucin missionary Bernardo da Gallo, who supported one of the other political factions; after her execution the Antonine movement continued for several decades. Renewal movements became increasingly common, and better documented, during the Free State era (1875–1908) as colonial labor recruitment, epidemic diseases, population decline, and renewed missionary efforts to defame traditional beliefs subjected the Kongo peoples to a loss of values and the disintegration of leaders' authority. By 1920 Kongo chiefs were generally ineffective; their judicial techniques were bypassed by the colonial authorities or banned. Especially important in the context of Kongo religious leaders is the twentieth-century Kongo prophet Simon Kimbangu, whose widely influential teachings eventually gave rise to the largest independent church in Africa. [*See the biography of Kimbangu.*]

Mission Christianity, implanted during the Free State and subsequent colonial era by British, Swedish, and American Protestant groups and by Belgian, French, and Portuguese Catholics has given rise to many congregations and conferences, as well as to schools, hospitals, seminaries, and other specialized institutions. Furthermore, it has brought about the far-reaching christianization of the Kongo populace. Many Kongo-speakers in the late twentieth century are nominal Christians. However, paradoxically, most Kongo Christians still subscribe to the fundamental tenets of the Kongo religion and worldview.

Kongo Beliefs and Practices Today. In the twentieth century large numbers of Kongo people migrated to the urban centers of Brazzaville, Kinshasa, Matadi, Pointe Noire, Luanda, and lesser towns, yet reverence for lineage ancestors and offerings made to them continue to be integrally tied to the maintenance of lineage land estates and to the guardianship of the matrilineal kin unit. Many of the eighteenth- and nineteenth-century initiatory and curing rites have been abandoned, yet many dimensions of life continue to be sacralized. For example, religious beliefs continue to revolve around providing assurance for women's reproductive capacity and male fertility; guaranteeing the legitimacy of authority roles at lineage and clan levels; presiding over rites of passage—naming, puberty, marriage, bride price payment, death; restoring ancestral ties where lineages have been segmented or where, in urban settings, lineage fragments seek to return to their roots.

Dealing with misfortune remains an important issue in Kongo religion, although the list of common occurrences has grown from hunting and gardening activities and related accidents (e.g., being gored by a wild boar, falling from a palm tree) to include accidents and misfortunes of industrial society (e.g., automobile crashes and factory accidents). The old desires for influence, love, justice, and success have remained current, along with the need to explain failures in these areas. Misfortunes, and the desire for good fortune, are dealt with in the perspectives of historical Kongo divining, mediumship, protective magic, and healing. The axioms of this worldview, apparently quite persistent over centuries, explain the fate of humans in terms of the priority of the invisible spirit world over the visible material world or the tendency of the former to regularly break in upon the latter. Normal events in the order of things and relationships created by Nzambi require no particular piety or devotion to continue. By contrast, abnormal or unusual events are considered to be caused by humans who, willfully or inadvertently, affect others' destinies (mostly for the worse) by spiritual or direct means. The Kongo word often translated as "witchcraft" or "sorcery" is *kindoki,* from *loka* ("to use charged words toward others"). The power of words in interpersonal discourse is greatly respected. Human ties, frequently polluted and muddled with ill will, malicious intentions, and envy, or the threat of becoming so, must regularly be renewed with gift exchanges, purification rites, and harmonious discourse.

When ordinary people cannot cope with their misfortunes and conflicts, they turn to the *nganga* (specialized priests and doctors). The *nganga* are diviners, religious specialists skilled in manipulating spirits, humans, and symbols; agents of power who inaugurate offices of authority; and healers who deal with sicknesses of mind and body. They use esoteric codes relating the visible realm of plants and substances and apply them to the invisible realm of emotions, society, and the beyond. These mediatory roles of the *nganga* (as well as those of chiefs, prophets, and other powerful people) require legitimation from the "white" otherworld *(mpemba),* the realm of ancestors and spirits. As a natural cosmology *mpemba* is most often associated with water, the realm of nature, and with ancestor spirits. Land, the abode of mundane human powers, is associated with "black," the realm of defective, partial, and evil forces. The sky is a third realm, not associated with any color; it is the abode of other spiritual forces. Redness, often used to describe the ambiguous or transitional areas of life, may be tied to power, or to the sun and other astral bodies, and it expresses the cycles and rhythms of natural and human life. This cosmology of natural realms and color qualities may be associated with the more explicit human ideology of matrilineal and patrilateral kinship, in a ritual grammar that amplifies the complementary dependencies of mother and child, father and child, siblings and spouses. At the most abstract level, the "white" may be contrasted to the "world" and used as a metaphor of renewal, postulating the ever-ready tendency of *mpemba* to pervade the human world, to replace, renew, and purify it.

Kongo religion is more complex and profound than any single doctrine or congregation represented within it. It is a set of perspectives about life, of symbolic traditions and roles that have formed over centuries of human experience at the mouth of the Kongo River. This experience includes the adversities of the slave trade, massive depopulation, epidemics, colonialism, and droughts, as well as the challenges of christianization and independence. Kongo religion is at the heart of one of the great historic, yet living, human civilizations.

BIBLIOGRAPHY

The English reader may begin a study of Kongo religion with John M. Janzen and Wyatt MacGaffey's *An Anthology of Kongo Religion: Primary Texts from Lower Zaire,* "Publications in Anthropology, University of Kansas," no. 5 (Lawrence, Kans., 1974), an introduction to several facets of the subject as seen in fifty-two translated texts. Wyatt MacGaffey's *Religion and Society in Central Africa: The BaKongo of Lower Zaire* (Chicago, 1986), is a major synthesis of all aspects of historical and current Kongo religion. Kongo religion as reflected in mortuary art is depicted in Robert Farris Thompson's *The Four Moments of the Sun: Kongo Art in Two Worlds* (Washington, D.C., 1981). The *double entendre* of Thompson's title, refering to the dichotomies of visible-invisible and Africa-New World in Kongo belief and ceremonial space, is derived from one of the clearest renderings of Kongo cosmology, A. Fu-kiau kia Bunseki-Lumanisa's *N'kongo ye Nza / Cosmogonie Kongo* (Kinshasa, 1969).

Classics in Kongo culture, including religion, are Jan van Wing's *Études baKongo* (Brussels, 1959), especially part 2 on religion and magic, and Karl Edward Laman's *The Kongo,* 4 vols., "Studia Ethnographica Upsaliensia," nos. 4, 8, 12, and 16 (Uppsala, 1953–1968). Specialized studies include, on Kongo messianism, Effraim Andersson's *Messianic Popular Movements in the Lower Congo* (Uppsala, 1958); on witchcraft and consecrated medicines, Tulu kia Mpansu Buakasa's *L'impensé du discours: "Kinodoki" et "nkisi" en pays kongo du Zaïre* (Kinshasa, 1973); on Christian missions in Kongo, Effraim Andersson's *Churches at the Grass Roots: A Study in Congo-Brazzaville* (London, 1968); and on historic healing cults, John M. Janzen's *Lemba, 1650–1930: A Drum of Affliction in Africa and the New World* (New York, 1981).

JOHN M. JANZEN

KONKŌKYŌ is a modern Japanese religion founded in 1859. In 1984 it boasted some 469,153 members. The founder of Konkōkyō, known by the honorary title Konkō Daijin (1814–1883), was born Kandori Genshichi to a peasant family in Ōtani village, Bitchū Province (present day Okayama Prefecture). Adopted at the age of twelve, he became head of the Kawate (later renamed Akazawa) family at twenty-three and took the name Akazawa Bunji. Under his direction, his family began to cultivate cotton in addition to the traditional rice crop, thereby raising their living standard above the norm of the local cultivating class. However, while Akazawa's diligence and initiative brought material benefit, he also experienced profound grief. Four of his children died of sickness, and in 1855 he himself became very ill.

As a young man, Akazawa was deeply religious and participated in the multifaceted religious life of rural Japan. While his village was principally affiliated with the Tendai school of Buddhism, it was also deeply influenced by the cult of sacred mountains, Shugendō. Shugendō ascetics *(yamabushi)* were prominent in village religion as healers, an activity from which they derived significant income. [*See* Shugendō.] In addition, priests of local Shintō shrines sponsored pilgrimages to the Ise Grand Shrines. Akazawa assisted traveling Ise priests *(oshi)* in distributing Ise talismans and almanacs in the village. He also joined village confraternities *(kō)* in pilgrimage to a circuit of eighty-eight temples on Shikoku island. He scrupulously observed horoscopic and geomantic prescriptions in planning any significant activity, such as travel or construction.

Teaching and Scripture. Akazawa's illness of 1855 was diagnosed as resulting from an offense against Konjin, who, according to local folk notions, was a malevolent deity ruling the northeast. It was believed that to offend Konjin was to precipitate his wrath in the form of possession or sickness. Akazawa's cure, thought to have been realized through earnest prayers to Konjin, marked the beginning of a complete reorientation of his life, culminating in a new understanding of humanity's relation to the deity Konjin and in the founding of Konkōkyō. Akazawa began to serve Konjin in 1858 and devoted increasing amounts of time to religion. Followers came to seek his advice and to have him mediate *(toritsugu)* Konjin's will to them. He received instructions *(shirase)* from the deity about agriculture, construction, sickness, and a host of other matters. From Konjin, Akazawa received a series of honorary titles marking his spiritual progress, and the deity revealed a corresponding set of titles of his own. Through Akazawa's spiritual development and earnest prayer the deity gradually manifested its true nature and desire for humanity's salvation.

While Akazawa originally conceived of Konjin as an evil being, he realized that the deity did not willfully cause suffering, and that the being he originally knew as Konjin was in fact the one, true God of the universe (Tenchi Kane no Kami), the source of all being. Akazawa's final title, Ikigami Konkō Daijin, reflects the concept that humanity and deity are originally united and indivisible.

In 1859 Akazawa, now called Konkō Daijin, gave up agriculture to devote himself fully to the service of Tenchi Kane no Kami (Great Living Deity Konkō); Konkōkyō dates its founding from that event. Two years later, Konkō Daijin began to record his consultations with followers, most of whom came from Okayama and Hiroshima. As the number of believers increased, the group encountered suppression and persecution from domain officials and *yamabushi*. Many followers believed they were healed by Konkō Daijin's mediation *(toritsugi)*, but as such healings detracted from the *yamabushi*'s prayer healings, and hence from their income, Konkō Daijin incurred considerable enmity from these powerful religious practitioners. In order to continue *toritsugi* and avert further persecution, Konkō Daijin took a license from the Shirakawa house of Shintō. Although this gave the organization limited recognition as a variety of Shintō, Tenchi Kane no Kami was not an authorized Shintō deity, nor did *toritsugi* bear any relation to the usual practices of the Shintō priesthood.

Konkōkyō's central doctrine is rooted in the concept of reciprocity between humanity and God. Both are said to be fulfilled through humanity's self-cultivation. The task of the religious life is to awaken to God's eternal love and to realize that everyone is endowed with life and sustained by Tenchi Kane no Kami and that all things in the universe derive from him. Because all people are believed to be the children of God, human equality is a fundamental tenet. Faith and spiritual strength, rather than healing rites or medication, are the keys to physical health. Konkō Daijin denied fatalistic ideas of horoscopy and geomancy and derided food taboos and pollution notions regarding women. The record of Konkō Daijin's *shirase* and *toritsugi*, as well as accounts of the lives and conversions of early followers, are collected in Konkōkyō's scripture, *Konkōkyō kyōten*.

Relation to Shintō. Konkōkyō's relation to Shintō is a complex and much debated issue among the ministry. Konkō Daijin's certification by the Shirakawa was acquired more in order to protect the group than as an expression of its faith. Between 1870 and 1884, during the Meiji government's campaign to promote Shintō (called the *taikyō senpu undō*), Konkō Daijin's son Hagio became a *kyōdōshoku* ("national evangelist") and his main disciple, Satō Norio, became a vigorous activist for the movement. It was Satō who was most influential in aligning the group's doctrine with State Shintō. In spite of the direct and repeated protests of Konkō Daijin, who denied that Konkōkyō was a variety of Shintō and refused to meet with local Shintō officials, Satō and other early leaders sought, and eventually gained, recognition for Konkōkyō as one of the thirteen sects of Shintō. The group accepted this designation, no doubt partially owing to their fear of suppression.

Since the early 1980s, however, the group has rejected Shintō rites and vestments, and many ministers repent the part Konkōkyō played in prewar Shintō. They see Shintō as having contributed to militarism and nationalism, traits they wholeheartedly reject. Yet a change of such magnitude, requiring a rejection of much of the group's history, is difficult for many to accept, even when carried out in the name of a return to the true spirit of the founder's teaching. At present, the group is in the midst of a true religious revolution, and the outcome seems sure to bring in a new order.

[*See also* New Religions, *article on* New Religions in Japan.]

BIBLIOGRAPHY

Articles of high scholarly merit often appear in *Konkōkyōgaku* (Konkō-machi), a journal published by Konkōkyō. In addition to this basic source, the following works may be profitably consulted.

Holtom, D. C. "Konkō Kyō—A Modern Japanese Monotheism." *Journal of Religion* 13 (July 1933): 279–300. General description and discussion of the group in terms of monotheism.

Konkō Churches of America. *Konkō Daijin: A Biography*. San Francisco, 1981. A shortened translation of the official biography of the founder.

Konkōkyō kyōten. Konkō-machi, 1983. A revised version of the sacred scriptures of the group plus much valuable information on the founder's life and those of early disciples.

The Sacred Scriptures of Konkōkyō. Konkō-machi. 1973. An abridged version of sacred texts.

Schneider, Delwin B. *Konkōkyō, a Japanese Religion: A Study in the Continuities of Native Faiths*. Tokyo, 1962. The only book-length study in a Western language, the book concentrates on the theology of the group.

HELEN HARDACRE

KOOK, AVRAHAM YITSḤAQ (1865–1935), a major figure in the history of Jewish spirituality. Kook was born in Greiva, Latvia, to a deeply pious Jewish family, and received his rabbinic education at the celebrated Talmudic Academy in Volozhin, Lithuania. He held rabbinical posts in the Lithuanian towns of Zaumel and Bausk, and in 1904 he was named chief rabbi of Jaffa in Palestine. Stranded in Europe by the outbreak of World War I, he served as a rabbi in London. At the end of the war he returned to Palestine to accept the position of chief rabbi of Jerusalem (1919) and later of the whole Jewish community in Palestine.

One of Kook's major activities was to interpret Talmudic law and apply it to the various problems that came before him. His mastery of Talmudic law is attested by several volumes of his legal decisions. But he often complained that this preoccupation with the law was too confining for his spirit. For him, all specialized disciplines of study were fragmented separations from a truth that, he believed, could be grasped only when seen in its comprehensive whole. He advocated the pursuit of general knowledge, of the sciences, of literature and poetry, and, above all, of the mystical tradition—the writings of Qabbalah and Hasidism.

Kook was himself a mystic, and his mystical illumination moved him to compose philosophical essays, spiritual meditations, moralistic tracts, and poetry. Perhaps the most significant work is the *Orot ha-qodesh* (Lights of Holiness), three volumes of which have been published. Written over a period of some fifteen years (1904–1919) as a spiritual diary, it is not an exposition of any one theme, nor is it structured in accordance with any conceptual development; rather, it consists of a series of meditations on various aspects of a life of holiness. Kook saw these as a series of illuminations that came to him from the mysterious realm of the divine. In *Major Trends in Jewish Mysticism* (1944), Gershom Scholem described this work as "a veritable *theologia mystica* of Judaism, equally distinguished by its originality and the richness of the author's mind."

The basic concept in Kook's thought is God's immanence in the entire order of existence, both its universal, comprehensive whole and its fragmented particulars. Since existence is a unity under God, people should rise above all divisiveness. Fragmentation is a temporary strategy to permit the full unfolding of the particulars, but it is only a step toward ultimate reunification. What we call evil is simply a condition afflicting the particular when it is detached from the whole.

According to Kook, there is something good in everything and everyone, and we are therefore called on to love everything and everyone: "The more the quest for God grows in a person's heart, the more does the love for all people grow in him, and he loves even wicked men and heretics, and he desires to perfect them, for he does indeed perfect them by his own great faith" (quoted in Bokser, 1978, p. 8). All things and all people assume the dimension of the holy when they are seen in the context of the entire unfolding drama of divine creation.

Kook was critical of the parochialism that led some Jews to disparage other faiths. In all religions, he held, there are authentic elements, "seeking after God and His ways in the world. . . . We must clarify the common elements of all religions, according to the degree of their development, and not be afraid of the customary and deep hostility that lurks in the soul against everything alien" (ibid., p. 12). As we rise toward universality we shall discover that the uniqueness of each religion is a source of enrichment and stimulation to all religions. Kook saw a measure of legitimacy even in atheism, since atheism challenges religion to purge itself of the dross of superstition and anthropomorphisms that mar its teachings. He called for openness to all the cultural creations of the past, but also for the cultivation of original, intuitive thought, which is God's gift to everyone ready to embrace it.

Seeing this vision of universality as the very essence of Judaism, Kook was saddened by what appeared to him as the arid state of the Jewish religion in its conventional expression. He found conventional Jewish piety characterized by legalism, parochialism, and a blind self-centeredness. In part he blamed this situation on the rabbis of his time who had shunned the mystical and moralistic elements in Judaism and focused only on the legal aspect; in part he attributed it to the persecution suffered by the Jews in the lands of their dispersion, making them defensive and blunting their larger vision. It was his hope that the renewal of Jewish life in the Holy Land, through the initiative of the Zionist movement, would redress this condition. He was an ardent supporter of the Zionist cause, even while acknowledging that some of the Zionist pioneers had broken with their religious faith. This position brought him fierce opposition from the ultrareligious circles in the country, to whom secular Zionism was anathema.

Kook's influence has been maintained through the Rabbi Kook Foundation (Mosad ha-Rav Kook), a research center and publishing house in Jerusalem. It has published Kook's writings, as well as other classic texts that are close to his spirit. Another channel of his influence has been the Jerusalem Yeshivat Merkaz ha-Rav, an academy of higher Jewish studies dedicated to his philosophy and led for many years by his son Tsevi Yehudah. Its disciples were trained to be ardent in their orthodoxy, militant in their Zionism, and consecrated to the love of the land and people of Israel.

BIBLIOGRAPHY

Agus, Jacob B. *The Banner of Jerusalem: The Life, Times, and Thought of Abraham Isaac Kuk.* New York, 1946.

Bokser, Ben Zion, trans. and ed. *Abraham Isaac Kook: The Lights of Penitence, the Moral Principles, Lights of Holiness, Essays, Letters, and Poems.* New York, 1978.

BEN ZION BOKSER

KORAN. *See* Qur'ān.

KORE. *See* Demeter and Persephone; *see also* Eleusinian Mysteries.

KOREAN RELIGION.

[*This entry discusses principally the indigenous religious system of Korea. For an overview of other traditions, see* Buddhism, *article on* Buddhism in Korea; Confucianism in Korea; *and* Christianity, *article on* Christianity in Asia.]

Confucianism, Taoism, and Buddhism, often said to be Korea's major religions, all came to Korea from or through China. Another faith, indigenous to Korea, has usually been considered superstition rather than religion because it lacks an explicitly formulated, elaborated, and rationalized body of doctrine. Yet this indigenous creed possesses a rich set of supernatural beliefs, a mythology, and a variety of ritual practices. In recent years, therefore, an increasing number of scholars have come to recognize this folk system of beliefs and rites as another of Korea's major religious traditions.

Little is known about the early history of Korea's indigenous religion. Few Korean records compiled before the latter half of the Koryŏ dynasty (918–1392 CE) survive today. Korea's earliest known myths, recorded in the twelfth and thirteenth centuries, are concerned with the creation of early kingdoms and bear little resemblance to the folk religion and oral mythology collected by folklorists in more recent times.

The importation from China of all three of Korea's elite religious traditions resulted not only from Korea's geographical proximity to the Middle Kingdom but also from the political relationship of these two nations prior to the twentieth century. China's cultural influence on its eastern neighbor began even before the Three Kingdoms period (fourth to seventh century CE); after the unification of the Korean Peninsula, regular exchanges with China continued, as Korea was a tributary state of the Chinese empire. Contacts with other nearby societies, principally Japan, were less frequent; Japanese culture never enjoyed the respect that Koreans held for Chinese civilization.

The three major religious traditions that came to Korea from China arrived more than fifteen hundred years ago and were selected, transformed, and adapted in varying degrees to the social and intellectual conditions prevailing on the Korean Peninsula. As a result, these elite traditions in Korea often differ from their Chinese counterparts. Korean Taoism, for example, is primarily early or philosophical Taoism. Lacking its own priests, temples, and rituals, its ideology is evident chiefly in fortune-telling and geomancy. Human longevity and magical transformations, themes characteristic of later or religious Taoism, are evident in Korean folktales, however. Similarly, Buddhism adapted itself to Korea by absorbing a number of native Korean deities into its pantheon and folk ritual practices into its liturgy. Even the fundamentalist approach to Neo-Confucianism taken by the Chosŏn (Yi) government (1392–1910) did not entirely prevent modifications of its ritual prescriptions to suit indigenous beliefs and social mores.

Affiliation with a traditional Korean religion entailed participation at some of its rites or acceptance of at least part of its ideology rather than exclusive membership in a church organization. As a result, participants at rituals usually include already existing social groups—such as family, village, or extended kinship group—rather than a specially constituted church congregation. Another result has been a religious eclecticism constrained not by feelings of commitment to one faith or sense of contradiction between disparate beliefs but by traditional role expectations of men and women. In many Korean families, men perform ancestor rites and consult geomancers whereas women make offerings to household gods and confer with fortune-tellers, but even this gender division of labor is not rigidly observed.

The absence of church congregations not only facilitated eclecticism and adaptation but also allowed significant regional, social, and even interpersonal variations in religious belief and practice. Nowhere is this more evident than in Korea's indigenous folk religion, where the lack of written scripture further encouraged diversity. In the sections below, I identify the most prevalent of the traditional ideas and rites, but variant forms can be found for many of these beliefs and practices.

During the nineteenth century, much of the traditional East Asian world order collapsed, and two major developments in Korean religion soon followed: the rise of Christianity and the emergence of various new religions. Christianity is unique in that it is difficult to characterize as a Korean religion, for the beliefs and rites of its major denominations have apparently not undergone significant indigenization. The adaptation of Christian rites and beliefs occurs readily in several of the new religions, however. These eclectic religious organizations draw upon Christianity as well as traditional Korean faiths in formulating their own respective doctrines and liturgies. Yet the established Christian churches, rather than the new religions, have attracted the larger following in South Korea. (Data on contemporary religion in North Korea are not readily available.) The greater success of Christianity compared with that of the new religions contrasts strikingly with their respective fates in Japan and presents one of the major puzzles of modern Korean religion.

Indigenous Folk Religion. Little can be known with certainty about the history of Korea's indigenous folk religion. Ancient Chinese histories, which occasionally mentioned customs or events in Korea, say nothing about this belief system or its rites. The *Samguk sagi* and the *Samguk yusa*, Korea's earliest histories, compiled in the twelfth and thirteenth centuries, respectively, contain extensive accounts of the Three Kingdoms period but reveal only that people called *mu* existed at that time. The word *mu* is written with the same Chinese character as the first syllable of the Korean word *mudang*, the term used in recent times to designate a ritual specialist of Korea's folk religion; the orthographic correspondence suggests some sort of relationship between the two terms. The early histories do not provide a clear description of the *mu*'s activities or functions, however, and much scholarly effort has been expended trying to interpret the relevant passages.

The earliest source on the rituals of Korea's folk religion appears in the *Tongguk Yi Sangguk chip*, a collection of poems and essays by Yi Kyu-bo (1168–1241). One of his poems describes some folk religious practices only briefly, but the description corresponds with the rites presently performed by *mudang* in Kyŏnggi Province, located in the western-central part of the Korean Peninsula. Historical documents from the Chosŏn dynasty contain frequent references to *mudang* and their activities, but these references are primarily condemnations of *mudang* or legal sanctions against their practices rather than descriptions of ethnographic value. Compiled by Confucian literati, these documents describe *mudang* as charlatans, assess heavy taxes on them in order to hinder their activities, and ascribe them to the lowest class of Chosŏn society. Despite these repressive sanctions, however, Korea's folk religion remained embedded in everyday life. New *mudang* continue to emerge today, and their rites still occur regularly in rural areas and frequently in urban areas as well.

Religious specialists. Though different regional terms also exist, the term *mudang* is used throughout Korea to designate the specialists of Korea's folk religion. It is usually translated into English as "shaman," but this translation is problematic because several different definitions have been advanced for the term *shaman*. Moreover, there are two types of *mudang*—possessed *(kangsin mu)* and hereditary *(sesŭp mu)*—and only the former fits some of the better-known definitions.

An apparently normal person, usually a woman, begins the process of becoming a *kangsin mu* when she exhibits some of the following symptoms: loss of appetite, the drinking only of water, use of crude language, violent behavior, unintelligible speech, and going off to mountains and subsequently not recalling her activities while there. When normal attempts at treatment fail, these symptoms are interpreted as signs of "spirit illness" *(sinbyŏng)*, an illness that can be relieved only by becoming a *mudang*.

A woman who is to become a *kangsin mu* is apprenticed to a senior *mudang* with whom she establishes a spiritual mother-daughter relationship. From her spiritual mother, the novice acquires ritual techniques, a more detailed knowledge of the supernatural, and other lore; by engaging in shamanistic activities in this way, the apprentice's spirit illness is relieved and her abnormal behavior ceases. After a period of apprenticeship, the spiritual mother performs an initiation ritual for the novice, who thereby becomes a full-fledged *mudang*. During the rites she performs throughout her career, various deities or ancestors "descend" or "come" to speak and act through her body. Should the new *mudang* abandon the role for any length of time, her spirit illness would return.

The other mode of recruitment into the profession of *mudang* entails heredity rather than spirit possession. *Mudang* and their families belonged to the lowest social stratum in the Chosŏn dynasty and thus frequently intermarried. A girl born of such a family usually married into another *mudang*'s household and then accompanied her mother-in-law's ritual performances, acquiring the latter's song texts, dances, and other ritual techniques. Unlike *kangsin mu*, *sesŭp mu* did not suffer from spirit illness, did not undergo initiation rites, did not become possessed at rituals, and were never men. A male born into a *sesŭp mu*'s family learned how to sing, play musical instruments, and perform acrobatic feats. With these skills he became an entertainer or assisted at his wife's and mother's rites.

Until recently, possessed and hereditary *mudang* occupied different regions of Korea. The Han River, which flows across the center of Korea, affords a rough dividing line between two of these major regions. To its north, *kangsin mu* prevailed; and to its south, *sesŭp mu* predominated. Cheju-do, Korea's largest island, located off the peninsula's southern coast, constituted a third region. There, both possessed and hereditary *mudang* were common. Today, however, these regional differences are disappearing rapidly and possessed *mudang* prevail everywhere in South Korea.

Pantheon. The pantheon of Korea's folk religion is polytheistic. A variety of gods are available to aid supplicants, bring them good fortune, and help them avoid misfortune. Some of these deities are known only in particular regions, but the following are known throughout Korea and are among those that most often receive rites: Mountain God, Earth God, Dragon King God, Smallpox God, Seven-Star God, God of Luck (Chesŏk), God of the House Site, Kitchen God, and Birth God. These represent only a small fraction of the total pantheon, however. More than three hundred names have been collected, and the number of Korean deities is even greater since several of them are often designated by the same term. A different mountain god exists for each mountain, for example.

Many of the folk deities have particular functions or territorial domains, but unlike the deities of Chinese folk religion, the Korean gods are not believed to be organized into a vast supernatural bureaucracy. Mountain God, for example, has for his domain a mountain's earth, rocks, trees, and landslides; Dragon King God is in charge of a lake, a sea, or a stream, and such activities as fishing and sailing. Similarly, God of the House Beam is charged with a household's prosperity, God of Luck with its property, and Seven-Star God with regulating each member's life span. With a few possible exceptions, each of these deities is autonomous. Indeed, they do not even consult or communicate with each other when carrying out their various functions.

A possible exception to the autonomy of Korean deities is implied by differences in ritual treatment accorded the various supernatural beings. Some are invited by the *mudang* to receive individual rites and food offerings not presented to others. Among the various household gods, for example, the god of the house beam and the god of the house site belong to the former category; the toilet god, the gate god, and the chimney god belong to the latter. The treatment of this latter category is not unlike that given to wandering and hungry ghosts, souls of the dead who have no descendants to care for them. Thus they gather at feasts to obtain a small handout. Some food is strewn about the ground for these supernaturals whenever *mudang* perform rites for the major deities.

The systematic differences in treatment offered to Korean deities imply differences in status and, in turn, authority. Yet even status differences are not expressed explicitly in *mudang*'s songs or articulated by believers. Neither are the deities equal, however. Some are more important than others because their domains cover activities that are particularly significant or frequently undertaken by believers. Perhaps *parallelotheism* is the best term for characterizing the autonomy, lack of hierarchy, and even lack of communication between Korean deities. Like parallel lines, each occupies its own space without meeting the others.

The deities are not thought to be inherently good or evil; whether they are helpful or harmful depends on the circumstances. If they are treated with regular offerings, they bring good fortune; otherwise, they inflict punishment. The god of the house beam, charged with taking care of the household's prosperity, and the god of luck, charged with its property, would seem to be purely helpful or protective deities. But if they are ignored, before long they will inflict poverty on the household. Nor is the smallpox god, who brings the disease to children, an entirely harmful deity. If taken care of properly and given food offerings, this god not only reduces the severity of the illness but may even bring good fortune as well.

The place where the deities reside is not clearly set forth in the indigenous belief system. Apparently the deities do not live in this world but inhabit an upper world, a higher plane than mortals, for the *mudang* invite them to "descend" and informants often say that "they look down on us." Yet the deities do not dwell in any specially designated or sacred area, such as the Mount Olympus of Greek mythology. Some informants say that a mountain god resides in a particular mountain, or a river god in a river; but whenever a *mudang* performs a rite for one of these deities, even at the site of its own domain, the god is invited to come to the rite, which would seem to imply that the god normally dwells elsewhere.

One characteristic of the Korean deities that stands out quite clearly is their dislike of dirt. Before invoking the gods at a major shamanistic rite, a great deal of effort is expended to clean the area where the ritual is to be performed. Dead animals and feces are removed, clean earth spread about, and straw rope used to cordon off the area. The food offerings, decorations, and other material objects used at the rite should be new, purchased on an auspicious date, and bought without haggling over their prices. Ritual participants should wash themselves and not taste the food offerings while they are being prepared. They should also be careful not to allow any spittle, hair, fingernail clippings, or dust to fall into the food. Prohibited from visiting the site of the ritual are people considered ritually "dirty," such as those in mourning, those who recently saw a dead body or attended a funeral, pregnant women, or those who have a swelling of any kind. Finally, the *mudang* usually performs a cleansing rite at the start of a major ritual. *Mudang* say that gods invited to a dirty place would inflict punishment instead of bringing good fortune.

The deities that figure in present-day rites of Korean *mudang* include not only those who originally belonged to Korea's indigenous religion but those who were added after the importation of Buddhism, Taoism, and Confucianism. Typically, these latter gods are thought to be male and have no special activity or function under their control. The indigenous deities, by contrast, are usually thought to be female and charged with major functions. Some of the originally female deities, however, appear to have changed their gender with the passage of time. Although it is far from conclusive, some evidence suggests that female deities were originally the most important in Korea's folk religion and that male deities came to be added as a result of centuries of pervasive Neo-Confucianism and male dominance.

Rituals. The rituals of Korean folk religion, generally known as *kut*, vary greatly in complexity, but three major categories can be identified. The simplest, called a *pison*, consists of no more than rubbing one's hands together to implore the assistance of a deity. The second type is called a *p'uttakkŏri* or *kosa*, depending on whether its purpose is to remove a present misfortune or seek a future benefit. At a *p'uttakkŏri* or *kosa*, food is offered to the deities.

The third and largest type of the major rituals, generally known as a grand *kut*, may involve as many as seven or eight *mudang* and musicians and may last from three to seven days and nights. A grand *kut* is a comprehensive rite offered to all the deities as well as to ancestors and ghosts. Several tables of food offerings are prepared, decorated with paper flowers, and furnished with candles and incense. The rite itself is usually composed of about fifteen to twenty-five sections (*kŏri, sŏk*), each comprising a *mudang*'s song, dance, instrumental music, and dialogue with supernatural beings.

The songs sung by the *mudang*, different for each of the *kut*'s sections, take anywhere from a half hour to three hours to perform. Their texts have been handed down orally, but the songs are not rigidly memorized and sung by rote. Though *mudang* usually adhere to their song's general content and structure, they often add, omit, or rearrange sections, depending on the purposes of the *kut*, the circumstances of the family or village sponsoring it, and other contingencies.

The contents of the *mudang*'s songs reveal much about the ideology of Korean folk religion. Rather than honor deities or thank them for past favors, the songs plead for good fortune or the removal of misfortune. Thus, the gods are perceived not primarily as objects of admiration and respect but as tools with which to satisfy one's desires. Related to this view is the timing of most *kut:* they are more often held when a specific need arises rather than on a regular or periodic basis.

The dialogue between the supernatural beings, speaking through the mouths of the *mudang*, and the persons who sponsor a *kut* is also instructive. Typically, the deities complain that their food offerings are inadequate; the sponsors respond by apologizing for being unable to prepare more, blame their poverty (and, by implication, the deities) for this inability, and promise to present larger offerings in the future if their economic situation improves. The gods then respond by saying that they will accept the offering this time and promise to bring good fortune to the supplicants.

Maintaining or improving the welfare of a household, either through economic aid or by relieving the illness of one of its members, is perhaps the most frequent motive for sponsoring a *kut*. Other common motives are promoting the welfare of a village and leading the soul of a recently deceased family member to the otherworld. A special *kut*, held when a child was afflicted with smallpox, was also very common in the past, but the eradication of this disease in Korea has obviated its *kut* as well.

Ancestor Worship. The history of Korean ancestor worship is better documented than the history of Korean folk religion, though it too suffers from a paucity of written records before the end of the Koryŏ dynasty (918–1392). Some form of rites for the dead probably existed in prehistoric times, and Buddhism was closely involved with such rites at the time of its importation from China in the fourth century CE. By the end of the Koryŏ dynasty, both Buddhist and *mudang* rites for the dead evidently existed. Such rites can still be seen today, and traces of Buddhist teachings are still evident in Korean funeral customs.

The establishment of the Chosŏn dynasty (1392–1910) brought the adoption of Neo-Confucianism as Korea's official ideology and government efforts to transform ancestor rites to a Neo-Confucian format. Particularly seminal was the *Chu-tzu chia-li*, a ritual manual attributed to the Chinese philosopher Chu Hsi. By the end of the Chosŏn dynasty, Neo-Confucian ancestor rites, with modifications, became generally accepted throughout most of the population. Even today, many Korean households have etiquette books with instructions for ancestor rites derived in some measure from the *Chu-tzu chia-li*.

The Chosŏn dynasty transformation of ideology and ancestor ritual procedures was accompanied by profound changes in Korean family and kinship organization as well as significant alterations in the structure of ancestor ritual obligations. As primogeniture and membership in patrilineal descent groups assumed greater importance toward the middle of the dynasty, women gradually lost their ritual responsibilities and eldest sons assumed a greater role in ancestor worship than any of their siblings.

Rituals. The kind of ritual activity directed toward an ancestor depends largely on the length of time that has elapsed since his or her death. A funeral usually begins with calling out the name of the deceased while setting forth shoes and rice for the death messenger(s) who come to escort the souls of the deceased along a difficult journey to face judgment in the underworld. The remainder of the funeral, during which visitors make condolence calls and the corpse is prepared for burial, usually lasts three days: the day of death, the following day, and the day of burial.

After the funeral is completed, a spirit shrine is erected at the home of the deceased. There his or her soul is said to reside for the duration of the formal mourning period. During this period interaction with the deceased is modeled closely on behavior appropriate toward living elderly parents. For example, portions of daily meals are placed at the spirit shrine, and visitors to the home are brought to the shrine to greet the deceased, just as they would be brought to greet elderly parents.

For the next four generations, ancestors receive rites at the home of their eldest son or subsequent primogeniture descendant (eldest son of the eldest son, etc.) on death anniversaries and holidays. Until recently, wooden ancestor tablets representing four generations of deceased paternal forebears and their wives were kept at the homes where the rites were offered, but in recent decades these have been almost entirely replaced by paper tablets, which are prepared for each ritual and later burned.

After four generations have passed, the primogeniture descendant is relieved of his obligations to offer an ancestor's death-anniversary and holiday rites. In their place, one ritual a year is offered at the ancestor's grave, usually in the fall. These grave rites are financed by a small piece of farmland acquired for this purpose by the ancestor's patrilineal descendants. It is rented out to a cultivator who, in return for its use, provides the food offerings and labor needed for the rite. By this method, the rites can be offered in perpetuity.

One of the striking features of Korean "ancestor" worship is that participants at these rites are not limited to patrilineal descendants of the commemorated ancestor but often include other agnatic kinsmen as well. This is especially true of holiday rites where several patrilineally related men reside together. In such communities, first, second, and even third cousins participate in the rites for each other's fathers, grandfathers, and great-grandfathers as well as in the rite for their common great-great-grandfather.

Not all of the dead receive the same complement of rites. A few famous people, granted the special privilege of permanent ancestor tablets by the Chosŏn government, receive death-anniversary rites perpetually. At the other end of the social scale are those whose descendants are dispersed and unorganized or too poor to provide grave rites for their ancestors beyond four generations. Others, who die without descendants, may receive only holiday rites from their next of kin or no rites at all. For these descendantless dead, rituals other than Neo-Confucian forms may also be offered: a tablet can be made and cared for by priests at a Buddhist temple or by a *mudang* in her shrine.

Even ancestors who receive standard Neo-Confucian rites also receive *mudang* rites. Shortly after death, such a rite may be offered to comfort the soul of the deceased and guide its transition to the otherworld. And most *kut* performed by *mudang* include a section for the benefit of the sponsoring household's deceased relatives. When performed by a *kangsin mu,* it takes the form of a séance.

Ritual attention is given to ancestors on yet other occasions. When a bride first enters her husband's family, for example, she bows before the tablets of the ancestors regularly commemorated by his household. A person's death may be reported to his ancestor, represented by a tablet; or an impending burial may be reported at the grave of the senior ancestor already interred on the same hill or mountain. And visits to ancestors' graves, usually to ensure their maintenance, are often accompanied by offerings of food and wine.

Ideas about the afterlife. Rites for ancestors take place in three different contexts, each implying a different location for the soul: before ancestor tablets, at graves, and at seances to which ancestors "come" from the otherworld. When pressed, individuals can justify these seemingly disparate practices by reciting the well-known saying that each person has three souls. In other situations, however, this multiplicity of souls is rarely mentioned.

With the exception of *mudang,* few people claim certain knowledge of the afterlife, but some basic ideas are prevalent. In general, the dead are thought to remain in the same condition as they were at the time of death and thus to retain the same need for clothing, shelter, and, especially, food. To meet these needs, sets of clothing are occasionally offered at *mudang* rites, graves are maintained, and food offerings are presented at Neo-Confucian rites. Those without offspring to provide for their needs, those whose offspring are negligent, or those who still retain some other pressing desire from their earthly existence and therefore cannot enter the otherworld are the dead who are most likely to afflict the living with illness or other misfortune in order to draw attention to their plight. Ancestors are generally thought to be benevolent, but when sudden illness or other misfortune arises, some consideration may be given to the possibility that a dead relative or other deceased person may have been the cause.

In cases of affliction, the ritual offering provided to the dead depends in large measure on his or her relationship to the living. Moving or repairing a grave is done only for patrilineal forebears and their wives. Any relative may be offered a Buddhist or *mudang* rite, however, though such rites are normally sponsored by descendants or, in their absence, next of kin. In general, responsibility for care of the dead falls on their closest living relatives, for nearest kin have the greatest obligation toward each other and thus are the most likely targets of retribution if care of the dead is inadequate. A dead stranger, by contrast, can afflict anyone but is given only a small food offering. Dead strangers, like beggars, can demand a small amount of food but not clothing, housing, or a large feast. In other words, obligations to the dead perpetuate obligations between the living.

Divination and Fortune-telling. A plethora of methods for fortune-telling and divination are known in Korea. Major differences can be seen in their philosophical foundations, practitioners, and scope, and even in the seriousness with which they are regarded. This section does not provide a systematic examination of all these characteristics for every technique but indicates the range of variation found among the more prevalent methods. Many others also exist, but they are more esoteric and less widely practiced.

Most of the divination practiced by professional fortune-tellers falls into two major categories: spirit divination and horoscope reading. The first is used by possessed *mudang* and possessed diviners. Though the latter, unlike *mudang*, do not perform *kut*, their divination techniques are the same. Speaking through the mouth of either a *mudang* or diviner, a supernatural being makes a revelation about the cause of a present misfortune or predicts a future event or condition. Often the fortune-teller mimics the spirit that is providing the revelation, speaking like a child, for example, when possessed by a dead child.

Mudang and spirit diviners also make predictions by interpreting patterns formed by grains of rice or tossed coins. Or they may have a client randomly select one of five colored flags. These methods, too, can be regarded as forms of spirit divination, for it is generally thought that a supernatural being shapes the patterns or causes a particular flag to be chosen.

Horoscope reading, the other major form of fortune-telling practiced by professional diviners, is especially prevalent in cities. Based on the theory that the time of a person's birth determines the main course of his or her life, horoscope reading utilizes the system of reckoning time according to the sexegenary cycle. Each year, month, day, and two-hour period is designated by one of sixty pairs of Chinese characters; and combining the four pairs associated with a person's year, month, day, and hour of birth yields eight characters. These are translated into predictions according to a variety of complex methods described in several printed manuals. Mastery of these complex methods is said to demand years of study, and their practice is limited to professional fortune-tellers who specialize in them. Since men enjoyed greater opportunities for study and the acquisition of literacy in traditional Korea, it is primarily they who practice horoscope reading. Most spirit diviners, by contrast, are women.

In addition to spirit divination and horoscope reading, professional fortune-telling includes less popular but still widely known methods. Most popular among these are reading hands and facial configurations or determining a person's fate from the number of strokes used to write his or her personal name. Like horoscope reading, these methods rely on learned techniques rather than on spirit possession. They are practiced either by professionals who specialize in them or by horoscope readers who utilize them as auxiliary methods. Any of these professional practitioners may also furnish their clients with charms to ward off present or future misfortunes.

Clients consult fortune-tellers in January in order to learn their fortunes for the coming year, or when a particular problem arises. Most clients are women, and their most frequently asked questions pertain to general marriage prospects, the compatibility of two potential marriage partners, future success in a business venture or college entrance examination, and the cause of a present illness. Married women often pose these questions on behalf of other members of their families, for the fate of any person usually affects the welfare of other members of a household.

Various forms of fortune-telling are also practiced by laymen. Typically, these methods require little specialized knowledge. Consulting the *Tojŏng pigyŏl*, a book of divination compiled by Yi Chi-ham (1545–1567), is one such method. It is especially popular in the month of January. After a person's year, month, and day of birth are each converted into a single digit and the digits are combined, the passage of the *Tojŏng pigyŏl* corresponding to that combined number is consulted. Each of the passages provides a general description of one's prospects for the coming year as well as month-by-month forecasts.

Almanacs are also used by laymen in Korea. Published annually, almanacs give day-by-day instructions regarding the auspiciousness of house repairs, marriages, changing one's residence, cutting down trees, funerals, and burials. Violating these prescriptions invites misfortune, but its nature is not specified by the almanac. Generally, the almanac is taken more seriously than other forms of fortune-telling also practiced by nonprofessionals. As with reading the *Tojŏng pigyŏl*, it is usually men who consult almanacs.

Geomancy. Geomancy *(p'ungsu)* is a method of finding propitious locations for houses, villages, Buddhist temples, capital cities, and graves. It is predicated on the belief that the site of a dwelling affects the well-being of its occupants, that of a capital city, the fortunes of its nation or dynasty, and that of a grave, the welfare of its occupant's patrilineal descendants. In actual practice, however, geomancy involves primarily the selection of grave sites.

Geomancy posits that a vital force *(saenggi)* travels under the surface of the earth and that individuals can avert misfortune or induce benefits by erecting their dwelling or burying an ancestor in one of the spots where this force congeals. Geomancy does not explain how the force influences human lives, however. Instead, it relies on analogy. In the case of graves, the bones of an ancestor are likened to the roots of a tree, and descendants are likened to the tree's leaves and branches; nourishing the tree's roots with the subterraneous force causes the leaves and branches to flourish also. The thrust of geomantic theory is not concerned with explaining how its effects are wrought but rather how to find and utilize propitious locations.

A geomantically favorable location is found primarily by examining the topography of the area in question, particularly its surrounding streams and mountains. Because water blocks the vital force, geomantically favorable sites usually have water just below them to restrain the force from flowing past. Wind, on the other hand, disperses the vital force, and thus the surrounding mountains should serve as shields to protect it. The configuration of the local mountains also indicates the strength of the force and the types of consequences that it will yield.

Other factors influencing the vital force are soil conditions, compass directions, and time, as calculated by the sexegenary cycle. For example, vital energy cannot congeal in stone, and too much moisture in the soil causes an ancestor's bones, conduits of the force, to decay. Associated with each compass direction and sexagenary couplet, moreover, is one of the five basic elements (fire, water, wood, metal, earth), and these should all be in harmony. A person born in a year designated by a couplet associated with wood, for example, should not be buried in such a way that his or her corpse is oriented along a direction associated with fire.

Reasoning by analogy is also used to infer the potential effects of a site. A mountain that is circular in shape and has a pointed top is said to resemble the tip of a writing brush, so burying an ancestor there will produce descendants who are good calligraphers or who are successful at passing the civil service examination. Similarly, wells should not be dug in a site shaped like a boat, for that would be analogous to sinking the boat and thereby destroying the site's geomantic benefits.

The methods of interpreting local configurations are so diverse that some feature in the local topography or time and place of burial can usually be found to explain a wide variety of subsequent events. In addition to all of the above considerations, an ancestor's discomfort in a grave site may also be advanced as the reason for that ancestor's inflicting misfortune on his or her descendants. The disparity between this interpretation of geomancy and its more conventional conception as an impersonal mechanism, a disparity noted in anthropological analyses of geomancy in China, is a matter of concern to neither informants nor geomantic manuals.

Known as the "theory of wind and water" *(p'ungsu)*, geomancy was originally developed in China (where it was known as *feng-shui*) and later spread to Korea, probably before the end of the Unified Silla dynasty (668–935 CE). Professional Korean geomancers appear to have adopted the Chinese system with little modification and even today use some of the manuals authored by Chinese geomancers. How well the Korean laymen's views match those of the professional, and how well these lay views correspond to those found in China, are matters that have yet to be investigated, however.

Christianity. Korea's first known contact with Christianity came during the late sixteenth century. A Jesuit missionary accompanied the Japanese army that invaded Korea at that time, but there is no evidence to indicate that his visit had any influence on Korean religion.

Christianity first had an influence in Korea during the following century, when Korean envoys to the Chinese court in Peking encountered some of the ideas brought there by Jesuit missionaries. A few of these attracted the interest of some noted Korean intellectuals of the seventeenth and eighteenth centuries. By the last quarter of the eighteenth century, a few Korean literati had formed study groups to examine and discuss Catholicism, and a few individuals even announced their conversion to the new religion.

The Chosŏn dynasty court soon viewed Catholicism as a threat to Korea's established social order, primarily because of Catholic opposition to ancestor rites. With Neo-Confucianism its official creed, the Chosŏn court viewed the father-son relationship not only as the basic paradigm for relations between subject and ruler but also as fundamental to the maintenance of social order. Any challenge to filial piety, whether toward living parents or deceased predecessors, had serious political implications. Thus the new religion was officially proscribed by the mid-1780s, and a few executions soon followed. This antipathy toward Catholicism was exacerbated in 1801 by the involvement of some Korean

Catholics in an attempt to draw Chinese and Western military forces into Korea in order to ensure freedom for their religion. The incident provoked further persecutions and imprisonment of Catholics. Yet despite bloody, if sporadic, persecutions, Catholicism continued to grow throughout the nineteenth century, largely through the efforts of French missionaries and church officials in Peking.

The growth of Catholicism in Korea was later eclipsed by the successes of Protestant missionaries. Though sustained Protestant missionary efforts began only in the penultimate decade of the nineteenth century, by the mid-1980s Protestants outnumbered Catholics by about four to one in South Korea. Though published statistics vary widely, depending on their sources, Catholics appeared to number about 1.5 million and Protestants about 5.5 million at that time.

The success of Christianity, particularly Protestantism, in South Korea is curious in view of the relative paucity of Christian converts in Japan and China, Korea's closest geographical and cultural neighbors. The success is all the more curious in view of the meager indigenization of Christian ideology and ritual in Korea. As a result, identifying the causes of Christianity's growth has emerged as one of the major issues in the study of Christianity. Three major causes have been advanced thus far: preexisting similarities between Christianity and Korean *mudang* practices, the ability of early Protestant missionaries to establish personal ties with members of the Korean court at the turn of the century, and the missionaries' sympathy toward Korean nationalism during the period of Japanese colonial rule (1910–1945). All of these may be valid, but none explains the remarkable growth of Christianity in South Korea during the 1970s and early 1980s. Wide variations in published statistics notwithstanding, both Catholicism and Protestantism apparently doubled their memberships in South Korea between 1972 and 1981. Perhaps this remarkable growth in recent years was fostered by South Korean industrialization and urbanization, the consequent dispersal of many of the social groups that participated at traditional Korean religious rites, and the widespread importation of nonreligious Western culture as well. Perhaps the growth was also fostered by the Christian churches' increasing involvement in the South Korean human rights movement.

New Religions. Like similar movements elsewhere in the world, Korea's new religions have tended to flourish in times of greatest personal distress and social disorder. The final decades of the Chosŏn dynasty and the years following World War II, during which many of these religions emerged and grew, were periods of especially intense social, economic, and political turmoil. In both eras, moreover, threatened or actual foreign military intervention exacerbated Korea's internal difficulties.

Continued foreign intervention in Korean affairs during the past one hundred years probably explains why nationalism has been a major theme of many new religions. The Eastern Learning (Tonghak) movement, the first of Korea's new religions, was at the forefront of anti-Japanese activities immediately prior to and during Japanese colonial rule. Some present-day new religions teach that Korea will eventually become the most important of the world's nations, or they display the South Korean flag prominently during their services.

In formulating their respective doctrines, the founders of Korea's new religions have most often been men who claimed to have received a supernatural revelation, but their teachings have drawn heavily upon Korea's traditional religions as well as upon Christianity. The particular blend of these sources varies greatly from one faith to the next, however, depending primarily on the personal religious background of their founders. Some groups, such as Wŏn Buddhism, are most similar to established Buddhism; others, such as Sun Myung Moon's Unification Church, draw more heavily upon Christianity.

Though the doctrines of the new religions vary, most are directed toward the resolution of economic or health problems rather than a concern for the afterlife. Many of the new religions offer their followers the promise of utopia on earth. As in Korean folk religion, wealth is not viewed as a hindrance to happiness but rather as a blessing to be actively sought.

After they were founded, many of Korea's new religions exhibited one of two common tendencies. Some grew and became established churches, shifted their emphasis away from magical cures and this-worldly concerns, and developed a rationalized, elaborated, and articulated body of teachings. Such was the fate of the Eastern Learning movement, which is now known as the Religion of the Heavenly Way (Ch'ŏndogyo), and of Sun Myung Moon's Unification Church. [*See* Ch'ŏndogyo *and* Unification Church.] Alternatively, some new religions did not grow but were plagued by continual segmentation, often precipitated by one of their members claiming to have received his or her own revelation and then establishing a separate church.

The total membership of Korea's new religions is difficult to determine with any precision, especially because many of the smaller religions have an ephemeral following. The most up-to-date and apparently accurate statistics, compiled by the South Korean government and as yet disseminated only through newspaper reports, estimates their total membership as of October

1983 at about one million, or about 3 percent of the South Korean population.

[*See also* Shamanism, *overview article, and* Ancestors, *article on* Ancestor Cults.]

BIBLIOGRAPHY

Korean-language scholarship on Korean religion is extensive. A good introduction to the entire field is *Min'gan sinang, chongyo,* "Han'guk minsok taegwan," vol. 3, edited by the Kodae minjok munhwa yŏn'guso (Seoul, 1983). This work covers the entire spectrum of Korean religion, including both folk religions and established faiths. It also contains footnotes that refer to much of the Korean-language scholarship and has a sixty-page English summary.

For the histories of the various Korean religions, much useful information can be found in Ki-baik Lee's *A New History of Korea,* translated by Edward W. Wagner with Edward J. Shultz (Seoul, 1984). Though some of his interpretations are controversial, Lee's work builds on that of several authors and thereby offers the best English-language survey of scholarship by Korean and other historians. Several chapter subsections, each one or two pages in length, chronicle each of the various faiths in different periods of Korean history.

The most comprehensive bibliography of Western-language works on Korean religion has been compiled by Kah-Kyung Cho and included in chapter 4 of *Studies on Korea: A Scholar's Guide,* edited by Han-Kyo Kim (Honolulu, 1980), pp. 120–133. With few exceptions, Cho's bibliography ends at 1970, but his classified listing of more than two hundred entries, many of them annotated, still provides the easiest entry to most of the Western scholarship.

Many of the best works on traditional Korean religion have appeared since 1970. Youngsook Kim Harvey's *Six Korean Women: The Socialization of Shamans* (Saint Paul, 1979) analyzes recruitment to the role of *kangsin mu* by identifying commonalities in their life histories and personalities. Laurel Kendall's *Shamans, Housewives, and Other Restless Spirits* (Honolulu, 1985) focuses on *mudang* rites and beliefs, relating these to the roles and social situations common to Korean women. *The Folk Treasury of Korea,* edited by Chang Duk-soon (Seoul, 1970), includes texts of *mudang*'s myths as well as a few myths from Korean literary sources compiled during the Koryŏ dynasty. *Ancestor Worship and Korean Society* (Stanford, Calif., 1982), by Roger L. Janelli and Dawnhee Yim Janelli, presents a description and analysis of rites for ancestors in terms of Korean family, kin group, and class structure. Alexandre Guillemoz's *Les algues, les anciens, les dieux* (Paris, 1983) surveys the diverse religious beliefs and rites of a single Korean village and points to their structural interrelationships.

Korean fortune-telling and geomancy have attracted far less scholarly attention than *mudang* rites and ancestor worship, but here again the best works have appeared within the past few years. For a brief but very informative survey of fortune-telling methods and topics of inquiry in Seoul, see Barbara Young's essay "City Women and Divination: Signs in Seoul," in *Korean Women: View from the Inner Room,* edited by Laurel Kendall and Mark Peterson (New Haven, Conn., 1983). Dawnhee Yim Janelli's "The Strategies of a Korean Fortuneteller," *Korea Journal* 20 (1980): 8–14, provides a brief description of consultation sessions with a horoscope reader in Seoul and identifies some of the techniques she employed to establish and maintain credibility in the eyes of her clients. For an account of Korean almanacs and their use in rural Korea, see M. Griffin Dix's "The Place of the Almanac in Korean Folk Religion," *Journal of Korean Studies* 2 (1980): 47–70. For a description of Korean geomancy, based on an examination of geomantic manuals, legends about geomancy, and interviews with professional geomancers, see Yoon Hong-key's Ph.D. dissertation, *Geomantic Relationships between Culture and Nature in Korea,* available as number 88 of the "Asian Folklore and Social Life Monograph Series" (Taipei, 1976).

Christianity has not enjoyed the same degree of recent growth in scholarly interest as have traditional Korean religions, and earlier books generally remain the most useful. The standard history of Protestantism in Korea is George L. Paik's *The History of Protestant Missions in Korea, 1832–1910* (1929; 3d ed., Seoul, 1980). For an account of Christianity's growth in terms of its relationships with Korean history and culture, see Spencer J. Palmer's *Korea and Christianity: The Problem of Identification with Tradition,* "Royal Asiatic Society, Korea Branch, Monograph Series," no. 2 (Seoul, 1967).

Among the more recent publications on Korean Christianity, two articles are especially noteworthy. The first is Donald L. Baker's "The Martyrdom of Paul Yun: Western Religion and Eastern Ritual in Eighteenth Century Korea," *Transactions of the Royal Asiatic Society, Korea Branch* 54 (1979): 33–58. Baker's study deals with the introduction of Catholicism into Korea and its perception by both early converts and the central government. The other is Frank Baldwin's "Missionaries and the March First Movement: Can Moral Men Be Neutral?," in *Korea under Japanese Colonial Rule,* edited by Andrew C. Nahm (Kalamazoo, Mich., 1973). Based on an examination of both Japanese and English sources, Baldwin's study depicts the Western missionaries' reluctance to participate in nationalist movements during the Japanese colonial era despite their personal sympathies toward the Korean cause.

Ch'ŏndogyo and the Unification Church have received far more attention than the other Korean new religions. *The New Religions of Korea,* edited by Spencer J. Palmer and published as volume 43 of the *Transactions of the Royal Asiatic Society, Korea Branch* (Seoul, 1967), is a collection of disparate but informative essays that deal with several of these faiths. It is still the best introduction to these religions.

YIM SUK-JAY, ROGER L. JANELLI, and
DAWNHEE YIM JANELLI

KOSMAS AITOLOS (1714–1779), also known as Father Kosmas; Christian saint, priest, monk, popular preacher, and educator. Kosmas was born in Aitolia, Greece, and received his elementary education in his home province. After spending some time as a teacher, he entered the theological academy on Mount Athos then headed by Eugerios Voulgares, one of the eminent Greek educators of the eighteenth century. Shortly afterward, Kosmas became a member of the monastery of Philotheou (one of the twenty monasteries of Mount Athos), where he later was ordained a priest.

Within a year, Kosmas felt called to leave the monastery and become an itinerant preacher. With the permission of the patriarch of Constantinople, Serapheim II (1761–1763), Kosmas began his preaching ministry, which lasted until his death by hanging in 1779 at the hands of the Ottoman authorities, who accused him of, among other things, being a Russian spy.

What alarmed the Ottoman authorities was the great popularity enjoyed by Kosmas. His honesty and direct manner of preaching in the language of the people, his reputation for sanctity, his frequent visits to remote villages and hamlets, and his total disregard for material possessions caused hundreds, sometimes thousands, of men and women to follow him while he traveled from village to village.

Kosmas preached a gospel of love and concern for the fair and just treatment of women and children. In addition, he laid great stress on education, founding ten secondary schools and over two hundred elementary schools. Often he secured both teachers and funds for these schools. He believed that an educated laity would be able to rise to a higher standard of moral and ethical living and thus be better prepared to resist the temptation, due to discrimination as well as social and economic pressures, to convert to Islam. Kosmas can truly be credited with effecting enormous changes in education and in the moral behavior of the people of western Greece and southern Albania.

Honored as a saint in his lifetime, Kosmas is today one of the most popular saints of the Greek Orthodox church. He has been given the sobriquet "teacher of the nation."

BIBLIOGRAPHY

A complete bibliography on Kosmas would include over two thousand items. The best work on him and his times is Markos A. Gkiokas's *Ho Kosmas Aitolos kai hē epochē tou* (Athens, 1972). The most complete account of his teachings in English is my own book *Father Kosmas, the Apostle of the Poor* (Brookline, Mass., 1977).

NOMIKOS MICHAEL VAPORIS

KOTLER, AHARON (1892–1962), rabbi and prominent educator in eastern Europe and the United States. A child prodigy, Kotler was sent as a youth to study in the famous *musar-yeshivah* of Slobodka (near modern-day Kaunas, Lithuania), which emphasized Talmudic studies as well as ethics and self-improvement. After his marriage to the daughter of Isser Zalman Meltzer, the head of the *yeshivah* in Slutsk, White Russia, Kotler moved to Slutsk and began to teach in the *yeshivah*. In the wake of World War I he moved the *yeshivah* from the Soviet-controlled area to Kletzk in Poland. There he became one of the best-known figures in Polish rabbinical circles. He was the youngest member of the Council of Scholars and Sages of Agudat Yisra'el.

In 1935 Kotler visited the United States, where he discussed the need for an American *yeshivah* that would be designed not for the training of rabbis and religious professionals but for the study of Torah for its own sake. The discussions came to naught and he returned to Poland.

Following the German occupation of Poland, Kotler immigrated in 1941 to the United States, where he was to have his most lasting influence. He was driven by the concern that with the destruction of the *yeshivot* in eastern Europe, new centers of Torah study would have to be established in America. Despite widespread doubt that the atmosphere of intense Torah study that had prevailed in eastern Europe could be re-created in the United States, Kotler persevered and in 1943 established the Beit Midrash Gevohah in Lakewood, New Jersey. The school was designed for students of post-high-school age, and its curriculum was made up solely of religious studies with no admixture of secular studies. The school grew rapidly and by the 1980s had more than eight hundred students. Active in the Jewish day-school movement as well, Kotler also helped to intensify Jewish education on the primary level. One result of his influence was a decrease of cooperation between Orthodox and non-Orthodox Jewish groups, for he was strongly opposed to the participation of Orthodox bodies in associations that included Reform or Conservative rabbis.

BIBLIOGRAPHY

There is no full-scale biography of Aharon Kotler. An interesting and highly complimentary study of the Beit Midrash Gevohah, which deals, of course, with Kotler, is Sidney Ruben Lewitter's "A School for Scholars" (Ph.D. diss., Rutgers University, 1981). Much relevant material can also be found in William B. Helmreich's *The World of the Yeshiva* (New York, 1982).

SHAUL STAMPFER

K'OU CH'IEN-CHIH (373–448), Celestial Master (*t'ien-shih*) at the Northern (T'o-pa) Wei court between the years 425 and 448, an office that marked a unique era of Taoist ascendancy in Chinese political history. A member of a traditionally Taoist gentry family of

Feng-i (Shensi), K'ou at an early age developed an intense interest in such occult sciences as astrology, alchemy, and knowledge of transcendental herbs. At about the age of thirty (c. 403) he went into reclusion on the western sacred peak of Mount Hua (Shensi) with his master the Taoist adept Ch'eng-kung Hsing (d. 412?), a student of the Buddhist monk and mathematician Shih T'an-ying (d. before 418), who had been a colleague of the great Central Asian translator Kumārajīva while the latter was in Ch'ang-an (modern Sian) between 402 and 413. After a brief sojourn on Mount Hua the two traveled to the central sacred peak, Mount Sung (in Honan). Ch'eng-kung died after seven years, and K'ou continued his cultivation of Taoist arts alone on the mountain. In 415 he was rewarded with a visitation from the deified Lao-tzu (T'ai-shang Lao-chün), who delivered to him a document labeled *Yün-chung yin-sung hsin-k'o chih chieh* (Articles of a New Code to Be Chanted to Yün-chung Musical Notation), which corresponds to the *Lao-chün yin-sung chieh-ching* of the present Taoist canon (Harvard-Yenching Index No. 784). At the same time the god revealed to him certain secret breathing and calisthenic techniques, and soon he began to attract disciples. Eight years later, in 423, when he was fifty, he was visited again by a divine being, this one a Li P'u-wen, who identified himself as Lao-tzu's great-great grandson *(hsüan-sun)*. Li P'u-wen presented K'ou with a second document, *Lu-t'u chen-ching* (The True Scripture of Talismanic Designs). It has not survived, but was probably similar to other collections of talismanic designs (fantastic characters) that can be found in the canon.

The *New Code* appears to have been influenced indirectly by translations of the Buddhist Vinaya that had recently appeared in China. It set forth rules for the selection and ceremonial roles of religious officers and the conduct of ceremonies, confessionals, and charitable feasts *(ch'u-hui)*, and laid down principles for moral behavior among the "chosen people" *(chung-min)*, that is, among the adherents of the Celestial Masters Sect (T'ien-shih Tao). The code seems to have been directed specifically at reforming certain practices that had emerged since the founding of the sect by Chang Tao-ling in the late second century and that were now felt to pose a threat to civic order in the Northern Wei state. These included the apocalyptic expectation of messianic deliverers (who often turned out to be fomenters of rebellion), the hereditary transmission of religious offices within particular families, and the extragovernmental levies of grain or silk *(tsu-mi)* to support them, which tended to create subgovernmental enclaves within the state. The code was also directed against the sexual ritual known as the "union of vital forces" *(ho-ch'i)*, which was seen as a threat to public morals. It is for these reasons that when in 424 K'ou Ch'ien-chih arrived in the Northern Wei capital of P'ing-ch'eng (in Shansi), he was eagerly welcomed by such diverse constituencies as the non-Chinese T'o-pa rulers and the Confucian-oriented minister Ts'ui Hao (381–450). It was Ts'ui Hao who sponsored K'ou's induction into the Northern Wei administrative hierarchy as Celestial Master in 425.

In his alliance with K'ou Ch'ien-chih, Ts'ui Hao had his own agenda. He was the scion of an old Chinese gentry family that looked forward to the restoration of a unified Han rule over the fragmented non-Chinese kingdoms of the north and the weakened Chinese exilic regimes of the south. Ts'ui utilized K'ou's essentially conservative *New Code* as a spiritual base from which he could promote his own goals. He saw to it that the *New Code* was promulgated to every corner of the T'o-pa empire, which at its peak included nearly all of China north of the Yangtze River and by 439 appeared ready to incorporate the south as well. He also took advantage of the confidence placed in him by Emperor T'ai-wu (424–452) to institute some reforms of his own. These culminated in the devastating purge of the Buddhist clergy and the proscription of the Buddhist religion and confiscation of its monasteries between the years 444 and 446. K'ou Ch'ien-chih has been accused of instigating the attacks in an attempt to eliminate a rival faith, but this is unlikely, although his acquiescence is probable. His own master, Ch'eng-kung Hsing, had studied with Buddhist teachers and had inculcated in his disciple a high regard for the foreign faith. K'ou seems to have acquiesced in Ts'ui Hao's purges primarily because they were also aimed at local heterodox cults *(yin-ssu)*. It was these pockets of popular religion where blood sacrifices and other unacceptable forms of worship were still practiced which K'ou, as head of an established Taoist orthodoxy, could not tolerate.

K'ou Ch'ien-chih's term as Celestial Master is sometimes compared to a theocracy because of the unique establishment of religion in the Northern Wei state, in which the Celestial Master as *pontifex maximus* mediated between the celestial divinities and the earthly ruler. The climax of K'ou's career was the inauguration of the reign period "Perfect Ruler of Grand Peace" (T'ai-p'ing Chen-chün), which lasted from 440 to 451. The title was unmistakably Taoist, recalling the ideal of universal peace proclaimed by the Yellow Turban leader Chang Chüeh in 184. His movement, known as the Way of Grand Peace (T'ai-p'ing Tao), was presumably based in turn on teachings found in the *Scripture of Grand Peace (T'ai-p'ing ching)*. In a magnificent public ceremony conducted on a newly constructed Taoist platform *(t'an)* south of the capital, on New Year's Day of the year 442 K'ou Ch'ien-chih, splendidly arrayed in Taoist robes, personally presented to Emperor T'ai-wu certain sacred talismans *(fu-lu)* in recognition of the emperor's sage virtue as "Perfect Ruler." The ceremony instituted a tradition of Taoist investiture that was continued by the T'o-pa states well into the next century. The "theocracy," however, ended with K'ou's death in 448. Four years later T'ai-wu was murdered by a palace eunuch. His successor, Wen-ch'eng (452–465), was an ardent Buddhist and in an orgy of penitential restitution reestablished Buddhism as the state religion. Under him began the construction of the monumental cave-temples of Yün-kang that have come down to the present day.

[*See also* Taoism, *overview article and article on* The Taoist Religious Community.]

BIBLIOGRAPHY

The primary source for K'ou Ch'ien-chih is the "Monograph on Buddhism and Taoism" *(Shih-Lao chih)* in fascicle 114 of the *Wei-shu* (Peking, 1974), pp. 3048–3055. The Taoist portion has been translated by James R. Ware in "The *Wei Shu* and the *Sui Shu* on Taoism," *Journal of the American Oriental Society* 53 (1933): 215–250. The most complete study of this text is found in Tsukamoto Zenryū's *Gisho Shakurōshi no kenkyū* (Kyoto, 1961), pp. 313–356. An annotated text of the "Articles of a New Code" attributed to K'ou Ch'ien-chih may be found in Yang Lien-sheng's *"Lao-chün yin-sung chieh-ching chiao-shih," Bulletin of the Institute of History and Philology, Academia Sinica* 28 (1956): 17–53. Two secondary studies are my own "K'ou Ch'ien-chih and the Taoist Theocracy at the Northern Wei Court, 425–451," in *Facets of Taoism,* edited by Holmes Welch and Anna Seidel (New Haven, 1979), and Anna Seidel's "The Image of the Perfect Ruler in Early Taoist Messianism: Lao-tzu and Li Hung," *History of Religions* 9 (1969–1970): 216–247.

RICHARD B. MATHER

KŌYA (903–972), also called Kūya, a charismatic Japanese monk who devoted himself to popularizing the Nembutsu (Chin., Nien-fo), the oral invocation of Amida Buddha. Kōya's origins are unknown, but some sources claim that he may have been a grandson of Emperor Ninmyō (810–850) or a son of Emperor Daigo (885–930). In his youth, as an itinerant lay priest *(ubasoku),* Kōya traveled in rural areas, directing and assisting in the repair of roads and bridges, improving wells and dikes, and supervising burials. In these activities he closely resembled Gyōgi (or Gyōki, 668–749), a revered monk of the Nara period. [*See the biography of Gyōgi.*]

In 924, Kōya formally entered the priesthood at the Kokubunji in Owari Province (modern Aichi Prefecture). He later spent periods of devotion and study at Mineaidera in Harima Province (modern Hyōgo Prefecture), at Yushima on the island of Shikoku, and perhaps in the far northern provinces as well. But beginning in about 938, his public demonstrations of the Nembutsu in the markets of Heiankyō, the capital city (modern Kyoto), began to attract a large following among the common people. He soon became known as *ichi no hijiri* ("the holy man of the markets") and *Amida hijiri* ("the holy man of Amida").

In 948 he received full ordination at Enryakuji, the headquarters of the Tendai school, and took the priestly name Kōshō. When an epidemic swept Heiankyō in 951, Kōya undertook several projects designed to ease the sufferings of the people, including the carving of images of the eleven-headed Kannon and other benevolent deities, the copying of the *Daihannyakyō (Mahāprajñāpāramitā Sūtra)* in gold letters, and the founding of a temple, originally named Saikōji, and now called Rokuharamitsuji. The temple, near Higashiyama in Kyoto, remains closely associated with Kōya, and it was also the site of his death, at age sixty-nine, in 972.

Kōya's Nembutsu, a chant accompanied by dancing to the beat of a small cymbal or drum, was probably an adaptation of shamanic practices. He also praised Amida and the Nembutsu in simple verses that were posted in the marketplace. Before Kōya, the Nembutsu was used as a magical charm, at funerals, and in the intense meditations of Tendai monks. Kōya was the first to prescribe it as a simple expression of faith to be used by the uneducated and the poor, and he is even said to have taught it to prostitutes and criminals. He thus contributed to the Heian-period developments that carried Buddhism beyond the confines of court and monastery and prefigured the founders of the Pure Land (Jōdo) schools that emerged in the Kamakura period (twelfth and thirteenth centuries), advocating exclusive devotion to the Nembutsu and appealing to persons from all social strata.

Like Gyōgi and the Kamakura innovators, Kōya functioned on the periphery of the ecclesiastical establishment while maintaining ties with influential, aristocratic patrons, and he was thus free to convey his teachings to a diverse audience. There are many legends about his deeds, and the wooden image of him enshrined at Rokuharamitsuji (done in the Kamakura period) emphasizes his *hijiri* character: he is clad as an ascetic and carries his cymbal and a staff topped with antlers; he leans forward as if to begin his dance, and from his mouth issue six tiny images of Amida Buddha, representing the six characters of the written Nembutsu.

[*For further discussion of the Nembutsu, called Nien-fo in Chinese, see* Nien-fo.]

BIBLIOGRAPHY

The most reliable account of Kōya's life and career is a memorial biography, *Kōya rui*, written in 972 (the year of his death) by Minamoto Tamenori. The biography in Yoshishige Yasutane's *Nihon ōjō gokuraku ki* (c. 986) and most other traditional versions are closely based on Tamenori's. These and other variants are reproduced and are the basis of the most comprehensive modern study in Japanese, Hori Ichirō's *Kōya* (Tokyo, 1963), no. 106 of "Jimbutsu sōsho." For the context of Kōya's activities in Heian Buddhism, see Hayami Tasuku's "Heian bukkyō to kizoku bunka," chapter 3 of *Ajia bukkyōshi, Nihon hen II: Heian bukkyō*, edited by Nakamura Hajime, Kasahara Kazuo, and Kanaoka Shūyū (Tokyo, 1974), pp. 192–194.

In Hori's English works, Kōya is discussed as one of several similar Heian period figures; see "On the Concept of *Hijiri* (Holy-Man)," *Numen* 5 (April 1958): 128–160 and (September 1958): 199–232; and *Folk Religion in Japan*, edited by Joseph M. Kitagawa and Alan L. Miller (Chicago, 1968), pp. 107ff. Two of Kōya's devotional poems are translated and discussed in *Sources of Japanese Tradition*, compiled by Ryusaku Tsunoda, Wm. Theodore de Bary, and Donald Keene (New York, 1958), vol. 1, pp. 187–188.

EDWARD KAMENS

KRAEMER, HENDRIK (1888–1965), Dutch historian of religions. Kraemer spent his professional career mainly in three significantly different settings: working with the Dutch Bible Society in Indonesia (1921–1935), serving as professor of the history and phenomenology of religions at the University of Leiden (1937–1947), and functioning as the first director of the Ecumenical Institute Chateau de Bossy in Switzerland (1948–1955). His guest lectureships included, among many others, a stay at Union Theological Seminary in New York (1956–1957), and the Olaus Petri Lectures at the University of Uppsala (February 1955).

Beginning with the Second International Missionary Conference held in Tambaram, India (December 1938), Kraemer played a major role in the ecumenical theological discussions on the relations between Christian faith and other religions. His works *The Christian Message in a Non-Christian World* (1938), *Religion and the Christian Faith* (1956), and *World Cultures and World Religions: The Coming Dialogue* (1960) explore this theme.

Among the less well known titles that are important for an assessment of Kraemer's work as a historian of religions and of how he viewed religio-historical data "in the light of Christ, the 'kritikos' of all things," four publications deserve special attention. The earliest of these is the article "Geloof en Mystiek" (Faith and Mysticism), which appeared in the missionary journal *Zendingstijdschrift "De Opwekker"* 79 (Bandeong, Netherlands Indies, 1934). Next is Kraemer's inaugural address in Leiden, *De Wortelen van het Syncretisme* (The Roots of Syncretism; 1937). Third is the study "Vormen van Godsdienstcrisis" (Forms of Crisis of Religion), originally published in *Mededelingen der Koninklijke Nederlandse Akademie van Wetenschappen, Afdeling Letterkunde*, n.s. 22 (1959): 103–134, and later reissued as a booklet (Nijkerk, n.d.); it is based on four lectures given in 1959 on the place of the history of religions in the faculty of theology. Finally, of particular interest are Kraemer's remarks on W. Brede Kristensen (who was his predecessor at Leiden) in the introduction to Kristensen's *The Meaning of Religion*, edited by John B. Carman (1960).

Without ever abandoning his earlier thesis of a discontinuity between the biblical revelation and all forms of religion—most radically expressed in his 1938 study for the Tambaram conference—Kraemer tried later, in his own words, "to improve upon" that view of "the non-Christian religions [as] . . . great human achievements" by paying careful attention to "the religious consciousness as the place of dialectic encounter with God" (*Religion and the Christian Faith*, p. 8). He affirmed religiosity as a fundamental aspect of human structure and as manifesting the permanence, amid various forms of religious crisis, of the *sensus divinitatis* and *semen religionis* "whatever the content of the 'divinitas' and whatever the quality of the 'semen'" ("Vormen van Godsdienstcrisis," p. 134). As the notion of "communication," including communications between people of different traditions, became a key concern for Kraemer in the later years, he stressed the need for participants in an interfaith dialogue to "be open to new insights through the instrumentality of contact with one another," and he called for "a real openness to truth wherever it may be found" (*World Cultures and World Religions*, pp. 356–365).

From 1938 onward the debate on Kraemer has focused on his theological views, and relatively little attention has been given to the question of the extent to which his theological perspectives and the categories derived from them influenced his description and analysis of world religions.

BIBLIOGRAPHY

Kraemer's extensive studies of Islam include his doctoral dissertation, *Een Javaansche Primbon uit de estiende eeuw* (Leiden, 1921); "Eenige grepen uit de moderne Apologie van de Islam," *Tijdschrift voor Indische Tall-, Land- en Volkenkunde* 75 (1935): 1–35, 165–217; and *Een nieuw geluid op het gebied der Koranexegese* (Amsterdam, 1962). Kraemer discussed Christian-Muslim relations in "L'Islam, une religion, un mode de vie: L'Islam, une culture; Points de confrontation entre l'Islam et le Christianisme," *Revue de l'évangélisation* 41 (1959): 2–38; "Die grundsätzlichen Schwierigkeiten in der Begegnung von Christentum und Islam," in *Neue Begegnung von Kirche und Islam,* edited by Walter Holsten (Stuttgart, 1960), pp. 15–27; and "Islamic Culture and Missionary Adequacy," *Muslim World* 50 (1960): 244–251.

For a bibliography of Kraemer's works, see Carl F. Hallencreutz's *Kraemer towards Tambaram* (Lund, 1965), pp. 309–317. A comprehensive list of biographies and works of appreciation can be found in Jacques Waardenburg's *Classical Approaches to the Study of Religion,* vol. 2, *Bibliography* (The Hague, 1974), pp. 133–135.

WILLEM A. BIJLEFELD

KRATOPHANY. *See* Power.

KRISHNA. *See* Kṛṣṇa.

KRISHNAMURTI, JIDDU (1895–1986), Indian spiritual leader. Jiddu Krishnamurti attained fame through his presentation of a unique version of Indian philosophy and mysticism in a charismatic, even mesmerizing, style of lecturing that attracted large audiences around the world.

Although Krishnamurti taught a philosophy that seemed to border on atheism, it is made clear in his authorized biography that throughout his life he was subject to a profound spiritual purgation. This purgation came to be called "the Process" and suggested to those who witnessed it that his "higher self" departed from his body and entered into what appeared to be a transcendent state of consciousness. This state was accompanied at times by severe pain in his head and back. Krishnamurti's experience has been likened to the awakening of the *kuṇḍalinī* power, practiced in some forms of Indian spirituality. The suffering accompanying this experience occurred only under certain circumstances and did not impede his teaching work; in fact, it contributed to the exalted state in which Krishnamurti knew the oneness with all life and the unconditioned freedom that he tried, through his continual lecturing and the books, tape recordings, and videotapes published by his organization, to convey to thousands of persons under his influence.

Krishnamurti was born in Madanapalle, a small town in what is now the state of Andhra Pradesh, north of Madras. He was of brahman caste. His father, Narianiah, was a rent collector and, later, a district magistrate under the British government. His mother, Sanjeevama, died when Krishnamurti was ten years old. His father cared for him and his brothers until he retired from government service and was granted permission to move to the estate of the Theosophical Society, located just outside Madras. This move occurred in January 1909, when Annie Besant was the international president of the Theosophical Society. Her close collaborator was Charles W. Leadbeater, whose clairvoyant powers, he claimed, enabled him to recognize Krishnamurti's potential for spiritual greatness when he observed the boy's aura as he was playing on the beach at the seaside edge of the Theosophical Society estate.

The teaching of theosophy, as promulgated by H. P. Blavatsky and H. S. Olcott, the founders of the Theosophical Society, held that the spiritual destiny of humanity was in the hands of "Masters," highly evolved human beings who had transcended material existence and lived on a higher plane. Leadbeater and Besant taught that the Lord Maitreya, the World Teacher, would become incarnate in this age in a manner similar to the way that Śrī Kṛṣṇa (the Hindu deity) and Jesus had appeared in the world in earlier eras. Krishnamurti was a likely candidate to become the vehicle for such a manifestation but it remained for him to be trained and tested before he could actually take on such a role.

Krishnamurti and his brother Nitya were "put on probation" (i.e., rigorously tested and prepared for spiritual leadership) by a Master named Kuthumi on 1 August 1909, when Krishnamurti was fourteen years old. From that time onward Krishnamurti was nurtured and financially supported by a circle of upper-class English and American men and women and was under the scrutiny of the larger group of Theosophists who saw him at public gatherings. An organization called the Order of the Star in the East was founded by George Arundale, a prominent Theosophist of the period, to promote Krishnamurti's projected vocation.

Krishnamurti and Nitya left India in 1911 for their first visit to England. After their return to India, Krishnamurti's father allowed Krishnamurti and Nitya to be taken back to England for education by Besant and signed a document to that effect in 1912. By the end of 1912 Narianiah had filed suit against Besant to regain custody and charged that Leadbeater and Krishnamurti were involved in a sexual relationship. In 1914, after a judgment against her in the Indian courts, Besant won an appeal to the Privy Council in London. Both she and Leadbeater were exonerated from the charges brought by Narianiah. Krishnamurti and Nitya remained in England during this period and were prepared by a tutor for university studies. However, Krishnamurti was not able to pass the entrance examinations for Oxford and never obtained a university degree, although he studied for many years privately and learned English, French, and some Sanskrit.

From about 1920 until the dissolution of the Order of the Star (formerly the Order of the Star in the East) in 1929, Krishnamurti's extraordinary gifts as a public lecturer and his independent viewpoint on the spiritual quest became evident. He spoke more and more frequently at gatherings of the Theosophical Society in India, the Netherlands, and North America. At some of these meetings he referred to himself in a way that implied he was speaking as the World Teacher. (Krishnamurti's brother and constant companion, Nitya, died of tuberculosis in Ojai, California, on 13 November 1925; Krishnamurti's struggle with the ensuing sorrow was formative of his judgment about the "bondages of the mind.") However, the articulation of his own special teachings alienated him from the inner circle of the leadership of the Theosophical Society, including Besant, Leadbeater, Arundale, and C. Jinarajadasa, each of whom claimed to have received communications from the Masters consisting of instructions for the Theosophical Society that were contrary to Krishnamurti's increasingly independent course. Besant's death in 1933 ended Krishnamurti's ties to the Theosophical Society, and for this break he was repudiated for some time by its leading officials. However, Jinarajadasa's successors to the presidency of the Theosophical Society, Nilakanta Sri Ram and Radha Burnier, sought cordial relations with Krishnamurti, who visited the Theosophical Society compound in the years before his death.

Krishnamurti's work as an independent teacher eventually combined two approaches. First, he traveled around the world on a schedule of lectures. In India he spoke often in Madras and Bombay, and occasionally in Delhi and Banaras. He lectured at Saanen in Switzerland, Brockwood Park in England, and New York City and Ojai (where he maintained his residence) in the United States. Second, he founded several schools in the United States, Canada, Europe, and India, where students through high-school age were instructed in ways to reduce aggression and to aid in acquiring Krishnamurti's universal insight. A noteworthy feature of Krishnamurti's later life was the interest he attracted from scientists. He participated in various dialogues with groups or individuals from the scientific community on the possible connection between his teachings and various contemporary theories of, for example, physics. One of the last books he published, *The Ending of Time* (1985), was cowritten with David Bohm, a professor of theoretical physics at Birkbeck College, University of London.

BIBLIOGRAPHY

Mary Lutyens's biographies of Krishnamurti, *Krishnamurti: The Years of Awakening* (New York, 1975) and *Krishnamurti: The Years of Fulfillment* (New York, 1983), were, according to Lutyens, read by Krishnamurti prior to their publication and their factual contents and interpretations approved by him. My article is based on these volumes, on discussions with personalities in the Theosophical Society, and on personal observation. *Candles in the Sun*, by Mary Lutyens's mother, Emily Lutyens (London, 1957), recounts its author's relationship with Krishnamurti during the time she and others took charge of his nurture in adolescence and early manhood. The bond between them was one of the closest in Krishnamurti's life. Krishnamurti's own *Krishnamurti's Notebook* (New York, 1976) contains firsthand descriptions of "the Process." *At the Feet of the Master* (Wheaton, Ill., 1970), by Alcyone (a pseudonym of Krishnamurti) has run to more than forty editions since it was first published in 1910. It recounts teachings from the Master Kuthumi that Krishnamurti received during astral projection while asleep and under the guidance of Leadbeater. Notes written by Krishnamurti after awakening in the morning during the five-month period of instruction were gathered together for the volume. Independent witnesses have attested that the only help Krishnamurti received in its composition was with spelling and punctuation, although he was only about fifteen at the time of its writing and was then still mastering English.

CHARLES S. J. WHITE

KRISTENSEN, W. BREDE (1867–1953), Norwegian historian of religions. From 1901 to 1937 William Brede Kristensen was professor of the history and phenomenology of religion at the University of Leiden. Virtually unknown outside of Scandinavia and the Netherlands during his lifetime, he was the teacher of many of the next generation of Dutch historians of religions and in the last twenty-five years has exerted some influence on methodological discussion through the posthumous publication in English translation of his class lectures at Leiden on the phenomenology of religion (*The Meaning of Religion*, 1960).

Kristensen was the son of a Lutheran minister, born in Kristiansand, Norway, on 21 June 1867. He went to the University of Kristiania (present-day Oslo) to study theology. After a year, however, he switched to the study of languages, which he later continued in Leiden and Paris. In addition to Latin, Greek, and Hebrew, he studied ancient Egyptian, Assyrian, Sanskrit, and Avestan. He did his dissertation research in the British Museum in London on Egyptian ideas of the afterlife and then returned to Kristiania to study and lecture on the ancient Zoroastrian text, the Avesta. In 1901 he was appointed to the chair of his teacher C. P. Tiele (1830–1902) at the University of Leiden, where he remained professor until his retirement in 1937; he lived in Leiden until his death in 1953. After World War II he returned briefly to Norway to give a course of introductory lectures on history of religions (posthumously published both in Norwegian as *Religionshistorisk studium,* 1954, and in a Dutch translation by Mevrouw Kristensen). Much of Kristensen's scholarly work consisted of papers dealing in some detail with various specific aspects of religious life in the ancient Near East. Many of the papers were presented at the annual meetings of the Dutch Royal Society. They were collected and published in two volumes in Dutch, *Verzamelde bÿdragen tot kennis der antieke godsdiensten* (Collected Contributions to the Knowledge of the Ancient Religions; 1947) and *Symbool en werkelÿkheid* (Symbol and Reality; 1954).

Kristensen rejected the prevailing evolutionist theory of his teacher and predecessor C. P. Tiele and tried to base his understanding of a given religion on its believers' own estimate of it; he found such estimates expressed in written documents, in languages he himself had learned to read. He believed that the religions of the ancient (preclassic) Mediterranean and Near East each had a distinctive nature but that all shared important underlying features basic enough to make comparison among them extremely fruitful. The aim of such comparison is not to define certain general ideas, such as the meaning of sacrifice, but to illuminate the meaning of some particular practice. In this respect the systematic work of the phenomenologist always remains in the service of the more particular investigation of the historian. For Kristensen, however, there was in practice very little difference, since he was interested neither in a philosophical theory of historical development in religion nor in tracing stages in the development of a particular religion. For him historical change becomes significant at the point that a particular religious apprehension comes to an end. The historian's task is thus not to focus on historical change but to find a bridge to understanding a vanished world of religious reality on the other side of the decisive change to the rationalistic consciousness of the modern world. Kristensen's work is full of polemics against this rationalism, not because he was antimodern, but because he felt that such rationalism led to the misunderstanding of ancient religions.

Kristensen did not regard informative comparison as a scientific method that would guarantee correct results. He sought to gain a certain inkling or intuition of what is important in the religion under examination, which requires in negative terms, that we not mix our praise or blame with what the believer tells us and, in positive terms, that we seek a sympathetic and loving understanding of the alien faith. Our understanding can be no better than approximate, because we cannot fully learn the alien religious language and because the other religion does not become a power in our own lives, but the effort is worthwhile, because across the barrier of languages and epochs and civilizations we can glimpse the truth perceived by believers in the alien religion. Thereby we can grow, Kristensen maintained, not only intellectually but religiously.

BIBLIOGRAPHY

Of Kristensen's many works, only one has been translated into English: *The Meaning of Religion: Lectures in the Phenomenology of Religion,* 2d ed. (The Hague, 1960). An extensive bibliography of Kristensen's works can be found in Jacques Waardenburg's *Classical Approaches to the Study of Religion,* vol. 2, *Bibliography* (The Hague, 1974).

JOHN B. CARMAN

KROCHMAL, NAḤMAN (1785–1840), Jewish philosopher and historian. A major figure in the Haskalah (Jewish Enlightenment movement), Krochmal is noted for his contributions to Jewish historiography and his program for a metaphysical understanding of Judaism using German idealist philosophy.

Born in the city of Brody in Galicia, Krochmal lived most of his life in the town of Żołkiew near Lvov. To supplement his traditional Talmudic education, he learned Latin, Syriac, Arabic, French, and German, giving him access to a broad range of medieval and modern philosophical literature. Despite an unsuccessful career as a merchant, Krochmal rejected the offer of a rabbinical post in Berlin and supported himself as a bookkeeper. His last years were spent in the Galician cities of Brody and Ternopol.

In the nineteenth century the large Jewish population of the Polish districts of the Hapsburg empire was an integral branch of the east European Jewish milieu both in its economic and social patterns and its traditional Jewish piety. Galicia was a center of Hasidism, as well as of rabbinic learning and leadership of Hasidism's opponents. Krochmal himself was a religiously observant Jew who was highly critical of the "delusions" and "folly" of the Ḥasidim, with whom he and his circle from time to time came into bitter conflict. Krochmal was one of the preeminent figures of the Galician phase of the Haskalah, then in its heyday and consisting of writers who advocated such reforms of Jewish life as the modernization of Jewish education and livelihood, a greater knowledge of natural sciences and European languages, and the introduction into Hebrew literature of the genres and ideas of modern European literature. A major aim of Krochmal's scholarship was to further the rapprochement between the modern rational, critical, and historical spirit and the Talmudic-rabbinic worldview.

Krochmal was a brilliant conversationalist but published little in his lifetime. After his death his papers were sent, according to his instructions, to the eminent German Jewish scholar Leopold Zunz, who edited and published them in 1851 as *Moreh nevukhei ha-zeman* (A Guide for the Perplexed of the Time), a title deliberately reminiscent of Moses Maimonides' *Guide for the Perplexed.*

Krochmal's book is an incompletely developed but suggestive work that covers the following topics: the connection between philosophy and religion, the philosophical significance of the Israelite conception of God, the cycles of Jewish history in relation to the cyclical history of nations, aspects of postbiblical Jewish literature (including a pioneering treatment of the evolution of the *halakhah* and *aggadah*), the logic of Hegel, and the philosophy of Avraham ibn 'Ezra'.

Like Hegel, Krochmal conceived of the dynamic totality of reality as an absolute Spirit whose nature is pure cognition, which for Krochmal was the philosophical meaning of the God of Judaism. Like Hegel, Krochmal believed that religion conveys through the faculty of imagination that which philosophy conveys through reason, so that it is the task of philosophers to make explicit what remains implicit in religious imagery. The extent of Krochmal's indebtedness to Vico, Herder, Schelling, and Hegel has been a matter of scholarly controversy: apart from his rendition of Hegel's logic and use of the terminology of post-Kantian idealism, Krochmal does not hold to a temporal unfolding of the absolute. Equally, if not more important to Krochmal's metaphysics were Maimonides, Abraham ibn 'Ezra', and Qabbalah.

Krochmal grounded the truth of Judaism in a general concept of religion and cultural nationalism. The intelligibility of reality and the lawfulness of nature derive from a system of spiritual powers which, in turn, is generated by an unconditioned absolute Spirit. All positive religions intuit some aspect of this supersensuous reality. Moreover, a particular national spirit expresses the unity and individuality of the nation during its history. All nations are finite organic entities, passing through a cycle of growth, maturity, and death. Only the people of Israel have avoided eventual extinction, because their singular, infinite God is the dynamic principle of absolute Spirit that generated all the particular spiritual powers. The people of Israel were the "eternal people" inasmuch as they worshiped and were sustained by the force that accounted for the entire cosmic process and that renewed the spiritual strength of Jewish culture after periods of stagnation and decline. The God of Judaism did not change as the Jewish people passed three times through the cycle of national historical existence. The first cycle of national growth, maturity, and decay extended from the time of the biblical patriarchs to the destruction of Judaea in 587/6 BCE. The second cycle began with the return from the Babylonian exile and ended with the failure of the Bar Kokhba Revolt in the second century CE. The third commenced with the codification of the Mishnah, culminated in the philosophical and mystical flowering of medieval Judaism, and declined in the late Middle Ages. Krochmal does not explicitly develop the notion of a fourth cycle of Jewish history, but he probably envisioned such a rebirth as beginning in the seventeenth century with the rise of the Haskalah. As the Jewish people passed through these cycles, the Jewish idea of God attained greater articulation and the meaning of the people's existence became transparent to reason.

Because Krochmal proposed a metaphysics that took Jewish history with the utmost seriousness, he can be seen as a pioneer both in Jewish religious thought and in modern theories of Jewish nationhood.

BIBLIOGRAPHY

The standard edition of Krochmal's works is *Kitvei RaNaK* (Writings of Rabbi Naḥman Krochmal), edited by Simon Rawidowicz (Berlin, 1924; reprint, Waltham, Mass., 1961). On Krochmal's place in Jewish thought, see Julius Guttmann's *Philosophies of Judaism*, translated by David W. Silverman (New York, 1964), pp. 321–344; Nathan Rotenstreich's *Jewish Philosophy in Modern Times* (New York, 1968), pp. 136–148; and Rotenstreich's *Tradition and Reality: The Impact of History on Modern Jewish Thought* (New York, 1972), pp. 37–48. Two articles of value are Ismar Schorsch's "The Philosophy of History of Nachman Krochmal," *Judaism* 10 (Summer 1961): 237–245, and Jacob Taubes's "Nachman Krochmal and Modern Historicism," *Judaism* 12 (Spring 1963): 150–164.

ROBERT M. SELTZER

KṚṢṆA, whose name means "black" or "dark," is customarily said to stand alongside Rāma in the Hindu pantheon as one of the two preeminent *avatāra*s of the great god Viṣṇu. Although present-day Hindus do not dispute such divine genealogy, they and most of their ancestors who have lived in the last millennium have found Kṛṣṇa more important to their faith than Viṣṇu. In Vaiṣṇava circles one often hears it emphasized, in a quote from the *Bhāgavata Purāṇa*, that "Kṛṣṇa is God himself" ("Kṛṣṇas tu bhagavān svayam"; 1.3.27), not merely a portion or manifestation of the divine fullness. In the devotion of contemporary Hindus, he more than any other figure symbolizes divine love *(prema)*, divine beauty *(rūpa)*, and a quality of purposeless, playful, yet fascinating action *(līlā)* that bears a peculiarly divine stamp. In recent centuries Kṛṣṇa has been adored principally as a mischievous child in the cowherd settlement (Vṛndāvana) where he chose to launch his earthly career and as a matchless lover of the women and girls who dwell there. In earlier times, however, heroic and didactic aspects of Kṛṣṇa's personality have played a more forceful role in his veneration.

Origins and History. Many scholars feel that Kṛṣṇa and Viṣṇu were originally two independent deities. On this view, Kṛṣṇa is to be understood as more closely associated with a warrior milieu than Viṣṇu, since most early information about him comes from epic texts. Viṣṇu, by contrast, appears in the Vedas, so knowledge about him would have been transmitted by brahmans. It is unclear at what point in time the two cults merged, if they were ever truly separate. Certainly this happened by the time of the *Viṣṇu Purāṇa* (c. fifth century CE), which declares Kṛṣṇa to be an *avatāra* of Viṣṇu; yet there are a number of indications that the interidentification was much older than that. A pillar at Ghoṣuṇḍi has often been interpreted as implying that Kṛṣṇa was worshiped alongside Nārāyaṇa, who in turn is closely related to Viṣṇu, in the first century BCE; and in a series of icons from the Kushan period (first and second centuries CE) Kṛṣṇa bears a series of weapons associated with Viṣṇu: the club, the disk, and sometimes the conch.

The Kṛṣṇa to whom reference is made in each of these cases is usually designated Vāsudeva. This patronymic title is one he inherits as head of the Vṛṣṇi lineage of Mathura. Vāsudeva Kṛṣṇa liberates the throne of Mathura from his evil kinsman Kaṃsa; he struggles with the Magadhan king Jarāsaṃdha for continued control of the Mathura region and apparently loses; he travels to the western city of Dvārakā on the shores of the Arabian Sea, there to establish a flourishing dynastic realm; and he serves as counselor to his cousins the Pāṇḍavas in their monumental battle with the Kauravas.

Early reports of these actions are found in various sections of the *Mahābhārata,* and reference is made to certain of them in Patañjali's *Mahābhāṣya* (c. second century BCE) and the Buddhist *Ghaṭa Jātaka.* None of them, however, is depicted in sculpture before the Gupta period. Instead one finds sets of icons that imply no narrative context. One group of sculptures from the Kushan period depicts Vāsudeva Kṛṣṇa in conjunction with his brother Saṃkarṣaṇa/Balarāma and adds a third figure, a sister Ekānaṃśā, whose role in the epic texts is minimal and not altogether clear. Another set enshrines a different grouping, wherein Vāsudeva is accompanied by his brother and two of his progeny. This set corresponds to a theological rubric in force in the Pāñcarātra and perhaps the Bhāgavata sects, according to which Vāsudeva is said to be the first in a series of four divine manifestations (*vyūhas*) of Nārāyaṇa in the human realm.

In addition to the many icons of Vāsudeva Kṛṣṇa that survive from pre-Gupta times, one finds a handful of narrative reliefs, and these depict quite another aspect of Kṛṣṇa. This is Kṛṣṇa Gopāla, the cowherd, and he seems as distinct from Vāsudeva Kṛṣṇa in the texts as he does in sculpture. The texts report that although Kṛṣṇa was born into the Vṛṣṇi lineage in Mathura, he was adopted by the simple Ābhīra herdspeople of the surrounding Braj countryside for the duration of his childhood and youth. Only as a fully developed young man did he return to Mathura to slay Kaṃsa. The involvements of Vāsudeva Kṛṣṇa and Kṛṣṇa Gopāla are sufficiently distinct that it has been suggested the two figures were initially separate. On this hypothesis, Kṛṣṇa Gopāla would originally have been worshiped by the Ābhīra clan, a nomadic group that extended its domain of activity from the Punjab and Indus regions to the Deccan and Gangetic plains by the third century CE. As the clan expanded its terrain, it moved into the Braj region and would have encountered the Vṛṣṇis, whose mythology of Vāsudeva Kṛṣṇa was then integrated with the Ābhīra cult of Kṛṣṇa Gopāla.

The Supremacy of Kṛṣṇa. The *Viṣṇu* and *Bhāgavata Purāṇas* (c. fifth and ninth centuries CE) clearly understood Kṛṣṇa in both his pastoral and royal roles to be an *avatāra* of Viṣṇu. In the *Bhāgavata,* however, which is the more important of the two, Kṛṣṇa occupies so much attention that the text is preeminently his. The same thing is true in the *Bhagavadgītā* (c. second century BCE), a portion of the *Mahābhārata* that vies with the *Bhāgavata Purāṇa* for the honor of being the most influential Vaiṣṇava text today. There, too, it is Kṛṣṇa who occupies center stage, not Viṣṇu. Indeed, Kṛṣṇa asserts that it is he who has issued forth in several *avatāras*, he who comprehends the many forms by means of which the divine makes itself manifest.

In the *Gītā* one has a glimpse of how Vāsudeva Kṛṣṇa could be interpreted as the supreme divinity. He enters the *Gītā* not as a combatant but as an adviser to his Pāṇḍava cousin Arjuna, who must fight. He himself is not implicated in the battle but is willing to serve as a resource. In the battle of life, similarly, one can act dispassionately by placing trust in the One who is too great to have any narrow interest in earthly conflict. Kṛṣṇa's oblique relation to the Pāṇḍavas' battle becomes a metaphor for his transcendence of the world altogether, and it enables Arjuna to transcend himself.

In the considerably later *Bhāgavata Purāṇa* one has a comparable vision of Kṛṣṇa's supremacy, but this time the supremacy of Kṛṣṇa Gopāla is more at issue than that of Vāsudeva Kṛṣṇa. Here the playful cowherd dances with all the milkmaids (*gopīs*) of Braj at once, multiplying himself so that each women feels he is dancing with her alone. This amorous dance *(rāsa līlā)* is an image of divinity and humanity wholly identified in one another, an absorption made possible by intense devotion *(bhakti)*. Like Arjuna's encounter with Kṛṣṇa, this meeting, too, relativizes the importance of worldly involvements. In the *rāsa līlā* the idyllic quality that always separated the pastoral life of Kṛṣṇa Gopāla from the royal world of Vāsudeva Kṛṣṇa attains its apotheosis.

The most important icon of Kṛṣṇa as the divine lover becomes prevalent in Orissa and Karnataka in the twelfth and thirteenth centuries and later spreads throughout the subcontinent. In this image Kṛṣṇa is shown with his neck tilted, waist bent, and ankles crossed as he plays his irresistible flute to summon the *gopīs*—symbolically, human souls—from their mundane preoccupations.

Two icons that enjoy a great prominence from Gupta times onward suggest still another way in which the supremacy of Kṛṣṇa Gōpala was experienced. One of these represents Kṛṣṇa lifting Mount Govardhana to protect the inhabitants of Braj from the angry, rainy torrents unleashed by Indra when at Kṛṣṇa's advice they turn their veneration away from that distant Vedic god and toward the symbolic center of the nourishing realm in which they live, Mount Govardhana itself. A second popular image shows Kṛṣṇa taming the evil snake Kāliya, whose presence had poisoned the Yamunā River upon whose waters all of Braj—humans and cattle alike—depend. In both moments Kṛṣṇa wrests order from chaos; in both he guarantees safe and habitable space; and in both he displaces and incorporates the powers earlier attributed to other figures in the pantheon. When he lifts the mountain he overcomes the sky gods captained by Indra, and when he tames the snake he subdues the nether spirits symbolized by snake deities *(nāgas)*. The preeminence of these images of Kṛṣṇa as cosmic victor is only gradually displaced by that of Kṛṣṇa as cosmic lover in the course of time.

Two Forms of Love. Kṛṣṇa is principally accessible to the love of his devotees in two forms—as a child and as a youth—and the affections elicited by each are distinct, though related. In systematic treatises such as the *Bhaktirasāmṛtasindhu* of the sixteenth-century theologian Rūpa Gosvāmī, these two are described by separate terms. The first is "calf love" *(vātsalya)*, the emotion felt by parents and especially mothers for their children, and the second is "sweet love" *(mādhurya)*, the emotion that draws lovers together. Kṛṣṇa serves as the ideal focus for both sets of feelings. As a child Kṛṣṇa is impish and irrepressible, and modern Hindus adore him as such, displaying his most lovable moments on the calendars and posters that provide India with a great proportion of its visual diet. As a youth he is charming and unabashed; and in Rajput miniature painting as well as a strand of love poetry broad enough to include the Sanskrit *Gītagovinda* of Jayadeva and the Hindi *Rasikapriyā* of Keśavdās, he serves as the "ideal hero" or "leading man" *(nāyaka)* known to secular erotic literature.

In both these roles there is an element of contrariness that sets Kṛṣṇa apart from others. His mischievous deeds in childhood contribute greatly to his fascination and are epitomized in his penchant for stealing the *gopīs*' freshly churned butter. Kṛṣṇa's naughtiness and outsized appetite further stimulate the *gopīs*' desire to have him as their own, yet he can never be possessed. As the young lover he remains unattainable. Though he makes himself present to all the *gopīs* in his *rāsa* dance, he does so on his own terms, never allowing himself to be brought within the confines of a domestic contract. The love he symbolizes exceeds the bounds set by any relationship that can be conceived in terms of *dharma*.

Child or adolescent, Kṛṣṇa is always a thief, for he is a thief of the heart. Hence even Rādhā, the maiden whom tradition recognizes as his special favorite, frequently and powerfully senses his absence. Much of the poetry that has been dedicated to Kṛṣṇa is in the nature of lamentation *(viraha)*. The women who speak in such poems give voice to the unquenched yearnings of the human heart, as in the following composition attributed to the sixteenth-century Hindi poet Sūrdās:

> Gopāla has slipped in and stolen my heart, friend.
> He stole through my eyes and invaded my breast
> simply by looking—who knows how he did it?—
> Even though parents and husband and all
> crowded the courtyard and filled my world.
> The door was protected by all that is proper;
> not a corner, nothing, was left without a guard.
> Decency, prudence, respect for the family—
> these three were locks and I hid the keys.
> The sturdiest doors were my eyelid gates—
> to enter through them was a passage impossible—
> And secure in my heart, a treasure immeasurable:
> insight, intelligence, fortitude, wit.
> Then, says Sūr, he'd stolen it—
> with a thought and a laugh and a look—
> and my body was scorched with remorse.

In this mode it is the elusiveness of Kṛṣṇa that gives evidence of his divine supremacy. Intimately accessible as he seems, whether as child or lover, he can never quite be grasped.

Cult and Ritual. Kṛṣṇa is worshiped in homes and temples throughout India and has become the devotional focus of the Hare Krishna movement (ISKCON) beyond Indian shores. Rituals vary from place to place and caste to caste, but some of the most impressive are those associated with the Gauḍīya and Puṣṭimārgīya Sampradāyas, which trace their lineage back to the fifteenth- and sixteenth-century divines Caitanya and Vallabha. In temples and homes belonging to these communities, Kṛṣṇa is worshiped in a series of eight daily *darśans* (ritual "viewings") in which the god allows himself to be seen and worshiped in image form by his devotees. His clothing, jewelry, and flower decorations may be altered many times in the course of a day, and different forms of devotional song are sung as the god's daily cowherding routine is symbolically observed. Vestments, food offerings, and musical accompaniment vary seasonally as well, with the festivals of Holī and Kṛṣṇajanmāṣṭamī occupying positions of special importance.

In the Braj country surrounding Mathura, which attracts pilgrims from all over India in festival seasons, these ceremonial observances are amplified by dramas in which Kṛṣṇa makes himself available in an especially vivid manner to his devotees through child actors. These brahman boys native to Braj are thought to become actual forms (*svarūpas)* of Kṛṣṇa and his companions as they present events in Kṛṣṇa's childhood life. A dancing of the *rāsa līlā* is the starting point for every performance, hence the genre as a whole is called *rāsa līlā*. In Sanskrit aesthetic theory, drama is thought to comprehend all the arts, and owing to his essentially aesthetic nature Kṛṣṇa is more frequently depicted in Indian art, dance, and music than any other god. Drama is a particularly appropriate mode in which to experience him, however, because Kṛṣṇa's antics so clearly embody the Hindu conviction that life itself is the product of divine play *(līlā)*. To surrender to play, to plays, and to the sense that all life is play, is to experience the world as it actually is.

[*For further discussion of the mythology of Kṛṣṇa, see* Avatāra; Viṣṇu; Rāma; Rādhā; *and* Vṛndāvana. *The worship of Kṛṣṇa is further discussed in* Kṛṣṇaism; Vaiṣṇavism; Bhagavadgītā; Holī; *and* Līlā.]

BIBLIOGRAPHY

Two works serve as basic references for the study of Kṛṣṇa. On the textual side there is the encyclopedic work of Walter Ruben, *Krishna: Konkordanz und Kommentar der Motive seines Heldenlebens* (Istanbul, 1944), and on the art historical side the somewhat more personal study of P. Banerjee, *The Life of Krishṇa in Indian Art* (New Delhi, 1978).

A broad study of materials relating to Vāsudeva Kṛṣṇa is provided in Suvira Jaiswal's *The Origin and Development of Vaiṣṇavism* (Delhi, 1967), critical portions of which are deepened by recent investigations on the part of Doris Srinivasan, including her "Early Kṛishṇa Icons: The Case at Mathurā," in *Kalādarśana*, edited by Joanna G. Williams (New Delhi, 1981). Alf Hiltebeitel lays out important new perspectives on Kṛṣṇa's role in the *Mahābhārata* in *The Ritual of Battle* (Ithaca, N.Y., 1976).

Two large thematic studies relating to Kṛṣṇa Gopāla have recently appeared. One is Friedhelm E. Hardy's *Viraha Bhakti* (Oxford, 1983), which emphasizes South Indian materials and focuses on Kṛṣṇa as a lover. The other is my work *Krishna, the Butter Thief* (Princeton, 1983), which emphasizes North Indian material and concentrates on the child Kṛṣṇa; the appendixes provide a digest of information relating to the iconography of Kṛṣṇa Gopāla.

Various aspects of the worship of Kṛṣṇa can be surveyed in *Krishna: Myths, Rites, and Attitudes*, edited by Milton Singer (Honolulu, 1966). My study *At Play with Krishna* (Princeton, 1981) gives an impression of the way Kṛṣṇa is celebrated in the most important pilgrimage site dedicated to him, particularly through the *rāsa līlā* dramas of the Braj region.

JOHN STRATTON HAWLEY

KṚṢṆAISM. The god Kṛṣṇa has been one of the most popular figures of Hinduism and of Indian culture generally. Episodes from his life story have found innumerable expressions in literature and art. Against this larger cultural background we witness a more specifically devotional and theological preoccupation with Kṛṣṇa that can be reduced to basically two different trends. On the one hand, we have the development of religious systems in which Kṛṣṇa is defined as an earthly *avatāra* (incarnation) of the god Viṣṇu. Here Viṣṇu plays the central role and we must thus speak of Vaiṣṇava (alternately, Vaiṣṇavite or Viṣṇuite) systems; these can be grouped together under the rubric "Vaiṣṇavism" ("Viṣṇuism"). But the global assumption that Kṛṣṇa is an *avatāra* of Viṣṇu is derived from an inadequate interpretation of the facts. This assumption has its origin in the Indian conceptualization of the religious situation and later came to be accepted uncritically by scholars. The concept "Vaiṣṇavism" has tended to subsume all Kṛṣṇaite phenomena and has thus proved to be far too wide. "Kṛṣṇaism" (along with parallel terms like "Rāmaism," "Rādhāism," "Sītāism," etc.) is a useful heuristic tool, as long as it is understood to denote not a single system but a whole range of systems.

The strictest definition of a system according to traditional Indian understanding is that of a *sampradāya*, a religious movement that proves its orthodoxy and orthopraxy through detailed exegesis of the Vedānta scriptures. In this sense, we find only three such Kṛṣṇaite systems (those of Nimbārka, Caitanya, and

Vallabha). On the other hand, there are many further instances in which Kṛṣṇa appears *de facto* as the central religious figure. Whether textual, theological, ritual, or devotional, such contexts can be described as types of Kṛṣṇaism, even when we are not dealing with a *sampradāya*. Finally, there are many examples of partial Kṛṣṇaism, whereby a religious system is Kṛṣṇaite on one level and, say, Vaiṣṇava on another. [*See also the biographies of Nimbārka, Caitanya, and Vallabha.*]

Early Kṛṣṇaism. The first Kṛṣṇaite system known to us is the theology of the *Bhagavadgītā*. When read as a self-contained work, and not automatically in the light of the Vaiṣṇava theology that pervades the *Mahābhārata* into which it was inserted, its Kṛṣṇaite character is unmistakable. There is no suggestion here that in the person of the physical Kṛṣṇa a different being, that is, an eternal, unmanifest Viṣṇu, is contained. Thus when it is said (in 4.7): "Whenever *dharma* is suffering a decline, I emit myself [into the physical world]," or (in 4.8): "In different ages I originate [in physical form]," there is not the slightest hint in the text that this "I" is different from that used in the previous verse (4.6): "I am without birth, of immutable self . . . ." Similarly, in the grand vision that Arjuna, by means of his "divine eye," has of Kṛṣṇa in his cosmic form, no change in person is suggested. Even more important are verses like 14.27 or 18.54, in which Kṛṣṇa's relationship to *brahman* is indicated: here *brahman* somehow is dependent on, and subsumed in, Kṛṣṇa. On the basis of these theological premises, the *Gītā* advocates a complex spiritual path leading ultimately to man's salvation. Attention to the demands of society is combined with the need for inner spiritual growth; but both must be carried out in total "loyalty" (the primary meaning of *bhakti*) to Kṛṣṇa. At the end appears "love" (called "highest *bhakti*") coupled with a sharing in Kṛṣṇa's "working" in the universe. [*See* Bhakti.]

The remaining portions of the epic, of which the *Bhagavadgītā* is but a minute part, are on the whole Vaiṣṇava. Eventually, by about the fourth or fifth century CE, the concept of the *avatāra* was introduced to clarify the relationship between Kṛṣṇa and Viṣṇu. This had very far-reaching consequences for the interpretation of Kṛṣṇaite material, including the *Gītā* itself. Thus our earliest source on the childhood and youth of Kṛṣṇa, the *Harivaṃśa* (third cent. CE?), an appendix to the *Mahābhārata*, presented the myths within a Vaiṣṇava framework, just as did the *Viṣṇu Purāṇa* (fifth cent. CE?), which contains a very much enlarged account of Kṛṣṇa's early life. By no means, however, did the *avatāra* concept acquire spontaneous, universal validity. [*See also* Bhagavadgītā.]

Developments in the South. When we turn our attention to southern India, the region where Tamil was spoken (modern Tamil Nadu, Kerala, and southernmost Andhra Pradesh), we find the figure of Māyōṉ documented from the beginning of the common era. Although he is assumed by some to have been an autonomous Dravidian god, no evidence for this theory can be found. Instead, a closer analysis of the sources shows that we are dealing here with Kṛṣṇa, or better, a god-figure of predominantly Kṛṣṇaite features who also incorporates elements of Viṣṇu. (Thus, strictly speaking we ought to use "Māyōṉism" rather than "Kṛṣṇaism" here). The name itself, and synonyms like Māl and Māyavaṉ, denote a person of black complexion—a precise translation into Tamil of the Sanskrit Kṛṣṇa. Different milieus deal with the situation differently. In the context of temple worship, the emphasis is on Viṣṇu-Nārāyaṇa. But in the area of folk religion, and, of central importance in later developments, among the (secular) literati, Māyōṉ appears as Kṛṣṇa, particularly the young Kṛṣṇa living among the cowherds, dallying with the girls and playing his tricks on the women. We also hear about his favorite, the milkmaid Piṉṉai, for whom he subdued seven vicious bulls. To the extent that we can infer from the literary allusions something about the religious situation during the first half of the first millennium CE, the songs, dances, and rituals celebrating those events appear decidedly Kṛṣṇaite. [*See also* Tamil Religions.]

With the Āḻvārs (sixth to ninth centuries), considerable changes in the conceptualization of Kṛṣṇa take place. Overall, a more pronounced Vaiṣṇava orientation emerges in their works. Yet even they do not introduce the conceptual distinction of Kṛṣṇa and Viṣṇu by means of the notion of *avatāra*, and the names by which they address their god fuse the Kṛṣṇaite with the Vaiṣṇava. The central range of myths that they develop in their poems and the eroticism that pervades their devotion have remained fundamentally Kṛṣṇaite. The emphasis is here on "love-in-separation." [*See* Āḻvārs.]

This situation changes only with the emergence of Rāmānuja's Śrī Vaiṣṇavism (from the eleventh century, with antecedents in the tenth). Although institutionally links with the Āḻvārs are maintained, the formation of a definite Vaiṣṇava theology, which in turn has close historical links with the Vaiṣṇava temple tradition of the Pāñcarātras (and Vaikhānasas), encouraged a very different form of *bhakti*. Even so, Kṛṣṇa remains here the central *avatāra*, only eventually to be overtaken by Rāma. [*See also* Śrī Vaiṣṇavas; Vaikhānasas; *and* Vaiṣṇavism, *article on* Pāñcarātras.]

Śrī Vaiṣṇavism was not the only heir to the devotional Kṛṣṇaism of the Āḻvārs. Two Sanskrit works have to be mentioned in this connection. One is the *Kṛṣṇa-karṇāmṛta* by one Vilvamaṅgala (also called "Līlāśuka," or "Playful Parrot"), of unknown date and possibly from Kerala. By 1200 the work is known in Bengal, and at a later stage was a favorite text of Caitanya. From ever-new angles, the erotic attraction of the youthful Kṛṣṇa is explored in this poem. Yet the importance of this work dwindles compared with the second text, the *Bhāgavata Purāṇa*. Written in the Tamil country around the ninth or early tenth century by an unknown poet, in Vedic-sounding and highly poetic language, this text is far more than a traditional *purāṇa*. It attempts to fuse a great variety of contemporary religious and cultural strands, and it does so in a decidedly Kṛṣṇaite manner. While for its "plot" it uses as its model the *Viṣṇu Purāṇa* (where Kṛṣṇa is an *avatāra* of Viṣṇu), in two important respects, devotional-literary and metaphysical, Kṛṣṇa is presented as the central deity. Book 10 and part of Book 11 comprise the structural center of the work: they have become the most famous source on the life of Kṛṣṇa among the cowherds of Vraja. Translating or paraphrasing here poems of the Āḻvārs (Periyāḻvār on Kṛṣṇa's childhood, Āṇṭāḷ, Nammāḻvār, and Parakālaṉ on his amours and on "love-in-separation"), Kṛṣṇaite *bhakti* finds here powerful expression. This devotional emphasis is complemented by a Kṛṣṇaite metaphysical framework. Thus in 1.3.28 we hear: "Kṛṣṇa is Bhagavān himself." Or in 10.33.36: "He who moves in the heart of all corporeal beings, here took on a body through playfulness." Kṛṣṇa is *brahman*, and—to make matters more complicated in this *purāṇa*—the ultimately sole real. Thus, an illusionist *advaita* teaching (in which Kṛṣṇa's love-play with the milkmaids can be compared to a child's playing with his own image seen in a mirror—10.33.17) is expounded in its metaphysical frame. Historically, this particular combination of *advaita* (metaphysical nondualism), sensuous *bhakti*, and the identification of Kṛṣṇa with *brahman* proved enormously influential. Most subsequent developments of Kṛṣṇaism in northern India are unthinkable without the *Bhāgavata Purāṇa*.

Early Developments in the North. Our knowledge of the situation in northern India during the first millennium CE is far more limited and patchy. No instances of Kṛṣṇaism can be cited, and yet a number of factors were essential in the formation of later types of Kṛṣṇaite religions. Numerous references in the various literatures of the period make it clear that Kṛṣṇa enjoyed enormous popularity. In predominantly secular works his amours with the milkmaids were explored and given a definite place in the imaginary landscape of classical Indian lovers. Moreover, already from the very beginning of the common era we hear about Rādhikā (later usually Rādhā) as his favorite beloved among the milkmaids. She is clearly different from the Tamil Piṉṉai, whom Sanskrit works present as Nīlā or Satyā. (Not that we have much of a story here, apart from the conventional amatory situations envisaged in the poetics of love.) But what was important was the inevitable association in the popular mind of Kṛṣṇa with Rādhikā. The religious works (the *Harivaṃśa*, Purāṇas, etc.) knew nothing about Rādhā, and broke the anonymity of the crowd of Kṛṣṇa's beloved ones only after his departure from Vraja, when he abducted and married the princess Rukmiṇī.

This whole popular interest in Rādhā and Kṛṣṇa reaches its culmination in Jayadeva's *Gītagovinda* (written in Bengal c. 1185 CE), a kind of libretto for a dance-drama about the lovers' quarrels due to Rādhā's jealousy, and about their eventual reconciliation and their passionate love-making. While the *Bhāgavata Purāṇa*, which became known during this period in the North, provided the metaphysical and devotional frame, the *Gītagovinda* acted as the focusing mechanism for mythical episodes in Kṛṣṇa's complex earthly life. [*See also the biography of Jayadeva.*]

A further contributory factor, *rasa* speculation, must be mentioned. Here we are dealing with academic aesthetics, which in India tended to focus on drama and poetry. By the ninth century CE a conceptual framework had evolved for the analysis of art and aesthetic experience that centered around the notion of *rasa* (literally, "flavor"). A good poem is supposed to contain one of eight possible emotions (love being by far the favorite among the poets) which, by means of poetic-linguistic devices can be transferred to the reader (listener), to appear in him now in a transformed state as his aesthetic relish, as *rasa*. Given that most of the sources on Kṛṣṇa's life were in poetry, that over the centuries an increasing concentration on his amours had taken place, and that in the devotee's emotions vis-à-vis Kṛṣṇa "aesthetic relish" could be found, it was perhaps natural for this to be developed systematically as *bhakti-rasa*. Particularly in the school of Caitanya, the scholastic exploration of *bhakti-rasa* (along with the production of Sanskrit poetry based on it) reached its climax.

Regional Trends in the North. Kṛṣṇaism makes its first documented appearance in the North with the beginning of the second millennium CE in a ritual context. This is the temple-culture of Paṇḍharpur in southern Maharashtra. The god in the temple is variously called Viṭṭhala or Viṭhobā. Although etymologies from *Viṣṇu* have been suggested, we are clearly dealing here, from at least a certain stage in the development onward, with Kṛṣṇa. His consort is Rakhumāī, the Marathi form of Rukmiṇī. Particularly through the popularizing activities of Marathi poets like Jñāneśvar, Nāmdev, and Tukārām, and many other (often pseudonymous) poets and texts, a markedly individual religious system of great popularity evolved in Maharashtra and also in Karṇāṭaka. Heaven and eternity, with Viṭhobā and Rakhumāī as king and queen, take visible form in Paṇḍharpur. Instead of the amorous episodes in Kṛṣṇa's earthly life (which do appear in numerous poems associated with this religious tradition), the emphasis is on secondary myths about the saints connected with Paṇḍharpur.

Maharashtra produced (from the thirteenth century onward) yet another type of Kṛṣṇaism, the very austere and idiosyncratic movement of the Mānbhāv (Mahānubhāva). Here five Kṛṣṇas are listed: Kṛṣṇa himself (husband of Rukmiṇī, etc.), who is closely connected with Parameśvara, the Absolute in the system; Dattātreya (a god-figure of Maharashtrian Hinduism); and three historical persons (Cakradhar, the founder of the movement, and two predecessors) who are identified with Kṛṣṇa. [*See also* Marathi Religions.]

As a further example of regional forms of Kṛṣṇaism centered around temples, mention may be made of Jagannātha in Puri, Orissa, the building of whose temple was started around 1100 CE. Accompanied by Baladeva and Subhadrā, he is evidently envisaged in a Kṛṣṇaite context. This connection was strengthened in the sixteenth century through the *bhakti* culture developed in the temple by Rāmānanda Rāya and Caitanya.

The first Kṛṣṇaite *sampradāya* was developed by Nimbārka. Unfortunately, very little reliable information is available on him and thus it is difficult to place him accurately in the history of Kṛṣṇaism. A date before the sixteenth century would emphasize his originality in terms of Kṛṣṇaite theology, but make his alleged residing in Bṛndāvan (a locality near Mathurā, thought to correspond to the mythical Vṛndāvana) very doubtful. For the first time in the Vedānta school-tradition we find here *brahman* identified with Kṛṣṇa (and not, as earlier on in Rāmānuja and also in Madhva, with Viṣṇu). Moreover, Kṛṣṇa is here envisaged in the company of Rādhā.

A further contributing factor to the increasing popularity of Kṛṣṇa throughout northern India was the appearance of vernacular poets who, in different languages and in varying approaches, dealt with Kṛṣṇa's amours and childhood pranks. While the Bengali poet Caṇḍīdās (1400 CE?) sang about his own tragic love in the imagery of Rādhā's separation, the Maithilī poet Vidyāpati (c. 1350 to 1450) fused the erotic culture of a royal court with the amours of Kṛṣṇa and the milkmaids.

But what about the locality on earth where myth places these amours, that is, Vṛndāvana? The Śrī Vaiṣṇavas had certainly listed it among their 108 primary places of pilgrimage (and in a prominent position) from the tenth century onward. But to what extent anybody from Tamil Nadu traveled all the way up to Mathurā during the period up to the sixteenth century is unknown. [*See also* Hindi Religious Traditions.]

Bṛndāvan. Toward the close of the fifteenth century, the longing to live in the actual place where Kṛṣṇa spent his childhood takes on concrete and documented form. Now we find a number of Kṛṣṇaite devotees, originating from various parts of India, settling in Bṛndāvan along with their disciples. Many temples are constructed on sites that had been (usually miraculously) "rediscovered" as the localities mentioned in Puranic episodes. These developments may well be connected with the transfer of the Mughal capital from Delhi to Agra (in 1506) and the construction of a major road between these two cities which passed through Mathurā. Certainly the tolerant reigns of Akbar (1556–1605) and Jahāngīr (1605–1627) were decisive factors as well.

While the claim that Nimbārka (at an earlier date) had lived in Bṛndāvan is of doubtful validity, both the Caitanyites and Vallabhites refer to an otherwise nebulous Mādhavendra Purī (late fifteenth century) as the original "rediscoverer" of the site of the mythical Vṛndāvana. He in turn appears to have inspired Caitanya to visit the place around 1516 and to settle his disciples there from 1516 onward. Vallabha (c. 1480–1533) and Haridās (c. 1500–1595) arrived somewhat later. During the sixteenth century a whole cluster of Kṛṣṇaite religious movements had their center in the locality of Bṛndāvan. These included Nimbārka's followers and Hit Harivaṃś (c. 1500–1552), who was native to the region. While as religious systems they preserved their separate identities, the common milieu nevertheless produced great similarity of theology and devotion. Although Vallabha himself, and then the branch of his movement that eventually arose in Gujarāt, ignored Rādhā and concentrated on the child Kṛṣṇa and his various pranks, through Vallabha's son Viṭṭhaladeva (c. 1518–1586) Rādhā gained prominence theologically, and through the vernacular poetry of Sūrdās (from c. 1480 to between 1560 and 1580), whom the Vallabhites consider as one of their poets, attention is focused upon Rādhā's and Kṛṣṇa's love-making. [*See the biography of Sūrdās.*] The poetry of Haridās and Hit

Harivaṃś is very similar to this. In contrast, the Caitanyites emphasized the *viraha* ("separation") of Kṛṣṇa and Rādhā.

This milieu shares generally the following features. The Absolute, namely, *brahman*, is Kṛṣṇa together with Rādhā (whom the Vallabhites, in this aspect, call Svāminī-jī). Their relationship may be formulated as that of *śaktimān* ("powerful") and *śakti* ("power"), which—according to the *advaita* stance employed—is one of "non-duality." The older, Upaniṣadic definition of *brahman* as *saccidānanda* ("being, consciousness, bliss") is transformed through emphasis on the "bliss" aspect (in which the other two become subsumed); Rādhā is Kṛṣṇa's *hlādinī-śakti*, the "bliss-causing power." Their love-making (and separation), which scriptures locate in the mythical Vṛndāvana, is on the one hand envisaged as denotative of the nature of *brahman* (ultimate unity of Kṛṣṇa and his *śakti*, differentiation within an *advaita* sense, etc.). On the other hand, it is perceived as taking place, more literally, in eternity, in a heaven usually called Goloka far above the world (and even above Viṣṇu's heaven, Vaikuṇṭha). Yet the earthly Bṛndāvan remains central, for here the eternal love mysteries and the events that took place in the mythical Vṛndāvana fuse invisibly. Thus, by living here and meditating through song and poetry on Kṛṣṇa and Rādhā—by cultivating *bhakti-rasa*—the devotee has direct access to the divine mysteries.

A large corpus of scriptures (devotional poetry along with learned treatises) evolved from all this. Even anonymous works like the *Brahmavaivarta Purāṇa* and the *Garga Saṃhitā*, or later sections of the *Padma Purāṇa*, show an affinity, if no direct connection, with this Bṛndāvan milieu. [*See also* Vṛndāvana.]

Further Diffusion. The centripetal forces that Bṛndāvan exerted on the North soon were balanced by a centrifugal diffusion of the type of Kṛṣṇaism developed here. Thus Vallabha's son Viṭṭhala moved to Gujarāt in about 1570, where the *sampradāya* acquired a large following. Kṛṣṇa's temple in Dvārakā served as ritual center and the *maharajas*—descendants of Vallabha and *gurus* of the community—as Kṛṣṇa's personal embodiments. A personal, devotional Kṛṣṇaism is expressed by the Rajput princess Mīrā Bāī (c. 1500–1565). In her famous poetry she sang about her love for Kṛṣṇa who is fused with her *guru*. [*See also the biography of Mīrā Bāī.*] A contemporary of hers was the Gujarāti poet Narsī Mehtā (c. 1500–1580), who wrote about Kṛṣṇa's and Rādhā's Vṛndāvana amours. In the east, the Caitanyites continued to flourish in Bengal and influenced Bengali poetry on Kṛṣṇa. Śaṅkardev (died c. 1570) and others introduced versions of Kṛṣṇaism into Assam. During the eighteenth century Calcutta witnessed the rise of the Sakhībhāvakas, whose members wore female dress in order to identify themselves even externally with the female companions of Rādhā. In modern times, the Hare Krishna movement exemplifies the continuation of devotional Kṛṣṇaism.

In Kerala ritual Kṛṣṇaism flourishes in connection with the temple of Guruvāyūr, which attracts nowadays large numbers of pilgrims from all over India. Popular texts such as the *Kṛṣṇavilāsa* (by Sukumāra, possibly thirteenth or fourteenth century) and the *Nārāyaṇīyam* (by Mēlpathūr Nārāyaṇa, 1560–1646)—both based on the *Bhāgavata Purāṇa*—provide a literary backing for it.

The term *Kṛṣṇaism*, then, can be used to summarize a large group of independent systems of beliefs and devotion that developed over more than two thousand years, through the interaction of many different cultural contexts. Given the composite nature of the Kṛṣṇa-figure itself (as prankish child, lover, king, fighter of demons, teacher of the *Bhagavadgītā*, etc.), the selective emphasis in these systems on such individual aspects is worth noting. No grand theological synthesis was attempted. Instead, we notice centralizing trends (on an abstract level, in the *Bhāgavata Purāṇa*, and in concrete form, in the influence of the Vṛndāvana milieu) which in turn produced localized expressions. As an overall trend, a concentration on Kṛṣṇa the lover can be recognized, and it is only in the twentieth century that people like Gandhi or Bal Gangadhar Tilak began to explore the role of Kṛṣṇa's teaching in relation to the demands of modern politics and society. The move "beyond Kṛṣṇa" in the direction of a "Rādhāism" (as found, for example, in the later teaching of the Rādhāvallabhīs or with the Sakhībhāvakas) was, on the other hand, tentative and of limited appeal.

[*For further discussion of related religious traditions, see* Vaiṣṇavism *and* Indian Religions, *article on* Rural Traditions. *For individual theographies, see* Kṛṣṇa; Rādhā; *and* Viṣṇu.]

BIBLIOGRAPHY

No single book has thus far surveyed the whole range of Kṛṣṇaism. William G. Archer's charming *The Loves of Krishna in Indian Painting and Poetry* (New York, 1957) can serve as a first introduction to the subject. Four more recent works explore different aspects of the Kṛṣṇa figure, but mainly of the earlier period. My *Viraha-Bhakti: The Early History of Kṛṣṇa Devotion in South India* (New Delhi, 1983), deals primarily with early North Indian material as received and developed in the South (particularly by the Āḻvārs and in the *Bhāgavata Purāṇa*). The Kṛṣṇa of the classical Purāṇas is envisaged in Benjamin Preciado-Solís's *The Kṛṣṇa Cycle in the Purāṇas: Themes and Motifs in a Heroic Saga* (New Delhi, 1984) in the context of heroic poetry and Indian art history, and in Noel Sheth's *The Divinity of Krishna* (New Delhi, 1984) from a theological point of view. In his *Krishna, the Butter Thief* (Princeton, 1983), John Stratton Hawley concentrates on the prankish child as treated in later Hindi poetry, but he includes earlier textual and art-historical material on the theme. Two collections of individual articles contain much relevant information: *Krishna: Myths, Rites, and Attitudes*, edited by Milton Singer (Honolulu, 1966), and *Bhakti in Current Research, 1979–1982*, edited by Monika Thiel-Horstmann (Berlin, 1983). Surendranath Dasgupta's *A History of Indian Philosophy*, vols. 3 and 4 (Cambridge, 1949–1955), may be consulted on the more technical side of the philosophical and theological discussion.

FRIEDHELM E. HARDY

KṢITIGARBHA, called Ti-tsang in China and Jizō in Japan, is, after Avalokiteśvara, the most important *bodhisattva* of Buddhist East Asia. Kṣitigarbha is also well known in Tibet. His name is usually interpreted to mean "receptacle (womb, storehouse) of the earth"; as such, he may be a Buddhist transformation of the Vedic earth goddess Pṛthivī.

Information about the cult of Kṣitigarbha in the esoteric and exoteric Buddhist traditions comes from a number of *sūtras*. Principal among these are two texts:

1. *Ta-sheng ta-chi ti-tsang shih-lun ching* (Mahāyāna Mahāsaṃnipāta Sutra on Kṣitigarbha and the Ten Wheels; T.D. no. 411). This *sūtra* was translated into Chinese by Hsüan-tsang (602–664) in the year 651, but there may have been an earlier translation of the same Sanskrit original made about 400. This scripture is the only exoteric *sūtra* concerning Kṣitigarbha whose pre-Chinese origin is undoubted.
2. *Ti-tsang p'u-sa pen-yüan ching* (Sutra of the Original Vow of the Bodhisattva Kṣitigarbha; T.D. no. 412). This *sūtra* is said to be translated from Sanskrit by Śikṣānanda (652–710), but in fact this attribution is impossible to substantiate. Many contemporary scholars believe that the *sūtra* was written in China as late as the tenth or eleventh century.

History in India. An independent cult of Kṣitigarbha apparently never developed in India. The seventh-century Chinese pilgrims to India do not mention Kṣitigarbha. *Maṇḍalas* in the cave-temples of Ellora do include Kṣitigarbha, but there are no separate images of him. We do find textual references to Kṣitigarbha as far back as the first or second century CE, as well as quotations from an *Ārya Kṣitigarbha Sūtra* in a text from the seventh or eighth century. In Central Asia, Kṣitigarbha was more important: separate images have been found in caves at Tun-huang in what is now Kansu Province.

According to the *Sutra on the Ten Wheels,* Kṣitigarbha's special characteristic is that Śākyamuni Buddha has entrusted him with the task of rescuing sentient beings during the Buddhaless interval between Śākyamuni's *parinirvāṇa* and the enlightenment of the next Buddha, Maitreya. For countless aeons, the scripture maintains, he has worked to lead sentient beings toward Buddhahood in worlds bereft of Buddhas. Kṣitigarbha is said to respond to those who call upon his name and rely on him singlemindedly, meeting their immediate needs, eliminating their suffering, and setting them firmly on the path to *nirvāna.* He softens the hearts of those mired in evil and brings them repentance. Similarly, those in hells obtain release through his intercession.

History in China. Knowledge of Kṣitigarbha (Ti-tsang) was probably introduced to China around 400, but there is no evidence that Ti-tsang became an object of widespread devotion there until much later. An important stimulus for the popularity of faith in Ti-tsang's vows seems to have come from the San-chieh Chiao, or Sect of the Three Stages, a group that believed that various of the teachings of the Buddha were designed to be beneficial in each of three historical ages. Hsin-hsing (540–594), the founder of the sect, promoted the worship of Ti-tsang as appropriate to the present, the third and most evil of the three ages. Judging from the number and dates of images in the Buddhist caves at Lung-men, worship of Ti-tsang became popular among the aristocracy, in tandem with that of the Buddha Amitābha, from 650 to 700. [*See the biography of Hsin-hsing.*]

The *Sutra of the Original Vow* and other texts very possibly written in China made central the notion of Kṣitigarbha's special intention to rescue those in the hells. Filial piety is another theme that emerges in these texts. Of four stories in the *Sutra of the Original Vow* that relate the origin of Kṣitigarbha's vow to rescue all beings from suffering, two tell of his previous births as women who are moved to take such a vow after they have learned that their own mothers are suffering in the Avīci hells. In certain "counterfeit" *sūtras* (i.e., *sūtras* whose provenance is clearly Chinese) showing obvious Taoist influence, Kṣitigarbha was linked to the "ten kings" who were the judges of the Chinese "dark regions," and prayed to specifically in order to lengthen life and ward off disaster. In these *sūtras*, Ti-tsang both judges and saves beings.

Reliance on Ti-tsang's vow remains part of Buddhist practice in Chinese cultural areas today. In the seventh lunar month the *Sutra of the Original Vow* is widely recited and special offerings made in gratitude for his rescuing of ancestors reborn in the various hells.

History in Tibet. Kṣitigarbha is known in Tibet as Saḥi-sñiṅ-po. There is a Tibetan translation of the *Sutra* *on the Ten Wheels* but not of the *Sutra of the Original Vow*. Kṣitigarbha is most frequently honored as one of the grouping of "eight great *bodhisattvas*" whose *maṇḍalas* are important in the Esoteric (i.e., Vajrayāna) tradition.

History in Japan. The first unquestioned evidence of the enshrining of an image of Jizō in Japan and the conducting of an offering service in his temple dates from the year 850. From the ninth century onward, ceremonies of offerings called Jizōkō were widely observed to avert illness and to rescue beings from the hells. Jizō also became honored throughout the country as a protector of children as well as a provider of various blessings sought by the common people. Jizō's festival (Jizōbon), on the twenty-fourth day of the seventh month, usually centers on prayers for the safety of children.

In Japan, many carved stone images of Jizō can still be found at roadsides or in the wild. (Some scholars say that these images gradually replaced an indigenous tradition of erecting stone phallic symbols by the roadside.) In this form, Jizō is the subject of many children's songs and folk songs from ancient times. Today, as in the past, when people mourn victims of war or traffic accidents, or pray for children or for the *mizunoko* (the souls of children who died before birth, usually by miscarriage and abortion), they still often dedicate a small Jizō image at a temple.

Iconography. Although Kṣitigarbha appears in the princely garb of a *bodhisattva* in the Esoteric tradition and in all traditions in China, in Japan he usually appears with the shaved head and monk's robes of a *śrāvaka*, or Hīnayāna monk, a devotee of the first of the "three vehicles" that, in Mahāyāna thought, comprehend the three soteriological paths recognized by the tradition. He usually carries a pearl and a staff. In the Japanese Shingon (Vajrayāna) tradition he appears in both the Taizōkai (Womb Realm Maṇḍala) and the Kongōkai (Diamond Realm Maṇḍala). Another highly developed tradition in Japan is the depiction of "six Jizōs," each with different attributes according to the path of rebirth in which he appears.

[*See also* Celestial Buddhas and Bodhisattvas.]

BIBLIOGRAPHY

In English, M. W. de Visser's *The Bodhisattva Ti-tsang (Jizō) in China and Japan* (Berlin, 1914), although somewhat dated, remains the best reference. The *Sutra of the Original Vow* has been translated into English by Heng Ching and the Buddhist Text Translation Society as *Sūtra of the Past Vows of Earth Store Boddhisattva: The Collected Lectures of Tripitaka Master Hsüan Hua* (San Francisco, 1974).

The literature in Japanese is extensive. Among the best works are Manabe Kōsai's *Jizō bosatsu no kenkyū*, 2d ed. (Kyoto, 1969), which includes a history of texts; Hayami Tasuku's *Jizō shinkō* (Tokyo, 1975), a well-researched, popular book with a good bibliography; and *Jizō shinkō*, edited by Sakurai Tokutarō (Tokyo, 1983), which includes essays on all aspects of the topic by a number of scholars.

Miriam Levering

KUAN-YIN. *See* Avalokiteśvara.

KUBRĀ, NAJM AL-DĪN (AH 540–618/1145–1221 CE), properly Abū al-Jannāb Aḥmad ibn ʿUmar; Iranian Ṣūfī. Known to posterity as the "great scourge" *(al-ṭāmmah al-kubrā)*, in reference to his sharp debating skills—hence his name Kubrā—Najm al-Dīn was born in the city of Khorezm (Khiva). He began Ṣūfī discipline by traveling to Egypt and then to Anatolia. His first master was Rūzbihān al-Wazzān (d. 1188), an Iranian resident in Egypt. The latter in turn had been a follower of Ḍiyāʾ al-Dīn Abū Najīb al-Suhrawardī (d. 1168), a founder of the Suhrawardīyah order *(ṭarīqah;* pl., *ṭuruq)* and author of *Ādāb al-murīdīn*, a widely read guide for Ṣūfī novices. Two other teachers of Najm al-Dīn were also students of Suhrawardī: ʿAmmār ibn Yāsir al-Bidlisī (d. 1200?) and Ismāʿīl al-Qaṣrī (d. 1193). Najm al-Dīn returned to Khorezm and established a Ṣūfī lodge *(khānagāh)* where numerous novices received training. Collectively, these students established a Ṣūfī line known to posterity as the Kubrawīyah, from which several orders emerged in later generations. Although these orders were of brief duration, their founders were to have a lasting influence among both Sunnīs and Shīʿah through disciples who carried Kubrā's teachings to Anatolia, Central Asia, and India. Najm al-Dīn himself died at the hands of the Mongols in the dreadful sack of Khorezm in 1221.

Kubrā's numerous works are primarily in Arabic; one notable exception is a guidebook for Ṣūfī novices in Persian *(Ṣifāt al-ādāb)* that marked an important stage in the development of Persian literature in the Ṣūfī vein. Of particular significance are his nine-volume Arabic commentary on the Qurʾān and, probably the most impressive of his works, the *Fawāʾiḥ al-jamāl wa-fawātiḥ al-jalāl*, which contains Kubrā's Ṣūfī psychology and descriptions of the mystical states that a novice may attain. These may briefly be described here. To Kubrā, the human being was a microcosm, incorporating all that exists in the macrocosm, except for the special qualities, the divine names, of God himself. With the exception of the quality *al-raḥmān al-raḥīm* ("the Merciful the Compassionate"), the qualities of God may be obtained through a process of spiritual ascent if the Ṣūfī follows ascetic practices of fasting, silence, prayer, and training by a master in this discipline of concentrating upon the divine names. Corresponding to the stages of spiritual ascent is a system of color symbols, ranging from black to green, the highest color in rank, which is associated with eternal life.

Kubrā's influence may be assessed from a summary listing of some famous Ṣūfīs who were his disciples, whose thought bore his imprint, or whose teachers came out of Kubrā's line of disciples. Among these masters were Farīd al-Dīn ʿAṭṭār (d. 1220?), Persian author of *Tadhkirat al-awliyā'*, a hagiography of Ṣūfīs, and *Manṭiq al-ṭayr*, a philosophical and poetic work; Najm al-Dīn Dāyā Rāzī (d. 1256), a disciple of Kubrā who carried the master's thought to Anatolia and, through his own disciples, to India; ʿAlā' al-Dawlah Simnānī (d. 1336), an important figure in the development of the Naqshbandī order in Central Asia; and Sayyid ʿAlī Hamadānī (d. 1385), a leading Ṣūfī figure in Kashmir.

BIBLIOGRAPHY

Kubra's principal works have been edited by Fritz Meier. *Die Fawā'iḥ al-ğamāl wa fawātiḥ al-ğalāl des Nağmad-dīn al-Kubrā* (Wiesbaden, 1957) contains an extensive introduction that is an essential work in its own right. See also Fritz Meier's, translation of *Ṣifāt al-ādāb*, "Ein Knigge für Sufi's," *Rivisti degli studii orientali* 32 (1957): 485–524, and his "Stambuler Handschriften dreier persischer Mystiker: ʿAin al-quḍāt al-Hamadānī, Nağm al-dīn al-Kubrā, Nağm al-dīn al-Dāja," *Der Islam* 24 (1937): 1–42. Other texts are found in Marijan Molé's "Traités mineurs de Nağm al-Dīn Kubrā," *Annales islamologiques* 4 (1963): 1–78. Molé also published the following studies of Kubrā and the Kubrawīyah: "Les Kubrawiya entre sunnisme et shiisme aux huitième et neuvième siècles de l'hégire," *Revue des études islamiques* 29 (1961): 61–142; "Professions de foi de deux Kubrawis: ʿAli-i Hamadānī et Muḥammad Nūrbaḫs," *Bulletin d'études orientales* 17 (1961–1962): 133–204; and "La version persane du Traité de dix principes de Najm al-Dīn Kobrá, par ʿAli b. Shihâb al-Din Hamadâni," *Farhang-e Īrān zamin*, 6 (1958): 38–51.

KARL BARBIR

K'UEI-CHI (632–682), religious name of the first patriarch of the Fa-hsiang school of Chinese Buddhism, also known by the titles Ta-sheng Chi and Tz'u-en Ta-shih. K'uei-chi was the foremost disciple of the great pilgrim-monk Hsüan-tsang, under whose tutelage he came to play an instrumental role in the second major transmission of Indian Yogācāra Buddhist thought into China.

Born into a family of famous generals, the Yü-chih, K'uei-chi received a classical Confucian education in preparation for the life of a court official, but decided while still in his teens to enter the Buddhist monastic order instead. In 645 Hsüan-tsang returned from his extended study of Buddhism in India and was commissioned by T'ai-tsung, the second T'ang emperor, to oversee the translation of the numerous Buddhist texts he had brought back to China. Upon his ordination several years later, K'uei-chi was assigned by imperial order to Hsüan-tsang's translation team and soon became one of his most capable students. As Hsüan-tsang's main assistant for much of the project, K'uei-chi appears to have been the actual editor of the influential *Ch'eng wei-shih lun*, a synopsis of early Indian scholarship on Yogācāra Buddhism.

After the death of Hsüan-tsang (664), K'uei-chi turned from translation to exegesis, writing extensive commentaries on most of the works translated by the imperial project, a corpus reflecting his interest in a wide range of Buddhist issues both philosophical and practical. He was especially concerned with the doctrine of *vijñaptimātratā*, which holds that the world as we know it is the result of a psychologically conditioned process of cognitive construction. K'uei-chi also devoted considerable literary effort to working out scholastic problems associated with the stages of progression along the path to liberation. In addition, he wrote important works on Buddhist logic and, consistent with his Yogācāra affiliation, his personal religious practice emphasized devotion to the *bodhisattva* Maitreya.

In spite of its early prominence, the Fa-hsiang school soon experienced a rapid decline, beginning with a shift in imperial patronage that was already apparent in K'uei-chi's lifetime. The conservative, highly technical, and very scholastic version of Indian Yogācāra thought represented by the school proved antithetical to the prevailing fashion of T'ang Buddhism, which had begun to develop independently of the continuing Indian tradition. To bridge this gap K'uei-chi sought to interpret unfamiliar Indian Yogācāra ideas in terms of contemporary Chinese Buddhist vocabulary (see especially his *Wei-shih chang*, or *Essay on Vijñaptimātratā*). His views became the subject of increasing polemic, however, and the school was soon eclipsed by the more indigenous Hua-yen and T'ien-t'ai doctrines. Particularly unacceptable to K'uei-chi's contemporaries was the Yogācāra affirmation of three distinct (and unequal) religious careers and its corollary that some beings, the *icchantikas*, were inherently incapable of any religious development and were thus forever barred from liberation.

Despite the eclipse of the Fa-hsiang school, K'uei-chi's commentaries and essays continued to be widely read throughout East Asia. His students introduced Fa-hsiang thought to Japan, where, as Hossō Buddhism, it became the basis for one of the historically most influential of the Nara schools. While the full range of K'uei-chi's contribution has not yet been fully assessed by modern scholarship, his greatest achievement may be seen in his effort to catalog and preserve details of the scholastic period of Indian Yogācāra thought, especially since he recorded material from texts that now no longer survive in the original Sanskrit.

[*See also* Yogācāra *and the biography of Hsüan-tsang.*]

BIBLIOGRAPHY

Besides his extensive commentaries, K'uei-chi wrote a number of essays, many of which were collected in his doctrinal compendium, the *Ta-sheng fa-yüan i-lin chang* (T.D. no. 1861). For a translation and study of the most important of these, his *Essay on Vijñaptimātratā (Wei-shih chang),* see my study "The Vijñaptimātratā Buddhism of the Chinese Monk K'uei-chi" (Ph.D. diss., University of British Columbia, 1980). On K'uei-chi's relation to the Indian Yogācāra tradition, see my article "The *Trisvabhāva* Doctrine in India and China: A Study of Three Exegetical Models," *Bukkyō bunka kenkyūjo kiyō* 21 (1982): 97–119. In his *Buddhist Formal Logic* (London, 1969), Richard S. Y. Chi has written an excellent study of early Indian Buddhist Nyāya in China based primarily on K'uei-chi's commentaries to the *Nyāyapraveśa.* The rather limited traditional sources for K'uei-chi's biography have been thoroughly analyzed and summarized by Stanley Weinstein in "A Biographical Study of Tz'ŭ-ên," *Monumenta Nipponica* 15 (April–July 1959): 119–149; and some further discussion of K'uei-chi's religious practice can be found in my chapter on "Fa-hsiang Meditation" in *Meditation Traditions in Chinese Buddhism,* edited by Peter Gregory (Honolulu, in press).

ALAN SPONBERG

KŪKAI (774–835), better known by his posthumous name, Kōbō Daishi; founder of the Shingon school of Esoteric (Tantric) Buddhism in Japan and an influential cultural figure—poet, calligrapher, artist, and educator. Kūkai's life covers the end of the Nara period (eighth century) and the beginning of the Heian period (ninth to twelfth century), two very important eras in Japanese cultural and religious history.

During the eighth century, the imperial regime actively exercised its prerogative, sanctioned by the native Shintō myths, to establish a centralized national community. The court welcomed Chinese art, learning, and technology to enrich Japanese society and culture. It also depended on Buddhism for the protection of the nation, as exemplified by the construction of the gigantic national cathedral, Tōdaiji (Eastern Great Temple), in the capital city, Nara. The Nara period witnessed the emergence of several religious phenomena: (1) a variety of unauthorized Buddhist clerics, ascetics, and healers, for instance, the *shidosō* ("private priests") and the *ubasoku* (Skt., *upāsaka;* unordained priests); (2) the Nature Wisdom tradition (Jinenchishū), whose adherents preferred to practice meditation in secluded mountain areas rather than in cloisters; and (3) the beginnings of the Shintō-Buddhist amalgam *(Shin-Butsu shūgō).*

Meanwhile, the cumulative effects of political corruption, ecclesiastical intrigue, and financial problems forced the government to move the capital, first from Nara to Nagaoka in 784, then from Nagaoka to Heiankyō (Kyoto) in 794. The Heian period ushered in new cultural and religious fashions, including the establishment of two Buddhist schools, the Tendai (Chin., T'ien-t'ai), founded by Saichō (Dengyō Daishi), and the Shingon (Chin., Chen-yen), founded by Kūkai.

Kūkai was born in 774 into the Saeki, a declining aristocratic family in Sanuki Province (the present Kagawa Prefecture) on the island of Shikoku. Tutored early in life in the Chinese classics by his maternal uncle, young Kūkai enrolled in the national college *(daigaku)* at the age of eighteen to pursue the study of Confucian classics, the standard requirement for government bureaucrats. Following a sudden conversion to Buddhism, however, he terminated his academic career and became an *ubasoku,* undergoing austere physical training on various mountains in order to acquire magical power. By chance he came across the *Mahāvairocana Sūtra (Dainichikyō),* an important scripture of Esoteric Buddhism. In 804, eager to learn the deep meaning of this scripture, he went to China as a government-sponsored student-monk, accompanying the Japanese envoy. His senior contemporary, Saichō, also went to China on the same occasion.

During the early ninth century, China reached the zenith of its cultural life under the T'ang dynasty. The capital, Ch'ang-an, was a colorful, cosmopolitan city. Although the T'ang court was hospitable to various religions, such as Nestorian Christianity, Zoroastrianism, and Islam, it gave special favor to Esoteric Buddhism, which had been transmitted from India by Śubhākarasiṃha (d. 735), Vajrabodhi (d. 741), and Amoghavajra (Pu-k'ung, d. 774). It was Pu-k'ung's successor, Hui-kuo (746–805), who transmitted the *dharma* of Esoteric Buddhism to Kūkai and made him the eighth patriarch of the Esoteric tradition. At the same time, Saichō received Esoteric teachings from Shun-hsiao, to whom the tradition of Śubhākarasiṃha had been transmitted by I-lin. Saichō returned to Japan in 805, but Kūkai stayed on in Ch'ang-an to pursue further studies in Sanskrit, art, literature, and calligraphy.

In 806, Kūkai returned to Japan with an impressive collection of Indian and Chinese scriptures, commentaries, ritual objects, and ornaments. The imperial court did not receive him immediately, but in 909 the newly ascended Emperor Saga (r. 809–823), himself an accomplished poet and calligrapher who admired Kūkai both as a man of culture and as a religious leader, invited him to reside at the Takaosanji, a temple near Kyoto. Later he appointed him to serve as administrator *(bettō)* of the Tōdaiji in Nara. It was Saga who granted Mount Kōya (in the present Wakayama Prefecture) to Kūkai so that he might build a monastic center. Emperor Junna (r. 823–833) made the Tōji (Eastern Temple) in Kyoto an establishment exclusively for Esoteric Buddhism under Kūkai's supervision. In doing so, he recognized *de facto* the official status of the Shingon school. Junna also appointed Kūkai to the successive ranks of junior ecclesiastical supervisor *(shōsōzu)* and senior ecclesiastical supervisor *(daisōzu)*. Illness obliged Kūkai to retire from official duties in 831, and his colorful life came to an end at Mount Kōya in 835.

Throughout his life Kūkai pursued a variety of activities. He was a prolific writer, a tireless philanthropist, a creative artist, and an advocate of liberal education, the last exemplified by his founding of the Shugei Shuchi-in (Academy of Arts and Sciences). His attitude toward the Shintō tradition was cordial and conciliatory. He thus prepared the ground for the subsequent development of Ryōbu Shintō, the Shingon form of the Shintō-Buddhist amalgam. Nevertheless, his primary objective was the promotion and expansion of Esoteric Buddhism among persons of all walks of life and in every region of Japan. His popularity was such that an amazing number of people, including members of the imperial family, Nara ecclesiastics, and even Saichō himself, sought Esoteric initiation from him.

For a time, Kūkai's relationship to Saichō was cordial, but it eventually became strained. Saichō regarded the Esoteric tradition as only a single, if important, dimension of his all-inclusive Tendai form of *ekayāna* ("one vehicle") Buddhism, but Kūkai was convinced that only the Esoteric tradition embodied the complete truth revealed by the Great Sun Buddha, Mahāvairocana, who was none other than the *dharmakāya*. As such, Kūkai felt that Esoteric Buddhism was the culmination and fulfillment of all other Buddhist schools and traditions. In his view, these other schools and traditions expounded only the exoteric teachings of Śākyamuni, a temporal incarnation of the timeless *dharmakāya* Mahāvairocana.

It is fair to say that even though Kūkai depended heavily on the philosophical, textual, cultic, and ecclesiastical framework of the Chinese Esoteric tradition, the basic structure of the Shingon school developed out of his own religious search and fertile reflection. Kūkai's cosmotheism was grounded in three epistemological components: (1) the intuitive function of the mind that enables it to determine moral choices *(shōtoku* or *shōgu)*, (2) knowledge acquired by learning and experience *(shūtoku)*, and (3) faith that gives certitude *(shinkō)*. Through the dialectic of these three epistemological components, Kūkai developed his schema: he distinguished Exoteric *(kengyō)* and Esoteric *(mikkyō)* teachings and classified and ranked various Buddhist schools in ascending order, placing Shingon at the apex. His system was not simply a philosophical-doctrinal exercise but was directed toward the goal of attaining Buddhahood in this very body *(sokushin jōbutsu)*.

This doctrine was a logical culmination of Kūkai's lifelong religious quest, begun during his days as an *ubasoku*. At that time, he was no doubt influenced by the tenets of the Nature Wisdom tradition, an admixture of the Buddhist and pre-Buddhist Japanese religious ethos. From this perspective Kūkai attempted to homologize religion and art, philosophy and literature, Buddhism and other religious traditions, and the spiritual and cultural life of Japan. As might be expected, Kūkai's death did not diminish his aura; rather, it deified him in the minds of his followers, who believe that he is still alive on Mount Kōya in an eternal trance of concentration, a savior to suffering humanity.

Kūkai's major works include *Sangōshīki* (The Goals of Three Teachings); *Jūjūshinron* (The Ten Stages of the Development of Mind); *Benkemmitsu nikyōron* (The Exposition of the Two Teachings, Esoteric and Exoteric); *Hizōhōyaku* (The Treasure Key to the Exoteric Store); *Sokushin jōbutsugi* (Attaining Buddhahood in This Very Body); and a work on the poetical theory and phonology of the Six Dynasties and early T'ang periods in China entitled *Bunkyō hifuron* (The Secret Treasure-house of the Mirrors of Poetry).

[*See also* Shingonshū.]

BIBLIOGRAPHY

Hakeda, Yoshito S. *Kūkai: Major Works.* New York, 1972. Contains an extensive bibliography.

Kitagawa, Joseph M. "Kōbō Daishi and Shingon Buddhism." Ph.D. diss., University of Chicago, 1951.

Kiyota, Minoru. *Shingon Buddhism: Theory and Practice.* Los Angeles, 1978.

Mikkyō Bunka Kenkyūjo, eds. *Kōbō Daishi zenshū* (1910). Reprint, Koyasan, 1965–1968. The collected works of Kūkai.

JOSEPH M. KITAGAWA

KULTGESCHICHTLICHE SCHULE. *See* Myth and Ritual School.

KULTURKREISELEHRE ("culture-circles teaching"), also called the cultural-historical method, refers to a model developed at the beginning of the twentieth century by German ethnologists in order to provide ethnology with a cultural-historical perspective and thus to secure for ethnology a place in the science of history. By setting up "culture circles," that is, various areas governed by the same or a dominant culture, ethnology ceased to be either the unsystematic collecting of artifacts or the binding of disparate artifacts under the concept of evolutionism, or unilinear development. It was thus possible to look not only at the differences between nonliterate peoples but also to examine chronologically the sequence of cultures.

Precursors of the cultural-historical method were the Russian naturalist N. Ia. Danilevskii (1822–1865) and the German geographer Friedrich Ratzel (1844–1904). In his *Anthropogeographie* (1882–1891) and *Völkerkunde* (1885–1888), Ratzel attempted to resolve the conflict between convergence theory (egregiously represented in Adolf Bastian's notion of *Elementargedanken*) and diffusionism in favor of the latter. Ratzel applied for the first time the zoological migration theory in order to explain the expansion, migration, and layering of cultures. In his analysis of individual cultures, Ratzel used what are called "form criteria" (i.e., material goods such as weapons) to confirm contacts, often across great distances, between cultures. Ratzel's pupil Leo Frobenius, however, is considered the founder of the culture-circle theory. With the aid of the "quantitative criterion," Frobenius proposed a "West African culture circle" in his *Der Ursprung der afrikanischen Kulturen* (1898). From this concept, however, he later developed the irrational notion of a "culture morphology" in which culture was conceived as a living organism whose development was determined by a soul *(paideuma)*.

Frobenius's work was joined by scholarship such as these articles that appeared in *Zeitschrift für Ethnologie* 37 (1905): Bernhard Ankermann's "Kulturkreise und Kulturschichten in Afrika" and Fritz Graebner's "Kulturkreise und Kulturgeschichten in Ozeanien." With his *Die Methode der Ethnologie* (1911), Graebner created the methodological basis for ethnology and introduced methods of historical inquiry, especially the methods developed in Ernst Bernheim's *Lehrbuch der historischen Methode* (5th ed., 1908). A majority of the young ethnologists of the period gathered under the banner of this cultural-historical method. In the United States, Franz Boas and his school made a substantial contribution to the historical analysis of data, despite their critical reservations with regard to the concept of culture circles.

It was the Viennese linguist and ethnologist Wilhelm Schmidt (1868–1954), however, who developed the concept of the culture circle into an extended system by unifying it and incorporating new elements. In his *Handbuch der Methode der kulturhistorischen Ethnologie* (1937), Schmidt writes, "If . . . a culture complex embraces all the essential and necessary categories of human culture, material culture, economic life, social life, custom, religion, then we call it a 'culture circle,' because returning into itself, like a circle, it is sufficient unto itself and, hence, also assures its independent existence" (Eng. ed., *The Culture Historical Method of Ethnology*, 1939, p. 176). Through the continuing scholarship of Wilhelm Koppers, Martin Gusinde, and Paul Schebesta, the concept of the culture circle acquired acceptance in the field of history of religion and, periodically, dominated discussion in the area of the ethnology of religion. In his twelve-volume work, *Der Ursprung der Gottesidee* (1912–1955), Schmidt used the culture-circle theory to support the theory of primordial monotheism *(Urmonotheismus)*.

In 1906, the periodical *Anthropos* became the mouthpiece of Schmidt's Viennese school. To quantitative and form criteria, Schmidt added the criteria of continuity and relatedness as a means of determining relatively uniform cultural complexes. He emphasized the temporal factor and the succession of cultural strata in time, and thus introduced the question of the origin and development of the culture circles. According to Schmidt, cultural elements can be compared only if they are related to each other or occur within the same culture circle. In determining the origin of the culture circle a double rule applies: a cultural element can be explained only within its own culture circle, and in this explanation, the oldest cultural forms are of primary significance. The culture circles proposed by Schmidt are as follows:

1. *Primitive cultures.* Characterized by preliterate hunters and gatherers
   - 1.1 Central primitive culture; exogamous and monogamous marriages
   - 1.2 Southern primitive culture; exogamous marriages and sex totems
2. *Primary cultures.* Characterized by preliterate agriculturalists
   - 2.1 Exogamous marriages, patrilineal kinship; totemism, higher stages hunting; "city" culture
   - 2.2 Exogamous marriages, matrilineal kinship; horticulturist; "village" culture
   - 2.3 Patrilineal kinship, undivided families; pastoral nomads who become ruling races
3. *Secondary cultures.* Characterized by picture writing
   - 3.1 Free patrilineal cultures (e.g., Polynesia, the Sudan, western India, western Asia, southern Europe)
   - 3.2 Free matrilineal cultures (e.g., southern China,

eastern India, Melanesia, the northeast of South America)

4. *Tertiary cultures.* Characterized by use of alphabet (the oldest civilizations of Asia, Europe, and America)

We can see that Schmidt presumes a succession that is distinguished from the older evolutionism schema but that assumes, in effect, a reverse evolution, or a "devolution." This reversal becomes particularly obvious in Schmidt's religious historical schema: in the primitive cultures the belief in a supreme being dominates; this belief is interpreted as primordial monotheism. It is within the next stage, or "primary cultures," that the belief in spirits (animism), magic, and totemism (animal worship) emerges. These beliefs increasingly stifle monotheism and eventually result in the polytheism of the higher cultures. This earlier monotheistic stage is finally revived by the biblical religions.

Without a doubt, Schmidt sought through the use of the culture-circle theory a historical proof of the existence of God. It is thus small wonder that this school has fallen into disrepute among ethnologists, since it appeared to serve the aims of Catholic theology more than those of unbiased research. The members of the Viennese school, especially Josef Haekel and Walter Hirschberg, have increasingly distanced themselves from Schmidt's ideas. The discussion surrounding the culture-circle theory continues, however, outside the Schmidt school: Hermann Baumann and Wilfred D. Hambly have presented different models for Africa, and Clark Wissler, Edward Sapir, Melville J. Herskovits, and A. L. Kroeber have done the same for America. The growing body of knowledge and increased specialization no longer permit a universal construction of culture circles. Especially problematic is the identification of the oldest nonliterate cultures (hunters and gatherers) with the prehistorical "primitive stage" *(Urstufe),* as found in Oswald Menghin's *Weltgeschichte der Steinzeit* (1931). The assumption that cultures could have survived over the millennia untouched by foreign influences and without internal change has no historical basis.

Today the influence of the higher cultures on the nonliterate cultures is taken into account to a greater extent and the complexity of the former is given greater attention. The heritage of the culture-circle theory is retained, however, in the continued use of the methods of historical inquiry in ethnology, and the broad application of the concept of culture.

[*For related discussion, see* Evolutionism *and the biographies of Frobenius, Graebner, and Schmidt.*]

BIBLIOGRAPHY

Baumann, Hermann, Diedrich Westermann, and Richard Thurnwald. *Völkerkunde von Afrika.* Essen, 1940.

Brandewie, Ernest. *Wilhelm Schmidt and the Origin of the Idea of God.* Lanham, Md., 1983.

Fiedermutz-Laun, Annemarie. *Der kulturhistorische Gedanke bei Adolf Bastian.* Wiesbaden, 1970.

Haekel, Josef, et al., eds. *Die Wiener Schule der Völkerkunde.* Vienna, 1956.

Kroeber, A. L. *Cultural and Natural Areas of Native North America.* Berkeley, 1939.

Langness, Lewis L. *The Study of Culture.* San Francisco, 1974.

Leser, Paul. "Zur Geschichte des Wortes Kulturkreis." *Anthropos* 58 (1963): 1–36.

Lowie, R. H. *The History of Ethnological Theory.* New York, 1937.

Muhlmann, Wilhelm E. *Geschichte der Anthropologie.* 3d ed. Wiesbaden, 1984.

Pinard de la Boullaye, Henri. *L'étude comparée des religions.* 4th ed. 3 vols. Paris, 1929–1931.

Schmidt, Wilhelm, and Wilhelm Koppers. *Völker und Kulturen,* vol. 1, *Gesellschaft und Wirtschaft der Völker.* Regensburg, 1924.

KURT RUDOLPH

Translated from German by William H. Snyder

KUMĀRAJĪVA (343–413; alternative dates: 350–409) renowned as the founder of the San-lun ("three treatise," i.e., Mādhyamika) school in China and as an adept translator into Chinese of many important and influential Mahāyāna Buddhist texts.

Kumārajīva was born of noble lineage in the Central Asian city of Kuchā. His father was an emigrant Indian brahman and his mother a Kuchean princess. During the fourth century Kuchā was a major city along the northern trade route of the Silk Road connecting China with India and the West. There is ample testimony from the travelogues of Fa-hsien and Hsüan-tsang that cities along this route were strongholds of Hīnayāna Buddhism, especially the Sarvāstivāda sect, which had been introduced from its center in Kashmir. The works of this sect were thus the first he was to study.

Kumārajīva became a novice monk at the early age of seven. His mother, who wanted to become a nun, also abandoned lay life at this time. He spent the next two years studying the Āgamas and Abhidharma texts. When he was nine he went with his mother to North India (to Chipin, in Kashmir), where for three years he studied the *Dirghāgama,* the *Madhyamāgama* and the *Kṣudraka* under the master Bandhudatta. At twelve he again set out with his mother for Kuchā. On the way they stopped for more than a year in Kashgar, where he studied the *Jñānaprasthāna Śāstra,* a Sarvāstivādin Abhidharma treatise, as well as the Vedas and the five sciences (grammar, logic, metaphysics, medicine, and the arts and crafts). While in Kashgar he met the Mahāyānist Sūryasoma, who converted him to the Mahāyāna. In Kashgar, Kumārajīva also met the Dharmagupta master Buddhayaśas. After returning to Kuchā, Kumārajīva received full ordination in the royal palace at age twenty. He studied the Vinaya of the Sarvāstivāda school with the North Indian master Vimalākṣa. More significantly, however, he spent the next twenty years concentrating on Mahāyāna *sūtra*s and *śāstra*s. His biography reports that he studied the three *śāstra*s of Nāgārjuna and Āryadeva that were later to become the central texts of the San-lun tradition, all of which he may have obtained in Kashgar. A Chinese account of 379 mentions Kumārajīva as an accomplished monk, and it is from this period that his fame reaches China.

Northern China at this time was ruled by the Former Ch'in dynasty. The most powerful ruler of this kingdom was a Tibetan named Fu Chien. Owing to his encouragement, many monks began to arrive in Ch'ang-an to train a corps of Chinese clerics who would serve in the translation bureaus of the capital. In 383 Fu Chien sent an expeditionary force under the general Lü Kuang to seize Kuchā. Kumārajīva was taken captive, but because Fu Chien had been killed in Ch'ang-an Lü Kuang decided to set up his own kingdom of Liang-chou in northwest China, where he detained Kumārajīva for seventeen years. During this period he learned Chinese. In 401, when the Later Ch'in defeated Lü, Kumārajīva was brought to Ch'ang-an. There he received the patronage of the ruler Yao Hsing, who put the Hsien-yao Garden translation center at his disposal. He was honored with the title "national preceptor" and was even assigned ten court women, with whom, Yao hoped, he would produce equally talented progeny. From 402 until his death Kumārajīva translated a large corpus of scriptures and trained an illustrious group of disciples, including Seng-chao and Seng-jui.

Kumārajīva's Translations. The *Ch'u san-tsang chi chi* (early sixth century) attributes thirty-five works in 294 fascicles to Kumārajīva. The central corpus of these works is well attested by contemporary prefaces, and dates of translation are known for twenty-three titles. The core of works translated by Kumārajīva shows that his main interest was in the Śūnyavādin *sūtra*s, particularly those of the Prajñāpāramitā class, and the Mādhyamika treatises. His interests were catholic, however, and he also translated pietist, Vinaya, and *dhyāna sūtras*, as well as the *Satyasiddhi Śāstra,* a Bahuśrutīya treatise by Harivarman.

Chief among the translated Śunyavādin works were the *Pañcaviṃśati* (T.D. no. 223), the *Aṣṭasāhasrikā* (T.D. no. 227), the *Vimalakīrtinirdeśa* (T.D. no. 475), the *Vajracchedikā* (T.D. no. 235), and the *Prajñāpāramitāhṛdaya* (T.D. no. 250). He also translated the three Mādhyamika treatises that form the basis for the San-lun school in China and Japan: the *Mūlamadhyamaka Śāstra,* a treatise consisting of verses by Nāgārjuna and commentary by Piṅgala (T.D. no. 1564; Chin., *Chung lun*); the *Śata Śāstra* of Āryadeva (T.D. no. 1569; Chin., *Po lun*); and the *Dvādaśanikāya Śāstra* of Nāgārjuna (T.D. no. 1568; Chin., *Shih-erh men lun*). Three other important Mādhyamika treatises that he translated are the *Daśabhūmivibhāṣā Śāstra* attributed to Nāgārjuna (T.D. no. 1521), the *Fa-p'u-t'i-hsin-ching lun* attributed to Vasubandhu (T.D. no. 1659), and the *Mahāprajñāpāramitā Śāstra* attributed to Nāgārjuna (T.D. no. 1509; Chin., *Ta chih-tu lun*). Four treatises on meditation are attributed to Kumārajīva; chief among them is the *Tso-ch'an san-mei ching* (T.D. no. 614), also called the *Bodhisattvadhyāna.* The major Vinaya works that he translated are the Sarvāstivāda *Prātimokṣa Sūtra* and, according to tradition, the *P'u-sa-chieh-pen (Bodhisattva-pratimokṣa).* His pietist translations include the *Saddharmapuṇḍarīka* (T.D. no. 262), the *Smaller Sukhāvativyūha* (T.D. no. 366), and two Maitreya texts (T.D. nos. 454 and 456). He also translated the *Daśabhūmika* (T.D. no. 286) in collaboration with his friend from Kashgar Buddhayaśas. All of these texts became central to the Chinese Buddhist community.

Kumārajīva, his chief assistants, and the translation bureau devised new transcriptions of names and Buddhist technical terms and utilized interpolated glosses when specific words could not be translated adequately. Although his translations betray careless editing, they are famous for their florid and elegant style. They may not preserve the original words of a Sanskrit *sūtra,* but they clearly express the intended meaning.

The most important evidence for Kumārajīva's religious thought is contained in the commentary on the *Vimalakīrtinirdeśa* (T.D. no. 1775) and the collection of correspondence (T.D. no. 1856) between Hui-yüan and Kumārajīva. From these works it is clear that Kumārajīva was an unqualified adherent of the Mādhyamika tradition. His critique of causation is the same as that of Nāgārjuna.

There is no evidence that Kumārajīva intended to found a lineage. Nevertheless, his influence in China, Korea, and Japan was pervasive. Although the *Saddharmapuṇḍarīka Sūtra,* the *Smaller Sukhāvativyūha Sūtra,* and the *Vimalakīrtinirdeśa Sūtra* had been translated earlier by Dharmarakṣa, Kumārajīva's more accurate translations further stimulated the growth and popularity of Mahāyāna Buddhism in the Far East: the *Saddharmapuṇḍarīka Sūtra* became the basic text of the T'ien-t'ai school and, later, of the Nichiren sect in Japan; the *Smaller Sukhāvatīvyūha* became one of the three major texts of the Pure Land Tradition; the *Vajracchedikā* continues to be esteemed as a basic text of the Ch'an school; the *Ta chih-tu lun* was very influential in the Chen-yen or Shingon (i.e., Vajrayāna) school in China and Japan; while the *Vimalakīrtinirdeśa* popularized the ideal of the *bodhisattva*. Other of his translations also helped shape the history of medieval Chinese Buddhism. The *Satyasiddhi Śāstra,* which had many commentaries written on it, became the most widely studied and influential work in the South during the Southern Ch'i (479–502) and Ling dynasties (502–557), and the Sarvāstivāda Vinaya became one of the two Vinaya systems prevalent in China and Japan. The old line transmission of the San-lun school persisted until the time of Chi-tsang (549–623) of the Sui dynasty (581–618). In summary, Kumārajīva's activities ushered in the second period of Chinese translations (fifth and sixth centuries), characterized by greater accuracy and widespread influence in the Chinese Buddhist community.

[*See also* Buddhism, Schools of, *article on* Chinese Buddhism; Mādhyamika; Buddhist Literature, *article on* Survey of Texts; *and the biographies of Hui-yüan, Seng-chao, and Nāgārjuna.*]

BIBLIOGRAPHY

The standard traditional account of the life of Kumārajīva can be found in Hui-chao's *Kao-seng chuan* (T.D. nos. 50. 330–333). For a German translation of the biography, see Johannes Nobel's "Kumārajīva," *Sitzungsberichte der preussischen Akademie der Wissenschaften* 26 (1927): 206–233. Erik Zürcher's *The Buddhist Conquest of China,* 2 vols. (1959; reprint, Leiden, 1979), treats the development of Buddhism in China through the end of the fourth century and thus provides an invaluable introduction to the religious and intellectual climate Kumārajīva encountered upon reaching Ch'ang-an. For a general survey of Kumārajīva's career see Kenneth Ch'en's *Buddhism in China: A Historical Survey* (Princeton, 1964). Other critical discussions include the following:

Kimura Eiichi, ed. *Eon kenkyū.* 2 vols. Kyoto, 1960–1962. Contains a translation of Kumārajīva's correspondence with Hui-yüan.

Koseki, Aaron K. " 'Later Mādhyamika' in China: Some Current Perspectives on the History of Chinese *Prajñāpāramitā* Thought." *Journal of the International Association of Buddhist Studies* 5 (1982): 53–62.

Liebenthal, Walter, ed. and trans. *The Book of Chao.* Peking, 1948.

Liebenthal, Walter. "Chinese Buddhism during the Fourth and Fifth Centuries." *Monumenta Nipponica* 11 (April 1955): 44–83.

Robinson, Richard H. *Early Mādhyamika in India and China.* New Delhi, 1976.

Sakaino Kōyō. *Shina bukkyō seishi* (1935). Tokyo, 1972. See pages 341–417.

T'ang Yung-t'ung. *Han Wei liang-Chin Nan-pei-ch'ao fo-chiao shih.* Shanghai, 1938.

Tsukamoto Zenryū. "The Dates of Kumārajīva and Seng-chao Re-examined." *Jinbum kagaku kenkyūsho* (Silver Jubilee Volume, 1954): 568–584.

Tsukamoto Zenryū, ed. *Jōron kenkyū.* Kyoto, 1955.

DALE TODARO

KUMAZAWA BANZAN (1619–1691), Japanese Confucian thinker of the Wang Yang-ming school. Born in Kyoto, the son of a *rōnin,* or masterless samurai, Banzan probably suffered deprivation during his early years. In 1634, however, he was employed as a page to Ikeda Mitsumasa (1609–1682), daimyo of Okayama, who was later acknowledged to be one of the enlightened rulers of his age. Banzan left the service of Mitsumasa in 1638. In 1641 and 1642 he studied under Nakae Tōju (1608–1648), the founder of the Wang Yang-ming school of Neo-Confucianism (Ōyōmeigaku) in Japan, an experience that permanently molded Banzan's attitude to the Confucian tradition.

Reentering Mitsumasa's service in 1645, Banzan appears to have been employed mainly as a Confucian adviser and teacher. He rose dramatically in the service of the domain, attaining the rank of *bangashira* (divisional commander) in 1650. Undoubtedly, his participation in domain adminstration further influenced his intellectual development, particularly his sense of the limited practicability of certain aspects of Confucianism to the Japanese social and intellectual condition. Banzan's resignation from Mitsumasa's service in 1657 probably resulted from a combination of internal domain rivalries and external pressure from the Tokugawa government to suppress *shingaku,* or "the learning of the heart," as Banzan's style of Confucianism was then known.

Banzan next lived for a number of years in Kyoto, where he associated with and taught court nobles and pursued a life of high culture. In 1667, however, his activities appear to have aroused the suspicion of the authorities and, subsequently, he was forced to leave the city. Thereafter, he lived under official surveillance in the castle towns of Akashi and Yada until finally he was placed under house arrest in Koga.

Banzan's extensive written works date mainly from the period of his retirement from service in Okayama. Among them are miscellanies relating to Confucianism in Japan and to contemporary affairs, including financial and economic matters; commentaries on the Confucian classics; an important treatise on contemporary political economy entitled *Daigaku wakumon* (Questions on the *Great Learning*); a series of dialogues in which speakers from different social groups discuss a wide range of issues; and a remarkable commentary on the *Tale of Genji.*

Banzan belonged to that generation of early Tokugawa-period thinkers who first explored seriously the practical relevance to their own society of Chinese Neo-Confucianism as established during the Sung (960–1279) and Ming (1368–1644) dynasties. He accepted in broad outline the metaphysical assumptions of that tradition, including the concept of a dualistically structured world of *li* (Jpn., *ri,* "principle") and *ch'i* (Jpn., *ki,* "ether"). He was also a proponent of the Neo-Confucian doctrine of the mind, asserting that it is man's duty to regenerate himself through self-cultivation. Like most of his Confucian contemporaries, he was anti-Buddhist and anti-Christian. Banzan's thought is further characterized by an eclecticism that is evident in his attempts to combine the intellectual traditions of Wang Yang-ming (1472–1529) and Chu Hsi (1130–1200). Banzan adhered to the former's emphasis on introspection as a technique for self-cultivation and on the subjective conscience in determining action. Following the thought of Chu Hsi, Banzan upheld the idea of *ri* as a rationally accessible and objective principle underlying the natural and social worlds. His pragmatism can be seen in his resolutely antidoctrinaire stance and his willingness to accommodate to Japanese conditions many conventional Chinese Confucian institutions such as earth burial of the dead, the prohibitions on nonagnatic adoption and agnatic marriage, and the rituals of mourning. This pragmatism was underpinned by sophisticated theories of history and geography that related national temperament to physical and historical environment.

Banzan's Confucianism, therefore, was not profoundly innovative or original. Rather, it bears the stamp of a vigorous and practical attempt to adapt the Chinese Neo-Confucian heritage to the complex realities of early Tokugawa Japan. Banzan himself had no major disciples, but his thought influenced the ideas of Ogyū Sorai (1666–1728) and several Confucian thinkers of the late Tokugawa period, including Yokoi Shōnan (1809–1869).

[*See also* Confucianism in Japan.]

BIBLIOGRAPHY

Gotō Yōichi and Tomoeda Ryūtarō, eds. *Kumazawa Banzan.* Nihon shisō taikei, vol. 30. Tokyo, 1971.

Taniguchi Sumio et al., eds. *Zōtei Banzan zenshū.* 7 vols. Tokyo, 1980.

I. J. McMullen

KUMBHA MELĀ. The Kumbha Melā is a Hindu pilgrimage fair that occurs four times every twelve years, once in each of four locations in North India: at Haridvār, where the Ganges River enters the plains from the Himalayas; at Prayāg, near Allahabad, at the confluence of the Ganges, Yamunā, and "invisible" Sarasvatī rivers; at Ujjain, in Madhya Pradesh, on the banks of the Kṣiprā River; and at Nāsik, in Maharashtra, on the Godavari River. Each twelve-year cycle includes the Mahā ("great") Kumbha Melā at Prayāg, which is the largest pilgrimage gathering in the world. These *melās* ("fairs"), also known as Kumbha Yoga or Kumbha Parva, occur during the conjunctions (Skt., *yoga, parva*) of celestial beings who performed important acts in the myth that forms the basis of the observance. In one version of the story, the gods and the antigods had concluded a temporary alliance in order to churn *amṛta* (the nectar of immortality, ambrosia) from the milky ocean. Among the "fourteen gems" they churned from the ocean was a pot *(kumbha)* of *amṛta.* One of the gods, Jayanta, took the pot and ran, chased by the antigods. For twelve divine days and nights (the equivalent of twelve human years) they fought over the *amṛta.* The Moon protected it from "flowing forth," the Sun kept the pot from breaking, Jupiter preserved it from the demons, and Saturn protected it from fear of Jayanta. During the battle, drops of *amṛta* fell at eight places in the inaccessible worlds of the gods and four places (Haridvār, Prayāg, Ujjain, and Nāsik) on the earth.

The Kumbha Melā is celebrated at the four earthly points where the nectar fell, during the conjunctions of planets *(graha)* with astrological houses *(rāśī)* that are characters in the story—for example, at Haridvār when Jupiter (Guru) is in Aquarius (Kumbha) and the Sun (Sūrya) is in Aries (Meṣa). It is popularly thought that a ritual bath (characteristic in all Hindu pilgrimages) at the Kumbha Melā confers extraordinary merit, not only by cleansing the pilgrim of "sin" *(pāpa),* but also by immersing him in waters infused with *amṛta.* Major baths are done at different times in each of the four Kumbha Melās, chiefly on new-moon and full-moon days.

The historical origin of the Kumbha Melā is an open and indeed almost uninvestigated question. The authenticity of its purported mention in the *Atharvaveda* has been challenged, although certain *khila* verses of unknown date in the *Ṛgveda* demonstrate familiarity with some of the sites and relevant astrological conjunctions. The Chinese Buddhist pilgrim Hsüan-tsang visited Prayāg in the seventh century, but there is no evidence that he witnessed a Kumbha Melā.

Traditions regarding the determination of the time of the Kumbha Melā are not unanimous. This is partly due to the absence of a single, authoritative scripture sanctioning the *melā*. It is mentioned only in late texts, notably the *Skanda Purāṇa*, which has several notoriously inconsistent recensions. Thus there are occasional disagreements between those who say that the Kumbha Melā should be held every twelve years and those who claim that, in exceptional instances, the precise astrological conjunction may occur in the eleventh year. Matters are complicated by the fact that Haridvār and Prayāg have traditions of *ardha* ("half") Kumbha Melās, which occur six years after the Kumbha Melās. Nevertheless, there is at present a rough consensus of learned opinion regarding the appropriate times of its occurrence.

Kumbha Melās are popularly understood to be not only pilgrimage fairs at which sins can be cleansed and merit gained but also religious assemblies at which doctrine is debated and standardized and Hindu unity affirmed. This is perhaps an apt characterization of present-day Kumbha Melās, but historical evidence indicates that in centuries past they were the scenes of bloody battles, chiefly between the militant sections of rival orders of Hindu monks. The main object of contention in these battles, which occurred as recently as 1807, was the right to bathe in the most auspicious place at the most powerful instant. The conflicts were so fierce that indigenous and British courts finally had to establish and enforce specific bathing orders at the various sites of the Kumbha Melā. The *sāīs*, processions of monks to the bathing place, are still focal events in the Kumbha Melās.

With the advent of modern transport and communications, contemporary Kumbha Melās are sometimes attended by several million people in a single day. The government of India provides safety, order, sanitation, and preventive inoculations for this multitude, which besides innumerable devout Hindus includes merchants, representatives of religious organizations, casual tourists, groups of monks, and others. Many of those who attend the Kumbha Melā hope to gain some specific "fruit," such as a job, a son, success in studies, and so on. The special power of the Kumbha Melā is often said to be due in part to the presence of large numbers of Hindu monks, and many pilgrims seek the *darśan* (Skt., *darśana*; "auspicious mutual sight") of these holy men. Others listen to religious discourses, participate in devotional singing, engage brahman priests for personal rituals, organize mass feedings of monks or the poor, or merely enjoy the spectacle. Amid this diversity of activities, the ritual bath at the conjunction of time and place is the central event of the Kumbha Melā.

[*See also* Pilgrimage, *article on* Hindu Pilgrimage.]

BIBLIOGRAPHY

An excellent description of a recent Kumbha Melā is given in Ved Mehta's *Portrait of India* (New York, 1970), pp. 77–111. A more scholarly analysis of the Kumbha Melā, based on Sanskrit sources, is Giorgio Bonazzoli's "Prayāga and Its Kumbha Melā," *Purāṇa* 19 (January 1977): 81–179. This article also discusses the scriptural glorifications (*mahātmyas*) of Prayāg at length and contains useful information regarding the history of the Kumbha Melā. A good example of a learned Hindu's ideas concerning the Kumbha Melā is Veṇīrāmaśarma Gauḍ's *Kumbhaparva Mahātmya* (Varanasi, n.d.) in Hindi. The best general introduction to Hindu pilgrimage is still Agehananda Bharati's "Pilgrimage Sites and Indian Civilization," in *Chapters in Indian Civilization*, edited by Joseph W. Elder, vol. 1, rev. ed. (Dubuque, 1970), pp. 84–126. The author discusses Hindu pilgrimage in general, the Kumbha Melā in particular, and also catalogs numerous pilgrimage places in India. For the significance of *parva*, see John M. Stanley's excellent article "Special Time, Special Power: The Fluidity of Power in a Popular Hindu Festival," *Journal of Asian Studies* 37 (November 1977): 27–43. This essay contains a clear exposition of Hindu astrological and astronomical ideas relating to *melās*.

WILLIAM S. SAX

KUNAPIPI. *See* Gadjeri.

KUṆḌALINĪ, or *kuṇḍalī* (from the Sanskrit *kuṇḍala*, "coil" of rope), is the name given in Tantric literature to the divine cosmic energy *(śakti)* as it is present both in the cosmos and in human beings, where it normally remains quiescent, coiled like a (female) serpent in the *mūlādhāra*, the lowest *cakra* of the subtle body. While thus enclosed in man, Kuṇḍalinī is also the Goddess in her cosmic activity: in yogic as in ritual practice, these two planes cannot be disjoined.

The notion of *kuṇḍalinī* is probably linked originally to archetypal beliefs, to the old Indian serpent lore and serpent cults, and to cosmogonic representations: between cosmic periods, Viṣṇu sleeps on a coiled serpent. *Kuṇḍalinī* rites and practices rest also on the ancient idea that the structure of man, both physical and subtle, parallels that of the cosmos, and so the movement of *kuṇḍalinī* in man not only mirrors that of cosmic energy but is also identical with it.

Kuṇḍalinī, when still "asleep" in the *mūlādhāra,* is coiled around a small *liṅga,* her head resting on its top. This "self-engendered" *(svayambhu) liṅga* is the eternal Śiva around whom sleeps the primeval energy. The masculine and feminine principles are thus both present in man in their unmanifest form, located in the *cakra* nearest to the genital organs. This underlines both the androgynous element in all human beings and the sexual aspect of *kuṇḍalinī.*

When "awakened" by means of psychophysical disciplines, *kuṇḍalinī* travels upward, along the central channel *(nāḍī) suṣumnā* located in the hollow of the cerebrospinal axis, to a spot on the top of the skull. As she ascends, she "pierces" in turn each of the *cakra*s tiered along the *suṣumnā* (in all of which a god and a goddess abide). She "awakens" and energizes them and thus opens to the mind of the adept new experiences, knowledge, and powers. She also transforms his body, since his condition is henceforth that of a man progressively being identified, body and mind, with the cosmos, which is nothing but an outward manifestation of the divine energy. When *kuṇḍalinī* reaches the topmost subtle center (usually the thousand-petaled lotus, *sahasrāra*), the adept attains full spiritual perfection. In that center, she, Kuṇḍalinī, is deemed to unite with the supreme God who symbolically abides there. This achieves in the human microcosm the archetypal union of the two cosmic principles of active and passive power. The adept experiences the ecstasy of that union while simultaneously participating in all the powers of the supreme godhead, transcending his limited self, merging into the deity and thus gaining liberation in life *(jīvanmukti),* which, in Tantrism, implies both the enjoyment of worldly and supernatural powers *(siddhi)* and total freedom from the world.

The method of awakening *kuṇḍalinī* is both physical and mental. Particular attitudes of the body and limbs *(āsana, bandha, mudrā)* and manipulations of the bodily functions (breath control, etc.) are used. These physical exercises are combined with mental (or psychosomatic) ones: enunciation *(uccāra)* or repetition *(japa)* of *mantra*s, and intense mental concentration *(bhāvanā),* by which the adept follows mentally the whole awakening process as he creates it, inwardly imagining and visualizing it vividly in all its details. *Kuṇḍalinī* is to be seen as a thin thread, or a flame of bright red color, throbbing and humming as it ascends. This sound is important since it is "unstruck" *(anāhata):* it is the eternal increate vibration of the godhead whose energy is the Word *(vāc).* Sexual practices are also used for this, with or without retention of semen, the total fusion of the adept with the ecstatic union of the god and his *śakti* being attained simultaneously with orgasm. These practices are very ritualized and complex; they have probably always been rather exceptional. This yoga is also called *layayoga* because the ascent of *kuṇḍalinī* causes the dissolution *(laya)* of the ordinary self into cosmic consciousness, a movement homologous to that of cosmic resorption.

Kuṇḍalinī, being a Tantric notion, is not found in classical Yoga but only in later texts, those of *haṭhayoga,* some Purāṇas, and in the later Upaniṣads. The impact of Tantric ideas and practices has, however, been such that this concept, with some at least of the related practices, although it probably originated among Tantric Śaiva ascetic groups, is now present also in non-Tantric Śaiva as well as in Tantric Vaiṣṇava circles. It is also found in Tantric Buddhism, which may in fact have contributed not inconsiderably to its earlier developments.

[*See also* Cakras *and* Jīvanmukti.]

BIBLIOGRAPHY

The basic work on *kuṇḍalinī* remains *The Serpent Power: Being the Shat-Chakra-Nirūpaṇa and Pādukā-Pañchakā, Two Works on Laya Yoga,* 7th ed. (Madras, 1964), by Arthur Avalon (Sir John Woodroffe). Also to be consulted are *The Haṭha Yoga Pradīpikā,* Sanskrit text with an English translation by Swami Svātmārāma (New York, 1974); *The Yoga Upaniṣads,* translated into English by T. R. Srinivasa Ayyangar (Adyar, 1977); and Lilian Silburn's *La kuṇḍalinī: L'énergie des profondeurs* (Paris, 1983).

ANDRÉ PADOUX

K'UNG-TZU. *See* Confucius.

KUNITOKODACHI, or Kuni no Tokotachi no Mikoto, is a Japanese cosmological deity. Kunitokodachi, whose name means "the earthly eternally standing deity," may be the personification of the process of the formation of solid earth from chaos. This deity is generally believed to be male, but to have no consort and no offspring. He is believed to be invisible. His name appears in Japanese creation myths, but there is no record of any shrine to him anywhere in Japan in ancient times.

The *Kojiki* and the *Nihonshoki,* the two ancient chronicles of Japan, give several different versions of this deity's origins. According to the *Kojiki,* in the beginning Ame-no-minaka-nushi ("master of the august center of heaven") and two other supreme deities appeared in primeval heaven. Then the deity Umashiashikabi-hikoji ("the pleasant reed-shoot prince elder") was born like a reed shoot from soft, floating earth. Next came the deity Ame no Tokotachi ("heaven eternally standing"). These five deities were called the Special Heavenly Deities. Kunitokodachi appeared after these five.

In the *Nihonshoki,* Kunitokodachi plays the more important role. According to the main version, when heaven and earth were not yet separated but were still a chaotic mass, the purer and clearer essence ascended and formed heaven, while the heavier, more solid element descended and became earth. Thereafter, divine beings appeared between the two. In those days, the soil of the earth moved to and fro like a fish on the surface of the primeval ocean. From such soft materials a reed-shoot-like being sprouted and was transformed into a deity. This was Kunitokodachi. Next came the two deities Kuni-no-satsuchi and Toyo-kumunu. All three deities were pure males and invisible. In another version of the *Nihonshoki,* Kunitokodachi appears first from the chaos.

Kunitokodachi does not appear in any other records of Japanese mythology, so it is often maintained that he is a product of the philosophical thought current at the imperial court in the seventh century, when the *Kojiki* and the *Nihonshoki* were compiled. Later, in medieval times, Kunitokodachi was adopted as the personification of the ontological substance by such Shintō theologians as Watarai Ieyuki (1256–1326) and Yoshida Kanetomo (1435–1511). They regarded this deity as the supreme god of the cosmos in a pantheistic, syncretic religion. Watarai Ieyuki, who was a priest of the Outer (Gekū) Shrine at Ise, maintained that the shrine was dedicated to Kunitokodachi and therefore deserved more respect and worship than the Inner (Naikū) Shrine of the sun goddess Amaterasu.

[*See also* Japanese Religion, *article on* Mythic Themes.]

BIBLIOGRAPHY

Aston, W. G., trans. *Nihongi: Chronicles of Japan from the Earliest Times to A.D. 697* (1896). Reprint, 2 vols. in 1, Tokyo, 1972.

Chamberlain, Basil Hall, trans. *Kojiki: Records of Ancient Matters* (1882). 2d ed. With annotations by W. G. Aston. Tokyo, 1932; reprint, Rutland, Vt., and Tokyo, 1982.

Matsumura Takeo. *Nihon shinwa no kenkyū,* vol. 2. Tokyo, 1955.

Ōsumi Kazuo. *Chūsei shintō ron.* Nihon shisō taikei, vol. 19. Tokyo, 1977.

Philippi, Donald L., trans. *Kojiki.* Princeton, 1969.

Matsumae Takeshi

KUO HSIANG (d. 312 CE), Chinese thinker associated with the *hsüan-hsüeh* ("dark learning" or "school of mystery") movement. A rationalist mystic and naturalist pantheist, Kuo Hsiang is the author of a commentary on the *Chuang-tzu,* the only text of his still extant and the best known and oldest of all the *Chuang-tzu* commentaries still in existence. Kuo Hsiang also edited the text of the *Chuang-tzu* itself. In establishing the version we have today he reduced the size of the text, chose what seemed to him to be "the best and most complete parts" to make a coherent whole, rejected some parts, and arranged the whole in thirty-three chapters. All the complete versions of the *Chuang-tzu* known at present are derived from his.

Kuo Hsiang's commentary both develops a personal philosophy and makes a radical reinterpretation of the *Chuang-tzu.* That the universe produces itself and is not produced by another is the starting point and the central concept of Kuo Hsiang's system. The universe contains all the attributes of the Absolute: it exists eternally and necessarily and is self-sufficient. Beings come into existence of themselves; their true nature is their self-beingness. They are defined as identical to themselves, and this identity is identical in each of them: thus Kuo Hsiang understands *Chuang-tzu*'s "identity of beings" as a type of monism. The Great One *(ta-i)* or, sometimes, the Ether *(ch'i)* is the universal force that is the source of the self-production of beings; every phenomenon represents a varying state of dispersion or condensation of the Ether. But Kuo Hsiang escapes complete monism by admitting the notion of *fen,* "allotment" or "limit." Beings are differentiated by the congenital limitations of their existential and social possibilities (their span of life, their natural endowment, their place in society). These limitations assign the place they must take in society and the universe, which place in turn actualizes and manifests their being. The relation that obtains between these limitations of beings *(fen)* follows a natural pattern *(li),* an immanent principle of order that is established spontaneously *(tzu-jan)* without any external agent. In order to achieve their own totality, individuals must accept the elements that compose their being: spontaneity (a universal, natural, and nonpersonal force that lies within each of us and is distinct from the ego), limitations in time and society *(fen),* and, finally, "daily renewal" (an incessant state of change characteristic of all beings). In this way, individuals enter into a "marvelous coincidence" with themselves and with the oneness of the world, into that mystic fusion with the immanent force that produces everything and has no beginning or end.

Kuo Hsiang was not a Confucian. He valued Confucian virtues after the fashion of Taoists; he did not believe in a life after death, a denial incompatible with the ancestor cult. He also advocated governing by *wu-wei* (noninterference), a Taoist emphasis. If he acknowledged a social life, it was because society was an inescapable fact, but he held that "names" (titles and official functions) in society were external aspects that must be "forgotten" in order to gain union with the unutterable reality. In avowing that names were an incomplete expression of the hidden source of existence, Kuo Hsiang was writing against the Confucian perspective as it developed in the "school of names" *(ming-chiao)*. The "determinism" Kuo Hsiang showed was nothing more than common sense: we must cope with what is unavoidable. Yet the participation in the world he advocated was a mystical one, very near the Taoist ideal. Kuo rejected everything supernatural and by so doing he came close to the Chinese "rationalists" such as Wang Ch'ung, but because he allotted a large place to *hsüan*, the Mystery, the undefinable, he is associated with *hsüan-hsüeh*. Nevertheless, in denying the central role of the concept of *wu* (nonbeing)—Kuo Hsiang maintains *wu* is a mere negation, that it simply serves to negate the existence of anything that gives birth to beings outside themselves, and that *wu* implies a total absence of a source other than an immanent one—he is at odds with Wang Pi, the movement's most prominent exponent. By his treatment of some of Chuang-tzu's terms, Kuo Hsiang prepared the way for the diffusion of the *Chuang-tzu* among Buddhist thinkers.

[*See also the biographies of Chuang-tzu and Wang Pi.*]

BIBLIOGRAPHY

Fukunaga Mitsuji. "Kaku Shō no Sōshi kaishaku." *Tetsugaku kenkyū* 37 (1954): 108–124, 166–177.

Fung Yu-lan. *Chuang-tzu: A New Selected Translation with an Exposition of the Philosophy of Kuo Hsiang* (1933). 2d ed. New York, 1964.

Nakajima R. "Kaku Shō no shisō ni tsuite." *Shūkan tōyōgaku* 24 (1970): 43–60.

Robinet, Isabelle. "Kouo Siang ou le monde comme absolu." *T'oung-pao* 69 (1983): 73–107.

Togawa Yoshio. "Kaku Shō no seiji shisō to sono Sōshi chū." *Nippon chūgoku gakkaihō* 18 (1966): 142–160.

Isabelle Robinet

KUROZUMIKYŌ is a popular charismatic religion founded in Japan in the early nineteenth century (the late Edo period) by Kurozumi Munetada (1780–1850). Kurozumi began to spread his teachings in 1814, and in the 1840s a formal religious body called Kurozumikyō was established. After the Meiji restoration the group was persecuted for a time, but in 1872 it received formal recognition from the government.

Its teachings include a belief in Amaterasu Ōmikami, the sun goddess and supreme deity of the universe. Another major tenet is that since all people are emanations of the *kami* (deities), they may themselves become *kami* through certain spiritual practices. Further, it is taught that when a person becomes one with the *kami* *(ikitōshi)* that person will achieve life without end. All are exhorted to "live cheerfully" and to obey the *kami*. At the time of its founding, the religion included a strong element of magic, including rituals for curing illnesses. Later, it came to stress the virtues of popular morality: frugality, diligence, filial piety, and harmony. The purpose of spiritual practices was to cultivate these virtues. The teachings of Kurozumikyō are characterized by a combination of popular morality and syncretic Shintō; believers seek immediate benefits in this world for the sake of popular salvation.

These beliefs, implying as they do that happiness may be garnered not by changing the realities of life but by changing one's spiritual attitude, tended to perpetuate a passive acceptance of the harsh realities of life. This is significant, given that most of the movement's followers were common people of subordinate status within the feudal order. On the other hand, they were also taught that all people have a kind of spiritual potentiality whereby life and death, poverty and wealth may be affected by pious practices. Furthermore, the idea of the spiritual independence and equality of all people was a part of Kurozumikyō's teachings. In this sense, the religion might be seen as the first step in the spiritual modernization of the late Edo period.

Kurozumi Munetada's proselytization was confined to the Okayama area, but thanks to the vigorous activities of his major disciples, the religion later extended from the Shikoku and Chugoku districts as far as the central Kyoto area. Akagi Tadaharu (1816–1867) in particular spread the teachings in Kyoto, and even converted aristocrats like Kujō Naotada, the imperial regent. Tadaharu, deeply influenced by the movement to restore direct imperial rule, envisioned a utopia in which all would be equal under the emperor. But his activities were so extreme that he was expelled from the religious organization.

In the 1880s Kurozumikyō grew dramatically and at one point boasted a membership of six or seven hundred thousand. In 1885, Munetada Shrine was established as its headquarters at Ōmoto in Okayama City. But as government control of religion tightened, the popular salvation aspect of Kurozumikyō gradually waned and the nationalistic component came to the fore.

After World War II, Kurozumikyō became chiefly a provincial religion based in western Japan. By the late 1970s its membership stood at around four hundred thousand. In 1974 a large *kami* hall (Shintōzan) was built in Okayama, and the organization's headquarters was moved there. The present and sixth-generation head is Kurozumi Muneharu. Three large religious festivals are held each year: the founder's festival on the first Saturday in April, a purification festival on 30 July, and the winter solstice festival. *Kuni no hikari* and *Keisei zasshi,* two magazines published by the group before the war, were followed by a third, *Nisshin,* published after the war.

[*See also* New Religions, *article on* New Religions in Japan.]

BIBLIOGRAPHY

Hirota Masaki. *Bunmei-kaika to minshū-ishiki.* Tokyo, 1980.

Murakami Shigeyoshi. *Kindai minshū shūkyōshi no kenkyū.* Kyoto, 1963.

Murakami Shigeyoshi and Yasamaru Yoshio. *Minshū shūkyō no shisō.* Tokyo, 1971.

HIROTA MASAKI

Translated from Japanese by Suzanne Gay

KURUKṢETRA, "the field of the Kurus," is today an important Hindu pilgrimage site *(tīrtha)* in Haryana state, about eighty-five miles north-northeast of Delhi. Its history can be traced from the period of the Brāhmaṇas to modern times; in 1014 CE its earliest shrines were destroyed by the invading Mahmud of Ghazni. The site forms part of the plain on which the two pivotal battles of Panipat were fought, marking the rise of the Mughals in 1526 and the defeat of the Marathas in 1761. Since at least the sixteenth century pilgrims have come to Sannihita Lake at Kurukṣetra at times of eclipses. According to contemporary *māhātmyas* ("glorifications" of the place that serve as pilgrims' manuals), a mendicant named Rāmācandra Swāmi came there several centuries after the early shrines had been destroyed and relocated the sites according to information he received in dreams. In all there are said to be 360 *tīrthas* within Kurukṣetra. Current lists include many sites associated by local tradition with the brave deeds and deaths of the heroes in the great war of the Bhāratas, which is said to have been fought at Kurukṣetra at the beginning of the present age. Other than these epic-related *tīrthas*, the pilgrim manuals of today mention much the same sites as are described in the *Mahābhārata* epic and the Purāṇas.

One of Kurukṣetra's traditional names, Samantapañcaka, indicates that the field is supposed to be "five [*yojanas*] on each side," or roughly a 160-mile circuit. The boundaries given in the *Mahābhārata* are little altered in Puranic sources and can be harmonized with this description. Kurukṣetra is thus bordered on the north and south by the rivers Sarasvatī and Dṛṣadvatī. Especially sacred, Sarasvatī is said to have gone underground at the Vināsana *tīrtha* within Kurukṣetra to avoid coming into contact with low castes. The epic mentions four *yakṣa* gatekeepers (*dvārapālas*) on the boundaries at the intermediate cardinal points. According to a nineteenth-century account (Cunningham, 1880), these *yakṣas* sang and danced during the great war of the Bhāratas and drank the blood of the slain.

The first texts to expound upon the sacredness of Kurukṣetra are the Brāhmaṇas, and it is likely Kurukṣetra was a heartland for Brahmanic learning in the period of both the Brāhmaṇas and early Upaniṣads. Thus *Śatapatha Brāhmaṇa* 14.1.1.2 describes it as "the gods' place of divine worship," and several passages speak of the gods' sacrificial performances there. It is also the territory of the Kurus and Pañcālas, or Kuru-Pañcālas, famed for their *brāhmaṇas*. These are the central peoples of the *Mahābhārata,* and several epic characters are already mentioned in Brāhmaṇa and Upaniṣadic texts.

It is through the *Mahābhārata,* however, that Kurukṣetra attains its renown. One passage ranks Kurukṣetra as the foremost *tīrtha* in the three worlds. Twice it is said that the dust of Kurukṣetra, blown by the wind, leads even those of bad *karman* to heaven. It is further described as the altar or northern altar *(vedī, uttaravedī)* of Brahmā or Prajāpati, and thus the preeminent place of sacrifice. Numerous sacrificial acts are said to have occurred there prior to the great war of the Bhāratas, including the destruction of the *kṣatriya* caste twenty-one times over by Rāma Jāmadagnya (later the *avatāra* Paraśurāma), which left in its wake five lakes of blood. But most significant is the legend told in the epic of the origins of Kurukṣetra. The field is named after King Kuru, ancestor of the epic heroes. Kuru had plowed the field for many years, seeking from Indra the boon that those who die there should go straight to heaven. The gods counseled Indra not to grant the boon, since it would mean that human beings could attain heaven without sacrificing to them, thus endangering the gods' existence. So Indra offered a compromise. Two types of beings could directly attain heaven there: yogins who practice *tapas* (asceticism), and *kṣatriyas* who were slain in battle. Thus the traditional Brahmanic sacrifices are dispensed with, but doubly transformed. *Kṣatriyas* will attain heaven by the epic's "sacrifice of battle," and yogins and pilgrims will do so by acts of *tapas,* which the epic repeatedly exalts above the traditional rites performed there. Indra's compromise is further sanctioned by Viṣṇu, Śiva, and Brahmā (the *trimūrti*), thus indicating the subordination of these transformed sacrificial acts to the higher ideals associated with *bhakti.* All this is thus in accord with the *Bha-*

gavadgītā, which begins with the proclamation that Kurukṣetra is a *dharmakṣetra* ("field of *dharma*"). There, Kṛṣṇa instructs Arjuna to perform the sacrifice of battle on Kurukṣetra as a *karmayogin,* and thus perform acts disciplined by *yoga* that are offered as if in sacrifice to God. Biardeau (1976) suggests that the name Kurukṣetra has come in the epic to mean the "field of acts," *kuru* being the imperative of the verb *to do*. It is thus analogous to the Puranic concept of the earth as the "world of acts" *(karmabhūmi).* The act of plowing, here undertaken by King Kuru, is further a common Indian metaphor for sowing the seeds of *karman.*

[*For further discussion of the significance of Kurukṣetra, see* Mahābhārata.]

BIBLIOGRAPHY

The main *Mahābhārata* passages are translated in *The Mahābhārata,* vol. 2, edited and translated by J. A. B. van Buitenen (Chicago, 1975), pp. 378–386, and in *The Mahabharata of Krishna-Dwaipayana Vyasa,* vol. 7, 2d ed., translated by P. C. Roy and K. M. Ganguli (Calcutta, 1970), pp. 158–159. For still the best on-site description, see Alexander Cunningham's *Report of a Tour in the Punjab in 1878–79,* vol. 14 (1880; reprint, Varanasi, 1970), pp. 86–106. On textual references, see Sasanka Sekhar Parui's *Kurukṣetra in the Vamana Purāṇa* (Calcutta, 1976). On symbolic overtones, see Madeleine Biardeau's "Études de mythologie hindoue, Chap. II, Bhakti et avatāra," *Bulletin de l'École Française d'Extrême Orient* 63 (1976): 111–263, esp. pp. 259–262.

ALF HILTEBEITEL

KUSHITE RELIGION. Kush was the name given in ancient times to the area of northeast Africa lying just to the south of Egypt. It is the Aethiopia of Herodotus and other classical writers, and it corresponds in a general way to the Nubia of today. Its peoples were and are African in race and language, but since very early times their culture has been strongly influenced by that of their northern neighbors.

The northern part of Kush was under direct Egyptian control during the New Kingdom (c. 1580–1000 BCE). Egyptians did not settle in the country in large numbers, but they oversaw the building of temples, towns, and fortresses and the inauguration of the typical pharaonic system of administration and of worship. When the colonial overlords departed, around 1000 BCE, they had laid the basis for an egyptianized successor-state that was to emerge a little later as the empire of Kush. The Kushite rulers assumed all the titles and trappings of the pharaohs, and for a brief period (751–656 BCE) were even accepted as rulers in Egypt itself. Kushite authority in Egypt was ended by an Assyrian invasion, but the empire later expanded southward at least as far as the confluence of the Blue and White Niles, and possibly much farther.

The original capital of Kush was at Napata, near the Fourth Cataract of the Nile, where a great temple of Amun had been erected during the Egyptian colonial regime. Later, as the empire expanded southward, the capital was moved to Meroe, near the mouth of the Atbara River. The earlier and later phases of Kushite civilization are often designated as Napatan and Meroitic, after the respective capitals. The empire of Kush was finally overrun and destroyed by barbarian invaders in the fourth century CE, but some of its traditions persisted until the coming of Christianity two centuries later.

Detailed information about the religion of Kush is scanty. The accounts of classical writers are unreliable, and the indigenous language of Kush (called Meroitic) is largely undeciphered. Most of our information is based on the interpretation of reliefs carved on temple and tomb walls and on votive objects.

In the beginning, the religion of Kush appears to have differed little from that of pharaonic Egypt. The principal state deity was Amun, whose cult was celebrated at the great state temples of Napata and Meroe, and at many other places. Other Egyptian deities who are depicted in Kushite temple reliefs include the moon god Khonsu, the ibis-headed Thoth, and the goddesses Isis, Hathor, and Mut. The ram-headed Khum, god of cataracts, was especially venerated in the cataract region of northern Kush. Horus, who in Egypt symbolized the pharaonic authority, was another deity especially popular in the north.

In Kush as in Egypt, mortuary ritual was associated with the Osirian family of deities: Osiris, his sister-wife Isis, and Nephthys, the sister of Isis. The jackal-headed Anubis also played an important part in mortuary ritual. In later centuries the cult of Isis became especially highly developed, and was no longer primarily a mortuary cult. Isis became the chief tutelary of the most northerly district of Kush (later known as Lower Nubia), but there were also Isis temples at Meroe and elsewhere in the south.

In the Meroitic period (c. 350 BCE–350 CE) the Kushite pantheon came to include a number of deities who were apparently not of Egyptian origin. The most important of them was Apedemak, a lion-headed male god who was a special tutelary of the ruling family. He was a god of victory and also of agricultural fertility. There were temples of Apedemak at Meroe and at several other towns in the southern part of Kush, but his cult seems to have been little developed in the more northerly districts, which were far from the seats of royal authority. Two other possibly indigenous deities were

Arensnuphis and Sebiumeker, who are sometimes depicted as guardians standing on either side of temple doors. There was, in addition, an enigmatic goddess with distinctly negroid features, whose name has not been recovered.

Cult animals were evidently important in Kushite religion, as they were in Egypt. Cattle are often depicted in temple procession scenes, and at the southern city of Musawwarat there was apparently a special cult of the elephant.

Kushite religious architecture shows very strongly the influence of Egypt, though with some distinctive local touches. Temples are of several types, but they fall into two broad categories. The largest temples, comprising from three to five rooms, are purely Egyptian in type, with pylon gate, forecourt, hypostyle hall, pronaos, and one or more sanctuaries. All of the temples dedicated to Amun are of this type. A much smaller type of temple comprises only a pylon gate and one or two adjoining chambers, with or without interior colonnading. Most if not all of the temples of Apedemak are of this type.

We know almost nothing about the details of ritual, but we can deduce from temple and tomb scenes that offerings of food and drink played an important role. Processions of priests and animals were probably also common. Pilgrimage was an important act of personal piety, to judge from the number of votive graffiti on temple walls and floors as well as on cliff faces. Funerary texts from northern Kush suggest that there were several ranks of priesthood attached to the temples, although the precise meaning of these texts is very far from clear.

As in Egypt, the afterlife was a major focus of concern. The Kushite rulers and their families were buried under steep-sided stone pyramids, each of which had attached to it a mortuary chapel like a miniature temple. Underground there were two or three chambers adorned with painted scenes of the afterlife. The royal dead were often laid out on a bed (a uniquely Kushite practice), accompanied by lavish offerings that sometimes included animal and human sacrifices. More ordinary folk were interred in an undecorated underground chamber, which might be surmounted by a brick platform or a miniature pyramid. These too usually had an adjoining chapel or at least an offering niche. A unique feature of mortuary ritual in the northern part of Kush was the making of *ba* statuettes, in the form of a bird with human head. These were placed outside the tomb superstructure, and symbolized that part of the soul (the *ba*) that remained on earth after death, while another manifestation of the soul (the *ka*) journeyed to the afterworld.

BIBLIOGRAPHY

There is no single, detailed work on the religion of Kush, as is to be expected in view of the scanty available evidence. Brief, popular summaries can be found in Peter L. Shinnie's *Meroe: A Civilization of the Sudan* (New York, 1967), pp. 141–152, and in my book *Nubia: Corridor to Africa* (Princeton, 1977), pp. 325–328, 336–338, 374–378. More technical discussions include those of Jean Leclant, "La religion Méroïtique," in *Histoire des religions*, edited by Henri-Charles Puech (Paris, 1970), vol. 1, pp. 141–153, and Nicholas B. Millet, "Meroitic Religion," in *Meroitische Forschungen 1980* (*Meroitica* 7), edited by Fritz Hintze (Berlin, 1984), pp. 111–121. L. V. Žabkar's *Apedemak, Lion God of Meroe* (Warminster, 1975) discusses at length one particular aspect of Kushite religion.

William Y. Adams

KU YEN-WU (*tzu*, Ning-jen; *hao*, T'ing-lin; 1613–1682), a founder of the "school of evidential research" *(k'ao-cheng)*. Ku Yen-wu was born to the scholarly life. He was from K'un-shan, Kiangsu Province, in Southeast China, a region renowned for its historians and philosophers. His forebears were distinguished intellectuals, passionate readers and collectors of books. From the age of eleven, Ku was taught to read the encyclopedic originals of historical works rather than the standard abridgments. His upbringing instilled in him the highest standards of Confucian moral conduct.

At an early age, Ku's parents sent him to be adopted as the heir of his father's cousin, who had died in his teens. He was raised by his adoptive grandfather and by the fiancée of the deceased cousin, who insisted on living as his widow. This woman's extraordinary devotion to her fiancé's family won her public recognition and an imperial title, "Chaste and Filial." Ku Yen-wu later expressed his admiration for his foster mother in a laudatory biography.

In 1644 the Manchus conquered North China, bringing an end to the Ming dynasty (1368–1644). The next year they drove south and conquered Kiangsu. During the siege, in which several of his relatives were killed or wounded, Ku fled with his foster mother to a remote village. When the Manchu victory was imminent, his mother starved herself to death as an act of loyalty to the Ming, exacting from her son a vow never to serve the Manchus.

In the early years of Manchu rule, Ku Yen-wu, like many in the Southeast, resented the Manchus and clung to the hope that the Ming might be restored. Ku may even have covertly aided the resistance government headed by an exiled Ming prince. As time passed, many accepted the finality of the Ming defeat and made their peace with the new regime. The Manchus, for their part, courted the holdouts by means of the *po-hsüeh hung-tz'u*, a special examination in 1679 to select candidates for a lavish imperial project on Ming history. The court invited the support of leading intellectuals to dissipate the last vestiges of resistance in the Southeast; the "invitation" was in fact a command performance. Ku Yen-wu was one of the few who did not take this examination; he escaped by working behind the scenes to have friends remove his name from the invitation list. Even after he had personally accepted the finality of the Ming defeat, he felt bound to honor his vow to his mother.

In 1657, Ku Yen-wu narrowly escaped assassination by a personal enemy with whom he had been embroiled in a land dispute. To avert further harassment, Ku moved north and spent the remainder of his life separated from family and regional friends. In earlier years, he had turned in times of trouble to ancestral veneration, both to honor the heritage of his ancestors and to seek their guidance. In the North, he worshiped regularly at the tombs of the Ming imperial family, ritually renewing his commitment never to serve the Manchus, and hence honoring the memory of his mother.

The values and ritual practices of Confucianism gave meaning and structure to the life of Ku Yen-wu. His scholarship was inspired and informed by his deep personal commitment to the Confucian Way.

Ku Yen-wu charged that Confucian scholarship of the Sung (960–1279) and Ming was so speculative and tainted by Buddhism that it lost sight of the core of the tradition. He echoed the scholars of the late Ming in their call for practical learning *(shih-hsüeh)*. Confucian scholarship could be effective only if it were solidly grounded in the authentic Way of the sages, which was expounded in the Confucian classics. For many centuries, however, Confucians, while venerating the classics as a kind of sacred canon, had distorted their true meaning by citing passages out of context or fabricating baseless interpretations. Inspired by Han dynasty (206 BCE–20 CE) commentaries, Ku advocated a close reexamination of the classics, seeking to reconstruct the actual pronunciations and meanings of the original texts. He built on late Ming scholarship in phonology and philology, broadening the method by bringing to bear an enormous range of evidence. His work became the benchmark of evidential research.

Ku extended the methodology of *k'ao-cheng* beyond classical studies. The broad-ranging collection of evidence and meticulous cross-checking of data were applied to such areas as water management, geography, and epigraphy. Ku did not limit his research to written materials; he made use of artifacts, interviews, and trips to the field. His energetic scholarship inspired several generations of intellectuals, many of whom did not appreciate the commitment to the Confucian Way that motivated his work.

Scholars have compared the legacy of *k'ao-cheng* to the European Renaissance (Liang, 1959, p. 11, and Yü, 1975, p. 128) or to the Reformation (Hou, 1962–1963, p. 250). A more appropriate comparison might be made to the historical-critical movement in biblical scholarship, which arose alongside the European Enlightenment. Both movements claimed that misinterpretations of the canon had obscured the true teachings and exposed their traditions to dangers and heresies. Both sought to recover the true core of the teachings by means of the most rigorous historical and critical tools available. Both were occasionally misconstrued as secularizations of their traditions. Ku Yen-wu devoted himself to rigorous scholarship in order to recover the solid foundations of the Way of the sages.

BIBLIOGRAPHY

Ku Yen-wu's *Yin-hsüeh wu-shu* in 38 *chüan* (1667), 8 vols. (Taipei, 1957), established a model for the method of evidential research. His broader scholarly approach is best embodied in his *Jih-chih lu* in 32 *chüan*, "Kuo-hsüeh chi-pen ts'ung-shu," vol. 14, edited by Wang Yun-wu (Taipei, 1968), a collection of erudite notes on a wide range of subjects that were revised throughout his life whenever he found a new bit of relevant information. The *Ku T'ing-lin shih wen-chi*, "Kuo-hsüeh chi-pen ts'ung-shu," vol. 317, edited by Wang Yun-wu (Taipei, 1968), contains important letters and prefaces that articulate in succinct form the principles behind his scholarly approach.

There are two standard sources for Ku Yen-wu's life. Fang Chao-ying's biography in *Eminent Chinese of the Ch'ing Period, 1644–1912*, 2 vols., edited by Arthur W. Hummel (Washington, D.C., 1943–1944), includes a valuable overview of Ku's scholarly contributions, pp. 421–426. Willard J. Peterson's "The Life of Ku Yen-wu, 1613–1682," *Harvard Journal of Asiatic Studies* 28 (1968): 114–156 and 29 (1969): 201–247, offers a thoughtful analysis of the historical and familial forces that shaped Ku's career.

On Ku's thought and scholarship, the best works are Hou Wai-lu's *Chung-kuo ssu-hsiang t'ung-shih*, vol. 5 (Peking, 1962–1963), pp. 204–250, and Ch'ien Mu's *Chung-kuo chin san-pai-nien hsüeh-shu shih*, 2 vols. (1937; reprint, Taipei, 1957), pp. 121–153. There is as yet little in Western languages. Liang Ch'i-ch'ao's *Intellectual Trends in the Ch'ing Period*, translated by Immanuel C. Y. Hsü (Cambridge, Mass., 1959), offers a brief introduction in English. Yü Ying-shih's article "Some Preliminary Observations on the Rise of Ch'ing Confucian Intellectualism," *Tsing-hua Journal of Chinese Studies*, n.s. 11 (1975): 105–146, is the most helpful source on the origins and significance of the *k'ao-cheng* movement.

JUDITH A. BERLING

KWOTH is the supreme deity of the Nuer, a Nilotic people who live in the southern part of the Republic of the Sudan. *Kwoth* (pl., *kuth*), generally translated as "god" or "spirit" also functions as a complex theological term in Nuer thought.

Like many supreme deities in African pantheons, Kwoth is associated with the sky. Kwoth is also known as *Kwoth Nhial* ("spirit of the sky") and *Kwoth a Nhial* ("spirit who is in the sky"). Celestial phenomena are associated with Kwoth: he is said to be in thunder and lightning and to fall in the rain; also, the Nuer call the rainbow "the necklace of God." Although there is no identification with celestial phenomena, the Nuer believe that Kwoth reveals himself through them. Other phenomena, such as certain species of birds, are also associated with Kwoth (and are called *gaat Kwoth*, "children of God"), as are twins.

Kwoth is the maker of all things—natural, spiritual, and human, yet only fragmentary creation myths are found among the Nuer. There is a separation between man and God, between earth and heaven, but Kwoth is not a distant, unapproachable deity. On the contrary, all Nuer rituals, prayers, and sacrifices are made to Kwoth. He is all-seeing, all-knowing, and ever present. The etymology of the word *kwoth* relates it to words such as "breath," "snorting," and "blowing out of air," and the Nuer say that Kwoth, like the air or wind, is ever present. Kwoth is also the giver of moral law, and it is he who punishes those who transgress the law.

Kwoth is a complex theological term, and its true nature can only by understood with reference to some other categories of spirits, notably *kuth nhial* ("spirits of the above") and *kuth piny* ("spirits of the below"). Even though the *kuth nhial* are believed to be of fairly new origin and borrowed from the neighboring Dinka, as the spirits of the above, they are in some ways "nearest" to Kwoth and thus are extremely powerful. The *kuth piny* are closely linked to lineages and family groups as totemic or totemistic spirits. These totems serve to define familial relationships and the relationship of particular totemic groups to God (Kwoth).

Even more interesting and complex in the relationship between Kwoth and man are the *colwic* spirits, who were once people but who were "taken by God into the sky" when they were killed by lightning or whirlwind. Such a death is feared by the Nuer, and the body is simply covered and abandoned, for, they say, God has already taken the "life," *yiegh*, leaving only the flesh. Kwoth's relationship to mankind, then, is both benevolent and dangerous, and the *colwic* spirits and the *kuth piny* symbolize the Nuer ambivalence toward Kwoth.

Thus, Kwoth is one being and yet many insofar as he is intimately associated with the *kuth nhial* and *kuth piny*. However, his various manifestations result from the fact that, for certain groups or occasions, he takes certain specific forms. Evans-Pritchard, the ethnographer of the Nuer, describes the relationship as follows:

> Since God is *kwoth* in the sense of all Spirit and the oneness of Spirit, the other spirits, whilst distinct with regard to one another, are all, being also *kwoth*, thought of as being of the same nature as God. Each of them, that is to say, is God regarded in a particular way; and it may help us if we think of the particular spirits as figures or representations or refractions of God in relation to particular activities, events, persons, and groups. (Evans-Pritchard, 1956, p. 107)

Kwoth, then, is a concept of divinity in which is incorporated, and somehow integrated, notions of one and many, of particularity and universality.

[*See also* Nuer and Dinka Religion.]

BIBLIOGRAPHY

Further discussion can be found in E. E. Evans-Pritchard's *Nuer Religion* (Oxford, 1956), the standard and definitive work on Nuer religion by one of the greatest ethnographers of Africa.

JAMES S. THAYER

L

LABOR. *See* Work.

LABYRINTH. The word *labyrinth* refers to a large variety of drawings and patterns, some intricate, some less so, ranging from prehistoric rock engravings to modern art, as well as to highly complex symbolic and mythological structures around which an immense richness of meaning has accumulated during the course of many centuries and civilizations. The word is used to describe:

1. a difficult path, or passage, or tunnel, often underground, through which it is extremely hazardous to find one's way without guidance
2. a seemingly unending building of innumerable rooms and galleries intended to confound intruders and lead them astray
3. metaphorically, any kind of complexity from which it is almost impossible to extricate oneself.

In this last and more general use, and under the pressure of the growing complexities of the contemporary world, the very old symbol of the labyrinth has come back with renewed vitality to haunt the subconscious of modern man and reenter the vocabulary of art and literature. What makes the labyrinth, in its wealth of analogical associations, so relevant today is the fact that it is an emblem of the existential dilemmas of modern urban man, who finds himself trapped in a prisonlike world and condemned to wander aimlessly therein. However, the labyrinth catches our imagination not just because it reminds us that we are lost in its bowels and about to be devoured by the Minotaur but also because it suggests that somewhere in the dark pit there must be an almost forgotten center from which, after the ultimate trial confronting terror and death, one may find the way out to freedom. These hints of fear and hope are, in fact, echoes of very ancient myths, among which stands the famous story of Theseus and the Minotaur.

The Myth of the Minoan Labyrinth. In concise terms the myth of the Minoan labyrinth tells of Minos, who became king of Crete when Poseidon, god of the sea, sent him a bull from the sea in answer to his prayers. But Minos failed to sacrifice the animal, as ordered by Poseidon, and so became sterile. Pasiphaë, daughter of the Sun and wife of Minos, conceived a passion for the bull; she placed herself inside an artificial cow, built for the purpose by Daedalus, and made love with the animal. The Minotaur, a monster half man and half bull, was born of this union. King Minos, appalled by this event, ordered Daedalus to build a labyrinth from which no one could escape and had the Minotaur hidden within it.

The town of Athens, which had been recently conquered by Crete, was ordered to send every eight years seven youths and seven maidens to be devoured by the Minotaur. The time came when the Athenian hero Theseus decided to put an end to this dreadful tribute and offered himself as one of the seven young men to be sacrificed. He entered the labyrinth and killed the monster, finding his way out again with the help of a ball of string he had spun out behind him, a gift to him from Ariadne, the enamored daughter of Minos.

After this triumph, however, things began to go wrong. First, on his way back to Athens, on the island of Naxos, the proud hero abandoned Ariadne while she was asleep and decided to marry her sister Phaedra—a decision that later proved disastrous. Then he forgot to substitute the black sails of his ship for white ones, as he had promised his father, King Aegeus, he would do if he had slain the Minotaur; the old Athenian king, on seeing the black sails in the distance, believed that Theseus was dead and so jumped off a cliff to his death. Meanwhile, the furious Minos punished Daedalus by incarcerating him and his son Icarus in the maze. Although Daedalus was the architect of the labyrinth, he could not find his way out. Therefore he decided to escape by the only possible route: upward. With feathers and wax he manufactured two pairs of wings; he warned his son not to ascend too high, and the two flew away. Icarus, however, intoxicated by the wonders of flight, forgot his father's advice and soared too near the sun; the wax of his wings melted, and he plunged into the sea and disappeared. The more cautious Daedalus landed safely in Sicily.

Many aspects of this story require careful study before one can fully grasp its meaning. Four of its more relevant themes are these:

1. There is the suggestion that the labyrinth is related to an unresolved conflict that carries a costly toll of guilt and fear—the annual sacrifice of the seven boys and girls—that can only be settled through the intervention of a "hero."
2. It is also suggested that the way out of this conflict depends on mnemonics and feats of memory—Ariadne's thread—and on the ability to "fly," that is, to achieve a higher level of consciousness.
3. The myth points to the ultimate failure of the hero. It is important that Theseus, apparently the hero, meets a dismal end when later he descends to hell, helped this time not by a loving woman but by a bandit named Peritoos, in an attempt to abduct Persephone, the wife of Hades; the project fails. Peritoos is dismembered by the three-headed dog Kerberos, and Theseus, lost in the labyrinth of Hades, is turned into a stone. This implies that the killing of the Minotaur is less heroic than it seems, for it involves the brutal suppression of a problem instead of the attempt at a harmonious solution.
4. Finally, the story of Theseus in the labyrinth can be seen as symbolizing the dangers of initiation according to a well-known pattern of *descensus ad inferos*, symbolic death and return to life. [*See* Descent into the Underworld.]

The Labyrinth as Symbol. I shall now briefly review some of the more significant connotations of the idea of the labyrinth itself. It should be kept in mind that all symbols and myths can be interpreted on many different levels and ask for a continuing effort of hermeneutics.

Descent into the unconscious. Entering the labyrinth stands for what a psychoanalyst would describe as a descent into the subconscious layers of the psyche, with its obscurities and terrors, its traumas, complexes, and unresolved emotional conflicts.

Regressus ad uterus. Entry into the labyrinth recalls as well a retreat into the bosom of Mother Earth, conceived also as *yoni*, grave, and magic oven, and related to the "V.I.T.R.I.O.L." injunction of alchemy attributed to Basilius Valentinus—"Visitabis Interiora Terrae Rectificando Invenies Occultum Lapidem" ("Visit the interior of the earth and by rectifying thou wilt find the secret stone"). This connotation is particularly strong in cave and underground labyrinths. In fact, many megalithic stone engravings seem to associate labyrinthine patterns simultaneously with the cult of the dead and symbols of fecundity, as for instance in the drawings in Val Camonica, Italy. In many cases prehistoric drawings show what seem to be the female genitalia; sometimes they show concentric circles with a straight or serpentine line running to the center, suggesting spermatozoa reaching the ovum (see figure 1). This is the kind of drawing Moritz Hoerner and Oswald Menghin called *Ringwallbilder* and considered the simplest and most common of labyrinthine patterns found in Europe. Explicit sexual symbolism can be found also in the Etruscan vase of Tragliatella (Museum of the Capitolium, Rome) and in connection with Knossos-type labyrinths.

Nekuia or the descent into Hades. In close association with the symbolism of a *regressus ad uterus* is that of a *nekuia*, or descent into Hades, to the underworld abode

FIGURE 1. *Ringwallbilder.* Engraving on a stone from Old Bewick, Northumberland, England.

of the dead where an invisible fire transforms all bodies that enter it. Inner fire destroys and melts, but as the *athanor* (the symbolic furnace of physical or moral transmutation) of the alchemist, it also purifies, regenerates, transmutes, and produces "gold."

Meeting the monster. Visiting the underworld entails meeting its guardians: Kerberos, old women and magicians, monsters and demons. Horned figures identical with the Minotaur can be found in many prehistoric drawings, as in Val Camonica, Italy, and the Cueva de los Letreros, Spain, as well as in ancient Egypt; they bring to mind the traditional images of the devil in Christian and other traditions.

The Minotaur's horns can be related to the idea of a crown, not only through etymology but also through symbolic associations. In Delos was an altar, named Keraton, made of the horns of bulls and goats and linked to the cult of Apollo Karneios, protector of horned animals. Another interesting link can be established between horns and the *labrus*, or the double ax. William H. Matthews (1922) reports that the German archaeologist Heinrich Schliemann, during his researches at Mycenae, unearthed from one of the graves an ox head of gold plate with a double ax between the upright horns. The double ax was the sign of the Zeus worshiped at Labraunda, and it occurs frequently in the Minoan palace of Knossos discovered by Arthur Evans; it was obviously an object of great importance and was linked with the cult of the bull. There was even a tomb shaped like a double ax that contained a big ax and some smaller ones. Arthur Evans, in the light of these and other discoveries, concluded that the palace of Knossos was the labyrinth, or "house of the Labrys," although some scholars dispute this. Confirming the initiatory symbolism of the labyrinth, some authors think that the ax signifies the "power of light" and is the equivalent to sword, hammer, and cross (Juan-Eduardo Cirlot); it corresponds to the Indian *vajra* and to Jupiter's lightning, symbols of the celestial illumination at the center, and as such it may reveal the symbolic reversal of polarities implied by Gemini (Luc Benois); in any case, the ax and the labyrinth respond to each other as representations of the supreme center and of a supreme principle (Mario Pasotti).

Temenos, or the enclosed space. Burying the dead and sowing seeds consecrates the ground. This creates a privileged place, a place of sacred mystery, of a *conjunctio oppositorum*, where life and death, light and darkness, male and female principles transform and melt into each other. Such a place is a *campo santo* and has to be protected from profane intrusion and invisible threat. In this connection the labyrinth acquires new symbolic functions, becoming a prophylactic device, a defensive wall, a trap for hostile invaders, while remaining at the same time, for those who know it, the secret path to the initiation chambers in which the "second birth" takes place. Both in magical terms and in actual fact, it comes to represent the protective ramparts of the most precious spiritual treasures of the clan. And then it becomes also the defense of the house of the living, the rampart of the town and the town itself. In southern India the Tamil women draw labyrinthine patterns on the threshold of their houses in the month of Margali, or Mṛgaśira, corresponding to the period of the winter solstice, during which the sun is "dead"; some of these patterns, called *kolams*, are named *brahmamudi* ("Brahma knot") and form a continuous line with no beginning and no end.

Daedalus. Labyrinthine defense develops with the rise of agrarian empires. The need to protect crops creates the need to build secure storage places; the silo foretells the stronghold. Soon the labyrinth becomes the emblem of the treasure house, of the king's palace (as in Knossos), of the defensive walls of the town, of the *urbs*. It is not surprising, thus, to find out that the name *Daedalus*, the inventor and mythic architect of the Minotaur's labyrinth, means "to build well"; Daedalus's ascendency is also significant, for we find as his ancestors Hephaistos, god of underground fire and an architect himself; Gaia, the earth, mother of all things; and Erecteion, their son, a half god whose nature is partly that of man, serpent, and wind.

According to Homer the ramparts of Troy were built by Apollo and Neptune disguised as humans; metaphorically, form-giving intelligence and solar reason combine with the energy-giving depths of the collective psyche to create the urban labyrinth symbol. In Indian myth the god of heavens, Varuṇa, whose power is symbolized by a knotlike emblem, commands the divine architect Visvakarman to build a castle of one hundred rooms where the sun woman Sutya shall be kept.

It is interesting, from this point of view, to recall some of the popular names of labyrinths current in Europe, like the Scandinavian "Ruins of Jerusalem," "City of Nineveh," "Walls of Jericho," and "Babylon," as well as the frequent names meaning "the castle of Troy," like *Trojin*, *Trojeburg*, *Troburg*, *Treiborg*, *Truberslot*, and so forth. This suggests that popular imagination sees the labyrinth as the symbol of a legendary town doomed to destruction. In contrast, the labyrinths that can still be seen on the floor of European churches and cathedrals, where penitents used to walk on their knees as the equivalent of a pilgrimage to the holy places (see figure 2) were called, among other names, La Lieue De Jeru-

FIGURE 2. *Floor Labyrinth.* Cathedral of Chartres, France.

salem ("the Jerusalem mile"). We find in them a clear symbol of the archetypal town, taken now as the promised celestial bride, the Heavenly Jerusalem glorified by the apostle John, as opposed to the doomed City of Destruction of the biblical apocalypse.

Ascent to the sacred mountain. If the labyrinth, as we have seen, denotes the underworld in its catharsis, in its descent "to the left" (the "sinister" direction), it also implies the meaning of an *anarsis,* or ascent to life and light in its turnings "to the right." These opposed movements are both comprised in the wholeness of the symbol. The link between them is evident in the wholeness of the symbol. The link between them is evident in the rapid passage from the maze's bottom, or from the pit of hell, into the mountain's ascent, or the liberating flight. In the legend of Minos, Daedalus escapes the prison by using artificial wings. In his *Commedia* Dante reaches the depths of hell only to find that he is at the bottom of the mountain of purgatory, which he subsequently climbs with his guide Vergil. Similarly, at the entrance of the cave leading to the Maya kingdom of the dead stands the stairway pyramid, symbolizing ascent to the heavens, and, according to Codex Borgia, after the terrifying journey to the abyss, the soul turns right into the realm of regenerating water and purifying fire, to be born again.

In the archetypal town the center represents this place of rebirth and ascent and is occupied by an empty space, which marks the vertical axis that links the different planes of the cosmos, or by a temple, which symbolizes the sacred mountain. The temple or the mountain's axis is again the central passage along which the underworld communicates with the world of man and the world of the gods. Such is the symbolism of the Temple of Solomon, built on Mount Moriah; of the sacred Mount Tabor; of the Samaritans' Mount Gerizim; of the Batu-Ribn, the cosmic rock of the Semang of Malacca, on which once stood a tree rising to heaven; of the subterranean temples of the Pueblo Indians of North America, in which a hole in the ground and a ladder to the ceiling link the netherworld to the worlds above; of the Ka'bah in Mecca, the sacred stone that fell from the sky, leaving a hole corresponding to the North Star that is known as the Door of Heaven; and so forth. The center of the labyrinth, the *axis mundi,* the vertical alignment of the centers of the abyss, of the earth and of the heavens, the temple, the sacred mountain, and the infinite number of variations on these themes—all are parts of the same symbolic constellation. [*See* Center of the World.]

Dance, playground, garden, and game. As we shall see below, there is a profound link between the labyrinth and dance. Legend says that Daedalus built in the agora of Knossos the first place for sacred dances. After the victory of Theseus over the Minotaur, the feat was reenacted on the island of Delos in a nightly dance dedicated to the goddess of love that was known by the name of *geranos,* a word coming from the Greek for "cranes," probably because these birds fly in a straight line.

Things sacred do not disappear with time, even when they are seemingly abandoned in favor of other traditions, beliefs, and cultures; they often survive in folklore, in popular and peasant festivals and traditions, in children's games, in plays and playgrounds. Labyrinthine games were extremely popular in England; witness the many surviving "turf-mazes," sometimes called "Troy towns" or "Caerdroia," which follow the pattern of the labyrinths seen on coins from Knossos. The art of trimming hedges of evergreens is very old; it made possible the creation of the hedge mazes in gardens that became popular in the seventeenth century, especially in Holland, France, and England. And the type of game in which a path must be followed to a center, like *jeu de l'oie,* snakes and ladders, and so many others everywhere is an example of how the symbol of the labyrinth has survived in children's games and puzzles.

Types of Labyrinth. Such a wealth of connotations and interlinked meanings combine in the single symbolic structure of the labyrinth. We can give only a pale idea of its riches. They show its antiquity and the accumulation of many layers of magical, religious, intuitive, rational, and metaphysical significance. Over the centuries the idea of the labyrinth has evolved and acquired new meanings that have influenced its design. In the discussion that follows, I shall attempt to categorize these different labyrinthine patterns.

The serpentine linear labyrinth. A type of protolabyrinthine pattern of wandering or undulating lines, sometimes going in one direction and then turning back in the opposite one, is frequent in prehistoric rock engravings (see figure 3); in some cases it appears in combination with spiral labyrinths. Serpentine lines evoke a voyage "to the left and to the right" and connote a fate decided by various opposing influences, visible and invisible—the path of the nomad or the hunter, the passage of man through space and time.

Ringwallbilder. A type of drawing known to scholarship as a *Ringwallbilder* consists basically of concentric circles penetrated by a straight or serpentine line (see figure 1). The central point corresponds to origin, to the *fiat*, to the manifestation of divine energy. In its dimensionless recesses is concealed the mysterious inmost womb of all creation and all creatures. Thus new life and fertility depend on the hidden center—of being, of the earth, of the mother. *Ringwallbilder* relate to a cosmogonic vision, to the mystery of life-generating processes, to fertility and sexual symbolism.

The spiral labyrinth. Basically the spiral labyrinth is made of a spiral line turning around a center; it implies a double movement, inward and outward, sometimes drawn into a double spiral. Many types of design are possible; the well-known representation of *yin* and *yang* and the Grecian motifs can be considered variations of the spiral. Because a spiral leaves no alternative paths, some authors prefer to call it a pseudolabyrinth. Spiral labyrinths are very frequent. Their first appearance is probably linked to man's revolutionary passage from neolithic nomadism to the settled agrarian life, a passage that forced a reappraisal of fertility, cosmic cycles, and earthly and motherly deities. Agriculture implies a fixed life and the creation of privileged loci, as well as the belief in the "resurrection" of seeds by invisible forces hidden in the earth, which is conceived as an inner fire capable of "digesting" whatever goes underground. It is not surprising, then, to find an ancient relation between the spiral and intestines, as in several drawings of the so-called Röntgen-style, frequent among Arctic populations, or in certain Japanese ceramics of the Jomon period. Károly Kerényi studied what he considered the first kind of labyrinth—the spiral—in the most ancient examples available: several clay plaquettes found during excavations in Babylon that show drawings of intestines. According to some scholars, the inscription on this drawing is *êkal tirâni* ("palace of viscera"); these plaquettes were probably used for divination. The bowels, through internal heat, or "fire," were supposed to create a form of energy that is analogous to the inner fire of the earth as shown in the slow "digestion" of seeds, ores, and crystals and in the sudden eruption of volcanoes.

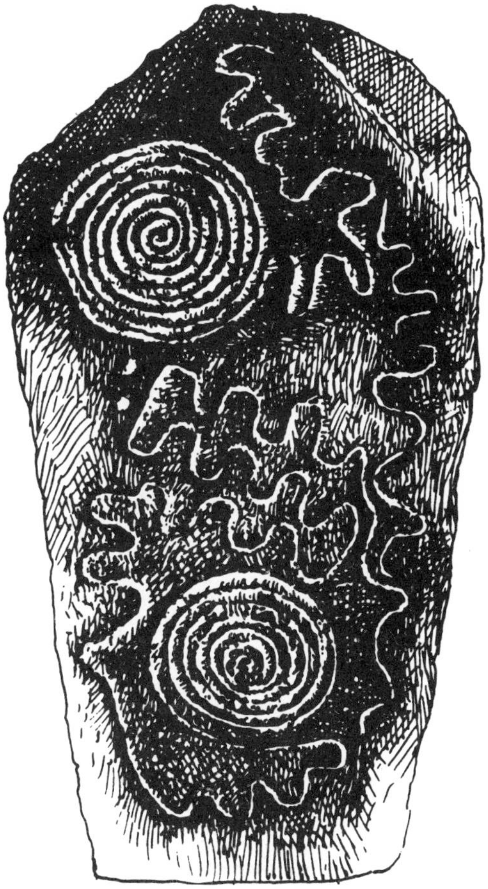

FIGURE 3. *Serpentine Linear Labyrinth.* At each of its ends, the serpentine line on this prehistoric rock engraving becomes a spiral. This example was found at Monte de Eiro (Marco de Canaveses), Portugal.

The spiral labyrinth is simultaneously the intestine, digestion, and energy, as we can see in some ancient documents—in the *Epic of Gilgamesh*, for example, the face of the horned monster Huwawa is made of viscera—as well as in much more recent ones—like the Romanesque paintings in which the abdomen of the figure of Christ in majesty displays the arms of a spiral and the frescoes that depict the triumph of Death in the Campo Santo of Pisa, in which a sinner's exposed bowels form a spiral. To eat and to be eaten are correlative moments in the cosmic balance; digestion in *viscera terrae* corresponds to death and dissolution, to the interchange of energies, to transmutation, and to promised resurrection. Jurgis Baltrusaitis says that until Carolingian times sepulchers often contained spiral-shaped snail shells, to symbolize a tomb from which man will rise again. Similarly, in Kansu, China, funerary urns of the Ma Chang period have been found decorated with cowrie patterns, also known as death patterns, spiral motifs that symbolize the promise of an afterlife. The earth, like an abdomen, ingests the seed, the dead, the sun, or the virgin before it allows the revival of plants, of souls, or of spring and fruits.

Several known myths of distinct areas and epochs follow an identical pattern of a virgin's sacrifice and burial that is necessary to ensure future crops. In one such myth, collected by Adolf E. Jensen from among the Maros of the island of Ceram in Indonesia, the virgin Hainuwele is put to death after a dance that lasts nine nights, during which men and women move along a big spiral centered upon a hole in the ground; the virgin is gradually pushed into that hole and, after the sacrifice, is buried in it; Malua Satene, probably a death divinity, infuriated by the murder of Hainuwele, forces every man to pass through a door decorated with a spiral of nine circumvolutions; those incapable of passing the portico are transformed into animals or spirits.

A definite link connects the spiral labyrinth with ritual dance. In Kerényi's opinion, all research into the labyrinth should take dance as its starting point. Peasants in many places still dance around a tree or pole (the maypole in Anglo-Saxon areas), often using bands or threads to create a spiral, as in the *geranos* dance performed in Delos in honor of Ariadne. The German *Bandltanze* are often performed inside a labyrinth made of stones aligned on the ground; such stone labyrinths are known in Germany as *Steintanz* and in Scandinavia as *jungfrudans* ("dance of the maidens"). There is also a possible link between the paramilitary ritual games of the Ludus Troiae in ancient Rome, corresponding to an equestrians' dance, and what became the tournaments of horsemen in the Middle Ages, as well as to the *ludus draconis* ("dragon's play") of France, Germany, and England, a feast related to the cult of Saint George and the return of the spring. In fact, a vast number of sacred dances of great antiquity were associated with funeral, fertility, and shamanistic rites and were performed around a center that symbolized the *axis mundi*, the entrance to hell, or "Jacob's ladder" to the heavens; in the *geranos* dance of Delos the women held a string or band and moved along a spiral, first to the left, into death, and then to the right, to rebirth. Many types of such dances could be mentioned, like the shamanistic ones of Central Asia, the first element of which is spinning around a center. According to the *Kojiki*, a collection of narratives and myths written in Japan at the beginning of the seventh century, the marriage of the male and female aspects of divinity was preceded by a dance around the "august celestial pilaster."

Spiral labyrinths connote symbolically also the serpent, as Indian tradition represents it implicitly in the first *cakra*, able to rise up the spine or *axis mundi*. The serpent motif, so charged with energy and meaning in Tantric as well as in Christian and many other cultures, is an ancient symbol connected with the earth that appeared on ceramics at the rise of agrarian civilization and spread to vast regions of Mesopotamia, India, and Mesoamerica. It is relevant to remember that in Vergil's *Aeneid*, after the description of the equestrian dances that closed the funerary feats in honor of Anchises, we are told that a serpent crept out of the tomb and twisted its body in seven knots.

The cross labyrinth. The cross labyrinth combines the spiral motif with the partition of space in four directions (see figure 4). The transition from spiral to cross labyrinth results perhaps from the psychic situation created by the rise of agrarian and subsequent urban cultures. The city becomes the privileged and protected area where wealth, knowledge, and power, both material and spiritual, are concentrated. The center of the city, as center of the labyrinth, is turned into a crossroads from which distances are measured and time calculated. Four is the basic number of directions: sunrise, sunset, north, and south. A cross is the sign of their spreading from the central heart. The square, which evolves from the cross, then becomes the emblem of the rational *urbs* and the dwelling place of the new urban man. The settlement of towns requires a mental revolution: man must make accurate forecasts and long-range plans; draw up laws and regulations, which implies a police force (the words *police* and *policy* both come from *polis*, "town"); and, last but not least, develop a "town memory" in the form of registers and archives, an act that requires the invention of writing. This change in thinking finds its visual expression in the orderly vertical and horizontal arms of the cross, which when repeated create geometric patterns based on squares. This type of geometric arrangement appeared in Mesopotamia and then, more suddenly, in Egypt in predynastic times, around the end of the fourth millennium; as René Huyghe points out, it served as a link in the passage from nomadism to settled life. The knife of Jebel el Arak, found near Dendera, a village on the Nile, is probably the first Egyptian example; the figures appear in parallel rows, not randomly, as in prehistoric art. This labyrinthine pattern eventually evolves into the classical model seen in the Knossos coins: a cross

FIGURE 4. *Cross Labyrinth.* This example is an uncommon combination of spiral and cross. Rock engraving from Rio Negro, Patagonia, Argentina.

with its arms bent and turning around the center in curvilineal or, more often, straight movements at right angles (see figure 5). Examples of this type occur most frequently, from antiquity to modern times.

A walled, strong, and organized city may reveal itself as a prison to its inhabitants, just as the labyrinth, after some authors, may have been used in a remote past to trap wild animals. Lost is the freedom of movement and direct contact with the spirits of nature. The mythical Minotaur is, thus, also the symbol of the repressed part of human nature, prerational and vital, which the new city hero wants to subdue; the artifices of Daedalus and the needs of the emerging state hide the "monster" in the underground, and Theseus, with the help of artful memory tricks, decides to suppress it. But this is a fatal mistake on the part of the hero, for the Minotaur is also the hidden source of his own energy and power; killing the monster brings tragic forgetfulness, loss of purpose, decay, and disaster. In fact, the Minotaur cannot die. He takes his revenge in the same labyrinth, which is turned now into hell, for the Minotaur is also the promise of the sun's rebirth (as the constellation Taurus brings back spring's vitality), and through the sun's rays Icarus is punished for his arrogance in trying to evade complexity and enjoy a new, marvelous freedom in the belief that he has to thank his own inflated ego alone.

The cross inside the spiral suggests a divine sacrifice necessary to redeem those who became lost in the "city of perdition"; Christ, like Theseus, descends to hell, but instead of killing the monster, he redeems the condemned. As an *iter mysticum* to salvation, the cross labyrinth was extensively used in Christian ethics and symbolical art, in illuminated manuscripts, on the floor of cathedrals, in painting, and in heraldic and esoteric emblems, especially after the twelfth century. In literature the connotations of this type of labyrinth have inspired poems, stories, and Hermetic and symbolic writings, from the cycle of the Holy Grail legends to the seventeenth-century writings of John Bunyan and Johannes Amos Comenius.

The cross is an immensely rich symbol. [*See* Cross.] It reconciles opposed directions and divided drives at its center, where the revolutions of the labyrinthine universe find their fixed axis, just as in one of the coins from Knossos we see the arms of a squared spiral turn around the polestar or the fixed sun (see figure 5).

The thread and the knot. The red thread of Ariadne is a symbol of memory, as we mentioned before; it symbolizes as well the sun's rays and the way to liberation. But the thread also binds when it turns and twists itself into knots, both as the cords tie the prisoner and as words compromise or the vow commits an honest man. The knots of Varuṇa are the symbol of the god's power to tie and untie, of the magic forces of sovereignty concentrated in the king or chief—justice, administration, public security, political decision, in fact, all the "powers," as Georges Dumézil established when he studied the Ouranos-Varuṇa symbolism. The knot contributes to the labyrinth as a tying device, a symbol of centralized urban power and "amazing" artifice, and as such is linked to Daedalus, the artist and the inventor. But the knot also symbolizes initiation and, through its intricate detours, the journey of the soul to salvation. [*See* Knots.]

The native peoples of the Malekula Islands in Vanuatu believe in a "journey of the dead," as John Layard (1937) has observed; according to one of the oldest variants of their myth, the soul must pass the "waters of death" and then, at the entrance of the cave leading to the kingdom of the souls, be confronted with the "female devouring ghost." This ghost has previously drawn with her finger on the sand of the floor of the cave, a geometric "knotty" pattern of considerable complexity: it is made of one uninterrupted line, named "the way" or "the path" (see figure 6). Half of the drawing has been erased by the ghost, however, and the soul must remake the missing half correctly before being admitted into the cave. The female devouring ghost will

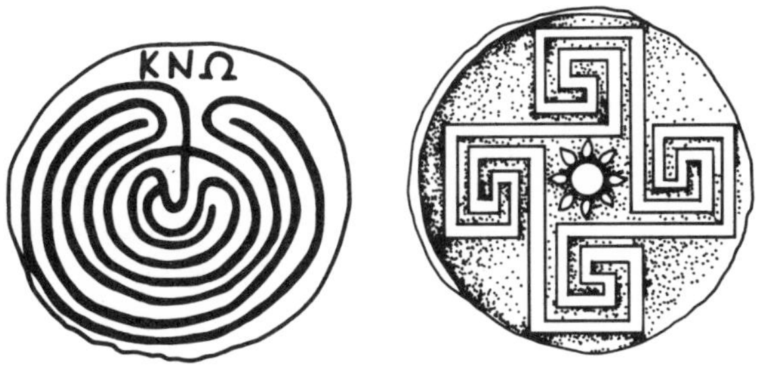

FIGURE 5. *Cross Labyrinths.* Coins from Knossos, Crete.

FIGURE 6. *Knot.* Drawing from Malekula Island, Vanuatu.

eat those who are unable to complete the drawing. In preparation for this journey the Malekula islanders practice the ritual drawing of difficult patterns on the sand.

We are reminded here of the cave of the sibyl of Cumae, in the sixth book of Vergil's *Aeneid*, and of the labyrinth drawn at its entrance. One-line, complex patterns evoke as well the famous *Concatenation* drawn by Leonardo da Vinci (see figure 7), Albrecht Dürer's *Sechs Knoten*, and the arabesques of Muslim art (in architecture, in frontispieces to the Qur'ān, in tile and carpet motifs). We also are reminded of many well-known Celtic labyrinthine designs sculpted on crosses and stones, such as the Carndonagm Cross at Donegal, in Ireland, and the Jelling Stone in Denmark (see figure 8).

The thread symbolizes guidance through a difficult path or through initiatory rites, the loving or charitable gift of secret knowledge, and the promise of freedom. In India the monks of Viṣṇu receive a sacred thread, and neophytes learn to perform symbolic exercises with it. Metaphysically, the thread is that with which God made all things, his divine logos; with it the sun, like a spider, unites the worlds. The *Śatapatha Brāhmaṇa* calls it the "wind" thread, and the *Bṛhadāraṇyaka Upaniṣad* comments that the knowledge of this thread and of *brahman* is the supreme knowledge of being in all its manifestations. Knowing that there is only one thread in spite of the infinite variety of its knots, as Ananda Coomaraswamy ponders, brings one safely to the end of the path, to the center, and to the cosmic architect, himself the way and the door.

FIGURE 7. *Knot.* Leonardo da Vinci's *Concatenation*, a *maṇḍala*-like drawing.

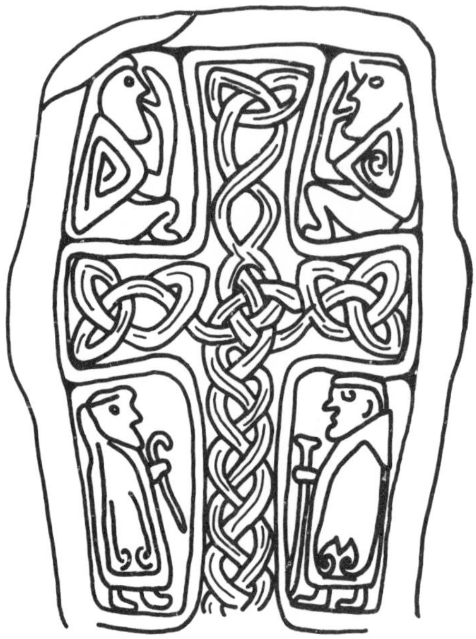

FIGURE 8. *Knot.* Celtic labyrinthine design on a slab from Drumhallagh, Donegal, Ireland.

The celestial city and the maṇḍala. Finding the way through a labyrinth, conceived as a mental, spiritual, and metaphysical enigma, corresponds to the successful conclusion of an *iter mysticum*. It can be expressed visually by transformation of the labyrinth drawing into what in Indo-Tibetan terms is known as *maṇḍala*. The *maṇḍala* (the more schematic linear variations are called *vantras*) basically consists of a circle enclosing a square divided into four triangles; in the center of each triangle, as well as in the center of the whole drawing, are circles that contain the images of deities. [*See* Maṇḍalas.] This pattern can take an infinite number of variations, some of which are similar to the classical pattern of the labyrinth: many *maṇḍalas* show bastions, ramparts, towers, and gardens. All are conducive to yogic meditation; they are meant to protect the meditator from distraction caused by unconscious impulses and lead him to a *descensus ad inferos* where he meets his "ghosts," and, recognizing their true nature, conquers them. Step by step he is lead out of the ocean of *saṃsāra*—the overpowering illusion of the complexity of appearances—to gain a new realization of being.

The *maṇḍala* is therefore a chart of the cosmos, including the *axis mundi*, the cosmic mountain of Sumeru, the palace of the *cakravartin* ("universal monarch"), and, according to the Tantric text, the *Sādhanamāla* ("city of liberation"). The city of liberation evokes the celestial Jerusalem that descends from the heavens at the end of time; like a *maṇḍala*, the celestial city expresses the final unification of opposites and the emergence of the transcendental ego—the "secret self" or *ātman* of the Vedānta, the Self in Jung's terminology. The rose windows in medieval churches and cathedrals of the West, considered one of the greatest achievements of European art, are *maṇḍalas*, symbolizing the process leading to the ultimate metamorphosis of man. Their colored light, circular shape, and geometric crystalization suggest the attained final radiance of the "adamantine body."

BIBLIOGRAPHY

Borgeaud, Philippe. "The Open Entrance to the Closed Palace of the King: The Greek Labyrinth in Context." *History of Religions* 14 (1974): 1–27.

Coomaraswamy, Ananda K. "The Iconography of Dürer's 'Knots' and Leonardo's 'Concatenation.'" *Art Quarterly* 7 (1944): 109–128. A brilliant essay on the symbolism of knots.

Cowen, Painton. *Rose Windows*. San Francisco, 1979. A valuable recent book on the history and, especially, the symbolism of the *maṇḍala*-type rose windows of Western churches.

Deacon, A. Bernard. "Geometrical Drawings from Malekula and Other Islands of the New Hebrides." *Journal of the Royal Anthropological Institute* 64 (1934): 129–175.

Deacon, A. Bernard. *Malekula: A Vanishing People of the New Hebrides*. London, 1934. See pages 552–579.

Deedes, C. N. *The Labyrinth: Further Studies in the Relation between Myth and Ritual in the Ancient World*. Edited by Samuel Henry Hooke. New York, 1935. An authoritative study on the subject, with emphasis on Egyptian seals and the use of labyrinths as a protection in Mesopotamian tombs.

Eliade, Mircea. *Images and Symbols: Studies in Religious Symbolism*. New York, 1961. See especially chapter 4.

Freitas, Lima de. *O labirinto*. Lisbon, 1975. A richly illustrated general essay on the symbolic meaning of the labyrinth.

Hocke, Gustav René. *Die Welt als Labyrinthe: Manier und Manie in der europäischen Kunst*. Hamburg, 1957. A scholarly conspectus of the labyrinthine complex through the evolution of Western art.

Kerényi, Karóly. *Labyrinth-Studien*. Amsterdam, 1941. A brilliant essay on the spiral labyrinth.

Knight, W. F. Jackson. *Cumaean Gates: A Reference of the Sixth Aeneid to the Initiation Pattern*. Oxford, 1936.

Layard, John. "Labyrinth Ritual in South India: Threshold and Tattoo Designs." *Folk-Lore* 48 (1937): 115–182.

Layard, John. "The Malekulan Journey of the Dead" (1937). In *Papers from the Eranos Yearbooks*, edited by Joseph Campbell, vol. 4, pp. 115–150. New York, 1960.

Matthews, William H. *Mazes and Labyrinths: Their History and Development* (1922). Reprint, New York, 1970. A classic general conspectus of the subject written with great care and scholarship.

Mumford, Lewis. *The City in History*. London, 1973. A masterly study of the evolution of towns. The first eight chapters are especially relevant to the understanding of the labyrinth.

Purce, Jill. *La spirale mystique*. Paris, 1974. A readable essay on the sacred meaning of the spiral.

Santarcangeli, Paolo. *Le livre des labyrinthes: Historie d'un mythe et d'un symbole*. Paris, 1974. A general overview of the development of the labyrinth through history, including a good bibliography.

Tucci, Giuseppe. *The Theory and Practice of the Mandala, with Special Reference to the Modern Psychology of the Subconscious*. London, 1969. An enlightening study by one of the world's leading authorities in the field.

LIMA DE FREITAS

LADY OF THE ANIMALS. The image of the lady of the animals is well known to readers of the classics: Aphrodite with her dove, Athena with her owl, and Artemis with her deer. But the image goes back much further than the Classical age of Greece (fifth and fourth centuries BCE), much further back than the time of Homer (before 700 BCE). It can be traced back to prehistory, certainly to the Neolithic era (began c. 9000 BCE in the Near East), if not to the Paleolithic (10,000 BCE and earlier). The lady of the animals is found in almost all cultures. [*See also* Lord of the Animals.]

A very early sculpture of a lady of the animals was found in Çatal Hüyük, a Neolithic site in central Anatolia (central Turkey), dating from 6500 to 5650 BCE. Made of baked clay, she sits on a chair, perhaps a birth chair or throne. She is full-breasted and big of belly, and she seems to be giving birth, for a head emerges from between her legs. Her hands rest on the heads of two large cats, probably leopards, that stand at her sides. From Sumer (c. 2000 BCE), a lady of the animals appears in a terra-cotta relief, naked and winged, with two owls at her sides and her webbed feet resting on the backs of two monkeys. This image is called Lilith. From Minoan Crete comes a small statue unearthed in the treasury of the palace of Knossos (c. 1700–1450 BCE). The depicted figure stares as if in trance, her outstretched arms holding two striped snakes; her breasts are exposed, and a small snake emerges from her bodice. Snakes encircle her headdress, and a small animal perches on her head.

In an image on a seal ring from Minoan Crete, a figure emerges bare-breasted from a mountaintop attended by two lions and a young male. In Ephesus, an enormous image of a lady of the animals dominated the great temple of Artemis, or Diana (rebuilt 334 BCE and known as one of the seven wonders of the ancient world). Her many egg-shaped breasts symbolized her life-giving power, while the signs of the zodiac forming her necklace expressed her cosmic power. Her arms were extended in gesture of blessing, and her lower body, shaped like the trunk of the tree of life, was covered with the heads of wild and domestic animals. At her feet were beehives; at her sides two deer. The city crowned her head. (This description is based on a small Roman copy of the lost original dating from the second century CE that is in the Ephesus museum.)

In Asia Minor the lady of animals is known as Kubaba or Cybele and is flanked by lions. In Egypt she is Isis the falcon or Isis with falcon wings and an uraeus emerging from her forehead; she is also Hathor the cow goddess or Hathor with the cow horns. In Canaan she is Ashtoret or Astarte holding snakes and flowers in her hands. In India she is Tārā or Pārvatī astride a lion or Durgā riding a lion into battle and slaying demons with the weapons in her ten arms. In Japan she is Amaterasu, the sun goddess, with her roosters that crow at dawn and her messengers the crows. To the Inuit (Eskimo) she is Sedna, goddess of the sea and sea animals, especially seals, walruses, and whales. To the Hopi she is Kokyanguruti, or Spider Woman, the creatrix and guardian of Mother Earth, who presides over emergence and return. To the Algonquin she is Nokomis, the Grandmother, who feeds plants, animals, and humans from her breasts. In Mexico she is Chicomecoate, Heart of the Earth, with seven serpent messengers. In Africa she is Ọṣun with peacocks and Mami Wata with snakes. In Christianity her memory remains in the images of Eve with the snake and Mary with the dove. She lingers, too, in such folk images as Mother Goose, the Easter Bunny, and the Stork.

Because prehistory has left no written records, interpretation of the meaning of the earliest images of the lady of the animals cannot be done with certainty. Thus we cannot know if she was known to her earliest worshipers as "Mother of All the Living" (a phrase used to refer to Eve in *Genesis* 3:20), as "Creatrix," "Goddess," "Clan Mother," "Priestess," or, simply, "Ma," or "Nana." Whatever she was called, the lady of the animals is an image of the awesome creative power of woman and nature.

Composed between 800 and 400 BCE, the Homeric Hymns, many of which reflect much earlier religious conceptions, provide two powerful written images of the lady of the animals that can help us interpret earlier drawn and sculpted images. In the *Hymn to Earth,* she is "well-founded Earth, mother of all, eldest of all beings. She feeds all creatures that are in the world, all that go upon the goodly land, and all that are in the paths of the seas, and all that fly." In the *Hymn to the Mother of the Gods,* she is "well-pleased with the sound of rattles and timbrels, with the voice of flutes and the outcry of wolves and bright-eyed lions, with echoing hills and wooded coombes."

In these songs the lady of the animals is cosmic power. She is mother of all. The animals of the earth, sea, and air are hers, and the wildest and most fearsome animals—wolves and lions, as well as human beings—praise her with sounds. The lady of the animals is also earth: she is the firm foundation undergirding all life. The hills and valleys echo to her. In these images she would not be called a "lady of the plants," which suggests that the conceptions reflected in these hymns may have originated in preagricultural times. Jane Harrison (1903) has suggested that the "lady of the wild things" becomes "lady of the plants" only after human beings become agriculturists.

The Paleolithic Age. Marija Gimbutas, Gertrude R. Levy, and E. O. James are among those who concur with Harrison in tracing the goddess symbolism of the Neolithic and later periods to the Upper Paleolithic, or Old Stone Age (c. 40,000–10,000 BCE). Therefore we must ask whether the image of the lady of the animals also goes back to the Paleolithic age.

Many small figures of so-called pregnant Venuses have been dated to the Upper Paleolithic. Abundantly fleshed with prominent breasts, bellies, and pubic triangles, they were often painted with red ocher, which seems to have symbolized the blood of birth, the blood of life. These images have been variously interpreted. [*See* Megalithic Religion, *article on* Prehistoric Evidence.]

These images must be interpreted in relation to the cave art of the Paleolithic era. Paleolithic peoples decorated the labyrinthine paths and inner recesses of caves with abstract line patterns and with drawings and paintings of animals, such as bison and deer. Small human figures, both male and female, were sometimes painted in the vicinity of the much larger animals. The drawings and paintings of these animals, and the rituals practiced in the inner reaches of the caves, have often been understood as hunting magic, done to ensure the capture of prey. But Gertrude R. Levy argues that the purposes of these rituals cannot have been simple "magic compulsion" but must have involved a desire for a "participation in the splendor of the beasts" (Levy, 1963, p. 20). If, as was surely the case later, Paleolithic peoples also understood the caves and their inner recesses to be the womb of Earth, then is it not possible to recognize the aniconic image of the lady of the animals in the womb-cave onto which the animals were painted? And can we not also see the lady of the animals in the well-known Paleolithic carving found in Laussel of an unclothed, apparently pregnant woman holding a bison horn? Must we not, then, interpret prehistoric rituals in the labyrinthine recesses of caves as a desire to participate in the transformative power of the creatrix, the lady of the animals?

Old Europe. Anthropomorphic images of the lady of the animals appear in abundance in the Neolithic, or early agricultural period, which began about 9000 BCE in the Near East. In *The Goddesses and Gods of Old Europe* (1982), Marija Gimbutas presents the results of her exhaustive study of the civilization of Old Europe (c. 7000–3500), a Neolithic and Chalcolithic (or Copper Age) civilization that included the lands surrounding the Aegean and Adriatic seas and their islands and extended as far north as Czechoslovakia, southern Poland, and the western Ukraine. [*See also Prehistoric Religions, article on* Old Europe.] There is reason to believe that Neolithic-Chalcolithic cultures developed along similar lines in other parts of the world, including, for example, Africa, China, the Indus Valley, and the Americas.

In Old Europe, Gimbutas found a pre–Bronze Age culture that was "matrifocal and probably matrilinear, agricultural and sedentary, egalitarian and peaceful" (Gimbutas, 1982, p. 9). This culture was presided over by a goddess conceived as the source and giver of all. Although originally this goddess did not appear with animals, she herself had animal characteristics. One of her earliest forms was as the snake and bird goddess, who was associated with water and represented as a snake, water bird, duck, goose, crane, diving bird, or owl or as a woman with a bird head or birdlike posture. She was the creator goddess, the giver of life.

The goddess of Old Europe was also connected with the agricultural cycles of life, death, and regeneration. Here she appeared as, or was associated with, bees, butterflies, deer, bears, hares, toads, turtles, hedgehogs, and dogs. The domesticated dog, bull, male goat, and pig became her companions. To the Old Europeans she was not a power transcendent of the earth but, rather, the power that creates, sustains, and manifests itself in the variety of life forms within the earth and its cycles. Instead of celebrating humanity's uniqueness and separation from nature, Old Europeans honored humanity's participation in, and connection to, nature's cycles of birth, death, and renewal. The creatrix manifested in animal form enhanced human understanding of her creative power. Many animals, such as the rapidly growing piglet, the caterpillar-chrysalis-butterfly, the bird that flies in the air and walks on the earth, and the snake that crawls above and below the earth, manifest the creative powers of the universe more fully than the human form alone. [*See* Animals.]

In Old Europe, the creator goddess who appeared as a lady of animals was the primary image of the divine. According to Gimbutas, the "male element, man and animal, represented spontaneous and life-stimulating—but not life-generating—powers" (Gimbutas, 1982, p. 9). Gimbutas believes that women were preeminent in the society and religion of Old Europe. It is generally conceded that women invented agriculture, for as the gatherers of plant foods in Paleolithic societies, women would have been the ones most likely to notice the connection between the dropping of a seed and the springing up of a new plant. If women were the first agriculturists—perhaps initially guarding the secrets from men—this might suggest social reasons for the preeminence of goddesses and women in the earliest agricultural societies.

Çatal Hüyük. The culture of Çatal Hüyük, excavated by James Mellaart, seems similar to that found by Gimbutas in Old Europe. Like Gimbutas, Mellaart found a culture where women and goddesses were prominent, a culture that he believed to have been matrilineal and matrilocal and peaceful and in which the goddess was the most powerful religious image. In Çatal Hüyük, the lady of the animals was preeminent. Wall paintings in the shrines frequently depict a goddess, with outstretched arms and legs, giving birth, sometimes to bulls' or rams' heads. Other shrines depict rows of bull heads with rows of breasts; in one shrine, rows of breasts incorporate the lower jaws of boars or the skulls of foxes, weasels, or vultures. Besides the small figure, mentioned earlier, of the seated goddess, hands on her leopard companions, giving birth, Mellaart also found a sculpture of a woman in leopard-skin robes standing in front of a leopard. One shrine simply depicts two leopards standing face to face.

Wall paintings of bulls were also frequent at the site. Mellaart believes that the religion of Çatal Hüyük was centered on life, death, and rebirth. The bones of women, children, and some men were found buried under platforms in the living quarters and in the shrines, apparently after having been picked clean by vultures. According to Mellaart, vultures were also associated with the goddess, thus indicating that she was both giver and taker of life.

As Mellaart states in *Earliest Civilizations of the Near East* (1965), the land-based matrifocal, sedentary, and peaceful agricultural societies of the Near East were invaded by culturally inferior northern peoples starting in the fifth and fourth millennia BCE. These invaders and others who followed set the stage for the rise of the patriarchal and warlike Sumerian state about 3500 BCE. According to Gimbutas, the patriarchal, nomadic, and warlike proto-Indo-Europeans infiltrated the matrifocal agricultural societies of Old Europe between 4500 and 2500 BCE. As a result, in both the Near East and Old Europe, the creator goddess was deposed, slain, or made wife, daughter, or mother to the male divinities of the warriors. The lady of the animals did not disappear (religious symbols linger long after the end of the cultural situation that gave rise to them), but her power was diminished. No longer understood to be the great power of the universe, she became subordinate to gods such as Zeus or Marduk, who claimed preeminent power.

Minoan Crete. In the islands, which were more difficult to invade, the goddess-centered cultures survived and developed into Bronze Age civilizations. In Crete, for example, the lady of the animals remained supreme until the Minoan civilization fell to the Mycenaeans about 1450 BCE. In the Old and New Palace periods of Minoan Crete (c. 2000–1450 BCE), a highly developed pre-Greek civilization, based on agriculture, artisanship, and trade, emerged. From existing archaeological evidence (Linear A, the written language of the Minoans, has not been translated), it appears that women and priestesses played the prominent roles in religious rituals. There is no evidence that they were subordinate in society. Indeed, the celebrated throne of King Minos, found by excavator Arthur Evans, is now thought by several scholars (including Jacquetta Hawkes, Stylianous Alexiou, Helga Reusch, and Ruby Rohrlich) to have been occupied by a priestess queen.

In Minoan Crete a goddess was worshiped at natural sites, such as caves or mountaintops, and in small shrines in the palaces and homes. She had attributes of both a "mountain mother" and a lady of the animals; in the seal ring mentioned earlier, she is both. In Crete the lady of the animals is commonly found in the company of snakes, doves, and trees, particularly the olive tree, which was cultivated by Minoan farmers. In a seal ring found in the cave at Dhíkti, the goddess appears with bird or snake head between two winged griffins, the same animals that flank the throne of Minos.

Other pervasive symbols in Crete include the stylized horns of consecration, which evoke not only the bull but also the crescent moon, the upraised arms of Minoan goddesses and priestesses, and the double ax, which Gimbutas interprets as a stylized butterfly. Heiresses and heirs to Neolithic religion, the Minoans continued to understand the divine as the power manifesting itself in the cycles of nature. Thus Cretan pottery and frescoes abound in rhythmical forms; images of waves, spirals, frolicking dolphins, undulating snakes, and graceful bull leapers are everywhere. The Minoans captured life in motion. Exuberant movement must have represented to them the dance of life, the dance of the lady of the animals.

Greece. Eventually all the Neolithic and (isolated) Bronze Age cultures where the creator goddess was supreme fell to patriarchal and warlike invaders. By the time of decipherable written records, we begin to see evidence that societies are ruled by warrior kings; goddesses are no longer supreme and women are subordinated by law to their husbands. On mainland Greece, Apollo took over the holy site of Delphi, sacred first to Earth and her prophetess, after slaying the python, the sacred snake that guarded the sanctuary. This act may be viewed as one record of the dethronement of the lady of the animals.

According to the Olympian mythology found in Homer's works and in the tragedies, Zeus, the Indo-European sky god, is named father and ruler of all the gods and goddesses. Hera, an indigenous goddess whose sanctuary at Olympia was older than that of Zeus, becomes his never fully subdued wife. Athena is born from the head of Zeus, but her mountain temples (e.g., the Parthenon) and her companions, the owl and snake, indicate her connection to the mountain mother and the lady of the animals. Aphrodite retains her connection to the dove and the goose. Artemis is the goddess of the untamed lands, mountain forests, and of wild animals such as bears and deer. Although she is named a virgin goddess, she aids both human and animal mothers in giving birth. Of all the Olympian goddesses, Artemis retains the strongest connection to the lady of the animals.

What happened to the goddesses in Greece happened everywhere. They were slain, tamed, made defenders of patriarchy and war, or relegated to a place outside the city. They were not allowed to challenge the patriarchal order that everywhere became the norm.

[*See also* Goddess Worship.]

BIBLIOGRAPHY

The best single book about prehistoric goddesses is Marija Gimbutas's *The Goddesses and Gods of Old Europe, 6500–3500 B.C.* (Berkeley, 1982) originally published as *The Gods and Goddesses of Old Europe, 7000–3500 B.C.* (Berkeley, 1974); a summary of her conclusions can be found in "Women and Culture in Goddess-Oriented Old Europe," in *The Politics of Women's Spirituality*, edited by Charlene Spretnak (Garden City, N.Y., 1982), pp. 22–31. The works of James Mellaart, particularly *Çatal Hüyük* (New York, 1967) and *Earliest Civilizations of the Near East* (London, 1965), are essential for understanding goddess symbolism in Neolithic civilization. Gertrude R. Levy's *Religious Conceptions of the Stone Age* (New York, 1963), originally titled *The Gate of Horn* (London, 1948), remains a valuable resource on prehistoric religion, especially on the question of cave symbolism. Jane E. Harrison's *Prolegomena to the Study of Greek Religion* (1903; reprint, Atlantic Highlands, N.J., 1981) has never been superseded as a comprehensive reference on Greek religion with particular emphasis on the prepatriarchal origins of goddesses. Jacquetta Hawkes presents the contrast between patriarchal and prepatriarchal Bronze Age societies in *Dawn of the Gods* (New York, 1968); Ruby Rohrlich provides a valuable feminist analysis in "Women in

Transition: Crete and Sumer," in *Becoming Visible*, edited by Renate Bridenthal and Claudia Koonz (Boston, 1977), pp. 36–59, and in "State Formation in Sumer and the Subjugation of Women," *Feminist Studies* 6 (Spring 1980): 76–102. For a general overview of goddess symbolism in many cultures, E. O. James's *The Cult of the Mother Goddess* (New York, 1959) remains extremely useful. Erich Neumann's *The Great Mother*, 2d ed., translated by Ralph Manheim (New York, 1963), contains a wealth of information mired in androcentric Jungian theory. Recent anthropological research on goddess symbolism and ritual in numerous cultures, most of them contemporary, can be found in *Mother Worship*, edited by James J. Preston (Chapel Hill, 1982). *The Book of the Goddess: Past and Present*, edited by Carl Olson (New York, 1983), presents recent research, some of it feminist, on historical and contemporary religions.

CAROL P. CHRIST

LĀHORĪ, MUḤAMMAD ʿALĪ (1874–1951), scholar of Islam and founder of the Lāhorī branch of the Aḥmadīyah movement. Born in Murar (Kapurthala), India, Lāhorī completed advanced degrees in English (1896) and law (1899) in Lahore. His life and works are closely intertwined with the Aḥmadīyah movement, a minor sect of Islam founded in 1899 by Ghulām Aḥmad (c. 1908), at whose suggestion Lāhorī undertook his two major works, a translation of the Qur'ān and *The Religion of Islam*. In 1902, Lāhorī was appointed co-editor of the Aḥmadīyah periodical, *Review of Religions*, through which he propagated the movement's news and views to the non-Muslim world. This appointment marked the beginning of Lāhorī's prolific career. He translated Ghulām Aḥmad's writings into English, defended his views in the face of the Sunnī majority's growing opposition, and wrote on various aspects of Islam.

In 1914, with the death of Ghulām Aḥmad's successor, Nūr al-Dīn—a prominent Qur'ān scholar considered the mastermind of the Aḥmadīyah movement by its opponents—the community split over doctrinal issues. Lāhorī headed an offshoot known as the Lāhorī group, which was more liberal and closer to the mainstream of Sunnī Islam, but also more aggressive in its outreach and more vocal in explaining its doctrinal differences with the parent group. Muḥammad ʿAlī was the main force behind the literary and missionary activities of this group, including the opening of new centers in western Europe and North America.

Lāhorī wrote profusely in Urdu and English. Equipped with Western research methodology and linguistic tools, he explained and defended various precepts of Islam to counterbalance criticism of Christian missionaries and to help develop a sense of pride in their heritage among Western-educated Muslims. He was the first Muslim to publish an English translation, with explanatory notes, of the entire text of the Qur'ān (1917). This was followed by a study, *Muhammad the Prophet* (1924), and a sequel, *Early Caliphate* (1932). He also addressed himself to current issues. Responding to the crisis of the Ottoman caliphate, for example, he wrote a short monograph entitled *The Khilafat in Islam* (1920), while his major work, *The Religion of Islam*, was written in response to a book of the same title published in 1906 by F. A. Klein.

The tenor of Lāhorī's writings reflects the mood of the times—polemical, apologetic, and missionary—and he clearly ranks with the intellectuals of the period, such as Sayyid Ahmad Khan, Syed Ameer Ali, Ḥālī, Chirāgh ʿAlī, and Shiblī. Among his followers he is considered the most prominent scholar of the century and, according to Mumtāz Aḥmad Farūqī, the "savior of the Aḥmadīyah movement." Through the efforts of various centers established in western Europe and North America, Lāhorī's works are well recognized there. It is claimed that a copy of his translated Qur'ān presented to Elijah Muhammad had far-reaching effects on the Black Muslim movement in North America. In the Indo-Pakistan subcontinent, however, the controversial character of the movement and ensuing polemic debates have adversely affected the popularity of his works among non-Aḥmadīyah Muslims.

BIBLIOGRAPHY

For Lāhorī's life and works, see Mumtāz Aḥmad Farūqī and Muḥammad Aḥmad's *Mujāhid-i kabīr* (Lahore, 1962), translated in an abridged version as *Muhammad Ali: The Great Missionary of Islam* (Lahore, 1966); and Muhammad Maulana Ali's *The Aḥmadiyyah Movement*, translated, with a biographical section and bibliography, by Muhammad Tufail (Lahore, 1973). For general discussion of the movement, see Spencer Lavan's *The Ahmadiyah Movement: A History and Perspective* (Delhi, 1974). See also A. H. A. Nadvi's critical work *Qādiyānīyat*, translated by Zafar Ishaq Ansari as *Qadianism: A Critical Study* (Lucknow, 1967); and Ehsan Elahi Zaheer's *Qadiyaniat, An Analytical Survey* (Lahore, 1972).

SAJIDA S. ALVI

LAIMA is one of the few goddesses of the Baltic peoples who can be said to personify a number of elemental concepts. She incorporates a wide variety of both individual and societal functions, of which two are particularly noteworthy: architect of destiny and agent of fertility. In connection with the former, the etymological link should be noted between the name *Laima* and the common noun *laime*, which in its general sense means "happiness." Notwithstanding the apparent restrictions of this definition, Laima embraces a wide range of functions. As goddess of destiny, Laima holds supreme power to determine an individual's life. Her decisions in this context are not rationally motivated; they are radical and unchangeable.

In Baltic religion, Laima's role became prominent at life's critical moments. The first and most significant of these was birth. Here Laima acted as determiner of the individual life of both mother and child. Her concern for the woman in childbirth began before the onset of labor. Traditionally, the place appointed for childbirth was the sauna, and in preparation for the event the woman was ritually cleansed, as was the route to the sauna, so that Laima could make her way unimpeded to aid the woman. As childbirth was frequently a life-threatening event, the woman would offer prayers to Laima before giving birth, asking her assistance in ensuring that both mother and infant would survive the birth. The prayer was accompanied by offerings to Laima (generally in the form of dyed threads and woven braids of wool or flax). On a religious level, the most significant moment occurred after successful childbirth: it took the form of a thanksgiving meal, held in the sauna and consisting of flat cakes, honey, and ale. Only married women were allowed to participate, with the place of honor reserved for Laima.

A similarly fateful moment was marriage, and Laima traditionally was held responsible for a happy as well as an unhappy married life. It is understandable, therefore, that an unmarried girl turned directly to the goddess with prayers that she be provided with a good and suitable husband so that her life might be happy. As determiner of the future, Laima alone was responsible if the girl was later unhappy because her husband was a drunkard or because he had died an untimely death, leaving her a young widow with sole responsibility for young children. In such cases, the conflict between the unfortunate woman and Laima could grow into an open feud. Folklore material shows that in these circumstances a woman might demand that Laima carry a heavy load of stones as punishment or even threaten to "drown" the goddess.

Laima also determined a person's death. Two forms of dialogue took place around the time of death. The first involved the dying person, who attempted to persuade Laima that it was not yet time to die because important work still had to be accomplished, of which the care of children was the most compelling. This form of appeal was generally unsuccessful. In the other type of dialogue, the dying person was represented by Dievs, the Baltic god of the heavens. An argument took place between Dievs and Laima over the issue of the person's death and whether it should occur at that particular moment. Clearly, Laima was one of the most rigid and extreme of the goddesses of destiny, and the extent of her radicalism was demonstrated by her inability to alter her own decisions. If the individual's future was determined at any one moment, it then remained unaltered, whatever the circumstances. If a man was destined to suffer all his life, then Laima could do no more than weep with him. A possible explanation for the evolution of this fatalist conception in Baltic religion is what many have seen as the centuries-long enslavement of these peoples by the German colonialist Christian church.

In addition to her role as determiner of the future, Laima's obligations included the encouragement of fecundity and of well-being in general. This is comprehensible in light of the structure of Baltic religion, which is that of an agrarian community. The basis of existence and well-being was determined by the fertility of the fields and animals. As Laima's name indicates, her primary *raison d'être* was happiness. Consequently she alone could make the farmer happy, and by dint of this she takes her place alongside the other fertility gods of Baltic religion. In this context she is further differentiated. Depending on which animals she was considered to aid, Laima was given an attributive qualification: thus she became Laima of Zirgu ("horses"), Laima of Govu ("cows"), Laima of Aitu ("sheep"). In the oldest agricultural tradition, the horse was held to be of particular worth; hence Laima was linked most closely with horse rearing. Yet she also aided crop cultivation by participating in hoeing and by circling the farmer's fields to protect them from evil spirits.

The iconography of Laima is very clearly delineated in the sources. She is represented as a beautiful young blonde woman dressed in clothes such as those worn by the wives of wealthy farmers on festive occasions. On her head is a splendid garland and on her shoulders a colorful shawl held together with one or more silver brooches. Only on rare occasions does she disguise herself as a poor old woman.

The interpretation of the essential qualities of Laima is nevertheless complicated by certain unresolved questions, one of which concerns the source of her frequent description as *Laimas māte* ("mother fortune"). On the one hand, it could be argued that the idea of "mother," one of the fundamental notions of religion, is clearly linked with Laima. Yet on the other hand, it is also true that for centuries the Baltic peoples were subject to the influence of Christianity, particularly the Marian cult. Hence it could be held that Laima's description as "mother" is a later development based on this influence.

Another problem concerns Laima's creative role. In the sources she is occasionally described as *laidēja* ("mainspring"), from the verb *laist* ("to let," in the dynamic sense of "to cause to happen"; its synonym is *radīt*, "to create"). The epithet *laideja* and the name *Laima* are etymologically derived from the same root (*lei*), and this common derivation suggests that the act of creation is one of Laima's basic functions. Precise statements to this effect are sparse, however.

BIBLIOGRAPHY

Biezais, Haralds. *Die Hauptgöttinnen der alten Letten.* Uppsala, 1955. An exhaustive critical monograph, including a bibliography.

Velius, Norbertas. *Mitines lietuvių sakmių butybes.* Vilnius, 1977. Analyzes the texts of Lithuanian legends and discusses relevant problems. An English summary is included on pages 294–302.

HARALDS BIEZAIS

LAITY is a term that has emerged in the Western religious and theological traditions to refer to those members of a religious community who, as a group, do not have the responsibilities of fulfilling the priestly functions appropriate to the offices of the clergy or ordained ministers.

Etymology and Origins of Concept. The adjective *lay* is derived from the Greek word *laikos* (Lat., *laicus*) meaning "of or from the people." In early Christianity the term came to connote "the chosen people of God," a meaning derived from the Greek *laos* ("people of unknown origin"). In the New Testament a distinction is made between the Jewish "people" *(laos)* and their priests and officials (as in, for example, *Acts of the Apostles* 5:26, the *Gospel of Matthew* 26:23, and the *Letter to the Hebrews* 7:5, 7:27).

Before the end of the first century CE the term *laos* took on a more ecclesiastical connotation. The term *laikos* is used by Clement of Alexandria (c. 200 CE) to distinguish a layman from a deacon and a presbyter. In the *Apostolic Canons,* laity *(laikoi)* are distinguished from clergy. The early Christian distinction between laity and clergy was informed by a political differentiation of Greek origin, that is, that between the *klēros* (from which *clergy* is derived) and "the people" *(laos),* the two groups that comprised the administration of the polis. As the Christian community continued to develop ecclesiastically, the *klēros,* the leaders or those with an "office," became the ones through whom the means of grace were extended to the believers, "the people" *(laos).* By the time of the Council of Nicaea (325) the organization and structure of the church was understood basically in terms of the clerical order, with authority vested in the bishops and the councils as distinguished from the laity.

While the notion of laity, derived as it is from Western sources, is not relevant to the study of all religious communities, it is a helpful heuristic category for the study of those traditions in which a fundamental distinction is drawn between two styles of the religious life, two modes of pursuing spiritual fulfillment. One mode, for the majority of persons within a given tradition, involves the religious quest in conjunction with full participation in the ordinary life of society. In this mode one will assume the responsibilities of some role as a member of a functioning society while at the same time pursuing the goals of the religious life. A second mode is characterized by a different way of life, involving total absorption in the religious quest, generally in association with a renunciation or turning away from full participation in the ordinary life of society. The following discussion will explore such a distinction in these two basic styles of the religious life as they are manifest in selected religious traditions: Christianity (Roman Catholic, Eastern Orthodox, Protestant), Theravāda Buddhism, and Jainism. I shall then proceed to suggest the possibilities and limits of the category "laity" with respect to some other traditions: Hinduism, the religions of Japan, and Islam.

Christianity. The Roman Catholic tradition makes a clear differentiation between "laity" and "religious." The religious are those who take orders, and they comprise two groups, priests and monastics. The ecclesiastical use of the term *order,* which had been a designation prevalent in Roman civil life, included reference in the time of Tertullian (c. 155–220 CE) to both clergy and laity. By the sixth century CE, however, *order* was used to specify appointment by a bishop to a given office, with both authorization and responsibility to carry out the duties thereof. The distinction between the clergy and the laity is held to be divinely established. The priesthood, set apart by the sacrament of "holy orders" or ordination, is commissioned to fulfill the threefold function of the priestly office: teaching, directing and administering, and sanctifying. Thus, the priest as a member of the episcopate fulfills the divinely established mission of the church as teaching authority and sacramental agent, making available to the laity the means of God's grace through the sacraments. The laity, in turn, receive the teaching and the grace of God by participation in the worship and liturgy of the church and share the responsibility of fulfilling the church's mission in the world, the sphere of their activity. Through their participation in the affairs of the world, the truth and values of the church are to permeate society.

The distinction between laity and clergy in the Roman Catholic tradition is correlative with a distinction between church and world. The church is conceived as a *societas perfecta* but *inequalis*, with the *status clericalis* and the *laicalis*, each group having its respective rights and responsibilities. The clergy, with the right and responsibility of administering the sacraments, is ordained to a sacred vocation. The laity, who are to receive the sacraments and teaching and to obey the teaching, are to pursue their work in the world, the profane realm. Ecclesiastically, the church, the realm of the sacred, is given priority over the profane. Implied in this distinction is a valorization of the office of the clergy. The monastics, who renounce ordinary participation in the world (i.e., the profane) by taking the vows of celibacy, poverty, and obedience, are committed to the pursuit of spiritual perfection and fulfillment.

In the Eastern Orthodox church a similar distinction is made between clergy and laity, with ecclesiastical authority and the responsibility for administering the sacraments residing in the clergy. The designated roles of clergy and laity are manifest during the weekly ritual drama of the Divine Liturgy, in which the most sacred area of the sanctuary behind the iconostasis is entered by the priest as mediator between God and the people but is not accessible to laypersons. In at least two regards, however, the demarcation between laity and clergy was qualified. First, the formulation of the interpretation and explanation of the truth affirmed to have been revealed by Jesus Christ and contained in the Bible is accomplished through the ecumenical councils. This truth comprises the "holy tradition," as distinguished from the church tradition that developed through the centuries of church life. The authority of the councils rests on the understanding that they represent the consensus of the faithful and the conscience of the entire church, viewed as a sacramental unity of love inclusive of the laity as well as the clergy. Second, although since the seventh century CE only the celibate clergy and monks have been eligible for the episcopate, ordination through the holy orders of the priesthood may be conferred on married men, thus qualifying the distinction between clergy and laity.

A significantly different approach to the status and role of laity was evident in the Protestant Reformation that began in the sixteenth century. Martin Luther (1483–1546), in his *To the Christian Nobility*, rejected the hierarchical structure of the Roman Catholic church as well as the distinction between clergy and laity. The principle of the universal priesthood of all believers, viewed as an essential teaching of the word of God, provided a basis for insistence on the preeminence of the laity in Protestant churches. The vocation of ministry, viewed as necessary for the life and practice of the church, was the delegated responsibility of persons from the community of believers who were commissioned by the congregation to teach, to preach, to lead in worship, and to administer Holy Communion and baptism.

Although the administering of Holy Communion and baptism were held to be the right of every baptized Christian, those who were commissioned to minister became the officiants for ritual occasions. John Calvin (1509–1564) stressed the importance for all members of the church, who collectively were the laity, to so live that the reality of their state of election by God would be evident in their work in the world, which was to be pursued diligently. While the theological principle of the universal priesthood of all believers has been central to Protestantism, in practice the ordained ministry is accorded a priority in keeping with the importance of its teaching, preaching, and liturgical responsibilities, for which special training and education were needed.

The changes associated with the Protestant Reformation in social and political as well as religious life required the exercise of power and authority on the part of political officials, providing opportunity for them, as laity, to exercise influence in church affairs. Also, it was necessary for practical reasons for those set apart (i.e., the ministers) to assume responsibility for church administration. It should be noted that in the churches of the more radical "left-wing" Reformation and in free and dissenting churches (Anabaptists, Baptists, Congregationalists, Methodists, Universalists, and Unitarians), even greater prominence was given to the laity.

Buddhism. The relationship between the *bhikkhu*s (monks) and the *upāsakas*/*upāsikās* (laymen/laywomen) in the Theravāda Buddhism of the countries of Southeast Asia (e.g., Thailand, Laos, Burma, and Sri Lanka) is characterized by a full measure of reciprocity. Just as the members of the *bhikkhu sangha* provide exemplary models for the laity, teach the Dhamma, and fulfill priestly functions by presiding at festival and ritual occasions, so the laity provide for the material support of the monastic community. [*See* Saṃgha.] Indeed, reliance of the *bhikkhu sangha* on the laity for daily provisions of food, for the erecting and maintenance of the buildings within the monastic compound, for the supplying of basic necessities (especially through lay offerings during the Uposatha rituals) provides cherished opportunities for merit making on the part of the laity. [*See* Merit, *article on* Buddhist Concept.]

The support of the laity, so rendered, invites the *bhikkhu*s to sustain and extend their compassionate service to society. In this way the life of the *sangha* (the all-encompassing Buddhist community) is sustained through the reciprocity of *bhikkhu*s and laity. The laity, by assuming responsibility for maintaining a stable civil and political order as well as by filling the basic needs of the monastics, provide the *bhikku*s with the opportunity to seek spiritual perfection (liberation, *mokkha, nibbāna*) by being free from the struggle to provide the necessities of samsaric existence. The laity, by their merit making, make progress toward fulfillment themselves by assuring a favorable rebirth. It should be noted that there are two orders of laity in Theravāda Buddhism, those who have never taken the full monastic orders and former *bhikku*s, who are extended higher status than laypersons of the first category. (It is customary in certain Southeast Asian societies for young men to be ordained for a brief period prior to assuming the economic and social responsibilities of adulthood.) Such former *bhikku*s preside at certain ritual occasions that do not require an active *bhikku* as officiant.

Jainism. In Jainism a definitive distinction is made between the laity and monastics, the vows of the latter requiring the practice of a rigorous asceticism in a disciplined effort over numerous existences to free the *jīva* (soul) from contaminating *karman.* Since this asceticism involves the practice of *ahiṃsā* (noninjury to any living thing), the support of the laity in providing the necessities of life for Jain monks and nuns is indispensable. The principles of Jainism necessitate the avoidance of professions or vocations that involve the violation of *ahiṃsā,* and the nurturing of the qualities of honesty and industry is commended. As a consequence, Jain laypersons have generally pursued business and professional occupations, at which they have been very successful. Among the vows taken by the laity are those commending the sharing of wealth and the providing of support for monks and nuns. Although they are a comparatively small religious community (between two and three million adherents) that has never spread beyond India, the Jains have maintained their tradition over a millennium and a half, largely because of the vital interdependent relationship of the monastics and the laity.

Other Traditions. As has been noted earlier, the category "laity" has limitations with respect to its capacity to illuminate the structures and dynamics of certain religious traditions. It has little to contribute, for example, to a discussion of Judaism in the common era. To be sure, there did develop among the ancient Israelites a priestly group (as members of the tribe of Levi came to be regarded, and later, at the time of the Babylonian exile, the Jerusalem priests, or Zadokites) distinct from those who were not involved in performing priestly functions, hence laity. After the destruction of the Temple by the Romans (70 CE), the continuity of a priestly order became moot, and the tradition of a rabbinate developed. The rabbinic tradition in Judaism is a learned tradition. Rabbis may be viewed as scholars of the Jewish texts and traditions—a learned laity—whose authority as teachers rests in their competence as scholars of the tradition.

With respect to Confucian China also, the notion of laity has limited applicability. Although religious Taoism and the schools of Mahāyāna Buddhism (especially Pure Land, T'ien-t'ai and Chen-yen) observed distinctions between priests and laity, the Confucian tradition looked upon the secular as sacred, and authority was vested in the sage and the educated Confucian gentry. However, it may be useful to explore briefly the relevance of the notion of laity with reference to Hinduism in traditional India, the religio-social context of Japan, and the tradition of Islam.

Hindu traditions. The most highly structured and hierarchical social organization in which there is a definitive distinction between those who have responsibility for specific and formal religious functions and other members of society who do not (hence, "laity") is the caste system of traditional India, a system that is inseparably interwoven with classical Hinduism. The four basic divisions of society had their roots in the Vedic era (1500–800 BCE) and assumed definitive form by the sixth century BCE. The *Mānava Dharmaśāstra* (Laws of Manu; 200 BCE–200 CE) is a codification of the normative behavior and duties of castes that has informed traditional Hindu society. The *varṇa*s are hereditary; one's birth in a particular caste is determined by a repository of karmic consequences from previous lives in accordance with the law of *karman* (often referred to as the law of moral retribution). Each caste has its duty *(dharma);* it is one's social as well as religious responsibility to fulfill the *dharma* of one's caste. Caste may thus be viewed as class undergirded by religious sanction and metaphysical principle.

The inequality of the castes is evident in the definition of rights and responsibilities of each as well as in the restrictions concerning the relationships between persons of different castes. The *brahmaṇa*s, for example, whose duty it is to study the sacred texts (the Vedas), to teach, to perform sacrifices and other rituals, and to see that the stipulations concerning caste are honored, are at the top of the religio-social hierarchy. They are thought to be superior by virtue of their karmic repository and spiritual accomplishment.

The other groups of the social structure comprise what may be termed the laity. The *kṣatriya*s, next in descending hierarchical order, are the ruling, bureaucratic, and warrior caste. The third caste, the *vaiśya*s, is composed of artisans, merchants, traders, and farmers (although farming has been largely turned over to the *śūdra*s). These three castes comprise the "twice-born" groups, that is, those who may study the Vedas as they pass through the four *āśramas*, or stages of spiritual progression: student, householder, forest dweller (one in retreat), and *saṃnyāsa* (holy person). Persons in each of these top three castes may pursue an occupation of a lower caste, should circumstances require it. The fourth caste, the *śūdras*, are to do the manual labor of society and to serve the needs of the castes above them.

There is considerable distance—social, economic, and religious—between the *vaiśyas* and the *śūdras*. For example, the *śūdras* are prohibited from participating in Vedic ceremonies, traditionally are not to marry persons of a higher caste, may not engage in the duties of other castes, are denied, along with outcastes and women, entry into the *āśramas*, and so forth. Below the *śūdras* are those outside the caste system altogether, whose work includes the undesirable occupations of leather worker, hunter, latrine cleaner, handler of corpses, etc.) Each of these social groupings is divided into subcastes or subgroups, each with its own duties and responsibilities. Although this religio-social structure appears to be rigidly entrenched, it must be remembered that it served traditional India well over many centuries, providing for stability, order, and the sure accomplishment of the many and diverse tasks essential to the effective functioning of society. In no society have differentiated groups of laity been addressed by more specifically assigned duties and responsibilities. While changes in the caste system are occurring in contemporary urban India, largely in the direction of increased fluidity, its major characteristics persist in Indian villages, which comprises about 75 percent of the subcontinent.

Japanese religions. The sociological expression of religious community in the distinctive religio-social context that is Japan invites an exploration of the possible relevance of the notion of laity in interpreting Japanese religious traditions. Although a diversity of religions has emerged in Japanese culture, there is among Japanese people a permeating and encompassing sense of sacred community that is coextensive with national identity. Rooted in the indigenous traditions of Shintō, a sense of the continuity between the people, the land, the ancestors, the nation, and *kami* (sacred and mysterious power) provides a cosmic orientation that sustains and informs the Japanese whatever the particularities of religious affiliation. To be Japanese is "to participate in the task of unfolding the underlying meaning of the national community which is their sacred trust" (Kitagawa, 1968, p. 309). There are, of course, priestly officials who are distinguished from lay members of the major religions, including Sectarian and Shrine Shintō, Pure Land (Jōdo and Shin), Shingon, Tendai, and Nichiren Buddhism, and Christianity. But the vitality of these particular religions is dependent upon the participation and support of the laity associated with each.

In addition to the sense of identity and meaning that is derived from participation in these particular religious communities, there is an encompassing sense of what it means to be Japanese. This feeling is grounded in a historic apprehension of Japan as "a communal manifestation of the sacred" (Kitagawa, 1968, p. 309). In this latter sense, all of the people of Japan can be viewed as participants in the corporate manifestation of sacrality. One question addressing contemporary Japan is whether this corporate sense with a cosmic dimension can be maintained alongside the continuing development of Japan as a modern nation-state within which there is a plurality of particular religions. A phenomenon of considerable interest has been the emergence of new religious movements *(shinkō shūkyō)* in Japan during the nineteenth and twentieth centuries, and especially after World War II. These new religions have been, in the main, lay movements. It is not incidental that they have developed during a time of rapid cultural and political change. The new religious movements, whether of Shintō (Tenrikyō, Konkōkyō, Tenshō Kōtai Jingukyō), Buddhist (Sōka Gakkai or Nichiren Shōshū, Reiyūkai, Risshō Kōseikai) or Christian origin, have frequently been inspired by a shamanistic manifestation of *kami* in a charismatic leader (who usually becomes a primary source of authority); they also provide a strong sense of corporate solidarity, emphasize the active participation of laity, and assure the realization of lay values (e.g., health and prosperity).

Islam. Since there is no clergy as such in Islam, there is technically no laity either. The sources of authority in Islam—Qur'ān, *sunnah*, analogical reasoning *(qiyās)*, and consensus *(ijmā')*—are the foundation of all Muslim teaching, and there is the need for commentary and interpretation of these authoritative sources as well as of the *sharī'ah* (divine law). For Sunnī Islam (the normative religion of about 85 percent of Muslims, dominant in the Muslim world outside of Iran and southern Iraq) there are the imams (preachers and teachers of the Muslim law) and the jurists (specialists in *fiqh*, or jurisprudence, and the study of the *sharī'ah*). They have a special responsibility to the *ummah* (the community of Muslims) but no special privileges before God.

For Shī'ī Islam (dominant in Iran and southern Iraq, with minorities in Yemen, India, Pakistan, and Lebanon) there is held to be a line of divinely ordained and authoritative successors (imams) of Muḥammad through his cousin and son-in-law, 'Alī, as teachers of the faithful. Although there are variations among the Shī'īs with respect to the specific figures accepted as legitimate in the line of succession, there is a general expectation that the authentic imam, now hidden, will return as the Mahdi to establish justice. Meanwhile, authority is vested in leaders of the various Shīʿī groups, who are thought, in the interim, to act on behalf of the hidden imam. All Muslims, in submission and commitment to God, are to be obedient to the revelation contained in the Qur'ān and are to follow "the straight path." All are equal before God, with no distinctions in this regard among those within the *ummah*. Thus, to speak of "laity" and "clergy" within the community of Islam is to introduce categories that are more likely to distort than to illuminate the religio-social dynamics of this tradition.

BIBLIOGRAPHY

Chatterjee, Satischandra. *The Fundamentals of Hinduism.* 2d ed. Calcutta, 1970. A basic discussion of the cardinal aspects of traditional Hinduism.

Fingarette, Herbert. *Confucius: The Secular as Sacred.* New York, 1972. A discerning interpretation of the formative influence of Confucius and Confucianism on traditional China.

Ghurye, G. S. *Caste and Class in India.* 2d ed. Bombay, 1950. A definitive presentation of the history and features of the caste system in India.

Glasenapp, Helmuth von. *Der Jainismus, eine indische Erlösungsreligion.* Berlin, 1925. A classic and unsurpassed treatment of the thought and practice of Jainism that is worthy of careful attention even though it does not profit from the findings of the most recent scholarship.

Hodgson, Marshall G. S. *The Venture of Islam.* 3 vols. Chicago, 1974. A comprehensive and accomplished treatment of Islam as a religion and of Islamic culture and history.

Kitagawa, Joseph M. *Religion in Japanese History.* New York, 1966. One of the most complete and authoritative accounts of the religions of Japan portraying their historical developments.

Kitagawa, Joseph M. *Religions of the East.* Enl. ed. Philadelphia, 1968. An interpretation of the major religions of Asia focusing on the theme of religious community.

Kraemer, Hendrik. *A Theology of the Laity.* Philadelphia, 1958. A Protestant interpretation of the role and status of the laity within the Christian tradition.

Latourette, K. S. *A History of Christianity.* New York, 1953. A competent and informative account; a work of careful scholarship and artful, judicious interpretation.

Lester, Robert C. *Theravada Buddhism in Southeast Asia.* Ann Arbor, 1973. This study, informed by field experience, depicts the modern situation and dominant features of Theravāda Buddhism in the countries in which it is strongest.

Maclean, A. J. "Laity, Laymen." In *Encyclopaedia of Religion and Ethics,* edited by James Hastings, vol. 7. Edinburgh, 1914. Although dated, this article presents in a concise and lucid manner the origins and derivations of the concept "laity" in early Christianity.

Rahman, Fazlur. *Islam.* 2d ed. Chicago, 1979.

Rahner, Karl. *Theology for Renewal: Bishops, Priests, Laity.* New York, 1964. A provocative theological statement about the responsibilities of and opportunities afforded the various offices and constituent groups of the Roman Catholic church in the contemporary era.

Seltzer, Robert M. *Jewish People, Jewish Thought: The Jewish Experience in History.* New York, 1980. An account of Jewish intellectual history by a foremost scholar of the basic texts and seminal figures of the tradition.

Zimmer, Heinrich. *Philosophies of India.* Edited by Joseph Campbell. Princeton, 1951. Zimmer's study remains one of the most illuminating treatments of the classical thought systems of India.

F. STANLEY LUSBY

LAKES. Water, essential to life on earth, has occupied a preeminent place in religious thought and imagery, together with the land and sky. In many cultures it is considered to be procreative, a source of forms and of creative energy. The life-giving property of water has been projected in its almost universal perception as *fons et origo,* "spring and origin," the element that preceeds solid form and is the support of all earthly creation. [*See* Water.] In this context, from remote times to the present, among peoples who have perceived the world in terms of sacred and profane phenomena, springs, ponds, and lakes have figured importantly in the realm of water symbolism. In many regions of the world where lakes are major geographic features, they often have been the setting of cosmogonic myths and have been invested with many meanings, historical associations, and ritual functions.

The importance of sacred lakes in cultural context will be discussed by examining the ritualistic and mythic significance of two American lakes, Titicaca and Texcoco, associated with the Andean and Mexican civilizations respectively. The areas around both these lakes have been heavily populated in ancient, colonial, and modern times. Accounts of the ancient ceremonial pageantry, mythology, and man-made or natural sacred places in and around these lakes have been reported since the sixteenth-century Spanish conquest. Their meanings and functions in the evolution of native American civilizations continue to form an expanding field of inquiry in archaeology, art history, and ethnology, as well as in the history of religions.

Lake Titicaca. Lake Titicaca lies between southern Peru and northwestern Bolivia, where the Peruvian intermontane valleys and rugged cordilleras give way, at the 12,500-foot level, to the spacious Altiplano. This lake is impressive in its size and is the highest navigable body of water in the world. It sustained the agricultural and economic life of the surrounding areas. As the mainstay of complex societies, the religious meaning of the lake was most dramatically defined in the case of the civilizations of the Tiahuanaco (c. 100 to 1000 CE) and the Inca (c. 1400 to 1532 CE). Near Lake Titicaca, the principal archaeological ruins are those of Tiahuanaco, located in Bolivia a few miles inland from the southern shore. This was an important political and religious center whose influence spread over large section of Bolivia and southern Peru. The Titicaca basin came again with the orbit of an imperial state during the fifteenth century, when the Inca nation extended political control from the capital of Cuzco, some 200 miles to the north. At this time the Inca nation affirmed a spiritual and historical connection with the earlier Tiahuanaco state, and the Inca ruler Tupac Yupanqui visited the islands of Titicaca and Koati on the lake and commissioned shrines there. Inca interest in the lake was expressed in religious art and architecture, the location of major shrines, and the incorporation of ancient myths concerning the lake into their own mythology. By these means the lake's ancient significance continued to remain part of an imperial sacred geography.

In Andean religion the border between the notion of deities and the phenomena of nature was entirely open, with emphasis placed on direct communication with the elements of nature. The worship of *huacas* and major nature deities was a basic theme of Andean religion. A *huaca* was an object or phenomenon that was perceived to have unusual presence or power beyond the range of everyday life, where the sacred may have been manifested or where the memory of some past momentous event resided. It could be the locus of an oracle, a cave, or a curiously indented boulder where a people were thought to have emerged from the earth during the time of creation. This belief system was closely tied to the formation of sacred geographies and formed part of a cosmological religion with an array of gods associated with natural epiphanies.

The island of Titicaca, about seven miles long, serves as a good example of how a lake figured in Andean sacred geography. Adolph Bandelier's explorations and interpretive report of 1910 remain fundamental to our understanding of the island and its ruins. Toward the northern end of the island there is a construction, and it was across this isthmus that a precinct wall was built to separate sacred from proface space. Early Spanish accounts record that three gates were arranged in succession here and that confessions were required of all who sought to pass through. The religious and ritual focus of the site lay beyond the gates. The sacred feature was comprised of a great rock about 25 feet high and 190 feet long, with a broad plaza or assembly ground built in front. This was the chief *huaca* of the island, named in Aymara *titi* ("wild cat") *kaka* ("rock"), the latter word a substitution for *kala* ("stone"). The shrine rock was thus the source for the name of the lake itself. Also included within this sacred precinct were burial cysts with offerings and paraphernalia, storehouses, and residences for cult priests, officers, and aides. In this context it is important to mention the Pilco-Kayma building on Titicaca Island, which corresponds to another structure called Inyak-Uyu on Koati Island nearby. The design and siting of these two buildings reveal an important aspect of Andean religion. Both buildings stand near the eastern shores of their respective islands, and the principal apartments in each ruin, with the most elaborate entrances and prominent niches, open toward the majestic snowcapped peaks of Sorata and its neighbors across the lake on the Bolivian (eastern) side. These grand mountains even today continue to be worshiped by the people in their vicinity. Considered in relation to Lake Titacaca and the island of Titicaca with its huge rock *huaca*, the mountains complete the *imago mundi* of Altiplano peoples.

The Inca people paid homage to Titicaca Rock as the dominant and central feature associated with the lake. This is illustrated by Spanish written accounts of an annual pilgrimage made to the island across the straits from a shrine on nearby Copacabana Peninsula. In that festival, which centered around solar events, two principal idols were brought in reed boats from Copacabana: a statue of the sun father, Inti, and one of the moon mother, Mama Quilla. These two effigies were regarded as husband and wife, and they were transported with other idols dedicated to thunder and other natural forces. The sun was represented in the form of an Inca of gold embellished with much brilliant jewelry; the moon was represented as a queen of silver; and thunder was a man of silver, also very brilliant. Once landed, they were placed in splendid litters decorated with flowers, plumage, and plates of gold and silver, and they were carried to the sacred enclosure. The idols were set up in a plaza, almost certainly in front of the sacred rock. After having placed the idols, the attendant Inca priests and nobles prostrated themselves, first worshiping the effigy of the sun, then that of the moon, afterward that of the thunder, and then the others. The prostrations were concluded by blowing kisses to the images and to the *huaca* itself. Dances, banquets, and amusements were then held to close the festival.

Even today, Titicaca Island is known as the "island of the sun," while Koati is the "island of the moon." Yet it is clear that, although the cult of these celestial bodies was maintained upon the islands by the Inca, they remained subordinate to the primary cult of Titicaca Rock itself.

What then, was the meaning of the sacred rock, the dominant icon of the island? What was its relationship to the surrounding waters of the lake? The answers lie in mythology. Bandelier's compilation of myths recorded by the sixteenth-century Spanish chronicler Cieza de León include a text in which the Indians tell of an event that occurred before the Incas ruled in these lands. Long ago, they went without seeing the sun for a long time and suffered greatly, so they prayed to their gods, begging them for light. The sun then rose in great splendor from the island of Titicaca, within the great lake of the Collao (the ancient name of province), so that all were delighted. Then from the south there came a white man of large size who showed great authority and inspired veneration. This powerful man made heights out of level plains and flat plains out of great heights, and created springs in live rock. Recognizing in him such power, they called him Maker of All Created Things, Beginning Thereof, and Father of the Sun. They also said that he gave men and animals their existence and that they derived from him great benefits. This being, called Ticciviracocha, was regarded as the supreme creator. Another myth, recorded by Juan de Betanzos before Ceiza, also connects two successive "creations" of the world by "Con Tici Viracocha" to Lake Titicaca (Bandelier, 1910, pp. 298–299). In yet another version, the sun and moon were said to have risen from Titicaca itself. In this mythological context, "wild cat rock" must be seen as a cosmogonic place of origin.

Rising from the windswept sheet of reflecting water, the island hills and promontories are removed from the sphere of ordinary life. On the ridges, marine fossil strata underscore the theme of aquatic emergence at this unusual site. The placement of the *huaca* and the relationship of buildings to the distant mountains are joined with ritual and mythic imagery in a powerful metaphor of man and land. The sense of place, of being "at the center," is also linked to notions of history, for the ancient myths and the architectural features of the Pilco-Kayma building (designed in an archaic style) reminded the Inca of Tiahuanaco and established a succession to that old imperial tradition. In this respect, the Inca shrine incorporated a sense of the past and signaled territorial possession. Woven into these levels of meaning was a still more fundamental theme. Most of all, the setting was designed to bring to mind the time and place of the beginnings. The sacred lake was the primordial natural icon, a reminder of *illud tempus*. Passive in the mythic imagery, the lake formed the fluid cosmogonic field from which all forms came forth in darkness. Upholding the island birthplace of the sun and moon, Lake Titicaca, as the home of Viracocha, who gave form to mountains, plains, and people, was the element from which the world itself was made.

Lake Texcoco and the Valley of Mexico. Rimmed by mountains and snowcapped volcanoes, the Valley of Mexico is a spacious basin that formerly contained a system of shallow interconnected lakes. The central lake, known as Texcoco, was saline from evaporation, but the southern lakes of Chalco-Xochimilco were fed by abundant aquafers that issued from the base of the steep Ajusco Mountains. To the north, lakes Zumpango-Xaltocán depended more on seasonal rain, but there is evidence that in ancient times the surrounding hills and open fields were watered by abundant springs and streams. In a collective sense, the entire set of lakes may be referred to as Lake Texcoco.

By the first century CE, the city of Teotihuacán began to dominate the lesser settlements in the Texcoco lakeshore region. A powerful manufacturing, trading, and religious center of some one hundred thousand people, Teotihuacán became the center of a trade network that ramified to the most distant parts of Mesoamerica. With the violent eclipse of this metropolis in the seventh century, power was transferred to other capitals throughout the neighboring highlands. The old ascendancy of the Valley of Mexico was not restored until the fifteenth century with the rise of the Méxica-Aztec capital of Tenochtitlán and its allied neighbor, the city of Texcoco. Built on an island and reclaimed marshes near the western shore of Lake Texcoco, Tenochtitlán became the most feared and powerful city, the seat of the most powerful empire in Mesoamerican history.

An agricultural economy, supplemented by fishing and the gathering of natural products, remained fundamental to urban life throughout the long history of the valley, and the problem of maintaining fruitful relationships between man and nature formed an underpinning of religious life. To express this relationship in symbolic form, monumental works of art and architecture were built as stage sets and memorials for seasonal rites as well as the important ceremonies of government and war. The ruined pyramids of Teotihuacán were the largest in Mesoamerica, and long after the city was destroyed they were visited in pilgrimage by the rulers of the later Méxica-Aztec state. In the middle of the Méxica-Aztec capital, Tenochtitlán, a new pyramid and attendant temples were built in a great quadrangular enclosure, with gates at the cardinal directions. The main pyramid, representing a symbolic mountain with dual shrines to the rain god, Tlaloc, and the Méxica national ancestor hero, Huitzilopochtli, established the vertical *axis mundi* of the cosmological design. A similar but smaller ritual center was constructed in the allied city of Texcoco.

In addition to such urban monuments, other shrines and temples were scattered throughout the valley on mountaintops, in caves, by springs and rivers, and in the waters of the lake itself. These places were the shrines of nature deities whose cults were also represented in the temples of the city. These cults, in addition to those of conquered nations, were woven into the religious fabric of the city in an effort to form an embracing state religion. The many divinities were impersonated by ritual performers on festival occasions. The costumes often visually corresponded to the cult names themselves: for example, Chalchiuhtlicue, a female deity of water on the ground, that is, a lake, river, or spring, would appear with a green-painted skirt or a skirt sewn with pieces of jade. *Chalchiuhtlicue* means "jade skirt" in the Nahuatl language. Thus the costume was an ideogram, and the impersonator became a living, moving metaphor naming the element of nature that she represented.

An illustration of this custom is recorded by the sixteenth-century chronicler Alvarado Tezozomoc, who describes a ceremony that took place to inaugurate an aqueduct built from mainland springs to the island of Tenochtitlán. The emperor Ahuizotl instructed two high priests to be attired as Chalchiuhtlicue and go welcome the incoming water. As the water arrived, they sacrificed quail and burnt copal incense. After drinking, the chief priest spoke directly to the water: "be very welcome, my lady, I come to receive you because you shall be coming to your home, to the middle of the reeds of Mexico-Tenochtitlan" (Alvarado Tezozomoc, 1975). The passage shows how a deity impersonator would also address the natural element whose symbolic form he represented. In this way of thought, the elements themselves were seen to have life-force and were considered inherently sacred. Lake Texcoco was spoken of as Tonanhueyatl, "our mother great water," a provider of moisture to agricultural fields who was teeming with edible algae, aquatic plants of various kinds, mosquito eggs (also edible), shrimp, a diversity of fish, as well as frogs, ducks, and other aquatic birds. As a sustainer of life, the lake was looked upon as the mother of Tenochtitlán.

Pilgrimages were made by the Aztec and their neighbors to sources of water at springs, streams, and lakes, as well as in hidden caves and ravines on cloudy mountaintops. [*See also* Caves.] At such places it was common practice to offer green stones and jewelry as well as sacrifices. A preoccupation with fertility was paramount among the reasons why water was so widely venerated. Nowhere was this more apparent than in an elaborate annual pilgrimage made by the ruler of Tenochtitlán and three allied rulers to shrines on the summit of Mount Tlaloc and in the middle of Lake Texcoco. The relationship between these two water shrines shows that no part of the natural setting could be considered in isolation, and that the imagery of sacred geography, based upon the ecological structure of the land, established fundamental integrating bonds between society and nature.

The bonds between man and nature are evident with the sequence of rituals, beginning at Mount Tlaloc. The archaeological ruins of the Tlaloc temple are located below the summit of this mountain, close by a grassy vale where springs are still located. Here the ruins of a square courtyard enclosed by masonry are entered via a long narrow walkway that had a controlling function in ritual procedure. Within, there was a flat-roofed chamber housing the main Tlaloc effigy, around which were clustered a group of lesser idols. These were intended to represent the other mountains and cliffs surrounding Mount Tlaloc. Thus the arrangement was a microcosm of the land itself, the symbol of a geographical setting where rain and springs were seen to originate.

This shrine was visited in late April, at the height of the dry season, by the ruler of Tenochtitlán and the allied rulers of Texcoco, Tlacopán, and Xochimilco (the number four was a ritual requirement). The pilgrimage was the duty and privilege of royalty alone. The ceremonies opened with the sacrifice of a male child, followed by a hierarchical procession in which the kings approached the idol in order of rank (Tenochtitlán first). One by one, they proceeded to dress the idols with splendid headdresses, breechcloths, various mantles, jewelry, and so on, according to the status of each monarch.

The next phase again involved a procession in order of rank, as the rulers approached with food for a sumptuous repast. After the food was put before the images, a priest entered to sprinkle everything with blood from the sacrificed child. The blood offering at Mount Tlaloc had a contractual function. As chief ritualists of their respective nations, the rulers set in motion a vital principle that unified the rain and mountains with their people, circulating life and energy throughout the social and ecological orders. Correspondingly, the structure of political alliances was reinforced through sacramental rites.

While these events were taking place, another rite was unfolding in the main religious precinct of Tenochtitlán. A large tree was brought in and erected in the courtyard of the dominating pyramid, on the side of the Tlaloc shrine. This tree, called Tota ("father"), was surrounded by four smaller trees in a symbolic forest designed according to the center and the cardinal directions. A girl attired as Chalchiuhtlicue to represent the great lake and other springs and creeks was brought to sit within the forest. A long chant with drums was then begun around the seated figure, until news was finally received that the rulers had completed the Mount Tlaloc offerings and were now at the Texcocan lakeshore, ready to embark in their canoes. At this time, the Chalchiuhtlicue impersonator was placed in a canoe at Tenochtitlán, and the Tota tree was also taken up and bound upon a raft. Accompanied by music and chanting, a vast fleet of canoes filled with men, women, and children embarked with the symbolic figures to a sacred place within the lake called Pantitlan. This was the site of a great spring, an aquifer that welled up from the lake bottom with remarkable turbulence. At this site the two processions met and, as the rulers and population watched, the Tota tree was unbound and set up in the muddy lake bottom by the spring. The Chalchiuhtlicue child was then sacrificed and her blood was offered to the waters, along with as much jewelry as had been given on Mount Tlaloc. The theme of water as *fons et origo* was strikingly expressed, incorporating the renewal of vegetation and of life itself at the height of the dry season. The ceremonies were then concluded and everyone departed, leaving the Tota to stand along with others of previous years. Diego Durán (1971) remarks that the peasantry went on to the preparation of the fields, continuing to make offerings at local springs and rivulets.

The imagery of this long and remarkable sequence of ceremonies was directly based on the ecological structure of the highland basin. The relationship of mountains to rain, mountains to springs, and springs to the great lake was symbolically acknowledged in covenants and pleas for water, crops, and vegetation. This communal ceremony, in which the major rulers and lords of the valley participated, affirmed a topographic metaphor: *atl tepetl* (lit., "water-mountain"), which means "city" or "community." In the Nahuatl language, the habitat of man was defined in terms of landscape elements that made life possible. The structure of the ceremony and the metaphor it brought to mind represent a powerful integrating principle that was known and recognized by everyone. Rooted in what was seen and experienced in the land itself, the imagery of the Tlaloc-Chalchihuitlicue rites represented a sense of order in the highland way of life and symbolically legitimized the governments with which it was identified. [*See also* Mountains.]

Conclusion. In the Andes and Mexico, sacred lakes formed part of religious systems that grew out of landscapes. The patterns become evident upon considering the ethnohistoric texts, archaeological monuments, and new ethnological reports of religious practices in the context of topography. At the time of the Inca and Méxica-Aztec empires, lakes were seen as sources of life where the generative, procreative qualities of water were especially concentrated. The properties of lakes were acknowledged in myths and metaphors, as in Andean cosmogonic stories and the *atl tepetl* theme of highland Mexico; in the powerful imagery of ritual; and in the design and disposition of monuments in the city and the country. These symbolic forms of representation celebrated the dynamic relationship of lakes and other features of the natural and man-made environment.

These concerns were fundamentally bound with fertility and agriculture, but the imagery of lakes was also creatively employed by ruling elites in building imperial domains. Myths, rites, and monuments affirmed territorial claims, consolidated alliances, and validated the larger interests and policies of state organizations. Rooted in cosmogony and the seasonal cycle, the symbolism of lakes was inseparably interwoven with the imagery of history. In New World Indian religions, the order of the cosmos and the structure of the state were inseparably bound.

BIBLIOGRAPHY

Alvarado Tezozomoc, Fernando de. *Crónica mexicana.* Mexico City, 1975.

Bandelier, Adolph F. *The Islands of Titicaca and Koati.* New York, 1910.

Barlow, Robert Hayward. *The Extent of the Empire of the Culhna Mexica.* Berkeley, 1949.

Bastien, Joseph W. *Mountain of the Condor: Metaphor and Ritual in an Andean Ayllu.* Saint Paul, 1978.

Bennett, W. C. *Excavations at Tihuanaco.* New York, 1934.

Betanzos, Juan de. *Suma y narración de los Incas.* Edited by Márcos Jiménez de la Espada. Madrid, 1880.

Boone, Elizabeth, ed. *The Aztec Templo Mayor.* Washington, D.C., forthcoming.

Carrión, Rebecca C. "El culto al agua en el antiguo Perú." *Revista del Museo Nacional de Antropología y Arqueología* (Lima) 11 (1955).

Cieza de León, Pedro de. *Segunda parte de la crónica del Perú, que trata del sēnorió de los Incas Yupanquis y de sus grandes hechos y gobernación,* vol. 5. Edited by Márcos Jiménez de la Espada. Madrid, 1880.

Cobo, Bernabé. *Historia del Nuevo Mundo.* 4 vols. Edited by Mŕcos Jiménez de la Espada. Seville, 1890–1895.

Demarest, Arthur Andrew. *Viracocha: The Nature and Antiquity of the Andean High God.* Cambridge, Mass., 1981.

Díaz del Castillo, Bernal. *The Discovery and Conquest of Mexico.* Translated by A. P. Mandslay. Edited by Eudora Garrett. Mexico City, 1953.

Durán, Diego. *Book of the Gods and Rites and The Ancient Calendar.* Translated and edited by Fernando Horcasitas and Doris Heyden. Norman, Okla., 1971.

Eliade, Mircea. *Patterns in Comparative Religion.* New York, 1958.

Kolata, Alan L. "The South Andes." In *Ancient South Americans,* edited by Jesse D. Jennings, pp. 241–285. San Francisco, 1983.

Million, René, ed. *Urbanization at Teotihuacán, Mexico,* vol. 1, *The Teotihuacán Map.* Austin, 1973.

Posnansky, Arthur. *Tiahuanacu, the Cradle of American Man.* 4 vols. Translated by James F. Shearer. New York, 1945–1958.

Reinhardt, Johan. *The Nazca Lines: A New Perspective on Their Origin and Meaning.* Lima, 1985.

Rowe, John Howland. "Inca Culture at the Time of the Spanish Conquest." In *Handbook of South American Indians,* vol. 2, pp. 183–330. Washington, D.C., 1946.

Sahagún, Bernardino de. *Historia general de las cosas de la Neuva Espana* (compiled 1569–1582; first published 1820). Translated by Arthur J. O. Anderson and Charles E. Dibble as *Florentine Codex: General History of the Things of New Spain.* 13 vols. in 12. Santa Fe, N.Mex., 1950–1982. See especially book 1, *The Gods;* book 2, *The Ceremonies;* and book 12, *The Conquest.*

Soldi, Ana Maria. "El agua en el pensamiento andino." *Boletín de Lima* (1980).

Sullivan, Thelma D. "Tlaloc: A New Etymological Interpretation of the God's Name, and What It Reveals of His Essence and Nature." In *Proceedings of the Fortieth International Congress of Americanists,* vol. 2, pp. 213–219. Rome, 1974.

Townsend, Richard F. "Pyramid and Sacred Mountain." In *Ethnoastronomy and Archaeoastronomy in the American Tropics,* edited by Anthony F. Aveni and Gary Urton, pp. 37–62. New York, 1982.

Townsend, Richard F. "Deciphering the Nazca World." *Museum Studies* 11 (1985): 116–139.

RICHARD F. TOWNSEND

LAKOTA RELIGION. *Lakota* is the native term for those Plains Indians conventionally known as the Teton or the Western Sioux, the latter of which is a pejorative name, meaning "snakes," applied to them by their Algonquian-speaking enemies, the Ojibwa. *Lakota,* the preferred term, also designates the language spoken by the seven divisions of the Teton: Oglala, Sicangu (or Brulé), Mnikowoju, Hunkpapa, Itazipco (or Sans Arcs), Oohenupa, and Sihasapa. These Lakota speakers, who occupied a number of semisedentary villages in Minnesota before moving onto the Great Plains in the early eighteenth century, represented the largest division of the political body known as the Oceti Šakowin ("seven fireplaces"). Their migration to the Great Plains coincided with the dissolution of the Seven Fireplaces.

Regarded as the "typical" Indians of the Plains, the Lakota were an equestrian, nomadic people who lived in tipis and hunted buffalo in what is now Montana, Wyoming, North and South Dakota, Nebraska, and parts of adjacent states. They participated in the great wars of the West under such leaders as Red Cloud, Crazy Horse, Sitting Bull, Gall, and Rain in the Face, and they were notably responsible for the annihilation of George Armstrong Custer's forces at the Battle of the Little Bighorn on 25 June 1876. The Lakota, along with other Plains tribes, signed a treaty with the federal government at Fort Laramie, Wyoming, in 1868, after which they were placed on reservations. As a result of their participation in the famous Ghost Dance movement of 1888–1890, several hundred Lakota men, women, and children were massacred at Wounded Knee, South Dakota, located on the Pine Ridge reservation. As of 1984, approximately one hundred thousand Lakota resided on reservations in South Dakota, North Dakota, Montana, and Saskatchewan.

The Religious System. The emigration from the Great Lakes to the Great Plains and the dissolution of the Seven Fireplaces resulted in a number of changes in Lakota religion. A cosmology that exhibited the characteristics of a village-dwelling, lacustrine culture remained integral to the religion of the eastern division of Dakota speakers (*L*akota and *D*akota are dialect markers), but the Lakota abandoned many of their earlier beliefs to accommodate a new nomadic way of life that often subjected them to long periods of starvation. The focal points of the new religion involved the propitiation of supernaturals in order to ensure success in buffalo hunting and protection from an unpredictable and often hostile environment.

Cosmology. The published works of James R. Walker, a physician at Pine Ridge, South Dakota, between 1896 and 1914, provide most of the information on Lakota cosmology, although some of his interpretations are specious. His reconstruction outlines a cosmological system in which prior to the creation of earth, gods resided in an undifferentiated celestial domain and humans lived in an indescribably subterranean world devoid of culture. Chief among the gods are the following: Takuškanškan ("something that moves"); the Sun, who is married to the Moon, with whom he has one daughter, Wohpe ("falling star"); Old Man and Old Woman, whose daughter Ite ("face") is married to Wind, with whom she has four sons, the Four Winds. Among numerous other named spirits, both benevolent and malevolent, the most important is Inktomi ("spider"), the devious trickster. Inktomi conspires with Old Man and Old Woman to increase their daughter's status by arranging an affair between the Sun and Ite. The discovery of the affair by the Sun's wife leads to a number of punishments by Takuškanškan, who gives the Moon her own domain and, in the process of separating her from the Sun, initiates the creation of time. Old Man, Old Woman, and Ite are sent to earth, but the latter is separated from Wind, who, along with the Four Winds and a fifth wind presumed to be the child of the adulterous affair, establishes space. The daughter of the Sun and the Moon, Wohpe, also falls to earth and later resides with South Wind, the paragon of Lakota maleness, and the two adopt the fifth wind, called Wamniomni ("whirlwind").

The emergence. Alone on the newly formed earth, some of the gods become bored, and Ite prevails upon Inktomi to find her people, the Buffalo Nation. In the form of a wolf, Inktomi travels beneath the earth and discovers a village of humans. Inktomi tells them about the wonders of the earth and convinces one man, Tokahe ("the first"), to accompany him to the surface. Tokahe does so and upon reaching the surface through a cave, now presumed to be Wind Cave in the Black Hills of South Dakota, marvels at the green grass and blue sky. Inktomi and Ite introduce Tokahe to buffalo meat and soup and show him tipis, clothing, and hunting utensils. Tokahe returns to the subterranean village and appeals to six other men and their families to travel with him to the earth's surface. When they arrive, they discover that Inktomi has deceived them: buffalo are scarce, the weather has turned bad, and they find themselves starving. Unable to return to their home, but armed with a new knowledge about the world, they survive to become the founders of the Seven Fireplaces.

The Seven Sacred Rites. Falling Star appears to the Lakota as a real woman during a period of starvation. She is discovered by two hunters, one of whom lusts for her. He is immediately covered by a mist and reduced to bones. The other hunter is instructed to return to his camp and tell the chief and people that she, Ptehincalaskawin ("white buffalo calf woman"), will appear to them the next day. He obeys, and a great council tipi is constructed. White Buffalo Calf Woman presents to the people a bundle containing the sacred pipe, and she tells them that in time of need they should smoke the pipe and pray to Wakantanka for help. The smoke from the pipe will carry their prayers upward. She then instructs them in the great Wicoȟ'an Wakan Šakowin ("seven sacred rites"), most of which continue to form the basis of Lakota religion.

1. *The Sweat Lodge.* Called Inikagapi ("to renew life"), the Sweat Lodge ceremony is held in a domical structure made of saplings, which is symbolic of the shape of the Lakota universe. Heated stones are placed in a central hole and water poured over them by a medicine man to create steam. The purpose of the ceremony is to revivify persons spiritually and physically, and during the ceremony benevolent spirits enter the darkened sweat lodge and instruct the medicine man about curing his patients.

2. *The Vision Quest.* Hanbleceya ("crying for a vision") is an ordeal undergone by an individual under the supervision of a medicine man. A person elects to go on a vision quest for personal reasons and pledges to stay on an isolated hill, usually lying in a shallow hole for one to four days without food or water. With only a blanket and a pipe, the individual prays for a vision, which usually comes toward the end of his ordeal. The significance of the vision is then later interpreted by the medicine man.

3. *Ghost Keeping.* It is believed that when a person dies his soul lingers for a year. Wanagi Wicagluha ("ghost keeping") is a ceremony performed by a mourner, especially one grieving for a favorite child. The spirit is ritually fed every day and after one year is finally freed in an elaborate ceremony.

4. *The Sun Dance.* The most important annual religious ritual, Wiwanyang Wacipi ("gaze-at-the-sun dance"), was held immediately before the communal buffalo hunt each summer. Principal dancers pledged to hang suspended from a sacred pole by skewers of wood inserted into their chests or to drag buffalo skulls skewered to the flesh over their scapulae. This was also a time when women offered bits of flesh from their arms, and medicine men pierced the ears of children. [*For further discussion, see* Sun Dance.]

5. *Making Relatives.* Hunka, the ritual for "making relatives," created an adoptive tie between two unrelated persons, one that was stronger than a kin tie. It was usually performed to unite an older and a younger person as ritual "father" and "son."

6. *Puberty Ceremony.* At the onset of a girl's first menses, the ritual called Išnati Awicalowanpi ("they sing over her menses") was performed to ensure that the girl would grow up to have all the virtues of a Lakota woman.

7. *Throwing the Ball.* Tapa Wankayeyapi ("throwing the ball upward") was a game in which a young girl threw a ball upward and several people vied to catch it. The winner was considered more fortunate than the others, for the ball was symbolically equated with knowledge.

Essential Beliefs. Lakota religion is reincarnative. Life is seen as a series of recurrent travels. People live through four generations: childhood, adolescence, maturity, and old age. When a person dies, one of his four "souls" travels along the Wanagi Tacanku ("spirit path," i.e., the Milky Way) southward, where it meets with an old woman who adjudicates its earthly virtues, directing it either to the spirit world, a hazy analog of earthly life where there is an unending supply of buffalo and where people rejoin their kin, or back to earth where they live as ghosts to haunt others and entice the living to join them. Other aspects of these four souls are invested into unborn fetuses, thus giving them life. Twins are particularly auspicious and are considered intellectually mature at birth.

The sacred lore is the domain of *wicaša wakan* ("sacred men"), locally known as medicine men, who conduct all the religious ceremonies. The most important symbol is the sacred pipe that is smoked to Wakantanka (sometimes translated as "Great Spirit" or "Great Mystery," but better left untranslated), a single name representing sixteen important supernatural beings and powers, half of which existed prior to the creation of the earth, half as a result of it. Wakantanka is metaphorically called Tobtob ("four times four") in the sacred language of the medicine men, underscoring the belief that all sacred things come in fours. The root *wakan* ("sacred") is a dynamic concept indicating the potentiality of anything to become transformed from a secular to a sacred state.

Inktomi, the trickster, named all things, taught culture to humans, and remains on the earth to continually deceive them. A set of Inktomi tales called *ohunkankan* ("myth"), in which Inktomi's pranks are ultimately turned against himself, serve as lessons in morality for young children.

Contemporary Religion. All of the Seven Sacred Rites are still performed, with the exception of Tapa Wankayeyapi. A more vital religious practice known as Yuwipi has become popular in the twentieth century. Based on a number of cultural concepts related to a buffalo-hunting way of life combined with problems confronting contemporary Indians on reservations, this ritual is performed in a darkened room under the supervision of a "Yuwipi man." The object of the ritual is to cure persons and at the same time to pray for the general welfare of all Indian people and for long life for the kinship group to which the adepts belong.

BIBLIOGRAPHY

Brown, Joseph Epes, ed. *The Sacred Pipe.* Norman, Okla., 1953. An interview with the Lakota medicine man Nickolas Black Elk on the Seven Sacred Rites, inspired by earlier interviews by John G. Neihardt.

Deloria, Ella C., ed. *Dakota Texts.* New York, 1932. The best bilingual compilation of Lakota mythological texts by an author who was both a Lakota and an anthropologist.

Densmore, Frances. *Teton Sioux Music.* Washington, D.C., 1918. Contains a number of interviews with Hunkpapa medicine men, transcriptions and translations of sacred songs, and vivid ethnographic accounts of most of the sacred ceremonies.

Hassrick, Royal B. *The Sioux: Life and Customs of a Warrior Society.* Norman, Okla., 1964. A comprehensive account of Lakota culture prior to the reservation period.

Neihardt, John G. *Black Elk Speaks* (1932). Reprint, Lincoln, Nebr., 1979. Although only a few chapters relate to Lakota religion, this interview between Nickolas Black Elk and the poet Neihardt has become an increasingly popular reference to American Indian spirituality in general. The problem lies in the reader's inability to distinguish between what is Neihardt's and what is Black Elk's. Brown's interview with Black Elk is much more authentically Lakota, but both Brown and Neihardt neglect to point out that Black Elk was a Catholic lay catechist at the time of the interviews.

Powers, William K. *Oglala Religion.* Lincoln, Nebr., 1977. A structural analysis of Oglala myth and ritual and their relationships to other aspects of Lakota culture such as kinship and political organization.

Powers, William K. *Yuwipi: Vision and Experience in Oglala Ritual.* Lincoln, Nebr., 1982. A translation of an entire Yuwipi ritual showing the relationship between Yuwipi and the Sweat Lodge ceremony and the vision quest. It also contains a chapter on the history of the development of Yuwipi at Pine Ridge.

Riggs, Stephen Return. *Tah-koo Wah-kan: The Gospel among the Dakotas.* Boston, 1869. Written by a missionary who spoke Dakota fluently, this account gives some indication of the early Dakota foundations of Lakota religion. Paternalistic, but insightful.

Walker, James R. *The Sun Dance and Other Ceremonies of the Oglala Division of the Teton Dakota.* New York, 1917. A seminal publication on the cosmology and rituals of the Oglala. Some of the myths should be read judiciously as some of them are obvious romantic reconstructions of Lakota myth from a classical Greco-Roman perspective.

Walker, James R. *Lakota Belief and Ritual.* Edited by Raymond J. DeMallie and Elaine Jahner. Lincoln, Nebr., 1980. Previously unpublished papers of J. R. Walker. Mainly interviews with Oglala men, some of whom were medicine men.

Wissler, Clark. *Societies and Ceremonial Associations in the Oglala Division of Teton Dakota.* New York, 1912. One of a number of monographs by the former curator of the American Museum of Natural History on Lakota religion. In particular, this monograph addresses the nature and function of "dream cults," and harbingers of the modern Yuwipi.

William K. Powers

LAKṢMĪ. *See* Goddess Worship, *article on* The Hindu Goddess.

LAMAISM. *See* Tibetan Religions.

LAMOTTE, ÉTIENNE (1903–1983), Belgian specialist in Indian Buddhist doctrine and history. A Roman Catholic priest, Lamotte was a professor at the Catholic University of Louvain. His two most significant achievements in the field of Buddhist studies were his *Histoire du bouddhisme indien des origines à l'ère Śaka* (1958), the most elaborate work thus far on the history of early Buddhism, and his *Le traité de la grande vertu de sagesse,* (1944–1980), an annotated translation of a large portion of the *Ta chih tu lun* (Skt., **Mahāprajñāpāramitopadeśa*), which is an encyclopedic treatise on Mahāyāna Buddhism attributed to Nāgārjuna and translated into Chinese by Kumārajīva.

His ten years of collaborative work with Louis de La Vallée Poussin (1869–1938) were more decisive in the formation of Lamotte's thought than were his short periods of study in Rome (1926–1927) and Paris (1931–1932). If the monumental writings of these two masters of the French-language school of Buddhist philology are compared, one realizes a great complementarity in their achievements. La Vallée Poussin's glittering genius is swift and full of illuminating and often paradoxical insights into every part of his field of study. Lamotte's genius is reflected in the remarkable organization of the exegetical work that formed his voluminous books. Each element of his books—chapter, paragraph, footnote (often constituting a comprehensive monograph)—contributes to the brightness of the synthesis of a broad range of information by diffusing its own particular light.

Lamotte's exegetical work centered on doctrinally important texts, mostly of the *śāstra* (treatise) type preserved primarily in Tibetan or Chinese. At first attracted to the Yogācāra (Idealist) school, he produced a study (1935) on the *Saṃdhinirmocana Sūtra* and a commentary (1938–1939) on Asaṅga's *Mahāyānasaṃgraha* entitled *La somme du grande véhicule d'Asaṅga (Mahāyānasaṃgraha).* His interest shifted to Vasubandhu's *Karmasiddhiprakaraṇa* and to the seventeenth chapter of Candrakīrti's *Prasannapadā*, a commentary to the *Madhyamakakārikās* by Nāgārjuna. This last work initiated his choice of Mādhyamika texts for the remainder of his career. In addition to the already mentioned *Traité (Mahāprajñāpāramitopadeśa),* he translated two related Mahāyāna *sūtras*: the *Vimalakīrtinirdeśa* (1962; translated into English as *The Teaching of Vimalakīrti,* 1976) and the *Śuramgamasamādhi* (1965).

Lamotte's *Histoire du bouddhisme indien des origines à l'ère Śaka* is an epoch-making synthesis based on multilingual documents (including Greek and Chinese) and incorporating the latest developments in Indian epigraphy, archaeology, and linguistics. The first volume traces the development of Buddhism up to the emergence of the Maitreya cult. The second volume was never finished. Some parts of this projected second volume, however, have been published separately, including "Mañjuśrī," *T'oung pao* 48 (1960): 1–96, and "Vajrapaṇi," in *Mélanges Demiéville,* vol. 1 (1966), pp. 156–168.

BIBLIOGRAPHY

Biographical and bibliographical information on Lamotte is available in the *Notice* published by the Imprimerie Orientaliste (Louvain, 1972). This work has been supplemented by D. Donnet's "L'œuvre de Mgr É. Lamotte," in *Indianisme et bouddhisme: Mélanges offerts à Mgr Étienne Lamotte* (Louvain, 1980), pp. vii–xvi.

HUBERT DURT

LANDVÆTTIR in Old Norse means literally "landwights," the guardian spirits of an area. The *Landnámabók* (the Icelandic "book of settlements," extant in thirteenth-century redactions but based on still older traditions) tells of a tenth-century settler who struck a deal with one of the *landvættir* and thereafter became a wealthy man. The same text cites an ancient law warning that the dragon head ornament on a ship's prow should be removed before land is sighted, so as to avoid frightening off the *landvættir.* The early thirteenth-century *Egilssaga* tells that Egill once erected a pole with a dragon's head and uttered a magic formula intended to arouse the *landvættir* to drive off the land's king. The *Óláfs saga helga* (the saga of Olaf the Saint in Snorri Sturluson's *Heimskringla*), reports that Harald II once sent a man of magic powers on an out-of-body journey to Iceland; there the man saw that the mountains and mounds were full of *landvættir,* both large and small.

The emphasis on *landvættir* in Icelandic sources, particularly the *Landnámabók,* may have to do with Iceland's status as a newly discovered and settled land where, according to folk tradition, the supernatural "owners" of nature had previously ruled unhindered by humans. The *Landnámabók* tells also about a man killed by the *landvættir.* Insofar as Iceland was unknown and hence mysterious, its supernatural beings were threatening; but as men settled the land and made it theirs, these beings became increasingly friendly and potentially helpful. The distinction may be viewed in the modern Scandinavian descendants of the *landvættir: nisser* and *tomtar* live on and about farms and are helpful if treated with respect, whereas trolls and similar creatures live in the uninhabited forests and mountains and are always dangerous.

Belief in the *landvættir* persisted even after the conversion to Christianity. This is indicated by a prohibition of such belief in medieval Norwegian law. Although one cannot truly speak of "worship" of the *landvættir*, ritual activity to ensure their cooperation and protection (such as leaving out food for them in uninhabited areas) persisted as part of this belief.

BIBLIOGRAPHY

There is no comprehensive treatment of the *landvættir*, although the literature on similar beings in recent Scandinavian lore is extensive. The fullest treatment is in the chapter "Landvættir," in Ólafur Briem's *Heiðinn siðor á Íslandi* (Reykjavík, 1945), pp. 71–90.

JOHN LINDOW

LANG, ANDREW (1844–1912), Scottish anthropologist and folklorist. Born in Selkirk, Scotland, Lang received his education at Saint Andrews, Glasgow, and Oxford universities. For seven years he was a fellow of Merton College, where he was regarded as a brilliant and promising classicist. After his marriage, he left Oxford, embarked upon a career as a literary journalist, and became widely known for his editions of fairy tales, his contributions to folklore and anthropology of religion, and his literary essays and reviews. Although Lang's range of interests and learning was considerable, his scholarly work was devoted to topical intellectual issues, and he made no major contribution to the development of knowledge. He was an astute critic of the theories of others rather than an original thinker. He was among the founders of the British Folklore Society and near the end of his life was president of the Society for Psychical Research.

As a professional man of letters, Lang wrote prodigiously. He was the author of 120 books (including pamphlets) and was involved in over 150 others either as editor or as contributor, and his periodical articles number in the thousands. At a time when the growing British and American intelligentsia were intensely interested in issues of science and scholarship, Lang's penetrating intellect and skillful writing made him a leading figure, especially in the newly developing fields of anthropology, folklore, and history of religions.

Lang is credited with demolishing the great Max Müller's philological approach to the study of myth and his popular theory that all myth was the result of a "disease of language." In *Modern Mythology* (1897) Lang used his extensive knowledge of comparative mythology to show that the themes in Indo-European mythology that Müller explained in terms of Indo-European philology, many of them concerning solar phenomena, were also present in myths from other parts of the world and could be accounted for by the more universal tendency to personify nature. Although Lang did not himself offer a new theory of myth, he regarded mythology as the key to the "actual condition of the human intellect" (*Myth, Ritual, and Religion*, 1887, vol. 1, p. 29), and he thought that myth had to be understood according to its own form of rationality. In this respect, Lang anticipated major developments in the contemporary study of myth in anthropology and history of religions.

In *Magic and Religion* (1901) Lang wrote a detailed criticism of the illustrious James G. Frazer's theory of magic and religion. He exposed the flaws in Frazer's evolutionary theory that magic preceded religion and that religion arose from the perceived failures of magic. Lang also took Frazer to task for explaining the divinity of Christ in terms of ritual king-killing and myths of dying-rising gods, and he produced a devastating criticism of Frazer's theory of ritual regicide and his comparative method in *The Golden Bough*, questions on which later scholarly opinion agreed.

Although Lang was a proponent of E. B. Tylor's evolutionary theory of animism, he rejected Tylor's view that the idea of God arose as a late development from the animistic notions of souls, ghosts, and spirits. He pointed out in *Myth, Ritual, and Religion* (1887) that the concept of a creator god who is moral, fatherly, omnipotent, and omniscient is found among the most culturally primitive peoples of the world. Hence, on the evolutionists' own grounds, the idea of God, having been found among the culturally simplest peoples, could not have arisen from ideas of ghosts and souls as a later development. Lang's criticism on this point was among the first of many that eventually led to the downfall of evolutionism in anthropology. Lang's own view was that the idea of the soul-ghost and the idea of God had totally different sources and that the idea of God may have preceded animism, though he recognized that the issue of priority could never be historically settled. Lang thought, however, that the idea of God may have been prior and that it may have been corrupted and degraded by later animistic ideas and pushed out of its originally central position. Although Lang's emphasis upon the presence of "high gods" among culturally primitive peoples was largely ignored in England, it was taken up by other scholars and made the subject of major investigation in anthropology (Wilhelm Schmidt, E. E. Evans-Pritchard) and history of religions (Nathan Söderblom, Raffaele Pettazzoni, Mircea Eliade). [*See* Supreme Beings.]

In later life, Lang developed an interest in psychic phenomena—ghosts, telepathy, crystal gazing, fire walking, apparitions, spiritualism—and he wrote two books on the subject. Although he treated ghost stories as a form of folklore, he thought that the psychological experience that gave rise to them might have some foundation in reality and that it might have been the original source of religious belief. In this matter, however, Lang stood alone and somewhat in disgrace among his folklore colleagues. What Lang seems to have been groping for was a way of documenting and exploring the experience of what Rudolf Otto was later to call "the numinous," which Otto and subsequent phenomenologists of religion held to be both the ancient source and the continuing foundation of religious belief.

BIBLIOGRAPHY

Noteworthy among Lang's many contributions to the study of religion and mythology are *Custom and Myth* (1885), 2d rev. ed. (1893; Oosterhout, 1970); *Myth, Ritual, and Religion,* 2 vols. (1887), rev. ed. (1899; New York, 1968); *Modern Mythology* (1897; New York, 1968); and *Magic and Religion* (1901; New York, 1969). His two works on parapsychological phenomena are *Cock Lane and Common-Sense* (1894; New York, 1970) and *The Book of Dreams and Ghosts* (1897), rev. ed. (1899; New York, 1970). A useful source for information regarding Lang's life and his enormous literary output is Roger L. Green's *Andrew Lang: A Critical Biography with a Short-Title Bibliography of the Works of Andrew Lang* (Leicester, 1946).

BENJAMIN C. RAY

LANGUAGE. [*This entry consists of two articles.* Sacred Language *is an overview of the sacral functions to which language is put and the ways in which language has been regarded as a manifestation of the sacred.* Buddhist Views of Language *surveys these same topics from the point of view of a tradition that has found them of exceptional religious significance.*]

Sacred Language

Language, as a fundamental form of human expression, is a central element in every religious tradition and can be examined from a variety of perspectives. This article will not be concerned with the theological issue of how to assess the truth of religious statements; that is, rather than dealing with language's function of making propositions about a sacred reality, the focus will be on the kinds of sacral functions to which language has been put, such as consecration and prayer, and on the ways in which language itself has been regarded as a manifestation of the sacred.

The enormous advances made in the disciplines of linguistics and the philosophy of language over the last few decades have provided the scholar of religion with the means for more precise characterization of sacred language and its functions. Traditional terms used to describe the forms of sacred language—such as *prayer, praise,* and *magic spell*—though they stand for important thematic concerns, are too broad and imprecise by themselves to express adequately the rich variety of religious functions performed by language and the complexities involved in accomplishing those ends. The key to the modern understanding of language is to see it as an integrated system of components that are concerned with form and purpose, as well as with meaning. Spoken language manifests itself in the speech act, a type of purposeful human activity that can be analyzed in terms of its intended effect within a social context. A speech act involves (1) a language in which to embody a message, (2) a speaker to send the message, (3) a hearer to receive it, (4) a medium by which it is transmitted, and (5) a context to which it makes reference. Sacred language can be examined in terms of how it gives distinctive treatment, in turn, to each of these elements of a speech act situation. Then we will see how these components are combined to achieve the various goals of sacred speech acts.

Language as a Manifestation of the Sacred. Perhaps the most interesting examples of the intersection of religion and language are those cases in which language has been viewed not just as a means for referring to or communicating with the sacred realm but as an actual manifestation of a sacred power. Some of the most sophisticated understandings of language as a sacred power entail the belief that it was a fundamental force in the creation of the cosmos. Such ideas are widespread.

Language and creation. The Karadjeri of Australia, for example, say that it was only from the moment that the first two humans gave names to all the plants and animals, on the first day of creation, that those things really began to exist. The texts of ancient Sumeria provide the first example of the commonly found Near Eastern doctrine of the creative power of the divine word. The major deities of the Sumerian pantheon first plan creation by thinking, then utter the command and pronounce the name, and the object comes into being. Well-known is the biblical version of this same theme, in which God brings order out of chaos by simply speaking ("Let there be light," *Gn.* 1:3) and by naming ("God called the light Day, and the darkness he called Night," *Gn.* 1:5). Adam's giving of names to the plants and animals in the second chapter of *Genesis,* like the Australian example above, confirms mere physical existence with linguistic existence. [*See* Names and Naming.]

The religions of India, extending back into the earliest recorded forms of Hinduism in the Vedic period (c. 1000

BCE), contain the most developed speculations about the cosmic role of language. Several of the Vedic texts record the story of a primordial contest between speech and mind to see which is the most fundamental and essential force. While mind always wins, there is still the acknowledgement that speech is a basic cosmic force. One Vedic god, Prajāpati, who in the Brāhmaṇas (c. 800 BCE) figures most prominently as the god of creation, speaks the primal syllables *bhūr, bhuvaḥ, svar* to create the earth, atmosphere, and heaven. He is said to give order to the world through name and form *(nāmarūpa)*, which are elsewhere called his manifest aspects. These two terms are key elements in much of later Hindu philosophy, standing for the two basic dimensions of reality. The single most important term from this earliest stratum of Indian thought on language is *vāc*. Meaning "speech," it has been personified as an independent deity, the goddess who is Prajāpati's wife and who is, in some places, given the role of the true active agent in creating or, more accurately, becoming the universe.

Among the Western religious traditions, a comparable idea has been expressed in the doctrine of the *logos*. It was developed in the ancient world through a combination of Platonic, Aristotelian, and Stoic ideas. *Logos* was viewed as the rational principle that pervaded and gave order to nature. It was a demiurge that mediated between the created cosmos and the transcendent god, in whose mind existed the eternal forms. This idea was taken over by Hellenistic Judaism (in the writings of Philo Judaeus, 30 BCE–50 CE), where *logos* was identified with the biblical "Word of God"; from there it came to influence Christianity, which around 150 CE began to refer to Jesus as the Logos. The Christian view of the Logos seems to stress its quality as language, word, and message, rather than as mere thought; and besides the world-ordering function, there is the idea that the Logos is a principle of salvation as well, delivering the message that shows the way to return to the condition of original cosmic purity. [*See* Logos.] Such a conception of the double movement of creative language is found within the Indian Tantric system also.

The widely influential Tantric philosophy (which began to reach its classical articulation around 1000 CE) developed earlier strands of Indian speculation on language into a full-blown cosmogonic and soteriological system. The supreme deity of Hindu Tantrism, Śiva, is pure consciousness and thus silent. But in his first manifest form he unites with his consort, Vāc ("speech"), who is also termed Śiva's *śakti* ("power"), the female agency through which the process of creation will proceed. Creation begins with a subtle vibration that develops into the "mothers of the letters" of the Sanskrit alphabet, then into the words of speech, and finally into the referents of those words, namely, the concrete objects of the world. Certain monosyllabic vocables, called *bāja mantras* (*mantras* are syllables, words, or whole sentences that serve as both liturgical utterances and meditational devices), are regarded as the primordial forms of this linguistic evolution and, therefore, as sonic manifestations of basic cosmic powers: literally "seeds" of the fundamental constituents of the universe. For example, *yāṃ* is equivalent to wind, *rāṃ* to fire. Importantly, the Tantric adept who masters the use of *mantras* is felt to know how to control the process of cosmic evolution, and to be able to reverse that process to take himself back to the condition of primordial unity and silence that constitutes the goal of Tantric practice.

A very similar conception of cosmic evolution as identical with linguistic evolution was developed in Qabbalah, the medieval tradition of Jewish mysticism. The main idea here was that God himself was totally transcendent, but flowing forth from him were a series of ten emanations of light *(sefirot)* that were his manifest and knowable aspects. However, parallel to the emanation doctrine existed the conception of creation as the unfolding of the divine language. Instead of realms of light, there issued forth a succession of divine names and letters, namely, the twenty-two consonants of the Hebrew alphabet. As in Indian Tantrism, such a belief led to a tradition of powerful word-magic; the initiate into the practices of Qabbalah was supposedly capable of repeating acts of cosmic creation through proper combination of the Hebrew letters.

Language as a sacred substance. A hallmark of the modern understanding of language is the realization that meaning rests on a conventional relationship between the signified and the signifier. The latter (e.g., a word) is comprised of both form (e.g., phonological and grammatical rules of proper formation) and substance (e.g., its sounds, if a spoken word). The meaning of a word, however, is not inherent in either its form or substance. In premodern attitudes toward language, such distinctions were not usually made. In particular, to regard some linguistic manifestation as sacred did not imply that it was exclusively, or even primarily, the meaning that was taken to be holy. More often it was the exact form or even the veritable substance in which it was expressed that was felt to be the locus of the sacrality. This is seen most clearly in the reluctance or refusal to allow translation of certain religious expressions into equivalent statements. Religious traditions have often held the position that synonymy does not preserve sacrality. After a brief look at some examples of language substance that are regarded as sacred, we will turn to some of the important ways in which language form has taken precedence over meaning in various religions.

The Dogon of Africa believe that the speech used by the priest during ritual action contains a life force, or *nyama,* that is conveyed by his breath and becomes mixed with the life force of the invoked gods and the sacrificial offerings that are to be redistributed for the benefit of all the people. The *nyama* is given to the priest by a snake deity who appears at night and licks his body, thereby conveying the moisture of the word—the same creative power used by God at the beginning of the world to fertilize the cosmic egg. The Chamula, a Maya community of Mexico, have a similar notion of the useful power inherent in the substance of sacred speech used in ritual, believing that this more formal and redundant language contains a "heat" that is consumed by the gods along with the other offered substances.

Sacred languages. It is well known that many religions have developed the idea that an entire language, usually other than the vernacular, is sacred. Such languages are then often reserved for liturgical or for other functions conveying sacred power, such as healing or magic. A sacred language usually begins as a vernacular through which a revelation is believed to have been received. This can lead to the belief that that language is particularly suited for revelation—that it is superior to other languages and thus inherently sacred. For example, Sanskrit, the language of the Vedas, the earliest sacred scriptures of Hinduism, means literally "perfected," or "refined" *(saṃskṛta).* In Islam, the Arabic wording of the Qur'ān is regarded as essential to its holiness; as is said in many passages of the book itself, "we have sent it down as an Arabic Qur'ān." This has sometimes led to the inference that translations of the Qur'ān are not themselves sacred scriptures, but more like mere commentaries. Such belief in the sacrality of what originally was a vernacular seem to be special cases of the widespread idea that one's people and culture are the best, superior to others by virtue of a special closeness to the gods. For example, the Chamula of Mexico say that the sun deity gave them the best of all the languages of mankind; thus they call it "true language."

Furthermore, the Chamula distinguish three different forms of their own language, the most important of which is "ancient words," those which were given to their ancestors during the first stages of world creation. These are the formal phrases used in ritual. This example well illustrates a general principle. Many traditional peoples, as well as high cultures, recite sacred doctrines and rituals in an archaic form of speech that is only barely comprehensible to contemporary speakers. But the language is regarded as sacred, not primarily because it is different from the vernacular, but because it contains the doctrines of revered figures from the past, such as gods, prophets, or ancestors. The desire to express the unchanging, eternal validity of some scripture or liturgy by not allowing any change over time in its language will necessarily result in the language becoming largely unintelligible to those without special training. Such is the case for many of the prayers *(norito)* that are spoken by the priests in Shintō shrines, having been preserved in their original classical Japanese of the tenth century CE. The further passage of time can yield a fully distinct, now "sacred," language, as the offspring vernaculars develop into independent forms. Such was the case for Sanskrit in relation to its vernacular offshoots, the Prakrits, as well as for Latin in relation to the Romance languages.

The most prominent place a sacred language will be found, aside from in the scriptures, is in the cult. Here the preservation of archaic forms of language is part of the general conservatism of liturgical practice. The inclusion in the Latin Mass of such ancient and foreign-sounding elements as the Hebrew and Aramaic formulas "Halleluja," "Amen," and "Maranatha" and the Greek prayer "Kyrie eleison" added an element of mystery and sense of connectedness to a religiously significant past, which even the Latin phraseology would eventually come to represent.

Whenever language has become mere form to the common person, having lost the ability to convey any message beyond its symbolic representation of a particular manifestation of sacrality, there will be a reaction by those who see a need for a scripture or liturgy that can once again speak and teach. Many religious movements have begun on this note, railing against frozen formalism and demanding—and usually producing—vernacular expressions of their religious feelings. Buddhism began in this manner, as did many *bhakti* movements in medieval India. The latter stressed vernacular compositions—devotional poetry—that often became the foundation for the flowering of literature in the regional language. In the West, Luther's insistence on hearing, understanding, and responding to the divine word led to the Protestant use of vernaculars and to the elevation of liturgical practices, such as the sermon, that stressed not just presentation of the scriptural forms but interpretation of the scriptural message.

Sets of sacred words. While not every religion develops the idea of an entire language as sacred, many—perhaps most—do regard some special subset of speech as an embodiment of the sacred. The mere uttering or hearing of words from this set, which usually takes the form of a collection of sacred scriptures, will be believed efficacious, whether or not the meaning is understood. This emphasis on formulaic, as opposed to spontaneous, language brings with it a stress on techniques of preservation and precise recitation of the given texts, rather than on methods for inspiration and creation of new expressions. The sacred words of scripture are a divine gift to man, which relieve him of the burden of inventing his own, merely human, response to the sacred.

Within the set of sacred scriptures, a single passage may stand out as the holiest of all, and therefore the most efficacious. Hinduism recognizes the mystic syllable *oṃ* as the essence of all the Vedas, and the hymn known as the Gāyatrī (*Ṛgveda* 3.62.10), has achieved a place of preeminence among all *mantras*. The smallest unit of sacred language is the single word, and there have been many candidates for the one that should be regarded as the holiest. However, the most widely recognized sacred word is the name of a god. This stems from a common association of the name of someone with that person's soul. Utterance of the name was felt to give power over the being. So the name of God in various religions has alternately been taboo—to be avoided because likely to incite the awesome power of the deity—and a focal point of prayer, meditation, or magic. The Igbo of Africa try to avoid using the names of gods they consider particularly capricious, employing instead such circumlocutions as "The One Whose Name Is Not Spoken." On the other hand, for the Ṣūfīs, the mystics of Islam, the intense repetition of the divine name over and over again in the practice of *dhikr* is regarded as one of the most effective means of achieving the highest state of pure, undivided consciousness of God.

The Speaker. Just as form may take precedence over content, so too the messenger may be a more important determinant of the sacrality of language than the message. Certainly the characteristics possessed by the speaker have often been regarded as significant factors contributing to, or detracting from, the sacral impact of the words uttered. The greatest impact comes when the speaker is regarded, in effect, as being a god. Very dramatic are those cases where a god is believed to talk directly and immediately through a person in the present. [*See* Oracles.] Here we have what has been called prophetic or charismatic speech, which stands in contrast to liturgical speech by representing a fresh and instantaneous infusion of sacrality. It may take such forms as speaking in tongues (glossolalia), or acting as a medium, oracle, or prophet.

For human speakers, in any case, their status will affect the sacrality attributed to their words; particular status may even be a necessary precondition for the use of sacred words. Priests, for example, may have exclusive rights to the use of liturgical utterances. In India, only the three upper classes were allowed to perform rites with Vedic *mantras*. Certainly high status will enhance the effectiveness of one's speech. Thus the Dinka of Africa believe that their priests' words are more effective in invoking, praying, and cursing because they have within themselves the power of the deity Flesh, who manifests himself in their trembling while they speak.

At some point in their history, most religions have struggled with the problem of keeping their tradition of rites and prayers from becoming an empty formalism. One approach has been to insist that a certain quality of heart or mind accompany the recitation of the sacred formulas. This usually involves a greater attention to the meaning of the language and requires a different attitude on the part of the speaker than does mere exactness in the repetition of the forms. In Vedic India, where precise articulation of the *mantras* became an essential ingredient of an effective ritual, there also developed the idea that the priest who had esoteric knowledge of the symbolic import of the ritual, and who silently rehearsed that knowledge during the performance, had the most effective ritual of all. In Indian Tantrism, the *mantra* became a meditational device that had to be uttered with the proper consciousness to be effective. The goal was to have the worshiper's consciousness blend with the thought-power represented by the *mantra*. A final example is the Jewish concept of *kavvanah*. In Talmudic writings, this was a state of mental concentration appropriate for prayer. But in the system of the Qabbalah, this became, during the recitation of a prayer, a form of single-minded meditation on the cosmic power to which the prayer was addressed. This gave one power over that cosmic element or allowed one's soul to ascend to that cosmic realm.

The Hearer. There may be a great difference in perspective on the issue of the sacrality of language between the speaker and the hearer or audience. The characterization of a sacred language as unintelligible and valued only for its form, discussed above, would apply, then, only to the untutored audience, and not to the priestly speaker who had been taught that language. Often, however, even a priest will be ignorant of the meaning of the words he uses, as is the case today, for example, among many of the Hindu brahmans who use Sanskrit recitations in their rituals, or the Buddhist monks who chant the Pali scriptures.

In many applications of sacred language, the intended hearer is a god. However, unlike the addressee in ordinary conversational situations, the addressed gods seldom speak back. The pattern of use most typical for sacred language—as in ritual or prayer—is not dialogue, with responsive exchanges between a speaker and hearer who alternate roles, but monologue. Or, in a ritual, there may be multiple speakers, but seldom are they responding to or addressing one another; rather they are prompted by cues of form to utter what the text calls for next, in a pattern that could be called orchestrated.

The Medium. The spoken word uses the medium of sound for its transmission. This gives it qualities that make it quite distinct from the written word, conveyed through the medium of print. This article focuses on sacred language as spoken, leaving to others the discussion of sacred forms of written language. [*See* Alphabets *and* Calligraphy.]

Many scholars in the past few decades have come to understand and emphasize the numerous differences between oral cultures and literate cultures. One key difference is that preliterate peoples regard the speaking of an utterance as an act that manifests power; the word is viewed as an active force that is immediately involved in shaping the world. In contrast, the written word comes to stand for lifeless abstraction from the world.

The medium of sound has a number of flexible qualities that can be manipulated to express nuances of power and sacrality in ways that go beyond the meaning of the words. These range from variation in tone and speed to the use of sound patterns such as rhythm and rhyme. The simplest of these vocal but nonverbal (or paralinguistic) features is variation in loudness. In the high cult of Vedic India, for example, three major variations were used for the *mantra*s: (1) aloud, for the priest who recited the hymns of praise; (2) muttered, for the priest who performed most of the physical handiwork; and (3) silent, for the priest who sat and watched for errors in the performance. The loud recitations of praise were further divided into high, medium, and low tones, with the louder portions also spoken at a faster pace. The instructions for the traditional (Tridentine) Mass of Catholicism also called for three different tones, from aloud to inaudible.

While heightened sacrality, as in a liturgical climax, is sometimes marked by the loudest dynamic, often it is just the opposite. Silent speech or pure silence have often been regarded as the highest forms of religious expression. Thus, many times in the history of the Mass, the Canon—the climactic hallowing and offering of the sacraments—has been recited inaudibly, or so softly that only those immediately around the celebrant can hear. In Indian Tantra an explicit doctrine developed according to which "prayer without sound is recommended as the most excellent of all." Among the Zuni of North America, a person's most prized prayers are said only "with the heart." [*See* Silence.]

Other modifications of sound may be used to set off some speech as particularly sacred. For example, the Zuni have another category of nonordinary language, used primarily in ritual, that they say is "raised right up." In this form they give strong stress and high pitch to ordinarily weak and low syllables. The most refined way of giving form to the sounds of language is to craft them into poetry or song. Adherents of many religions have felt that these forms possessed more magical power than prose or are more fitting modes of expression for the very solemn. For example, the traditional distinction between low and high mass is based primarily on the use in the latter of a sung or chanted liturgy. In the Vedic high cult, the more lavish and important rituals were marked by the addition of a sung portion taken from the *Sāmaveda*.

The Context. Full understanding of any speech act requires knowledge of the context in which it occurs. Language regarded as sacred quite often has for its context a ritual setting. In that case, the intended effects of the speech acts are largely confined to the domain of the ritual. Some rituals do, of course, intend their effects to carry over into the nonritual environment as, for example, when the priest says "I now pronounce you man and wife." Sacred language may also find expression in settings other than ritual, in the case of spontaneous prayers or the occasional use of magic spells, for example.

The relationship between ritual language and its context is much different from that between ordinary language and its context. Since ritual language is, for the most part, the repetition of a fixed text, it precedes and, in effect, creates its context rather than reflecting and re-presenting in speech a context regarded as prior and already defined. Therefore, much ritual language is directed toward defining the characteristics of the participants and the nature of the ritual situation. The rich symbolism of both object and action that marks off ritual behavior from ordinary behavior will add yet another distinctive trait to ritual language. Its message is often paralleled in the symbolic systems of those other media—the visual and tactile properties of the physical objects, the kinesthetic sensibilities of gesture and movement—which then serve to reinforce, enhance, or even complete the verbal meaning. For example, as the Dinka priest recites an invocation over the animal victim during a sacrifice, he accompanies each phrase with a thrust of his sacred spear to ensure that his words "hit the mark" and weaken the beast for the final physical act of killing. During the reciting of the Institution in the Mass, the priest breaks bread and offers the cup of wine to reenact the Last Supper and, thus, give parallel reinforcement to the words that make reference to the same event.

Language in Sacred Function. The several speech act components just surveyed, from language itself to the context in which it is spoken, combine to achieve the final product of the sacred utterance. There has been a wide variety of terms used to describe the possible intended effects (or, in linguistic terminology, illocutionary forces) of words used in the service of religious ends. However, it seems possible to reduce this multiplicity to two basic categories of purpose: (1) transforming some object or state of affairs and (2) worshiping spiritual beings. These categories correspond, in some measure, to the traditional views of sacred language as either magic spell, the self-effective word of power, or prayer, the petitionary communication with a god. That phrasing, however, overstates the dichotomy. It is all too customary to regard the formulas in one's own religion as prayers and those of another's as spells.

There is, in fact, an important trait held in common by both transforming and worshiping forms of language when they are employed in the context of ritual. As remarked earlier, most ritual language comes from a preexisting text and is repeated verbatim during the performance. It conveys little or no information to any of the ritual participants, since nothing new is being said. Therefore, it might be best to characterize the overall purpose of ritual language as creating and allowing participation in a valorized situation, rather than communicating information.

Language and transformation. It has already been noted above that there is a significant difference between sacred language uttered within the context of a ritual and that spoken outside of such a setting. A ritual is a self-contained and idealized situation in which the participants and objects momentarily take on changed identities in order to play out sacred roles. The words of the liturgy are the chief instruments by which these transformations take place.

The human participants. First of all, the human observants need to express their pious qualifications for undertaking the ritual. First-person indicative utterances are most frequently used to accomplish this task. In Christianity, for example, the proper identity of a repentant sinner and believer in the correct doctrine becomes manifest through the recitation of the Confession, "I confess to almighty God . . . that I have sinned," and the Creed, "I believe in one God . . ."

Some ritual traditions involve transforming the human into a divine being, in many cases by using language that states an identity between parts of their bodies. This is a common theme in Navajo healing rites. One prayer, for example, describes the deeds of two Holy People at the time of creation, and then continues: "With their feet I shall walk about; . . . with their torso I shall walk about." The priest in a Vedic ritual must also establish his partial identity with the gods, using such *mantras* as, "I pick you [grass bundle] up with the arms of Indra."

The ritual objects. The transmundane character of the ritual objects is, in a parallel fashion, often conferred or made explicit by indicative phrases. Most of the implements at a Vedic sacrifice are addressed by the priest with second-person utterances, such as this one to a wooden sword: "You are the right arm of Indra." The words spoken over the sacraments of the Christian Eucharist ("This is my body") also typify utterances of this category, whose function could appropriately be labeled consecration.

The ritual goals. Once the ritual setting has been transformed into an assemblage of divine or cosmic personages and forces, the transforming language of the liturgy will be directed to the task of prompting those powers to bring about some desired end. At the simplest level, there are the wishes that the ritual will produce a positive result. These may be first-person optatives (the optative is the grammatical mood for expressing a wish) of a condition one desires for oneself, as in this mantra said by the patron of a Vedic sacrifice: "By the sacrifice to the gods for Agni may I be food-eating." The patron will utter a wish in the same form after each offering is poured onto the fire. A similar connection between ritual activity and desired end is expressed in the Catholic Mass by a third-person optative: "May the body of our Lord Jesus Christ preserve my soul for everlasting life." This is said by the priest when he takes communion himself. But when he offers the sacrament to others he turns the wish into a blessing: "May the body of our Lord Jesus Christ preserve your soul for everlasting life." When one utters a wish that some negative condition may come about for another, it is a curse.

One may also direct the ritual objects to bring about a goal, as when the Vedic priest calls on the firmly fixed baking tile: "You are firm. Make the earth firm. Make life firm. Make the offspring firm." Or, finally, past-tense indicative utterances may be used simply to declare that the wished-for state of affairs has indeed come about. Navajo blessing prayers regularly conclude on such a note of verbal accomplishment.

There are some transformations that are supposed to carry over into, or take place in, nonritual settings. The marriage pronouncement is one such instance. These verbally accomplished acts that bring about a change in status were closely studied first by the philosopher J. L. Austin, who called them "performative utterances." Following his lead, some scholars have interpreted the magic spell as a simple case of a performative act that is felt to bring about a change in condition through the proper application of wholly conventional rules—just as turning two single people into a married couple requires only the recitation of the correct set of words under stipulated circumstances. Others, however, have pointed out that there is a difference between the conventional, socially recognized condition of being married and the brute, physical facts of illness or even death, which magic spells have regularly been employed to bring about. Thus when the priest at a Vedic sacrifice thrusts a wooden sword into the ground and says "O gods, he who hates me . . . his head I cut off with Indra's thunderbolt," words are being used to connect a ritual or magical action with a desired end that is more than just a conventional reality. [*See* Magic.]

Language and worship. The most prominent sacred task to which language is put is the worship of the gods. The transformation of the ritual setting is usually an activity preparatory to the climactic offering of praise. The service of the gods demands a complex verbal etiquette. Interaction with the gods cannot be a matter of simple manipulation; instead, every act must be cushioned with words of explanation and concern. Furthermore, the intangible nature of the gods demands a linguistic means to make their presence take on a more concrete reality.

Most religious traditions have decided that worship of the gods must follow a particular form. The topics of the liturgy have a proper order. In Judaism there is the principle enunciated by the rabbis: "A man should always utter the praises of God before he offers his petitions." The opening lines of the official worship service dedicated to the Chinese earth god display a typical pattern: "She [the earth god] defends the nation and shelters the people. . . . Now during the mid-spring, we respectfully offer animals and sweet wine in this ordinary sacrifice. Deign to accept them." Indicative statements of the god's praiseworthy activity are followed by a first-person announcement of the act and objects of offering. Last comes the request to the god to accept the sacrifice. Most of the fundamental themes of worship will be found within the structure: invocation, praise, offering, and petition.

Invocation. Logically the first topic of any service of worship, securing the gods' presence at the rite—usually with second-person imperatives requesting them to come—will form an elaborate early portion of many liturgies. Hindu Tantric ritual, for example, uses an invocation to bring about the presence of the god in the concrete image that is the focus of worship: "O Lord who protects the world, graciously be present in this lingam [phallic image of Śiva] until the end of worship."

Praise. Essentially *to praise* means to pronounce publicly and thereby acknowledge recognition of a god's praiseworthy characteristics. If these involve deeds accomplished in the past that were of benefit, one expresses thanksgiving. There is always the hope, and probably expectation, that mentioning such deeds of benevolence will prompt the deity to act again on the celebrant's behalf. Certainly uttering praise is intended to make the god favorably disposed, or even to fill the god with renewed energy.

The simplest way to give linguistic expression to praise is to say "I praise," as in the Christian Gloria: "We praise thee, we bless thee, we adore thee, we glorify thee. . . ." Also typical are optative phrases, hoping that praise will become the universal response to the god. There is, for example, the Lesser Doxology: "Glory be to the Father, the Son, and the Holy Ghost." That is a common form for Hindu mantras of praise as well. The most basic verbal expression of piety for followers of Śiva is the "root *mantra*" *(mūlamantra)*, "Namo Śivāya," meaning "[Let there be] reverence to Śiva." This Sanskrit form was carried by Buddhism all the way to Japan, where the favorite way of showing devotion in the Pure Land sects became the constant repetition of "Namu Amida Butsu," meaning "[Let there be] reverence to Amida Buddha."

A further development of the theme of praise comes through indicative statements of a god's praiseworthy characteristics, either present-tense declarations of constant attributes or past-tense statements of a god's great deeds. Both help to give a vivid sense of the god's actual presence, especially when made in the intimate form of second-person direct address. The Jewish *berakhot* ("blessings") combine the two methods of praise just presented. They usually have the form "Blessed are You O Lord, who has done [or does] such-and-such." The phrase "Blessed are You O Lord" ("Barukh attah Adonai") is equivalent to the optative expression "Let there be reverence (or glory) to you."

Offering. The high point of many worship services is the act of offering some gift to the invoked and praised gods. Words are necessary accompaniments to the physical act to define it as an act of offering, motivated by the appropriate intention on the part of the worshiper. There must also be statements expressing the proper concern for the god's feelings. Again, the simplest way to establish an act as one of offering is to say "I offer." This is usually accompanied by an enumeration and description of the objects offered. Almost always there will be a request that the god accept the offerings. In the Mass one finds "Holy Father . . . accept this unblemished sacrificial offering." Hindu worship includes such phrasing as "What has been given with complete devotion, . . . do accept these out of compassion for me."

Petition. The logically final act of worship, petition is in many cases the motive force behind the entire service. There are religious traditions, however, that downplay this goal. The worship service *(pūjā)* of Hindu Tantra, for example, is intended primarily as a spiritual discipline to be valued in its own right, rather than for any boon that might be obtained by prayer to the worshiped deity. The liturgy of Islam also has little in the way of petition. However, in the standard weekday service of rabbinic Judaism, the central element, the ʿAmidah, contains a set of twelve supplications, the *tefillot,* accompanied by praise. And in the traditional Mass, the most prominent single type of utterance is a second-person imperative addressed to God the Father—for example, "Deliver us from every evil" or "Grant us this day our daily bread." The term *prayer,* though often used in the widest sense to refer to almost any form of language used in dealing with the gods, might best be restricted to this function of petition.

[*Sacred forms of language are discussed also in* Mantra *and* Glossolalia; *for treatments of language that serves a sacred function, see* Incantation *and* Prayer.]

BIBLIOGRAPHY

General Works. Still the only major general and cross-cultural treatment of forms of sacred language is Friedrich Heiler's *Prayer: A Study in the History of Psychology and Religion* (London, 1932). Its usefulness is limited, however, because it gives primary emphasis to the psychology of spontaneous prayers and downplays the worth of liturgical compositions. Overviews of the traditional ways of characterizing religious conceptions and uses of language, with examples drawn from around the world, can be found in Heiler's *Erscheinungsformen und Wesen der Religion* (Stuttgart, 1961), chap. 7, "Das Heilige Wort"; and in a number of chapters in Gerardus van der Leeuw's *Religion in Essence and Manifestation,* 2d ed., 2 vols. (Gloucester, 1967).

Theoretical Studies. In order to appreciate the newer studies of sacred language that employ the insight of modern linguistics, it would be useful to consult the seminal work on speech acts by J. L. Austin, *How to Do Things with Words,* 2d ed. (Cambridge, Mass., 1975), or the sophisticated development of his ideas in John Searle's *Speech Acts: An Essay in the Philosophy of Language* (London, 1969). One of the first and most successful attempts to clarify the category of prayer, using contemporary linguistic tools, is Antti Alhonsaari's *Prayer: An Analysis of Theological Terminology* (Helsinki, 1973). Some of the most insightful applications of speech act theory to religious language have come from anthropologists. Of particular significance is the work being done by Stanley J. Tambiah, particularly his article "The Magical Power of Words," *Man,* n.s. 3 (June 1968): 175–208, and chapter 12, "Liberation through Hearing," in *Buddhism and the Spirit Cults in North-East Thailand* (Cambridge, 1970). The former gives some important new discussion to the concept of the magic spell, and the latter proposes useful ways for understanding sacred languages and sacred scriptures. The relevance of much linguistic theory to the understanding of ritual language is summarized in Wade T. Wheelock's "The Problem of Ritual Language: From Information to Situation," *Journal of the American Academy of Religion* 50 (March 1982): 49–71. Groundbreaking work in examining the factors that make sacred language distinctive in its actual context of use, in both tribal societies and high cultures, has been done in the several fine studies in *Language in Religious Practice,* edited by William Samarin (Rowley, Mass., 1976).

Studies of Specific Traditions. Sam D. Gill's *Sacred Words: A Study of Navajo Religion and Prayer* (Westport, Conn., 1981) represents both an important theoretical study on methods for the thematic analysis of liturgical texts and a fine introduction to Navajo religious practices. The fascinating and complex theory of sacred language of the Dogon of West Africa is presented in Marcel Griaule's *Conversations with Ogotemmêli* (London, 1965). Pedro Laín Entralgo's *The Therapy of the Word in Classical Antiquity,* edited and translated by L. J. Rather and John M. Sharp (New Haven, 1970), gives a comprehensive discussion of the views on the power of charms and prayers in ancient Greece and Rome. The language theory of the Jewish mystical tradition is best presented in Gershom G. Scholem's *On the Kabbalah and Its Symbolism* (New York, 1965). The best discussion of the difficult philosophy of language of Indian Tantrism, as well as a useful overview of other Indian speculations on language, is André Padoux's *Recherches sur la symbolique et l'énergie de la parole dans certaines textes tantriques* (Paris, 1963).

WADE T. WHEELOCK

Buddhist Views of Language

Any tradition that seeks mystical silence becomes intensely involved with the question of the role of language in religion. Silence presupposes speech; concern with the former reflects a concern with the latter. Even a brief survey of Buddhism would reveal a number of important strands within its tradition that depend heavily, or focus primarily, on some concept of sacred language.

Doctrinal Background. Pre-Mahāyāna Buddhist literature tends to subsume all forms of discourse into the category of discursive thought. At this early stage there is already a tendency to identify language with "discursive or conceptual thought," and to identify the latter with erroneous knowledge. The Nikāyas and Āgamas suggest—certainly not as strongly as in Mahāyāna—the ineffable character of the Buddhist religious goal. The Buddha is beyond the "paths of speech" (*Suttanipāta* 1076), he cannot be conceived in visual or auditory images (*Theragāthā* 469).

Buddhist scholastics, on the other hand, downplay the nonconceptual. For them, liberating wisdom *(prajñā)* has discursive, as well as nondiscursive, dimensions. Still, their view of Buddhism unquestionably pictures the religion as a critique of conventional perceptions and descriptions of reality. The *dharma* theory of the Abhidharma can be interpreted as an attempt to establish a technical language of liberation—a set of concepts that will replace the misconceptions inherent in our ways of speaking about the world. These reflections find expression in the Abhidharmic concept of *prajñapti*, as developed in particular in the Sautrāntika school. *Prajñapti*, or "conventional designation," is the term used to explain the role and function of conventional language in contrast to the language of truth *(paramārtha)*, which describes accurately the nature of reality as seen by the enlightened.

Prajñapti is also the key link between Abhidharmic thought and the philosophy of the Mādhyamika school. In the latter school human experience of reality is seen as being of two kinds: conventional views and the perception of ultimate reality. Language is an important aspect of the former, and as such it is perceived as a tool for the construction of a mock reality. Yet language also serves to express, or point at, the nonlinguistic sphere, that is, at the nature of things.

The Sautrāntika logicians also sought to attack what they perceived as reification of language in the philosophy of their Hindu rivals. The extremes to which these Buddhist philosophers went in trying to show the deceptive nature of language are particularly obvious in their theory of *apoha*—language as "exclusion." According to this theory, words do not correspond or refer to objects, for their meaning is the exclusion of whatever is not the object of reference. The word *cow*, for instance, means only "the absence of non-cow." Among Buddhist philosophers after the eighth century (e.g., Śāntirakṣita, Kamalaśīla, Ratnakīrti) several refinements and qualifications of this view became the standard theories of meaning. Application of these theories to the religious sphere, however, does not seem to have occurred to their formulators. [*See* Sautrāntika; Mīmāṃsā; *and the biographies of Śāntirakṣita and Kamalaśīla.*]

Nevertheless, it is difficult to imagine that doctrines of meaning and negation could remain unconnected to Buddhism as a religious practice—that is, as a type of apophatic mysticism. In the Sūtra literature the connection is established explicitly. For instance, the *Laṅkāvatāra Sūtra* sees the world of speech as the world of delusion, which is identical with the world of the disturbed and illusory mind. Accordingly, the Buddha is said to have abided in "the silence of the sage." He never spoke a word. The *Vimalakīrtinirdeśa Sūtra* likewise, while asserting that everything is language, claims that only silence can express ultimate reality.

It is impossible, however, to remain in the realm of pure silence yet claim to practice a religion in a religious community. The Buddhist must therefore find a doctrinal bridge that will reach out beyond the sphere of mystical silence. Two doctrines are selected for this purpose by the scriptural and scholastic traditions: the doctrines of conventional truth *(saṃvṛti)* and "skillful means" *(upāya)*. These are in part a theoretical recognition of the fact that Buddhism as a living religion is seldom a practice of literal silence. The silence of the Buddha is manifested in his speech; his words take the form that is understood by his listeners. Language is therefore not necessarily false. It is not misleading under all circumstances, because it can be used "skillfully" as a "means" *(upāya)*. This is the ultimate statement on language made in texts such as the *Laṅkāvatāra Sūtra* and the *Tathāgataguhya Sūtra*.

Religious Practice. Concern with the sacred word and acceptance of language as a practical tool play a much more significant role in Buddhist religious life than does the philosophical understanding of Buddhist silence, although they are never understood as contradicting the apophatic doctrine.

The importance of language and "the word" in the general history of religions in India is well attested (e.g., the Hindu *kirtan*, the pan-Indian *mantra*, and the school of Mīmāṃsā). What is characteristic of Buddhism is its concern with a critique of language. This concern is often found mixed, paradoxically, with a strong sense of the importance of the invariant word, the holy manifested in utterance, silence embodied in words. There are, however, many instances in which the sacred word is just that—its immutable character endowing it with power to protect and redeem.

Typology of the word. One can speak of a typology of the sacred word in Buddhism as ranging from the canon of scriptures, through the book, the sacred phrase, the (single) sacred word, the sacred syllable, and the sacred sound or letter. The following are a few major examples of the use of sacred words in Buddhism.

The vow. Perhaps the most important of these beliefs are the Mahāyāna doctrines of the *bodhisattva*'s solemn utterance of a vow *(praṇidhāna)*, to follow the path of Buddhahood, and the ritual formulation of the vow and the precepts *(saṃvara-grahaṇa)*. The vow is a kind of "act of truth," in which the will of an extraordinarily virtuous human being cooperates with the power of truth inherent in any statement of fact.

The book. Even in the sober Theravāda there is a strong sense of the authority of scriptural pronouncement as the *ipsissima verba* of Gautama the Buddha. As such, the sacred text is sacred regardless of the devotee's capacity to understand the conceptual content of the text. Concrete manifestations in ritual of this Buddhist reverence for the sacred word—including the literal text and the material book—are also well attested in Mahāyāna traditions. For example, the "perfection of wisdom" *(prajñāpāramitā)* stands not only for the "highest experience" of absolute nonduality, but also represents the expression of this experience in words. The words themselves, and even the material "book" in which the words are preserved, embody the *prajñāpāramitā,* they *are* the *prajñāpāramitā.* Thus, scripture, as the "embodiment" of the Buddha as Dharma, becomes a living relic of the Buddha, so that every place where the text is made known becomes a sacred location, a reliquary, as it were (*Vajracchedikā* 12.15c; *Aṣṭasāhasrikā Prajñāpāramitā* 3.57). The preservation of the sacred word, therefore, is tantamount to the preservation of the Buddha's own being.

The ritual recitation of the scriptures as a source of merit is a common practice throughout Buddhist Asia. This practice can extend from the actual study and expounding of the Sūtra as doctrinal discourse to the cult of the collection of scriptures (cult of the Tripiṭaka), from the study of extensive collections of texts to the symbolic repetition of the text by copying it, or merely by turning a revolving bookcase containing the whole canon of scriptures or a praying wheel with copies of a short incantation. The enshrinement of texts—a common practice in Tibetan Buddhism—is not qualitatively different from the acceptance of a single fragment of text as an embodiment of the Dharma.

Incantation. The concept of words as summary or embodiment of the sacred has its most extreme manifestation in the symbolization of the Dharma in short segments of speech that are either fragments of natural expressions (the title of *sūtra*s, the *Prajñāpāramitā in a Single Syllable*), or strings of phonemes with little or no signification in the natural language *(mantra, dhāraṇī).* These texts are also regarded as a condensation of the sacred power of the enlightened, and can be protective formulas as well as instruments of meditation. The latter function is reserved primarily, although not exclusively, for the *mantra.*

The use of sacred texts or fragments of sacred speech (e.g., *paritta* and *dhāraṇī*) as incantations to guard off evil or eliminate negative influences or as propitiatory formulas plays an important role in both popular and "great tradition" Buddhist practice. A mysterious Dhāraṇī Piṭaka seems to have formed part of the canon of the Dharmaguptaka Buddhists in Andhra (in Southeast India), and may have been the repository of many of these formulas, otherwise attested in inscriptions, in anthologies (e.g., Śāntideva's *Śikṣāsamuccaya*), and as part of *sūtras* (e.g., the *dhāraṇī* sections of the *Saddharmapuṇḍarīka,* chap. 21, and *Laṅkāvatāra,* chap. 9). In the same way that the book comes to stand for the source of Buddhahood, the *dhāraṇī,* as epitome of the wisdom and power of the Dharma, can be conceived as a protective deity. The word becomes personified power in the mythology of figures, for example, the "Five Protective Deities" *(pañcarakṣā).*

Sectarian manifestations. The importance of these religious phenomena becomes even more obvious when one considers their central role in the development of some of the most successful sectarian traditions of Buddhist Asia. In all of the examples given below, a practice connected with the sacred word has become the characteristic doctrinal or practical axis of a distinct school.

Pure Land. Pure Land Buddhism, as a generalized religious ideal in India, epitomizes Buddhist doctrines of grace and the sacred word. The *bodhisattva* or the Buddha is the source of grace, the savior who can be reached by merely calling his name. The classical examples of this tradition are the chapters on the *bodhisattva* Avalokiteśvara in the *Gaṇḍavyūha Sūtra* and the *Saddharmapuṇḍarīka Sūtra.*

The practice of the recitation of the name of Buddha Amitābha, on the other hand, is usually not separated from the traditions of faith and meditation, as found, for instance in the *Sukhāvatīvyūha.* The mythology behind the practice reveals that it can be conceived as something more than faith in the magical power of words. Amitābha, in a former existence as the *bodhisattva* Dharmākara, pronounced a solemn vow, the power of which is such that it can produce the effect (the goals sought by the vow) by the sheer power of the truth of the words uttered. This vow and its effects are embodied, and can be evoked or reached by another sacred word—the name of Amitābha. The power is not in the name as such, but in the intention of the Buddha's former vows.

Nevertheless, a belief that the repetition of the names of Buddhas is intrinsically meritorious is amply attested. In China, the incantation of the name of Amitābha Buddha became an independent religious form. The most extreme example of the mechanical application of this practice is the custom of keeping accurate accounts of how many times one repeats the name of Amitābha. Whether one is attempting to visualize the Buddha or not is irrelevant; the merit accrues regardless of the state of mind or degree of spiritual advancement of the believer.

In the Pure Land traditions of Japan the repetition of

the name of Amitābha (Jpn., Amida) is divorced from the doctrine of merit altogether. [*See especially* Jōdo Shinshū.] The invocation itself becomes the primary practice, the only access to Amida's saving grace. The simplicity of this practice (known as the Nembutsu) is such that many believers would even deny that it is a ritual of invocation. Rather, it is conceived as the simple enunciation of the formula "Namu Amida Butsu" (the Japanese pronunciation of the Chinese phrase "Namo O (or A)-mi-t'o-fo," itself an attempt to reproduce the Sanskrit sentence: "Namo 'mitābhāya buddhāya"). This short phrase is considered equivalent to the "true name" of the Buddha—that is to say, the essence of the Buddha as Buddha. [*See also* Amitābha; Nien-fo; Ching-t'u; *and* Jōdoshū.]

Nichirenshū. Related to this faith in the power of the name is the Buddhist trust in the power of particular *sūtras*. The most successful development of this belief is the Japanese sect founded by Nichiren (1222–1282). For him, the title *(daimoku)* of the *Lotus Sutra* recited in the formula "Namu *Myōhōrengekyō*" becomes the powerful source of all spiritual and material well-being. Nichiren himself is said to have inscribed the phrase on a scroll. This inscription is considered the primary object of veneration in the sect. It is conceived—following Japanese esoteric tradition—as a *maṇḍala*. [*See* Nichirenshū.]

Tantra. Perhaps the most obvious manifestation of concern with the sacred character of language within Buddhism is in the phenomena encompassed by the broad term "Buddhist Tantra" or "Tantric Buddhism." [*See* Tantrism, *overview article; and* Buddhism, Schools of, *article on* Esoteric Buddhism.] In the Tantric tradition the sacred word is at the same time the embodiment of multiple dimensions of the holy. Tantric texts such as the *Guhyasamāja Tantra* develop homologies linking the Buddha's silence (the ineffable), his mind (the experience of meditation), his speech (the expression of his experience), and his power (apotropaic formulas).

The sacred formula *(mantra)* or syllable *(bīja)* serves both as a powerful tool of incantation and a vehicle for visualization. A sacred and esoteric language or code *(saṃdhā-bhāṣā, saṃdhyā-bhāṣā)* is developed to convey the meaning of ritual symbolism as the embodiment of religious experience. The latter use of sacred language is perhaps an interpretive device that tends to reduce the sacred word to the experience of meditation. The reduction takes place by means of homologies similar to the ones at the heart of the mystical tradition of the Brāhamaṇas and the early Upaniṣads. Thus, the *mantra* conveys meaning primarily as a code—a multivalued icon embodying a system of sacred identities.

Therefore, one can rightly speak of "the word as icon" in the Tantric tradition. In Tibet, for instance, the sacred word acquires a life of its own. The sacred *mantra* of the *bodhisattva* Avalokiteśvara, "Oṃ maṇi padme huṃ," is inscribed on building walls, on rooftops, and on stones in the road. It is inserted in praying wheels, where the mere mechanical turning of the inscribed syllables is supposed to invoke the presence of the *bodhisattva*, and allow the devotee to gain access to his grace or visualize his image.

The Japanese Kūkai (774–835), the founder of the esoteric tradition of Japanese Tantra, regarded all language as sacred, although he also adopted the philosophical critique of language. He regarded *mantras* as the primary form of the sacred (the "true word," *shingon*), but at the same time he considered that all words, even syllables and letters, stood ultimately for the silent meditation of Vairocana Buddha. Words, but above all Sanskrit sounds, were the embodiment of the highest reality. [*See* Mantra; Oṃ; Shingonshū; *and the biography of Kūkai.*]

Zen. Ch'an or Zen Buddhism also represents an important manifestation of both a concern with language and a predilection for the development of specialized sacred languages. The Zen tradition is avowedly the Buddhism of Vimalakīrti's silence—a claim that is explicitly reinforced by the practice of silent meditation. However, the excesses of blank mental concentration have been criticized in the sect since its inception in the eighth century, and an important segment of the tradition also practices meditation on "words"—*kanna-zen*. The use of the *kōan* (Chin., *kung-an*) or *mondō* as sacred text (even in ritual contexts) is well attested; the *kōan* collections became the sacred canon of the sect. Nevertheless, even as the tradition concedes the immutable character of the sacred utterance it emphasizes the critical function of the *kōan* as expression of the dialectic nature of the enlightenment experience. For the *kōan* is also regarded as the embodiment of the enlightenment experience of the great masters of the past and a test case for the aspirant to that experience—hence its name, "public *(kung)* case or precedent *(an)*." [*See* Ch'an *and* Zen.]

The general category of "sacred language," however, does not exhaust or explain the specific meanings of the sacred word in Pure Land, Tantra, and Zen. Each one has a particular context. They represent only polarities in a wide range of possibilities within the Buddhist tradition. The three types of sacred word—*nembutsu*, *kōan*, and *mantra*—share a common element insofar as they represent forms of nonnatural linguistic expression, but the analogy ends there. On the one hand, the *mantra* and the *dhāraṇī* express or embody the enlightenment experience as the manifestation in sound of a nonlinguistic sphere. They usually convey sacred meaning with only a token or minimal regard for linguistic sense. The title of a *sūtra* or the name of a Buddha, on the other hand, are clearly exact names that correspond to well-formed names in the natural language. The Nembutsu may embody Amida's enlightenment and true nature, but only by way of the actual name found in the myth of Dharmākara. Last, the *kōan* also claims to contain the actual linguistic form of a sacred, yet natural utterance "attested" in the quasi-historical context of hagiography; unlike the title of a *sūtra,* however, it alludes explicitly to the mythic context, and unlike the calling on the name of a Buddha, it claims to preserve a segment of meaningful, albeit paradoxical discourse.

Interpretive Frameworks. Among the religious traditions, explicit discussion of the nature of language occurs mainly within the Tantra, which in Tibetan and late Indian Buddhism constitutes the practical branch of the eclectic philosophical schools. In conformity with its philosophical roots Tantrism falls back on two Mādhyamika principles that are no doubt the most important hermeneutic devices in Buddhist philosophy—the concept of "two truths" and the concept of "explicit" and "implicit" meanings *(nīta-* and *neya-artha).* As convention, language has a certain validity, but its claim to represent something more than convention or to depict reality are spurious. The experience of reality as such, or of things as they are "before language," is the experience of the highest goal, the ultimate meaning, or the most real object *(paramārtha).* Although this experience lies beyond all linguistic procedures or operations, beyond all conceptualization, it is accessible only through some form of linguistic index. Thus, linguistic convention, while merely conventional and relative, is necessary for liberation as well as for everyday practical activities.

Furthermore, the rejection of linguistic convention and conceptual thought is seldom unconditional or unqualified. In some Buddhist traditions the conventional world is not to be rejected because it is convention. The linguistic realm is deceptive and false only when it claims to be something more than a conventional construct. Therefore, certain forms of linguistic convention—everyday use of language and special sacred language tools or substitute linguistic conventions—are acceptable. This is especially clear in late Mādhyamika thought, where the realm of the conventional is further divided to distinguish a "true" conventional from a "false" conventional usage. For instance, the Indian philosopher Kamalaśīla (fl. eighth century) regards the logic of everyday transactions as true in a certain manner of speaking. It is in fact the only logic possible, and discourse about the absolute only serves to clear away metaphysical language games. Thus, even the ultimate reality of emptiness is subject to a critique that corrects its apparent isolation from the world. Conventional and religious discourse alike may be illusions, but so is talk about the silence of emptiness. This is the theoretical context in which religious practices such as Tantra see themselves as a means to a practical and effective resolution of the tension between absolute and relative, silence and speech, liberating knowledge *(prajñā)* and skillful application of liberating means *(upāya).*

[*See also* Buddhist Literature, *article on* Exegesis and Hermeneutics; Prajñā; *and* Upāya.]

BIBLIOGRAPHY

Bharati, Agehananda. *The Tantric Tradition.* London, 1965. A study of Indian Tantrism in general, and Hindu Tantra in particular.

Bhattacharyya, Benoytosh. *An Introduction to Buddhist Esotericism* (1932). Reprint, Varanasi, 1964. A work of uneven quality, but still indispensable. The reprint edition contains a new preface by the author, but chapter 7, "The Mantras," is unfortunately too short.

Blacker, Carmen. "Methods of Yoga in Japanese Buddhism." In *Comparative Religion: The Charles Strong Trust Lectures, 1961–1970,* edited by John Bowman, pp. 82–98. Leiden, 1972. An accessible, yet scholarly comparison of the practice of the *kōan* method of Rinzai Zen, and the *mantra*s of Shingon Buddhism.

Dasgupta, Shashibhusan. *An Introduction to Tantric Buddhism* (1958). Reprint, Berkeley, 1974. The reprint edition of this work contains a forward by H. V. Guenther, in which he points to some of the book's shortcomings. Like Bhattacharyya, this work is still one of the standard surveys, in spite of its problems.

Gómez, Luis O. "Liberation from Language and the Language of Liberation." In *The Word,* edited by Jan Swearingen. Tucson, forthcoming. Discusses the role of sacred words and sacred language as a tool of liberation from language.

Hakeda, Yoshito S., trans. *Kūkai: Major Works.* New York, 1972. A study of Kūkai, and a translation of some of his works. Includes his most important work on the meaning of language and the sacred word, the *Shōji jissō gi.*

Hamlin, Edward. "Discourse in the Laṅkāvatāra-Sutra." *Journal of Indian Philosophy* 11 (September 1983): 267–313. An original interpretation of the *sūtra*'s view of language as *upāya.*

Hopkins, Jeffrey, ed. and trans. "The Great Exposition of the Secret Mantra." Hopkins' translation of Tsoṅ-kha-pa's classical treatise on the Tantric path, *Sṅags rim chen po,* was published in two volumes under two different titles: *Tantra in Tibet: The Great Exposition of the Secret Mantra,* "Wisdom of Tibet Series," no. 3 (London, 1977), and *The Yoga of Tibet: The Great Exposition of the Secret Mantra, 2 and 3,* "Wisdom of Tibet Series," no. 4 (London, 1981).

Huntington, C. W., Jr. "A 'Nonreferential' View of Language and Conceptual Thought in the Work of Tsoṅ-Kha-pa." *Phi-*

losophy East and West 33 (October 1983): 325–340. Highlights the elements of "linguistic philosophy" found in Tsoṅ-kha-pa's interpretation of Indian Mādhyamika. With Williams (1980), this paper adds to the strength of the linguistic interpretation of Mādhyamika.

Ñāṇananda, Bhikkhu. *Concept and Reality in Early Buddhist Thought.* Kandy, 1971. An imaginative interpretation of the Buddhist critique of conceptual thought in the Pali tradition.

Padoux, André. *Recherches sur la symbolique et l'énergie de la parole dans certains textes tantriques.* Paris, 1963. A general discussion of sacred language in Hindu Tantra. Many of the authors interpretations could apply to Buddhist Tantra.

Saunders, E. Dale. "Some Tantric Techniques." In *Studies in Esoteric Buddhism and Tantrism,* pp. 167–177. Koyasan, 1965. Surveys various Tantric ritual and meditation styles, including the use of *mantras* in meditation.

Schopen, Gregory. "The Phrase *'sa pṛthivīpradeśaś caityabhūto bhavet'* in the *Vajracchedikā:* Notes on the Cult of the Book in Mahāyāna." *Indo-Iranian Journal* 17 (November–December 1975): 147–181. This essay lays the groundwork for Schopen's views on the cult of the book in Mahāyāna. Schopen's forthcoming article, "The Buddha and the Book: The Text as a Sacred Object and Source of Power in Indian Mahāyāna Buddhism," brings his thesis into sharper focus.

Sen, Sukumar. "On Dharani and Pratisara." In *Studies in Esoteric Buddhism and Tantrism,* pp. 67–72. Koyasan, 1965. A study of *pratisarā* as emblematic of the so-called "deified" utterances.

Sharma, Dhirendra. *The Differentiation Theory of Meaning in Indian Logic.* The Hague, 1969. An edition and translation of Ratnakīrti's (fl. 1070) *Apohasiddhi.*

Snellgrove, David L., ed. and trans. *The Hevajra Tantra: A Critical Study.* 2 vols. London, 1959. An edition and translation of an important Tantric text of the Indo-Tibetan tradition.

Tambiah, Stanley J. "The Magical Power of Words." *Man* 3 (June 1968): 175–208. The role of nonhuman language forms in the "little tradition" of Theravāda.

Ueda, Yoshifumi, ed. *Notes on Once-calling and Many-calling: A Translation of Shinran's Ichinen-tanen mon'i.* Kyoto, 1980. An annotated translation of one of Shinran's most lucid expositions on the meaning of Nembutsu practice.

Waddell, L. Austine. " 'Dharani,' or Indian Buddhist Protective Spells." *Indian Antiquary* 43 (1914): 37–42, 49–54. This essay contains translations of Tibetan *dhāraṇīs*. See also the same author's "The Dhāraṇī Cult in Buddhism, Its Origin, Deified Literature and Images," *Ostasiatische Zeitschrift* 1 (1912): 155–195, which is dated, but remains the most complete attempt to establish a history of Buddhist *dhāraṇī*. Includes a discussion of the personified protective formulas *(pañcarakṣā).*

Waldschmidt, Ernst. "Das Paritta: Eine magische Zeremonie der buddhistischen Priester auf Ceylon." *Baessler-Archiv* 17 (1934): 139–150. Reprinted in *Von Ceylon bis Turfan: Schriften zur Geschichte, Literatur, Religion und Kunst des indischen Kulturraumes von Ernst Waldschmidt* (Göttingen, 1967), pp. 465–478. Analysis of the use of *parittā* in Sri Lanka, and its sources in the Pali tradition.

Wayman, Alex. "Concerning *saṃdhā-bhāṣā/saṃdhi-bhāṣā/saṃdhyā bhāṣā.*" In *Mélanges d'indianisme à la mémoire de Louis Renou,* pp. 789–796. Paris, 1968. Summarizes earlier research on the subject and proposes Wayman's theory of "twilight language." This thesis is developed further in "Twilight Language and a Tantric Song," chapter 11 of Wayman's *The Buddhist Tantras: Light on Indo-Tibetan Esotericism* (New York, 1973). Other aspects of the problem of language in Buddhism have been explored by Wayman in "The Hindu-Buddhist Rite of Truth: An Interpretation," in *Studies in Indian Linguistics,* edited by Bhadriraju Krishnamurti (Poona, 1968), pp. 365–369. In this essay the author considers the connections between the "act of truth" and other "pan-Indian" notions of the "true word." Wayman studies early instances of the tension between the ideals of silence and truth in Indian religious thought in "Two Traditions of India—Truth and Silence," *Philosophy East and West* 24 (October 1974): 389–403. He has also written extensively on the *Guhyasamāja* and the symbolism of the *mantra* in *Yoga of the Guhyasamājatantra: The Arcane Lore of Forty Verses: A Buddhist Tantra Commentary* (Delhi, 1977).

Williams, Paul M. "Some Aspects of Language and Construction in the Madhyamaka." *Journal of Indian Philosophy* 8 (March 1980): 1–45. Summarizes, with new data and insight, the linguistic aspects of Mādhyamika dialectic.

LUIS O. GÓMEZ

LAO RELIGION. The Lao people inhabit both banks of the Middle Mekong, from Louang Phrabang in the north to Khong Island in the south. Properly speaking, they represent only half of the population in the country that bears their name; the number of Lao in neighboring Thailand is five times as great. A variety of influences have contributed to the religious contours of the Lao. Tai-speaking peoples from south of the Chinese empire introduced into the autochthonous Austroasiatic culture of the region a variety of myths and rites exhibiting Chinese influence. In the ensuing process of assimilation elements of both cultures were preserved. [*See map accompanying* Southeast Asian Religions, *article on* Mainland Cultures.] The dominant cultural vector, however, stems ultimately from the Indian subcontinent. When asked his or her religion, a Lao invariably will answer that he is a Buddhist, more specifically, a follower of the Theravāda ("doctrine of the elders") school. The center and symbol of the rural collectivity, indeed, of all action that is communal in Lao society, remains the *vat* (Pali, *vatthu;* Skt., *vāstu*) or Buddhist monastery. Within its precincts matters both sacred and secular—religious instruction, public meetings, community rituals, the election of a village chief—are conducted. Conversion to Buddhism remains the principal means of assimilation of minorities into the sphere of Lao culture.

Coextensive with Buddhism, and functionally integrated with it, is the so-called *phī* cult, or cult of local spirits. While belief in local spirits predates the introduction of Buddhism, it is important to recognize that it is impossible to extrapolate from contemporary practice the contours of Lao religion prior to the introduction of Buddhism. Nor is it consistent with the society's own understanding of its religious system to see the *phī* cult as formally or functionally distinct from Buddhism. Centuries of syncretization have forged an internally consistent religious ideology that has rationalized the mutual interdependence of both systems. The separate consideration of the two in the discussion that follows is merely a heuristic device, designed to illuminate the prevailing religious concerns of each.

The Phī Cult. The term *phī* is common to all Tai-speaking populations (one finds the term *fī* among certain non-Buddhist Tai in northern Vietnam) and typically designates an ensemble of various entities such as "souls," ancestors, evil spirits, and celestial deities. The cult probably originated in pre-Buddhist Tai society, enriched by contact with Austroasiatics, the previous inhabitants of the region. The influence of the *phī* cult is seen in the concern to maintain the integrality of the person, as it is held that the departure of one (or several) "souls" provokes sickness and death. Here, it is the therapeutic aspect that dominates, Buddhism having appropriated the funerary rites. The performance of *sū khwan* ("calling back the souls") is mandated at times of risk: illness, before a voyage or examination, or at the passage to another stage of life. This "call" is accompanied by invocations and the recitation of votive formulas and is concluded by the tying of ligatures of cotton threads to the wrist, thus connecting the souls to the body.

The Lao have recourse equally to specialist healers *(mǭ)* and occasionally to female mediums *(nāng thiam)*. The most powerful among the former is the *mǭ thēvadā*, or "master of divinities," a shaman who invokes the aid of his auxiliary spirits, the *phī thēvadā*. The *mǭ thēvadā* have a double competence, as shamans and as mediums, as demonstrated by the "sacrifice to the talisman protectors" *(liang khǭng haksā)*. In this ceremony, master and disciples stage a séance of successive possessions by diverse deities, among them a class of spirits known as *khā*, said to include both Austroasiatic authochthones and Vessantara, the Buddha in his last rebirth prior to that in which he achieved enlightenment as Gautama. Richard Pottier (1973) has exposed this same double competence among the *nāng thiam* of the Louang Phrabang region, who undergo possession in public rites but act as shamans in the course of healing consultations. However, the *nāng thiam* function principally on the level of the collectivity, where they intervene in ceremonies honoring the guardian deity of the territory *(phī muang)* or of the individual village *(phī bān)*.

The cult of the tutelary deity of the village is headed by a master of ritual known as a *caw cam*, a position that is gained through village elections. It is the role of the *caw cam* to announce to the *phī* all events affecting the life of the collectivity, notably events in which the *phī* is directly implicated. He addresses to the spirits the personal requests of the villagers; when these requests are granted it is his duty to officiate at the *kę̄ba*, or sacrifice of thanksgiving. His principal task, however, is to organize and execute the annual sacrifice to the tutelary deity, the *liang phī bān*, or "nourishing of the village spirit," in which all households participate.

Buddhist Influences. Buddhism and the *phī* cult are not simply juxtaposed in Lao popular religion; over the course of several centuries they have become syncretized. Those who compiled the royal annals have presented the introduction of Buddhism at the time of the Lao kingdom's foundation as a victory over the *phī* cult that had predominated. They recall the vigorous campaign carried against the *phī* by King Pothisarath, who passed an edict in 1527 prohibiting them and ordering the destruction of all sanctuaries consecrated to the *phī*. His successors showed more understanding toward the *phī*, and Buddhism had to accomodate itself to the persistence of the cult's hold on the population. Some concepts and practices were "civilized" by assuming an outwardly Hindu form—it is likely that this phenomenon predates the arrival of Hīnayāna Buddhism.

This syncretism shows up constantly in daily life and in grand public celebrations. For example, one utilizes Buddhist formulas for magical purposes and seeks without hesitation the knowledge of a monk before drawing a number in the lottery. It would never enter anyone's mind to reproach the *caw cam phī bān* for indulging in acts contrary to *tham* (Pali, *dhamma;* Skt., *dharma*), because one generally elects to this position a man known for his devotion to the Perfect One; in fact, before going to officiate at this altar of the tutelary deity, this ritual master first prays at the pagoda. We see within the very compound of the *vat* the presence of a replica in miniature of the altar of the tutelary deity: this altar, the *hǭ phī khun vat*, is dedicated to the spirit benefactor of the monastery, the monk who was its founder. The tutelary deity, in the majority of cases, is also the founder of the village, and it happens frequently that the master of the *phī bān* ritual is the same as that of the *phī khun vat*.

One of the great village feasts is the Bun Bang Fai ("rocket festival"). There is no need to overemphasize the sexual symbolism of the giant rockets that are shot against the sky just before the coming of the monsoon with its fecundating rains; moreover, the carnavalesque processions with their ribald songs and provocative exhibition of enormous wooden phalluses for the benefit of young maidens points more explicitly to the nature of the festival. That the Buddhist clergy sanctions and effectively participates in this festival is evidenced by the fact that the rockets are placed within the compound of the pagoda under the supervisions of the monks. It is also in the monastic compound that the dancing *nāng thiam* enter into trances and where rockets of invited neighboring pagodas are collected for the rites. In numerous villages the festival of Bun Bang Fai is connected with the feast of the tutelary deity. Fertility, bawdiness, the drinking of alcoholic beverages, entering into trances, gambling (with betting on the rockets)—all of these are against Buddhist law. However, in the eyes of the Lao farmer, the festival of the rockets commemorates the Visākhā Pūjā—the triple anniversary of the birth, the enlightenment, and the death of the Buddha.

The Buddhist notion that has most profoundly permeated Lao popular religion seems to be that of *bun* (Pali, *puñña*), "merit." One must acquire merit to enrich one's *kam* (Pali, *kamma;* Skt., *karman*), which permits the attainment of spiritual liberation in the cycles of transmigration. The Lao thinks very little of *niphān* (Pali, *nibbāna;* Skt., *nirvāṇa*), but remains concerned with a mundane counterpart of merit: prestige, wealth, power. It should be noted that the Lao layman preoccupies himself even less with the inverse notion, that of *bāp* (Pali, Skt., *pāpa*), "error." He is particularly concerned with the acquisition of merits, best obtained through gift giving. Moreover, the gift most laden with merit is that which has as its beneficiary the *pha sang* (Pali, *sangha;* Skt., *saṃgha*), the community of monks. Thus, one who has chosen monastic asceticism by his sacrifice enriches not only his own *kam* but offers to others the possibility of acquiring merit, even if only through the food alms that he must collect each day. To this daily source of *bun* must be added the massive enrichment procured through offerings of paraphernalia for the ordination of a monk or for the celebration of Buddhist feasts. Moreover, it should not be forgotten that at least once in his life every man must wear the saffron robe, a trial that constitutes a sort of initiation and preparation to adult life. [*See* Merit, *article on* Buddhist Concepts.]

Another outwardly Buddhist component of Lao society that also serves non-Buddhist functions is the *vat*, or monastery, mentioned above. The monastery rises and grows with the collective it represents. After having cleared a section of the forest and forming a sufficiently autonomous hamlet, a group of farmers may decide to establish a hermitage (*vat pā*, "forest pagoda") for a monk. This small wooden house on stilts becomes the first *kutdī* (Skt., *kutī;* monks' quarters) and grows with the hamlet itself. Consequently, this growth brings an increase in voluntary manpower and thus the construction of a more sophisticated building, the *sālā*, a public hall. Once this grand square hall on short stilts has been completed, the collective is able to invite a greater number of monks and laity to the village's religious ceremonies. The *sālā* does not function solely as a religious center, however. It serves also as a forum for meetings where the local inhabitants convene to debate on matters concerning the entire collective, such as the election of village chief, common works to undertake, and feasts to celebrate. It also serves as a warehouse for materials needed for the realization of these projects, a shelter for hawkers and travelers, and as classroom for any occidental-type schools built in the rural area. When a village attains a degree of development and reputation such that it has at its disposal the means to pay hired labor (thanks to collections made during feasts or gifts offered by individuals), it undertakes the construction of a sanctuary (*sim;* Pali, Skt., *sīmā*). We see, therefore, that the monastery is the center not only of the religious life of the rural collective but also, by virtue of its multifunctional role, of all activity that is communal in character.

The two currents of Buddhist and indigenous folk religious belief intermingle to form Lao religion, but their respective proportions vary with the epochs and regions. As the reigning power reinforces itself and develops the teaching of Buddhism, the *phī* cult's influence tends to diminish. Despite this, Lao farmers do not completely abandon this recourse to nature's forces, which guarantee them the resources necessary for the maintenance and renewal of life. Even when they concern the whole village, the *phī* ceremonies take place beyond the sight of strangers. On the other hand, the monastery bears witness to the adherence of its members to a universalistic religion. The individual finds therein refuge for the most important phases of his spiritual life. But the *vat* is not there to serve the spiritual activities of Buddhism only; it caters also to all aspects of collective life. By its openness, it bears testimony to a social space comprising the totality of peasant system of relations: state officials on inspection tours hold meetings there, monks whom it shelters come from a hierarchy paralleling that of state administrative divisions, and festivals held in the monastery take all forms, sacred or profane, of Lao culture.

[*For an overview of Lao culture in the context of mainland Southeast Asia as a whole, see* Southeast Asian Religions, *article on* Mainland Cultures. *The Buddhist com-*

ponent of Lao religion is discussed in Buddhism, *article on* Buddhism in Southeast Asia, *and* Theravāda. *See also* Worship and Cultic Life, *article on* Buddhist Cultic Life in Southeast Asia.]

BIBLIOGRAPHY

First and foremost, a portion of the many but dispersed publications of Charles Archaimbault has been compiled in one volume, *Structure religieuses lao: Rites et mythes* (Vientiane, 1973). Archaimbault's article "Les ceremonies en l'honneur des phi f'à (phi celestes) et des phi t'ai (phi précieux) à Basăk," appears in *Asie du Sud-Est et monde insulindien* 6 (1975): 85–114. Richard Pottier's "Notes sur les chamanes et médiums de quelques groupes thaï," *Asie du Sud-Est et monde insulindien* 4 (1973): 99–103, is supplemented by his very important dissertation, "Le système de santé lao et ses possibilités de développement" (Ph.D. diss., University of Paris, 1979), which he is currently preparing for publication. Another indispensible work on Lao religion is Marcel Zago's *Rites et cérémonies en milieu bouddhiste lao* (Rome, 1972). For more details, I refer the reader to my own essay, "Notes sur le bouddhisme populaire en milieu rural lao," which appeared in consecutive issues of *Archives de sociologie des religions* 13 (1968): 81–110, 111–150. A small section of this essay has been translated into English under the title *"Phībān* Cults in Rural Laos," in *Change and Persistence in Thai Society: Essays in Honor of Lauriston Sharp*, edited by G. William Skinner and A. Thomas Kirsch (Ithaca, N.Y., 1975), pp. 252–277.

Concerning the Thai-Lao of Phaak Isaan, see Stanley J. Tambiah's *Buddhism and the Spirit Cults in North-East Thailand* (Cambridge, 1970). A useful general bibliographical reference is Frank E. Reynolds's "Tradition and Change in Theravāda Buddhism: A Bibliographical Essay Focused on the Modern Period," in *Contributions to Asian Studies*, edited by Bardwell L. Smith, vol. 4 (Leiden, 1973), pp. 94–104.

GEORGES CONDOMINAS
Translated from French by
Maria Pilar Luna-Magannon

LAO-TZU, a quasi-historical figure who came to be revered as a supreme godhead in Chinese Taoist and popular religious traditions. His divinity is understood to be both transcendent and immanent. The *Tao-te ching,* also known simply as the *Lao-tzu,* is traditionally attributed to him. By mid-Han times (206 BCE–220 CE), this text and the *Chuang-tzu* (c. fourth to third century BCE) were regarded as the cornerstones of early Taoist thought.

Lao Tan, the Teacher of Confucius. There is no textual evidence that the *Tao-te ching* itself existed prior to about 250 BCE, although various sayings in the text were in circulation somewhat earlier. It is thought that those who valued this literary heritage as an alternative to the teachings associated with Confucius began to attribute it only retrospectively to a Lao-tzu. The source of inspiration for this hypothetical spokesman was a presumably historical figure known only as Lao Tan, "Old Tan." According to the *Li chi* (Book of Rites; c. 100 BCE), Lao Tan's reputation as an expert on mourning rituals was well established. On four occasions, Confucius is reported to have responded to inquiries about ritual procedure by quoting Lao Tan. It was knowledge he had apparently gained firsthand, for Confucius recalls how he had once assisted Lao Tan in a burial service. Lao Tan, on the other hand, is quoted as addressing Confucius by his given name, Ch'iu, a liberty only those with considerable seniority would have taken. It is no mere coincidence that those at odds with the Confucian tradition should have found a spokesman in someone said to be a mentor of Confucius, for Lao Tan is in fact the only teacher of Confucius about whom there is any documentation.

Unlike the *Book of Rites,* texts outside the Confucian legacy drew on an oral tradition that emphasized the humiliation rather than the enlightenment of Confucius before his teachers. Chief among his detractors was none other than Lao Tan. The *Chuang-tzu,* which is the earliest text to speak of Lao Tan and Lao-tzu as one, appears to have taken the lead in presenting this version of the education of Confucius. There is one allusion to Confucius as a pupil of Lao Tan in the *nei-p'ien* ("inner chapters") of this text. The passage is particularly significant, for the inner chapters are the only portion ascribable to a Chuang-tzu (c. 320 BCE), and the characterizations given here for both Lao Tan and Confucius differ substantially from those recorded in the *Book of Rites.* Lao Tan is no longer presented as a specialist in ritual protocol, nor is Confucius regarded as an exemplar of his teachings. Rather, Lao Tan here counsels a way of life that Confucius is thought too dull to master.

This difference between Confucius and Lao Tan is expanded upon in the *wai-p'ien* ("outer chapters") of the *Chuang-tzu,* the product of heterogeneous authorship. Seven episodes supposedly document instances when Confucius sought advice from Lao Tan on various principles of the Tao. In one of the passages, Lao Tan is identified for the first time as an archivist in retirement from the court of Chou (c. 1046–221 BCE). On each encounter, Confucius is invariably made to look the fool, slow to grasp the subtleties of the Tao. Internal evidence suggests that some of these accounts were perhaps not composed until after the beginning of the Han dynasty. It may have been only a few decades earlier that this reputed superior of Confucius became associated with the *Tao-te ching.* Although the text is never mentioned by title in the *Chuang-tzu,* the outer chapters do draw occasionally on its sayings and twice ascribe them to Lao Tan. Both the *Han Fei–tzu* (third century BCE) and *Huai-nan–tzu* (c. 130 BCE) are more specific, and attribute citations from a *Lao-tzu* text to Lao Tan. By the first century BCE, the legend that Lao-tzu was the author of the *Tao-te ching* had entered the annals of Chinese history as accepted fact.

Li Erh and the Journey West. Ssu-ma Ch'ien (145–86 BCE) is the first known to have attempted a biography of Lao-tzu. His *Shih chi* (Records of the Historian, c. 90 BCE) gives Lao-tzu's full name as Li Erh or Li Tan. The Li clan is identified as native to Hu district, modern Lu-i near the eastern border of Honan Province. In specifying the surname Li, Ssu-ma appears to have had no authority other than an imperial tutor named Li who traced his ancestry to Lao-tzu. Only two episodes are recorded from the life of Lao-tzu. One appears to have drawn on the legacy of both the *Book of Rites* and *Chuang-tzu*. Confucius is said to have sought out Lao-tzu explicitly for instruction on ritual *(li)*, a venture that left him befuddled as well as in awe of the archivist. The second episode centers on Lao-tzu's disappearance. It is said that after living in the domains under Chou rule for a considerable time, Lao-tzu took his leave when he perceived the imminent downfall of the regime. Heading west, he left the central plains of China, but at the Han-ku Pass he was detained by a gatekeeper named Yin Hsi and asked to compose a text on the concepts of *tao* and *te*.

The text Lao-tzu completed was reported to have contained altogether five thousand words filling two folios. That Ssu-ma Ch'ien incorporates this legend on the origins of the *Tao-te ching* into Lao-tzu's biography suggests that the text was fairly well established by his time. The earliest extant versions of a *Te ching* and a *Tao ching* were in fact found among silk manuscripts unearthed in 1973 at a Han tomb known as Ma-wang-tui, located outside modern Ch'ang-sha in Hunan Province. One of the manuscripts appears to have been made sometime prior to 195 BCE and the other sometime between 180 and 168 BCE, both predating Ssu-ma's *Records* by a century or so.

Apocryphal though the attribution to Lao-tzu may be, the *Tao-te ching* became a fundamental text not only for students of pre-Han thought but also for those who came to venerate Lao-tzu as a divine being. Ssu-ma himself says no more about the history of the text or its following. He appears instead to have been genuinely puzzled as to the true identity of Lao-tzu and what writings he may have left behind. His main conclusion seems to be that Lao-tzu was a recluse who, according to popular traditions, may have had a life span of 160 to over 200 years. Such supernatural longevity Lao-tzu presumably attained by an ascetic cultivation of the Tao. So although Ssu-ma does not ascribe a divine status to Lao-tzu, he does retain in his account the suggestion of otherworldly characteristics. This motif and that of the journey west, with its apocalyptic implications of the fall of the Chou, came to be two of the predominant features in the lore that developed around Lao-tzu.

Lao-tzu and Yin Hsi, Master and Disciple. Among the earliest texts to expand upon Ssu-ma's account is the *Lieh-hsien chuan* (Lives of the Immortals), ascribed to Liu Hsiang (77–6 BCE). This work, the current redaction of which dates to no earlier than the second century CE, includes separate entries for Lao-tzu and the gatekeeper Yin Hsi. As the exemplary disciple of Lao-tzu, Yin was also eventually revered as a Taoist patriarch. The *Lives* makes special note of how master and disciple were each aware of the other's uniqueness. Not only did Yin Hsi reportedly recognize Lao-tzu as a *chen-jen* ("true man"), but Lao-tzu is also said to have seen in Yin the rare qualities that made him deserving of instruction.

The master-disciple relationship between them served as a model for generations. According to the hagiographic lore, Yin begged to accompany Lao-tzu on his westward trek. This he could not do, he was told, until he had cultivated the Tao as his master had. Thus it seems that the supernatural qualities that had permitted Lao-tzu to undertake his vast travels abroad were regarded as equally within the reach of his disciple. After an appropriate period of concentrated study, Yin had but to wait his master's summons at the Ch'ing-yang marketplace in what came to be known as the Szechwan city of Ch'eng-tu. The Ch'ing-yang Kung (Palace of the Blue Lamb), newly restored in Ch'eng-tu, stands today in testimony to this ideal discipleship.

The Divinization of Lao-tzu. An equally important shrine in the history of the veneration of Lao-tzu lies far to the northeast of Ch'eng-tu, at Lu-i, his putative birthplace. It is at this site, the T'ai-ch'ing Kung (Palace of Grand Clarity), that Emperor Huan (r. 147–167) of the Latter Han dynasty is known to have authorized sacrifices to Lao-tzu in the years 165–166. Commemorating the imperial offerings is the *Inscription on Lao-tzu (Lao-tzu ming)*, composed by a contemporary local magistrate named Pien Shao. While Pien honors Lao-tzu as a native son of his district, he goes far beyond Ssu-ma's *Records* to convey for the first time something about popular beliefs regarding his apotheosis. He describes Lao-tzu as coeval with primordial chaos, from which he emerged prior to the evolution of the universe itself. After a series of cosmic metamorphoses, Lao-tzu is said to have finally achieved an incarnate form and thus to have begun his descent as savior to the mortal realm. He then became, according to Pien, counselor to successive generations of the great sage-kings of China. It is clear from Pien's inscription that by the late Han, Lao-tzu was viewed as a cosmic force capable of multiple reincarnations in the role of preceptor to the ruling elite. The messianic purpose of his descent became the single most important theme in Lao-tzu's divinization, one that subsequently served all classes of Chinese society, from emperor to revolutionary.

Lao-tzu as Buddha. At the time that Emperor Huan ordered sacrifices at Lu-i, he also presided over an elaborate ritual at court held in honor of both Lao-tzu and the Buddha. An academician named Hsiang K'ai was moved to comment on this service in a memorial that he submitted to the throne in 166. Hsiang alludes in his address to a belief that Lao-tzu transformed himself into the Buddha after having ventured west of his homeland. Thus did the legend of Lao-tzu's disappearance at Han-ku Pass lead to the claim that the Buddha was none other than Lao-tzu, and that his journey was a mission to convert all mortals to the "way of the Tao." This is what came to be known as the *hua-hu* ("conversion of barbarians") theory. Initially, the proposal that Lao-tzu was the Buddha seems to have reflected no more than an amalgamation of Taoist and Buddhist traditions in their formative stages. But as the Buddhist heritage became better articulated and more firmly established on Chinese soil, this notion served as a point of dispute.

By the early fourth century, debates between a prominent Buddhist monk named Po Yüan (d. 304) and the polemicist Wang Fou appear to have inspired the first full treatise on Lao-tzu as the Buddha. Following his defeat in these debates, Wang is said to have composed the *Lao-tzu hua-hu ching* (Scripture on Lao-tzu's Conversion of the Barbarians). Not surprisingly, those who sought to assert the preeminence of Lao-tzu took every opportunity to enlarge upon the legacy of the *hua-hu* myth. Such efforts did not go unchallenged. Twice during the T'ang dynasty *hua-hu* literature was proscribed by imperial command. The decrees were clearly issued at times when defenders of the Buddha's uniqueness held the upper hand at court. Their influence was felt even more strongly during the Mongol regime, when formal debates on the subject were conducted before the throne. The success of the Buddhist monks over the Taoist priests led, in 1281, to the burning of all Taoist texts deemed forgeries. Officially, only the *Tao-te ching* itself was to be spared.

Lao-tzu as a Messiah. The vision of Lao-tzu as a messiah, moving freely between the celestial and mundane realms, inspired a large body of sacred literature. Just as the motives of the authors of these texts varied, so too did their conceptions of what was meant by a deified Lao-tzu. One of the earliest and most enigmatic sources to take up the soteriological theme is the *Lao-tzu pien-hua ching* (Scripture on the Transformations of Lao-tzu). This text was among the manuscripts recovered by Sir Aurel Stein in 1907 at Tun-huang in Kansu Province. Although fragmentary, the work can be identified as the tract of a popular sect in the Ch'eng-tu region, dating to the end of the second century CE.

The *Lao-tzu pien-hua ching* reflects some of the same beliefs articulated in the contemporary "Inscription" of Pien Shao. Lao-tzu is seen as coeval with primordial chaos, circulating in advance of the creation of the universe. He is portrayed as the ultimate manifestation of spontaneity *(tzu-jan)*, the source of the Tao itself, and as the "sovereign lord" *(ti-chün)* of the spirit realm. Such is his transubstantiality that Lao-tzu, according to this text, not only nourishes his own vital principle within the cosmos, but also emerges at various times as an imperial counselor. His series of corporeal transformations is enumerated from legendary times down to the year 155. The final passage appears to be a sermon of Lao-tzu himself, addressed to the faithful masses awaiting his reappearance. He promises them relief from all their tribulations and at the same time vows to overthrow the Han. Precisely what politico-religious sect produced this text is not known, but it was unmistakably intended to set the scene for the reincarnation of Lao-tzu in a charismatic figure who harbored dynastic aspirations. This messianic vision of Lao-tzu's imminent physical transformation continued to inspire generations of rebel leaders, most notably those who also bore the surname Li.

In the Name of Lao-tzu. The documents available on the early Celestial Master tradition (T'ien-shih Tao), which originated in the same area of Szechwan Province as the sect associated with the *Pien-hua ching*, suggest a distinctly different view of Lao-tzu. To the founder, Chang Tao-ling (c. 142), and his successors, Lao-tzu was known as Lord Lao the Most High (T'ai-shang Lao-chün). Although Lord Lao was thought capable of manifesting himself at times of political unrest, the Celestial Masters apparently never entertained the possibility of his reincarnation. Rather than assume a worldly identity, Lord Lao was seen as a transmitter of sacred talismans and registers and, eventually, newly revealed scriptures. He thereby designated the Celestial Masters as his personal envoys and gave them alone responsibility for restoring order on earth.

As agents of their Lord Lao, the Celestial Masters themselves often assumed the role of imperial preceptor that Lao-tzu was traditionally thought to have fulfilled for the sage-kings. Thus Chang Lu (c. 190–220) and K'ou Ch'ien-chih (d. 448), for example, served the monarchs of the Wei and Northern Wei regimes, respectively. Crucial to their success as counselors to the throne was the emperor's perception of his own divine rank. It was advantageous, in other words, to identify the head of state as a deity incarnate, just as K'ou proclaimed the emperor T'ai-wu (r. 423–452) to be the T'ai-p'ing Chen-chün ("true lord of grand peace"). As the influence of the Celestial Masters declined, the T'ang imperial lineage, surnamed Li, laid claim to being the direct descendants of Lao-tzu. In support of this assertion, there seems to have been a renewed interest during the T'ang in witnessing the epiphanies of Lord Lao. [*See also the biographies of Chang Tao-ling, Chang Lu, and K'ou Ch'ien-chih.*]

Lao-tzu as a Focus of History. The histories of the faith that survive in the Taoist canon *(Tao-tsang)* are remarkably uniform in that they are organized as chronicles of Lao-tzu's unending transmigrations. An early example of this annalistic approach is found in the *Li-tai ch'ung-tao chi* (A Record of Historical Reverence for the Tao), compiled by the preeminent ritual specialist Tu Kuang-t'ing (850–933) in 884. The T'ang portion of this chronicle is devoted primarily to a record of Lao-tzu's providential manifestations, from the founding of the dynasty to the suppression of the Huang Ch'ao rebellion (c. 878–884).

Later historians also sought to link the vitality of their age to the beneficence of Lao-tzu. Chia Shan-hsiang (c. 1086), for example, paid special tribute to the favors Lord Lao granted during the early part of the Sung dynasty. He wrote his lengthy treatise, the *Yu-lung chuan* (Like unto a Dragon), while stationed at the Palace of Grand Clarity in Lu-i, the site to which Lao-tzu reputedly made many return visits following his "historical" birth there. While Chia writes extensively about the mythical manifestations of Lao-tzu, it is to his incarnation as Li Erh that he devotes an unprecedented amount of detail, much of it parallel to the legends surrounding the Buddha. Just as Śākyamuni was, according to some traditions, born of his mother's right armpit, so was Lao-tzu said to have emerged from his mother's left armpit. Lao-tzu was also conceived to be equally precocious for, according to legend, he, too, took his first steps immediately after birth. The latter episode is among those given further elaboration in the *Hun-yüan sheng chi* (A Chronicle of the Sage from the Primordiality of Chaos), compiled a century later. The compiler of this work, Hsieh Shou-hao (1134–1212), extends the chronology of Lao-tzu's manifestations down to the end of the Northern Sung dynasty (960–1126) and offers a thoughtful commentary on many controversial points such as the *hua-hu* theory.

Of note in the writings of both Chia and Hsieh is the wide range of revealed literature associated with the successive rebirths of Lao-tzu. Chronicles of this type also typically record the honorary titles bestowed upon Lord Lao by imperial decree, thus calling attention to the periods when state patronage was at its height. The title of Hsieh's work is in fact based on the epithet granted Lao-tzu in 1014.

Lao-tzu Embodied. The feature of the hagiographic lore that came to serve as a primary focus of Taoist meditative practice is the process by which Lao-tzu came to his earthly incarnation. An early account of his "historical" nativity appears in the late second-century *Scripture on the Transformations of Lao-tzu.* There it is said that by a metamorphosis of his spirit *(shen),* Lao-tzu assumed the form of his mother and then within her womb, after a long gestation, he achieved carnal form. This concept of Lao-tzu as his own mother is ultimately derived from the *Tao-te ching,* where the Tao that bears a name is said to be the mother of all things. It is understood, in other words, that Lao-tzu is the body of the Tao itself. The transformations he undergoes prior to his incarnation are thought to be analogous to the evolutionary stages of the universe. Lao-tzu arises from primordial chaos as the Tao incarnate to become the mother of all things, the source of creation. The reenactment of this process of Lao-tzu's birth is precisely what lies at the heart of the early manuals on meditative practices associated with "nourishing the vital principle" *(yang-hsing).* Just as Lao-tzu, the embodiment of the Tao, is himself perceived to be a microcosm of the universe, so too does the Taoist adept view his own body as a vast kingdom. Within this internal landscape, the adept strives to transform his vital forces into the image of a newborn babe, a homunculus modeled after Lao-tzu.

In the legacy of *nei-tan,* physiological alchemy, this creation has come to be referred to as the enchymoma, or inner macrobiogen. The generation of an enchymoma is achieved by a variety of psycho-physiological means, including respiratory exercises, visualization procedures, and controlled sexual practices. It is as if the adept strives to replicate within his body the elixir of immortality that alchemical reaction vessels were designed to produce. Consequently, to attain physiological rejuvenation through the enchymoma is to attain longevity and to become impervious to any external threats from demonic sources. Some manuals spell out even higher goals, including liberation from the bonds of mundane existence and promotion to the ranks of heavenly transcendents.

Such techniques of regeneration are also commonly applied by a Taoist priest in the liturgies, such as the Chiao ceremony, held on behalf of the living and dead he serves. By re-creating the "sovereign lord" embryo within, the priest promotes not only his own transcendent status but that of his entire parish as well. Thus does the embodiment of the cosmogonic image of Lao-tzu lead to the salvation of all. [*See also* Chiao.]

Patterns of Devotion. The importance of the *Tao-te ching* in various scriptural guides to the Taoist way of life cannot be overemphasized. In a preface to his analysis of the work, the thirty-ninth Celestial Master Chang Ssu-ch'eng (d. 1343) laments the fact that many who regarded themselves as disciples of Lord Lao had no understanding of his teachings. Many such commentaries to the *Tao-te ching* were compiled upon imperial command, following the model of the emperor's personal exegesis. The opaque language of the text easily lent itself to countless reinterpretations and metaphorical applications.

As early as the Han dynasty, the *Tao-te ching* was apparently recited not only for magico-religious purposes, but also as a guide to deportment. Additionally, a number of separate tracts appeared, offering advice to the adept on how to conduct one's life in accordance with the principles of the *Tao-te ching,* namely, limited activity *(wu-wei),* pure quiescence *(ch'ing-ching),* and noncontention *(pu-cheng).* According to hagiographic lore, it was not unusual for exemplars of these principles to find themselves bearing witness to an epiphany of Lao-tzu, an experience that in turn frequently presaged their own spiritual transcendence. From at least the thirteenth century, Lao-tzu was ritually evoked as the primary patriarch of the Ch'üan-chen lineage on the putative date of his birth, the fifteenth day of the second lunar month. It was also customary, according to the Ch'üan-chen tradition established by Wang Che (1112–1170), to call upon Lord Lao to preside over ritual commemorations of immortals sacred to the lineage. These ceremonies no doubt drew large crowds of clergy and laity alike. [*See also the biography of Wang Che.*]

To the individual lay believer, Lao-tzu appears to have offered a wide range of solace. The texts of stone inscriptions preserved from the sixth to the thirteenth century attest to the various demands devotees put on their compassionate messiah. Two inscriptions dating to the Northern Ch'i (550–577), which mark the crafting of an image of Lao-tzu, express the hope that the deceased will be granted ascent to the heavenly realm. By the T'ang dynasty, many images and shrines to Lao-tzu had been created as talismans to ensure the welfare of the emperor, reflecting thereby the close relation between church and state.

Large quantities of newly revealed scriptures written in the name of T'ai-shang Lao-chün took equal account of both this-worldly and otherworldly concerns. These texts, especially popular during the T'ang and Sung, purport to be the Lord Lao's personal instructions on everything from the art of prolonging life to the quelling of all the malevolent forces thought to threaten mankind. As was the case with the *Tao-te ching,* it was believed that the full efficacy of the new scriptures could only be realized after repeated recitation. To Lao-tzu were also attributed very specific behavioral codes, designed to reinforce traditional Chinese values as well as to promote the goals of a utopian, socialist society. Lao-tzu, in other words, was a source of inspiration for many special interests from all levels of society. During waves of spiritual innovation, many shrines to Lord Lao arose throughout the countryside, while others were restored or enlarged. Worshipers at these shrines were often rewarded by visions of their Lord, appearing in response to individual pleas for divine intervention. According to one inscription dated 1215, Lord Lao was expressly evoked by Taoist priests in an elaborate ritual to exorcise a victim of possessing spirits.

Images of Lao-tzu. In his *Pao-p'u–tzu,* a compilation of southern Chinese religious beliefs and practices, Ko Hung (283–343) offers one of the earliest descriptions of Lao-tzu's appearance. According to a passage in the *nei-p'ien* ("inner chapters"), one was to envision Lord Lao as a figure nine *ch'ih* (about seven feet) tall, invested with cloudlike garments of five colors, a multitiered cap, and a sharp sword. Among the distinctive facial features he is reputed to have are a prominent nose, extended eyebrows, and long ears, a physiognomy typically signifying longevity. Ko Hung concludes that the ability to call forth this vision of Lord Lao gave one assurance of divine omniscience, as well as everlasting life. [*See also the biography of Ko Hung.*]

Later resources propose a far more elaborate scheme of visualization. For example, nearly an entire chapter of a seventh-century anthology, the *San-tung chu-nang* (A Satchel of Pearls from the Three Caverns) of Wang Hsüan-ho (fl. 682), is devoted to citations on the salient features of supramundane beings. Among the more notable passages is one from the *Hua-hu ching* that asserts that Lao-tzu is endowed with seventy-two distinguishing attributes, an obvious parallel to the Buddha's thirty-two *lakṣaṇa.* The specification of these divine features varies according to the meditation guide quoted. One manual speaks of meditating on the nine transformations of Lao-tzu, the last and most imposing of which bears all seventy-two attributes. In this ultimate vision, the cosmogonic body of Lao-tzu is said to emerge as a radiant simulacrum of the heavens above and earth below.

A variation on this visualization technique is found in an anonymous account of the Lord Lao of the early eleventh century, the *Hun-yüan huang-ti sheng chi* (A Chronicle of the Sage and Majestic Sovereign from the Primordiality of Chaos). Two meditative techniques prescribed in this text invite comparison with the changing conceptualizations of the Buddha's *dharmakāya.* The initial procedure is based on a recall of each of the seventy-two attributes of Lao-tzu's "ritual body," or *fa-shen,* which is the standard translation of the term *dharmakāya.* The focus of the second type of meditation is on the "true body" or *chen-shen* of Lao-tzu, as he is perceived suspended in the cosmos, utterly tranquil, beyond all transmigrations. The *Hun-yüan huang-ti sheng chi* also discusses the settings in which the ever-radiant Lord Lao may be envisioned, for example, seated Buddha-fashion on a lotus throne or in command of a jade chariot harnessed to divine dragons. The vividness of these descriptions suggests that they may very well have served as guides to those who crafted images of Lao-tzu or painted temple murals.

Later hagiographic accounts supplement the teachings on visualization with reports on the miraculous impressions of Lord Lao upon both natural and man-made landmarks. Although these visions commonly proved to be equally ephemeral, their memory was often reportedly preserved in works of art. Details on early icons are otherwise scarce, for even in the epigraphic records little more is specified than the choice of material to be worked, such as stone, jade, or clay. A T'ang dynasty rendition of Lao-tzu in stone, now housed in the Shansi Provincial Museum of T'ai-yüan, is one of the few such images to survive. The right hand of this seated figure, dating to 719, holds a short-handled fan in the shape of a palm leaf. This type of fan became the defining feature of the Lord Lao as he is most commonly depicted in a grouping of the Celestial Worthies of the Three Clarities (San-ch'ing T'ien-tsun). A remarkable representation of this trinity in wood is once more on view in the upper story of the rear pavilion at the Pai-yün Kuan (White Cloud Abbey) in Peking, a Ch'üan-chen shrine that is now home to the Chinese Taoist Association.

[*See also* Taoism; Millenarianism, *article on* Chinese Millenarian Movements; *Huang-lao Chün; and the biography of Confucius.*]

BIBLIOGRAPHY

Tao Te Ching, rev. ed., translated by D. C. Lau (Hong Kong, 1982), includes a translation of the Wang Pi text of the *Lao-tzu,* together with a rendition based on the Ma-wang-tui manuscripts. Of special interest in this work are Lau's introductions on Lao-tzu and the Ma-wang-tui texts, and two appendixes on "The Problem of Authorship" and "The Nature of the Work." *Chuang-tzu; The Seven Inner Chapters and Other Writings from the Book Chuang-tzu,* translated by A. C. Graham (London, 1981), includes a thoughtful analysis of the passages that bear on Lao-tzu's encounters with Confucius. Annotated translations of Liu Hsiang's biographies of Lao-tzu and Yin Hsi are found in *Le Lie-sien tchouan: Biographies légendaires des Immortels taoïstes de l'antiquité,* edited and translated by Max Kaltenmark (Peking, 1953). Anna K. Seidel's *La divinisation de Lao tseu, dans le taoïsme des Han* (Paris, 1969) is an invaluable monograph based on a critical reading of the *Lao-tzu ming* and the *Lao-tzu pien-hua ching.* For a comprehensive study of the *hua-hu* issue from the second to the sixth century, Erik Zürcher's *The Buddhist Conquest of China,* 2 vols. (1959; Leiden, 1972), remains unsurpassed. Outstanding documentation of the techniques for prolonging life with which Lao-tzu became associated is available in Henri Maspero's *Le taoïsme et les religions chinoises* (Paris, 1971), translated by Frank A. Kierman, Jr., as *Taoism and Chinese Religion* (Amherst, Mass., 1981). Norman J. Girardot's *Myth and Meaning in Early Taoism* (Berkeley, 1983) examines the mythology of Lao-tzu's transformations as it pertains to early cosmogonic theory. His analysis is based in large part on Seidel's work, taken together with Kristofer Schipper's "The Taoist Body," *History of Religions* 17 (1978): 355–386. Schipper offers a more detailed interpretation of Lao-tzu's "cosmogonic body" in *Le corps taoïste* (Paris, 1982). Extensive documentation of the *nei-tan* tradition is found in Joseph Needham and Lu Gwei-Djen's *Science and Civilisation in China,* vol. 5, pt. 5 (Cambridge, 1983). For a survey of pertinent hagiographies, historical chronologies, and exegeses on the *Tao-te ching,* see my *A Survey of Taoist Literature, Tenth–Seventeenth Centuries* (Berkeley, 1986).

JUDITH MAGEE BOLTZ

LAPP RELIGION. *See* Saami Religion; *see also* Arctic Religions *and* Finno-Ugric Religions.

LARES. The Latin word *lares* does not have a clear etymology. It is used in the singular *(lar, laris)* and, more often, in the plural *(lares, larum)* to designate the protective gods of a parcel of land. "In their basic meaning, the *lares* should be considered as divinities attached to a place" (Wissowa, 1912, p. 169). The definition, which cultic evidence supports, was obscured by the glosses of ancient scholars and then recovered to some extent by modern experts. Thus, the *lares* were perceived by some as "infernal spirits" (Paulus-Festus, ed. Lindsay, 1913, p. 273 L.). This confusion with the *manes* is a product of arbitrary speculation. While the religion of the earliest Roman period does not know genealogical ties, there was concocted a "mother of the *lares,*" who was called Mania by Varro (*De lingua Latina* 9.67) and Macrobius (*Saturnalia* 1,7.35), Lara by Ovid (*Fasti* 2.615.), and Mater Larum in the imperial liturgy of the Arval Brothers. Mania was understood by others as a "mother of the *larvae*" ("evil spirits"; Paulus-Festus, op. cit., p. 115 L.). Some here ventured equally fanciful connections with the name **Larenta*, borrowed from the name of the funerary feast, *Larentalia*, or even from the "Sabine" *Larunda* (Varro, *De lingua Latina* 5.74).

Better evidence is obtained by examining the cultic data. In the plural, the *lares* were invoked (under the form *lases*, from an age when the first *s* had not yet yielded to the *r*) as protectors of the *ager Romanus* ("the cultivated fields of Rome") in the archaic hymn of the Arval Brothers. They were venerated as the *lares compitales* at the crossroads *(compita)* at the time of the Compitalia, a movable feast at the beginning of January. Protectors of the site of the City (Rome), they were honored as *lares praestites* on 1 May (Ovid, *Fasti* 5.129–136). Their range could extend even out to sea. As the *lares permarini* they were honored by a temple that was vowed during the naval battle against Antiochus in 190 BCE by the praetor L. Aemilius Regillus.

In the singular, the *lar familiaris* was the protector of the family domain, both of freemen and of slaves. It was to him that the *pater familias* would offer a wreath "so that this abode might be for us a source of wealth, blessing, happiness, and good fortune" (Plautus, *Trinummus* 40–47). It was he who the master would first salute upon arriving at his villa (Cato, *De agricultura* 2.7). One recent discovery has brought to light an archaic inscription—transcribed "Lare Aenea d[ono]"—from a stone of the fourth or third century BCE, found at Tor Tignosa near Lavinium. It is the earliest example of the use of *lar* with a proper noun and should attest as well to the existence of a cult rendered to Aeneas.

BIBLIOGRAPHY

Dumézil, Georges. *La religion romain archaïque*. 2d ed. Paris, 1974. See pages 346–350. This work has been translated from the first edition by Philip Krapp as *Archaic Roman Religion*, 2 vols. (Chicago, 1970).

Latte, Kurt. *Römische Religionsgeschichte*. Munich, 1960. See pages 90–94 on *lares larentalia*.

Schilling, Robert. *"Cippo di Tor Tignosa."* In *Enciclopedia Virgiliana*. Rome, forthcoming. Apropos of *lar Aeneas*.

Schilling, Robert. *Rites, cultes, dieux de Rome*. Paris, 1979. See pages 401–414 on *lares grundiles*.

Wissowa, Georg. *Religion und Kultus der Römer*. 2d ed. Munich, 1912. See pages 166–175.

ROBERT SCHILLING
Translated from French by Paul C. Duggan

LAS CASAS, BARTOLOMÉ DE (1474–1566), Christian missionary. Las Casas was born in Seville, Spain. In 1502 he went to the island of Hispaniola (present-day Dominican Republic and Haiti), where he participated in the conquest of the Indians. As a reward he received lands and Indians under the *encomienda* system, a kind of indentured servanthood. He exercised the lay office of catechist, worked to evangelize the Indians, and was ordained a priest about 1512. His commitment to evangelization did not keep him from participating in the bloody conquest of Cuba, for which he received additional lands and Indians. However, in 1514, at forty years of age, he was converted to concern for the plight of the Indians while reading *Ecclesiasticus (Ben Sira)* 34:22. Four months later he preached his famous sermon in the Church of the Holy Spirit, denouncing the grave injustices being committed, and turned his Indians over to the governor of Cuba. Until his death at ninety-two, he was the tireless "Defender of the Indians," a title conferred on him in Madrid in 1516.

Las Casas returned to Spain four times, in attempts to save the Indians from the cruelties of the Spanish conquest and to find new methods to convert them to Christianity. In his efforts he became a court reformer in Spain (1515); the leader of the unsuccessful colony of peace in Curmaná, Venezuela (1520), which attempted to establish agricultural communities of Spanish and Indian workers; a Dominican monk and prior in Santo Domingo (1523); the unrelenting foe of the unjust wars of suppression in Nicaragua (1535); a defender of the Indians against ecclesiastics in Mexico (1532); a promoter and participant in the project to colonize and Christianize the natives of Guatemala by peaceable means (1537); a successful attorney for the Indians before Charles V, urging the adoption of the New Laws (1542), which, for example, negated the rights of the *encomienda* over Indian children; and the rejected bishop of Chiapas (1545). When he returned to Spain for the last time in 1547, it was as a legal adviser and theologian in defense of Indian rights.

In his prophetic crusade, alternately encouraged and denounced by creoles and clerics, Las Casas doggedly and dogmatically followed what he conceived to be his life's purpose. With a missionary conviction that his truth could not be negotiated, he proclaimed, "All peoples of the earth are men." He categorically denied the claims of Juan Ginés de Sepúlveda that "the Indians are inferior to the Spanish as are children to adults, women to men, and . . . almost as monkeys to humans." Rather, he lauded the cultural and artistic achievements of Indian cultures, which he considered equal to that of ancient Egypt. In some respects, he declared in his *Apologetic History*, Indians are superior to Spaniards.

Las Casas wrote in reaction to what he viewed as horrible inhumanities committed with hypocritical religious justification. Must people be converted by slavery and the sword? In his *Only Method of Attracting All People to the True Faith* (1537), he argued for means that persuade by exhortation and gentle attractions of the will. With furious verbal assaults and chilling realism, he recounted the relations of the Indians with their European conquerors in his *History of the Indies*, on which he worked from 1527 to 1566. Equally brutal in exposing the grave crimes against the Indian race, his *Very Brief Account of the Destruction of the Indies* (1542) and eight more tracts for public dissemination (1552) raised storms of protest against Las Casas. But the prophet was unbending: his *Advice and Regulations for Confessors* (1545) advocated denial of the sacraments of the church to all who had Indians and did not "pay a just wage." In later years British royalists, New England colonists, French rationalists, and Latin American nationalists freely used his condemnation of the Spanish atrocities as propaganda for their own causes.

Crusader, traitor, prophet, paranoiac, servant of God, anarchist, visionary, pre-Marxist, egalitarian—these are but a few of the epithets hurled at his memory. The issues Las Casas raised are dangerously modern.

BIBLIOGRAPHY

An admirable collection of the principal writings of Las Casas is *Orbras escogidas*, 5 vols., edited by Juan Pérez de Tudela (Madrid, 1957–1958). The missionary's view that the gospel requires a peaceful evangelization of the Indians without the use of arms is contained in his *Del único modo de atraer a todos los pueblos a la verdadera religión*, edited by Augustín Millares (Mexico City, 1942). Two of his principal works are available in English: *Devastation of the Indies: A Brief Account*, translated from Spanish by Herman Briffault (New York, 1974), and *In Defense of the Indians*, edited and translated from Latin by Stafford Poole with Lewis Hanke, V. Friede, and Benjamin Keen (De Kalb, Ill., 1974). The first work defends the thesis that the cause of the destruction of an "infinite number of souls" by Christians is solely the latter's thirst for gold and "to become fat with riches in a few brief days." The second work denounces the imperialistic exploitation of the Indians inspired by the conquistadors' greed and ambition; as such, it may be considered a tract for all times against economic and social exploitation.

A useful bibliography is Lewis Hanke and Manuel Giménez Fernández's *Bartolomé de las Casas, 1474–1566: Bibliografía crítica y cuerpo de materiales para el estudio de su vida* (Santiago de Chile, 1954). Though dated, this work gives a valuable accounting of studies on historical background and additional bibliographical sources. Manuel Giménez Fernández's *Bartolomé de las Casas*, 2 vols. (Seville, 1953–1960), is an excellent, though unfinished, biography of the first part of his life.

SIDNEY H. ROOY

LATTER-DAY SAINTS. *See* Mormonism.

LATVIAN RELIGION. *See* Baltic Religion.

LA VALLÉE POUSSIN, LOUIS DE (1869–1938), Belgian Indologist and specialist in Buddhist philosophy. Educated in Liège, Louvain, Paris, and Leiden, La Vallée Poussin became professor at the University of Ghent. He entered his field of research at a time when Buddhist studies were dominated by the study of the Pali canon and Sanskrit narrative literature with an emphasis either on psychological and ethical aspects or on mythology and social concerns. (A more doctrinal approach did exist, mostly in the French and Russian traditions.) La Vallée Poussin dedicated all the strength of his philological genius to this field and thus contributed to a reorientation of Buddhist studies toward the languages of northern Buddhism (Sanskrit and Tibetan) and toward Buddhist philosophy considered in its historical perspective. He produced two main types of studies: scholarly editions, and translations with exegeses. These correspond roughly to the two periods of his activity, that before and that after World War I.

During the first period, there was a need for accurately edited texts. It remains La Vallée Poussin's major contribution to Buddhist studies that he gave us several text editions, some published in Belgium, others in the classical series "Bibliotheca Indica," Calcutta, and others in the series "Bibliotheca Buddhica," Saint Petersburg. He began with some of the then-neglected Tantric texts, *Pañcakrama* (1896) and *Adikarmapradīpa* (1898), and continued with important Mādyamika writings, among them Nāgārjuna's *Mādyamikasūtras* (1903–1913) and Prajñākaramati's *Pañjikā* commentary on the *Bodhicaryāvātara* of Śāntideva (1901–1905). Other texts he edited included some fragments then newly discovered by Aurel Stein.

Besides this editorial oeuvre, La Vallée Poussin produced numerous translations, exegetical studies, and text analyses. He also wrote several essays (including some that were to appear in Christian publications) that show his preoccupation with and perpetual reassessment of what he called Buddhist dogmatics.

After World War I, La Vallée Poussin, who had in the meantime mastered the languages of the Chinese Buddhist translations, undertook the enormous enterprise of translating and critically annotating two *summae* of Buddhist scholastics: Vasubandhu's *Abhidharmakośa*, the masterwork of the northern Hīnayāna *abhidharma* school, and Hsüan-tsang's *Vijñaptimātratāsiddhi*, the best compendium of the tenets of the Yogācāra, or Idealist, current of the Mahāyāna. For his *Abhidharmakośa* (1923-1931), La Vallée Poussin had to master the huge Kashmirian *Mahāvibhāsā,* which even today has not been translated into a Western language. With his *Vijñaptimātratāsiddhi: La Siddhi de Hiuan-tsang* (1928–1929) he took the lead in the study of Idealist Buddhism, a field in which Sylvain Lévi had laid the foundation and which Paul Demiéville and La Vallée Poussin's pupil Étienne Lamotte were to continue.

These exegetical exercises did not keep La Vallée Poussin from pursuing other areas of Buddhist thought. Paradoxically, La Vallée Poussin was both fascinated and reticent regarding the Mādhyamika; he was attracted by the critical stance of Mādhyamika thought, but this attraction was resisted by his strong personal convictions. His attitude is reflected in numerous publications on the meaning of *nirvāṇa* (annihilation or bliss?) and in his polemics with Theodore Stcherbatsky on the interpretation of *śūnyatā* (emptiness or relativity?). La Vallée Poussin submitted the ancient history of India to his Nagarjunian criticism in three volumes: *Indo-Européens et Indo-Iraniens* (1924), *L'Inde aux temps des Mauryas* (1930), and *Dynasties et histoire de l'Inde* (1935).

BIBLIOGRAPHY

Besides the writings mentioned in this article, the thirty-six articles La Vallée Poussin contributed to the *Encyclopaedia of Religion and Ethics,* edited by James Hastings (Edinburgh, 1908–1926), yield much information on the results of the studies of his first period. A good overview of his second period can be gained from his "Notes bouddhiques" in the *Bulletin de la classe des lettres* of the Académie Royale de Belgique (Brussels, 1921–1929) and from his numerous contributions to the first five volumes (Brussels, 1932–1937) of the publication series he founded in 1931, the "Mélanges chinois et bouddhiques."

Works on La Vallée Poussin include Marcelle Lalou's article "Rétrospective: L'œuvre de Louis de la Vallée Poussin," in *Bibliographie bouddhique,* fasc. annexe 23 bis (Paris, 1955), pp. 1–37; and Étienne Lamotte's article "Notice sur Louis de la Vallée Poussin," *Annuaire de l'Académie Royale des Sciences, des Lettres et des Beaux-arts* 131 (1965): 145–168.

HUBERT DURT

LAW, WILLIAM (1686–1761), English devotional writer. Born at King's Cliffe, Northamptonshire, William Law came from a family "of high respectability and of good means." He entered Emmanuel College, Cambridge, in 1705 to prepare for the Anglican ministry; he achieved the B.A. in 1708 and the M.A. in 1712, the same year in which he received a fellowship and ordination. He read widely from the classics, the church fathers, and the early mystics and devotional writers, and he studied science and philosophy as well. Law's refusal to take oaths of allegiance and abjuration upon the accession of George I deprived him of his fellowship and his right to serve as minister in the Church of England. He remained loyal to the state church, however, throughout his life. After an extended period as tutor to Edward Gibbon, father of the historian, Law took up permanent residence at his birthplace, King's Cliffe, where he served as spiritual adviser to many, engaged in acts of charity to the deprived of the community, and wrote the nine volumes that make up his major works.

Law's early writings include *Remarks upon the Fable of the Bees* (1723), a refutation of Bernard Mandeville's work; *The Unlawfulness of Stage Entertainment* (1726); *The Case of Reason or Natural Religion* (1731); and two better-known works, *Treatise upon Christian Perfection* (1726) and *A Serious Call to a Devout and Holy Life* (1729). These latter contribute significantly to a tradition of devotional prose literature that includes such writers as Augustine, Richard Baxter, Jeremy Taylor, John Donne, and Lancelot Andrewes. Law's devotional writing has as its controlling purpose the aiding of man in his quest of the "godly life," and it reveals several distinguishing themes: preoccupation with the scriptures and Christ as the bases and models for perfection; self-denial as a necessary antidote to vainglory and passion; prayer and meditation; and ways and means for implementing Christian doctrine in practical affairs.

Among Law's later work were responses to various religious writers: *The Grounds and Reason for Christian Regeneration* (1739), *An Appeal to All Who Doubt the Truths of the Gospel* (1740), *An Answer to Dr. Trapp's Discourse* (1740), and *A Refutation of Dr. Warburton's Projected Defense of Christianity* (1757). More influential, however, were the mystical writings *The Spirit of Prayer* (1749), *The Spirit of Love* (1752), and *The Way to Divine Knowledge* (1752). These three works reveal the influence of Jakob Boehme, who professed visionary encounters with God. Many Christian critics have objected to the oversubjectivism and implicit universalism in Law's later writings, branding them as "mystical," a term often held as opprobrious by traditional religious thinkers. However, if one considers an intuitive approach to reality, awareness of unity in diversity, and a passion for a spiritual reality that underlies and unifies all things to be typical of mysticism, one realizes that this desire for union with God lies at the root of all religious devotion. In this light, Law's "mystical" works reflect his earlier theological beliefs and have a close kinship with his *Christian Perfection* and *A Serious Call.*

Many readers have paid tribute to Law's simple, clear, and vivid prose style, and scholars have pointed to his pronounced religious influence on such minds as

Samuel Johnson, John Wesley, John Henry Newman, Charles Williams, and C. S. Lewis. His intellectual power, incisiveness, and piety wielded a marked influence both within and without organized church ranks. Law's major achievement lay in his significant contribution to the English tradition of devotional prose literature.

BIBLIOGRAPHY

Primary Source

Law, William. *The Works of the Reverend William Law, M.A.* (1762). Reprint, 9 vols. in 3, London, 1892–1893.

Secondary Sources

Baker, Eric. *A Herald of the Evangelical Revival.* London, 1948. Examines basic views of Law and Jakob Boehme and shows how Law kindled in Wesley a passion for an unimpaired "ethical ideal."

Hopkinson, Arthur. *About William Law: A Running Commentary on His Works.* London, 1948. Recognizes works with different subjects: religious controversy, morality, mysticism, and theology. Sketchy but informative.

Overton, John H. *William Law: Nonjuror and Mystic.* London, 1881. Still the best single source for Law's life and thought.

Rudolph, Erwin P. *William Law.* Boston, 1980. Examines the range of Law's thought and contribution to devotional prose literature.

Walker, Arthur K. *William Law: His Life and Thought.* London, 1973. Examines Law's intellectual biography, focusing on the people whom Law knew and the writings with which he was familiar. Sometimes digressive and biased but generally useful.

ERWIN P. RUDOLPH

LAW AND RELIGION. [*This entry concerns the interactions between religious traditions and legal systems, and it explores the ways in which religion has influenced the development of law in several of the world's major cultural areas. It consists of five articles:*

An Overview
Law and Religion in South Asia
Law and Religion in East Asia
Law and Religion in the West
Religion and the Constitution of the United States

For discussion of the place of law within the Israelite, Jewish, and Islamic traditions, see Israelite Law; Halakhah; *and* Islamic Law.]

An Overview

If law and religion are viewed narrowly—law as rules of conduct promulgated and enforced by political authorities, and religion as beliefs and practices relating to the supernatural—the two may be treated as largely independent of each other, at least in most cultures. If, however, each is viewed more broadly, they will be seen to be closely interrelated. In virtually all societies the established legal processes of allocating rights and duties, resolving conflicts, and creating channels of cooperation are inevitably connected with the community's sense of, and commitment to, ultimate values and purposes.

The religious dimension of law is apparent in at least four elements found in all legal systems: (1) *ritual,* that is, the ceremonial procedures that symbolize the objectivity of law; (2) *tradition,* that is, the language and practices handed down from the past that symbolize the ongoing character of law; (3) *authority,* that is, reliance on written or spoken sources that are considered to be decisive in themselves and that symbolize the binding power of law; and (4) *universality,* that is, the claim to embody universally valid concepts or insights that symbolize the law's connection with all-embracing morality. All four of these elements connect a society's legal order to its belief in a reality beyond itself.

In some societies law and religion, even in their narrowest sense, are expressly identified with each other. This is true of those rudimentary societies in which persons with religious authority play a dominant role in governing, and where there is no distinct class of lawgivers or judges or lawyers. In many of these societies magical and mechanical legal procedures, such as ordeals and ritual oaths, are used in punishing misconduct and resolving disputes. In an early stage of development of Roman law, the priesthood (pontiffs) played a dominant role and the methods of proof were highly formalistic. In an early stage of the development of law in Greece, judgment, retribution, custom, and apportionment of losses were all hypostatized as Olympian gods whose decrees were divined in the oracles.

A different interconnection between law and religion exists in the Hebrew and Muslim civilizations, where a sophisticated system of law is found in sacred writings, namely the Torah and the Qur'ān. There the observance of law is itself a religious act.

In societies where jurisdiction has eventually been transferred from religious to secular authorities, a certain desanctification of legal rules and procedures has inevitably resulted. In Greece and Rome, however, this process was accompanied by the development of a philosophy of natural law in which religious assumptions played a major part. Furthermore, a great deal of Greek and Roman law continued to concern itself with the regulation of religious ceremonies.

Even in cultures where law is most sharply distinguished from religious beliefs, the distinction itself is usually thought to have a religious significance. Thus in traditional China, which considered law *(fa)* to be ad hoc, mechanistic, and based on mere expediency—in contrast to virtue or "principle" *(li)*, which is rooted in nature—*fa* was nevertheless thought to be directed ultimately by the natural (heavenly) world order.

In the West, the interdependence of law and religion took on a different significance in the late Middle Ages with the separation of ecclesiastical and secular polities, each with its own law. Both the canon law of the Roman Catholic church and the various systems of secular law that existed alongside it were supposed to promote the good life. However, the canon law had the still higher purpose of permitting the obedient to be in communion with God. This conception of a spiritual law of the church was rejected by Luther and Calvin and their followers who removed all law to the earthly realm of sin and death. In the original Protestant conception, nevertheless, law remained linked with faith, since faithful Christians—and especially Christian rulers—were called upon to use the law in order that justice be done and the world reformed. Neither Luther nor Calvin shared the antinomian view that the Christian community can live in a state of grace without law. Nor did they or their followers make a contrast, such as some twentieth-century theologians have made, between law and love; they understood both the moral law and the civil law to be directed toward the realization of *caritas* in social relationships.

Undoubtedly there has been a decline, during the twentieth century, of direct religious influences on the legal systems of western Europe and the United States. This has been the result, in part, of the widespread privatization of religion, which has helped produce a tension, and even an antagonism, between religion and law, the two being seen primarily as a matter of personal psychology and social action respectively. This view recognizes that law may ultimately stem from religious beliefs (the usual formula is that law is based on morality, and morality on religion), but considers it important to distinguish between religion and law to the maximum extent possible, partly to maintain both the freedom of religion from legal controls and the freedom of law from religious influences.

The privatization of traditional religions has sometimes been accompanied by the pouring into nontheistic belief systems (ideologies, "isms") of universal theory, apocalyptic vision, and sacrificial passion such as formerly characterized Western Christian movements. In communist countries this has led not only to an extreme separation of church and state (involving virtual withdrawal of public support from the churches, and virtual exclusion of religious believers from participation in political life), but also to an extreme identification of the state with the official belief system. The socialist legal systems of the Soviet Union and other communist countries are intended to directly reflect the belief systems to which those countries are committed. In that broad sense, one might speak of them as (nontheistic) religious legal systems.

[*See also* Marxism.]

BIBLIOGRAPHY

For general surveys of law and religion, see my books *The Interaction of Law and Religion* (Nashville, 1974) and *Law and Revolution: The Formation of the Western Legal Tradition* (Cambridge, Mass., 1983); Karl Bünger's *Religiöse Bindungen in frühen und orientalischen Rechten* (Wiesbaden, 1952); Christopher H. Dawson's *Religion and Culture* (London, 1948); Ze'ev W. Falk's *Law and Religion: The Jewish Experience* (Jerusalem, 1981); Henry Sumner Maine's *Ancient Law: Its Connection with the Early History of Society and Its Relation to Modern Ideas*, 3d ed. (New York, 1879); and *Religion and the Law*, a special issue of *Hastings Law Journal* 29 (July 1978).

On the interrelation of Greek and Roman law and religion, see Werner W. Jaeger's *Paideia: The Ideals of Greek Culture*, 3 vols. (Oxford, 1939–1944); and Pierre Noailles's *Fas et jus: Études de droit romain* (Paris, 1948) and *Du droit sacré au droit civil* (Paris, 1949). On communism as a secular religion and on religious dimensions of Soviet law, see my *Justice in the U.S.S.R.*, rev. ed. (Cambridge, Mass., 1963).

HAROLD J. BERMAN

Law and Religion in South Asia

[*This article treats the notion of* dharma *with respect to its role in the formation of the legal system of classical India. For a discussion of the Islamic sources of Indian law, see* Islamic Law.]

The distinction between law and religion is one that does not exist in classical Hindu thought. Instead, both law and religion are parts of the single concept known as *dharma*. This fact is the key to understanding the legal system of classical India and its eventual acceptance and adaptation in Southeast Asia. *Dharma*, the basis for the legal system, is a system of natural laws in which specific rules are derived from an ideal, moral, and eternal order of the universe. The fact that the laws are based on this eternal order is their source of validation and authority. The king was charged with the responsibility of seeing to it that the populace adhered to its *dharma*, but this charge of the king's was itself a part of his *dharma*, so it is difficult to distinguish between the political, legal, and religious aspects of the South Asian legal tradition.

The pervasive idea of *dharma* influences all aspects of a Hindu's life. It is a natural and moral order, and its disturbance has grave consequences for individuals and society. In theory, at least, every act of every Hindu's life should be done in accordance with this natural and moral order, so a righteous person would wish to perform every act in accordance with *dharma*. There are four sources of *dharma* enumerated in the legal literature (see, for example, *Manusmṛti* 2.12 and 1.108): the Veda, *smṛti*, custom (i.e., *sadācāra;* literally, "the practice of the good"), and whatever seems correct to one's conscience *(ātmatuṣṭi)*. The Veda is the ultimate source; all of the statements concerning *dharma* are theoretically traceable to the Veda. Both *smṛti* and custom are, according to the commentators, dependent on the Veda, in that the practices described in *smṛti* and followed in the customs of various groups and localities can all be traced, at least theoretically, to the Veda. The last source of *dharma*—whatever seems correct to one's conscience—is the most vague and least discussed, but it seems to have been included to cover those circumstances where no specific rule exists. In this last case it is presumed that the individual in question is one who has been instructed in *dharma* and is familiar with the sacred tradition. In all four of these cases, the connection with the Veda is the validation of their teachings on *dharma*.

The enormous corpus of Sanskrit literature called *smṛti* ("what has been remembered") attempted to teach the rules for conducting a righteous life. The ways in which this literature taught *dharma*, that is, taught righteousness as reflected in the conduct of one's life, varied considerably. One subcategory of *smṛti*, the Purāṇas, is made up of narrative texts that relate mythological stories focused on the incarnations of various gods. The great epics of India, the *Mahābhārata* and the *Rāmāyaṇa*, constitute another branch of *smṛti* literature and contain large amounts of didactic teaching. These two genres are designed to convey *dharma* by the examples of the characters in their stories.

A much more technical and strictly "legal" literature that constitutes a subcategory of *smṛti* is the Dharmaśāstra, or literally, the "science of *dharma*." These Dharmaśāstra texts are all presumed by Hindus to teach the eternal and immutable *dharma* contained in the Vedas. The presumption of these texts was that the reader was familiar with the ritual texts and was a practitioner of the Vedic ritual. It was the purpose of the literature on *dharma* to unify the Hindu's world. This was done by enabling the members of society to harmonize their existence with the universal order. Precisely because this literature dealt with *dharma*, its rules and regulations were held to be inviolable: the fact that *dharma* is itself the order of the universe validates rules pertaining to it. In an ideal sense the literature on *dharma* served to define who and what a righteous believer in the Veda was. [*See also* Vedas.] The Dharmaśāstra literature comprises four types: (1) the earliest, aphoristic texts, the Dharmasūtras, each of which are attributed pseudonymously to a famous sage of antiquity; (2) later metrical texts, also pseudonymous, often referred to by the term "metrical *smṛti*s" and (somewhat confusingly) when in opposition to the Dharmasūtras by the term *dharmaśāstra*; (3) commentaries (*bhāṣyas*) on both of the preceding; and (4) legal "digests" called *nibandhas*.

The earlier texts, the Dharmasūtras, were taught as part of the literature of a particular Vedic school *(cāraṇa)*, whereas the later texts, the metrical *smṛti*s, were not connected with any particular school. This fact indicates that the study of *dharma* had become much broader and more specialized than it was at the time of the Dharmasūtras. The *dharma* literature is often very difficult to date (for the earlier texts, especially, we are only able to establish tentative relative chronologies), but the extant texts range in date from the sixth century BCE to the late eighteenth century CE. It is in this body of literature that we find the most explicit descriptions of the legal system of classical India. The most authoritative of these explicitly legal writings is the earliest metrical *smṛti*, the *Mānava Dharmaśāstra* or *Manusmṛti*, (c. 200 BCE–200 CE), which is atrributed to the semidivine mythical figure Manu Svayambhu.

Both the Dharmasūtras and the metrical *smṛti*s claim to be the teachings of great sages who have made *dharma* known to mankind. The rules contained in these texts are specific statements of the principles of righteousness *(dharma)* and world order *(ṛta)* that are contained in the Veda. While the Veda is the theoretical source for all of the law contained in the *smṛti* literature, very little of what is contained in Vedic literature could itself be called "law." The exact way in which specific laws are derived from the largely ritual, sacerdotal literature of the Vedas is never made clear; therefore the connection between the Vedas and *smṛti* is not obvious except for their shared theoretical concern for *dharma*. The test of the orthodoxy of any *smṛti* or interpretation of *smṛti* was its acceptance in practice by the educated and righteous men of the community.

Acceptance of a rule did not always mean that its purpose was clearly understood by the educated and righteous men of the community. Indeed, the very obscurity of the reason for some rules is an important interpretative device. Since *dharma* is not "visible" or apparent to ordinary human beings, and since the *smṛti* literature teaches *dharma*, whenever there is "no visible purpose" *(adṛṣṭārtha)* for a rule, then that rule is of greater importance than a rule for which there is an obvious purpose *(dṛṣṭārtha)*. Rules with an obvious purpose relate to the realm of the practical *(artha)* or that of the pleasant *(kāma)* and are therefore of less consequence to the metaphysical well-being of a person than rules that relate to *dharma*. For example, the metrical *smṛti* of the sage Yājñavalkya (at 1.352) states that the king should strive to make friends because friends are worth more than material possessions. This is a rule with an obvious purpose—the welfare of the king. The same text (at 2.1) later states that the king must administer his judicial court impartially and according to Dharmaśāstra. The purpose of this rule is not apparent *(adṛṣṭārtha)*, except that to fulfill this rule is to engage in righteous behavior *(dharma)*; thus, it is a rule which is more compelling than the earlier one advising the king to make friends. The sum of these rules, then, is that the king is not allowed to use his position as administrator of justice to cultivate friends. Indeed, when he is in court, he must be equally impartial to both friends and enemies (*Yājñavalkyasmṛti* 2.2). This principle of the superiority of rules relating to *dharma* is stated explicitly in several places in the *smṛti* literature (see, for example, *Yājñavalkyasmṛti* 2.21).

It is important to make a distinction between the rules contained in the *smṛti* literature and what we might call "the law of the land." In general, we have such limited evidence for daily practice that we cannot say with much certainty what the actual law was in a given place in the subcontinent at a given moment in history. All that we can say is that the Dharmaśāstras and the Dharmasūtras record the theoretical foundation on which the legal system was based. The level of technical sophistication of the Dharmaśāstra was considerable, however, and it seems likely that the adjective law found in the texts was born of a long process of actual practice that resulted in the elaborate legal procedure described there.

The commentators and digest writers (and to some extent the texts themselves) tell us that local custom was of overriding authority. This means that the Dharmaśāstras and the Dharmasūtras were not statements of substantive law as actually applied; rather, they were theoretical guidelines that conveyed in specific statements the ways that members of society might adhere to *dharma*. The actual implementation of these guidelines was fragmentary and localized. Local custom played a significant part in these variations. The Dharmasūtras and the Dharmaśāstras explicitly provide for variations in local custom and also indicate that these local customs are valid sources for knowledge of *dharma*. There was no concern for precedent, and although the decisions of courts were recorded, the records, as far as we know, were then usually given to the litigants themselves, who were responsible for the maintenance of the documents of their respective trials.

The fragmentary nature of the administration of the Hindu legal system was in part a function of the fact that there was no centralized legal hierarchy that had the capacity to uniformly enforce "the law." The king had appellate jurisdiction, and there were very few matters that he could prosecute on his own initiative without first having had a case brought to him by a plaintiff. The purpose of the entire legal system was not so much to deliver justice as it was to ensure that the entire populace adhered to the duties and obligations of *dharma*. The administration of law courts and the enforcement of "law" was not a purely political matter (although it had a political dimension); it was a religious concern. The fact that there is no central ecclesiastical authority in the Hindu tradition also contributed to the fragmentariness of the development of this legal tradition. This fragmentary and localized administration was also a result of the idea that every individual has a unique *dharma* and therefore a unique set of responsibilities. Since accordingly the circumstances of every case would be unique, there would be no reason to record for reference the previous deliberations of a court.

The validation of the "laws" in this system was to be found in the religious belief that the world is organized according to the natural and moral order of *dharma*. The enforcement of the laws was primarily the responsibility of the king, who was viewed as semidivine (see *Manusmṛti* 7.4–5), and this semidivine nature legitimized his temporal power. Within this natural and moral universal order, any polity without a king was one that suffered calamities; thus the monarchy was essential to the well-being of the people. The reason that a polity without a king suffered calamities is that the primary task of the king was to protect his subjects. The most important part of his protection was seeing to it that *dharma* was adhered to by all of his subjects. Therefore the king was the punisher of violators of *dharma* and the ultimate guarantor that *dharma* was adhered to in his kingdom. The *Mahābhārata*, for example, states in several places that the king's *dharma* is the culmination and sum of all other *dharmas*. His court was the court of final jurisdiction. There was no appeal from a judgment of the king's court. The king himself was the judge, but he was also urged to appoint a number of experts in Dharmaśāstra (preferably *brāhmaṇas*) to serve as judges in his court. One of these could be appointed the chief judge, and this judge would preside in the king's absence. Even though he had the assistance of these experts, and even though he could appoint them to serve in his absence, the king was still ultimately responsible for the adherence to *dharma;* if there were wrong judgments handed down by his court, the judges were liable to punishment, but so was the king.

Though the king was seen as semidivine—he is even addressed as *deva* ("god") in Sanskrit drama—there was no real idea of the "divine right of kings." To be sure, the monarch was endowed with extraordinary powers, but the literature contains references to kings who were dethroned for their failure to adhere to their own *dharma* or who had failed to see to it that others did so. The *smṛti* literature recognized this as a legitimate response of the people to an unrighteous king.

The concept of punishment was closely tied to the concept of penance. Any violation of *dharma* means that the violator incurred sin. To expunge this sin it was necessary to undergo some penance. The punishment meted out for a crime was thus viewed as purifying (*Manu* 8.318). It was also possible to mitigate the corporal or financial punishment of a crime by undergoing a specific penance (*Manu* 9.240). Neither punishment nor penance is described as a deterrent or as a way of compensating for injury or tort, but they are ways of compensating for the violation of the natural and moral order of *dharma.*

The Dharmaśāstras and the Dharmasūtras are the most succinct statements of *dharma,* but, as in all legal systems, the power to interpret the law is the power to make the law. In classical India this power was in the hands of the king and his judges, but we have very little record of their rulings. There has been controversy among scholars over the question of whether or not the king had the power to "legislate." The texts tell us that any ruling of the king had to be obeyed, but at the same time there are indications that existing custom had such a superior claim to validity that the king was bound not to interfere with it (so long as it was not depraved) but to enforce it.

Commentators on the *smṛti*s and digest writers were also interpreters of the law, and we have a huge corpus of literature recording their views. The function of interpretation served to keep the legal texts attuned to the changing needs of society. It was the task of the commentators and the digest writers to relate the general principles found in the texts to the current society in which the commentator was writing. Interpretation of Dharmaśāstras and the Dharmasūtras was regulated by two factors. First, an interpreter had to use the codified hermeneutical techniques of the *Mīmāṃsā* school of philosophy. [*See* Mīmāṃsā.] These techniques were originally developed for interpretation of Vedic texts to determine the exact procedures for the ritual. Since the *smṛti* literature is seen as a sort of continuation of the Vedic tradition, it is appropriate that the same techniques of interpretation be applied to it. The second factor controlling the interpretation of *smṛti* was the acceptance/implementation or rejection/ignoring of any interpretation by the community. The validation of any interpretation was to be found in its implementation.

The contents of the Dharmaśāstras and the Dharmasūtras may be divided into three broad categories: rules for "good conduct" *(ācāra),* those for legal procedure *(vyavahāra),* and those for penance *(prāyaścitta).* It was the design of these texts to prescribe rules that would guide each member of society so that he might live his life as fully in accordance with *dharma* as possible. This meant that as society changed, the prescriptions for righteousness contained in the texts needed to be adapted to those changes. This adaptation was done by the commentators on the Dharmasūtras and the Dharmaśāstras and by the digest writers. Because it was their responsibility to adapt the teachings of the Dharmasūtras and the Dharmaśāstras, their role as arbiters of *dharma* (righteousness) became central in the development of classical Hindu law.

In classical Hindu society, the rights and responsibilities of an individual were determined by status. In general, the role and place of women were of marginal concern in the legal texts. The texts were composed by men, and they deal with matters of concern to men. In addition to gender, the determiners of one's status are caste *(varṇa* or *jāti),* stage of life *(āśrama),* age, and so forth. Every caste, age group within that caste, and stage of life has certain generic responsibilities that must be fulfilled *(varṇāśramadharma).* These are a part of the concept of *dharma.* [*See* Varṇa and Jāti *and* Rites of Passage, *article on* Hindu Rites.] Every individual has a *dharma* which is a constellation of duties and responsibilities that are unique to him. This *svadharma* ("own *dharma*") is unique to each individual, because each individual has different capacities for righteousness. An individual's capacity for righteousness is determined by his birth, and his birth is determined by his *karman.* Because every individual has a different capacity for righteousness, every individual cannot be expected to meet the same standard. In broad terms, a *brāhmaṇa* and a *śūdra* (the highest and lowest *varṇa*s, respectively) are therefore qualitatively different members of society. The social, religious, and legal expectations and requirements of a *brāhmaṇa* and a *śūdra* were different in accordance with their qualitative differences. For example, the killing of a *brāhmaṇa* was a very serious crime requiring harsh penances lasting twelve years (*Manu* 11.73–82), while the killing of a *śūdra* was a minor offense requiring a penance that lasts only six months; this penance was the same one prescribed for the killing of lizards (*Manu* 11.131, 11.141). Thus, to kill a *brāhmaṇa* was to do greater violence to the universal order than to kill a *śūdra* because of their qualitative differences in ritual purity. The same reasoning is employed in the standards of behavior applied to members of society. A *brāhmaṇa* must take great care to perform penance for offenses, whether committed knowingly or unknowingly (*Manu* 11.45–46), but many of the things for which a *brāhmaṇa* would be outcasted are not even offenses for a *śūdra* (*Manu* 10.126).

It was this aspect of the Indian legal tradition that most alienated the British when, in 1772, they decided that they should assume the responsibility for the enforcement of laws in the territories controlled by them. They mistrusted the traditional *paṇḍitas* because they appeared to discriminate between litigants on the basis of "religious" matters such as caste. Only after they had instituted sweeping changes in personal laws (such as those dealing with inheritance, marriage, adoption, etc.) did the British come to understand that the concept of *dharma* was different from the concepts of justice and equity found in the common-law tradition. In their defense it must be said that the traditional lack of concern for precedent, the fragmentary nature of the legal system, and the reliance on largely uncodified custom made the task of British administrators of Hindu law extremely difficult. It was the intention of the British to remove these uncertainties by providing a codified "Hindu Law." The British commissioned such a code, the *Vivādārṇavasetu*, and for a time the English translation of this code (*A Code of Gentoo Laws*, first published in 1776) served as the basis for the British courts adjudication of Hindu personal law. Eventually, by the mid-nineteenth century, British scholarship had learned enough about the Dharmaśāstra to point out the errors that had been committed by the British-Indian judiciary, but by that time the corpus of judicial precedent was so large that it had an inertia of its own, and it was not possible to retrace all the steps that had been taken in the name of justice and equity. This corpus of judicial precedent continued to grow and was inherited by the judiciary of independent India so that the Hindu personal law of modern India is only nominally based upon *smṛti*. Having created it judicially, the British and their heirs in independent India were left with the task of legislatively reforming this new "Hindu Law."

Since the Indian "legal" tradition is so integral a part of the religious and philosophical ideas of the Hindu tradition, it was inevitable that it would be exported to Southeast Asia when it became "indianized" (a process lasting for centuries, but beginning in the early centuries of the common era). The indianization of Southeast Asia involved the adoption of Indian culture and religion (Hinduism and Buddhism), including the use of the Sanskrit language, the mythology of the Purāṇas and the epics, the concept of kingship, and the reliance on the Dharmaśāstra as a statement of a generalized standard of conduct.

As a result of the adoption of these Indian religious and philosophical ideas by the Southeast Asian countries, the idea of *dharma* came to be central in the legal systems of this region as well. Burma, Thailand, Cambodia, Java, and Champa all adopted the Hindu ideal of law based on a natural and moral order of the universe. As an integral part of this idea of *dharma* the Hindu concept of kingship was also adopted in these regions of Southeast Asia. [*See* Kingship, *article on* Kingship in Southeast Asia.] Though these were originally Hindu ideas, they were integrated into Buddhist kingdoms by the convention of explaining in the introductions to legal texts that a sage by the name of Manu was inspired by the Buddha to discover the eternal laws and to make them available to the world. In some texts of the Southeast Asian tradition, the organization of the Indian *Mānava Dharmaśāstra* is followed fairly closely, but in other texts it is not adhered to at all. There is generally less concern with the technical aspects of law in the Southeast Asian tradition, and unlike the Indian Dharmaśāstra the texts do not recognize and incorporate custom as a source of law. This fact probably contributed to the role assumed by these texts, which function much more as exemplary statements of general standards of conduct than as statements of actual law.

Each of the cultures of Southeast Asia adopted the Indian legal tradition in slightly different ways. There are significant variations in the formal aspects of each legal system, and generally it may be said that the further the geographical distance from India, the greater the formal differences. In every case, however, the religio-philosophical basis of the Indian legal system was accepted: namely, that *dharma* is the natural, moral order of the universe and that it is this concept that defines and validates the law.

[*For elucidation of terms and texts discussed in this article, see* Dharma, *article on* Hindu Dharma; Śāstra Literature; Ṛta; *and* Sūtra Literature.]

BIBLIOGRAPHY

Bühler, Georg. *The Laws of Manu* (1886). Sacred Books of the East, vol. 25. New Delhi, 1964.

Coedès, George. *The Indianized States of Southeast Asia*. Trans-

lated by Susan Brown Cowing and edited by Walter F. Vella. Canberra, 1968.
Derrett, J. D. M. *Hindu Law Past and Present.* Calcutta, 1957.
Derrett, J. D. M. *Religion, Law and the State in India.* New York, 1968.
Direck Jayanama. *The Evolution of Thai Laws.* Bonn, 1964.
Forchhammer, Emanuel. *The Jardine Prize: An Essay on the Sources and Development of Burmese Law.* Rangoon, 1885.
Gharpure, Jagannatha Raghunatha. "*Yājñavalkya smṛti,* or the *Institutes of Yājñavalkya,* Together with the Commentary Called the *Mitākṣarā* by Śrī Vijñaneśvara, Book the Second: An English Translation." In *Collections of Hindu Law Texts,* vol. 2. Bombay, 1914.
Hoadley, Mason C., and M. B. Hooker. *An Introduction to Javanese Law.* Tucson, 1981.
Hooker, M. B. *A Concise Legal History of South-East Asia.* Oxford, 1978.
Jolly, Julius. *Hindu Law and Custom* (1928). Translated by Batakrishna Ghosh. Varanasi, 1975.
Kane, P. V. *History of Dharmaśāstra.* 2d ed., rev. & enl. 5 vols. Poona, 1968–1975.
Lingat, Robert. *The Classical Law of India.* Translated by J. D. M. Derrett. Berkeley, 1973.
Rocher, Ludo. "Hindu Law and Religion: Where to Draw the Line." In *Malik Ram Felicitation Volume,* edited by S. A. J. Zaidi, pp. 167–194. New Delhi, 1972.
Sarkar, Upendra Chandra. *Epochs in Hindu Legal History.* Hoshiarpur, 1958.
Sen Gupta, Nares Chandra. *Evolution of Ancient Indian Law.* London, 1953.

Richard W. Lariviere

Law and Religion in East Asia

From the earliest period of recorded history, law *(fa)* in China was conceived as standing independently of religious beliefs, as a system of penal sanctions *(hsing)* which at the beginning were held applicable only to the lower orders of society, while the nobles and officers were bound by a complex system of social conventions and ethics (*li*, usually translated as "ritual"). It is often said that *li* derived from the Confucians and *fa* from the Legalists. But this is a misleading oversimplification.

Law And Ethic. The system of penal law can be traced back to the earliest written texts in Chinese, perhaps dating from the tenth century BCE, which show the king adjudicating over a range of criminal offenses. The texts of simple sets of laws were cast on bronze vessels to ensure permanence. The first detailed systems of codified law seem to have appeared in the fifth century BCE. They were systematized especially in the northwestern state of Ch'in during the fourth and third centuries BCE by a school of thinkers collectively known as the Fa-Chia (School of Law) who were also experts in administrative practice. They built up a detailed and complex code of carefully defined offenses matched by precisely prescribed sanctions, rules which were applicable to all members of society. It was a system based upon fear and naked deterrence, its object the strengthening of the state's authority, the preservation of order, and a rigidly disciplined society.

In time *li* came to be the special sphere of expertise of self-professed Confucians, and the major ritual compendiums, which took final form under the Han dynasty (206/202 BCE–220 CE), became part of the Confucian scriptural canon. But the *li* themselves long antedated Confucius, and the system of *li* existed apart from Confucianism, as a complex set of norms covering all aspects of familial, social, and interpersonal behavior, manners, and ritual gradually became a system which penetrated to varying degrees all of society, not only the noble elite.

The system of *li* and *fa* imposed by the state coexisted through most of Chinese history but gradually lost the sharp distinction of early times. By the time of the first Chinese law code to survive in its entirely, that of the T'ang (compiled 624, and revised repeatedly until 737), which was also adopted in early eighth-century Japan, the whole system of penal law was permeated by the ideas, practices, and prescriptions of *li*. These paved the way in which hierarchical differences of status between parties helped define the penalty for an offense: offenses by an inferior against a superior, by a son against his parents, by a wife against her husband were more heavily punished than the same offenses between equals. Ideas derived from *li* were also embodied in great detail in those sections of the codified administrative law (the *ling*, or statutes) which regulated ritual, religious observance of major festivals, dwellings, dress, carriages, and the way of life allowable to persons of differing social status. Moreover, the law codes regularly contained general provisions by which offenses against the *li* could be punished as infractions of criminal law.

Even as *li* and law came to form parallel but linked systems of normative conduct, there remained many contradictions between them. *Li* were generally accepted and respected in society as the "rules of civilized behavior," while the penal law *(fa)* was the province of state power, involvement with which was to be avoided at all costs. But the two not only enjoyed a difference of esteem and respect; they also sometimes came into direct and unresolved conflict. One notable issue, in the Middle Ages, was that of vendetta, which was enjoined upon the victims of injustice by some of the canonical *li* texts but was strictly forbidden by penal law. In one famous case the defendant was given honors for his observance of the ritual prescription for vengeance and was simultaneously condemned to death for homicide.

Another clear influence of ethical thinking on law was the emergence of a category of particularly abhorrent crimes, the "ten abominations," which involved especially severe punishment. Considered unpardonable, these crimes arose from either major offenses against the state (rebellion, treason, etc.), or from offenses in ritually defined relationships: cruel injustice toward one's inferiors, lack of respect toward the religious symbols of the state or toward the emperor's person, lack of filial obedience, causing discord among kinsmen, injuring those having authority over one, incest, black magic, and sorcery.

Basic Concepts Of Law . The law as it developed in China not only incorporated many of the basic ideas articulated in the *li* but also reflected other very deep-seated religious ideas concerning the relation of man and the universe. The basic concept behind the early rigorous systems of law, as these were formulated in the fourth and third centuries CE, was that any criminal offense could upset the fundamental equilibrium of man and the universe, and further that the function of a penal system should be to impose a sanction that would balance the disturbance caused by the offense and restore the natural equilibrium. This general idea is seen in the earliest texts from the ninth century CE, but there the sanctions were either supernatural, imposed by the gods, or personal, imposed by the king. The idea behind law, especially as it was developed by the Fa-chia writers associated with the state of Ch'in, was that the operation of law, and thus the restoration of social equilibrium would be a function of the state. It should be as nearly automatic as possible, eliminating all supernatural intervention and, as far as possible, all arbitrary human judgment.

Other fundamental religious ideas affected the law and its operation. Law was function of the state, and the state was believed to rule thanks to its possession of the mandate of Heaven, which in effect meant that a regime's legitimacy depended on its acceptance of a system of common ideals. Although China is often described as having been a purely secular state, this is quite incorrect. The exercise of power in China took place in a setting of complex symbols, rituals, and observances suffused with religious awe, all of which were prescribed by codified legislation and in the context of deeply held religious beliefs. Some of these ideas directly affected the operation of the penal law. For example, the year, with its calendar of state religious observance, was divided into two halves; the winter, dominated by the dark, female force of *yin*, and the summer, dominated by the light, male principle *yang*. Until the beginning of this century, executions of the capital sentences, with the exception of especially heinous crimes, were forbidden during the summer *yang* months, because execution would offend the general principles of growth.

The penal law did not embody many provisions directly concerning religious belief and practice. In general the law confined itself to the proscription of magical practices, especially black magic, to the prohibition of heterodox doctrines (which in effect meant doctrines potentially hostile to the state or social stability and capable of provoking rebellion), and to the prevention of private persons from performing religious functions proper to the state. The law was particularly anxious to ban predictions and prophecies and the making of charms and amulets. In practice, however, in a society where prognostication, divination, and fortune-telling were commonplace at every level of society these general bans were not enforceable, and they were limited to prophecies and charms with political implications, which might be used by potential rebels.

The State and Organized Religion. During the centuries when Chinese law was taking shape there were various systems of religious belief and many philosophical schools but no organized religion separate from the state, no church, and no clergy. It was only in the first and second centuries CE that the state, thus the law, first found itself in conflict with organized religion.

In the late second century CE the messianic rebel movements of the Five Pecks of Rice and the Yellow Turbans, which seriously disrupted the Later Han empire from 184 to 190, were organized by religious groups professing a system of beliefs derived from an egalitarian form of Taoism, the T'ai-p'ing. These sects were organized into parishes and local cells and led by self-professed patriarchs. From these movements there gradually evolved in the following centuries the various powerful and organized sects of Taoism.

Slightly earlier, in the first century CE, Buddhism had entered China from India by way of Central Asia, and had gradually taken hold, first as a religion of the elite and later as a mass religion in which a large proportion of the Chinese population was involved. Buddhism introduced a number of ideas and institutions which were in sharp conflict with the interests of the state. The foremost of these was monasticism. For the Buddhists the body of religious, the *saṃgha*, was conceived of as an autonomous institution, a perpetual corporation of celibate religious that denied the normal obligations of its members both to the state and to the society. Every monastic community had its own officers and its own hierarchy. Each held its own property, and many owned slaves and controlled many subordinate households. There was no precedent in Chinese law for a perpetual corporation of this kind.

The Buddhist clergy was expected to cut all ties with lay society, including ties with family and state. In China, status relationships binding an individual with family, society, and the state were crucial to the law, deeply affecting the individual's responsibility and liablities in every way. The idea that a son on ordination opted out of his obligations to the state and ceased to obey his father was anathema. The result was constant tension: during the period of weak state authority and political division between North and South between 220 and 589 CE; during periods when the monastic establishment asserted its claims to autonomy; and at other times when the state attempted to establish firm control over the clergy, sometimes by incorporating its higher echelons into the bureaucratic establishment. Several times the state attempted to strictly control or even to proscribe Buddhism. There were two great proscriptions, the first in 574–577 CE under the Northern Chou, the second in 843–845 CE under the T'ang. On both occasions vast numbers of monks and nuns were returned to lay life, thousands of temples demolished, and enormous amounts of wealth confiscated. On both occasions, however, the Buddhist temples were soon restored, and the Buddhist religion reemerged as strong as before.

Some measure of the problem is given by the numbers of clergy. Under the Northern Chou in 574–577, 3 million clerics are said to have been returned to lay life, an obvious exaggeration, but in 518 there were 1,367 temples in the northern capital Lo-yang alone and some 30,000 in the northern Wei empire. Under the T'ang (618–907 CE) the power and wealth of the Buddhist monasteries reached their apogee. In 845 there were said to have been 260,000 registered clergy in addition to which there were tens of thousands of novices and innumerable households of slaves and laymen attached to the temples and the slaves.

Gradually the codified law was extended to cover those areas where the clergy and state came into conflict. In the early eighth century the *Tao-seng ko*, a special category of laws relevant to the Buddhist and Taoist clergy, was drawn up. This sharply defined the jurisdiction of the *saṃgha*, which was allowed to punish infractions of religious discipline. It also detailed other cases where monks or nuns would be subject to the normal penal law in the same way as the laity. Laws were also incorporated into the statutes in T'ang and Sung times covering the property of individual monks and nuns and their relations with the state and their temples.

In Japan, where T'ang codified law was adopted wholesale, but where the temples were even more powerful, the rules for Buddhist monks covering disciplinary offenses (the *Sōniryō*) were actually incorporated into the main body of the statutes.

In China the state began, from the eighth century, to control the ordination of monks and nuns, to limit their number, and to keep separate registers of all clergy. The state also began formally to approve the establishment of new temples. This continued through later dynasties.

In addition to being subject to laws imposed by the state, the clergy was also subject to the strict rules of behavior laid down in the Vinaya, the collections of monastic rules originally drawn up in India but somewhat changed in China, which formed a separate section of the Buddhist canonical writings. These rules were enforced on its members by the *saṃgha*, not by the state. [*See* Vinaya.]

From time to time the state attempted to set up government bodies or officials specifically to control the clergy. During the T'ang period, Buddhist affairs were placed under the aegis of the *hung-lu ssu* ministry dealing with foreign affairs (because Buddhism was a foreign religion), and Taoist affairs were placed under the ministry of the imperial clan (because the T'ang house claimed descent from Lao-tzu). There were also, during the seventh and eighth centuries, special official titles given to Zoroastrian priests in the T'ang hierarchy. But in general, church and state remained separate in China. No Chinese government succeeded in completely dominating the Buddhist orders, and at no time did the Buddhist or Taoist clergy achieve real freedom from control by the state.

[*See also* Confucian Thought, *article on* The State Cult; Legalism; *and* Li.]

BIBLIOGRAPHY

Bodde, Derk. "Authority and Law in Ancient China." *Journal of the American Oriental Society*, supp. vol. 17 (1954): 46–55.

Bodde, Derk. "Basic Concepts of Chinese Law: The Genesis and Evolution of Legal Thought in Traditional China." *Proceedings of the American Philosophical Society* 107 (October 1963): 375–398. Treats Confucian, Taoist, and Buddhist influences on Chinese law.

Bodde, Derk, and Clarence Morris. *Law in Imperial China*. Cambridge, Mass., 1967.

Ch'ü T'ung-tsu. *Law and Society in Traditional China*. Paris, 1961.

Hsu Dau-lin. "Crime and Cosmic Order." *Harvard Journal of Asian Studies* 30 (1970): 111–125.

Li Tsu-yin et al., comps. *Chung-kuo fa-chih-shih ts'an-k'ao shu-mu chien-chieh*. Peking, 1968. A bibliography of works on Chinese legal history and legal practice before 1949.

Needham, Joseph. "Human Law and the Laws of Nature in China and the West." In his *Science and Civilisation in China*, vol. 2, pp. 518–583. Cambridge, 1956.

Sun Tsu-chi, comp. *Chung-kuo li-tai fa-chia chu-shu k'ao* (1934).

Reprint, Taipei, 1970. A descriptive bibliography of over five hundred works on Chinese law.

DENIS TWITCHETT

Law and Religion in the West

From the perspective of Western history, the interrelationship of religion and law appears in large part as a series of challenges to power made by the Christian church, in various stages of its development—and also, increasingly in the last two centuries, by secular faiths derived from Christianity—to shape legal rules, concepts, and procedures to serve human needs. The basic theme of this part of the story is Jesus' claim, "The sabbath was made for man, not man for the sabbath" (*Mk.* 2:27). But there is also an opposing theme: human aspirations become identified with established institutions, religious and secular, and church and state cooperate with each other in attributing to law a sanctity and an authority independent of its ultimate purposes. This theme, too, has biblical support, especially in Paul's injunction to Christians to obey the law because "there is no authority except from God, and those that exist have been instituted by God" (*Rom.* 13:1).

Early Christianity. The ambivalence of Christianity toward law was severely tested when the law of the Roman empire prohibited Christian worship. Civil disobedience became a first principle of Christian jurisprudence; this fact had a considerable significance for the future, when Christians were confronted with unconscionable laws enacted by their own Christian rulers—laws that were often imposed in the name of the church itself. It was then sometimes recalled that the Christian era began with the assertion of a right and duty to violate law that conflicts with divine will. Thus, in Western Europe in the twelfth century John of Salisbury taught, for the first time, the right and duty of tyrannicide, and in the sixteenth and seventeenth centuries followers of John Calvin taught the duty of community leaders to overthrow a tyrannical regime.

With the conversion of the Roman emperors to Christianity, the church came to operate within the existing power structure. Emperors now declared it their Christian responsibility to revise the laws "in the direction of greater humanity": among other reforms, increased rights were given to wives and children and to slaves. The great legal collections compiled by the Byzantine emperor Justinian in the sixth century and by his successors in the seventh and eighth centuries were inspired in part by the belief that Christianity required that law be systematized as a necessary step in its humanization.

The Middle Ages. Among the Germanic, Celtic, and other peoples of western Europe, autonomous legal systems in the modern sense did not exist before the late eleventh century. There were no professional lawyers or judges, no law books, no law schools; law remained, for the most part, embedded in custom. Occasionally, the rulers of major tribal peoples, from Anglo-Saxon England to Kievan Russia, usually after their conversion to Christianity, promulgated written collections of tribal laws and introduced various reforms, especially in connection with family relations, slavery, protection of the poor and oppressed, and the safeguarding of church property and the rights of clergy. The laws of Alfred (c. 890), for example, began with a recitation of the Ten Commandments and excerpts from the Mosaic law, and in restating and revising native Anglo-Saxon customs Alfred announced such great principles as "Doom [i.e., judge] very evenly; doom not one doom to the rich, another to the poor; nor doom one to your friend, another to your foe." During this period, monasteries in the West applied an elaborate system of punishments for offenses against God's commands, and the books ("penitentials") in which these offenses and penances were defined formed an important part of the contemporary folk law.

The medieval church, subordinate as it was to emperors, kings, and lords, sought to limit violence by establishing rules to control blood feuds. In the tenth and eleventh centuries the great abbey of Cluny, with branches all over western Europe, had some limited success in establishing the rules known as the Peace of God, which exempted the clergy and peasantry from warfare, and the Truce of God, which prohibited warfare on weekends.

Starting in about 1050, a campaign was waged in western Europe to free the clergy from domination by monarchy and nobility and to transform the church of Rome into an independent, corporate, political, and legal entity, under the papacy. Separation and expansion of the "spiritual" jurisdiction required a new legal analysis of the canons of the church, and their eventual systematization and rationalization as a "body of canon law" *(corpus juris canonici)*. The *jus canonicum* served to legitimate and effectuate papal authority as well as to secure the separate corporate identity of the clergy as a whole. It was also essential to the maintenance of the church's relations with the various secular polities, which, in turn, needed relatively autonomous and rational systems of secular law (imperial law, royal law, feudal law, urban law) in order to legitimate and effectuate their own newly developing secular powers and to maintain their relations with the church and with each other.

The Beginnings of Secular Law. In this period the manuscripts of Justinian's collections of Roman law were rediscoverd in Italy, and the first European university was established at Bologna primarily in order to study, gloss, and systematize them. Within two generations the first great legal treatise was written: Gratian's *Concordance of Discordant Canons* (c. 1140); this remained the fundamental work on canon law until the twentieth century. In the twelfth century there also appeared the first important scholarly works on secular law, as well as the first important legislation promulgated by central ecclesiastical and secular authorities. In their development both canon law and secular law borrowed from the Roman law studied in the universities.

Late medieval theorists saw the need for legal systems as not only practical and political but also moral and intellectual. "God is himself law, and therefore law is dear to him," wrote the author of the *Sachsenspiegel*, the first German law book (c. 1220). Law was seen as a way of fulfilling the mission of Western Christendom, under the leadership of the church of Rome, to realize the kingdom of God on earth. The "spiritual sword" itself was represented in a consciously systematized body of canon law. The great lawyer-popes of the twelfth and thirteenth centuries developed within the church the institutions of a professional judiciary, treasury, chancery, and, indeed, an entire governmental apparatus, intended, in part, to make the new ecclesiastical legal system work. This was the first modern Western system of government and law. It was emulated by the secular polities that took form throughout Europe in the same period.

Protestantism and Law. Prior to the sixteenth century the church taught that human law is derived from natural law, which in turn reflects divine law; that by the exercise of reason and will, man is capable of achieving justice; and that if he combines good deeds with faith he can achieve salvation itself—albeit not until he has paid a heavy price, in this life and the next, for his sins. These beliefs were closely connected with the jurisdiction of the ecclesiastical hierarchy over a large part of the life of Christendom.

In 1517 Martin Luther inaugurated a revolutionary movement that rejected all these teachings. Luther substituted a new "two kingdoms" doctrine for the earlier "two swords" doctrine; he sharply divided the heavenly kingdom of grace and faith from the earthly kingdom of sin and death, and he placed all law, including both moral and civil law, in the earthly kingdom. The church, for Luther, was an invisible community of believers, without a legal character. The implication was that all legislative and judicial power—all jurisdiction, including jurisdiction over the church itself—was vested in the secular authorities.

Superficially understood, Luther's doctrine seems to take a negative view of law and, indeed, of social institutions generally. Law and politics are not paths to the heavenly kingdom; faith alone "justifies" a person. Yet Luther also taught that one who has faith will inevitably exercise his reason and his will to do good works. In his relations with God, he wrote, each believer is a "private person," "a person for himself alone," but in his social relations he is a "public person," "a person for the sake of others." Indeed, Luther extended the doctrine of the Christian calling, which previously had been applied only to the clergy, to all occupations. He was particularly concerned that the ruler, the Christian prince, should use his lawmaking authority to promote order and justice.

More specifically, Luther developed a new conception of the "uses" of the law, including both the moral law and the civil law. Law, he wrote, has a "political use," namely, to deter recalcitrant people from misconduct by threat of penalties. It also, however, has a "theological use," namely, to make people conscious of their obligations, and hence repentant of their sins. Some Lutherans, at least, and most Calvinists accepted a third "pedagogical use" of the law: to guide faithful people in the paths of virtuous living.

The immediate political effect of the Lutheran Reformation was to transfer to secular rulers the legal authority previously exercised by the ecclesiastical hierarchy. Lutheranism also played an important part in fostering the attitudes and values that were reflected in the new secular law. Examples of Lutheran influence may be seen in the laws providing (liberally) for public education and for poor relief, and in those punishing (strictly) vagrancy, begging, and sumptuousness of dress. Lutheran influence may also be seen in the movement to humanize German criminal law and in the emphasis on written law, on scholarly systematization, and on the use of the vernacular in legislation, legal proceedings, and legal literature.

The Puritans. A century after Luther, English Puritans invoked similar theological doctrines to support the overthrow of the Stuart monarchy and the establishment of Parliamentary supremacy. Under Calvinist influence, however, they placed even more stress on the role of law in achieving the reformation of the world. This was connected with their ecclesiology: they saw each local church as a visible, corporate, political-legal body, with elected ministers and elders, who were to govern it by law. This local church polity was to be balanced against the civil authority. Calvinists also—more than Lutherans—stressed the positive role of both moral and civil law in teaching man to walk in the paths that God had set for him.

When the English Puritans came to power in 1640 they proposed a multitude of reforms, not only of constitutional law but also of criminal, civil, and other branches of law. Of these reforms many were not adopted, and many proved short lived, but others were lasting in their consequences. In constitutional law, limitations were placed on the monarchy, and supremacy was vested in the Parliament. Royal prerogative courts were abolished, and the common law was established as the supreme law of the land. Civil rights earlier demanded by the Puritans—including the privilege against self-incrimination, the writ of habeas corpus, bail, and the independence of the jury from judicial domination—became accepted as basic principles of English law. A substantial rationalization of the common law took place, in response not only to secular forces but also to the Puritan emphasis on order, discipline, and rationality. A new emphasis on analogy of cases and on historical precedent owed much to Puritan casuistry and Puritan historicism.

Anglicanism and Calvinism. Not only Puritanism but also Anglicanism influenced English legal developments in this period. For example, the historicism of seventeenth-century English common lawyers was much more akin to the historicism of Bishop Richard Hooker and of the Church of England than to that of Calvin and his English followers. The English Calvinists looked first to biblical history and biblical examples, although they added to them a vision of England as an "elect nation" destined to fulfill God's plan of history. The Anglicans, though influenced by Calvinism, taught the fiction of a continuously developing Anglican church, never really Roman, founded not on doctrinal consistency but on historical continuity. This kind of historicism found expression in the English common law, with its emerging doctrine of precedent.

Calvinism in England and America, and its counterparts elsewhere in Europe, constituted the last great movement within the institutional church to influence the development of Western law in any fundamental sense. In the eighteenth and nineteenth centuries Roman Catholicism and Anglicanism as well as the various forms of Protestantism continued, of course, to exert pressures upon law in various directions. Undoubtedly, prophetic Christianity continued to play an important part in bringing about law reform—for example, in the abolition of slavery, in the protection of labor, in the struggle for equality of women, and in the promotion of welfare legislation generally. Undoubtedly, on the other side, organized religion continued to support the status quo, whatever that happened to be. But more significant than these influences was the gradual reduction of traditional religion to the level of a personal, private matter, without public influence on legal development, while other belief systems—new secular ideologies—were raised to the level of fighting faiths.

Enlightenment and Revolution. The American and French revolutions set the stage for pouring into secular political and social movements the religious psychology, as well as many of the religious ideas, that had previously been expressed in various forms of Catholicism and Protestantism. Such leaders of the eighteenth-century Enlightenment as Voltaire, Rousseau, Franklin, and Jefferson postulated the creation of the world by a "supreme artisan" or "Supreme Being," who, having given nature its direction and its laws, ceased to intervene further. These theological tenets, called deism, lay at the core of the belief that there is a cosmic order, that it was designed to operate harmoniously for the benefit of mankind, and that the laws by which it operates are accessible to rational observation and to analysis by the individual.

The individualism and rationalism, as well as the optimism, implicit in deism had important implications for law. The *philosophes* of the Enlightenment attacked the privileges of the aristocracy, advocated freedom of speech, called for the separation of the legislative, judicial, and executive branches of government, and denounced the barbarism of the prevailing system of criminal law as well as the irrationality of the legal system as a whole. These ideas eventually became embodied in written constitutions providing for democratic institutions, and in comprehensive legislation that protected rights of private property and of contract and that rationalized trial procedure.

Nationalism and State Socialism. The American and French revolutions added to the philosophy of the Enlightenment a faith in the nation. The individual was a citizen, and public opinion was not the opinion of mankind but the opinion of Frenchmen, the opinion of Americans, the opinion of Germans, and so forth. Liberal democracy, operating within the nation, became the first great secular faith in Western history. It was soon confronted, however, with a rival: revolutionary socialism. And by the time, after a century of revolutionary activity throughout Europe, that a form of communism seized power in Russia in 1917, the doctrines of socialism had acquired the sanctity of authoritative revelation and its leadership the charisma of high priests.

The jural postulates of socialism, though they differ in many respects from those of liberal democracy, show a common ancestry in Christian doctrine. The Soviet Moral Code of the Builder of Communism, for example, which is taken as a basis for Soviet legal policy, contains such principles as "conscientious labor for the good of society—he who does not work, neither shall he eat"; "concern on the part of everyone for the preservation and growth of public wealth"; "collectivism and comradely mutual assistance—one for all and all for one"; "honesty and truthfulness, moral purity, modesty, and unpretentiousness in social and personal life"; "an uncompromising attitude toward injustice, parasitism, dishonesty, careerism, and money-grubbing." Soviet law is strikingly reminiscent of the Puritan code of the Massachusetts Bay Colony, the Body of Liberties of 1641, in its punishment of ideological deviation, idleness, and personal immorality. In addition, the Soviet system places a strong emphasis on the educational role of law and on popular participation in legal proceedings and in law enforcement—through Comrades' Courts and People's Patrols, and through placing offenders in the care of the collective of the factory or the neighborhood. Moreover, this is done in the name of an eschatology that foresees the ultimate disappearance of coercion and of law itself as a communist society is created in which every person will treat every other—again, in the words of the Moral Code of the Builder of Communism—as "comrade, friend, and brother." It is by no means seen as inconsistent with this utopian vision that strong measures of coercion and of formal law are used to bring it about.

In many noncommunist countries of the West, the twentieth century has witnessed a revival of older Roman Catholic and Protestant (especially Calvinist) theories of law, and a movement among some lawyers and legal scholars to rediscover the religious roots of the Western legal tradition. In addition, the United States has experienced a grass-roots movement among rapidly growing fundamentalist groups to support, on biblical grounds, particular legal measures such as prohibition of abortions, authorization of prayer in elementary schools, and the banning of certain kinds of publications. This movement invokes Calvinist teachings but lacks the larger vision of the interaction of law and religion that inspired the Puritans of the seventeenth century.

[*See also* Canon Law; Civil Religion; Deism; Enlightenment, The; Evangelical and Fundamental Christianity; Marxism; Modernity; Natural Law; Papacy; *and* Puritanism.]

BIBLIOGRAPHY

Berman, Harold J. *Law and Revolution: The Formation of the Western Legal Tradition.* Cambridge, Mass., 1983.

Bohatec, Josef. *Calvins Lehre von Staat und Kirche.* Aalen, 1961.

Cranz, F. Edward. *An Essay on the Development of Luther's Thoughts on Justice, Law, and Society.* Cambridge, Mass., 1959.

Ellul, Jacques. *The Theological Foundation of Law.* New York, 1969.

Hertz, Karl H. *Two Kingdoms and One World.* Minneapolis, 1976.

Little, David. *Religion, Order, and Law: A Study in Pre-Revolutionary England.* New York, 1969.

Religion and the Law. A special issue of *Hastings Law Journal* 29 (July 1978).

Shaffer, Thomas L. *On Being a Christian and a Lawyer.* Provo, Utah, 1981.

Tellenbach, Gerd. *Church, State, and Christian Society at the Time of the Investiture Contest* (1959). Reprint, New York, 1979.

Tierney, Brian. *The Crisis of Church and State 1050–1300, with Selected Documents.* Englewood Cliffs, N.J., 1964.

Walzer, Michael. *The Revolution of the Saints: A Study in the Origins of Radical Politics.* New York, 1965.

HAROLD J. BERMAN

Religion and the Constitution of the United States

Unlike most of the constitutions that had been adopted by the states on their declaration of independence from England in 1776, the United States Constitution, adopted in 1787, contained no bill of rights. True enough, it did guarantee a few rights of individuals, such as the right to a jury trial in criminal proceedings (Article III), and it banned religious tests for public office (Article VI). These provisions, however, did not satisfy the states, and the Constitution won approval only after its supporters promised that a bill of rights would be promptly added by amendment. The promise was kept, and such a bill, set forth in the first ten amendments, was adopted in 1791. Its opening words were "Congress shall make no law respecting an establishment of religion or prohibiting the free exercise thereof."

The authors of the First Amendment, in specifying "Congress," manifested an intent to limit the amendment's effect to the federal government, but in *Cantwell* v. *Connecticut* (1940) the United States Supreme Court ruled that the free-exercise mandate was equally applicable to the states by reason of the Fourteenth Amendment, adopted in 1868, which forbade states from depriving any person of life, liberty, or property without due process of law. Seven years later, in *Everson* v. *Board of Education,* the Court ruled that the ban on establishment of religion (known popularly as the guaranty of separation of church and state) was likewise equally applicable to the states.

Even in respect to the federal government, the amendment, on its face, is limited to "Congress," thus implying exclusion of the executive and judicial branches. Nevertheless, the amendment has been interpreted by the courts to be equally applicable to the other branches of government. Thus, governmental military academies, part of the Department of Defense in the executive branch, may not require cadets to attend religious services, and the Department of Justice may not disqualify atheists from testifying as witnesses or serving as jurors.

There are times when the mandate of free exercise dictates or seems to dictate what the establishment clause forbids, requiring the courts to favor one clause over the other. Historically, those who framed the amendment did not deem the two clauses possibly contradictory, but rather saw them as two facets of one comprehensive right or duty. Thus, when in 1785 the state of Virginia was considering a measure to appropriate funds for the support of religion, James Madison, generally considered to be the major draftsman of what was later to be the national constitution and shortly thereafter the First Amendment, issued a memorial and remonstrance against the measure, arguing that it tended toward an establishment of religion and an abridgment of its free exercise. The same thought had earlier been expressed by Thomas Paine in *Common Sense* (1776). In appealing for independence, Paine stated that as "to religion, I hold it to be the indispensable duty of government to protect all conscientious professors thereof, and I know of no other business which government hath to do therewith." The same idea had been expressed even earlier in the writings of Roger Williams, who in the mid-seventeenth century founded what later became the state of Rhode Island, and by the English philosopher John Locke, who in the late seventeenth century asserted in his first *Letter Concerning Toleration* that the jurisdiction of the magistrate extended only to civil concerns and not to the salvation of souls.

On the other hand, a substantial number of constitutional law scholars assert that the ban on establishment and the mandate of free exercise are separable and may point to contrary determinations of a particular controversy. There are, they argue, many democratic nations—Great Britain and the Scandinavian states are prominent examples—that do not separate church and state and yet accord full religious freedom to all. These scholars maintain that the First Amendment forbids establishment because in most cases it curtails free exercise. The ban on establishment therefore is a means but not an end in itself, and in those instances in which it frustrates achievement of that end, it must yield. For example, the government would ordinarily violate the establishment clause if it paid clergymen to perform religious services beyond opening legislative sessions with prayers, a long-standing custom that the Supreme Court upheld in *Marsh* v. *Chambers* (1983). (Long-standing practice was, again, one of the bases for the Supreme Court's 1984 decision, in *Lynch* v. *Donnelly,* to allow state financing of a crèche during the Christmas season.) But this is not the case if the clergyman is a military chaplain engaged to provide religious services for men who have been conscripted into the armed forces and thereby deprived of their free-exercise right to attend the church of their choice.

In its earlier decisions the Supreme Court had not recognized a possible conflict between nonestablishment and free exercise, but on more recent occasions it has done so, and in those cases it has favored free exercise. In *Wisconsin* v. *Yoder* (1972), the Court stated that the danger of violating the establishment clause cannot be allowed to prevent any exception, no matter how vital it may be, to the protection of values promoted by the right to free exercise. Earlier, in *Abington School District* v. *Schempp* (1963), Justice William Brennan in his concurring opinion pointed to employment of army chaplains as an instance in which possible violation of the establishment clause would have to yield for the security of free exercise. However, in *Larson* v. *Valente* (1982), Justice Brennan, speaking for the majority of the Court, stated that the constitutional prohibition of establishment is inextricably connected with the continuing vitality of the free-exercise clause. The Court thus apparently returned to the earlier assumption that both are aspects of one fundamental freedom, affirming what Justice Wiley Rutledge had stated in his dissenting opinion in *Everson:* "establishment" and "free exercise" were correlative and coextensive facets or ideas, representing only different facets of the single great and fundamental freedom.

Ban on Establishment. In *Everson* v. *Board of Education* (1947), the Supreme Court had the first occasion to spell out in detail what was meant by the ban on establishment. It meant at least, the Court said, that the government may not set up a church, pass laws that aid all religions or prefer one over another, force or influence a person to attend or to remain away from church, punish anyone for entertaining or professing religious beliefs or attending or not attending church, use tax-raised funds to support religious activities or institutions, participate in the affairs of any religious organization, or allow religious organizations as such to participate in governmental affairs. In *Walz* v. *Tax Commission of New York* (1970) and later cases, the Court worded the establishment clause somewhat differently. A law violates the clause, it said, if its purpose or principal effect is to advance or inhibit religion or if it results in excessive governmental entanglement with religion. Although the wording is different, an examination of the decisions indicates that the substance is the same: no case using either test would be decided differently if the other had been used, and in decisions relying on the test used in *Walz*, reference is often made to the *Everson* decision.

Education and religion. More than in any other area, the question of applying the establishment clause has arisen in cases concerning education. In respect to public schools, these cases involve religious instruction, prayer, religious symbols, and religious tests for personnel: in religious, commonly called parochial, schools they involve governmental financial aid to the schools, their personnel, or the pupils' parents.

The first case to reach the Supreme Court challenging religion in public schools was *McCollum* v. *Board of Education of Champaign, Illinois* (1948). As Justice Felix Frankfurter noted in his concurring opinion, traditionally the organized education of children in America, as elsewhere in the Western world, had been church-sponsored education. Toward the end of the eighteenth century and in the first half of the nineteenth, the concept of universal public education controlled by civic authorities and free of sectarianism or sectarian control was urged by statesmen such as Thomas Jefferson of Virginia and Thaddeus Stevens of Pennsylvania and by educators like Horace Mann in New York. Gradually the principle became accepted with the enactment of compulsory school attendance laws in every state of the Union. In many instances the states originally discharged their responsibility by taking over existing church schools, but as the population increased, state-established new schools became the norm. Yet even in these it was quite natural that religion should play some role in the instruction, notwithstanding provisions in state constitutions and laws expressly forbidding sectarian teaching.

To avoid these prohibitions—and at the same time to overcome the objections of the Roman Catholic church and of Catholic parents to Protestant-oriented instruction—the released-time program for religious education was introduced. The first such program was established in Gary, Indiana, in 1914, and thereafter similar plans were adopted in the majority of other states. The program in Champaign, Illinois, as well as its background, typical of similar programs in other communities, was described by the Court in the *McCollum* case as follows. In 1940, interested members of the Protestant, Catholic, and Jewish faiths formed an association called the Champaign Council on Religious Education and obtained from the board of education permission to offer classes in religious instruction to public school pupils during regular school hours. At the beginning of each term, the teachers distributed cards on which parents could indicate consent to the enrollment of their children in the religious instruction classes. Children obtaining consent were released from secular work for a period of thirty to forty-five minutes weekly to participate in the instruction. They were divided into three groups, Protestant, Catholic, and Jewish, and received instruction in separate classrooms from teachers provided, without cost to the school system, by the local council on religious education. Applying the establishment test that had been set forth in *Everson* the Supreme Court in 1948 held the program violative of the First Amendment. It did not matter, the Court stated, whether enrollment was voluntary; the clause was violated because of the use of tax-supported property to aid religion and because the program was assisted by and integrated into the state's compulsory education system.

The *McCollum* decision outlawed religious instruction programs within the public schools. It did not pass upon statutes or regulations authorizing the release of pupils, usually for an hour once or twice weekly, to participate, with parental consent, in instruction conducted in off-school premises while children of nonconsenting parents remained in school and continued their regular studies. However, the constitutionality of these programs was upheld in *Zorach* v. *Clauson* (1952). They involved, the Court noted, neither religious instruction in the public schools nor the expenditure of public funds, since the costs of busing the pupils to the off-school premises and providing parental consent blanks were paid by the religious organizations, with the public school system's contribution limited to the release of the enrolled pupils. This no more violated the free-exercise or the establishment clause than did releasing Catholics to attend Mass on a holy day of obligation, permitting Jews to attend synagogue on Yom Kippur, or allowing Protestants to attend family baptismal ceremonies. To construe the First Amendment as prohibiting public institutions from making any adjustment of their schedules to accommodate the religious needs of the people would be to read into the Bill of Rights a philosophy of hostility to religion.

The *Zorach* ruling applied only to off-school religious instruction; it was not intended to overrule the *McCollum* decision barring religious instruction within the public school at the elementary or secondary school levels, or to authorize devotional Bible reading, school-sponsored prayer recitation, or even the placing of religious symbols such as crucifixes or the Ten Commandments on the walls of public school classrooms. All of these practices were declared unconstitutional in the Court's later decisions, the first of which was *Engel* v. *Vitale* (1962). That case arose out of an effort by the New York Board of Regents, the state's highest educational body, to encourage prayer recitation in a public school system encompassing Protestant, Catholic, and Jewish pupils. Accordingly, the regents formulated what they deemed to be a nonsectarian prayer: "Almighty God, we acknowledge our dependence upon Thee, and beg Thy blessings upon us, our parents, our teachers, and our country." This prayer the regents issued with a "policy statement" urging, although not mandating, its daily use in public schools. Because the American people have always been religious, the regents observed, a program of religious inspiration in the schools would ensure that children would acquire "respect for lawful authority and obedience to law [and that] each of them will be properly prepared to follow the faith of his or her father, as he or she receives the same at mother's knee or father's side and as such faith is expounded and strengthened by his or her religious leaders." The Supreme Court ruled that the action violated the First Amendment's guaranty of church-state separation, even though the prayer might be denominationally neutral and its recitation voluntary. Nothing could be more wrong, the Court added, somewhat defensively, than the argument that the prohibition of religious services in public schools indicates hostility toward religion or prayer.

A year later, in *Abington School District* v. *Schempp* (1963), the Supreme Court passed upon the constitutionality of a daily religious program in public schools that included devotional Bible-reading exercises and the recitation of the Lord's Prayer, in which the pupils were asked to join. The evidence at the trial showed that although the school furnished only the King James Version (that is, a Protestant version) of the Bible, the pupils selected to do the reading could use a different version, and at times Catholic and Jewish versions were used. There were no prefatory statements; no questions were asked, solicited, or answered; and no interpretation was given at the exercise. The pupils (and parents) were advised that they might absent themselves from the classroom if they so elected. The Court held this program unconstitutional, repeating in its decision what it had earlier said in other cases: that the establishment clause did not forbid the objective study of the Bible for its literary and historical qualities, or of religion or religious art or music presented as part of a secular program of education. The Court banned only traditional religious instruction or exercises provided by the state in violation of the First Amendment's command that the government maintain strict neutrality, neither aiding nor opposing religion.

In *Stone* v. *Graham* (1980), the Court struck down a Kentucky statute requiring the posting of the Ten Commandments, financed with private contributions, on the wall of each public school classroom in the state. The statute, the Court held, had no secular purpose since the first part of the Ten Commandments concerns not secular but religious duties—worshiping God, avoiding idolatry, not using the Lord's name in vain, and observing the Sabbath.

Cases heretofore considered in this section involved efforts to introduce religious teachings or practices into the public schools. *Epperson* v. *Arkansas* (1968) presented the converse: the religiously motivated exclusion of secular instruction from the school curriculum. The Court held violative of the establishment clause a statute that forbade teaching "the theory or doctrine that mankind ascended or descended from a lower order of animals." The impermissible statutory purpose, the Court found, was to protect religious orthodoxy from what the legislature considered dangerous and inconsistent secular teaching.

"Effect" and "excessive entanglement." The other education-related issue that reached the Supreme Court dealt with the use of tax-raised funds to finance, in whole or part, the operations of parochial schools that provide both secular and religious instruction. There is no doubt that the First Amendment forbids governmental financing of Sunday schools or other institutions that offer only religious instruction; other cases reaching the Supreme Court, however, dealt with schools offering both types of instruction. Did the First Amendment allow governmental financing in these cases?

The controversy here encompasses only the educational aspects of parochial schools' activities. As early as 1899 the Supreme Court, in *Bradfield* v. *Roberts*, handed down a decision that has generally been interpreted as sanctioning governmental financing of hospitals conducted under the auspices of religious groups. On the authority of this ruling, it may be assumed that the Constitution does not forbid governmental financing of such noneducational benefits to parochial-school pupils as medical and dental care and meals. This distinction, the Court held in *Everson*, justifies statutes appropriating tax-raised funds to finance the busing of children to parochial schools. The legislative purpose is to protect the children from the hazards of traffic; the benefit to the schools, on the assumption that if the protection were not afforded some parents would elect not to send their children there, is incidental or secondary. This reasoning was followed in *Board of Education* v. *Allen* (1968), in which the Court upheld a state statute authorizing the loan of nonreligious textbooks to pupils in parochial schools. The primary beneficiaries of the law were the pupils, and it was immaterial that, as in the *Everson* case, some parents might not enroll their children if secular textbooks were not provided. In later decisions, however, the Court manifested some unhappiness about both the *Everson* and *Allen* rulings, limiting them to the specific facts of the cases. In *Meek* v. *Pittenger* (1975), it refused to extend *Allen* to encompass instructional equipment or materials other than textbooks, and in *Wolman* v. *Walter* (1977) it held that *Everson* did not justify bus transportation during school hours to governmental, industrial, cultural, and scientific centers in order to enrich the students' secular studies.

More important was the joint decision (1971) in *Lemon* v. *Kurtzman* and *Earley* v. *DiCenso*. In the former, the Court invalidated a statute under which the state "purchased" from parochial school management the "secular educational services" of the teachers; in the latter, it held equally unconstitutional another state's statute seeking to supplement by 15 percent the salaries of parochial school teachers as partial compensation for their secular teaching services. The Court held that both statutes violated the establishment clause because they fostered excessive entanglement between government and religion. A comprehensive and continuing state surveillance would be required, reasoned the Court, to ensure that the teachers did not seek to advance religion in their teaching.

Applying these principles, the Court in *Levitt* v. *Committee for Public Education and Religious Liberty* (1973) invalidated a statute appropriating funds to compensate parochial schools for the costs of preparing, conducting, and grading periodic examinations to measure pupils' achievement in secular subjects. However, in *Committee for Public Education and Religious Liberty* v. *Regan* (1979), it limited the 1973 decision by allowing the use of public funds to reimburse parochial schools for the cost of providing the state-mandated services involved in taking and reporting to state educational officials daily pupil attendance, as well as for conducting uniform state-approved objective achievement tests in secular subjects.

Simultaneously with its decision in *Levitt*, the Court, in *Committee for Public Education and Religious Liberty* v. *Nyquist*, struck down in its entirety a three-pronged statute aimed at partially financing the costs of parochial school education. The first part of the law provided that in order to ensure the health and safety of the pupils grants were to be made to the schools to finance "maintenance and repair" expenses, a term defined to include the costs of heat, light, water, ventilation, sanitary facilities, fire and accident prevention, and other expenditures deemed necessary. The second part provided grants, not to exceed 50 percent of tuition, to low-income non-taxpaying parents who presented receipted tuition bills from the nonpublic schools. For upper-income parents, the law provided what was in effect tuition credit on income taxes paid to the state. All three aspects of the statute, the Court said, had the effect of advancing religion in violation of the establishment clause. Thereafter, in *Meek* v. *Pittenger* (1975), the Court held unconstitutional under the establishment clause a state statute providing "auxiliary services," defined primarily as remedial and accelerated instruction for below- and above-average pupils, respectively. In *Mueller* v. *Allen* (1983), however, the Court upheld laws allowing parents to deduct tuition paid for parochial school attendance from their gross taxable income.

The cases discussed here all involved aid to education at the elementary and secondary levels. In *Tilton* v. *Richardson* (1971), *Hunt* v. *McNair* (1973), and *Roemer* v. *Board of Public Works* (1976), the court manifested a more tolerant position in respect to aid at the college level. In these cases it upheld aid in the form of interest-favorable loans or (in *Roemer*) outright grants to educational institutions that, although owned and operated by church-affiliated institutions, did not award exclusively seminarian or theological degrees and did not use the funds to finance religious instruction. Although the three-pronged purpose-effect-entanglement test is not limited to elementary and secondary schools, the basis for the distinction in applying it probably was a recognition that at the college level the separation of religious from secular instruction is feasible and that college students are less likely to be influenced in their religious commitments.

Tax exemption. Subsidies and loans to educational institutions are not the only avenues of governmental aid to religious institutions; more substantial aid takes the form of tax exemptions accorded to them or to their contributors. The practice, which can be traced to biblical times (*Gn.* 47:26, *Ezr.* 7:24), was challenged in *Walz* v. *Tax Commission* (1970). There the Court rejected the contention that exempting from real estate taxes property used for religious purposes violated the establishment clause. It noted that from the time the nation was established by the Declaration of Independence up to the present all the states, including those that adopted the First Amendment in 1791, have accorded tax exemptions for church-owned property (and subsequently granted income tax benefits to church contributors). This, the Court indicated, was strong evidence that exemptions have not been considered constitutionally impermissible as violating the no-aid or purpose-effect-entanglement tests. Exemption, unlike subsidization, did not entail sponsorship or excessive governmental entanglement; indeed, in respect to the latter, it avoided rather than fostered the governmental intrusion that would result from auditing and scrutinizing church affairs.

Intrachurch disputes. Governmental intervention into intrachurch disputes, like many other issues, reflects an aspect of both the establishment and free-exercise clauses. It is treated here because it involves most prominently entanglement by government (particularly through its courts) in religious affairs.

As early as 1872, the Court stated in *Watson* v. *Jones* that governmental agencies—judicial, legislative, or executive—are constitutionally forbidden to make theological judgments as to what is orthodox and what is heretical in any faith. Yet when a schism occurs and both factions claim church-owned property, secular courts have no choice but to intervene so that the controversy may be resolved peaceably. Intervention, however, must be kept to the minimum. Generally this means that a court should determine whether the polity of the church is hierarchical (as in Catholicism or Presbyterianism) or congregational (as among Baptists or Jews). If the former, the courts will enforce the decision of the highest ecclesiastical authority or tribunal; if the latter, that of the congregation's membership. What the First Amendment forbids a court to do is determine which faction is orthodox and which heretical. Basically these guidelines were followed in later Supreme Court decisions, such as *Kedroff* v. *St. Nicholas Cathedral* (1952) and *Presbyterian Church* v. *Hull Church* (1968). However, in *Jones* v. *Wolf* (1979) the Court modified the *Watson* v. *Jones* rule. Resort to ecclesiastical polity, it said, should be avoided if the controversy can be resolved by neutral principles of law, such as the language of the deeds that initially conveyed the property to the local church, the terms of local church charters, or state statutes expressly governing church property. Of course, nothing in the decision precluded a general church from including in a resolution accepting local affiliation an express provision of general church ownership of all local church property, a practice that by reason of *Jones* v. *Wolf* is now widespread.

Protection of Free Exercise. As previously noted, it was not until the Supreme Court's 1940 decision in *Cantwell* v. *Connecticut* that the free-exercise clause in the First Amendment was held applicable to the states no less than to the federal government. Thus, in *Permoli* v. *New Orleans* (1845) the Court had rejected an appeal from the conviction of a priest who conducted funeral services at a chapel that was not licensed in accordance with a state statute; the priest claimed that his right to the free exercise of religion was thereby violated. The First Amendment, the Court declared, guaranteed a citizen's right only against the federal government, allowing the states to forbid free exercise as they saw fit. (Of course, every state constitution secured free exercise, but violations thereof could be dealt with only in state courts.) After the *Cantwell* decision, the Court applied the same free-exercise test to both state and federal actions.

For fifteen years before *Cantwell* the Court necessarily dealt with state impairment of free exercise as infringements on freedom of speech because the latter had been held applicable to the states in the 1925 case of *Gitlow* v. *New York.* Quite naturally, therefore, in determining constitutionality the Court used the test made applicable to speech in *Schenck* v. *United States* (1919). This test, known popularly as the clear-and-present-danger test, sought to discover whether words—religious as well as secular—were spoken in such circumstances as to create a clear and present danger to the government or people of the United States. In later cases, however, the Court has applied a somewhat differently worded test, known as the compelling-interest rule. Only those interests of the highest order and those not otherwise served, the Court said in *Wisconsin* v. *Yoder* (1972), can overbalance the legitimate claim to the free exercise of religion. It is probable, however, that in most instances the Court would reach the same conclusion in respect to the particular case before it no matter which test was used.

In examining the Supreme Court's decisions under the free-exercise clause, it is convenient to consider them in the light of the purposes set forth in the preamble to the Constitution. These purposes are to form a more perfect union, establish justice, assure domestic tranquillity, provide for the common defense, promote the general welfare, and secure the blessings of liberty for the American people. The liberty referred to, of course, includes religious liberty. Unfortunately, however, fulfillment of another of the purposes often conflicts with upholding religious liberty, and it is the function of the courts, and ultimately the Supreme Court, to resolve these conflicts.

Conscientious objectors. Probably no interest of any nation is deemed more important than its defense against foreign enemies; the development of nuclear weaponry that can destroy the world testifies to this. It is hardly surprising, therefore, that the Supreme Court has consistently ruled that an individual's constitutional liberties must yield to the nation's security. The Thirteenth Amendment's ban of involuntary servitude, the Court held in the *Selective Draft Law Cases* (1918), was not intended to override the nation's power to conscript an army without regard to religious beliefs forbidding armed service. Exemption from military service accorded to Quakers, Mennonites, Adventists, Brethren, and others who by religious conviction may not participate in war is not a constitutional right, only a privilege granted by Congress and therefore, like the tax exemption of churches, subject to revocation at any time. Like tax exemption, too, the roots of this privilege can be traced to biblical times; exemption was allowed to the newly betrothed, the newly married, the fainthearted, and others (*Dt.* 20:8). (Since all biblical wars were divinely commanded, religious exemption would have been self-contradictory.) In seventeenth-century England, Oliver Cromwell believed that those whose religious doctrine forbade them to participate in armed conflict should not be compelled to do so. The legislatures in some of the American colonies thought likewise, and as early as 1789 a congressional resolution was introduced, but not adopted, that the Constitution be amended to exempt religious objectors from compulsory military service. The first national measure for the exemption of conscientious objectors was adopted by Congress during the Civil War, and like its colonial precedents it was limited to members of well-recognized religious denominations whose articles of faith forbade the bearing of arms.

The Selective Service Act of 1917 likewise accorded exemption to members of recognized religious denominations whose doctrines and discipline declared military service sinful. The Selective Service Act of 1940 liberalized the exemption by making it applicable to anyone who by reason of religious training and belief possessed conscientious scruples against participation in armed conflict in any form. In 1948, however, the law was amended. A claim of conscientious objection was denied to those whose refusal to participate in war was based on essentially political, sociological, and philosophical views or on a mere personal code, and religion was defined as a belief in a supreme being.

In *Torcaso* v. *Watkins* (1961), the Court held that the Constitution forbade disqualifying for public office (including that of notary public) persons who refused to take an oath of belief in God. It noted that there were ancient, well-recognized religions, such as Buddhism, Taoism, and Confucianism, that were not theistic and that, unlike Christianity and Judaism, did not require belief in a personal deity. From this it follows that limiting the conscientious-objection exemption to theists would likely be deemed unconstitutional, even if exemption were adjudged not a right but only a privilege accorded by the legislature, since so too is the license to act as notary public.

The Court faced the problem of allowing nontheists to claim conscientious objection in the three 1965 cases decided under the title *United States* v. *Seeger*. Seeger, in applying for exemption, admitted his "skepticism or disbelief in the existence of God," but he avowed a "belief in and devotion to goodness and virtue for their own sakes and a religious faith in a purely ethical creed," citing Plato, Aristotle, and Spinoza in support of such belief. Jakobson, another applicant, stated a belief in "Godness horizontally through Mankind and the World" rather than "vertically, towards Godness directly." The third applicant, Peter, avowed a commitment to religion defined as "the supreme expression of human nature; man thinking his highest, feeling his deepest, living his best." The Court adjudged all three applicants entitled to exemption since all had the requisite training and belief in relation to a "Supreme Being." By using that term instead of "God," the Court said, Congress intended something broader than the traditional personal deity. As for the phrase "religious belief," the Court construed it to mean a belief that is sincere and meaningful and occupies a place in the life of its possessor parallel to that filled by the orthodox belief in God of one who clearly qualifies for the exemption.

The exemption accorded by Congress was conditional upon conscientious objection to all wars; it did not encompass selective objection limited to wars deemed sinful or immoral. However, in *Sicurella* v. *United States* (1955), the Court held that the willingness of a Jehovah's Witness to fight as a soldier of Christ at Armageddon if Jehovah so commanded him did not deprive him of his claim to exemption in pre-Armageddon wars between nations of the world. On the other hand, in *Gillette* v. *United States* (1971), the Court held that the refusal of Congress to exempt persons who would not serve in what they deemed immoral wars (such as that in Vietnam) but would fight in moral wars (such as the one against Nazi Germany) did not violate the free-exercise clause of the First Amendment.

Clergymen's exemption from military service can be traced back to the Bible (*Nm.* 1:3, 1:47), as can the employment of military chaplains (*Dt.* 20:1–4): both were held constitutional in the *Selective Draft Law Cases* of 1918. In 1972, on the other hand, compulsory chapel attendance in national military academies was held violative of the First Amendment, notwithstanding the claim that such attendance was "a vital part of the leadership package" *(Laird* v. *Anderson)*.

National loyalty. Closely related to national defense is the idea of national loyalty. Governments generally demand that the people manifest loyalty by such overt acts as saluting the flag and pledging allegiance to it. Jehovah's Witnesses, however, refuse to participate in such manifestations, deeming them forbidden by the biblical prohibition of idolatry. The issue of whether a public school may constitutionally oust a pupil who refuses to participate in the flag salute ceremony was passed upon and upheld in *Minersville School District* v. *Gobitis* (1940). The Supreme Court ruled that a valid general law commanding, regulating, or forbidding a secular practice such as flag salute (or military service, polygamous marriages, or the drinking of intoxicating liquors even at Mass) does not violate the Constitution simply because it might violate the conscience of some to obey it. Three years later, however, in *West Virginia State Board of Education* v. *Barnette,* the Court overruled the *Gobitis* decision and held that freedom of expression, including religious expression, might not be restricted in the absence of a clear and present danger to a substantial governmental interest.

Domestic tranquillity. Peace in the streets is probably the arena in which the vigorous missionary efforts of Jehovah's Witnesses played a major role in the shaping of constitutional law relating to the free exercise of religion. Attacks upon the Witnesses, both physical and legal, were widespread and intense for a number of reasons. Their refusal to salute the flag was considered unpatriotic, if not treasonable. Their denunciations of the conventional Christian churches infuriated many churchgoers, particularly but not exclusively Roman Catholics. Persistently the Witnesses brought their grievances to the Supreme Court. They were not alone in this. In *Kunz* v. *New York* (1951), for example, the Court held that a Baptist preacher could not be denied renewal of a permit for evangelical street meetings on the grounds that his preachings, scurrilously attacking Catholicism and Judaism, had led to disorder. There were, the Court said, appropriate remedies to protect communities from violence, but these did not include advance suppression.

Jehovah's Witnesses, however, were the major target of efforts to circumscribe religious liberty in the two decades between 1935 and 1955. During that period they brought to the Supreme Court a host of cases challenging a variety of laws, such as those against littering the streets, disturbing the peace, peddling without a license, using sound trucks, obstructing traffic, using child labor, and withholding tax revenues. The Supreme Court's decisions relating to aspects of domestic tranquillity can be summarized as follows.

The First Amendment guarantees the right to teach and preach religion in the public streets and parks and to solicit contributions or the purchase of religious materials. Although a prior municipal permit may be required, its grant or denial may not be based on the substance of what is taught, preached, or distributed, but only upon the need to regulate—in the interest of traffic control—the time, place, and manner of all public meetings *(Cantwell* v. *Connecticut,* 1940*)*. This right, so construed, encompasses religious processions, although in all cases a fee may be imposed to cover administrative expenses and the added cost of maintaining public order *(Cox* v. *New Hampshire,* 1941*)*. The Constitution, however, does not immunize from prosecution persons who in their missionary efforts use expressions that are lewd, obscene, libelous, insulting, or "fighting"—words that by their very utterance inflict injury or tend to incite an immediate breach of peace *(Chaplinsky* v. *New Hampshire,* 1942*)*. The right to solicit contributions or distribute handbills in streets and publicly owned railroad or bus terminals is likewise secured *(Jamison* v. *Texas,* 1943*)*, as is the right to ring doorbells in order to offer house occupants religious literature, although this does not, of course, include the right to force oneself into the house for that purpose *(Martin* v. *City of Struthers,* 1943*)*.

Related to the Jehovah's Witnesses' claims in respect to public streets and parks are the demands of other feared or unpopular minority religious groups (often referred to as "sects" or "cults," such as the Unification Church and the Church of Scientology) for free access in publicly controlled areas. However, the Supreme Court held, in *Heffron* v. *International Society for Krishna Consciousness* (ISKCON) (1981), that a state rule limiting to specific booths on public fair grounds the sale or distribution of merchandise, including religious materials, did not violate the free-exercise clause when applied to ISKCON, which required its members to distribute or sell its religious literature and solicit donations in all public places. Discriminatory treatment, on the other hand, is not permissible. Thus in *Cruz* v. *Beto* (1972) the Supreme Court upheld the claim of a Buddhist prisoner that his constitutional rights had been violated in that he had been denied use of the prison chapel, had been punished for sharing his Buddhist religious materials with other prisoners, and had been denied other generally available privileges, such as enhancement of eligibility for early parole by reason of attendance at religious services.

The power and duty of the police to ensure domestic tranquillity encompasses protecting the public not only from violent crimes but also from the unlawful, albeit peaceful, deprivation of property. A difficult problem arises when the courts are called upon to decide between religious freedom and the state's duty to punish persons who obtain property through falsehoods in religious matters. The leading case on this subject is *United States* v. *Ballard* (1944), originating in a prosecution for using the mails to defraud. The indictment charged that the defendents, organizers of a cult called "I Am," had mulcted money from elderly and ill persons by falsely representing that they had supernatural powers to heal and that they themselves had personally communicated with heaven and with Jesus Christ. The Supreme Court held that the free-exercise clause would be violated if the state were allowed to prove that the representations were false. Neither a jury nor any other organ of government, the Court said, had the power to pass on whether alleged miraculous religious experiences had actually occurred. Courts could constitutionally determine only whether the defendants themselves genuinely believed that what they recounted was true. Only if a jury determined that the defendants did not believe their own claims could they be convicted of obtaining money under false pretenses.

Conflicts between principles. The power to establish justice will on occasion conflict with a claim to religious freedom. In providing for "affirmation" as an alternative to "oath" by federal officers, Article Six of the Constitution recognized that religious convictions may forbid some persons (specifically Quakers) to take oaths. By so providing, the constitutional convention manifested its intention that no person in the federal judicial system—judge, lawyer, court official, or juryman—be disqualified because of religion or lack of religion. In *Torcaso* v. *Watkins* (1961), the Court reached the same conclusion in respect to state offices (such as that of notary public), and in the case of *In re Jenison* (1963) the Justices refused to uphold a conviction for contempt of court of a woman who would not serve on a jury because of the biblical command "Judge not that ye not be judged."

The phrase "promote the general welfare" is not defined in the Constitution. Generally one may assume that the phrase refers to the protection of life, liberty, and property, but under the American federal system that responsibility rests with the states, with federal intervention allowable only where some power specifically allocated to the federal government is endangered. (For example, under the clause empowering Congress to regulate interstate commerce, laws have been enacted criminalizing the interstate transportation of women, including the wives of Mormons committed to plural marriages, for immoral purposes.) However, as already noted, the First Amendment's guaranty of religious freedom is equally applicable to the states in their attention to the general welfare.

Where communal health conflicts with an individual's religious conscience, there is little doubt that religion must yield. Thus, as the Court held in *Jacobsen* v. *Massachusetts* (1905), compulsory vaccination against communicable diseases is enforceable notwithstanding religious objections to the procedure. So, too, fluoridation of municipal water supplies to prevent tooth decay cannot be judicially forbidden because of objection by those who consider the drinking of fluoridated water to be sinful.

The constitutional principles are also fairly clear when the life, health, or safety of individuals rather than communities at large is involved. Where, for example, the individuals are children who require blood transfusions to preserve their lives, the procedure may be undertaken notwithstanding the objection by parents (usually Jehovah's Witnesses) who consider transfusions to be a biblically forbidden drinking of blood. Similarly, the Court held in *Prince* v. *Massachusetts* (1944) that Jehovah's Witnesses can be prosecuted for violations of child labor laws by allowing their children to engage in selling the sect's literature in the streets. However, in *Wisconsin* v. *Yoder* (1972) the Court held that in some instances what may be considered the welfare of children must yield to the parents' free exercise of religion. In this decision the Court ruled that although a state may enforce its compulsory school-attendance law in respect to children up to the age of sixteen, it may not do so where the (Amish) parents consider attendance at secondary schools sinful. The state's interest in universal secondary school education, the Court held, must be balanced against the parents' right to the free exercise of religion and their traditional interest in the religious upbringing of their children. In so balancing, the Court ruled for the free-exercise right, notwithstanding the state's argument that if the children later leave their church they should not have to make their way in the world without the education available in the one or two additional years required by state.

Another instance relating to the balancing of competing interests concerns the enforcement of compulsory Sunday closing laws against those whose religious conscience forbids labor or trade on the seventh rather than the first day of the week. In *McGowan* v. *Maryland* (1961) and *Two Guys from Harrison* v. *Allentown* (1961) the Court upheld the general validity of these laws under the establishment clause. The Justices argued that although the origin of these laws may have been religious, their present purpose was the secular one of ensuring a weekly day for rest, relaxation, and family togetherness. Simultaneously, in two other cases, *Gallagher* v. *Crown Kosher Super Market* and *Braunfeld* v. *Brown*, the Court rejected the argument that the free-exercise clause was violated by requiring Orthodox Jews either to abstain from engaging in trade two days weekly or to sacrifice their religious conscience, whereas their Sunday-observing competitors were required to abstain only one day without impairing their conscience. Exempting sabbatarians, the Court held, might be administratively difficult, might benefit nonsabbatarians motivated only by a desire for a competitive advantage over merchants closing on Sundays, and might frustrate the legitimate legislative goals of ensuring a uniform day of rest for all. Although state legislatures could constitutionally elect to exempt sabbatarians, the free-exercise clause did not require them to do so.

In *Sherbert* v. *Verner* (1963), the Court reached a conclusion difficult to reconcile with that reached in *Gallagher* and *Braunfeld.* Denial of unemployment insurance benefits to a Seventh Day Adventist who refused to accept tendered employment that required working on Saturday, the Court held, placed an impermissible burden on the free exercise of religion. Governmental imposition of such a choice puts the same kind of burden upon free exercise as would a fine imposed for Saturday worship. Similarly, in *Thomas* v. *Review Board* (1981) the Supreme Court invalidated a state law denying unemployment compensation benefits to one who for religious reasons refused to work in a plant manufacturing armaments. On the other hand, in *United States* v. *Lee* (1982) the Court held that the free-exercise clause did not mandate exemption from social security and unemployment insurance contributions by Amish employers whose religious conscience (based on *1 Timothy* 5:8: "But if any provide not . . . for those of his own house, he hath denied the faith, and is worse than an infidel") forbade them to participate in the program. Compulsory contribution, the Court said, could be justified by a showing that it is essential in order to accomplish the overriding governmental interest in the effective operation of the social security system.

Finally, in *Murdock* v. *Town of McCormack* (1944) the Court ruled that under the free-exercise clause a revenue-raising tax for the privilege of canvassing or soliciting orders for articles could not be applied to Jehovah's Witnesses who sold their literature from door to door. In the same case, however, it stated that the income tax statute could constitutionally be applied to clergymen whose income came solely from salaries received for performing clerical duties. As previously noted, however, the validity under the establishment clause of the privilege of tax exemptions accorded to church-owned real estate was upheld in *Walz* v. *Tax Commission* (1970).

[*For discussion of the history of church-state relations, religious toleration, and religious freedom, see* Church and State. *For information regarding some recent legal controversies involving religious groups, see* New Religions, *article on* New Religions and Cults in the United States.]

BIBLIOGRAPHY

The standard history of religious freedom and church-state relations in the United States is the work by Anson Phelps Stokes, *Church and State in the United States,* 3 vols. (New York, 1950); a revised and updated one-volume edition, written by Stokes and myself, has been published (New York, 1964). Although this edition, prepared after Reverend Stokes's death, includes a summary of all major court decisions on the subject up to that time, it remains primarily a historical rather than a juridical account. Other, but shorter, works include Sanford H. Cobb's *The Rise of Religious Liberty in America* (New York, 1902), Franklin H. Littel's *From State Church to Pluralism* (Garden City, N.Y., 1977), William Warren Sweet's *Religion in Colonial America* (New York, 1942) and *Religion in the Development of American Culture: 1765–1840* (New York, 1952), and Elwyn A. Smith's *Religious Liberty in the United States: The Development of Church-State Thought since the Revolutionary Era* (Philadelphia, 1972).

The major work on constitutional issues of religious freedom and church-state relationships is my own *Church, State, and Freedom,* 2d ed., rev. & enl. (Boston, 1967); my *God, Caesar and the Constitution* (Boston, 1975) is essentially an abridged version of the earlier work. I have further updated my work in *Religion, State, and the Burger Court* (New York, 1984). Although I seek in these works to relate and explain the courts' relevant decisions objectively and to present impartially the arguments for and against each contested issue, I leave no doubt of my belief that, as stated in *Church, State and Freedom,* "complete separation of church and state is best for the church and best for the state, and secures freedom for both." In a shorter work, *Freedom from Federal Establishment: Formation and Early History of the First Amendment Religious Clauses* (Milwaukee, 1964), Chester J. Antieau and the volume's other authors insist, from a Catholic viewpoint, that the Supreme Court has misinterpreted the true intent of the authors of the First Amendment, which was only to bar exclusivity, preference, and compulsion. Basically the same premise, that the Court has misinterpreted the authors' intent by construing the amendment in a manner hostile rather than friendly to religion, is set forth in Mark DeWolfe Howe's *The Garden and the Wilderness: Religion and Government in American Constitutional History* (Chicago, 1965) and in Robert L. Cord's *Separation of Church and State* (New York, 1982).

Lawrence H. Tribe's *American Constitutional Law* (Mineola, N.Y., 1978; plus supplements) devotes only seventy-five of its twelve hundred pages to the subject of religion, but it is often cited in court decisions as authoritative in respect to the amendment's religion clauses; its technical legal style, however, makes it difficult reading for the nonlawyer. In *Religion and the Law: Of Church, State and the Supreme Court* (Chicago, 1962), Philip B. Kurland holds that free exercise and nonestablishment should be read together as a single precept requiring government to be religion-blind in respect to both conferring benefits and imposing burdens upon churches. Milton R. Konvits's *Religious Liberty and Conscience: A Constitutional Inquiry* (New York, 1968) argues that the term *religion* in the First

Amendment cannot be satisfactorily defined and that it should be kept open-ended in order to encompass each person's conscience. Richard E. Morgan, in *The Supreme Court and Religion* (New York, 1972), expresses agreement with the Supreme Court's decisions barring ritual practices from the public schools, but he asserts that the Court has gone too far in protecting religious minorities and barring aid to parochial schools. David Fellman's *Religion in American Public Law* (Boston, 1965) is an expository summary of court decisions; although a strong separationist, the author recognizes that a complete and uncompromising separation is, in the nature of things, altogether unattainable. M. Searle Bates's *Religious Liberty: An Inquiry* (New York, 1945) is still a valuable exposition of religious freedom and church-state relations throughout the world. E. R. Norman's *The Conscience of the State in North America* (Cambridge, 1968) presents this British historian's comparative study of the development of church-state relations in the United States and Canada. Treating the subject of interreligious tensions and conflict from a historical and sociological approach is Herbert Stroup's *Church and State in Confrontation: A Sociological Study of Church-State Relations from Old Testament Times to the Present* (New York, 1967). *Religious Freedom in America: Essays in Historical Interpretation* is the title of a special issue of the *Union Seminary Quarterly Review* 38 (1984), which brings together papers originally presented at a symposium on religious toleration and religious freedom held in Newport, Rhode Island, in 1978; the collection contains essays by John E. Smith, William G. McLoughlin, David Little, Gillian Lindt, and others. Finally, mention should be made of my *Creeds in Competition* (New York, 1958), a comparative exposition of the positions taken by American Protestantism, Catholicism, Judaism, and secular humanism on such controversial subjects as church-state separation, religion in the public schools, aid to parochial schools, Sunday closing laws, and birth control through contraception and abortion; it concludes that such competition, although occasionally bitter, is nevertheless of great value to the American democratic system.

LEO PFEFFER

LEADERSHIP. The concept of religious leadership, although indispensable to general discourse, has been of limited value to the social scientific study of religion, which has advanced little beyond the pioneering studies of Max Weber and Joachim Wach. While we know a great deal about individual religious leaders and have accumulated a reservoir of case studies of such leaders, we know far less about the phenomenon of leadership. Indeed, what is lacking at present is a generally accepted concept of religious leadership. Scholars working in different religious traditions use diverse modes of theorizing and analysis and do so in pursuit of differing and often unrelated questions. Important but largely unrecognized work in the psychology of leadership in small groups, social exchange models of interaction processes developed by sociologists, and shifts in focus from power to leadership in political science thinking all provide new bases for generalizations about religious leadership across differing cultures and times.

Religious leadership may be defined as the process by which leaders induce followers to act for certain transcendental goals that embody the values, motivations, and aspirations of both leaders and followers. Such leadership involves the exercise of power in religious collectivities, but its domain is more limited than that of power. Unrestricted power over others is exercised to realize the goals of the power-wielder whether or not these goals are shared by the followers. The essence of leadership lies in the manner in which leaders perceive and act on their own and their followers' values and needs (Burns, 1978).

Weber's Typology of Religious Leadership. The groundwork for a comparative study of religious leadership was laid by the German sociologist Max Weber in his *Wirtschaft und Gesellschaft* (1925), the first strictly empirical comparison of the social structure and normative order of societies in world-historical depth. He contributed the outlines of a typology of religious leaders as well as a major statement on forms of domination and the bases of legitimization of authority underlying different types of leadership. In spite of his stress on the independent significance of religious values and ethics, he acknowledged the importance of the social vehicles through which the impact of religion is effected. His analysis of religious groups, as one instance of a variety of nearly universal types of human groups found at differing phases of historical development, highlights the crucial importance of religious leadership as a vehicle of religiosity and religious change.

Weber isolates the features peculiar to three major types of leaders—magicians, prophets, and priests—through a comparison with each other as well as with the subsidiary leadership roles of lawgivers, teachers of ethics, and mystagogues. The emergence of priests as distinct from practitioners of magic centers on several points of differentiation: (1) priests influence the gods by means of worship, whereas magicians coerce demons by magical means; (2) priests are "functionaries of a regularly organized and permanent enterprise concerned with influencing the gods," whereas magicians engage in "individual and occasional efforts"; (3) priests are actively associated with some type of social organization by which they are employed, in contrast to magicians who are typically self-employed; and (4) the priest exerts influence by virtue of his professional expertise in fixed doctrine and his vocational qualifications, whereas magicians exert their influence by virtue of personal gifts and charisma made manifest in miracles. The nature of the learning of these leadership roles differs; priests undergo rational training and discipline and magicians are prepared through an "awakening" using nonrational means and proceeding in part as a training in purely empirical lore.

Weber recognized that in reality the contrasts just noted are fluid and by no means unequivocally determinable so that empirically the two contrasted types often flow into one another. The crucial feature of the priesthood is centered on "the specialization of a particular group of persons in the continuous operation of a cultic enterprise permanently associated with particular norms, places, and times and related to specific social groups."

Building on Adolf von Harnack's typology, Weber isolates the sociologically distinctive traits of the prophet as a "purely individual bearer of charisma who by virtue of his mission proclaims a religious doctrine or divine commandment." For Weber, it is this personal call that is the decisive element distinguishing prophet from priest. It is the latter who claims authority by virtue of his service in a sacred tradition, whereas the prophet's claim is based on personal revelation and charisma. It is no accident that almost no prophets have emerged from the priestly class. The priest typically dispenses salvation by virtue of his office even in instances in which personal charisma may be involved. It is the hierarchical office that confers legitimate authority upon the priest as a member of an organized collectivity.

A second and closely linked point is Weber's focus on the prophet as an agent of change who takes personal responsibility for breaking with the established normative order, declaring this break to be morally legitimate. The leadership role of the priest by contrast is exercised typically in the service of an established order.

Unlike the magician, the prophet claims definitive revelations, the core of his mission being doctrine or commandment, not magic. Again, Weber acknowledged that this distinction was fluid; magicians are frequently knowledgeable experts in divination and prophets often practice divination as well as magical healing and counseling like the *nevi'im* mentioned in the Old Testament. What distinguishes the prophet from both the magician and the priest in this regard is an economic factor, namely, that prophecy is unremunerated. Weber further differentiates prophets from the religious leadership roles of lawgivers, epitomized in the Greek *aisumnētai*, teachers of ethics, and mystagogues. While the transition historically from prophet to each of these types is not clearly defined, Weber separated out from the category of prophet these other types, treating them as analytically distinguishable leadership roles for "sundry purveyors of salvation." Of these, only the mystagogue—Weber's neologism for the religious counterpart of the demagogue—shared with the prophet a leadership role that demands a break with the established order. But whereas the prophet legitimates that break in ethical and moral terms, the bases of legitimation for the mystagogue are primarily magical.

Central to Weber's delineation of the role of prophet was his differentiation of two subtypes. One was the *ethical* prophet, who preaches as one who has received a commission from God and who demands obedience as an ethical duty. He is represented most clearly by Muḥammad and Zarathushtra (Zoroaster). The Buddha by contrast typified the *exemplary* prophet, who by his personal example demonstrates to others the way to religious salvation.

A discussion of Weber's typology of religious leaders is distorted unless it includes reference to his discussion of the laity whom prophets and priests sought to influence. For a prophecy is successful only if the prophet succeeds in winning permanent helpers. These include the *amaga*, or members of the inner circle of devotees of Zoroastrianism; the disciples of the Hebrew Bible and of the New Testament; and the intimate companions of Hinduism and Islam. The distinctive characteristic in all these cases is that these are personal devotees of the prophet who, in contrast to those of the priest, are not organized into guilds or office hierarchies. In addition to these most active co-workers, there is a widening circle of followers who support the prophet and expect to obtain their salvation through his mission. These followers may engage in intermittent action or associate themselves continuously in a congregation. The latter community does not arise in connection with every type of prophecy; generally it is the result of routinization, that is, of a process securing the permanence of the prophet's preaching and the congregation's role as distributor and recipient of grace.

Weber reserves the term *congregation* for situations in which the laity has been organized permanently in such a manner that it becomes an active participant. Thus a mere administrative unit that delimits the jurisdiction of priests is a parish but not yet a congregational community. From this point of view, one finds that in medieval Christianity in the West and Islam in Near East the parish was essentially a passive ecclesiastical tax unit with the laity generally lacking the character of a congregation. By contrast, it is the distinctive characteristic of sects that they are based on a restricted association of individual local congregations. In such circumstances the relationship between priesthood and laity becomes of crucial significance for the practical consequences of religion and for the exercise of religious leadership.

Weber here argues that every type of priesthood is to some extent in a similar position: to maintain its own power it must meet the needs of the laity to a very considerable degree. Since as a rule both the ethical and the exemplary prophet are themselves laymen, the prophet's power position depends in both cases also on that of his lay followers. To what extent the prophet would succeed as a leader depended on the outcome of a struggle for power. All prophets made use of the prestige of their prophetic charisma and the support it gained them among the laity. The sacredness of the radically new revelation was continuously opposed to that of tradition. Depending on the success of the propaganda by each side, the priesthood might compromise with the new prophecy, outbid its doctrine, eliminate it, or be subjugated itself. Religious leadership, in short, is exercised typically in competition or conflict with others in which the different leaders contend for the support of their potential followers.

In Weber's ensuing discussion of the major social classes and their affinities for religion, he provides a comparative frame of reference for assessing the influence of class factors in conditioning the outcome of specific religious leaders' claims for support by the laity. This includes a discussion of intellectuals and of the conditions under which priests and monks become intellectual elaborators of religion, as was true, for example, in India, Egypt, and Babylonia. In the religions of the ancient city-states, however, notably among the Phoenicians, Greeks, and Romans, the development of all metaphysical and ethical thought became the province of nonpriests. Weber further emphasized the predominance of high-status intellectuals as religious innovators and leaders. [*See also* Priesthood; Prophecy; Shamanism; *and* Intellectuals.]

The Bases of Legitimation of Authority. Weber's typology of religious leadership is intricately linked to his sociological analysis of forms of domination, with its threefold typology of the bases of legitimation of authority to which such leaders made claim. [*See* Authority.] Domination was defined by Weber as "the probability that certain specific commands (or all commands) will be obeyed by a given group of persons." Domination ("authority") for Weber could be based on diverse motives of compliance "all the way from simple habituation to the most purely rational calculation of advantage." But he makes clear that every form of domination implies at least a minimum of voluntary compliance and thus represents obedience based on self-interested calculation.

For Weber, the key to leadership had to be found in the kind of legitimacy claimed by the leader, the type of obedience demanded, the kind of administrative support developed to guarantee its success, and the modes by which such authority is exercised. All of these would differ fundamentally depending upon which of three types of legitimization was most prevalent. The validity of claims to legitimacy, according to Weber, were based on (1) rational grounds, resting on a belief in the legality of enacted rules and the right of those elevated to authority under such rules to issue commands, that is, legal authority; (2) grounds resting on an established belief in the sanctity of traditions and the legitimacy of those exercising authority under them, that is, traditional authority; and (3) charismatic grounds "resting on devotion to the exceptional sanctity, heroism, or exemplary character of an individual person and of the normative patterns or order revealed or ordained by him, i.e., charismatic authority."

The concept of charisma, "gift of grace," was taken from the vocabulary of early Christianity and drew heavily on writings of the church and legal historian Rudolf Sohm, in particular his *Kirchenrecht* (1892). The term *charisma* as elaborated by Weber refers to "a certain quality of an individual personality by virtue of which he is considered extraordinary and treated as endowed with supernatural, superhuman, or at least specifically exceptional powers or qualities. These . . . are regarded as of divine origin or as exemplary and on the basis of them the individual concerned is treated as a 'leader'." What is crucial is how the individual is regarded by those subject to charismatic authority, that is, by the leader's followers or disciples. Such recognition is freely given and guaranteed by "what is held to be proof, originally always a miracle, and consists in devotion to the corresponding revelation, hero worship, or absolute trust in the leader."

Weber notes that where charisma is genuine, the basis lies not in such proof per se but rather in the conception that it is the duty of those subject to charismatic authority to recognize its genuineness and to act accordingly. Psychologically, such recognition is a matter of complete personal devotion to the possessor of the quality, arising out of enthusiasm or alternately out of despair or of hope. The charismatic leader's legitimacy to act is thus not derived from the follower's consent or from custom or law, but from a transcendental realm.

The right of the leader to rule is determined by the follower's recognition of the godlike qualities either imputed to him by the follower or bestowed on him through ascension to a charismatic office. The success of the charismatic leader in developing a community of disciples or followers gives rise to the charismatic community. But if that community is to take on a degree of permanence—a matter of considerable interest to the disciples and followers if their own positions are to be put on a stable, everyday basis—it becomes necessary for the character of the original charismatic authority to be altered radically.

The problem of leadership transfer from the charismatically endowed leader to his successor is thus inherently unstable. How this problem is met, if it is met at all, is amenable to a range of solutions. These include the search for a new leader, using as criteria qualities that will fit him for the position of authority, as has historically been so with the search for a new Dalai Lama; revelation manifested in the use of lots or divine judgment or other techniques of selection; designation on the part of the original charismatic leader of his own successor (a very common form); designation of a successor by the charismatically qualified administrative staff together with his recognition by the community; and transmission of charisma by heredity or by ritual means. In the last case, charisma becomes disassociated from a particular individual, is objectified, and becomes a transferable entity that may be transformed into a charisma of office. A critical example is the transmission of priestly charisma by anointing, consecration, or the laying on of hands.

The Weberian typology of religious leadership was subsequently enlarged by Joachim Wach in his *Einführung in die Religionssoziologie* (1931). Wach attempts to classify the variety of types of religious authority "according to the principle of personal and official charisma," although he recognizes that a given type can include a combination of both elements. [*See* Charisma.] Even though the critical issue of leadership as deriving from different forms of charismatic authority is never explicitly addressed by Wach, his typology has generally been presumed to constitute both a delineation of types of religious leaders and an analysis of the underlying types of legitimation of their rule. In addition to the categories of priest, prophet, and magician already developed by Weber to which Wach's delineation provides little that is analytically new, Wach adds the following types: founder, reformer, seer, diviner, saint, and *religiosus*. As with Weber, Wach's analysis is directed not only to an examination of the charismatic basis of their claims to authority, but also to an elaboration of the variety of religious roles played by such leaders. Even as a classificatory tool, however, Wach's typology needs to be substantially enlarged if it is to encompass the diversity of religious leadership known to contemporary scholars. Still more crucial is the fact that with Wach, the emphasis shifted from typology as a tool of analysis and explanation to a tool of description and classification. It is to these analytic and explanatory concerns to which we must now return.

Current Theories in the Social Sciences. Research in the fields of psychology, political science, and sociology may be drawn on to suggest a number of new directions for the study of religious leadership.

Origins of religious leadership. One key to understanding leadership lies in recent findings and concepts in psychology, psychiatry, and psychohistory. Despite its cultural limitations, psychobiography can be an important tool in analyzing the formative influences on religious leadership, as Erik H. Erikson's studies of Luther and Gandhi have documented. Viewing some of the influences in the early years of great religious leaders, we may come to better understand the powerful influences of family, peer group, class, and adolescent experience. Such studies, however, will always be inadequate, since they deal with only one segment and tend to slight the effects of religious learning, political and institutional contexts, and the role of followers in shaping the behavior of leaders.

Social sources of leadership. Typologies of leadership by virtue of their abstraction tend to disassociate leadership from its social-situational context. Leadership occurs, as Weber's discussion of hierocracy, theocracy, and caesaropapism documents, in an immensely complex social network of structured and patterned relationships. The psychology of small-group research documents, moreover, how leadership adheres not in an individual but in a role that is imbedded within some specified social system. Variations in the social context within which religious leadership is deemed to be critical represent an important historical variable. Thus, studies of religious organizations that have focused on their leadership in modern industrial societies in the period since World War II rarely if ever address the kinds of issues dealt with by Weber. The study of religious leadership in these contexts typically involves an analysis of personnel recruitment, socialization, professionalization, training for the ministerial or priestly role, and delineation of the various role segments of administrator, preacher, counselor, teacher, and pastor. A recent review of the literature by the American sociologist Edgar W. Mills (1985) decried the absence of a concern with leadership in most contemporary studies of the ministry. These themes reflect, as Roland Robertson (1970) has noted, organizational constraints upon the exercise of leadership in societies in which religion has become increasingly differentiated and compartmentalized.

Personal traits. Religious leadership like other forms of leadership cannot be reduced to some specific set of abilities or personal attributes. Even the prophet is not born with "the gift of grace"; he must claim it. Natural endowment, intellectual or emotional predisposition, and training are only accessory, and they vary considerably.

A mixing of variables. Typologies of leadership, including those of religious leadership, have too often drawn on a variety of analytical and theoretical considerations without adequately differentiating the specific variables according to which a given religious leader is classified within one type rather than another. Indeed the very delineation of these types and their nomenclature suggest a mixing of variables. Thus a delineation of religious leaders as founders, reformers, revolutionaries, and conservationists focuses on the role of such leadership in challenging, revitalizing, or maintaining the existing social and religious order. By contrast, a typological distinction between expressive and instrumental types of leaders emphasizes differences in the ways in which leadership is exercised and followers exhorted, as was also true of Weber's original distinction between exemplary and ethical forms of prophetic leadership. Other typologies have focused on segmental roles or functions assumed by specific religious leaders, such as miracle workers, exorcists, moral teachers, mediators, ritual specialists, administrators, and scribes, as well as intellectual leaders and educators.

Revised Assumptions. Underlying the Weberian approach to religious leadership, and subscribed to equally by Wach, are a number of assumptions that recent research has either seriously questioned or forced to abandon altogether. Classic sociological treatments of religious leadership have leaned heavily on conceptions applying to elites, to authoritarian systems and to rigid caste- and class-based societies. The literature on religious leaders (and on leadership in general) has generally been committed to images of strong-willed leaders and mindless masses. Weber emphasized the authoritarian character of such leadership, especially charismatic leadership, by focusing on the exclusive prerogative of leaders to command and the unquestioning obligation of subordinates to obey. As a result there has been an unfortunate emphasis on the "great man" theory of leadership.

The role of gender—to the extent to which it enters into these studies of religious leadership at all—has simply reinforced the sterotyped image of religious leaders as male. The conditions under which women claim and successfully exercise such leadership has only recently become a topic of serious scholarly investigation. The focus on the great men who exercised religious leadership has moreover ignored the vital network of secondary, tertiary, and even "lower" leadership in most societies and most religious communities.

Weber's delineation of charismatic leadership has been a source of considerable confusion. This confusion has arisen because he integrated two distinct analytic components, the one social-structural and the other psychological, into his discussion of charismatic legitimations of authority. Each of them highlights different aspects of leaders and of their relationships to their followers. Yet, in focusing on the personal and affective dimensions of the relationship between charismatic leaders and their followers, Weber himself tilted the balance toward an emphasis on personality. The dominant thrust of his analysis was toward linking charisma with certain structural strains that are likely to be pronounced during periods of accelerated social change. But his analysis of the social conditions that give rise to charismatic leadership remained sketchy. These ambiguities in Weber's own discussion of charismatic leadership are reflected and magnified in the recent literature dealing with charisma, which has often used historical materials in an undiscriminating way to refer to almost all nonbureaucratic forms of leadership.

Although Weber never adopted the traditional image of leadership as unilateral—one was either leader or follower—his analysis of the relationship between the two, seen in the light of more recent research findings from the social sciences, tends to underplay the degree to which followers condition, shape, and mold both their leaders and the religious movements of which they form a part.

Similarly, Wach's discussion of the groups "corresponding to religious authority" is entitled "the audience" and includes references to the ephemeral audience of the migrating preacher or prophet, the crowd attending a religious celebration, and the permanent circle accompanying the founder and prophet. Such labeling of the group of followers as an audience betrays the passivity with which they are presumed to function and relate to their leader. While past studies of religious leaders generally portrayed their followers as a passive audience or mere aggregation minus the leader, more recent psychological and sociological research drawing on interaction theory and social exchange theory has demonstrated conclusively that the concepts of leading and following are reciprocal. Thus, religious leaders are by no means exclusively and always engaged in acts of leading. Leaders and followers do at times exchange roles, with the most active followers and disciples initiating acts of leadership. The expectations of followers and the acceptance accorded the leader may be as influential in shaping the character and consequences of that leadership as the resources of the leader himself. A more systematic attention to followers is likely to lead to the development of typologies not only of followers but of various models of leader-follower relationships.

The topic of religious leadership needs to draw on the empirical findings, concepts, and theoretical insights of recent research by social scientists working for the most part outside the realm of religious studies. The rapid proliferation of case studies of individual religious leaders, both past and present, has yet to be systematically integrated into a conceptual framework capable of subsuming the complex character of religious leadership. Greater integration is necessary if we are to move beyond description and classification to a level of analysis that will incorporate the determinants, processes, character, and consequences of such leadership.

BIBLIOGRAPHY

Bendix, Reinhard. "Reflections on Charismatic Leadership." In *State and Society: A Reader in Comparative Political Sociology*, edited by Reinhard Bendix, pp. 616–629. Boston, 1968.

Bierstedt, Robert. "The Problem of Authority." In *Freedom and Control in Modern Society*, edited by Morroe Berger, Theodore Abel, and Charles H. Page, pp. 67–81. New York, 1954.

Burns, James MacGregor. *Leadership*. New York, 1978.

Erikson, Erik H. *Young Man Luther: A Study in Psychoanalysis and History*. New York, 1958.

Erikson, Erik H. *Gandhi's Truth: On the Origins of Militant Nonviolence*. New York, 1969.

Gibb, Cecil A. "Leadership: Psychological Aspects." In *International Encyclopedia of the Social Sciences*, edited by David L. Sills, vol. 9, pp. 91–101. New York, 1968.

Mills, Edgar W. "The Sacred in Ministry Studies." In *The Sacred in a Secular Age*, edited by Phillip E. Hammond. Berkeley, 1985.

Robertson, Roland. *The Sociological Interpretation of Religion*. New York, 1970.

Sohm, Rudolf. *Kirchenrecht*. Leipzig, 1892.

Tannenbaum, Arnold S. "Leadership: Sociological Aspects." In *International Encyclopedia of the Social Sciences*, edited by David L. Sills, vol. 9, pp. 101–107. New York, 1968.

Wach, Joachim. *Einführung in die Religionssoziologie* (1931). Translated by the author as *Sociology of Religion*. Chicago, 1944.

Weber, Max. *Wirtschaft und Gesellschaft: Grundriss der verstehenden Soziologie* (1922). 2 vols. Translated by Ephraim Fischoff et al. as *Economy and Society*, edited by Guenther Roth and Claus Wittich. Berkeley, 1978

Willner, Ann Ruth. *The Spellbinders: Charismatic Political Leadership*. New Haven, 1984.

GILLIAN LINDT

LEAH. *See* Rachel and Leah.

LEAVEN. The Hebrews and other peoples of the Middle East were taught to use leaven by the Egyptians, who may have discovered its use as early as 2600 BCE. Although leavened bread took on importance as a religious symbol during the Azyme Controversy that finally divided Eastern and Western Christianity in 1054, the use of unleavened bread has had far greater significance in religious ritual. As a consequence, the ritualistic use of unleavened bread and the symbolic meaning of leaven merit special attention.

The best-known use of unleavened bread is described in the twelfth chapter of *Exodus*, where Ḥag ha-Matsot, the Feast of Unleavened Bread, and Passover are interfused in a historical commemoration of Israel's deliverance from Egypt. Other texts in the Hebrew scriptures indicate that the two feasts had different origins (*Dt.* 16:1–8, *Lv.* 23:5–6). Whereas Passover was a pastoral festival, the Feast of Unleavened Bread was agricultural. Since natural dough, a harvest gift of Yahveh, was considered holy, the addition of yeast would profane it. In addition, fermentation may have been viewed as a form of corruption.

Unleavened bread was prescribed for the night of Passover also to remind the Hebrews of the great haste with which they ate during their anxious flight from Egypt. During the Feast of Unleavened Bread, which began on the day following Passover and lasted seven days, the Israelites were directed to destroy all leavened bread that remained in their homes and eat only the "bread of misery." [*See* Passover.]

When the Israelites celebrated Shavuʿot, the Feast of Weeks (or Pentecost), at the end of the wheat harvest, they offered leavened bread as first fruits because it had become their common bread in Canaan. Although they associated leavened bread with the giving of the Law of Moses, the ritual for communion sacrifices stipulated that unleavened cakes mixed with oil and unleavened wafers smeared with oil be used. Leavened bread, however, was also to be given to the priest for the sacrificial meal (*Lv.* 7:11–15).

The Israelites seem to have been ambivalent about adding leaven to dough. Although its use conflicted with their eating habits as nomads, once they settled in Egypt and Canaan they routinely consumed leavened bread.

In the New Testament, leaven has at least three symbolic meanings: it is a sign of the Old Covenant that must yield to the New Covenant; it is symbolic of corrupting influences; and it typifies small beginnings that have enormous potential for growth. Paul instructed the Corinthians to rid themselves of the old yeast of evil and wickedness and to become instead the unleavened bread of sincerity and truth (*1 Cor.* 5:8). In this way, they would be united with the risen Christ in an unending Passover. Paul thus turned the cultic practice of the Israelites into an ethical injunction. The suggestion that leaven corrupts is also found in the admonition of Jesus to be on guard against the yeast of the Pharisees, that is, their hypocrisy (*Lk.* 12:1). Like many other symbols, yeast had a positive as well as a negative aspect. The parable comparing the kingdom of heaven to a yeast that spreads through three measures of flour (*Mt.* 13:33) refers to the fact that something as small and unpretentious as yeast can have astonishing potential.

Plutarch recounts that in Greco-Roman culture, the priest of Jupiter was forbidden to touch unleavened bread because it was unclean and corrupt. For Philo Judaeus, unleavened bread was a symbol of humility and leavened bread a symbol of pride.

The bread used for the Eucharist was leavened in the Eastern church and unleavened in the Western rite. These geographical variations caused no difficulty until the Middle Ages, when the discrepancy gradually became a point of contention. It reached a climax in 1054 in the Azyme Controversy preceding the Great Schism that divided the Eastern and Western churches. Mohlan Smith, tracing the controversy in his book *And Taking Bread,* suggests that Eastern and Western liturgical traditions involving different types of eucharistic bread are based on an apparent disagreement in the scriptures about the date of the Last Supper. The synoptic Gospels seem to indicate that the Last Supper took place on the first day of the Feast of Unleavened Bread. A reading of *John,* on the other hand, suggests that Jesus was crucified on the Day of Preparation. If this interpretation of *John* is accepted, the Last Supper would not have been a Passover meal, and leavened bread would have been used. The Eastern church's liturgical use of leavened bread also has theological overtones: it accentuates the break between the Old and New Covenants. Western rituals, on the other hand, emphasize the continuity of Hebrew and Christian traditions.

[*See also* Bread.]

BIBLIOGRAPHY

Smith, Mohlan H. *And Taking Bread: Cerularius and the Azyme Controversy of 1054.* Paris, 1978. An excellent study of the correspondence concerning the use of leaven in the eucharistic bread that was one of the issues in the schism between the Eastern and Western churches in 1054.

Wambacq, Benjamin N. "Les Maṣṣôt." *Biblica* 61 (1980): 31–54. A scholarly work that questions whether the Feast of Unleavened Bread was an agricultural feast.

JAMES E. LATHAM

LEE, ANN (1736–1784), English visionary and founder of the American Shakers. Growing up in a poor, working-class family in Manchester, England, Ann Lee was attracted in 1758 to the Shakers, a religious group that engaged in ecstatic dancing and other charismatic activities. Married in 1762, Lee had four children, all of whom died in infancy or early childhood. She interpreted these losses and the pain that she experienced in childbirth as a judgment on her concupiscence. In 1770 a vision convinced her that lust was the original sin in the Garden of Eden and the root of all human evil and misery. Only by giving up sexual intercourse entirely, following the heavenly pattern in which "they neither marry nor are given in marriage," could humankind be reconciled to God.

The Shakers and the celibate message that Ann Lee introduced among them experienced little success in England, where the group was sporadically persecuted but generally ignored. In 1774 Lee and eight of her followers emigrated to America and two years later settled at Niskeyuna (now Watervliet), New York, near Albany. Between 1781 and 1783, during the troubled aftermath of the American Revolution, Lee and the Shakers undertook a major proselytizing effort in New York and New England in the course of which they attracted support primarily from Free Will Baptists. Ensuing persecution, including brutal beatings and harassment, weakened Ann Lee and her brother William, contributing to their premature deaths in 1784.

Although Ann Lee's involvement with the Shakers in America lasted only a decade, her influence at that time was profound and has continued to be so during the groups's subsequent two-hundred year history. Intelligent, dynamic, and loving, she was revered by her followers. They came to believe that in "Mother Ann," as they affectionately called her, God's spirit had been incarnated in female form just as they believed that in Jesus, God's spirit had been incarnated in male form. Whether Lee herself ever claimed such quasi divinity—except in ecstatic utterances subject to symbolic interpretation—is questionable. Yet the conviction that Ann Lee was the second embodiment of Christ's spirit and the inaugurator of the millennium is central to the Shaker faith.

[*See also* Shakers.]

BIBLIOGRAPHY

The most thorough scholarly treatment of Ann Lee is presented in Edward Deming Andrews's *The People Called Shakers,* new enl. ed. (New York, 1963). Anna White and Leila S. Taylor's *Shakerism: Its Meaning and Message* (Columbus, Ohio, 1904) provides a perceptive Shaker assessment of the life and spirit of Ann Lee. The most valuable primary source on Ann Lee's life and beliefs is the rare *Testimonies of the Life, Character, Revelations, and Doctrines of Our Ever Blessed Mother Ann Lee and the Elders with Her* edited by Rufus Bishop and Seth Y. Wells (Hancock, Mass., 1816). An analysis that compares the Shakers under Ann Lee with other radical sectarian movements is Stephen A. Marini's *Radical Sects of Revolutionary New England* (Cambridge, Mass., 1982).

LAWRENCE FOSTER

LEENHARDT, MAURICE (1878–1954), French Protestant missionary and ethnographer. In the French ethnographic tradition of the era before World War II, Leenhardt stands out as a fieldworker of uncommon depth. From 1902 until 1926 he was a liberal evangelist in New Caledonia. His active defense of the Melanesians against colonial abuses and his stress on vernacular education and on the growth of autonomous local churches anticipated what would later be called liberation theology. His extremely subtle work in linguistics and Bible translation led him to ethnography. He had a relativist's understanding of cultural process and invention that brought him to challenge the notion of religious conversion as a discrete event. Leenhardt envisaged a longer, locally rooted historical development leading to a fresh articulation of Christianity, an experience of personal authenticity that would transcend, not abolish, Melanesian totemism and myth.

Upon leaving his mission field in 1926, after a successful, albeit embattled and unorthodox, career, Leenhardt turned his attention more directly to ethnographic description and ethnological theory. With the help of Lucien Lévy-Bruhl and Marcel Mauss he obtained a professorship at the École Pratique des Hautes Études and a post at the Musée de l'Homme. He published four works of detailed New Caledonian cultural description: *Notes d'ethnologie néo-calédonienne* (1930), *Documents néo-calédoniens* (1932), *Vocabulaire et grammaire de la langue houailou* (1935), and *Langues et dialectes de l'Austro-Mélanésie* (1946). He also wrote a synthetic ethnography, *Gens de la grande terre* (1937; rev. ed., 1952), and what is perhaps his best-known work, *Do Kamo: La personne et le mythe dans le monde mélanésien* (1947; translated into English as *Do Kamo: Person and Myth in the Melanesian World,* 1979). These works are characterized by rigorous attention to issues of linguistic and conceptual translation, by an emphasis on cultural expressivity and change over structure and system, and by an analytic focus on the person.

Leenhardt's chief ethnological contribution is his experiential concept of myth. In this view, myth should be freed from the status of a story or even of a legitimating social charter. Myth is not expressive of a "past." Rather, myth is a particular kind of engagement with a world of concrete presences, relations, and emotional participations. It is a "mode of knowledge" accessible to all human experience. There is nothing mystical, vague, or fluid about this way of knowing; it does not preclude logical, empirical activities, as Lévy-Bruhl tended to assume. Myth is fixed and articulated by a "socio-mythic landscape." For Leenhardt, place has a density inaccessible to any map; it is a superimposition of cultural, social, ecological, and cosmological realities. (The valleys of New Caledonia provided his most potent examples.) Orienting, indeed constituting, the person, this complex spatial locus is not grasped in the mode of narrative closure by a centered, perceiving subject. Rather, the person "lives" a discontinuous series of socio-mythic "times"—less as a distinct character than as a loose bundle of relationships. This *mythe vécu* ("lived myth") calls into question a Western view of the self as coterminous with a discrete body, a view that values identity at the expense of plenitude.

BIBLIOGRAPHY

For a full account of Leenhardt's life and writings, see my work *Person and Myth: Maurice Leenhardt in the Melanesian World* (Berkeley, 1982). Useful collections assessing his career appear in the *Journal de la société des océanistes* 10 (December 1954) and 34 (March–June 1978) and in *Le monde non chrétien* 33 (January–March 1955). On his work in the light of liberation theology, see Jean Massé's "Maurice Leenhardt: Une pédagogie libératrice," *Revue d'histoire et de philosophie religieuse* 1 (1980): 67–80, and Pierre Teisserenc's "Maurice Leenhardt en Nouvelle Calédonie: Sciences sociales, politique coloniale, stratégies missionnaires," *Recherches de science religieuse* 65 (July–December 1977): 389–442.

JAMES CLIFFORD

LEESER, ISAAC (1806–1868), American rabbi, writer, and leader of Jewish traditionalism. Born in Neunkirchen, Westphalia (Prussia), Leeser was orphaned at an early age. He received his secular education at a *Gymnasium* in Münster, and his religious tutelage from Benjamin Cohen and Abraham Sutro. At the age of eighteen he joined his uncle Zalman Rehiné in Richmond, Virginia, where he began to prepare for a business career and assisted the local religious functionary, Isaac B. Seixas. An article he published in defense of Judaism brought him to public attention and resulted in an invitation to occupy the pulpit of Philadelphia's congregation Mikveh Israel in 1829. During the next forty years he was the most prolific American Jewish writer and the most creative communal architect.

Leeser's *Instruction in the Mosaic Law* (1830) was followed by *The Jews and Mosaic Law* (1834), "a defence of the Revelation of the Pentateuch"; *Discourses, Argumentative and Devotional* (1837), "delivered at the Synagogue Mikveh Israel"; and *The Form of Prayers According to the Custom of the Spanish and Portugese Jews*, 6 vols. (1837–1838), edited and translated by Leeser, as was *The Book of Daily Prayers . . . According to the Custom of the German and Polish Jews* (1848). An edition of the Pentateuch in 1845 was followed by a translation of the entire Hebrew Bible into English in 1853, the first to be done by a Jew. In 1867 his collected sermons and essays, *Discourses on the Jewish Religion*, were published in ten volumes. His chief literary monument is *The Occident and American Jewish Advocate*, which he edited for twenty-five years (1843–1868).

Leeser inspired the establishment of the first Jewish Sunday school in America (1837), helped establish the Hebrew Education Society of Philadelphia (1848), and founded and headed the first rabbinical seminary in the New World, Maimonides College (1867). "His far seeing vision," Mayer Sulzberger wrote in 1868, "years and years ago projected a Hebrew College, a Jewish Hospital, a Foster home, a Union of Charities, a Board of Delegates of American Israelites, an Educational Society, an American Publication Society. . . ."

Religiously, Leeser was a staunch traditionalist who resisted and battled the rising Reform movement. His Orthodoxy, however, kept him neither from fully partaking of world culture nor from introducing the English sermon. Both Conservative and modern Orthodox Jews claim him and acknowledge his influence.

BIBLIOGRAPHY

Davis, Moshe. *The Emergence of Conservative Judaism*. Philadelphia, 1963. See pages 347–349.

Korn, Bertram W. "Isaac Leeser: Centennial Reflections." *American Jewish Archives* 19 (November 1967): 127–141.

Morais, Henry Samuel. *Eminent Israelites of the Nineteenth Century*. Philadelphia, 1880. See pages 195–201.

Seller, Maxine S. "Isaac Leeser's Views on the Restoration of a Jewish Palestine." *American Jewish Historical Quarterly* 58 (1968): 118–135.

Whiteman, Maxwell. "Isaac Leeser and the Jews of Philadelphia." *Publications of the American Jewish Historical Society* 48 (1959): 207–244.

Abraham J. Karp

LEEUW, GERARDUS VAN DER (1890–1950),

Dutch historian of religions, theologian, and phenomenologist.

Life. Born and raised in the Hague, van der Leeuw studied theology at the University of Leiden (1908–1913), with history of religions as his main field and W. Brede Kristensen as his principal teacher. The faculty also included P. D. Chantepie de la Saussaye, who himself had taught history of religions at the University of Amsterdam and who influenced the young man. Van der Leeuw specialized in ancient Egyptian religion and studied for a year in Germany (1913–1914), first in Berlin under Adolf Erman and Kurt Sethe, and then in Göttingen under Wilhelm Bousset. He obtained his doctorate in 1916 from Leiden. After having been a minister in the Dutch Reformed church for two years, van der Leeuw was called to Groningen in 1918 to occupy the chair of history of religion and history of the doctrine of God, with responsibility for the "theological encyclopedia" in the faculty of theology. He also taught Egyptian language and literature in the literary faculty. "History of the doctrine of God" was later dropped from his chair's title and after World War II phenomenology of religion was added to van der Leeuw's official assignment; after 1940 he also taught liturgics.

Van der Leeuw was active in the Dutch Reformed church where, like Chantepie de la Saussaye, he adhered to the so-called ethical theology, which stressed the value of religion as a reality of the heart and as an existential datum. Later he was particularly active in the liturgical movement in his church and in attempts to reform it. From 1945 to 1946 he was minister of education, arts, and sciences. In 1950 van der Leeuw became the first president of the newly founded International Association for the History of Religions; this put the seal on his international reputation. He died shortly afterward in Utrecht.

Principal Works. Van der Leeuw's books that are relevant to the study of religion fall into a number of categories. Most of his scholarly work was in the field of comparative studies and phenomenology, for which he wrote an introductory work, *Inleiding tot de godsdienstgeschiedenis* (1924), later completely revised as *Inleiding tot de phaenomenologie van den godsdienst* (1948), and the famous handbook entitled *Phänomenologie der Religion* (1933), subsequently translated into English as *Religion in Essence and Manifestation* (1938). Further, he produced articles and books on subjects as varied as sacrifice, mysticism, representations of Paradise, children in worship, the image of God, and the God-man relationship as well as articles on myth and mythology and on immortality.

In other categories, van der Leeuw's works are almost as numerous. His major historical studies concern ancient Egyptian religion, although he also wrote on ancient Greek religion and produced studies of ancient calling-songs and lamentations and on the meeting of early Christianity and paganism. Also important are his books on liturgics, on religious art, and on music and religion—including books treating the works of Bach and the history of church hymns—and his several theological works, which often derive their insights from the history and phenomenology of religion. Another category of van der Leeuw's works comprises his writings on his phenomenological method and on issues of philosophical and theological anthropology. He also wrote extensively on Christian topics and on various literary and cultural subjects. The total number of his publications amounts to about 650.

Major Contributions. Van der Leeuw's most original contribution may be his phenomenological approach to the study both of religious data and of the phenomenon of religion itself. Guided by a particular vision of religion as a whole, he looked for structure and meaning in the multitude of religious data. With this approach van der Leeuw rejected certain parochial theological schemes of interpretation, evaluation, and judgment that were current in his time. He thus cleared the terrain for new kinds of inquiries into the various meanings pertaining to religious data and into the potential religious meaning of basic natural and human phenomena. Van der Leeuw's phenomenology was characterized by its psychological orientation and its status as a theological discipline.

In his approach, van der Leeuw leans heavily on psychology and in particular on structural psychology in Dilthey's sense, as he states himself in 1928. He was then even prepared to speak of the "psychology" instead of the "phenomenology" of religion. His concept of psychology, however, is not that of present-day empirical psychology; he sees it instead as a way of approaching a subject through one's own experience. Understanding rather than explanation should be the aim of the study of religion, he believes, echoing a similar aim formulated in psychology in the 1920s by such scholars as Karl Jaspers, Eduard Spranger, and Ludwig Binswanger. In this psychological understanding-through-experience, the "subjectivity" of the researcher is an indispensable datum. In order to understand a religious phenomenon as a human expression, the researcher should allow it to affect him in its wholeness, and van der Leeuw contends that this should be done methodically, in the field of religion as well as in such other humanistic fields as history and psychology. This particular way of understanding implies that the researcher interpolates the religious phenomenon into his own life and "experiences" it, while bracketing *(epochē)* both its factual and ultimate reality. Van der Leeuw describes this procedure in the "Epilegomena" of his handbook and adds that such a psychological understanding should be followed by empirical research to control and correct what has been understood. It is precisely the subjective nature of the experience of understanding, as propounded by van der Leeuw, that has given rise to scholarly objections, because this approach may lead to abuse in hermeneutical investigations. The discussion of the value for hermeneutics of van der Leeuw's psychologically oriented phenomenology is still continuing.

Phenomenology of religion had a theological foundation for van der Leeuw. The "sacramental" experience of reality on the one hand and the tension between subject and object of religious experience on the other, which are at the basis of his phenomenology of religion, find their theological basis, according to him, in the doctrine of the Incarnation. As a discipline, phenomenology of religion had for van der Leeuw a theological status; he did, in fact, also speak of it as "phenomenological theology." Basically, it was a theological discipline concerned with the meaning of religious data in the experience of the believers, and van der Leeuw wanted to see this phenomenological theology as an intermediary stage between "historical" theology, concerned with literary and historical facticity, on one hand and "systematic" theology, concerned with ultimate truth and reality, on the other. Since it leaves open the status of the phenomenon with regard to ultimate values, phenomenological theology limits itself to the problem of "meaning" and "significance." In practice, however, a theological phenomenologist will interpret the meaning of religious phenomena finally in the light of the "true" religious meaning known in faith, and van der Leeuw's *Religion in Essence and Manifestation* bears witness in fact to its author's faith as a Christian. This book describes religious phenomena in five parts. The first three parts represent the classical structure given by Chantepie de la Saussaye: the object of religion, the subject of religion, and object and subject in their reciprocal operation. Part 4 deals with "the world" and part 5 with "forms" (religions and founders). Religion, for van der Leeuw, is man's encounter with "power," and it implies being "overpowered," for he understood "power" as a philosophical category with theological overtones. Philosophically, in van der Leeuw's view, religion is one of the consequences of the fact that man does not accept life as given to him: he seeks power in life, something that is superior, and he tries to find meaning in life and to arrange this into a significant whole. For van der Leeuw, consequently, religion is intimately linked to culture as man's creative effort.

Appraisal of Oeuvre. Theological schools have not been prepared to accept van der Leeuw's theological vision, and its most elaborate expression, his *Sacramentstheologie* (1949), has had little resonance. Nor have scholars of religion, whatever their orientation and persuasion, been prepared to accept van der Leeuw's subordination of the phenomenological enterprise to theology. Further objections have been raised against van der Leeuw's relative neglect of the historical and social realities in which religious phenomena are embedded, and against his notion of "understanding."

Apart from the information it offers and the insights contained in it, one of the definite contributions of van der Leeuw's erudite oeuvre is the attention it draws to the problem of the scholar's role in research in the humanities in general and in religious studies in particular. In his phenomenological work there is an evident tension between the researcher's "participation" and his "distance" with regard to the subject matter; these stances he even considered as representative of two basic anthropological structures, the "primitive" and the "modern" mentality. In many respects van der Leeuw anticipated problems that were to be explored by postwar existential and hermeneutical philosophy in Germany and France. His own presuppositions were largely determined by Dutch theological thought of the beginning of this century, and this allowed him to be receptive to the ideas of Dilthey, Husserl, Spranger, Lucien Lévy-Bruhl, and others. In his search for the right view of human phenomena he protested against any idealistic interpretation of man.

Throughout van der Leeuw's oeuvre is a broad mosaic of statements that bear witness to his sensitivity, realism, and open mind. Even now, his insights into his materials sometimes must be recognized as brilliant, and that is why his work, mostly in Dutch, still counts: suddenly, connections are revealed in an original, striking, and somehow convincing way.

BIBLIOGRAPHY

The following books by van der Leeuw are available in English: *Religion in Essence and Manifestation: A Study in Phenomenology* (1938), rev. ed. (1963; reprint, Gloucester, Mass., 1967); and *Sacred and Profane Beauty: The Holy in Art* (London, 1963), a translation of the third edition, completely revised by E. L. Smelik, of *Wegen en grenzen: Studie over de verhouding van religie en kunst* (Amsterdam, 1955).

A bibliography of van der Leeuw's publications up to 1950 was compiled by Wiebe Vos, "Dr. G. van der Leeuw: Bibliografie zijner geschriften," in *Pro Regno, Pro Sanctuario,* edited by Willem Jan Kooiman and Jean Marie van Veen (Nijkerk, Netherlands, 1950), pp. 553–638. For lists of works about van der Leeuw and of van der Leeuw's main publications in religious studies, see my *Classical Approaches to the Study of Religion,* vol. 2, *Bibliography* (The Hague, 1974), pp. 149–156. Further bibliographical information can be found in my article "Gerardus van der Leeuw," in *Biografisch lexicon voor de geschiedenis van het Nederlandse Protestantisme,* vol. 1, edited by D. Nauta and others (Kampen, Netherlands, 1978), pp. 114–120, and in my *Reflections on the Study of Religion* (The Hague, 1978), which volume also contains my essay "Gerardus van der Leeuw as a Theologian and Phenomenologist," pp. 186–253. See also Jan Hermelink's *Verstehen und Bezeugen: Der theologische Ertrag der 'Phänomenologie der Religion' des G. van der Leeuw* (Munich, 1960). For an autobiographical statement by van der Leeuw, see his "Confession scientifique," *Numen* 1 (1954): 8–15.

JACQUES WAARDENBURG

LEFT AND RIGHT. Symbolic differentiations of left and right are virtually universal cultural classifications among humankind. Research interest in the asymmetrical functioning of the left and right hemispheres of the brain and in the dominance of right-sided dexterity arose about a century ago. From a growing body of clinical evidence a variety of theories have evolved about the presumed physiological and neurological causes of right versus left preferences and performances in human behavior. Less well studied is the significance of right and left in the matrix of textual and contextual symbols that comprise a given culture. In 1909, French sociologist Robert Hertz established the first genuine social-science approach in his article "The Preeminence of the Right Hand: A Study of Religious Polarity" by making the following observation: "To the right hand go honors, flattering designations, prerogatives: it acts, orders, and *takes.* The left hand, on the contrary, is despised and reduced to the role of a humble auxiliary: by itself it can do nothing; it helps, it supports, it *holds*" (Hertz, in Needham, 1973, p. 3). Since Hertz's pioneering study, social scientists have explored the religious polarity of left and right in both literate and nonliterate societies, although the bulk of research has been on nonreligious aspects. As E. E. Evans-Pritchard has observed, much work on the cultural significance of left and right symbolism remains to be done.

The views advanced by Hertz on left and right have been affirmed by Émile Durkheim, Marcel Mauss, E. E. Evans-Pritchard, and Rodney Needham, among others, and may be summarized as follows. First, a preference for the right hand or foot to perform the noble tasks of life, in religious rituals as well as ordinary social intercourse, is widely observable among world cultures, both civilized and primitive. Conversely, the left hand and foot are regularly assigned secondary, converse, and even debasing tasks. From these widely observed sets of asymmetrical behavior it is often concluded that it is characteristic of human beings to regard the right side as exalted and auspicious and the left, by contrast, as despised and inauspicious.

A second characteristic of much of the ethnographic literature on left and right is the general tendency to see their opposition as part of a generic capacity in humans to classify the world around them and to derive the meanings of things in relation to their opposites. Thus, the binary oppositions of right and left, male and female, positive and negative, cooked and raw, up and down, noble and ignoble, and sacred and profane, indicate some of the fundamental modes human groups use to organize the world and to determine how to act within it. The structural properties of these schemata become more complex and interesting when, for example, sacrality, right-sidedness, and maleness are associated in some contexts. Is asymmetrical binary opposition a fundamental feature of the mind and of social symbolization and thus a key to unlock the cultural codes of left- versus right-sidedness in those religions where it appears?

Associated with the question of asymmetrical binary oppositions, of which left and right differentiation is presumed to be a species, are other issues that still divide scholars. One is the cultural versus the physiological (or neurological) question of origins. Are humans primarily and by preference right-handed because the corresponding left hemisphere of the brain predominates, or do the left hemisphere and right hand function as they do in most cases because of cultural conditioning? Another issue concerns the differences among societies regarding left-and-right symbolism and the increasing amount of evidence that in some cases the left is considered to be more auspicious than the right.

It is not the primary task of religious studies to attempt to answer these questions, however important they may be in establishing or confuting theories propounded by neurologists, psychologists, and ethnographers. The historian of religions works with a variety of textual and contextual materials, such as sacred texts and rituals, religious worldviews, and symbols. In this regard the interest of religious studies in left and right symbolism lies more in the interface of textual and cognitive valuations of left versus right with contextual and behavioral patterns.

The evidence for left and right symbolism in Islam was examined by Joseph Chelhod in a 1964 essay entitled "A Contribution to the Problem of the Right, Based upon the Arabic Evidence" (Chelhod, in Needham, 1973). As Chelhod and other Near Eastern specialists have shown, the differential roles of the left and right hands were already entrenched in ritual practices among Arabs at the sacred shrine in Mecca prior to the seventh century CE and shared some common characteristics with ancient Near Eastern practices. Much of the scholarship on pre-Islamic Arabian culture has adduced the probability that a solar cult gave directional orientation to ritual activities at the Ka'bah in Mecca, where one would face toward the east in ritual activities. Correspondingly, the Arabic word for "right" is *yamīn* (root, *ymn*), whose cognates include terms that mean "south," the prosperous land of the Yemen, and "felicity" *(yumn);* the word for "left," on the contrary, is *shimāl,* whose cognates and synonyms include terms for "bad luck," "north," and Syria, a land associated with ill omen.

The Qur'ān assigns auspiciousness to the right side, including a person's right hand and foot and the symbolic circumstance of being situated on the right side of God. Corresponding inauspiciousness and servility are assigned to the left. As in other civilizations, so in the early Islamic culture of Arabia certain ambiguities clouded a clear-cut association between right and left with good and evil, respectively. For example, Chelhod points out that the Qur'anic term *yasār* means both "left" and "prosperity." Does this constitute evidence of the inversion of values that W. Robertson Smith and others saw in the sacred as distinct from secular realms? Whether or not this is so, the solution to the problems raised by linguistic evidence lies in a study of the semantic fields of terms for "right" and "left" that would determine in what contexts such terms are used, especially in cases where single lexical items seem on the surface not to conform to general cultural pairings of right with good and auspiciousness and left with bad and inauspiciousness.

Early Islamic textual and more recent ethnographic evidence further attest to such practices as setting out for the mosque or on the pilgrimage to Mecca on the right foot but setting out on the return trip from these places on the left foot; eating and drinking with the right hand but touching the genitals for toilet activities with the left hand; seating one's honored guest to one's right, and so forth. Today, non-Arab Muslims of Africa and Asia generally adhere to the normative Islamic patterns for behavior involving the right and the left side. Thus, for example, in Indonesia it is considered offensive to pass food to another with the left hand. The fact is, however, that in both Africa and Asia forms of left-and-right cultural symbolism preceded the historical arrival of Islam, and hence the role of Islam was probably that of linking local meanings and myths about left-and-right symbolism with the more universal meanings of the great tradition.

The application of Hertz's thesis on the religious polarity of left and right in China was discussed by the French sociologist Marcel Granet in 1933 (trans. in

Needham, 1973). The Chinese textual and ethnographic evidence differs from that of the Western monotheistic religions insofar as the Chinese regard the left side as a place of honor even though right-handedness is encouraged by social convention. Granet found that preference for the left or right varies in traditional Chinese culture, depending upon the context. For example, children are taught to eat with the right hand, but males greet others by bowing, presenting the left hand and covering the right, while females reverse the pattern, concealing the left hand and exposing the right. Male/female differentiation of right-and-left symbolic acts corresponds to the *yin/yang* metaphysical polarity. Left, *yang*, and male are associated symbols in opposition to right, *yin*, and female. The opposition is not diametric, however, but circumstantial, conforming to strict social codes and rites that determine etiquette throughout society. Thus, at the levels of the universe (cosmos), society as a whole (etiquette), and the human body (physiology), left and right are differentiated, though both are valued in their symbolic association with *yin* and *yang*, sky and earth, male and female as opposing but complementary forces in the universe. The Chinese case differs from most others, because neither side of the interactive polarity is consistently valued over the other; preference is determined by context.

Tribal societies exhibit left-and-right symbolic differentiation at the levels of cosmic myth, social interaction, and physiological performance. In Africa, for example, there is greater similarity to the patterns described in Islamic culture. South of the Sahara, ethnic groups tend to associate the right side with male sexuality, moral good, good fortune, and auspicious directions and orientations, while the left side is associated with female sexuality, evil, misfortune, and inauspicious or bad places. H. A. Wieschhoff provided several examples of these patterns, noting that in Cameroon and parts of northeast Africa some ethnic groups regard the left hand as symbolic of good fortune and the right of misfortune (Wieschhoff, in Needham, 1973).

Although the Chinese evidence fits less well with Hertz's widely accepted "exalted right / debased left" theory, Granet's approach to right-and-left symbolism in Chinese culture illumines more appropriately the religious significance of right-and-left differentiation. Continuing research on the different roles of the right and left hemispheres of the brain in neurology and cognitive psychology may eventually reveal the extent to which right- or left-handedness is physiologically determined. The religious character of such symbolism lies, however, in the combined cultural media of cosmology, ritual performance, and social interaction. The study of right-and-left religious symbolism must take all of the textual and contextual fields into account in order to appreciate the full dynamics of the symbolism for each group studied.

BIBLIOGRAPHY

The articles referred to above can be found in *Right and Left: Essays on Dual Symbolic Classification*, edited by Rodney Needham (Chicago, 1973). Still valuable is Ira S. Wile's *Handedness: Right and Left* (Boston, 1934). Bibliographic references to right and left symbolism and physiological differentiation are generally classified under the heading "right and left," while "left and right" normally designates political subject matters.

RICHARD C. MARTIN

LEGALISM is an ancient Chinese school of political philosophy that developed during the last centuries of the Chou dynasty (1121–221 BCE) and reached maximum influence in the short-lived Ch'in dynasty (221–206 BCE). It was a product of a period when the old aristocratic order had weakened. Independent states were emerging from the originally dependent feudatories, and these states were engaged in intense competition with one another for limited economic resources. Such conditions spawned a new spirit of political realism that challenged the ritual, morality, and political philosophy of the declining Chou aristocracy. The most extreme and uncompromising challenge of this type came from Legalism. As the Chinese name for this school of philosophy implies (Fa-chia, "school of law"), Legalism is the culmination of a growing belief that written law, rather than custom, ritual, or morality, is the most effective means to control human behavior and to enhance governmental power.

Shang Yang. Legalism, unlike Confucianism or Moism, cannot be traced to a single founder. Traditional Chinese bibliographic scholarship has classified as Legalist such disparate figures as Kuan-tzu (d. 645 BCE), Shang Yang (d. 338 BCE), and Shen Pu-hai (d. 337 BCE). While all three of these figures contributed ideas to the great Legalist synthesis of Han Fei-tzu (d. 233 BCE), only Shang Yang is unequivocally a Legalist. Shang Yang was born in the state of Wei. When his talent as a political philosopher was not utilized by his own government, he left for the state of Ch'in, where he served as an officer for more than twenty years and eventually rose to the position of chancellor. His policies are associated with the growth of Ch'in power, growth that was to culminate in the Ch'in unification of China in 221 BCE.

Shang Yang supposedly wrote a book in twenty-six chapters entitled *Shang-chün shu* (The Book of Lord Shang). Although most authorities believe that the text dates from a period of time later than Shang Yang and is not the work of a single author, its basic philosophical message can probably be traced to the teachings of the Ch'in chancellor.

Shang Yang regards the state and the people as antagonistic forces. Law exists primarily to protect the power of the state from the people, not to shield the people from the state. To maintain and enhance the power of the state, governmental leaders must articulate laws clearly and enforce them ruthlessly. Shang Yang held an extremely pessimistic view of human nature. Consequently, law, in his view, should be little more than rules for rewards and punishments, with the greater emphasis on punishment. There is no "natural law" in his thought; rather, law is established arbitrarily by man to preserve power. As such, it need pay no heed to precedent. Indeed, Shang Yang, and Legalists in general, break with the strong Chinese tendency to find support in the past. Each ruler must respond to the circumstances of his own time; the rules of earlier Sage-Kings carry no authority.

Shang Yang rejects all notions of "virtue" or "goodness." The state, concerned only with "obedience," sets the standards, and people must follow without concern for traditional morality. He repeatedly castigates those intellectuals who talk obsessively about the way things "used to be" and quibble over right and wrong. They pose a serious threat to the state, confusing the people and eventually fostering rebellion. Indeed, only two legitimate pursuits need occupy people: agriculture and warfare. Those who produce and those who protect serve the interest of the state and should gain rewards, while those who only talk and speculate must be cast aside.

Han Fei–tzu. The Legalist position was articulated more comprehensively and persuasively one century after Shang Yang by the brilliant Han Fei–tzu, who was born as the prince of a royal family in the state of Han. Han Fei–tzu studied with the famous Confucian philosopher Hsün-tzu (c. 298–238 BCE), who taught that man was by nature evil and needed the "straightening" that moral education could provide. Han Fei–tzu rejected his teacher's emphasis upon Confucian morality as a corrective to human weakness and became a Legalist. However, he failed in his attempts to influence the king of Han and eventually traveled to Ch'in, where he had a short but important political career as an adviser to the same king of Ch'in who would eventually unify China.

Unlike the repetitive and lackluster writings of Lord Shang, the book which bears the name of the second great Legalist philosopher, *Han Fei–tzu,* is one of the great prose masterpieces of classical Chinese. This work contains fifty-five sections. Most of these sections are probably written by Han Fei–tzu himself, but some may come from later Legalist thinkers.

Han Fei–tzu welds several earlier philosophical ideas into a grand Legalist synthesis. He is, of course, deeply indebted to Shang Yang's emphasis upon law, but goes even further to advocate that "in the state of the intelligent ruler, there is no literature of books and records, but the laws serve as teachings." To him any writings beyond official law are not only superfluous but also dangerous. From *Kuan-tzu,* writings identified with the famous early minister of the state of Ch'i, he extracts the concept of "power" *(shih),* or more specifically, the governmental power that grows out of taking proper advantage of the situation. From the writings of Shen Pu-hai, which currently exist only in fragments, he borrows the concept of "methods" *(shu).* This concept refers to administrative methods of handling ministers that ensure the maintenance of the ruler's power. However, the most important single influence on the writings of Han Fei–tzu comes from Taoism. Indeed, he recasts the concepts of both power and method into a Taoist mold. Power, in the opinion of Han Fei, should be hidden and should operate dispassionately. The wise ruler does not reveal his desires, knowing that this will lead to an attempt by ministers to skew information and curry favor. Rather, "he waits, quiet and still, letting names define themselves and affairs reach their own settlement." This is essentially a government of Taoist "non-action" *(wu-wei),* but it is hardly laissez-faire. Han Fei–tzu believes that laws and institutions should be so well organized that everything would operate quite automatically—and ruthlessly. Such a system dissociates the efficacy of rule from the wisdom of the ruler. One need not await the coming of a "sage-king" in order to have effective government; if all is organized properly, even a mediocre talent can govern effectively and bring peace to the empire. Here Legalism breaks radically with Confucianism. The key to good governance is not a moral leader, for law, power, and proper administrative techniques make irrelevant the personal morality of the ruler.

Han Fei–tzu argues that the government must guard itself tenaciously against all opponents. The Confucians, in his opinion, are "vermin" who use their learning to throw the laws into confusion. People, Han Fei teaches, are not moved in the direction of obedience by Confucian "righteousness" but by "authority." In fact, he rejects all of those who would use the past as a corrective to the present. Sages of earlier years were sages because they adapted their rule to the concrete realities of their age. Perhaps "moral virtue" worked then, for in earlier years there was a surplus of natural resources, but Han Fei–tzu recommends strength and power as the only appropriate means to rule in an era of intense rivalries between competing groups for limited resources. All those who would question this principle and suggest that government be founded on any basis other than power must be eradicated. [*See also the biography of Han Fei–tzu.*]

Later History of Legalism. Legalist influence reached its apogee during the Ch'in dynasty. As noted previously, both Shang Yang and Han Fei–tzu, the two most significant members of this philosophical school, deeply influenced the government of the state of Ch'in. Still another Legalist, Li Ssu (d. 208 BCE), rose to the position of prime minister under the reign of the First Ch'in Emperor (221–210 BCE) and recommended policies in accord with Legalist principles. These recommendations accomplished three goals: the elevation of the ruler, symbolized by the new imperial title "August Emperor" *(huang-ti)*; the centralization of authority, which led to the creation of a directly administered commandery-county system, a system that was to prevail in China for the next two thousand years; and a prohibition of any private learning. The last and most extreme of these recommendations led to a ban on all books other than those dealing with medicine, divination, and agriculture, and resulted in the infamous book burning that took place in 213 BCE.

The rapid fall of the Ch'in dynasty, and its reputation for extraordinary harshness, was a serious blow to Legalism. Thereafter, one could count oneself a Legalist only at the peril of identifying with a dynasty that Confucian historians consistently excoriated. However, Legalist influence was strong throughout the Han dynasty and exerted considerable impact on later Chinese history as well. Indeed, the famous "Debates on Salt and Iron," which culminated in a record compiled in 81 BCE, indicate that strife between Confucians and Legalists was still strong in the first century of the Han dynasty. Although the ostensible issue of these debates was whether or not the state should have monopolies on salt and iron, with the Confucians in strong opposition to this example of centralization, the fundamental philosophical disagreement underlying all argument was whether the government was to rely primarily on penalties and laws or on ethical teachings. While Confucianism supposedly prevailed on this issue, and subsequent Chinese leaders for the most part proclaimed the centrality of Confucian ethics, Legalism left a permanent mark on Chinese government. First of all, the administrative centralism advocated by Legalists was to continue; second, the view of law as primarily penal and aimed at protecting the interests of the government lived on in traditional Chinese legal codes.

Interest in Legalism has grown in the present century. The members of the May Fourth generation, who repudiated much of the Chinese tradition, sometimes praised the Legalists for their bold innovations and attacks on Confucian conservatism. In fact, Mao Tse-tung regarded himself as a modern-day First Ch'in Emperor, bent upon forging a new Chinese unity based on antitraditional policies. When Mao launched the anti-Confucianism campaign of 1973, a campaign that was directed at Lin Piao and other political opponents, the country was admonished not just "to criticize Confucius" but also "to praise the Ch'in dynasty." As a result of these political trends, modern scholarship in the People's Republic of China has been rather sympathetic to Legalism, reversing the frequently negative view that has prevailed in China since the fall of the Ch'in dynasty.

[*See also* Law and Religion, *article on* Law and Religion in East Asia.]

BIBLIOGRAPHY

Excellent general surveys of Legalist thought can be found in Hsiao Kung-ch'uan's *A History of Chinese Political Thought*, translated by F. W. Mote (Princeton, 1979), pp. 368–424 and 427–468, and in Fung Yu-lan's *A History of Chinese Philosophy*, vol. 1, *The Period of the Philosophers*, 2d ed., translated by Derk Bodde (Princeton, 1952), pp. 312–336. The initial chapters of J. J. L. Duyvendak's translation of Shang Yang, *The Book of Lord Shang* (London, 1928), also provide a good introduction to Legalism. *Han Fei–tzu* has been translated in its entirety by W. K. Liao in *The Complete Works of Han Fei Tzŭ*, 2 vols. (London, 1939–1959). A translation of the most critical chapters can be found in Burton Watson's *Han Fei Tzu: Basic Writings* (New York, 1964). The writings of Shen Pu-hai, with a comprehensive discussion of his relationship to Legalism, can be found in Herrlee G. Creel's *Shen Pu-hai* (Chicago, 1974). *Kuan-tzu* has been translated in part by W. Allyn Rickett as *Guanzi* (Princeton, 1985).

STEPHEN W. DURRANT

LEGITIMATION is a process in which new situations in society are sought, or current ones sustained, through reference to widely shared values and/or qualities. Law and order, tradition, justice, patriotism, class affiliation, and ethnic identity are common legitimating values; charismatic leadership, the status quo experience of success, and the sting of oppression are common legitimating qualities. Legitimation is a feature of all formal governance but must not be construed exclusively as such. Nongovernmental groups also seek to preserve or alter social arrangements, and their success similarly depends upon their capacity to link goals with common values and qualities, somtimes for and sometimes against the interests of governments. By "social action" we mean efforts by nongovernmental groups to promote or resist social change. It is not our task here to discuss legitimation of and by governments in general or social action promoted by secular, nongovernmental groups, although in both cases religious and parareligious values and qualities are sometimes used as legitimating references. The scope of this article is social action undertaken by religious communities and legitimated by reference to values and qualities preferred within their own traditions. Religiously legitimated social action can refer to actions undertaken by religious hierarchies, denominational agencies, local congregations, groups within congregations, or church members who act through voluntary associations outside their religious institutions.

The fact that social action is promoted by religious groups and is religiously legitimated does not insure its positive worth. Religious social action, as we understand it, injects into a situation new sensitivity to issues and attempts to undercut spurious legitimations of power. Spurious legitimations often have appeared in the interests of nationalism, and the church often has become a legitimating authority for imperial power.

The examination of legitimation is largely a study of ambiguity, of value orientations amenable to a variety of meanings or interpretations. The reasons for this include the variety of situations in which ostensibly the same sanctions are appealed to, the variety of interests that come into play in a single situation, the mixture of good and evil, the conflict among values, and the difficulty of providing a rational, unambiguous formulation of the legitimation claimed.

Social Action. The unique context of social action is the modern community in which diverse groups coexist under the rubrics of freedom of association, freedom of assembly, and freedom of speech. Within pluralistic society, government is generally viewed as the one association that holds a monopoly on legitimated coercion. Modern pluralism implies that associations may hold conflicting values. In an open society, where change and conflict are common, dissent is entitled to a hearing and to constitutional protection. In fact, one role of associations (James Madison called them factions) is to guard the state against demonic usurpation of authority by any group; they do so by means of an ongoing dialogue among rival conceptions of what is legitimate. The growth of voluntary associations in modern society has enhanced the importance of public opinion as a factor in social reality. Social action, therefore, is concerned to affect public opinion.

The means for social change are viewed differently by different parties. Some prefer subjective means aimed at modifying larger social realities through the power of transformed persons and the spread of influence from person to person and from persons to social structures. This approach depends upon good character rather than organized planning and action by groups. A second approach, philanthropy, offers assistance to persons and groups whose efforts show signs of positive outcome for the larger society. This approach, important as it sometimes is, aims more at remedying the consequences of social (structural) dysfunction than at criticism and change of social structures. Finally, some believe that meaningful social change must occur at the level of socioeconomic and political structures. It is this approach that we call social action.

Social action is concerned with what H. Richard Niebuhr (1954) calls the macro, meso, and micro levels or dimensions of human experience. It is concerned primarily with the macro and meso levels although changes in these levels affect and are affected by the micro level. Ernst Troeltsch (1968), through his distinction between subjective and objective values, deals with these same conceptions in a somewhat different way. For Troeltsch, subjective values spring from an individual's direct relation to God, one's direct relation to other persons, and one's internal dialogue in the striving for integrity. Here truthfulness, openness, benevolence, and loyalty are characteristic values. Objective values, on the other hand, are the social-ethical claims that inform or guide action in the realm of "history"—the structured sphere of group life with its particular roles and rules. Objective values attach to the structures of society, the family (especially in its relation to other spheres), the state, the community, property and production, education, science, art, and "organized" religion.

Moral life, then, comprises both subjective and objective values, and they are of course interrelated. Social action must relate to all these levels. Martin Luther King, Jr., Mohandas Gandhi, and current theologians of liberation all agree that there is a clear and direct link between personal spirituality and a person's social praxis.

Values sometimes are widely held and are central for an entire society, while others are held only by a few and are marginal for the society. Marginality, however, is not irrelevance. Radical transforming insights frequently originate at the margins of society, calling into question central values while also expressing a desire for community based on alternative values. This was true of ancient prophecy and is true as well of many modern movements. Most Western monasticism, for example, may be understood as socially marginal, subjective withdrawal from the social community. But, as many have observed, monasticism has often reentered the community at large in objective, world-affirming ways: service, reform, intellectual leadership, and contemplative inspiration. This two-sidedness has existed in the Gandhian ashrams, in the black churches that supported the civil rights movement, in contemporary Latin American base communities, and in many communitarian experiments of the past two centuries. There is a dynamic interaction of values back and forth, between the margins of society and the center.

The Decline of Authority. Legitimation is aligned with authority and is dependent on it. [*See* Authority.] Many would agree, however, with Hannah Arendt's disconsolate view that "authority has vanished from the world." The modern world has an authority crisis, therefore a legitimation crisis (see Arendt, 1958; Habermas, 1975). Since Plato, it has been understood that power rests on authority outside the present situation: nature, God, eternal ideas, custom, or some historical event of great importance. These outside authorities have been referred to by some as elements of "numinous" legitimation (see Sternberger, 1968). In past times of effective authority such as the Roman empire and the Christian Roman empire, those authoritative elements have been persuasive, legitimating whole societies. In modern times, they are undercut and we are left in a myopic state of individualistic want-orientation with far-reaching implications for all realms of life from the most public to the most private, including political organization and religion (see Tribe, 1976; Arendt, 1958). The value that most frequently replaces traditional legitimating values is the state. In modern Western states, the problem of authority is complicated by the fact that individualism carries within itself seeds of dissonance; capitalistic individualism and democratic individualism contradict one another in theory and practice (Troeltsch, 1968). The goal of the latter is freedom, whereas that of the former is want-satisfaction. The latter leads toward a broadening recognition of personhood and rights with attendant pluralism and a stress on community; the former leads toward bureaucratization of production and suppression of opportunities for democratic expression of individuality.

The impact of social change is greater in the modern epoch than in former ones. The rapid rate of change in recent generations is unique in history and destabilizes enduring values. Legitimation is more difficult in the context of unprecedented change.

Likewise, the impact of modern pluralism and responses to it have raised other problems for legitimation. [*See* Religious Pluralism.] In Roman Catholicism, for example, Vatican II has been a watershed, opening the way for a more pluralistic emphasis in the church. At the same time, the Roman church is experiencing strong internal conflict on some key issues such as human sexuality, the roles of women, and the place of popular religious movements within the church. The Vatican is faced with a dilemma about whether to impose traditional monolithic authority upon its increasingly pluralistic and worldwide constituency; the issues of liberation theology and popular religion in Latin America are current cases in point. Protestant evangelicals are experiencing analogous difficulties. They no longer can claim unity of political goals. A progressive wing attacks the conservative political values and programs of right-wing evangelicals.

Nationalism and Civil Religion. When the "constitution of the everyday world" is examined in terms of its "preferred and pre-eminent modes of being," there are "structures of faith and reason" that express the actual religious commitments of cultures, their orientations toward what is deemed by them to be sacred, "with or without the benefit of a transcendent referent or supervening unity" (Pickering, in press). Seen in this light, nationalism has become a dominant form of religion in the modern world, preempting a void left by the deterioration of traditional religious values. What appear to be conflicting legitimations often are evidences of rival nationalisms. Nationalism, devotion to nation as an ultimate reality or to one nation to the exclusion of others, must not be confused with civil religion, values transcending a nation by which that nation is both legitimated and judged (see Mead, 1975; Bellah, 1967). Indeed, nationalism and civil religion may often conflict. Nationalism, without any means for self-transcending criticism, is inclined toward the demonic. Its primary interest is unquestioning loyalty. Civil religion, on the other hand, tests present reality by reference to transcending values that represent the ideals and values of a nation.

Carl Schmitt (1932), saw that nationalism is fueled by the fear of an enemy. Hitlerism was promoted as a means for saving Germany from bolshevism. The lengthening conflict between the Soviet Union and the United States in this century may be understood, at least in part, by the same dynamic. But nationalism is ambiguous. Gandhi appealed to national interests, or "home rule," both as a way of overcoming the unwieldiness of deep-seated village sovereignty and as a way of uniting India against British rule. And Martin Luther King, Jr., effectively appealed to the national interest by forcing issues into federal jurisdiction in order to overcome the segregationism that dominated Southern state and local courts. In the sections that follow, the thread of nationalism as a major legitimating value runs through virtually every situation examined.

Praxis. In 1851, Stephen Crowell, a trustee of Princeton Theological Seminary, in his volume *New Themes for the Protestant Clergy* (Philadelphia, p. 15), asserted, "The whole socialist movement is one of the greatest events of this age. . . . The works of socialists have exposed this hideous skeleton of selfishness—they have pursued it with unfaltering hatred; and this constitutes our main obligation to them" (cited in Stackhouse, 1985). This exposure, he argued, calls for a new application of Christian principles to the economic order. The book was published three years after the *Communist Manifesto* and three years after the appearance of the Christian Socialists sponsored in England by Frederick Denison Maurice and Charles Kingsley "to socialize Christianity and Christianize socialism."

Earlier in the nineteenth century, Roman Catholic writers had mounted a similar attack. Social action in the following period of well over a century concerned itself not only with a critique of the legitimacy of the industrial system but also with experiments in alternative social groupings. These experiments presupposed new conceptions of legitimacy.

Growth of the idea of social salvation. The search for alternative societies may be traced to the writings of Plato, Thomas More, and Tommaso Campanella, and also to the heretical sects of the Middle Ages and the withdrawing as well as the aggressive sects of the Reformation. [*See* Utopia.] Most influential of all have been the monastic communities from which the concept of sainthood emerged. In these efforts, one can see the deliberate formation of nonoppressed, marginal groups in contrast to the oppressed margins in which the labor movements were born as well as the U.S. civil rights movement and grass-roots liberation movements in the Third World.

Of special character and significance were the social actions associated with communitarian movements in the United States and Europe. The fantastic schemes of Samuel Taylor Coleridge and Robert Southey are familiar. In the United States these experiments, religious and secular, appeared from New Hampshire to Oregon, from the Rappites and the Owenites to the Shakers and Brook Farm. In the nineteenth century, there were over a hundred known communities of more than one hundred thousand men, women, and children. Writing to Carlyle in 1840, Emerson said, "We are all a little wild here with numberless projects of social reform. Not a reading man but has a draft of a new community in his waistcoat pocket."

Egalitarianism was a major nerve of these movements. Their conceptions of legitimacy issued in the demand for equality of sex, nationality, and color, the abolition of private property, the abolition of slavery, the humane treatment of domestic animals, and the practice of nonresistance.

Experiments have continued into the present century, for example, the interracial community Koinonia Farm in Americus, Georgia, and the mainly Roman Catholic Focolare ("fireplace") movement. The latter, an international group with four thousand members, emphasizes face-to-face "family" groups stressing unity toward the end of transforming structures of domination through praxis rather than doctrine, and uses mass media for wider communication. Especially significant too are the *kibbutsim* in Israel, the oldest extant communal experiments among marginal, alternative societies.

In England, the philosophy of individualism may be traced to left-wing Puritanism, with its attack on chartered monopoly and its promotion of the dispersion of power in church and state. Legitimation was found in the alleged congregational polity of primitive Christianity. Here was the birth of the bourgeois revolt against feudalism. Later, the work of Adam Smith gave birth to belief in automatic harmony issuing from a free market. This hope for automatic harmony constituted an eschatological form of legitimation. This eschatology was fueled by the belief in progress, a restatement of the doctrine of providence. Marxism in dialectical fashion, centering attention on economic analysis and on the hope for a classless society, also adopted an optimistic eschatology.

Automatic harmony failed to appear. Smith had not anticipated the advent of large corporations and the coalitions among them. nor had he foreseen greater success in production than in the capacity to expand markets, maintain employment levels, and encourage consumption. This economic system left in its wake a residue of faceless poverty that over a long period has remained undiminished in proportion to the middle class. Legitimation became more difficult to maintain as prebourgeois social solidarity eroded. In this century, as New Deal politics shifted from the older individualism, Roscoe Pound would speak of a return to features of feudalism. The legal system, however, stood in opposition, concerned about order more than justice.

In an environment of individualistic pietism and privatization, the idea of "social salvation" appeared in the United States and Europe. From the ecumenical movement and the World Council of Churches arose the idea of "a responsible society." The secular articulation of these new religiously conceived ideas helped to legitimate the welfare state.

Meanwhile, the deprivations of Third World peoples were coming into sharper focus and it rapidly became evident that bureaucratization of business and the welfare state was inimical to training for democratic citizenship. For example, the percentage of eligible voters in the United States who participate in presidential elections has diminished by nearly half in this century. As these conflicts became more obvious, the crisis of legitimations became more acute. In this period of attacks upon prevailing legitimations, increasing appeals were made to the teachings of Jesus as a final authority, for example, by Walter Rauschenbusch in the earlier years of this century and later by John Bennett, Walter Muelder, Reinhold Niebuhr, and others (see Stackhouse, 1985).

The movement Christians for Socialism in Europe, North America, and Latin America is more pluralistic in goals and methods. Here there is recognition of the church as an economic and political power sometimes inimical to a socialist reorganization of society. Marxist tools of analysis have been employed, but the major thrust is against inequality among classes, regions, and production sectors. The emergence of new "base communities," especially but not only in Latin America, has provided grass-roots support with a new religious awareness in the face of institutional concentrations of power, ecclesiastical or economic.

This trend has continued, for example in papal encyclicals since the end of the nineteenth century and, in the period since Vatican II, in the official statements issued by councils of bishops in Latin America and the United States. These Protestant and Catholic views in part have rearticulated a century-old religious socialism with its numinous legitimation of freedom in community.

Gandhi's appeal to religion. Mohandas Gandhi was born to a political father and a religious mother. The Gandhis were *vaiśya* Hindus, though both mother and father, according to Gandhi's reflections, were tolerant and actively interested in persons and ideas outside their own religious tradition. Gandhi's mature religious views, consequently, were grounded in Hindu wisdom but also mingled with non-Hindu, especially Christian wisdom. With this beginning, it is not surprising that, for Gandhi, God is greater than any concept of God, Hindu or Christian. Gandhi interchangeably used terms like truth, life, light, and love to describe God. In his view, one draws close to God by struggling against evil in the world, even at the risk of death. He saw no distinction between religion and politics. Whereas many saw him as a religious figure involved in politics, he saw himself as a political individual trying to be religious.

The motivating vision for Gandhi was *Rāma rājya*, an ideal state of harmony in which the "welfare of all" *(sarvodaya)* would characterize the systemic interconnections of society. There would be "rights alike of prince and pauper," "sovereignty of the people based on pure moral authority," and "self-rule." Human relations in *Rāma rājya*, therefore, will manifest the principle of "noninjury" *(ahiṁsā)*. *Ahiṁsā* is more than refraining from hurting by active aggression; it is subtle harmony of all living things; it is love in action. Because truth is beyond human grasp, one is bound to respect the truth claims of others. One may not inflict injury *(hiṁsā)* upon others in the name of one's own truth. Truth is larger than any person's or group's comprehension of it; it is always beyond, judging every human truth. One must "hold on to truth" *(satyāgraha)* in the latter sense, that is, one must be committed to the truth one knows with humility, knowing that one's commitment is ultimately to the greater, unseen truth (see Chatterjee, 1983).

In the Gandhian movement, we find the three legitimating forces discussed by German sociologist Max Weber: tradition, charisma, and law. Gandhi himself was charismatic; Hindu values were traditional; and Gandhi, an attorney by training, believed in law even when he took exception to it through civil disobedience.

Gandhi met many forms of resistance to his work, even from some who shared his general desires for transformation. His differences with Rabindranath Tagore are well known; both were religious, but Tagore seriously disliked many of Gandhi's methods. Gandhi's conflict with B. R. Ambedkar over how to deal with the issue of untouchability was even more serious. Ambedkar, born an untouchable himself, saw Gandhi's approach as bourgeois, therefore ineffective and even harmful in perpetuating the very oppressions in question. The final irony is that Gandhi's assassin belonged to a Hindu group whose members resented Gandhi's openness to Muslims.

Transformations in recent Buddhism. In Japan since World War II, numerous new religions (voluntary associations) have enjoyed phenomenal growth. From among these we select the lay Buddhist movements Sōka Gakkai and Risshō Kōseikai for a brief account. Both these new religions trace their heritage to the Buddhist "Nichiren sect" stemming from the thirteenth century.

Literally translated, the name *Sōka Gakkai* means "the value-creating society." The movement, characterized by family membership, has claimed to have sixteen million on its rolls. Its mushroom growth sprang from the ashes of the second world war. These value preferences, it is claimed, can be traced to Nichiren who seven centuries ago brought Buddhism to the common people and who traced authority to the *Lotus Sutra* of the fourth century.

The characteristic ideas of this *sūtra* are that every living being possesses the Buddha in embryo and should, through meditation and discipline, achieve the enlightenment of Buddhahood and also assist others on the *bodhisattva* path. All are heirs of the Buddha who engage in *bodhisattva* practice that leads to happiness in this world and the next.

The basic faith issues from worship of the mandala and the repetition of prescribed words of prayer enabling one to get rid of delusion, to achieve merit toward happiness in this world and the next, to enter the state of Buddhahood, and also to contribute to world peace. Happiness consists in material satisfaction (promised to everyone) such as economic prosperity, freedom from bad personal habits and adversity, sound health, peace of mind, and a bubbling over with joy—a markedly utilitarian, cash-value religion. The search for Buddhahood in Sōka Gakkai is the sign of the one and only true religion; other religions are to be uprooted. Conversion of nonmembers requires "a stern strategy" of pummeling ("breaking and subduing") the unbeliever, which is the highest form of compassion. There is confidence that inner reform (subjective virtue) will move outward to infuse politics, economics, art, and all spheres of life with new value.

Sōka Gakkai has been politically active, at one time establishing a political party and gaining several representatives in the national legislature. Its successful international missionary efforts have generated mass peace rallies. In a volume sponsored by the rapidly growing Youth Division, *Peace Is Our Duty* (1977), many individual statements recount vividly the brutalities of war and the callousness of former military training. It is not quite clear what the work for peace is apart from rallies; economic questions relating to world peace are not taken into account.

The fundamental motivation (or legitimation) of this "value-creating" movement resides in Buddhahood, though legitimation has been scarcely a pressing matter; the possession of truth suffices. The authoritarian, nationalist ethos and concern for individual happiness are readily evident. But still more evident is the transformation from early Buddhism's escape from history to a dynamic, utilitarian this-worldliness, yet with no social action in the strict sense.

Risshō Kōseikai, possessing six million members, also traces its heritage to Nichiren and earlier Mahāyāna Buddhism. Oriented to the *Lotus Sutra,* members of Risshō Kōseikai interpret the way of the *bodhisattva* as the path of those who, in compassion, strive to achieve salvation for themselves and others "who shed tears of sorrow." All people have the potentiality of attaining Buddhahood; conflict prevails in the world because people have forgotten this potentiality. One aims to be loyal to one's own country, but through religious faith one hopes to be united with other peoples in a spirit transcending national boundaries.

This movement was founded in 1934 by Niwano Nikkyō, who was thoroughly familiar with the *Lotus Sutra,* and by a prophetess, Naganuma Myōkō, who from time to time received revelations regarding immediate situations. They tirelessly visited the sick, claimed miraculous healings, and offered pastoral counseling; these elicited personal transformation and public testimonials. In all situations, they emthasized the reading of the *sūtra;* later Niwano published numerous articles of commentary on it. As Risshō Kōseikai has grown in size, close interpersonal relations of the early days have been retained in the form of the *hōza,* small groups in which personal, family, neighborhood, and business problems are discussed with the assistance of leaders who are appointed and trained by the hierarchy.

The general ethos is authoritarian, reflecting the charismatic and administrative leadership of Niwano.

Institutionalized dissent is unknown. Various social activities are encouraged, including community projects and also vigorous assistance to the "boat people" in Southeast Asia. These philanthropic concerns, however, have not led to political-social action, though there is some educational interest in such matters; young members going abroad are studying international affairs and social sciences (and other world religions). Risshō Kōseikai, like Sōka Gakkai, has aroused widespread interest in world peace, stimulated of course by the memory of the American destruction of Hiroshima and Nagasaki.

Niwano has vigorously promoted an international thrust, for example, becoming active in the International Association for Religious Freedom and in the World Conference on Religion and Peace. he has served as president of both these organizations with their global constituencies, searching in world religions for common bonds conducive to peace. It should be noted, in addition, that concern for world peace is widely prevalent in Japanese society and not only in these new religions.

Legitimation is provided in general by the *Lotus Sutra* and to some extent by modern conceptions of tolerance and interfaith cooperation. One does not, however, discern any tendency to alter the authoritarian, hierarchical structure of Risshō Kōseikai itself. The question of legitimation, though not fully formulated in Risshō Kōseikai, is becoming more important, as is evident in Niwano's personal growth, which is centered in traditional Buddhism but reaches out to Western and Eastern non-Buddhist concepts, including the New Testament and the writings of Gandhi.

It can be seen, from this brief discussion, that social action within the group is still largely undeveloped. To be sure, some new Buddhist groups are interested in philanthropic effort. However, in Risshō Kōseikai as well as in Sōka Gakkai, political participation is not explicitly promoted. We can see how objective values are beginning to engage attention in the Nichiren groups but more in practical, microcosmic, and mesocosmic (e.g., neighborhood) ways than in systematic macrocosmic ways—that is, apart from the peace movements. Yet, in all this a return to this-worldliness is markedly evident.

In recent decades a turn toward this-worldliness is increasingly apparent in Theravāda Buddhism, too, especially in Burma, though not without tensions that render the outlook ambiguous. This turn is taking place at both the macrocosmic and the microcosmic levels. Indeed, the evaluation of the world has become so positive that escape from it in complete detachment is not a primary or immediate goal.

This change of outlook has appeared strikingly in the sphere of objective, institutional values. Winston L. King, in his writings, has delineated these changes of recent decades. In his article "Samsara Re-Valued" (1964), he succinctly defines *saṃsāra,* the round of births and deaths, as a synonym for "all that is evil," as compounded in the impermanence, suffering, and insubstantiality of the world, as well as in the "no-souledness of individuatedness of space-time existence," a malady from which one escapes through complete detachment. Yet today practical changes are being sought, for example, emancipation from "economic strangulation." The inspiration for this stance is found in the career of the Buddha himself, who realized during the course of ascetic practices that privation did not conduce to spiritual liberation, or, in other words, that *dharma* can be better practiced on a full stomach. This emancipation will bring freedom from want, economic well-being for the entire people, an end to exploitation of man by man. In short, what is required is a Buddhist national socialism—adumbrated by U Nu, the first premier of independent Burma in 1948, (though his effort was aborted, to be resumed by the revolutionary government). Other changes are also demanded, for example, a new role for the meditating lay person, who should have equality with the monks. Meditation is useful for both this world and *nirvāṇa,* maintaining detachment for both worlds. A new meaning for *karman* makes room for change of the self and for self-reliance. The *bodhisattva* ideal from Mahāyāna Buddhism is reinterpreted to give sanction for public service in the community, to be sure not without a strong element of nationalism. Detachment can accompany activity in the world toward achieving *nirvāṇa* peace in daily life. For the understanding and enhancement of daily existence, the study of the sciences is encouraged, something traditionally found in the teachings of Buddha.

In these ways, *saṃsāra* is being revalued. Legitimation for this way of life is claimed by appeal to the intentions of the true Lord Buddha for the sake of otherworldliness within this world. Since thousands of lives lie ahead of us, there need be no hurry about striving for the achievement of *nirvāṇa.* King (1964) describes this paradox as having one's cake and eating it, too. With an absolutely straight face, the defender can say that these developments provide a new hope for transformation in this world in preparation for the next, while at the same time maintaining the rule of *dharma* against false consciousness and greed. In all this, one can detect influences from the West and from Marxism.

The civil rights movement in the United States. The civil rights movement of the 1950s and 1960s in the United States is significant for our present purposes because the movement claimed legitimations that were largely, though not entirely, religious in a traditional sense. The movement was a religiously legitimated mass social-action movement. Black church networks provided the talent, energy, and institutional connections that were determinative for the wisdom, strength, and durative power of the movement.

Martin Luther King, Jr., added a charismatic presence to the movement and became its focal personality and symbolic leader. As one whose father, grandfather, and great-grandfather had been Baptist ministers, whose father and grandfather had been civil rights leaders in Atlanta, and as one who had himself earned a doctorate in systematic theology, King was well prepared in many respects to lead a social-action movement legitimated by religious values and based in churches. Within the black church tradition, King knew the symbolism, the characteristic networking, and the style of male-oriented, charismatic leadership. He also knew the ins and outs of the liberal Protestant social theology that echoed in many Northern churches and seminaries. He could preach extemporaneously from his thorough familiarity with the ideas of Walter Rauschenbusch, Paul Tillich, Reinhold Niebuhr, Henry Nelson Wieman, and the Boston University personalist theologians, as well as the rich theological heritage of the black church.

From his church tradition and theological education,

King emphasized community ("beloved community," he called it), faith in a personal God who struggles in history side by side with those who suffer and work for justice, an eschatological vision of liberation, and a doctrine of human personality rooted in God as personal. With these he interpreted the significance of being free and fully human of the one hand, and the destruction of human personality by racism on the other. The means of social transformation and liberation had to be in accord with the goal of the beloved community. For King only nonviolence, rooted in Christian love and influenced by the example of Gandhi's nonviolent *satyāgraha* campaigns in South Africa and India, could produce change and create "beloved community." For King, these values were grounded in a willingness to suffer and a belief that unmerited suffering can be redemptive. These legitimating values were the heart of the movement.

In spite of religious values at the center of the movement, many in the churches did not follow King's lead. In his famous 1963 "Letter from Birmingham Jail" King lamented the failure of churches, especially white church leaders, to support the movement. Even before 1966, there was tension within the movement when King and his supporters were challenged by a group of younger black leaders who wished to move ahead faster and with greater militancy. In 1966, this challenge within the movement became public and serious when the cry of "black power," supported by Stokely Carmichael and Floyd McKissick, struck a resonant note among civil rights workers and created a legitimation crisis in the movement, a crisis that was not resolved at the time of King's murder and is not yet resolved in liberation struggles around the world. The struggle against apartheid in South Africa and the revolutionary struggle against poverty in Latin America are current examples of the same crisis over which values will legitimate and guide social transformation.

The civil rights movement also precipitated an old tension in American life between the legitimating ideals of the Constitution and federal courts on the one hand, and persistent attempts of regions to resist federal domination on the other. On both sides of the conflict, people felt they were in a moral struggle. One of King's most repeated aphorisms was "The moral arc of the universe is long but it bends ultimately toward justice." On the other hand, some supporters of Jim Crow also believed their struggle was a moral one. It was part of King's genius to understand their feelings and the history from which such feelings come into being. This moral element, despite its ambiguity, helps to explain the depth of feeling, commitment, and sacrifice that characterized the movement on all sides but especially among the inner ranks of the nonviolent workers.

We find again Weber's three kinds of legitimation—tradition, charisma, and law. The black church and liberal theology were traditional elements; the black minister model of leadership was charismatic, and King was its consummate manifestation; and civil rights work in the South before 1955, especially the work of the National Association for the Advancement of Colored People (NAACP), focused very often on legal redress and on respect for the courts and bringing pressure to bear on them. Most interpretation of this movement overemphasizes the role of charisma, mistakenly following Weber's thesis that charisma is the chief legitimating force that produces social change. Such a view distorts the role of King even as it intends to elevate his importance, and it also undervalues the importance of indigenous leadership in southern black church communities (see Morris, 1984).

Theologies of liberation. Since 1960, theologies of liberation have emerged from theologians identified with the experiences of oppressed groups, groups that have been pushed to the margins of society by economic and political systems. From this new perspective, earlier traditional theologies too often have been unwitting expressions of privileged interests that serve to further the oppression of groups such as women, the chronically poor, and black people. This section will concentrate primarily on Latin American theologies of liberation. Feminist theologies, black theologies, and liberation theologies from Africa and Asia also offer much to this conversation as they challenge traditional legitimating values.

One thing is common to Latin American theologies of liberation—the view that theology is never ideologically neutral, that no theology is Christian if it is aligned ideologically with privileged groups and against the welfare of already oppressed groups. Theology, these theologians believe, must serve as an element of liberation rather than oppression.

In most liberation theologies, scripture is placed side by side with the suffering of the poor. The God of scripture is one who liberates, who is on the side of the poor against their oppressors. In the faces of the poor one meets God in history; the liberation of the poor in history is the work of God. Liberation praxis is the way of meeting and serving God in history; it is the way of discipleship.

In light of the strong emphasis on scripture as a primary legitimating authority for many liberation theologians, it is important to note that some feminist theologians believe that scripture is so thoroughly accommodated to past cultures of oppression which produced it, that it cannot legitimate liberation; legitimations for liberation, especially the liberation of women, must be sought elsewhere. It is at this point that certain feminist theologians suggest such alternative sources as goddess traditions to legitimate theology and social praxis. Among black theologians also, there is debate about the role of scripture as a legitimating source. In the black churches of the United States, there is no doubt that scripture has been central; some, however, believe it would be better to draw more of African culture as a central source of liberating praxis. But in Latin American theologies of liberation, scripture is fundamental.

There are areas of ambiguity in these theologies. For instance, if God favors the oppressed, how is the concept of the church as God's people to be reconciled with the historical reality of the church in which there are both oppressed and oppressors? This has been a central question for liberation leaders such as Oscar Romero, Helder Camara, and Camilo Torres. If social transformation is legitimated by appeal to God's preference for the poor and oppressed, does that introduce partisan divisions into the body of the church? On the other hand, appeal is made to an image of the church as a harmonious whole, as one body in Christ, undisturbed by historical injustices. History has shown, however, how the church denies and rationalizes the bitter conditions of the poor and oppressed in order, with a clear conscience, to sustain the ideal of wholeness as a credible legitimating ideal. One can see these ambiguities in current discussions surrounding the Vatican instruction on liberation theology and the Vatican's silencing of the Brazilian theologian Leonardo Boff.

In the Ecumenical Association of Third World Theologians (EATWOT), which includes among its members many of the Latin American theologians of liberation, there has been disagreement about the order of importance of legitimating principles. Oppression, and therefore liberation, are viewed by some as matters of class, by others as matters of race, and by still others as matters of culture. These differences, serious as they are, should not divert attention from the wide agreement among these theologians about liberation as the essence of the gospel: liberation from sin, of course, but also liberation in history from the oppressions of history.

The social form of theology of liberation in Latin America is the base community movement. Concerns are largely practical—work, food, health care, freedom from political oppression and terror, and empowerment for political participation. Liberation thought stresses the primacy of social transformation at the macro level, but is also keenly aware of the interconnectedness of the personal with the sociohistorical, the micro with the macro level. Objective virtue is valued above subjective virtue, although the connections between them are clearly seen and appreciated (see Gutiérrez, 1984). Marginality is a key feature of the liberation movements. The poor are the central subjects of this historical process and theology. The phrase "the irruption of the poor" points to that process by which the poor in the margins of society are speaking, organizing, and acting for themselves in a new way.

The Weberian elements are visible in the liberation movement in Latin America. Scripture and the church, the two great elements of Catholic authority, continue to be affirmed even when reinterpreted; they are traditional elements. There are charismatic leaders, heroes, and martyrs in the movement—Helder Camara, Camilo Torres, Gustavo Gutiérrez, Rutillo Grande, and Oscar Romero among others; but there is no one person who marks this movement as King marked the civil rights movement in the United States or Gandhi marked the work in India. This is a more diffuse, more people-oriented movement in which democratic organization and participation transcend the role of charisma. The result is a different kind of people empowerment. The element of law can be seen in the ongoing role of church authority; it can be seen also in the desire to transform society, if possible, by lawful means.

Concluding Remarks. In the so-called secular, modern world of the past century and a half, the role of religious legitimation has been highly ambiguous. Progressive secularization has driven religion to the margins of contemporary culture. Some have lamented this while others have welcomed "a world come of age." This article has noted several major movements of social transformation whose primary legitimating values are religious.

The social-reform movements represent a focus on world affirmation or social salvation. In the case of Gandhian applications of Hindu values and new Buddhist socialism, world affirmation is a reversal of traditional world negation or contempt for the world. In the case of Latin American liberation movements, world affirmation is the reclaiming of a prophetic tradition that until recently was recessive in the Latin American church. In the civil rights movement, prophetic world affirmation was a continuation of the black church's traditional emphasis on historical liberation. However, scholars of black religions maintain that, from the United States Civil War until the civil rights movement, the prophetic edge of black church theology, so common in the antebellum period, was in recession.

In spite of these recent examples of religiously legitimated social action, the barriers to such change remain substantial. Bureaucratization of military, governmental, and economic powers increases the difficulty of effective social action. The global extent of these problems is only now becoming fully apparent. In addition, religious groups generally are divided about social action.

What characterizes the present situation is a movement, by no means universal, toward world affirmation in the religious legitimation of social action. This is not a recent turn, parallel with the birth of the so-called postmodern era, but rather a slowly spreading phenomenon with roots in the nineteenth century. It represents an extension of the modern emphasis on the world, with a peculiar twist that world affirmation in these movements is religious, not secular (see Cox, 1984). This change is occurring in Eastern and Western religious traditions. Even pietistic religious groups have taken an interest in social transformation. Cases in point are the recent emergence in the United States of the "moral majority" as well as socially minded evangelical theology (see Mott, 1982). Especially interesting is the recent legitimation of "democratic capitalism" with religious sanctions and, at the same time and by the same writers, a sharp criticism of recent statements on the economy issued by the Catholic bishops of the United States.

The growth of prophetic, world-affirming religiousness is one manifestation, a notable one, of the search for moral meaning in a modern world (see Tipton, 1982). It is not the only one, however; modernism is pluralistic and the search for moral meaning is drawn in many directions, especially by the lure of nationalism. It would seem, however, judging from the vitality of world-affirming religious movements during the past 150 years, that religious legitimation of social action is destined to play a continuing role in the struggles for social transformation in both East and West. It is worth noting, in this connection, the Catholic church's historic transition toward world affirmation in the events of Vatican II (see *Gaudium et Spes*, documents of the Consejo Episcopal Latino-americano conferences at Medellín, 1968, and Puebla, 1979, and the declarations of the Conference of United States Bishops on Nuclear Weapons and the American Economy.) Secularization has contributed to that expansion by helping to clarify the conflict of rival legitimations inherent in it. The future of social action legitimated by traditional religious values, when pitted against powerful rival religions or rival structures of faith and reason such as nationalism, remains to be seen.

[*See also* Religious Communities, *article on* Religion, Community, and Society.]

BIBLIOGRAPHY

Arendt, Hannah. "What Was Authority?" In *Authority*, edited by Carl J. Friedrich, pp. 81–112. Cambridge, Mass., 1958.

Bellah, Robert N. "Civil Religion in America." *Daedalus* 96 (Winter 1967): 1–21.

Bellah, Robert N., and Phillip E. Hammond. *Varieties of Civil Religion*. San Francisco, 1980.

Berger, Peter L. *The Sacred Canopy: Elements of a Sociological Theory of Religion*. Garden City, N.Y., 1967. This is an especially useful book for consideration of the complex issues of legitimation.

Berger, Peter L., and Thomas Luckmann. *The Social Construction of Reality: A Treatise on the Sociology of Knowledge*. Garden City, N.Y., 1966.

Boulding, Kenneth. *The Organizational Revolution*. New York, 1953.

Chatterjee, Margaret. *Gandhi's Religious Thought*. South Bend, Ind., 1983.

Cox, Harvey. *Religion in the Secular City: Toward a Post-Modern Theology*. New York, 1984.

Gerth, Hans H., and C. Wright Mills, eds. and trans. *From Max Weber*. Oxford, 1958. See especially chapters 4 and 11.

Gutiérrez, Gustavo. *A Theology of Liberation*. Maryknoll, N.Y., 1973.

Gutiérrez, Gustavo. *We Drink from Our Own Wells*. Translated by Matthew J. O'Connel. Maryknoll, N.Y., 1984.

Habermas, Jürgen. *Legitimation Crisis*. Translated by Thomas McCarthy. Boston, 1975.

Hartshorne, Charles. "Toward a Buddhisto-Christian Religion." In *Buddhism and American Thinkers*, edited by Kenneth K. Inada and Nolan P. Jacobson, pp. 1–130. Albany, N.Y., 1984.

King, Winston L. "Samsara Re-Valued." In *Midwest Conference on Asian Affairs*. Carbondale, Ill., 1964.

Mead, Sidney E. *The Nation with the Soul of a Church*. New York, 1975.

Mead, Sidney E. *The Old Religion in the Brave New World*. Berkeley, 1977.

Morris, Aldon. *The Origins of the Civil Rights Movement*. New York, 1984.

Mott, Stephen C. *Biblical Ethics and Social Change*. New York, 1982.

Niebuhr, H. Richard. "The Idea of Covenant and American Democracy." *Church History* 23 (June 1954): 126–135.

Niebuhr, Reinhold. *Moral Man and Immoral Society*. New York, 1932.

Niebuhr, Reinhold. *An Interpretation of Christian Ethics*. New York, 1935.

Niebuhr, Reinhold. *The Nature and Destiny of Man*. 2 vols. New York, 1941, 1943.

Parsons, Talcott. "Authority, Legitimation, and Political Action." In *Authority*, edited by Carl J. Friedrich, pp. 197–221. Cambridge, Mass., 1958.

Pickering, George. "Reflections on the Task of Social Ethics." *Journal of the Interdenominational Theological Center* (in press).

Schmitt, Carl. *The Concept of the Political* (1932). Translated and edited by George Schwab. New Brunswick, N.J., 1976.

Stackhouse, Max L. "Jesus and Economics: A Century of Christian Reflection on the Economic Order." In *The Bible in American Law, Politics, and Political Rhetoric,* edited by James T. Johnson. Chico, Calif., 1985.

Sternberger, Dolf. "Legitimacy." In *International Encyclopedia of the Social Sciences,* edited by David L. Sills, vol. 9, pp. 244–248. New York, 1968. Contains an interesting discussion of the history of the concept of legitimation.

Tillich, Paul. "Kairos." In his *The Protestant Era.* Chicago, 1948.

Tillich, Paul. *Love, Power, and Justice.* New York, 1954.

Tipton, Steven M. *Getting Saved from the Sixties: Moral Meaning in Conversion and Cultural Change.* Berkeley, 1982.

Tribe, Laurence H. "Ways Not to Think about Plastic Trees." In *When Values Conflict,* edited by Laurence H. Tribe et al. Cambridge, 1976.

Troeltsch, Ernst. "Fundamental Problems of Ethics." In *The Shaping of Modern Christian Thought,* edited by Warren F. Groff and Donald E. Miller. Cleveland, 1968.

JAMES LUTHER ADAMS and THOMAS MIKELSON

LEHMANN, EDVARD (1862–1930), Danish historian of religions. Born in Copenhagen, Edvard Johannes Lehmann began studying theology at the university there in 1880. Frants Buhl, in Old Testament, and Karl Kroman, in philosophy, exercised the greatest influence on the young scholar. In 1886 he obtained his theological degree, and until 1892 he earned his living as a schoolteacher while continuing his theological and philosophical studies.

In 1890 he received the gold medal of the University of Copenhagen for his treatise *Den religiøse Følelses Natur og psychologiske Oprindelse og dens etiske Betydning* (The Nature and Psychological Origin of the Religious Feeling and Its Ethical Importance). He had already conceived an interest in the history of religions and felt the need to acquire knowledge of Near Eastern languages. The gold medal provided a scholarship that enabled him to study in Germany, Holland, England, and France.

In Holland, Lehmann became closely acquainted with scholars in the comparative study of religion and the history of religions, including C. P. Tiele and P. D. Chantepie de la Saussaye. Lehmann was invited by Chantepie to write on Greek, Indian, and Persian religion in the second edition of Chantepie's *Lehrbuch der Religionsgeschichte,* which appeared in 1897. (Lehmann later became the coeditor, with Alfred Bertholet, of the fourth edition of the *Lehrbuch,* 1925.) The immediate result of Lehmann's studies abroad was his doctoral thesis of 1896, "Om Foroldet mellem Religion og Kultur i Avesta" (On the Relationship between Religion and Culture in the Avesta). In this work, Lehmann addressed the problem of the animosity toward culture that he found characteristic of religion in general. According to Lehmann himself, however, this little work is to be considered only a preliminary study to his *magnum opus, Zarathustra: En Bog om Persernes ganmle Tro* (Zarathustra: A Book on the Ancient Faith of the Persians), 2 vols. (1899–1902).

The first volume of this work made such an impression on the academic authorities that Lehmann in 1900 was made docent at the University of Copenhagen. In 1904 he published *Mystik i Hedenskab og Kristendom,* which was translated into a number of languages, including English, and in 1907 *Buddha: Hans lære og dens gærning* (Buddha: His Teaching and Work), dedicated to Nathan Söderblom. Both works, though widely read and of no small influence, reveal a weak point in Lehmann's scholarship: his profound attachment to the ideals of Protestantism and his conviction of its superiority, which he thought was confirmed by the study of other religions.

In 1910 Lehmann was invited by the theological faculty of the University of Berlin to take the post of professor ordinarius of the history and the philosophy of religion, but only three years later he left Berlin to accept to a similar invitation from the University of Lund in Sweden. He held the latter chair until his retirement in 1927; from then on he lived in Copenhagen until his death in 1930.

With the passage of time, Lehmann's interest in strictly religio-historical studies gradually receded into the background. In 1914 he published (with Johannes Pedersen) the treatise "Der Beweis für die Auferstehung im Koran" (The Proof of the Resurrection in the Koran) in *Der Islam,* vol. 5, pp. 54–61; but his *Stället och vägen: Ett religionshistorisk perspektiv* (1917), on the static and dynamic elements in the history of religions, marks a turning point in his activity. He now felt his most important role to be that of a folk-educator who was to rouse interest in general cultural (including religio-historical) matters and problems; to this end he wrote a number of books on cultural themes and current social issues.

BIBLIOGRAPHY

Only one of Lehmann's books is available in English: *Mysticism in Heathendom and Christendom* (London, 1910) is the English version of *Mystik i Hedenskab og Kristendom* (Copenhagen, 1904). Lehmann's contributions to a number of encyclopedias and other collective works are important in that they call attention to his inspired style, breadth of view, and strong endeavors to promote the study of world religions. These include "Die Religion der primitiven Völker," in *Die Kultur der Gegenwart,* part 1, section 3 (Leipzig, 1906), pp. 8–29; several articles on Iranian religion and one on Christmas customs in the *Encyclopaedia of Religion and Ethics,* edited by James Hastings, vol. 3 (Edinburgh, 1910); "Erscheinungswelt der Religion," in *Die Religion in Geschichte und Gegenwart* (Tübingen, 1910); and articles in *Textbuch zur Religionsgeschichte* (Leipzig, 1912). Lehmann also edited and was a contributor to *Illustreret Religionshistorie* (Copenhagen, 1924).

A bibliography of Lehmann's works can be found in *Festskrift udgivet af Københavns Universitet i anledning af universitetets aarsfest, November 1930* (Copenhagen, 1930), pp. 148ff. A biography, written by Arild Hvidtfeldt and Johannes Pedersen, appears in *Dansk biografisk leksikon,* vol. 8 (Copenhagen, 1981), pp. 657–659.

JES P. ASMUSSEN

LEIBNIZ, GOTTFRIED WILHELM (1646–1716), German polymath. Leibniz was born in Leipzig on 1 July 1646. Trained in the law, he earned his living as a councillor, diplomat, librarian, and historian, primarily at the court of Hanover. Leibniz made important intellectual contributions in linguistics, geology, historiography, mathematics, physics, and philosophy. Although he did not view himself primarily as a theologian, he devoted considerable time and energy to church reunion projects, engaging in extended efforts to provide a basis for reunion among Catholics and Protestants, and, that project having failed, attempting to provide a basis for reunion between Lutherans and Calvinists.

Leibniz completed the arts program at Leipzig University in 1663 with a philosophical dissertation entitled *Metaphysical Disputation on the Principle of Individuation.* He then entered a program at the university leading to the doctorate of law. By virtue of a quota system, he was not awarded the doctorate in 1666, although his final dissertation was written. Offended, Leibniz enrolled in the law program at the University of Altdorf in October 1666 and almost immediately submitted his completed dissertation, *Disputation concerning Perplexing Cases in the Law,* which was accepted. He was awarded the doctorate in 1667.

After declining a teaching position offered at Altdorf, Leibniz was employed first by Baron Johann Christian von Boineburg, and, then, by Boineburg's sometime employer, Johann Philipp von Schönborn, elector of Mainz. While in the employ of the elector he initially worked on a project aimed at a codification of German civil law, and later as an officer in the court of appeal. During his time in Mainz Leibniz produced work in physics, the law, and philosophy, especially philosophy of religion. It was in this period that he formulated the idea of writing a definitive apology for Christianity, under the title *The Catholic Demonstrations.* While at Mainz he outlined the entire project and filled in some of the details. The aims of the project included proofs of the propositions of natural theology, proofs of the possibility of Christian dogmas not included in natural theology, and the adumbration of a philosophical system that would provide a basis for reunion among the Christian churches.

In the winter of 1671–1672 Leibniz drew up a plan for the French conquest of Egypt, which appealed to his German superiors because, if carried out, it would have provided Louis XIV with a task they assumed to be incompatible with his attacking Germany. Leibniz was sent to Paris to present his plan to Louis. He was never granted an audience with the French king, but during his protracted stay there (spring 1672 to December 1676) he met and conversed with some of the leading intellectuals of Europe, including Antoine Arnauld, Nicolas Malebranche, and Christian Huygens. Huygens became Leibniz's mentor in mathematics. When Leibniz arrived in Paris his mathematical knowledge was out of date and superficial; by the time he left he had developed the basic theory of calculus, which he first published in 1684. Later in his life a storm of controversy was to arise over whether he or Isaac Newton deserved credit for laying the foundations of calculus. Modern scholarship seems to have reached the verdict that Leibniz and Newton both developed the idea of calculus independently. Newton was the first to develop calculus, Leibniz was the first to publish it. A time of intensive effort in mathematics, Leibniz's Paris period was also a period of serious work in philosophy and, in particular, philosophy of religion. During the Paris years he wrote *The Faith of a Philosopher,* apparently for Arnauld, a work that considers many of the same problems treated in his only philosophical monograph published in his lifetime, *The Theodicy.*

Leibniz left Paris in October 1676 to accept a position as councillor and librarian to Duke Johann Friedrich in Hanover. During the trip from Paris to Hanover Leibniz had a four-day visit with Spinoza, which generated Leibniz's particular contribution to the ontological argument for the existence of God. He believed that the ontological argument, as formulated by Descartes, for example, established the conditional proposition that if the existence of God is possible, then the existence of God is necessary. Leibniz set out to prove the antecedent, that is, that the existence of God is possible. The main idea of the proof is that God may be characterized as a being having all and only perfections; perfections are positive simple qualities, and, hence, collections of them must be consistent.

During his years of service to Johann Friedrich, a convert to Catholicism, and his early years of service to Ernst August, a Lutheran, Leibniz was deeply involved in reunion projects, first with the apostolic vicar Nicholas Steno, who read and commented on Leibniz's *The Faith of a Philosopher,* and then with Cristobal de Rojas y Spinola, the representative of the emperor Leopold I, who, with papal approval, engaged in extensive negotiations in Hanover in an effort to find compromise positions acceptable to both Catholics and Protestants. Although not an official party to the negotiations, Leibniz produced various documents intended to further their progress, including *A System of Theology,* a document that has generated considerable debate about Leibniz's attitude toward Catholicism. What is clear is that the work considers some of the problems relating to church reunion from the Catholic standpoint. What is less clear is the extent to which Leibniz accepted its contents.

Much of Leibniz's intellectual effort went into his extensive correspondence. The most famous of his irenic correspondences was with Jacques-Bénigne Bossuet, bishop of Meaux and leading French prelate, a correspondence that began in earnest in 1691 and continued with some interruptions until 1702. Leibniz aimed at compromise, Bossuet at capitulation. Neither succeeded.

Leibniz himself dated his philosophical maturity from 1686 and the writing of *The Discourse on Metaphysics.* Leibniz's original work in dynamics, begun prior to *The Discourse on Metaphysics* and reaching its culmination in the *Specimen Dynamicum* of 1695, and his original work in logic, begun in 1679 and reaching a high point in the *General Inquiries concerning the Analysis of Concepts and Truth* of 1686, partially motivate the metaphysics of *The Discourse on Metaphysics.* But so do the theological aims of *The Catholic Demonstrations,* previously mentioned. Thus it is plausible to see *The Discourse on Metaphysics* as attempting to provide a philosophical framework adequate to permit a satisfactory account of the relation of human freedom to divine causality. Indeed, the major project of *The Discourse on Metaphysics* is an attempt to provide a theory of individual created substances that will permit a distinction between those actions properly attributed to creatures and those properly attributed to God, yet a distinction so drawn that it is consistent with God's universal conservative causation.

Much of Leibniz's philosophical work in the mature period may be seen as a contribution to the aims of *The Catholic Demonstrations.* Thus, in *The Theodicy* (1710), Leibniz set out to show, contrary to the claims of Pierre Bayle, that the tenets of Christianity are not contrary to the dictates of reason; in particular, that the Christian view that God is omnipotent, omniscient, omnibenevolent, and the creator of the world is consistent with the fact that there is evil in the world. He believed that his views about the structure of possible worlds, composed of independent possible substances, from which God chose at creation in accordance with the principle of sufficient reason, provided a suitable framework for resolving the problem of evil, as well as the problem of the relation of human freedom to divine grace. The basic idea of Leibniz's solution to the problem of evil is this: God's choice among possible worlds, like every choice of every agent, is subject to the principle of sufficient reason. God's reason in connection with creation is based on the principle of perfection; hence, God chooses the best possible world. There is evil in the world and there are possible worlds containing no evil. Still, this is the best possible world, so the evil it contains must be necessary for good things without which the overall perfection of the world would be diminished.

Leibniz's major metaphysical thesis, articulated in his mature period, is that there is nothing in the world except simple substances (monads) and, in them, nothing except perceptions and appetites. He believed that monads, although capable of spontaneous action, could not causally interact, but that they were so programmed by their creator that they appeared to interact in accordance with the principle of preestablished harmony. An extensive correspondence with Bartholomew des Bosses, a Jesuit professor of theology in Hildesheim, dating from 1706 until Leibniz's death, considers, among other things, whether Leibniz's major metaphysical thesis is consistent with the Catholic dogma of transubstantiation and the Christian understanding of the incarnation.

Leibniz traveled extensively in connection with his historical research and on various diplomatic missions, particularly to Berlin and Vienna. During the same period he made efforts to bring about the establishment of scientific academies, particularly at Berlin, Dresden, Vienna, and Saint Petersburg. Of these proposals, only the plan for an academy at Berlin came to fruition in his lifetime. In 1700 the Brandenburg Society of Sciences was founded in Berlin, with Leibniz its president for life.

The later period of Leibniz's life produced important philosophical work in addition to *The Theodicy,* for example, *The Monadology* (1714); *The New Essays on Human Understanding* (1703–1704), a commentary in dialogue form on John Locke's philosophy; and the correspondence with Samuel Clarke, a disciple of Isaac Newton, on the nature of space and time.

BIBLIOGRAPHY

Works by Leibniz. Much of the material Leibniz wrote on philosophical and theological topics was not published in his lifetime, in part, because it was not intended for publication.

Some remains unpublished. The work of producing a definitive edition has been undertaken jointly by various German academic groups. The "academy edition," as it is usually called, is being produced under the title *Gottfried Wilhelm Leibniz: Sämtliche Schriften und Briefe*. Until that grand project reaches fruition it will be necessary to rely on partial editions, among which the most useful is Charles James Gerhardt's *Die philosophischen Schriften von G. W. Leibniz*, 7 vols. (Berlin, 1875–1890). The most complete edition available in English is Leroy E. Loemker's *Philosophical Papers and Letters*, 2d ed. (Dordrecht, 1969).

Works about Leibniz. The Leibniz manuscript material available in Hanover is cataloged in two volumes by Eduard Bodemann: *Der Briefwechsel des Gottfried Wilhelm Leibniz* (1895; reprint, Hildesheim, 1966) and *Die Leibniz: Handschriften* (1889; reprint, Hildesheim, 1966). Two major works of Leibniz bibliography are Émile Ravier's *Bibliographie des œuvres de Leibniz* (1937; reprint, Hildesheim, 1966) and Albert Heinekamp and Kurt Müller's *Leibniz Bibliographie: Verzeichnis Der Literatur über Leibniz bis 1980* (Frankfurt, 1983).

A scholarly exploration of some aspects of Leibniz's theological thinking is Gaston Grua's *Jurisprudence universelle et théodicée selon Leibniz* (Paris, 1953). On the specific topic of Leibniz's reunion efforts, see Paul Eisenkopf's *Leibniz und die Einigung der Christenheit: Überlegungen zur Reunion der evangelischen und katholischen Kirche* (Munich, 1975). Two penetrating studies of his philosophy in English are Bertrand Russell's *A Critical Exposition of the Philosophy of Leibniz*, new ed. (London, 1937), and G. H. R. Parkinson's *Logic and Reality in Leibniz's Metaphysics* (Oxford, 1965). An excellent introduction to Leibniz's philosophy is Nicholas Rescher's *Leibniz: An Introduction to His Philosophy* (Totowa, N.J., 1979). The scholarly journal *Studia Leibnitiana* (Wiesbaden, 1969–) is devoted to the study of Leibniz.

R. C. Sleigh, Jr.

LEMMINKÄINEN is one of the heroes of the Finnish national epic, the *Kalevala*. Elias Lönnrot, who published his redaction of the *Kalevala* in 1835, composed those sections concerning the adventures of Lemminkäinen by combining elements from the stories of five other heroes, a process already begun by the traditional rune singers on whose songs his work was largely based. Lemminkäinen thus came to play such diverse roles as Don Juan, belligerent adventurer, skier, sailor, and witch.

The only poem incorporated into the *Kalevala* having Lemminkäinen as its original hero describes his journey as an uninvited guest to a place variously named Luotola ("homestead of the archipelago"), Pohjola ("homestead of the north"), or Päivölä ("homestead of the sun"). There he overcomes various supernatural obstacles: the fiery grave, the rapids, the fence coiled with snakes (or one giant serpent), and the fettered beasts that guard the yard. His host there serves him a flagon of beer with snakes hidden beneath the foam, which he nevertheless drinks. After this he kills his host in a battle of magical skills.

The description of Lemminkäinen's journey has features in common with medieval vision poetry and the visionary journeys described by arctic shamans. It also finds close parallels in the oral traditions of the Saami (Lapps) and others, which include poems about battles of magic between shamans of different communities.

A few of the three hundred variants of the Lemminkäinen poem contain a sequel that has attracted the attention of many scholars of mythology and religion. In one of its episodes a herdsman shoots (or, in some versions, stabs) Lemminkäinen with the only weapon against which he has taken no magical precautions and throws him into the black river of Tuonela (the realm of death). As Lemminkäinen dies, his mother notices that a brush has begun oozing blood, fulfilling Lemminkäinen's prophesy of his own death. Taking this as a sign that her son is in danger, she sets out in search of him. She rakes parts of his body out of the river, but, according to most versions, does not succeed in restoring him to life.

Scholars have noted the similarity of this story to the ancient Egyptian myth of Osiris, as well as to the religious legends concerning the death of Christ and Balder. The poem contains clear influences from the Russian bylina *Vavilo i skomorokhi*, a poem through which it is believed motifs from the Osiris myth were conveyed from Byzantium to northern Europe.

A Christian poet-singer has reshaped the poem, adding to it, among other things, a passage describing Lemminkäinen's power to cure the blind and the crippled. At the end of the poem, Lemminkäinen delivers a homily on the horrors that await the wrongdoer in the world beyond.

[*See also* Finnic Religions; Tuonela; Ilmarinen; *and* Väinämöinen.]

BIBLIOGRAPHY

Krohn, Kaarle. "Lemminkäinens Tod < Christi > Balders Tod." *Finnisch-ugrische Forschungen* 5 (1905–1906): 83–138. Includes a German translation of the last portion of the poem.

Kuusi, Matti, Keith Bosley, and Michael Branch, eds. and trans. *Finnish Folk Poetry: Epic; An Anthology in Finnish and English.* Helsinki, 1977. Pages 205–223 and 538–540 contain three extensive variants with translations and comments in English.

Matti Kuusi

LENSHINA, ALICE (c. 1919–1978), founder of the African prophetic movement referred to as the Lumpa church. A barely literate peasant woman, Alice Lenshina Mulenga, from Kasomo village, Chinasali district, in the northern province of Northern Rhodesia, started the movement among the Bemba, a matrilineal Bantu-speaking people of Northern Rhodesia (now Zambia). In 1953, Lenshina claimed to have had a spiritual experience in which she died, went to heaven, and met a Christian spirit, described variously as Jesus, God, or an angel, who told her to return to earth to carry out God's works. She told her story to the minister of the nearby Church of Scotland mission at Lubwa (founded by David Kaunda, the father of Kenneth Kaunda, the president of Zambia) and was baptized into the church, taking the name Alice. In 1954, she began holding her own services and baptizing her followers. Her meetings drew large crowds, and by 1955 her following was more or less distinctive from the Church of Scotland mission. One characteristic feature of Lenshina's movement was the singing of hymns, many of which were closer in form to traditional Bemba music than were the hymns of the Church of Scotland. Moreover, Lenshina's followers believed that she could provide protection against witchcraft, the existence of which the Church of Scotland denied.

By 1956 the Lenshina movement, with a membership of over 50,000, could be considered a church of its own. As the movement grew it drew members from different ethnic and religious backgrounds—matrilineal and patrilineal peoples, urban workers and rural subsistence farmers—and from a range of social statuses, although its appeal was strongest among the poorer, less educated sections of Northern Rhodesian society. The movement spread along the line of the railroad into the towns of the Copper Belt, one of the main urban, industrial regions of central Africa. It also spread to the remote rural areas of the northern and eastern provinces, and poor peasants would walk hundreds of miles to contribute their labor and money to construct the monumental cathedral at Kasomo, Lenshina's religious headquarters. Lenshina's followers became known as *Lumpa* (a Bemba term meaning "excelling," "the most important").

In its early years, from the mid-1950s to the early 1960s, the Lumpa church, with its anti-European stance, was viewed as a political ally of the independence movement in Northern Rhodesia, and Lumpa meetings incorporated nationalist propaganda. Afterward, however, the church became increasingly nonpolitical and otherworldly in its outlook, and conflicts developed with the United National Independence Party, a political party founded under the leadership of Kenneth Kaunda and the main political contender to establish Zambian independence from colonial rule. In 1957 the Lumpa church, in its constitution, had stated that it was not opposed to the laws of the country; its solution to the problem of colonialism, African political nationalism, and rapid economic change was withdrawal. By 1963 church members refused to obey the laws of the colonial state or to join political parties. They believed that the end of the world was at hand, and they withdrew from the secular world and built their own separate communities in anticipation of the end. These communities were believed to be sacred domains, immune from the evils of the external world, which was thought to be under the control of Satan and his evil influence and agents.

By 1964, at a time when Northern Rhodesia's independence was imminent, both the colonial administration and the African independence movement attempted to control the Lumpa church. This led to fighting between church members and the recently elected Northern Rhodesia government, and between July and October 1964 over 700 people were killed. The Lumpa, armed with indigenous weapons such as spears, axes, and muzzle loaders, confronted soldiers with automatic weapons. As the Lumpa attacked they shouted, "Jericho!" in the belief that the walls of evil would tumble down and that they would triumph in battle. As they were shot they shouted, "Hallelujah!" in the belief that they would be transported directly to heaven, only to return to rule the world. The Lumpa were defeated, the church was banned, and Lenshina herself was imprisoned. Some of her followers fled to Zaire, where the Lumpa church continued to exist.

In its beliefs and practices, the Lumpa church combined both African and European elements. Movements of this type were and are characteristic of southern and central Africa. At the core of such movements is a prophet who is believed to have had a Christian experience. As is typical of such movements, Lenshina's prophecy was ethical in that it imposed a strict, puritanical moral code upon her followers. She forbade adultery, polygamy, divorce, dancing, and drinking. Lenshina herself was the ultimate source of authority, and some Lumpa hymns even represented Lenshina as the savior. Baptism, the most important rite of the church, could only be performed by Lenshina herself, using water which she claimed to have received from God himself. Baptism was believed to wash away sins and ensure salvation.

In Lumpa theology, God was viewed as the creator of all things. Satan was thought to have been created by

God as a good spirit who turned against God. Witchcraft, thought to stem from Satan, could be safeguarded against by church membership. Unlike the European mission churches, the Lumpa church did not deny the existence of witchcraft; instead it gave its members a means of combating it. Lenshina was believed to be the personification of good and to provide protection against evil. For the Lumpa, evil came to be the world outside their church, including the colonial administration, and the United National Independence Party represented evil.

The movement gradually acquired a structure, with Lenshina, her disciples, and spiritual and secular advisers at the center. Deacons supervised congregations, and within congregations preachers and judges ministered to the needs of local members and adjudicated their disputes. The church was itself a complete community, meeting its own spiritual, social, judicial, and economic requirements. In the historical context of the struggle for Zambian independence, a movement that demanded the complete allegiance of its members was bound to come into conflict with secular authorities. The Lenshina cult was not an atypical African religious expression; what brought it into prominence and led to its destruction was its unfortunate timing and conflict with the movement for Zambia's independence.

BIBLIOGRAPHY

Binsbergen, Wim van. "Religious Innovation and Political Conflict in Zambia: The Lumpa Rising." In his *Religious Change in Zambia.* Boston, 1981.

Bond, George Clement. "A Prophecy That Failed: The Lumpa Church of Uyombe, Zambia." In *African Christianity,* edited by George Clement Bond, Walton Johnson, and Sheila S. Walker, pp. 137–160. New York, 1979.

Calmettes, J.-L. "The Lumpa Sect, Rural Reconstruction, and Conflict." M.Sc. (Econ.) thesis, University of Wales, 1978.

Roberts, Andrew D. "The Lumpa Church of Alice Lenshina." In *Protest and Power in Black Africa,* edited by Robert I. Rotberg and Ali A. Mazrui. Oxford, 1970.

Rotberg, Robert I. "The Lenshina Movement of Northern Rhodesia." *Rhodes-Livingston Journal* 29 (June 1961): 63–78.

Taylor, John Vernon, and Dorothea A. Lehmann. *Christians of the Copperbelt.* London, 1961.

GEORGE CLEMENT BOND

LEO I (d. 461), pope of the Roman Catholic church (440–461), called "the Great." Nothing is known for certain about Leo's early life, although according to the *Liber pontificalis,* he was born in Tuscany probably at the turn of the fourth to the fifth century. Leo is one of the most important Roman pontiffs and one of the architects of papal authority. He served as a deacon of the Roman church under both Celestine I (422–432) and Sixtus III (430–440), and in that position exercised great influence. He took an active role in the theological controversies with the Nestorians and the Pelagians and was also involved with institutional matters. While Leo was on a mission to Gaul in early 440, Sixtus died, and the legate returned to Rome to find himself elected pope. He was consecrated as bishop of Rome on 29 September 440.

The energy that Leo had devoted to religious questions before he became pope carried into his pontificate. In the first decade of his papacy, Pelagians, Manichaeans, and Priscillianists were at different times condemned in his writings and even in public debate. Of Leo's undoubtedly extensive homiletical and epistolary production, only 96 sermons and 123 indisputably authentic letters survive. Yet even this legacy is unusually large for a pope prior to Gregory I (590–604) and permits insight not only into Leo's papal activities, but also into his ideas and beliefs.

Leo considered himself to be, as bishop of Rome, the successor of Peter in a transhistorical sense. When Leo spoke it was the apostle who spoke. Just as all bishops are responsible for the care of their own flocks, so, in Leo's conception, the successor of Peter in the Roman church is charged with the care of all churches, for it was to Peter that Christ gave the keys of binding and loosing in heaven and on earth (*Mt.* 16:16–19). Just as it was for Peter's faith alone that Christ prayed when all the apostles were threatened (*Lk.* 22:32), so firmness to the apostolic tradition of the Roman church will strengthen all bishops. With a strikingly deep sense of the traditions both of his office and of Roman law, and with a conviction about the presence of apostolic authority in his words and actions, Leo stands out among other fourth- and fifth-century architects of papal claims, such as, for example, Celestine I and Damasus I (366–384). With deft use of such a dossier, it is small wonder that notions such as the contrast between *plenitudo potestatis* ("fullness of power") and *pars solicitudinis* ("part of the responsibility")—terms that emerge from a letter of Leo's to Anastasius, his vicar in Illyricum—became central in the tradition of describing the powers of Rome vis-à-vis other churches.

Leo was, however, not merely a theoretician of papal claims. He was deeply committed to effective action, whether in a pastoral role at Rome or in the larger sphere of empirewide ecclesiastical politics. He promoted the claims of Roman authority in various ways: for example, negotiating in the West with barbarian invaders, or dealing with issues in regions as far removed as Egypt and Gaul. In the former instance, although he acknowledged Dioscorus as successor of Cyril on the patriarchal throne of Alexandria, Leo urged uniformity between the two churches in certain liturgical practices. Tradition stated that the evangelist Mark had founded the Alexandrian church, and Mark was a disciple of Peter, who had "received the apostolic principate [*apostolicum principatum*] from the Lord, and the Roman church preserves his teachings" (*Regesta pontificum Romanorum,* JK406). Leo reasoned that teacher and disciple ought not to represent disparate traditions.

The pope asserted papal authority in Gaul in the face of staunch opposition. The archbishop of Arles had been granted a primacy over the Gallican church by Zosimus I (417–418). The vigorous exercise of that privilege and the objection of local churchmen gave Leo an opportunity to exercise prerogatives of the Roman church. The pope restored to Besançon a bishop who had been deposed by Bishop Hilary of Arles and was able to gain support from Emperor Valentinian III against Hilary. When the latter challenged Leo's authority, the pontiff had him confined in 445 to his diocese by an imperial decree in which the primacy of the bishop of Rome was acknowledged.

The most famous instance in which Leo's claims were manifest involved the renewed christological dispute in the East in the 440s. When the troubles over Eutyches began at Constantinople, Leo felt that they should have been referred to Rome at once. In 449 the pope sent to Bishop Flavian of Constantinople his famous *Tome* in the custody of legates destined for the synod held at Ephesus, a synod that Leo later condemned as a *latrocinium* (a band of robbers, or an act of banditry), rather than a *concilium.* The problem with Ephesus as Leo saw it was that the gathering was controlled by Dioscorus of Alexandria and concluded by condemning Flavian and rehabilitating Eutyches and his Alexandrian monophysite Christology.

The events of 449 were reversed through the concerted efforts of Leo, in association with powerful allies in Constantinople, both in the imperial household and in the church. The Roman pontiff's legates and *Tome* had been ignored in Ephesus. When a new synod was convened at Chalcedon in 451 by the recently elevated emperor Marcian, the opponents of the Alexandrians were firmly in charge. Leo's *Tome* was received, to quote Henry Chadwick, "with courteous approval" (*The Early Church,* 1967, p. 203), and it became the basis of the Chalcedonian definition of faith (not a new creed, in deference to the tradition that no faith different from that of the Council of Nicaea, 325, should be proclaimed). The definition set forth a Christology of two natures, divine and human, in Christ, within one person, and represented a triumph for Western views and Roman authority within the complex Eastern world. Chalcedon also, in its twenty-eighth canon, which was enacted without the approval of the Roman legates, elevated the see of Constantinople to a rank in ecclesiastical dignity equal to that of Rome. The pope was furious, refused to accept this decree into the Latin canonical tradition, and even delayed affirming the council's theological decisions.

With Leo, Roman ecclesiastical authority became both a concept and a force to be taken seriously in the Christian world. Scholars debate the extent of his contributions to the sacramentary that bears his name, although Leo may have composed some of the material. There can be no question, however, of Leo's contribution to the papacy as a religious and political force. Together with Damasus I, Gelasius I, and Gregory I, he stands out as one of the most important Roman pontiffs of antiquity, and throughout papal history only Leo and Gregory have been remembered with the sobriquet "the Great."

BIBLIOGRAPHY

Readers should begin with the sections on Leo by Karl Baus and others in *The Imperial Church from Constantine to the Early Middle Ages,* "History of the Church," no. 2 (New York, 1980), pp. 264–269, with a bibliography. The best guide to Leo's letters is still *Regesta pontificum Romanorum,* vol. 1, 2d ed., edited by Phillip Jaffé (Leipzig, 1885). The letters are usually cited by number preceded by J(affé) K(altenbrunner); an English translation of Leo's letters and sermons by Charles Lett Feltoe is in "A Select Library of Nicene and Post-Nicene Fathers," 2d series, vol. 12 (New York, 1895). Useful still is the informative article by G. N. Bonwetsch in *The New Schaff-Herzog Encyclopedia of Religious Knowledge,* 13 vols., edited by Samuel M. Jackson (Grand Rapids, Mich., 1953). See also Henry Chadwick's *The Early Church* (Harmondsworth, 1967).

ROBERT SOMERVILLE

LEO XIII (Vincenzo Giaocchino Pecci, 1810–1903), pope of the Roman Catholic church (1878–1903). The sixth child of noble parents, Giaocchino Pecci was born in Carpineto in the Papal States on 2 March 1810. Educated at the Jesuit college in Viterbo (1818–1824), the Roman College (1825–1832), and the Roman Academy of Noble Ecclesiastics (1832–1837), he was made a domestic prelate in 1837 and began a career as a papal civil servant.

Following his ordination as a priest in late 1837, he held the post of papal delegate (provincial governor) successively at Benevento (1838–1841), Spoleto (briefly in 1841), and Perugia (1841–1843). As a result of his success as an administrator, in 1843, Pope Gregory XVI made him papal nuncio to Belgium and promoted him to the rank of bishop. At the request of King Leopold I, he was recalled to Rome and named to the vacant see of Perugia in 1846.

During his long Perugian tenure (1846–1878), he developed and displayed the complex attitude toward modernity (combining a principled resistance to the currents of the age with a pragmatic accommodation to the same for the church's welfare) that was later to mark his pontificate. Thus, on the one hand, he identified with Pius IX's program calling for the definition of papal infallibility and the convening of an ecumenical council to solidify the church's teaching authority. He also reflected Pius's views in condemning both the Sardinian annexation of Perugia (1860) and the anticlerical legislation that followed it. On the other hand, he revamped the seminary curriculum of his diocese to include the study of modern developments, founded the Academy of Saint Thomas to help the church meet the philosophical challenges of the age, praised the advances of modern science, technology, and scholarship in a series of pastoral letters (1874–1877), and sought accommodation with the Sardinian regime.

Pecci's complex stance toward modernity produced mixed reactions. Giacomo Antonelli, the cardinal secretary of state, distrusted him, while some bishops hailed his perspicacity. Although he did not sympathize with him entirely, Pius IX recognized Pecci's abilities. Consequently, in 1853 he made him a cardinal, and in 1877 he appointed him the camerlengo, the cardinal to whom fell the responsibilities of governing the church and organizing the electing conclave during a papal interregnum.

Following Pius's death in 1878, Pecci was elected pope. At the time of his election, the church's prospects were not very promising. Leo's sympathy with Pius's attitudes toward modernity led him to continue or at least to echo some of the latter's sentiments and policies, most notably concerning compensation for the loss of church lands (the Roman Question), the centralization of church authority, and a distaste for modern political developments (which in 1878 he voiced in the encyclical *Inscrutabili*). But his contribution to modern Catholicism lay in his discerning that Pius's strident hostility to modernity had not won for the church the influence that both men desired.

With a pragmatism that his detractors interpreted as rank opportunism, Leo realized that the church had to come to terms with the intellectual, political, and socioeconomic conditions of the times. Although his statesmanship succeeded both in ending German repression of the Catholic church *(Kulturkampf)* and in establishing correct relations with Britain and cordial ties with the United States, it was Leo's revitalization of the church's philosophical tradition that allowed Catholicism effectively to come to terms with the two major currents of the age: democracy and industrial life.

In 1879, Leo issued *Aeterni patris* and called for a Catholic return to the study of Thomism. As time went on, it became clear that in his plan for a revival of Thomas, Leo revered him above all as a methodological mentor who pointed the way to a reconciliation of church and world. As Thomas had used the intellectual advances and categories of his day to reconcile faith and reason, enhancing the teaching prestige of the church by giving it a philosophy that was solid, plausible, and useful, so also Leo wished to enhance the prestige of the modern church by advancing a philosophical system that was solid because it was based on natural-law principles and both plausible and useful because these same principles could be translated into modern terms. Once this translation had been made, Leo believed that the church would be able to understand the modern world, converse with the natural-law adherents of the Enlightenment, and offer plausible and lasting solutions to the problems of contemporary society.

In Leo's hands, Neo-Thomism proved a remarkably supple and useful instrument for confronting the political and socioeconomic conditions of the age. Spurred on by crises in the French church, Leo used his new philosophical method to rehabilitate democracy for the church. In a series of encyclicals running from *Diuturnum illud* (1881) to *Au milieu des sollicitudes* (1892), he used natural-law thought to distinguish between the forms and functions of states. Although he never personally reconciled himself with the idea of popular sovereignty or the revolutionary aspects of modern democracies, he was able to accept democratic republics as long as they fulfilled the functions assigned them by natural law and did not interfere in the religious sphere.

Leo likewise used his Neo-Thomist method to frame a universal Catholic response to the problems of worker unrest, unionization, and socialism. Building on the work of ecclesiastics such as Henry Manning (d. 1892) and Wilhelm von Ketteler (d. 1877), in 1891 Leo issued *Rerum novarum*. In this encyclical, he used natural-law social thought to condemn both liberalism and socialism and to champion the rights of workers both to earn a living wage and to organize in unions. In addition, he used the natural-law understanding of the positive function of the state (i.e., the promotion of the common good) to sanction state intervention for the alleviation of worker distress. Although Leo's encyclical came relatively late in the history of European industrial growth, and although it was frequently construed as a purely antisocialist document, it earned for him the sobriquet Pope of the Workingman, and its sympathy for the rights of labor was generally credited with stopping or at least slowing the exodus of industrial workers from the church.

Although he met with defeats (most notably his failure to interest European governments in his plans for the return of the papacy's temporal power) and although he never gained for the church that degree of power for which he yearned, Leo XIII did, through his diplomacy, his revitalization of Catholic scholarship, his social concern, and his sincere desire to touch the world, leave the church more secure, more respected, and more able to deal with the modern world than it had been at the time of his accession to the papal throne in 1878.

BIBLIOGRAPHY

Camp, Richard L. *The Papal Ideology of Social Reform: A Study in Historical Development, 1878–1967.* Leiden, 1969. Deals with the growth of sophistication in papal social documents from Leo XIII to Paul VI. Helpful for seeing Leo's long-term influence on the church.

Gargan, Edward T., ed. *Leo XIII and the Modern World.* New York, 1961. A collection of essays marking the sesquicentennial of Leo's birth. Joseph N. Moody's contribution on Leonine social thought and James Collins's article on Leo's philosophical program are especially helpful.

Jedin, Hubert, and John Dolan, eds. *The Church in the Industrial Age,* vol. 9 of *The History of the Church.* New York, 1981. This work benefits from the contributions of Oskar Kohler, which place Leo in his historical context.

Moody, Joseph N., et al., eds. *Church and Society: Catholic Social and Political Thought and Movements, 1789–1950.* New York, 1953. Has the virtue of gathering together extended essays and primary sources that, among other things, shed light on the development of Catholic social thought.

Murray, John Courtney. "Leo XIII on Church and State: The General Structure of the Controversy," "Leo XIII: Separation of Church and State," "Leo XIII: Two Concepts of Government," *Theological Studies* 14 (1953): 1–30, 145–214, 551–567; and "Leo XIII: Government and the Order of Culture," *Theological Studies* 15 (1954): 1–33. A series of four important articles that offer a progressive and historically sophisticated interpretation of the political thought of Leo XIII.

Soderini, Eduardo. *The Pontificate of Leo XIII.* 2 vols. London, 1934–1935. Written with the aid of the Vatican Archives. Only two of the original volumes have been translated into English.

Wallace, Lillian P. *Leo XIII and the Rise of Socialism.* Durham, N.C., 1966. Argues that the rise of socialism forced the church to come to terms with the problems of industrialization, and that the church's entrance into the field of economics blunted the advance of socialism.

JOSEPH M. MCSHANE, S.J.

LEONTIUS OF BYZANTIUM (c. 500–c. 543), Orthodox Christian monk and theologian, author of a brief corpus in the christological controversies of the Greek East just before the Second Council of Constantinople (553). The manuscript tradition calls Leontius only "monk" and "eremite," but modern scholarship identifies him as Leontius of Byzantium, an Origenist monk of Palestine, who appears in the *Life of Sabas* by the sixth-century hagiographer Cyril of Scythopolis. This Leontius, born probably in Constantinople, entered the monastery called the New Laura near Tekoa in Palestine around 520 with his spiritual master Nonnus, a disciple of the Origenist monk Evagrios of Pontus (345–399). Coming to Constantinople in 531, he became the nucleus of an Origenist party led by his friend Theodore Askidas (d. 558), which defended the Council of Chalcedon against the monophysites. Back in Palestine in 537, Leontius returned to Constantinople around 540 to defend the Origenists against charges of heresy. In 543 the emperor Justinian condemned Origenism. Leontius's polemic against Theodore of Mopsuestia (c. 350–428) probably initiated the campaign that led to Justinian's publication of the "Three Chapters" edict (a collection of condemned texts attributed to three representatives of the school of Antioch: Theodore of Mopsuestia, Theodoret of Cyrrhus, and Ibas of Edessa), which persuaded the Second Council of Constantinople (553) to condemn the school as teaching the heresy of Nestorius (that in Jesus exist two distinct "sons" or persons, the one divine, the other human).

Three of Leontius's works survive, all defending and interpreting the christological formula of Chalcedon. The first work collects three different treatises but is usually called by the name of the first: *Against the Nestorians and Eutychians.* This treatise, the best known of Leontius's works, defends the formula of Chalcedon both against those who "divide" or "separate" (and not simply "distinguish") Christ's divine and human natures (that is, the Nestorians) and against those who collapse the two natures into "one incarnate nature of God the Word" (the formula of the Orthodox father Cyril of Alexandria adopted by the monophysites). Leontius represents Chalcedon as a middle way between heresies, defending it by means of a common metaphor: just as soul and body, although different by nature, are united to form a single human being, so also the Son of God (bearing the divine nature) is united with human nature to form Jesus Christ.

The second treatise, *Dialogue Against the Aphthartodocetists,* attacks the monophysite Julian of Halicarnassus (d. after 518), who had taught that the body of Jesus had become incorruptible not at his resurrection (the

Orthodox view) but at the very moment of the Son's entering it. The third treatise, *Critique and Triumph over the Nestorians,* argues that Theodore of Mopsuestia was the spiritual father of the heretic Nestorius. Leontius's other works include *Resolution of the Arguments Opposed by Severus, Thirty Propositions against Severus,* and *Against the Frauds of the Apollinarists,* the last work attested to be genuine (on the strength of only a single manuscript).

The Origenism ascribed to Leontius of Byzantium by Cyril of Scythopolis derived not from Origen (c. 184–c. 254) himself but from Evagrios of Pontus, who taught that Jesus was not, strictly speaking, the Son of God, but rather an eternally spiritual intellect (nous) who had, without losing his primordial unity with the Son, transformed himself into a soul capable of uniting its flesh to the Son. Modern scholarly interpretations divide over the question whether the Christology of Leontius reflects this Origenism. The best-known of Leontius's teachings is the formula "one person in two natures," in which the term nature is understood as an "enhypostasized nature." The traditional scholarly view maintains that for Leontius only the human nature of Jesus is enhypostasized; it exists only in the hypostasis or person of the Son of God. Leontius is therefore a "strict Chalcedonian" who rejected the extremes of both Alexandria and Antioch. Others interpret Leontius as an Origenist: both natures of Christ are enhypostasized in a third entity, the "intellect" Jesus.

Although known to Maximos the Confessor (580–662) and John of Damascus (c. 645–c. 749), Leontius's works exercised almost no influence in the later Byzantine tradition and were unknown in the Latin West until Heinrich Canisius published a Latin translation by Francisco Torres in 1603.

BIBLIOGRAPHY

Daley, Brian. "The Origenism of Leontius of Byzantium." *Journal of Theological Studies* 27 (October 1976): 333–369.

Evans, David B. *Leontius of Byzantium: An Origenist Christology.* Washington, D.C., 1970.

Evans, David B. "Leontius of Byzantium and Dionysius the Areopagite." *Byzantine Studies* 7 (1980): 1–34.

Gray, Patrick T. R. *The Defense of Chalcedon in the East, 451–553.* Leiden, 1979.

Guillaumont, Antoine. *Les "Kephalaia gnostica" d'Evagre le Pontique et l'histoire de l'Origénisme chez les Grecs et chez les Syriens.* Paris, 1962.

Loofs, Friedrich. *Leontius von Byzanz und die gleichnamigen Schriftsteller der griechischen Kirche.* Leipzig, 1887.

Richard, Marcel. "Léonce de Byzance était-il origéniste?" *Revue des études byzantines* 5 (1947): 31–66.

DAVID B. EVANS

LESSING, G. E. (1729–1781), German dramatist, historian, and essayist. Born in Kamenz, the son of a Lutheran pastor, Gotthold Ephraim Lessing went to university in Leipzig in 1746 to study theology, which his interest in drama soon caused him to abandon. He moved to Berlin in 1748 and there became acquainted with noted Enlightenment figures. Between 1755 and 1760 Lessing spent time in Leipzig and Berlin as a journalist. In 1760 he took up residence in Breslau, where he wrote his famous drama *Minna von Barnhelm* (1767–1777) and his treatise comparing literary and visual arts criticism, *Laokoon* (1766). In 1766 Lessing became resident critic for a new theater in Hamburg and composed the *Hamburg Dramaturgy* (1767). The theater soon failed, and Lessing finally became librarian at the library of the duke of Brunswick in Wolfenbüttel. Here he pursued intently his heretofore intermittent theological and historical studies. His publication of anonymous fragments from a manuscript by Samuel Reimarus (1694–1768), attacking Christianity, provoked heated opposition from orthodox Lutherans, and Lessing eventually became embroiled in polemics with the Hamburg pastor Johann Melchior Goeze (1717–1786). Upon being placed under censorship by the duke in 1778, Lessing answered with his famous play *Nathan the Wise* (1779), which pleads for religious toleration. He died in Braunschweig in 1781. Lessing's theological tracts include *Vindication of Hieronymous Caradanus* (1754); *Leibniz on Eternal Punishments* (1773); *Berengarius Turonesis* (1770); "Editor's Counterpropositions," prefacing Reimarus's fragments (1777); *New Hypotheses Concerning the Evangelists Seen as Merely Human Historians* (1778); *Axiomata* (1778); and *The Education of Mankind* (1780).

Lessing's theological reflections have produced divergent interpretations. He is variously seen as an Enlightenment rationalist, basing knowledge upon mathematical models, or as an irrationalist influenced by British empiricism. There are sound textual grounds for both positions, but both presuppose a consistent and relatively complete theory on Lessing's part. Lessing is most effectively interpreted not as a consistent theorist, however, but as one caught up in the cognitive crisis of precritical philosophy between 1750 and 1781. Rationalistic and empiricist paradigms are evident as organizational principles in his handling of religious data.

Religion, specifically revealed religion, became an acute problem for Lessing because its medium is history. "Accidental truths of history can never become the proof of necessary truths of reason," he wrote in *On the Proof of the Spirit and the Power* (1777). Reason, he argued, posits a mathematical mode for all reality. The inner truth of being evinces the formal features of necessity, universality, and intelligibility; truth about God must accord with the formal structure of reason. Historical truth is, on the other hand, always concerned with what, empirically, has occurred. But empirical events are structurally accidental, that is, their contradiction is always possible; this generates the accidental essence of the historical. To base metaphysical and moral truth about God and human relation to God on accident would accordingly constitute *metabasis eis allo genos* (passage into another conceptual realm). Lessing does not flatly deny, for instance, the historical truth of Christ's resurrection. Letting it be accepted as historically possible, he nevertheless balks at drawing a conclusion of salvational importance from such an "accidental" event. History would thereby become a "spider's thread," too weak for the weight of eternity.

Because Lessing freed himself from orthodox dependence upon the literal word of the Bible, he was able to entertain various theses concerning the purely historical origins of the books of the New Testament. He can thus be considered an early exponent of higher criticism.

Through Lessing's reflections there runs an empiricist, if not irrationalist, counterthesis: man as he really is—in history and as a historical being—is not a rationalist, grounding moral activity on rational insight into the nature of God. From his youthful poetic fragment "Religion" to his late "collectanea to a book," *The Education of Mankind,* Lessing complained of the benightedness of human consciousness. Indeed, he sometimes viewed reason as a destructive force that has removed man from a primitive innocence. At any rate, man, left to his own powers, would wander about for "many millions of years" in error, without reaching moral and religious perfection. *De facto,* man has fallen from a primordial state (be it in fact or only in allegory) and is cognitively limited. *De facto,* man does not possess a rational consciousness; he is limited to "unclear" ideas. In short, human consciousness is sensate-empirical. Along with man's benighted cognition goes his essentially emotional psychology. Images, not abstract ideas, move him to action.

Lessing clearly separated himself from Lutheran orthodoxy, but he expressed his appreciation for it: historical Christianity at least addresses man as he *de facto* is. Neological and rationalist theologies, on the other hand, assume man to be rational; this, history proves false. Lessing thus repeatedly opposed theological "liberals" such as J. A. Eberhard (1738–1809).

Lessing reconciled rationalism and Christianity by distinguishing between Christianity as history and Christianity's contemporary meaning; he then brought the two together through the notion of the progressivity of history. Man, clearly incapable of reaching moral perfection, is in need of a directional impulse from beyond. Lessing accordingly accepts hypothetically the basic Christian position that God has entered history. But for Lessing, God enters history as an educator who uses prerational means (e.g., miracles) to stimulate man's evolution toward rational self-sufficiency. The Old and New Testaments are thus stages leading to a new eternal covenant, not unlike that envisioned by some rationalists, in which man will reach perfection.

In the modern period, revealed religion is valid independent of any historical proofs because it has the function to stimulate man's progressively improving capacity for rational self-reflection. The effects (still evident) of a maturing Christianity, not its historical miracles, become the criterion of the inner truth of Christianity. True religion improves man.

Lessing's theology does not constitute a worked-out philosophy; rather, it evinces a laborious and painful encounter with revolutionary tendencies of the modern world. His progressive view of history constitutes an early link in the great theodicies of historical evolution developed in the eighteenth and nineteenth centuries, particularly by Hegel.

Lessing's influence on posterity has been ambiguous. He founded no school and had no followers, yet his theological efforts encompass and epitomize the theological currents of the eighteenth century, currents that influenced subsequent developments critically. In addition, he was a master stylist and rhetorician. Lessing's writings are masterfully, even dramatically, constructed. Here is the source of his lasting influence. He has historical importance because of the content of his theologizing and enduring appeal because of the creative form of his writing.

BIBLIOGRAPHY

An agreed-upon interpretation of Lessing's theology is lacking, and great divergencies among scholars are evident. In the twentieth century some have found Lessing to be a secular rationalist. In this connection, see Martin Bollacher's *Lessing: Vernunft und Geschichte; Untersuchungen zum Problem religiöser Aufklärung in den Spätschriften* (Tübingen, 1978) and Martin Haug's *Entwicklung und Offenbarung bei Lessing* (Gütersloh, 1928). Bollacher's study is a particularly good presentation of this view. Since the 1930s some scholars have found Lessing to be a theist, even Christian to a degree—at any rate, at least receptive to the idea of revelation. For two very important works concerning this thesis, see Arno Schilson's *Geschichte im Horizont der Vorsehung: G. E. Lessings Beitrag zu einer Theologie der Geschichte* (Mainz, 1974) and Helmut Thielicke's *Offenbarung, Vernunft und Existenz: Studien zur Religionsphilosophie Lessings*, 3d ed. (Göttingen, 1957). My study *G. E. Lessing's Theology: A Reinterpretation* (The Hague, 1977) is an attempt to integrate the two traditions by viewing Lessing not as a systematic thinker but as one who evinced contradictions and hovered between secularism and Christianity. For two introductions in English to Lessing's theology, see Henry Allison's *Lessing and the Enlightenment* (Ann Arbor, 1966) and Henry Chadwick's "Introduction," in *Lessing's Theological Writings* (Stanford, Calif., 1957), pp. 9–49.

L. P. WESSELL, JR.

LEUBA, JAMES H. (1868–1946), American psychologist and one of the leading figures of the early phase of the American psychology of religion movement (1880–1930). Born in Switzerland, Leuba came to the United States as a young man and studied at Clark University under G. Stanley Hall. In 1895 he graduated from Clark and became a fellow there, and in 1896 he published the first academic study of the psychology of conversion. In 1889 he had begun teaching at Bryn Mawr College, where he spent all his active academic life. His numerous publications on the psychology of religion gave him a position of prominence in the field through the 1930s.

Leuba was responsible for the classic study on religious beliefs among scientists and psychologists. He found that the more eminent the scientist, the less likely he was to profess religious beliefs. The same finding held for psychologists. The results accorded with Leuba's own sympathies, for he was a critic of religion, a skeptic reporting on other skeptics. In his book *The Psychology of Religious Mysticism* (1926) he emphasized the importance of sexual impulses in motivating religious rituals and of the sexual symbolism of religious ecstasy. Leuba's work has been described as empiricist, reductionist, and antireligious. There is no doubt that in his time he was the least inclined among the leading psychologists to show any respect for conventional religion.

As Leuba himself reported, his early experiences in Switzerland led him to his critical views regarding religion and religious people. Raised in a Calvinist home, he began to have doubts, but then came under the influence of the Salvation Army and had a conversion experience. After he began his scientific studies he became an atheist. He remained, throughout the rest of his life, a critic of religion, much in the same vein as Freud, and a critic of religious hypocrites. He accused Hall and others of keeping up the appearance of religiosity for the sake of their social standing, or as a way of maintaining the authority of religious institutions in order to keep the "ignorant masses" under control. The current standing of Leuba's contribution can be gauged by the fact that of the six books he published during his lifetime, four are still in print, and one of them *(The Psychology of Religious Mysticism)* was reissued as recently as 1972. His brilliant ideas regarding the origins of religion and magic presaged those of Freud and Malinowski, and should keep Leuba numbered among the true greats of the study of religion.

BIBLIOGRAPHY

Argyle, Michael, and Benjamin Beit-Hallahmi. *The Social Psychology of Religion.* Boston, 1975.

Beit-Hallahmi, Benjamin. "Psychology of Religion, 1880–1930: The Rise and Fall of a Psychological Movement." *Journal of the History of the Behavioral Sciences* 10 (1974): 84–90.

Leuba, James H. *A Psychological Study of Religion.* New York, 1912.

Leuba, James H. *The Belief in God and Immortality.* Chicago, 1921.

Leuba, James H. *The Psychology of Religious Mysticism* (1926). Boston, 1972.

BENJAMIN BEIT-HALLAHMI

LÉVI, SYLVAIN (1863–1935), French Sanskritist, Orientalist, and cultural historian. "Sylvain was—always and from the very first—my second uncle," Marcel Mauss declared, recalling his fateful introduction to Sylvain Lévi in 1895; "I owe to Sylvain the new directions of my career." Many other scholars, European and Asian, owed Sylvain Lévi similar debts, and twentieth-century studies of South and East Asia's cultural and religious legacy owe numerous insights and new directions to Lévi's scholarship and personal example.

Just as Marcel Mauss was indebted to Sylvain Lévi for crucial advice, so Lévi owed a similar debt to Ernest Renan, who urged that he sit in Abel Henri Joseph Bergaigne's Sanskrit course at the École des Hautes Études in 1882. Born in Paris, 28 March 1863, Lévi was nineteen when he took Renan's advice, and his career was set after the first hour with Bergaigne. Three years later, in 1885, he was appointed to the second Sanskrit post at the École, and the following year he also took up a lectureship in the newly established section on *sciences religieuses.* In 1889, the year after Bergaigne's death, he became head of Sanskrit instruction at the École. He resigned that post to become professor of Sanskrit language and literature at the Collège de France in 1894, a position he held until his death, 30 October 1935.

Initially fascinated by the possible impact of Greek culture on ancient India, Lévi remained captivated by the nature and extent of cross-cultural influences in Asia. The extensive domain of his own scholarship on primary sources ranged from the first systematic study of Sanskrit drama to Buddhist studies, in which he was, in effect, the successor of Eugène Burnouf. In pursuit of these latter studies, he learned Chinese, Tibetan, and Japanese, and also mastered the Tocharian dialects of Central Asia. Broad and imaginative in his scholarly vision and speculation, Lévi remained a versatile specialist who insisted that the discovery of a single text, the confirmation of a single historical fact, the decipherment of a single stanza, was more significant than any theoretical construct.

Having become a close friend of two young Japanese while still a student, Lévi always sought to strengthen living cross-cultural associations and to recover dimensions of cultural heritage for the benefit of all. These humanistic concerns were evident not only in his scholarship but in his numerous activities as an unofficial cultural ambassador. Instrumental in establishing the École Française d'Extrême Orient, the Institut de Civilisation Indienne, and the Musée Guimet, Lévi founded the Maison Franco-Japonaise and was its first director. His close friendship with the ruling family of Nepal resulted in his classic three-volume work, *Le Népal.* As a friend and adviser of such Indians as Rabindranath Tagore and as a teacher of students, such as Takakusu Junjirō, who came to him from Japan, India, and other Asian countries, Lévi internationalized Asian religious studies and was perhaps Europe's first "postcolonial" Orientalist.

An important element in Lévi's background as a scholar was his abiding interest in Judaism of the Diaspora. The son of Alsatian Jewish immigrants, he worked tirelessly on behalf of world Jewry, becoming the president of the Alliance Israélite Universelle. In the last years of his life, efforts on behalf of Jewish refugees from Germany consumed much of his energy. Clearly, he saw parallels between the adventure of Buddhism in Asia and the impact of Jewish life and thought in Europe. The one historical verity reinforced the other; together the two helped shape and direct a career that changed European Orientalism and inaugurated an epoch in scholarship and in the human interaction between Europe and Asia. Lévi was, as one of his admirers put it, more than an Orientalist: he was a humanist.

BIBLIOGRAPHY

Lévi's writings remain untranslated from the French. A fairly complete bibliography concludes Victor Goloubew's tribute, "Sylvain Lévi et l'Indochine," *Bulletin de l'École Française d'Extrême Orient* 35 (1935): 551–574. The volume *Mémorial Sylvain Lévi,* edited by Louis Renou (Paris, 1937), contains forty-two articles by Lévi that eloquently illustrate the nature and range of his interests and scholarship. Renou's preface to this collection, "Sylvain Lévi et son œuvre scientifique" (first published in the *Journal asiatique*), is an informative and affectionate evaluation of the scholar and the man.

The essays (including an address in English) published as *L'Inde et le monde* (Paris, 1925) may be the most accessible introduction to Lévi's thought. Of his longer works, three are indisputable classics: *Le théâtre indien,* 2 vols. in 1 (Paris, 1890), *La doctrine du sacrifice dans les Brāhmaṇas* (Paris, 1898), and *Le Népal: Étude historique d'un royaume hindou,* 3 vols. (Paris, 1905–1908). Among his numerous editions, translations, and studies, two that remain especially important are *Asaṅga: Mahāyāna-sūtrālaṃkāra; Exposé de la doctrine du Grand Véhicule selon le système Yogācāra,* 2 vols. (Paris, 1907–1911), and *Un système de philosophie bouddhique: Matériaux pour l'étude du système Vijñaptimātra* (Paris, 1932).

G. R. WELBON

LEVI BEN GERSHOM, (1288–1344), known by the hellenized name of Gersonides and, in rabbinic texts, by the acronym RaLBaG (Rabbi Levi ben Gershom); French mathematician and philosopher. Born in Bagnols, Gersonides lived most of his life in Orange and Avignon; little is known about his life other than where he resided in Provence under the protection of the popes. Given the nature of his writings and where he lived, it is not unreasonable to speculate that in addition to his involvement with the Jewish community (he may have been a rabbi) he taught astronomy/astrology in the papal university, medical school, and court. Gersonides is generally acknowledged to be the greatest and most independent medieval Jewish philosopher after the death of Moses Maimonides (Mosheh ben Maimon, 1135/8–1204). Of those rabbis who based their religious thought on the philosophy of Aristotle, Gersonides is the most thorough and rigorous; his major work in this area is *The Wars of the Lord* (1329). Gersonides also dealt with rabbinics, philosophy, mathematics, medicine, and astronomy.

In rabbinics Gersonides wrote commentaries on the Pentateuch, the Former Prophets, *Proverbs, Job, Song of Songs, Ruth, Ecclesiastes, Esther, Daniel, Ezra, Nehemiah,* and *1* and *2 Chronicles,* as well as a commentary on the thirteen hermeneutic rules of Yishma'e'l ben Elisha' (a tanna of the first and second centuries) and a commentary on the tractate *Berakhot* of the Babylonian Talmud. In philosophy he published a treatise on direct syllogisms and supercommentaries on the *Middle Commentaries* and *Résumés* of Ibn Rushd (1126–1198). In medicine he is known to have written a remedy for the gout. In mathematics he composed a treatise on algebra and a commentary on parts of Euclid's *Elements.*

Finally, Gersonides published a major treatise on astronomy (1340), called *Sefer tekhunah* by Moritz Steinschneider, which consists of 136 chapters. (A summary of this more detailed work is contained in the second part of the fifth book of *The Wars of the Lord.*) What is of particular interest to historians of science is that the work contains significant modifications of the systems of Ptolemy and al-Biṭrūjī as well as useful astronomical tables. The work also includes a description of an instrument, which he calls a *magalleh 'amuqqot* ("detector of depths"), that he invented for making precise astronomical observations. The work was praised and extensively quoted by Pico della Mirandola in his *Disputationes in astrologiam.* In general Gersonides' instrument was considered the most useful tool developed to assist measurements in astronomy prior to the development of the telescope, and historians of science regard Gersonides as one of the most important European astronomers before Galileo.

The Wars of the Lord deals only with those questions that Maimonides either resolved in direct opposition to Aristotelian principles or explained so vaguely that Maimonides' own view cannot be determined. These questions are discussed in six treatises on (1) the nature of the soul (i.e., psychology), (2) prophecy, (3) God's knowledge, (4) divine providence, (5) the nature of the celestial spheres (i.e., cosmology), and (6) the eternity of matter (i.e., cosmogony).

In each treatise, every question is systematically discussed. First, Gersonides lists all of the different positions that had previously been taken on the issue in question. Second, he presents a critical analysis of each view; in so doing he lists every form of argument for each position and judges the extent to which each argument is and is not valid. Third, he states his own view. Fourth, he shows how each of the arguments given for other positions, to the extent to which they are valid, supports his own position. Fifth, he demonstrates that his position is in agreement with the correct meaning of the Torah.

Gersonides' theory of divine knowledge was the single most controversial part of his work. In the subsequent history of philosophy it led some Jewish thinkers to condemn his work (e.g., Shem Ṭov ibn Shem Ṭov, c. 1390–1440) and others to follow him (e.g., Barukh Spinoza, 1632–1677). Gersonides argued that all terms correctly predicated of God and man are such that those terms apply primarily to God and derivatively to humans. Hence, the term *knower* refers primarily to how God knows, and by reference to divine knowledge the term is applied to human beings. As their creator, God knows all things as they are essentially in and of themselves. In contrast, human beings, with the assistance of the Active Intellect, know these creations through their senses as effects. God knows everything, but he knows it in a single act of knowledge. The content of divine knowledge is expressible in human terms as an infinite conjunction of distinct universal, conditional propositions. Concerning each entity and fact, whereas human beings may know it accidentally, as a particular, through sense reports, God knows it essentially, as a unique individual, through his intellect. Gersonides' opponents interpreted this thesis to amount to a denial that God knows particulars with the consequence that God is limited in knowledge and power.

Possibly the most original part of Gersonides' work was his cosmology. The concluding treatise of *The Wars of the Lord* consists of a detailed demonstration, based on astronomy and physics, of the existence of the different heavenly intelligences (angels) and the uniqueness of the ultimate intelligence (God). In terms of philosophy and science this treatise constitutes the most sophisticated work of theology in the history of Judaism. In it he argues that this unending universe was created in time, not out of the remains of some previously existing universe but out of nothing. However, the "nothing" from which the world was created is not absolutely nothing; instead, it is an eternal, unformed matter, unlike any other matter of which we can conceive. Gersonides' account of this matter may be the most original part of the work. It is significantly different from the theory of prime matter found in any other work of Jewish, Muslim, or Christian philosophy. But to give an adequate account of it involves a technical discussion that goes beyond the confines of this essay. Suffice it to say that Gersonides' theory of prime matter bears some resemblance to the use by Hermann Cohen (1842–1918) of the term *origin* in his application of the infinitesimal calculus to ontology, and/or it may have parallels with the kind of high-energy radiation from which the universe originated, according to those astrophysicists who support the "Big Bang" theory.

[*For further discussion, see* Jewish Thought and Philosophy, *article on* Premodern Philosophy.]

BIBLIOGRAPHY

A full list of the published writings of Gersonides can be found in Bernhard Blumenkranz's *Auteurs juifs en France médiévale* (Toulouse, 1975), pp. 65–69. An extensive bibliography of secondary sources is given in Menachem M. Kellner's "Gersonides, Providence, and the Rabbinic Tradition," *Journal of the American Academy of Religion* 42 (1974): 673–685. An English translation of the entire *Wars of the Lord* is currently being prepared by Seymour Feldman for the Jewish Publication Society. In addition, there are three English translations of separate treatises, each of which contains valuable commentaries: on treatise 3, see my own *Gersonides' The War of the Lord, Treatise Three: On God's Knowledge* (Toronto, 1977); on treatise 4, see J. David Bleich's *Providence in the Philosophy of*

Gersonides (New York, 1973); and on treatise 6, see Jacob J. Staub's *The Creation of the World According to Gersonides* (Chico, Calif., 1982).

Gersonides' positions on divine knowledge and providence as well as his cosmogony are inherently connected with his cosmology. As yet no one has undertaken the difficult task of translating his treatise on astronomy. However, some light on his cosmology can be gleaned from Bernard R. Goldstein's "Preliminary Remarks on Levi Ben Gerson's Contribution to Astronomy," *Proceedings of the Israel Academy of Sciences and Humanities* 3 (1969): 239–254.

A useful introduction to the body of Gersonides' thought is Charles Touati's *La pensée philosophique et théologique de Gersonide* (Paris, 1973).

NORBERT M. SAMUELSON

LEVITES. [*This entry discusses the role of the* leviyyim *("Levites") and* kohanim *("priests") in Israelite religion and in Judaism. For further discussion of the concept of priesthood in Judaism, see* Priesthood, *article on* Jewish Priesthood.]

The origin of the Levites remains obscure despite considerable scholarly attention. Without contemporary documentation of the sort available on the larger societies of the ancient Near East, scholars must rely largely on the Hebrew Bible and later Jewish sources for information, making it difficult to trace the early development of this priestly group. What is known is that religious life in antiquity, from an institutional point of view, always required special places of worship with priests who were trained to perform cultic rites, make oracular inquiry, record temple business, and instruct worshipers on religious matters. Like the scribe, the priest had a set of skills unknown to most other members of society, and the need for skilled personnel generated a system of "schools" attached to temples and other cult centers to recruit, support, and educate priests. In ancient societies three factors interact: training and skill, family and clan, and place of residence. The family provided an ideal setting for teaching priestly skills and retaining exclusive control over them. In Israel, as elsewhere, families and clans tended to concentrate in certain locales, where their members lived in proximity to each other. Clans were not strictly ancestral, contrary to the impression made by certain biblical texts, and it was not uncommon to admit an outsider to learn the skills practiced by the clan, and eventually to grant clan membership as well.

Some biblical traditions regard the Levites as one of the original twelve tribes, whose members were collectively consecrated to cult service; other less systematic but perhaps more authentic biblical evidence regards them as a professional group, whose members came from various tribes and clans. Initially, priestly groups may have formed along professional lines, subsequently developing into clans and even larger units. Biblical writers probably began to regard the Levites as a tribe only after the interaction of training, locale, and family affiliation had progressed to a considerable degree. Biblical historiography has shown a strong tendency toward fitting social groups into neat, genealogical categories, which may account for the traditional identity of the Levites as a tribe.

Of the professional titles and terms used in Hebrew sources to designate priests of different types, the most common is *kohen* (pl. *kohanim*), cognates of which are found in the Ugaritic, Aramaic, Phoenician, and Arabic languages. The term *komer* ("priest"), with cognates in Akkadian, the el-Amarna dialect, and again Aramaic, is used in Hebrew scriptures only for pagan priests, and then rarely (*2 Kgs.* 23:5, *Hos.* 10:5, *Zep.* 1:4).

There is no feminine form for *kohen* because there was no role for women in the official Yahvistic cult of Israel. And yet there is a term for priestess, *qedeshah*, which literally means a (female) "consecrated person." (The masculine equivalent, *qadesh*, also occurs.) Based upon biblical evidence, these terms would be considered solely derogatory (e.g., *Dt.* 23:18, *Hos.* 4:14). However, in Ugaritic, *qadishuma* is an administrative term for priests and in Akkadian, *qadishtu* designates a priestess class widely known in the Old Babylonian period. Thus, biblical usage of *qedeshah* and *qadesh* as terms of derision to designate improper or pagan priests is more a matter of attitude than of nomenclature. The terms *kohen*, *komer*, and *qadesh/qedeshah* are professional titles.

A bigger problem arises in defining the term *levi* (Levite). A number of etymologies have been posed along professional lines, ranging from the notion of "carrying, bearing," to camping "around" the sanctuary. Poor documentation aside, what these etymologies are actually positing is more logical than linguistic, reflecting known cultic functions, such as carrying cultic artifacts, guarding temples, and so on. If the term derives from a single verbal root, it is not presently established and any definition must be according to context and usage.

Early History in Biblical Tradition. The earliest biblical reference to a *levi* is probably to be found in *Judges* 17–18. Micah, a man who lived somewhere in the Ephraimite hills before there was a monarchy in Israel, built a temple and installed in it several cult objects. He appointed one of his sons as priest. About that time, "a young man from Bethlehem, from the clan of Judah, who was a *levi*" (*Jgs.* 17:7), arrived at Micah's residence while en route to seek his fortune in northern Israel. After conversing with him, Micah invited him to live in his household and serve as priest in his temple; more precisely, to be a father (*av*) and priest (*kohen*). Micah offered him ten shekels of silver a year, clothing, and room and board. The *levi* accepted, and Micah was assured that God would grant him good fortune now that he had a *levi* of his own.

Chapter 18 opens with the tribe of Dan, then living in the southern plain, seeking territory elsewhere because of pressure from the Philistines. The Danites sent spies to northern Israel, where they stopped at Micah's home, and the *levi* assured them that God was with them. They later found suitable land in upper Galilee, and when the entire tribe began its migration northward, they once again stopped at Micah's home. The spies informed the others that valuable cult objects were to be found in the local temple, and they persuaded the young *levi* to abandon Micah and serve as priest for their tribe. The Danites stole Micah's cult objects, including a statue, an *efod* (a vestment with pockets, containing lots used in oracular divination), and *terafim* (statuettes that probably served as family gods). Then they proceeded to Laish, took it without an attack, and renamed it Dan, and thus the cult of Dan was established.

The story has all the earmarks of authenticity precisely because it does not conform to traditional notions about Yahvistic religion. The *levi* was of the clan of Judah and from Bethlehem. But it was his profession, as distinct from clan affiliation, that was valued all over the country, affording him a certain degree of mobility. He was appointed *av* and *kohen,* the former a term sometimes used to designate a "teacher" or "master," quite apart from its use in a familial sense.

From this story it could be concluded that a *levi* was a mobile professional who might have come from any tribe or clan, employed by a family or at a temple or other cult site, supported by them and serving at their pleasure. In contrast to other members of clans, who normally tended agricultural lands, a *levi* could move about. This portrait, probably more accurate for the early period of Israelite settlement than for the later, sheds light on the question of origins, and corrects the traditional and less historical picture found in biblical priestly literature.

Hebrew scriptures tell little about the status of Micah himself except that he owned a temple, which indicates that he was a local leader. Leading residents of towns built temples, appointing members of their own families as priests. Some biblical historians claim that in the early Israelite period the head of the clan or household was the priest, an image that seems to fit the patriarchs of Israel, who built altars and endowed cults.

An early story about the training of a priest is preserved in *1 Samuel* 1–3. Samuel, a cult prophet, officiated at sacrifices but also spoke with the authority of a prophet who communicated God's word to the people. Before his birth, he was dedicated to temple service by his mother, pledged as a *nazir* ("Nazirite") to serve all his life in the temple at Shiloh. This form of cultic devotion, which parents might perform for a variety of reasons, was one of the ways of recruiting priests. With Samuel the motive given was the gratitude of his onetime barren mother, but in reality economic deprivation often prompted parents to seek security for their sons in the priesthood. *1 Samuel* 2:36 intimates as much in predicting that the sinful priests of the House of Eli would beg to be accepted in a priestly group just to have bread to eat.

It was Eli, the chief priest of Shiloh, to whom young Samuel was brought by his mother. Samuel's prophetic role is anticipated by a divine theophany whose message Eli does not fail to comprehend. Samuel is taught the priestly arts by Eli, whose own sons were greedy and improper in the conduct of the sacrificial cult. Here we see an instance in which an outsider rose to prominence at a major temple, while the family that had controlled the priesthood lost power. The hereditary succession did not always work and one adopted into the priesthood might assume leadership if he had superior gifts. In *1 Chronicles* 6:13, the name of Samuel is inserted in a Levitical genealogy. At that late period, it would have been inconceivable that a legitimate priest and leader of the people such as Samuel would not have been the descendant of a Levitical clan.

The story of the Canaanite king of Salem, Melchizedek, characterized as "a priest of El, the most high," adds yet another dimension to the status of priests in early Israel. In *Genesis* 14 (by all accounts an early biblical text), Melchizedek greets the patriarch Abram (later Abraham) after a victorious battle fought against foreign kings. He blesses Abram in the name of his own god, El ʿElyon. Here the king of a Canaanite city-state serves as a priest, showing the priestly office to be a corollary of civil status.

Little else is known about priests, generally, in the premonarchic period. Quite coincidentally, *Judges* 19:1 reports that the man whose concubine was raped and murdered in Gibeah of Benjamin was a *levi* living in the Ephraimite hills. That he had originally taken a concubine from Bethlehem suggests that he, like Micah's *levi,* may also have been from Bethlehem.

Curiously, the term *levi* most often appears in north

Israelite literature. Indeed, it may be a north Israelite term for "priest," which would explain its general absence from Judahite sources and its occurrence in *Deuteronomy*, a book essentially northern in origin.

Monarchic period. The biblical narratives about Saul, the first king of Israel, reveal two aspects of the role of priests during the early monarchy. Saul employed an elderly professional priest, a descendant of Eli, from Shiloh (it having since been destroyed by the Philistines), who made oracular inquiry for Saul and the Israelite forces using the *efod* (*1 Sm.* 14). There is also the recurring theme of Saul's own involvement in priestly functions. At one point, Saul officiated at a sacrifice when, after seven days of waiting, Samuel failed to arrive (*1 Sm.* 13). Although Samuel was enraged over what Saul had done, it was probably in accordance with contemporary custom: kings often assumed sacral roles.

David also employed professional priests, appointing and dismissing them at will. The first priest he encountered was Ahimelech, priest of Nob—the town of priests (*1 Sm.* 21). Ahimelech sided with David against Saul, offering him and his band comfort and aid. Saul eventually murdered the priests of Nob, but one escaped, Abiathar, Ahimelech's son (*1 Sm.* 22:20f.), who joined David's forces and regularly undertook oracular inquiry for David (*1 Sm.* 23:10f., 30:7f.). Later, David had two priests with him, Ahimelech and Zadok, whose origins are not revealed (*2 Sm.* 8:17, 15:24). These two lines of priests continued to serve David throughout his career until a priest of the Abiathar line sided with David's son, Adonijah, in an attempt to claim the succession and this line of priests was rejected (*1 Kgs.* 1:7, 1:19). Solomon banished the priest to his hometown, and henceforth only the line of Zadok served the Judahite royal house (*1 Kgs.* 2:35). The list preserved in *1 Kings* 4:25, which still mentions Abiathar, is apparently a later source, showing how literary tradition often ignores historical sequence.

In priestly families, as in many royal lines, sons were named after their grandfathers, a method known as "papponymy," so that names like Zadok reappear in subsequent generations (*Ez.* 40:46).

The narratives of David and Solomon reveal how certain priestly families were appointed under the monarchy and were expected to be loyal to their royal sponsors. At one point David used the priest Zadok to spy for him and to report on Absalom's activities (*2 Sm.* 15:26f.).

Considerable information is found in the Bible about priestly families during the period of the Judahite and northern Israelite monarchies, but there is hardly any mention of Levites. *1 Kings* 12:31 states that Jeroboam I did a wicked thing by appointing non-Levitical priests to officiate at his heterodox temples, but this statement occurs in a later insertion into the text. For the most part, *Samuel* and *Kings* know nothing about a tribe of Levi.

The reference to Nob as a town of priests introduces the factor of locale. The law of *Leviticus* 25:32–34 provides tax exemptions for Levitical towns, justifying such exemptions by the fact that the Levites had no territory of their own. The same justification underlies the provisions in *Numbers* 35:1–8. Both are late texts.

The lists of *Joshua* 21 and *2 Chronicles* 6 present a different problem because they specifically name forty-eight Levitical towns, most of which have been located. Benjamin Mazar argues that these lists ultimately reflect the situation under the united monarchy of the tenth century BCE. According to Mazar, these towns were first established by David and Solomon as part of a system of royal outposts, especially in newly conquered territories.

Aside from the fact that these lists show signs of lateness, there is some difficulty in ascertaining whether the sites listed were actually settled by Israelites in the tenth century BCE. Recent archaeological surveys in Israel show a different pattern of early settlement. Then too Mazar must rest his case on the traditions of *Chronicles,* to the effect that Levites specifically were involved with David and Solomon. Given the generally biased character of *Chronicles,* these traditions may not reflect an earlier reality. In any event, the concentration of Levites in certain locales is logical in the earlier periods of biblical history, as is the existence of certain towns of asylum, often located where priests lived (*Nm.* 35:9f.).

Deuteronomy, essentially derived from the northern Israelite kingdom of the eighth century BCE, refers to all priests as Levites. Its classic designation is "the Levitical priests, the entire tribe [Heb., *shevet*] of Levi" (*Dt.* 18:1). Clearly, in the north Levites were regarded as having a tribal identity: all legitimate priests were Levites, and all Levites were priests.

From what *Deuteronomy* says about Levites elsewhere we note that the tribe of Levi was not like other tribes. Levites lived throughout the land (*Dt.* 14:26f.) and had no territory of their own, relying on cultic service for support (*Dt.* 18:6f.). The concern in *Deuteronomy* with the Levitical priests stems from its doctrine, expressed in chapters 12 and 16, that sacrifice is proper only at one central temple in a town to be selected by God. The habitation patterns of the Levites had corresponded to the decentralized pattern of worship at local and regional centers. Tithes and votaries remitted at these centers henceforth were to be collected only at a central temple. Once *Deuteronomy* legislated against the customary, decentralized pattern, provision had to be made for those Levitical priests who had served throughout the land. They therefore were granted the right to be maintained at the central Temple in Jerusalem, and assigned to cultic duties there.

The "Tribe of Levi." Current scholarship is only able to explain the traditions concerning a tribal origin for the Levites in broad, sociological terms. The biblical record of twelve tribes, into which that set of traditions fits, is questionable historically. The number twelve is maintained quite artificially in various tribal lists that sometimes include a tribe named Levi, sometimes not.

Apart from the genealogical recasting of the early Israelites, so characteristic of Priestly literature, the tradition of a tribe named Levi occurs in two poetic passages. In *Genesis* 49, Levi, the eponym of one of Jacob's sons, is the head of a tribe like all the others. Nothing is said about any cultic function associated with Levi, but there is the telling threat to disperse Levi throughout the Land of Israel, suggesting what came to be the real situation of the Levites.

In *Deuteronomy* 33, the Levites are a tribe, but a tribe of priests. This same chapter, verses 8 through 11, contains an oblique reference to the incident of the golden calf, recounted first in *Exodus* 32:26–29, and again in *Deuteronomy* 9:16f. Of all the Israelites, the Levites alone rallied to Moses' side. For their loyalty to God they were rewarded by being granted the Israelite priesthood. The cult of Yahveh was threatened when the golden calf, an allusion to the calves installed by Jeroboam I at Dan and Bethel, became the object of worship (*1 Kgs.* 12:29f.). The Levites are not characterized as a tribe, but rather as a group bound by the commitment to a proper Yahvistic cult that superseded their various tribal affiliations.

The reference to a tribe of Levi in *Genesis* 49 is less readily explained. Some historians have suggested that *Genesis* 49 is a very ancient passage that proves the early existence of a tribe called Levi. This is doubtful, because the incident of Shechem, recounted in *Genesis* 35, may be a late story of priestly origin.

Priests and Levites. The distinction between priest and Levite, basic to certain Priestly traditions, may have first emerged during the Babylonian exile. In *Ezekiel* 44:9f., the prophet, in his vision of a restored Temple in Jerusalem, favored the priestly line of Zadok exclusively. The Levites who had turned away from Yahveh (when, is not clear) were no longer to officiate at the cult, but were demoted (as it were) to supporting tasks in maintaining the Temple. In effect, the Levites were to take over tasks formerly performed by foreign workmen (or, perhaps, foreign Temple slaves), whose presence in the Temple was condemned by Ezekiel.

This is the first indication outside of the Priestly texts of the Torah of a differentiation between Levitical priests and ordinary Levites, laying the groundwork for the postexilic system wherein priests were considered superior to Levites. Most biblical historians have explained this distinction as a consequence of Josiah's edict (c. 622). Josiah had closed down the local *bamot* ("high places") and summoned the priests serving them to Jerusalem (*2 Kgs.* 23). The reconstruction that Ezekiel's heterodox Levites were, in fact, these priests is logical but still only conjecture.

Classes of priests, with differentiated functions, were characteristic of Near Eastern temples, and undoubtedly applied to the Temple in Jerusalem at one time or another. Conceivably, the poem of *Genesis* 49 served to explain the demotion of the Levites, which is attributed to some outrageous act.

Postexilic references to priests and Levites appear in *Ezra, Nehemiah,* and *Chronicles,* a pattern continuing through and even subsequent to the destruction of the Second Temple in Jerusalem in 70 CE. In *Kings,* as in *Jeremiah* with its strong historical orientation, priests are in charge of the First Temple, before the exile. Recent archaeological discoveries have added to information on the succession of high priests from the eve of the exile through to the Hellenistic and Roman periods. By correlating postexilic writings with the works of Josephus Flavius and apocryphal books such as *1 Esdras,* Frank Moore Cross (1975) uses the Aramaic Samaria papyri of the fourth century BCE to propose an uninterrupted succession of high priests. From Jehozadak, who served on the eve of the Babylonian exile, Cross moves forward to Simeon I, born in 320. Based on the custom of "papponymy," Cross traces the priestly names.

High-born priestly families, like those recorded in the lists of returning exiles in *Ezra* 2 and *Nehemiah* 7, owned estates outside of Jerusalem and probably derived their income from sources other than mere priestly emoluments. It can be logically assumed that of all the Jewish exiles in Babylonia, priestly families may have been particularly motivated to return to the Holy Land. By contrast, the Levites seem a deprived group in the early postexilic period. Ezekiel's differentiation between Zadokite priests and Levites may, in the last analysis, reflect the different economic standing of priestly families.

Thus far the history and formation of priestly groups in Israel have been discussed, but scripture highlights Priestly traditions on the origin and character of the priesthood that cannot be regarded historically, certainly not in detail. It would be fruitful to attempt a synthesis of history and tradition, both subjects for the historian but each requiring different methods in studying the past.

The Priestly traditions trace the origin of the priesthood, as well as the origin of the Yahvistic cult, to the time of Moses, prior to the settlement of Canaan. When we first encounter Aaron in the earliest traditions of *Exodus* (in the source known as JE, which combines Judean and north Israelite texts), he is Moses' brother certainly, but serves as a spokesman and emissary, and not as a priest. In *Exodus* 2:1f., Moses is affiliated with a Levitical family, and 4:14 refers to Aaron as "your brother, the *levi*," but these references are the work of the Priestly editors. The identification of Moses and Aaron as Levites was part of the overall Priestly historiography, linking the cult and the priesthood to the Sinai theophanies. [*See* Aaron.]

The consecration and investiture of Aaron and his sons as priests are themes woven into the Tabernacle texts of *Exodus* 24:12–31:18 and 35–40, and into *Numbers*, especially 1–10:28, and 26, as well as in the descriptions of the investiture of Aaron and his sons in *Leviticus* 8–10. G. B. Gray (1971) regarded Moses as a priest, primarily on the basis of Psalm 99:6. It is preferable, however, to interpret the Priestly traditions of the Torah as a mirror image of reality: Moses, like other leaders and like the Judahite and northern Israelite kings, is portrayed as a priest maker, not a priest. He oversees the transfer of priestly authority to Eleazar, Aaron's son, before Aaron's death (*Nm.* 20:22f.); Moses never actually performs cultic functions, apart from the investiture of the first priests. As for Psalm 99, it is actually a late, postexilic composition and it endorses the Aaronic priesthood.

Aaron the priest, as opposed to Aaron the person, is nowhere mentioned in *Deuteronomy*. A Priestly addendum in *Deuteronomy* 32:50 speaks of his death, and *Deuteronomy* 9:20f. merely retells the episode of the golden calf. Even in that episode, with its cultic context, Aaron functions as leader of the people. The Aaronic priesthood is never referred to in the historical books of the Bible—*Judges, Samuel, Kings*—except in a few interpolated passages (such as *Jgs.* 20:28).

It is in *Chronicles*, however, that Aaronic genealogies are presented in detail, much in the spirit of the Priestly writings of the Torah (*1 Chr.* 5–6, 23–24, etc.). In this fourth-century BCE recasting of early Israelite history, Aaronic priests are projected into the preexilic period of the Judahite monarchy, as though to compensate for their absence in *Samuel* and *Kings*. Julius Wellhausen (1957) was logical in concluding that the Priestly Torah traditions originated in the period of *Chronicles*, but it would be more precise to place them somewhat earlier in the postexilic period, the fifth century BCE.

Ezra, Nehemiah, and *Chronicles* present a dual situation: on the one hand, the Aaronic tradition, and on the other, evidence of a more historical character on the history of the priesthood. In *1 Chronicles* 5:27–41 Aaron and his sons launch the priestly line, but then the narrative returns to historical reality, listing known priestly families. In *1 Chronicles* 6:1–27 the names are entirely different, and generally match those in *Numbers*. Thus even within *Chronicles* a distinction must be drawn between history and tradition. The same is true in *Ezra* and *Nehemiah*.

This and other information confirms the unreliability of the Aaronic genealogy, while at the same time confirming the postexilic books as the repository of historical information, as well as tradition.

Yehoshu'a Ben Sira, a sage very much in the priestly tradition, writing in the late third or early second century BCE, endorses the Aaronic line (*Ben Sira* 50). Ellis Rivkin (1976) conjectures that beginning in the time of Ezra, around the mid-fifth century, a group of priests claimed descent from Aaron, and it was this group who promulgated the tradition of the Aaronic priesthood continued by Ben Sira.

The Torah also preserves Priestly traditions on the consecration of the Levites. In *Numbers* 8–10 the description of Levitical devotion parallels that of priestly investiture in *Leviticus* 8–10. The tasks of the Levites are set forth in *Numbers* 3–4 according to clans.

In the Priestly tradition, priests and Levites shared a common descent. All priests were of the tribe of Levi, but not all Levites were priests. *Nehemiah* 10 has the population registered in a stratified way: priests, Levites, and the people at large.

Organization. The internal organization of the Israelite priesthood probably changed little over the centuries, from the inception of the monarchies to the destruction of the Second Temple. A priest was usually in charge of a temple/cult center, and he was referred to simply as *ha-kohen* ("the priest") or as the priest of a particular locality or temple. The chief priest of Jerusalem in the near-exilic period was called *kohen ha-ro'sh* ("the head priest," *Jer.* 19:1), and the second in charge *kohen ha-mishneh* ("the deputy head"). The title *ha-kohen ha-gadol* ("the high priest") that occurs in several passages in *Kings* (*2 Kgs.* 22:10, 23:3f.) is probably a later designation based on the characterization of the head priest in the Holiness Code (*Lv.* 21:10) as *ha-kohen ha-gadol me-eḥav* ("the priest who is higher than his kinsmen"). From the fifth-century BCE Jewish mercenary community at Elephantine comes the Aramaic counterpart, *khn' rb'* ("the high priest"), and it is entirely possible that the Hebrew *ha-kohen ha-gadol* is a translation from the Aramaic. The Torah includes the epithet *ha-kohen ha-mashiaḥ,* "the anointed priest" (*Lv.* 4, 6), reflecting a Priestly tradition that has only Aaron receiving unctions, not his sons (*Lv.* 8:12). The rabbinic tradition has the additional title *ha-segan,* or *segan ha-kohanim* ("the director of the priests"); the term *segan* is a cognate of the Akkadian *shaknu* ("govern"). This terminology reflects the widely attested practice of applying political and administrative nomenclature to cultic offices (*Yoma'* 3.9, 4.1; *Tam.* 7.3). In *2 Kings* 19:2 we find the designation *ziqnei ha-kohanim* ("the elders of the priests"), perhaps the "curia" of the priesthood. In rabbinic literature, apprentice priests were called *pirḥei kehunah* ("the budding flowers of the priesthood," *Yoma'* 1.7, *Tam.* 1.1). Certain postexilic sources refer to *sarei ha-kohanim* ("the leaders of the priests," *Ezr.* 8:24) who had a role in governing the people.

The Mishnah (*Tam.* 3.1) mentions *ha-memunneh* ("the appointed priest"), who served either as an "officer of the day," or was in charge of a specific bureau or set of rites. In short, the priesthood of the Temples of Jerusalem was organized along royal, administrative lines.

From early times priests likely were assigned to Temple duty for one-week periods. Nehemiah is said to have instituted these *mishmarot* (*Neh.* 13:20; cf. *1 Chr.* 7:6) and indications are that this was the arrangement in the Jerusalem Temple during the monarchy. In *2 Kings* 11:5f., groups of priests are designated as *ba'ei ha-shabbat* ("going on duty on that Sabbath") and *yots'ei ha-shabbat* ("going off duty on that Sabbath"), suggesting weekly tours of duty for the priests.

Support Systems. While on duty, priests lived in the Temple complex, apart from their families; this arrangement helped ensure a state of purity.

Priests were supported by levies and donations, and enjoyed the privilege of partaking of sacred meals; their families also benefitted from Temple support. [*See* Tithes.] There is evidence, however, that as time went on, prominent priestly families amassed independent wealth and owned large estates.

Functions. The skills required for the priestly functions (see below) were learned from masters and based on written "instructions" (or manuals) called *torot* (sg. *torah*). The term *torah,* which has enjoyed wide applications in the Jewish tradition, derives from the priestly context: it is the priest who knows the *torah,* as is indicated in many biblical characterizations of the priesthood (*Jer.* 18:18, *Ez.* 7:26, *Hg.* 2:11). [*See* Torah.] In the Priestly laws of the Pentateuch captions such as *zo't ha-torah* ("this is the instruction," *Nm.* 19:2) and *zo't torat* ("this is the instruction for," *Lv.* 6:2) introduce guides for purification and sacrifices.

The Mishnah describes how priests were guided or directed step by step in the celebration of cultic rites. In ancient Egypt, officiating priests were actually followed around by a "lector priest" who held before him a tablet with precise instructions that he read aloud to the officiant. Failure to carry out the specific instructions could render the rite ineffective, disqualify the priest, and in severe cases defile the sanctuary.

In addition to their roles as skilled professionals, priests were consecrated persons. The Torah preserves detailed descriptions of the procedures followed in consecration (*Lv.* 8–10, *Ex.* 28–29), including prophylactic rites (involving the use of blood and oil), ablutions, and investiture—all accompanied by purification or expiatory sacrifices. Once consecrated, the priest officiated for the first time and partook of expiatory sacrifice.

The priestly vestments are described in *Exodus* 28 and are referred to in *Leviticus* 8 and 16. The high priest (Aaron was the first) wore distinctive garb; linen was used extensively, as was dyed cloth, and both were embroidered with gold. The high priest wore an *efod* decorated with twelve gemstones symbolizing the tribes of Israel, a breastpiece on which were sewn the binary oracles Urim and Tummim (two small stones), a headdress, diadem, robes, and pantaloons. These vestments were worn only while officiating, or when present in a sacred precinct.

Ezekiel's vision of the restored Temple (44:15f.) includes more information on priestly vestments as well as grooming: wool was to be avoided, and priests were to crop their hair but refrain from shaving their head. They probably officiated barefoot.

The priesthood was bound by a rigid law of purity. First were fitness requirements for officiating priests, who had to be free of blemishes, as were the sacrifices. Priests at all times were to avoid impurity, and as necessary would undergo purification in order to be readmitted to the Temple and allowed to officiate once again. The most severe impurity was contact with dead human bodies. According to their law, priests were forbidden to attend burials, which removed the cult of the dead from the priesthood's functions. An ordinary priest was permitted to attend the burial of his most immediate, consanguineous relatives, but even that was denied the high priest. Purity involved marriage law as well. A priest was forbidden to marry a divorced woman, since adultery was originally the basis of divorce; similarly unfit (at least in later law) was a woman who had committed harlotry, or whose fathers had been pronounced unfit for the priesthood. An improper wife would disqualify a priest's son from cultic service. A priest could only marry an Israelite, and the high priest only a virgin. [*For a cross-cultural discussion, see* Purification.]

All of these regulations originate in the Priestly laws of the Pentateuch and were expanded and variously applied by the rabbinic authorities of a later age. How early they applied is not certain, but they were in force during the early postexilic period. In late Second Temple times, priestly families kept marriage records and were presumed to adhere to a stricter code. *Ezra* 2 and *Nehemiah* 7 mention priests who had been declared impure, and removed from the priesthood on that account, an obvious reference to violations of the priestly marriage code.

Sacrificial and cultic functions. The primary responsibility of the priest was to officiate at sacrificial worship; quite possibly, others than priests may have officiated at certain periods in biblical history. As stated earlier, the priestly laws of the Pentateuch include the *torot* ("instructions") for this function, spelled out in detail. Apart from actually officiating, priests were undoubtedly responsible for sacrificial *matériel*—mixing spices and incense, preparing flour for grain offerings, and preparing proper oils for various purposes, including lighting of the *menorah* ("candelabra") and the like. According to the later pattern, Levites attended to certain of the preparations, but actual slaughtering of sacrificial animals was a priestly function.

The function of the priest as officiant was indispensable to the efficacy of the sacrificial cult, and priests were required to partake of sacrifices in sacred meals. Certain sacrifices were not valid if the priest failed to partake of them. The priests invoked God's blessing of the people on certain occasions; *Numbers* 6:24–26 preserves the text of the benediction. "May the Lord bless you and watch over you. May He cause the light of His countenance to shine over you, and may He be gracious to you. May the Lord lift His face toward you and grant you peace." The benediction was usually pronounced at the end of the sacrifice, when the priest emerged from the Temple and its inner courtyard to face the people. This blessing is one of the rare instances of recitation in the priestly laws of the Torah, which otherwise fails to preserve the many formulas employed by priests in the Israelite cult.

In addition to sacrificial *matériel,* priests were clearly responsible for maintaining the purity of the Temple and of all cultic utensils, vestments, and such. The Torah's priestly laws assign some of these "maintenance" tasks (*mishmeret*) to the Levites, but they usually required priestly supervision.

Oracular functions. Again, some of the earliest biblical references to priests are in connection with oracular activity. Micah and the Danites were served in this way by a young Levite, and the priests who accompanied Saul and David into battle provided similar service. Very likely the laws of *Deuteronomy* 20 are to be understood against the background of oracular inquiry. Before battle the Israelites were addressed by the priest, undoubtedly the high priest, who assured them that God would stand at the side of his people and grant them victory. The priest then stipulated certain deferrals and exemptions from military service, an act reminiscent of the ancient custom of "clearance" (in Akkadian, *tebibtu*), known from the archives of Mari, a Syrian capital of the eighteenth century BCE. Soldiers had to be "cleared" by checking to see if their obligations on the "home front" had been met. Presumably, the priest was asked whether the contemplated military venture had God's support. While priests provided such services most of the time, in some instances prophets advised kings in this way, as in *1 Kings* 22, a reflection of the overlapping of priestly and prophetic functions.

Most forms of divination were expressly forbidden in official Israelite religion, but surprisingly the casting of lots was not. The best known form of this practice was using the Urim and Tummim. Comparative evidence suggests that the Urim and Tummim consisted of two somewhat flat stones similar to the *puru* ("lots") known in Mesopotamia. The Tummim, a term derived from *tamam* ("perfect, without blemish"; hence, "innocent, right"), probably indicated an affirmative response, or a response establishing innocence. It is therefore assumed that Urim was negative, establishing guilt, although its precise meaning remains unclear. Casting lots was intended to yield a response: either the stones were similar to dice, each with affirmative and negative markings, or one was affirmative, the other negative.

The Urim and Tummim were kept by the priest in a pouch sewn into an embroidered cloth breastpiece. They are mentioned also in connection with the *efod,* a finely embroidered garment. In the depiction of the vestments of the high priest (*Ex.* 28, *Lv.* 8), the two stones were carried in a separate breastpiece, called *ḥoshen,* fastened to the *efod,* but it is quite obvious that they were an important part of the *efod,* the essential oracular vestment. The depiction of carved gemstones, symbolizing the tribes of Israel, further indicates the vestments' oracular function. The term *ḥoshen ha-mishpaṭ* ("breastpiece of judgment," *Ex.* 28:15, *Lv.* 8:8) reflects the use of the Urim and Tummim in determining guilt and innocence, a process also indicated by the phrase *mishpaṭ ha-urim* ("the judgment of the Urim," *Nm.* 27:21).

The casting of lots *(goral)* by priests was not always directly associated with the Urim and Tummim, at least not explicitly. In the Yom Kippur ritual (*Lv.* 16), the high priest cast lots to determine which of two goats was to be designated the scapegoat and which the sin offering. Priestly traditions, found primarily in *Numbers* and *Joshua,* portray the division of the Promised Land among the tribes by casting lots (*Nm.* 26, 33–36; *Jos.* 17–21). Priests again conducted the proceedings.

Oracular inquiry is generally viewed as characteristic of the earlier period of Israelite history, fading out as time went on, an opinion not borne out, however, in the priestly writings that give prominence to oracular, priestly functions. *Ezra* (2:63) and *Nehemiah* (7:65) each include a curious statement about the disqualification of certain priestly families among the returning Judahite exiles that, unable to produce genealogical records, were denied the right to partake of sacrificial meals, "until a priest with Urim and Tummim should appear."

It would be erroneous to minimize the lasting importance of oracular inquiry in early religion, a function shared by priests and prophets. The term *darash* (to inquire) often connotes oracular inquiry in biblical Hebrew, perhaps more often than is generally realized. Other than the casting of lots, very little is known about the mechanics of oracular inquiry in Israelite Jewish religion. [*See* Prophecy, *article on* Biblical Prophecy; *see also* Oracles.]

Therapeutic functions. *Leviticus* 13–15 prescribes a quasi-medical role for priests in the treatment of skin ailments that were considered contagious, and that in similar form appeared as blight on leather, cloth, and plaster-covered buildings and stones. Such a role was assigned to priests in other parts of the ancient Near East; Mesopotamian magical texts, for instance, speak of the activities of the *ashipu* ("magical practitioner") who combined magical and sacrificial activity with medical methods to heal the afflicted, often "purifying" them through exorcism. In *Leviticus* the priest orders quarantine, examines patients, shaves the hair of the afflicted, and diagnoses skin ailments on the basis of a set of given symptoms, observing the course of the disease. Along with these procedures, he conducts expiatory rites, involving the utilization of sacrificial blood in magic, as well as making sanctuary offerings. It is the priest who declares one either "impure" or "pure."

Such functions were akin to the instructional and juridical roles of the priest: all involved interpreting the contents of the priestly *torot* ("instructions"). As with oracular inquiry, these functions were probably shared by prophets and other "men of God."

Instructional and juridical functions. The cult role of the priest cast him in a sacred, somewhat detached light, for he officiated within sacred precincts from which the people at large were excluded. In contrast, the instructional and juridical functions of the priesthood, like the less known therapeutic ones just discussed, brought the priesthood into contact with the people. The same applies to its administrative role discussed later.

The instructional and juridical roles were, of course, closely interrelated. *Ezekiel* 44:23–24 gives a fairly comprehensive definition of these priestly functions:

> They [the Zadokite priests] shall declare to My people what is sacred and what is profane, and inform them what is pure and what is impure. In lawsuits, too, it is they who shall act as judges: they shall decide therein in accordance with My rules. They shall preserve My teachings and My laws regarding all My fixed occasions, and they shall maintain the sanctity of My Sabbaths.

In *Deuteronomy* 17:8f., we read that a court was to be located in the central temple of the land where priests and magistrates could hear cases referred to them by local and regional courts. The high court of the Jews, the Sanhedrin, convened in the Temple complex and was composed largely of priests. The early Pharisees, members of a lay movement, eventually gained predominance in the courts, but not until after the destruction of Jerusalem's Second Temple.

The epitome of the instructional role of the priest is preserved in *2 Kings* 17:24f. Foreigners settling in northern Israel (Samaria) following its annexation by the Assyrians in 722 suffered misfortunes, and they attributed their sad state to not knowing how to worship "the god of the land" properly. Sargon, the Assyrian king, sent back an Israelite priest who established residence in Bethel. "He went about instructing the people how they should worship Yahveh" (*2 Kgs.* 17:28). The verb *horah* is most often used to convey the instructional role of the priests, who answered the questions brought to them by the people and their leaders.

The early exilic prophecy of Haggai (*Hg.* 2:11–13) contains an actual inquiry that, although it was rhetorical and symbolic in the prophetic context, is worded precisely; it is dated to 520:

> Inquire of the priests *torah* ["instruction"] as follows: If a person should carry sacrificial flesh in a fold of his garment, and if this fold should touch bread, stew, wine or oil, or any other foodstuffs, would it [that foodstuff] become sacrificial?
>
> The priests responded by saying, "No!"
>
> Haggai continued: Should a person impure by reason of contact with a dead human body touch any of these materials, would it [that foodstuff] be rendered impure?
>
> The priests responded by saying, "It would become impure!"

An entire body of ancient Near Eastern literature of priestly texts has to do with the interpretation of dreams, often a function of the priest. Indeed, the instructional and juridical roles of the priesthood would be clearer if similar Israelite texts had survived. [*For discussion of dream interpretation in a cross-cultural context, see* Dreams.]

Administrative and political functions. In addition to conducting the cult of worship, priests were responsible for the overall administration of the Temple and its affairs.

Temple business. The Temples of Jerusalem were hubs of activity: worshipers often purchased sacrifices in the Temple bureaus; they remitted votary pledges (the so-called vows); they paid their dues (tithes to the Levites, and in later times priestly levies, the firstlings of the herd and flocks). In *2 Kings*, chapters 12 and 22, we learn that Temple business was administered by the priests often in collaboration with agents of the king. In the postexilic recasting of these earlier accounts, such as in *2 Chronicles* 24, priests and Levites are sent out to collect dues from the people, as well as voluntary contributions for the Temple.

Maintenance. Cult vessels had to be replaced and purified from time to time, as did the Temple. The Temple complex had to be kept in good repair, and priestly vestments fashioned. Temple maintenance meant not only repair but purifi ation, and the priesthood was in charge of these activities.

In the postexilic period when Jerusalem and Judah were under foreign domination, the high priest and heads of other important priestly families often served as heads of the Jewish community, especially in conducting its relations with the imperial authorities. This political arrangement is referred to as "hierocracy," government by priests. Something of this atmosphere colors the *Letter of Aristeas,* which reports on delegations to the high priest of Jerusalem, and the writings of Josephus of the first century CE.

Throughout most of the period of the Second Temple the power of the priesthood was more than it had been in the preexilic period. In the wake of the Hasmonean Revolt (167–164 CE) the priests assumed both political and spiritual power, a situation that lasted for about a century and correlated well with the imperial policy of various foreign rulers throughout their empires.

The political function of the priesthood is more specific during the postexilic period, although it is likely that, as in most societies, leading priests had exercised power and influence under Judahite and northern Israelite kings as well. Whereas such earlier historic books as *Samuel* and *Kings* are primarily concerned with the monarchy, and therefore say little about priestly power, it is the later *Chronicles* that create the myth of deep cooperation between the two establishments—the royal and the sacerdotal—especially during the reign of the "upright" Judahite kings.

In the postexilic period, Levites had specific functions distinct from priests. In *Numbers* 1–4, Levites are assigned the task of guarding the sanctuary, in addition to "bearing" its appurtenances, and other duties. They are encamped around it, barring entry to all unfit to approach the sacred precincts. This role coincides with the postexilic *Ezra, Nehemiah,* and *Chronicles* concerning Levitical "gatekeepers" (*Neh.* 7:1, *1 Chr.* 9:18). In the later literature Levites are also the Temple singers and musicians, a role further suggested by some of the captions in *Psalms,* attributing them to Levitical authors, members of musical guilds, and affiliates of the Levitical clans, such as "the sons of Koraḥ."

Postexilic traditions also speak of Levites as "teachers, interpreters" (*Ezr.* 8:16, *Neh.* 8:7, *2 Chr.* 35:3), thereby endorsing the ancient instructional role of priestly and Levitical groups as teachers. Levitical names have turned up at Arad, in the Negev, during the late preexilic period, thus affirming that such families were assigned to royal outposts where there were also temples.

Worship was never the end-all of religious life in biblical and later Jewish traditions, and prophets continually criticized the common belief that God was more desirous of praise than of obedience to his laws. The prophet Samuel put the matter as follows (*1 Sm.* 15:22): "Does the Lord delight in burnt offerings and sacrifices, as much as in obedience to the Lord's command?" And yet, it was through the institution of religion, as conducted by sanctified and trained priests, that the people of Israel were able to secure the presence of God, in sacred places and in celebration. No institution was more volatile, more subject to abuse and exploitation than the priesthood (except, perhaps, the monarchy and political leadership), and none was more indispensable to the expression of Israel's unique religion. Whereas the Hebrew scriptures and later Jewish literature never spared priests from criticism and rebuke and faithfully recorded their misdeeds from Aaron to Menelaus, the same tradition held forth the idea of the devout and learned priest:

> True teaching was in his mouth,
> Nothing perverse was on his lips.
> He served Me with complete loyalty,
> And held the many back from iniquity.
> For the lips of a priest preserve knowledge,
> And men seek instruction from his mouth.
> For he is a messenger of the Lord of Hosts!
> (*Mal.* 2:6–7)

[*For further discussion of the priestly functions, see* Biblical Temple. *For the context within which the priesthood functioned, see* Israelite Religion.]

BIBLIOGRAPHY

The higher critical point of view regarding the development of Israelite religion and its priestly institutions, according to which these are relatively late phenomena in biblical history, is best presented in Julius Wellhausen's *Prolegomena to the History of Ancient Israel,* translated by J. Sutherland Black (1885; reprint, New York, 1957). In contrast, Yeḥezkel Kaufmann's *The Religion of Israel,* translated and abridged by Moshe Greenberg (Chicago, 1960), offers a learned argument against the higher position, insisting on the greater antiquity of priestly institutions.

The best, and virtually the only, overall history of the Israelite priesthood is Aelred Cody's *A History of Old Testament-Priesthood* (Rome, 1969). G. B. Gray's *Sacrifice in the Old Testament* (1925), reissued with a prolegomena by myself (New York, 1971), devotes a section to the priesthood (pp. 179–270), analyzing its character primarily on the basis of the biblical textual evidence, and that of postbiblical ancient sources.

Several recent encyclopedia articles summarize and assess scholarly research. They include: Menahem Haran's "Priests and Priesthood," in *Encyclopaedia Judaica* (Jerusalem, 1971); my own "Priests," and Ellis Rivkin's "Aaron, Aaronides," in *Interpreter's Dictionary of the Bible: Supplementary Volume* (Nashville, 1976).

New light is shed on the history of the high priesthood by Frank Moore Cross in his "A Reconstruction of the Judean Restoration," *Journal of Biblical Literature* 94 (1975): 4–18, drawing on the evidence of the Samaria Papyri of the fourth century BCE. The religious and political roles of the postexilic priesthood, in particular, are discussed with considerable insight in Morton Smith's *Palestinian Parties and Politics That Shaped the Old Testament* (New York, 1971). The less explored functions and status of the Levites, as distinct from priests, are investigated, on the basis of biblical terminology, in Jacob Milgrom's *Studies in Levitical Terminology,* 2 vols. (Los Angeles and Berkeley, 1970–1974). All of the above references provide extensive bibliographical information.

The reader will also want to consult ancient sources outside the Bible referred to in this article. The best available English translation of the Mishnah is Herbert Danby's *Mishnah* (Oxford, 1933). The writings of the ancient historian Josephus Flavius, translated by Henry St. J. Thackeray and Ralph Marcus, are available in volumes 1–5 and 7 of the "Loeb Classical Library" (Cambridge, Mass., 1950–1961). *The Apocrypha and Pseudepigrapha of the Old Testament,* 2 vols., edited by R. H. Charles (Oxford, 1913), includes such works as *Ben Sira. Aristeas to Philocrates, or the Letter of Aristeas* has been edited and translated by Moses Hadas (New York, 1951).

The discoveries at Arad, a Negev site principally excavated by the late Yohanan Aharoni, have been carefully summarized in the article by Ze'ev Herzog and others, "The Israelite Fortress at Arad," *Bulletin of the American Schools of Oriental Research* 254 (Spring 1984): 1–34. The inscriptions, originally published with a Hebrew commentary by Aharoni, have been translated by Judith Ben-Or and edited and revised by Anson F. Rainey as *Arad Inscriptions* (Jerusalem, 1981). These inscriptions and the information received from the excavations shed light on the functioning of Levitical priests at such royal outposts as Arad in the late preexilic period.

BARUCH A. LEVINE

LEVI YITSḤAQ OF BERDICHEV (c. 1740–1810), Hasidic master and among the best-beloved figures of the east European Jewish folk tradition. Born into a distinguished rabbinical family, Levi Yitsḥaq joined the circle of disciples around Dov Ber of Mezhirich (Międzyrzecz, Poland) in 1766. He served as rabbi of Richwal, Żelechów, and Pinsk before being appointed to the important Ukrainian rabbinate of Berdichev in 1785. As both statutory rabbi and Hasidic *rebe* of that city for twenty-five years, he made Berdichev a center of Hasidic influence and played an important role as a leader of Russian Jewry. While in his earlier rabbinical positions he had been hounded by the *mitnaggedim* (the "opponents" of Hasidism; he was apparently deposed in both Żelechów and Pinsk), his strong position in Berdichev allowed him to serve as convener of rabbinical conferences, author of important communal legislation, and defender of Hasidism from attack. He also worked to ameliorate the oppression of the Jews by their newly acquired Russian masters, but to little avail. Better known are his reputed attempts to "storm the gates" of heaven, demanding of God, sometimes in harsh terms, that he better the lot of his beloved Israel. It is this image of Levi Yitsḥaq as defender of Israel and advocate of individual Jews before the heavenly tribunal that is especially prevalent in the later folk literature. The relationship between the Levi Yitsḥaq of these tales and the actual historical figure has yet to be tested.

Widely revered among the Ḥasidim even in his own day, Levi Yitsḥaq worked to stem the growing discord within the Hasidic movement at the turn of the nineteenth century. He served as intermediary in the disputes between his friend, Shne'ur Zalman of Lyady, and Barukh of Medzhibozh, as well as in Barukh's dispute with his own nephew, the young Naḥman of Bratslav.

The homilies of Levi Yitsḥaq, *Qedushat Levi,* were issued in two parts; the extended treatises on the meaning of Ḥanukkah and Purim were published during his lifetime (Slavuta, U.S.S.R., 1798), while the better-known treatment of the weekly Torah portions were edited after his death and appeared in Berdichev in 1811. This work was largely a popularization of Dov Ber's teachings but in a readable and homiletically creative setting.

Levi Yitsḥaq was a sounding board for all the major ideas of Dov Ber's circle, and all are well represented in *Qedushat Levi.* The call for ecstatic self-negation in *devequt* (communion with God) is adumbrated but is coupled with warnings about its potentially antinomian implications. Levi Yitsḥaq was well aware of the more radical implications of Hasidic teaching and sought to warn against them. Thus he places in the mouth of the snake in Eden the notion that since all things are created by God there can be no category of the forbidden; he saw the authority of the *mitsvot* (commandments) potentially challenged by the notion, so loudly and uncompromisingly proclaimed in the early Hasidic movement, that all is holy. He agreed with the elevation of the *tsaddiq* (holy man) to a place of primacy in Hasidic Judaism and speaks of the cosmic power such a figure has in the ongoing development of Torah. The sense of communal responsibility he felt as rabbi is frequently reflected in his homilies, in which there is also to be seen a touch of regret about the fate of his own intense spiritual life, as he was forced to devote his energies to communal matters.

[*For further discussion of Levi Yitsḥaq in his historical and religious context, see* Hasidism, *overview article.*]

BIBLIOGRAPHY

The biography by Samuel H. Dresner, *Levi Yitzhaq of Berditchev: Portrait of a Hasidic Master* (New York, 1974) retells the traditional tales but also contains notes of scholarly interest. Michael J. Luckens's "Rabbi Levi Yitzhak of Berdichev" (Ph.D. diss., Temple University, 1974) surveys both the life and thought of Levi Yitsḥaq.

Arthur Green

LÉVY-BRUHL, LUCIEN (1857–1939), French philosopher and sociologist. Lévy-Bruhl devoted most of his attention to the analysis of the human mind in primitive societies. He studied mental functions and mystical experience, symbols and myths, and notions of the soul and of the supernatural.

Lucien Lévy-Bruhl was born in Paris. A student at the École Normale Supérieure, he passed his *agrégation* in philosophy in 1870. He then taught successively at three *lycées*. In 1884 he was awarded the *docteur ès-lettres* with a thesis on the idea of responsibility. At the École des Sciences Politiques, he gave a remarkable course of lectures on the history of ideas in Germany since Leibniz. As senior lecturer (1895) and then professor (1907) at the Sorbonne, he taught the history of modern philosophy and developed his ideas about primitive peoples. He became the editor of the *Revue philosophique* in 1916, was elected to the Académie des Sciences Morales et Politiques in 1917, and, with Paul Rivet and Marcel Mauss, founded the Institute d'Ethnologie.

Without ever openly disagreeing with Émile Durkheim, Lévy-Bruhl diverged from the leader of the French sociological school—a divergence that was made apparent when his book *La morale et la science des mœurs* (1904) criticized Durkheim's theory of *métamorales* and what he took to be Durkheim's confusion of moral philosophy with the sociology of moral life. In *Les fonctions mentales dans les sociétés inférieures* (1910), Lévy-Bruhl examined what he took to be fundamentally different kinds of mental activity. This work sought to establish the existence of a "primitive" mentality, an attitude of mind characterized by mystic participations and exclusions and by alogical liaisons not subject to the principle of contradiction.

In *La mentalité primitive* (1922), he emphasized the difference between the "primitive mind" and the "civilized mind." These terms describe the distinctive tone or quality of the "collective representations" of two basic types of society. A society finds representation in the concepts and beliefs of its members; the members share a mental attitude and hence a manner of experiencing the world.

According to Lévy-Bruhl, the "primitive" mentality and the "civilized" mentality each embodies its own irreducible logic: respectively, the magico-religious and the critical. Differing conceptions of causality and representations of time and space define these contrasting modes of thought. The magico-religious, or "prelogical" mentality, judges no event (e.g., accident, sickness, death) to be natural and fortuitous but instead attributes it to the direct action of supernatural powers belonging to an invisible extraspatial and extratemporal world. Dreams, omens, divinatory practices, and ordeals are given great importance as signs of a primary mystic causality, the only truly efficient cause. Without the critical mentality's concern for the causal interconnections of phenomena, the "primitive" mind is indifferent to secondary causation. Immediate and intuitive, the "primitive" concept of causation does not employ the inductive method of the scientific West.

In *L'âme primitive* (1927) Lévy-Bruhl argues that the "primitive" personality appears stronger than the "civilized" personality, because the ego and the cosmos are integrated there through a network of mystic relations. In his later works, Lévy-Bruhl develops the notion of the "law of participation," according to which various aspects of reality comprise a single mystical unity based on resemblance, contrast, or contiguity and thereby enable a being to be simultaneously himself and something other. This "law of participation" is a way of living, of acting, and of being acted upon. Lévy-Bruhl attempts to show that symbols are the vehicles of participation; he claims that extrarational reality does not permit itself to be systematized into a conceptual framework.

Lévy-Bruhl's theories were controversial in their day and met criticism from a variety of perspectives. Most contemporary anthropologists have rejected the notion of a specifically primitive mentality. In his posthumous *Carnets* (1949), Lévy-Bruhl himself considerably tempers the difference between prelogical and logical mentalities, showing that they coexist to various degrees in all kinds of societies and that participatory thought is never entirely eclipsed by pure rationality.

BIBLIOGRAPHY

Several works by Lévy-Bruhl have been translated. These works include *Les fonctions mentales dans les sociétés inferieures* (Paris, 1910), translated as *How Natives Think* (London, 1926); *La mentalité primitive* (Paris, 1922), translated as *Primitive Mentality* (New York, 1923); *L'âme primitive* (Paris, 1927), translated as *The "Soul" of the Primitive* (New York, 1928); and *Le surnaturel et la nature dans la mentalité primitive* (Paris, 1932), translated as *Primitives and the Supernatural* (New York, 1935). Two additional works, though not translated, deserve to be mentioned: *La mythologie primitive* (Paris, 1935) and *L'experience mystique et les symboles chez les primitifs* (Paris, 1938).

For a brief assessment of the context and application of Lévy-Bruhl's theories, see the chapter entitled "Lévy-Bruhl" in E. E. Evans-Pritchard's *Theories of Primitive Religion* (Oxford, 1965). The repercussions of Lévy-Bruhl's notion of mystic participation are examined in Jonathan Z. Smith's article, "I Am a Parrot (Red)," *History of Religions* 11 (May 1972): 391–413. For discussions of his life and work, see Jean Cazeneuve's *Lucien Lévy-Bruhl* (Paris, 1963), translated under the same title (New York, 1972); and Georges Davy's *Sociologues d'hier et d'aujourd'hui*, 2d ed. (Paris, 1950).

Claude Rivière
Translated from French by G. P. Silverman-Proust

LEWIS, C. S. (1898–1963), Anglican scholar, novelist, and theologian. Clive Staples Lewis was born in Belfast on 29 November 1898. As a boy he read omnivorously and wrote remarkably imaginative stories about a world he called Boxen. He was educated at Malvern College, and then privately. Soon after discovering Celtic and Norse mythology, in 1913, he became convinced that Christianity was one of the inferior mythologies of the world and that God, if he existed, was a cosmic sadist. After one term at University College, Oxford, in 1917, he went to France with the Somerset Light Infantry, and on 15 April 1918 he was wounded in the Battle of Arras. Upon his return to Oxford in 1919 he took First class degrees in classics, philosophy, and English. Between 1925 and 1954 he was the fellow of English language and literature at Magdalen College, Oxford, and he won acclaim as a medievalist for *The Allegory of Love* (1936).

Lewis's efforts to keep God at bay gave way slowly as he began to find his own arguments philosophically untenable. His friend and colleague J. R. R. Tolkien (1892–1973) did much to unsettle his atheism when he convinced Lewis that the Christain myth differed from all others in that it ended in the Word made flesh. After his conversion in 1931, Lewis published the partly autobiographical *The Pilgrim's Regress* (1933), whose main theme is that our experiences of inconsolable longing (which he was later to call "joy") are longings for and pointers to God. Another theme of the book—afterward developed in his *Miracles* (1947)—is that, while all mythologies contain hints of divine truth, Jewish mythology was chosen by God and culminates in myth becoming fact. A clearer account of Lewis's almost purely philosophical conversion is his autobiography, *Surprised by Joy* (1955).

Lewis was happiest with a few male friends, and especially at the weekly meetings of the "Inklings," a group that included his brother Warren (1895–1973), Tolkien, Merton College English scholar Hugo Dyson (1896–1975), the novelist Charles Williams (1886–1945), the philosopher Owen Barfield (b. 1898), and a few others. The influence of these men on Lewis was important, as they read and criticized one another's writings.

Lewis relished "rational opposition," and in debate his inexorable logic was unanswerable. His *Abolition of Man* (1943) is considered one of the most carefully reasoned defenses of natural law ever formulated. Able to adapt to any audience, Lewis became well known in Britain from his talks over the BBC in 1941–1944, which were expanded into the book *Mere Christianity* (1952). One of his most popular works, *The Screwtape Letters* (1942), was rapturously received in America. These and many other books established him as a brilliant and lucid defender of orthodox, supernatural Christianity, and through them he won a wide hearing for Christianity. A great many people have been introduced to Christian ideas through Lewis's three science fiction novels, of which the first is *Out of the Silent Planet* (1938), and his seven fairy tales of the mythical land of Narnia, beginning with *The Lion, the Witch and the Wardrobe* (1950). A brilliant popularizer of the faith and an apologist acceptable to an exceptionally wide spectrum of Christians, Lewis, through his books, sheds light from unexpected angles on the faults and foibles of men and women. Lewis was made professor of medieval and Renaissance literature at Cambridge University in 1955. In 1956 he married Joy Davidman Gresham, who died in 1960. Lewis died at Oxford on 22 November 1963.

BIBLIOGRAPHY

For a complete list of C. S. Lewis's writings, see my "Bibliography of the Writings of C. S. Lewis," in *C. S. Lewis at the*

Breakfast Table, and Other Reminiscences, edited by James T. Como (New York, 1979), pp. 250–276. *Miracles: A Preliminary Study,* rev. ed. (New York, 1960), is Lewis's most solid work of theology, and *Mere Christianity* (London, 1952) is his most popular. For information about Lewis, see his *Surprised by Joy: The Shape of My Early Life* (London, 1955) and *C. S. Lewis: A Biography,* by Roger Lancelyn Green and myself (London, 1974).

WALTER HOOPER

LI. The homophones *li* and *li,* two distinct Chinese graphs, are seminal concepts in Chinese moral philosophy and metaphysics. Although they are both pronounced the same in the modern Peking dialect, they differed in ancient pronunciation and were originally unrelated: one *li,* meaning "principle," terminated in the consonant sound *g,* according to Karlgren's reconstruction, while the other, meaning "rites," ended in the consonant sound *r.* While the meaning and usage of these terms converge to some extent, they will be discussed separately in this article.

Li as Principle. The root graph for this *li* combines the elements "field divided into sections for planting" with "earth," and means "village." To this is added the element "jade," in consequence of a derived meaning—thought by later philosophers to be the original sense—"cut and polish jade" so as to make its inner pattern of veins visible. The original meaning as found in the *Shih ching* (Classic of Odes), however, apparently was to mark out divisions in a field for planting, and so to organize it for agricultural work. Thus *li* has the senses "put in order," "govern," and the resulting (good) "order" in society, as well as "inner structure." In antiquity these senses already converge in the sense "natural order or structure."

In the *Meng-tzu* the word occurs in a moral sense in the term *li-i,* "order and right," which Meng-tzu says is what "all human hearts have in common" and what naturally "pleases" our moral sensibility (6A.7). By the early Han dynasty, the term had gone through a semantic evolution: from just "patterns observable here and now" to patterns in temporal extention; hence a pattern developing through history; hence potential or ideal as well as what is actual; hence not only patterns observed in particulars but also general patterns in types or classes; and hence also one overarching pattern through time, branching out from a simple beginning to the complexity of observables in the present; thus both one and many, both explanatory and normative. The *Huainan-tzu* (c. 130 BCE) says, "As for the *tao,* when unity is established the myriad creatures are produced. For this reason, the *li* of unity permeates the entire world, and the expansion of unity reaches the bounds of Heaven and earth." This sense is further developed by Wang Pi (226–249), who speaks of *chih li* ("ultimate *li*"), and Kuo Hsiang (d. 312). However, one already finds the expression *t'ien li* ("heavenly" or "natural" *li*) in *Chuang-tzu* and in the *Li chi. Li* thus approaches the sense of a single first "principle," intelligible but distinct from sensible phenomena, linked with *tao* and Heaven. It was not yet, perhaps, an object of religious awe.

The word acquired this religious sense when Buddhists, realizing its importance, appropriated it to refer to the primary object (and state) of saving contemplation. The *Sutra in Forty-two Sections* (c. 100 CE) says that the saint who has cut ties to the world "attains to the deep *li* of Buddhahood," gaining enlightenment and *nirvāṇa.* Chih Tun (314–366) uses the word interchangeably with the Taoist *wu* ("nothing" or "nonbeing") and the Buddhist *k'ung* (Skt., *śūnyatā;* "emptiness"), the ultimately real character ("divine *li*") of things. Still later, proponents of Hua-yen Buddhism such as Tu-shun (557–640), retreating from the negativistic Mādhyamika terminology of *k'ung* and *se* ("phenomena"), offered a dualism of *li* ("principle"?) and *shih* (things and events), in which *li* are both one and many, "pervading" and "pervaded by" *shih,* so that the one-and-many *li* of everything is instanced, for example, in each mote of dust.

The word next is repossessed by the Confucians of the Sung and following dynasties; *li* is now both one and many, it becomes the object of religious veneration insofar as it is identified with their first principle, under various names and aspects—*t'ai chi* ("supreme ultimate"), *tao* ("way"), *t'ien* ("heaven"), and *hsing* ("human nature"). In the dualism of Ch'eng I (1033–1108), *li,* "principle(s)," sometimes redescribed as *tao,* is "above form" *(hsing erh shang),* while *ch'i,* "embodiments," are "within form" *(hsing erh hsia).* Different attempts were made to overcome this dualism by such thinkers as Lu Hsiang-shan, Wang Yang-ming, and Tai Chen; some of them (Lu, Wang, but also even Ch'eng I himself) identified *li* with *hsin* ("mind"). *Li* is (are) both normative *(tang-jan)* and explanatory-descriptive *(so-i-jan).* As described by Ch'eng I and Chu Hsi, after long study *(ko-wu,* "investigating things") the Confucian sage attains a sudden unitary vision of all *li.* The concept is often illustrated by reference to natural objects; however, the Confucians usually have in mind the "principles" of social institutions and relationships.

Li as Rites. The graphic root of this *li* represents a type of ritual vessel (called a *li*), to which is added the graph for "altar stand," an element commonly marking graphs for religious objects or activities. The basic sense was "religious rite." By the time of the earliest moral-philosophical writings the term had already taken on an expanded meaning: not merely a rite in a religious ceremony, but formal, patterned behavior of any kind, from court ceremonial—and hence, the functions and duties of officials—to the ordinary forms of everyday polite behavior. In early Confucian writings great attention was paid to *li* in all senses; Confucius frequently complained about eminent people's use of ceremonials to which they were not by rank entitled. Some schools of his followers specialized in the study and practice of *li*. Of particular importance were observances for the dead, such as the three-year period of mourning for parents *(Meng-tzu* 3A.1–3).

As the meaning evolved during the first millennium BCE two concurrent tendencies developed. First, there was a progressive secularization of certain originally religious concepts, not only "rite" but also Heaven *(t'ien)*. This latter term originally denoted an anthropomorphic deity, but by the third century BCE it had become for many simply the physical heaven and the order of nature. [*See* T'ien.] The other tendency was a persisting sacralization of the concept of ordinary civilized behavior (Fingarette, 1972). Both of these developments came to fruition in the subtle moral philosophy of Hsün-tzu, in whose writings the ubiquitous term *li-i* ("rites-and-right") means in effect "morality," much like *jen-i* in Mencian thought. [*See* Jen and I.] Hsün-tzu was cognitively and explicitly atheist, yet attitudinally deeply religious, devoting a major chapter to the utility, beauty, and cosmic appropriateness of *li*. Earlier, Meng-tzu had taken *li*, in the sense of a disposition to propriety, as one of man's four natural virtues.

The different sorts and aspects of *li* were explained and cataloged in a group of the Confucian classics that probably date from Han times (with older material): the *Chou li*, on the organization of the early Chou state and functions of its officers; the *I li*, on ceremonies in everyday life; and the *Li chi*, which contains miscellaneous treatises on ritual and related moral-philosophical matters, and which was probably the cumulative product of Han court specialists on ritual.

Li has continued to have a double importance in Confucian moral thought. On the one hand, its observance is evidence of the moral health of society or of the individual. On the other hand, observing the rites is thought to develop moral character and the moral health of society (see Ou-yang Hsiu's *Pen lun*). The *li*, therefore, are thought of as the patterns of behavior of a good society, a good government, or a good life.

In this sense the concept overlaps with the *li* meaning "pattern" or "principle." The convergence of *li* and *li* was noticed by Hsün-tzu: "Music [i.e., the standard modes and traditional pieces] is harmonies that are unchangeable; rites [*li*] are patterns [*li*] that are unalterable" (*Hsün-tzu*, chap. 20). That is, the rites are forms of social behavior that are valid throughout history. Much later, Wang Yang-ming offers a very different idea. In his *Ch'uan-hsi lu* (Instructions for Practical Living) Wang argues that "*li* [rites] means *li* [principle]," because "restraining oneself with *li* [rites]" means that "this mind" must become completely identified with the "principle of nature," the *li* of Heaven (3.9).

[*For further discussion of both terms, see* Confucian Thought, *articles on* Foundations of the Tradition *and* Neo-Confucianism.]

BIBLIOGRAPHY

Chan, Wing-tsit. "The Evolution of the Neo-Confucian Concept of *Li* as Principle." *Tsing-hua Journal of Chinese Studies*, n.s. 4 (February 1964): 123–148.

Demiéville, Paul. "La pénétration du bouddhisme dans la tradition philosophique chinois." *Cahiers d'histoire mondiale* 3 (1956): 19–38.

Fingarette, Herbert. *Confucius: The Secular as Sacred.* New York, 1972.

Gimello, Robert M. "Apophatic and Kataphatic Discourse in Mahāyāna: A Chinese View." *Philosophy East and West* 26 (April 1976): 117–136.

Graham, A. C. *Two Chinese Philosophers: Ch'êng Ming-tao and Ch'êng Yi-ch'uan.* London, 1958.

Moran, Patrick Edwin. "Explorations of Chinese Metaphysical Concepts: The History of Some Key Terms from the Beginnings to Chu Hsi (1130–1200)." Ph.D. diss., University of Pennsylvania, 1983.

Waley, Arthur, trans. and ed. *The Analects of Confucius.* London, 1938.

DAVID S. NIVISON

LIANG WU-TI (464–549), or Emperor Wu of the Liang dynasty, also known as Hsiao Yen; first emperor of the Liang dynasty (502–557), man of letters, and patron of Buddhism. Although from a Taoist family and versed, like all educated gentlemen of his time, in the Confucian principles of morality and statecraft, Hsiao Yen came to be fascinated by Buddhism through exposure as a young man to the teachings of Buddhist monks at the court of Prince Ching-ling, Hsiao Tzu-liang, of the Southern Ch'i dynasty (479–502). Hsiao Yen later overthrew the Ch'i and declared himself emperor of the Liang dynasty, but he maintained his interest in Buddhism and became a full convert after three years on the throne.

Endeavoring to fashion state policy according to Buddhist ideals, Emperor Wu softened the traditionally harsh penal code by minimizing the application of torture, capital punishment, and other excesses of government. He also forswore meat and alcohol and built numerous temples, including the T'ung-t'ai Ssu, where he often sponsored a kind of Buddhist symposium, known as an "open assembly" *(wu-che ta-hui),* so called because it was open to men and women, clergy and laity, regardless of class. The emperor, who sometimes delivered lectures on Buddhist doctrine at these assemblies, four times used the occasion to announce that he was surrendering himself to voluntary servitude to the T'ung-t'ai temple. He of course expected his imperial officials to ransom him, and so they did, each time for prodigious sums. Each ransoming was followed by a full reenactment of the imperial enthronement ceremony. Emperor Wu's behavior, which had precedents in the history of Indian Buddhism and may have been suggested by the newly translated *Aśokāvadāna* (Legend of King Aśoka), was intended to raise money for the propagation of the Buddhist religion. The emperor also established "inexhaustible treasuries" *(wu-chin tsang),* institutions that provided safe-deposit vaults and repositories for donations made to the religion. These funds were often used in financial transactions the profits of which reverted to the church.

Emperor Wu was overthrown by the rebel Hou Ching in 548. Some anti-Buddhist critics attributed his fall to the slackening effect of Buddhist principles on governmental control. Such a view unjustifiably ignores the political complexities of the period. Nor are his deeds to be comprehended merely in terms of whether or not they conform to Buddhist principles. Although versed in Buddhist doctrine beyond the level of the ordinary layman, Emperor Wu also devoted an important part of his energies to his literary work, much of which is still preserved and admired. This artistic bent, as much as his religious proclivities, must be taken into account in any effort to assess his fitness to rule.

BIBLIOGRAPHY

Annals of the reign of Emperor Wu can be found in fascicles 1 to 3 of the *Liang shu* and in fascicles 6 and 7 of the *Nan shih.* His writings are collected in Yen K'o-chün's *Ch'üan shang-ku san-tai Ch'in Han san-kuo liu-ch'ao wen* (1930, available on microfilm at the University of Chicago library). See also Mori Mikisaburō's *Ryō no Butei* (Kyoto, 1956).

Miyakawa Hisayuki

LIBATION is one of the oldest and perhaps least understood religious rituals, the sacrificial pouring out of liquid. Its primary importance seems to lie in the act of pouring, since the liquids that are poured out (wine, milk, honey, water, oil, and in some cases even blood) and the places where this is done (on the ground, into chasms, upon the altar, over the sacrificial victim, into a sacrificial bowl) vary and change. Libation can be traced back as far as the Bronze Age by means of libation pitchers and bowls discovered in excavations or depicted in stone reliefs and vase paintings or on gems, seals, and rings. The ritual is found in almost every culture and geographical area, but the kinds of libations and their performance, place in the cult, relations to other rituals, sacrificial materials, and possible meanings and functions differ from one religion to another and even within the same religion.

In spite of a wealth of evidence, many of the basic problems have remained unsolved. The information about Greek religion is extraordinarily complicated, but the situation may have been just as confusing in other religions where data have not been as fully preserved. Further, in this regard there is a remarkable degree of similarity between religions that otherwise have little connection, as for instance the sacrificial rites of Classical Greece and the Priestly tradition of the Old Testament.

Name and Terminology. The word *libation* is derived from the Latin *libatio* ("sacrificial offering of drink"). The word is connected with the Greek noun *loibē* ("libation") and the verb *leibō* ("to pour out a libation"), used since Homer. More common than these poetic terms, however, are the synonyms *spendō, spondē* (Hittite, *shipand-;* Latin, *spondeo;* German, *spenden;* English, *spend*) and *cheō, choē.* The word-field points to an Indo-European religious ritual with the wider range of social and legal functions.

Meaning. The meaning of the libation offering can vary as much as the way it was performed. It is not known for certain what the original meaning of the ritual was, if, in fact, there was only one original meaning. Perhaps the original meaning or meanings are still found among the many seemingly secondary applications and developments. The ritual itself, being rather simple and of no great interest, may have attracted what appeared to be deeper interpretations and connections with other rituals. In these matters history may provide some clues.

The most ancient sources treat libations as separate gift offerings, and this is probably what they originally were. In Babylonian and Assyrian religion, it was primarily the king's office to offer libations to the gods. Libations were part of the meals presented to the gods on altar tables, around which the divinities gathered eagerly. In purifications and magic, however, the purpose of libations was different. The ancient Egyptian sources provide a similar picture, so that the common performances of the ritual may not have changed much over the centuries down to the Greco-Egyptian period, when libations are found in all their variety in the Greek Magical Papyri. These sources show libations of wine, honey, milk, water, and oil as standard features of most religious rites, either separately or in connection with other ceremonies. Originally they seem to have been separate from animal sacrifices, with which they were often later connected. If at the beginning libations were gift offerings, they were most likely understood as gifts to the deity in return for benefits received. By the seemingly wasteful giving up of some vital resources, libations constituted fundamental acts of recognition and gratitude as well as hope for future benefits. Thus they were part of the communication with the divine sphere of life through the exchange of gifts. This may also explain why the gods themselves are often shown offering libations.

Greek Religion. Libations were common as early as the Minoan-Mycenaean period (c. 2000 BCE). Gems often depict sacrificial scenes with libation pitchers and offering tables laden with bread and fruit. While these pictures generally separate such gift offerings from animal sacrifices, there is at least one noted exception: the Hagia Triada sarcophagus from the late Minoan period (c. 1500 BCE; Long, 1974). Here one scene shows a procession of women and men carrying buckets of liquid; the first person, a priestess, is pouring her bucket into a krater (mixing bowl). This scene probably depicts the mixing of wine and water as preparation for the libation. In another scene altars are shown in a tree sanctuary. A priestess officiates before one of these altars, on which stand a libation pitcher and a basket of bread and fruit. Behind this altar, however, appears a table bearing a newly slaughtered bull, his blood flowing from his throat into a vessel on the floor. The data provided by these pictures suggest that later Greek sacrifice dates back to this Archaic period, when the originally separate gift offerings had already become associated with animal sacrifice.

It is difficult to understand the relationship between libations and the special blood sacrifices performed in funerary rites for heroes (see Pindar, *Olympian Odes* 1.90, with the technical expression *haimakouria,* "a fill of blood"; Homer, *Iliad* 23.34; Plutarch, *Aristides* 21). Whether these blood rites are to be regarded as different from libations, or in some instances as adaptations to libations, is far from clear.

While the gift offerings continued in Classical Greek religion, libations also made their way into a variety of other rituals and became a part of them. Animal sacrifice had libations as part of its preliminary sacrifice (as in Aristophanes' *The Peace* 431–435) and used libation as well in its conclusion, when wine was poured into the fire that consumed the remains of the victim. Wine drinking at symposiums involved libations by all participants, together with invocations and prayers. Concern for protection and a safe return is evident in libations made just prior to sea voyages (Thucydides, 6.32.1–2; Pindar, *Pythian Odes* 4.193–200) and battle (*Iliad* 16.220–252). Libations in connection with legal agreements had a different meaning, signifying the entering into obligation. The more magically oriented libations for the dead, of which we possess literary accounts, were again different, but their specific role and function, despite ancient attempts at explanation, remain somewhat ambiguous (e.g., the epithet *gapotos,* "to be drunk up by Earth," in Aeschylus, *The Libation Bearers* 97, 164, and *The Persians* 621). A reflection of popular beliefs is found in Lucian's remark (*On Funerals* 9) that the souls of the dead receive nourishment from libation. Libations of oil, another very old custom, develop more in a magical direction: anointing stones and funerary stelae was customary in much of the ancient world.

Whatever the original purpose of water libations may have been, they were later understood mostly in terms of purification. This is true especially of the ablution of hands *(chernips)* at the beginning of the offering ceremonies. Yet water libations were also performed at tombs by putting the water on them or pouring it into them. Mythology may have provided secondary explanations: they are bathwater *(loutra)* from the underworld (Sophocles, *Electra* 84.434) or a fresh drink for the thirsty dead (cf. *Luke* 16:24). The origins of water-carrying festivals *(hudrophoria),* which existed since ancient times, were different still, the purpose perhaps originally being purification. Yet another water ritual found its way into the mysteries of Eleusis, when at their conclusion two jugs were filled and then overturned, one toward the east and the other toward the west. This probably happened while the initiates shouted "Hue kue," telling the heavens, "Rain!" and the earth, "Conceive!"

Israelite Religion. Israelite libations, as known from the Hebrew scriptures and the Mishnah (*Suk.* 4.9), were remarkably similar in appearance to ancient Greek rituals. Similar too are some of the ambiguities, such as the role of blood in relation to libations (see McCarthy, 1973; Kedar-Kopfstein, 1978). The formation of the composite sacrifice in the Priestly texts can be compared to the formation of the Greek sacrifice. No attempt is made in the Hebrew scriptures to explain the purpose of the libations. If reasons are given, they apply as caricatures of foreign religions and express sarcasm (*Is.* 1:11; *Ps.* 50:13). Together with other parts of the sacrificial cult, libation was taken over from the Canaanites. The root of the term designating libation *(nsk)* also occurs in Ugaritic and Phoenician-Punic. Direct takeover of a foreign ritual including libations is reported in connection with King Ahaz's imitation of the royal cult of Damascus (*2 Kgs.* 16:10–18) and in Artaxerxes' decree to Ezra (*Ezr.* 7:17). The sharp polemics by the prophets also reflect the non-Israelite origin of libations (*Jer.* 7:18, 19:13, 32:29; *Ez.* 20:28; *Dt.* 32:38; *Ps.* 16:4). Texts dealing with libations mention them either alone (*Gn.* 28:18, 35:14; *Jer.* 7:18, 19:13, 32:29, 44:17–19, 44:25; *Ez.* 20:28; *Ps.* 16:4) or in connection with the *minḥah*, the gift offering of cereals (*Jl.* 1:9, 1:13, 2:14; *Is.* 57:6). The Priestly legislation shows the combination of *minḥah* ("gift offering") and *nesekh* ("libation") with the burnt offering (*'olah*) (*Lv.* 23:13, 23:18, 23:37; *Nm.* 6:15, 6:17, 15:10, 28:7–31, 29:39), as do the morning and evening offerings in *Exodus* 29:40–41. References to libation utensils confirm what is known from excavations (*Ex.* 25:29, 30:9; *Nm.* 4:7; *1 Chr.* 29:21; *2 Chr.* 29:35). Anointing of stones with oil was perhaps traditional at Bethel (*Gn.* 28:18, 35:14); water libations are also mentioned (*1 Sm.* 7:1; *2 Sm.* 23:16; *1 Chr.* 11:18). The notion of wine symbolizing blood is late (*Sir.* 50:15).

Special Developments. Some religions and cultures have developed special forms of libation offerings, several of which should be mentioned. The Iranian cult of *haoma* goes back to great antiquity. This drink of immortality was encountered by Zarathushtra (Zoroaster, c. 600 BCE), who attacked it. Its later revival suggests that he reformed the ritual and thus continued it. The *haoma* cult corresponds to the Vedic cult of *soma*. *Soma* is at once a deity and the plant from which the juice comes that, when pressed and then mixed with water and milk, makes the *soma* drink. This drink is offered to the gods, but it is also consumed by the people during feasts and conveys immortality (*Ṛgveda* 8:48).

Ancient Chinese religion developed the festival of Shih-tien ("pouring a drink offering"). The cult seems to have its origin in ancestral worship and is connected with the veneration of Confucius and his pupil Yen Hui. It consisted of a sacrifice and a banquet. During the Ming dynasty (1368–1644), the Shih-tien ritual was greatly expanded along with the Confucius cult.

The sacrifice of the legendary first emperor, Jimmu, in Shintō religion is also interesting because of its antiquity. The offering includes the essential means for life, food, and drink and is followed by a feast. Ceremonial beer-drinking rituals were conducted by the Vikings of Scandinavia. The *drykkeoffer* was a sumptuous beer party with three ceremonial cups of mead offered to Óðinn (Odin), Þórr (Thor), and Freyja. The three offerings have a curious parallel in Greek sacrifice, but beer-drinking rituals are found elsewhere as well, as for instance in Southeast Asia.

For different reasons, several major religions have discontinued libations altogether. Buddhist religion is opposed to external sacrifices in principle. Jewish religion was compelled to abandon its sacrificial ritual, and with it libations, because of the destruction of the Jerusalem Temple in 70 CE. Christianity has no room for libations in its cult. It uses water in baptism; sees in wine the blood of Christ, the sacramental drink of the Eucharist (substituted in some instances by milk or honey), which is offered not to but by the deity, and certainly must not be spilled; and uses oil for sacramental anointing. Islam has no sacrifices in the proper sense of the term. The pre-Islamic libations of milk, predominant among the Arabs, were discontinued, but in some quarters those offerings persist.

BIBLIOGRAPHY

No scholarly investigation exists that takes adequate account of the libations in the various religions, nor do most encyclopedias include a separate article on this important ritual. The following bibliography lists items that summarize the evidence of specific religions, provide surveys, or contain bibliographies.

Asmussen, Jes P., and Jørgen Laessøe, eds. *Handbuch der Religionsgeschichte.* 2 vols. Göttingen, 1971–1975. Sections on the various religions give attention to libations; see the index, s.v. *Opfer (Trink-, Libations-).*

Bonnet, Hans, ed. *Reallexikon der ägyptischen Religionsgeschichte.* 2d ed. Berlin, 1952. See pages 424–426, s.v. *Libation.* Surveys the evidence in Egyptian religion; includes a useful bibliography.

Borghouts, J. F. "Libation." In *Lexikon der Ägyptologie,* vol. 3. Wiesbaden, 1980. Presents evidence for Egyptian religion on the basis of current research.

Burkert, Walter. *Homo Necans: The Anthropology of Ancient Greek Sacrificial Ritual and Myth.* Berkeley, 1983. Basic study of Greek sacrificial rituals and their prehistory.

Burkert, Walter. *Greek Religion.* Cambridge, Mass., 1985. Best account of the current state of research on Greek religion, with sections on libation. Contains a wealth of bibliographical, textual, and archaeological references.

Gill, David. "*Trapezomata:* A Neglected Aspect of Greek Sacrifice." *Harvard Theological Review* 67 (1974): 117–137. Discusses Greek gift offerings set up for the gods on tables.

Graf, Fritz. "Milch, Honig und Wein: Zum Verständnis der Libation im griechischen Ritual." In *Perennitas: Studi in onore di Angelo Brelich,* pp. 209–221. Rome, 1981. Important study of the complexities of the Greek ritual, especially with regard to the substances of milk, honey, and wine. Bibliographic references.

Hanell, Krister. "Trankopfer, Spenden, Libationen." In *Real-Encyclopädie der klassischen Altertumswissenschaft,* 2d series, vol. 6. Stuttgart, 1937. Collection of the evidence of libations in Greek religion.

Herrmann, Wolfram. "Götterspeise und Göttertrank in Ugarit und Israel." *Zeitschrift für die alttestamentliche Wissenschaft* 72 (1960): 205–216. Compares the evidence from Ugarit and the Old Testament.

Kedar-Kopfstein, Benjamin. *"dam"* (Blood). In the *Theological Dictionary of the Old Testament,* vol. 3. Grand Rapids, Mich., 1978. Deals with the evidence and literature on blood sacrifice in the ancient Near East and the Old Testament.

Latte, Kurt. *Römische Religionsgeschichte.* Munich, 1960. Summary of the evidence in Roman religion.

Long, Charlotte R. *The Ayia Triadha Sarcophagus: A Study of Late Minoan and Mycenaean Funerary Practices and Beliefs.* Göteborg, 1974. Investigation of the sacrificial scenes on the sarcophagus from Hagia Triada (Crete), with good photographic material.

McCarthy, Dennis J. "The Symbolism of Blood and Sacrifice." *Journal of Biblical Literature* 88 (1969): 166–176.

McCarthy, Dennis J. "Further Notes on the Symbolism of Blood and Sacrifice." *Journal of Biblical Literature* 92 (1973): 205–210. Discusses the evidence and possible meaning of blood sacrifice in the ancient Near East and Israel and in Greek religion.

Meuli, Karl. "Griechische Opferbräuche." In *Phyllobolia für Peter von der Mühll zum 60. Geburtstag,* edited by Olof Gigon and Karl Meuli, pp. 185–288. Basel, 1946. Reprinted in Meuli's *Gesammelte Schriften,* vol. 2, edited by Thomas Gelzer (Basel, 1975). A seminal study.

Michel, Otto. *"Spendomai, spendō."* In the *Theological Dictionary of the New Testament,* vol. 7. Grand Rapids, Mich., 1971. Surveys the evidence in the Old Testament, Judaism, and Christianity. Contains a rich bibliography, for which also see the supplement in *Theologisches Wörterbuch zum Neuen Testament,* vol. 10, pt. 2 (Stuttgart, 1979).

Mitropoulou, Elpis. *Libation Scenes with Oinochoe in Votive Reliefs.* Athens, 1975. Collects evidence from the perspective of art history.

Nilsson, Martin P. *The Minoan-Mycenaean Religion and Its Survival in Greek Religion* (1950). 2d rev. ed. New York, 1971. Especially important for the pictorial material.

Nilsson, Martin P. *Geschichte der griechischen Religion.* 3d ed. 2 vols. Munich, 1967–1974. A monumental work, especially important for bibliographical references.

Rendtorff, Rolf. *Studien zur Geschichte des Opfers im alten Israel.* Neukirchen-Vluyn, West Germany, 1967. The only modern critical study of the Old Testament traditions concerning libations. Contains a comprehensive bibliography.

Smith, W. Robertson. *Lectures on the Religion of the Semites: The Fundamental Institutions* (1889). 3d ed. New York, 1969. This nineteenth-century classic is still indispensable.

Stengel, Paul. *Opferbräuche der Griechen.* Leipzig, 1910. Basic study of the Greek sacrificial terminology and practices.

Stengel, Paul. *Die griechischen Kultusaltertümer.* 3d ed., rev. Munich, 1920. Standard work concerning Greek cultic practices. See pages 103–105 on libations.

Wachsmuth, Dietrich. "Trankopfer." In *Der Kleine Pauly,* vol. 5, edited by Konrat Ziegler. Munich, 1975. Update of the articles by Krister Hanell and Ludwig Ziehen with additional references.

Wendel, Adolf. *Das Opfer in der israelitischen Religion.* Leipzig, 1927. A basic study that is still of value.

Ziehen, Ludwig. *"Nēphalia."* In *Real-Encyclopädie der klassischen Altertumswissenschaft,* vol. 16. Stuttgart, 1935. Surveys wineless libations in Greek religion.

HANS DIETER BETZ

LIBERAL JUDAISM. *See* Reform Judaism.

LIBERATION. *For discussion of Hindu concepts of liberation, see* Mokṣa; *see also* Jīvanmukti.

LIBERATION THEOLOGY. *See* Political Theology; *see also* Christianity, *article on* Christianity in Latin America.

LIEH-TZU, personal name Yu-k'ou; reputedly a Taoist thinker of the fifth and early fourth centuries BCE and alleged author of the work that bears his name. Both the authenticity of the work and the existence of the author have for centuries been in doubt. To be sure, Lieh-tzu's name is mentioned in the *Chuang-tzu,* where he is credited with the power of riding on the wind. Furthermore, a book of eight chapters entitled *Lieh-tzu* was submitted to the throne in 14 BCE by Liu Hsiang, the imperial historian and librarian. On the other hand, the philosopher Lieh-tzu is not once mentioned in the several summaries of contemporary thought that survive from ancient times. Most conspicuously, his name never appears in Ssu-ma Ch'ien's highly reliable *Shih chi.* Such omissions make Lieh-tzu's historicity a matter of considerable doubt.

Without going into the intricate arguments surrounding this point, I feel justified in saying that there was very likely an ancient philosopher with Taoist inclinations known as Lieh-tzu, who lived decades before Chuang-tzu (369?–286? BCE) and left a work behind him. The *Lieh-tzu* that we now have, however, is not the same book. Around the year 300 CE, several centuries after a *Lieh-tzu* was presented at court in 14 BCE, the now extant *Lieh-tzu* appeared. A full commentary by Chang Chan (fl. fourth century CE) followed some decades later. Still composed of eight chapters, but with as much as a quarter of the contents consisting of passages copied from known sources, the newly surfaced *Lieh-tzu,* the edition known to us today, is generally considered a forgery. Only fragments from the original *Lieh-tzu*, if indeed they are such, have been preserved.

Though a forgery, the *Lieh-tzu* is not an insignificant work. The time in which the *Lieh-tzu* reappeared, known in Chinese history as the Southern and Northern Dynasties period (Nan-pei-ch'ao), was an era of political fragmentation and recurring civil strife during which both Buddhism and Taoism flourished. The formation of a Taoist church was one of the more notable events of the era. In the tradition of this Taoist religion, Lieh-tzu the author was known as Ma Tan of the Ti clan, and was ranked among its apotheosized philosophers. According to hagiographic sources, Lieh-tzu perfected himself through long years of religious cultivation until he became a Taoist immortal *(hsien)*, able to walk in the heavens on the wings of the wind.

Forgery or not, the *Lieh-tzu* was eagerly embraced by the Taoist religion and was ranked next only to the *Tao-te ching* and the *Chuang-tzu* in the Taoist canon. Particularly in the common mind, the *Lieh-tzu* is often more highly esteemed than the more contemplative and sophisticated *Tao-te ching* and *Chuang-tzu*. In 742 CE, the T'ang emperor Hsüan-tsung honored the *Lieh-tzu* with the imperially bestowed title of *Ch'ung-hsü chen-ching* (The True Classic of Vacuity), and in 1007 an imperial decree from the Sung emperor Chen-tsung elaborated the title further as *Ch'ung-hsü chih-te chen-ching* (The True Classic of Supreme Virtue and Vacuity).

Without trying to reach great philosophical depth, the *Lieh-tzu* is filled with delightful anecdotes, fables, and folk tales. One of them tells of a man who is worried that the heavens will fall; another tells of a slave who, in a dream, enjoys the ease and pleasures of the master, while the master, in his dream, is suffering the pain and hardships of the slave. The *Lieh-tzu* emphatically champions egalitarianism and the cause of the common man. It declares that "all things in the world are born together with us as one kind, with no distinction of noble and mean." The utopia depicted in the *Lieh-tzu* is a place where old and young live together as equal comrades, where there are neither rulers nor subjects, and where men and women associate freely instead of meeting through go-betweens or in brothels. It has been said that Taoism has inculcated in the Chinese people a moderate degree of skepticism, fatalism, and indulgence in the pleasures of life. To this achievement Lieh-tzu has made a notable contribution.

The seventh chapter of the *Lieh-tzu* bears the heading "Yang Chu." This chapter is evidently a separate work, or a remnant of a larger work, left by Yang Chu (440–360? BCE) and somehow incorporated in the *Lieh-tzu*. Written in a compact and brisk style, the monograph presents a notably refreshing point of view on life and reality, advocating as it does a free-spirited and essentially hedonistic self-interest that is at variance with the normative Chinese outlook on human behavior.

BIBLIOGRAPHY

For a recent and highly reliable translation of the *Lieh-tzu*, see A. C. Graham's *The Book of Lieh-tzu: A New Translation* (London, 1961). Graham's "The Date and Composition of *Liehtzyy*," *Asia Major*, n.s. 8 (1961): 139–198, offers a comprehensive discussion of the problems surrounding the textual history of the work. Herlee G. Creel's "The Changing Shapes of Taoism," in volume 1 of the section on philosophy and history of thought of *Kuo-chi Han-hsüeh-hui i-lun wen-chi*, the proceedings of Academica Sinica's 1980 International Conference on Sinological Studies (Taipei, 1981), contains a penetrating though brief treatment of the *Lieh-tzu* on pages 1–35.

Y. P. MEI

LIFE. Throughout the ages, humanity has exhibited, through myths, rituals, religious and cultural institutions, and various other modes of symbolic expression, a central and overriding preoccupation with the creation, prolongation, and felicitous consummation of life. The truth of this claim is demonstrated by the fact that most of the human cultures known to us today possess one or more terms to designate life, being, existence, or other cognate concepts, and these concepts have occupied a core position in the intellectual life of each tradition. Even the Chinese language, which does not possess an exact equivalent of the term *life*, does contain a number of other words to describe the seat of life or basis of the life process (e.g., *yu*, "being," and its counterpart, *wu*, "nonbeing").

Among the impressive array of terms for "life" that are to be found in both ancient and modern languages, the following illustrative examples might be mentioned: *nefesh/ruaḥ* (Heb.), *psuchē/pneuma* (Gr.), *spiritus* (Lat.), *ātman/jīva/prāṇa/puruṣa* (Skt.), *'umr/'īshah* (Arab.), and *yiegh* (Nuer).

The identity of the human faculty or function that is regarded as an undeniable indication of the presence of life in an animated organism varies from one culture to another. By and large, however, the seal of life has been identified with the tangible signs of the presence of breath, with consciousness or mental functioning, and with physical movement or—in the modern scientific fields of physiology and neurology—pulsebeat and measurable brain-wave activity.

In both archaic and historical cultures, it is, perhaps, breath, more than any other single human function, that has been designated as the most dependable sign of life. That this is the case is confirmed by the fact that in many languages, both ancient and modern, the words for "life" and "breath" are one and the same. A particularly intriguing illustration of this phenomenon appears in one of the most ancient texts in Hindu scripture, the *Bṛhadāraṇyaka Upaniṣad* (chap. 6), where a debate as to which of the human faculties is indispensable to the maintenance of life is resolved in favor of breath *(prāṇa)*. [*See* Breath and Breathing.]

Even a cursory survey of the religions of the world indicates that a majority of traditions attributed the existence of the world and its entire population of living inhabitants to the creative act of God or gods at the beginning of time. According to various cosmologies, representing both tribal and complex societies, the divine creator fashioned the universe as we know it either out of nothing or from some type of preexistent *materia prima* (e.g., water, earth, fire, mind, human spittle, etc.). Because of its divine origins, the cosmos is believed to be sacred, suffused with and supported by the sacred energies of the creator deity.

By virtue of this primordial act of creation, human life is linked physically and spiritually with the life of the cosmos as a whole. That is, the human realm is established within, informed, and directed by a cosmic, celestial, or divine dimension of reality, of either a personal or a transpersonal nature. As a consequence, human existence is believed to possess both a human and a divine, a temporal and an atemporal dimension, with the latter being both logically and metaphysically prior to the former.

In addition, most religions and philosophies make a qualitative distinction between two contrasting and mutually exclusive modes or styles of life. The two categories of existence have been characterized variously as profane and sacred, impure and pure, fallen and redeemed, ignorant and enlightened, bound and liberated, alienated and authentic.

The first category pertains to life in a state of separation from or in opposition to the will of God or gods in theistic systems or in opposition to the natural law or the principle of ultimate reality within nontheistic systems (e.g., *dharma* in Hinduism and Buddhism, *moira* or *logos* in ancient Greece, and *tao* in China and Japan). Life in this state is depicted as a realm of sin and ignorance, suffering and misery, and death (linked, in certain cases, with rebirth).

Achievement of the second, more salutary state of existence (conceived as one of wholeness, physical and spiritual integration, redemption, or liberation), is realized by living in compliance with the cosmic law or the will of God.

Primitive Societies. From the perspective of most tribal cultures, human existence is viewed as real and meaningful only insofar as it is experienced as organically rooted in a divine realm of existence. This divine realm is conceived to be a celestial abode of God or the gods or the shadowy domain of the cultural ancestors. It is the function of the network of myths and symbols, cultic rituals, and cultural customs to preserve and strengthen the connection between the human and divine realms and, thereby, to guarantee to human beings the sense of reality and value that makes life not only bearable but fulfilling.

The Aboriginal inhabitants of Arnhem Land in Australia believe that the world existed from the beginning; only human beings were lacking. Human life originated with the peregrinations of a primal ancestor and his two sisters. They wandered about the landscape, paused from time to time, engaged in sexual intercourse, and thereby produced human offspring and various totemic emblems known as Dreamings (i.e., the world as it now is). The peoples who inhabit this territory trace the origin of all entities that constitute the world in which they live back to a "Dreaming period." It was, therefore, during this timeless, mythical epoch that the life-world as we know it was established.

According to the people of West Ceram in the Sulawesi Islands, human beings emerged from bananas that grew at the base of a sacred mountain. Living beings of all sorts, together with various foodstuffs and diverse sources of wealth, resulted from the sacrifice (lit., "murder") of a coconut maiden, Hainuwele, and the implantation of the several parts of her body in the surrounding landscape. By this means, her bodily parts became sources of sustenance for all living creatures. But this primal murder was also the occasion for the advent of death. Hence, death is understood to be a necessary precondition for the creation and maintenance of life.

According to the Nuer, a tribe of cattle keepers in the southern Egyptian Sudan, life is bestowed upon the universe and all its inhabitants by the cosmic spirit (Kwoth), invoked variously as "spirit of the sky," "grandfather of the universe," or "spirit who created the ancestors." This omnipresent spirit of the sky is credited with creating the world and its offspring and determining the course of its operations. From his lofty perch, he rewards and punishes human actions and upholds the moral order of the universe, by which all life is governed.

In addition, there are smaller and more localized spirits *(kuth)* of the sky, atmosphere, and earth, through whose mediating powers the life energies of Kwoth are transmitted to animals and human beings. Specifically, this transmission of power is effectuated by the killing and partaking of the flesh and blood of the ox, the totemic ancestor of the Nuer. Even as birth necessitates a temporary separation from the primordial spirit, death is the return of the individual soul to the great spirit and its near-complete isolation from the realm of the living. The deceased are transmuted into ghosts at the moment of death but retain the capacity to return to the living in dreams, visions, and various types of misfortune.

Judaism. In the *Book of Genesis,* the world is created by divine fiat. For the compiler of the Yahvist (J) tradition, life comes from God. He breathed the breath of life (*Gn.* 2:7) into the nostrils of the inert human organism. In contrast, the writer of the Priestly materials (P), in accordance with most of the Hebrew tradition, identifies the basis of human life as the blood (*Lv.* 17:14).

The writers of the various books in the Hebrew scriptures are in general agreement that the relative length of life is determined by human virtues and vices. It was not death that Adam's sin brought upon the human race, but rather shortness of life, the pangs of birth, and the shame of sexuality. God is the lord of life and death by virtue of his sovereign rulership over the book of life.

In classical Judaism, therefore, life reveals its presence through breath *(ruaḥ)* and blood. Hence, God is the prototypical living being whose life is eternal, whereas the existence of all created beings and entities is fragile and perishable, "like the grass of the field" (*Ps.* 103:15, *Is.* 40:6). Truly vigorous and authentic life is filled with hope, with possibilities for physical and spiritual growth; such life is, therefore, open to the future.

God's life is manifested through action and creativity. He is the creator and therefore the lord of life (*Jb.* 43:14f.). Hence, to live in rebellion against his will is equivalent to experiencing death in the midst of life (*Jb.* 3:11–26, *Jon.* 4:9). Such an existence will be filled, inwardly, with misfortune and misery, however favorable the external circumstances may be.

The realization that death is the fate of all living beings brings into question the ultimate value of life and its various aspects (*Eccl.* 1:1–11), but in the final analysis the judgment is rendered that those who live in submission to God's will can expect to enjoy a long and happy life and, in the end, be gathered to the fathers (*Gn.* 15:15, *Jb.* 42:17). All persons, therefore, face a choice between the way of life and the way of death (*Prv.* 5:6, 14:12).

In the belief of ancient Judaism, the life of Israel is maintained and revitalized through sacrifice. The community of Israel as a whole appropriates the divine power resident within the sacrificial oblation and shares in the sanctity created by the sacrifice. Likewise, by offering the sacrifice to God, the sacrificer also strengthens both God's nature and, through his revitalization, that of the world and its inhabitants. [*See* Sacrifice.]

In the writings of the great prophets of Israel, life is the natural and inevitable outcome of righteousness, for on righteousness the Israelite establishes his confidence in life. Such a belief is based upon the covenant between God and his people and is maintained by a faithful fulfillment of the terms of the agreement by both parties.

Christianity. A true understanding of the New Testament concept of life rests upon an accurate grasp of the distinction between mere existence, or natural life (*bios,* as the ancient Greeks used the term), and true or authentic life in Christ. In the first instance, human life is finite, fragile, and mortal. As in the Old Testament, to be alive is to possess the capacity to perform one's intended function and act efficaciously (*Acts* 7:38) and to do so in a state of health (*Mk.* 5:23). While animal life is sustained by nourishment, human life is dependent upon the continued presence of the soul *(psuchē),* or life breath *(pneuma),* which is a gift of God. Since God is the only being who possesses life inherently (*Jn.* 5:26) and, hence, alone lives eternally, it follows that all living creatures derive their existence from him. In recognition of the fact that life is a divine dispensation, the believer does not live for himself, nor primarily for his fellow creatures, but for his creator and redeemer (*Rv.* 14:7f., *Gal.* 2:19). He who lives for his own selfish pleasure will come, in the end, to sin and death (*2 Cor.* 5).

While the life of redemption is available in the present as a consequence of the establishment of the new regime of faith through Christ's resurrection as the second Adam (*1 Cor.* 15:20–22), its complete realization must await the end of time, when Christ is to deliver the kingdom of God and, thereby, put "all enemies under his feet." The last enemy to be destroyed is death (*1 Cor.* 15:24–27). For the time being, Christians must be contented with faith in the signs of future fulfillment that are presented through the message of life and love (*1 Cor.* 13:12) and hope for that day when all believers will come to a full realization of life in Christ (*2 Cor.* 5:8, *1 Cor.* 15).

Since life in its truest and most efficacious form lies in the future, beyond the grave, then all present conduct is but a preparation for that eventuality. But, in the final analysis, this indestructible form of life is the result of divine grace (*Jn.* 3:16, *Rom.* 8:1–11), extended to those who repent past sins and accept the promise of salvation (*Lk.* 13:3, *Acts* 2:38, *Rom.* 2:4). The doctrine of the immortality of the soul is entirely foreign to the New Testament. [*See* Soul, *article on* Christian Concept.]

In contrast to the Old Testament view of life, the New

Testament writers declare that authentic life is based not upon God's nature in general but rather upon God's expression of his love and compassion for the sufferings of humanity and his readiness to forgive and redeem all those who seek his forgiveness through the life, death, and resurrection of his only son, Jesus, the Christ (*Jn.* 3:16, *1 Pt.* 1:18–19). According to Paul, the consummate realization of the benefits of the "life in Christ" will occur only after the Day of Resurrection. Hence, true life can be appropriated in the present time only in the form of hope (*Rom.* 5:1–11, *1 Cor.* 15). Whereas the letter of the law kills (i.e., destroys the freedom of life in the spirit), the spirit gives life (*2 Cor.* 3:6). Where the spirit is present there is life, eternal and indestructible (*2 Cor.* 3:17f.). This life is embodied in and offered through the preached word *(kērugma)*, the "power of God for salvation to all those who have faith" (*Rom.* 1:16).

According to Augustine, the wide panorama of living beings is distinguished by the divine creator according to a hierarchical order of existence. At the lowest level are the merely nutritive life forms such as plants, devoid of sensibility or consciousness. Then come sentient forms of life, devoid of mind or soul, such as cattle, birds, and fishes. Third, there is man, the crown of God's created order by virtue of his possession of mind and will. Ultimately, transcendent to man, whose life is conditioned by the vicissitudes of change and death, there is the eternal, unchanging, absolute existent, God, "who is wisdom itself."

For Augustine, as for other Christian writers who followed him, God is to be understood as living in a highly exceptional, and indeed, absolute sense. He possesses the capacity to give life to the multitude of creatures that inhabit the world. He is the boundless and inexhaustible reservoir of power from which all other living beings derive their existence. He is, in short, the alpha and omega, the source and final resting place for all living beings.

Hinduism. In the Vedas, the earliest strata of Hindu scripture, the creation of the life-world is attributed to a variety of divine agents or cosmogonic entities, with no apparent compulsion toward consistency among the many theories of creation. The cosmos was believed to have originated from the primordial sacrifice of a cosmic superman *(Puruṣa)* and the distribution of his bodily parts throughout the universe to form the sun, moon, stars, sky, earth, and so forth (*Ṛgveda* 10.90). Alternatively, the universe arose from the mysterious breathing, windlessly, of "That One" *(tad ekaṃ)* within the realm where "there was neither existence nor nonexistence" (*Ṛgveda* 10.12), or it resulted from the fragmentation of a primordial "Golden Germ" *(hiraṇyagarbha)* floating upon the cosmic ocean (*Ṛgveda* 10.121). At least one sage expressed skepticism that the origins of the world can be known even to the highest deity (*Ṛgveda* 10.129.7).

In the Brāhmaṇas, liturgical manuals employed by Brahmanic priests, creation of the universe and its multitudinous inhabitants is attributed to a high god, addressed as Prajāpati ("lord of creatures"). In the later traditions recorded in the Hindu epics and Purāṇas, the life process is subdivided into three stages (creation, duration, and destruction), with causation and surveillance of each stage assigned to Brahmā, Viṣṇu, and Śiva, respectively.

In the Upaniṣads, the scriptural basis of Vedānta, the focus shifts from cosmology to spiritual psychology, from accounts of the origin and operations of the universe to the birth, death, and rebirth of the human soul *(ātman)*. It is also here that the Hindu doctrines of *karman* and rebirth burst into full flower. From the Vedantic perspective, creaturely existence (including that of the gods) is the direct result of action *(karman)* performed in past lives in a state of metaphysical ignorance *(avidyā)*. This ignorance, which pervades the existence of all creatures and is the cause of transmigration *(saṃsāra)*, results from the confusion of the finite and evanescent self *(jīva)* with the absolute, unchanging self of the universe *(ātman-brahman)*. This phenomenal self or human personality is composed of five sheaths or layers of faculties, which account for a person's conscious existence and which, if identified egoistically as the ultimate basis of reality, serve as the causal basis of rebirth *(saṃsāra)*. The cyclical recurrence of rebirth is terminated and permanent liberation is achieved only after the person has come to a transformative knowledge *(prajñā)* of the quintessential identity of the human self *(ātman)* and the self of the universe *(brahman)*.

The *Bhagavadgītā*, also a scriptural foundation of Vedānta, attempts a synthesis of Vedic and Upaniṣadic conceptions of the world and creaturely existence. The *Gītā* embraces the view that the life of the cosmos and all its inhabitants is the result of the formative activities of God (i.e., Kṛṣṇa). Kṛṣṇa is both the womb of the universe and its final resting place (*Bhagavadgītā* 7.6). He is the primal spirit *(puruṣa)*, the source of all beings (10.8), the seed of all creatures (7.10, 10.39), and the universal father who plants the seeds from which all living entities arise. The world, in turn, is God's body (11.7). All beings abide in him (9.6). Hence, all states of existence arise from God alone (10.5). Abiding within the hearts of all beings and by means of his celestial power of creation *(māyā)*, he causes them to revolve *(saṃsāra)* around the circuit of rebirth as though they were mounted on a machine (18.61).

As the creator and sovereign ruler over the universe, God is also the divine embodiment of time, the destroyer of creatures and of worlds. It is he, not human warriors, who slays enemies on the battlefield. Humans serve merely as instruments of death (11.32–33).

When the life process is viewed *sub species aeternitatis,* God projects creatures into being, time after time, by means of his material nature *(prakṛti)* through the instrumentality of his magical power *(māyā).* He implants spirit *(puruṣa)* within the physical organism as the basis for the experience of pleasure and pain. The human being, in turn, appropriates the material nature of God by identifying with the three strands (*guṇa*s) of creaturely existence (i.e., passion, lethargy, and mental clarity), rather than with the *ātman,* which is the spiritual essence of the divine nature.

Human beings, then, are bound to the factors of material nature. Their emotional and appetitive attachment to these factors provokes them to perform egoistical actions *(karman),* which bind them to self-deluding ignorance and, thereby, to the round of death and rebirth. They are bound by their own past actions and also, paradoxically, by the will of God, who controls the ultimate course of events throughout the universe.

Once the embodied soul transcends the three strands that arise from physical existence, it is freed from bondage to death and rebirth and, in the end, it achieves immortality in God. Those persons who renounce the fruits of their actions and submit themselves completely to the divine will pass beyond the sphere of sorrow and death and arrive at the final termination of the cyclical life process to enjoy eternal bliss *(ānanda)* in perfect union with the godhead.

Buddhism. The Buddha himself declared that the search for answers to all metaphysical questions concerning life (Was the universe created by God or is it eternal? Is the source of birth and death traceable to a divine agent? Does the human soul survive the death of the body?) is detrimental to the human quest for lasting peace and contentment. The sole *raison d'être* of the whole of his life and teachings was the identification of the cause of human misery and the means to its permanent eradication. In one sense, therefore, it could be said that the Buddha was perhaps the first proponent of a philosophy of life.

The Buddha declared that creaturely existence is characterized by three distinguishing marks or factors: impermanence *(anitya),* suffering or unsatisfactoriness *(duḥkha),* and no-selfhood *(anātman/anatta).* With this teaching, the Buddha undercut, by a single stroke, the Hindu Vedantic conviction that the life-world *(nāma-rūpa),* with its myriad of arising and perishing creatures, is established upon a single, universal, eternal, and unchanging reality *(ātman-brahman).*

While the Buddha embraced the twin Hindu beliefs in *dharma/dhamma* (the universal law that governs the operations of the entire life-world) and *karman* (the principle that all past actions condition all current life situations), he radically redefined both concepts by rejecting the notion of an eternally enduring and unchanging soul or self. In place of the Vedantic notion of soul, or *ātman,* he declared that the human personality is constituted of five aggregates (*skandha*s) or clusters of physical and psychological factors that form the core of human consciousness and behavior. The five groups of factors are: (1) the body *(rūpa),* or physical context of sentient existence; (2) the feelings *(vedanā),* or physical and psychological sensibilities; (3) the perceptual group *(saṃjñā),* from which arise the perceptions of physical objects; (4) the mental factors (*saṃskāra*s), or tendencies of mind and will in combination; and (5) the consciousness proper *(vijñāna),* the property of awareness in the fullest personal sense of the term and the factor that binds together the other elements to form a unified personality.

It is these five collections of psychosomatic factors, therefore, that constitute the functional apparatus of all human beings, the operations of which account for the birth, existence, death, and rebirth of each person. Nor are these factors to be thought of as real and permanent entities. They are rather physical and mental components of life that condition the multitude of situations under which a person exists within each moment of consciousness. Ultimately, viewed against the backdrop of the one, unchanging reality (i.e., *nirvāṇa,* "cessation," or *śūnyatā,* "emptiness"), the aggregates or components of life are discovered to be an ever-fluctuating (hence, unreal) succession of psychosomatic events.

But the Buddha'ṣ teaching concerning the nature of creaturely existence becomes fully comprehensible only when interpreted within the context of the doctrine of causality or the universal law of karman. The Buddhist view of causation, succinctly stated, is as follows: "When this is present, that comes to be; from the arising of this, that arises; when this is absent, that does not come to be; on the cessation of this, that ceases" (*Saṃyutta Nikāya* 2.28).

The law of causation, which governs the coming to be and passing away of all forms of life, is depicted through the image of the wheel of life and death *(saṃsāra-maṇḍala).* The wheel is composed of two causally interlocking aspects or links in a chain of causes and effects. Each of the pairs of links in the chain is dependent, causally, upon the one or ones preceding it, and each, in turn, is a precondition for the link or links that follow it. In this way, the two aspects of existence form a closed circle.

Again, properly understood, the doctrine of causation (or dependent co-origination) is to be viewed not as a set of abstract metaphysical principles but as the theoretical basis of a therapeutic system by means of which the infirmities of sentient existence can be diagnosed and an antidote administered. By demonstrating that the miseries of existence (i.e., death followed by rebirth) arise out of a series of finite conditions governed by a state of ignorance *(avidyā)*, the teaching of causation defines the various points at which the succession of causally related symptoms can be broken and a cure achieved.

According to the teachings of Buddhism, therefore, the ultimate objective of human existence is to suppress all witless desires, obliterate the causes of ignorance, suffering, and rebirth, and thereby terminate the ever-recurrent cycle of death and rebirth in the bliss of *nirvāṇa*. [*See* Nirvāṇa.]

Conclusion. *Homo sapiens* is that creature within the biosphere who not only exists but also is conscious of his existence. Or, more accurately stated, he is the being who realizes the aims of his existence through the medium of self-consciousness. His possession of the faculty of self-consciousness enables him to exercise the capacity to transcend the sheer flux and flow of sensual experience and to reflect upon the nature of his existence, its origins, and the direction he wishes it to take. Hence, he can imagine other ideal states of existence that are preferable to that in which he finds himself at any given moment. He can, then, exercise his will in choosing among preferred states in hopes of bringing those states closer to realization.

In the view of *Homo sapiens*, mere physical survival has never stood as an adequate legitimation of human life. Indeed, it should be said that human existence is found to be acceptable only when it can be experienced within the framework of a meaningful and purposeful order.

For *homo religiosus*, a meaningful life is predicated upon the confidence that the world and all the creatures who inhabit it are the handiwork of divine creative forces or beings, who also, in some cases, are believed to provide a cosmic milieu that is hospitable to the growth of plant, animal, and human species.

Thus, humans everywhere look to a transhuman order of being for the revelation of the basic structure of the universe and of the moral and spiritual laws that govern its various operations. Even the performance of such commonplace activities as eating and defecating, working and sleeping, marriage and reproduction is patterned after celestial or transtemporal models. [*See* Archetypes.]

Further, it is evident from the study of the history of religions that life and death are inextricably interconnected aspects of a single reality and that all beings exist under the inexorable law of mortality. In all probability, therefore, every religious and cultural institution that composes the fabric of the social life of a people (from temple or church to family and educational system, from fertility and puberty rites to funeral and ancestral ceremonies) is established in response to the universal recognition that finitude and death are inescapable realities. The religious community sanctions these and all other institutions in the belief that the *élan vital* that undergirds and nourishes all living beings can be augmented and either the event of death can be postponed or the remaining period of life can be enriched by means of these performative rites.

Again, almost all religious traditions distinguish between an imperfect and ultimately unsatisfactory state in which human existence is set and a more satisfying, long-lasting, and fulfilling state beyond the grave (variously referred to as Heaven, Paradise, the Pure Land, the Land of the Blessed, the state of enlightenment, or *nirvāṇa*), toward which human life, in response to its loftiest aspirations, is striving. Among the world's religions, the so-called salvation religions (Judaism, Christianity, Islam, Hinduism, and certain sects of Mahāyāna Buddhism) believe that access to this loftier, purer, and more enduring postmortem existence comes in the form of a gift or an act of grace on the part of God or other celestial bearer of salvation.

In the end, the question reemerges: what is life? The very act of posing the question produces an initial sense of bafflement and perplexity. Augustine's statement to the effect that he knows the meaning of the term *love* until asked to define it could be echoed in this context. Almost anyone who has been asked to specify the meaning of the term *life* might well feel insulted. Yet, on surveying the vast array of semantic values that have been attributed to the word for "life" in the various languages of mankind, one is inevitably led to conclude that a precise, distinct, and universally acceptable concept does not accompany the use of the term. Instead, the posing of the query brings in its wake a sense that life is an inexhaustible storehouse of mysteries, a realm of endlessly self-perpetuating novelties, in which the solution to any given problem gives rise to a plethora of other questions that beckon the always-restless, never-contented mind of *Homo sapiens* to seek further for additional answers or, at least, to search out more intellectually refined, morally elevating, and spiritually salutary ways of pursuing the quest.

[*See also* Afterlife.]

BIBLIOGRAPHY

Creation

Ditfurth, Hoimar von. *The Origins of Life: Evolution as Creation.* San Francisco, 1982.

Freund, Philip. *Myths of Creation.* New York, 1965.

Long, Charles H. *Alpha: The Myths of Creation* (1963). Reprint, Chico, Calif., 1983.

Sproul, Barbara C. *Primal Myths: Creating the World.* San Francisco, 1979.

Primitive Societies

Eliade, Mircea. *Birth and Rebirth.* New York, 1958.

Eliade, Mircea. *From Primitives to Zen.* New York, 1967. A thematic sourcebook on the history of religions.

Evans-Pritchard, E. E. *Nuer Religion.* Oxford, 1956.

Griaule, Marcel. *Conversations with Ogotemmêli: An Introduction to Dogon Religious Ideas.* New York, 1965.

Judaism

Pederson, Johannes. *Israel: Its Life and Culture.* 2 vols. Oxford, 1926–1947.

Rad, Gerhard von. *Old Testament Theology.* 2 vols. New York, 1962–1965.

Christianity

Bultmann, Rudolf. *Theology of the New Testament.* 2 vols. New York, 1951–1955.

Kittel, Gerhard, ed. *Theological Dictionary of the New Testament,* vol. 10. Grand Rapids, 1964.

Hinduism

Long, J. Bruce. "Death as a Necessity and a Gift in Hindu Mythology." In *Religious Encounters with Death,* edited by Frank E. Reynolds and Earle H. Waugh. University Park, Pa., 1977. See pages 73–96.

Radhakrishnan, Sarvepalli, and Charles A. Moore, eds. *A Source Book in Indian Philosophy.* Princeton, 1957.

Buddhism

Conze, Edward. *Buddhist Thought in India.* London, 1962.

Kalupahana, David J. *Buddhist Philosophy: A Historical Analysis.* Honolulu, 1976.

J. Bruce Long

LIGHT AND DARKNESS. One need not be a structuralist of the Lévi-Straussian persuasion in order to realize that humanity has always perceived and structured its world (cosmos, society, value systems) in dual, namely "binary," oppositions: male-female, right-left, heaven-earth, day-night, sacred-profane, exogamous-endogamous, and so on. Sometimes these oppositions have developed into full-fledged metaphysical, ethical, or other kinds of symbolic dualisms (spirit-matter, soul-body, good-evil, pure-impure). One of the most "obtrusive," universal, omnipresent, and impressive oppositions encountered in human experience is that between light and darkness. Like many other oppositions, that of light and darkness is experienced in rhythmical alternation. Very often these oppositions are correlated in series of symbolic equations (e.g., light = day = heat = spirit = good = divine = male versus darkness = night = cold = matter = evil = demonic = female, etc.), and hence light and darkness can stand symbolically for many other realities.

History of Religion. Many cosmologies begin their accounts of the creation with the emergence of light (or the sun, or an equivalent light principle) out of a primeval darkness, and conversely many mythologies describe the end of the world as a twilight or darkness of the gods, that is, the disappearance of light in a final darkness that engulfs all. There is an obvious connection between light and the sun as the source of light, though not all gods of light are always and necessarily solar deities. Nevertheless, perhaps because of the conspicuous presence of sun, moon, and stars, these celestial bodies often appear as manifestations of the gods. [*See* Sun; Moon; *and* Stars.] There seems to be a correlation between light and the "ouranic" gods of the heavens, on the one hand, and between darkness and the "chthonic" gods of the earth and the underworld, on the other. Originally, there appears to have been no ethical evaluation of the opposition between light and darkness, but since the sun above is also all-seeing, he (i.e., the god connected with the sun) becomes guardian of the law, of the faithful keeping of treaties, of justice, and ultimately also of the ethically good.

Generally speaking, light serves as a symbol of life, happiness, prosperity, and, in a wider sense, of perfect being. As a symbol of life, light can also serve as a symbol of immortality. Darkness, on the other hand, is associated with chaos, death, and the underworld. When light is personified and worshiped, it tends to become associated with the sun. Solar worship was central in ancient Egyptian religion. Thus the ancient Egyptian god Amun became identified, in due course, with the sun god Re as Amun-Re (whose predecessor may have been Re-Atum). As the sun god, Amun-Re was threatened every day to be swallowed by Apopis, the serpent monster of darkness (the night). Amunhotep IV (Akhenaton; fourteenth century BCE) even attempted—unsuccessfully—to impose on Egypt a near-monotheistic sun cult. Sun worship and symbolism also figured in Mesopotamian religion and established themselves—probably because of Asian influences—in later Roman religion, with the great Roman festival of the Sol Invictus ("invincible sun") subsequently becoming the date of the Christian celebration of the Nativity. [*See* Sol Invictus.]

Light is an attribute of many divinities. As regards the religious history of the West, the eastern Mediterranean area (Egypt, Syria, Mesopotamia) seems to have been the cradle of many gods of light who regained considerable importance in the Hellenistic period and played a major role in the mystery cults of the period, though here too it is difficult to make sharp distinctions between light and solar deities. Most mystery rites performed their function of mediating salvation by having the sun/light deity bring the "initiate" *(mustēs)* "from darkness unto light." Divine manifestations are usually described as epiphanies of light.

Light symbolism in Western religions (including Islam) was decisively influenced by Greek philosophy, which gave to light a simultaneously intellectual and ethical connotation. Here, again, it is difficult to distinguish sharply between light and sun symbolism, or to evaluate the precise extent of the influence of Syrian and Egyptian sun cults. The sun as the "light of the world" represents cosmic reason. Light also represents Wisdom since it is through her that things are apparent. According to Plato (*Republic* 506d), the idea of the Good (which illuminates the soul) corresponds in the supersensual world with Helios (the sun) as the light of the physical world. The opposition of light and darkness is thus not so much an ethical one as a distinction of degrees of purity between the higher world of ideas and its copy, the lower world. Already pre-Socratic philosophy (e.g., Parmenides, Pythagoras) associated light and darkness with the light and heavy elements respectively and hence ultimately with spirit (soul) and matter (body).

According to some thinkers, it was the fire of the heavenly bodies that begot human souls. The ascent from a low, material, "dark" existence to a higher, spiritual, and divine level of being is expressed in terms of illumination (Gr., *phōtismos*)—a concept that came to play an increasingly important role in mysticism. The main connecting link between philosophy and mysticism in the Hellenistic world, especially regarding the terminology and symbolism of light, was Neoplatonism. Light symbolism spilled over from the mystery cults and the philosophical traditions to influence magic, Hermetism, and gnosticism.

In the Magical Papyri, the gods frequently are endowed with light attributes, and in the collection of writings known as the Hermetic Corpus, spirit and light are practically identical. In fact, as man rises to greater spiritual heights "he is turned into light" (*Corpus Hermeticum* 13). The identification of the inner self as light and its experience of identity with Absolute Being as light experiences are frequently mentioned in Indian sources (e.g., *Bṛhadāraṇyaka Upaniṣad* 4.37).

The Hermetic, but especially the gnostic, type of dualism equates the opposition of light and darkness with that of spirit and matter, and hence tends to develop a hostile attitude to "this world," which is the creation of an inferior or even evil power. Salvation consists in leaving behind this lower world of darkness and rejoining the principle of light. Often salvation is brought about by the supernal light principle (or a part of it) descending from above in order to redeem the particles of light (e.g., souls) from the realm of darkness into which they have fallen and in which they are imprisoned. Of all the gnostic-type religions, Manichaeism emphasizes the light symbolism most. Since Manichaeism also penetrated Central Asia and even farther east, as far as China, it is not impossible that certain forms of Buddhist light symbolism (especially Amida, the Buddha of Eternal Light) owe much to Manichaean influence. Certain aspects of Manichaeism have analogies in Christianity, but the exact nature of these analogies and of the relationship between Christianity and gnosticism in general are still a matter of scholarly controversy. Surprising analogies with the gnostic systems can also be found in the medieval Jewish Qabbalah, especially in the form that it assumed in the sixteenth century. [*See the biography of Isaac Luria.*]

A very different type of light-darkness dualism characterizes ancient Iranian religion. The principles of light and dark, that is, the gods representing them—Ahura Mazdā and Angra Mainyu—are locked in a cosmic combat. But here the opposition is not between spirit and matter but between good and evil. Matter, too, is the creation of the good god and belongs to the realm of light. But creation as a whole has to be defended against the onslaught of the forces of darkness. This struggle (and man, too, was originally created in order to assist the forces of light in their struggle against the powers of darkness) will end with the final triumph of light. Many scholars consider Iranian dualism to have had a crucial influence on Hellenistic and gnostic systems. In the rituals of contemporary Parsi religion, lights and fire play a major role.

The Hebrew Bible begins with an account of the creation of light, followed by that of the creation of the sun and the celestial bodies, but it has no original light or solar mythology. In due course, however, light became a symbol of divine presence and salvation: "The Lord is my light and my salvation" (*Ps.* 27:1); "In thy light we shall see light" (*Ps.* 36:10); "Let us walk in the light of the Lord" (*Is.* 2:5); sun and moon will no longer be the sources of light, for "the lord shall be unto thee an everlasting light" (*Is.* 60:19). The association of light and sun is preserved in many other biblical passages, especially *Malachi* 4:20: "The sun of righteousness shall arise."

Early Christianity inherited both the biblical and the contemporaneous Hellenistic (philosophical as well as religious) light symbolism. Christ was the *sol iustitiae* (see *Mal.* 4:20), and hence there was nothing incongruous about celebrating the Nativity on the date of the pagan Roman festival of the "invincible sun." According to the *Gospel of John* (8:12), Jesus said of himself, "I am the light of the world," and his followers would possess the "light of life." Easter is therefore celebrated with fire and light rituals. In the Roman Catholic rite, the paschal candle is carried into a pitch dark church with the thrice-repeated exclamation "Lumen Christi." In fact, the equation of God with the Absolute and the pure light essence finds expression also in the creed where the Son (Christ) is defined as "God of God, Light of Light, very God of very God." The Logos is also described as light in the prologue to the *Gospel of John.* Paul's experience on the road to Damascus was a typical light experience.

Already the Jewish Qumran community had divided Israel into "children of light" (to be ultimately saved) and "children of darkness" (doomed to eternal damnation)—a distinction that was subsequently taken over by Christianity. The Prince of Evil and Darkness, Satan, was originally an angel of light and hence one of his names is Lucifer (Gr., Phosphoros), literally "bearer of light." The imagery is derived from *Isaiah* 14:12, where the king of Babylonia, who in his overweening pride fell from glory to destruction, is called the morning star who fell from heaven. But the same term (*phōsphoros,* "morning star") is also applied to Christ in the *Second Letter of Peter.* The expectation of the advent of Christ was like "a light that shineth in a dark place until . . . the daystar arose" (*2 Pt.* 1:19).

Practically all religions give symbolic expression—in mythology, worship, and iconography—of their valuation of light as a symbol of blessing. Even when light and darkness are not diametrically opposed as two hostile principles but are conceived as complementary cosmic modes and creative agents (the Chinese *yin* and *yang*), there is a marked preference for light. Thus *yang* is light, heaven, positive, constructive, masculine, while *yin* is the opposite. Chinese religious history, too, has its goddesses of light as well as its sects and religious movements (including secret societies) in which light symbols play a role. There even was a women's sect—officially classified as a "heterodox sect"—called the Light of the Red Lamp, which gained some notoriety through its connections with the Boxer Rebellion around 1900.

The significance of light is also illustrated by the ritual use of lamps or candles in temples, on altars, in or near tombs, near holy images, or in processions, and by the lighting of fires on special occasions. Christmas has become a festival of light; so is the Jewish Ḥanukkah, the Hindu Dīvālī, and many other rituals, festivals, and customs in both the ancient (cf., e.g., the ancient Greek torch race known as Lampadedromia or Lampadephoria) and the modern world.

Light symbolism is also conspicuous in religious iconography: saints or divine figures have a halo surrounding their head or their whole body or a flame above their head. [*See* Nimbus.] This is particularly conspicuous in Buddhist iconography, especially in its Mahāyāna forms (e.g., in many *maṇḍalas*). Amida is easily identifiable by the halo of "infinite" rays emanating from his head. Similarly, the Buddha Mahāvairocana (Jpn., Dainichi-nyorai), the "Great Illuminator," who radiates the most intense light, appears in many Tibetan *maṇḍalas* as the radiant center. For many Buddhist sects (e.g., the Japanese Shingon), he is the supreme reality. In Japanese Buddhist-Shintō syncretism, he was also identified with Amaterasu, the sun goddess (and chief goddess) of the Shintō pantheon. The holy city of Banaras in North India is also called Kāśī, "city of light." From the seven-branched candelabrum in the Temple in Jerusalem to the secularized ritual of a permanently burning flame at the Tomb of the Unknown Soldier, the symbolism of light has shown a power and persistence unparalleled by most other symbols.

The Qur'ān, too, has its famous "light verses." In due course, there developed a prophetic and ultimately metaphysical doctrine of light. With the assimilation of Neoplatonic philosophy into Islam after the ninth century, light began to be identified with the divine light principle (i.e., the intellect, according to some philosophical thinkers) emanating into this world, a process corresponding to the elevation of the human soul to the divine light. The ultimate goal of the mystic is to behold the pure light and beauty of God. Light speculations are to be found among orthodox Muslim theologians, mystics, and gnostics (including those that were suspected of gnosticizing heresies).

Mysticism. Enough has now been said to indicate the special role of ideas and experiences of light (illumination, *phōtismos*) in mystical systems. It seems that mysticism almost automatically resorts to a terminology of light. Greek Orthodox mystical theology emphasizes the doctrine of the divine, "uncreated light" through which the mystic achieves union with God. The New Testament account of the transfiguration of Christ (*Lk.* 9) supplied the basis for this mystical theology, and hence Mount Tabor is one of its central symbols. The doctrine, rejected as heretical by the Roman Catholic church, exhibits some interesting analogies with the qabbalistic doctrine of the *sefirot*.

But while mysticism of light and illumination (cf. the technical term *via illuminativa*) is a commonplace that hardly calls for a detailed account—also Buddhist meditation systems lead through innumerable light spheres and worlds—there is one noteworthy and highly paradoxical exception. That is the doctrine of mystical darkness. The doctrine appears first in the writings of Dionysius the Areopagite (probably c. 500 CE), a pseudonymous writer whose mysticism combined Neoplatonic and Christian elements. His influence, mediated to the medieval West by John Scottus Eriugena, became strongly felt in the later Middle Ages. Already Philo Judaeus had declared that the divine splendor was so radiant as to be blinding. For Dionysius, God is so utterly unknowable, and his essence so utterly beyond our reach, that all our knowledge of him is perforce "negative." [*See* Via Negativa.] The experience that he expounds in his *Mystical Theology* is essentially an "unknowing." It is beyond human thought. It is not light but, from the point of view of human understanding, utter darkness. (This doctrine reappears in the famous fourteenth-century English mystical treatise *The Cloud of Unknowing*.) Echoes of this notion can be found also in non-Christian mystical literature (e.g., in the Qabbalah), but it should not be confused with Indian and Chinese concepts of *śūnyatā*, or "emptiness," and the like.

The sixteenth-century Spanish mystic John of the Cross similarly describes the path of the soul to total union with God as the ascent through two "dark nights": that of the senses (i.e., loss of all discursive thought, feeling, and images) and that of the spirit. In other words, mysticism is not the enjoyment of charismatic graces, illuminations, or supernaturally infused higher knowledge. Using an Old Testament image, it is not the Pillar of Fire that went before the camp of the Children of Israel at night, but rather the Cloud of Darkness. In this tradition, we do not, however, deal with an option for darkness as against light in the ordinary sense, but rather with a dialectically paradoxical response to the traditional and commonplace "mysticism of light," which is here represented as totally inadequate to describe the nature of the mystical union with the utterly unknowable absolute divine transcendence. [*See also* Mystical Union.]

BIBLIOGRAPHY

In addition to the entry "Light and Darkness" by J. A. MacCulloch et al. in the *Encyclopaedia of Religion and Ethics*, edited by James Hastings, vol. 8 (Edinburgh, 1915), and Sverre Aalen's "Licht und Finsterniss," in *Die Religion in Geschichte und Gegenwart*, 3d ed., vol. 4 (Tübingen, 1960), much valuable material can be found in the voluminous writings of Mircea Eliade and Georges Dumézil. The following texts provide further useful reading.

Aalen, Sverre. *Die Begriffe Licht und Finsterniss im Alten Testament im Spätjudentum und im Rabbinismus*. Oslo, 1951.

Bousset, Wilhelm. *Hauptprobleme der Gnosis*. Göttingen, 1907.

Bultmann, Rudolf. "Zur Geschichte der Lichtsymbolik im Altertum." *Philologus* 97 (1948): 1–36.

Cumont, Franz. *Lux perpetua* (1949). Reprint, New York, 1985.

Dodd, C. H. *The Interpretation of the Fourth Gospel*. Cambridge, 1953.

Goodenough, Erwin R. *By Light, Light: The Mystic Gospel of Hellenistic Judaism*. New Haven, 1935. On Philo.

Reitzenstein, Richard. *Das iranische Erlösungsmysterium*. Bonn, 1921.

Wetter, G. P. *Phōs*. Uppsala, 1915.

R. J. Zwi Werblowsky

LĪLĀ is a Sanskrit noun meaning "sport" or "play." It has been the central term in the Hindu elaboration of the idea that God in his creating and governing of the world is moved not by need or necessity but by a free and joyous creativity that is integral to his own nature. He acts in a state of rapt absorption comparable to that of an artist possessed by his creative vision or to that of a child caught up in the delight of a game played for its own sake. The latter comparison is the basis for speaking of God's acts as *līlā*, or sport. Although the translation is the best available, the English word *sport* is a rough rendering that suggests a frivolity not necessarily implied by the word *līlā*. In the Hindu thought world in which this term arose, the description of God's acts as sport was intended to negate any notion that they are motivated, like the acts of human beings, by acquisitive desire *(kāma)* or are necessitated by the retributive impetus of the actor's previous deeds *(karman)* or by the requirements of duty. Since God forever possesses all, he has no wants and no desires. His ever-desireless acts entail no retribution. He is not the instrument of duty but duty's creator. The spontaneity and autonomy of his actions are absolute.

The word *līlā*, used in this theological sense, began to appear in Hindu religious literature in about the third or fourth century CE. Partial sources of the concept are found in earlier writings that mention, even in the Vedic age, the frolicsome nature of the gods and the ease and freedom of their acts. The attribution of joyous freedom to the one supreme being made its appearance in the Upaniṣads in reports of experiences of unity with the Divine that were expansive states of blissful release from care. It was not in the monistic systems, however, but in the great Hindu monotheisms that the notion of divine sportiveness became a major concept. Even the worshipers of Śiva—a violent and dangerous deity not easily credited with playfulness—explained the universe as formed in the gyrations of a cosmic dance in which, as Naṭarāja, or Lord of Dancers, Śiva ecstatically creates and sustains and destroys. The elaboration of the idea of *līlā* into a studied doctrine has been primarily the work of the Vaiṣṇava tradition; in particular, the cult of Kṛṣṇa as Gopāla, the young cowherd, carried the teaching of *līlā* to its most advanced development. This later Kṛṣṇaism was shaped decisively by the idea of *līlā* in almost every aspect of its religious system—in its theology, its mythology, its mysticism, and its conception of salvation.

The Theology of Līlā. The first appearance of *līlā* as a theological term is apparently a use of the word in the *Vedānta Sūtra* of Bādarāyaṇa (third century CE?). In 2.1.33 of that work the author defends belief in a personal Creator against an objection that the God of monotheistic belief who is all and has all cannot be credited with creation, because persons create only in order to come into possession of something that they do not already have. The author replies that, even in the ordinary world, some people carry out creative acts not for the satisfaction of any wants, but merely sportively, for the sheer joy of the activity itself. Faith in a personal Creator is thus reasonable and possible.

The theological literature on *līlā* consists primarily of the commentarial writings on this passage that have been written by the founders and other recognized scholars of the various Vaiṣṇava sects. In the twelfth century, for example, Rāmānuja illustrates the meaning of *līlā* by the example of a great monarch who, though he has no unsatisfied desire, sports enthusiastically on the playing field just for the amusement of the game. The Caitanyaite commentator Baladeva compares the Creator's activity to that of a healthy man just awakened in the morning from deep sleep, who breaks into a dance simply to express his own exuberance.

Since all schools of Vedānta accept the *Vedānta Sūtra*, in some fashion they must accept also its teaching on divine sportiveness. The adherents of the illusionist school of Advaita Vedānta have been obliged, of course, to understand the sports of God to have only such reality as belongs to the personal God himself. For them, the absolute being is not in truth a person, nor in reality has any world been created, nor have any sports been performed. The teaching of *līlā* is provisional only, expressing how unenlightened persons must understand the course of the apparent world so long as they remain under the influence of the deluding cosmic ignorance *(māyā)* that creates the appearance of a world that is false. Over against this illusionist cosmology those who fully embraced the *līlā* teaching were able to maintain that the creative process is real and that the creation is not an obscuration but a manifestation of the nature of God. Indeed, some Hindus have been able to use the *līlā* doctrine to support appreciation of the world in a spirit of religious wonder and to sustain a joy in living. But the general world-weariness of medieval India did not encourage such positive applications. It was more common to use the idea of divine sportiveness to domesticate the tragedies of life by reflecting that wealth and poverty, health and sickness, and even death itself are apportioned to creatures by God in his mysterious play. The reasons for such fateful interventions are beyond human comprehension, but devotees who understand their fortunes to be the sport of God will know that it is not blind fate that controls their lot, and hence they will accept their condition as providential.

Some tension exists between the conception of God's sportiveness and the older picture presented in the *Bhagavadgītā* (3.21–25, 4.5–14) of God as acting in order to assist devotees, to maintain righteousness, and to preserve the integrity of the world. Thinkers of the school of Caitanya (1486–1533) have gone so far as to insist that God acts solely for his own sport and without thought of benefiting his creatures; creatures are in fact benefited by God's sportive acts, but only because those acts are the pleasure of a supreme being whose nature includes compassion. In other Vaiṣṇava circles it has been more common to see no difference between the two explanations of the divine motivation: God's sportive acts and his supportive acts are one because both are done without calculation of any selfish gain that might be made through them. Both are therefore desireless *(niṣkāma)* in terms of the ethical ideal of the *Bhagavadgītā*, and between God's *līlā* and his grace there is no inconsistency.

Līlā Mythology. Although such Vaiṣṇava reasonings could reconcile the old and new views of the divine motivation to each other at the level of theological doctrine, a lavish new mythology was arising in the same period that could not be reconciled so easily with the narratives of earlier forms of Kṛṣṇa worship. The theological development of the *līlā* idea was overshadowed in mass and influence by a profuse literature that expressed the new conception of the deity in myth. A diversion of attention away from the earnest Kṛṣṇa of the *Bhagavadgītā* is evident in the *Harivaṃśa Purāṇa,* composed about 300 CE. Chapters 47 to 77 of that work relate for the first time a famous set of tales about how Kṛṣṇa as a child disobeyed his parents, played tricks on his elders, spread lighthearted havoc in his cowherd village, disposed of demons with jocular nonchalance, and flirted with the cowherdesses with a daring naughtiness. About a century later these whimsical stories were retold in the fifth book of the *Viṣṇu Purāṇa,* where Kṛṣṇa's antics are called *līlā*s and the whole of his earthly career is described as his *manuṣyalīlā,* or human sport (5.7.38). About the ninth century CE these pranks were fully elaborated in the tenth book of the *Bhāgavata Purāṇa,* a text that remains the foremost scripture of the family of Vaiṣṇava sects that worship Kṛṣṇa in the form of Gopāla. The stories contained in the *Bhāgavata Purāṇa* have been retold endlessly in dependent literature in the regional languages of India. The major poets of Hindi, of whom Sūrdās was the greatest, have created in the Braj dialect an especially honored literature on the sport of the child Kṛṣṇa. The attractiveness of these myths has made the worship of Gopāla Kṛṣṇa one of the most prominent forms of Hinduism throughout the past thousand years.

In the Gopāla cult's portrayal of Kṛṣṇa's childhood behavior, the flouting of Hindu moral codes was a prominent element already in the *Viṣṇu Purāṇa,* and the antinomian tendency increased steadily thereafter. The stories of the god's infancy have remained relatively innocent in spirit, but the tales of his childhood and youth soon focused particularly upon his lying, stealing, violation of sexual taboos, and other mischievous tricks. His nocturnal flirtations in the *rāsa* dance with the *gopī*s, or cowherdesses, and in particular with a *gopī* named Rādhā, became more and more explicitly sexual. In recent centuries a major stream of Bengal Vaiṣṇavism has insisted that Kṛṣṇa's amours must be construed as adulterous. At the same time the story of Kṛṣṇa's dance with the *gopī*s has become ever more important, a central and revelatory mystery of the faith. The lesson that Kṛṣṇa worshipers have drawn from this myth has been purely devotional, however: the ideal devotee must surrender the self to God with a passion as total as that of the straying Hindu wife who, love-mad, sacrifices reputation and home and security in her ruinous devotion to a paramour.

Līlā in Meditation. The myths of Kṛṣṇa's *līlā*s provide the mental material for most of the religious observances of the Gopāla cults. The purpose of their characteristic practices is to preoccupy the consciousness with visionary perception of the *līlā*s of Kṛṣṇa. Simple conditioning begins with participation in assemblies where the stories are presented in dance, drama, the singing of narrative poetry, or the chanting of sacred texts. Brahman actors called *rāsdhārī*s enact the sports of Kṛṣṇa in a Hindi drama called the *rāslīlā.* Professional declaimers called *kathaka*s, *purāṇika*s, or *kathāvācaka*s read out the scriptural tales and explain them publicly. Devotees move toward a more inward absorption in the *līlā*s by quiet and reflective reading of mythological books. Aspiration to yet deeper Kṛṣṇa consciousness leads some further into elaborate meditational practices analogous to yoga, carried out under the spiritual direction of a sectarian teacher. Because yogic instruction has traditionally been confidential, and particularly because meditation in this tradition focuses upon matter that is shockingly erotic by usual Hindu standards, the pattern of these disciplines has remained secret to an exceptional degree. A little can be learned from manuscript works of early scholastic writers of the Bengal school, however.

One plan of meditation requires the devotee to follow in imagination the erotic interplay between Rādhā and Kṛṣṇa through all the eight periods of the traditional Hindu day, from their arising in the morning to their retiring at night. Another requires long focus of the inner imagination upon one or another mythical meeting of the divine lovers in the bowers, the meditator assuming the role of one of the female attendants (*sakhī*s) whose names are mentioned in late Vaiṣṇava legends. The hope of the meditator is to perceive his chosen *līlā* no longer merely in his imagination but in its ongoing celestial reality. By meditating on the manifested *(prakaṭa) līlā*s that are known to all because Kṛṣṇa performed them in the light of history when he descended to earth as an *avatāra,* it is possible to develop a spiritual eye and to attain vision *(darśana)* of the same sports as they are being played eternally in Kṛṣṇa's transcendent paradise in unmanifested *(aprakaṭa)* form. It helps one's meditation to take up residence in the holy region of Mathurā because that earthly city stands directly beneath the celestial city of that name where Kṛṣṇa sports unceasingly, and is its shadow and a point of special contact between the two. Such contemplations focus upon divine acts that have the form of human sexual activities, and success in meditation involves the deliberate arousal and sublimation and use of the meditator's own erotic sensibility. However, the divine love sports that meditators sometimes see are not understood to be acts of lust *(kāma),* but acts of spiritual love *(prīti).* It is believed that they will remain forever invisible to those who cannot rise above longings that are carnal.

The religious experience that is idealized by this tradition is exemplified in Narsī Mehtā, a Kṛṣṇa devotee of sixteenth-century Gujarat. His career as a major poet sprang from a vision in which he found himself in a celestial region at night, an attendant holding a blazing torch in his hand and privileged to see the heavenly sports of Rādhā, Kṛṣṇa, and the *gopīs*. So fascinated did he become as he witnessed their eternal dance that his torch burned down through his hand, he said, without his having taken any notice. In visions such as this, intense devotion to Kṛṣṇa is produced and devotees receive assurance of divine assistance and of final liberation.

Līlā in Salvation. The idea of Kṛṣṇa's eternal sport dominates the Gopāla worshipers' understanding of the nature of ultimate blessedness also. They do not expect a merging with the deity but participation forevermore in his celestial sports. It is a state of liberation that can be achieved by attaining on earth a state of total mental absorption in the *līlā*s. The schools of Vallabha and of Caitanya hold that such raptness of attention is not a mere means of liberation but is the state of liberation itself, and say that those who truly attain this ecstatic state do not care whether they shall be taken into transcendency on death or shall be reborn forever into the world. The usual anticipation, however, is mythological in its imagery. According to the *Brahmavaivarta Purāṇa* (4.4.78ff.), the sainted visionary will rise not merely to Vaikuṇṭha, the paradise of Viṣṇu, but to its highest level, Goloka, the paradise of Kṛṣṇa. There the liberated become cowherdesses belonging to the sportive entourage of Kṛṣṇa. As delighted observers and helpers, they attend forever upon the love sports of Rādhā and Kṛṣṇa, expressing through their joyful service their love for Kṛṣṇa as the center of all existence.

Hindu critics of the notion of *līlā* have felt that it trivializes God's motives and obscures his active benevolence as savior. Rāmānuja avoids the use of the word when not obliged to explain it in his role as a commentator on a sacred text, and never mentions the mythology of the *Bhāgavata Purāṇa*, which was already widely known in his day. The Śaiva theologian Umāpati in section 19 of his *Śivap Pirakācam* declares that all five classes of divine activities recognized in the system of Śaiva Siddhānta must be understood to spring from God's gracious concern for the deliverance of souls, and that it is not permissible to say that Śiva's acts of creation, preservation, destruction, and so forth, are his sports. Nor have the chief spokesmen of modern Hinduism been attracted generally by the conception of *līlā* or by its myths. Swami Dayananda in his *Satyārthaprakāśa* denounces the sportive Kṛṣṇa and his supposed acts as immoral human fabrications. Moved by their social and civic concerns and influenced by the ethical stress in Christian theology, most modern Hindu leaders have preferred the morally earnest Kṛṣṇa of the *Bhagavadgītā* to the pleasure-seeking Gopāla. Yet a few have responded to the world-affirming implications of *līlā* as a cosmological idea and have used it in interpreting the natural and human realms. In his book *The Life Divine,* Aurobindo teaches that the Lord as a free artist creates real worlds and real beings, and sports with souls and in souls in order to lead his creatures to ever-higher levels of consciousness. Rabindranath Tagore uses the language of traditional *līlā* teaching in testifying to his intuitions that a joyful, ever-creative God is continually revealing himself in the play of natural forces and in the interactions of human beings (see his *Gitanjali,* poems 56, 59, 63, 80, and 95).

Appraisals of the *līlā* doctrine have usually recognized its contribution to theology in providing a solution to an important question in cosmology and in supporting a positive appreciation of the world and of life. On the other hand, the *līlā* idea has been condemned widely as a negative development in Hindu ethics. The judgment assumes that thinking about God arises necessarily out of moral concern and must be applied immediately to the governing of the moral life. The *līlā* literature is entirely separate, however, from the *dharma* literature that is the repository of moral guidance for Hindus. The worshipers of the young Kṛṣṇa have never understood the sports of the god to be models for their own actions. Indeed, the *Bhāgavata Purāṇa* itself in 10.33.32f. admonishes ordinary mortals never to behave as Kṛṣṇa does, not even in their minds. The Kṛṣṇa cults have been orthodox in their submission to the social patterns prescribed in the Dharmaśāstras and the folk codes. Their sportiveness has manifested itself in cultic matters that are marginal to social ethics: in the exuberance of their religious assemblies, in the easy emotionality of their pathway of salvation through devotion, in the madcap behavior that they tolerate in their saints, and in the spirit of abandon that pervades their fairs and pilgrimages and a few saturnalian festivals like the licentious Holī. The great problem with which this religion deals is not a chaotic world's struggle for order, but the struggle for emotional freedom in a world already firmly and tryingly regulated. There is a clear correlation between the religion of sportiveness and the closed world of caste, as confirmed by the contemporaneity of their historical origins.

Fascination with Kṛṣṇa's *līlā*s became strong in the fourth century CE, when the writing of mature Dharmaśāstras had become a full tide and the rules of caste were being systematically enforced for the first time by brahmanical dynasties after centuries of foreign rule. Thereafter Hindus found little meaning in the *Bhagavadgītā*'s call to save an anarchic world from disintegration; instead, they sought release from bondage, and found it in new tales about Kṛṣṇa as an irresponsible and irrepressible child. Seeking in the supernatural what was most desperately lacking in their lives, what they now cherished most in Kṛṣṇa was the spirit of sport. For many centuries, imaginative participation in the frolics of a boy-god helped them to endure the restrictions of the life of caste.

[*The religious sects that developed around Kṛṣṇa and the concept of* līlā *are discussed in* Kṛṣṇaism *and in* Vaiṣṇavism, *article on* Bhāgavatas. *The reenactment of* līlā *in sacred dance drama is discussed in* Drama, *article on* Indian Dance and Dance Drama. *For further discussion of their various mythic and religious roles, see* Rādhā *and* Kṛṣṇa.]

BIBLIOGRAPHY

Banerjea, Akshay Kumar. "The Philosophy of Divine Leela." *Prabuddha Bharata* 49 (1944): 275–281, 311–316.

Banerjea, Akshay Kumar. "The Conception of the Sportive Absolute." *Prabuddha Bharata* 56 (1951): 170–173, 216–218, 258–261, 290–296. Banerjea's articles provide the beginner with a useful philosophical introduction to the concept of *līlā.*

Bäumer, Bettina. "Schöpfung als Spiel: Der Begriff Līlā im Hinduismus, seine philosophische und theologische Deutung." Ph.D. diss., Ludwig-Maximilians-Universität, Munich, 1969. This work is the sole monograph on the theological conception of *līlā.* In her conclusion, the author provides a comparison with Christian cosmogonies.

Coomaraswamy, Ananda K. "Līlā." *Journal of the American Oriental Society* 61 (1941): 98–101. An inconclusive etymological study of the word *līlā* and the associated verbal root *krīḍ-* or *krīḷ-,* "play."

Kinsley, David R. *The Divine Player: A Study of Kṛṣṇalīlā.* Delhi, 1979. A loose survey of the concept of *līlā* and of some of the Hindu narratives in which it finds expression. Includes notes on related extra-Indian materials.

NORVIN HEIN

LILITH. Identified in postbiblical Judaism as a female demon who seduces men and kills unsuspecting children, Lilith (Heb., Lilit) also became identified as Adam's first wife, created from dust to be her husband's equal. As the name of a demon, *Lilit* is etymologically related to the Sumerian *lil* ("wind") and not, as some once supposed, to the Hebrew *laylah* ("night"). Yet like the Sumerian wind demon and her later Babylonian counterpart, Lilitu, a succuba who seduces men in their sleep, Lilith is active at night, seizing men and forcing them to copulate with her. Although as child slayer Lilith bears greatest resemblance to the Babylonian demon Lamashtu, Lamashtu eventually became confused in the popular imagination with the succuba Lilitu.

In the Hebrew scriptures, there is only one clear reference to Lilith. *Isaiah* 34:14, describing the devastation of Edom, maintains that Lilith shall be at rest in the desert, among wild animals, screech owls, and satyrs. This reference to Lilith as demon is more fully developed in postbiblical Jewish literature, where Lilith is associated with the *lilin,* one of three classes of demons that appear in rabbinic writings. In the Babylonian Talmud Lilith is portrayed as having a woman's face, long hair (*'Eruv.* 100b), and wings (*Nid.* 24b) like the cherubim. Her identity as demon is underscored in *Bava' Batra'* 73a, referring to the demon Hormiz or Ormuzd as Lilith's son, and in *Shabbat* 171b, where men are warned against sleeping alone lest they be seized by Lilith.

Pesaḥim 112b, warning men not to go out alone on Wednesday and Sabbath evenings because of the presence of "Agrat, the daughter of Maḥalat," has been taken by some commentators as a further reference to Lilith. However, as Gershom Scholem maintains in his essay on Lilith in the *Encyclopaedia Judaica* (New York, 1971), the identification of Lilith with Agrat, although both are night demons, seems to have no real foundation. In one early Midrashic commentary on the Bible (*Nm. Rab.* 16.25), Lilith is portrayed as a child killer, slaying her own children when no others are available to her. Raphael Patai (1967) points out that Aramaic incantation texts from Nippur in Babylonia (present-day Iraq) dating from the seventh century CE also describe Lilith as endangering women at various times in their sexual life cycle, especially during childbirth.

All of these views are given greater expression in the *Alphabet of Ben Sira,* a biblical commentary written sometime between the seventh and tenth centuries CE. Here in the first fully developed account of Lilith, we find earlier descriptions of her as night demon and child killer combined with a number of rabbinic *midrashim.* According to the *Alphabet of Ben Sira,* when God created Adam, he realized that it was not good for man to exist alone, and so he created a woman out of the earth, just as he had created Adam, and he called this woman Lilith. Immediately, Lilith and Adam began to quarrel. Insisting that they were equals, Lilith refused to lie beneath Adam, while he argued that it was proper for him, as a man, to lie on top. Uttering God's ineffable name, Lilith flew away. In response to Adam's complaints, God sent three angels—Sennoi, Sansanui, and Samangaluf—to bring Lilith back, telling them that if she refused, one hundred of her demon children would die each day. The angels found Lilith at the Red Sea and implored her to return. She refused to do so. When informed of her impending punishment, she vowed to inflict harm on male infants up until the eighth day after birth, presumably until their circumcision, and on females up until the twentieth day (perhaps an allusion to some now-forgotten ritual for girls; see Trachtenberg, 1939). Lilith made one additional vow: if she saw an amulet bearing the name of the three angels, she would not harm the infant in any way.

Illustrations of such amulets can be found in the *Sefer Ratsi'el,* first printed in 1701 but largely based on the writings of El'azar of Worms, a mystic of the late twelfth and early thirteenth centuries. Describing certain mysteries supposedly revealed to Adam by the angel Ratsi'el, this work includes several incantations to Lilith that identify her as: *Ḥavvah ri'shonah* (the "first Eve"), the one who seeks to harm newly born infants and women in childbirth. In other medieval mystical works, most notably the *Zohar,* Lilith once again appears, both as child killer and night demon. For the first time, she also appears as wife of the demon Sama'el and, as such, is recognized as Queen of the Underworld. The thirteenth-century qabbalist Yitsḥaq ha-Cohen, and most qabbalists after him, speak of two Liliths: Lilith the Elder, the wife of Sama'el, and Lilith the Younger, the wife of Asmodeus (Ashmed'ai), another demon king.

Other suggestions found in the *Zohar* are further developed in later qabbalistic texts. These include the view that Lilith, along with the demon Na'amah or Agrat, was one of two harlots who stood in judgment before Solomon and that the Queen of Sheba was actually Lilith, a claim first made in the Targum to *Job* 1:15. Belief in Lilith as child killer persisted in traditional European Jewish communities at least through the nineteenth century. According to Scholem (1971), protective amulets would be placed either above the bed of a woman about to give birth, or on all four walls of the room in which she lay.

Erich Neumann, in his psychological study *The Great Mother* (2d ed., New York, 1963), views Lilith as an archetype of the Terrible Mother, an image within the human psyche of the mother—and, more generally, of woman—as destroyer. This ahistorical suggestion, however, does not explain why Lilith is no longer an object of either fear or desire. Indeed, for most Jews, Lilith has been relegated to the realms of rabbinic *midrash* and medieval superstition. Since the mid-1970s, however, she has reappeared in various guises, in Jewish poetry and fiction alike, and has been reclaimed by American Jewish women as a model of female strength and independence. A Jewish feminist magazine named *Lilith* has been in print since 1976, and a number of Jewish feminist theologians, reexamining the accounts of creation in *Genesis* 1:27ff., have worked to create *midrashim* of their own. In one such *midrash,* Judith Plaskow (in Koltun, 1976) restores Lilith's independence and belief in her equality with Adam, as portrayed in *The Alphabet of Ben Sira,* and replaces the myth of Lilith's supercession by Eve with an optimistic vision of the two first rejecting, then returning to, the garden of Eden to rebuild it together. These reclamations of Lilith may, therefore, be seen as a part of a more general awakening of interest in female images and symbols within Jewish tradition.

[*For further discussion of Jewish demonology, see* Folk Religion, *article on* Folk Judaism; *for the rise of feminist theology, see* Women's Studies.]

BIBLIOGRAPHY

A relatively brief, but accurate, description of the myth of Lilith based on the *Alphabet of Ben Sira* can be found in volume 1 of Louis Ginzberg's *The Legends of the Jews,* translated by Henrietta Szold *et al.* (1909; reprint, Philadelphia, 1946). For an examination of Lilith's origins, see *The Mythology of All Races,* vol. 5, *Semitic* (New York, 1964), by Stephen H. Langdon. A fuller treatment of Lilith in Jewish demonology, including her appearance in qabbalistic literature, is given in Raphael Patai's *The Hebrew Goddess* (New York, 1967), which, despite some questionable assertions, remains the most detailed study of Lilith in English to date. Those wishing to discover non-Jewish parallels to the Lilith myth should consult Joshua Trachtenberg's *Jewish Magic and Superstition* (1939; reprint, New York, 1982) and Moses Gaster's *Studies and Texts in Folklore, Magic, Mediaeval Romance, Hebrew Apocrypha, and Samaritan Archaeology,* vol. 2 (1926; reprint, New York, 1971). *Voices within the Ark,* edited by Howard Schwartz and Anthony Rudolph (New York, 1980), is an example of the resurgence of interest in Lilith, under various guises, in Jewish poetry and fiction. Judith Plaskow's *midrash* about Lilith and Eve is found in her essay "The Jewish Feminist: Conflict in Identities," in *The Jewish Woman,* edited by Elizabeth Koltun (New York, 1976).

ELLEN M. UMANSKY

LIMINALITY. *See* Flow Experience *and* Rites of Passage.

LIN-CHI (d. 867 CE), known also by his initiatory name I-hsüan; Chinese Buddhist monk of the Ch'an school. Lin-chi (Jpn., Rinzai) is considered the eponymous "ancestor" (founder) of the Lin-chi sect, one of five major Ch'an schools. In Japan, Lin-chi's Ch'an was transmitted though the Rinzai lineage, one of the principal Zen schools there.

Like most Ch'an monks, Lin-chi studied the canonical teachings of Buddhism while still in his youth and eventually progressed from doctrinal to practical studies. An early source of Ch'an history, the *Tsu t'ang chi,* suggests that he took particular interest in the doctrines of the

Wei-shih (Skt., Vijñāptimātratā, or Representation Only) school. Some of the emphases in his own teaching, his concern to expose the mental nature of the actualities underlying Buddhist doctrines and the artificiality of their formulations, are reminiscent of Wei-shih Buddhism. In Lin-chi's teaching, the notion of nonattachment as a means of freedom is extended to include intellectual and spiritual matters as well as emotional and material concerns. In common with many Ch'an teachers, he pointed out that striving for higher attainments may be no more than a disguised form of greed, a kind of agitation that in fact inhibits realization of enlightenment. Lin-chi recommended nonseeking, in the sense of noncontrivance, contending that the spiritual noble is the one who is free from obsessions, not the theoretician or the devotee of transic exercises. In Lin-chi's terms, the task of Ch'an is to be free, to be immune to psychological coercion by practices or ideas, people or circumstances; the fundamental experience he called for is what he referred to as "the true human being without status," the original, "ordinary" human being, of which all states, mundane or spiritual, are merely, in Lin-chi's terms, "clothing." To this end he repeatedly called attention to what he called the formless light of the mind, the giver of names and definitions, which itself cannot be defined or grasped but only experienced through itself.

Lin-chi's recorded sayings include descriptions of the teacher-student interaction, an important part of Ch'an activity, which outline the perceptive capacity needed in a genuine teacher, various didactic strategies, and typical barriers to understanding. This aspect of Lin-chi's work provides valuable material for understanding processes of Ch'an Buddhist teaching as relational or situational rather than dogmatic.

In his own teaching, Lin-chi was famed for his shout, which he described as a technique that might be used in a number of ways, such as to interrupt a train of thought, dislodge fixed attention, test a student by observing the reaction, draw a student into an interchange, or express the nonconceptuality of being in itself. Such was the impact of this method that it was extensively imitated, to the point that certain of Lin-chi's heirs expressly denounced such mimetic behavior as void of true understanding. Nonetheless, "Lin-chi's shout" became a stock expression in Ch'an lore, and continued to be employed ever after.

Lin-chi's sayings contain elaborations of themes and structures used by his predecessors; several of these became standard items of later Ch'an teaching material. Among the most famous of Lin-chi's formulations is his "four views," in which he sums up basic processes of Ch'an in terms of (1) effacing the environment while leaving the person, (2) effacing the person while leaving the environment, (3) effacing both person and environment, and (4) effacing neither person nor environment. Like other Ch'an devices, these views allude to actual experiences to be undergone by the practitioner in accordance with need.

Although most of Lin-chi's twenty-odd spiritual successors are obscure and his lineage did not flourish until more than half a century after his death, he became one of the outstanding figures of tradition. The record of his sayings, *Lin-chi lu* (T.D. no. 1958), is one of the great classics of Ch'an Buddhism. Excerpts from this collection appear in numerous Ch'an books of later times, used as illustrative stories or points for meditation. Less well known materials of a somewhat different tradition also appear in the tenth-century *Tsu t'ang chi* and *Tsung ching lu.*

[*See also* Ch'an.]

BIBLIOGRAPHY

Lin-chi's recorded sayings, the *Lin-chi lu,* have been edited by Takahashi Shinkichi as the *Rinzairoku* (Tokyo, 1970). Paul Demiéville's translation of Lin-chi's sayings, *Entretiens de Lin-tsi* (Paris, 1972), is informed by the translator's own superb Sinological and Buddhological skills and contains much valuable commentarial material. Readers of English will want to consult Ruth Fuller Sasaki's *The Recorded Sayings of Ch'an Master Lin-chi Hui-chao of Chen Prefecture* (Kyoto, 1975).

THOMAS CLEARY

LINGAM. *See* Phallus; *see also* Śiva *and* Iconography, *article on* Hindu Iconography.

LIṄGĀYATS. *See* Śaivism, *article on* Vīraśaivas.

LINGUISTIC ANALYSIS. *See* Analytic Philosophy.

LINGUISTIC THEORY. *See* Study of Religion *and the biography of F. Max Müller.*

LIONS. Largest of the cat family and feared by most wild animals, the lion is almost universally known as the "king of beasts." Its physical appearance, size, strength, dignified movements, and fierceness in killing other animals have, since early times, left a deep imprint on the human psyche. Associations with the concept of royalty (i.e., power, majesty, control of others) have elevated the status of the lion as symbol; such figures as Richard the Lion-Hearted; various Catholic popes who have taken the name of Leo; the Buddha, who was known as the "Lion of the Śākya Race"; and Christ, called the "Lion of Judah," have all been identified with this animal through their imputed possession of certain heroic qualities. Sekhmet, Gilgamesh, Herakles, Samson, David, Daniel, Aeneas, and Aphrodite all share some of the "lionlike" qualities of ferocity, strength, valor, dignity, and nobility.

In astrology, such connotations of royalty were taken a step further: the lion was equated with the solar principle, which is often identified as the illumination of consciousness. The constellation of Leo was assigned the sun as its ruler, and the zodiacal sign of Leo appearing during the hottest time of the year (July–August). This relationship between the sun and Leo is central to an understanding of the major role played by the solar principle in this complex symbolism.

In early Western mythology, sun/lion attributes were identified as powerful cosmic forces, eventually replacing the moon/bull themes that had dominated earlier myths. In Sumer and Crete, the lion was associated with the blazing sun, which slays the moon and parches vegetation. In Egyptian art and mythology, representations of lions were frequently stationed at the end of tunnels and placed at palace doors and tombs to protect against evil spirits. Sekhmet appears as a lion-headed woman holding a sun disk. She was known as a war goddess and became associated with the Temple of Mut during the reign of Amunhotep II (1450–1425 BCE). In his study *The Great Mother,* (New York, 1963), Erich Neumann sees Sekhmet as a symbol of fire—the devouring, negative aspect of the solar eye that burns and judges.

In the Hebrew scriptures (Old Testament), the lion appears as a symbol of strength and power and an object of fear intended as a catalyst in man's relationship to God. The allusion in *Judges* 14:18—"What is stronger than a lion?"—and the story in *Daniel* 6 of the prophet who was sent into the lion's den as a test of his faith in God exemplify the awe-inspired associations of the lion with God's power to judge humankind.

In Christian iconography Mark the evangelist is depicted as a winged lion, perhaps because the first chapter of the *Gospel of Mark* refers to "the voice of one crying in the wilderness" (*Mk.* 1:3), a voice that reputedly resembled a lion's roar. The lion is also symbolic of Christ's royal dignity. The *Book of Revelation* contains a reference to the lion as symbolic of Christ, particularly his ability to conquer evil and overcome darkness: "Weep not, the Lion of Judah, the Root of David, has conquered" (*Rv.* 5:5). The lion also came to symbolize resurrection. According to popular legend, lion cubs, when born in litters of three, were stillborn; they were brought back to life by their father, who after mourning for three days, revived them with his breath. Similarly, Jesus, three days after his death, was resurrected by God the Father.

Royal and superhuman qualities are also reflected in the portrayal of the Hindu Great Mother goddess, Śakti, who rides upon a lion. In one of Viṣṇu's many incarnations, he manifests himself in the form of Narasiṃha, the "man-lion," to defeat the demon Hiraṇyakaśipu. Numerous references in the *Bhagavadgītā* demonstrate the importance of the lion as a symbol. In battle scenes, Bharata, chief of warriors, is compared to Indra and described as an "invincible lion of a man."

Well-known representations of the lion in Indian Buddhist art include the Aśoka pillar, capped by a four-faced lion, and the Sarnāth pillar, crowned by a lion upholding a great wheel or disk indicative of the solar principle. In Tantric Buddhist art, the *bodhisattvas* Avalokiteśvara and Mañjusrī are seated on lions, and the fierce goddess Siṃhamukha is depicted as having the head of a lioness. The stylized posture called The Buddha Entering *Nirvāṇa* is also known as the Lion Posture and forms part of the ritual for disciples being initiated into certain ceremonies.

In addition to its function as a representation of the solar principle, the lion symbol has also been variously used to depict contemplation and the solitary life. These qualities are best illustrated in the lives of certain Christian saints, especially Euphemia, Ignatius, Jerome, Paul the Hermit, and Mary of Egypt.

Rebirth motifs have also focused on the lion. In the Mithraic cult, the lion-headed god Aion (Deus Leontocephalus) is associated with time and the shedding of light so that rebirth may ensue. C. G. Jung regarded the lion, as discussed in alchemical literature, as a "synonym for mercurius . . . or a stage in transformation." "The fiery lion," he concludes, "is intended to express passionate emotionality that precedes recognition of unconscious contents."

According to Heinrich Zimmer, the insatiable qualities of the lion as devourer are demonstrated in Śiva's creation of a lion-headed monster. The *Book of Job* (4:10) also notes the destructive, fear-inspiring characteristics of the lion in epitomizing its roar as the "voice of the fierce."

BIBLIOGRAPHY

Bleek, W. H. I., and L. C. Lloyd, eds. *Specimens of Bushman Folklore* (1911). Reprint, Cape Town, 1968.

Goodenough, Erwin R. "The Lion and Other Felines." In his *Jewish Symbols in the Greco-Roman Period,* vol. 7, *Pagan Symbols in Judaism,* pp. 29–86. New York, 1958.

Gray, Louis H., et al., eds. *The Mythology of All Races.* 13 vols. Boston, 1916–1932. Consult the index, s.v. *Lions.*

Gubernatis, Angelo de. "The Lion, the Tiger, the Leopard, the

Panther, and the Chameleon." In his *Zoological Mythology, or The Legends of Animals*, vol. 2, pp. 153–161. London, 1872.

Thompson, Stith. *Motif-Index of Folk Literature.* 2d ed., rev. & enl. 6 vols. Bloomington, Ind., 1955–1958. Consult the index, s.v. *Lions.*

KATHRYN HUTTON

LI SHAO-CHÜN (second century BCE), magician and alchemist at the court of the Chinese emperor Han Wu-ti (140–87 BCE). According to a contemporary history, the *Shih chi,* Li, like many earlier magicians, first gained prominence in the northeastern coastal area of China, present-day Shantung. There he won a reputation among the nobility for his magical remedies and especially for warding off old age. Though he never explicitly claimed to be more than seventy himself, he let it be known that he had witnessed events decades or even centuries earlier than would have been possible for a septuagenarian. In 133 BCE Li attracted the attention of the emperor himself. He recommended that Wu-ti should worship the God of the Stove (Tsao-chün) as a preliminary to transforming cinnabar into gold; this gold was then to be used to make eating utensils that would confer on the food served from them longevity-producing powers. Eating these foods was in turn a precondition for sighting the immortal beings of the magic isle of P'eng-lai, off the Shantung coast. Only then would Wu-ti's performance of the imperial *feng* and *shan* sacrifices on the sacred Mount T'ai win immortality for himself as well. Li claimed that he had already visited P'eng-lai and there had met the immortal Master An-ch'i.

Although Li's career at court was cut short by his death before the emperor had succeeded in encountering immortals himself, Wu-ti continued to send out expeditions in search of Master An-ch'i, on the assumption that Li had in fact not died but had himself been transformed into an immortal. A legend (attested in the fourth century CE) claims that before Li's death, the emperor dreamed that an emissary riding on a dragon flew down and announced that Li had been summoned by the god T'ai-i. Some time after Li's death, Wu-ti had his coffin opened and found in it only his gown and hat. According to another account, Li came to court only in order to acquire for his own use the ingredients for an elixir of immortality too expensive for an impoverished private citizen. The emperor's well-attested concern with the supernatural inspired further legends during the period of disunion that followed the fall of the Han in 220 CE. These elaborated on Li's career in yet greater detail. In some he is confused with the necromancer Shao-weng, a later thaumaturge at Wu-ti's court.

To modern scholars Li remains a significant figure as the first recorded alchemist in Chinese history, the first devotee of the pursuit of immortality who was said to have feigned death, and the first of many known to have worshiped the God of the Stove. The *Shih chi* account also states that Li practiced the avoidance of cereal foods, a discipline that would figure prominently in later ages as a means of achieving longevity or even immortality. Later hagiography is probably correct, however, in depicting him as but one among many magicians of his day with similar preoccupations.

[*See also* Alchemy, *article on* Chinese Alchemy.]

BIBLIOGRAPHY

The *Shih chi* account of Li Shao-chün's activities is translated in volume 2 of Burton Watson's *Records of the Grand Historian of China* (New York, 1963), pp. 38–39. For a translation of some early legends, see James R. Ware's *Alchemy, Medicine, and Religion in the China of A.D. 320: The Nei P'ien of Ko Hung* (Cambridge, Mass., 1967), p. 47. A modern assessment of Li Shao-chün is Holmes Welch's *Taoism: The Parting of the Way*, rev. ed. (Boston, 1965), pp. 99–102.

T. H. BARRETT

LITERATURE. [*This entry is composed of three articles that discuss the importance of literature and literary criticism in the study of religion:*

Literature and Religion
Religious Dimensions of Modern Literature
The Novel as Secular Literature

Particular religious literatures and mythic themes of particular religions are discussed in separate entries on the religions and on their bodies of literature.]

Literature and Religion

The most apparent and apposite justification for the inclusion of literary materials in the study of religion is the historical one. What is most obvious, however, is often overlooked, and thus even the familiar in this case bears rehearsal. In virtually every high-cultural system, be it the Indic, the Islamic, the Sino-Japanese, or the Judeo-Christian, the literary tradition has, though in vastly different forms and guises, developed in intimate—indeed, often intertwining—relation to religious thought, practice, institution, and symbolism. Without paying due heed to Greek myth and thought, to Hebrew saga and wisdom, and to Christian symbolism and piety, the twenty-five-hundred-year "drama of European literature," as Erich Auerbach calls it, simply cannot be understood. Conversely, our knowledge of these three religious traditions, of their self-expression and cultural impact, would be grossly truncated without specific consideration of their literary legacy in both canonical and extracanonical writings. In a similar way, Taoist rituals, Buddhist dogmas, and Confucian ethics joined, in imperial China, to shape and sustain the classic forms of Chinese lyric poetry, drama, and prose fiction. The itinerant Buddhist priest and his exorcistic exploits in medieval Japan have provided numerous plots for *nō* drama, while subtle debates on the Buddhahood of trees and plants *(sōmoku jōbutsu)* underlie many of the exquisite *waka* of Saigyō, the twelfth-century poet. In Hinduism, Judaism, Christianity, and several major divisions of Buddhism, sacred and secular hermeneutics have developed, at various periods, in a parallel or mutually influential manner. To ignore this interrelatedness of holy and profane texts and the interdependence of their interpretive sciences is to distort large segments of the world's literary and religious history.

The Testimony of Literature. Scholars have frequently suggested that certain genres of literature, notably poetry and drama, may have arisen directly from religious rituals. [*See* Poetry *and* Drama.] While such a view may not be applicable to all forms of literature, there is little question that the origin of some types of epic is traceable to the practice of shamanism (Mircea Eliade, *Shamanism: Archaic Techniques of Ecstasy,* 1964). [*See* Shamanism *and* Epics.] One of the most important and conspicuous features of literature's relation to religion is thus that of affirmation, in the sense that literature—both oral and written, both elite and demotic—functions to preserve and transmit religious ideas and actions. Witness the detailed description of Sibylline prophecy in Vergil (*Aeneid* 6.77–102) or haruspicy in Seneca (*Oedipus* 303ff.). Sometimes in a particular culture, as in the case of ancient India, literature may be the principal record of a religious tradition.

It is commonly recognized that "the question of the relation between gods and men is central in the world of Homer" (Albin Lesky, *Geschichte der griechischen Literatur,* 2d ed., 1963), but to an even greater extent this observation is relevant to a vast amount of ancient Near Eastern and Indian literature. Dubbed "une initiation manquée" by Eliade (*Histoire des croyances et des idées religieuses,* vol. 1, 1976), the *Epic of Gilgamesh,* in its Sumerian and Old Babylonian versions, is already a classic example of religious materials commingling with entertainment and adventure, the accepted hallmark of secular literature. Although its action is concerned with the ostensibly human quest for knowledge and escape from mortality, and though there is no firm evidence that the poem was ever recited as part of religious ritual (as was *Enuma elish,* the Babylonian poem of creation), *Gilgamesh* itself nonetheless provides its readers with a full and intricate view of Mesopotamian cosmology and theogony. As the story of Gilgamesh and Enkidu unfolds through its several extant episodes—the siege of a city, a forest journey, the routing of a fickle goddess, the lamented death of a tutelary companion—we encounter at the same time the character and activity of a host of deities. The vast pantheon and the important role these deities play in the poem serve to reveal to us important conceptions of the divine in this ancient civilization. Moreover, the story of the Deluge and vivid accounts of the underworld have, understandably, elicited illuminating comparison with Hebraic notions of creation and eschatology (cf. Thorkild Jacobsen, *The Treasures of Darkness: A History of Mesopotamian Religion,* 1976; Jeffrey H. Tigay, *The Evolution of the Gilgamesh Epic,* 1982). [*See also* Enuma Elish; Gilgamesh; *and* Drama, *article on* Ancient Near Eastern Ritual Drama.]

To students of the Indian tradition, it is entirely appropriate, indeed even commonplace, to assert that religion provides both form and substance for virtually all of its classical literary culture. So indivisible are the two phenomena that the authors of a modern introduction to Indian literatures feel compelled to state that "until relatively modern times in India—meaning by India the Indo-Pakistan subcontinent—it is sometimes difficult to distinguish literature from religious documentation. This is not because there has been an imposition of a system of religious values on the society; it is rather because religion in India is so interwoven with every facet of life, including many forms of literature, that it becomes indistinguishable" (Edward C. Dimock, Jr., et al., *The Literatures of India: An Introduction,* 1974). The truth of such a sweeping declaration is to be found first and foremost in the exalted doctrine of the spoken word in Indian antiquity, in every sense a potent equal to the Hebraic *davar* or the Johannine *logos.* This is the view that literary speech, not that of home or court but one deliberately cultivated, is virtually identical with divinity, "the Goddess herself, the first utterance of Prajāpati, Lord of Creation, and herself coterminous with creation" (Dimock). Literary speech is the language enshrined in the Vedas, four collections of hymns with origins harking back to the second millennium BCE. Although these hymns are themselves magnificent and majestic ruminations on man's place in the cosmos, on his relation to his fellow creatures, and on the great questions of life and death, it is the language itself that was supremely revered long before the texts were transcribed. It is as if the serene sublimity of the text, called *śruti* ("revelation" or "that which one has sacramentally heard"), demands of its earthly celebrants a method of transmission that would defy the corrosive power of time. To the long line of priests entrusted with this awesome responsibility, this means the obsessive concern for letter- and accent-perfect recitation of these sacred hymns and sacrificial incantations. This profound respect for the word not unexpectedly gave rise also to a science of linguistic analysis, in which detailed etymological investigation complements the exhaustive, minute dissections of words and their linguistic components. The grammar of Pāṇini (fl. around 400 BCE), comparable in effect to the minister Li Ssu's codification of the Chinese radical system (c. 213 BCE) and Hsü Shen's compilation of the first great dictionary, *Shuo-wen Chieh-tzu* (c. 121), was a culmination of this science and served to standardize Sanskrit as a national literary language.

That language, of course, is also the mother tongue of many of India's major literary monuments. As the texts of the Vedas have led to the development of philosophical speculations later embodied in the Āraṇyakas and the Upaniṣads, so the literature in Sanskrit, as defined according to Pāṇini's grammar, encompasses the two monumental epics, the *Mahābhārata* (compiled between 500 BCE and 400 CE) and the *Rāmāyaṇa*, authored by the poet Vālmīki in the first century. The length of the former is unique in world literature; it is a 100,000-line poem about the protracted conflict between two rival brothers, Dhṛtarāṣṭra and Pāṇḍu, and their descendents, the Kauravas and the Pāṇḍavas. Sometimes called "the fifth Veda," it is also a massive compendium of mythologies, folk tales, discourses, and dogmas (the *Bhagavadgītā* is an insertion in the sixth book of the poem) which exhibits more than any other of its genre what Northrop Frye has termed "the encyclopedic form." Unlike its companion, the *Rāmāyaṇa* is a shorter work with a more unified perspective, a romantic tale in which the hero, Rāma, assisted by a host of magical monkeys led by Hanuman, their simian leader, routs the god Rāvaṇa, abductor of Rāmā's wife. Similar to the compendious nature of the two epics are the Purāṇas, a repository of "stories and tales and sayings that document the thoughts, the religious attitudes, and the perceptions of self and world of the Indian peoples" (Dimock). The first century CE, which saw the *Rāmāyaṇa*'s composition, also witnessed the birth of the *kāvya* style of writing, the poetic expressions of which include both the longer narrative form (the *mahākāvya*) and the short lyric (the *subhāṣita*). [*See also* Vedas; Brāhmaṇas and Āraṇyakas; Upaniṣads; Mahābhārata; Rāmāyaṇa; Bhagavadgītā; Poetry, *article on* Indian Religious Poetry; *and the biography of Pāṇini.*]

It should be remembered that Sanskrit is but one of the major linguistic and literary currents in the history of India. Other significant tributaries which must be mentioned even in so brief a survey include the Dravidian literatures, of which the four primary languages are Tamil, Telugu, Kannada, and Malayalam, each having its own forms and conventions and its own epic, lyric, and narrative works. There are also rich and varied specimens of Hindi and Bengali religious lyric, and for students of Buddhism, Pali and Prakrit literatures constitute the indispensable vehicle for both canonical and extracanonical writings. Though the scholar of Indian religions, like all scholars of religions, must perforce study art and architecture, rites and institutions, icons and cults, social structures and cultural patterns, the length and breadth of that nation's literary history offers a magnificent panoply of virtually all the salient topoi of religion: cosmology and eschatology, theogony and theomachy, *dharma* and *karman*, sin and redemption, pollution and purification, fertility and immortality, initiation and apotheosis, brahamanical austerity and *bhakti* piety, and the thousand faces of the divine. The studies of Georges Dumézil (*Mythe et épopée*, 2 vols., 1968–1971) demonstrate the inextricable link between the gods and heroes in an epic like the *Mahābhārata*. The five Paṇḍava heroes primarily, but also countless others, are bonded to the mythic by divine parentage. These heroes replicate on earth the tripartite function of their parents: sovereignty, force, and fecundity. Moreover, whole mythological scenarios have been "transposed," according to Dumézil, onto the human level to undergird the characters and their actions in the epic. The eschatological conflict at the end of the world becomes the great battle of the *Mahābhārata* and numerous other Indo-European epics. The ancient opposition between the Sun and the Storm God in the Vedas is transplanted in the famous duel between Karna (son of the Sun) and Arjuna (son of Indra). To understand this aspect of the epic characters and their exploits is therefore to recognize "an entire archaic mythology," displaced but nonetheless intact. For this reason also, Dumézil can claim that what we know of the formation of such epics is equivalent "to the same thing in many societies, the formation of 'the history of origins'" (*Du mythe aux roman*, 1970).

India is not, of course, the only culture wherein a developed body of literary texts serves as a fundamental datum for the scholar of religion. In a well-known passage Herodotus has observed that "Homer and Hesiod are the poets who composed our theogonies and described the gods for us, giving them all their appropriate titles, offices, and powers" (*Histories* 2.15). [*See the biographies of Homer and Hesiod.*] This claim is not in dispute, though the picture drawn by these two poets must be supplemented by the Homeric Hymns and the works of Stesichorus, Pindar, and the tragedians.

Theogony, a work attributed to Hesiod and composed soon after 700 BCE, contains meticulous descriptions of the underworld. Not only does this feature indicate the Greeks' deep interest in the condition and physical locale of the departed, but also the thematic resonance of the subject would, through book 11 of the *Odyssey*, spread beyond Hellenic culture to touch such subsequent Western poets as Vergil and Dante. As befits its name, however, *Theogony* is centrally concerned with the process of divine emergence, differentiation, and hierarchy. Since it purports to trace the successive stages by which Zeus (a sky and storm god of unambiguously Indo-European origin) attained his unchallenged supremacy, the poem devotes greater attention to those immediately related to this deity and his dynastic struggles (Kronos, Hekate, Prometheus, and a motley crew of monsters and giants) than to other prominent members of the Olympian circle of Twelve Gods. While the earlier portion of the work focuses on cosmogonic development in which Ouranos and Gaia, sky and earth, were first enveloped and then separated by Chaos, the latter part chronicles among other events the series of Zeus's marriages—to Metis, Themis, Eurynome, Mnemosyne, and Hera. The significance of these multiple unions and erotic adventures is discernibly both religious (hierogamy) and political. "By taking to himself the local, pre-Hellenic goddesses, worshiped since time immemorial, Zeus replaces them and, in so doing, begins the process of symbiosis and unification which gives to Greek religion its specific character" (Eliade, *Histoire*, vol. 1, 1976). This portrait of Zeus's growth and triumph has its literary counterpart in the depiction of the central heroes of the *Iliad* and *Odyssey*, who are also transformed by Homeric epos from local cultic figures to the Panhellenic heroes of immortal songs (L. R. Farnell, *Greek Hero Cults and Ideas of Immortality*, 1920; Erwin Rohde, *Psyche*, 2d ed., trans. W. B. Hillis, 1925).

The Homeric poems offer what may be the earliest and is certainly the fullest account of the gods once they have achieved their permanent stations and functions. Throughout the two epics the presence is felt not only of Zeus but also of martial and tutelary deities like Athena, Hera, Apollo, and Poseidon and of gods with particular functions like Hermes and Hephaistos. The critical roles such deities assume and their unpredictable behavior confer on the relation between gods and men its characteristic antinomies: distance and nearness, kindness and cruelty, justice and self-will (Lesky, *Geschichte*, 1963).

Of the heroes of Greece, Herodotus has said that they "have no place in the religion of Egypt," implying that the worship of noteworthy dead men and women, real or imaginary, is peculiar to Hellenic culture. Though we know now that such a class of individuals does populate other Indo-European literatures, their presence in Homer sheds an odd, distinguishing light on these poems as both literary masterpieces and religious documents. The fact that they are local cultic figures celebrated by a pan-Hellenic epic tradition means that the central heroes "cannot have an overtly religious dimension in the narrative" (Gregory Nagy, *The Best of the Acheans*, 1979). On the other hand, it is not the near-divinity of the Greek heroes—their cultic background, their fully or semidivine parentage, their elicitation of subsequent speculation on how virtuous humans can become gods (Plutarch, *De defectu oraculorum* 415b)—that makes them impressive. It is, rather, the "disconcerting ambiguity" of their humanity—"to be born of gods, and yet to be human" (Paolo Vivante, *The Homeric Imagination*, 1970)—that sets apart figures like Achilles and Prometheus (in Aeschylus's trilogy) and endows them with problematic magnitude.

The Homeric poems are famous for their portrayals of the deities in the image of human virtues and vices, of precipitous actions and petulant emotions. This anthropomorphic feature, however, cannot obscure the one profound feeling pervading all classical Greek literatures, that between gods and men there is indeed a great gulf fixed. Whereas the blessed Olympians are immortal *(aphthitoi, athanatoi)*, humans are miserable creatures of a day *(brotoi, ephemeroi)* who, in the words of Apollo, may "glow like leaves with life as they eat the fruits of the earth and then waste away into nothing" (*Iliad* 21.463).

Only against this background of life's brevity and human insignificance can the strivings of heroic virtue *(aretē)* be seen in their greatest intensity and special poignance. Only in the light of the constant injunction against excess and aspiration to divinity, that one should not forget one's mortality *(mē thnēta phronein)*, can the heroic epithet "godlike" *(theoides, theoeikelos)* attain its fullest ironic impact. In Homer and in the tragedians, the gods are free to uphold or to dispose, to confirm or to deceive, to enable or to destroy. They may even be tied to particular individuals (Apollo and Hector, Athena and Odysseus) by means of an affinity that is both natural and ideal; yet at no point in this "divine-human encounter" are the gods to be trusted. "The gods have made us suffer," declares Penelope to her husband at their long-awaited reunion, "for they are jealous to think that we two, always together, should enjoy our youth and arrive at the threshold of old age" (*Odyssey* 23.210–212). The pathos of this utterance notwithstanding, the mood of this epic is not one of bitter regret for what fulfillment life might have brought had the divine powers been more benign. The *Odyssey* is, rather, a celebration of the exercise of human intelligence, resourcefulness, courage, and loyalty in the presence of overwhelming odds, as is the *Iliad* also in Hector's farewell and departure for battle, or in Priam's solitary confrontation of Achilles. For this reason we can justly cherish "the totality of Homer, the capacity of the *Iliad* and *Odyssey* to serve as repertoire for most of the principal postures of Western consciousness—we are petulant as Achilles and old as Nestor, our homecomings are those of Odysseus" (George Steiner, *After Babel,* 1975).

To speak of the gods' jealousy and self-will is to confront the character of their morality, already a problem disturbingly felt in the Homeric poems but reserved for the keenest scrutiny by the tragic dramatists. At bottom the issue is whether human suffering is an affair of crime and punishment, as when Paris in his sin brought down divine wrath on his city (*Iliad* 13.623), or whether the gods themselves are arbitrarily complicitous.

Tragedy's enduring bequest to Western civilization is the arresting but troubling spectacle of the failure of an extraordinary individual. This is its first paradox. Men and women like Ajax, Philoctetes, Oedipus, Antigone, Medea, and Deianira, because of their exalted station in life and nobility of character, should in all likelihood enjoy success. Tragedy, however, disabuses us of that expectation by showing us that "virtue is insufficient to happiness" (James Redfield, *Nature and Culture in the "Iliad,"* 1975). Its second paradox stems from our recognition that such a spectacle can be intensely pleasing. Aristotle's *Poetics,* attempting to explain both these phenomena, concentrates on the ideal properties of tragedy's internal structure and its designed effect on the audience. Whatever its precise meaning, catharsis, in the view of modern interpreters, is to be regarded as the key to the Aristotelian understanding of tragic pleasure. The aesthetic appeal of tragedy lies in its capacity to neutralize or purge the tragic emotions of pity and fear aroused by the incidents in the plot, much as the mimetic medium itself delights by working to remove the repugnance caused by certain natural objects (*Poetics* 1448b). The realization of tragedy's aesthetic power, however, hinges on the proper resolution of the first paradox. Hence Aristotle brings to the fore the concept of hamartia: an essentially good man, not perfect, fails not out of his own vice or crime but through error or ignorance.

Such a formulation clearly reflects the philosopher's perception of the necessarily unequal balance between culpability and consequence. The protagonist must not be wholly innocent or wholly wicked, for his suffering should neither revolt nor exhilarate. Only undeserved suffering or the kind that is disproportionate to one's offense can arouse the requisite tragic emotion of pity (cf. *Rhetoric* 1386b). The audience's cognitive and emotive response thus depends on its accurate assessment of the hero's situation, which in turn depends on how a drama unravels the causes *(aitia)* of faulty knowledge or ignorance of circumstance that can initiate a disastrous sequence of action. Although Aristotle's explanation stresses human motivation and action, the literary texts themselves are more ambiguous, for they frequently point to the complementary image of divine interference as the ultimate cause of evil in human existence.

Whereas *atē* in Homeric religion invariably implies the awful delusion instigated by capricious deities, writers such as Hesiod, Solon, Theognis, and Pindar tend to see it also as a form of punishment for human arrogance and violence. Both strands of emphasis converge in the theology of the dramatists. In Aeschylus's *The Persians,* for example, Xerxes is both victimized by a daemon, which exacerbates his actions, and guilty of hubris, for which he is afflicted by *atē.* In the *Oresteia,* Zeus is extolled as the all-seeing, the all-powerful, the cause of all, and the bearer of justice. Against such a high view of the godhead, nonetheless, there is at the same time the discordant and jarring emphasis, notably in *Prometheus Bound,* on Zeus as a cruel and truculent despot, one who is hardhearted (160) and not open to reason or entreaty (184–185). The string of testimonies on divine malevolence extends even further in the plays of Sophocles and Euripides. Perhaps the extreme expression of the god who blinds and dooms is to be found in the latter's *Heracles* when Lyssa at Hera's command appears in palpable form to madden the pious hero, who kills his wife and children, mistaking them for the sons of Eurystheus.

Even in the dramas which make no use of such sensational devices as the *deus ex machina,* there is a constant depiction of "an arbitrary and malicious interference of the gods with human action, causing infatuation in man and resulting in disaster" (Jan Bremmer, *Hamartia: Tragic Error in the "Poetics" of Aristotle and in Greek Tragedy,* 1969). *Atē* in the language of the dramatists has consequently been interpreted by contemporary scholars (Bremmer, R. D. Dawe, T. C. W. Stinton) as the counterbalance to Aristotle's concept of hamartia. Though it neither exculpates the guilty nor exempts the person from accountability, *atē* functions to help us think the unthinkable. The momentous error leading to disaster cannot be "explained" fully by human irrationality, excess of passion, or finitude of knowledge alone. "When adverse circumstance seems to give evidence of a hidden pattern hostile to man" (Redfield, 1975), the dramatists invariably invoke the deed of the striking god *(plēges dios)* for producing the ironic perversion of purposive action (Oedipus's desperate moves to save his city, Deianira's gift to her husband, Phaedra's tactics under the influence of Aphrodite). This aspect of tragedy is what shocks Plato, for its explicit formulation, as Paul Ricoeur succinctly points out (*Symbolism of Evil,* 1967), "would mean self-destruction for the religious consciousness." Therefore, the notion of evil's divine origin cannot be adumbrated and made explicit in reflective wisdom, cultic worship, or the reasoned discourse of formal theology. It can come into thought, as it were, only through the concrete, albeit circuitous, medium of art. That the figure of the wicked god is not, however, an isolated cultural aberration of ancient Greece may be seen in the fact that the Indian tradition also embodies many paths of theodicy and antitheodicy (Wendy Doniger O'Flaherty, *The Origins of Evil in Hindu Mythology,* 1976). The literary data that enshrine tragic theology, scandalous though its implications may be, will therefore always be pertinent to the study of certain types of religious phenomena—from primitive sacrifices to the modern anomaly of a Jonestown (cf. René Girard, *La violence et le sacré,* 1972; *Le bouc emissaire,* 1982; Jonathan Z. Smith, *Imagining Religion: From Babylon to Jonestown,* 1982). [*See* Evil.]

If Greek religion has had lasting impact on major genres of classical literature, the effect of the Christian religion on Western literary tradition is even more pronounced and far-reaching. In the incisive observation by E. R. Curtius, "it was through Christianity that the book received its highest consecration. Christianity was a religion of the Holy Book. Christ is the only god whom antique art represents with a book-scroll. Not only at its first appearance but also throughout its entire early period, Christianity kept producing new sacred writings—documents of the faith such as gospels, letters of apostles, apocalypses; acts of martyrs; lives of saints; liturgical books" (*European Literature and the Latin Middle Ages,* trans. Willard R. Trask, 1953). There is, however, one crucial difference between Classical Greek literature and Christian writing. Whereas the former is largely reflective of a religious ethos peculiar to one culture, the latter is by no means the unique product of one solitary community. Even the language and form of Christian canonical writings bear the imprint of antecedent religious milieus, notably the Jewish and the Greco-Roman. In his zeal to defend Christian particularism, the second-century apologist Tertullian once posed the famous question "What has Athens to do with Jerusalem?"—thereby conveniently forgetting that Jerusalem as a sacred city and a symbol of faith was hardly a Christian creation alone. Throughout its long history, Christianity and its environing culture have always developed in a dialectical fashion of discreteness and syncretism, invention and adaptation, disjunction and harmony.

Such a process is apparent at the outset of Christian literary history, in those twenty-seven documents that make up the New Testament. [*See* Biblical Literature, *article on* New Testament, *and* Gospel.] Virtually all four major literary types found in the canon—gospel, acts, letters, and apocalypse—possess the paradoxical features of distinctiveness and newness in utterance on the one hand and affinity and alliance with local literary cultures on the other. In its formal totality the gospel may be regarded as a novel genre created by the early Christian community, since its synthetic amalgamation of narrative, biography, history, dialogue, and sermonic materials defies easy classification. When analyzed in the light of historical and form criticism, however, many of the gospel's smaller, constitutive units are demonstrably comparable to other verbal forms and expressions found in the religious and philosophical movements of the Hellenistic world. There are, for example, elements of the biographical apothegm, which chronicles the life of a sage climaxing in pregnant sayings or dramatic dialogues; and there are tales of the miracle worker or healing hero common to Mediterranean religions of that era. The permanent legacy of Jesus as master teacher may well have been his highly individualized use of the parable, but the form itself was long known in rabbinic instruction. The content of Jesus' teachings on many occasions again may show striking originality or deviation from tradition, but the language in which his teachings and actions are cast (e.g., the marked series of anaphoras that introduce the Beatitudes, the deliberately crafted introduction to *Luke* and *Acts*) can also significantly reveal the author or redactor's familiarity with classical rhetoric and literary form.

This phenomenon of originality joined with conventionality also characterizes the named, anonymous, or pseudonymous epistolary writings of the New Testament. Students of the apostle Paul's letters are understandably prone to stress their distinctive features: the Christian transformation of the opening and address; the special use of the diatribe; the vivid autobiographical accounts; the intimate, personal tone of his concerns; and the powerful texture woven out of both kerygmatic and paraenetical elements of his faith. To balance such an emphasis, it must be pointed out that these apostolic documents are not isolated instances of letter writing. Letters in the ancient world were used, among other purposes, as a medium for the exposition of ideas, and such writings as those of Epicurus on philosophy, Archimedes and Eratosthenes on science, and Dionysius of Halicarnassus on literary criticism still provide an illuminating context for the study of Christian epistolary achievement (H. Koskenniemi, *Studien zur Idee und Phraseologie des griechischen Briefes bis 400 nach Christentum,* 1956). Increasingly, contemporary New Testament scholarship has come to recognize that Paul's education may well have included exposure to the rhetoric of Roman law courts, the practices of itinerant Greek philosophers, and the conventions of Greek letter-writers. While one scholar has analyzed the letter to the churches in Galatia in terms of the classical "apology" (Hans Dieter Betz, *Galatians,* 1979), with exordium, narration, proposition, proof, and conclusion, another sees in *1 Corinthians* 13 a possible imitation of a Greek encomium on virtue, and in the peristasis catalog of *2 Corinthians* 11 traces of the Cynic-Stoic diatribe and the imperial *res gestae* (Wayne A. Meeks, *The Writings of St. Paul,* 1972).

As one moves into the subsequent centuries of the Christian era in the West, the tension between "pagan learning" and an emergent Christian literary culture continues to be evident. Anticipating by more than a millennium some of the sentiments of Milton's Christ in *Paradise Regained,* the *Didascalia apostolorum* (Teachings of the Apostles, 12) solemnly instructs the faithful:

> But avoid all books of the heathen. . . . If thou wouldst read historical narratives, thou hast the Book of Kings; but if philosophers and wise men, thou hast the Prophets, wherein thou shalt find wisdom and understanding more than that of the wise men and philosophers. And if thou wish for songs, thou hast the Psalms of David; but if thou wouldst read of the beginning of the world, thou hast the Genesis of the great Moses; and if laws and commandments, thou hast the glorious Law of the Lord God. All strange writings therefore which are contrary to these wholly eschew.

The persistence of Greco-Roman *paideia* in the schools and the gradual increase of educated converts, however, rendered it inevitable that a narrow parochialism had to modify itself. Augustine epitomizes the alternate attitude in a rhetorical question: "While the faculty of eloquence, which is of great value in urging either evil or justice, is in itself indifferent, why should it not be obtained for the uses of the good in the service of truth?" (*On Christian Doctrine* 4.2). Once Christians had settled on this prosaic but potent justification for art, realizing that beauty could be enlisted for the cause of faith, incentive for both adaptations of alien cultural forms and original productions multiplied. Echoing Augustine's sentiments, George Herbert in the seventeenth century asked of his God:

> Doth poetry
> Wear Venus' livery, only serve her turn?
> Why are not sonnets made of thee, and lays
> Upon thy altar burn?

In view of such zealous concern, it is not surprising that Catholic meditative techniques and Protestant biblical poetics combined to produce in the late English Renaissance an abundance of the finest Christian devotional lyrics.

Although the bulk of patristic prose literature remains in the categories of dogmatic treatises, apologetics, exegetical and hermeneutical writings, homiletics, and pastoral disquisitions, Christian writers of the early centuries have also contributed to noteworthy and lasting changes in literary language. While the likes of Minucius Felix (d. about 250) and Cyprian (d. 258) faithfully and skillfully emulated classical models, Tertullian forged a new style through translation, word-borrowing (Greek to Latin), and the introduction of new Latin diction based on vernacular usage (E. Norden, *Die antike Kunstprosa,* reprint, 1909; F. T. Cooper, *Word Formation in the Roman Sermo Plebius,* 1895). By means of extensive translations (of both sacred scriptures and other Christian writers), letters, lives of saints, travelogues, and the continuation of Eusebius's chronicle, Jerome (c. 347–419/20) also mediated between classical antiquity and Christian letters.

Within this context of continuity and change, Augustine of Hippo (354–430) justifiably occupies a place of pivotal importance. Not only did he set forth a profound and mature theological vision that across the centuries has exerted abiding influence on both Catholic and Protestant thought in the West, but his mercurial mind and voluminous speculations also directly funded such divergent developments as medieval literature, science, and aesthetics. More than any other figure in early Christian history, Augustine exemplifies the near-perfect fusion of pagan wisdom and Christian invention, of thought and style, of ideology and language. [*See the biography of Augustine.*]

As the astute analysis of Erich Auerbach has shown, the sermons of Augustine are masterful transformations of the Ciceronian model of oratory. To the ornate abundance of rhetorical figures and tropes at his disposal, the bishop of Hippo brought new depths of passion, piety, and inwardness. Of the three styles *(magna, modica,* and *parva)* that defined the ancient gradations of writing, the last and the lowliest is now endowed with unprecedented dignity and employed with new flexibility, precisely because *sermo humilis* is structured to mirror the threefold *humilitas* of the Incarnation, the culture of the Christian community, and the relative linguistic simplicity of scripture (Auerbach, *Literary Language and Its Public in Late Latin Antiquity and in the Middle Ages*, trans. Ralph Manheim, 1965).

Just as Augustine's *Confessions* exists for all posterity as the undisputed prototype of both spiritual and secular autobiographies, and his *City of God* as an unrivaled exemplum of Christian philosophy of history and historiography, so his *On Christian Doctrine* remains a milestone in the history of interpretation theory and homiletics. [*See* Autobiography.] The Augustinian understanding of rhetoric, hermeneutics, poetry, and allegory pervades medieval formulations of literary theory, notable in the works of Isidore of Seville (c. 560–636), Vergil of Toulouse (fl. seventh century), Bede (c. 673–735), Alcuin (730/40–804), Rabanus Maurus (c. 780–856), John Scottus Eriugena (fl. 847–877), and Thomas Aquinas (c. 1225–1274). The grand themes of his theology—creation, the human image as analogy to the divine, the Fall, the Incarnation, election, redemption, history, providence, temporality, and eternity—and his particular mapping of the *ordo salutis* find reverberations and echoes not only in such specifically Christian poets as Spenser and Milton but also in some of the Romantics and moderns.

Unlike writing in prose, poetry had a discernibly slower development within Christianity. Although three of the largest works in the Hebrew canon are essentially poetical—*Job*, *Psalms*, and *Proverbs*—and long passages of poetry stud the historical and prophetic books, what can pass for verse in the New Testament amounts to no more than bits and fragments. [*See* Biblical Literature, *article on* Hebrew Scriptures.] Christians had to wait for over a thousand years before they can be said to have produced devotional and liturgical verse of comparable intensity and complexity to "the songs of David." The author of *Colossians* in a well-known passage (3:16) bids his readers to sing "psalms, hymns, and spiritual songs," and hymn singing was apparently a common act of worship among the early Christians (cf. *1 Cor.* 14:26, *Eph.* 5:19, *Mk.* 14:26, *Acts* 16:25). But the texts of such hymns or songs are all but unknown. Even the so-called Magnificat preserved in the first chapter of *Luke* displays greater indebtedness to Hebraic sentiment and diction than to Christian feeling. Beyond the canonical corpus, examples of early Christian versification in classical languages may be found in such diverse contexts as the pseudo-Sibylline Oracles (additions by Judaic Christians in the late first to third centuries); an anonymous poem at the end of *Paidagōgos* by Clement of Alexandria (early third century); the partly allegorical *Symposium of the Ten Virgins* by Methodius (fourth century); the *Peristephanon*, *Cathemerinon*, and *Psychomachia* by the Spaniard Prudentius (late fourth century); the *Carmen Paschale* by Sedulius (mid-fifth century); and in such verse paraphrases of the Bible as Juvencus's *Historia evangelica* (fourth century) and Marius Victor's *Alethia* (fifth century). With the possible exception of those by Prudentius, these works are now read more for their historical than for their literary merit. The ensuing Carolingian age produced verse (both accentual and quantitative) on a variety of subjects, which would eventually fill four massive volumes (in *Monumenta Germaniae Historica*), but no poet ranking with the immortals. As for vernacular literature, such poems as the *Chanson de Roland*, *Beowulf*, and the *Víga-Glúmssaga* continue to fuel scholarly debate about the extent to which Christian conceptions of virtue and piety colored pagan notions of heroism and fate.

In contrast to the relative crudity and simplicity of their predecessors' accomplishments, the poetic genius of Dante, Spenser, and Milton seems all the more remarkable, for the Christian tradition would be immeasurably impoverished if it did not possess their writings. These eminent *poetae theologi*, however, are so well known and their works have been the subject of so much sustained commentary that any utterance one may presume to make about them risks superfluity. Yet, their permanent greatness in the annals of Western religious poetry surely rests on their creation of original, large-scale works of art that are at the same time monuments in the history of religions. Neither ponderous paraphrases of scripture or doctrinal treatises nor the unassimilated union of poetic forms and religious substance, the texts of the *Commedia*, *The Faerie Queene*, and *Paradise Lost* represent the fullest, most systematic exploration and embodiment of the poets' faith. Each in its respective manner is, as Dante said of his own masterpiece, "a sacred song / To which both Heaven and Earth have set their hand" (*Paradiso* 25.2–3). Their luminous, mellifluous sacrality is to be measured not simply by the extent to which they faithfully reflect or document tradition but by the creativity and acuity wherewith they challenge and revise tradition. Dante, for example, claims for his poem "the cognitional function Scholasticism denied to poetry in general" (Curtius, *European Literature*, 1953) and reverses the *Summa* by disclosing "divine truth as human destiny, as the element of Being in the consciousness of erring man" (Erich Auerbach, *Dante: Poet of the Secular World*, trans. Ralph Manheim, 1961). Milton's attempted theodicy significantly alters patristic and reformed dogmas

(Christology, election, creation, hamartology) to stress a dynamic conception of the *imago dei* and the import of free will and human love in the drama of fall and redemption. Their distinctive elucidation of scripture and embroidery of tradition render these articulate canticles part of Christian exegesis and theology, for they participate as much as any work of "the doctors of faith" in seeking to comprehend and interpret the original mystery of faith, of revelation itself. [*See also* Poetry, *article on* Christian Poetry, *and the biography of Dante.*]

The Study of Literature. The foregoing survey of religious and literary history has sought to demonstrate how individual texts, figures, genres, movements, and periods may provide crucial data for the student of religion. The survey has been deliberately focused on more traditional materials, since the applicability of its principal thesis is manifestly more restricted in the modern era, given the undeniable shifts in historical development and cultural climate. However, inasmuch as the study of religion frequently, if not exclusively, involves the study of verbal texts, the discipline is even more indissolubly bound with the study of literature. Both disciplines at that juncture entail the deepest and most wide-ranging engagement with the analysis of language, and this engagement implicates all the concerns expressive of the human sciences. [*See also* Scripture; Hermeneutics; Biblical Exegesis; Buddhist Literature; *and* Aesthetics, *article on* Philosophical Aesthetics.]

Prior to any textual interpretation there must be an acceptable text. This truism forcefully reminds us that textual criticism, the science developed since the Renaissance for the establishment of the so-called proper text, already locates the unavoidable convergence of classical scholarship, biblical criticism, and the techniques of literary analysis. Most religious communities are not so fortunate as the Church of Jesus Christ of Latter-Day Saints, which has in its possession both partial and complete versions (the latter in the church's reorganized branch) of the *Book of Mormon*'s original manuscript. For Jews, Christians, and Buddhists, to cite obvious examples, the original documents of revelation exist only in a scholarly construct called the "urtext" and, if even that seems an impossible ideal, in a family or group of the best texts, critically ascertained and adjudged to approximate the original form. Of necessity, therefore, the study of sacred texts at its most fundamental level already utilizes procedures and methods that transcend the provenance of any particular religious tradition or community. The author of *2 Timothy* may claim that "all scripture is inspired by God" (3:16), but all scripture is not thereby protected from wayward readings by errant mortals or the corruptions of temporal transmission. "To repair the wrecks of history" requires the use of "a historical method" (Jerome J. McGann, *A Critique of Modern Textual Criticism,* 1983), and any religion of the book or books must rely on this most venerable of humanistic disciplines (that is, textual criticism, which for McGann depends on the historical method) for its continuance and propagation.

Were textual criticism merely an affair of the mechanical activities of editing, collation, and application of the canons of textual criticism, the consequence of its pursuit might not appear to be immediately relevant. But scholars have long recognized that in many instances textual criticism does bear powerfully on textual interpretation, that stemmatics inevitably intrudes upon hermeneutics (e.g., *New Testament Textual Criticism: Its Significance for Exegesis,* ed. Eldon Jay Epp and Gordon D. Fee, 1981). On the one hand, the modes of critical reasoning employed in the determination of variant readings are identical with or similar to those engaged in the determination of verbal meaning, in exegesis, and in translation. On the other hand, the difference of a single word or of an entire edition can drastically alter the construal of textual meaning. Whether Christians, as a result of their "justification by faith," are told that they in fact have peace with God or that they are to have peace with God depends on the selection of either the indicative *(echomen)* or the hortatory subjunctive *(echōmen)* found in different manuscript traditions of *Romans* 5:1. "Soiled fish of the sea," a phrase lodged in the Constable Standard Edition of Melville's *Works,* has led the great American critic F. O. Matthiessen to speak unwittingly of "the *discordia concors,* the unexpected linking of the medium of cleanliness with filth, [which] could only have sprung from an imagination that had apprehended the terrors of the deep," only to have such eloquence vitiated by the cruel discovery of a typesetter's oversight, when *coiled,* not *soiled,* is proved to be in both the English and American first editions. The publication in 1984 of *Ulysses: A Critical and Synoptic Edition,* with five thousand corrections and additions heretofore unavailable, has led critics to reexamine and revise many previous interpretations of this modern classic.

Because textual criticism wishes to retrieve a text as free as possible of historical corruptions, its goal is often taken as the starting point for textual interpretation. Paradoxically, however, such criticism can also set one kind of limit for interpretation. The "pure" authoritative text in such a discussion means that which is closest to the author's final intentions, whether those intentions are perceived to be identified with a manuscript or one of the first printed editions. Although such considerations are germane to many modern texts, they become unsuitable for editing (and thus *a fortiori* for interpreting) many medieval and older texts, particularly those with polygenous stemmas. In *A Critique of Modern Textual Criticism* (1983), Jerome G. McGann notes:

> In their earliest "completed" forms these texts remain more or less wholly under the author's control, yet as a class they are texts for which the editorial concept of intention has no meaning. These texts show, in other words, that the concept of authorial intention only comes into force for criticism when (paradoxically) the artist's work begins to engage with social structures and functions. The fully authoritative text is therefore always one which has been socially produced; as a result, the critical standard for what constitutes authoritativeness cannot rest with the author and his intentions alone.

In the example from *Romans* 5 cited above, even the recovery of the original manuscript may not be decisive enough to decipher authorial intention, since the fact that the Greek words are homonyms could easily have dictated the particular spelling of the amanuensis known to have been used by the apostle. Short of questioning Paul himself, we are left with two perhaps equally plausible readings, but with definitely different meanings. We can recover, independently and without difficulty, the meaning of these two Greek words, but no amount of attention paid to "shared experiences, usage traits, and meaning expectations" (E. D. Hirsch, *Validity in Interpretation*, 1967) can now tell us exactly what it is that Paul wished to convey by this particular sequence of linguistic signs. Inability to discern final intention in this instance is also synonymous with inability to discern original intention, but the indeterminancy of textual meaning is not caused so much by the historicity of our understanding as it is by the historicity of the text.

In his effort to elevate the discourse of contemporary literary criticism, Geoffrey Hartman wants to make it "participate once more in a living concert of voices, and to raise exegesis to its former state by confronting art with experience as searchingly as if art were scripture" (*Beyond Formalism*, 1970). This noble proposal unfortunately does not make clear how searchingly scriptural exegesis, in whatever former state, has been confronted with experience. More importantly, it overlooks the fact that scriptural exegesis itself throughout its history, much as any other kind of exegesis, has always had to struggle with the question of how a verbal text is to be read, how its language—from a single word to an entire book—is to be understood. If biblical critics of late "have been looking over the fence and noting the methods and achievements of the secular arm" (Frank Kermode, *The Genesis of Secrecy*, 1979), this tendency is not radically different from the Alexandrian school's appropriation of Philonic allegory to interpret Christian scriptures or the Protestant reformers' use of humanistic philology to advance their own grammatical-historical mode of exegesis. Wary of misreadings through willful or unintended anachronism, some contemporary biblical scholars are justifiably skeptical of the current movement in certain quarters to read the Bible as literature, to expound sacred writ by means of secular norms and literary classifications.

While it may be true that the comparison of Hebrew narrative with Homeric epic or the analysis of a parable of Jesus in terms of plot and character can lead only to limited yields, the reverent affirmation that scripture must be read as revelation or the word of God does not itself explain how language is used in such divine literature. The confusion here arises from the too ready identification of literature with fiction or fictionality, itself a common but nonetheless a particular view of the nature of literature. The rejection of this view, on the other hand, in no way absolves the biblical reader from wrestling with the linguistic phenomenon that is coextensive with the text. Does the Torah or the New Testament or the *Lotus Sutra* use language as human beings do, and if not, what other contexts are there for their readers to consider and consult? What sort of literary competence or what system of conventions ought to be operative in reading sacred texts? [*See* Language.]

The history of Christian biblical exegesis is filled with examples of how interpretation changes along with different reading assumptions and conventions. A particular view of language has led patristic writers to understand in a certain way the terms *image* and *likeness* (Heb., *tselem, demut;* Gr., *eikona, homoiōsin;* Lat., *imaginem, similitudinem*), used in the first creation narrative of *Genesis*. For Irenaeus, in the second century, the former has come to signify the *anima rationalis* in human nature, whereas the latter refers to the *donum superadditum supernaturale* which will be lost in the Fall. Later interpreters, notably the Protestant reformers, have challenged this developed Catholic doctrine of the *imago dei* on the ground that it has missed the Hebraic convention of linguistic parallelism, though the reformed interpretation itself is by no means free of dogmatic presupposition. The precise meaning of one fundamental Christian assertion—the Eucharistic formula, "This is my body . . . this is my blood"—has eluded interpreters and divided Christendom for centuries because the issue of whether it is a literal or a figurative statement is as much a linguistic one as it is a theological one.

These examples of biblical exegesis serve to reinforce one basic insight of Friedrich Schleiermacher: namely, that special or sacred hermeneutics "can be understood only in terms of general hermeneutics" (MS 2, in *Hermeneutics: The Handwritten Manuscripts,* ed. H. Kimmerle, 1977). For this very reason, every significant turn or development in literary theory and the culture of criticism should, in principle, be of interest to scholars of religion. Because verbal texts are more often than not the objects of their inquiry, they must know "the manifold varieties of minutely discriminating attention to the artful use of language, to the shifting play of ideas, conventions, tone, sound, imagery, syntax, narrative viewpoint, compositional units, and much else" (Robert Alter, *The Art of Biblical Narrative,* 1981). That last amorphous category, in the light of the American and European critical discourse of the last three decades, would certainly include such large and controversial subjects as phenomenology, philosophical hermeneutics, feminist criticism, genre theory, reception theory, communication and information theory, linguistics, structuralism, deconstructionism, and psychoanalysis. Although space does not permit extensive treatment of any single facet of this new "armed vision," a brief review of the problem of where to locate textual meaning may be instructive.

In the heyday of New Criticism, distinguished by its apologetic zeal to honor literature's intrinsic worth and mode of being, meaning was virtually identical with the text. In contrast to scientific denotative language, literary language was held to be reflexive and self-referential; hence the perimeters of a single text constituted its most proper context. Meaning was generated by the text's essential form or verbal structure, which was said to resemble "that of architecture or painting: it is a pattern of resolved stresses" (Cleanth Brooks, *The Well Wrought Urn,* 1947). Because the poem represented the most felicitous union of ontology and praxis—"it is both the assertion and the realization of the assertion"—its meaning was thus paradoxically comprehensible but supposedly could not be paraphrased. Similarly, the act of interpretation was itself something of a paradox. On the one hand, the aim of interpretation was to ascertain "the way in which the poem is built . . . the form it has taken as it *grew* in the poet's mind." Since interpretation was thought to be determined by no factor other than that single object of the text, even the consideration of its origin or effect (the celebrated "intentional" and "affective fallacies") was deemed extraneous and irrelevant. Because the text was taken as the privileged vehicle of meaning, its integrity could be preserved only if the interpreter were purged as much as possible of his or her own assumptions, prejudices, beliefs, and values. Despite such noble effort, the New Critics confessed, the interpreter's act carries the pathos of a quixotic quest, for the adequacy of criticism will always be surpassed by the adequacy of the poem.

In various ways the history of literary theory over the past thirty years may be regarded as a steady and increasingly stringent attack on such New Critical doctrines of the text and the interpreter. The Heideggerian notion of *Vorverstädnis,* mediated by the translated writings of Rudolf Bultmann and Hans Gadamer, demonstrated the impossibility of unprejudiced, objective interpretation, because no act of knowing can be undertaken without a "pre-knowing" that is necessarily bound by the person's history and culture. In fact, both texts and the historical "horizon" of the interpreter, when scrutinized by such hermeneuticians of suspicion as Marxists, neo-Marxists (cf. Jürgen Habermas's critique of Gadamer), and Freudians (Jacques Lacan and followers), are inevitably obscured by ideology, false consciousness, or the subversive language of repression. In place of the "closed readings" in which purity and objectivity are ensured by an innocent, submissive critical consciousness, the languages of both text and critic seem more likely to wear the masks of deceit and desire (René Girard), as well as of domination and violence. Instead of the text being the bearer of authorially structured meaning (E. D. Hirsch), textual meaning is regarded as a product either of readers or communities of readers (Stanley Fish, Frank Kermode) or of the dialectical interplay of the text and the reading process (H. R. Jauss, Wolfgang Iser, the later writings of Roland Barthes). Meaning may be actualized by uncovering the deep structures—the equivalences and oppositions—buried within a poem's semantic, syntactic, and phonological levels (Roman Jakobson and Claude Lévi-Strauss), by the delineation of the vision and world projected "in front of" the text (Paul Ricoeur), or by the perception of generic codes that at once familiarize and defamiliarize (Victor Shklovsky).

The most radical treatment of the problem of text and meaning is certainly that fashioned by Jacques Derrida and his followers. The traditional view of language in Western civilization has been essentially a mimetic one: language can faithfully and fruitfully mirror the interchange between mind, nature, and even God. The agenda of deconstructionism, however, is to undertake the most trenchant and skeptical questioning of the symmetrical unity between signifiers and signifieds posited by Saussurean linguistics. "For the signified 'boat' is really the product of a complex interaction of signifiers, which has no obvious end-point. Meaning is the spin-off of a potentially endless play of signifiers, rather than a concept tied firmly to the tail of a particular signifier. . . . I do not grasp the sense of the sentence just by mechanically piling one word on the other: for the words to compose some relatively coherent meaning at all, each one of them must, so to speak, contain the trace of the ones which have gone before, and hold itself open to the trace of those which are coming after" (Terry Eagleton, *Literary Theory: An Introduction,* 1983). For this reason meaning in the Derridean view must be qualified by the characteristics of *différance* (in the sense of both difference and deferral), absence (in the sense that signs are forever inadequate to "make present" one's inward experiences or phenomenal objects), and decentering (in the sense of rejecting the "transcendental signified" and reconceptualizing any notion of the fixed origin or metaphysical *Urgrund* as the product of desire). To speak of the stability and determinancy of textual meaning is therefore meaningless, just as it is futile to refer to a poem's language as its proper context. The context of a poem, rather, is the entire field of the history of its language, or, in Jonathan Culler's apt dictum, "Meaning is context bound, but context is boundless" (*On Deconstructionism: Theory and Criticism after Structuralism,* 1982). Meaning is thus finally coincidental with the Nietzschean concept of free play, both labyrinthine and limitless; and interpretation, far from being an affair of passive mimesis, is another form of mediation and displacement, of substituting one set of signifiers for another (cf. Jacques Derrida, *Writing and Difference,* 1978; *Of Grammatology,* 1976; *Dissemination,* 1982).

The merit of deconstructionism for literary study is already hotly debated; whether it is of use to the study of religion must await scholarly lucubrations. To a discipline committed to investigating the infinite varieties and morphologies of "the irreducibly sacred," a program replete with logocentrism, the challenge posed by the uncanny, Cassandra-like utterances of Derrida seems all too apparent.

[*See also* Biography; Cosmogony; Heroes; Myth; Quest; *and the biographies of writers, religious thinkers, and philosophers mentioned herein.*]

BIBLIOGRAPHY

Auerbach, Erich. *Mimesis: The Representation of Reality in Western Literature.* Princeton, 1953.

Booth, Wayne C. *A Rhetoric of Irony.* Chicago, 1974.

Fairchild, Hoxie N. *Religious Trends in English Poetry.* 6 vols. New York, 1939–1968.

Frye, Northrop. *The Great Code: The Bible and Literature.* New York, 1982.

Gunn, Giles B. *The Interpretation of Otherness: Literature, Religion, and the American Imagination.* Oxford, 1979.

Handelman, Susan A. *The Slayers of Moses: The Emergence of Rabbinic Interpretation in Modern Literary Theory.* Albany, N.Y., 1982.

Kennedy, George A. *Classical Rhetoric and Its Christian and Secular Tradition from Ancient to Modern Times.* Chapel Hill, N.C., 1980.

LaFleur, William R. *The Karma of Words: Buddhism and the Literary Arts in Medieval Japan.* Berkeley, 1983.

Lewalski, Barbara Kiefer. *Protestant Poetics and the Seventeenth-Century Religious Lyric.* Princeton, 1979.

Lieb, Michael. *Poetics of the Holy: A Reading of "Paradise Lost".* Chapel Hill, N.C., 1981.

Miner, Earl, ed. *Literary Uses of Typology from the Late Middle Ages to the Present.* Princeton, 1977.

O'Flaherty, Wendy Doniger, ed. *The Critical Study of Sacred Texts.* Berkeley, 1979.

Poland, Lynn M. *Literary Criticism and Biblical Hermeneutics: A Critique of Formalist Approaches.* Chico, California, 1985.

Ramsaran, John A. *English and Hindi Religious Poetry.* Leiden, 1973.

Redmond, James, ed. *Drama and Religion.* Cambridge, 1983.

Ricoeur, Paul. *Time and Narrative.* 2 vols. Chicago, 1984–1986.

Scott, Nathan A., Jr. *The Poetics of Belief.* Chapel Hill, N.C., 1985.

Shaffer, E. S. *"Kubla Khan" and the Fall of Jerusalem: The Mythological School in Biblical Criticism and Secular Literature, 1770–1880.* Cambridge, 1975.

Sternberg, Meir. *The Poetics of Biblical Narrative.* Bloomington, Ind., 1984.

Strier, Richard. *Love Known: Theology and Experience in George Herbert's Poetry.* Chicago, 1983.

Wilder, Amos N. *Early Christian Rhetoric: The Language of the Gospel.* Cambridge, Mass., 1972.

ANTHONY C. YU

Religious Dimensions of Modern Literature

In the West, the major literature of the modern period forms a canon reaching from Stendhal to Faulkner, from Leopardi to Stevens, from Gogol to Malraux, from Rimbaud to Rilke and Yeats and Montale; and this is a canon that, in its predominant tone and emphasis, is secular. Indeed, the modern writer, in his characteristic manifestations, is commonly regarded (in the phrase from Wallace Stevens's *Esthétique du Mal*) as a "shaken realist" who, in a time left darkened by the recession of traditional codes and patterns of belief, has had to steer his own course without compass or guiding star. The Christian mythos has, of course, steadily retained its power to offer certain figures a controlling vision of the world; and, in this connection, one will think of such poets and novelists and dramatists of the present century as Georges Bernanos, Paul Claudel, François Mauriac, Gertrud von le Fort, T. S. Eliot, David Jones, W. H. Auden, R. S. Thomas, Graham Greene, and Flannery O'Connor. But these and numerous others who might also be spoken of are writers who, for all the immense distinction of an Eliot or an Auden, form nevertheless a minority tradition that does not carry (in Matthew Arnold's phrase) "the tone of the centre."

This is by no means, however, to say that the literature of the modern period is without significant religious interest. For even when it has thrown away, as Stevens would say, all the lights and definitions of the past and when it will no longer use "the rotted names" for what it vaguely and agnostically descries of *theos* "in the dark," it may, by the very radicality of its unbelief, awaken sensibilities of a contrary order, so that by way of a kind of *coincidentia oppositorum* it becomes an instrument of religious recovery. One classic case in point is Paul Claudel's testimony (in his preface to the *Œuvres de Rimbaud,* Paris, 1924) about how his early admiration for the poet of *Une saison en enfer* came to be a decisive *praeparatio* in his own life for a deeper entrance into the Christian faith. And similar testimonies have been made by others about the poetry of Baudelaire and the fiction of Kafka and the theater of Beckett.

The analysis of the interrelations in the modern period between religious and literary forms finds its greatest challenge, however, in the kind of subterranean life that religious modalities often have in literature that announces itself as radically secular. Remarking this paradox often provokes, to be sure, a certain vexation among those literary scholars and critics who like a tidier state of affairs. So when, for example, a Christian interpreter of culture detects in this body of poetry or in that body of drama phases of Christian thought and feeling that have, as it were, gone underground and taken on strange new accents and guises, he may be irritatedly told that it is appropriate for literary criticism to make reference to the Christian firmament of value only when it is dealing with a literature that explicitly relies on a particular tradition of Christian orthodoxy, on its symbolism and conceptual structures and cultic forms and all its protocol. But (as Amos Wilder reminds us, in his book *Modern Poetry and the Christian Tradition*) it ought to be regarded as one of the great lessons of the Incarnation that a faith grounded in a divine act of self-*emptying* (kenosis) will itself always be an affair of diaspora—dying in order to live, wedding itself to changing forms and sensibilities "in a daring surrender of life, and [thus introducing] creative energies and perspectives which then make their appearance in secular form," and in ways undistinguished by any evangelical stamp.

The chief paradigm here is, of course, that of the Romantics, that "visionary company" of such people as Blake and Wordsworth and Chateaubriand and Hölderlin and Schiller. For these and numerous other strategists of the Romantic insurgency, though they were seeking a way out of the wilderness that had been created by Enlightenment iconoclasm, had yet lived through the Enlightenment, which meant that, eager as they were to retrieve the religious *possibility,* they could not simply reinstate without revision the traditional dogmatic system of Christian belief. Just as Romantic philosophers like Schelling and Hegel were adapting biblical themes and categories to the new requirements of speculative metaphysics, so, too, their literary counterparts were approaching their religious inheritance as in Wallace Stevens's phrase, a "poem of the mind in the act of finding / What will suffice" *(Of Modern Poetry,* in *The Collected Poems).* But, now that "the theatre was changed," if the poem of the mind were "to learn the speech of the place" and "to face the men of the time," it had "to construct a new stage." So, inevitably, it underwent the sort of profound hermeneutic transformation that had to be administered, if the received heritage of faith were to be so reconstituted as to be intellectually and emotionally appropriable in an altered climate. And very often (as M. H. Abrams has shown in his book *Natural Supernaturalism*) the result proved to be one or another kind of project for naturalizing the supernatural and for humanizing the divine.

Yet in Blake's *The Four Zoas* as in Hölderlin's *Hyperion,* in Wordsworth's *Prelude* as in Novalis's *Hymnen an die Nacht,* the pressure of biblical forms and categories is manifest: the central realities are alienation and reunion, death and rebirth, hell and heaven, paradise lost and paradise regained. And we can discern the formative influence of the archetypes of the old Christian story of man as an exiled pilgrim who, having lost an original state of felicity through a tragic fall, must undertake a difficult *Bildungsweg,* a circuitous journey in search of a new Jerusalem.

Now, it is this Romantic pattern—of the religious heritage being submitted to a process of revision and secularization but of the themes and issues of that heritage retaining a powerful underground life—that, improbable as it may at first seem, is frequently to be encountered in the literature of the modern period. It may well be, therefore, that in this connection we ought not to use the term *secularization.* True, the idea of the world as the creation of a *deus faber,* of some sort of immaterial Person behind the myriad phenomena of experience who periodically perforates or breaks into the realm of nature and history to set things aright, is, indeed, an idea in which the modern writer does not characteristically take any great interest, and his tendency has been to endorse something like the famous word that the French astronomer Laplace offered Napoleon, when he said, "I have no need of that hypothesis." Which is not, however, to say that the literary imagination has not regularly sought to assure itself that the world is something more than the inert blankness of what Coleridge called "fixities and definites": on the contrary, again and again it searches for evidence that things are charged (in Stevens's phrase) with "a kind of total grandeur at the end," for evidence that, inconceivable though the idea of Grace "overhead" may be, the world does itself tabernacle grace and glory. Transcendence, in other words, is to be found in and through the secular, or, to borrow the terms of the French philosopher Jean Wahl, the route to be taken toward felicity and plenitude is not "transascendence" but "transdescendence"—or, in the familiar formulation of Dietrich Bonhoeffer's *Letters and Papers from Prison,* the "Beyond" is to be found "in the midst of our life." It is such an axiom as this that comes close to forming the basis of the period style in large ranges of twentieth-century literature, and it may be descried to be a guiding principle for writers as various as William Butler Yeats and Wallace Stevens, D. H. Lawrence and William Carlos Williams, Jorge Guillén and René Char, Marianne Moore and Charles Olson, Elizabeth Bishop and Gary Snyder, Jules Supervielle and Czeslaw Milosz.

The poetry of Stevens, for example, provides a great case of this relocation of transcendence into the dimension of immanence. Taking it for granted, as he does, that "the author of man's canons is man, / Not some outer patron" (*Conversation with Three Women of New England,* in *Opus Posthumous*), he is, to be sure, a "shaken realist" who finds it impossible to avoid the conclusion that something *else* "must take the place / Of empty heaven and its hymns" *(The Man with the Blue Guitar,* in *The Collected Poems).* So, as he says, "We seek / Nothing beyond reality" *(An Ordinary Evening in New Haven,* in *The Collected Poems),* since the "essential integrity" of things must be found within "The actual landscape with its actual horns / Of baker and butcher blowing." But this actual landscape is by no means for Stevens merely a huge *res extensa,* silent and dead and immeasurable. On the contrary, the "Is-ness" of everything that exists is invested with a most extraordinary radiance and presence: in the poem *Metaphor as Degeneration* he says, "It is being." This it is that lights up the things and creatures of earth—"mere Being," which is, as he says in *The Sail of Ulysses,* that

> life lighter than this present splendor,
> Brighter, perfected and distant away,
> Not to be reached but to be known,
> Not an attainment of the will
> But something illogically received. . . .
> (*Opus Posthumous,* p. 101;
> used by permission)

So we need not, therefore, cast about for some *scala sacra* leading up beyond the phenomenal world into the timelessness of eternity, since that which is steadfast and reliable, which is gracious and deserving of our trust, is already at hand in "the vulgate of experience," in the uncreated Rock of reality—"mere Being"—which offers us "the imagination's new beginning." And most especially in the great poems of his last years—in *Chocorua to Its Neighbor, Credences of Summer, Notes toward a Supreme Fiction, A Primitive like an Orb, An Ordinary Evening in New Haven, To an Old Philosopher in Rome, The Rock*—all his "edgings and inchings" appear to be calculated at the end to speak of "the final goodness" of things, of a holiness indwelling every nook and cranny of the world, which invites "a fresh spiritual," one untouched by any sort of supernaturalist figuralism. It is a poetry of immanence. But, for all Stevens's impatience with traditional metaphysical theism, it can hardly be declared to be a poetry that fails to line itself up behind any significantly religious outlook, and its accent and emphasis require us to pay deference to what he himself on one occasion wanted to insist upon when, in a Christmas letter of 1951 to the critic Sister M. Bernetta Quinn, he said, "I am not an atheist although I do not believe to-day in the same God in whom I believed when I was a boy."

Yet, however much modern literary sensibility may be distinguished by the determination of such a writer as Stevens to find the possibility of transcendence in and through the secular, many of the old paradigms and archetypes of the Judeo-Christian story continue to endure with a remarkable persistence. More than three hundred years after the first publication of Milton's *Paradise Lost* the myth of the Fall, for example, has lost none of its power to captivate and focalize the literary imagination. In part, this is no doubt consequent upon the disclosures that have come from modern psychology of the furies of unreason that rage deep within the human interior. And in the twentieth century the gas ovens and concentration camps that have been devised for the obliteration of millions of people and the nightmares of nuclear warfare have surely provided the most compelling incentive for subsuming the human condition at large under this ancient apologue. But, for whatever reason, it has been used almost endlessly as a framing structure for narrative, and not only by writers sustained by some mode of religious orthodoxy but by, say, the Conrad of *Heart of Darkness*, the Hesse of *Demian*, the Camus of *La chute*.

Indeed, the English novelist William Golding is so obsessed by what is broken and deformed in the human situation that in book after book—in *Lord of the Flies*, in *Free Fall*, in *The Spire*—he uses in one way or another imagery of "fallenness." In, for example, his novel of 1954, *Lord of the Flies*, he builds his narrative around a group of English schoolboys who survive a plane crash on a tropical island. But this remote fastness turns out not at all to be any sort of Isle of the Blessed: its shoreline is "torn everywhere by the upheavals of fallen trees," the heat is felt as "a threatening weight," and the forests roar and flail, the thorny underbrush is a reminder of how nearly the adjacent jungle presses in, and the fruits of the place induce diarrhea. Such is the uncongenial precinct amid which the little company of refugee schoolboys must undertake to organize a makeshift confederation for their common welfare. But, almost immediately, their life together is so perverted by the will to power that it collapses into a savage kind of depravity. They invent absurd taboos and barbaric blood-rituals. And their cruel aggrandizements against one another erupt at last into murder. Golding was for many years a teacher in Bishop Wordsworth's School, Salisbury; so, as an ex-schoolmaster, he has the requisite experience of boys for making the whole tale fully plausible. But his novel does not want to say "You see? This is what *boys* are like, once they escape the civilizing disciplines of family and church and school." On the contrary, it intends to say "Here is the naked reality of elemental human nature itself." Nowhere, to be sure, is any explicit reference made to the story about the garden of Eden in *Genesis*, but Golding's very refusal to submit the Fall to anything resembling logical or historical analysis is an indication that he, like the numerous other modern writers who work with this theme, takes for granted the lesson laid down by the English theologian John Seldon Whale (in his book *Christian Doctrine*), when he says: "Eden is on no map, and Adam's fall fits no historical calendar. Moses is not nearer to the Fall than we are, because he lived three thousand years before our time. The Fall refers not to some datable aboriginal calamity in the historic past of humanity, but to a dimension of human experience which is always present. . . . Everyman is his own 'Adam,' and all men are solidarily 'Adam.' "

Or, again, like the myth of the Fall, the Christic image is frequently invoked in the literature of recent decades. What is here being referred to is not, however, the kind of fictionalized biography of Jesus that occasionally provides the focus for historical novels in the mode of Robert Graves's *King Jesus* and Nikos Kazantzakis's *The Last Temptation of Christ*. Nor is reference being made to the various literary presentations—as in Gerhart Hauptmann's *Hanneles Himmelfahrt* or Upton Sinclair's *They Call Me Carpenter*—of Christ in modern garb, of the figure whom Theodore Ziolkowski (in his book *Fictional Transfigurations of Jesus*) speaks of as the *Jesus redivivus*. Nor, again, to insert still another negative, is reference being made to the phenomenon that Ziolkowski denominates as "Christomania," the condition that is being explored (as in Nathanael West's *Miss Lonelyhearts* or Kazantzakis's *The Greek Passion*) when the novelist takes as his subject a personage who, often under the pressure of a pathological psychology, commits himself to the exactions of an *imitatio Christi*. What is rather in view are the various examples in modern literature of sanctity and of redemptive suffering that are rooted in the archetype of Christ, in the same manner that other dramatic patterns are grounded in the archetypes of Prometheus and Orpheus and Parzival and Faust.

When poets and novelists and dramatists begin, out of whatever framework of personal belief, to explore what is involved in life releasing itself as an offering to other life, surely it is inevitable that this *leitourgia* should be apprehended, even if unconsciously, within the terms of the Passion story, since this is the most familiar and the most pervasive narrative in Western culture of what Dietrich Bonhoeffer (in his book *Ethics*) called "deputyship." When we act *for* others—as, said Bonhoeffer, when a "father acts for the children, working for them, caring for them, interceding, fighting and suffering for them" and thus undertaking to be "their deputy"—something is being given up: what is one's own is being handed over to another, for the sake of the human communion. And, at least on one level, it is of such sacrificial service that Christ stands in our culture as the primary archetype. So, when "deputyship" forms a part of the experiential reality with which the literary imagination seeks to deal, it ought not to be regarded as surprising that the figure of Christ should often be found hovering in the background.

One will not, of course, be surprised to find the Christic image being invoked by a Roman Catholic novelist like François Mauriac (in the character of Xavier Dartigelongue in *L'agneau*) or Graham Greene (in "the whiskey priest" of *The Power and the Glory*). But it is also to be encountered over and again in the fiction of many writers who, if not representing some mode of secular humanism, stand in at least a very ambiguous relation to Christian doctrine.

In American literature one will think, for example, in this connection of John Steinbeck's *The Grapes of Wrath*. Its moving account of the flight to California of a family of tenant farmers from an Oklahoma ruined by the dust storms of the 1930s established it as the dominant social novel of its period on the American scene, and it remains a minor classic. On their long and difficult journey the Joads are accompanied by Jim Casy, an ex-preacher who has lost his faith and who, in his lighthearted womanizing, does not conform in any conventional way to a saintly norm. But, in his steadfast loyalty to the Joads throughout all their hazardous journeying to the Promised Land (not unlike the journeying of the ancient Israelites) and in his sympathy for all those who are in need of succor and encouragement, he proves his role in the design of the novel to be that of showing that, indeed, the Good Place is not so much a particular region or tract of land as it is that space among human beings that is made radiant by reverence for the sacrality of the neighbor. And, not unnaturally, his fidelity to the insulted and the injured leads to his death at the hands of strikebreakers in California who are sent to hunt him down for the part he has played in leading a strike. Tom Joad, who kills the man who struck Casy, becomes a fugitive, and, when Ma Joad reaches him in his place of hiding, he says:

> "Lookie, Ma. I been all day an' all night hidin' alone. Guess who I been thinkin' about? Casy! He talked a lot. Used ta bother me. But now I been thinkin' what he said, an' I can remember—all of it. Says one time he went out in the wilderness to find his own soul, an' he foun' he didn' have no soul that was his'n. Says he foun' he jus' got a little piece of a great big soul. Says a wilderness ain't no good, 'cause his little piece of a soul wasn't no good 'less it was with the rest, an' was whole. Funny how I remember. Didn' think I was even listenin'. But I know now a fella ain't no good alone."

So it seems that this Christlike man in death has at least one disciple, for Tom Joad appears to have mastered Casy's great lesson, that "two are better than one."

Nor will it be forgotten how regularly the Passion of Jesus guided William Faulkner's imagination. Though the principal action of *The Sound and the Fury* occurs in the year 1928, the chronology of the novel is, clearly, that of Passion Week. At the center of *Light in August* is not only Joanna Burden but also Joe Christmas, who is marked by the invisible "cross" of the Negro blood that flows in his veins and who, after a lifetime of being badgered and abused, is finally slaughtered on a Friday, at the same age of Christ at the time of his crucifixion. And he, too, achieves a kind of apotheosis, for, after being castrated by a white racial maniac while he is dying of gunshot wounds, "from out the slashed garments about his hips and loins the pent black blood . . . seemed to rush out of his pale body like the rush of sparks from a rising rocket; upon that black blast the man seemed to rise soaring into their memories forever and ever." Or, again, Ike McCaslin in *The Bear* and Nancy—"Negro, dopefiend, whore"—in *Requiem for a Nun* want in various ways to say, as Nancy puts it, "Trust in Him." And the book of 1954, *A Fable,* presents the culminating instance of Faulkner's dependence upon the imagery of the Passion, for his central protagonist here is an obscure pacifist corporal who, by the manner of his death in the attempt to bring to an end the carnage in the French theater of World War I, appears unmistakably to be an analogue of Christ.

Steinbeck and Faulkner are, of course, but two of many other writers who might be cited in this context, for, from the time of Melville's *Billy Budd* on to the present, the American literary imagination has been repeatedly drawn to the archetype of Christ. Nor does modern European literature represent any great difference in this respect. The fiction of the Italian novelist Ignazio Silone, for example—*Bread and Wine, The Seed beneath the Snow, The Secret of Luca*—recurrently presents a dramatic economy that is knit together by its parallels to the gospel of the New Testament, and Silone's play *And He Hid Himself,* which is essentially a dramatization of *Bread and Wine,* makes explicit how much Pietro Spina, the protagonist of the novel and of *The Seed beneath the Snow,* is intended to be a figure of Christ.

Or, again, odd as it may at first seem in the work of a writer apparently so distant from any sort of Christian position, the great climactic moment of André Malraux's last novel, *Les noyers de l'Altenburg,* is nothing if it is not a rehearsal of the Passion of Christ. The action occurs on 12 June 1915 on the Eastern Front, where the narrator's father Vincent Berger (a native of Alsace, then a part of Germany), as an officer of the German intelligence service, is observing a bombardment being launched by German troops against the Russians. A newly developed poisonous gas is to be used, and, once it is released and begins to float down the adjacent valley toward the Russian trenches, the German troops wait and wait, and continue to wait, but they can discern through their binoculars no trace of any activity in the neighborhood of the enemy's advance positions. So, after a long interval, they decide to move forward; but no fire comes from the Russian artillery. And, finally, Berger and the other staff officers begin to wonder why it is that, long after plunging into the Russian trenches, the foot soldiers in their advance guard do not reappear. At last they are seen, but instead of continuing their advance, they return in a great swarm, and the officers, as they peer through their binoculars, are baffled by what they seem to be carrying, which, at a distance of a mile or so, appear to be only white spots. As it turns out, the Germans, in making their way back to their own lines, are carrying the bodies of gassed Russian infantrymen. "No," says one, "man wasn't born to rot!" Berger, as he contemplates the scene, slowly realizes that this mutiny is not merely an expression of pity, that it attests to "something a good deal deeper, an impulse in which anguish and fraternity were inseparably mingled." And, as he passes a German infantryman struggling to carry on his shoulders a dying Russian out of "the sordid world of the liquefied forest," he notices that the two together in silhouette form an outline like that of the Descent from the Cross.

So the old images and myths and archetypes of the Christian story persist in the secular literature of the modern period, although often in altered form. But not only do these protoplastic forms continue to have a significant subterranean life; so, too, do certain habits of spiritual perception. The works, for example, of D. H. Lawrence—the Lawrence of *Women in Love* and *The Plumed Serpent* and *Lady Chatterley's Lover*—are a case in point. T. S. Eliot laid it down (in *After Strange Gods*) that Lawrence was "an almost perfect example of the heretic," that his vision was "spiritually sick," and that it could appeal only "to the sick and debile and confused." And no doubt Lawrence's quest of "mindlessness" and the "dark gods" and his commitment to "savage pilgrimage" will still prompt many to blurt out some such impatient dismissal as Eliot ejaculated. But such a response will only reflect, as it did in Eliot, a failure of intelligence, for Lawrence's whole emphasis on "phallic consciousness," as it was combined with his polemic against "mental consciousness," was intended to rescue human carnality from the kind of "scientific" reductionism that, in the manner of a Marie Stopes, would make it merely an affair of calculation and mechanism (as it is for "the young man carbuncular" of Eliot's *Waste Land*). In Lawrence's short story *Glad Ghosts,* Lord Lathkill is speaking to Colonel Hale about the latter's wife, now deceased, and he says: "You may have been awfully good to her. But her poor woman's body, were you ever good to that? . . . That's the point. If you understand the marriage service: with my body I thee worship. That's the point. No getting away from it." And in his richest work—in *The Rainbow,* in *Women in Love,* in *St. Mawr,* in many of his finest poems—it is precisely his purpose to advance such a sacramental view of the sexual act as may indeed be far more authentically Christian than the frequent tendency of the theological tradition, in both its Catholic and Protestant phases, to pronounce *concupiscentia* as valid only insofar as, within the bond of marriage, it is instrumental toward procreation.

Or, in another direction, we may turn to a writer as different from Lawrence in style of vision as Ernest Hemingway, and, immediately, the common tendency will be to think of him as having been a votary of *nada,* as one who was prepared to say (in the language of his famous story *A Clean, Well-Lighted Place*), "Our nada who art in nada, nada be thy name thy kingdom nada thy will be nada in nada as it is in nada. Give us this nada our daily nada and nada us our nada as we nada our nadas and nada us not into nada but deliver us from nada; pues nada. Hail nothing full of nothing, nothing is with thee." And many of Hemingway's readers may be inclined to posit—not, indeed, without some reason—that it is this "nothing full of nothing" that defines the basic metaphysical situation forming the background of his fiction. But, then, one may remember the glorious interlude of those five days that Jake Barnes and Bill Gorton in *The Sun Also Rises* spend together fishing in waters up in the Pyrenees, where the air is crisp and clean and where they exchange, as it were, a smile of complicity with the golden Basque uplands, with the clear trout streams and the dense beech woods and the untraveled sandy roads and the rising sun—and one will remember that the novel's epigraph from *Ecclesiastes* speaks of how "the earth abideth forever." Or one will remember Santiago in *The Old Man and the Sea* and his reverential amazement at how beautiful and wondrous are the creatures of the sea and the sky. Though he beseeches the Holy Mother after he has hooked his great marlin to "pray for the death of this fish," he thinks to himself, "Never have I seen a greater, or more beautiful, or a calmer or more noble thing than you, brother." And he is "glad we do not have to kill the stars." Or, again, in a similar vein, one will think of the Nick Adams stories in Hemingway's first major book, *In Our Time,* and of how Nick is touched by the healing power of the good earth as he fishes deep in the back country of the north woods of Michigan, sometimes tenderly unhooking the barb from the mouth of a trout he has caught and dropping it back into the water. And, throughout the novels and the short stories, there is so much else in this mode that it is difficult finally not to conclude that this writer often sounds one of the most primitive meanings of the Christian doctrine of Creation, that the world at hand is touched by a transcendent glory, that indeed (as it is said by the canticles of the Morning Office) the mountains and the hills, the nights and the days, the dews and the frosts, the sun and the moon, and all the things of earth "uttereth speech" and "sheweth knowledge" and are exalted forever.

Now it is into this general order of discrimination that we shall be taken when we begin to reckon with, say, Joyce's *Portrait of the Artist as a Young Man*, with many of Pound's *Cantos*, with Kafka's *Das Schloss*, with Brecht's *Der gute Mensch von Sezuan*, with Beckett's *En attendant Godot*, with William Carlos Williams's *Paterson*, and with a vast number of other focal modern texts. Which is not at all to say that, for all its secularity, the characteristic literature of the modern period reveals itself to be somehow controlled by an *anima naturaliter Christiana*. What requires rather to be acknowledged is that the great symbolic forms of Christendom never (as Mircea Eliade says of symbols generally, in *Images and Symbols*) simply disappear from the reality of the psyche: "the aspect of them may change, but their function [often] remains the same; one has only to look behind their latest masks." And it is the uncovering of what is hidden and disguised that constitutes the difficult effort to be undertaken when literature in the age of Joyce and Kafka and Sartre begins to be viewed from the standpoint of its relation to our religious inheritance.

BIBLIOGRAPHY

Abrams, M. H. *Natural Supernaturalism: Tradition and Revolution in Romantic Literature.* New York, 1971.

Brooks, Cleanth. *The Hidden God.* New Haven, 1963.

Killinger, John. *The Fragile Presence: Transcendence in Modern Literature.* Philadelphia, 1973.

Moseley, Edwin M. *Pseudonyms of Christ in the Modern Novel: Motifs and Methods.* Pittsburgh, 1962.

Otten, Terry. *After Innocence: Visions of the Fall in Modern Literature.* Pittsburgh, 1982.

Scott, Nathan A., Jr. *Negative Capability: Studies in the New Literature and the Religious Situation.* New Haven, 1969.

Scott, Nathan A., Jr. *The Wild Prayer of Longing: Poetry and the Sacred.* New Haven, 1971.

Turnell, Martin. *Modern Literature and Christian Faith.* London, 1961.

Webb, Eugene. *The Dark Dove: The Sacred and Secular in Modern Literature.* Seattle, 1975.

Wilder, Amos N. *Modern Poetry and the Christian Tradition: A Study in the Relation of Christianity to Culture.* New York, 1952.

Ziolkowski, Theodore. *Fictional Transfigurations of Jesus.* Princeton, 1972.

NATHAN A. SCOTT, JR.

The Novel as Secular Literature

The novel is a genre of literary art that rarely takes religion as its obvious and principal theme. Some books that read like novels do so, but they are better described as works of edification; although they may possess grace of style or persuasive power, their inspiration is not artistic but propagandist. A true novel, even in modest categories of this genre, seeks to show man in society; any teaching that may be inherent in it, or any moral conclusion it may point to, is secondary to this artistic impulse. The great novelists frequently write on themes that have religious implications, but these are approached indirectly and shown in action or reflection rather than direct admonition. To form any notion of the connection between the novel and religion, we must look below the surface of the work of art, and we must not expect wholehearted assent to any version of orthodoxy.

This is not to set the novel at odds with religion, if we accept the latter word in terms of its derivation as implying the careful consideration of forces, laws, ideas, or ideals that are sufficiently powerful to inspire awe or devotion. The novel seeks to show man, confused and fallible, meeting the complexities of life, among which are likely to be those elements describable as numinous. If indeed man is naturally religious, the novel cannot avoid religion, though its principal theme will continue to be man.

The novel came into being roughly four hundred years ago, as a successor to the epic, which dealt with man as a heroic being, and the romance, which was free of any necessity for its characters to obey the broad laws of probability, or for stated causes to bring their usual consequences. The novel, entering the world of letters as a consequence of the Renaissance and strongly influenced by the Reformation, required that a story should be, in broad terms, probable, and its characters believable in terms of common experience. The novel was expected to be a story about what most readers would accept as real life, and as ideas of real life are inseparably associated with what mankind, at any period of history, is inclined to take for granted without much reflection, the novel became a mirror of society and thus a mirror of the nature of the era for which it was written. Although the novel does not seek to avoid issues that are properly religious, its principal energy in this area is better described as moral.

The morality put forward by novelists may be reduced to a number of broad precepts. "God is not mocked, for whatsoever a man soweth, that shall he also reap"; "Vengeance is mine, I will repay, saith the Lord"; "The dog is returned to his vomit again; and the sow that was washed to her wallowing in the mire"; "If a man think himself to be something, when he is nothing, he deceiveth himself." These are but a few of the more minatory precepts found in the Bible that underlie scores of novels. That these general laws may be seen at work in daily life, in the uttermost variety of circumstances, and that they are psychological truths, makes them the natural guides of the novelist, who must be, like any artist, an undeluded observer. He may deal with these grim truths humorously, and some of the most truly religious novels are seen by the world as funny books, but their underlying morality is far from funny.

This is not the place for a historical consideration of the novel, but it is useful to begin with *Don Quixote* (1605), by Miguel de Cervantes, often spoken of as the first true novel. Its story is of the fortunes of a Spanish gentleman whose wits have been turned by reading old books of romance and chivalry; he equips himself absurdly as a knight, and rides forth in search of adventures; in a rambling and sometimes coarse and perfunctory tale he is mocked, beaten, and humiliated until, on his deathbed, he understands the folly of his delusion.

The book is often read superficially, or not read at all, by many people who are nevertheless aware of it, as the story is familiar from stage, film, and operatic versions and as the word *quixotic*, meaning "actuated by impracticable ideals of honor," is in common use. A careful reading of the novel reveals the mainspring of the book's extraordinary power. It is the first instance in popular literature of the profoundly religious theme of victory plucked from defeat, which has strong Christian implications. The Don, who is courteous and chivalrous toward those who ill use him, and who is ready to help the distressed and attack tyranny or cruelty at whatever cost to himself, is manifestly a greater man than the dull-witted peasants and cruel nobles who torment and despise him. We love him, because his folly is Christlike, his victory is not of this world.

The theme is repeated in countless novels. One of the greatest is Dickens's *Pickwick Papers* in which Mr. Pickwick, whom we first meet as a foolish and almost buffoonlike character, is deepened by an unjust imprisonment to a point where he is truly aware of the misery that is part of the society in which he lives. It is of importance to our theme that Mr. Pickwick is dependent on his valet, Sam Weller, as Don Quixote is dependent on his peasant squire, Sancho Panza, for a measure of common sense and practical wisdom that saves him from disaster. Faith, hope, charity, justice, and fortitude are exemplified in the masters, but without the prudence and temperance of the servants they would be lost. A character who possessed all the seven great virtues would never do as the hero of a novel, but when a hero who has most of them is complemented by a helper and server who has what he lacks, great and magical fiction may result.

As the mighty virtues appear in numerous, though often disguised, forms in great novels, so also do the capital sins. To provide an equivalent for each suggests a list that inevitably means the exclusion of many others equally cogent. When we think of pride, however, we remember how brilliantly it is deployed in Dickens's *Domby and Son* (1846); wrath recalls *The Brothers Karamazov* (1880) and *Moby Dick* (1851); envy is the mainspring of Balzac's *La cousine Bette* (1846); lust has many exemplars, some of them presenting the vice in a refined form, as in Richardson's *Clarissa Harlowe* (1747), and others explicit, as in Cleland's *Fanny Hill* (1748); gluttony is a less popular theme, though drunkenness, which might be regarded as one of its forms, is very common, and is explored in Zola's *L'assommoir* (1877); avarice is popular, and Balzac's *Le cousin Pons* (1847) shows it in the guise of the collector's mania, linked in Sylvain Pons with a greed that exemplifies gluttony in the guise of gourmandise, the gourmet's refinement of the uglier word; sloth recalls Goncharov's *Oblomov* (1857), in which that sin is explored to its depth. The list is certainly not meant to be definitive, and the Seven Deadly Sins do not include cruelty, of which Dickens affords many examples, nor stupidity, which Flaubert displays subtly in *Madame Bovary* (1857), nor snobbism, which, though hardly a sin, is a deep preoccupation of the bourgeois world, and has never been more searchingly anatomized than in Proust's *À la recherche du temps perdu* (1913–1917). Virtually any attribute, exaggerated, may become a vice, and in some circumstances vice may take on the color of virtue. This makes heavy work for the moralist, but is the delight of the novelist who thrives on delicate distinctions and on that enantiodromia, or tendency of attributes and emotions to run into their opposites, which is familiar in psychology.

When novelists choose churches and churchmen as their theme, they frequently dwell on faults that are undeniable, but paint an ungenerous picture of the whole. This is particularly the case when the sort of religion portrayed is of the evangelistic, nonsacramental kind. In such religion, popular opinion expects that the evangelist or the parson will exemplify in himself the virtues he urges on others; in Sinclair Lewis's term, he is a Professional Good Man. His failure to be wholly good makes diverting reading, for hypocrisy provides livelier fiction than virtue. In Lewis's *Elmer Gantry* (1927), all the shams of vulgar religiosity are exposed, and its appeal to naive and unreflective people held up to ridicule.

A truer depiction of the religious life as it is lived by well-intentioned but not spiritually gifted priests is to be found in the novels of Anthony Trollope. In *The Warden* (1855), the principal character, the Reverend Septimus Harding, is a good man, but timid and weak, and his dilemma when he is accused of holding a sinecure is a choice between Christian precept and the way of the world; obedient to public opinion, he resigns his wardenship. In its sequel, *Barchester Towers* (1857), we meet the warden's son-in-law, Archdeacon Grantly, who dearly longs to succeed his father as bishop, for he is a man of strong worldly ambition; but in the first chapter of that book Grantly must decide whether he desires the bishopric at the cost of his father's life. His decision is made in terms of his faith rather than his ambition. The scene in which he prays for forgiveness at his father's bedside is moving and finely realized. Not a crumb of religiosity or false sentiment is to be found in it. Grantly is no saint but he is a man of principle. In the same fine novel we meet the bishop's chaplain, Mr. Slope, who cloaks inordinate ambition under evangelistic piety, and the Reverend Dr. Vesey Stanhope, who draws his salary as a clergyman but lives a fashionable life in Italy, and leaves his work to curates. Trollope parades before us a wide variety of clergy, some of whom are saved from moral ignominy by the fact that the Church of England, through its catholicism, separates the priestly function from the man who discharges it, though abuse of this distinction is frowned upon. But such characters as Mr. Harding, the warden; the Reverend Francis Arabin, an exemplar of the scholar-priest and intellectual; and the Reverend Josiah Crawley, in whom his creator combines pride with humility, manliness with weakness, and acute conscience with bitter prejudice, redeem Trollope's clergy and emphasize his very English, very Victorian conviction that a clergyman is not required to be a saint, but should unquestionably be a man of principle and a gentleman. This is a long way from Elmer Gantry, who was neither.

No discussion of this subject can escape some consideration of the part the intellectual and artistic character of the novelist plays in his depiction of religion, and its influence on his characters. All generalizations are suspect, but it may be stated broadly that the temperament that makes a writer a novelist is unlikely to be friendly to orthodoxy, and that the Manichaean struggle between darkness and light is more friendly to his purpose (the depiction of man in society) than is an unwavering adherence to a creed. Inevitably there are important exceptions. Calvinist predestination is the mainspring of James Hogg's fine *The Private Memoirs and Confessions of a Justified Sinner* (1824). There is no mistaking the Roman Catholic thought behind all the work of James Joyce, of Graham Greene, of Anthony Burgess, and the monolithic Orthodoxy that informs the novels of Aleksandr Solzhenitsyn. But more often the theme of *Don Quixote* is repeated: the good man exhibits weaknesses that betray him, but the forces that oppose him—which are more likely to be stupidity, conventionality, and self-seeking than determined evil—succeed in the short view. It is the reader who understands and appreciates the goodness of the hero, and whereas in a work of inferior artistic merit this may simply flatter the reader's ego, in a great novel it may leave him with a larger vision of life and an appreciation of the weight of religious feeling that he did not have before.

The good novelist manages this by indirect means; his aim is not to teach but to entertain, and thus to persuade. His chief purpose, from which he strays at his peril as an artist, is to depict life as he sees it, and his own temperament will color whatever he touches. The temperament of the artist is not unwaveringly noble; wholeness of spirit, not perfection, is his aim. Many novelists, of whom Sinclair Lewis may serve as an example, are disappointed idealists, angry with life because it does not conform to the best they can conceive, and their strictures on religion, as on other great themes, are apt to be bitter. The calm observation of Trollope is a rarer gift.

Examples could be cited to the point of weariness, without achieving very much. Let it suffice to say that a turbulent and tormented spirit like Dostoevskii will not see religion as it is seen by a stronger, more deeply and often more narrowly moral writer like Tolstoi. [*See the biographies of Dostoevskii and Tolstoi.*] Neither exhibits the philosophical, ironic, but finally positive spirit of Thomas Mann. To look for what is called "real life" in the novels of these and countless others is to search for something definable only in vague terms. As Vladimir Nabokov says, "a masterpiece of fiction is an original world and as such is not likely to fit the world of the reader." The serious reader enters such original worlds as he encounters any work of art—in search of enlargement and enlightenment. If the novel has this effect the reader's concept of "real life" has been changed.

Serious readers, however, are not a majority, nor are serious writers. We must beware of the critical error that tries to define art solely in terms of the best. Below the level of greatness are innumerable novels that cannot be dismissed as having no merit; they may be lesser works of art, or on a level below that, or they may be widely popular and thus in some measure influential. The best-seller should not be brushed aside simply because many people like it; its very popularity is a strong clue to what a multitude of people will accept as a depiction of man in society, and therefore as an indication of what those people believe society to be. Even more than what these readers believe to be true, popular literature displays what they wish were true, about religion as about many other things.

What many readers seem to wish is that religion should not obtrude into a novel, either directly or in some awareness of the numinous. Writers who ignore their wish feel the lash of their resentment. Aldous Huxley, who seemed to a large and eager group of readers to be the perfection of the cynicism of the period following World War I, astonished and displeased them when, in 1936, he published *Eyeless in Gaza,* in which the voice of the moralist and explorer of faith that had been earlier evident in *Brave New World* (1932) could no longer be ignored. A similar experience befell Evelyn Waugh, whose works, being both witty and funny (for the two are not interchangeable terms), had secured him a delighted following of readers who, although they knew him to be a Roman Catholic, did not appreciate how determinedly Catholic he was until 1945, when *Brideshead Revisited* demanded that Catholic orthodoxy be taken with the uttermost seriousness. The deathbed repentance of the earl of Marchmain was ridiculed by those critics who could not bring themselves to believe that it might be true. That the wit, the funnyman, should also be religious was unbearable to multitudes of religious illiterates, many of them critics.

It is significant that when Huxley revealed the quester beneath the cynic he was forty; when Waugh forced his readers to face an embarrassing fact he was forty-two. Both men had reached the midpoint in life, when radical psychological change presents problems that can no longer be dismissed, or dissembled before the artist's audience. The lives of virtually all novelists of the serious sort reveal some such alteration in the thrust of their work. If not religion in some readily identifiable form, the religious spirit of awe and a moral conviction asserts itself and shows in the work that is most characteristic.

In fiction on the most popular level, that of the best-seller, religion or the trappings of religion may be used (not necessarily cynically) by an author to induce in his readers an impression that they are thinking about and weighing serious problems. The familiar tale of the priest who falls in love lies beneath many plots, an example of which is *The Thorn Birds* (1977), by Colleen McCullough, hailed as admirable and even profound by innumerable readers. The priest cannot deny his love, for to do so would be to reject something necessary to his wholeness; in time, as a cardinal, he receives his unacknowledged son into the priesthood.

There may lie beneath McCullough's book, and others like it, something that should not be ignored: Christianity has never wholly accepted man's sexuality as a potentially noble part of his being. Such books are a protest against that attitude, a demand that religion should include sexuality and the distinctively feminine element in the human spirit as it shows itself in both sexes. The conflict between a high feminine spirit and a torturing, wholly masculine morality is finely explored in Hawthorne's *The Scarlet Letter* (1850); Hester Prynne's greatness is opposed to the orthodoxy of her secret lover, the Reverend Arthur Dimmesdale, and there can be no doubt which spirit is the more truly religious.

Innumerable books have dealt with this question in a manner that may have been the best possible to their authors but that can only be called slight and in some cases cynically frivolous. An early example is the immensely popular novel by Matthew Gregory Lewis, called *Ambrosio, or The Monk* (1795), in which the externals of Catholicism are exploited in a tale of nymphomania, murder, magic, and unappeasable lust spangled with hints of homosexuality. Unquestionably it is lively reading, but its notions of numinosity reach no higher than scenes with the Inquisition and a trumpery pact with the Devil. (For a fine example of the theme of the pact with the Devil, one may turn to Thomas Mann's *Dr. Faustus,* 1947.) Lewis's Gothic shocker is mentioned here because it is the forerunner of many such tales in which religion serves indecency in the manner Shakespeare describes as "to have honey a sauce to sugar." But they are popular, and it cannot be denied that they represent what religion means to many people. Victor Hugo's *Notre Dame de Paris* (1831) offers an artistically superior example. Eugène Sue's *Le juif errant* (1844) is a lesser work in which the supposed unscrupulous intellectualism of the Jesuits is exploited.

Some reference must be made to the large category of books that make use of the occult as part of the paraphernalia of their stories, employing a romantic Satanism to produce an atmosphere of evil and decadence. Two works of Joris-Karl Huysmans have been admired: *À rebours* (1884), in which Catholicism is embraced as a remedy against a blighting pessimism, and *Là-bas* (1891), in which the hero searches for a consoling faith through the path of black magic. On a lower level of artistic achievement is the long-lived romance by Bram Stoker, *Dracula* (1897), in which the popular theme of vampirism is the mainspring of the action. These books are relevant to any discussion of religion and the novel because they are evidence of a yearning in a large reading public for something to balance the apparent spiritual barrenness of the world that has emerged from the industrial and scientific revolution. That the public responds to the negative spirit of black magic rather than to something more hopeful is not surprising. Where religion loses its force, superstition is quick to supplant it, and it would need a strong new religious impulse or revelation to reverse that movement.

It is not surprising that when religion appears in this class of literature it is usually Catholicism, Orthodoxy, Jewish mysticism (Qabbalah) that accommodate naive or unevolved religious feeling more sympathetically than Protestantism. The reformed versions of Christianity in their eagerness to banish superstition appear sometimes to have banished any sense of the numinous along with it, and it may be argued that man cannot live comfortably without some elements of belief that a stern moralist would class as superstitious. The human psyche cannot relate wholly toward the positive and the light side of life; it must have some balancing element of the dark, the unknown, and the fearful.

It is because of this unrecognized pull toward the numinous in its dark side that it is so difficult, even for a great literary artist, to portray a wholly good and admirable character. Dickens's villains have a power not found in his good men and women, and the great artist usually provides a balance, as he does in *The Old Curiosity Shop* (1841), where the innocent and saintly Little Nell is opposed to the grotesque villainy of the dwarf Quilp. This opposition provides the tension that gives the novel life, and would slacken if Nell had things too much her own way. In *The Brothers Karamazov* (1880), Dostoevskii cannot, by his finest art, make the saintly Alyosha as real to us as the man divided between his good and evil, his brother Ivan. Modern man is aware of this tension as a demanding element in his own life, and responds to it in fiction.

When Tolstoi wrote *War and Peace* (1868) and *Anna Karenin* (1878), his powerful depiction of this tension makes him a literary artist of the highest achievement; when he was impelled later to write works determinedly improving in tone, that splendor did not survive. But we must sympathize with Tolstoi's deep conviction that art should be religious in its impulse and make religious feeling at its highest available to a public neither devout nor philosophical. This is a conviction recognizable in many novels of the first rank.

In vast areas of popular literature a defensible, if sometimes crude, morality asserts itself, greatly to the satisfaction of its readers. In Westerns the Good Guy, and the values he stands for, triumphs over the Bad Guy, who is corrupt, cruel, and frequently cynical in his attitude toward women. For the Bad Guy to win in the struggle would topple the myth of worthiness and decency that readers of Westerns value. The same simple morality informs much science fiction.

This is significant. In the words of G. K. Chesterton, "men's basic assumptions and everlasting energies are to be found in penny dreadfuls and halfpenny novelettes" (*Heretics,* 1905). Great numbers of readers of detective stories are, without ever defining their attitude, devoted to the morality of "Vengeance is mine, I will repay, saith the Lord," or the bleaker law of *Exodus*— "If any mischief follow then thou shalt give life for life, eye for eye, tooth for tooth, hand for hand, foot for foot." Who is the instrument of the Lord's vengeance, who brings the murderer or the thief to his just reward? The Great Detective, of course. Be he the cold reasoning-machine Sherlock Holmes; or the man of pity, Chesterton's own Father Brown; or the high-born, donnish Peter Wimsey, or the immobile, intellectual Nero Wolfe; he is always the figure recognizable from medieval religious drama, sometimes called Divine Correction. He is the restorer of balance, the dispenser of justice, working on behalf of a higher authority.

The same pattern is observable in the spy story, which is the principal rival of the detective novel. However attractive or extenuating may be the temptations that make the spy betray his country, and however plodding, weary, disillusioned, and dowdy the spy-catcher may be, in the end the betrayer of the highest values must be found and brought to some sort of justice. Often the tone is cynical; often the secret service is represented as no more than a game; but behind every game lies the desire to win, and thereby to establish or reaffirm some superiority. What superiority? That of an overriding morality.

How far is morality from religion? To the novelist it sometimes looks like the religion that people profess who wish to ignore God, or keep him behind a veil as being too grand for common concerns. It may be the religion of people who find an ever-present God embarrassing company, because they are aware that they cannot live always on the heights, and they do not believe that God understands their insufficiencies. But to support a system of morality without some reference to numinous values is uphill work for a philosopher, and beyond the scope of even a highly intelligent general reader.

The novel is a work of literary art at its best, and a form of entertainment at all levels, concerned with man in every aspect of his life including, but not necessarily approving, his religious life. That its connection with religion should be in the main through morality rather than through faith or revelation should therefore surprise no one. Whatever pinnacles it may achieve in morality or philosophy, its character remains secular.

BIBLIOGRAPHY

Many books of criticism that deal with the novel make passing reference to religious concerns when these are relevant, but not all critics are even-handed in their treatment of religion, and some of them seem almost to be religious illiterates, who either stand in foolish awe of what they have not examined or ignorantly decry it. The reader who wishes to pursue the train of thought suggested in the preceding article might well reread the novels it mentions with special attention to their religious implication. A valuable background to some aspects of religious feeling as it is shown in literature is provided by Mario Praz's classic study *The Romantic Agony*, 2d ed., translated by Angus Davidson (London, 1951). Profitable reading also are *The Abolition of Man* by C. S. Lewis (Oxford, 1943) and *Man in Modern Fiction* by Edmund Fuller (New York, 1958).

A work of particular value to the general reader is *Literature and Western Man* by J. B. Priestley (London, 1960); it has been unfairly neglected by the scholarly community, but it possesses a breadth of understanding and a critical shrewdness that most academic critics might envy. Another valuable book is *Creative Mythology*, vol. 4 of *The Masks of God*, by Joseph Campbell (New York, 1968); it traces the great themes of modern literature as they relate to religion and mythology and is particularly illuminating about the work of James Joyce and Thomas Mann. Like Priestley's book, it is based on a broader learning and a more humane concept of life than most academic scholarship, and without being Jungian texts, both books show the influence of the thought of C. G. Jung.

ROBERTSON DAVIES

LITHUANIAN RELIGION. *See* Baltic Religion.

LITURGICAL DANCE. *See* Dance, *article on* Theatrical and Liturgical Dance.

LITURGY. [*This entry, drawing examples from various religious traditions, presents the definition and function of liturgy as a system or set of rituals prescribed for collective performance. For a historical and theological discussion of Christian liturgy, see* Worship and Cultic Life, *article on* Christian Worship.]

The term *liturgy* is derived from the Greek *leitourgia*, which refers to an act or work *(ergon)* performed by or for the people *(laitos)*. In the Greek city-states the term often had the technical political sense of referring to the obligation placed upon wealthy citizens to undertake tasks relating to the common good (building a monument, outfitting a ship, helping to supply an army). It could also be used in a wider sense to refer to any service that one person performed for another. Related to this more general sense of service, *liturgy* acquired a new technical meaning within the cultic sphere of a service performed for a deity, especially among the mystery cults of Eleusis, Isis, and so on. The Septuagint follows this usage, employing *leitourgia* only to designate cultic actions. The earlier political meaning is retained, however, in that these cultic actions always have in view the responsibility and welfare of the people as a whole, the whole understood as the people of God.

In early Christianity *liturgy* retained this primarily cultic significance and was used especially to refer to the Eucharist. In Eastern and grecophone Christianity this sense has been retained to the present day. But in Western Christendom the term disappeared with the abandonment of the Greek language. Only in the nineteenth century did it emerge again as a way of designating particular ritual actions. Its reemergence is closely related to a variety of movements for the reform of Christian worship or ritual. These movements for liturgical reform have emphasized two distinct principles on which they seek to revise the practice of worship. On the one hand, especially within Roman Catholicism, these movements have emphasized the importance of increasing lay participation in the ritual activity of the church, thereby stressing the corporate character of Christian worship. On the other hand, especially within Protestantism, movements of liturgical reform have sought to amplify and diversify the ritual expression of congregational life. Within this context, then, *liturgy* suggests the articulation of a ritual structure or calendar. Because both directions of liturgical reform have had a common orientation toward the historical sources of Christian ritual, the term *liturgics* is often used to designate the historical investigation of such sources.

Definition. On the basis of this historical background, it seems appropriate to use the term *liturgy* to designate any system or set of rituals that is prescribed for public or corporate performance. Thus for phenomenological or comparative purposes we may emphasize both the corporate character of liturgy and its articulation as a set of ritual performances.

Corporate character. Emphasis on the corporate character of liturgy serves to distinguish liturgical rituals from other types: those employed only by and for individuals (as in many forms of magic), the esoteric rituals of cult societies, and the household rituals so important in China and India.

In practice there are a number of transitional examples that may also serve to clarify the specificity of liturgical actions. The Christian Eucharist, for example, has historically been performed not only corporately and publicly but also privately or in solitude. Only in the former case is the sacrament liturgical in the sense here employed. The esoteric rituals of the Antelope and Snake cult societies of the Hopi of the southwestern United States serve also as preparation for the public performance of their dances, which are therefore liturgical in character. In China the household ancestral cult terminates in a public and corporate (i.e., liturgical) performance in celebration of a new year. Initiation rites typically have an esoteric character, but since they eventually include all members of a society (or all males), they closely approximate this definition of liturgy. The Sun Dance of the American Plains Indians is an interesting case, since it quite closely combines initiation rites with a public and corporate performance.

These and similar transitional phenomena stand at the boundary of the domain of ritual action that is specifically liturgical in character, a domain constituted by the set of rituals prescribed for corporate participation and public performance or that are explicitly performed on behalf of the community as a whole by its designated representatives. It is important to notice that liturgy by no means plays the same role for all religions or peoples. It does play an important role in the religious life of the ancient Near East, of Christianity, of many African groups, and of certain high cultures of ancient Mexico and Peru, the Maya, the Aztec, and the Inca. It plays a much reduced role in Islam, in modern Judaism, in Brahmanic Hinduism, and in China.

Systematic character. A striking feature of liturgical rituals is their deployment in a cycle of such rituals, a cycle characterized by both variety and integration. The liturgy of a group consists of its entire system of public ritual. The system may comprise both calendrical rituals governed by solar or lunar cycles and rituals that are occasioned by specific crises or turning points in the life of the community (preparations for war, coronations, the dedication of a major temple, etc.). While there is some merit in restricting the term *liturgy* to the former (calendrical) set of rituals, both the regular (although not calendrical) character and the corporate nature of the occasional rituals warrant their inclusion in liturgical systems.

Since the cycle of liturgical rituals has a systematic character, the individual rituals that compose the system may be appropriately studied in relation to other component rituals of the cycle as a whole. In this way it is possible to avoid distortions in interpretation that arise from the isolation of a particular ritual from the set of which it is naturally a member. Thus *liturgy* should be understood as referring primarily to the set of corporate rituals that form a coherent structure, and only secondarily to the structure of a particular ritual within this complex. In Christianity the ambiguity of the term results from the possibility of understanding the liturgical calender as a set of variations upon the Eucharist and of understanding the Eucharist as a concentration of the liturgical system as a whole.

Understanding liturgy as an articulate system of prescribed corporate action raises the question of how such systems are generated. From a historical perspective it is clear that they are produced through processes of internal elaboration and interaction with the ritual systems of other cultures. Illustrations of this process include the appropriation of agrarian rituals by ancient Israel and its transformation of them into commemorations of historical events. Victor Turner has cited a number of illustrations from Africa in which the ritual systems of autochthonous peoples have been assimilated into the ritual structure of conquering groups to produce a new structure. The most familiar illustration, however, is the development of the early Christian liturgical calendar, which was produced through the appropriation of Jewish and Hellenistic ritual practices. This interactive development of a liturgical structure did not cease with early centuries of Christian expansion but continues into the modern era with such additions to the liturgical calendar as Thanksgiving in the United States and the festival of the Virgin of Guadalupe in Mexico.

This selection of examples from among the many that might be cited indicates that a liturgical system is by no means a timeless entity but is in the process of development, interaction, and transformation. Thus the study of liturgy may benefit from a synchronic perspective that views a particular ritual as an integral component within the whole of the liturgical system, as well as from a diachronic perspective that attends to the processes of elaboration, interaction, transformation, and harmonization that produce and alter such liturgical systems.

Functions. While a number of different and conflicting theories have been developed to identify the function of ritual in general and of the liturgical system of corporate rituals in particular, it does seem possible to isolate at least four functions or effects of liturgy upon which there may be some agreement.

Temporalization. The tendency for liturgy to acquire an elaborate articulation distributed through time indicates that one of its principal functions or effects is the ordering or structuring of time. The periodization that is a necessary basis for the experience of time is one of the principal contributions of liturgical elaboration. Thus in many societies astronomical and calendrical development is closely associated with priestly endeavor. The ancient Babylonian and the pre-Columbian Maya religious traditions, for example, generated and were in turn governed by precise astronomical observation and calendrical prediction.

While most religious traditions organize their liturgical calendar on an annual cycle, a cycle especially appropriate for agrarian societies, additional forms of periodization, including lunar and diurnal, are used. In some religious traditions this temporalization extends to include, for example, three-year cycles (as in the Christian lectionary). Judaism, at least in theory, calls for a fifty-year cycle (*Lv.* 25), while the Aztec and other Mesoamerican groups made use of a fifty-two-year cycle, and the Vedic system of rites is theoretically extended over an even longer time.

In the West the sense of history is generated at least in part by apocalyptic speculation concerning a sequence of "ages" that reduces history to an ordered periodicity. This apocalyptic speculation is rooted in priestly reflection, the traces of which are clearly discernible in the liturgical imagery of much apocalyptic literature (the biblical books *Daniel* and *Revelation*, the work of Joachim of Fiore, etc.).

A principal effect of liturgy, then, is to structure time, thereby making it available for conscious experience and intellectual comprehension. This in turn makes possible the further elaboration of liturgical action.

Socialization. In addition to the tendency of liturgy to be distributed through and so regularize temporality, it also has, as we have seen, a decisively corporate character. While the sociologist Émile Durkheim argued that religion in general designated an essentially social reality, this appears to be especially true of the cycle of corporate action that is liturgy.

Thus the social or corporate identity of a people is closely associated with its liturgical practice. To be Ndebele or Aztec or Christian or Vaiṣṇava is to participate in the designated corporate actions that both reflect and engender this corporate identity. Indeed, the possibility of experiencing the group or community as such appears to be dependent on participation in its significant corporate action as elaborated through liturgy. Liturgical action, then, serves to focus corporate identity in such a way as to make it available for conscious appropriation.

The perception of a close correlation between liturgical practice and corporate identity has produced a number of theories of ritual action that stress its social function. Such theoreticians as Émile Durkheim, A. R. Radcliffe-Brown, Mary Douglas, and René Girard have developed markedly differing interpretations of ritual, all of which are based on this correlation.

Coordination. A particularly striking feature of liturgical rituals is their tendency to coordinate a variety of dimensions of experience. While their correlation to social reality is especially noticeable, owing to the public and corporate character of their performance, this should not be so emphasized as to obscure from view the presence of a variety of other dimensions of experience and interaction that are focused within the liturgical system. Liturgical systems typically exhibit an interplay of symbols and actions drawn from dimensions of experience as divers as the psychological-emotive (sexuality, mortality), the domestic (hearth), the socioeconomic (authority and exchange), the natural (relation to animals, to agriculture, to seasons), and the celestial.

In the *Ṛgveda* 10.90 *(Puruṣasūkta)* the fire sacrifice is exhibited as a coordination of phenomena that are bodily (ears, eyes, thighs, feet, etc.), social (the various castes), cosmic (earth, atmosphere, heaven), and natural (spring, summer, fall, equated with butter, firewood, oblation). In the Christian Eucharist, elements of human interaction with nature (bread and wine) and domesticity (eating and drinking) are woven together with the individualized themes of guilt and forgiveness and the historico-apocalyptic themes of the death of Jesus and his expected return. Thus the sacrament coordinates disparate dimensions of experience.

This coordination of different types of experience makes possible, while at the same time placing a limit on, the success of attempts to provide psychoanalytic or politico-economic interpretations of liturgical systems. The complex mirroring of individual, social, and natural or cosmic bodies gives to ritual its evocative power and rich content. In this way liturgy generates the world of shared human experience. Indeed, the reason often given for the performance of liturgical rituals, whether the fire sacrifice of the Vedas or the human sacrifice of the Aztec, is that thereby the cosmos is sustained, is both brought into being and maintained in being. With respect to the shared world of meaning, this claim is scarcely an exaggeration.

Liturgical paradigms. The coordination and concentration of disparate regions of experience enables liturgical action to serve as a set of paradigms for actions that occur outside the sphere of liturgy itself and even outside the immediate sphere of religion. Thus the liturgical repertoire of a group provides a set of shared patterns of action that are available as common models of what appropriate or significant action is like. This effect may be illustrated from a variety of cultures.

The formal and solemn Vedic fire sacrifice serves as a pattern for the less formal domestic, or hearth, rites of the householder. In combination these rites serve to shape the decorum that is appropriate for all acts of welcome and hospitality, acts that also exhibit and reinforce the structuring of society along the lines of caste. In yet another direction of development, the external ritual of the fire sacrifice becomes the pattern for the interior discipline of yoga, which self-consciously appropriates the essential structure of the public action while eschewing the external act itself. Finally, in the *Bhagavadgītā* the climactic action of renunciation (*tyāga*) in the sacrifice is taken to be a model for the renunciation of the fruits of all worldly action (*karma-phala-tyāga*).

In Christianity the corporate or liturgical recitation of the Lord's Prayer is taken to be the pattern of all prayer, including prayer that in principle renounces any external manifestation; conversely, prayer thus publicly modeled and inwardly appropriated may be understood as the shape or structure of all action, including worldly or secular action.

These two examples from the many made available by the disciplines of comparative religion and phenomenology of religion illustrate the importance of the liturgical paradigm for shaping both nonliturgical religious action and the extrareligious action of individuals and groups who participate in the liturgical action.

Authority and Tradition. The capacity of liturgy to structure time and so provide the basic framework for shared experience, to manifest the community as the context of experience and action, to coordinate the varied dimensions of individual, domestic, social, and cosmic experience, and to provide shared paradigms for all meaningful action—all contribute to the sense of liturgy as authoritative, and as action that generates and legitimates authority.

While liturgy may sometimes be legitimated by apparent reference to something outside itself—the gods have required this, or this is what we have always done, or this sustains the cosmos—it is by reference to the inherent character of liturgical action that its own authority may perhaps best be understood. Thus, for example, the sense that liturgy is timeless or that it persists from the origin of time owes as much to its capacity to produce, structure, or "invent" time as it does to any actual antiquity. Similarly, the legitimation of liturgy by reference to the authority of the community may have a comparably circular character since the community is manifested and, indeed, constituted by these same liturgical performances.

The cultural value of liturgy ensures that its forms will be assiduously preserved, even though its inherently conservative nature by no means precludes innovation or modification.

[*For related discussion in a broader context, see* Ritual. *For discussion of the use of religious rites in secular settings, see* Ceremony. *For discussions of specific liturgical cycles, see* Buddhist Religious Year; Christian Liturgical Year; Hindu Religious Year; Jewish Religious Year; *and* Islamic Religious Year.]

BIBLIOGRAPHY

Helpful information with respect to the history of the term *liturgy* may be found in the appropriate articles of the *Theological Dictionary of the New Testament*, edited by Gerhard Kittel and translated by Geoffrey W. Bromiley (Grand Rapids, Mich., 1964–), and the *Encyclopedia of Theology*, edited by Karl Rahner (New York, 1975).

Standard discussions of liturgy within the Christian context may be found in Dom Gregory Dix's *The Shape of the Liturgy*, 2d ed. (New York, 1982) and Alexander Schmemann's *Introduction to Liturgical Theology*, translated by Asheleigh E. Moorhouse (London, 1966). Discussions of ritual, with particular bearing on the understanding of liturgy, include Mary Douglas's *Natural Symbols* (New York, 1970), Ronald L. Grimes's *Beginnings in Ritual Studies* (Washington, D.C., 1982), Roy A. Rappaport's *Ecology, Meaning and Religion* (Berkeley, 1979), and Victor Turner's *The Ritual Process* (1969; reprint, Ithaca, N.Y., 1977). The collection of materials in *Reader in Comparative Religion*, 4th ed., edited by William A. Lessa and Evon Z. Vogt (New York, 1979), is also helpful. Information on rituals in Hinduism can be found in Thomas J. Hopkins's *The Hindu Religious Tradition* (Encino, Calif., 1971), and Åke Hultkrantz's *Religions of the American Indians*, translated by Monica Setterwall (Los Angeles, 1979), contains useful information on the religious practices of the indigenous peoples of North and South America.

THEODORE W. JENNINGS, JR.